Software and Internet Law

Software and Internet Law

Second Edition

Mark A. Lemley
Professor of Law
University of California at Berkeley

Peter S. Menell
Professor of Law
University of California at Berkeley

Robert P. Merges
Wilson, Sonsini, Goodrich, and Rosati
Professor of Law and Technology
University of California at Berkeley

Pamela Samuelson
Professor of Law and Information Management
University of California at Berkeley

ASPEN
PUBLISHERS

1185 Avenue of the Americas, New York, NY 10036
www.aspenpublishers.com

Permissions
Aspen Publishers
1185 Avenue of the Americas
New York, NY 10036

Printed in the United States of America

1 2 3 4 5 6 7 8 9 0

ISBN 0-7355-3654-6

Library of Congress Cataloging-in-Publication Data

Software and internet law / Mark A. Lemley ... [et al.].—2nd ed.
    p. cm.
    Includes index.
    ISBN 0-7355-3654-6 (alk. paper)
    1. Software protection—Law and legislation—United States. 2. Internet—Law and legislation—United States. I. Lemley, Mark A.

KF3024.C6S617 2003
343.7309'944—dc21

2002043887

About Aspen Publishers

Aspen Publishers, headquartered in New York City, is a leading information provider for attorneys, business professionals, and law students. Written by preeminent authorities, our products consist of analytical and practical information covering both U.S. and international topics. We publish in the full range of formats, including updated manuals, books, periodicals, CDs, and online products.

Our proprietary content is complemented by 2,500 legal databases, containing over 11 million documents, available through our Loislaw division. Aspen Publishers also offers a wide range of topical legal and business databases linked to Loislaw's primary material. Our mission is to provide accurate, timely, and authoritative content in easily accessible formats, supported by unmatched customer care.

To order any Aspen Publishers title, go to *www.aspenpublishers.com* or call 1-800-638-8437.

To reinstate your manual update service, call 1-800-638-8437.

For more information on Loislaw products, go to *www.loislaw.com* or call 1-800-364-2512.

For Customer Care issues, e-mail CustomerCare@aspenpublishers.com; call 1-800-234-1660; or fax 1-800-901-9075.

Aspen Publishers
A Wolters Kluwer Company

For Rose, as ever.

M.A.L.

For Ralph, Nancy, Devon, Carol, and Jeffery;
and Claire, Dylan, and Noah

P.S.M.

For Jo, Robbie, and James

R.P.M.

For Bob, who has made so many
things possible.

P.S.

Summary of Contents

Contents

2   *Copyright Law*   *33*

5   *Sui Generis Protection of Computer Technology*   *261*

6   *Software Licensing*   *299*

7 Antitrust in the Computer Industry 387

8 *International Protection of Computer Technology* *467*

II   INTERNET LAW   581

9   *Jurisdiction and Choice of Law*   583

Preface

Lawyers serve the software industry and Internet firms in many significant roles. They often draft or review license agreements for acquiring software or other information products. They may monitor ongoing licensing arrangements. They sometimes draft or negotiate agreements for the custom development of software to be performed by other firms. They may conduct intellectual property audits to enable their clients to understand better how to protect the firm's overall intellectual capital. Lawyers also help design electronic ordering systems or review Web sites to ensure that no illegal content is posted there. They may provide assessments about legal or policy developments likely to affect their clients. Finally, when necessary, they litigate claims or otherwise work to settle disputes between their clients and other firms. To play these multiple roles successfully, lawyers need a considerable understanding of the law, how it has been applied in the past, and how it is evolving.

Although one might obtain this understanding by taking a standard curriculum in intellectual property, antitrust, contract, and tort law, perhaps with some constitutional or criminal law mixed in, there are several reasons why studying software and Internet law in one course may offer a better framework for providing sound advice to information technology clients. The most obvious reason to study software and Internet law as a special course is that the practice of law in this field will often require the kind of integrative thinking that this book will facilitate. A software entrepreneur may develop an innovative user interface and ask her lawyer: "Should I patent it? Can I copyright it? How else might I protect the look and feel?" Such questions may be easier to answer when the lawyer has studied intellectual property law as it has specifically been applied to software.

There are, however, at least three other reasons to study software and Internet law. A course on these subjects not only is useful because it covers cases that involve the application of different kinds of laws to computers, software, or the Internet; more importantly, a course of this sort raises fundamental questions about the adequacy of existing laws to adapt to the challenges posed by computer software and the Internet.

Computer software was the first digital subject matter to raise such challenges, and several chapters (Chapter 2 on copyright, Chapter 3 on patent, and Chapter 5 on sui generis laws) address them. However, as will become apparent in Chapter 10, those challenges are not confined to software. Why did software pose challenges for the law? The answer lies in the very nature of software. It is a *utilitarian text*. Copyright law has a long history of protecting literary and artistic works, but not utilitarian works. Patent and trade secret laws, on the other hand, have a long history of protecting useful physical devices but not writings or innovations embodied in textual form. Given the traditional bounds of both copyright and patent law, the hybrid nature of computer programs has made it difficult to integrate this new subject matter into the existing intellectual property regimes.

A second reason to study software and Internet law is that economic considerations, especially those deriving from network effects, complicate the application of existing laws to these industries. When the value of a product depends critically on its compatibility with other products, the absolute character of traditional intellectual property rights can block access to networks, thereby creating particularly serious impediments to competition and new challenges for antitrust law. In addition, firms need to plan their development and marketing strategies with network effects in mind; this may mean planning to give away some software or other digital products or services in order to establish market share, build brand, and take advantage of network effects. *See* Carl Shapiro and Hal Varian, Information Rules (1998).

A third reason to study software and Internet law is that the needs of these emerging industries are bringing about legal developments that once might have seemed unlikely or unthinkable. In the 1970s or 1980s it might have seemed absurd to think that firms could use licensing agreements to distribute mass-marketed information products. Developers of computer software started using "shrinkwrap" licenses for this purpose (that is, putting inside a box of packaged software a document that states, among other things, that the purchaser of the software is a licensee; that the purchaser's rights to use the software are restricted in certain ways; and that the purchaser's opening of the package or installing the software constitutes agreement to the terms of the "license"). Yet the ubiquity of such licenses in the software marketplace has paved the way for an increased use of licensing as a means to control distribution of commercially valuable information in other venues and has led to proposals for laws to validate mass-market licensing agreements. Other new legal regimes have been devised to respond to other perceived threatened market failures to information technology industries, one for the design of semiconductor chips and another to protect the contents of databases. New laws of this sort may best be understood in the information industry context out of which they arose.

The goal of this book is to provide students with a comprehensive treatment of the law of computer software and the Internet, with a particular focus on intellectual property, licensing, antitrust, tort, and constitutional law. By their nature, both software and especially Internet law will change rapidly. Indeed, the second edition differs radically from the first, particularly in the Internet chapters. We have greatly expanded our treatment of jurisdiction, Internet intellectual property disputes, and computer crime and added a new chapter on unauthorized access to Internet servers. Our goal in this book is not to freeze the development of the law at one particular point in time, but to provide a base of fundamental principles and issues on which subsequent developments will build. Those subsequent developments will be reflected in future supplements to this book and, perhaps more importantly, in our Web site, http://www.law.berkeley.edu/institutes/bclt/pubs/swbook/. We encourage those who use the book to refer to the Web site for up-to-date developments before planning their course of study.

Finally, as always, a book of this magnitude would not be possible without the assistance of many people. We would like to thank Ryan Garcia, Peter Huang, Rebecca Lubens, John Sasson, Leah Theriault, and Larry Trask for their work on the first edition; Colleen Chien, Laura Quilter, Chris Ridder, and Helaine Schweitzer for their work on the second edition; and Dan Burk, Stacey Dogan, Paul Heald, and several anonymous reviewers for their comments on earlier versions.

Mark A. Lemley
Peter S. Menell
Robert P. Merges
Pamela Samuelson
Berkeley, California

January 2003

Acknowledgments

We acknowledge the copyright owners of the following images and excerpts used in this volume with their permission (this list does not include works by the authors of this book):

Jane Kaufman Winn, The Emerging Law of Electronic Commerce.
J. Bradford De Long & A. Michael Froomkin, The Next Economy, in Internet Publishing and Beyond: The Economics of Digital Information and Intellectual Property (D. Hurley ed., 1998).
David Johnson & David Post, And How Shall the Net Be Governed? A Meditation on the Relative Virtues of Decentralized, Emergent Law, in Coordinating the Internet (Brian Kahin & James Keller, eds., 1997).
Bernadine Trompenaars, IVIR Report.
Dennis Karjala, The Protection of Operating Software Under Japanese Law, 12 Eur. Intell. Prop. Rev. 359 (1998).
Ward S. Bowman Jr., Patent and Antitrust Law (1973), reprinted by permission of the University of Chicago Press.
Lauren Fisher Kellner, Trade Dress Protection for Computer User Interface "Look and Feel", 61 U. Chi. L. Rev. 1011 (1994).
Michael Meurer, Price Discrimination, Personal Use and Piracy, 45 Buff. L. Rev. 845 (1997).
Andrea Migdal, Shrinkwrap Licenses Abroad, Journal of Internet Law (1999).

Note: We have selectively omitted citations and footnotes from cases without the use of ellipses or other indications. All footnotes are numbered consecutively within each chapter, except that footnotes in cases and other excerpts correspond to the actual footnote numbers in the published reports.

Many of the problems in this text are taken from actual cases. However, in many instances we have altered the facts of the case. In most cases we have also altered the names of the parties involved. In a few cases, however, particularly in the trademark and antitrust chapters, we felt that it was important to the problem to use the name of a product or company with which the reader would be familiar. Readers should understand that the problems are hypothetical in nature and that we do not intend them to represent the actual facts of any case or situation.

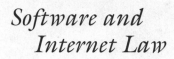

Software and Internet Law

1

SOFTWARE PROTECTION

Part I deals largely with the legal protection of computer software. Most of the chapters concern intellectual property protection for computer software, both in the United States and abroad. Other chapters deal with closely related subjects: the use of contracts and licenses to create alternative forms of protection for software, and the limits that antitrust law places on both intellectual property and contract protection.

The law of computer software is still evolving, though some clear patterns have emerged in the last decade. Part I approaches intellectual property protection in roughly chronological order, beginning with early efforts to protect computer programs as trade secrets. It traces the rise (and partial fall) of copyright law as a primary means of protecting the code and structure of computer programs. Part I then considers the more recent application of both patent and trademark law to protect various aspects of computer programs. Finally, after tracing this chronological development, Chapter 5 explores whether software would be better served by some sui generis form of intellectual property protection. Subsequent chapters explore recent trends toward "protecting" computer programs through contract law, the internationalization of software IP law, and the limits that antitrust law imposes on the software industry.

Because new cases are being decided and statutes created all the time in this field, the picture this book offers of computer software protection will necessarily be incomplete. But a number of principles in this field now seem well settled, and this Part explores those principles.

1

Trade Secret Protection

In the early days of computing, computer companies often bundled software "free" with the hardware they sold to customers to encourage them to buy and use the hardware. Other groups, especially in the government and academia, provided software for free because they were not motivated by profit. As the demand for computing grew, purchasers increasingly had specific needs that could only be filled with customized computer programs. While many companies developed these custom programs in-house, increasingly specialized software development firms realized that many companies needed the same basic sorts of data-processing programs. These firms undertook to develop more general-purpose software that could be sold to multiple clients. As programs became marketable commodities, rather than services provided to a particular client, the need for some sort of intellectual property protection became clear.

Today, the main contours of legal protection for computer technology are relatively clear. Copyright law protects computer software, and it is generally acknowledged that it is not acceptable behavior to make multiple copies of someone else's software without permission, with important exceptions and qualifications discussed later. Patent law protects computer hardware and new processes or "structures" embodied in computer software. But in the late 1970s and early 1980s, things were very different. Whether copyright protected computer programs at all was an open question, debated by the federal Commission on New Technological Uses of Copyright (CONTU)[1] and not finally resolved until the enactment of the 1980 Amendments to the Copyright Act. During this period, and even after the 1980 Amendments, courts disagreed over such fundamental issues as the copyrightability of object code and whether copyright protected computer programs against nonliteral infringement.

---

1. Final Report of the National Commission on New Technological Uses of Copyrighted Works (U.S. Gov't Printing Office 1978).

At the same time, a similar debate was raging in the federal courts over the patentability of computer software. The Supreme Court had held computer programs unpatentable in the 1972 decision of Gottschalk v. Benson, 409 U.S. 63 (1972), and it did not reopen the door *Gottschalk* closed until 1981. Even after 1981, the patentability of "pure" computer software was open to dispute. The issue was sufficiently clouded in 1994, for example, that the Federal Circuit took In re Alappat en banc in an attempt to clarify the standards for issuing software patents. 33 F.3d 1526 (Fed. Cir. 1994) (en banc). It was not until 1998 that the Federal Circuit unambiguously permitted patents on "pure" software. While software patents appear to be here to stay, their status has been uncertain until quite recently.

Against this backdrop, it was important for software vendors in the 1970s and early 1980s to establish their rights vis-à-vis users. One way for vendors to prevent users from freely copying their computer programs was to claim a program as a trade secret. Trade secrecy was a particularly viable alternative in the early days of the computer industry, because most computer software was customized and sold to a limited number of customers, generally large companies, rather than distributed in the mass market. Trade secrets have also been important in the computer industry as a means of protecting projects under development from being taken by departing employees.

As a mass market in software products became a reality, it became clear that software would need more legal protection than trade secrecy alone could provide. However, commercial software vendors did not abandon trade secrecy, even as they began to rely increasingly on copyright and patent protection. In part, this was due to the uncertainty described above, and in part, it is because trade secrecy offers some advantages to vendors that copyright and patent protection alone do not provide. This chapter explores the benefits and limitations of trade secret law as a form of legal protection for computer systems, and investigates the further challenges Internet distribution models pose for trade secret protection.

Today, every one of the 50 states protects trade secrets in one form or another. Improper use or disclosure of a trade secret is generally a common law tort. In the last century, the principal document setting forth the law of trade secrets was the Restatement of Torts, published in 1939. Sections 757 and 758 of the Restatement set forth basic principles of trade secret law, which were quickly adopted by courts in most states. Those sections (and accompanying comments) are reproduced in the statutory appendix, which the reader is encouraged to review now. The Restatement protected as a trade secret any information "used in one's business" which gives its owner "an opportunity to obtain an advantage over competitors who do not know or use it," so long as the information was in fact a secret. Restatement §757, comment *b*.

When the Restatement (Second) of Torts was published in 1979, the authors made the decision not to include sections 757 and 758 on the grounds that the law of trade secrets had developed into an independent body of law that no longer relied on general principles of tort law. The influence of the original Restatement remained, however, because it had been adopted by so many courts. The main principles of the Restatement of Torts relating to trade secrets have been adopted in the Restatement (Third) of Unfair Competition, published in 1994.

Beginning in 1979, the National Conference of Commissioners on Uniform State Laws promulgated a model state statute, the Uniform Trade Secrets Act, which differed in some respects from the common law. This Act has now been enacted (in one form or another) by 41 states and the District of Columbia. Because of its importance, we reproduce its primary provisions here.

Uniform Trade Secrets Act, with 1985 Amendments

§1. Definitions

As used in this [Act], unless the context requires otherwise:

(1) "Improper means" includes theft, bribery, misrepresentation, breach or inducement of a breach of a duty to maintain secrecy, or espionage through electronic or other means;

(2) "Misappropriation" means:

(i) acquisition of a trade secret of another by a person who knows or has reason to know that the trade secret was acquired by improper means; or

(ii) disclosure or use of a trade secret of another without express or implied consent by a person who

(A) used improper means to acquire knowledge of the trade secret; or

(B) at the time of disclosure or use, knew or had reason to know that his knowledge of the trade secret was

(I) derived from or through a person who had utilized improper means to acquire it;

(II) acquired under circumstances giving rise to a duty to maintain its secrecy or limit its use; or

(III) derived from or through a person who owed a duty to the person seeking relief to maintain its secrecy or limit its use; or

(C) before a material change of his [or her] position, knew or had reason to know that it was a trade secret and that knowledge of it had been acquired by accident or mistake. . . .

(4) "Trade secret" means information, including a formula, pattern, compilation, program, device, method, technique, or process, that:

(i) derives independent economic value, actual or potential, from not being generally known to, and not being readily ascertainable[2] by proper means by, other persons who can obtain economic value from its disclosure or use, and

(ii) is the subject of efforts that are reasonable under the circumstances to maintain its secrecy.

COMMENTS AND QUESTIONS

While there once was a question as to the availability of copyright and/or patent protection for computer technology, there is no longer. In view of this fact, to what extent should hardware and software manufacturers be able to rely on trade secret protection? Are there disadvantages to trade secret law as a means of protection for innovations in computer technology? On this point, see the Final Report of the Commission on New Technological Uses of Copyright (1978), at 34-35 [hereinafter CONTU Final Report]:

---

2. Some states, including California, do not include the "readily ascertainable" language in the definition of "trade secret." See Cal. Civ. Code §3426.1.—EDS.

Although many proprietors feel secure when using trade secrecy, there are several problems they must face with respect to its use in protecting programs. Because secrecy is paramount, it is inappropriate for protecting works that contain the secret and are designed to be widely distributed. Although this matters little in the case of unique programs prepared for large commercial customers, it substantially precludes the use of trade secrecy with respect to programs sold in multiple copies over the counter to small businesses, schools, consumers and hobbyists. Protection is lost when the secret is disclosed, without regard to the circumstances surrounding the disclosure. The lack of uniform national law in this area may also be perceived by proprietors as reducing the utility of this method of protection.

From the user's standpoint, there are additional drawbacks. Users must cover the seller's expenses associated with maintaining a secure system through increased prices. Their freedom to do business in an unencumbered way is reduced, since they may need to enter into elaborate nondisclosure contracts with employees and third parties who have access to the secrets and to limit that access to a very small number of people. Since secrets are by definition known to only a few people, there is necessarily a reduced flow of information in the marketplace, which hinders the ability of potential buyers to make comparisons and hence leads to higher prices.

Experts in the computer industry state that a further problem with respect to trade secrecy is that there is much human effort wasted when people do for themselves that which others have already done but are keeping secret.

In his dissent to the CONTU Report, Commissioner Hersey speculated (correctly, as it turns out) that permitting copyright protection for computer programs would not stop companies from relying on trade secret protection as well.

Does it make sense to permit both copyright and trade secret to protect the same works?

A. THE SECRECY REQUIREMENT

Even at a very early stage in the history of computer law, there was no serious question that computer hardware and software *could* be protected by the trade secrets laws. See, e.g., University Computing Co. v. Lykes-Youngstown Corp., 504 F.2d 518 (5th Cir. 1974) (plaintiff's computer system was a protectable trade secret). Cases such as *Lykes-Youngstown* involved a fairly typical trade secrets situation—people with access to a secret program still under development attempting to use or sell their own product based in part on the program. See also Cybertek Computer Products v. Whitfield, 203 U.S.P.Q. 1020 (Cal. Super. 1977).

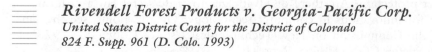

Rivendell Forest Products v. Georgia-Pacific Corp.
United States District Court for the District of Colorado
824 F. Supp. 961 (D. Colo. 1993)

FINESILVER, Chief Judge.
This is a case involving alleged misappropriations of trade secrets. This matter comes before the Court on the motion for summary judgment filed by the defen-

dants, Georgia-Pacific Corporation and Timothy L. Cornwell (collectively, "Georgia-Pacific") and the subsequent cross-motion for summary judgment by the plaintiff, Rivendell Forest Products, Ltd. ("Rivendell"). Jurisdiction is based on 28 U.S.C.A. §1332 (West 1992). The parties have fully briefed the matter.

For the reasons stated below, Georgia-Pacific's motion is GRANTED and Rivendell's is DENIED.

I. Background

Plaintiff Rivendell, now out of business, was a reload wholesaler in the lumber industry. It purchased milled lumber from Canadian mills and had that lumber shipped to and unloaded at any of about ten lumber yards it leased. Defendant Timothy Cornwell went to work for Rivendell in January 1987 and worked there until March 1990. While at Rivendell, Cornwell supervised employees using Rivendell's price quoting screen (the "Quote Screen") to quote prices to customers. He had no involvement in the development of the Quote Screen program's software. By using the Quote Screen, Rivendell was able to instantaneously quote to customers lumber prices, including freight, thereby allowing Rivendell to become more efficient in handling customer inquiries and eliminating the need for time-consuming manual calculations. Rivendell claims the "Quote Screen" system allowed it to be 20 to 30 times faster and to generate two to three times more sales, giving it a huge advantage over competitors, like Georgia-Pacific, who were still using much slower manual systems. Apparently in part to protect the Quote Screen system, Rivendell asked all employees to sign a confidentiality agreement in 1988 and Rivendell claims all employees did so. Rivendell further advised its employees that the business practices of Rivendell were trade secrets.

Defendant Georgia-Pacific is a supplier and wholesaler of lumber and lumber products. After Cornwell left Rivendell in March 1990, Georgia-Pacific hired Cornwell as marketing manager of Canadian lumber for Georgia-Pacific's distribution division. Rivendell alleges that soon after Cornwell arrived at Georgia-Pacific, he helped them to develop a "Quick Quote" system that borrowed heavily from trade secrets embodied in Rivendell's own Quote Screen. Rivendell alleges that shortly after Cornwell began work at Georgia-Pacific, he received an orientation from Georgia-Pacific employees Ken Porter and Dean Johnson. During the orientation, Cornwell was shown a demonstration of Georgia-Pacific's Noranda computer program. He allegedly stated he had a much better program, went to his office, and returned with a far more sophisticated program. Porter recalled in his deposition that the name "Rivendell" was mentioned in connection with the program. Rivendell cites this as both a clear violation of the confidentiality agreement Cornwell signed with Rivendell and evidence of a misappropriation of trade secrets.

Rivendell brought this suit two years after Cornwell left its employment, alleging tortious interference with contract, breach of contract, and theft of trade secrets. Rivendell alleges that while Cornwell worked for Rivendell, he had access to and gained knowledge of its highly sophisticated and customized computer software system. After reading a description of Georgia-Pacific's "Quick Quote" system, L.G. Broderick, Rivendell's former owner and chief executive officer, claimed the two systems were "virtually identical." . . .

III.   Misappropriation of Trade Secrets

Georgia-Pacific does not dispute that trade secrets may exist in the implementation or expression, that is, in the computer source code, of Rivendell's Quote Screen software. The questions we must address, then, are whether either Georgia-Pacific copied Rivendell's source code, or Rivendell's Quote Screen contained a protectible combination of concepts or ideas used by Georgia-Pacific. Rivendell has adduced no facts tending to show that Georgia-Pacific copied its source code. Rather, Rivendell relies on the inference that Georgia-Pacific must have misappropriated the trade secret it defines as the Quote Screen's unique method of integrating various concepts and ideas, even though those concepts and ideas were already in existence in the computerization of the lumber industry. . . .

In a letter to Georgia-Pacific's counsel, Rivendell's counsel outlined what Rivendell considered its trade secrets. Behind the Quote Screen, Rivendell stated, were several databases:

1.   Customer master file—all information on the customer
2.   All current credit information on the customer
3.   All current sales prices on all inventory items at all distribution facilities
4.   "Real-time" inventories on all items at all distribution facilities
5.   "Real-time" delivery status on all inventory "in transit" or on order with mills
6.   Current lowest truck transportation rates and mileage from all distribution facilities to the thousands of known customer or prospective customer destinations
7.   Bundle sizes of each item at all distribution facilities
8.   Weight per MBF of all items, at all yards, by specie[s] and dryness

Furthermore, interacting with these databases was software which made the following calculations:

1.   Automatic board footage conversions
2.   Automatic calculation of the dollar value per item, per thickness/width, and on entire inquiry
3.   Automatic calculation of FOB yard delivered customer destination prices
4.   Automatic calculation of weights per bundle, per thickness/width, and on entire inquiry
5.   Automatic calculation of inventory availability by item
6.   Automatic calculation of real dollar premium or discount to list price being offered by or to customer

Georgia-Pacific claims all of the concepts and ideas (e.g., the databases and functions performed) claimed by Rivendell as its trade secrets were known to and collectively already used by Georgia-Pacific before the alleged misappropriation and before Cornwell was hired. In particular, prior to Cornwell's hiring, two other divisions of Georgia-Pacific were using computer systems that, between them, performed nearly all the functions identified by Rivendell as constituting its trade secrets. Moreover, Georgia-Pacific has provided an exhibit showing that its Quick Quote system has in common with Rivendell's Quote Screen only two attributes:

display of bundle sizes and calculation of board-footage conversions. Bundle size is a constant set by the supplying mill; board-footage calculations are standard industry calculations necessary for selling lumber. Rivendell does not dispute Georgia-Pacific's assertion that both functions are "functional constraints of the lumber industry." Accordingly, neither function is a trade secret in and of itself. Georgia-Pacific concludes that the concepts and ideas embodied in Rivendell's Quote Screen were well known throughout the lumber industry and in particular by Georgia-Pacific. In any event, Georgia-Pacific claims, its own Quick Quote system used only two, unprotectable functions.

Rivendell's responses to this argument are generally unpersuasive. Rivendell first places great weight on Georgia-Pacific's failure to show that Georgia-Pacific's allegedly similar, publicly available systems were ever seen by Cornwell prior to developing the Quick Quote system. There is no relevance to such information. Where a defendant claims that a so-called "trade secret" is in fact public knowledge, it makes no difference whether the defendant obtained that knowledge from the plaintiff, the defendant's own information, or the public library. Rivendell next asks rhetorically why, if Georgia-Pacific had such computer capability, it had to hire Cornwell to "develop[] a new computer system." Such rhetorical questions do little to advance Rivendell's burden of going forward on summary judgment. Rivendell also states, incorrectly, that Georgia-Pacific's Quick Quote has more than two similar functions. Regardless, it is clear that protection could not be extended merely to the publicly available functions or elements of Rivendell's Quote Screen. Finally, Rivendell states that Georgia-Pacific has misunderstood Rivendell's trade secret claim, and that the trade secret is Rivendell's software, while the concepts and ideas embodied in the software are merely what makes it so important and valuable to Rivendell.

This argument puts us back where we began. Much of the confusion in Rivendell's arguments stems from the fact that when it argues for the existence of a trade secret, it points generally to its software, secure in the knowledge that some part of that software, whether or not appropriated by Georgia-Pacific, contains a trade secret. By contrast, when Rivendell argues that Georgia-Pacific has used its trade secrets, unable to claim the software has been copied or otherwise compromised, Rivendell focuses broadly on the concepts and ideas contained in the software.

But the concepts and ideas are not protectible, and by declaring its trade secret to be its software, Rivendell makes the unsupportable, contradictory suggestion that Georgia-Pacific appropriated its source code. However, Rivendell has long admitted and does not now deny that Georgia-Pacific did not copy its source code. Furthermore, Rivendell's expert examined the parties' source codes, display screens, file layouts, and detailed program designs without rendering an opinion as to any similarity between the programs. Fortunately, Rivendell ultimately returns to its true claim: the combination of these concepts and their integration into a single, workable and highly sophisticated computer software package is its trade secret. Georgia-Pacific's existing systems were not so expertly integrated as Rivendell's, and thus did Georgia-Pacific come to require the services of Cornwell.

In the terminology of trade secret law, Rivendell appears to be claiming not that Georgia-Pacific misappropriated its concepts and ideas, which are not protectible anyway, but their integration or implementation. Although Rivendell at times inconsistently disputes whether trade secret law contains such a distinction, the case law, including cases cited by Rivendell, is replete with it. . . .

The Tenth Circuit in Kodekey Electronics, Inc. v. Mechanex Corporation, 486 F.2d 449 (10th Cir. 1973) noted that "'novelty and invention are not requisite for a trade secret as they are for patentability. . . . The protection is merely against breach of faith and reprehensible means of learning anothers [sic] secret.'" *Id.* at 455, quoting Restatement of Torts §757, comment b at 6-7. When we say that Rivendell must show some special, protectible attribute of its combination of commonly available concepts and ideas, then, we are not saying that it must show them to be novel, but rather it must point to some justification for their secrecy. It would make little sense to allow individuals to throw veils of secrecy around the most common things, all in an attempt to establish their claim to a trade secret and then to prohibit others from appropriating their "secret." But "simply to assert a trade secret resides in some combination of otherwise known data is not sufficient, as the combination itself must be delineated with some particularity in establishing its trade secret status." Jostens, Inc. v. National Computer Systems, Inc., et al., 318 N.W.2d 691, 699 (Minn. 1982).

It is here that Rivendell fails to bear its summary judgment burden of designating specific facts showing genuine issues for trial on any element challenged by the motion. Its conclusory allegations that it holds a secret method of combining concepts and ideas for computerization of the lumber business, without more, do not establish issues of fact sufficient to defeat summary judgment. Rivendell offers no facts to suggest either that it had a protectible methodology for implementing the combination of concepts and ideas; that Georgia-Pacific appropriated any protected implementing methodology, rather than the unprotectible elements or functions common to both programs; or that Georgia-Pacific's resulting program is similar to Rivendell's in protected particulars. Rivendell makes only bare, unsupported allegations on every point, yet even these bare allegations are refuted with specificity by Georgia-Pacific.

B. Unauthorized Use of a Trade Secret

. . . Trade secret misappropriation can be established despite the lack of any copying or physical appropriation. Knowledge attained while working for the holder of the trade secret or memory alone are sufficient. However, contrary to what Rivendell told its employees, business practices hold at best a tenuous claim to being trade secrets. In Fishing Concepts v. Ross, et al., 226 U.S.P.Q. (BNA) 692, 695, 1985 WL 1549 (D. Minn. 1985), for example, the Court held that concepts regarding how to market Canadian fishing lodges were not trade secrets but merely "sound business practices." By Rivendell's failure either to make a claim that Cornwell physically appropriated Rivendell's source code; that he held in his mind Rivendell's source code and later gave it to Georgia-Pacific; that he relayed to Georgia-Pacific some relatively novel method of combining commonly known concepts; or that Georgia-Pacific ended up with a very similar system, Rivendell is unable to establish any more than that Cornwell took to Georgia-Pacific his knowledge that certain databases and business techniques lend themselves to speedy customer service. We could not hold as valid an agreement that absolutely prohibited a person from carrying on his or her career by taking generalized business knowledge from job to job. For these reasons and the reasoning we employed to find Rivendell failed to make out a claim for the existence of a trade secret, we find that nothing protectible was used. . . .

Rivendell Forest Products v. Georgia-Pacific Corp.
United States Court of Appeals for the Tenth Circuit
28 F.3d 1042 (10th Cir. 1994)

SETH, Circuit Judge.

. . . This computer software system in issue, Rivendell asserts, took it nine years to develop at a cost of nearly a million dollars. Mr. Cornwell worked for Rivendell in this development, knew it well, and had a significant role although he was not a computer expert. While working for Rivendell he was contacted by an executive of G.P., and two months thereafter was hired by G.P. with a job description to develop a new computer software system for G.P. This new system had become necessary with the decision by G.P. to consolidate its entire Distribution Division which consisted of about 100 distribution centers. G.P. had no need before the consolidation decision for such a new system, and there had been none in place. After the decision to consolidate G.P. contacted Cornwell and he was offered the task to develop a system quickly to permit the consolidation.

Rivendell's system was the only one Cornwell had been familiar with, and was the only one then in the industry which could provide immediate answers on all aspects of the customers' needs. He was not a computer expert, as mentioned, but immediately after being hired by G.P. he went to work on a computer system for G.P. This system was very soon developed, and it was for all practical purposes the same as the one at Rivendell.

. . . [I]n our view, the basic issue was and is whether the computer system of Rivendell was a "trade secret" appropriated by G.P. As mentioned, the authorities hold that what constitutes a trade secret and whether one exists, as claimed, is an issue of fact. Whether Rivendell's computer system was a "trade secret" was sought to be resolved in the summary judgment proceedings. . . .

. . . This issue as to whether there was a trade secret was complicated by the trial court's method for its factual examination of the asserted trade secret. The court required that the software system be examined bit by bit with the further requirement that Rivendell demonstrate protectability of its elements or some of them rather than the protectability of the software system as a whole. The trial court at page 11 of its order states the basic analysis it applied: "Without a showing that the two systems are similar in some protectable particular, there is no such clarity in Rivendell's claim." The authorities recognize that a trade secret such as the one here claimed can consist of a combination of elements which are in the public domain. This was held originally in Imperial Chemical Indus., Ltd. v. Nat'l Distillers & Chemical Corp., 342 F.2d 737 (2d Cir.). The same court again considered the issue in Integrated Cash Management Serv., Inc. v. Digital Transactions, Inc., 920 F.2d 171 (2d Cir.), and in substance adopted the following quotation from *Imperial Chemical Industries* that the case was covered by the operation of

> the general principle that a trade secret can exist in a combination of characteristics and components, each of which, by itself, is in the public domain, but the unified process, design and operation of which, in unique combination, affords a competitive advantage and is a protectable secret.

(Citations omitted.) See also Cybertek Computer Products, Inc. v. Whitfield, 203 U.S.P.Q. (BNA) 1020 (Cal. Super. Ct.).

The trial court also did not apply the doctrine described as follows in *Kode-key*, again:

> "Novelty and invention are not requisite for a trade secret as they are for patentability . . . (here a discussion of patent law). . . . The protection is merely against breach of faith and reprehensible means of learning another[']s secret."

. . . We must disagree with the trial court's first statement above that Rivendell had not shown it had a protectable methodology. In our view, the record demonstrates that such a methodology implementing the combination of concepts and ideas was shown. The record establishes the production by Rivendell's software system of immediate final pricing by the integration of the many computations as to size of lumber, type of lumber, location of the lumber, size of bundles, freight charges, time of delivery, and other factors to permit the immediate quotation of a total price. This was a basic factual demonstration of the integration obtained by the software, and it was a total package for immediate use. It was the only system in the industry which could accomplish this. G.P. had nothing comparable before the Defendant Cornwell was hired away from Rivendell. At best G.P. had a scattering of unrelated elements in the 100+ offices, and had no need for an integrated system until it decided to consolidate its offices. The evidence as to the quick development (four months) after Cornwell went to work for G.P. with the affidavits that the G.P. employees used Cornwell's ideas and the fact that Cornwell had never seen G.P.'s scattered systems before he developed G.P.'s Quick Quote integrated system were important because they demonstrated that he and G.P. relied entirely on Rivendell's system. He was not a computer expert at Rivendell or G.P. The position of G.P. and apparently of the trial court was that throughout G.P.'s large organization with many offices there could be found separately the elements of the Rivendell system. But the fact remained and the testimony of Gary Mote, a G.P. employee, showed there was no prior interest in G.P. to develop a new system. The company decision to integrate its many offices led to the hiring of Cornwell for the purpose of developing a new system; from the fact that the G.P. system was almost identical, the conclusion could well be reached at a trial that G.P. appropriated Rivendell's system.

The trial court in the above quotation refers to unprotected elements or functions, and so would examine the separate elements rather than the combination. We hold that the doctrine has been established that a trade secret can include a system where the elements are in the public domain, but there has been accomplished an effective, successful and valuable integration of the public domain elements and the trade secret gave the claimant a competitive advantage which is protected from misappropriation. . . .

The case must be REVERSED and REMANDED for further proceedings consistent with this opinion.

IT IS SO ORDERED.

COMMENTS AND QUESTIONS

1. Which opinion is more persuasive? Should Rivendell be entitled to protect the basic concepts of organizing a price quote against misappropriation by others? On the one hand, the District Court is surely correct that if Rivendell's ideas are not in fact secret, Georgia-Pacific is free to copy them. On the other hand, the Court of Appeals points out that basic concepts are protectable under trade secret law in certain combinations, if those combinations are not generally known in the industry. On this issue, compare Integrated Cash Mgmt. Serv. v. Digital Transactions, Inc., 920 F.2d 171 (2d Cir. 1990) (the combination of publicly known utility programs into a specific arrangement is protectable as a trade secret) with Comprehensive Technologies, Inc. v. Software Artisans, Inc., 3 F.3d 730 (4th Cir. 1993) (combination of known elements did not qualify as a trade secret where the particular combination was logically required and common in the industry). Cf. Vermont Microsystems Inc. v. Autodesk Inc., 88 F.3d 142 (2d Cir. 1996) (shading algorithm could be protected as a trade secret even though other developers had independently created similar algorithms, because defendant got value from using plaintiff's algorithm).

A related problem has to do with the identification of the trade secret before trial. The appellate court in *Rivendell* took a very flexible approach toward identifying exactly what constituted a trade secret. Other courts, by contrast, have refused to let plaintiffs simply identify the program containing the trade secret. They have demanded a detailed listing of what the plaintiff claims as a trade secret and why. See, e.g., IDX Systems v. Epic Systems, 285 F.3d 581 (7th Cir. 2002); ECT Int'l v. Zwerlein, 594 N.W.2d 479 (Wis. Ct. App. 1999); Cal. Code Civ. Proc. §2019(d) (requiring disclosure of a "trade secrets list" before trial).

2. Note the interaction between the definition of "trade secret" and the question of misappropriation. Like copyright law, trade secret law enters a gray area when what is alleged is not literal copying but similarity of general concepts. While such concepts may sometimes be protected, the case for misappropriation is usually not as clear as when computer code has been literally copied. We discuss this issue in more detail in Section C.

3. Suppose that Rivendell had widely sold its program to lumber companies but required each of its purchasers to keep the program confidential. Can Rivendell protect the basic ideas behind its program as trade secrets? Does your answer differ if what Rivendell seeks to protect is its literal object code? Does it matter that Rivendell's "basic ideas" are not contained in unintelligible 1s and 0s? That they may in fact be obvious to anyone using the program?

A closely related question involves attempts by the owners of information to "contract around" the requirement of secrecy. If the parties agree to treat a piece of information as secret, is the licensee bound not to use or disclose the information under contract principles regardless of whether it is in fact in the public domain? We discuss this issue in more detail in Chapter 6.

B.   DISCLOSURE OF TRADE SECRETS

While it was established early on that the secret elements of a computer program could be protected from misappropriation, computer companies that wanted to protect their intellectual property still had a problem. It is a fundamental principle of trade secret law that the thing protected must remain a secret. If the secret is disclosed to the public, protection is forever lost. Computer companies did not want to keep their hardware or software "secret"—they wanted to sell it![3] An influential early case held that they could do both. Key to this conclusion is the fact that software developers generally distribute their programs only in object code form and keep the source code and the design documentation as trade secrets, licensing them only rarely and only under agreements of confidentiality.

Data General Corp. v. Digital Computer Controls, Inc.
Delaware Court of Chancery
297 A.2d 433 (Del. Ch. 1971), aff'd, 297 A.2d 437 (Del. S. Ct. 1972)

MARVEL, Vice Chancellor:

Data General Corporation seeks an order preliminarily enjoining the defendant Digital Computer Controls from making use of claimed trade secrets allegedly contained in design drawings which accompany certain sales of plaintiff's Nova 1200 computer, defendant having acquired such a computer with accompanying drawings from one of plaintiff's customers. This is the decision of the Court on plaintiff's motion for a preliminary injunction as well as on defendants' cross-motion for summary judgment of dismissal of the present action.

The relevant facts thus far adduced are as follows: During the past several years plaintiff has developed and marketed successfully small general-purpose computers to which they have given the name Nova, a large part of plaintiff's research and development budget for the past several years having been allocated to the development of such small computers, which, the parties agree, are the only ones of their type presently being profitably marketed, there having been no device on the market comparable to plaintiff's machines until defendant's entry on the scene.

When a sale of a Nova 1200 computer is made, plaintiff makes available at no extra cost to those customers who wish to do their own maintenance the design or logic drawings of the device sold, in this case a Nova 1200 computer. Such type of maintenance has been found to be desired by some customers in order to avoid

---

3. Of course, some computer code is written for internal use only, and that code can be protected as a secret fairly easily, since it need not leave the company.

periods of unproductive delay while waiting for repairs to be made by plaintiff's trained personnel.

Design drawings made available to customers are furnished subject to the terms of a non-disclosure clause contained in a paper which accompanies a purchase agreement. Furthermore, all drawings bear a legend to the effect that they contain proprietary information of the plaintiff which is not to be used by a purchaser for manufacturing purposes. However, the Nova 1200 is not patented, and its design drawings have not been copyrighted.

In April, 1971, the defendant Ackley, the president of Digital, purchased for his company from a customer of Data General, namely Mini-Computer Systems, Inc., a Nova 1200 computer which the latter had earlier acquired from plaintiff. Although the exact circumstances surrounding such sale are not entirely clear on the present record, the corporate defendant's president, in consummating such purchase, acquired a set of design drawings of the Nova 1200, said drawings having been furnished to MiniComputer by the plaintiff in order to facilitate maintenance by the former of its Nova 1200's. The corporate defendant thereafter proceeded to use such design drawings as a pattern for the construction of a competing machine which it is now about to market, the corporate defendant's president conceding that only minor changes have been made in the basic design of plaintiff's device in the course of the development of defendant's comparable computer.

I.

[The court held that plaintiff's trade secret claims are not preempted by the federal intellectual property or antitrust laws.]

II.

Defendants' other arguments are accordingly based on the law of trade secrets. Thus, in order for the plaintiff to establish its right to relief here, it must demonstrate (1) the existence of a trade secret and that the corporate defendant has either (2) received the information within the confines of a confidential relationship and proposes to misuse the information in violation of such relationship, or (3) that the corporate defendant improperly received the information in question in such a manner that its confidential nature should have been known to it and that it nonetheless proposes to misuse such information.

Trade secrets have been defined in Restatement, Torts §757, comment b. as follows:

> A trade secret may consist of any formula, pattern, device or compilation of information which is used in one's business, and which gives him an opportunity to obtain an advantage over competitors who do not know or use it.

Defendants insist, however, that plaintiff has not maintained that degree of secrecy which will preserve its right to relief, either by publicly selling an article alleged to contain a trade secret, or by failing to restrict access to the design drawings for its device, arguing that matters of common knowledge in an industry may not be claimed as trade secrets.

It has been recognized in similar cases that even though an unpatented article, device or machine has been sold to the public, and is therefore subject to examination and copying by anyone, the manner of making the article, device or machine may yet constitute a trade secret until such a copy has in fact been made, Schulenburg v. Signatrol, Inc., 33 Ill.2d 379, 212 N.E.2d 865, and Tabor v. Hoffman, N.Y., 118 N.Y. 30, 23 N.E. 12.

Defendants contend, however, that the issuance by plaintiff of copies of design drawings to its customers was made without safeguards designed properly to maintain the secrecy requisite to the existence of a trade secret. In other words, it is contended that plaintiff's attempts to maintain secrecy merely consisted of (1) not giving copies of the design drawings to those customers who did not need them for maintenance of their computer, (2) obtaining agreements not to disclose the information from those customers who were given copies of the drawings, and (3) printing a legend on the drawings which contained the allegedly confidential information which identified the drawing as proprietary information, the use of which was restricted. Plaintiff argues, however, that disclosure of the design drawings to purchasers of the computer is necessary properly to maintain its device, that such disclosure was required by the very nature of the machine, and that reasonable steps were taken to preserve the secrecy of the material released. I conclude at this preliminary stage of the case that it cannot be held as a matter of law that such precautions were inadequate, a factual dispute as to the adequacy of such precautions having clearly been raised. Defendants' motion for summary judgment must accordingly be denied.

Finally, I am satisfied that if plaintiff were to prevail at final hearing, it would only be entitled to injunctive relief during that undetermined period of time which would be required for defendants substantially to reproduce to plaintiff's device without its accompanying drawings. Such period of time would, on the present record, vary according to the number of man hours devoted to so-called reverse engineering. Thus, the granting of a preliminary injunction at this juncture would grant plaintiff all the relief it might hope ultimately to obtain after final hearing. Compare Thomas C. Marshall, Inc. v. Holiday Inn, Inc., 40 Del.Ch. 77, 174 A.2d 27. In addition, while plaintiff has presented evidence of its attempts to preserve the secrecy of the alleged secrets it now seeks to have protected by injunction, it has not adduced sufficient evidence to establish that likelihood of ultimate success on final hearing which would entitle it to the issuance of a preliminary injunction.

On notice, an order may be presented denying defendants' motion for summary judgment as well as plaintiff's motion for a preliminary injunction, which order shall also include a provision that all drawings issued by the corporate defendant in connection with the sale of its Nova-type computer contain a restrictive legend of the type now set forth on plaintiff's drawings here in issue.

COMMENTS AND QUESTIONS

1. For background on Data General and the development of the Nova computer, see Tracy Kidder, The Soul of a New Machine (1981).

2.   The plaintiff in *Data General* sold over 500 Nova computers to the general public. Each purchaser who requested one got a copy of the "confidential" design drawings. Why are these drawings still considered a secret? Does widespread disclosure compromise the secrecy claim at some point, even though all disclosures are made under an agreement of confidentiality? This issue arises frequently today in the software industry. As computers have become ubiquitous in business and quite common in the home, the numbers of "secret" programs in circulation may be counted in the millions rather than in the hundreds. *Data General* implicitly concludes that even a relatively widespread disclosure to customers does not compromise the secrecy of the computer design. For cases addressing this issue in the context of computer software, compare Management Science of Am. v. Cyborg Sys., Inc., 1977-1 Trade Cas. (CCH) ¶61,472 (N.D. Ill. 1977) (distribution of 600 copies of a program under a confidentiality agreement did not destroy secrecy) with Young Dental Mfg. Co. v. Q3 Special Prods., Inc., 891 F. Supp. 1345 (E.D. Mo. 1995) (characterizing as "completely frivolous" plaintiff's claim that its publicly sold software was a trade secret).

As we shall see, customers who buy a product on the open market are entitled to break it apart to see how it works. This process is called "reverse engineering" the product. Trade secret law does not protect owners against legitimate purchasers who discover the secret through reverse engineering. But does the possibility that a product might be reverse engineered foreclose *any* trade secret protection? At least one court has said no. In Data General Corp. v. Grumman Systems Support Corp., 825 F. Supp. 340, 359 (D. Mass. 1993), the court upheld a jury's verdict that Grumman had misappropriated trade secrets contained in object code form in Data General's computer program, despite the fact that many copies of the program had been sold on the open market. The court reasoned: "With the exception of those who lawfully licensed or unlawfully misappropriated MV/ADEX, Data General enjoyed the exclusive use of MV/ADEX. Even those who obtained MV/ADEX and were able to *use* MV/ADEX were unable to discover its trade secrets because MV/ADEX was distributed only in its object code form, which is essentially unintelligible to humans." The court noted that Data General took significant steps to preserve the secrecy of MV/ADEX, requiring that all users of the program sign licenses agreeing not to disclose the program to third parties.

The *Data General* cases suggest that reasonable efforts to protect the secrecy of an idea contained in a commercial product—such as locks, black boxes, or the use of unreadable code—may suffice to maintain trade secret protection even after the product itself is widely circulated. Does this result make sense? For a different approach, see Videotronics v. Bend Electronics, 564 F. Supp. 1471, 1476 (D. Nev. 1983) (software cannot be a trade secret if it is publicly distributed and can be readily copied).

3.   One way in which computer software cases may be distinguished from other trade secret cases has to do with the nature of what is being distributed. While a particular computer program may be widely distributed, in fact all that is sold to the consumer is a disk containing object code, which is virtually impossible for humans to read without machine assistance.[4] Because of this, computer soft-

---

4. To be sure, it is possible to reverse-engineer object code in some cases to create a kind of rough estimate of what must have been in the original source code. The process, however, is demanding and time-consuming even for expert programmers. See, e.g., Andrew Johnson-Laird, Reverse Engineering of

ware is in some sense unlike a physical product whose design is evident to the casual observer. Even after it is publicly distributed, object code is meaningless to the casual observer. Only a complex process of reverse engineering (sometimes called "disassembly" or "decompilation") can enable the user to decipher the source code that was originally written for the program.

Should it matter that a computer program is distributed only in object code form? Consider the following case, in which the defendant was accused of misappropriating a computer program in object code form.

> The source code can and does qualify as a trade secret. . . .
> Whether the object code is a trade secret is a more difficult question.[4] Atkinson first contends that the object code cannot be a trade secret because it does not derive independent economic value from its secrecy, and therefore fails the first definitional requirement of a trade secret. This argument has no merit. Trandes generates most of its revenues by providing computer services. . . . Armed with a copy of the object code, an individual would have the means to offer much the same engineering services as Trandes. . . .
> Atkinson next argues that the object code cannot be a trade secret because Trandes did not keep it secret. . . . Atkinson asserts that the Tunnel System has been widely disclosed as a mass-marketed product and that its existence and its abilities are not secret. [The court concluded that the object code remained secret because it had only been distributed to two customers, and both of them signed licenses agreeing to keep the program a secret].

Trandes Corp. v. Guy F. Atkinson Co., 996 F.2d 655, 663-664 (4th Cir. 1993). Consider the court's footnote. Can object code be a trade secret, if it can easily be duplicated (whether or not the copier understands what he is copying)? Is the plaintiff in this case really trying to leverage copyright protection out of a trade secret claim?

Why might a company want to maintain both its source code and its object code as a secret?

Some companies may want to distribute not only their object code but also their source code. For example, if a company is in the business of selling software components for reuse by others, it needs to transfer not just the executable code, but at least that portion of the source code that will permit the buyer to build a truly inter-operable component. *See* Mark A. Lemley & David W. O'Brien, Encouraging Software Reuse, 49 Stan. L. Rev. 255, 271-272 (1997). Still other companies distribute their source code in order to encourage users to help them improve it. For example, the "open source" movement operates on the belief that making source code available to everyone produces better code as users cooperate to improve the product. Trade secret protection is much harder to obtain if the source code is freely transferred.

Software: Separating Legal Mythology from Actual Technology, 5 Software L.J. 331, 342-343 (1992) ("[d]eciphering computer-executable programs is extremely tedious and error-prone").

4. This case presents an unusual set of facts. In the ordinary case, the owner of trade secret computer software will maintain the secrecy of the source code but freely distribute the object code. See, e.g., Q-Co Indus. v. Hoffman, 625 F. Supp. 608, 617 (S.D.N.Y. 1985) (program secret where source code secret, even though object code not secret). In such cases, the owner of the software cannot claim trade secret protection for the object code because its disclosure to the public destroyed its secrecy. In this case, however, Trandes maintained the secrecy of the source code *and* the object code, as we explain below.

4. Trade secrets may be publicly disclosed (through publication or the sale of a product) by someone other than the trade secret owner. Commonly, this occurs when someone other than the owner has independently developed or discovered the secret. Call the first trade secret "owner" *A*, and the independent developer *B*. *A* has no control over what *B* does with her independent discovery; if she chooses to disclose the secret, she defeats not only her rights to trade secret protection, but *A*'s rights as well.

Suppose that *B* had not developed the secret independently of *A* but in fact had stolen it from *A*. What happens if *B* publishes the secret—can *A* still protect it? If so, what happens to *C*, who begins using the secret after reading the publication? This issue was addressed in Religious Technology Center v. Lerma, 908 F. Supp. 1362 (E.D. Va. 1995). In that case, the Church of Scientology sued (among others) The Washington Post, which had quoted from part of the church's confidential "scriptures." The court concluded that the fact that the scriptures were posted on a Usenet newsgroup for 10 days defeated any claim of trade secrecy:

> [For 10 days, the documents] remained potentially available to the millions of Internet users around the world.
>
> As other courts who have dealt with similar issues have observed, "posting works to the Internet makes them generally known" at least to the relevant people interested in the news group. Once a trade secret is posted on the Internet, it is effectively part of the public domain, impossible to retrieve. Although the person who originally posted a trade secret on the Internet may be liable for trade secret misappropriation, the party who merely down loads Internet information cannot be liable for misappropriation because there is no misconduct involved in interacting with the Internet.

Id. 908 F. Supp. at 1368. See also American Red Cross v. Palm Beach Blood Bank Inc., 143 F.3d 1407 (11th Cir. 1998) (holding that a donor list could not be a trade secret because the plaintiff posted it on a computer bulletin board, destroying its confidentiality); Weigh Sys. South v. Mark's Scales & Equip., 68 S.W.3d 299 (Ark. 2002) (data held disclosed because some of it could be found on the Internet, and plaintiff had not protected its passwords).

PROBLEM

Problem 1-1. Microsoft Corp.'s Windows operating system has become an industry standard for personal computer operating systems. Microsoft sells tens of millions of copies of Windows each year; there are estimated to be upwards of 125 million copies in circulation worldwide. Further, Windows is normally "pre-installed" on most new personal computers, so that PC purchasers automatically purchase the operating system as well. Assuming that Microsoft has taken reasonable efforts to require both hardware manufacturers and end users to keep the program confidential, is Microsoft entitled to protect Windows as a trade secret? What efforts would be "reasonable" under these circumstances?

C. MISAPPROPRIATION

Misappropriation of trade secrets can occur in one of two ways: where the defendant acquires the trade secret through improper means, such as by theft or some forms of espionage; and where the defendant uses or discloses the trade secret in breach of a confidential relationship, usually but not necessarily involving a contractual agreement limiting the use of the secret. The legal issues concerning misappropriation are well established in the general law of trade secrets; thus we do not cover them in detail here. For a good summary with a focus on cases in the computer industry, see Gale R. Peterson, Trade Secrets in an Information Age, 32 Hous. L. Rev. 385 (1995). However, there are certain problems that arise specifically in the context of computer software.

Comprehensive Technologies International, Inc. v. Software Artisans, Inc.
United States Court of Appeals for the Fourth Circuit
3 F.3d 730 (4th Cir. 1993)

WILLIAMS, Circuit Judge:

Comprehensive Technologies International, Inc. (CTI), brought this action for copyright infringement against former employees Dean Hawkes, Igor A. Filippides, Randall L. Sterba, Richard T. Hennig, and David R. Bixler (the Defendant employees). CTI also named as defendants Alvan S. Bixler and Software Artisans, Inc. (SA), a corporation formed by Alvan Bixler and several of the Defendant employees shortly after their departure from CTI. CTI contended that "Transend," a computer program developed by the Defendants, infringed upon the copyrights CTI held in its "Claims Express" and "EDI Link" computer programs. CTI appended numerous state law causes of action, including trade secret misappropriation, breach of confidentiality, and breach of contract. CTI also alleged that Hawkes breached his covenant not to compete with CTI by performing services for SA, soliciting CTI's customers, and hiring CTI's former employees. After a bench trial, the district court entered judgment for the Defendants on all counts.

CTI now appeals. . . .

With regard to CTI's copyright infringement and trade secret misappropriation claims, we affirm the judgment for the Defendants. We agree, however, with CTI's contention that Hawkes's covenant not to compete is enforceable. We therefore vacate the judgment for Hawkes on CTI's claim for breach of contract, and remand for the district court to determine whether Hawkes has breached his covenant not to compete. . . .

I. Factual Background

CTI, a California corporation with its principal place of business in Chantilly, Virginia, is engaged in defense related services. CTI was founded in 1980 by Celestino Beltran, who at the time of trial served as CTI's president, chief executive officer, and chairman of the board of directors. By 1988 Beltran was hoping to diversify CTI's operations into newly emerging technologies. At that time, Beltran's next door neighbor, Alvan Bixler, worked for the Electronic Data Interchange Association (EDIA). Electronic data interchange, or EDI, is the computer-to-computer transmission of business transactions in proprietary or standard formats. After discussing EDI with Alvan Bixler and conducting his own research on the subject, Beltran concluded that EDI technology presented substantial growth potential in the small business market.

With the approval of his board of directors, Beltran established a Software Products Group and designated Dean Hawkes to lead it. Hawkes was given the responsibility to design, develop, test, and market software that would enable clients to process and transmit data through EDI technology. CTI selected Igor Filippides as the Software Products Group's Acting Vice President for Sales and gave him primary responsibility for marketing the software. Other members of the Software Products Group included Sterba, Hennig, and David Bixler, who together wrote the actual software. To boost the marketability of its products, CTI obtained an agreement from EDIA to assist CTI in the development of its software. Pursuant to that agreement, Alvan Bixler collaborated with CTI as a consultant on EDI technology.

Each of the Defendant employees except Hawkes signed CTI's standard Confidentiality and Proprietary Information Agreement. Under the Agreement, each employee agreed not to disclose or use, directly or indirectly, during his employment and for three years thereafter any confidential, proprietary, or software-related information belonging to CTI. The Agreement specifically identified the Claims Express and EDI Link projects as confidential. Although Hawkes did not sign a Confidentiality and Proprietary Information Agreement, he did sign an Employment Agreement that contained similar but more restrictive provisions. In addition to promising confidentiality, Hawkes agreed that during the term of his employment he would not compete with CTI, solicit CTI's customers, or employ CTI's current or former employees.

The Software Products Group undertook to develop two software packages for personal computers. The first, Claims Express, is an electronic medical billing system. Claims Express transmits information that conforms to two specific insurance claims forms, the "HFCA 1500" and the "UB 82." The program has been successfully marketed. CTI's second software package, EDI Link, is not specific to the health care industry. It is designed to permit users to create generic forms, enter data on the forms electronically, test that data for errors, and store both the forms and the data on a computer. Although CTI expended substantial effort on EDI Link, at the time of trial the program had not been completed and had never been sold or marketed. Trial testimony indicated that between 35 and 85 percent of the program had been completed.

In February 1991, all of the Defendant employees left CTI. Hawkes executed a formal Termination Agreement with CTI. In that Agreement, Hawkes agreed to rescind his Employment Agreement in return for $50,000 and more than $20,000 worth of equipment. Hawkes also agreed that he would not disclose or use CTI's confidential information, and that, for a period of one year following his departure, he would not (1) compete with CTI, (2) solicit CTI's customers, or (3) hire CTI's employees.

In April 1991, the Defendants incorporated Software Artisans, Inc., located in Fairfax, Virginia. By July 1991, SA had developed and begun to market its own program called Transend. According to its User's Manual, Transend creates a "paperless office environment" by enabling its users to process business forms on a computer. Transend is similar to Claims Express and EDI Link in that it is designed to prepare forms for transmission by EDI. Transend permits the user to input data, check the data for errors, and prepare the data for transmission by EDI. . . .

III.

. . . In denying CTI's claim for trade secret misappropriation, the district court found that CTI did not possess any trade secrets and that, even if CTI did possess trade secrets, the Defendants had not misappropriated them. The court found no evidence that CTI's purported trade secrets—the organization of Claims Express and EDI Link, the database access techniques of the two programs, and the unique identifiers of the two programs—derived independent economic value from not being generally known or were not readily ascertainable by proper means. Consequently, the court concluded that CTI's purported trade secrets failed to satisfy all of the elements necessary to prove a trade secret. The district court also concluded that the Defendants did not "copy" any trade secrets, implying that Defendants did not "use" or otherwise misappropriate them. . . .

CTI reads the district court's opinion as ruling as a matter of law that the organization of a database, its database access techniques, and its unique identifiers could not constitute trade secrets because each of their composite elements was in the public domain. CTI argues vociferously (and correctly) that although a trade secret cannot subsist in information in the public domain, it can subsist in a *combination* of such information, as long as the combination is itself secret. According to CTI, each of its alleged trade secrets is just such a combination of publicly available information.

In making this argument, CTI misreads the district court's opinion. The district court did not rule that unique combinations or arrangements of publicly available information cannot receive protection as trade secrets. Rather, the district court held that CTI failed to present any evidence that its database organization, its access techniques, and its identifiers were not themselves publicly available. The court specifically found that the arrangement and interaction of the functions of Claims Express and EDI Link were "common to all computer programs of this type." Information that is generally known cannot qualify as a trade secret. Consequently, the district court did not misapply the law; it simply found insufficient evidence to support CTI's claim. The district court correctly concluded that CTI failed to prove that the organization, database access techniques, and identifiers of CTI's software constituted trade secrets.

Even if CTI had demonstrated that these items constituted trade secrets, CTI has not convinced us that the district court clearly erred in finding that the Defendants did not misappropriate any of CTI's alleged trade secrets. CTI points to the short development time and the complete lack of design documentation for Transend as strong circumstantial evidence of misappropriation. Although this evidence does raise some suspicions, Defendants provided a colorable explanation for the absence of design documentation. First, Defendant's expert, Dr. Rotenstreich, testified that it was not atypical for small software companies to neglect to prepare extensive design documentation. Second, Sterba testified that he and the others disliked the amount of paperwork involved in documenting their designs, that they preferred to use a "whiteboard" for their design work, and that they placed much of the information that would ordinarily appear in design documentation in the code itself. In light of this testimony, CTI's circumstantial evidence is not enough to convince us that the district court clearly erred in finding that the Defendants did not copy (or "use") any of CTI's.alleged trade secret information.

We find instructive the Fifth Circuit's decision in Plains Cotton Cooperative Ass'n v. Goodpasture Computer Service, 807 F.2d 1256 (5th Cir. 1987):

> [T]he trade secrets allegedly involved here are particular implementations of software functions. . . . [T]he misuse of these implementations can occur only through copying the particular software designs on a sufficiently specific level. . . . [The trade secrets] are matters of design, where *the issue of misuse boils down to evidence of copying.* If no copying occurred on any level, appellant cannot demonstrate that appellees misused the trade secrets they allegedly possessed. . . .
>
> . . . If appellees did not in any way "copy" any part of appellant's protected idea or expression, then appellant cannot demonstrate trade secret misappropriation any more than it can show copyright infringement.

(Emphasis added). As the district court noted, CTI produced insufficient evidence that Transend copied any unique designs or functions of either Claims Express or EDI Link. Without proof of copying at the functional (or ideational) level, CTI has not proved that Defendants "used" and thereby misappropriated any of its trade secret information. The district court correctly concluded that the Defendants did not misappropriate any trade secret information belonging to CTI.

COMMENTS AND QUESTIONS

1. Compare the result in Integrated Cash Mgmt. Serv. v. Digital Transactions, Inc., 920 F.2d 171 (2d Cir. 1990):

> As discussed above, the district court properly found a cognizable trade secret in the manner in which ICM combined various non-secret utility programs to create its software product. The court further found that the defendants made use of this information in designing similar software. Newlin and Vafa "ma[de] use of information learned while at ICM concerning which functions and relationships among the modules would and would not work in the generic program." Contrary to defendants-appellants' suggestion, the court's statement that Vafa "was certainly capable of writing the source code in his own right" does not contradict the finding that Vafa and Newlin, in fact, used ICM's trade secrets. ICM is, therefore, entitled to injunctive relief.

Id. at 174-175. Is this result consistent with *CTI*? With *Plains Cotton*? In particular, consider the role of circumstantial evidence of misappropriation. Should the court in *CTI* have presumed misappropriation from the defendants' short product development time? From their failure to produce a "paper trail" documenting their software development efforts? On the other hand, should the court presume independent development if there is no evidence the defendants took documents or disks with them when they left? What incentives would each presumption create for strategic behavior on the part of parties who might be involved in litigation?

2. In both *CTI* and *ICM*, the alleged trade secret at issue was not the source or object code of the computer program itself, but certain high-level design features of the program (its "architecture"). Suppose that, rather than using what they had learned of the architecture of the program while employed by the company, ICM's former employees had copied the object code of the program altogether. (Leave aside for the moment questions of copyright infringement and consider only the trade secrets issue.) Would they be liable for misappropriating the trade secrets contained in the program architecture on the grounds that copying the program in its entirety necessarily copied the architecture? Or would the fact that the object code was publicly disclosed protect them from liability? How would the courts in *Trandes* and the *Data General* cases answer this question? Does the answer suggest a problem with relying on trade secrecy to protect computer programs?

3. Employees inevitably learn a great deal about a business while on the job. They may learn the trade secrets of their employer, but they may also learn basic information such as how many people it takes to make a product, who is likely to buy the product, where to advertise, etc. Further, employees develop personal relationships with vendors, customers, and others that are immensely useful in business. For this reason, many employers would like to prevent their employees from competing against them at all. Such employers often ask their employees to sign noncompetition agreements, which prevent the employee from competing with his former employer for customers for a set period of time. *Comprehensive Technologies* involved such an agreement. Despite finding (above) that the employees took no trade secrets, the court enforced an agreement signed by one of the employees, Dean Hawkes. The agreement provided that for a period of 12 months after he left CTI, Hawkes would not

> engage directly or indirectly in any business within the United States (financially as an investor or lender or as an employee, director, officer, partner, independent contractor, consultant or owner or in any other capacity calling for the rendition of personal services or acts of management, operation or control) which is in competition with the business of CTI. For purposes of this Agreement, the "business of CTI" shall be defined as the design, development, marketing, and sales of CLAIMS EXPRESS and EDI LINK type PC-based software with the same functionality and methodology. . . .

The court stated the general legal standard governing covenants not to compete:

> Virginia has established a three-part test for assessing the reasonableness of restrictive employment covenants. Under the test, the court must ask the following questions:
>
>> (1) Is the restraint, from the standpoint of the employer, reasonable in the sense that it is no greater than is necessary to protect the employer in some legitimate business interest?
>> (2) From the standpoint of the employee, is the restraint reasonable in the sense that it is not unduly harsh and oppressive in curtailing his legitimate efforts to earn a livelihood?
>> (3) Is the restraint reasonable from the standpoint of a sound public policy?

Blue Ridge Anesthesia & Critical Care, Inc. v. Gidick, 239 Va. 369, 389 S.E.2d 467, 469 (Va. 1990). If a covenant not to compete meets each of these standards of reasonableness, it must be enforced. As a general rule, however, the Virginia courts do not look favorably upon covenants not to compete, and will strictly construe them against the employer. The employer bears the burden of demonstrating that the restraint is reasonable.

Id. at 738. The court found that Hawkes' agreement, which prevented him from competing with CTI anywhere in the United States, was reasonable because CTI had offices, clients, or prospects in many (though not all) states throughout the country. Further, the court noted that

> . . . As the individual primarily responsible for the design, development, marketing and sale of CTI's software, Hawkes became intimately familiar with every aspect of CTI's operation, and necessarily acquired information that he could use to compete with CTI in the marketplace. When an employee has access to confidential and trade secret information crucial to the success of the employer's business, the employer has a strong interest in enforcing a covenant not to compete because other legal remedies often prove inadequate. It will often be difficult, if not impossible, to prove that a competing employee has misappropriated trade secret information belonging to his former employer. *Eden Hannon,* 914 F.2d 556 at 561 (applying Virginia law). On the facts of this case, we conclude that the scope of the employment restrictions is no broader than necessary to protect CTI's legitimate business interests.

Id. at 739. There seems to be no question in the court's mind that none of the defendants misappropriated any CTI trade secrets, infringed any copyrights, or otherwise "took" anything belonging to CTI in starting Software Artisans. Why didn't that dispose of the case? What social purpose is served by enjoining former employees from pursuing their livelihood?

Some courts have limited the enforcement of noncompetition agreements to situations where trade secrets are likely to be used or disclosed if an employee is allowed to compete. The New York Court of Appeals, for example, took the following view:

> Undoubtedly judicial disfavor of these covenants is provoked by "powerful considerations of public policy which militate against sanctioning the loss of a man's livelihood" (Purchasing Assoc. v. Weitz . . .). Indeed, our economy is premised on the competition engendered by the uninhibited flow of services, talent and ideas. Therefore, no restrictions should fetter an employee's right to apply to his own best advantage the skills and knowledge acquired by the overall experience of his previous employment. This includes those techniques which are but "skillful variations of general processes known to the particular trade" (Restatement, Agency 2d, §396, Comment b; see, also, Customer List—as Trade Secret-Factors, Ann., 28 ALR3d 7).
>
> Of course, the courts must also recognize the legitimate interest an employer has in safeguarding that which has made his business successful and to protect himself against deliberate surreptitious commercial piracy. Thus restrictive covenants will be enforceable to the extent necessary to prevent the disclosure or use of trade secrets or confidential customer information (e.g., Lepel High Frequency Labs. v. Capita, 278 NY 661; Carpenter & Hughes v. De Joseph, 10 NY2d 925). In addition injunctive relief may be available where an employee's services are unique or extraordinary and the covenant is reasonable (e.g., Lumley v. Wagner, 42 Eng Rep 687; Frederick Bros.

Artists Corp. v. Yates, 271 App Div 69, *aff'd* 296 NY 820). This latter principle has been interpreted to reach agreements between members of the learned professions (e.g., Karpinski v. Ingrasci, 28 NY2d 45).

Reed Roberts Assoc. v. Strauman, 40 N.Y.2d 303, 353 N.E.2d 590 (N.Y. Ct. App. 1976).

Other states, notably California, have an even more restrictive rule. For example, Cal. Bus. & Prof. Code sec. 16600 provides that "every contract by which anyone is restrained from engaging in a lawful profession . . . is to that extent void." California courts have interpreted this statute to bar noncompetition agreements in employee contracts but to permit such agreements if they are ancillary to the sale of a business, so long as the terms of the agreement are "reasonable." See Monogram Indus., Inc. v. SAR Indus., Inc., 64 Cal. App. 3d 692, 134 Cal. Rptr. 714, 718 (1976). Further, while California courts will not enforce a noncompetition agreement, they will prevent departing employees from using or disclosing their former employer's trade secrets. See State Farm Mutual Automobile Ins. Co. v. Dempster, 344 P.2d 821 (Cal. App. 1959); Gordon v. Landau, 49 Cal. 2d 690, 321 P.2d 456 (Cal. 1958).

4. Covenants not to compete are enforceable in most jurisdictions only if they are reasonably limited in time and geographic scope. How should these restrictions apply in the context of the Internet? Is there any way to impose an effective noncompetition agreement on an employee of an Internet company that is less than worldwide? See National Business Servs. v. Wright, 2 F. Supp.2d 701 (E.D. Pa. 1998) (mobile nature of Internet business justified nationwide restriction). Some courts have taken the dynamic nature of the Internet into account, concluding that a reasonable period of time is shorter in a fast-paced industry than in a more traditional industry. See, e.g., EarthWeb, Inc. v. Schlack, 71 F. Supp.2d 299 (S.D.N.Y. 1999) (one year too long); Sprint Corp. v. DeAngelo, 12 F. Supp.2d 1188 (D. Kan. 1998) (18 months too long). Cf. Doubleclick, Inc. v. Henderson, 1997 WL 731413 (N.Y. Sup. Ct. 1997) (one-year agreement reduced to six months and enforced).

5. Shouldn't the mobility and liberty of individuals be the paramount consideration, as California courts have suggested? See Diodes, Inc. v. Franzen, 260 Cal. App.2d 244 (1968). One author has suggested that there is a more practical economic motivation for precluding such noncompetition agreements. She argues that the relative success of California's Silicon Valley compared to Boston's Route 128 is directly attributable to the prevalence of noncompetition agreements in Route 128 companies, which prevented the free movement of employees and therefore discouraged start-up companies. *See* Annalee Saxenian, Regional Advantage: Culture and Competition in Silicon Valley and Route 128 (1994).

PROBLEM

Problem 1-2. Software Incorporated (SI), the developer of application software, possesses a valid trade secret on the proprietary computer code in its CALCUTEC program and has taken reasonable steps to protect its secrecy. *Q*, a disgruntled employee of USER Inc., a licensee of the CALCUTEC program, wrongfully makes the proprietary code widely available by posting it on

BBS, an electronic bulletin board service, from which it can be easily copied. SI learns of this unauthorized disclosure within a few weeks and notifies BBS. BBS promptly removes CALCUTEC and posts a notice of the unauthorized disclosure of CALCUTEC on the bulletin board but not before Software Distributors, Inc., among other companies, downloads the program and distributes it. Software Distributors sells CALCUTEC, without designation of source or copyright, to TECH Corp.

- What actions does SI have against *Q*, USER, BBS, and Software Distributors, and TECH?
- What difficulties might SI encounter in maintaining such an action?
- Does "wrongful publication" of the CALCUTEC code on the BBS negate its status as a secret, thereby placing it in the public domain?
- What does this problem suggest about the viability of trade secret as a means for protecting widely distributed software products?

D. REVERSE ENGINEERING

One issue requires special attention in the computer context: reverse engineering.

Reverse engineering of a legally obtained product to discover the trade secrets it contains is legal under the Uniform Trade Secrets Act. The Commissioners' Comment to section 1 of the Act provides

> Proper means include: . . .
>   2. Discovery by "reverse engineering", that is, by starting with the known product and working backward to find the method by which it was developed. The acquisition of the known product must, of course, also be by a fair and honest means, such as purchase of the item on the open market for reverse engineering to be lawful. . . .

COMMENTS AND QUESTIONS

1. Why is reverse engineering lawful? If, as the Commissioners suggested, one purpose of trade secrets law is to promote standards of commercial ethics, doesn't there seem to be something wrong with taking apart a competitor's product in order to figure out how to copy it—or, in some cases, how to render it useless? See Vault Dev. Corp. v. Quaid Software, 847 F.2d 255 (5th Cir. 1988) (defendant permitted to reverse-engineer plaintiff's encryption program in order to figure out how to defeat that program). Does reverse engineering benefit only those competitors who are not smart enough to develop ideas or products for themselves?

In the computer context, reverse engineering arguably serves a very important commercial purpose. Decompilation of a computer program may be a necessary first step in analyzing it. As the Manifesto authors explain,

[m]ost copyrighted works reveal their contents to anyone seeking to read them, which makes it unnecessary to reproduce the texts to get access to the ideas, techniques, methods and information they contain. By contrast, the unprotectable elements embodied in computer programs can only be discerned by decompilation. If decompilation is forbidden, software developers could use copyright law to get de facto monopolies on functional process and systems embodied in programs that have not met patent standards.

Pamela Samuelson et al., A Manifesto Concerning the Legal Protection of Computer Programs, 94 Colum. L. Rev. 2308, 2390 n.329 (1994). For a more detailed discussion of the economics of reverse engineering, see Pamela Samuelson & Suzanne Scotchmer, The Law and Economics of Reverse Engineering, 111 Yale L.J. 1575 (2002).

A more general argument for permitting reverse engineering law may be that it serves to differentiate trade secret law from patent law. As we shall see, patent law grants stronger protection than trade secret law (including protection against reverse engineering), but only if the patent holder meets relatively stringent standards. Reverse engineering may be a legal rule designed to weaken trade secret protection relative to patent protection. Can you think of reasons why we would want to weaken trade secret protection? On this point, see Bonito Boats v. Thunder Craft Boats, 489 U.S. 141 (1989), in which the Court held that the defense of reverse engineering in trade secrets law was an important part of what allowed patents and trade secrets to coexist.

2. Reverse engineering of computer software is not easy. Software is generally found in object code form. To reverse engineer it, experts often try a process generally known as "decompilation"—that is, the attempt to translate the 1s and 0s into some form of assembly language and then into readable source code. This process is expensive and time-consuming and can produce imperfect results. See, e.g., Andrew Johnson-Laird, Reverse Engineering of Software: Separating Legal Mythology from Actual Technology, 5 Software L.J. 331, 342-343 (1992). Further, as we see in the next chapter, reverse engineering a computer program almost always involves making one or more intermediate copies of that program, which might be problematic under the copyright laws. Does the difficulty (both technical and legal) of reverse engineering a computer program from object code affect the balance of rights that *Kewanee*, supra, considered so important?

An alternative means of reverse engineering a computer program is called "black box" analysis. In this process, the analyst does not try to take the software apart to see how it works. Rather, she tests the software by feeding it instructions or commands to see what comes out. While the code of the program cannot be discovered using black box analysis, it is sometimes possible to puzzle out the logical structure of the program by feeding it the right data.

3. One rationale for reverse engineering is to achieve compatibility. Is this a legitimate reason to permit the defendants to use secret information they could not otherwise obtain? In United States Golf Ass'n v. St. Andrews Systems, 749 F.2d 1028 (3d Cir. 1984), the U.S.G.A. sued the defendant for copying its formula for handicapping golf scores and implementing it in a commercial product. Because the formula was not a secret, the court decided the case on the related grounds of misappropriation of ideas. But its final paragraphs are instructive:

The public acceptance of the U.S.G.A.'s handicap formula stems from the golfing public's desire to have a uniform system of quantifying recent performances in a way that will allow equitable competition among golfers of differing abilities. The U.S.G.A., in furtherance of its role as the governing body of amateur golf, has provided such a system and, in the absence of a better system, the public has apparently accepted it. Under this state of affairs, the emergence of a single standard becomes largely a function of the need for uniformity. To require Data-Max to use a different formula would effectively destroy its ability to provide a handicapping service, since the U.S.G.A. formula is widely accepted by the golfing public. The purpose of a handicap is comparison between golfers, and handicaps based on different formulas cannot be readily compared.

Because the U.S.G.A. formula is the equivalent of an "industry standard" for the golfing public, preventing other handicap providers from using it would effectively give the U.S.G.A. a national monopoly on the golf handicapping business. Where such a monopoly is unnecessary to protect the basic incentive for the production of the idea or information involved, we do not believe that the creator's interest in its idea or information justifies such an extensive restraint on competition. This case provides a good example of why such a restraint would harm the golfing public. Data-Max has expended time and creative energy in devising its own products and services. It has not only created the program used to calculate handicaps by computer, but has devised a handicapping service which improves on that provided by the U.S.G.A., at least to the extent that Data-Max provides a golfer with a fresh handicap faster than the U.S.G.A. does. In addition, the U.S.G.A. has not been completely deprived of the opportunity to be compensated for its "good will" in connection with the handicap formula. To the extent that the approval of the U.S.G.A. would enhance the value of "instant handicaps," the U.S.G.A. has an opportunity, if it wishes to exercise it, of offering either Data-Max or other companies the use of the U.S.G.A. name in marketing its products and services.

Id. at 1040-1041. Can a similar argument be made for a computer program that provides the only means of communicating with a mainframe computer?

4. Under what circumstances should the owner of a trade secret be able to "contract around" the reverse engineering rule? Contracts that purport to do so are relatively common in the software industry, but their enforceability is open to some question. We discuss this issue in more detail in Chapter 6.

5. While reverse engineering clearly is not an infringement of civil trade secrets statutes, its status under the new Economic Espionage Act (EEA) is less clear. Some commentators have argued that, read literally, the EEA makes reverse engineering a crime.

The most troubling thing about 18 U.S.C. §1831(a)(2) is that it arguably prohibits many forms of heretofore lawful reverse engineering activity. While reverse engineering is not expressly prohibited under this section, neither is it expressly permitted. Rather, its legality appears to be judged according to whether the reverse engineer engages in any of the prohibited acts.[103] To be sure, some types of reverse engineering, such as looking at or tasting a lawfully acquired product in order to determine what is in it, will not be illegal under the EEA. On the other hand, several of the restrictions in section (2) will if read literally encompass some forms of reverse engineering. For example, reverse engineering of computer software by "decompila-

103. See S. Rep., 142 Cong. Rec. S12212.

tion" almost always involves the making of a prohibited "copy" of the program. Reverse engineering of mechanical devices and computer hardware may well involve prohibited "sketching, drawing, or photographing" of the trade secret contained in the publicly sold device. And it is even possible that the prohibition against "altering" a trade secret will be interpreted to prevent chemical analysis of a trade secret product if such analysis involves the use of chemical reactants which bond to secret chemicals or which precipitate out certain elements from the formula.

The legislative history of the EEA is not encouraging to reverse engineers. The Senate Report suggests that "the important thing is to focus on whether the accused has committed one of the prohibited acts of this statute rather than whether he or she has 'reverse engineered.' If someone has lawfully gained access to a trade secret and can replicate it without violating copyright, patent *or this law*, then that form of 'reverse engineering' should be fine."[106] The Report goes on to suggest that observing a lawfully purchased product, or drinking a Coca-Cola, are legitimate activities.[107] On the other hand, there appears to be no reverse engineering defense protecting any of the forms of analysis suggested above. A computer programmer has the right to decompile a software program in certain circumstances under the Uniform Act, copyright law, and the common law without fear of civil liability. Under the EEA, though, that programmer has apparently committed a felony.

James H.A. Pooley et al., Understanding the Economic Espionage Act of 1996, 5 Tex. Intell. Prop. L.J. 177 (1997). On the other hand, other commentators have pointed out that abolishing reverse engineering would work a radical change in the structure of trade secret law, and it is unlikely Congress intended to enact such a change sub rosa. And even Pooley et al. go on to argue that criminalizing reverse engineering would be unwise and that reverse engineering cases are not appropriate for prosecution. To date, no case has been brought that would test the proposition.

Note on Encryption

Of late, two very popular topics of discussion on the Internet have been encryption technology and the problems with patent and, to a lesser degree, copyright law. Recently some have even synthesized the two, suggesting that encryption, or "crypto-bottling," replace patent and copyright as the means for defining intellectual property rights in cyberspace. See, e.g., John P. Barlow, The Economy of Ideas, Wired, Mar. 1994, at 84, 129 (suggesting encryption as a means to protect intellectual property in the digital age). While cryptography may be extremely useful in establishing high electronic security barriers to unauthorized access, it is hardly a new paradigm destined to supplant the entirety of intellectual property law. Instead, cryptography simply establishes more credible barriers to reverse engineering (in this case decryption) than does embedding a program in object code. Fundamentally, trade secret law is at work, but with more powerful tools. Even assuming that the technique provides perfect security, which it does not, the encryption merely shifts the problems of trade secret law to focus on the end user. Software must be decrypted to be valuable to purchasers and finally to end users of the integrated software system. While encryption may enhance the vendor's protection against unauthorized *access* to the software, it can do nothing

---

106. 142 Cong. Rec. at S12212-13 (emphasis added).
107. *Id.* at S12213. Cf. Mason v. Jack Daniels Distillery, 518 So. 2d 130 (Ala. Civ. App. 1987).

about unauthorized use or disclosure of the component by those who have legitimately acquired and decrypted it.

Thus, encryption may be a useful way of restricting reverse engineering by those who have access to the program only in encrypted form. It may also constitute a "reasonable precaution" that helps preserve the secrecy of the encrypted program. It is an imperfect barrier, however, that alone can do nothing about either reverse engineering or misappropriation by end users who know how to decrypt the program.

A recent case involves the secrecy of encryption algorithms themselves and presents many of the issues we have discussed in this chapter. In DVD Copy Control Assoc. v. Bunner, 113 Cal. Rptr. 2d 338 (Ct. App. 2001), *review granted* 117 Cal. Rptr. 2d 167 (Sup. Ct. 2002), a California Court of Appeal reversed a preliminary injunction prohibiting defendant Andrew Bunner from posting to the Internet the computer program DeCSS, source code that describes how to overcome access controls placed on DVDs. The preliminary injunction had been awarded based on a theory of trade secret misappropriation, but the appeals court held that the code was pure speech protected by the First Amendment and that the trade secret provisions "must bow to the protections offered by the First Amendment." In lifting the preliminary injunction, the court was careful to note the narrowness of its decision, noting that legal actions alleging copyright infringement or unlawful conduct rather than speech, or that claimed damages for trade secret misappropriation, might still be possible. Cf. Mark A. Lemley & Eugene Volokh, Freedom of Speech and Injunctions in Intellectual Property Cases, 48 Duke L.J. 147 (1998) (suggesting that preliminary injunctions in IP cases may be prior restraints on speech).

Ironically, it is not clear that the court had to reach the constitutional question. DeCSS was first posted on the Internet in October 1999 by Jon Johansen, a 15-year old Norwegian programmer, and was apparently obtained through reverse engineering the CSS code despite shrinkwrap licensing terms that prohibited reverse engineering. Bunner and many others subsequently republished the code on their web sites, and at the time of trial DeCSS was widely available around the world. Did Johansen act legitimately in reverse engineering a computer program to obtain the trade secrets contained therein? Even if he didn't, does the broad subsequent publication of DeCSS invalidate the trade secret?

We return to the issue of encryption and circumvention in the next chapter, when we consider the Digital Millennium Copyright Act, a 1998 law that makes decryption illegal in many circumstances.

PROBLEM

Problem 1-3. Return to Problem 1-1, above. Assume for the moment that Microsoft has succeeded in maintaining the secrecy of its computer operating system, and has taken reasonable efforts to protect that secrecy. Are competing applications programmers entitled to decompile the operating system in order to prepare applications programs that will run on Microsoft's OS? Is there anything Microsoft can do that will prevent its competitors from legally reverse engineering its product?

2

Copyright Law

A. THE ORIGINS OF COPYRIGHT PROTECTION FOR COMPUTER SOFTWARE

Computer software, by its very nature as written work intended to serve utilitarian purposes, defies easy categorization within our intellectual property system. The copyright law has traditionally served as the principal source of legal protection for original literary work, whereas the patent system and trade secret law have been the primary means for protecting novel utilitarian works.

During the early stages of the computer industry (through 1965), most computer software was provided by computer manufacturers along with the hardware. By bundling software in this way, computer manufacturers could fully recoup their investments in developing computer programs. Computers were highly specialized machines that were not sold through retail channels of distribution, and manufacturers could adequately protect their technology through contractual agreements and trade secrecy protections. There was little or no interest in protecting software technology separately, because patent protection for computer hardware adequately rewarded innovation.

As computers became more powerful and versatile, specialty software firms emerged to provide customized and general-purpose software in direct competition with the mainframe manufacturers. The contract/trade secrecy model continued to meet the needs of most firms in the nascent industry. Programming continued to be a highly specialized field in which programs were customized to the specific machine, customer, and tasks. A software company could tailor a contract to the specific customer and monitor and enforce the agreement.

As computer technology advanced, computers proliferated, and specific models emerged as market leaders, it became feasible for software companies to offer systems and particular application programs to a wider market. The advent of minicomputers in the mid-1960s furthered this development. As a result, the market for software expanded from service and custom programming to the development and marketing of software products that could be installed with relatively little customization to the user's computer system. The unbundling of application software products from IBM hardware in 1970 as a result of antitrust pressures further spurred the market for software products.

It became evident to many that trade secret licensing alone would not be a viable way to protect software products, especially if a mass market in software were to develop. When computer programmers first approached the U.S. Copyright Office about protecting programs by copyright law in the mid-1960s, the Office expressed some doubts about whether machine-executable forms of programs could be protected by copyright law on account of their utilitarian character. The Office viewed the difference between source and object code versions of programs to be akin to the difference between engineering drawings (copyrightable as a drawing) and a bridge design depicted therein (not copyrightable because of its utilitarian character). Eventually the Office began issuing copyright registration certificates to computer programs under its "rule of doubt." (Such certificates indicated that the Copyright Office had doubts about the copyrightability of machine-readable versions of the claimed program but would leave the legal question to the courts in case litigation occurred.) See Cary, Copyright Registration and Computer Programs, 11 Bull. Copyright Soc'y 362 (1964). Although "rule of doubt" registrations might have discouraged some software developers from applying to the Office for a certificate of registration, a more powerful deterrent to registration was the Copyright Office's requirement that the full text of the source code be deposited with the Office. Like other deposit copies, this source code would be made available for public inspection. Such public availability of source code posed a threat to the trade secret status of the contents of software. Between 1966 and 1978, only about 1200 copyright registration certificates were issued.

Because a number of controversial new technology issues were holding up enactment of a major revision of the 1909 Copyright Act, Congress decided in 1974 to establish the Commission on New Technological Uses of Copyrighted Works (CONTU) to investigate and make recommendations on these issues. One such issue was whether computer programs could be copyrighted. After conducting hearings and receiving expert reports, a majority of the panel of copyright authorities and interest group representatives concluded that "computer programs, to the extent that they embody an author's original creation, are proper subject matter of copyright." National Commission on New Technological Uses of Copyrighted Works, Final Report 1 (1979) (hereinafter cited as "CONTU Report"). CONTU was clear, however, that the fundamental limitation reflected in the idea/expression dichotomy that copyright law cannot protect "any idea, procedure, process, system, method of operation, concept, principle, or discovery" should apply with equal force with regard to computer programs. CONTU Report at 20. "[C]opyright protection for programs does not threaten to block the use of ideas or program language previously developed by others when that use is necessary to achieve a certain result. When other language *is* available, programmers are free to read copyrighted programs and use the ideas embodied in them in preparing their own works." *Id.* (emphasis in original). "One is always free to make the machine do the same thing as it would if it had the copyrighted work placed in it, but only by one's own creative effort rather than by piracy." *Id.* at 21. A majority of the CONTU Commissioners concluded that computers programs already were copyrighted under the Copyright Act of 1976, but it recommended some changes to this Act to make appropriate rules for programs.

Congress implemented CONTU's recommendations in 1980 by adding a definition of "computer program" to §101 of the Copyright Act and amending §117 of the Act to authorize the owner of a copy of a computer program to make another copy or adaptation of the program for the purpose of running the program on a computer. See H.R. Rep. No. 1307, 96th Cong., 2d Sess. 23, reprinted in 1980 U.S.C.C.A.N. 6460, 6482 (noting that the 1980 Amendments to the Copyright Act were intended to implement CONTU's recommendations). Congress defined "computer program" as "a set of statements or instructions to be used directly or indirectly in a computer in order to bring about a certain result."

In light of the computer software industry's relative youth and anticipated rapid growth, CONTU's rough empirical judgment that copyright would best promote the invention, development, and diffusion of new and better software products was, by necessity, highly speculative. See, e.g., Pamela Samuelson, CONTU Revisited: The Case Against Copyright Protection for Computer Programs in Machine-Readable Form, 1984 Duke L.J. 663 (criticizing some misleading statements in the CONTU Report about the way computer programs work, and how copyright law could protect them). As CONTU recognized, it was impossible in 1978 to establish a precise line between copyrightable expression of computer programs and the uncopyrightable processes that they implement. Yet the location of this line—the idea/expression dichotomy—was critical to the rough cost-benefit analysis that guided CONTU's recommendation. Drawing the line too liberally in favor of copyright protection would bestow strong monopolies upon those who develop operating systems that become industry standards and would thereby inhibit other creators from developing improved programs and computer systems. Drawing the line too conservatively would allow programmers' efforts to be copied easily, thus discouraging the creation of all but modest incremental advances. The wisdom of Congress's decision to bring computer programs within the scope of copyright law thus depends critically upon where the courts draw this line. See generally Peter S. Menell, An Epitaph for Traditional Copyright Protection of Network Features of Computer Software, 43 Antitrust Bull. 651 (1998).

We begin with the first generation of copyright infringement suits under the 1980 amendments, which focus on whether and to what extent literal copying of computer software violates copyright law. The next section examines the second generation of copyright infringement suits, focusing on the extent to which nonliteral forms of copying constitute copyright infringement. We then turn to protection for program outputs and user interfaces. Finally, we discuss a number of issues related to infringement and fair use. A distinct set of issues relating to the role of copyright on the Internet is reserved for Chapter 10.

B. THE SCOPE OF SOFTWARE COPYRIGHT

1. Protection for Literal Elements of Program Code

The first questions about copyright for computer programs involved the simplest form of copyright infringement—direct copying of the program code. Because the copying in these early cases was "literal"—that is, the accused infringer took the actual text of the work, not merely the structure, organization, or output of the programs—there is no question of scope of protection or "substantial similarity." Rather, the disputed issue in these early cases was whether computer programs could be protected by copyright at all.

The first major case confronting this issue involved Apple Computer. By 1981, Apple had established a strong market for its Apple II computers, thereby attracting competitors seeking to sell "compatible" products capable of functioning with peripheral equipment and software designed for the Apple platform. One such company, Franklin Computer Corporation, copied Apple's operating system program as well as several of its application programs nearly verbatim. Proof of actual copying was easily established by the many lines of identical code and the presence of the names of some of Apple's programmers in comment portions of Franklin's code. Franklin conceded that it had copied Apple's programs, but argued that Apple's operating system programs are not protectable under copyright law. Among the arguments put forth to support this proposition were that object code (binary expression of computer code) cannot be copyrighted because it is not intended to be read by a human, programs embedded in read-only memory cannot be copyrighted (because they are merely utilitarian objects (machine parts)), and that operating system programs are excluded from copyright protection under section 102(b) as processes, systems, or methods of operation. Based upon legislative history of the 1976 Act and Congress's endorsement of the CONTU Report in the 1980 Amendments, the Third Circuit rejected these arguments. See Apple Computer v. Franklin Computer Corp., 714 F.2d 1240, 1246-48 (3d Cir. 1983), *cert. dismissed*, 464 U.S. 1033 (1984).

COMMENTS AND QUESTIONS

1. *Distinguishing Operating Systems and Application Programs.* Is there any legal basis for drawing a distinction between operating system code and application program code? What would be the policy basis for such a distinction? Are there any drawbacks to such an approach?

There are arguably some important differences between the two. First, operating systems are designed to communicate with other computer elements, not with people. Some scholars have suggested that the absence of a "communicative function" should render an operating system uncopyrightable. See, e.g. David Luettgen, Functional Usefulness vs. Communicative Usefulness: Thin Copyright Protection for the Nonliteral Elements of Computer Programs, 4 Tex. Intell. Prop. L.J. 233 (1996). But the 1976 Copyright Act seems to reject this argument, offering protection to works even if they can be perceived or reproduced only with the aid of a computer or other device.

Still, one might reasonably suggest that there is a difference between a videotape or CD, which encodes information that can only be read by a machine, but that the machine translates into words, pictures, or sounds that people can understand, and an operating system component, which *never* communicates information to a human recipient. Does it make sense to extend copyright protection to the latter sorts of programs?

Commissioner Hersey, in his dissent to the CONTU Report, highlighted the fact that computer "[p]rograms are profoundly different from the various forms of 'works of authorship' secured under the Constitution by copyright. Works of authorship have always been intended to be circulated to human beings and to be used by them—to be read, heard, or seen, for either pleasurable or practical ends. Computer programs, in their mature phase, are addressed to machines." Hersey argued that copyright protection should "not extend to a computer program in the form in which it is capable of being used to control computer operations." Do you agree with Commissioner Hersey's critique of bringing computer software, in all of its forms, within the copyright law? Does the Constitution limit copyright protection for "works of authorship" solely to works intended to be directly "read, heard, or seen" by humans? Should protection for computer software be limited in this way? Would Hersey's proposed limitation on the scope of copyright protection for software better balance the social interests affected by legal protection for software? What might justify CONTU's decision to accord software full inclusion within the copyright law, irrespective of whether it is directed toward operating machines or communicating with humans?

For a detailed discussion of the problems raised by Commissioner Hersey in his dissent, see Pamela Samuelson, CONTU Revisited: The Case Against Copyright Protection for Computer Programs in Machine-Readable Form, 1984 Duke L.J. 663 (1984).

A second difference between operating systems and applications programs is that the operating systems market is characterized by significant network effects. Operating systems markets tend toward standardization around a single product, because consumers benefit from using the same operating system that everyone else uses. Some scholars have suggested that strong copyright protection for operating systems is inappropriate because of these market characteristics. See Peter S. Menell, An Epitaph for Traditional Copyright Protection of Network Features of Computer Software, 43 Antitrust Bull. 651 (1998); Peter S. Menell, An Analysis of the Scope of Copyright Protection for Computer Programs, 41 Stan. L. Rev. 1045, 1101 (1989).

2. *Distinguishing Object Code and Source Code.* The court rejects the contention that object code (the actual implementation of the program in 1s and 0s in magnetic memory or on a circuit) cannot itself be copyrightable. The idea that object code is copyrightable is not terribly controversial today. In part, copyrightability of object code stems from what might be thought a slippery-slope argument: Since source code is copyrightable, and since source code can readily be translated into object code, object code must also be copyrightable. See Dan L. Burk, Software as Speech, 8 Seton Hall Const. L.J. 683, 687-88 (1998) (discussing this rationale).

But this argument has some troubling implications. One of the fundamental rules of computing is that anything that can be implemented in software can in principle be implemented in hardware too. Indeed, "software" itself is nothing more than a temporary (rather than permanent) way of ordering circuit switches in hardware. So, if object code is copyrightable, why not more permanent instantiations in hardware—the microcode instructions embedded in computer chips, for example, or the layout of a circuit board itself?

Copyright law does sometimes protect the design elements of utilitarian objects; the sculpture/lamp of Mazer v. Stein, 347 U.S. 201 (1954), is a prominent example. But while courts have had difficulty at times separating the artistic from the utilitarian, they have steadfastly refused to extend copyright protection to the utilitarian aspects of three-dimensional objects such as lamps, jewelry, and manne-quins. Protecting object code and microcode raises many of the same troubling issues. How should courts separate the unprotectable utilitarian aspects of a computer program from the protectable expressive aspects? In the sections that follow we will see how the courts have dealt with this issue.

3. *Achieving Compatibility and the Scope of Copyright Protection for Interface Specifications.* The *Apple* court concludes that the "idea" of Apple's operating system is to run the Apple computer, and that the particular way in which Apple runs its computer is protectable expression. Because it defines the idea of the program in very broad terms, the decision gives broad protection to Apple's operating system. In addressing the issue of whether achieving interoperability would justify some limited copying, the court commented that

> The idea which may merge with the expression, thus making the copyright unavail-able, is the idea which is the subject of the expression. The idea of one of the operat-ing system programs is, for example, how to translate source code into object code. If other methods of expressing that idea are not foreclosed as a practical matter, then there is no merger. *Franklin may wish to achieve total compatibility with independently developed application programs written for the Apple II, but that is a commercial and competitive objective which does not enter into the somewhat metaphysical issue of whether particular ideas and expressions have merged.*

714 F.2d at 1253 (emphasis added). Since two entirely different programs may achieve the same "certain result[s]" (e.g., generate the same set of protocols needed for interoperability), was the court justified in making such an expansive statement about the scope of copyright protection for computer programs? Doesn't this statement essentially deny a right to use a program in order to achieve compatibility with it? We return to both of these issues in greater detail below.

PROBLEM

Problem 2-1. LETNI Corp. produces microprocessors, the central component of microcomputer systems. These "computers on a chip" are integrated circuits capable of performing arithmetic functions, manipulation of data, and other operations in response to object code instructions. At one time, LETNI's 684 microprocessor commanded a 70 percent market share of the microcomputer market. LETNI's 684 chip utilizes a single "bus" or path for transferring data. It features 512 lines of microcode, each of which is 21 bits long, that enable the microprocessor to interpret 133 assembly instructions.

CEN Corp., a competing microprocessor manufacturer, seeks to sell semiconductor chips capable of running the same software as LETNI's 684 microprocessor. A prior patent cross-licensing agreement entitles CEN to du-plicate LETNI's 684 microarchitecture and hardware to the extent comprehended by the LETNI's patent. In order to increase processing speed and capability relative to LETNI's 684 chip, CEN designed its U2 microprocessor with a dual bus system and a larger microinstruction word size (29 bits). The 1,024 lines of microcode enable the microprocessor to interpret 156 assembly instructions. Five hundred fifty-two of these lines carry out the instruction set of the LETNI 684 microprocessor. The remaining lines perform other functions not carried out by the 684 chip. Because of the dual bus architecture and larger word size, CEN was able to write shorter and more efficient microcode.

Nonetheless, there were a number of similarities in the microcodes of the two microprocessors. LETNI brought suit, alleging: (1) Microprograms are computer programs and hence protected by the Copyright Act; and (2) CEN's U2 microcode infringed the copyright of LETNI's 684 chip.

Applying the analysis of Apple v. Franklin, how should this case be resolved? Should microcode be copyrightable? If so, what should be the scope of protection?

Can a hardware manufacturer obtain copyright protection for the configuration of the hardwiring of its computer? If so, under what theory? If your answer is different from that for microcode, what explains the distinction?

2. Protection for Nonliteral Elements of Program Code

The *Apple* decision established an important baseline principle: that exact copying of computer program code was copyright infringement. It was almost inevitable, however, that software developers would test whether copyright protection for computer programs would extend to other aspects of programs, such as their "look and feel" or their structure, sequence, and organization. This subsection will explore how courts have assessed such claims for nonliteral copying of internal structural details of software design, user interface elements, or the interactive behavior of programs.

A few years after its decision in *Apple*, the Third Circuit confronted copyright protection for nonliteral elements of application programs. In Whelan Associates, Inc. v. Jaslow Dental Laboratory, Inc., 797 F.2d 1222 (3d Cir. 1986), *cert. denied*, 479 U.S. 1031 (1987), the owner of a dental laboratory hired a custom software firm to develop a computer program that would organize the bookkeeping and administrative tasks of its business. Whelan, the principal programmer, interviewed employees about the operation of the laboratory and then developed a program to run on the laboratory's IBM Series One computer. Under the terms of an agreement, Whelan retained the copyright in the program and agreed to use its best efforts to improve the program, while Jaslow Laboratory agreed to use its best efforts to market the program. Rand Jaslow, an officer and shareholder of the laboratory, set out to create a version of the program that would run on other computer systems. Whelan sued for copyright infringement. At trial, the evidence showed that the Jaslow program did not literally copy Whelan's code, but there were overall structural similarities between the two programs. As a means of distinguishing protectable expression from unprotectable idea, the court reasoned:

[T]he purpose or function of a utilitarian work would be the work's idea, and everything that is not necessary to that purpose or function would be part of the expression of the idea. Where there are many means of achieving the desired purpose, then the particular means chosen is not necessary to the purpose; hence, there is expression, not idea.

Id. at 1236 (emphasis in original; citations omitted). In applying this rule, the court defined the idea as "the efficient management of a dental laboratory," for which countless ways of expressing of the idea would be possible. Drawing the idea/expression dichotomy at such a high level of abstraction implies an expansive scope of copyright protection. Furthermore, the court's conflation of merger analysis and the idea/expression dichotomy implicitly allows the protection under copyright of procedures, processes, systems, and methods of operation, which are expressly excluded under §102(b). Although the case did not directly address copyright protection for computer code establishing interoperability protocols for computer systems, the court's mode of analysis dramatically expanded the scope of copyright protection for computer programs. If everything below the general purpose of the program was protectable under copyright, then it would follow that particular protocols were protectable because there would be other ways of serving the general purpose of the program. Such a result would effectively bar competitors from developing interoperable programs and computer systems.

The *Whelan* test was roundly criticized by commentators,[1] and other courts began developing alternative approaches to the scope of copyright protection that better comported with the fundamental principles of copyright protection. A few months after the *Whelan* decision, the Fifth Circuit confronted a similar claim of copyright infringement based upon structural similarities between two programs designed to provide cotton growers with information regarding cotton prices and availability, accounting services, and a means for conducting cotton transactions electronically. Plains Cotton Cooperative Assoc. v. Goodpasture Computer Service, Inc., 807 F.2d 1256 (5th Cir. 1987). In declining to follow the *Whelan* approach, the court found that the similarities in the programs were dictated largely by standard practices in the cotton market (which the court called "externalities"), such as the "cotton recap sheet" for summarizing basic transaction information, which constitute unprotectable ideas.[2]

1. See, e.g., 3 Melville B. Nimmer & David Nimmer, Nimmer on Copyright §§13.03[F] (1991); Peter S. Menell, An Analysis of the Scope of Copyright Protection for Computer Programs, 41 Stan. L. Rev. 1045, 1074 (1989); David Nimmer, Richard L. Bernacchi, & Gary N. Frischling, A Structured Approach to Analyzing the Substantial Similarity of Computer Software in Copyright Infringement Cases, 20 Ariz. St. L.J. 625 (1988).

2. The court found persuasive the decision in Synercom Technology, Inc. v. University Computing Co., 462 F. Supp 1003 (N.D.Tex. 1978), in which Judge Higginbotham analogized the "input formats" of a computer program (the organization and configuration of information to be inputted into a computer) to the "figure-H" pattern of an automobile stick shift.

Several different patterns may be imagined, some more convenient for the driver or easier to manufacture than others, but all representing possible configurations. . . . The pattern (analogous to the computer "format") may be expressed in several different ways: by a prose description in a driver's manual, through a diagram, photograph, or driver training film, or otherwise. Each of these expressions may presumably be protected through copyright. But the copyright protects copying of the particular expressions of the patterns, and does not prohibit another manufacturer from marketing a car using the same pattern. Use of the same pattern might be socially desirable, as it would reduce the retraining of drivers.

Id. at 1013.

Computer Associates International v. Altai, Inc.
United States Court of Appeals for the Second Circuit
982 F.2d 693 (2d Cir. 1992)

WALKER, Circuit Judge: . . .

This appeal comes to us from the United States District Court for the Eastern District of New York, the Honorable George C. Pratt, Circuit Judge, sitting by designation. By Memorandum and Order entered August 12, 1991, Judge Pratt found that defendant Altai, Inc.'s ("Altai"), OSCAR 3.4 computer program had infringed plaintiff Computer Associates' ("CA"), copyrighted computer program entitled CA-SCHEDULER. Accordingly, the district court awarded CA $364,444 in actual damages and apportioned profits. Altai has abandoned its appeal from this award. With respect to CA's second claim for copyright infringement, Judge Pratt found that Altai's OSCAR 3.5 program was not substantially similar to a portion of CA-SCHEDULER called ADAPTER, and thus denied relief. . . .

II. Facts . . .

The subject of this litigation originates with one of CA's marketed programs entitled CA-SCHEDULER. CA-SCHEDULER is a job scheduling program designed for IBM mainframe computers. Its primary functions are straightforward: to create a schedule specifying when the computer should run various tasks, and then to control the computer as it executes the schedule. CA-SCHEDULER contains a sub-program entitled ADAPTER, also developed by CA. ADAPTER is not an independently marketed product of CA; it is a wholly integrated component of CA-SCHEDULER and has no capacity for independent use.

Nevertheless, ADAPTER plays an extremely important role. It is an "operating system compatibility component," which means, roughly speaking, it serves as a translator. An "operating system" is itself a program that manages the resources of the computer allocating those resources to other programs as needed. The IBM System 370 family of computers, for which CA-SCHEDULER was created, is, depending upon the computer's size, designed to contain one of three operating systems: DOS/VSE, MVS, or CMS. As the district court noted, the general rule is that "a program written for one operating system, e.g., DOS/VSE, will not, without modification, run under another operating system such as MVS." Computer Assocs., 775 F. Supp. at 550. ADAPTER's function is to translate the language of a given program into the particular language that the computer's own operating system can understand.

The district, court succinctly outlined the manner in which ADAPTER works within the context of the larger program. In order to enable CA-SCHEDULER to function on different operating systems, CA divided the CA-SCHEDULER into two components:

- a first component that contains only the task-specific portions of the program, independent of all operating system issues, and
- a second component that contains all the interconnections between the first component and the operating system.

In a program constructed in this way, whenever the first, task-specific, component needs to ask the operating system for some resource through a "system call", it calls the second component instead of calling the operating system directly.

The second component serves as an "interface" or "compatibility component" between the task-specific portion of the program and the operating system. It receives the request from the first component and translates it into the appropriate system call that will be recognized by whatever operating system is installed on the computer, e.g., DOS/VSE, MVS, or CMS. Since the first, task-specific component calls the adapter component rather than the operating system, the first component need not be customized to use any specific operating system. The second, interface, component insures that all the system calls are performed properly for the particular operating system in use. *Id.* at 551. ADAPTER serves as the second, "common system interface" component referred to above.

A program like ADAPTER, which allows a computer user to change or use multiple operating systems while maintaining the same software, is highly desirable. It saves the user the costs, both in time and money, that otherwise would be expended in purchasing new programs, modifying existing systems to run them, and gaining familiarity with their operation. The benefits run both ways. The increased compatibility afforded by an ADAPTER-like component, and its resulting popularity among consumers, makes whatever software in which it is incorporated significantly more marketable.

Starting in 1982, Altai began marketing its own job scheduling program entitled ZEKE. The original version of ZEKE was designed for use in conjunction with a VSE operating system. By late 1983, in response to customer demand, Altai decided to rewrite ZEKE so that it could be run in conjunction with an MVS operating system.

[At that time, James P. Williams, then an employee of Altai and now its president, recruited Claude F. Arney, III, a long-standing friend and computer programmer who worked for CA, to assist Altai in designing an MVS version of ZEKE. Unknown to Williams, Arney was intimately familiar with CA's ADAPTER program and he took VSE and MVS source code versions of ADAPTER with him when he left CA to join Altai. Without disclosing his knowledge of ADAPTER, Arney persuaded Williams that the best way to modify ZEKE to run on an MVS operating system was to introduce a "common system interface" component, an approach that stemmed from Arney's familiarity with ADAPTER. Arney subsequently developed a component-program named OSCAR using the ADAPTER source code. Approximately 30 percent of the first generation of OSCAR was copied from CA's ADAPTER program. In mid-1988, CA discovered the copying from ADAPTER and brought this copyright infringement and trade secret action. Altai learned of its employees' copying from the complaint.]

Upon advice of counsel, Williams initiated OSCAR's rewrite. The project's goal was to save as much of OSCAR 3.4 as legitimately could be used, and to excise those portions which had been copied from ADAPTER. Arney was entirely excluded from the process, and his copy of the ADAPTER code was locked away. Williams put eight other programmers on the project, none of whom had been involved in any way in the development of OSCAR 3.4. Williams provided the programmers with a description of the ZEKE operating system services so that they could rewrite the appropriate code. The rewrite project took about six months to complete and was finished in mid-November 1989. The resulting program was entitled OSCAR 3.5.

From that point on, Altai shipped only OSCAR 3.5 to its new customers. . . .

Discussion

[The district court concluded that version 3.5 was not substantially similar to CA-ADAPTER.]

I. *Copyright Infringement . . .*

As a general matter, and to varying degrees, copyright protection extends beyond a literary work's strictly textual form to its non-literal components. As we have said, "[i]t is of course essential to any protection of literary property that the right cannot be limited literally to the text, else a plagiarist would escape by immaterial variations." Nichols v. Universal Pictures Co., 45 F.2d 119, 121 (2d Cir. 1930) (L. Hand, J.), *cert. denied,* 282 U.S. 902, 51 S. Ct. 216, 75 L. Ed. 795 (1931). Thus, where "the fundamental essence or structure of one work is duplicated in another," 3 Nimmer, §13.03[A][1], at 13-24, courts have found copyright infringement. . . . This black letter proposition is the springboard for our discussion.

A. Copyright Protection for the Non-Literal Elements of Computer Programs

It is now well settled that the literal elements of computer programs, i.e., their source and object codes, are the subject of copyright protection. . . . Here, as noted earlier, Altai admits having copied approximately 30% of the OSCAR 3.4 program from CA's ADAPTER source code, and does not challenge the district court's related finding of infringement.

In this case, the hotly contested issues surround OSCAR 3.5. As recounted above, OSCAR 3.5 is the product of Altai's carefully orchestrated rewrite of OSCAR 3.4. After the purge, none of the ADAPTER source code remained in the 3.5 version; thus, Altai made sure that the literal elements of its revamped OSCAR program were no longer substantially similar to the literal elements of CA's ADAPTER.

According to CA, the district court erroneously concluded that Altai's OSCAR 3.5 was not substantially similar to its own ADAPTER program. CA argues that this occurred because the district court "committed legal error in analyzing [its] claims of copyright infringement by failing to find that copyright protects expression contained in the non-literal elements of computer software." We disagree.

CA argues that, despite Altai's rewrite of the OSCAR code, the resulting program remained substantially similar to the structure of its ADAPTER program. As discussed above, a program's structure includes its non-literal components such as general flow charts as well as the more specific organization of inter-modular relationships, parameter lists, and macros. In addition to these aspects, CA contends that OSCAR 3.5 is also substantially similar to ADAPTER with respect to the list of services that both ADAPTER and OSCAR obtain from their respective operating systems. We must decide whether and to what extent these elements of computer programs are protected by copyright law.

The statutory terrain in this area has been well explored. . . . While computer programs are not specifically listed as part of the statutory definition, the legislative history leaves no doubt that Congress intended them to be considered literary works. See H.R. Rep. No. 1476, 94th Cong., 2d Sess. 54, reprinted in 1976 U.S.C.C.A.N. 5659, 5667 (hereinafter "House Report"); *Whelan*, 797 F.2d at 1234; *Apple Computer*, 714 F.2d at 1247.

The syllogism that follows from the foregoing premises is a powerful one: if the non-literal structures of literary works are protected by copyright; and if computer programs are literary works, as we are told by the legislature; then the non-literal structures of computer programs are protected by copyright. See *Whelan*, 797 F.2d at 1234 ("By analogy to other literary works, it would thus appear that the copyrights of computer programs can be infringed even absent copying of the literal elements of the program."). We have no reservation in joining the company of those courts that have already ascribed to this logic. See, e.g., Johnson Controls, Inc. v. Phoenix Control Sys., Inc., 886 F.2d 1173; 1175 (9th Cir. 1989); Lotus Dev. Corp., 740 F. Supp. at 54; Digital Communications Assocs., Inc. v. Softklone Distrib. Corp., 659 F. Supp. 449, 455-56 (N.D.Ga. 1987); Q-Co Indus., Inc. v. Hoffman, 625 F. Supp. 608, 615 (S.D.N.Y. 1985); SAS Inst., Inc. v. S & H Computer Sys., Inc., 605 F. Supp. 816, 829-30 (M.D. Tenn. 1985). However, that conclusion does not end our analysis. We must determine the scope of copyright protection that extends to a computer program's non-literal structure.

As a caveat, we note that our decision here does not control infringement actions regarding categorically distinct works, such as certain types of screen displays. These items represent products of computer programs, rather than the programs themselves, and fall under the copyright rubric of audiovisual works. . . . In this case, . . . we are concerned not with a program's display, but the program itself, and then with only its non-literal components. In considering the copyrightability of these components, we must refer to venerable doctrines of copyright law.

1) Idea vs. Expression Dichotomy

It is a fundamental principle of copyright law that a copyright does not protect an idea, but only the expression of the idea. . . .

Drawing the line between idea and expression is a tricky business. Judge Learned Hand noted that "[n]obody has ever been able to fix that boundary, and nobody ever can," *Nichols*, 45 F.2d at 121. Thirty years later his convictions remained firm. "Obviously, no principle can be stated as to when an imitator has gone beyond copying the 'idea,' and has borrowed its 'expression,'" Judge Hand concluded. "Decisions must therefore inevitably be ad hoc." Peter Pan Fabrics, Inc. v. Martin Weiner Corp., 274 F.2d 487, 489 (2d Cir. 1960).

The essentially utilitarian nature of a computer program further complicates the task of distilling its idea from its expression. See *SAS Inst.*, 605 F. Supp. at

829; cf. Englund, at 893. In order to describe both computational processes and abstract ideas, its content "combines creative and technical expression." See Spivack, at 755. The variations of expression found in purely creative compositions, as opposed to those contained in utilitarian works, are not directed towards practical application. For example, a narration of Humpty Dumpty's demise, which would clearly be a creative composition, does not serve the same ends as, say, a recipe for scrambled eggs—which is a more process-oriented text. Thus, compared to aesthetic works, computer programs hover even more closely to the elusive boundary line described in §102(b).

[The court reviewed the facts and holding of Baker v. Selden.]

To the extent that an accounting text and a computer program are both "a set of statements or instructions . . . to bring about a certain result," 17 U.S.C. §101, they are roughly analogous. In the former case, the processes are ultimately conducted by human agency; in the latter, by electronic means. In either case, as already stated, the processes themselves are not protectable. But the holding in *Baker* goes farther. The Court concluded that those aspects of a work, which "must necessarily be used as incident to" the idea, system or process that the work describes, are also not copyrightable. 101 U.S. at 104. Selden's ledger sheets, therefore, enjoyed no copyright protection because they were "necessary incidents to" the system of accounting that he described. *Id.* at 103. From this reasoning, we conclude that those elements of a computer program that are necessarily incidental to its function are similarly unprotectable.

While Baker v. Selden provides a sound analytical foundation, it offers scant guidance on how to separate idea or process from expression, and moreover, on how to further distinguish protectable expression from that expression which "must necessarily be used as incident to the work's underlying concept." In the context of computer programs, the Third Circuit's noted decision in *Whelan* has, thus far, been the most thoughtful attempt to accomplish these ends.

[The court quoted from the Whelan v. Jaslow decision reproduced above.]

So far, in the courts, the *Whelan* rule has received a mixed reception. While some decisions have adopted its reasoning, see, e.g., Bull HN Info. Sys., Inc. v. American Express Bank, Ltd., 1990 Copyright Law Dec. (CCH) ¶26,555 at 23,278 (S.D.N.Y. 1990); Dynamic Solutions, Inc. v. Planning & Control, Inc., 1987 Copyright Law Dec. (CCH) ¶26,062 at 20,912 (S.D.N.Y. 1987); Broderbund Software Inc. v. Unison World, Inc., 648 F. Supp. 1127, 1133 (N.D.Cal. 1986), others have rejected it. See Plains Cotton Co-op v. Goodpasture Computer Serv. Inc., 807 F.2d 1256, 1262 (5th Cir.), *cert. denied*, 484 U.S. 821, 108 S. Ct. 80, 98 L. Ed.2d 42 (1987); cf. Synercom Technology, Inc. v. University Computing Co., 462 F. Supp. 1003, 1014 (N.D. Tex. 1978) (concluding that order and sequence of data on computer input formats was idea not expression).

Whelan has fared even more poorly in the academic community, where its standard for distinguishing idea from expression has been widely criticized for being conceptually overbroad. See, e.g., Englund, at 881; Menell, at 1074, 1082; Kretschmer, at 837-39; Spivack, at 747-55; Thomas M. Gage, Note, Whelan Associates v. Jaslow Dental Laboratories: Copyright Protection for Computer Software Structure—What's the Purpose?, 1987 Wis. L. Rev. 859, 860-61 (1987). The leading commentator in the field has stated that, "[t]he crucial flaw in [*Whelan*'s] reasoning is that it assumes that only one 'idea,' in copyright law terms, underlies any computer program, and that once a separable idea can be identified, everything else must be expression." 3 Nimmer §13.03[F], at 13-62.34. This criticism focuses not upon the program's ultimate purpose but upon the reality of its structural design. As we have already noted, a computer program's ultimate function or purpose is the composite result of interacting subroutines. Since each subroutine is itself a program, and thus, may be said to have its own "idea," *Whelan*'s general formulation that a program's overall purpose equates with the program's idea is descriptively inadequate.

Accordingly, we think that Judge Pratt wisely declined to follow *Whelan*. See *Computer Assocs.*, 775 F. Supp. at 558-60. In addition to noting the weakness in the *Whelan* definition of "program-idea," mentioned above, Judge Pratt found that *Whelan*'s synonymous use of the terms "structure, sequence, and organization," see *Whelan*, 797 F.2d at 1224 n. 1, demonstrated a flawed understanding of a computer program's method of operation. See *Computer Assocs.*, 775 F. Supp. at 559-60 (discussing the distinction between a program's "static structure" and "dynamic structure"). Rightly, the district court found *Whelan*'s rationale suspect because it is so closely tied to what can now be seen—with the passage of time—as the opinion's somewhat outdated appreciation of computer science.

2) Substantial Similarity Test for Computer Program Structure: Abstraction-Filtration-Comparison

We think that *Whelan*'s approach to separating idea from expression in computer programs relies too heavily on metaphysical distinctions and does not place enough emphasis on practical considerations. Cf. *Apple Computer*, 714 F.2d at 1253 (rejecting certain commercial constraints on programming as a helpful means of distinguishing idea from expression because they did "not enter into the somewhat metaphysical issue of whether particular ideas and expressions have merged"). As the cases that we shall discuss demonstrate, a satisfactory answer to this problem cannot be reached by resorting, *a priori*, to philosophical first principles.

As discussed herein, we think that district courts would be well-advised to undertake a three-step procedure, based on the abstractions test utilized by the district court, in order to determine whether the non-literal elements of two or more computer programs are substantially similar. This approach breaks no new ground; rather, it draws on such familar copyright doctrines as merger, *scenes a faire*, and public domain. In taking this approach, however, we are cognizant that computer technology is a dynamic field which can quickly outpace judicial decisionmaking. Thus, in cases where the technology in question does not allow for a literal application of the procedure we outline below, our opinion should not be read to foreclose the district courts of our circuit from utilizing a modified version.

In ascertaining substantial similarity under this approach, a court would first break down the allegedly infringed program into its constituent structural parts. Then, by examining each of these parts for such things as incorporated ideas, expression that is necessarily incidental to those ideas, and elements that are taken from the public domain, a court would then be able to sift out all non-protectable material. Left with a kernel, or possibly kernels, of creative expression after following this process of elimination, the court's last step would be to compare this material with the structure of an allegedly infringing program. The result of this comparison will determine whether the protectable elements of the programs at issue are substantially similar so as to warrant a finding of infringement. It will be helpful to elaborate a bit further.

Step One: Abstraction

As the district court appreciated, see *Computer Assocs.*, 775 F. Supp. at 560, the theoretic framework for analyzing substantial similarity expounded by Learned Hand in the *Nichols* case is helpful in the present context. In *Nichols*, we enunciated what has now become known as the "abstractions" test for separating idea from expression:

> Upon any work . . . a great number of patterns of increasing generality will fit equally well, as more and more of the incident is left out. The last may perhaps be no more than the most general statement of what the [work] is about, and at times might consist only of its title; but there is a point in this series of abstractions where they are no longer protected, since otherwise the [author] could prevent the use of his "ideas," to which, apart from their expression, his property is never extended.

Nichols, 45 F.2d at 121.

While the abstractions test was originally applied in relation to literary works such as novels and plays, it is adaptable to computer programs. In contrast to the *Whelan* approach, the abstractions test "implicitly recognizes that any given work may consist of a mixture of numerous ideas and expressions." 3 Nimmer §13.03[F] at 13-62.34-63.

As applied to computer programs, the abstractions test will comprise the first step in the examination for substantial similarity. Initially, in a manner that resembles reverse engineering on a theoretical plane, a court should dissect the allegedly copied program's structure and isolate each level of abstraction contained within it. This process begins with the code and ends with an articulation of the program's ultimate function. Along the way, it is necessary essentially to retrace and map each of the designer's steps—in the opposite order in which they were taken during the program's creation.

As an anatomical guide to this procedure, the following description is helpful:

> At the lowest level of abstraction, a computer program may be thought of in its entirety as a set of individual instructions organized into a hierarchy of modules. At a higher level of abstraction, the instructions in the lowest-level modules may be replaced conceptually by the functions of those modules. At progressively higher levels of abstraction, the functions of higher-level modules conceptually replace the implementations of those modules in terms of lower-level modules and instructions, until finally, one is left with nothing but the ultimate function of the program. . . . A program has structure at every level of abstraction at which it is viewed. At low levels of abstraction, a program's structure may be quite complex; at the highest level it is trivial.

Englund, at 897-98. Cf. Spivack, at 774.

Step Two: Filtration

Once the program's abstraction levels have been discovered, the substantial similarity inquiry moves from the conceptual to the concrete. Professor Nimmer suggests, and we endorse, a "successive filtering method" for separating protectable expression from non-protectable material. See generally 3 Nimmer §13.03[F]. This process entails examining the structural components at each level of abstraction to determine whether their particular inclusion at that level was "idea" or was dictated by considerations of efficiency, so as to be necessarily incidental to that idea; required by factors external to the program itself; or taken from the public domain and hence is non-protectable expression. See also Kretschmer, at 844-45 (arguing that program features dictated by market externalities or efficiency concerns are unprotectable). The structure of any given program may reflect some, all, or none of these considerations. Each case requires its own fact specific investigation.

Strictly speaking, this filtration serves "the purpose of defining the scope of plaintiff's copyright." Brown Bag Software v. Symantec Corp., 960 F.2d 1465, 1475 (9th Cir.) (endorsing "analytic dissection" of computer programs in order to isolate protectable expression), *cert. denied*, 113 S. Ct. 198 (1992). By applying well developed doctrines of copyright law, it may ultimately leave behind a "core of protectable material." 3 Nimmer §13.03[F][5], at 13-72. Further explication of this second step may be helpful.

(a) Elements Dictated by Efficiency

The portion of Baker v. Selden, discussed earlier, which denies copyright protection to expression necessarily incidental to the idea being expressed, appears to be the cornerstone for what has developed into the doctrine of merger. See Morrissey v. Procter & Gamble Co., 379 F.2d 675, 678-79 (1st Cir. 1967) (relying on *Baker* for the proposition that expression embodying the rules of a sweepstakes contest was inseparable from the idea of the contest itself, and therefore were not protectable by copyright); see also *Digital Communications*, 659 F. Supp. at 457. The doctrine's underlying principle is that "[w]hen there is essentially only one way to express an idea, the idea and its expression are inseparable and copyright is no bar to copying that expression." Concrete Machinery Co. v. Classic Lawn Ornaments. Inc., 843 F.2d 600, 606 (1st Cir. 1988). Under these circumstances, the expression is said to have "merged" with the idea itself. In order not to confer a monopoly of the idea upon the copyright owner, such expression should not be protected. See Herbert Rosenthal Jewelry Corp. v. Kalpakian, 446 F.2d 738, 742 (9th Cir. 1971).

CONTU recognized the applicability of the merger doctrine to computer programs. In its report to Congress it stated that:

> [C]opyrighted language may be copied without infringing when there is but a limited number of ways to express a given idea. . . . In the computer context, this means that when specific instructions, even though previously copyrighted, are the only and essential means of accomplishing a given task, their later use by another will not amount to infringement.

CONTU Report at 20. While this statement directly concerns only the application of merger to program code, that is, the textual aspect of the program, it reasonably suggests that the doctrine fits comfortably within the general context of computer programs.

Furthermore, when one considers the fact that programmers generally strive to create programs "that meet the user's needs in the most efficient manner," Menell, at 1052, the applicability of the merger doctrine to computer programs becomes compelling. In the context of computer program design, the concept of efficiency is akin to deriving the most concise logical proof or formulating the most succinct mathematical computation. Thus, the more efficient a set of modules are, the more closely they approximate the idea or process embodied in that particular aspect of the program's structure.

While, hypothetically, there might be a myriad of ways in which a programmer may effectuate certain functions within a program—i.e., express the idea embodied in a given subroutine—efficiency concerns may so narrow the practical range of choice as to make only one or two forms of expression workable options. See 3 Nimmer §13.03[F][2], at 13-63; see also *Whelan*, 797 F.2d at 1243 n. 43 ("It is true that for certain tasks there are only a very limited number of file structures available, and in such cases the structures might not be copyrightable. . . ."). Of course, not all program structure is informed by efficiency concerns. See Menell, at 1052 (besides efficiency, simplicity related to user accommodation has become a programming priority). It follows that, in order to determine whether the merger doctrine precludes copyright protection to an aspect of a program's structure that is so oriented, a court must inquire "whether the use of *this particular set of modules* is necessary efficiently to implement that part of the program's process" being implemented. Englund, at 902. If the answer is yes, then the expression represented by the programmer's choice of a specific module or group of modules has merged with their underlying idea and is unprotected. *Id.* at 902-03.

Another justification for linking structural economy with the application of the merger doctrine stems from a program's essentially utilitarian nature and the competitive forces that exist in the software marketplace. See Kretschmer, at 842. Working in tandem, these factors give rise to a problem of proof which merger helps to eliminate. Efficiency is an industry-wide goal. Since, as we have already noted, there may be only a limited number of efficient implementations for any given program task, it is quite possible that multiple programmers, working independently, will design the identical method employed in the allegedly infringed work. Of course, if this is the case, there is no copyright infringement. See Roth Greeting Cards v. United Card Co., 429 F.2d 1106, 1110 (9th Cir. 1970); *Sheldon*, 81 F.2d at 54.

Under these circumstances, the fact that two programs contain the same efficient structure may as likely lead to an inference of independent creation as it does to one of copying. See 3 Nimmer §13.03[F][2], at 13-65; cf. *Herbert Rosenthal Jewelry Corp.*, 446 F.2d at 741 (evidence of independent creation may stem from defendant's standing as a designer of previous similar works). Thus, since evidence of similarly efficient structure is not particularly probative of copying, it should be disregarded in the overall substantial similarity analysis. See 3 Nimmer §13.03[F][2], at 13-65. . . .

(b) Elements Dictated by External Factors

We have stated that where "it is virtually impossible to write about a particular historical era or fictional theme without employing certain 'stock' or standard literary devices," such expression is not copyrightable. Hoehling v. Universal Studios,

Inc., 618 F.2d 972, 979 (2d Cir.), *cert. denied*, 449 U.S.1 841, 101 S. Ct. 42, 66 L. Ed.2d 1 (1980). . . .

Professor Nimmer points out that "in many instances it is virtually impossible to write a program to perform particular functions in a specific computing environment without employing standard techniques." 3 Nimmer §13.03[F][3], at 13-65. This is a result of the fact that a programmer's freedom of design choice is often circumscribed by extrinsic considerations such as (1) the mechanical specifications of the computer on which a particular program is intended to run; (2) compatibility requirements of other programs with which a program is designed to operate in conjunction; (3) computer manufacturers' design standards; (4) demands of the industry being serviced; and (5) widely accepted programming practices within the computer industry. *Id.* at 13-65-71. . . .

(c) Elements Taken from the Public Domain

Closely related to the non-protectability of *scenes à faire*, is material found in the public domain. Such material is free for the taking and cannot be appropriated by a single author even though it is included in a copyrighted work. See E.F. Johnson Co. v. Uniden Corp. of America, 623 F. Supp. 1485, 1499 (D. Minn. 1985); see also *Sheldon*, 81 F.2d at 54. We see no reason to make an exception to this rule for elements of a computer program that have entered the public domain by virtue of freely accessible program exchanges and the like. See 3 Nimmer §13.03[F][14]; see also *Brown Bag Software*, 960 F.2d at 1473 (affirming the district court's finding that "[p]laintiffs may not claim copyright protection of an . . . expression that is, if not standard, then commonplace in the computer software industry."). Thus, a court must also filter out this material from the allegedly infringed program before it makes the final inquiry in its substantial similarity analysis.

Step Three: Comparison

The third and final step of the test for substantial similarity that we believe appropriate for non-literal program components entails a comparison. Once a court has sifted out all elements of the allegedly infringed program which are "ideas" or are dictated by efficiency or external factors, or taken from the public domain, there may remain a core of protectable expression. In terms of a work's copyright value, this is the golden nugget. See *Brown Bag Software*, 960 F.2d at 1475. At this point, the court's substantial similarity inquiry focuses on whether the defendant copied any aspect of this protected expression, as well as an assessment of the copied portion's relative importance with respect to the plaintiff's overall program. See 3 Nimmer §13.03[F][5]; *Data East USA*, 862 F.2d at 208 ("To determine whether similarities result from unprotectable expression, analytic dissection of similarities may be performed. If . . . all similarities in expression arise from use of common ideas, then no substantial similarity can be found.").

3) Policy Considerations

We are satisfied that the three step approach we have just outlined not only comports with, but advances the constitutional policies underlying the Copyright

Act. Since any method that tries to distinguish idea from expression ultimately impacts on the scope of copyright protection afforded to a particular type of work, "the line [it draws] must be a pragmatic one, which also keeps in consideration 'the preservation of the balance between competition and protection. . . .'" *Apple Computer,* 714 F.2d at 1253 (citation omitted).

CA and some amici argue against the type of approach that we have set forth on the grounds that it will be a disincentive for future computer program research and development. At bottom, they claim that if programmers are not guaranteed broad copyright protection for their work, they will not invest the extensive time, energy and funds required to design and improve program structures. While they have a point, their argument cannot carry the day. The interest of the copyright law is not in simply conferring a monopoly on industrious persons, but in advancing the public welfare through rewarding artistic creativity, in a manner that permits the free use and development of non-protectable ideas and processes.

In this respect, our conclusion is informed by Justice Stewart's concise discussion of the principles that correctly govern the adaptation of the copyright law to new circumstances. In Twentieth Century Music Corp. v. Aiken, he wrote:

> The limited scope of the copyright holder's statutory monopoly, like the limited copyright duration required by the Constitution, reflects a balance of competing claims upon the public interest: Creative work is to be encouraged and rewarded, but private motivation must ultimately serve the cause of promoting broad public availability of literature, music, and the other arts. The immediate effect of our copyright law is to secure a fair return for an "author's" creative labor. But the ultimate aim is, by this incentive, to stimulate artistic creativity for the general public good. . . . When technological change has rendered its literal terms ambiguous, the Copyright Act must be construed in light of this basic purpose.

422 U.S. 151, 156 (1975) (citations and footnotes omitted).

Recently, the Supreme Court has emphatically reiterated that "[t]he primary objective of copyright is not to reward the labor of authors. . . ." Feist Publications, Inc. v. Rural Tel. Serv. Co., —U.S.—, 111 S. Ct. 1282, 1290 (1991). While the *Feist* decision deals primarily with the copyrightability of purely factual compilations, its underlying tenets apply to much of the work involved in computer programming. *Feist* put to rest the "sweat of the brow" doctrine in copyright law. *Id.* 111 S. Ct. at 1295. The rationale of that doctrine "was that copyright was a reward for the hard work that went into compiling facts." *Id.* 111 S. Ct. at 1291. The Court flatly rejected this justification for extending copyright protection, noting that it "eschewed the most fundamental axiom of copyright law —that no one may copyright facts or ideas." *Id.*

Feist teaches that substantial effort alone cannot confer copyright status on an otherwise uncopyrightable work. As we have discussed, despite the fact that significant labor and expense often goes into computer program flow-charting and debugging, that process does not always result in inherently protectable expression. Thus, *Feist* implicitly undercuts the *Whelan* rationale, "which allow[ed] copyright protection beyond the literal computer code . . . [in order to] provide the proper incentive for programmers by protecting their most valuable efforts. . . ." *Whelan,* 797 F.2d at 1237 (footnote omitted). We note that *Whelan* was decided prior to *Feist* when the "sweat of the brow" doctrine still had vitality. In view of the Supreme Court's recent holding, however, we must reject the legal basis of CA's disincentive argument.

Furthermore, we are unpersuaded that the test we approve today will lead to the dire consequences for the computer program industry that plaintiff and some amici predict. To the contrary, serious students of the industry have been highly critical of the sweeping scope of copyright protection engendered by the *Whelan* rule, in that it "enables first comers to 'lock up' basic programming techniques as implemented in programs to perform particular tasks." Menell, at 1087; see also Spivack, at 765 (*Whelan* "results in an inhibition of creation by virtue of the copyright owner's quasi-monopoly power").

To be frank, the exact contours of copyright protection for non-literal program structure are not completely clear. We trust that as future cases are decided, those limits will become better defined. Indeed, it may well be that the Copyright Act serves as a relatively weak barrier against public access to the theoretical interstices behind a program's source and object codes. This results from the hybrid nature of a computer program, which, while it is literary expression, is also a highly functional, utilitarian component in the larger process of computing.

Generally, we think that copyright registration—with its indiscriminating availability—is not ideally suited to deal with the highly dynamic technology of computer science. Thus far, many of the decisions in this area reflect the courts' attempt to fit the proverbial square peg in a round hole. The district court, see *Computer Assocs.*, 775 F. Supp. at 560, and at least one commentator have suggested that patent registration, with its exacting up-front novelty and non-obviousness requirements, might be the more appropriate rubric of protection for intellectual property of this kind. See Randell M. Whitmeyer, Comment, A Plea for Due Processes: Defining the Proper Scope of Patent Protection for Computer Software, 85 Nw.U. L. Rev. 1103, 1123-25 (1991); see also Lotus Dev. Corp. v. Borland Int'l, Inc., 788 F. Supp. 78, 91 (D. Mass. 1992) (discussing the potentially supplemental relationship between patent and copyright protection in the context of computer programs). In any event, now that more than 12 years have passed since CONTU issued its final report, the resolution of this specific issue could benefit from further legislative investigation—perhaps a CONTU II.

In the meantime, Congress has made clear that computer programs are literary works entitled to copyright protection. Of course, we shall abide by these instructions, but in so doing we must not impair the overall integrity of copyright law. While incentive based arguments in favor of broad copyright protection are perhaps attractive from a pure policy perspective, see *Lotus Dev. Corp.*, 740 F. Supp. at 58, ultimately, they have a corrosive effect on certain fundamental tenets of copyright doctrine. If the test we have outlined results in narrowing the scope of protection, as we expect it will, that result flows from applying, in accordance with Congressional intent, long-standing principles of copyright law to computer programs. Of course, our decision is also informed by our concern that these fundamental principles remain undistorted.

B. The District Court Decision . . .

2) Evidentiary Analysis

The district court had to determine whether Altai's OSCAR 3.5 program was substantially similar to CA's ADAPTER. . . .

The district court took the first step in the analysis set forth in this opinion when it separated the program by levels of abstraction. The district court stated:

> As applied to computer software programs, this abstractions test would progress in order of "increasing generality" from object code, to source code, to parameter lists, to services required, to general outline. In discussing the particular similarities, therefore, we shall focus on these levels.

Computer Assocs., 775 F. Supp. at 560. While the facts of a different case might require that a district court draw a more particularized blueprint of a program's overall structure, this description is a workable one for the case at hand.

Moving to the district court's evaluation of OSCAR 3.5's structural components, we agree with Judge Pratt's systematic exclusion of non-protectable expression. With respect to code, the district court observed that after the rewrite of OSCAR 3.4 to OSCAR 3.5, "there remained virtually no lines of code that were identical to ADAPTER." *Id.* at 561. Accordingly, the court found that the code "present[ed] no similarity at all." *Id.* at 562.

Next, Judge Pratt addressed the issue of similarity between the two programs' parameter lists and macros. He concluded that, viewing the conflicting evidence most favorably to CA, it demonstrated that "only a few of the lists and macros were similar to protected elements in ADAPTER; the others were either in the public domain or dictated by the functional demands of the program." *Id.* As discussed above, functional elements and elements taken from the public domain do not qualify for copyright protection. With respect to the few remaining parameter lists and macros, the district court could reasonably conclude that they did not warrant a finding of infringement given their relative contribution to the overall program. See Warner Bros., Inc. v. American Broadcasting Cos., Inc., 720 F.2d 231, 242 (2d Cir. 1983) (discussing de minimis exception which allows for literal copying of a small and usually insignificant portion of the plaintiff's work); 3 Nimmer §13.03[F][5], at 13-74. In any event, the district court reasonably found that, for lack of persuasive evidence, CA failed to meet its burden of proof on whether the macros and parameter lists at issue were substantially similar. See *Computer Assocs.*, 775 F. Supp. at 562.

The district court also found that the overlap exhibited between the list of services required for both ADAPTER and OSCAR 3.5 was "determined by the demands of the operating system and of the applications program to which it [was] to be linked through ADAPTER or OSCAR. . . ." *Id.* In other words, this aspect of the program's structure was dictated by the nature of other programs with which it was designed to interact and, thus, is not protected by copyright.

Finally, in his infringement analysis, Judge Pratt accorded no weight to the similarities between the two programs' organizational charts, "because [the charts were] so simple and obvious to anyone exposed to the operation of the program[s]." *Id.* CA argues that the district court's action in this regard "is not consistent with copyright law"—that "obvious" expression is protected, and that the district court erroneously failed to realize this. However, to say that elements of a work are "obvious," in the manner in which the district court used the word, is to say that they "follow naturally from the work's theme rather than from the author's creativity." 3 Nimmer §13.03[F][3], at 1365. This is but one formulation of the *scenes a faire* doctrine, which we have already endorsed as a means of weeding out unprotectable expression. . . .

Since we accept Judge Pratt's factual conclusions and the results of his legal analysis, we affirm his dismissal of CA's copyright infringement claim based upon OSCAR 3.5. We emphasize that, like all copyright infringement cases, those that involve computer programs are highly fact specific. The amount of protection due structural elements, in any given case, will vary according to the protectable expression found to exist within the program at issue. . . .

COMMENTS AND QUESTIONS

1. How does the *Altai* court distinguish idea from expression? Compare this method to that proposed and applied in *Whelan*. How would the *Whelan* case have come out if the *Altai* test had been applied? How would Baker v. Selden be decided under the *Altai* approach?

2. *Computer Associates* seems to ask courts to analytically dissect a computer program to determine what is protectable and copied and compare this to the entire program, rather than to the protectable uncopied elements, to determine substantial similarity. Does this suggest that a program with relatively little protectable material can be freely copied?

One limitation on such copying may be the copyright protection afforded to *compilations* of uncopyrightable material. Even though all of the individual elements of a computer program may themselves be uncopyrightable, the expressive selection and arrangement of those uncopyrightable pieces may itself qualify for copyright protection. Indeed, the Second Circuit acknowledged this in Softel Inc. v. Dragon Medical and Scientific Communications Inc., 118 F.3d 955 (2d Cir. 1997), where it held that the "comparison" step was required even where all of the elements of a program had been filtered out. The court remanded the case "so that the district court may enter a finding as to whether the manner in which Softel combined the various design elements in its software was protectable expression, and, if it was, whether Dragon infringed that expression." *Id*.

If the elements of a computer program are all unprotectable—for example, because they are driven by functional considerations, how likely is it that the selection and arrangement of those elements will be expressive rather than functional? Won't the constraints of programming dictate not only which modules are chosen, but how they must interact with respect to each other?

3. Which approach—*Whelan* or *Altai*—comports better with section 102(b) and Baker v. Selden? Is there a more appropriate way of distinguishing idea from expression in the context of application program code?

4. The *Altai* case has been warmly praised by most commentators. See, e.g., David Bender, Computer Associates v. Altai: Rationality Prevails, Computer Law., Aug. 1992, at 1; Pamela Samuelson et al., The Nature of Copyright Analysis for Computer Program: Copyright Law Professors' Brief Amicus Curiae in Lotus v. Borland, 16 Hastings Comm and Ent. L.J. 657 (1994) (brief of 24 copyright law professors endorsing *Altai*). However, the decision has also been bitterly attacked by lawyers and scholars representing large computer companies. See Jack Brown, Analytical Dissection of Copyrighted Computer Software—Complicating the

Simple and Confounding the Complex, 25 Ariz. St. L.J. 801 (1993); Anthony L. Clapes & Jennifer M. Daniels, Revenge of the Luddites: A Closer Look at Computer Associates v. Altai, Computer Law., Nov. 1992, at 11. Professor Arthur Miller, a CONTU Commissioner, has expressed apprehension about the implications of the *Altai* approach:

> [A] court must employ considerable caution in excluding efficient or speedy program expression lest it undermine the effective protection of computer programs. For example, the mere fact that the expression is efficient should not, without more, bar protection for original authorship in the programming context any more than it does in prose work. An uncritical application of *Altai*'s language would penalize the most effective (and in some senses the most artistic) programmers.

Miller, Copyright Protection for Computer Programs, Databases, and Computer-Generated Works: Is Anything New Since CONTU?, 106 Harv. L. Rev. 977, 1004-1005 (1993) (footnotes omitted). Do you agree with Miller's view of the scope of copyright protection for the efficient elements of program structure? Is protection of decisions dictated by efficiency consistent with copyright cases outside the computer context? Or would it mean protecting function rather than expression?

    5. The *Altai* test was rapidly adopted by most courts. Judicial convergence on the abstraction-filtration-comparison test has been so complete that every court to confront the issue since 1992 has chosen the *Altai* approach over the *Whelan* approach. See ILOG, Inc. v. Bell Logic, LLC, 181 F. Supp.2d 3 (D. Mass. 2002); O.P. Solutions v. Intellectual Property Network, Ltd., 50 U.S.P.Q.2d 1399 (S.D.N.Y. 1999); Bateman v. Mnemonics, Inc., 79 F.3d 1532, 1543-1545 (11th Cir. 1996); Apple Computer v. Microsoft Corp., 35 F.3d 1435 (9th Cir. 1994); Engineering Dynamics, Inc. v. Structural Software, Inc., 26 F.3d 1335 (5th Cir. 1994); Kepner-Tregoe, Inc. v. Leadership Software, 12 F.3d 527 (5th Cir. 1994); Gates Rubber Co. v. Bando Chemical Indus., 9 F.3d 823 (10th Cir. 1993); Atari Games Corp. v. Nintendo, 975 F.2d 832 (Fed. Cir. 1992); Control Data Systems, Inc. v. Infoware, Inc., 903 F. Supp. 1316 (D. Minn. 1995); CMAX/Cleveland, Inc. v. UCR, Inc., 804 F. Supp. 337 (M.D. Ga. 1992); Mark A. Lemley, Convergence in the Law of Software Copyright, 10 High Tech. L.J. 1 (1995). See also Brown Bag Software v. Symantec Corp., 960 F.2d 1465, 1475-1476 (9th Cir. 1992) (endorsing "analytic dissection" of the elements of a computer program prior to the *Altai* decision). Cf. MiTek Holdings Inc. v. Arce Engineering Co., 89 F.3d 1548 (11th Cir. 1996) (upholding *Altai* approach but allowing plaintiff to skip abstraction step by identifying in advance those elements it considers to be protectable and infringed). In addition, courts in Canada, the United Kingdom, and France have endorsed the *Altai* filtration analysis.

    Not all of these courts have approached the abstraction-filtration-comparison analysis in precisely the same way, however. The Tenth Circuit decision in *Gates Rubber* is particularly notable for its elaboration of the test beyond the parameters of *Altai*. The *Gates Rubber* court acknowledged that "[a]pplication of the abstractions test will necessarily vary from case-to-case and program-to-program. Given the complexity and ever-changing nature of computer technology, we decline to set forth any strict methodology for the abstraction of computer programs." Nonetheless, the court identified six levels of "generally declining abstraction":

(1) the main purpose of the computer program; (2) the structure or architecture of a program, generally as represented in a flowchart; (3) "modules" that comprise particular program operations or types of stored data; (4) individual algorithms or data structures employed in each of the modules; (5) the source code that instructs the computer to carry out each necessary operation on each data structure; and (6) the object code that is actually read by the computer. The court used these levels of abstraction to facilitate its analysis of the program at issue.

The *Gates Rubber* court also gave further content to the filtration part of the *Altai* analysis. The court filtered out six unprotectable elements: ideas, the processes or methods of the computer program,[2] facts, material in the public domain, expression that has "merged" with an idea or process, and expression that is so standard or common as to be a "necessary incident" to an idea or process.[3] Finally, the *Gates Rubber* court indicated that comparison of the protected elements of a program should be done on a case-by-case basis, with an eye toward determining whether a substantial portion of the protectable expression of the original work has been copied.

Is this analysis consistent with *Altai*? Is a court applying *Gates Rubber* likely to give more or less protection to a computer program than would the *Altai* court? Note that applying *Altai* does not mean that the nonliteral elements of computer programs get no protection at all. For example, in the Fifth Circuit, which has expressly adopted the *Gates Rubber* approach, one district court has concluded that a set of threshold values set by a computer manufacturer to indicate a failure threshold for replacement of a hard drive were copyrightable, because the business and engineering decisions that went into setting those values showed sufficient original expression to be protected. Compaq Computer v. Procom Technology, 908 F. Supp. 1409 (S.D. Tex. 1995). The court held that the merger and *scenes à faire* doctrines did not bar copyrightability, because the precise values Compaq chose were not necessary for competing manufacturers. See also Harbor Software Inc. v. Applied Systems Inc., 925 F. Supp. 1042 (S.D.N.Y. 1996) (finding nonliteral elements of a computer program protectable at a fairly low level of abstraction under the *Altai* test).

6. Note that while both *Whelan* and *Altai* are nominally about the scope of protection afforded computer programs under the copyright laws, both courts merge the analysis of infringement into the protectability analysis. This is particularly evident in *Altai*'s filtration analysis, where the comparison step involves identifying the similarities between the copyrighted program and the accused program.

---

2. *Gates Rubber*, 9 F.3d at 836-837. The court cited the legislative history accompanying section 102(b) of the Copyright Act, which clearly indicates that the actual processes or methods used in a computer program are not entitled to copyright protection. *Id*. The court noted that processes were most commonly found in the program architecture, module structure, and algorithms used. *Id*. at 837.

3. *Id*. This is the *scenes à faire* doctrine. The court held that such standard devices in computer programs include "those elements of a program that have been dictated by external factors," such as hardware and software standards, specifications, or compatibility requirements, customer design specifications, and basic industry practices. *Id*.

PROBLEMS

Problem 2-2. The Midwest Corn Cooperative Association (MCCA) is a nonprofit agricultural cooperative comprising approximately 15,000 corn farmers in the midwestern states. MCCA's purpose is to assist its members in the growing and marketing of corn. During the mid-1970s, MCCA developed a computer software system called "CornMart," which provides users with information regarding corn prices and availability, accounting services, and a means for electronically completing actual sales. The Cornmart system is used by corn farmers and buyers through terminals connected to MCCA's large central computer by telephone lines.

CornMart was developed by a team of programmers that included George Cusher and Ben Fishman. In the early 1980s, after the program had been up and running for a number of years, Cusher and Fishman decided that the system would have much greater usefulness if the CornMart program could be operated on personal computers, which were by then increasingly used by members of MCCA. Cusher and Fishman took a complete source code version of CornMart and supporting program documentation when they departed MCCA.

In 1985, Cusher and Fishman formed Cornware, Inc., and began work on a personal computer version of CornMart. By early 1986, they succeeded in writing this version, which they marketed as Cornware. Soon after they began marketing their new software, MCCA sued, alleging copyright infringement.

Expert testimony at trial established that Cornware and CornMart were very similar in terms of functional specification, overall structure, and documentation. The main difference between the systems is that CornMart is designed to run on a mainframe computer and Cornware is designed to run on a personal computer. There was, however, no literal copying of code. Cusher and Fishman testified that they had not copied or modified the CornMart program but instead had "drawn on their knowledge of the corn industry and expertise in computer programming and design gained over many years." Expert testimony at trial indicated that it would take significant effort to modify a program as complex as CornMart to run on a personal computer—perhaps more effort than rewriting the program entirely. Nonetheless, there remained significant structural similarities between the programs, although two experts testified that residual similarity between the programs reflected features of the corn market and that different programmers knowledgeable about the corn industry could conceivably make similar judgments. For example, both programs were designed to present the same information as is contained on a corn recap sheet, a standard form used for corn transactions.

How would you argue the case for MCCA? For Cornware? How would this case be resolved under the *Whelan* test?

Problem 2-4. Demento Corporation (Demento) produces Demento II, the leading home video game system. The Demento II consists of a console, which runs game cartridges and attaches to a monitor or standard television, and a control device, which enables the user to manipulate characters or other images of particular games on the screen. Demento licenses a limited number of games per year.

In order to prevent unauthorized game producers from manufacturing games to run on the Demento II console, Demento developed a "lock-out" device that governs access to the console. The console contains a "master chip" or "lock" that will only run game cartridges that contain an appropriate "slave chip" or "key." When a user inserts an authorized game cartridge into the Demento II, the slave chip transmits an arbitrary data stream key, which is received by the master chip and unlocks the console, allowing the game to be played. The unlocking device is a sophisticated software program encoded in the master and slave chips. There is a multitude of different programs capable of generating the data stream that unlocks the console, although it would be almost impossible to decipher the "key" by trial and error. It would be like trying to find a needle in a haystack.

The rapid growth of the home video game market eroded the revenue base of Mutant Corporation (Mutant), a leading maker of arcade video games. Mutant sought to license the right to produce game cartridges for the Demento II system, but was put off by the limits on the number of new games that Demento would license per year and the high cost of each license. Mutant decided instead to develop its own slave chip that would unlock the Demento II game cartridge.

Mutant engineers first chemically peeled the layers of the Demento II chips to allow microsopic examination of the circuitry. Through this means, they were able to decipher the object code and construct the series of pulsating signals that unlock the master chip. Mutant discovered that only a relatively small portion of the coded message was necessary to unlock the Demento II console. From this information, Mutant software designers built a slave chip that successfully unlocked the Demento II console and enabled Mutant's game cartridges to run. It included the entire coded message for fear that Demento might later alter new versions of the Demento II system in such a way as to make Mutant's cartridges inoperable on newer units seeking the fuller coded message. In order to differentiate its product, the Mutant slave program was written in a different computer language and employed a microprocessor different from the Demento II system. Since the Mutant microprocessor operated at a faster speed than the Demento II chip, the Mutant program included numerous pauses.

Despite these differences, Demento promptly sued Mutant for copyright infringement after Mutant introduced its first game cartridge for the Demento II system. What is the unprotectable idea of the Demento II system? What is the protectable expression? Is the lockout code functional? How would this case be resolved in a jurisdiction adhering the *Whelan* test? The *Altai* test?

3. Protection for Functional Elements and Protocols

Many software copyright cases involve the taking of particular pieces of a plaintiff's program. Defendants in these cases may be those who attempt to clone the plaintiff's program, writing their own code to create a functionally equivalent program. See Lotus Dev. Corp. v. Paperback Software, 740 F. Supp. 37 (D. Mass. 1990). The defendants may also be those who simply attempt to reproduce the internal program interface necessary to make two programs compatible. Whether functional program elements could be protected under copyright law was tested in a series of cases involving the Lotus 1-2-3 spreadsheet.

Lotus Development Corp. v. Borland International
United States Court of Appeals for the First Circuit
49 F.3d 807 (1st Cir. 1995)

STAHL, Circuit Judge.

This appeal requires us to decide whether a computer menu command hierarchy is copyrightable subject matter. In particular, we must decide whether, as the district court held, plaintiff-appellee Lotus Development Corporation's copyright in Lotus 1-2-3, a computer spreadsheet program, was infringed by defendant-appellant Borland International, Inc., when Borland copied the Lotus 1-2-3 menu command hierarchy into its Quattro and Quattro Pro computer spreadsheet programs. See Lotus Dev. Corp. v. Borland Int'l, Inc., 788 F. Supp. 78 (D. Mass. 1992) ("*Borland I*"); Lotus Dev. Corp. v. Borland Int'l, Inc., 799 F. Supp. 203 (D. Mass. 1992) ("*Borland II*"); Lotus Dev. Corp. v. Borland Int'l, Inc., 831 F. Supp. 202 (D. Mass. 1993) ("*Borland III*"); Lotus Dev. Corp. v. Borland Int'l, Inc., 831 F. Supp. 223 (D. Mass. 1993) ("*Borland IV*").

I. Background

Lotus 1-2-3 is a spreadsheet program that enables users to perform accounting functions electronically on a computer. Users manipulate and control the program via a series of menu commands, such as "Copy," "Print," and "Quit." Users choose commands either by highlighting them on the screen or by typing their first letter. In all, Lotus 1-2-3 has 469 commands arranged into more than 50 menus and submenus.

Lotus 1-2-3, like many computer programs, allows users to write what are called "macros." By writing a macro, a user can designate a series of command choices with a single macro keystroke. Then, to execute that series of commands in multiple parts of the spreadsheet, rather than typing the whole series each time, the user only needs to type the single pre-programmed macro keystroke, causing the program to recall and perform the designated series of commands automatically. Thus, Lotus 1-2-3 macros shorten the time needed to set up and operate the program.

Borland released its first Quattro program to the public in 1987, after Borland's engineers had labored over its development for nearly three years. Borland's objective was to develop a spreadsheet program far superior to existing programs, including Lotus 1-2-3. In Borland's words, "from the time of its initial release . . . Quattro included enormous innovations over competing spreadsheet products."

The district court found, and Borland does not now contest, that Borland included in its Quattro and Quattro Pro version 1.0 programs "a virtually identical copy of the entire 1-2-3 menu tree." *Borland III*, 831 F. Supp. at 212. In so doing, Borland did not copy any of Lotus's underlying computer code; it copied only the words and structure of Lotus's menu command hierarchy. Borland included the Lotus menu command hierarchy in its programs to make them compatible with Lotus 1-2-3 so that spreadsheet users who were already familiar with Lotus 1-2-3 would be able to switch to the Borland programs without having to learn new commands or rewrite their Lotus macros.

In its Quattro and Quattro Pro version 1.0 programs, Borland achieved compatibility with Lotus 1-2-3 by offering its users an alternate user interface, the "Lotus Emulation Interface." By activating the Emulation Interface, Borland users would see the Lotus menu commands on their screens and could interact with Quattro or Quattro Pro as if using Lotus 1-2-3, albeit with a slightly different looking screen and with many Borland options not available on Lotus 1-2-3. In effect, Borland allowed users to choose how they wanted to communicate with Borland's spreadsheet programs: either by using menu commands designed by Borland, or by using the commands and command structure used in Lotus 1-2-3 augmented by Borland-added commands.

Lotus filed this action against Borland in the District of Massachusetts on July 2, 1990, four days after a district court held that the Lotus 1-2-3 "menu structure, taken as a whole—including the choice of command terms [and] the structure and order of those terms," was protected expression covered by Lotus's copyrights. Lotus Dev. Corp. v. Paperback Software Int'l, 740 F. Supp. 37, 68, 70 (D. Mass. 1990) ("*Paperback*").[1] . . .

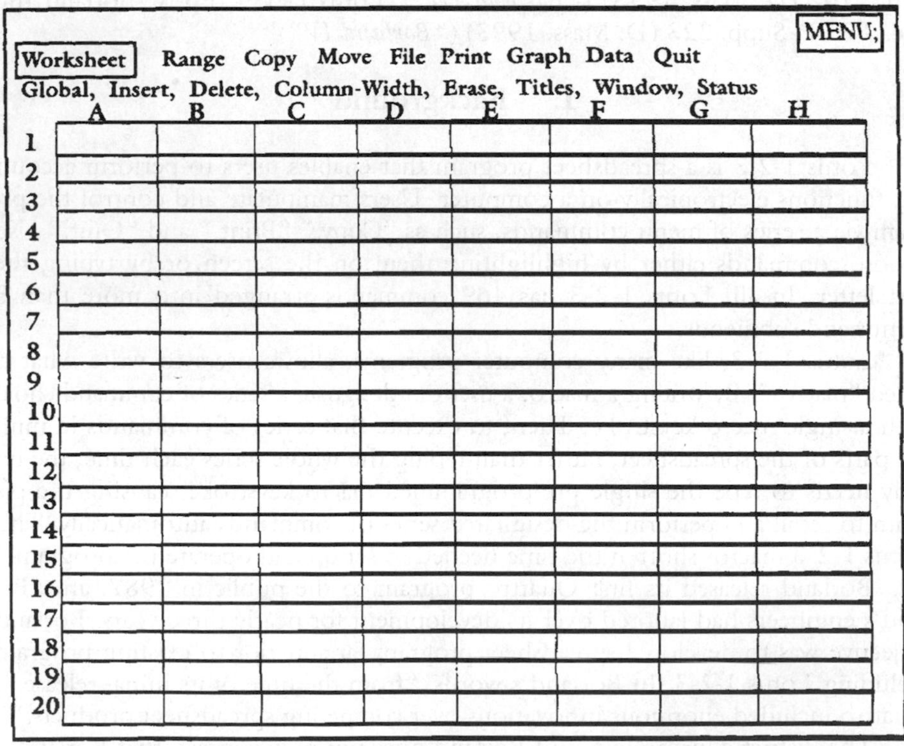

FIGURE 2-1
Facsimile of a Lotus 1-2-3 screen display.

1. Judge Keeton presided over both the *Paperback* litigation and this case.

On July 31, 1992, the district court denied Borland's motion [for summary judgment] and granted Lotus's motion in part. The district court ruled that the Lotus menu command hierarchy was copyrightable expression because

> [a] very satisfactory spreadsheet menu tree can be constructed using different commands and a different command structure from those of Lotus 1-2-3. In fact, Borland has constructed just such an alternate tree for use in Quattro Pro's native mode. Even if one holds the arrangement of menu commands constant, it is possible to generate literally millions of satisfactory menu trees by varying the menu commands employed.

Borland II, 799 F. Supp. at 217. The district court demonstrated this by offering alternate command words for the ten commands that appear in Lotus's main menu. *Id.* For example, the district court stated that "the 'Quit' command could be named 'Exit' without any other modifications," and that "the 'Copy' command could be called 'Clone,' 'Ditto,' 'Duplicate,' 'Imitate,' 'Mimic,' 'Replicate,' and 'Reproduce,' among others." *Id.* Because so many variations were possible, the district court concluded that the Lotus developers' choice and arrangement of command terms, reflected in the Lotus menu command hierarchy, constituted copyrightable expression.

In granting partial summary judgment to Lotus, the district court held that Borland had infringed Lotus's copyright in Lotus 1-2-3 . . . . *Borland II*, 799 F. Supp. at 223. The court nevertheless concluded that while the Quattro and Quattro Pro programs infringed Lotus's copyright, Borland had not copied the entire Lotus 1-2-3 user interface, as Lotus had contended. . . .

Immediately following the district court's summary judgment decision, Borland removed the Lotus Emulation Interface from its products. Thereafter, Borland's spreadsheet programs no longer displayed the Lotus 1-2-3 menus to Borland users, and as a result Borland users could no longer communicate with Borland's programs as if they were using a more sophisticated version of Lotus 1-2-3. Nonetheless, Borland's programs continued to be partially compatible with Lotus 1-2-3, for Borland retained what it called the "Key Reader" in its Quattro Pro programs. Once turned on, the Key Reader allowed Borland's programs to understand and perform some Lotus 1-2-3 macros. With the Key Reader on, the Borland programs used Quattro Pro menus for display, interaction, and macro execution, except when they encountered a slash ("/") key in a macro (the starting key for any Lotus 1-2-3 macro), in which case they interpreted the macro as having been written for Lotus 1-2-3. Accordingly, people who wrote or purchased macros to shorten the time needed to perform an operation in Lotus 1-2-3 could still use those macros in Borland's programs. The district court permitted Lotus to file a supplemental complaint alleging that the Key Reader infringed its copyright.

The parties agreed to try the remaining liability issues without a jury. The district court held two trials, the Phase I trial covering all remaining issues raised in the original complaint (relating to the Emulation Interface) and the Phase II trial covering all issues raised in the supplemental complaint (relating to the Key Reader). . . .

In its Phase I trial decision, the district court found that "each of the Borland emulation interfaces contains a virtually identical copy of the 1-2-3 menu tree and that the 1-2-3 menu tree is capable of a wide variety of expression." *Borland III*, 831 F. Supp. at 218. The district court also rejected Borland's affirmative defenses of laches and estoppel. *Id.* at 218-23.

In its Phase II trial decision, the district court found that Borland's Key Reader file included "a virtually identical copy of the Lotus menu tree structure, but represented in a different form and with first letters of menu command names in place of the full menu command names." *Borland IV*, 831 F. Supp. at 228. In other words, Borland's programs no longer included the Lotus command terms, but only their first letters. The district court held that "the Lotus menu structure, organization, and first letters of the command names . . . constitute part of the protectable expression found in [Lotus 1-2-3]." *Id*. at 233. Accordingly, the district court held that with its Key Reader, Borland had infringed Lotus's copyright. *Id*. at 245. The district court also rejected Borland's affirmative defenses of waiver, laches, estoppel, and fair use. *Id*. at 235-45. The district court then entered a permanent injunction against Borland, *id*. at 245, from which Borland appeals. . . .

II. Discussion

On appeal, Borland does not dispute that it factually copied the words and arrangement of the Lotus menu command hierarchy. Rather, Borland argues that it "lawfully copied the unprotectable menus of Lotus 1-2-3." Borland contends that the Lotus menu command hierarchy is not copyrightable because it is a system, method of operation, process, or procedure foreclosed from protection by 17 U.S.C. §102(b). Borland also raises a number of affirmative defenses.

A. Copyright Infringement Generally

. . . In this appeal, we are faced only with whether the Lotus menu command hierarchy is copyrightable subject matter in the first instance, for Borland concedes that Lotus has a valid copyright in Lotus 1-2-3 as a whole and admits to factually copying the Lotus menu command hierarchy. As a result, this appeal is in a very different posture from most copyright-infringement cases, for copyright infringement generally turns on whether the defendant has copied protected expression as a factual matter. Because of this different posture, most copyright-infringement cases provide only limited help to us in deciding this appeal. This is true even with respect to those copyright-infringement cases that deal with computers and computer software.

B. Matter of First Impression

Whether a computer menu command hierarchy constitutes copyrightable subject matter is a matter of first impression in this court. While some other courts appear to have touched on it briefly in dicta, see, e.g., Autoskill, Inc. v. National Educ. Support Sys., Inc., 994 F.2d 1476, 1495 n.23 (10th Cir.), cert. denied, 126 L. Ed. 2d 254, 114 S. Ct. 307 (1993), we know of no cases that deal with the copyrightability of a menu command hierarchy standing on its own (i.e., without other elements of the user interface, such as screen displays, in issue). Thus we are navigating in uncharted waters.

Borland vigorously argues, however, that the Supreme Court charted our course more than 100 years ago when it decided Baker v. Selden, 101 U.S. 99, 25 L. Ed. 841 (1879). In Baker v. Selden, the Court held that Selden's copyright over the textbook in which he explained his new way to do accounting did not grant him a monopoly on the use of his accounting system. Borland argues:

> The facts of Baker v. Selden, and even the arguments advanced by the parties in that case, are identical to those in this case. The only difference is that the "user interface" of Selden's system was implemented by pen and paper rather than by computer.

. . . We do not think that Baker v. Selden is nearly as analogous to this appeal as Borland claims. Of course, Lotus 1-2-3 is a computer spreadsheet, and as such its grid of horizontal rows and vertical columns certainly resembles an accounting ledger or any other paper spreadsheet. Those grids, however, are not at issue in this appeal for, unlike Selden, Lotus does not claim to have a monopoly over its accounting system. Rather, this appeal involves Lotus's monopoly over the commands it uses to operate the computer. Accordingly, this appeal is not, as Borland contends, "identical" to Baker v. Selden.

C. *Altai*

Before we analyze whether the Lotus menu command hierarchy is a system, method of operation, process, or procedure, we first consider the applicability of the test the Second Circuit set forth in Computer Assoc. Int'l, Inc. v. Altai, Inc., 982 F.2d 693 (2d Cir. 1992). The Second Circuit designed its *Altai* test to deal with the fact that computer programs, copyrighted as "literary works," can be infringed by what is known as "nonliteral" copying, which is copying that is paraphrased or loosely paraphrased rather than word for word. See *id.* at 701 (citing nonliteral-copying cases); see also 3 Melville B. Nimmer & David Nimmer, Nimmer on Copyright §13.03[A][1] (1993). When faced with nonliteral-copying cases, courts must determine whether similarities are due merely to the fact that the two works share the same underlying idea or whether they instead indicate that the second author copied the first author's expression. The Second Circuit designed its *Altai* test to deal with this situation in the computer context, specifically with whether one computer program copied nonliteral expression from another program's code. . . .

In the instant appeal, we are not confronted with alleged nonliteral copying of computer code. Rather, we are faced with Borland's deliberate, literal copying of the Lotus menu command hierarchy. Thus, we must determine not whether nonliteral copying occurred in some amorphous sense, but rather whether the literal copying of the Lotus menu command hierarchy constitutes copyright infringement.

While the *Altai* test may provide a useful framework for assessing the alleged nonliteral copying of computer code, we find it to be of little help in assessing whether the literal copying of a menu command hierarchy constitutes copyright infringement. In fact, we think that the *Altai* test in this context may actually be misleading because, in instructing courts to abstract the various levels, it seems to encourage them to find a base level that includes copyrightable subject matter that, if literally copied, would make the copier liable for copyright infringement.[8] While that base (or literal) level would not be at issue in a nonliteral-copying case like *Altai*, it is precisely what is at issue in this appeal. We think that abstracting menu command hierarchies down to their individual word and menu levels and then filtering idea from expression at that stage, as both the *Altai* and the district court tests require, obscures the more fundamental question of whether a menu command hierarchy can be copyrighted at all. The initial inquiry should not be whether individual components of a menu command hierarchy are expressive, but rather whether the menu command hierarchy as a whole can be copyrighted. But see Gates Rubber Co. v. Bando Chem. Indus., Ltd., 9 F.3d 823 (10th Cir. 1993) (endorsing *Altai*'s abstraction-filtration-comparison test as a way of determining whether "menus and sorting criteria" are copyrightable).

D. The Lotus Menu Command Hierarchy: A "Method of Operation"

Borland argues that the Lotus menu command hierarchy is uncopyrightable because it is a system, method of operation, process, or procedure foreclosed from copyright protection by 17 U.S.C. §102(b). Section 102(b) states: "In no case does copyright protection for an original work of authorship extend to any idea, procedure, process, system, method of operation, concept, principle, or discovery, regardless of the form in which it is described, explained, illustrated, or embodied in such work." Because we conclude that the Lotus menu command hierarchy is a method of operation, we do not consider whether it could also be a system, process, or procedure.

We think that "method of operation," as that term is used in §102(b), refers to the means by which a person operates something, whether it be a car, a food processor, or a computer. Thus a text describing how to operate something would not extend copyright protection to the method of operation itself; other people would be free to employ that method and to describe it in their own words. Similarly, if a new method of operation is used rather than described, other people would still be free to employ or describe that method.

We hold that the Lotus menu command hierarchy is an uncopyrightable "method of operation." The Lotus menu command hierarchy provides the means by which users control and operate Lotus 1-2-3. If users wish to copy material, for example, they use the "Copy" command. If users wish to print material, they use the "Print" command. Users must use the command terms to tell the computer what to do. Without the menu command hierarchy, users would not be able to access and control, or indeed make use of, Lotus 1-2-3's functional capabilities.

8. We recognize that *Altai* never states that every work contains a copyrightable "nugget" of protectable expression. Nonetheless, the implication is that for literal copying, "it is not necessary to determine the level of abstraction at which similarity ceases to consist of an 'expression of ideas,' because literal similarity by definition is always a similarity as to the expression of ideas." 3 Melville B. Nimmer & David Nimmer, Nimmer on Copyright §13.03[A][2] (1993).

The Lotus menu command hierarchy does not merely explain and present Lotus 1-2-3's functional capabilities to the user; it also serves as the method by which the program is operated and controlled. The Lotus menu command hierarchy is different from the Lotus long prompts, for the long prompts are not necessary to the operation of the program; users could operate Lotus 1-2-3 even if there were no long prompts. The Lotus menu command hierarchy is also different from the Lotus screen displays, for users need not "use" any expressive aspects of the screen displays in order to operate Lotus 1-2-3; because the way the screens look has little bearing on how users control the program, the screen displays are not part of Lotus 1-2-3's "method of operation." The Lotus menu command hierarchy is also different from the underlying computer code, because while code is necessary for the program to work, its precise formulation is not. In other words, to offer the same capabilities as Lotus 1-2-3, Borland did not have to copy Lotus's underlying code (and indeed it did not); to allow users to operate its programs in substantially the same way, however, Borland had to copy the Lotus menu command hierarchy. Thus the Lotus 1-2-3 code is not an uncopyrightable "method of operation."

The district court held that the Lotus menu command hierarchy, with its specific choice and arrangement of command terms, constituted an "expression" of the "idea" of operating a computer program with commands arranged hierarchically into menus and submenus. *Borland II*, 799 F. Supp. at 216. Under the district court's reasoning, Lotus's decision to employ hierarchically arranged command terms to operate its program could not foreclose its competitors from also employing hierarchically arranged command terms to operate their programs, but it did foreclose them from employing the specific command terms and arrangement that Lotus had used. In effect, the district court limited Lotus 1-2-3's "method of operation" to an abstraction.

Accepting the district court's finding that the Lotus developers made some expressive choices in choosing and arranging the Lotus command terms, we nonetheless hold that that expression is not copyrightable because it is part of Lotus 1-2-3's "method of operation." We do not think that "methods of operation" are limited to abstractions; rather, they are the means by which a user operates something. If specific words are essential to operating something, then they are part of a "method of operation" and, as such, are unprotectable. This is so whether they must be highlighted, typed in, or even spoken, as computer programs no doubt will soon be controlled by spoken words.

The fact that Lotus developers could have designed the Lotus menu command hierarchy differently is immaterial to the question of whether it is a "method of operation." In other words, our initial inquiry is not whether the Lotus menu command hierarchy incorporates any expression. Rather, our initial inquiry is whether the Lotus menu command hierarchy is a "method of operation." Concluding, as we do, that users operate Lotus 1-2-3 by using the Lotus menu command hierarchy, and that the entire Lotus menu command hierarchy is essential to operating Lotus 1-2-3, we do not inquire further whether that method of operation could have been designed differently. The "expressive" choices of what to name the command terms and how to arrange them do not magically change the uncopyrightable menu command hierarchy into copyrightable subject matter.

Our holding that "methods of operation" are not limited to mere abstractions is bolstered by Baker v. Selden. In *Baker*, the Supreme Court explained that the teachings of science and the rules and methods of useful art have their final end in application and use; and this application and use are what the public derive from the publication of a book which teaches them. . . . The description of the art in a book, though entitled to the benefit of copyright, lays no foundation for an exclusive claim to the art itself. The object of the one is explanation; the object of the other is use. The former may be secured by copyright. The latter can only be secured, if it can be secured at all, by letters-patent.

Baker v. Selden, 101 U.S. at 104-05. Lotus wrote its menu command hierarchy so that people could learn it and use it. Accordingly, it falls squarely within the prohibition on copyright protection established in Baker v. Selden and codified by Congress in §102(b).

In many ways, the Lotus menu command hierarchy is like the buttons used to control, say, a video cassette recorder ("VCR"). A VCR is a machine that enables one to watch and record video tapes. Users operate VCRs by pressing a series of buttons that are typically labelled "Record, Play, Reverse, Fast Forward, Pause, Stop/Eject." That the buttons are arranged and labeled does not make them a "literary work," nor does it make them an "expression" of the abstract "method of operating" a VCR via a set of labeled buttons. Instead, the buttons are themselves the "method of operating" the VCR.

When a Lotus 1-2-3 user chooses a command, either by highlighting it on the screen or by typing its first letter, he or she effectively pushes a button. Highlighting the "Print" command on the screen, or typing the letter "P," is analogous to pressing a VCR button labeled "Play."

Just as one could not operate a buttonless VCR, it would be impossible to operate Lotus 1-2-3 without employing its menu command hierarchy. Thus the Lotus command terms are not equivalent to the labels on the VCR's buttons, but are instead equivalent to the buttons themselves. Unlike the labels on a VCR's buttons, which merely make operating a VCR easier by indicating the buttons' functions, the Lotus menu commands are essential to operating Lotus 1-2-3. Without the menu commands, there would be no way to "push" the Lotus buttons, as one could push unlabeled VCR buttons. While Lotus could probably have designed a user interface for which the command terms were mere labels, it did not do so here. Lotus 1-2-3 depends for its operation on use of the precise command terms that make up the Lotus menu command hierarchy. . . .

Computer programs, unlike VCRs, are copyrightable as "literary works." 17 U.S.C. §102(a). Accordingly, one might argue, the "buttons" used to operate a computer program are not like the buttons used to operate a VCR, for they are not subject to a useful-article exception. The response, of course, is that the arrangement of buttons on a VCR would not be copyrightable even without a useful-article exception, because the buttons are an uncopyrightable "method of operation." Similarly, the "buttons" of a computer program are also an uncopyrightable "method of operation."

That the Lotus menu command hierarchy is a "method of operation" becomes clearer when one considers program compatibility. Under Lotus's theory, if a user uses several different programs, he or she must learn how to perform the same operation in a different way for each program used. For example, if the user wanted the computer to print material, then the user would have to learn not just one method of operating the computer such that it prints, but many different methods. We find this absurd. The fact that there may be many different ways to operate a computer program, or even many different ways to operate a computer program using a set of hierarchically arranged command terms, does not make the actual method of operation chosen copyrightable; it still functions as a method for operating the computer and as such is uncopyrightable.

Consider also that users employ the Lotus menu command hierarchy in writing macros. Under the district court's holding, if the user wrote a macro to shorten the time needed to perform a certain operation in Lotus 1-2-3, the user would be unable to use that macro to shorten the time needed to perform that same operation in another program. Rather, the user would have to rewrite his or her macro using that other program's menu command hierarchy. This is despite the fact that the macro is clearly the user's own work product. We think that forcing the user to cause the computer to perform the same operation in a different way ignores Congress's direction in §102(b) that "methods of operation" are not copyrightable. That programs can offer users the ability to write macros in many different ways does not change the fact that, once written, the macro allows the user to perform an operation automatically. As the Lotus menu command hierarchy serves as the basis for Lotus 1-2-3 macros, the Lotus menu command hierarchy is a "method of operation." . . .

We also note that in most contexts, there is no need to "build" upon other people's expression, for the ideas conveyed by that expression can be conveyed by someone else without copying the first author's expression. In the context of methods of operation, however, "building" requires the use of the precise method of operation already employed; otherwise, "building" would require dismantling, too. Original developers are not the only people entitled to build on the methods of operation they create; anyone can. Thus, Borland may build on the method of operation that Lotus designed and may use the Lotus menu command hierarchy in doing so.

Our holding that methods of operation are not limited to abstractions goes against *Autoskill*, 994 F.2d at 1495 n.23, in which the Tenth Circuit rejected the defendant's argument that the keying procedure used in a computer program was an uncopyrightable "procedure" or "method of operation" under §102(b). The program at issue, which was designed to test and train students with reading deficiencies, *id.* at 1481, required students to select responses to the program's queries "by pressing the 1, 2, or 3 keys." *Id.* at 1495 n.23. The Tenth Circuit held that, "for purposes of the preliminary injunction, . . . the record showed that [this] keying procedure reflected at least a minimal degree of creativity," as required by *Feist* for copyright protection. *Id.* As an initial matter, we question whether a programmer's decision to have users select a response by pressing the 1, 2, or 3 keys is original. More importantly, however, we fail to see how "a student selecting a response by pressing the 1, 2, or 3 keys," *id.*, can be anything but an unprotectable method of operation.[14] . . .

Reversed.

---

14. The Ninth Circuit has also indicated in dicta that "menus, and keystrokes" may be copyrightable. Brown Bag Software v. Symantec Corp., 960 F.2d 1465, 1477 (9th Cir.), *cert. denied*, BB Asset Management, Inc. v. Symantec Corp., 121 L. Ed. 2d 141, 113 S. Ct. 198 (1992). In that case, however, the plaintiff did not show that the defendant had copied the plaintiff's menus or keystrokes, so the court was not directly faced with whether the menus or keystrokes constituted an unprotectable method of operation. *Id.*

BOUDIN, Circuit Judge, concurring.

The importance of this case, and a slightly different emphasis in my view of the underlying problem, prompt me to add a few words to the majority's tightly focused discussion.

I.

Most of the law of copyright and the "tools" of analysis have developed in the context of literary works such as novels, plays, and films. In this milieu, the principal problem—simply stated, if difficult to resolve—is to stimulate creative expression without unduly limiting access by others to the broader themes and concepts deployed by the author. The middle of the spectrum presents close cases; but a "mistake" in providing too much protection involves a small cost: subsequent authors treating the same themes must take a few more steps away from the original expression.

The problem presented by computer programs is fundamentally different in one respect. The computer program is a means for causing something to happen; it has a mechanical utility, an instrumental role, in accomplishing the world's work. Granting protection, in other words, can have some of the consequences of patent protection in limiting other people's ability to perform a task in the most efficient manner. Utility does not bar copyright (dictionaries may be copyrighted), but it alters the calculus.

Of course, the argument for protection is undiminished, perhaps even enhanced, by utility: if we want more of an intellectual product, a temporary monopoly for the creator provides incentives for others to create other, different items in this class. But the "cost" side of the equation may be different where one places a very high value on public access to a useful innovation that may be the most efficient means of performing a given task. Thus, the argument for extending protection may be the same; but the stakes on the other side are much higher.

It is no accident that patent protection has preconditions that copyright protection does not—notably, the requirements of novelty and non-obviousness—and that patents are granted for a shorter period than copyrights. This problem of utility has sometimes manifested itself in copyright cases, such as Baker v. Selden, 101 U.S. 99, 25 L. Ed. 841 (1879), and been dealt with through various formulations that limit copyright or create limited rights to copy. But the case law and doctrine addressed to utility in copyright have been brief detours in the general march of copyright law.

Requests for the protection of computer menus present the concern with fencing off access to the commons in an acute form. A new menu may be a creative work, but over time its importance may come to reside more in the investment that has been made by users in learning the menu and in building their own mini-programs—macros—in reliance upon the menu. Better typewriter keyboard layouts may exist, but the familiar QWERTY keyboard dominates the market because that is what everyone has learned to use. See P. David, CLIO and the Economics of QWERTY, 75 Am. Econ. Rev. 332 (1985). The QWERTY keyboard is nothing other than a menu of letters.

Thus, to assume that computer programs are just one more new means of expression, like a filmed play, may be quite wrong. The "form"—the written source code or the menu structure depicted on the screen—look hauntingly like the familiar stuff of copyright; but the "substance" probably has more to do with problems presented in patent law or, as already noted, in those rare cases where copyright law has confronted industrially useful expressions. Applying copyright law to computer programs is like assembling a jigsaw puzzle whose pieces do not quite fit. . . .

II.

In this case, the raw facts are mostly, if not entirely, undisputed. Although the inferences to be drawn may be more debatable, it is very hard to see that Borland has shown any interest in the Lotus menu except as a fall-back option for those users already committed to it by prior experience or in order to run their own macros using 1-2-3 commands. At least for the amateur, accessing the Lotus menu in the Borland Quattro or Quattro Pro program takes some effort.

Put differently, it is unlikely that users who value the Lotus menu for its own sake—independent of any investment they have made themselves in learning Lotus' commands or creating macros dependent upon them—would choose the Borland program in order to secure access to the Lotus menu. Borland's success is due primarily to other features. Its rationale for deploying the Lotus menu bears the ring of truth.

Now, any use of the Lotus menu by Borland is a commercial use and deprives Lotus of a portion of its "reward," in the sense that an infringement claim if allowed would increase Lotus' profits. But this is circular reasoning: broadly speaking, every limitation on copyright or privileged use diminishes the reward of the original creator. Yet not every writing is copyrightable or every use an infringement. The provision of reward is one concern of copyright law, but it is not the only one. If it were, copyrights would be perpetual and there would be no exceptions.

The present case is an unattractive one for copyright protection of the menu. The menu commands (e.g., "print," "quit") are largely for standard procedures that Lotus did not invent and are common words that Lotus cannot monopolize. What is left is the particular combination and sub-grouping of commands in a pattern devised by Lotus. This arrangement may have a more appealing logic and ease of use than some other configurations; but there is a certain arbitrariness to many of the choices.

If Lotus is granted a monopoly on this pattern, users who have learned the command structure of Lotus 1-2-3 or devised their own macros are locked into Lotus, just as a typist who has learned the QWERTY keyboard would be the captive of anyone who had a monopoly on the production of such a keyboard. Apparently, for a period Lotus 1-2-3 has had such sway in the market that it has represented the de facto standard for electronic spreadsheet commands. So long as Lotus is the superior spreadsheet—either in quality or in price—there may be nothing wrong with this advantage.

But if a better spreadsheet comes along, it is hard to see why customers who have learned the Lotus menu and devised macros for it should remain captives of Lotus because of an investment in learning made by the users and not by Lotus. Lotus has already reaped a substantial reward for being first; assuming that the Borland program is now better, good reasons exist for freeing it to attract old Lotus customers: to enable the old customers to take advantage of a new advance, and to reward Borland in turn for making a better product. If Borland has not made a better product, then customers will remain with Lotus anyway.

Thus, for me the question is not whether Borland should prevail but on what basis. Various avenues might be traveled, but the main choices are between holding that the menu is not protectable by copyright and devising a new doctrine that Borland's use is privileged. No solution is perfect and no intermediate appellate court can make the final choice.

To call the menu a "method of operation" is, in the common use of those words, a defensible position. After all, the purpose of the menu is not to be admired as a work of literary or pictorial art. It is to transmit directions from the user to the computer, i.e., to operate the computer. The menu is also a "method" in the dictionary sense because it is a "planned way of doing something," an "order or system," and (aptly here) an "orderly or systematic arrangement, sequence or the like." Random House Webster's College Dictionary 853 (1991).

A different approach would be to say that Borland's use is privileged because, in the context already described, it is not seeking to appropriate the advances made by Lotus' menu; rather, having provided an arguably more attractive menu of its own, Borland is merely trying to give former Lotus users an option to exploit their own prior investment in learning or in macros. The difference is that such a privileged use approach would not automatically protect Borland if it had simply copied the Lotus menu (using different codes), contributed nothing of its own, and resold Lotus under the Borland label.

The closest analogue in conventional copyright is the fair use doctrine. E.g., Harper & Row, Publishers, Inc. v. Nation Enters., 471 U.S. 539, 85 L. Ed. 2d 588, 105 S. Ct. 2218 (1985). Although invoked by Borland, it has largely been brushed aside in this case because the Supreme Court has said that it is "presumptively" unavailable where the use is a "commercial" one. See *id.* at 562. In my view, this is something less than a definitive answer; "presumptively" does not mean "always" and, in any event, the doctrine of fair use was created by the courts and can be adapted to new purposes.

But a privileged use doctrine would certainly involve problems of its own. It might more closely tailor the limits on copyright protection to the reasons for limiting that protection; but it would entail a host of administrative problems that would cause cost and delay, and would also reduce the ability of the industry to predict outcomes. Indeed, to the extent that Lotus' menu is an important standard in the industry, it might be argued that any use ought to be deemed privileged.

In sum, the majority's result persuades me and its formulation is as good, if not better, than any other that occurs to me now as within the reach of courts. Some solutions (e.g., a very short copyright period for menus) are not options at all for courts but might be for Congress. In all events, the choices are important ones of policy, not linguistics, and they should be made with the underlying considerations in view.

COMMENTS AND QUESTIONS

1. The issues raised by the *Lotus* decision remain unsettled. The Supreme Court granted certiorari in the case, but deadlocked 4-4, and therefore affirmed the First Circuit, but produced no precedential opinion. Lotus Dev. Corp. v. Borland Int'l, 516 U.S. 233 (1996). Note that the First Circuit concedes that its opinion is at odds with the Tenth Circuit's decision in Autoskill, Inc. v. National Educational Support Systems, 994 F.2d 1476, 1495 n.23 (10th Cir. 1993), and dictum from the Ninth Circuit's decision in Brown Bag Software v. Symantec Corp., 960 F.2d 1465, 1477 (9th Cir. 1992). It is also arguably inconsistent with the Fifth Circuit's decision in Engineering Dynamics, Inc. v. Structural Software Inc., 26 F.3d 1335 (5th Cir. 1994), which gave broad copyright protection to program interfaces and relied extensively on Judge Keeton's prior decision in Lotus Dev. Corp. v. Paperback Software, 740 F. Supp. 37 (D. Mass. 1990).

On the other hand, the *Lotus* approach seems consistent with the legislative history of 17 U.S.C. section 102(b). The House Report accompanying that section states:

> Section 102(b) is intended, among other things, to make clear that the expression adopted by the programmer is the copyrightable element in a computer program, and that the actual processes or methods embodied in the program are not within the scope of the copyright law.

H.R. Rep. No. 1476, 94th Cong., 2d Sess. 57 (1976), *reprinted in* 1976 U.S.C.C.A.N. 5659, 5670. Further, most commentators seem to agree with the ultimate result in *Lotus*, though many are troubled by the court's reasoning. See, e.g., Brief Amicus Curiae of Copyright Law Professors in Support of Respondent in Lotus v. Borland, No. 94-2003 (U.S. 1995) (brief submitted by 34 copyright professors urging affirmance for a variety of reasons); Mark A. Lemley, Convergence in the Law of Software Copyright, 10 High Tech. L.J. 1 (1995); Glynn S. Lunney Jr., Lotus v. Borland: Copyright and Computer Programs, 70 Tul. L. Rev. 2397 (1996); Peter S. Menell, The Challenges of Reforming Intellectual Property Protection for Computer Software, 94 Colum. L. Rev. 2644, 2653 (1994). Finally, at least one court has followed the First Circuit's ruling in *Lotus*. The court used section 102(b) to reject a copyright claim to a menu tree structure, noting that granting copyright on such a structure would infringe on the province of patent law. MiTek Holdings v. Arce Engineering Co., 89 F.3d 1548 (11th Cir. 1996). But see Mitel, Inc. v. Iqtel, Inc., 124 F.3d 1366 (10th Cir. 1997) ("We conclude that although an element of a work may be chararcterized as a method of operation, that element may nevertheless contain expression that is eligible for copyright protection. . . . Thus, we decline to adopt the *Lotus* court's approach to section 102(b), and continue to adhere to our abstraction-filtration-comparison approach.").

2. Contrast the analysis of section 102(b) and Baker v. Selden in the *Lotus* case with that in Apple v. Franklin. Applying the *Lotus* court's logic, isn't object code a "method of operation" for instructing a CPU how to process information? If so, how can the copyrightability of computer programs be reconciled with the exclusion from copyright of "methods of operation"?

3. Note that the *Lotus* court chose to reject the filtration test adopted by the Second Circuit in Computer Associates v. Altai and followed by most other circuits. Is the holding in *Lotus* really incompatible with *Altai*'s abstraction-filtration-comparison test? One possible way to reconcile *Lotus* and *Altai* is to treat *Lotus* not as a case involving "literal" copying of a menu structure but as a case involving nonliteral copying of the program itself. Lotus distributed object code that in certain combinations produces physical images on a screen that represent certain words and that have certain effects. Borland did not copy that code; rather, it wrote its own code, which produced similar images and had the same effects as the Lotus code. The court could then have applied *Altai*'s abstraction-filtration-comparison analysis. Perhaps this is in effect what the *Lotus* court did—although when it reached the "filtration" step, it determined that the entire program was unprotectable at the menu command hierarchy level. See Mark A. Lemley, Convergence in the Law of Software Copyright?, 10 High Tech. L.J. 1, 21-22 (1995).

Do the *Altai* and *Lotus* cases present analogous issues? Is a "filtration" analysis that filters out the entire copyrighted work at one level of abstraction within the contemplation of the *Altai* court?

4. The *Lotus* court compares the 1-2-3 menu command hierarchy to the buttons on a VCR, which it says are uncopyrightable because they are methods of operation. But is this the right analogy? Lotus claimed that Borland had infringed its copyright by copying the structure, sequence, and organization of its menu hierarchy, not the words of the menus themselves. This "structure, sequence and organization" seems the equivalent of the location and arrangement of the VCR buttons rather than the buttons themselves. Would an original way of arranging the buttons on a VCR be copyrightable? Should it? Is the question one of originality and the idea-expression dichotomy, or is there some reason not to copyright the arrangement of buttons on a VCR even if it were original and expressive?

5. In the predecessor case to Lotus v. Borland, defendant Paperback Software argued that the command structure of the Lotus program is in essence an uncopyrightable language. It can be used to create macros and to run the spreadsheet. Is this a fair characterization? The district court attacked this analogy (which it called "strained") on two basic grounds: that Lotus 1-2-3 was not in fact a language, and that languages could be copyrightable. The first conclusion is certainly debatable: one's definition of a language (or, alternatively, a "system") will go a long way toward answering this question. But consider the court's second premise —that languages might be copyrightable. Is copyrighting "natural" (i.e., human) languages consistent with what you know of copyright law? Is a language functional, or does it express? Does it matter whether the plaintiff is claiming the creation of certain words or the entire system of grammar and interaction between words? Cf. Reiss v. National Quotation Bureau, 276 F. 717 (S.D.N.Y. 1921) (suggesting in dictum that Esperanto could be copyrighted). On this point, compare Ronald Johnson & Allen Grogan, Copyright Protection for Command Driven Interfaces, 8:6 Computer Law. 1 (June 1991) (advocating copyright protection for languages) with Pamela Samuelson, How to Interpret the Lotus Decision; And How Not To, 33:11 Communications of the ACM 27 (Nov. 1990), and Elizabeth G. Lowry, Comment, Copyright Protection for Computer Languages: Creative Incentive or Technological Threat, 39 Emory L.J. 1293 (1990) (both opposing such protection).

Does the First Circuit's decision in Lotus v. Borland shed any light on this issue? Are languages "systems" or "methods of operation" that are denied protection under section 102(b)? An Australian case, Data Access Corp. v. Powerflex Services Pty., No. VG473 (Fed. Ct. Aus., Melbourne 1996), may prove instructive. The Federal Court in that case (the trial court) held that even a single word serving a menu command function may be copyrightable, because it is a concatenation of letters. Copyright protection therefore clearly extended to the computer language at issue in that case, which consisted of 225 words. But the appellate panel reversed, concluding that the words in that case were not themselves sufficiently creative to be deserving of copyright protection.

6. Both the majority and Judge Boudin's concurrence express concern over the harm that would be done to users of Lotus 1-2-3 if they could not copy their macros for use on Quattro Pro. Certainly, users have invested time and effort in using Lotus 1-2-3, and this may make them reluctant to change spreadsheet programs, even if Borland's program really is superior. But is this the sort of problem with which the copyright law should be concerned? Why isn't a customer preference for a known and trusted product part of the reward that the copyright owner is entitled to reap?

Is the QWERTY keyboard protectable by copyright? Why or why not? Does the answer depend on timing—whether the QWERTY keyboard has just been introduced or whether it is well-established as the industry standard for typewriters? How would you apply section 102(b) in each case?

7. In his concurrence, Judge Boudin proposes (although he does not necessarily adopt) an alternative rationale for the *Lotus* decision: that Lotus's menu command hierarchy was copyrightable but that Borland's use of the menu hierarchy in this case was privileged because it was done for the purpose of making the two programs compatible. The "privileged use" rationale is narrower than the majority's "method of operation" rule. Because the majority holds the menu command hierarchy entirely uncopyrightable, Lotus has no power to prevent anyone from copying its menu structure, regardless of the circumstances in which the copying occurs.

Suppose that, without taking any protected source or object code, a small company managed to acquire an early copy of Lotus 1-2-3. It replicated the menu command hierarchy and began to sell "clone" programs that looked and worked just like Lotus 1-2-3. Cf. Lotus Dev. Corp. v. Paperback Software, 740 F. Supp. 37 (D. Mass. 1990), a prior decision by Judge Keeton that is apparently overruled by the First Circuit's decision. In such a case, the equities might seem to tilt towards *Lotus* more than they did in the *Borland* case. Nonetheless, under the majority's rule, the clone manufacturer has the right to make such copies. By contrast, the "privileged use" rationale might not protect the clone manufacturer from a copyright infringement suit. Does Judge Boudin's "privileged use" approach better address this circumstance? Some commentators have argued for the First Circuit's result in *Lotus* on these narrower grounds—that in the particular circumstances of this case Borland's improvement on the Lotus 1-2-3 program was sufficiently great that it should justify the taking. See Mark A. Lemley, The Economics of Improvement in Intellectual Property Law, 75 Tex. L. Rev. 989 (1997). For a more detailed discussion of a privilege to copy certain aspects of a computer program in order to achieve compatibility, see Section E below.

For an argument that the effort that goes into program design should be protected against misappropriation, though not by copyright law, see Pamela Samuelson et al., A Manifesto Concerning the Legal Protection of Computer Programs, 94 Colum. L. Rev. 2308 (1994).

8. In *Lotus*, the menu command hierarchy served both as a functional part of the program (structuring the way the program itself functioned) and as a user interface. Borland's emulation products (though not its Key Reader feature) copied this user interface and under certain conditions therefore presented the same appearance to the user as the Lotus 1-2-3 program. It might therefore be appropriate to think of *Lotus* as a user interface copyright case as well as a protocol copyright case. We discuss the protection of user interfaces in subsection B.5 below.

Note on the Protection of Computer Protocols After *Lotus*

The *Lotus* decision—and those rejecting it—are directly relevant to the copyright protection that will be afforded various software protocols governing data communication, applications program interfaces (APIs), and numerous other operational components of computer programs. The First Circuit's opinion in *Lotus* would seem to suggest that such APIs are, as a system of operation, themselves uncopyrightable in their entirety. As noted above, however, most courts do not take this absolute approach.

Even if an interface protocol is eligible for copyright protection, however, it may still lose protection against all but the most literal copying if a court concludes during its filtration analysis that virtually all of the elements of the interface are unprotectable. For example, in *Mitel*, the Tenth Circuit concluded that the arbitrary selection of code numbers in the operation of telephone call controllers was not sufficiently original to qualify for copyright protection. *Mitel* supra, 124 F.3d at 1366. But see Atari Games Corp. v. Nintendo of America, 975 F.2d 832, 840 (Fed. Cir. 1992) (arbitrary string of numbers in a lock-out device was not dictated by function and therefore could be copyrighted); American Dental Ass'n v. Delta Dental Plans, 126 F.3d 977 (7th Cir. 1997) (listing of code numbers assigned to each element was a copyrightable part of a taxonomy of information, because different numbers could have been chosen).

Program interface elements will also be uncopyrightable if they are dictated by external factors, such as the requirements of compatibility with a particular hardware or software platform. Thus, the Tenth Circuit concluded that the selection of values matched to codes in Mitel's call controllers, while sufficiently original to qualify for copyright protection, could not be protected because they were dictated by the needs of the industry. *Mitel*, supra, 124 F.3d at 1366. See also *Altai*, 982 F.2d at 707-709. On the other hand, other courts have found similar program elements to be copyrightable—e.g., *Atari*, 975 F.2d at 845; *Engineering Dynamics*, 26 F.3d at 1347; CMAX/Cleveland, Inc v. UCR, Inc., 804 F. Supp. 337, 355-56 (M.D. Ga. 1992).

Initially, it makes considerable difference which approach a court takes. The program implementing the protocols may well contain a significant amount of code. Even if facts and other unprotectable elements were to be filtered out of both the program and the documentation, it is evident that there is ample protectable expression remaining in both to allow the copyright owner to prevent literal copying of either the program itself or the documentation that accompanies it. Factual books, compilations of data, and computer programs that contain much less detailed expressive information than these programs have nonetheless been protected under copyright law—e.g., *Apple Computer*, 714 F.2d at 1240 (protecting early Apple operating system containing relatively few lines of code by modern standards); *American Dental*, supra, 126 F.3d at 977 (protecting individual words and numbers in a taxonomy containing short descriptions of dental treatments); Lipton v. Nature Co., 71 F.3d 464 (2d Cir. 1995) (protecting short list of "terms of venery"). The words chosen in the documentation to explain the program, and the actual code written to implement the program, necessarily contain myriad expressive choices, and those choices are protectable under the idea-expression dichotomy. Indeed, the program and the documentation are clearly protectable not only against literal copying, but even against the copying of a substantial part of the works. See Central Point Software v. Nugent, 903 F. Supp. 1057, 1060 (E.D. Tex. 1995) (copying of 50 percent of program code held infringement). By contrast, a court applying the *Lotus* approach might well circumvent this process, concluding that the entire protocol (including the supporting code) was unprotectable.

Nonetheless, *Mitel* suggests that even courts applying the abstraction-filtration-comparison approach may conclude that the protocol as a whole is uncopyrightable. However, not all courts follow *Mitel*'s approach. In particular, two decisions find that even the seemingly logical selection of a few number options can be copyrightable expression. In *Autoskill*, for example, the court protected a procedure under which reading test subjects keyed 1, 2, or 3 on the keyboard in response to material displayed on the screen. The court rejected the argument that this process was an uncopyrightable "method of operation." 994 F.2d at 1495 and n.23. While the program used in *Autoskill* contained many elements other than the three-key user input, the decision clearly indicates that the input system itself is protectable.

To similar effect is Compaq Computer Corp. v. ProCom Technology, 908 F. Supp. 1409 (S.D. Tex. 1995). In that case, Compaq successfully claimed copyright in a set of five numerical parameters that it used to warn of potential hard drive failure. The court distinguished *Feist* on the grounds that the selection of five parameters to monitor, and the choice of threshold values indicative of drive failure for each of those parameters, reflected expressive "selection and arrangement" entitling Compaq to copyright protection. This was true despite the fact that the selection of the parameters to be used was dictated by the function of the software and that "a third party seeking compatibility with [Compaq's system] has no choice but to use those five parameters as well." *Id.* at 1421. Accord *Atari Games*, 975 F.2d at 843-844; *American Dental Ass'n*, 126 F.3d at 977. These cases provide some support for the copyrightability of protocol elements themselves.

Further, even if individual elements of the protocol are determined to be uncopyrightable because they are dictated by function, the entire protocol may be copyrightable as a compilation of uncopyrightable elements. *Compaq*, 908 F. Supp. at 1418 ("Compaq's compilation of the five threshold values meets the standard announced in *Feist*."). Cf. Apple Computer v. Microsoft Corp., 35 F.3d 1435, 1446 (9th Cir. 1994) (compilation of uncopyrightable elements protectable against virtually identical copying); *MiTek*, 89 F.3d at 1558-59 (same). On the other hand, at least one court following *Lotus* has concluded that data structures are uncopyrightable as a whole. See Baystate Technologies v. Bentley Systems, Inc., 946 F. Supp. 1079 (D. Mass. 1996). That court concluded that the selection and arrangement of data file elements was "dictated mainly by external factors," notably the need for compatibility and programming efficiency, and was therefore not protectable.

Of course, even if the protocol is copyrighted, not all uses of copyrighted data will be infringing. In particular, a number of courts have held that in appropriate circumstances the copying of elements of a computer program for purposes of achieving interoperability may be a "fair use." For a more detailed discussion of this issue, see Section D below.

COMMENTS AND QUESTIONS

Should APIs be copyrightable? Why or why not? Do we need to provide protection to program interfaces in order to encourage the creation of new ones? Do network effects mean that protecting APIs is likely to give too much control to the copyright owner?

4. Protection for Program Outputs: Screen Displays

Many computer programs generate graphic images, audio, and audiovisual outputs, which copyright law has long protected. Video games incorporating all of these elements have been among the most popular consumer products made possible by computer technology, and disputes over the scope of copyright protection in such works have frequently arisen.

One of the first such cases focused on the originality and "fixation" requirements of copyright law. 17 U.S.C. §102(a). In order to be eligible for copyright protection, a work must be both original—independently created and exhibiting a modicum of creativity—and "fixed" in a tangible medium of expression. Under the Copyright Act, a work is "fixed" when "its embodiment in a copy . . . is sufficiently permanent or stable to permit it to be perceived, reproduced, or otherwise communicated for a period of more than transitory duration." 17 U.S.C. §101. As further explained in the legislative history, "the definition of 'fixation' would exclude from the concept purely evanescent or transient reproductions such as those projected briefly on a screen, shown electronically on a television or other cathode ray tube, or captured momentarily in the 'memory' of a computer." H.R. Rep. 94-1476 52-53 (1976).

In Stern Electronics v. Kaufman, 669 F.2d 852 (2d Cir. 1982), the owner of rights in an arcade video game sued a competitor for infringing the copyright in the audiovisual work comprising the game. The competitor defended on the ground that it had not copied the underlying computer code, but rather had imitated the screen display images, which failed to satisfy the fixation and originality requirements of the Copyright Act. Since the player of the game affects the displayed image through manipulation of the game controller, the owner of the copyright in the underlying code could not, in the view of the defendant, establish that the displayed image is "fixed" or "original." Judge Newman acknowledged this nuance, but noted that

> many aspects of the sights and the sequence of their appearance remain constant during each play of the game. These include the appearance (shape, color, and size) of the player's spaceship, the enemy craft, the ground missile bases and fuel depots, and the terrain over which (and beneath which) the player's ship flies, as well as the sequence in which the missile bases, fuel depots, and terrain appears. Also constant are the sounds heard whenever the player successfully destroys an enemy craft or installation or fails to avoid an enemy missile or laser. It is true, as appellants contend, that some of these sights and sounds will not be seen and heard during each play of the game in the event that the player's spaceship is destroyed before the entire course is traversed. But the images remain fixed, capable of being seen and heard each time a player succeeds in keeping his spaceship aloft long enough to permit the appearances of all the images and sounds of a complete play of the game. The repetitive sequence of a substantial portion of the sights and sounds of the game qualifies for copyright protection as an audiovisual work.

Id. at 855.

COMMENTS AND QUESTIONS

1. Why are computer programs entitled to two different types of copyright protection—protection of the code (and nonliteral structural elements) as a literary work and protection of the output as a pictorial or audiovisual work? One possible answer lies in the unique nature of computer programs. The "literary work" protected by copyright is not actually readable by humans. When it is read by the computer, what the computer displays is not the code itself, but a screen display that is based on that code. Because what goes into the computer bears no physical resemblance to what comes out, limiting copyright protection to the code of a program would leave software vulnerable to being "copied" by other programmers, who would be free to write *their own* code to produce similar or even identical screen displays. Because the screen display is all that is visible to the user, allowing the display to be copied would significantly undermine the value of copyright protection.

Could we solve this problem by applying the rules of nonliteral code infringement to cases where what is alleged to have been copied is the screen display? How would the *Lotus* court resolve such a claim?

For an argument that infringement of screen displays (and the broader but overlapping category of "user interfaces," discussed below) should be treated as a subset of the more general question of whether the program itself has been infringed, see Pamela Samuelson, Computer Programs, User Interfaces, and Section 102(b) of the Copyright Act of 1976: A Critique of Lotus v. Paperback, 6 High Tech. L.J. 209, 264-69 (1991).

2. How broad is the scope of protection for screen displays? Many computer audiovisual works—particularly video games—often display sequences of vivid and fanciful images accompanied by music and other sounds. Because of their highly expressive content, these video screen displays enjoy the broad scope of copyright protection that is accorded cartoon movies and similar works. On the other hand,

copyright protection for video displays treated as an audiovisual work does not extend to the underlying game or program itself. See generally LaST Frontier Report on Copyright Protection of Computer Software, 30 Jurimetrics J. 15, 32 (1989).

3. How should video game manufacturers register their works with the Copyright Office—as literary works or as audiovisual works? Are two separate copyright registrations required? The Copyright Office has ruled that

> all copyrightable expression owned by the same claimant and embodied in a computer program, or first published as a unit with a computer program, including computer screen displays, is considered a single work and should be registered on a single application form. . . . Ordinarily, where computer program authorship is part of the work, literary authorship will predominate, and one registration should be made on application Form TX. Where, however, audiovisual authorship predominates, the registration should be made on Form PA.

Registration and Deposit of Computer Screen Displays, 53 Fed. Reg. 21,817-18 (1988). What is the importance of the type of form on which a work is registered? Cf. Jefferson Airplane v. Berkeley Systems, 32 U.S.P.Q.2d 1632 (N.D. Cal. 1994) (registration of sound recordings did not extend to art contained on album cover).

Does it matter whether a computer program is treated as a literary work or an audiovisual work? On this point, see Manufacturers Technologies, Inc. v. CAMS, Inc., 706 F. Supp. 984, 992-93 (D. Conn. 1989), approaching the protectability of screen displays by treating "the single registration of a computer program as accomplishing two interrelated yet distinct registrations; one of the program itself and one of the screen displays or user interface of that program, to the extent that each contains copyrightable subject matter."

PROBLEM

Problem 2-5. Atari Games Corp. seeks to register BREAKOUT, a video game program. The game simulates a ball and paddle game. BREAKOUT's audiovisual display features a wall formed by red, amber, green, and blue layers of rectangles representing bricks. The screen shows the two players' scores at the top. The player manipulates a control knob that causes a rectangular "paddle" to hit a square "ball" against the brick wall. When the ball hits a brick, that brick disappears from its row, the player scores points, and a brick on a higher row becomes exposed. A "breakout" occurs when the ball penetrates through all rows of bricks to the empty space beyond, where it ricochets at greatly increased speed until it reemerges. The game produces four different tones as the ball touches different objects or places on the screen. The ball's movement depends on where it contacts the paddle. The size of the paddle diminishes and the motion of the ball accelerates as the game is played.

Should the Copyright Office register BREAKOUT as an audiovisual work?

Note on the Copyrightability
of Computer-Generated Works

Who is the author of a computer-generated work? In *Stern Electronics*, Judge Newman comments that the player's participation does not nullify copyright protection for a video game. But in that case the court acknowledged that the exact video output being protected varied with each game, depending on the particular person playing the game and what actions she took. Who is the author of the images created on the video game? The creator of the program? The user? Both the creator of the program and the user as joint authors? The computer?

CONTU took a traditional copyright approach to the question of copyrightability of computer-generated works. "If a work created through application of computer technology meets th[e] minimal test of originality, it is copyrightable." CONTU Report at 45. With regard to authorship, CONTU reasoned as follows:

> Computers are enormously complex and powerful instruments which vastly extend human powers to calculate, select, arrange, display, design, and do other things involved in the creation of works. However, it is a human power they extend. The computer may be analogized or equated with, for example, a camera, and the computer affects the copyright status of a resultant work no more than the employment of a still or motion-picture camera, a tape recorder, or a typewriter. Hence, it seems clear that the copyright problems with respect to the authorship of new works produced with the assistance of a computer are not unlike those posed by the creation of more traditional works. . . .
>
> Finally, we confront the question of who is the author of a work produced through the use of a computer. The obvious answer is that the author is one who employs the computer. The simplicity of this response may obscure some problems, though essentially they are the same sort of problems encountered in connection with works produced in other ways.
>
> One such problem is that often a number of persons have a hand in the use of a computer to prepare, for example, a complex statistical table. They may have varying degrees and kinds of responsibility for the creation of the work. However, they are typically employees of a common employer, engaged in creating a work-for-hire, and the employer is the author. When the authors work together as a voluntary team and not as employees of a common employer, the copyright law with respect to works of joint authorship is as applicable here as to works created in more conventional ways, and the team itself may define by agreement the relative rights of the individuals involved.
>
> To be used in the creation of a work, a computer must be controlled by a program and must ordinarily utilize data input from other sources. Both the program and the data may be copyrighted or parts of copyrighted works. The question has been raised whether authorship or proprietorship of the program or data base establishes or may establish a claim of authorship of the final work. It appears to the Commission that authorship of the program or of the input data is entirely separate from authorship of the final work, just as authorship of a translation of a book is distinct from authorship of the original work. It is, of course, incumbent on the creator of the final work to obtain appropriate permission from any other person who is the proprietor of a program or data base used in the creation of the ultimate work. The ultimate use of a program or data base might limit or negate the author's claim of copyright in the ultimate work, just as a failure of a translator to obtain a license from the proprietor of the translated work might prevent securing copyright in and making use of the

translation. But this is not a question of authorship itself, and the author of the original work does not become the author of a translation merely because it is made from the original work without permission. Here, too, the situation with respect to works produced by the use of a computer does not appear to differ from that with respect to works otherwise created. . . .

However, the Commission recognizes that the dynamics of computer science promise changes in the creation and use of authors' writings that cannot be predicted with certainty. The effects of these changes should have the attention of Congress and its appropriate agencies to ensure that those who are the responsible policy makers maintain an awareness of the changing impact of computer technology on both the needs of authors and the role of authors in the information age. . . .

CONTU Report at 45-46.

COMMENTS AND QUESTIONS

1. The UK Copyright and Design Patent Act of 1988 provides that in the case of a computer-generated work, "the author shall be taken to be the person by whom the arrangements necessary for the creation of the work are undertaken." §9(3).

2. On the copyright ownership implications of "artificial intelligence" programs, see generally Arthur Miller, Copyright Protection for Computer Programs, Databases, and Computer-Generated Works: Is Anything New Since CONTU? 106 Harv. L. Rev. 977, 1042-72 (1993); Pamela Samuelson, Allocating Ownership Rights in Computer-Generated Works, 47 U. Pitt. L. Rev. 1185 (1986).

One case has addressed the issue of nonhuman creativity, albeit in a different context. In Urantia Foundation v. Maaherra, 114 F.3d 955 (9th Cir. 1997), the plaintiff was a church that claimed that its sacred text was written by a divine being, as channeled through a psychiatric patient. When it sued the defendant (a church splinter group) for copying the text, the defendant claimed that "there can be no valid copyright in the Book because it lacks the requisite ingredient of human creativity, and that therefore the Book is not a 'work of authorship' within the meaning of the Copyright Act." The court seemed to agree that human authorship was required: "it is not the creations of divine beings that the copyright laws were intended to protect . . . in this case some element of human creativity must have occurred in order for the Book to be copyrightable. At the very least, for a worldly entity to be guilty of infringing a copyright, that entity must have copied something created by another worldly entity." *Id*. Nonetheless, the court found that the Book was copyrightable because humans had "compiled" the teachings of the divine being in question.

What does *Urantia* suggest for computer-generated works? Are they ineligible for copyright protection? Or could a computer program be a "worldly entity" within the language of the court?

3. Is the CONTU report on ownership consistent with the court's decision in *Stern*? In particular, CONTU emphasizes that "authorship of the program or of the input data is entirely separate from authorship of the final work." The Report goes on to suggest that it is the user of the computer, not the author of the program, who owns the final work. In some contexts, this makes perfect sense. It would be unreasonable to suggest, for example, that the creator of a

word-processing program owned the documents written using that program. But what does this suggest about the ownership of video game screen displays? If the programmer merely set up some possible screen elements and the game player put them together into the actual screen displays shown, why should the programmer own those screen displays? Does it matter whether the actual displays shown are "fixed" in a tangible medium of expression other than the screen itself?

4. *Ownership of Human-Authored Software.* Disputes sometimes arise regarding authorship and ownership of software that is unquestionably human authored, often in the context of programs written by employees.

- *Works Made for Hire*—One scenario involves employees who are not hired primarily as programmers but nonetheless write programs to assist in their work. Consider the case of an IP lawyer who develops a software program for automating trademark prosecution or a website for managing document retrieval. Does such work fall within the "work made for hire doctrine"? See Quinn v. City of Detroit, 23 F. Supp.2d 741 (E.D. Mich. 1998).

- *Authorship*—Another scenario involves the authorship of programs where a supervisor defines the project and a programmer merely produces code. Who is the author? Are both joint authors? Cf. Medforms, Inc. v. Healthcare Management Solutions, Inc., 290 F.3d 98 (2d Cir. 2002).

PROBLEMS

Problem 2-6. Analyze the copyrightability and authorship of the output generated by the computer programs described below. Assume that there is no prior agreement between the program creator and the user.

(a) The user of a video game for home computers controls the movement of characters with a joystick. The user decides to write a book about strategies for mastering the game. She prints out a number of visual displays that she arranged through placement of game characters for her book.

(b) SoftDesign, a computer program for architects, depicts floor plans in three-dimensional perspective. In addition, the program allows architects to see how sunlight will reflect through structures over the course of the day. Users enter the dimensions of a structure into the program either by tracing floor plans onto the screen or by entering dimensions directly.

(c) Instant Poet is a sophisticated computer program that enables users to develop poems for a variety of occasions. The basic program contains 120 vocabularies of 30 to over 5,000 words. Each vocabulary contains a particular type of word, such as articles, verbs in the imperative mode, or nouns. The program structures the relationship among categories in order to generate poems. Users select a number of variables—such as type of poem (romance, comedy, birthday), name of object, key attributes of object (e.g., age, interests). The program then generates a poem, prompting the user with a variety of choices along the way.

(d) Composer enables novice musicians to compose sophisticated musical compositions by combining digital samples of different instrument tracts.

(e) Car Repair is a diagnostic tool for evaluating car automotive problems. The computer asks the user a series of questions. Depending on how the user answers, the computer guides the user through a decision tree, eventually diagnosing the particular problem.

(f) Weatherware enables users to develop weather forecasts for a particular geographical area. The program is based on correlation analysis. The user first defines the geographical area by entering a set of six cities and their locations with respect to the location for which forecasts are sought. The user then enters daily information on temperature, wind speed, cloud cover, and precipitation for each of the cities. After the computer has a statistically significant body of data, it can generate up to four-day forecasts, along with margins for error.

(g) Translator is a sophisticated program for translating from English to French and French to English. The user merely enters the text to be translated. The program generates the translated text.

(h) PoMo is an automatic "postmodern literary theory paper generator." At the click of a button, PoMo generates prose similar in style to much postmodern literary criticism. The prose is "original" in the sense that it is not copied from anywhere else, although because PoMo is designed to mimic an existing genre, it uses words and phrases that commonly appear in that genre.

Problem 2-7. FractalArt is a computer graphics company that writes artistic software for the computer. In particular, FA's new program generates fractal patterns that partially replicate those found in nature at a microscopic level. The software includes a set of pseudo-random number generators which create new fractal patterns that are not stored anywhere in the program itself. The fractal patterns are displayed on a computer screen for approximately five minutes each as screen savers. After five minutes, the fractals are replaced by a new image. Because of the number of fractals that the program is capable of generating, it is extremely unlikely that a precise image will ever be repeated. FA has registered a copyright in its program.

A purchaser of the FA program likes the fractals displayed on his computer. Upset that he cannot "save" particularly attractive fractals, he photographs a number of the images, develops the photos, and publishes them in an art book without FA's permission. Is the purchaser liable for copyright infringement?

Data East USA, Inc. v. Epyx, Inc.
United States Court of Appeals for the Ninth Circuit
862 F.2d 204 (9th Cir. 1988)

TROTT, Circuit Judge:

[Data East, a video game manufacturer, received audio-visual copyright certificates for arcade and home computer versions of its video game "Karate Champ." Epyx subsequently commenced distribution of a video game designed to run on Commodore computers called "World Karate Championship."]

Each competing product . . . consists of the audio-visual depiction of a karate match or matches conducted by two combatants, one clad in a typical white outfit and the other in red. Successive phases of combat are conducted against varying stationary background images depicting localities or geographic scenes. The match is supervised by a referee who directs the beginning and end of each phase of combat and announces the winning combatant of each phase by means of a cartoon-style speech balloon. Each game has a bonus round where the karate combatant breaks bricks and dodges objects. Similarities also exist in the moves used by the combatants and the scoring method.

Data East alleged that the overall appearance, compilation, and sequence of the audio-visual display of the video game "World Karate Championship" infringed its copyright for "Karate Champ" as embodied in the arcade and home versions of the video game. Data East also charged Epyx with trademark and trade dress infringement.

The district court found that except for the graphic quality of Epyx's expressions, part of the scoreboard, the referee's physical appearance, and minor particulars in the "bonus phases," Data East's and Epyx's games are qualitatively identical. The district court then held that Epyx's game infringes the copyright Data East has in "Karate Champ." . . .

II. Discussion

A district court's determination of findings of fact is subject to the clearly erroneous standard of review. . . .

As in most infringement cases of this kind, no direct evidence was developed that [Epyx or the company from whom Epyx licensed its game] copied any version of Data East's product. There seldom is any direct evidence of copying in these matters. Therefore, copying may be established instead by circumstantial evidence of (1) the defendant's access to the copyrighted work prior to defendant's creation of its work, and (2) the substantial similarity of both the general ideas and expression between the copyrighted work and defendant's work. *Id.*; Baxter v. MCA, Inc., 812 F.2d 421, 423 (9th Cir. 1987), *cert. denied*, 108 S. Ct. 346 (1987). In essence, the question of copying becomes a matter of reasonable inferences. Because we find no substantial similarity, we decline to address the issue of access. . . .

B. *Substantial Similarity*

"To show that two works are substantially similar, plaintiff must demonstrate that the works are substantially similar in both ideas and expression." Frybarger v. International Business Machines Corp., 812 F.2d 525, 529 (9th Cir. 1987). Although plaintiff must first show that the ideas are substantially similar, the ideas themselves are not protected by copyright and therefore, cannot be infringed. It is an axiom of copyright law that copyright protects only an author's expression of an idea, not the idea itself. Mazer v. Stein, 347 U.S. 201, 217-18 (1954). There is a strong public policy corollary to this axiom permitting all to use freely ideas contained in a copyrightable work, so long as the protected expression itself is not appropriated. Landsberg v. Scrabble Crossword Game Players, Inc., 736 F.2d 485,

488 (9th Cir. 1984), *cert. denied*, 469 U.S. 1037 (1984). Thus, to the extent the similarities between plaintiff's and defendant's works are confined to ideas and general concepts, these similarities are noninfringing.

The Ninth Circuit has developed a two-step test for the purposes of determining substantial similarity. *McCulloch*, 823 F.2d at 319; *Krofft*, 562 F.2d at 1164. First, an "extrinsic" test is used to determine whether two ideas are substantially similar. This is an objective test which rests upon specific criteria that can be listed and analyzed. *Krofft, id.* Second, an "intrinsic" test is used to compare forms of expression. This is a subjective test which depends on the response of the ordinary reasonable person. *Id.*

In applying the extrinsic test, the district court found that the idea expressed in plaintiff's game and in defendant's game is identical. The idea of the games was described by the court as follows:

> . . . a martial arts karate combat game conducted between two combatants, and presided over by a referee, all of which are represented by visual images, and providing a method of scoring accomplished by full and half point scores for each player, and utilizing dots to depict full point scores and half point scores.

The district court further found that:

> In each of the games, the phases of martial arts combat are conducted against still background images purporting to depict geographic or locality situses and located at the top of the screen as the game is viewed. The action of the combatants in each of the games takes place in the lower portion of the screen as the game is viewed, and is against a one color background in that portion of the screen as the game is viewed.

Once an idea is found to be similar or identical, as in this case, the second or intrinsic step is applied to determine whether similarity of the expression of the idea occurs. This exists when the "total concept and feel of the works" is substantially similar. Aliotti v. R. Dakin & Co., 831 F.2d 901 (9th Cir. 1987). Analytic dissection of the dissimilarities as opposed to the similarities is not appropriate under this test because it distracts a reasonable observer from a comparison of the total concept and feel of the works. *Id.*

The rule in the Ninth Circuit, however, is that "[n]o substantial similarity of expression will be found when 'the idea and its expression are . . . inseparable,' given that 'protecting the expression in such circumstances would confer a monopoly of the idea upon the copyright owner.'" *Id.* (quoting Herbert Rosenthal Jewelry Corp. v. Kalpakian, 446 F.2d 738, 742 (9th Cir. 1971)); see also *Landsberg*, 736 F.2d at 489 (factual works); see v. Durang, 711 F.2d 141, 143 (9th Cir. 1983) (*scenes a faire* doctrine); *Krofft*, 562 F.2d at 1168.

Nor can copyright protection be afforded to elements of expression that necessarily follow from an idea, or to "*scenes a faire*," i.e., expressions that are "as a practical matter, indispensable or at least standard in the treatment of a given [idea]." *Aliotti*, 831 F.2d at 901 (quoting Atari, Inc. v. North American Phillips Consumer Elecs. Corp., 672 F.2d 607, 616 (7th Cir. 1982), *cert. denied*, 459 U.S. 880 (1982)).

To determine whether similarities result from unprotectable expression, analytic dissection of similarities may be performed. If this demonstrates that all similarities in expression arise from use of common ideas, then no substantial similarity can be found. *Id.*

The district court performed what can be described as an analytic dissection of similarities in its findings of fact and stated:

Plaintiff's and defendant's games each encompass the idea of depicting the performance of karate martial arts combat in each of the following respects:

A. Each game has fourteen moves.
B. Each game has a two-player option.
C. Each game has a one-player option.
D. Each game has forward and backward somersault moves and about-face moves.
E. Each game has a squatting reverse punch wherein the heel is not on the ground.
F. Each game has an upper-lunge punch.
G. Each game has a back-foot sweep.
H. Each game has a jumping sidekick.
I. Each game has low kick.
J. Each game has a walk-backwards position.
K. Each game has changing background scenes.
L. Each game has 30-second countdown rounds.
M. Each game uses one referee.
N. In each game the referee says "begin," "stop," "white," "red," which is depicted by a cartoon-style speech balloon.
O. Each game has a provision for 100 bonus points per remaining second.

The district court found that the visual depiction of karate matches is subject to the constraints inherent in the sport of karate itself. The number of combatants, the stance employed by the combatants, established and recognized moves and motions regularly employed in the sport of karate, the regulation of the match by at least one referee or judge, and the manner of scoring by points and half points are among the constraints inherent in the sport of karate. Because of these constraints, karate is not susceptible of a wholly fanciful presentation. Furthermore, the use of the Commodore computer for a karate game intended for home consumption is subject to various constraints inherent in the use of that computer. Among the constraints are the use of sprites,[5] and a somewhat limited access to color, together with limitations upon the use of multiple colors in one visual image.

The fifteen features listed by the court "encompass the idea of karate." These features, which consist of the game procedure, common karate moves, the idea of background computer graphics, and bonus points, result from either constraints inherent in the sport of karate or computer restraints. After careful consideration and viewing of these features, we find that they necessarily follow from the *idea* of a martial arts karate combat game, or are inseparable from, indispensable to, or even standard treatment of the idea of the karate sport. As such, they are not protectable. "When idea and expression coincide, there will be protection against

---

5. A "sprite" involves the use of a special technique for creating mobile graphic images on a computer screen that is appropriate for animation. An increase in sophistication of sprite techniques used in the computer program will increase the graphic quality of the game's animation.

nothing other than identical copying." *Krofft*, 562 F.2d at 1168. A comparison of the works in this case demonstrates that identical copying is not an issue.

Accordingly, we hold that the court did not give the appropriate weight and import to its findings which support argument that the similarities result from unprotectable expression. Consequently, it was clear error for the district court to determine that protectable substantial similarity existed based upon these facts.

The lower court erred by not limiting the scope of Data East's copyright protection to the author's contribution—the scoreboard and background scenes. In actuality, however, the backgrounds are quite dissimilar and the method of scorekeeping, though similar, is inconsequential. Based upon these two features, a discerning 17.5 year-old boy[6] could not regard the works as substantially similar. Accordingly, Data East's copyright was not infringed on this basis either. . . .

COMMENT AND QUESTION

Data East, like most software copyright cases (but unlike many more traditional copyright cases) seems to combine the copyrightability and substantial similarity inquiries, identifying similarities between the two works and then attempting to determine if the similarities were copyrightable. See also Interactive Network v. NTN Communications, 875 F. Supp. 1398 (N.D. Cal. 1995), *aff'd*, 57 F.3d 1083 (Fed. Cir. 1996) (NTN's interactive football game was not infringed by similar IN game, since most of the copying of the game was a result of the rules of football and the idea of an interactive prediction game). We have seen this combined approach before in *Altai*'s abstraction-filtration-comparison test. Is this also the correct analytical approach to a screen display case?

5. Protection for Program Outputs: User Interfaces

Source and object code (as well as the nonliteral elements of program structure) are protectable as literary works. Screen displays (the output of the computer program) are protectable as audiovisual or pictorial works. Given these two rules, it might be considered evident that user interfaces—the screen displays that mediate the input to and output from a computer program—should also be protected by copyright.

Acknowledging this does not, however, tell us what *portions* of the user interface can be considered copyrightable expression. To a greater extent than other types of screen displays, user interfaces are dictated by market standards and functional considerations. As a result, assessing claims of copyright infringement is a challenging task.

---

6. The district court found that the average age of individuals purchasing "Karate Champ" is 17.5 years, that the purchasers are predominantly male, and comprise a knowledgeable, critical, and discerning group.

Apple Computer, Inc. v. Microsoft Corp.
United States Court of Appeals for the Ninth Circuit
35 F.3d 1435 (9th Cir. 1994)

RYMER, Circuit Judge:

Lisa and Macintosh are Apple computers. Each has a graphical user interface ("GUI") which Apple Computer, Inc. registered for copyright as an audiovisual work. Both GUIs were developed as a user-friendly way for ordinary mortals to communicate with the Apple computer; the Lisa Desktop and the Macintosh Finder are based on a desktop metaphor with windows, icons and pull-down menus which can be manipulated on the screen with a hand-held device called a mouse. When Microsoft Corporation released Windows 1.0, having a similar GUI, Apple complained. As a result, the two agreed to a license giving Microsoft the right to use and sublicense derivative works generated by Windows 1.0 in present and future products. Microsoft released Windows 2.03 and later, Windows 3.0; its licensee, Hewlett-Packard Company (HP), introduced NewWave 1.0 and later, NewWave 3.0, which run in conjunction with Windows to make IBM-compatible computers easier to use. Apple believed that these versions exceed the license, make Windows more "Mac-like," and infringe its copyright. This action followed.

[The district court held that the only triable issue of fact was whether certain minor parts of the Windows interface were "virtually identical" to the Apple GUI. Apple appealed.]

Apple asks us to reverse because of two fundamental errors in the district court's reasoning. First, Apple argues that the court should not have allowed the license for Windows 1.0 to serve as a partial defense. Second, Apple contends that the court went astray by dissecting Apple's works so as to eliminate unprotectable and licensed elements from comparison with Windows 2.03, 3.0 and NewWave as a whole, incorrectly leading it to adopt a standard of virtual identity instead of substantial similarity. We disagree. . . .

III

Apple makes a number of related arguments challenging the district court's copyright analysis. It contends that the district court deprived its works of meaningful protection by dissecting them into individual elements and viewing each element in isolation. Because the Macintosh GUI is a dynamic audiovisual work, Apple argues that the "total concept and feel" of its works—that is, the selection and arrangement of related images and their animation—must be compared with that of the Windows and NewWave GUIs for substantial similarity. Apple further asserts that in this case, the court had no occasion to dissect its works into discrete elements because Microsoft and HP virtually mimicked the composition, organization, arrangement and dynamics of the Macintosh interface, as shown by striking similarities in the animation of overlapping windows and the design, layout and animation of icons. Apple also argues that even if dissection were appropriate, the district court should not have eliminated from jury consideration those elements that are either licensed or unprotected by copyright. Though stated somewhat differently, all of these contentions boil down to the same thing: Apple wants an overall comparison of its works to the accused works for substantial similarity rather than virtual identity.

The fact that Apple licensed the right to copy almost all of its visual displays fundamentally affects the outcome of its infringement claims. Authorized copying accounts for more than 90% of the allegedly infringing features in Windows 2.03 and 3.0, and two-thirds of the features in NewWave. More than that, the 1985 Agreement and negotiations leading up to Microsoft's license left Apple no right to complain that selection and arrangement of licensed elements make the interface as a whole look more "Mac-like" than Windows 1.0.

Thus, we do not start at ground zero in resolving Apple's claims of infringement. Rather, considering the license and the limited number of ways that the basic ideas of the Apple GUI can be expressed differently, we conclude that only "thin" protection, against virtually identical copying, is appropriate. Apple's appeal, which depends on comparing its interface as a whole for substantial similarity, must therefore fail. . . .

Although this litigation has raised difficult and interesting issues about the scope of copyright protection for a graphical user interface, resolving this appeal is a matter of applying well-settled principles. In this, as in other cases, the steps we find helpful to follow are these:

(1) The plaintiff must identify the source(s) of the alleged similarity between his work and the defendant's work.

(2) Using analytic dissection, and, if necessary, expert testimony, the court must determine whether any of the allegedly similar features are protected by copyright. Where, as in this case, a license agreement is involved, the court must also determine which features the defendant was authorized to copy. Once the scope of the license is determined, unprotectable ideas must be separated from potentially protectable expression; to that expression, the court must then apply the relevant limiting doctrines in the context of the particular medium involved, through the eyes of the ordinary consumer of that product.

(3) Having dissected the alleged similarities and considered the range of possible expression, the court must define the scope of the plaintiff's copyright—that is, decide whether the work is entitled to "broad" or "thin" protection. Depending on the degree of protection, the court must set the appropriate standard for a subjective comparison of the works to determine whether, as a whole, they are sufficiently similar to support a finding of illicit copying. . . .

B

It is not easy to distinguish expression from ideas, particularly in a new medium. However, it must be done, as the district court did in this case. Baker v. Selden, 101 U.S. 99, 25 L. Ed. 841 (1879). As we recognized long ago in the case of competing jeweled bee pins, similarities derived from the use of common ideas cannot be protected; otherwise, the first to come up with an idea will corner the market. Herbert Rosenthal Jewelry Corp. v. Kalpakian, 446 F.2d 738, 742 (9th Cir. 1971). Apple cannot get patent-like protection for the idea of a graphical user interface, or the idea of a desktop metaphor which concededly came from Xerox. It can, and did, put those ideas together creatively with animation, overlapping windows, and well-designed icons; but it licensed the visual displays which resulted.

The district court found that there are five other basic ideas embodied in the desktop metaphor: use of windows to display multiple images on the computer screen and to facilitate user interaction with the information contained in the windows; iconic representation of familiar objects from the office environment; manipulation of icons to convey instructions and to control operation of the computer; use of menus to store information or computer functions in a place that is convenient to reach, but saves screen space for other images; and opening and closing of objects as a means of retrieving, transferring and storing information. *Apple V*, 799 F. Supp. at 1026. No copyright protection inheres in these ideas. Therefore, substantial similarity of expression in unlicensed elements cannot be based on the fact that the Lisa, the Finder, Windows 2.03, 3.0 and NewWave all have windows, icons representing familiar objects from the office environment that describe functions being performed and that can be moved around the screen to tell the computer what to do, menus which give easy access to information or functions without using space on the screen, or objects that open and close.

Well-recognized precepts guide the process of analytic dissection. First, when an idea and its expression are indistinguishable, or "merged," the expression will only be protected against nearly identical copying. *Krofft*, 562 F.2d at 1167-68; *Kalpakian*, 446 F.2d at 742. For example, in this case, the idea of an icon in a desktop metaphor representing a document stored in a computer program can only be expressed in so many ways. An iconic image shaped like a page is an obvious choice.

The doctrine of *scenes a faire* is closely related. As we explained in Frybarger v. International Business Machines Corp., 812 F.2d 525 (9th Cir. 1987), when similar features in a videogame are "'as a practical matter indispensable, or at least standard, in the treatment of a given [idea],'" they are treated like ideas and are therefore not protected by copyright. Id. at 530 (quoting Atari, Inc. v. North Am. Philips Consumer Elecs. Corp., 672 F.2d 607, 616 (7th Cir.), *cert. denied*, 459 U.S. 880, 74 L. Ed. 2d 145, 103 S. Ct. 176 (1982)). Furthermore, as Frybarger holds, "the mere indispensable expression of these ideas, based on the technical requirements of the videogame medium, may be protected only against virtually identical copying." *Id.;* see also *Data East*, 862 F.2d at 209 (visual displays of karate match conducted by two combatants, one of whom wears red shorts and the other white as in the sport, and who use the same moves, are supervised by a referee and are scored alike as in the sport, are inherent in the sport of karate itself and as such are unprotectable). In this case, for example, use of overlapping windows inheres in the idea of windows. A programmer has only two options for displaying more than one window at a time: either a tiled system, or an overlapping system. As demonstrated by Microsoft's *scenes a faire* video, overlapping windows have been the clear preference in graphic interfaces. Accordingly, protectable substantial similarity cannot be based on the mere use of overlapping windows, although, of course, Apple's particular expression may be protected.

Apple suggests that *scenes a faire* should not limit the scope of its audiovisual copyright, or at least that the interactive character of GUIs and their functional purpose should not outweigh their artistry. While user participation may not negate copyrightability of an audiovisual work, see, e.g., Midway Mfg. Co. v. Artic Int'l, Inc., 704 F.2d 1009, 1011-12 (7th Cir.), *cert. denied*, 464 U.S. 823, 78 L. Ed. 2d 98, 104 S. Ct. 90 (1983); Stern Elecs., Inc. v. Kaufman, 669 F.2d 852, 856 (2d Cir. 1982), the district court did not deny protection to any aspect of Apple's works on this basis. In any event, unlike purely artistic works such as novels and plays, graphical user interfaces generated by computer programs are partly artistic and partly functional. They are a tool to facilitate communication between the user and the computer; GUIs do graphically what a character-based interface, which requires a user to type in alphanumeric commands, does manually. Thus, the delete function is engaged by moving an icon on top of a trash can instead of hitting a "delete" key. In Apple's GUI, the ability to move icons to any part of the screen exemplifies an essentially functional process, indispensable to the idea of manipulating icons by a mouse.

To the extent that GUIs are artistic, there is no dispute that creativity in user interfaces is constrained by the power and speed of the computer. See Manufacturers Technologies, Inc. v. Cams, Inc., 706 F. Supp. 984, 994-95 (D. Conn. 1989) (denying protection to formatting style of plaintiff's screen displays because of constraints on viable options available to programmers). For example, hardware constraints limit the number of ways to depict visually the movement of a window on the screen; because many computers do not have enough power to show the entire contents of the window as it is being moved, the illusion of movement must be shown by using the outline of a window or some similar feature. Design alternatives are further limited by the GUI's purpose of making interaction between the user and the computer more "user-friendly." These, and similar environmental and ergonomic factors which limit the range of possible expression in GUIs, properly inform the scope of copyright protection.

Originality is another doctrine which limits the scope of protection. As the Supreme Court recently made clear, protection extends only to those components of a work that are original to the author, although original selection and arrangement of otherwise uncopyrightable components may be protectable. Feist Publications, Inc. v. Rural Tel. Serv. Co., 499 U.S. 340, 348-51, 113 L. Ed. 2d 358, 111 S. Ct. 1282 (1991). Apple's argument that components should not be tested for originality because its interface as a whole meets the test, see Roth Greeting Cards v. United Card Co., 429 F.2d 1106, 1109 (9th Cir. 1970) ("The originality necessary to support a copyright merely calls for independent creation, not novelty."), is therefore misplaced. Beyond that, Apple admits that it borrowed heavily from the iconic treatments in the Xerox Star and an IBM Pictureworld research report but disputes several of the district court's individual determinations. For instance, Apple claims that its file folder and page icon designs are original. Even if they are, these particular icons add so little to the mix of protectable material that the outcome could not reasonably be affected.

In sum, the district court's analytic dissection was appropriately conducted under the extrinsic portion of our test for whether sufficient copying to constitute infringement has taken place. We are not persuaded to the contrary by Apple's arguments that the district court shouldn't have dissected at all, or dissected too much; that it "filtered out" unprotectable and licensed elements instead of viewing the Macintosh interface as a whole; and that it should have recognized protectability of arrangements and the "total concept and feel" of the works under a substantial similarity standard.

First, graphical user interface audiovisual works are subject to the same process of analytical dissection as are other works. We have dissected videogames, which are audiovisual works and therefore closely analogous, see, e.g., *Data East*, 862 F.2d at 208-09 (performing analytic dissection of similarities to determine whether similarities resulted from unprotectable expression); *Frybarger*, 812 F.2d at 529-30 (district court correctly concluded that similar features in videogames were unprotectable ideas and that no reasonable jury could find expressive elements substantially similar), and we have dissected nonliteral elements of computer programs, which are somewhat analogous, see, e.g., *Brown Bag*, 960 F.2d at 1475-77 (rejecting argument similar to Apple's about propriety of analytic dissection of computer program components such as screens, menus and keystrokes); Johnson Controls, Inc. v. Phoenix Control Sys., Inc., 886 F.2d 1173, 1176 (9th Cir. 1989) (noting special master's detailed analysis of similarities). Other courts perform the same analysis, although articulated differently. See, e.g., Computer Assocs. Int'l, Inc. v. Altai, Inc., 982 F.2d 693, 706-11 (2d Cir. 1992) (adopting "abstraction-filtration-comparison" test for analyzing nonliteral structure of computer program, relying in part on our own approach); Gates Rubber Co. v. Bando Chem. Indus., 9 F.3d 823, 834, 841 (10th Cir. 1993) (adopting *Altai* test, but suggesting that comparison of works as a whole may be appropriate as preliminary step before filtering out unprotected elements); Engineering Dynamics, Inc. v. Structural Software, Inc., 26 F.3d 1335, 1342-43 (5th Cir. 1994) (adopting *Gates Rubber/Altai* test to analyze scope of copyright protection for user interface, input formats and output reports); Lotus Dev. Corp. v. Borland Int'l, Inc., 788 F. Supp. 78, 90, 93 (D. Mass. 1992) (describing similar three-part test); cf. Whelan Assocs. v. Jaslow Dental Lab., Inc., 797 F.2d 1222, 1236 (3d Cir. 1986) (defining idea of utilitarian work as its purpose or function, and everything not necessary to that purpose as expression), *cert. denied*, 479 U.S. 1031, 93 L. Ed. 2d 831, 107 S. Ct. 877 (1987).

Nor did the district court's dissection run afoul of the enjoinder in such cases as *Johnson Controls*, 886 F.2d at 1176, *Krofft*, 562 F.2d at 1167, and *Roth*, 429 F.2d at 1110, to consider the "total concept and feel" of a work. Here, the court did not inappropriately dissect dissimilarities, and so did nothing to distract from subjectively comparing the works as a whole. See Aliotti v. R. Dakin & Co., 831 F.2d 898, 901 (9th Cir. 1987) (indicating that as the concern of *Krofft*).

As we made clear in *Aliotti*, the party claiming infringement may place "no reliance upon any similarity in expression resulting from" unprotectable elements. *Id.* (Similarities between competing stuffed dinosaur toys on account of posture and body design, and being cuddly, stem from the physiognomy of dinosaurs or from the nature of stuffed animals and are thus unprotectable.) Otherwise, there would be no point to the extrinsic test, or to distinguishing ideas from expression. In this case, it would also effectively rescind the 1985 Agreement. This does not mean that at the end of the day, when the works are considered under the intrinsic test, they should not be compared as a whole. See McCulloch v. Albert E. Price, Inc., 823 F.2d 316, 321 (9th Cir. 1987) (contrasting artistic work at issue, where decorative plates were substantially similar in more than the one unprotectable element (text), with factual works which have many unprotectable elements and very little protectable expression). Nor does it mean that infringement cannot be based on original selection and arrangement of unprotected elements. However, the unprotectable elements have to be identified, or filtered, before the works can be considered as a whole. See *Harper House*, 889 F.2d at 207-08 (reversing because "total impact and effect" test of jury instruction did not distinguish between protectable and unprotectable material, thereby improperly making it possible for jury to find copying based on unprotected material instead of selection and arrangement); see also *Pasillas*, 927 F.2d at 443 (copyright holder could not rely on unprotectable elements to show substantial similarity of expression); *Frybarger*, 812 F.2d at 529 (to extent that similarities between works were confined to ideas and general concepts, they were noninfringing).

C

The district court's conclusion that the works as a whole are entitled only to limited protection and should be compared for virtual identity follows from its analytic dissection. By virtue of the licensing agreement, Microsoft and HP were entitled to use the vast majority of features that Apple claims were copied. Of those that remain, the district court found no unauthorized, protectable similarities of expression in Windows 2.03 and 3.0, and only a handful in NewWave. Thus, any claim of infringement that Apple may have against Microsoft must rest on the copying of Apple's unique selection and arrangement of all of these features. Under *Harper House* and *Frybarger*, there can be no infringement unless the works are virtually identical.

Apple, however, contends that its audiovisual work with animation and icon design cannot be analogized to factual works such as game strategy books, see Landsberg v. Scrabble Crossword Game Players, Inc., 736 F.2d 485, 488 (9th Cir.) ("Similarity of expression may have to amount to verbatim reproduction or very close paraphrasing before a factual work will be deemed infringed."), *cert. denied*, 469 U.S. 1037, 83 L. Ed. 2d 403, 105 S. Ct. 513 (1984), accounting systems, see Selden, 101 U.S. at 104 (copyright in book describing new accounting system not infringed when defendant copied ledger sheets used in system), or organizers, see *Harper House*, 889 F.2d at 205 (as compilations consisting largely of uncopyrightable elements, plaintiff's organizers entitled only to protection against "bodily appropriation of expression"), which are afforded only "thin" protection because the range of possible expression is narrow. See *Feist*, 499 U.S. at 349. Rather, it submits that the broader protection accorded artistic works is more appropriate. See, e.g., *McCulloch*, 823 F.2d at 321 (artistic work like a decorative plate receives broader protection because of endless variations of expression available to artist).

Which end of the continuum a particular work falls on is a call that must be made case by case. We are satisfied that this case is closer to *Frybarger* than to *McCulloch*. See also Atari Games Corp. v. Oman, 298 U.S. App. D.C. 303, 979 F.2d 242, 245 (D.C. Cir. 1992) (analogizing audiovisual work like a videogame to compilation of facts). Accordingly, since Apple did not contest summary judgment under the virtual identity standard on the merits, judgment was properly entered. . . .

We therefore hold that the district court properly identified the sources of similarity in Windows and NewWave, determined which were licensed, distinguished ideas from expression, and decided the scope of Apple's copyright by dissecting the unauthorized expression and filtering out unprotectable elements.

Having correctly found that almost all the similarities spring either from the license or from basic ideas and their obvious expression, it correctly concluded that illicit copying could occur only if the works as a whole are virtually identical.

COMMENTS AND QUESTIONS

1. What is the appropriate standard for testing infringement of the user interfaces of computer programs? The traditional test for evaluating copying has been the "substantial similarity" standard. *Apple*'s "virtual identicality" test comes from a number of cases, including Hoehling v. Universal City Studios, Inc., 618 F.2d 972 (2d Cir. 1980), that deal with "thin" copyrights. It has been endorsed by at least one software case as well. See MiTek Holdings, Inc. v. ARCE Engineering Co., 89 F.3d 1548, 1558 (11th Cir. 1996) ("we join the Ninth Circuit in adopting the 'bodily appropriation of expression' or 'virtual identicality' standard" for claims of software infringement based on a compilation of uncopyrightable elements). See also Mark A. Lemley, Convergence in the Law of Software Copyright?, 10 High Tech. L.J. 1 (1995) (endorsing this test for "high-level" copying of program elements).

Is it appropriate to vary the standard for infringement with the scope of copyright protection, or does that "double count" the results of the filtration analysis?

2. To what extent is user interface design constrained by utilitarian considerations? As discussed in the introductory chapter, many programmers think of interface design as a "science" governed by fundamental principles of desirability. If certain goals are indeed inherently desirable—the "what you see is what you get" principle, say—what impact does that have on copyright protection for user interfaces?

3. In certain nonliteral software infringement cases, as well as in *Apple*, the vast majority of the copied work is determined to be uncopyrightable for one reason or another. If only a few "kernels" of copyrightable expression are mixed in with a large amount of public domain material, how should the courts test the "substantiality" of copying? Put another way, suppose that at trial Apple could prove only that a defendant had copied its "trash can" icon used for deleting files. Should copying of that one piece be sufficient to find infringement? If not, why not?

4. Consider the effect of dissection on copyright incentives. Does the fragmented protection that copyright affords to functional works such as computer programs really encourage creation of more programs? Does it encourage programmers to be more expressive when writing programs? If so, is that a desirable goal?

Before *Apple* and *Lotus*, a number of courts had given protection to relatively small individual elements of a user interface that they considered "artistic." See, e.g., Broderbund Software, Inc. v. Unison World, 648 F. Supp. 1127, 1134 (N.D. Cal. 1986) (choice of typeface on user interface screen and choice of words "Choose a Font" as title for a Print Shop screen were examples of audiovisual displays "dictated primarily by artistic and aesthetic consideration, and not by utilitarian or mechanical ones"); Lotus Dev. Corp. v. Paperback Software, 740 F. Supp. 37 (D. Mass. 1990) (choice of particular words to describe interface commands was expressive and therefore protectable). Is *Apple* inconsistent with protecting such microlevel design choices? Or is it simply harder to do so now?

5. Is Lotus Dev. Corp. v. Borland Int'l, reprinted above, really a case about command structures or about user interfaces? If the court approached it as a user interface case, should it reach the same result? Would it? Cf. Mitel Inc. v. Iqtel, Inc., 896 F. Supp. 1050 (D. Colo. 1995), where the district court followed the First Circuit's decision in *Lotus* and in addition rejected the plaintiff's claim that its command codes were protectable as a user interface. On appeal, the Tenth Circuit affirmed, but it expressly refused to rely on *Lotus*, turning instead to *Altai*'s filtration approach. Mitel, Inc. v. Iqtel, Inc., 124 F.3d 1366 (10th Cir. 1997).

One court has held that user interfaces are really a species of nonliteral computer program elements and are not separately copyrightable. See O.P. Solutions Inc. v. Intellectual Property Network, 50 U.S.P.Q.2d 1399 (S.D.N.Y. 1999).

PROBLEM

Problem 2-8. Pueblo Graphics sells software that produces a variety of word processing fonts. (Fonts control the appearance of letters and numbers in typesetting.) The software allows the fonts to appear on the screen in exactly the same way they will appear on the printed page. Pueblo's software contains a number of "classic" print fonts, such as Geneva, Helvetica, and Times Roman Bold. In addition, however, Pueblo has designed several new fonts that look significantly different from any fonts previously produced.

Pueblo would like to assert a copyright infringement suit against a competitor who has copied its fonts. The competitor wrote its own program to implement those fonts, so Pueblo wants to know if it can get copyright protection in the fonts themselves. How would you advise Pueblo? Is their company's claim appropriately characterized as one for a "user interface"? Why or why not?

C. EXCLUSIVE RIGHTS IN COMPUTER PROGRAMS

1. The Right to Make "Copies"

Most of the cases we have considered in this chapter have involved the copying of all or part of a program by a company that sold a competing program. "Copying" has a potentially broader meaning in the computer context, however. The use of any modern computer program necessarily involves the creation of transitory copies in the RAM memory of a computer, and because running a computer program necessarily involves copying the program from long-term memory (ROM, CD-ROM, or disk) into the short-term memory of the computer, it is virtually impossible to use any computer program without making a "copy" of the entire program. However, that copy is not saved; it is erased whenever the application is exited or the computer is turned off. Whether such copies are fixed—and therefore potentially violate the copyright owner's rights under section 106(1)—has been a matter of some debate.

In 1993, the Ninth Circuit held that loading a computer program into RAM involved making a copy for purposes of section 106. MAI Systems Corp. v. Peak Computer, Inc., 991 F.2d 511, 518 (9th Cir. 1993). The court reasoned:

> The district court's grant of summary judgment on MAI's claims of copyright infringement reflects its conclusion that a "copying" for purposes of copyright law occurs when a computer program is transferred from a permanent storage device to a computer's RAM. This conclusion is consistent with its finding, in granting the preliminary injunction, that: "the loading of copyrighted computer software from a storage medium (hard disk, floppy disk, or read only memory) into the memory of a central processing unit ('CPU') causes a copy to be made. In the absence of ownership of the copyright or express permission by license, such acts constitute copyright infringement." We find that this conclusion is supported by the record and by the law.
>
> Peak concedes that in maintaining its customer's computers, it uses MAI operating software "to the extent that the repair and maintenance process necessarily involved turning on the computer to make sure it is functional and thereby running the operating system." It is also uncontroverted that when the computer is turned on the operating system is loaded into the computer's RAM. As part of diagnosing a computer problem at the customer site, the Peak technician runs the computer's operating system software, allowing the technician to view the systems error log, which is part of the operating system, thereby enabling the technician to diagnose the problem.
>
> Peak argues that this loading of copyrighted software does not constitute a copyright violation because the "copy" created in RAM is not "fixed." However, by showing that Peak loads the software into RAM and is then able to view the system error log and diagnose the problem with the computer, MAI has adequately shown that the representation created in the RAM is "sufficiently permanent or stable to permit it to be perceived, reproduced, or otherwise communicated for a period of more than transitory duration."
>
> After reviewing the record, we find no specific facts (and Peak points to none) which indicate that the copy created in the RAM is not fixed. . . .
>
> We have found no case which specifically holds that the copying of software into RAM creates a "copy" under the Copyright Act. However, it is generally accepted that the loading of software into a computer constitutes the creation of a copy under the Copyright Act. See, e.g., Vault Corp. v. Quaid Software, 847 F.2d 255, 260 (5th Cir. 1988) ("the act of loading a program from a medium of storage into a computer's memory creates a copy of the program"); 2 Nimmer on Copyright, §8.08 at 8-105 (1983) ("Inputting a computer program entails the preparation of a copy."); Final Report of the National Commission on the New Technological Uses of Copyrighted Works, at 13 (1978) ("the placement of a work into a computer is the preparation of a copy"). We recognize that these authorities are somewhat troubling since they do not specify that a copy is created regardless of whether the software is loaded into the RAM, the hard disk or the read only memory ("ROM"). However, since we find that the copy created in the RAM can be "perceived, reproduced, or otherwise communicated," we hold that the loading of software into the RAM creates a copy under the Copyright Act.

COMMENTS AND QUESTIONS

1. If the Ninth Circuit is correct, every use of a computer or any computer program involves the making of at least one (and probably multiple) copies of the computer program. The fact that it is impossible to read or use a computer pro-

gram without making such copies means that the application of the copyright laws to computer software is potentially far broader than to other types of works. While you can "use" a book without making a copy, under *MAI* any use of a computer program—even turning the computer on!—necessarily implicates the copyright laws. But cf. NFLC, Inc. v. Devcom Mid-America, Inc., 45 F.3d 231 (7th Cir. 1995) (suggesting that the use of dumb terminals to view a work located elsewhere might not make an infringing copy of that work).

Perhaps in recognition of this problem, Congress enacted section 117 of the Copyright Act in 1980. Section 117 makes it possible for users of computer programs to make certain copies without fear of liability. It was amended in 1998 to permit RAM copies specifically for the purpose of hardware maintenance (and therefore to overturn, at least in a narrow sense, the holding of *MAI*). We discuss section 117 in detail in the next Section; for now, keep in mind that making a copy is not always a violation of the copyright laws.

Does the specific enactment by Congress of a statutory provision permitting a user to make copies "necessary" to run a program suggest that Congress agreed that RAM copies were "fixed" for copyright purposes?

2. *MAI* is arguably inconsistent with both prior case law and the intent of Congress. In Apple Computer v. Formula Int'l, 594 F. Supp. 617, 621-22 (C.D. Cal. 1984), a case cited with apparent approval in *MAI*, the court indicated that copies stored in RAM, unlike those loaded in ROM, were only "temporary." And the House Report discussing the definition of "fixed" in section 101 of the Act had this to say on the subject of computer memory: "[T]he definition of 'fixation' would exclude from the concept purely evanescent or transient reproductions such as those projected briefly on a screen, shown electronically on a television or other cathode ray tube, or captured momentarily in the 'memory' of a computer." H.R. Rep. No. 94-1476, 94th Cong., 2d Sess. 52-53 (1976).

On the other hand, a number of courts have followed *MAI*'s lead in holding that copies loaded in RAM are fixed for purposes of copyright infringement. See Triad Systems v. Southeastern Express Co., 64 F.3d 1330 (9th Cir. 1995); Stenograph L.L.C. v. Bossard Assocs., 144 F.3d 96 (D.C. Cir. 1998); In re Independent Service Organizations Antitrust Litigation, 910 F. Supp. 1537, 1541 (D. Kan. 1995); MAI v. ACS, 845 F. Supp. 356 (E.D. Va. 1994).

Is RAM memory perceivable for "more than a transitory duration"? Is it more like movies projected on a screen or like movies stored on videotape?

3. Most commentators have been critical of the *MAI* decision. See, e.g., Niva Elkin-Koren, Copyright Law and Social Dialogue on the Information Superhighway: The Case Against Copyright Liability of Internet Providers, 13 Cardozo Arts & Ent. L.J. 345, 381-82 (1995); Michael E. Johnson, Note, The Uncertain Future of Computer Software Users' Rights in the Aftermath of MAI Systems, 44 Duke L.J. 327 (1994); Ronald Katz & Janet S. Arnold, An Unprecedented Opinion with Sparse Analysis, Computer Law., May 1993; Mark A. Lemley, Dealing with Overlapping Copyrights on the Internet, 22 U. Dayton L. Rev. 547, 550-52 (1997); Katrine Levin, Note, MAI v. Peak: Should Loading Operating System Software Into RAM Constitute Copyright Infringement?, 24 Golden Gate U.L. Rev. 649 (1994); Jessica Litman, The Exclusive Right to Read, 13 Cardozo Arts & Ent. L.J. 29, 41-43 (1994); David Nimmer, Brains and Other Paraphernalia of the Digital Age, 10 Harv. J.L. & Tech. 1 (1997); Carol G. Stovsky, Note, MAI Systems Corp. v. Peak Computer, Inc.: Using Copyright Law to Prevent Unau-

thorized Use of Computer Software, 56 Ohio St. L.J. 593 (1995). On the other hand, the Clinton administration enthusiastically endorsed *MAI* in its White Paper on copyright and the Internet. See NII Working Group on Intellectual Property, Intellectual Property and the National Information Infrastructure (August 1995). The White Paper read *MAI* as authority for the proposition that reading a book online was an act of copyright infringement.

4. A few courts have held that copyright owners committed "copyright misuse" by attempting to extend their control over copyrights to RAM copies. Alcatel USA, Inc. v. DGI Technologies Inc., 166 F.3d 772 (5th Cir. 1999). DSC Communications Corp. v. DGI Technologies, Inc., 81 F.3d 597 (5th Cir. 1996); Tricom v. EDS, 902 F. Supp. 741 (E.D. Mich. 1995); see also Nimmer, supra (arguing that *MAI* should really have been a copyright misuse case). Presumably these cases implicitly reject the finding of MAI v. Peak, since it is hard to see how making a legitimate assertion of copyright infringement could be "misuse" of the copyright. Cf. 35 U.S.C. §271(d)(3) (not a misuse of patent rights to bring suit against infringers). On this point, see Mark A. Lemley, Beyond Preemption: The Law and Policy of Intellectual Property Licensing, 87 Cal. L. Rev. 111 (1999). The Fifth Circuit seemed to strengthen this inference in Hogan Systems Inc. v. Cybresource Int'l, 158 F.3d 319 (5th Cir. 1998), when it held that accessing a computer program from a remote location did not make a copy of the program. While the court did not discuss *MAI*, its conclusion was inconsistent with that case.

Note on the "Special" Problem of Multimedia

In the early 1990s, "multimedia" became an industry buzzword used to refer to the vast domain of products made possible through the integration of sound, graphics, film, and other works in modern interactive computer systems. Virtually everyone in the legal community and the popular press seemed to agree that the future of education and entertainment lies in multimedia. With this attention came a significant focus on the legal issues surrounding the creation of multimedia products. By and large, these are copyright issues.

The term "multimedia" itself refers to a rather amorphous group of actual or planned products that use computer technology to transcend the categories of traditional copyright law. For example, a multimedia CD-ROM might contain text, audio recordings, audiovisual works, and computer graphics and animation, along with hypertext search capabilities. Each of these elements has been digitized and placed onto a computer disk. Multimedia products are often (but not always) "interactive," which means that (like a video game) what occurs on the computer screen is a function of the choices made by the user of the software.

Despite the intense legal and industry interest in the law of multimedia, there are relatively few *legal* issues specific to multimedia, and most of those are well-settled principles of copyright law. Multimedia law might fairly be described as copyright law, only more so. The legal difficulties that plague producers of multimedia works result not from the novelty of the medium but from the aggregation of copyright issues already present in a number of old media.[3]

3. One exception to this statement is the unification of different types of copyrighted works as digital content. Pictorial works, literary works, audiovisual works, and even architectural works can all be reduced to 1s and 0s in the digital medium. Arguably, therefore, they all become literary works. Since

The typical multimedia program will incorporate dozens, if not hundreds, of "clips" or samples of preexisting works. The genius of the multimedia program lies in the collection and organization of these prior works—putting different pieces relating to a single subject in the same place, and designing a hypertext network that allows the user to "jump" from one piece to another in both predictable and spontaneous ways. Such programs present two types of copyright issues. First, program authors must get permission to use each of the copyrighted works in their program. Second, authors who have "compiled" these works into a unique format would like to copyright their compilation in order to prevent others from copying it.

Neither of these copyright issues is new. The process of obtaining copyright permissions for sound recordings, audiovisual works, photographs, text, and works of art is straightforward—copyright licensing has been going on as long as copyright law has been in existence. While the fact that the multimedia product takes only a small "sample" from each preexisting work may distinguish multimedia from many copyright infringement cases, copyright has dealt with sampling before, notably in the context of rap music. See, e.g., Tin Pan Apple v. Miller Brewing Co., 30 U.S.P.Q.2d 1791 (S.D.N.Y. 1994); Jarvis v. A&M Records, 827 F. Supp. 282 (D.N.J. 1993); Grand Upright Music v. Warner Bros. Records, 780 F. Supp. 182 (S.D.N.Y. 1991). Whether a particular sample infringes the copyright on the original work depends on whether the taking from the original is substantial rather than de minimis.

Likewise, the protection of multimedia works can be treated according to well-established copyright principles. Program authors who write their own hypertext code or search engines can protect that code (and the nonliteral elements of the program) in the same way that they could protect any other computer program. And if the author has exercised creativity and originality in selecting preexisting materials for her multimedia program, she is entitled to a "compilation" copyright protecting that creativity against one who would copy her selection outright. 17 U.S.C. §103(a).

The problem copyright lawyers seem to have with multimedia is an eminently practical one—it is extraordinarily expensive and time-consuming to obtain hundreds of copyright permissions in order to put out a single product. Further, missing or intractable copyright owners can create "holdout" problems by leaving critical gaps in a multimedia work or charging exorbitant fees for the final pieces of a work. But these difficult problems inhere in the idea of copyright as a property right granted to authors and backed up by the force of injunctive relief.

The solution to these problems—if there is one—will take one of three forms. First, multimedia products may just be hard to produce or be incomplete and expensive. No novel interpretation of copyright law is required to achieve this result; it follows naturally from the economics of the copyright system.

Second, Congress could change the law to encourage the development of multimedia. The obvious candidate for legislative reform is the creation of some form of compulsory license that allows multimedia programmers to take works

---

copyright law has historically given different rights to different types of works, this unification creates some potential problems. For a discussion of these issues, see Pamela Samuelson, Fair Use for Computer Programs and Other Copyrightable Works in Digital Form: The Implications of *Sony, Galoob,* and *Sega,* 1 J. Intell. Prop. L. 49 (1993).

freely as long as they pay a set (or easily determinable) fee to the original copyright owner. This outcome seems unlikely, however. Multimedia by its nature would require a broad compulsory license governing most if not all types of copyrightable works. Unless the compulsory license were somehow limited to use in multimedia (a prospect that seems unworkable in practice), Congress could not accommodate the multimedia industry without revamping all of copyright law in a significant way.

Finally, it is possible that private organizations will develop that facilitate licensing of multiple works on a voluntary basis. Precursors of such groups already exist in some industries: American Society for Composers, Authors and Publishers (ASCAP) and Broadcast Music, Inc. (BMI) administer public performance rights to musical compositions, and the Copyright Clearance Center (CCC) grants the right to photocopy literary works, for example. See Robert P. Merges, Contracting Into Liability Rules: Institutions Supporting Transactions in Intellectual Property Rights, 84 Cal. L. Rev. 1293 (1996) (intellectual property rights support the development of private licensing organizations). But for multimedia to thrive, these voluntary organizations would have to expand into other areas (particularly with sound recordings and audiovisual works), and a significant percentage of copyright owners would have to sign on to the idea of automatically licensing their works to strangers. Unless and until that happens, the development of multimedia works will be hampered (though not prevented) by the problem of copyright licenses.

2. Copies and Section 117

As noted above, making copies is an essential part of using computer programs. Because of this important difference between computer software and other types of copyrightable material, Congress followed the recommendations of CONTU and passed section 117. That section provides in relevant part:

> Notwithstanding the provisions of section 106, it is not an infringement for the owner of a copy of a computer program to make or authorize the making of another copy or adaptation of that computer program provided:
>
> (1) that such a new copy or adaptation is created as an essential step in the utilization of the computer program in conjunction with a machine and that it is used in no other manner, or
>
> (2) that such new copy or adaptation is for archival purposes only and that all archival copies are destroyed in the event that continued possession of the computer program should cease to be rightful.

17 U.S.C. §117.

Section 117's right to make archival copies has not been controversial. It allows computer users to make backup copies of their programs as well as to load the programs onto hard drives from a floppy disk. See Vault Corp. v. Quaid Software Ltd., 847 F.2d 255 (5th Cir. 1988); ProCD, Inc. v. Zeidenberg, 908 F. Supp. 640 (W.D. Wis. 1996), *rev'd on other grounds*, 86 F.3d 1447 (7th Cir. 1996). The language of the statute also contemplates that multiple archival copies may be made of a single computer program. It clearly does *not* allow users of a program to make copies and distribute them to others for commercial purposes. See, e.g.,

Allen Myland Inc. v. IBM, 746 F. Supp. 520 (E.D. Pa. 1990); Apple Computer v. Formula Int'l, 594 F. Supp. 617 (C.D. Cal. 1984).

The right to make "essential" copies has proven more controversial. The basic intention of the section seems to be to allow copies like those made in *MAI v. Peak,* above. Further, the language of section 117(1) extends not only to identical copies, but to such "adaptation" of programs as is necessary to use them with a particular computer. In *Vault,* the Fifth Circuit held that such adaptations were not limited to those intended by the software vendor. In that case, Vault sold a computer program called PROLOK, which was used to "copy-protect" software.[4] Quaid reverse engineered Vault's program in order to create its own program, called RAMKEY, which disabled PROLOK's copy protection. In the course of writing RAMKEY, Quaid loaded the PROLOK program into its computer memory. The Court rejected Vault's claim of copyright infringement:

> In order to develop RAMKEY, Quaid analyzed Vault's program by copying it into its computer's memory. Vault contends that, by making this unauthorized copy, Quaid directly infringed upon Vault's copyright. The district court held that "Quaid's actions clearly fall within [the §117(1)] exemption. The loading of [Vault's] program into the [memory] of a computer is an 'essential step in the utilization' of [Vault's] program. Therefore, Quaid has not infringed Vault's copyright by loading [Vault's program] into [its computer's memory]." *Vault,* 655 F. Supp. at 758.
>
> Section 117(1) permits an owner of a program to make a copy of that program provided that the copy "is created as an essential step in the utilization of the computer program in conjunction with a machine and that it is used in no other manner." Congress recognized that a computer program cannot be used unless it is first copied into a computer's memory, and thus provided the §117(1) exception to permit copying for this essential purpose. See CONTU Report at 31. Vault contends that, due to the inclusion of the phrase "and that it is used in no other manner," this exception should be interpreted to permit only the copying of a computer program for the purpose of using it for *its intended purpose.* Because Quaid copied Vault's program into its computer's memory for the express purpose of devising a means of defeating its protective function, Vault contends that §117(1) is not applicable.
>
> We decline to construe §117(1) in this manner. Even though the copy of Vault's program made by Quaid was not used to prevent the copying of the program placed on the PROLOK diskette by one of Vault's customers (which is the purpose of Vault's program), and was, indeed, made for the express purpose of devising a means of defeating its protective function, the copy made by Quaid was "created as an essential step in the utilization" of Vault's program. Section 117(1) contains no language to suggest that the copy it permits must be employed for a use intended by the copyright owner, and, absent clear congressional guidance to the contrary, we refuse to read such limiting language into this exception. We therefore hold that Quaid did not infringe Vault's exclusive right to reproduce its program in copies under §106(1).

Vault Corp. v. Quaid Software Ltd., 847 F.2d at 261.

To whom does section 117 apply? By its terms, the statute authorizes copies or adaptations made by "the owner of a copy of a computer program" or persons she authorizes to make such copies. In its Final Report, the CONTU Commission

---

4. Copy protection, which was common during the early 1980s, refers to programs that attempt to prevent unauthorized copies of software—for example, by disabling a copy from running at all or by requiring a user to enter a key word from the manual before each operation.

indicated its intention "that *persons in rightful possession of copies of programs* be able to use them freely without fear of exposure to copyright liability." CONTU Final Report at 13 (emphasis added). The report seems to indicate that section 117 applies to anyone who has not obtained the program by improper means.

Without discussion or explanation, Congress changed "persons in rightful possession of copies" to "owners of copies." Does this mean that section 117 doesn't benefit licensees—a group that on some readings encompasses *all* users of a computer program? Or should the phrase "owner of a copy of a computer program" be interpreted to refer to the rightful possessor of the physical copy, regardless of who retains the copyright in the program itself? This issue was addressed at length by the Federal Circuit in DSC Communications Corp. v. Pulse Communications Inc., 170 F.3d 1354 (Fed. Cir. 1999):

> The district court concluded that making copies of the POTS-DI software (in the resident memory of POTS cards) was an "essential step in the utilization" of the POTS-DI software and that there was no evidence that the RBOCs used the software in any other manner that would constitute infringement. Accordingly, under the district court's theory of the case there was no direct infringement (and thus no contributory infringement) if the RBOCs were section 117 "owners" of copies of the POTS-DI software.
>
> The district court then held that the RBOCs were "owners" of copies of the POTS-DI software because they obtained the software by making a single payment and obtaining a right to possession of the software for an unlimited period. Those attributes of the transaction, the court concluded, made the transaction a "sale."
>
> DSC challenges the district court's conclusion that, based on the terms of the purchase transactions between DSC and the RBOCs, the RBOCs were "owners" of copies of the POTS-DI software. In order to resolve that issue, we must determine what attributes are necessary to constitute ownership of copies of software in this context.
>
> Unfortunately, ownership is an imprecise concept, and the Copyright Act does not define the term. Nor is there much useful guidance to be obtained from either the legislative history of the statute or the cases that have construed it. The National Commission on New Technological Uses of Copyrighted Works ("CONTU") was created by Congress to recommend changes in the Copyright Act to accommodate advances in computer technology. In its final report, CONTU proposed a version of section 117 that is identical to the one that was ultimately enacted, except for a single change. The proposed CONTU version provided that "it is not an infringement for the rightful possessor of a copy of a computer program to make or authorize the making of another copy or adaptation of that program. . . ." Final Report of the National Commission on New Technological Uses of Copyrighted Works, U.S. Dept. of Commerce, PB-282141, at 30 (July 31, 1978). Congress, however, substituted the words "owner of a copy" in place of the words "rightful possessor of a copy." See Pub.L. No. 96-517, 96th Cong., 2d Sess. (1980). The legislative history does not explain the reason for the change, see H.R.Rep. No. 96-1307, 96th Cong., 2d Sess., pt. 1, at 23 (1980), but it is clear from the fact of the substitution of the term "owner" for "rightful possessor" that Congress must have meant to require more than "rightful possession" to trigger the section 117 defense.
>
> In the leading case on section 117 ownership, the Ninth Circuit considered an agreement in which MAI, the owner of a software copyright, transferred copies of the copyrighted software to Peak under an agreement that imposed severe restrictions on Peak's rights with respect to those copies. See MAI Sys. Corp. v. Peak Computer, Inc., 991 F.2d 511, 26 USPQ2d 1458, 1462 (9th Cir. 1995). The court held that

Peak was not an "owner" of the copies of the software for purposes of section 117 and thus did not enjoy the right to copy conferred on owners by that statute. The Ninth Circuit stated that it reached the conclusion that Peak was not an owner because Peak had licensed the software from MAI. See *id.* at 518 n. 5. That explanation of the court's decision has been criticized for failing to recognize the distinction between ownership of a copyright, which can be licensed, and ownership of copies of the copyrighted software. See, e.g., 2 Melville B. Nimmer, Nimmer on Copyright ¶8.08[B][1], at 8-119 to 121 (3d ed. 1997). Plainly, a party who purchases copies of software from the copyright owner can hold a license under a copyright while still being an "owner" of a copy of the copyrighted software for purposes of section 117. We therefore do not adopt the Ninth Circuit's characterization of all licensees as non-owners. Nonetheless, the MAI case is instructive, because the agreement between MAI and Peak, like the agreements at issue in this case, imposed more severe restrictions on Peak's rights with respect to the software than would be imposed on a party who owned copies of software subject only to the rights of the copyright holder under the Copyright Act. And for that reason, it was proper to hold that Peak was not an "owner" of copies of the copyrighted software for purposes of section 117. See also Advanced Computer Servs. of Mich. v. MAI Sys. Corp., 845 F. Supp. 356, 367, 30 USPQ2d 1443, 1452 (E.D. Va. 1994) ("MAI customers are not 'owners' of the copyrighted software; they possess only the limited rights set forth in their licensing agreements"). We therefore turn to the agreements between DSC and the RBOCs to determine whether those agreements establish that the RBOCs are section 117 "owners" of copies of the copyrighted POTS-DI software. [The court concluded after a detailed analysis of the facts of the transaction that certain agreements in that case did not transfer ownership of the particular copies of the program at issue but that other transactions did involve a transfer of ownership.]

Id. at 1359-62. It is worth noting that *DSC* involved a negotiated agreement between sophisticated parties—the buyers were the regional Bell operating companies. By contrast, in the mass-market context, most (though by no means all) cases that have considered the issue have concluded that mass-market, over-the-counter transfers of computer programs at retail stores constitute "sales of goods" subject to the Uniform Commercial Code rather than license agreements. See Chapter 6 (discussing these cases).

The Digital Millennium Copyright Act, passed by Congress in 1998, reversed the holding of MAI v. Peak but in a very narrow way. Rather than declare that section 117 applies to rightful possessors of a computer program, as CONTU intended, the DMCA altered section 117 to create a particular exemption from liability for the owner or lessee of a computer to make or authorize the making of a copy of a computer program for purposes of maintenance or repair of the computer hardware. However, the copy thus made must be made solely by turning the machine on and be used for no other purpose; and no other programs can be copied. Further, the new provision does not apply to maintenance or repair of software—just hardware.

Does this solve the problem created by the *MAI* case? Or does it give legislative sanction to the idea that RAM copies are not permitted except in the narrow circumstances covered by the new Act? One might read this new exemption as creating a negative implication that all other copies made by lessees or licensees were illegal, even if they fell within subsections 117(1) or (2). Thus, this change may benefit independent service organizations that service computer hardware, but it does nothing for computer users in general.

Is there a social interest in maintaining a competitive market for hardware and software maintenance? One way of thinking about the issue is to determine whether the copyright in a computer program should permit its owner to control the markets for hardware and software maintenance, or whether using the copyright to prevent competition in that market would expand copyright protection beyond its intended boundaries. For a discussion of the competitive interest in software maintenance, see Pamela Samuelson, Modifying Copyrighted Software: Adjusting Copyright Doctrine to Accommodate a Technology, 28 Jurim. J. 179 (1988).

3. Derivative Works

Copyright Act section 106(2) grants the copyright owner the exclusive right to prepare "derivative works" based on the original copyrighted work. (This right, like the right to make copies, is subject to section 117.) Because computer programs are inherently easy to modify, the "derivative works" right has taken on particular significance in the computer context.

Midway Manufacturing Co. v. Artic International, Inc.
United States Court of Appeals for the Seventh Circuit
704 F.2d 1009 (7th Cir. 1983), cert. denied, 464 U.S. 923 (1983)

CUMMINGS, Chief Judge. . . .

Plaintiff manufactures video game machines. Inside these machines are printed circuit boards capable of causing images to appear on a television picture screen and sounds to emanate from a speaker when an electric current is passed through them. On the outside of each machine are a picture screen, sound speaker, and a lever or button that allows a person using the machine to alter the images appearing on the machine's picture screen and the sounds emanating from its speaker. Each machine can produce a large number of related images and sounds. These sounds and images are stored on the machine's circuit boards—how the circuits are arranged and connected determines the set of sounds and images the machine is capable of making. When a person touches the control lever or button on the outside of the machine he sends a signal to the circuit boards inside the machine which causes them to retrieve and display one of the sounds and images stored in them. Playing a video game involves manipulating the controls on the machine so that some of the images stored in the machine's circuitry appear on its picture screen and some of its sounds emanate from its speaker.

Defendant sells printed circuit boards for use inside video game machines. One of the circuit boards defendant sells speeds up the rate of play—how fast the sounds and images change—of "Galaxian," one of plaintiff's video games, when inserted in place of one of the "Galaxian" machine's circuit boards. Another of defendant's circuit boards stores a set of images and sounds almost identical to that stored in the circuit boards of plaintiff's "Pac-Man" video game machine so that the video game people play on machines containing defendant's circuit board looks and sounds virtually the same as plaintiff's "Pac-Man" game.

Plaintiff sued defendant alleging that defendant's sale of these two circuit boards infringes its copyrights in its "Galaxian" and "Pac-Man" video games. . . .

The final argument of defendant's that we address is that selling plaintiff's licensees circuit boards that speed up the rate of play of plaintiff's video games is not an infringement of plaintiff's copyrights. Speeding up the rate of play of a video game is a little like playing at 45 or 78 revolutions per minute ("RPM's") a phonograph record recorded at 33 RPM's. If a discotheque licensee did that, it would probably not be an infringement of the record company's copyright in the record. One might argue by analogy that it is not a copyright infringement for video game licensees to speed up the rate of play of video games, and that it is not a contributory infringement for the defendant to sell licensees circuit boards that enable them to do that.

There is this critical difference between playing records at a faster than recorded speed and playing video games at a faster than manufactured rate: there is an enormous demand for speeded-up video games but there is little if any demand for speeded-up records. Not many people want to hear 33 RPM records played at 45 and 78 RPM's so that record licensors would not care if their licensees play them at that speed. But there is a big demand for speeded-up video games. Speeding up a video game's action makes the game more challenging and exciting and increases the licensee's revenue per game. Speeded-up games end sooner than normal games and consequently if players are willing to pay an additional price-per-minute in exchange for the challenge and excitement of a faster game, licensees will take in greater total revenues. Video game copyright owners would undoubtedly like to lay their hands on some of that extra revenue and therefore it cannot be assumed that licensees are implicitly authorized to use speeded-up circuit boards in the machines plaintiff supplies.

Among a copyright owner's exclusive rights is the right "to prepare derivative works based upon the copyrighted work." 17 U.S.C. §106(2). If, as we hold, the speeded-up "Galaxian" game that a licensee creates with a circuit board supplied by the defendant is a derivative work based upon "Galaxian," a licensee who lacks the plaintiff's authorization to create a derivative work is a direct infringer and the defendant is a contributory infringer through its sale of the speeded-up circuit board. See, e.g., Gershwin Publishing Corp. v. Columbia Artists Mgmt., Inc., 443 F.2d 1159, 1162 (2d Cir. 1971); Universal City Studios, Inc. v. Sony Corp. of America, 659 F.2d 963, 975 (9th Cir. 1981), *certiorari granted*, 457 U.S. 1116, 102 S. Ct. 2926, 73 L. Ed.2d 1326 (1982).

Section 101 of the 1976 Copyright Act defines a derivative work as "a work based upon one or more preexisting works, such as a translation, musical arrangement, dramatization, fictionalization, motion picture version, sound recording, art reproduction, abridgment, condensation, or any other form in which a work may be recast, transformed, or adapted." It is not obvious from this language whether a speeded-up video game is a derivative work. A speeded-up phonograph record probably is not. Cf. Shapiro, Bernstein & Co. v. Jerry Vogel Music Co., 73 F. Supp. 165, 167 (S.D.N.Y. 1947) ("The change in time of the added chorus, and the slight variation in the base of the accompaniment, there being no change in the tune or lyrics, would not be 'new work'"); 1 Nimmer on Copyright §3.03 (1982). But that is because the additional value to the copyright owner of having the right to market separately the speeded-up version of the recorded performance is too trivial to warrant legal protection for that right. A speeded-up video game is a substantially different product from the original game. As noted, it is more exciting to play and it requires some creative effort to produce. For that reason, the owner of the copyright on the game should be entitled to monopolize it on the same theory that he is entitled to monopolize the derivative works specifically listed in Section 101. The current rage for video games was not anticipated in 1976, and like any new technology the video game does not fit with complete ease the definition of derivative work in Section 101 of the 1976 Act. But the amount by which the language of Section 101 must be stretched to accommodate speeded-up video games is, we believe, within the limits within which Congress wanted the new Act to operate. Cf. *WGN Continental Broadcasting Co.*, *supra*, 693 F.2d at 627; *Williams Electronics, Inc.*, supra, 685 F.2d at 873-874; *Atari, supra*, 672 F.2d at 614-620. . . .

———————————

Recall Vault Corp. v. Quaid Software Ltd., 847 F.2d 255 (5th Cir. 1988), discussed above. Early versions of RAMKEY had contained some characters from the original Vault program. The court found that this copying of characters was insufficient to make RAMKEY a derivative of the original PROLOK program:

> Section 106(2) of the Copyright Act provides the copyright owner exclusive rights "to prepare derivative works based on the copyrighted work." Section 101 defines a derivative work as:

>> a work based on one or more preexisting works, such as a translation, musical arrangement, dramatization, fictionalization, motion picture version, sound recording, art reproduction, abridgment, condensation, or any other form in which a work may be recast, transformed, or adapted. A work consisting of editorial revisions, annotations, elaborations or other modifications which, as a whole, represent an original work of authorship is a "derivative work."

> To constitute a derivative work, "the infringing work must incorporate in some form a portion of the copyrighted work." Litchfield v. Spielberg, 736 F.2d 1352, 1357 (9th Cir. 1984), *cert. denied*, 470 U.S. 1052, 105 S. Ct. 1753, 84 L. Ed.2d 817 (1985). In addition, the infringing work must be substantially similar to the copyrighted work. *Id.*

> The 1984 version of RAMKEY contained approximately 30 characters of source code copied from Vault's program. Vault's program contained the equivalent of approximately 50 pages of source code, and the 1984 version of RAMKEY contained the equivalent of approximately 80 pages of source code. By all accounts, the 30 character sequence shared by RAMKEY and Vault's program constituted a quantitatively minor amount of source code. In response to Vault's contention that RAMKEY constitutes a derivative work, the district court found that "the copying in 1984 was not significant" and that "there has been no evidence . . . that there has been any further duplication." Holding that "RAMKEY is not a substantially similar copy of PROLOK," the court concluded that "RAMKEY is not a derivative work." *Vault*, 655 F. Supp. at 759.

> Vault now contends that the district court, in evaluating the 1984 version of RAMKEY, incorrectly emphasized the *quantity* of copying instead of the *qualitative* significance of the copied material, and cites Whelan Assoc's., Inc. v. Jaslow Dental Laboratory, Inc., 797 F.2d 1222 (3d Cir. 1986), *cert. denied*, — U.S. —, 107 S. Ct. 877 (1987), for the proposition that a "court must make a qualitative, not quantitative, judgment about the character of the work as a whole and the importance of the substantially similar portions of the work." *Id.* at 1245. See Midway Mfg. Co. v. Artic

Int'l, Inc., 704 F.2d 1009, 1013-14 (7th Cir.), *cert. denied*, 464 U.S. 923 (1983). The sequence copied, Vault asserts, constituted the identifying portion of Vault's program which interacts with the "fingerprint" to confirm that the original PROLOK diskette is in the computer's disk drive. Vault contends that, because this sequence was crucial to the operation of Vault's program and RAMKEY's ability to defeat its protective function, the copying was qualitatively significant.

The cases upon which Vault relies, *Whelan* and *Midway*, both involved situations where the derivative work performed essentially the same function as the copyrighted work. In this case, Vault's program and RAMKEY serve opposing functions; while Vault's program is designed to prevent the duplication of its customers' programs, RAMKEY is designed to facilitate the creation of copies of Vault's customers' programs. Under these circumstances, we agree with the district court that the 1984 copying was not significant and that this version of RAMKEY was not a substantially similar copy of Vault's program.

While Vault acknowledges that the latest version of RAMKEY does not contain a sequence of characters from Vault's program, Vault contends that this version is also a derivative work because it "alters" Vault's program. Vault cites *Midway* for the proposition that a product can be a derivative work where it alters, rather than copies, the copyrighted work. The court in *Midway*, however, held that the sale of a product which speeded-up plaintiff's programs constituted contributory infringement because the speeded-up programs were derivative works. 704 F.2d at 1013-14. The court did not hold, as Vault asserts, that defendant's product itself was a derivative work. We therefore reject Vault's contention that the latest version of RAMKEY constitutes a derivative work.

COMMENTS AND QUESTIONS

1. What is the scope of the derivative works right under *Midway* decision? The court suggests that any nontrivial variation that would result in added revenues constitutes a derivative work. Is this consistent with the case law on derivative works outside the computer context? See Litchfield v. Spielberg, 736 F.2d 1352 (9th Cir. 1984) (works cannot be derivative unless they are substantially similar to the underlying work). In United States v. Manzer, 69 F.3d 222 (8th Cir. 1995), the court held that a 70 percent similarity between the code of two programs was sufficient to support a finding that one was an infringing derivative of the other. Would application of the *Litchfield* rule provide an easy way to resolve the "derivative works" issue in *Vault*?

It is also possible to criticize the *Midway* decision for reading the scope of derivative works too narrowly. After all, why should it matter whether there is a market for a particular derivative work? Shouldn't the property right of the program's owner include the right to prevent modifications whether or not they turn out to be commercially successful?

2. To what extent does the first-sale doctrine (17 U.S.C. §109(a)) protect makers of "add-on" software and hardware? Should it matter whether the underlying computer program is sold or licensed? See H.R. Rep. No. 94-1476, 94th Cong., 2d Sess. (1976) (licensors can control or prevent exercise of first sale rights by users).[5]

5. Note that a user's rights under the first-sale doctrine are limited in the computer context. Under the Software Rental Amendments Act of 1990, section 109 of the Act was amended to preclude those in

Note on Derivative Works and Section 117

In many circumstances, computer system and software manufacturers encourage the development of "add-on" software so as to make their products more attractive to users and to build large networks of users. As the *Midway* and *Vault* cases highlight, however, the interests of add-on developers and original program manufacturers can conflict, making the scope of the derivative-works right critical to the innovative environment. Whose rights should prevail in such a conflict may depend on your evaluation of the economics of software development. Preventing independent derivative works will certainly give a greater reward to the originator of the initial program, but by giving a monopoly on subsequent development it may slow the creation of improvements or add-ons to the program.

In certain cases, such as *Vault*, the entire point of an add-on is to defeat or render useless the original program. In such cases, is there some policy goal that would be served by giving the copyright owner a veto right over such "improvements" to his program? Is the *Vault* case more like the mutilation or destruction of a work of art, which many countries prohibit under moral rights statutes, or like a parody that should be legal precisely *because* copyright owners will refuse to license it?

The Copyright Act provides that the owner of a copy of a computer program has the right to adapt that program "provided that such . . . adaptation is created as an essential step in the utilization of the computer program in conjunction with a machine." 17 U.S.C. §117. To what extent does section 117 give the owners of computer programs the right to make derivative works for their own use? In *Aymes v. Bonnelli*, 47 F.3d 23 (2d Cir. 1995), the Second Circuit held that the rightful owner of a copy of a computer program had the right under section 117 "to add features to the program that were not present at the time of rightful acquisition," and to modify it for internal use, but not to distribute the work to others. The court relied on CONTU's explanation of section 117: "Buyers should be able to adapt a purchased program for use on the buyer's computer because without modifications, the program may work improperly, if at all."

Does *Aymes* justify the production of new versions of software? The translation of a program to run on a different operating system?

Some commentators have argued for a narrow scope for the derivative-works right in the context of computer program add-ons. See Richard Stern, Copyright Infringement by Add-On Software: Beyond Deconstruction of the Mona Lisa Moustache Paradigm and Not Taking Video Game Cases Too Seriously, 31 Jurimetrics J. 205 (1991); Christian H. Nadan, Comment, A Proposal to Recognize Component Works: How a Teddy Bears on the Competing Ends of Copyright Law, 78 Cal. L. Rev. 1633 (1990). Stern argues that allowing the creator of the original program to control add-ons not incorporated within that product would provide little additional incentive to develop the product, while inhibiting subsequent developers of add-on programs. Are there any other adverse effects of a narrow derivative-works right for add-on software? To what extent would Stern's argument apply to other fields of copyrightable works? On this issue, see Mark A.

---

possession of a copy of a computer program from "disposing of" it "by rental, lease, or lending, or by any other act or practice in the nature of rental, lease or lending." See Central Point Software Inc. v. Global Software & Accessories, 880 F. Supp. 957 (E.D.N.Y. 1995) ("Deferred Billing Plan" amounted to a de facto rental of software and was prohibited).

Lemley, The Economics of Improvement in Intellectual Property Law, 75 Tex. L. Rev. 989 (1997).

COMMENTS AND QUESTIONS

1. The Ninth Circuit took a much more limited view of add-on programs and enhancements in Micro Star v. Formgen, 154 F.3d 1107 (9th Cir. 1998). There, the copyright infringement plaintiff was Formgen, the owner of a popular computer game called "Duke Nukem 3D," in which characters adventured on multiple "levels." Players of the game had an established practice of writing and trading their own levels. Writing a level involved writing certain specifications that called on established graphics in the copyrighted game itself. However, the programs (MAP files) that created these add-on levels did not actually incorporate any of the code or graphics of the original computer game directly. Formgen permitted this practice so long as the levels were not sold. When Micro Star tried to compile and market add-on levels for the game, Formgen sued. The Ninth Circuit held that the levels were infringing derivative works, despite the fact that they did not themselves incorporate any aspect of the game in fixed form.[6]

Does this result make sense? Is it consistent with *Vault*? With *Aymes*? Note that the effect of this case is to give the copyright owner control over add-on works that merely interoperate with, rather than directly incorporate, the original copyrighted works. But see Lewis Galoob Toys v. Nintendo of America, 964 F.2d 965 (9th Cir. 1992) (concluding that a similar device that allowed users to alter the play of a video game was not a derivative work at all and in addition was fair use).

PROBLEM

Problem 2-9. Evaluate whether the following products would be deemed within the section 106(2) exclusive right to prepare derivative works.

(a) Demento Corporation (Demento) produces Demento II, the leading home video game system. The Demento II consists of a console, which runs game cartridges and attaches to a monitor or standard television, and a control device, which enables the user to manipulate characters or other images of particular games on the screen. Demento licenses a limited number of games per year.

Users of the Demento II, principally teenagers, quickly master the existing games. Without obtaining a license from Demento, MC Corporation developed a device to enable users to get more enjoyment out of the Demento

---

6. When a user played the game, Formgen's graphics would be incorporated, but only for a brief and arguably unfixed period of time. The court concluded that some sort of quasi-fixation was indeed a requirement for derivative works, but that the audiovisual works produced during game play were sufficiently fixed to qualify as derivative works because the audiovisual displays were described in exact detail in the user-created level specifications (MAP files). Note, however, that the MAP files themselves did not copy any of Formgen's protected program code, but merely told the game which files to display from the 'Duke Nukem' graphics library.

games. Its product, Master Controller, allows users to alter the speed of play and the capabilities of characters within Demento games. Master Controller functions by altering the data sent from the game cartridge to the console. It does not alter the data within the game cartridge and cannot be used without both the Demento II console and game cartridges.

(b) ACME Software Inc. has developed a program called Speechwriter that works in conjunction with a number of leading word processing programs. When a user selects keywords within a document and enters "Alt Q," Speechwriter displays a series of famous quotations related to the selected keywords. The program is geared to the visual presentation format of the particular word processing program. Once in the Speechwriter mode, the program offers users a variety of convenient ways to search among quotations. The program allows the user to download the quotation into the document. The actual program is stored on a separate floppy disk or can be loaded onto the computer's hard drive. It contains some program code from the word processing programs needed to interact with the word processing software and the graphical interface of the computer.

D. FAIR USE

§107. Limitations on Exclusive Rights: Fair Use

Notwithstanding the provisions of section 106, the fair use of a copyrighted work, including such use by reproduction in copies or phonorecords or by any other means specified by that section, for purposes such as criticism, comment, news reporting, teaching (including multiple copies for classroom use), scholarship, or research, is not an infringement of copyright. In determining whether the use made of a work in any particular case is a fair use the factors to be considered shall include —

(1) the purpose and character of the use, including whether such use is of a commercial nature or is for nonprofit educational purposes;

(2) the nature of the copyrighted work;

(3) the amount and substantiality of the portion used in relation to the copyrighted work as a whole; and

(4) effect of the use upon the potential market for or value of the copyrighted work.

The fact that a work is unpublished shall not itself bar a finding of fair use if such finding is made upon consideration of all the above factors.

It is well established that both the list of potential fair uses and the factors to be considered in determining fair use are illustrative rather than exhaustive. The House Report accompanying section 107 describes the four factors—and the list of possible fair uses—as "the result of a process of accretion" during the judicial development of the fair use doctrine at common law. According to the report, section 107 is designed to "offer some guidance" in determining fair use, not to formulate "exact rules." H.R. No. 94-1476, at 66 (1976).

Section 107 represents the first attempt to codify what has been a common law doctrine for some time. The first reference to fair use (albeit by a different name) is thought to be in Folsom v. Marsh, 9 F. Cas. 342 (C.C. Mass. 1841). The court there focused on the loss in value to the plaintiff from copying to determine whether the defendant had engaged in what it called a "justifiable use" of plaintiff's copyrighted work. However, more recent cases have also looked to the purpose of the use and the "public benefit" conferred thereby. See Rosemont Enterprises v. Random House, Inc., 366 F.2d 303 (2d Cir. 1966). Indeed, *Folsom* itself involved the publication of George Washington's private letters, and therefore contained a strong public interest component as well.

The inability of the courts or Congress even to articulate a complete list of the factors to be applied in determining fair use is evidence of the difficulty courts have had in applying the doctrine. Judge Learned Hand described the fair use doctrine as "the most troublesome in the whole law of copyright." Dellar v. Samuel Goldwyn, Inc., 104 F.2d 661 (2d Cir. 1939).

Lewis Galoob Toys, Inc. v. Nintendo of America, Inc.
United States Court of Appeals for the Ninth Circuit
964 F.2d 965 (9th Cir. 1992)

FARRIS, Circuit Judge:

Nintendo of America appeals the district court's judgment following a bench trial (1) declaring that Lewis Galoob Toys' Game Genie does not violate any Nintendo copyrights and dissolving a temporary injunction and (2) denying Nintendo's request for a permanent injunction enjoining Galoob from marketing the Game Genie. Lewis Galoob Toys, Inc. v. Nintendo of America, Inc., 780 F. Supp. 1283, 20 U.S.P.Q.2D (BNA) 1662 (N.D. Cal. 1991). We have appellate jurisdiction pursuant to 15 U.S.C. §1121 and 28 U.S.C. §§1291 and 1292(a)(1). We affirm.

Facts

The Nintendo Entertainment System is a home video game system marketed by Nintendo. To use the system, the player inserts a cartridge containing a video game that Nintendo produces or licenses others to produce. By pressing buttons and manipulating a control pad, the player controls one of the game's characters and progresses through the game. The games are protected as audiovisual works under 17 U.S.C. §102(a)(6).

The Game Genie is a device manufactured by Galoob that allows the player to alter up to three features of a Nintendo game. For example, the Game Genie can increase the number of lives of the player's character, increase the speed at which the character moves, and allow the character to float above obstacles. The player controls the changes made by the Game Genie by entering codes provided by the Game Genie Programming Manual and Code Book. The player also can experiment with variations of these codes.

The Game Genie functions by blocking the value for a single data byte sent by the game cartridge to the central processing unit in the Nintendo Entertainment System and replacing it with a new value. If that value controls the character's strength, for example, then the character can be made invincible by increasing the value sufficiently. The Game Genie is inserted between a game cartridge and the Nintendo Entertainment System. The Game Genie does not alter the data that is stored in the game cartridge. Its effects are temporary.

Discussion

[The court concluded that the Game Genie was not a derivative work, because it did not itself incorporate the copyrighted work. The court also distinguished Midway v. Artic, reproduced above, and apparently concluded that the end user does not create a derivative work either. Nonetheless, the court went on to discuss fair use by the end user.]

2. Fair Use

"The doctrine of fair use allows a holder of the privilege to use copyrighted material in a reasonable manner without the consent of the copyright owner." Narell v. Freeman, 872 F.2d 907, 913, 10 U.S.P.Q.2D (BNA) 1596 (9th Cir. 1989) (citations omitted). The district court concluded that, even if the audiovisual displays created by the Game Genie are derivative works, Galoob is not liable under 17 U.S.C. §107 because the displays are a fair use of Nintendo's copyrighted displays. "Whether a use of copyrighted material is a 'fair use' is a mixed question of law and fact. If the district court found sufficient facts to evaluate each of the statutory factors, the appellate court may decide whether defendants may claim the fair use defense as a matter of law." Abend v. MCA, Inc., 863 F.2d 1465, 1468, 9 U.S.P.Q.2D (BNA) 1337 (9th Cir. 1988), *aff'd sub nom.* Stewart v. Abend, 495 U.S. 207, 109 L. Ed. 2d 184, 110 S. Ct. 1750, 14 U.S.P.Q.2D (BNA) 1614 (1990).

Section 107 codifies the fair use defense. . . .

Much of the parties' dispute regarding the fair use defense concerns the proper focus of the court's inquiry: (1) Galoob or (2) consumers who purchase and use the Game Genie. Nintendo's complaint does not allege direct infringement, nor did it try the case on that theory. The complaint, for example, alleges only that "Galoob's marketing advertising [sic], promoting and selling of Game Genie has and will contribute to the creation of infringing derivatives of Nintendo's copyrighted . . . games.". Contributory infringement is a form of third party liability. See Melville B. Nimmer & David Nimmer, 3 Nimmer on Copyright ¶12.04[A]2, at 12-68 (1991). The district court properly focused on whether consumers who purchase and use the Game Genie would be infringing Nintendo's copyrights by creating (what are now assumed to be) derivative works.

Nintendo emphasizes that the district court ultimately addressed its direct infringement by authorization argument. The court concluded that, "because the Game Genie does not create a derivative work when used in conjunction with a copyrighted video game, Galoob does not 'authorize the use of a copyrighted work without the actual authority from the copyright owner.'" *Galoob*, 780 F. Supp. at 1298 (quoting *Sony*, 464 U.S. at 435 n.17). Although infringement by authorization is a form of direct infringement, this does not change the proper focus of our inquiry; a party cannot authorize another party to infringe a copyright unless the authorized conduct would itself be unlawful.

The district court concluded that "a family's use of a Game Genie for private home enjoyment must be characterized as a non-commercial, nonprofit activity." *Galoob*, 780 F. Supp. at 1293. Nintendo argues that Game Genie users are supplanting its commercially valuable right to make and sell derivative works. Nintendo's reliance on Harper & Row Publishers, Inc. v. Nation Enters., 471 U.S. 539, 562, 85 L. Ed. 2d 588, 105 S. Ct. 2218, 225 U.S.P.Q. (BNA) 1073 (1985), is misplaced. The commercially valuable right at issue in Harper & Row was the right of first publication; Nation Enterprises intended to publish the copyrighted materials for profit. See id. at 562-63. See also *Sony*, 464 U.S. at 449 ("If the Betamax were used to make copies for a commercial or profit-making purpose, such use would presumptively be unfair."). Game Genie users are engaged in a non-profit activity. Their use of the Game Genie to create derivative works therefore is presumptively fair. See *Sony*, 464 U.S. at 449.

The district court also concluded that "the [Nintendo] works' published nature supports the fairness of the use." *Galoob*, 780 F. Supp. at 1293. Nintendo argues that it has not published the derivative works created by the Game Genie. This argument ignores the plain language of section 107: "the factors to be considered shall include . . . the nature of the copyrighted work." The argument also would make the fair use defense unavailable in all cases of derivative works, including "criticism, comment, news reporting, teaching . . . , scholarship, or research." 17 U.S.C. §107. A commentary that incorporated large portions of *For Whom the Bell Tolls*, for example, would be undeserving of fair use protection because the incorporated portions would constitute an unpublished derivative work. This cannot be the law.

The district court further concluded that the amount of the portion used in relation to the copyrighted work as a whole "cannot assist Nintendo in overcoming the presumption of fair use." *Galoob*, 780 F. Supp. at 1293. The video tape recorders at issue in *Sony* allowed consumers to tape copyrighted works in their entirety. The Supreme Court nevertheless held that, "when one considers . . . that [video tape recording] merely enables a viewer to see such a work which he had been invited to witness in its entirety free of charge, the fact that the entire work is reproduced does not have its ordinary effect of militating against a finding of fair use." 464 U.S. 449 at 449-50 (citations omitted). Consumers are not invited to witness Nintendo's audiovisual displays free of charge, but, once they have paid to do so, the fact that the derivative works created by the Game Genie are comprised almost entirely of Nintendo's copyrighted displays does not militate against a finding of fair use.

Nintendo would distinguish *Sony* because it involved copying copyrighted works rather than creating derivative works based on those works. In other words, the consumers in *Sony* could lawfully copy the copyrighted works because they were invited to view those works free of charge. Game Genie users, in contrast, are not invited to view derivative works based on Nintendo's copyrighted works without first paying for that privilege. *Sony* cannot be read so narrowly. It is difficult to imagine that the Court would have reached a different conclusion if Betamax purchasers were skipping portions of copyrighted works or viewing denouements before climaxes. *Sony* recognizes that a party who distributes a copyrighted work cannot dictate how that work is to be enjoyed. Consumers may use a Betamax to view copyrighted works at a more convenient time. They similarly may use a Game Genie to enhance a Nintendo Game cartridge's audiovisual display in such a way as to make the experience more enjoyable.

"The fourth factor is the 'most important, and indeed, central fair use factor.'" *Stewart*, 495 U.S. at 238 (quoting 3 Nimmer on Copyright ¶13.05[A], at 13-81). The district court concluded that "Nintendo has failed to show any harm to the present market for its copyrighted games and has failed to establish the reasonable likelihood of a potential market for slightly altered versions of the games at suit." *Galoob*, 780 F. Supp. at 1295. Nintendo's main argument on appeal is that the test for market harm encompasses the potential market for derivative works. Because the Game Genie is used for a noncommercial purpose, the likelihood of future harm may not be presumed. See *Sony*, 464 U.S. at 451. Nintendo must show "by a preponderance of the evidence that some meaningful likelihood of future harm exists." *Id.*

Nintendo's argument is supported by case law. Although the Copyright Act requires a court to consider "the effect of the use upon the potential market for or value of the copyrighted work," 17 U.S.C. §107(4), we held in *Abend* that "although the motion picture will have no adverse effect on bookstore sales of the [underlying] novel—and may in fact have a beneficial effect—it is 'clear that [the film's producer] may not invoke the defense of fair use.'" 863 F.2d at 1482 (quoting 3 Nimmer on Copyright ¶13.05[B], at 13-84). We explained: " 'If the defendant's work adversely affects the value of any of the rights in the copyrighted work . . . the use is not fair even if the rights thus affected have not as yet been exercised by the plaintiff.'" *Id.* (quoting 3 Nimmer on Copyright ¶13.05[B], at 13-84 to 13-85 (footnotes omitted)). The Supreme Court specifically affirmed our finding that the motion picture adaptation "impinged on the ability to market new versions of the story." *Stewart*, 495 U.S. at 238.

Still, Nintendo's argument is undermined by the facts. The district court considered the potential market for derivative works based on Nintendo game cartridges and found that: (1) "Nintendo has not, to date, issued or considered issuing altered versions of existing games," *Galoob*, 780 F. Supp. at 1295, and (2) Nintendo "has failed to show the reasonable likelihood of such a market." *Id.* The record supports the court's findings. According to Stephen Beck, Galoob's expert witness, junior or expert versions of existing Nintendo games would enjoy very little market interest because the original version of each game already has been designed to appeal to the largest number of consumers. Mr. Beck also testified that a new game must include new material or "the game player is going to feel very cheated and robbed, and [the] product will have a bad reputation and word of mouth will probably kill its sales." Howard Lincoln, Senior Vice President of Nintendo of America, acknowledged that Nintendo has no present plans to market such games.

The district court also noted that Nintendo's assertion that it may wish to re-release altered versions of its game cartridges is contradicted by its position in various other lawsuits:

> In those actions, Nintendo opposes antitrust claims by using the vagaries of the video game industry to rebut the impact and permanence of its market control, if any. Having indoctrinated this Court as to the fast pace and instability of the video game industry, Nintendo may not now, without any data, redefine that market in its request for the extraordinary remedy sought herein. . . . While board games may never die, good video games are mortal.

Galoob, 780 F. Supp. at 1295. The existence of this potential market cannot be presumed. See *Sony*, 464 U.S. at 451. See also Wright v. Warner Books, Inc., 953 F.2d 731, 739, 20 U.S.P.Q.2D (BNA) 1892 (2d Cir. 1991) (affirming district court's finding of no reasonable likelihood of injury to alleged market because "plaintiff has offered no evidence that the project will go forward"). The fourth and most important fair use factor also favors *Galoob*.

Nintendo's most persuasive argument is that the creative nature of its audiovisual displays weighs against a finding of fair use. The Supreme Court has acknowledged that "fair use is more likely to be found in factual works than fictional works." *Stewart*, 495 U.S. at 237. This consideration weighs against a finding of fair use, but it is not dispositive. See *Sony*, 464 U.S. at 448 (fair use defense is an "equitable rule of reason"). The district court could properly conclude that Game Genie users are making a fair use of Nintendo's displays. . . .

AFFIRMED.

COMMENTS AND QUESTIONS

1. Suppose that Nintendo had announced its intention to sell add-on devices to its entertainment system that would perform the same function as the Game Genie. Should this fact change the fair use analysis? Certainly Nintendo could prove that it was losing money to Galoob in this example. Does this fact sway the fourth factor in Nintendo's favor? What if Nintendo could show the existence of a "market" for *licensing* devices like the Game Genie? Is Galoob depriving Nintendo of a royalty payment? On this issue, cf. American Geophysical Union v. Texaco, 37 F.3d 881 (2d Cir. 1994) (existence of "market" for royalty payments of copies undercuts fair use argument); Princeton University Press v. Michigan Document Servs., 99 F.3d 1381 (6th Cir. 1996) (en banc) (same); *contra* Williams & Wilkins Co. v. United States, 487 F.2d 1345 (Ct. Cl. 1973) (en banc).

2. One of the reasons people play video games is for the challenge of overcoming obstacles. Does a device that gives a game character "super powers" or an infinite number of lives defeat this purpose? It is certainly possible that owners of the Game Genie will more quickly grow bored with video games than those without it.[7] If Nintendo can prove that the Game Genie will cut into its sales of games by making the games less challenging, should that affect its copyright argument?

Alternatively, does Nintendo have some "moral right" in the integrity of its audiovisual work that is being violated by Galoob's device?

3. Most of Nintendo's games are not written by Nintendo itself, but by independent authors who write and sell them for use on the Nintendo system. Isn't

---

7. Of course, this might induce them to buy more Nintendo games, rather than fewer. If that is the case, it is hard to see how Nintendo has been injured.

it the authors, rather than Nintendo itself, who should be bringing this action? On this point, see Vault v. Quaid:

> Vault contends that, because purchasers of programs placed on PROLOK diskettes use the RAMKEY feature of CopyWrite to make unauthorized copies, Quaid's advertisement and sale of CopyWrite diskettes with the RAMKEY feature violate the Copyright Act by contributing to the infringement of Vault's copyright and the copyrights owned by Vault's customers. Vault asserts that it lost customers and substantial revenue as a result of Quaid's contributory infringement because software companies which previously relied on PROLOK diskettes to protect their programs from unauthorized copying have discontinued their use. . . .
>
> . . . The district court held that Vault lacked standing to raise a contributory infringement claim because "it is not Vault, but the customers of Vault who place their programs on PROLOK disks, who may assert such claims. Clearly the copyright rights to these underlying programs belong to their publishers, not Vault." *Vault,* 655 F. Supp. at 759. [The Court of Appeals did not reach this issue because it found that RAMKEY was capable of a substantial noninfringing use, and therefore Quaid could not be liable for contributory infringement in any event].

847 F.2d 255, 261-62 (5th Cir. 1988).

4. In Sony v. Bleem, 214 F.3d 1022 (9th Cir. 2000), the court held that copying screen shots from a television display to use in comparative advertising constituted fair use. By contrast, a district court held that digital manipulation of a photograph to produce a new work fell outside the scope of fair use. See Tiffany Design v. Reno-Tahoe Specialty (D. Nev. 1999).

▆▆
▆▆ *Micro Star v. Formgen Inc.*
▆▆ *United States Court of Appeals for the Ninth Circuit*
▆▆ *154 F.3d 1107 (9th Cir. 1998)*

KOZINSKI, Circuit Judge.

Duke Nukem routinely vanquishes Octabrain and the Protozoid Slimer. But what about the dreaded Micro Star?

I

FormGen Inc., GT Interactive Software Corp. and Apogee Software, Ltd. (collectively FormGen) made, distributed and own the rights to Duke Nukem 3D (D/N-3D), an immensely popular (and very cool) computer game. D/N-3D is played from the first-person perspective; the player assumes the personality and point of view of the title character, who is seen on the screen only as a pair of hands and an occasional boot, much as one might see oneself in real life without the aid of a mirror. Players explore a futuristic city infested with evil aliens and other hazards. The goal is to zap them before they zap you, while searching for the hidden passage to the next level. The basic game comes with twenty-nine levels, each with a different combination of scenery, aliens, and other challenges. The game also includes a "Build Editor," a utility that enables players to create their own levels. With FormGen's encouragement, players frequently post levels they have created on the Internet where others can download them. Micro Star, a computer software distributor, did just that: It downloaded 300 user-created levels and stamped them onto a CD, which it then sold commercially as Nuke It (N/I). N/I is packaged in a box decorated with numerous "screen shots," pictures of what the new levels look like when played.

Micro Star filed suit in district court, seeking a declaratory judgment that N/I did not infringe on any of FormGen's copyrights. FormGen counterclaimed, seeking a preliminary injunction barring further production and distribution of N/I. Relying on Lewis Galoob Toys, Inc. v. Nintendo of Am., Inc., 964 F.2d 965 (9th Cir. 1992), the district court held that N/I was not a derivative work and therefore did not infringe FormGen's copyright. The district court did, however, grant a preliminary injunction as to the screen shots, finding that N/I's packaging violated FormGen's copyright by reproducing pictures of D/N-3D characters without a license. The court rejected Micro Star's fair use claims. Both sides appeal their losses. . . .

III

To succeed on the merits of its claim that N/I infringes FormGen's copyright, FormGen must show (1) ownership of the copyright to D/N-3D, and (2) copying of protected expression by Micro Star. See Triad Systems Corp. v. Southeastern Express Co., 64 F.3d 1330, 1335 (9th Cir. 1995). FormGen's copyright registration creates a presumption of ownership, see *id.*, and we are satisfied that FormGen has established its ownership of the copyright. We therefore focus on the latter issue.

FormGen alleges that its copyright is infringed by Micro Star's unauthorized commercial exploitation of user-created game levels. In order to understand FormGen's claims, one must first understand the way D/N-3D works. The game consists of three separate components: the game engine, the source art library and the MAP files. The game engine is the heart of the computer program; in some sense, it is the program. It tells the computer when to read data, save and load games, play sounds and project images onto the screen. In order to create the audiovisual display for a particular level, the game engine invokes the MAP file that corresponds to that level. Each MAP file contains a series of instructions that tell the game engine (and, through it, the computer) what to put where. For instance, the MAP file might say scuba gear goes at the bottom of the screen. The game engine then goes to the source art library, finds the image of the scuba gear, and puts it in just the right place on the screen.[3] The MAP file describes the level in painstaking detail, but it does not actually contain any of the copyrighted art itself; everything that appears on the screen actually comes from the art library. Think of the game's audiovisual display as a paint-by-numbers kit. The MAP file might tell you to put blue paint in section number 565, but it doesn't contain any blue paint

---

3. Actually, this is all a bit metaphorical. Computer programs don't actually go anywhere or fetch anything. Rather, the game engine receives the player's instruction as to which game level to select and instructs the processor to access the MAP file corresponding to that level. The MAP file, in turn, consists of a series of instructions indicating which art images go where. When the MAP file calls for a particular art image, the game engine tells the processor to access the art library for instructions on how each pixel on the screen must be colored in order to paint that image.

itself; the blue paint comes from your palette, which is the low-tech analog of the art library, while you play the role of the game engine. When the player selects one of the N/I levels, the game engine references the N/I MAP files, but still uses the D/N-3D art library to generate the images that make up that level.

FormGen points out that a copyright holder enjoys the exclusive right to prepare derivative works based on D/N-3D. See 17 U.S.C. §106(2) (1994). According to FormGen, the audiovisual displays generated when D/N-3D is run in conjunction with the N/I CD MAP files are derivative works that infringe this exclusivity. Is FormGen right? The answer is not obvious.

The Copyright Act defines a derivative work as

> a work based upon one or more preexisting works, such as a translation, musical arrangement, dramatization, fictionalization, motion picture version, sound recording, art reproduction, abridgment, condensation, or any other form in which a work may be recast, transformed, or adapted. A work consisting of editorial revisions, annotations, elaborations, or other modifications which, as a whole, represent an original work of authorship, is a "derivative work."

Id. §101. The statutory language is hopelessly overbroad, however, for "[e]very book in literature, science and art, borrows and must necessarily borrow, and use much which was well known and used before." Emerson v. Davies, 8 F. Cas. 615, 619 (C.C.D.Mass. 1845) (No. 4436), quoted in 1 Nimmer on Copyright, §3.01, at 3-2 (1997). To narrow the statute to a manageable level, we have developed certain criteria a work must satisfy in order to qualify as a derivative work. One of these is that a derivative work must exist in a "concrete or permanent form," *Galoob*, 964 F.2d at 967 (internal quotation marks omitted), and must substantially incorporate protected material from the preexisting work, see Litchfield v. Spielberg, 736 F.2d 1352, 1357 (9th Cir. 1984). Micro Star argues that N/I is not a derivative work because the audiovisual displays generated when D/N-3D is run with N/I's MAP files are not incorporated in any concrete or permanent form, and the MAP files do not copy any of D/N-3D's protected expression. It is mistaken on both counts.

The requirement that a derivative work must assume a concrete or permanent form was recognized without much discussion in *Galoob*. There, we noted that all the Copyright Act's examples of derivative works took some definite, physical form and concluded that this was a requirement of the Act. See *Galoob*, 964 F.2d at 967-68; see also Edward G. Black & Michael H. Page, Add-On Infringements, 15 Hastings Comm/Ent. L.J. 615, 625 (1993) (noting that in *Galoob* the Ninth Circuit "re-examined the statutory definition of derivative works offered in section 101 and found an independent fixation requirement of sorts built into the statutory definition of derivative works"). Obviously, N/I's MAP files themselves exist in a concrete or permanent form; they are burned onto a CD-ROM. See ProCD, Inc. v. Zeidenberg, 86 F.3d 1447, 1453 (7th Cir. 1996) (computer files on a CD are fixed in a tangible medium of expression). But what about the audiovisual displays generated when D/N-3D runs the N/I MAP files—i.e., the actual game level as displayed on the screen? Micro Star argues that, because the audiovisual displays in *Galoob* didn't meet the "concrete or permanent form" requirement, neither do N/I's.

In *Galoob*, we considered audiovisual displays created using a device called the Game Genie, which was sold for use with the Nintendo Entertainment System.

The Game Genie allowed players to alter individual features of a game, such as a character's strength or speed, by selectively "blocking the value for a single data byte sent by the game cartridge to the [Nintendo console] and replacing it with a new value." *Galoob*, 964 F.2d at 967. Players chose which data value to replace by entering a code; over a billion different codes were possible. The Game Genie was dumb; it functioned only as a window into the computer program, allowing players to temporarily modify individual aspects of the game. See Lewis Galoob Toys, Inc. v. Nintendo of Am., Inc., 780 F. Supp. 1283, 1289 (N.D.Cal. 1991).

Nintendo sued, claiming that when the Game Genie modified the game system's audiovisual display, it created an infringing derivative work. We rejected this claim because "[a] derivative work must incorporate a protected work in some concrete or permanent form." *Galoob*, 964 F.2d at 967 (internal quotation marks omitted). The audiovisual displays generated by combining the Nintendo System with the Game Genie were not incorporated in any permanent form; when the game was over, they were gone. Of course, they could be reconstructed, but only if the next player chose to reenter the same codes.[4]

Micro Star argues that the MAP files on N/I are a more advanced version of the Game Genie, replacing old values (the MAP files in the original game) with new values (N/I's MAP files). But, whereas the audiovisual displays created by Game Genie were never recorded in any permanent form, the audiovisual displays generated by D/N-3D from the N/I MAP files are in the MAP files themselves. In *Galoob*, the audiovisual display was defined by the original game cartridge, not by the Game Genie; no one could possibly say that the data values inserted by the Game Genie described the audiovisual display. In the present case the audiovisual display that appears on the computer monitor when a N/I level is played is described—in exact detail—by a N/I MAP file.

This raises the interesting question whether an exact, down to the last detail, description of an audiovisual display (and—by definition—we know that MAP files do describe audiovisual displays down to the last detail) counts as a permanent or concrete form for purposes of *Galoob*. We see no reason it shouldn't. What, after all, does sheet music do but describe in precise detail the way a copyrighted melody sounds? See 1 William F. Patry, Copyright Law and Practice 168 (1994) ("[A] musical composition may be embodied in sheet music. . . ."). To be copyrighted, pantomimes and dances may be "described in sufficient detail to enable the work to be performed from that description." *Id*. at 243 (citing Compendium II of Copyright Office Practices §463); see also Horgan v. Macmillan, Inc., 789 F.2d 157, 160 (2d Cir. 1986). Similarly, the N/I MAP files describe the audiovisual display that is to be generated when the player chooses to play D/N-3D using the N/I levels. Because the audiovisual displays assume a concrete or permanent form in the MAP files, *Galoob* stands as no bar to finding that they are derivative works.

---

4. A low-tech example might aid understanding. Imagine a product called the Pink Screener, which consists of a big piece of pink cellophane stretched over a frame. When put in front of a television, it makes everything on the screen look pinker. Someone who manages to record the programs with this pink cast (maybe by filming the screen) would have created an infringing derivative work. But the audiovisual display observed by a person watching television through the Pink Screener is not a derivative work because it does not incorporate the modified image in any permanent or concrete form. The Game Genie might be described as a fancy Pink Screener for video games, changing a value of the game as perceived by the current player, but never incorporating the new audiovisual display into a permanent or concrete form.

In addition, "[a] work will be considered a derivative work only if it would be considered an infringing work if the material which it has derived from a preexisting work had been taken without the consent of a copyright proprietor of such preexisting work." Mirage Editions v. Albuquerque A.R.T. Co., 856 F.2d 1341, 1343 (quoting 1 Nimmer on Copyright §3.01 (1986)) (internal quotation marks omitted). "To prove infringement, [FormGen] must show that [D/N-3D's and N/I's audiovisual displays] are substantially similar in both ideas and expression." Litchfield v. Spielberg, 736 F.2d 1352, 1356 (9th Cir. 1984) (emphasis omitted). Similarity of ideas may be shown by comparing the objective details of the works: plot, theme, dialogue, mood, setting, characters, etc. See *id*. Similarity of expression focuses on the response of the ordinary reasonable person, and considers the total concept and feel of the works. See *id*. at 1356-57. FormGen will doubtless succeed in making these showings since the audiovisual displays generated when the player chooses the N/I levels come entirely out of D/N-3D's source art library. Cf. Atari, Inc. v. North Am. Philips Consumer Elec. Corp., 672 F.2d 607, 620 (7th Cir. 1982) (finding two video games substantially similar because they shared the same "total concept and feel").

Micro Star further argues that the MAP files are not derivative works because they do not, in fact, incorporate any of D/N-3D's protected expression. In particular, Micro Star makes much of the fact that the N/I MAP files reference the source art library, but do not actually contain any art files themselves. Therefore, it claims, nothing of D/N-3D's is reproduced in the MAP files. In making this argument, Micro Star misconstrues the protected work. The work that Micro Star infringes is the D/N-3D story itself—a beefy commando type named Duke who wanders around post-Apocalypse Los Angeles, shooting Pig Cops with a gun, lobbing hand grenades, searching for medkits and steroids, using a jetpack to leap over obstacles, blowing up gas tanks, avoiding radioactive slime. A copyright owner holds the right to create sequels, see Trust Co. Bank v. MGM/UA Entertainment Co., 772 F.2d 740 (11th Cir. 1985), and the stories told in the N/I MAP files are surely sequels, telling new (though somewhat repetitive) tales of Duke's fabulous adventures. A book about Duke Nukem would infringe for the same reason, even if it contained no pictures.[5]

Micro Star nonetheless claims that its use of D/N-3D's protected expression falls within the doctrine of fair use. . . .

As a preliminary matter, Micro Star asks us to focus on the player's use of the N/I CD in evaluating the fair use claim, because—according to Micro Star—the player actually creates the derivative work. In *Galoob*, after we assumed for purposes of argument that the Game Genie did create derivative works, we went on to consider the fair use defense from the player's point of view. See *Galoob*, 964 F.2d at 970. But the fair use analysis in *Galoob* was not necessary and therefore is clearly dicta. More significantly, Nintendo alleged only contributory infringement—that *Galoob* was helping consumers create derivative works; FormGen here alleges direct infringement by Micro Star, because the MAP files encompass new Duke stories, which are themselves derivative works.

---

5. We note that the N/I MAP files can only be used with D/N-3D. If another game could use the MAP files to tell the story of a mousy fellow who travels through a beige maze, killing vicious saltshakers with paper-clips, then the MAP files would not incorporate the protected expression of D/N-3D because they would not be telling a D/N-3D story.

Our examination of the section 107 factors yields straightforward results. Micro Star's use of FormGen's protected expression was made purely for financial gain. While that does not end our inquiry, see Campbell v. Acuff-Rose Music, Inc., 510 U.S. 569, 584, 114 S. Ct. 1164, 127 L. Ed.2d 500 (1994), "every commercial use of copyrighted material is presumptively an unfair exploitation of the monopoly privilege that belongs to the owner of the copyright." Sony Corp. of Am. v. Universal City Studios, Inc., 464 U.S. 417, 451, 104 S. Ct. 774, 78 L. Ed.2d 574 (1984).[6] The Supreme Court has explained that the second factor, the nature of the copyrighted work, is particularly significant because "some works are closer to the core of intended copyright protection than others, with the consequence that fair use is more difficult to establish when the former works are copied." Campbell, 510 U.S. at 586, 114 S. Ct. 1164. The fair use defense will be much less likely to succeed when it is applied to fiction or fantasy creations, as opposed to factual works such as telephone listings. See United Tel. Co. v. Johnson Publ'g Co., 855 F.2d 604, 609 (8th Cir. 1988); see also Stewart v. Abend, 495 U.S. 207, 237, 110 S. Ct. 1750, 109 L. Ed.2d 184 (1990). Duke Nukem's world is made up of aliens, radioactive slime and freezer weapons—clearly fantasies, even by Los Angeles standards. N/I MAP files "expressly use[] the [D/N-3D] story's unique setting, characters, [and] plot," Stewart, 495 U.S. at 238, 110 S. Ct. 1750; both the quantity and importance of the material Micro Star used are substantial. Finally, by selling N/I, Micro Star "impinged on [FormGen's] ability to market new versions of the [D/N-3D] story." Stewart, 495 U.S. at 238, 110 S. Ct. 1750; see also Twin Peaks Productions, Inc. v. Publications Int'l, Ltd., 996 F.2d 1366, 1377 (2d Cir. 1993). Only FormGen has the right to enter that market; whether it chooses to do so is entirely its business. "[N/I] neither falls into any of the categories enumerated in section 107 nor meets the four criteria set forth in section 107." Stewart, 495 U.S. at 237, 110 S. Ct. 1750. It is not protected by fair use.

Micro Star also argues that it is the beneficiary of the implicit license FormGen gave to its customers by authorizing them to create new levels. Section 204 of the Copyright Act requires the transfer of the exclusive rights granted to copyright owners (including the right to prepare derivative works) to be in writing. See 17 U.S.C. §204(a); Effects Assocs., Inc. v. Cohen, 908 F.2d 555, 556 (9th Cir. 1990). A nonexclusive license may, however, be granted orally or implied by conduct. See Effects, 908 F.2d at 558. Nothing indicates that FormGen granted Micro Star any written license at all; nor is there evidence of a nonexclusive oral license. The only written license FormGen conceivably granted was to players who designed their own new levels, but that license contains a significant limitation: Any new levels the players create "must be offered [to others] solely for free." The parties dispute whether the license is binding, but it doesn't matter. If the license is valid, it clearly prohibits commercial distribution of levels; if it doesn't, FormGen hasn't granted any written licenses at all.

In case FormGen didn't license away its rights, Micro Star argues that, by providing the Build Editor and encouraging players to create their own levels,

---

6. Of course, transformative works have greater recourse to the fair use defense as they "lie at the heart of the fair use doctrine's guarantee of breathing space within the confines of copyright . . . and the more transformative the new work, the less will be the significance of other factors, like commercialism, that may weigh against a finding of fair use." Campbell, 510 U.S. at 579, 114 S. Ct. 1164 (citations omitted). N/I can hardly be described as transformative; anything but.

FormGen abandoned all rights to its protected expression. It is well settled that rights gained under the Copyright Act may be abandoned. But abandonment of a right must be manifested by some overt act indicating an intention to abandon that right. See Hampton v. Paramount Pictures Corp., 279 F.2d 100, 104 (9th Cir. 1960). Given that it overtly encouraged players to make and freely distribute new levels, FormGen may indeed have abandoned its exclusive right to do the same. But abandoning some rights is not the same as abandoning all rights, and FormGen never overtly abandoned its rights to profit commercially from new levels. Indeed, FormGen warned players not to distribute the levels commercially and has actively enforced that limitation by bringing suits such as this one.

IV

Because FormGen will likely succeed at trial in proving that Micro Star has infringed its copyright, we reverse the district court's order denying a preliminary injunction and remand for entry of such an injunction.

COMMENTS AND QUESTIONS

1. Exactly what protected expression did Micro Star copy? The MAP files produced by game players themselves contain entirely new program code, and contain no code at all copied from Formgen. It is true that these files are designed to run with Formgen's game engine and art library and, indeed, would be useless without them. But does it follow from that that the MAP files themselves are "copies" of the original Duke Nukem game?

The real basis of the court's argument seems to be that the MAP files are guides to produce an infringing work. If a user buys the Micro Star CD and runs the game using the MAP files, he will generate on his screen a new Duke Nukem "level" that incorporates Micro Star's protected art. That might possibly be an infringing act that Micro Star has contributed to or induced. But if that is the complaint, the court was wrong to distinguish *Galoob*. Indeed, *Galoob* looks precisely analogous: the defendant makes a product that does not itself contain any copyrighted expression but that end users can employ to generate altered versions of the copyrighted work. The same analytic problem infects the court's analysis of the third fair use factor, in which the court concluded that the use copied substantially from Duke Nukem. While the game played by the end user does copy substantially from Formgen's original, it is hard to see how anyone could argue that the MAP files themselves did so.

2. Does the court's analogy to a movie sequel support its result? Why exactly are sequels considered derivative works? If it were possible to imagine a sequel that didn't itself include any copyrighted expression, would it be infringing? Should it be? How does the court square its result with Litchfield v. Spielberg, cited in the case, which held that a work could not be an infringing derivative work unless it was substantially similar in protected expression to the original?

3. The court's fair use analysis has a number of problems. First, the court disposes of the first factor entirely by reference to the *Sony* "presumption" that commercially motivated uses are unfair. This approach was specifically rejected by

the Supreme Court in Campbell v. Acuff-Rose Music, Inc., 510 U.S. 569, 584 (1994), which flatly rejected the use of any such presumption.

Second, the court suggests in a footnote that there is nothing transformative about the MAP files Micro Star sold. Why not? Aren't these files creative additions to the Duke Nukem universe?

Third, the court disposes of the market-effect factor by asserting that Micro Star's use interferes with Formgen's right to sell additional Duke Nukem levels. Does it matter whether Formgen has made any effort to do so? Whether it plans to do so in the future? Neither fact is considered in the court's opinion. It is also worth considering how Formgen's license to users to distribute their own levels for free on the Internet would affect the market for additional levels.

4. Is this case really about the scope of the license Formgen admittedly granted to the individual users who wrote the MAP files at issue? It appears that Micro Star could have collated and distributed those MAP files for free without running afoul of Formgen's license restriction. If the only basis for the suit is that Micro Star charged money for doing what it had a right to do for free, isn't this case better resolved under contract law than under copyright law?

For a more detailed discussion of the uncertain issue whether exceeding the scope of a license agreement constitutes copyright infringement or merely breach of contract, see Chapter 6.

5. We discuss one specific type of fair use—reverse engineering—in the next Section. For a discussion of a variety of other activities that may qualify for fair use in the digital environment, see Pamela Samuelson, Fair Use for Computer Programs and Other Copyrightable Works in Digital Form: The Implications of *Sony, Galoob*, and *Sega*, 1 J. Intell. Prop. L. 49 (1993).

E. REVERSE ENGINEERING

In view of the network externalities in many software-related industries and the cumulative nature of innovation in software, two critical issues in the computer industry are the extent to which and manner by which competitors can develop compatible or interoperable programs, competitive programs, and enhancements of programs. Of particular relevance is the permissibility of reverse engineering. "Reverse engineering" is loosely defined as "starting with the known product and working backward to divine the process which aided in its development or manufacture." Kewanee Oil Co. v. Bicron Corp., 416 U.S. 470 (1974). It typically involves two phases: (1) disassembly or decompilation of the program in order to create human-readable source code that may be analyzed; and (2) using the results of this analysis to create a commercially viable program.

Most computer programs are distributed only in object code form, a fact that makes it difficult to discover the ideas and principles contained in a program without reverse engineering. In addition, some programs have special devices designed to prevent inspection. Nonetheless, reverse engineering of software, while difficult, is possible in some limited circumstances and may be growing easier with time. There are a variety of approaches to reverse engineering of computer programs. One is referred to as "black box" testing. By systematically inputting instructions, a computer programmer can learn how the program processes information and can construct a program that produces the same outputs for given instructions. Because of the complexity of most programs today, however, this approach is often infeasible. A second method is to study the technical specifications and user manuals. These materials, however, often do not contain the information necessary to achieve compatibility and interoperability. In order to feasibly achieve these objectives, it is often necessary to take a machine apart and directly observe its operation or, as is more common with regard to software, to decompile the program. After a program is understood, the competitor can use the results of the analysis to create a commercially viable program.

Patent and trade secret laws treat reverse engineering very differently. Reverse engineering a patented product necessarily constitutes infringement if it involves making, using, or selling the patented invention. There is no statutory defense for reverse engineering. By contrast, the Uniform Trade Secrets Act expressly provides that reverse engineering a commercially available product is a legitimate means of discovering a trade secret. See Chapter 1. (Of course, many companies have tried to avoid this rule by contract, as discussed in Section I.B).

Copyright occupies an intermediate position on the legality of reverse engineering.

≡≡ *Sega Enterprises Ltd. v. Accolade, Inc.*
≡≡ *United States Court of Appeals for the Ninth Circuit*
≡≡ *977 F.2d 1510 (9th Cir. 1992)*

REINHART, Circuit Judge:

I. Background

Plaintiff-appellee Sega Enterprises, Ltd. ("Sega"), a Japanese corporation, and its subsidiary, Sega of America, develop and market video entertainment systems, including the "Genesis" console (distributed in Asia under the name "Mega-Drive") and video game cartridges. Defendant-appellant Accolade, Inc., is an independent developer, manufacturer, and marketer of computer entertainment software, including game cartridges that are compatible with the Genesis console, as well as game cartridges that are compatible with other computer systems.

Sega licenses its copyrighted computer code and its "SEGA" trademark to a number of independent developers of computer game software. Those licensees develop and sell Genesis-compatible video games in competition with Sega. Accolade is not and never has been a licensee of Sega. Prior to rendering its own games compatible with the Genesis console, Accolade explored the possibility of entering into a licensing agreement with Sega, but abandoned the effort because the agreement would have required that Sega be the exclusive manufacturer of all games produced by Accolade.

Accolade used a two-step process to render its video games compatible with the Genesis console. First, it "reverse engineered" Sega's video game programs in order to discover the requirements for compatibility with the Genesis console. As part of the reverse engineering process, Accolade transformed the machine-readable object code contained in commercially available copies of Sega's game cartridges into human-readable source code using a process called "disassembly" or "decompilation".[2] Accolade purchased a Genesis console and three Sega game cartridges, wired a decompiler into the console circuitry, and generated printouts of the resulting source code. Accolade engineers studied and annotated the printouts in order to identify areas of commonality among the three game programs. They then loaded the disassembled code back into a computer, and experimented to discover the interface specifications for the Genesis console by modifying the programs and studying the results. At the end of the reverse engineering process, Accolade created a development manual that incorporated the information it had discovered about the requirements for a Genesis-compatible game. According to the Accolade employees who created the manual, the manual contained only functional descriptions of the interface requirements and did not include any of Sega's code.

In the second stage, Accolade created its own games for the Genesis. According to Accolade, at this stage it did not copy Sega's programs, but relied only on the information concerning interface specifications for the Genesis that was contained in its development manual. Accolade maintains that with the exception of the interface specifications, none of the code in its own games is derived in any way from its examination of Sega's code. In 1990, Accolade released "Ishido", a game which it had originally developed and released for use with the Macintosh and IBM personal computer systems, for use with the Genesis console.

Even before Accolade began to reverse engineer Sega's games, Sega had grown concerned about the rise of software and hardware piracy in Taiwan and other Southeast Asian countries to which it exported its products. Taiwan is not a signatory to the Berne Convention and does not recognize foreign copyrights. Taiwan does allow prosecution of trademark counterfeiters. However, the counterfeiters had discovered how to modify Sega's game programs to blank out the screen display of Sega's trademark before repackaging and reselling the games as their own. Accordingly, Sega began to explore methods of protecting its trademark rights in the Genesis and Genesis-compatible games. While the development of its own trademark security system (TMSS) was pending, Sega licensed a patented TMSS for use with the Genesis home entertainment system.

The most recent version of the Genesis console, the "Genesis III", incorporates the licensed TMSS. When a game cartridge is inserted, the microprocessor contained in the Genesis III searches the game program for four bytes of data consisting of the letters "S-E-G-A" (the "TMSS initialization code"). If the Genesis III finds the TMSS initialization code in the right location, the game is rendered compatible and will operate on the console. In such case, the TMSS initialization code then prompts a visual display for approximately three seconds

---

2. Computer programs are written in specialized alphanumeric languages, or "source code". In order to operate a computer, source code must be translated into computer readable form, or "object code". Object code uses only two symbols, 0 and 1, in combinations which represent the alphanumeric characters of the source code. A program written in source code is translated into object code using a computer program called an "assembler" or "compiler", and then imprinted onto a silicon chip for commercial distribution. Devices called "disassemblers" or "decompilers" can reverse this process by "reading" the electronic signals for "0" and "1" that are produced while the program is being run, storing the resulting object code in computer memory, and translating the object code into source code. Both assembly and disassembly devices are commercially available, and both types of devices are widely used within the software industry.

which reads "PRODUCED BY OR UNDER LICENSE FROM SEGA ENTER-PRISES LTD" (the "Sega Message"). All of Sega's game cartridges, including those disassembled by Accolade, contain the TMSS initialization code.

Accolade learned of the impending release of the Genesis III in the United States in January, 1991, when the Genesis III was displayed at a consumer electronics show. When a demonstration at the consumer electronics show revealed that Accolade's "Ishido" game cartridges would not operate on the Genesis III, Accolade returned to the drawing board. During the reverse engineering process, Accolade engineers had discovered a small segment of code—the TMSS initialization code—that was included in the "power-up" sequence of every Sega game, but that had no identifiable function. The games would operate on the original Genesis console even if the code segment was removed. Mike Lorenzen, the Accolade engineer with primary responsibility for reverse engineering the interface procedures for the Genesis console, sent a memo regarding the code segment to Alan Miller, his supervisor and the current president of Accolade, in which he noted that "it is possible that some future Sega peripheral device might require it for proper initialization."

In the second round of reverse engineering, Accolade engineers focused on the code segment identified by Lorenzen. After further study, Accolade added the code to its development manual in the form of a standard header file to be used in all games. The file contains approximately twenty to twenty-five bytes of data. Each of Accolade's games contains a total of 500,000 to 1,500,000 bytes. According to Accolade employees, the header file is the only portion of Sega's code that Accolade copied into its own game programs. In this appeal, Sega does not raise a separate claim of copyright infringement with respect to the header file.

In 1991, Accolade released five more games for use with the Genesis III, "Star Control", "Hardball!", "Onslaught", "Turrican", and "Mike Ditka Power Football." With the exception of "Mike Ditka Power Football", all of those games, like "Ishido", had originally been developed and marketed for use with other hardware systems. All contained the standard header file that included the TMSS initialization code. According to Accolade, it did not learn until after the Genesis III was released on the market in September, 1991, that in addition to enabling its software to operate on the Genesis III, the header file caused the display of the Sega Message. All of the games except "Onslaught" operate on the Genesis III console; apparently, the programmer who translated "Onslaught" for use with the Genesis system did not place the TMSS initialization code at the correct location in the program.

[Sega sued Accolade for copyright infringement].

III. Copyright Issues

Accolade raises four arguments in support of its position that disassembly of the object code in a copyrighted computer program does not constitute copyright infringement. First, it maintains that intermediate copying does not infringe the exclusive rights granted to copyright owners in section 106 of the Copyright Act unless the end product of the copying is substantially similar to the copyrighted work. Second, it argues that disassembly of object code in order to gain an understanding of the ideas and functional concepts embodied in the code is lawful under section 102(b) of the Act, which exempts ideas and functional concepts from copyright protection. Third, it suggests that disassembly is authorized by section 117 of the Act, which entitles the lawful owner of a copy of a computer program to load the program into a computer. Finally, Accolade contends that disassembly of object code in order to gain an understanding of the ideas and functional concepts embodied in the code is a fair use that is privileged by section 107 of the Act.

Neither the language of the Act nor the law of this circuit supports Accolade's first three arguments. Accolade's fourth argument, however, has merit. . . .

A. Intermediate Copying

We have previously held that the Copyright Act does not distinguish between unauthorized copies of a copyrighted work on the basis of what stage of the alleged infringer's work the unauthorized copies represent. Walker v. University Books, 602 F.2d 859, 864 (9th Cir. 1979) ("[T]he fact that an allegedly infringing copy of a protected work may itself be only an inchoate representation of some final product to be marketed commercially does not in itself negate the possibility of infringement."). Our holding in *Walker* was based on the plain language of the Act. Section 106 grants to the copyright owner the exclusive rights "to reproduce the work in copies", "to prepare derivative works based upon the copyrighted work", and to authorize the preparation of copies and derivative works. 17 U.S.C. §106 (1)-(2). Section 501 provides that "anyone who violates any of the exclusive rights of the copyright owner as provided by sections 106 through 118 . . . is an infringer of the copyright." Id. §501(a). On its face, that language unambiguously encompasses and proscribes "intermediate copying". *Walker*, 602 F.2d at 863-64.

In order to constitute a "copy" for purposes of the Act, the allegedly infringing work must be fixed in some tangible form, "from which the work can be perceived, reproduced, or otherwise communicated, either directly or with the aid of a machine or device." 17 U.S.C. §101. The computer file generated by the disassembly program, the printouts of the disassembled code, and the computer files containing Accolade's modifications of the code that were generated during the reverse engineering process all satisfy that requirement. The intermediate copying done by Accolade therefore falls squarely within the category of acts that are prohibited by the statute.

Accolade points to a number of cases that it argues establish the lawfulness of intermediate copying. Most of the cases involved the alleged copying of books, scripts, or literary characters. See v. Durang, 711 F.2d 141 (9th Cir. 1983); Warner Bros. v. ABC, 654 F.2d 204 (2d Cir. 1981); Miller v. Universal City Studios, Inc., 650 F.2d 1365 (5th Cir. 1981). In each case, however, the eventual lawsuit alleged infringement only as to the final work of the defendants. We conclude that this group of cases does not alter or limit the holding of *Walker*.

The remaining cases cited by Accolade, like the case before us, involved intermediate copying of computer code as an initial step in the development of a competing product. Computer Assoc. Int'l v. Altai, Inc., [*supra*] (2d Cir. 1992) ("CAI"); NEC Corp. v. Intel Corp., 10 U.S.P.Q.2D (BNA) 1177 (N.D. Cal. 1989); E.F. Johnson Co. v. Uniden Corp., 623 F. Supp. 1485 (D. Minn. 1985). In each case, the court based its determination regarding infringement solely on the degree of similarity between the allegedly infringed work and the defendant's final product. A close reading of those cases, however, reveals that in none of them was the legality of the intermediate copying at issue. Sega cites an equal number of cases involving intermediate copying of copyrighted computer code to support its assertion that such copying is prohibited. Atari Games Corp. v. Nintendo of America, Inc., 18 U.S.P.Q.2D (BNA) 1935 (N.D. Cal. 1991); SAS Institute, Inc. v. S&H Computer Systems, Inc., 605 F. Supp. 816 (M.D. Tenn. 1985); S&H Computer Systems, Inc. v. SAS Institute, Inc., 568 F. Supp. 416 (M.D. Tenn. 1983); Hubco Data Products v. Management Assistance, Inc., 219 U.S.P.Q. (BNA) 450 (D. Idaho 1983). Again, however, it appears that the question of the lawfulness of intermediate copying was not raised in any of those cases.

In summary, the question whether intermediate copying of computer object code infringes the exclusive rights granted to the copyright owner in section 106 of the Copyright Act is a question of first impression. In light of the unambiguous language of the Act, we decline to depart from the rule set forth in *Walker* for copyrighted works generally. Accordingly, we hold that intermediate copying of computer object code may infringe the exclusive rights granted to the copyright owner in section 106 of the Copyright Act regardless of whether the end product of the copying also infringes those rights. If intermediate copying is permissible under the Act, authority for such copying must be found in one of the statutory provisions to which the rights granted in section 106 are subject.

B. The Idea/Expression Distinction

Accolade next contends that disassembly of computer object code does not violate the Copyright Act because it is necessary in order to gain access to the ideas and functional concepts embodied in the code, which are not protected by copyright. 17 U.S.C. §102(b). Because humans cannot comprehend object code, it reasons, disassembly of a commercially available computer program into human-readable form should not be considered an infringement of the owner's copyright. Insofar as Accolade suggests that disassembly of object code is lawful *per se*, it seeks to overturn settled law.

Accolade's argument regarding access to ideas is, in essence, an argument that object code is not eligible for the full range of copyright protection. Although some scholarly authority supports that view, we have previously rejected it based on the language and legislative history of the Copyright Act. Johnson Controls, Inc. v. Phoenix Control Sys., Inc., 886 F.2d 1173, 1175 (9th Cir. 1989). . . .

Nor does a refusal to recognize a *per se* right to disassemble object code lead to an absurd result. The ideas and functional concepts underlying many types of computer programs, including word processing programs, spreadsheets, and video game displays, are readily discernible without the need for disassembly, because the operation of such programs is visible on the computer screen. The need to disassemble object code arises, if at all, only in connection with operations systems, system interface procedures, and other programs that are not visible to the user when operating—and then only when no alternative means of gaining an understanding of those ideas and functional concepts exists. In our view, consideration of the unique nature of computer object code thus is more appropriate as part of the case-by-case, equitable "fair use" analysis authorized by section 107 of the Act. See infra Part III(D). Accordingly, we reject Accolade's second argument.

C. Section 117

Section 117 of the Copyright Act allows the lawful owner of a copy of a computer program to copy or adapt the program if the new copy or adaptation "is created as an essential step in the utilization of the computer program in conjunction with a machine and . . . is used in no other manner." 17 U.S.C. §117(1). Accolade contends that section 117 authorizes disassembly of the object code in a copyrighted computer program.

Section 117 was enacted on the recommendation of CONTU, which noted that "because the placement of any copyrighted work into a computer is the preparation of a copy [since the program is loaded into the computer's memory], the law should provide that persons in rightful possession of copies of programs be able to use them freely without fear of exposure to copyright liability." CONTU Report at 13. We think it is clear that Accolade's use went far beyond that contemplated by CONTU and authorized by section 117. Section 117 does not purport to protect a user who disassembles object code, converts it from assembly into source code, and makes printouts and photocopies of the refined source code version.

D. Fair Use

Accolade contends, finally, that its disassembly of copyrighted object code as a necessary step in its examination of the unprotected ideas and functional concepts embodied in the code is a fair use that is privileged by section 107 of the Act. Because, in the case before us, disassembly is the only means of gaining access to those unprotected aspects of the program, and because Accolade has a legitimate interest in gaining such access (in order to determine how to make its cartridges compatible with the Genesis console), we agree with Accolade. Where there is good reason for studying or examining the unprotected aspects of a copyrighted computer program, disassembly for purposes of such study or examination constitutes a fair use.

1.

As a preliminary matter, we reject Sega's contention that the assertion of a fair use defense in connection with the disassembly of object code is precluded by statute. First, Sega argues that not only does section 117 of the Act *not* authorize disassembly of object code, but it also constitutes a legislative determination that any copying of a computer program *other* than that authorized by section 117 cannot be considered a fair use of that program under section 107. That argument verges on the frivolous. Each of the exclusive rights created by section 106 of the Copyright Act is expressly made subject to all of the limitations contained in sections 107 through 120. 17 U.S.C. §106. Nothing in the language or the legislative history of section 117, or in the CONTU Report, suggests that section 117 was intended to preclude the assertion of a fair use defense with respect to uses of computer programs that are not covered by section 117, nor has section 107 been amended to exclude computer programs from its ambit.

Moreover, sections 107 and 117 serve entirely different functions. Section 117 defines a narrow category of copying that is lawful *per se.* 17 U.S.C. §117. Section 107, by contrast, establishes a *defense* to an otherwise valid claim of copyright infringement. . . .

Second, Sega maintains that the language and legislative history of section 906 of the Semiconductor Chip Protection Act of 1984 (SCPA) establish that Congress did not intend that disassembly of object code be considered a fair use. Section 906 of the SCPA authorizes the copying of the "mask work" on a silicon chip in the course of reverse engineering the chip. 17 U.S.C. §906. The mask work in a standard ROM chip, such as those used in the Genesis console and in Genesis-compatible cartridges, is a physical representation of the computer program that is embedded in the chip. The zeros and ones of binary object code are represented in the circuitry of the mask work by open and closed switches. Sega contends that Congress's express authorization of copying in the particular circumstances set forth in section 906 constitutes a determination that other forms of copying of computer programs are prohibited.

The legislative history of the SCPA reveals, however, that Congress passed a separate statute to protect semiconductor chip products because it believed that semiconductor chips were intrinsically utilitarian articles that were not protected under the Copyright Act. H.R. Rep. No. 781, 98th Cong., 2d Sess. 8-10, reprinted in 1984 U.S.C.C.A.N. 5750, 5757-59. Accordingly, rather than amend the Copyright Act to extend traditional copyright protection to chips, it enacted "a sui generis form of protection, apart from and independent of the copyright laws." Id. at 10, 1984 U.S.C.C.A.N. at 5759. Because Congress did not believe that semiconductor chips were eligible for copyright protection in the first instance, the fact that it included an exception for reverse engineering of mask work in the SCPA says nothing about its intent with respect to the lawfulness of disassembly of computer programs under the Copyright Act. Nor is the fact that Congress did not contemporaneously amend the Copyright Act to permit disassembly significant, since it was focusing on the protection to be afforded to semiconductor chips. Here we are dealing not with an alleged violation of the SCPA, but with the copying of a computer program, which is governed by the Copyright Act. Moreover, Congress expressly stated that it did not intend to "limit, enlarge or otherwise affect the scope, duration, ownership or subsistence of copyright protection . . . in computer programs, data bases, or any other copyrightable works embodied in semiconductor chip products." *Id.* at 28, 1984 U.S.C.C.A.N. at 5777. Accordingly, Sega's second statutory argument also fails. We proceed to consider Accolade's fair use defense.

2.

. . . In determining that Accolade's disassembly of Sega's object code did not constitute a fair use, the district court treated the first and fourth statutory factors [of 17 U.S.C. section 107, reprinted above] as dispositive, and ignored the second factor entirely. Given the nature and characteristics of Accolade's direct use of the copied works, the ultimate use to which Accolade put the functional information it obtained, and the nature of the market for home video entertainment systems, we conclude that neither the first nor the fourth factor weighs in Sega's favor. In fact, we conclude that both factors support Accolade's fair use defense, as does the second factor, a factor which is important to the resolution of cases such as the one before us.

(a)

With respect to the first statutory factor, we observe initially that the fact that copying is for a commercial purpose weighs against a finding of fair use. *Harper & Row*, 471 U.S. at 562. However, the presumption of unfairness that arises in such cases can be rebutted by the characteristics of a particular commercial use. Hustler Magazine, Inc. v. Moral Majority, Inc., 796 F.2d 1148, 1152 (9th Cir. 1986); see also Maxtone-Graham v. Burtchaell, 803 F.2d 1253, 1262 (2d Cir. 1986), *cert. denied*, 481 U.S. 1059, 95 L. Ed. 2d 856, 107 S. Ct. 2201 (1987). Further "the commercial nature of a use is a matter of degree, not an absolute. . . ." *Maxtone-Graham*, 803 F.2d at 1262.

Sega argues that because Accolade copied its object code in order to produce a competing product, the *Harper & Row* presumption applies and precludes a finding of fair use. That analysis is far too simple and ignores a number of important considerations. We must consider other aspects of "the purpose and character of the use" as well. As we have noted, the use at issue was an intermediate one only and thus any commercial "exploitation" was indirect or derivative.

The declarations of Accolade's employees indicate, and the district court found, that Accolade copied Sega's software solely in order to discover the functional requirements for compatibility with the Genesis console—aspects of Sega's programs that are not protected by copyright. 17 U.S.C. §102(b). With respect to the video game programs contained in Accolade's game cartridges, there is no evidence in the record that Accolade sought to avoid performing its own creative work. Indeed, most of the games that Accolade released for use with the Genesis console were originally developed for other hardware systems. Moreover, with respect to the interface procedures for the Genesis console, Accolade did not seek to avoid paying a customarily charged fee for use of those procedures, nor did it simply copy Sega's code; rather, it wrote its own procedures based on what it had learned through disassembly. Taken together, these facts indicate that although Accolade's ultimate purpose was the release of Genesis-compatible games for sale, its direct purpose in copying Sega's code, and thus its direct use of the copyrighted material, was simply to study the functional requirements for Genesis compatibility so that it could modify existing games and make them usable with the Genesis console. Moreover, as we discuss below, no other method of studying those requirements was available to Accolade. On these facts, we conclude that Accolade copied Sega's code for a legitimate, essentially non-exploitative purpose, and that the commercial aspect of its use can best be described as of minimal significance.

We further note that we are free to consider the public benefit resulting from a particular use notwithstanding the fact that the alleged infringer may gain commercially. See *Hustler*, 796 F.2d at 1153 (quoting MCA, Inc. v. Wilson, 677 F.2d 180, 182 (2d Cir. 1981)). Public benefit need not be direct or tangible, but may arise because the challenged use serves a public interest. *Id.* In the case before us, Accolade's identification of the functional requirements for Genesis compatibility has led to an increase in the number of independently designed video game programs offered for use with the Genesis console. It is precisely this growth in creative expression, based on the dissemination of other creative works and the unprotected ideas contained in those works, that the Copyright Act was intended to promote. See Feist Publications, Inc. v. Rural Tel. Serv. Co., — U.S. —, 111 S. Ct. 1282, 1290, 113 L. Ed. 2d 358 (1991) (citing *Harper & Row*, 471 U.S. at 556-57). The fact that Genesis-compatible video games are not scholarly works, but works offered for sale on the market, does not alter our judgment in this regard. We conclude that given the purpose and character of Accolade's use of Sega's video game programs, the presumption of unfairness has been overcome and the first statutory factor weighs in favor of Accolade.

(b)

As applied, the fourth statutory factor, effect on the potential market for the copyrighted work, bears a close relationship to the "purpose and character" inquiry in that it, too, accommodates the distinction between the copying of works in order to make independent creative expression possible and the simple exploitation of another's creative efforts. We must, of course, inquire whether, "if [the challenged use] should become widespread, it would adversely affect the potential market for the copyrighted work," Sony Corp. v. Universal City Studios, 464 U.S. 417, 451 (1984), by diminishing potential sales, interfering with marketability, or usurping the market, *Hustler*, 796 F.2d at 1155-56. If the copying resulted in the latter effect, all other considerations might be irrelevant. The *Harper & Row* Court found a use that effectively usurped the market for the copyrighted work by supplanting that work to be dispositive. 471 U.S. at 567-69. However, the same consequences do not and could not attach to a use which simply enables the copier to enter the market for works of the same type as the copied work.

Unlike the defendant in *Harper & Row*, which printed excerpts from President Ford's memoirs verbatim with the stated purpose of "scooping" a *Time* magazine review of the book, 471 U.S. at 562, Accolade did not attempt to "scoop" Sega's release of any particular game or games, but sought only to become a legitimate competitor in the field of Genesis-compatible video games. Within that market, it is the characteristics of the game program as experienced by the user that determine the program's commercial success. As we have noted, there is nothing in the record that suggests that Accolade copied any of those elements.

By facilitating the entry of a new competitor, the first lawful one that is not a Sega licensee, Accolade's disassembly of Sega's software undoubtedly "affected" the market for Genesis-compatible games in an indirect fashion. We note, however, that while no consumer except the most avid devotee of President Ford's regime might be expected to buy more than one version of the President's memoirs, video game users typically purchase more than one game. There is no basis for assuming that Accolade's "Ishido" has significantly affected the market for Sega's "Altered Beast", since a consumer might easily purchase both; nor does it seem unlikely that a consumer particularly interested in sports might purchase both Accolade's "Mike Ditka Power Football" and Sega's "Joe Montana Football", particularly if the games are, as Accolade contends, not substantially similar. In any event, an attempt to monopolize the market by making it impossible for others to compete runs counter to the statutory purpose of promoting creative expression and cannot constitute a strong equitable basis for resisting the invocation of the fair use doctrine. Thus, we conclude that the fourth statutory factor weighs in Accolade's, not Sega's, favor, notwithstanding the minor economic loss Sega may suffer.

(c)

The second statutory factor, the nature of the copyrighted work, reflects the fact that not all copyrighted works are entitled to the same level of protection. The protection established by the Copyright Act for original works of authorship does not extend to the ideas underlying a work or to the functional or factual aspects of the work. 17 U.S.C. §102(b). To the extent that a work is functional or factual, it may be copied, Baker v. Selden, 101 U.S. 99, 102-04, (1879), as may those expressive elements of the work that "must necessarily be used as incident to" expression of the underlying ideas, functional concepts, or facts, id. at 104. Works of fiction receive greater protection than works that have strong factual elements, such as historical or biographical works, *Maxtone-Graham*, 803 F.2d at 1263 (citing Rosemont Enterprises, Inc. v. Random House, Inc., 366 F.2d 303, 307 (2d Cir. 1966), *cert. denied*, 385 U.S. 1009 (1967)), or works that have strong functional elements, such as accounting textbooks, *Baker*, 101 U.S. at 104. Works that are merely compilations of fact are copyrightable, but the copyright in such a work is "thin." *Feist Publications*, 111 S. Ct. at 1289.

Computer programs pose unique problems for the application of the "idea/expression distinction" that determines the extent of copyright protection. To the extent that there are many possible ways of accomplishing a given task or fulfilling a particular market demand, the programmer's choice of program structure and design may be highly creative and idiosyncratic. However, computer programs are, in essence, utilitarian articles—articles that accomplish tasks. As such, they contain many logical, structural, and visual display elements that are dictated by the function to be performed, by considerations of efficiency, or by external factors such as compatibility requirements and industry demands. Computer Assoc. Int'l, Inc. v. Altai, Inc. In some circumstances, even the exact set of commands used by the programmer is deemed functional rather than creative for purposes of copyright. "When specific instructions, even though previously copyrighted, are the only and essential means of accomplishing a given task, their later use by another will not amount to infringement." CONTU Report at 20; see *CAI*, 23 U.S.P.Q. 2d at 1254.

Because of the hybrid nature of computer programs, there is no settled standard for identifying what is protected expression and what is unprotected idea in a case involving the alleged infringement of a copyright in computer software. We are in wholehearted agreement with the Second Circuit's recent observation that "thus far, many of the decisions in this area reflect the courts' attempt to fit the proverbial square peg in a round hole." *CAI*, 23 U.S.P.Q. 2d at 1257. In 1986, the Third Circuit attempted to resolve the dilemma by suggesting that the idea or function of a computer program is the idea of the program as a whole, and "everything that is not necessary to that purpose or function [is] part of the expression of that idea." Whelan Assoc., Inc. v. Jaslow Dental Laboratory, Inc., 797 F.2d 1222, 1236 (3d Cir. 1986) (emphasis omitted). The *Whelan* rule, however, has been widely—and soundly—criticized as simplistic and overbroad. See *CAI*, 23

U.S.P.Q. 2d at 1252 (citing cases, treatises, and articles). In reality, "a computer program's ultimate function or purpose is the composite result of interacting subroutines. Since each subroutine is itself a program, and thus, may be said to have its own 'idea,' Whelan's general formulation . . . is descriptively inadequate." *Id.* For example, the computer program at issue in the case before us, a video game program, contains at least two such subroutines—the subroutine that allows the user to interact with the video game and the subroutine that allows the game cartridge to interact with the console. Under a test that breaks down a computer program into its component subroutines and sub-subroutines and then identifies the idea or core functional element of each, such as the test recently adopted by the Second Circuit in *CAI*, 23 U.S.P.Q.2D (BNA) at 1252-53, many aspects of the program are not protected by copyright. In our view, in light of the essentially utilitarian nature of computer programs, the Second Circuit's approach is an appropriate one.

Sega argues that even if many elements of its video game programs are properly characterized as functional and therefore not protected by copyright, Accolade copied protected expression. Sega is correct. The record makes clear that disassembly is wholesale copying. Because computer programs are also unique among copyrighted works in the form in which they are distributed for public use, however, Sega's observation does not bring us much closer to a resolution of the dispute.

The unprotected aspects of most functional works are readily accessible to the human eye. The systems described in accounting textbooks or the basic structural concepts embodied in architectural plans, to give two examples, can be easily copied without also copying any of the protected, expressive aspects of the original works. Computer programs, however, are typically distributed for public use in object code form, embedded in a silicon chip or on a floppy disk. For that reason, humans often cannot gain access to the unprotected ideas and functional concepts contained in object code without disassembling that code—i.e., making copies.[8] Atari Games v. Nintendo of America, 975 F.2d 832 (Fed. Cir. 1992).

Sega argues that the record does not establish that disassembly of its object code is the only available method for gaining access to the interface specifications for the Genesis console, and the district court agreed. An independent examination of the record reveals that Sega misstates its contents, and demonstrates that the district court committed clear error in this respect.

First, the record clearly establishes that humans cannot *read* object code. Sega makes much of Mike Lorenzen's statement that a reverse engineer can work directly from the zeros and ones of object code but "it's not as fun." In full, Lorenzen's statements establish only that the use of an electronic decompiler is not absolutely necessary. Trained programmers can disassemble object code by hand. Because even a trained programmer cannot possibly remember the millions of zeros and ones that make up a program, however, he must make a written or computerized copy of the disassembled code in order to keep track of his work. See generally Johnson-Laird, Technical Demonstration of "Decompilation," *reprinted*

---

8. We do not intend to suggest that disassembly is always the only available means of access to those aspects of a computer program that are unprotected by copyright. As we noted in Part III(B), *supra,* in many cases the operation of a program is directly reflected on the screen display and therefore visible to the human eye. In those cases, it is likely that a reverse engineer would not need to examine the code in order to understand what the program does.

in Reverse Engineering: Legal and Business Strategies for Competitive Design in the 1990's 102 (Prentice Hall Law & Business ed. 1992). The relevant fact for purposes of Sega's copyright infringement claim and Accolade's fair use defense is that *translation* of a program from object code into source code cannot be accomplished without making copies of the code.

Second, the record provides no support for a conclusion that a viable alternative to disassembly exists. The district court found that Accolade could have avoided a copyright infringement claim by "peeling" the chips contained in Sega's games or in the Genesis console, as authorized by section 906 of the SCPA, 17 U.S.C. §906. Even Sega's amici agree that this finding was clear error. The declaration of Dr. Harry Tredennick, an expert witness for Accolade, establishes that chip peeling yields only a physical diagram of the *object code* embedded in a ROM chip. It does not obviate the need to translate object code into source code. *Atari Games Corp.*, slip op. at 22.

The district court also suggested that Accolade could have avoided a copyright infringement suit by programming in a "clean room". That finding too is clearly erroneous. A "clean room" is a procedure used in the computer industry in order to prevent direct copying of a competitor's code during the development of a competing product. Programmers in clean rooms are provided only with the functional specifications for the desired program. As Dr. Tredennick explained, the use of a clean room would not have avoided the need for disassembly because disassembly was necessary in order to discover the functional specifications for a Genesis-compatible game.

In summary, the record clearly establishes that disassembly of the object code in Sega's video game cartridges was necessary in order to understand the functional requirements for Genesis compatibility. The interface procedures for the Genesis console are distributed for public use only in object code form, and are not visible to the user during operation of the video game program. Because object code cannot be read by humans, it must be disassembled, either by hand or by machine. Disassembly of object code necessarily entails copying. Those facts dictate our analysis of the second statutory fair use factor. If disassembly of copyrighted object code is *per se* an unfair use, the owner of the copyright gains a de facto monopoly over the functional aspects of his work—aspects that were expressly denied copyright protection by Congress. 17 U.S.C. §102(b). In order to enjoy a lawful monopoly over the idea or functional principle underlying a work, the creator of the work must satisfy the more stringent standards imposed by the patent laws. Bonito Boats, Inc. v. Thunder Craft Boats, Inc., 489 U.S. 141, 159-64, 103 L. Ed. 2d 118, 109 S. Ct. 971 (1989). Sega does not hold a patent on the Genesis console. Because Sega's video game programs contain unprotected aspects that cannot be examined without copying, we afford them a lower degree of protection than more traditional literary works. See *CAI*, 23 U.S.P.Q.2d at 1257. In light of all the considerations discussed above, we conclude that the second statutory factor also weighs in favor of Accolade.

(d)

As to the third statutory factor, Accolade disassembled entire programs written by Sega. Accordingly, the third factor weighs against Accolade. The fact that an entire work was copied does not, however, preclude a finding a fair use. *Sony*

Corp., 464 U.S. at 449-50; *Hustler*, 795 F.2d at 1155 (*"Sony Corp.* teaches us that the copying of an entire work does not preclude fair use per se."). In fact, where the ultimate (as opposed to direct) use is as limited as it was here, the factor is of very little weight. Cf. Wright v. Warner Books, Inc., 953 F.2d 731, 738 (2d Cir. 1991).

(e)

In summary, careful analysis of the purpose and characteristics of Accolade's use of Sega's video game programs, the nature of the computer programs involved, and the nature of the market for video game cartridges yields the conclusion that the first, second, and fourth statutory fair use factors weigh in favor of Accolade, while only the third weighs in favor of Sega, and even then only slightly. Accordingly, Accolade clearly has by far the better case on the fair use issue.

We are not unaware of the fact that to those used to considering copyright issues in more traditional contexts, our result may seem incongruous at first blush. To oversimplify, the record establishes that Accolade, a commercial competitor of Sega, engaged in wholesale copying of Sega's copyrighted code as a preliminary step in the development of a competing product. However, the key to this case is that we are dealing with computer software, a relatively unexplored area in the world of copyright law. We must avoid the temptation of trying to force "the proverbial square peg into a round hole." *CAI*, 23 U.S.P.Q.2d at 1257.

In determining whether a challenged use of copyrighted material is fair, a court must keep in mind the public policy underlying the Copyright Act. "'The immediate effect of our copyright law is to secure a fair return for an "author's" creative labor. But the ultimate aim is, by this incentive, to stimulate artistic creativity for the general public good.'" *Sony Corp.*, 464 U.S. at 432 (quoting Twentieth Century Music Corp. v. Aiken, 422 U.S. 151, 156 (1975)). When technological change has rendered an aspect or application of the Copyright Act ambiguous, "'the Copyright Act must be construed in light of this basic purpose.'" *Id*. As discussed above, the fact that computer programs are distributed for public use in object code form often precludes public access to the ideas and functional concepts contained in those programs, and thus confers on the copyright owner a de facto monopoly over those ideas and functional concepts. That result defeats the fundamental purpose of the Copyright Act—to encourage the production of original works by protecting the expressive elements of those works while leaving the ideas, facts, and functional concepts in the public domain for others to build on. *Feist Publications*, 111 S. Ct. at 1290.

Sega argues that the considerable time, effort, and money that went into development of the Genesis and Genesis-compatible video games militate against a finding of fair use. Borrowing from antitrust principles, Sega attempts to label Accolade a "free rider" on its product development efforts. In *Feist Publications*, however, the Court unequivocally rejected the "sweat of the brow" rationale for copyright protection. 111 S. Ct. at 1290-95. Under the Copyright Act, if a work is largely functional, it receives only weak protection. "This result is neither unfair nor unfortunate. It is the means by which copyright advances the progress of science and art." *Id*. at 1290; see also *id*. at 1292 ("In truth, 'it is just such wasted effort that the proscription against the copyright of ideas and facts . . . [is] designed to prevent.'") (quoting Rosemont Enterprises, Inc. v. Random House,

Inc., 366 F.2d 303, 310 (2d Cir. 1966), *cert. denied* 385 U.S. 1009, 87 S. Ct. 714, 17 L. Ed. 2d 546 (1967)); *CAI*, 23 U.S.P.Q.2d at 1257. Here, while the work may not be largely functional, it incorporates functional elements which do not merit protection. The equitable considerations involved weigh on the side of public access. Accordingly, we reject Sega's argument.

(f)

We conclude that where disassembly is the only way to gain access to the ideas and functional elements embodied in a copyrighted computer program and where there is a legitimate reason for seeking such access, disassembly is a fair use of the copyrighted work, as a matter of law. Our conclusion does not, of course, insulate Accolade from a claim of copyright infringement with respect to its finished products. Sega has reserved the right to raise such a claim, and it may do so on remand.

COMMENTS AND QUESTIONS

1. Virtually all recent courts, as well as most commentators, have endorsed reverse engineering in some circumstances. In addition to *Sega*, see DSC Communications v. DGI Technologies, 81 F.3d 597, 601 (5th Cir. 1996); Bateman v. Mnemonics, Inc., 79 F.3d 1532, 1539 n.18 (11th Cir. 1995); Lotus Dev. Corp. v. Borland Int'l, 49 F.3d 807, 817-18 (1st Cir. 1995) (Boudin, J., concurring); Atari Games Corp. v. Nintendo of America, 975 F.2d 832, 843-44 (Fed. Cir. 1992); Sega, Inc. v. Accolade, 977 F.2d 1510, 1527-28 (9th Cir. 1992); Vault v. Quaid, 847 F.2d 255, 270 (5th Cir. 1988); Mitel Inc. v. Iqtel Inc., 896 F. Supp. 1050 (D. Colo. 1995), *aff'd on other grounds*, 124 F.3d 1366 (10th Cir. 1997); Pamela Samuelson & Suzanne Scotchmer, The Law and Economics of Reverse Engineering, 111 Yale L.J. 1575 (2002); Jonathan Band & Masanobu Katoh, Interfaces on Trial (1995); Julie Cohen, Reverse Engineering and the Rise of Electronic Vigilantism: Intellectual Property Implications of "Lock-Out" Technologies, 68 S. Cal. L. Rev. 1091 (1995); Lawrence D. Graham & Richard O. Zerbe Jr., Economically Efficient Treatment of Computer Software: Reverse Engineering, Protection, and Disclosure, 22 Rutgers Computer & Tech. L.J. 61 (1996); Dennis S. Karjala, Copyright Protection of Computer Documents, Reverse Engineering, and Professor Miller, 19 U. Dayton L. Rev. 975, 1016-18 (1994); David A. Rice, Sega and Beyond: A Beacon for Fair Use Analysis . . . At Least as Far as It Goes, 19 U. Dayton L. Rev. 1131, 1168 (1994).

On the other hand, some early decisions rejected compatibility as a justification for copying. See Apple Computer v. Franklin Computer, 714 F.2d 1240 (3d Cir. 1983); Digital Communications Assoc. v. Softklone Distributing Corp., 659 F. Supp. 449 (N.D. Ga. 1987). See also Anthony Clapes, Confessions of an Amicus Curiae: Technophobia, Law and Creativity in the Digital Arts, 19 U. Dayton L. Rev. 903 (1994) (no right to reverse engineer software should exist) and Arthur Miller, Copyright Protection for Computer Programs, Databases, and Computer-Generated Works: Is Anything New Since CONTU?, 106 Harv. L. Rev. 977 (1993) (same). Most of these decisions, unlike *Sega*, involve copied code that appears in the defendant's final product, rather than just intermediate copying. Should the courts treat intermediate copying differently from copying for compatibility in a final product?

In DSC Communications Corp. v. Pulse Communications Inc., 170 F.3d 1354 (Fed. Cir. 1999), the court seemed to acknowledge that reverse engineering could be a fair use but held that it was not always fair. It wrote:

> The district court dismissed DSC's direct copyright infringement claim on the ground that Pulsecom's conduct was excused by the affirmative defense of fair use for reverse engineering, as discussed in Sega Enterprises, Ltd. v. Accolade, Inc., 977 F.2d 1510, 1520, 24 USPQ2d 1561, 1569 (9th Cir. 1992). The *Sega* case, however, does not stand for the proposition that any form of copyright infringement is privileged as long as it is done as part of an effort to explore the operation of a product that uses the copyrighted software. On the basis of DSC's evidence at trial, Pulsecom's activities in creating copies of the POTS-DI software on its POTS cards by using the RBOCs' Litespan systems does not qualify as "fair use" under the *Sega* analysis. DSC's evidence showed that Pulsecom representatives made copies of the POTS-DI software on Pulsecom POTS cards as part of the ordinary operation of those cards, not as part of an effort to determine how the Litespan system worked. Rather than being part of an attempt at reverse engineering, the copying appears to have been done after Pulsecom had determined how the system functioned and merely to demonstrate the interchangeability of the Pulsecom POTS cards with those made and sold by DSC.

Id. at 1363. Why isn't there a valid social purpose in testing one's system to make sure it is compatible with the plaintiff's system? Does Pulse's use have a market-destroying effect here? If so, what is it? For a result in some tension with *Pulse*, see Alcatel USA Inc. v. DGI Technologies Inc., 166 F.3d 772 (5th Cir. 1999) (holding that it was copyright misuse for DSC to attempt to prevent a competitor from testing the compatibility of its cards with DSC's).

2. Do you agree with the *Sega* court's analysis of the fourth fair use factor? Hasn't Sega been injured because it can no longer control who produces games for its machine? Won't it lose the ability to charge a fee to game writers?

3. *Sega* suggests that the very nature of computer programs entitles them to less protection than other literary works, since programs must be copied in order for the user to have access to the uncopyrightable ideas and facts they contain. Does this reasoning apply only to copying to achieve compatibility, or does it suggest that *any* copying is more likely to constitute fair use?

4. In Sony Computer Entertainment, Inc. v. Connectix Corp., 203 F.3d 596 (9th Cir.), *cert. denied*, 531 U.S. 871 (2000), the Ninth Circuit took the *Sega* doctrine a significant step further. This case concerned Sony's successful Playstation game platform. Unlike the situation in *Sega*, where Accolade had reverse engineered the Sega platform for purposes of manufacturing games that could be run on Sega machines, Connectix reverse engineered the interoperability specifications for Sony's platform in order to enable games to be run on the Apple iMac microcomputer platform. In essence, Connectix enabled the porting of Playstation games from the Sony console to another platform. In this way, Connectix directly competed with Sony in the platform technology. Should this difference matter under the fair use test? Cf. Pamela Samuelson & Suzanne Scotchmer, The Law and Economics of Reverse Engineering, 111 Yale L.J. 1575, 1621-26 (2002) (distinguishing between incentives to develop games within a platform and incentives to innovate new platforms).

5. Is standardization a valid rationale for copying? Menell suggests that even arbitrary elements of user interfaces that become de facto industry standards should lose copyright protection in order to foster network externalities. Peter Menell, An Analysis of the Scope of Copyright Protection for Computer Programs, 41 Stan. L. Rev. 1045, 1101 (1989). He argues that the high premium that consumers place on widely learned standards makes compatibility with such standards critical to entering the marketplace. In effect, what began as an arbitrary element has become functional due to widespread consumer learning. See also Frederick Warren-Boulton et al., The Economics of Intellectual Property for Software: The Proper Role for Copyright, Computer Law. (Feb. 1995); Mark A. Lemley & David McGowan, Legal Implications of Network Economic Effects, 86 Cal. L. Rev. 479 (1998).

On the other hand, not every case requires standardization. The *Sega* court is careful to note that intermediate copying qualifies as fair use only if it is necessary to produce an interoperable program. At least one court has rejected a claim of fair use on the grounds that the copyrighted material taken was not needed for interoperability. Compaq Computer v. Procom Technology, 908 F. Supp. 1409 (S.D. Tex. 1995).

6. Is the fair use doctrine an appropriate means of encouraging compatibility or standardization? Does accommodating those policy goals require stretching the doctrine too far? A number of commentators have suggested that encouraging compatability is best accomplished by legislating a right to reverse engineer, analogous to the right provided in the Semiconductor Chip Protection Act of 1984.[10] See, e.g., Timothy S. Teter, Merger and the Machines: An Analysis of the Pro-Compatibility Trend in Computer Software Copyright Cases, 45 Stan. L. Rev. 1061, 1089-97 (1993).

7. Is Sega entitled to control not only the sales of its copyrighted software-hardware package but also video games that will run on the Sega system? The court's decision obliquely suggests that there are antitrust (or possibly copyright misuse) problems with giving Sega such power: "an attempt to monopolize the market by making it impossible for others to compete runs counter to the statutory purpose of promoting creative expression and cannot constitute a strong equitable basis for resisting the invocation of the fair use doctrine." *Sega*, 977 F.2d at 1523-24. Is this concern properly addressed in the fair use doctrine? Are there other limits on Sega's ability to control the creation of compatible programs? See infra (discussing the copyright misuse doctrine).

8. At the time *Sega* was decided, reverse engineering a computer program was a difficult and time-consuming task. If reverse engineering were simple and flawless, should it still be legal? For an argument that "easy" reverse engineering would be problematic, see Pamela Samuelson et al., A Manifesto Concerning the Legal Protection of Computer Programs, 94 Colum. L. Rev. 2308 (1994).

Note on Reverse Engineering and the Digital Millennium Copyright Act

Congress enacted the Digital Millennium Copyright Act in 1998. That act, which creates an entirely new cause of action against people who circumvent "copy

---

10. This statute is discussed in detail in Chapter 5.

protection" schemes or make devices that enable others to do so, is discussed in detail in Chapter 10. One provision is particularly important for reverse engineering, however. While the statute generally outlaws any activity that involves bypassing or disabling a copy protection system, there is an exception for certain sorts of reverse engineering. 17 U.S.C. section 1201(f) provides in part:

> (1) Notwithstanding the provisions of subsection (a)(1)(A), a person who has lawfully obtained the right to use a copy of a computer program may circumvent a technological measure that effectively controls access to a particular portion of that program for the sole purpose of identifying and analyzing those elements of the program that are necessary to achieve interoperability of an independently created computer program with other programs, and that have not previously been readily available to the person engaging in the circumvention, to the extent any such acts of identification and analysis do not constitute infringement under this title.

Subsections (2) and (3) further provide that people can develop tools to permit such reverse engineering, and can share the information they learn with others, subject to the same conditions identified in paragraph (1).

Is this provision an endorsement of *Sega?* On the one hand, Congress clearly determined that reverse engineering could serve valuable social purposes and protected it from liability. But the last clause of the statute seems to contemplate the possibility that reverse engineering even for such a laudable social purpose might be infringing. Cf. DSC v. Pulse, discussed *supra.* The statute does not appear to change the law in that case.

PROBLEM

Problem 2-10. Return to the Demento v. Mutant problem (Problem 2-4). Suppose that Mutant deciphered Demento's "key" program by decompilation. How would a court rule on the issue of fair use?

F. COPYRIGHT MISUSE

Lasercomb America, Inc. v. Reynolds
United States Court of Appeals for the Fourth Circuit
911 F.2d 970 (4th Cir. 1990)

SPROUSE, Circuit Judge:

Appellants Larry Holliday and Job Reynolds appeal from a district court judgment holding them liable to appellee Lasercomb America, Inc., for copyright infringement and for fraud, based on appellants' unauthorized copying and marketing of appellee's software. We affirm in part, reverse in part, and remand for recomputation of damages.

I. Facts and Proceedings Below

Appellants and defendants below are Larry Holliday, president and sole shareholder of Holiday Steel Rule Die Corporation (Holiday Steel), and Job Reynolds, a computer programmer for that company. Appellee is Lasercomb America, Inc. (Lasercomb), the plaintiff below. Holiday Steel and Lasercomb were competitors in the manufacture of steel rule dies that are used to cut and score paper and cardboard for folding into boxes and cartons. Lasercomb developed a software program, Interact, which is the object of the dispute between the parties. Using this program, a designer creates a template of a cardboard cutout on a computer screen and the software directs the mechanized creation of the conforming steel rule die.

In 1983, before Lasercomb was ready to market its Interact program generally, it licensed four prerelease copies to Holiday Steel which paid $35,000 for the first copy, $17,500 each for the next two copies, and $2,000 for the fourth copy. Lasercomb informed Holiday Steel that it would charge $2,000 for each additional copy Holiday Steel cared to purchase. Apparently ambitious to create for itself an even better deal, Holiday Steel circumvented the protective devices Lasercomb had provided with the software and made three unauthorized copies of Interact which it used on its computer systems. Perhaps buoyed by its success in copying, Holiday Steel then created a software program called "PDS-1000," which was almost entirely a direct copy of Interact, and marketed it as its own CAD/CAM die-making software. These infringing activities were accomplished by Job Reynolds at the direction of Larry Holliday.

There is no question that defendants engaged in unauthorized copying, and the purposefulness of their unlawful action is manifest from their deceptive practices. For example, Lasercomb had asked Holiday Steel to use devices called "chronoguards" to prevent unauthorized access to Interact. Although defendants had deduced how to circumvent the chronoguards and had removed them from their computers, they represented to Lasercomb that the chronoguards were in use. Another example of subterfuge is Reynolds' attempt to modify the PDS-1000 program output so it would present a different appearance than the output from Interact.

When Lasercomb discovered Holiday Steel's activities, it registered its copyright in Interact and filed this action against Holiday Steel, Holliday, and Reynolds on March 7, 1986. . . .

Holliday and Reynolds raise several issues on appeal. They do not dispute that they copied Interact, but they contend that Lasercomb is barred from recovery for infringement by its concomitant culpability. They assert that, assuming Lasercomb had a perfected copyright, it impermissibly abused it. This assertion of the "misuse of copyright" defense is based on language in Lasercomb's standard licensing agreement, restricting licensees from creating any of their own CAD/CAM die-making software. . . .

II. Misuse of Copyright Defense

A successful defense of misuse of copyright bars a culpable plaintiff from prevailing on an action for infringement of the misused copyright. Here, appellants claim Lasercomb has misused its copyright by including in its standard licensing agreement clauses which prevent the licensee from participating in any manner in the creation of computer-assisted die-making software. The offending paragraphs read:

> D. Licensee agrees during the term of this Agreement that it will not permit or suffer its directors, officers and employees, directly or indirectly, to write, develop, produce or sell computer assisted die making software.
>
> E. Licensee agrees during the term of this Agreement and for one (1) year after the termination of this Agreement, that it will not write, develop, produce or sell or assist others in the writing, developing, producing or selling computer assisted die making software, directly or indirectly without Lasercomb's prior written consent. Any such activity undertaken without Lasercomb's written consent shall nullify any warranties or agreements of Lasercomb set forth herein.

The "term of this Agreement" referred to in these clauses is ninety-nine years.

Defendants were not themselves bound by the standard licensing agreement. Lasercomb had sent the agreement to Holiday Steel with a request that it be signed and returned. Larry Holliday, however, decided not to sign the document, and Lasercomb apparently overlooked the fact that the document had not been returned. Although defendants were not party to the restrictions of which they complain, they proved at trial that at least one Interact licensee had entered into the standard agreement, including the anticompetitive language.

The district court rejected the copyright misuse defense for three reasons. First, it noted that defendants had not explicitly agreed to the contract clauses alleged to constitute copyright misuse. Second, it found "such a clause is reasonable in light of the delicate and sensitive area of computer software." And, third, it questioned whether such a defense exists. We consider the district court's reasoning in reverse order.

A. Does a "Misuse of Copyright" Defense Exist?

We agree with the district court that much uncertainty engulfs the "misuse of copyright" defense. We are persuaded, however, that a misuse of copyright defense is inherent in the law of copyright just as a misuse of patent defense is inherent in patent law.

The misuse of a patent is a potential defense to suit for its infringement, and both the existence and parameters of that body of law are well established. Although there is little case law on the subject, courts from time to time have intimated that the similarity of rationales underlying the law of patents and the law of copyrights argues for a defense to an infringement of copyright based on misuse of the copyright. The origins of patent and copyright law in England, the treatment of these two aspects of intellectual property by the framers of our Constitution, and the later statutory and judicial development of patent and copyright law in this country persuade us that parallel public policies underlie the protection of both types of intellectual property rights. We think these parallel policies call for application of the misuse defense to copyright as well as patent law. . . .

Although a patent misuse defense was recognized by the courts as early as 1917, most commentators point to Morton Salt Co. v. G.S. Suppiger, 314 U.S.

488, 62 S. Ct. 402, 86 L. Ed. 363 (1942), as the foundational patent misuse case. In that case, the plaintiff Morton Salt brought suit on the basis that the defendant had infringed Morton's patent in a salt-depositing machine. The salt tablets were not themselves a patented item, but Morton's patent license required that licensees use only salt tablets produced by Morton. Morton was thereby using its patent to restrain competition in the sale of an item which was not within the scope of the patent's privilege. The Supreme Court held that, as a court of equity, it would not aid Morton in protecting its patent when Morton was using that patent in a manner contrary to public policy. Id. at 490-92, 62 S. Ct. at 404-05. . . .

3. The "Misuse of Copyright" Defense

Although the patent misuse defense has been generally recognized since *Morton Salt*, it has been much less certain whether an analogous copyright misuse defense exists. This uncertainty persists because no United States Supreme Court decision has firmly established a copyright misuse defense in a manner analogous to the establishment of the patent misuse defense by Morton Salt. The few courts considering the issue have split on whether the defense should be recognized, see Holmes, Intellectual Property §4.09 (collecting cases), and we have discovered only one case which has actually applied copyright misuse to bar an action for infringement. M. Witmark & Sons v. Jensen, 80 F. Supp. 843 (D.Minn. 1948), *appeal dismissed*, 177 F.2d 515 (8th Cir. 1949).

We are of the view, however, that since copyright and patent law serve parallel public interests, a "misuse" defense should apply to infringement actions brought to vindicate either right. As discussed above, the similarity of the policies underlying patent and copyright is great and historically has been consistently recognized. Both patent law and copyright law seek to increase the store of human knowledge and arts by rewarding inventors and authors with the exclusive rights to their works for a limited time. At the same time, the granted monopoly power does not extend to property not covered by the patent or copyright. *Morton Salt*, 314 U.S. at 492, 62 S. Ct. at 405; *Paramount Pictures*, 334 U.S. at 156-58, 68 S. Ct. at 928-29; cf. Baker v. Selden, 101 U.S. 99, 101-04, 25 L. Ed. 841 (1880).

Thus, we are persuaded that the rationale of *Morton Salt* in establishing the misuse defense applies to copyrights. In the passage from Morton Salt quoted above, the phraseology adapts easily to a copyright context:

> The grant to the [author] of the special privilege of a [copyright] carries out a public policy adopted by the Constitution and laws of the United States, "to promote the Progress of Science and useful Arts, by securing for limited Times to [Authors] . . . the exclusive Right . . . " to their ["original" works]. United States Constitution, Art. I, §8, cl. 8, [17 U.S.C.A. §102]. But the public policy which includes [original works] within the granted monopoly excludes from it all that is not embraced in the [original expression]. It equally forbids the use of the [copyright] to secure an exclusive right or limited monopoly not granted by the [Copyright] Office and which it is contrary to public policy to grant.

Cf. *Morton Salt*, 314 U.S. at 492, 62 S. Ct. at 405.

Having determined that "misuse of copyright" is a valid defense, analogous to the misuse of patent defense, our next task is to determine whether the defense should have been applied by the district court to bar Lasercomb's infringement action against the defendants in this case.

B. *The District Court's Finding that the Anticompetitive Clauses Are Reasonable*

In declining to recognize a misuse of copyright defense, the district court found "reasonable" Lasercomb's attempt to protect its software copyright by using anticompetitive clauses in their licensing agreement. In briefly expressing its reasoning, the court referred to the "delicate and sensitive" nature of software. It also observed that Lasercomb's president had testified that the noncompete language was negotiable.

If, as it appears, the district court analogized from the "rule of reason" concept of antitrust law, we think its reliance on that principle was misplaced. Such reliance is, however, understandable. Both the presentation by appellants and the literature tend to intermingle antitrust and misuse defenses. E.g., Holmes, Intellectual Property, at §4.09. A patent or copyright is often regarded as a limited monopoly—an exception to the general public policy against restraints of trade. Since antitrust law is the statutory embodiment of that public policy, there is an understandable association of antitrust law with the misuse defense. Certainly, an entity which uses its patent as the means of violating antitrust law is subject to a misuse of patent defense. However, *Morton Salt* held that it is not necessary to prove an antitrust violation in order to successfully assert patent misuse. . . .

So while it is true that the attempted use of a copyright to violate antitrust law probably would give rise to a misuse of copyright defense, the converse is not necessarily true—a misuse need not be a violation of antitrust law in order to comprise an equitable defense to an infringement action. The question is not whether the copyright is being used in a manner violative of antitrust law (such as whether the licensing agreement is "reasonable"), but whether the copyright is being used in a manner violative of the public policy embodied in the grant of a copyright.

Lasercomb undoubtedly has the right to protect against copying of the Interact code. Its standard licensing agreement, however, goes much further and essentially attempts to suppress any attempt by the licensee to independently implement the idea which Interact expresses. The agreement forbids the licensee to develop or assist in developing any kind of computer-assisted die-making software. If the licensee is a business, it is to prevent all its directors, officers and employees from assisting in any manner to develop computer-assisted die-making software. Although one or another licensee might succeed in negotiating out the noncompete provisions, this does not negate the fact that Lasercomb is attempting to use its copyright in a manner adverse to the public policy embodied in copyright law, and that it has succeeded in doing so with at least one licensee. Cf. Berlenbach v. Anderson & Thompson Ski Co., 329 F.2d 782, 784-85 (9th Cir.), *cert. denied*, 379 U.S. 830, 85 S. Ct. 60, 13 L. Ed.2d 39 (1964).

The language employed in the Lasercomb agreement is extremely broad. Each time Lasercomb sells its Interact program to a company and obtains that company's agreement to the noncompete language, the company is required to forego utilization of the creative abilities of all its officers, directors and employees in the area of CAD/CAM die-making software. Of yet greater concern, these creative abilities are withdrawn from the public. The period for which this anticompetitive restraint exists is ninety-nine years, which could be longer than the life of the copyright itself.

. . . Again, the analysis necessary to a finding of misuse is similar to but separate from the analysis necessary to a finding of antitrust violation. The misuse arises from Lasercomb's attempt to use its copyright in a particular expression, the Interact software, to control competition in an area outside the copyright, i.e., the idea of computer-assisted die manufacture, regardless of whether such conduct amounts to an antitrust violation.

C. The Effect of Appellants Not Being Party to the Anticompetitive Contract

In its rejection of the copyright misuse defense, the district court emphasized that Holiday Steel was not explicitly party to a licensing agreement containing the offending language. However, again analogizing to patent misuse, the defense of copyright misuse is available even if the defendants themselves have not been injured by the misuse. In *Morton Salt*, the defendant was not a party to the license requirement that only Morton-produced salt tablets be used with Morton's salt-depositing machine. Nevertheless, suit against defendant for infringement of Morton's patent was barred on public policy grounds. Similarly, in *Compton*, even though the defendant Metal Products was not a party to the license agreement that restrained competition by Compton, suit against Metal Products was barred because of the public interest in free competition. See also *Hensley Equip. Co.*, 383 F.2d at 261; cf. *Berlenbach*, 329 F.2d at 784-85.

Therefore, the fact that appellants here were not parties to one of Lasercomb's standard license agreements is inapposite to their copyright misuse defense. The question is whether Lasercomb is using its copyright in a manner contrary to public policy, which question we have answered in the affirmative.

In sum, we find that misuse of copyright is a valid defense, that Lasercomb's anticompetitive clauses in its standard licensing agreement constitute misuse of copyright, and that the defense is available to appellants even though they were not parties to the standard licensing agreement. Holding that Lasercomb should have been barred by the defense of copyright misuse from suing for infringement of its copyright in the Interact program, we reverse the injunction and the award of damages for copyright infringement.[22] . . .

COMMENTS AND QUESTIONS

1. A number of cases have applied copyright misuse to bar enforcement of the copyright, though many others have refused to do so. For cases applying the misuse doctrine, see, e.g., in addition to *Lasercomb* and DSC Communications v.

---

22. This holding, of course, is not an invalidation of Lasercomb's copyright. Lasercomb is free to bring a suit for infringement once it has purged itself of the misuse. Cf. United States Gypsum Co. v. National Gypsum Co., 352 U.S. 457, 465 (1957); *Hensley Equipment Co.*, 383 F.2d at 261, 386 F.2d at 443.

DGI Technologies, 81 F.3d 597 (5th Cir. 1996), which is discussed below, see Alcatel USA Inc. v. DGI Technologies, 166 F.3d 772 (5th Cir. 1999); Practice Management Info. Corp. v. American Med. Ass'n, 121 F.3d 516, 520-21 (9th Cir. 1997), *as amended* Jan. 9, 1998 (finding that AMA license of its works to government agency on the condition that they did not use a competing work was copyright misuse, even though the clause was not enforced); PRC Realty Sys. v. National Ass'n of Realtors, 1992 U.S. App. LEXIS 18017 (4th Cir. 1992) (unpublished) (invalidating a license agreement for copyright misuse because it precluded competition by licensees); F.E.L. Publications, Ltd. v. Catholic Bishop, 214 U.S.P.Q. 409, 413 n.9 (7th Cir. 1982) (noting that "it is copyright misuse to exact a fee for the use of a musical work which is already in the public domain"; dictum); Tamburo v. Calvin, 1995 WL 121539 (N.D. Ill. Mar. 17, 1995) (holding that a software license agreement that prevents the development of competing products, whether or not based in software, constituted patent misuse); qad, Inc. v. ALN Assocs., 770 F. Supp. 1261, 1267-69 (N.D. Ill. 1991) (holding that wrongly asserting copyright infringement on the basis of material that in fact plaintiff copied from another was copyright misuse, precluding plaintiff from asserting even the original portions of the copyrighted work), *aff'd,* 974 F.2d 834 (7th Cir. 1992); Broadcast Music, Inc. v. Moor-Law, Inc., 527 F. Supp. 758, 772 n.24 (D. Del. 1981) ("Copyright misuse and antitrust analysis in this area are not necessarily coextensive."); Vogue Ring Creations, Inc. v. Hardman, 410 F. Supp. 609, 615-16 (D.R.I. 1976) (finding that material misstatements in copyright registration form constituted copyright misuse); cf. Coleman v. ESPN, Inc., 764 F. Supp. 290, 295 (S.D.N.Y. 1991) (holding that defendant could proceed to trial on its copyright misuse defense).

Of course, in many other cases courts have refused to find copyright misuse in the circumstances before them. See Herbert Hovenkamp et al., IP and Antitrust Law, §3.4a (discussing cases). And a few older decisions took the position that there was no such thing as a copyright misuse defense at all, but no courts have done so recently.

2. The *Lasercomb* court relies heavily on the patent law analogy. Patent misuse is generally tested according to antitrust (or at least antitrust-related) principles. Should copyright misuse likewise be limited to cases in which the copyright owner engages in the sort of conduct that brings antitrust scrutiny? Courts that have found misuse are likely to do so on principles that go beyond antitrust law and arise instead from copyright policy. See Practice Management Info. Corp. v. American Med. Ass'n, 121 F.3d 516 (9th Cir. 1997), *as amended* Jan. 9, 1998 (suggesting that copyright misuse need not constitute an antitrust violation); Lasercomb Am., Inc. v. Reynolds, 911 F.2d 970, 978 (4th Cir. 1990) (describing misuse as "an equitable defense to an infringement action" that applies where "the copyright is being used in a manner violative of the public policy embodied in the grant of a copyright"); cf. Bateman v. Mnemonics, Inc., 79 F.3d 1532, 1547 (11th Cir. 1996) (suggesting that copyright misuse might be appropriate to prevent a copyright owner from capturing protection for an idea in violation of 17 U.S.C. §102(b)). But see Reed-Union Corp. v. Turtle-Wax, Inc., 77 F.3d 909 (7th Cir. 1996) (suggesting that copyright misuse is limited to cases in which the antitrust laws are violated).

Commentators too are divided on whether copyright misuse is broader than antitrust law but lean heavily toward the view that it is. See Sean Michael Aylward,

The Fourth Circuit's Extension of the Misuse Doctrine to the Area of Copyright: A Misuse of the Misuse Doctrine?, 17 U. Dayton L. Rev. 661 (1992) (copyright misuse doctrine is broader than antitrust law but shouldn't be); Julie E. Cohen, Reverse Engineering and the Rise of Electronic Vigilantism: Intellectual Property Implications of "Lock-Out" Technologies, 68 S. Cal. L. Rev. 1091 (1995) (arguing for application of misuse outside the antitrust context); Timothy H. Fine, Misuse and Antitrust Defenses to Copyright Infringement Actions, 17 Hastings L.J. 315 (1965) (arguing that misuse can occur without an antitrust violation); Marshall Leaffer, Engineering Competitive Policy and Copyright Misuse, 19 U. Dayton L. Rev. 1087, 1099 (1994) ("Most courts have declared that the misuse defense does not require proof of an antitrust violation."); John G. Mills, Possible Defenses to Complaints for Copyright Infringement and Reverse Engineering of Computer Software: Implications for Antitrust and I.P. Law, 80 J. Pat. & Trademark Off. Soc'y 101, 119 (1998) (arguing that copyright misuse does not require a showing of injury to competition); Maureen A. O'Rourke, Drawing the Boundary Between Copyright and Contract: Copyright Preemption of Software Licensing Terms, 45 Duke L.J. 479, 534 (1995) ("it seems that the quantum of proof is somewhat less" in a copyright misuse than in an antitrust case); Troy Paredes, Copyright Misuse and Tying: Will Courts Stop Misusing Misuse?, 9 High Tech. L.J. 271 (1994) (arguing that copyright misuse should be abolished, and only antitrust violations should be considered); David Scher, The Viability of the Copyright Misuse Defense, 20 Fordham Urb. L.J. 89 (1993) (arguing that misuse should cover all extensions of copyright); Richard Stitt, Copyright Self-Help Protection as Copyright Misuse: Finally, the Other Shoe Drops, 57 UMKC L. Rev. 899 (1989) (arguing that misuse is distinct from antitrust); Toshiko Takenaka, Extending the New Patent Misuse Limitation to Copyright, 5 Software L.J. 739, 746-48 (1992) (arguing for an antitrust-based approach to misuse); James A.D. White, Misuse or Fair Use? That Is the Software Copyright Question, 12 Berkeley Tech. L.J. 251, 302-05 (arguing that "misuse is independent of antitrust" and should be, at least for software); Philip Abromats, Comment, Copyright Misuse and Anticompetitive Software Licensing Restrictions, 52 U. Pitt. L. Rev. 629 (1991) (arguing for antitrust-based treatment of misuse); Ramsey Hanna, Note, Misusing Antitrust: The Search for Functional Copyright Misuse Standards, 46 Stan. L. Rev. 401 (1994) (arguing that misuse should be independent of but narrower than antitrust); Note, Clarifying the Copyright Misuse Defense: The Role of Antitrust Standards and First Amendment Values, 104 Harv. L. Rev. 1289 (1991) (arguing that copyright misuse should properly have both antitrust and pro-dissemination objectives).

For an interesting argument that network effects in the software industry support reliance on misuse principles independent of antitrust, see White, *supra*, at 277-80; cf. Mark A. Lemley & David McGowan, Could Java Change Everything? The Competitive Propriety of a Proprietary Standard, 43 Antitrust Bull. 715 (1998).

Does it make sense to test copyright misuse by principles other than those derived from antitrust law? If so, what should those guiding principles be? Many of the cases finding copyright misuse are vulnerable to the criticism that the challenged practices were really alleged antitrust violations to which the court applied a more lenient standard (refusing to require a showing of market power in the *Lasercomb* case, for example).

3.   To what extent can the copyright misuse doctrine do the work of doctrines like fair use? A recent application of the copyright misuse doctrine in a context analogous to Sega v. Accolade is DSC Comm. Corp. v. DGI Technologies, 81 F.3d 597, 601 (5th Cir. 1996). In that case, the Fifth Circuit held that a plaintiff was not likely to prevail on a claim of copyright infringement stemming from the creation of RAM copies of its operating system because the plaintiff's assertion of such a copyright claim was likely to constitute copyright misuse. The court reasoned:

> DSC seems to be attempting to use its copyright to obtain a patent-like monopoly over unpatented microprocessor cards. Any competing microprocessor card developed for use on DSC phone switches must be compatible with DSC's copyrighted operating system software. In order to ensure that its card is compatible, a competitor such as DGI must test the card on a DSC phone switch. Such a test necessarily involves making a copy of DSC's copyrighted operating system, which copy is downloaded into the card's memory when the card is booted up. If DSC is allowed to prevent such copying, then it can prevent anyone from developing a competing microprocessor card, even though it has not patented the card. The defense of copyright misuse "forbids the use of the copyright to secure an exclusive right or limited monopoly not granted by the Copyright Office, including a limited monopoly over microprocessor cards."

See also Tricom v. EDS, 902 F. Supp. 741 (E.D. Mich. 1995) (attempting to enforce copyright law against RAM copying constituted copyright misuse). In Sega v. Accolade is it reasonable to argue that Sega was misusing its copyright? Would application of the misuse doctrine provide a narrower rationale on which to decide the case? Is such a narrower rationale desirable? See Julie E. Cohen, Reverse Engineering and the Rise of Electronic Vigilantism: Intellectual Property Implications of "Lock-Out" Technologies, 68 S. Cal. L. Rev. 1091 (1995) (suggesting that such a misuse-based approach may be warranted); David Nimmer, Brains and Other Paraphernalia of the Digital Age, 10 Harv. J. L. & Tech. 1 (1997) (arguing that the *MAI* decision should have been reversed on misuse grounds).

3

Patent Protection

A. IS SOFTWARE PATENTABLE SUBJECT MATTER?

The computing industry has always relied on patents to a substantial degree. Patents on computer hardware have generally proved uncontroversial. Given the high level of innovation and the industry's prosperity, there is reason to think that the patent system has contributed to the success of this industry. Given the technological equivalence of hardware and software, it may be surprising to know that patents for software or software-related inventions have been controversial for about four decades. For most of this time, substantial questions existed about whether programs or program-related inventions were patentable subject matter. Indeed, an early Supreme Court case suggested that important categories of computer software were not patentable at all. More recently, courts have at first grudgingly, and then enthusiastically, accepted software patents, and the debate about software patents has focused on how sound are examiner judgments about the novelty and nonobviousness of claimed software inventions. Notwithstanding this debate, software developers have increasingly come to rely on patents (if for no other reason than to have something to trade).

Although the debates over patenting software have subsided to some degree, it is still useful to understand why software inventions have been regarded as troublesome for the patent system, because remnants of these arguments still surface from time to time in the United States and elsewhere. Further, the early unwillingness of the U.S. Patent Office (PTO) and courts to grant patents on software set the stage for the next two decades of legal protection for computer software, bringing trade secrets and copyright to the forefront. And finally, the history of software patents has influenced the nature of legal protection to this day. We therefore begin with some historical perspective on the patentability of software.

1. The Patentability of Mathematical Algorithms

On several notable occasions, early programmer/applicants brought their fight to patent software to the Supreme Court. These early cases—and, indeed, the vast majority of software patent cases to date—focused on the question of whether an "invention" consisting of the use of a mathematical algorithm could be patentable subject matter under 35 U.S.C. section 101. Although the Federal Circuit has radically rewritten the law of section 101 in the last decade, the older Supreme Court cases are still relevant as the most recent authority from the highest court in the patent arena. We begin with the first Supreme Court opinion on this issue.

Gottschalk v. Benson
Supreme Court of the United States
409 U.S. 63, 175 U.S.P.Q. (BNA) 673 (1972)

MR. JUSTICE DOUGLAS delivered the opinion of the Court.

Respondents filed in the Patent Office an application for an invention which was described as being related "to the processing of data by program and more particularly to the programmed conversion of numerical information" in general-purpose digital computers. They claimed a method for converting binary-coded decimal (BCD) numerals into pure binary numerals. The claims were not limited to any particular art or technology, to any particular apparatus or machinery, or to any particular end use. They purported to cover any use of the claimed method in a general-purpose digital computer of any type. Claims 8 and 13 were rejected by the Patent Office but sustained by the Court of Customs and Patent Appeals.

The question is whether the method described and claimed is a "process" within the meaning of the Patent Act.[2]

A digital computer, as distinguished from an analog computer, operates on data expressed in digits, solving a problem by doing arithmetic as a person would do it by head and hand. Some of the digits are stored as components of the computer. Others are introduced into the computer in a form which it is designed to recognize. The computer operates then upon both new and previously stored data. The general-purpose computer is designed to perform operations under many different programs.

The representation of numbers may be in the form of a time series of electrical impulses, magnetized spots on the surface of tapes, drums, or discs, charged spots on cathode-ray tube screens, the presence or absence of punched holes on paper cards, or other devices. The method or program is a sequence of coded instructions for a digital computer.

---

2. Title 35 U.S.C. §100(b) provides:

The term "process" means process, art or method, and includes a new use of a known process, machine, manufacture, composition of matter, or material.

Title 35 U.S.C. §101 provides:

Whoever invents or discovers any new and useful process, machine, manufacture, or composition of matter, or any new and useful improvement thereof, may obtain a patent therefor, subject to the conditions and requirements of this title.

The patent sought is on a method of programming a general-purpose digital computer to convert signals from binary-coded decimal form into pure binary form. A procedure for solving a given type of mathematical problem is known as an "algorithm." The procedures set forth in the present claims are of that kind; that is to say, they are a generalized formulation for programs to solve mathematical problems of converting one form of numerical representation to another. From the generic formulation, programs may be developed as specific applications.

The decimal system uses as digits the 10 symbols 0, 1, 2, 3, 4, 5, 6, 7, 8, and 9. The value represented by any digit depends, as it does in any positional system of notation, both on its individual value and on its relative position in the numeral. Decimal numerals are written by placing digits in the appropriate positions or columns of the numerical sequence, *i.e.*, "unit" (10^0), "tens" (10^1), "hundreds" (10^2), "thousands" (10^3), etc. Accordingly, the numeral 1492 signifies $(1\times10^3)+(4\times10^2)+(9\times10^1)+(2\times10^0)$.

The pure binary system of positional notation uses two symbols as digits—0 and 1, placed in a numerical sequence with values based on consecutively ascending powers of 2. In pure binary notation, what would be the tens position is the twos position; what would be hundreds position is the fours position; what would be the thousands position is the eights. Any decimal number from 0 to 10 can be represented in the binary system with four digits or positions as indicated in the following table.

Shown as the sum of powers of 2

	2^3		2^2		2^1		2^0		
Decimal	*(8)*		*(4)*		*(2)*		*(1)*		*Pure Binary*
0 =	0	+	0	+	0	+	0	=	0000
1 =	0	+	0	+	0	+	2^0	=	0001
2 =	0	+	0	+	2^1	+	0	=	0010
3 =	0	+	0	+	2^1	+	2^0	=	0011
4 =	0	+	2^2	+	0	+	0	=	0100
5 =	0	+	2^2	+	0	+	2^0	=	0101
6 =	0	+	2^2	+	2^1	+	0	=	0110
7 =	0	+	2^2	+	2^1	+	2^0	=	0111
8 =	2^3	+	0	+	0	+	0	=	1000
9 =	2^3	+	0	+	0	+	2^0	=	1001
10 =	2^3	+	0	+	2^1	+	0	=	1010

The BCD System using decimal numerals replaces the character for each component decimal digit in the decimal numeral with the corresponding four-digit binary numeral, shown in the righthand column of the table. Thus decimal 53 is represented as 0101 0011 in BCD, because decimal 5 is equal to binary 0101 and decimal 3 is equivalent to binary 0011. In pure binary notation, however, decimal 53 equals binary 110101. The conversion of BCD numerals to pure binary numerals can be done mentally through use of the foregoing table. The method sought to be patented varies the ordinary arithmetic steps a human would use by changing the order of the steps, changing the symbolism for writing the multiplier used in some steps, and by taking subtotals after each successive operation. The mathematical procedures can be carried out in existing computers long in use, no new machinery being necessary. And, as noted, they can also be performed without a computer.

The Court stated in Mackay Co. v. Radio Corp., 306 U.S. 86, 94 [1939], that "[w]hile a scientific truth, or the mathematical expression of it, is not a patentable invention, a novel and useful structure created with the aid of knowledge of scientific truth may be." That statement followed the longstanding rule that "[a]n idea of itself is not patentable." "A principle, in the abstract, is a fundamental truth; an original cause; a motive; these cannot be patented, as no one can claim in either of them an exclusive right." Le Roy v. Tatham, 14 How. [55 U.S.] 156, 175 [1853]. Phenomena of nature, though just discovered, mental processes, and abstract intellectual concepts are not patentable, as they are the basic tools of scientific and technological work. As we stated in Funk Bros. Seed Co. v. Kalo Co., 333 U.S. 127, 130 [1948], "He who discovers a hitherto unknown phenomenon of nature has no claim to a monopoly of it which the law recognizes. If there is to be invention from such a discovery, it must come from the application of the law of nature to a new and useful end." We dealt there with a "product" claim, while the present case deals with a "process" claim. But we think the same principle applies.

Here the "process" claim is so abstract and sweeping as to cover both known and unknown uses of the BCD to pure binary conversion. The end use may (1) vary from the operation of a train to verification of drivers' licenses to researching the law books for precedents and (2) be performed through any existing machinery or future-devised machinery or without any apparatus.

In O'Reilly v. Morse, 15 How. [56 U.S.] 62 [1853], Morse was allowed a patent for a process of using electromagnetism to produce distinguishable signs for telegraphy. *Id.*, at 111. But the Court denied the eighth claim in which Morse claimed the use of "electro magnetism, however developed for marking or printing intelligible characters, signs, or letters, at any distances." *Id.*, at 112. The Court in disallowing that claim said, "If this claim can be maintained, it matters not by what process or machinery the result is accomplished. For aught that we now know, some future inventor, in the onward march of science, may discover a mode of writing or printing at a distance by means of the electric or galvanic current, without using any part of the process or combination set forth in the plaintiff's specification. His invention may be less complicated—less liable to get out of order— less expensive in construction, and in its operation. But yet, if it is covered by this patent, the inventor could not use it, nor the public have the benefit of it, without the permission of this patentee." *Id.*, at 113.

In *The Telephone Cases*, 126 U.S. 1, 534 [1887], the Court explained the *Morse* case as follows: "The effect of that decision was, therefore, that the use of magnetism as a motive power, without regard to the particular process with which it was connected in the patent, could not be claimed, but that its use in that connection could." Bell's invention was the use of electric current to transmit vocal or other sounds. The claim was not "for the use of a current of electricity in its natural state as it comes from the battery, but for putting a continuous current in a closed circuit into a certain specified condition suited to the transmission of vocal and other sounds, and using it in that condition for that purpose." *Ibid.* The claim, in other words, was not "one for the use of electricity distinct from the particular process with which it is connected in his patent." *Id.*, at 535. The patent was for that use of electricity "both for the magneto and variable resistance methods." *Id.*, at 538. Bell's claim, in other words, was not one for all telephonic use of electricity.

In Corning v. Burden, 15 How. [56 U.S.] 252, 267-268 [1853], the Court said, "One may discover a new and useful improvement in the process of tanning, dyeing, etc., irrespective of any particular form of machinery or mechanical device." The examples given were the "arts of tanning, dyeing, making waterproof cloth, vulcanizing India rubber, smelting ores." *Id.*, at 267. Those are instances, however, where the use of chemical substances or physical acts, such as temperature control, changes articles or materials. The chemical process or the physical acts which transform the raw material are, however, sufficiently definite to confine the patent monopoly within rather definite bounds.

Cochrane v. Deener, 94 U.S. 780 [1876], involved a process for manufacturing flour so as to improve its quality. The process first separated the superfine flour and then removed impurities from the middlings by blasts of air, reground the middlings, and then combined the product with the superfine. *Id.*, at 785. The claim was not limited to any special arrangement of machinery. *Ibid.* The Court said,

> That a process may be patentable, irrespective of the particular form of the instrumentalities used, cannot be disputed. If one of the steps of a process be that a certain substance is to be reduced to a powder, it may not be at all material what instrument or machinery is used to effect that object, whether a hammer, a pestle and mortar, or a mill. Either may be pointed out; but if the patent is not confined to that particular tool or machine, the use of the others would be an infringement, the general process being the same. A process is a mode of treatment of certain materials to produce a given result. It is an act, or a series of acts, performed upon the subject-matter to be transformed and reduced to a different state or thing.

Id., at 787-88.

It is argued that a process patent must either be tied to a particular machine or apparatus or must operate to change articles or materials to a "different state or thing." We do not hold that no process patent could ever qualify if it did not meet the requirements of our prior precedents. It is said that the decision precludes a patent for any program servicing a computer. We do not so hold. It is said that we have before us a program for a digital computer but extend our holding to programs for analog computers. We have, however, made clear from the start that we deal with a program only for digital computers. It is said we freeze process patents to old technologies, leaving no room for the revelations of the new, onrushing technology. Such is not our purpose. What we come down to in a nutshell is the following.

It is conceded that one may not patent an idea. But in practical effect that would be the result if the formula for converting BCD numerals to pure binary numerals were patented in this case. The mathematical formula involved here has no substantial practical application except in connection with a digital computer, which means that if the judgment below is affirmed, the patent would wholly preempt the mathematical formula and in practical effect would be a patent on the algorithm itself.

It may be that the patent laws should be extended to cover these programs, a policy matter to which we are not competent to speak. The President's Commission on the Patent System rejected the proposal that these programs be patentable:

> Uncertainty now exists as to whether the statute permits a valid patent to be granted on programs. Direct attempts to patent programs have been rejected on the ground

of nonstatutory subject matter. Indirect attempts to obtain patents and avoid the rejection, by drafting claims as a process, or a machine or components thereof programmed in a given manner, rather than as a program itself, have confused the issue further and should not be permitted. The Patent Office now cannot examine applications for programs because of a lack of a classification technique and the requisite search files. Even if these were available, reliable searches would not be feasible or economic because of the tremendous volume of prior art being generated. Without this search, the patenting of programs would be tantamount to mere registration and the presumption of validity would be all but nonexistent.

It is noted that the creation of programs has undergone substantial and satisfactory growth in the absence of patent protection and that copyright protection for programs is presently available.[1]

If these programs are to be patentable, considerable problems are raised which only committees of Congress can manage, for broad powers of investigation are needed, including hearings which canvass the wide variety of views which those operating in this field entertain. The technological problems tendered in the many briefs before us indicate to us that considered action by the Congress is needed. Reversed.

Appendix to Opinion of the Court

Claim 8 reads:

"The method of converting signals from binary coded decimal form into binary which comprises the steps of
"(1) storing the binary coded decimal signals in a re-entrant shift register,
"(2) shifting the signals to the right by at least three places, until there is a binary 1 in the second position of said register,
"(3) masking out said binary 1 in said second position of said register,
"(4) adding a binary 1 to the first position of said register,
"(5) shifting the signals to the left by two positions,
"(6) adding a 1 to said first position, and
"(7) shifting the signals to the right by at least three positions in preparation for a succeeding binary 1 in the second position of said register."

COMMENTS AND QUESTIONS

1. Recall the idea-expression merger doctrine in copyright law, which is invoked to refuse protection to otherwise copyrightable expression if it will allow the author to effectively appropriate the idea underlying the work. Does *Benson* create a similar merger doctrine in patent law? Is this approach consistent with other patent cases?

---

1. "To Promote the Progress of . . . Useful Arts," Report of the President's Commission on the Patent System 13 (1966). [—EDS.]

2. Prior to the *Benson* case, the Court of Customs and Patent Appeals (CCPA) had heard eight appeals from applicants claiming computer program-related inventions. According to an in-depth analysis of these cases and other matters pertaining to *Benson*,

> [a] curious thing about these eight pre-*Benson* cases is that none of them, not even the CCPA's decision in the *Benson* case, makes any more than an incidental use of the word "algorithm" in discussing the patentability issue. Hence, none of the analysis contained in these lower court decisions focused on the patentability of "algorithms." It was the Supreme Court's decision in *Benson* that shifted the focus of attention to "algorithms."

Pamela Samuelson, Benson Revisited: The Case Against Patent Protection for Algorithms and Other Computer Program-Related Inventions, 39 Emory L.J. 1025, 1042-1043 (1990). After *Benson*, Samuelson states, the case law "is focused almost exclusively on algorithms." *Id.*, at 1059.

3. Donald Chisum, the author of the authoritative patent law treatise, has criticized the *Benson* decision and called for it to be overruled. The result in the case, he argues, "stemmed from an antipatent judicial bias that cannot be reconciled with the basic elements of the patent system established by Congress." Donald Chisum, The Future of Software Protection: The Patentability of Algorithms, 47 U. Pitt. L. Rev. 959, 961 (1986). Chisum states that the "awkward distinctions and seemingly irreconcilable results of the case law since *Benson* . . . are the product of the analytical and normative weakness of *Benson* itself." *Id.*, at 961-962. Professor Chisum believes there are strong policy reasons to favor the patentability of computer algorithms.

Consider the section 101 cases outside the computer context, such as Diamond v. Chakrabarty, 447 U.S. 303 (1980) (holding that section 101 encompasses "anything under the sun made by man"). Is this a fair criticism? Has the *Benson* Court treated software differently than it does other inventions?

Note on the "Mental Steps" Doctrine

In *Benson*, Justice Douglas states: "Phenomena of nature, though just discovered, *mental processes*, and abstract intellectual concepts are not patentable, as they are the basic tools of scientific and technological work." 409 U.S. at 67 (emphasis added). The Court's invocation of what had been known as the "mental steps" doctrine followed the lead of several software-related cases that had been decided by the CCPA prior to the 1972 decision in *Benson*. See, e.g., In re Prater, 415 F.2d 1378 (C.C.P.A. 1968), *modified on reh'g*, 415 F.2d 1393 (C.C.P.A. 1969). Indeed, the pre-*Benson* cases were primarily concerned with the application of the "mental process" or "mental steps" doctrine, and only tangentially referred to the concept of an algorithm. The mental steps doctrine was eventually repudiated by the C.C.P.A. in In re Musgrave, 431 F.2d 882 (C.C.P.A. 1970), but the Supreme Court's reference to "mental processes" in the passage above makes it unclear whether the doctrine has been entirely eliminated from current law. In any event, the issues that were debated under the banner of "mental steps" are still very much with us, so a brief review of some of the cases and concepts connected with it is in order.

In its 1968 *Prater* decision the CCPA affirmed the Patent Office's rejection of process claims for identifying the optimal set of equations for determining the gaseous composition of materials subjected to spectrographic analysis—i.e., analysis based on radiation reflected off a sample. The CCPA noted that the applicant in *Prater I* had failed to limit his claims to machine implementations of his method. If the claims were allowed, said the court, then merely working through the claimed procedure by hand or in one's head would constitute infringement. This would run afoul of the "mental steps" doctrine developed in earlier cases. See, e.g., In re Shao Wen Yuan, 188 F.2d 377 (C.C.P.A. 1951) (finding mathematical means to determine optimal profile of airfoil exhibiting desired aerodynamic characteristics not patentable); In re Heritage, 150 F.2d 554 (C.C.P.A. 1945) (finding method of color-coating fiber board not patentable because the only novel feature of the method was in its process of selecting the amount of coating material to be used); Halliburton Oil Well Cementing Co. v. Walker, 146 F.2d 817 (9th Cir. 1944) (finding method of computing to determine depth of oil well not patentable), *rev'd on other grounds,* 329 U.S. 1 (1946); Don Lee, Inc. v. Walker, 61 F.2d 58 (9th Cir. 1932) (finding unpatentable formula for computing the centrifugal force of engine shafts to determine the appropriate mass and positions of counter balances). See also Diamond v. Diehr, 450 U.S. 175, 195-96 nn.6-9 (1981) (Stevens, J., dissenting) (citing other "mental step" or mental process" cases). See generally 1 Donald Chisum, Patents §1.06[6] (1978 & Supp. 1998).

The earlier "mental steps" cases are aptly summarized by Professor Samuelson in her article, *Benson* Revisited: The Case Against Patent Protection for Algorithms and Other Computer Program-Related Inventions, 39 Emory L.J. 1025, 1034-35 (1990):

> These decisions involved claims for patenting processes in which human beings took measurements about something, and after making calculations with data derived from these measurements, learned useful information about how to solve a problem in a technological field. The measurements, calculations, and interpretations of data are the "mental processes" or "mental steps" to which the cases refer.
>
> One of these cases, In re Abrams, endorsed a set of "rules" by which to judge processes involving mental steps. [*Abrams*, 188 F.2d at 166.] The first rule is that if a process is "purely mental," it is not patentable. The second is that if a process contains both mental and physical steps, but the advance over the prior art is found in the mental steps, it too is not patentable. The third is that if both mental and physical steps have been claimed and there is some novelty in the physical as well as the mental steps, then the process is patentable. The courts deciding *Abrams* and the other "mental process" cases, although they spoke frequently about "mental processes" and "mental steps," largely seemed to be concerned not with the "mental" character of the invention (all inventions, after all, are mental conceptions). Instead, these courts concentrated on not granting patent protection to data collection and analysis, just as the courts deciding the "printed matter" cases concentrated on not granting patent protection to data representation or presentation.

Although, as mentioned, the "mental steps" doctrine has faded into obscurity since the *Benson* case, it contains the kernel of an objection to software patents that many observers feel is very important: the sacrosanct legal status of human think-ing. To claim a thought process, the objection goes, is to assert ownership over something that should simply not be owned. (Note the similarity to the "gut-level" objection many people have to patenting living organisms.) Indeed, First Amendment objections were raised in some of the earliest software patent cases—the thought being that these patents might infringe a person's right to think cer-tain thoughts. See Samuelson, *supra,* at 1044 n.60 (discussing Patent Office brief in the first *Prater* case, discussed above).

A prominent computer scientist and pioneer in the field of machine or "artifi-cial" intelligence, Professor Alan Newell, voiced this objection in a response to the article by Professor Chisum cited earlier.

> Next consider algorithms and mental steps. The main line of progress in psy-chology for the last thirty years (called cognitive psychology) has been to describe human behavior as computational. We model what is going on inside the thinking human brain, as the carrying out of computational steps. Therefore, humans think by means of algorithms. Sequences of mental steps and algorithms are the same thing. Any attempt in the law to make distinctions that depend upon contrasting mental steps versus algorithms is doomed to eventual confusion. It is not important whether you accept this computational view of human thinking. There can be controversy about whether such an approach is the correct one for psychology. What is important is that such a view is a major one in the study of the human mind—that many psy-chologists see the mind this way and that thousands of technical papers are written from within this view, covering large expanses of psychological phenomena. Any at-tempt to erect a patent system for algorithms that tries to distinguish algorithms as one sort of thing and mental steps as another, will ultimately end up in a quagmire.
>
> Just avoiding the use of this distinction is only half the story. *An identity between algorithms and mental steps leads to such questions as whether you can keep people from thinking patented thoughts.* You might attempt to avoid such an untenable position by invoking a doctrine of fair use. Indeed, I found the comments by Professor Chisum on the problem of fair use interesting. But the implications of this identity go much fur-ther. We are talking about people who engage in those patented thoughts daily and hourly—even every few seconds—in the pursuit of their business and who make their money and their livelihood by so doing. I expect that any doctrine of fair use would experience substantial strain under such challenges.

Alan Newell, The Models Are Broken, The Models Are Broken!, 47 U. Pitt L. Rev. 1023, 1025 (1986) (emphasis added).

Later in the same article, Professor Newell considers a series of problems with the legal status of software patents, and comments on the problems that would attend the use of a basic algorithm that had been patented:

> [C]ertainly one might contemplate patenting addition. . . . [I]f you want actually to do addition—that requires doing a sequence of things, not to the integers, which are abstract (so you cannot do things to them anyhow), but to some representation of the integers. Doing addition is accomplished by carrying out an algorithm. If algorithms are patentable, then I can keep you from doing addition with the algorithms invented for it. There would be ever so many things that the poor would not be able to do, such as add up their grocery bill.

Id., at 1027.

COMMENTS AND QUESTIONS

1. What exactly is wrong with patenting addition? It seems strange to us, but isn't that simply because addition is so well established in the prior art? Didn't the first person to come up with the idea of addition make a significant advance for the world, one that ought to be encouraged?

2. For examples of the "printed matter" rule referred to in the preceding excerpt, see In re Rice, 132 F.2d 140 (C.C.P.A. 1942) (holding pictorial method of writing sheet music not patentable); In re Russell, 48 F.2d 668 (C.C.P.A. 1931) (holding method of arranging directories in a phonetic order not patentable); Guthrie v. Curlett, 10 F.2d 725 (2d Cir. 1926) (holding consolidated tariff index not patentable). In Boggs v. Robertson, 13 U.S.P.Q. (BNA) 214 (D.C. Cir. 1931), which involved a patent for a map projection system, the court regarded printed matter as unpatentable when it merely reduces an abstract idea to written form. See Note, The Patentability of Printed Matter: Critique and Proposal, 18 Geo. Wash. L. Rev. 475 (1950).

3. Some scholars have argued that the "mental steps" rule should be rejected. See McClaskey, The Mental Process Doctrine: Its Origin, Legal Basis, and Scope, 55 Iowa L. Rev. 1148 (1970); Comment, The Mental Steps Doctrine, 48 Tenn. L. Rev. 903 (1981). But several scholars argue that the mental steps doctrine may serve a function beyond that of a narrow subdoctrine under 35 U.S.C. §101. See Dan L. Burk, Patenting Speech, 79 Tex. L. Rev. 99 (2000); Dan L. Burk, Software as Speech, 8 Seton Hall Const. L. J. 683, 690 (1998) (arguing that the mental steps doctrine previously limited patent rights so as to avoid patent restrictions that would raise First Amendment issues, and that weakening of the doctrine means that patent laws may now limit free use of mental processes in ways that will violate the First Amendment). See also Robert A. Kreiss, Patent Protection for Computer Programs and Mathematical Algorithms: The Constitutional Limitations on Patentable Subject Matter, 29 N.M. L. Rev. 31, 86 (1999) (giving as an example of an unpatentable mental process a claim to a method of visualizing a gymnastics routine prior to performing it).

4. The patent office has issued a number of "pure" algorithm patents. The most notable of these are the Karmarkar patent on improvements to the "simplex method" algorithm in the field of operations research, U.S. Patent No. 4,744,028; and the Bracewell patent on the Discrete Bracewell Transform, a replacement for the Fast Fourier Transform in signal processing that does not require the use of complex numbers, U.S. Patent No. 4,646,256. Other pure algorithm patents include those issued to Diffie-Hellman and RSA for the application of large-number factoring methods in public-key cryptography.

Do the policy justifications for protecting software algorithms extend to these "pure" algorithm patents?

Diamond v. Diehr
Supreme Court of the United States
450 U.S. 175, 209 U.S.P.Q. (BNA) 1 (1981)

REHNQUIST, J.
We granted certiorari to determine whether a process for curing synthetic rubber which includes in several of its steps the use of a mathematical formula and a programmed digital computer is patentable subject matter under 35 U.S.C. §101.

I

The patent application at issue was filed by the respondents on August 6, 1975. The claimed invention is a process for molding raw, uncured synthetic rubber into cured precision products. The process uses a mold for precisely shaping the uncured material under heat and pressure and then curing the synthetic rubber in the mold so that the product will retain its shape and be functionally operative after the molding is completed.[1]

Respondents claim that their process ensures the production of molded articles which are properly cured. Achieving the perfect cure depends upon several factors including the thickness of the article to be molded, the temperature of the molding process, and the amount of time that the article is allowed to remain in the press. It is possible using well-known time, temperature, and cure relationships to calculate by means of the Arrhenius equation[2] when to open the press and remove the cured product. Nonetheless, according to the respondents, the industry has not been able to obtain uniformly accurate cures because the temperature of the molding press could not be precisely measured, thus making it difficult to do the necessary computations to determine cure time. Because the temperature inside the press has heretofore been viewed as an uncontrollable variable, the conventional industry practice has been to calculate the cure time as the shortest time in which all parts of the product will definitely be cured, assuming a reasonable amount of mold-opening time during loading and unloading. But the shortcoming of this practice is that operating with an uncontrollable variable inevitably led in some instances to overestimating the mold-opening time and overcuring the rubber, and in other instances to underestimating that time and undercuring the product.

---

1. A "cure" is obtained by mixing curing agents into the uncured polymer in advance of molding, and then applying heat over a period of time. If the synthetic rubber is cured for the right length of time at the right temperature, it becomes a usable product.

2. The equation is named after its discoverer Svante Arrhenius and has long been used to calculate the cure time in rubber-molding presses. The equation can be expressed as follows:

$$\ln v = CZ + x$$

wherein ln v is the natural logarithm of v, the total required cure time; C is the activation constant, a unique figure for each batch of each compound being molded, determined in accordance with rheometer measurements of each batch; Z is the temperature in the mold; and x is a constant dependent on the geometry of the particular mold in the press. A rheometer is an instrument to measure flow of viscous substances.

Respondents characterize their contribution to the art to reside in the process of constantly measuring the actual temperature inside the mold. These temperature measurements are then automatically fed into a computer which repeatedly recalculates the cure time by use of the Arrhenius equation. When the recalculated time equals the actual time that has elapsed since the press was closed, the computer signals a device to open the press. According to the respondents, the continuous measuring of the temperature inside the mold cavity, the feeding of this information to a digital computer which constantly recalculates the cure time, and the signaling by the computer to open the press, are all new in the art.

The patent examiner rejected the respondents' claims on the sole ground that they were drawn to nonstatutory subject matter under 35 U.S.C. §101.[5] . . .

II

Last Term in Diamond v. Chakrabarty, 447 U.S. 303 (1980), this Court discussed the historical purposes of the patent laws and in particular 35 U.S.C. §101. As in *Chakrabarty*, we must here construe 35 U.S.C. §101.

In cases of statutory construction, we begin with the language of the statute. Unless otherwise defined, "words will be interpreted as taking their ordinary, contemporary, common meaning," and, in dealing with the patent laws, we have more than once cautioned that "courts 'should not read into the patent laws limitations and conditions which the legislature has not expressed.'" Diamond v. Chakrabarty, supra, at 308, quoting United States v. Dubilier Condenser Corp., 289 U.S. 178, 199 (1933).

The Patent Act of 1793 defined statutory subject matter as "any new and useful art, machine, manufacture or composition of matter, or any new or useful im-

---

5. Respondents' application contained 11 different claims. [Two] examples are claims 1 [and] 2, which provide:

"1. A method of operating a rubber-molding press for precision molded compounds with the aid of a digital computer, comprising:
"providing said computer with a data base for said press including at least,
"natural logarithm conversion data (ln),
"the activation energy constant (C) unique to each batch of said compound being molded, and
"a constant (x) dependent upon the geometry of the particular mold of the press,
"initiating an interval timer in said computer upon the closure of the press for monitoring the elapsed time of said closure,
"constantly determining the temperature (Z) of the mold at a location closely adjacent to the mold cavity in the press during molding,
"constantly providing the computer with the temperature (Z),
"repetitively calculating in the computer, at frequent intervals during each cure, the Arrhenius equation for reaction time during the cure, which is
"ln v=CZ+x
"where v is the total required cure time,
"repetitively comparing in the computer at said frequent intervals during the cure each said calculation of the total required cure time calculated with the Arrhenius equation and said elapsed time, and
"opening the press automatically when a said comparison indicates equivalence."
"2. The method of claim 1 including measuring the activation energy constant for the compound being molded in the press with a rheometer and automatically updating said data base within the computer in the event of changes in the compound being molded in said press as measured by said rheometer."

provement [thereof].'" Act of Feb. 21, 1793, ch. 11, §1, 1 Stat. 318. Not until the patent laws were recodified in 1952 did Congress replace the word "art" with the word "process." It is that latter word which we confront today, and in order to determine its meaning we may not be unmindful of the Committee Reports accompanying the 1952 Act which inform us that Congress intended statutory subject matter to "include anything under the sun that is made by man." S. Rep. No. 1979, 82d Cong., 2d Sess., 5 (1952); H.R. Rep. No. 1923, 82d Cong., 2d Sess., 6 (1952).

Although the term "process" was not added to 35 U.S.C. §101 until 1952, a process has historically enjoyed patent protection because it was considered a form of "art" as that term was used in the 1793 Act.

. . . [W]e think that a physical and chemical process for molding precision synthetic rubber products falls within the §101 categories of possibly patentable subject matter. That respondents' claims involve the transformation of an article, in this case raw, uncured synthetic rubber, into a different state or thing cannot be disputed. The respondents' claims describe in detail a step-by-step method for accomplishing such, beginning with the loading of a mold with raw, uncured rubber and ending with the eventual opening of the press at the conclusion of the cure. Industrial processes such as this are the types which have historically been eligible to receive the protection of our patent laws.

III

Our conclusion regarding respondents' claims is not altered by the fact that in several steps of the process a mathematical equation and a programmed digital computer are used. This Court has undoubtedly recognized limits to §101 and every discovery is not embraced within the statutory terms. Excluded from such patent protection are laws of nature, natural phenomena, and abstract ideas. Only last Term, we explained:

> [A] new mineral discovered in the earth or a new plant found in the wild is not patentable subject matter. Likewise, Einstein could not patent his celebrated law that $E=mc^2$; nor could Newton have patented the law of gravity. Such discoveries are "manifestations of . . . nature, free to all men and reserved exclusively to none."

Diamond v. Chakrabarty, 447 U.S., at 309, quoting Funk Bros. Seed Co. v. Kalo Inoculant Co., supra, at 130.

Our recent holdings in Gottschalk v. Benson, supra, and Parker v. Flook, supra, both of which are computer-related, stand for no more than these long-established principles. In *Benson*, we held unpatentable claims for an algorithm used to convert binary code decimal numbers to equivalent pure binary numbers. The sole practical application of the algorithm was in connection with the programming of a general purpose digital computer. We defined "algorithm" as a "procedure for solving a given type of mathematical problem," and we concluded that such an algorithm, or mathematical formula, is like a law of nature, which cannot be the subject of a patent.

Parker v. Flook presented a similar situation. The claims were drawn to a method for computing an "alarm limit." An "alarm limit" is simply a number and the Court concluded that the application sought to protect a formula for computing this number. Using this formula, the updated alarm limit could be calculated if several other variables were known. The application, however, did not purport to explain how these other variables were to be determined, nor did it purport "to contain any disclosure relating to the chemical processes at work, the monitoring of process variables, or the means of setting off an alarm or adjusting an alarm system. All that it provides is a formula for computing an updated alarm limit." 437 U.S., at 586.

In contrast, the respondents here do not seek to patent a mathematical formula. Instead, they seek patent protection for a process of curing synthetic rubber. Their process admittedly employs a well-known mathematical equation, but they do not seek to pre-empt the use of that equation. Rather, they seek only to foreclose from others the use of that equation in conjunction with all of the other steps in their claimed process. These include installing rubber in a press, closing the mold, constantly determining the temperature of the mold, constantly recalculating the appropriate cure time through the use of the formula and a digital computer, and automatically opening the press at the proper time. Obviously, one does not need a "computer" to cure natural or synthetic rubber, but if the computer use incorporated in the process patent significantly lessens the possibility of "overcuring" or "undercuring," the process as a whole does not thereby become unpatentable subject matter.

Our earlier opinions lend support to our present conclusion that a claim drawn to subject matter otherwise statutory does not become nonstatutory simply because it uses a mathematical formula, computer program, or digital computer. In Gottschalk v. Benson we noted: "It is said that the decision precludes a patent for any program servicing a computer. We do not so hold." 409 U.S., at 71. Similarly, in Parker v. Flook we stated that "a process is not unpatentable simply because it contains a law of nature or a mathematical algorithm." 437 U.S., at 590. It is now commonplace that an *application* of a law of nature or mathematical formula to a known structure or process may well be deserving of patent protection. As Justice Stone explained four decades ago:

> While a scientific truth, or the mathematical expression of it, is not a patentable invention, a novel and useful structure created with the aid of knowledge of scientific truth may be.

Mackay Radio & Telegraph Co. v. Radio Corp. of America, 306 U.S. 86, 94 (1939).

We think this statement in *Mackay* takes us a long way toward the correct answer in this case. Arrhenius' equation is not patentable in isolation, but when a process for curing rubber is devised which incorporates in it a more efficient solution of the equation, that process is at the very least not barred at the threshold by §101.

In determining the eligibility of respondents' claimed process for patent protection under §101, their claims must be considered as a whole. It is inappropriate to dissect the claims into old and new elements and then to ignore the presence of the old elements in the analysis. This is particularly true in a process claim because a new combination of steps in a process may be patentable even though all the constituents of the combination were well known and in common use before the combination was made. The "novelty" of any element or steps in a process, or even of the process itself, is of no relevance in determining whether the subject matter of a claim falls within the §101 categories of possibly patentable subject matter.

IV

We have before us today only the question of whether respondents' claims fall within the §101 categories of possibly patentable subject matter. We view respondents' claims as nothing more than a process for molding rubber products and not as an attempt to patent a mathematical formula. We recognize, of course, that when a claim recites a mathematical formula (or scientific principle or phenomenon of nature), an inquiry must be made into whether the claim is seeking patent protection for that formula in the abstract. A mathematical formula as such is not accorded the protection of our patent laws, Gottschalk v. Benson, and this principle cannot be circumvented by attempting to limit the use of the formula to a particular technological environment. Similarly, insignificant postsolution activity will not transform an unpatentable principle into a patentable process. To hold otherwise would allow a competent draftsman to evade the recognized limitations on the type of subject matter eligible for patent protection. On the other hand, when a claim containing a mathematical formula implements or applies that formula in a structure or process which, when considered as a whole, is performing a function which the patent laws were designed to protect (*e.g.*, transforming or reducing an article to a different state or thing), then the claim satisfies the requirements of §101. Because we do not view respondents' claims as an attempt to patent a mathematical formula, but rather to be drawn to an industrial process for the molding of rubber products, we affirm the judgment of the Court of Customs and Patent Appeals.

Note on "Floppy Disk" Claims

The *Diehr* approach emphasizes that software runs on hardware, and in some sense each program creates a unique piece of hardware. This approach reached its logical limit in 1995, when IBM appealed the PTO's rejection of a claim to "software contained on a floppy disk" to the Federal Circuit. See In re Beauregard, 53 F.3d 1583 (Fed. Cir. 1995). While the appeal was pending, the PTO decided not to oppose the claim and promised the court that it would shortly issue new examining guidelines for software patents. After several false starts, the PTO did issue final Examination Guidelines for Computer-Implemented Inventions in January of 1996. These Guidelines direct examiners as follows:

> The subject matter courts have found to be outside the four statutory categories of invention is limited to abstract ideas, laws of nature and natural phenomena. While this is easily stated, determining whether an applicant is seeking to patent an abstract idea, a law of nature or a natural phenomenon has proven to be challenging. These three exclusions recognize that subject matter that is not a *practical application or use* of an idea, a law of nature or a natural phenomenon is not patentable. . . .

Claims to computer-related inventions that are clearly non-statutory fall into the same general categories as non-statutory claims in other arts, namely natural phenomena such as magnetism, and abstract ideas or laws of nature which constitute "descriptive material." Descriptive material can be characterized as either "functional descriptive material" or "non-functional descriptive material." In this context, "functional descriptive material" consists of data structures and computer programs which impart functionality when encoded on a computer-readable medium. "Non-functional descriptive material" includes but is not limited to music, literary works and a compilation or mere arrangement of data.

Both types of "descriptive material" are non-statutory when claimed as descriptive material *per se*. When functional descriptive material is recorded on some computer-readable medium it becomes structurally and functionally interrelated to the medium and will be statutory in most cases. When non-functional descriptive material is recorded on some computer-readable medium, it is not structurally and functionally interrelated to the medium but is merely carried by the medium. Merely claiming non-functional descriptive material stored in a computer-readable medium does not make it statutory. Such a result would exalt form over substance. Thus, non-statutory music does not become statutory by merely recording it on a compact disk. Protection for this type of work is provided under the copyright law. . . .

Data structures not claimed as embodied in computer-readable media are descriptive material *per se* and are not statutory because they are neither physical "things" nor statutory processes. Such claimed data structures do not define any structural and functional interrelationships between the data structure and other claimed aspects of the invention which permit the data structure's functionality to be realized. In contrast, a claimed computer-readable medium encoded with a data structure defines structural and functional interrelationships between the data structure and the medium which permit the data structure's functionality to be realized, and is thus statutory.

Similarly, computer programs claimed as computer listings *per se*, *i.e.*, the descriptions or expressions of the programs, are not physical "things," nor are they statutory processes, as they are not "acts" being performed. Such claimed computer programs do not define any structural and functional interrelationships between the computer program and other claimed aspects of the invention which permit the computer program's functionality to be realized. In contrast, a claimed computer-readable medium encoded with a computer program defines structural and functional interrelationships between the computer program and the medium which permit the computer program's functionality to be realized, and is thus statutory. Accordingly, it is important to distinguish claims that define descriptive material *per se* from claims that define statutory inventions. . . .

Since a computer program is merely a set of instructions capable of being executed by a computer, the computer program itself is not a process and Office personnel should treat a claim for a computer program, without the computer-readable medium needed to realize the computer program's functionality, as non-statutory functional descriptive material. When a computer program is claimed in a process where the computer is executing the computer program's instructions, Office personnel should treat the claim as a process claim. When a computer program is recited in conjunction with a physical structure, such as a computer memory, Office personnel should treat the claim as a product claim. . . .

Where certain types of descriptive material, such as music, literature, art, photographs and mere arrangements or compilations of facts or data, are merely stored so as to be read or outputted by a computer without creating any functional interrelationship, either as part of the stored data or as part of the computing processes performed by the computer, then such descriptive material alone does not impart functionality either to the data as so structured, or to the computer. Such "descriptive material" is not a process, machine, manufacture or composition of matter.

The policy that precludes the patenting of non-functional descriptive material would be easily frustrated if the same descriptive material could be patented when claimed as an article of manufacture. For example, music is commonly sold to consumers in the format of a compact disc. In such cases, the known compact disc acts as nothing more than a carrier for non-functional descriptive material. The purely non-functional descriptive material cannot alone provide the practical application for the manufacture.

Office personnel should be prudent in applying the foregoing guidance. Non-functional descriptive material may be claimed in combination with other functional descriptive material on a computer-readable medium to provide the necessary functional and structural interrelationship to satisfy the requirements of §101. The presence of the claimed non-functional descriptive material is not necessarily determinative of non-statutory subject matter. For example, a computer that recognizes a particular grouping of musical notes read from memory and upon recognizing that particular sequence, causes another defined series of notes to be played, defines a functional interrelationship among that data and the computing processes performed when utilizing that data, and as such is statutory because it implements a statutory process. . . .

Office personnel must treat each claim as a whole. The mere fact that a hardware element is recited in a claim does not necessarily limit the claim to a specific machine or manufacture. If a product claim encompasses *any and every* computer implementation of a process, when read in light of the specification, it should be examined on the basis of the underlying process. Such a claim can be recognized as it will:

- define the physical characteristics of a computer or computer component exclusively as functions or steps to be performed on or by a computer, and
- encompass *any and every* product in the stated class (*e.g.*, computer, computer-readable memory) *configured in any manner* to perform that process.

. . . If a claim is found to encompass any and every product embodiment of the underlying process, and if the underlying process is statutory, the product claim should be classified as a statutory product. By the same token, if the underlying process invention is found to be non-statutory, Office personnel should classify the "product" claim as a "non-statutory product." If the product claim is classified as being a non-statutory product on the basis of the underlying process, Office personnel should emphasize that they have considered all claim limitations and are basing their finding on the analysis of the underlying process. . . .

A claim that requires one or more acts to be performed defines a process. However, not all processes are statutory under §101. To be statutory, a claimed computer-related process must either: (1) result in a physical transformation outside the computer for which a practical application in the technological arts is either disclosed in the specification or would have been known to a skilled artisan (discussed in (i) below), or (2) be limited by the language in the claim to a practical application within the technological arts (discussed in (ii) below). The claimed practical application must be a further limitation upon the claimed subject matter if the process is confined to the internal operations of the computer. If a physical transformation occurs outside the computer, it is not necessary to claim the practical application. A disclosure that permits a skilled artisan to practice the claimed invention, *i.e.*, to put it to a practical use, is sufficient. On the other hand, it is necessary to claim the practical application if there is no physical transformation or if the process merely manipulates concepts or converts one set of numbers into another. . . .

There is always some form of physical transformation within a computer because a computer acts on signals and transforms them during its operation and changes the state of its components during the execution of a process. Even though such a physical transformation occurs within a computer, such activity is not determinative of whether the process is statutory because such transformation alone does not distinguish a statutory computer process from a non-statutory computer process. What is determinative is not how the computer performs the process, but what the computer does to achieve a practical application.

A process that merely manipulates an abstract idea or performs a purely mathematical algorithm is non-statutory despite the fact that it might inherently have some usefulness. For such subject matter to be statutory, the claimed process must be limited to a practical application of the abstract idea or mathematical algorithm in the technological arts. For example, a computer process that simply calculates a mathematical algorithm that models noise is non-statutory. However, a claimed process for digitally filtering noise employing the mathematical algorithm is statutory. . . .

If the "acts" of a claimed process manipulate only numbers, abstract concepts or ideas, or signals representing any of the foregoing, the acts are not being applied to appropriate subject matter. Thus, a process consisting solely of mathematical operations, *i.e.*, converting one set of numbers into another set of numbers, does not manipulate appropriate subject matter and thus cannot constitute a statutory process.

COMMENTS AND QUESTIONS

1. The law of software patents in the last fifteen years can be criticized as exalting form over substance, allowing patent attorneys to circumvent the limitations of section 101 through artful drafting. See Julie E. Cohen & Mark A. Lemley, Patent Scope and Innovation in the Software Industry, 89 Calif. L. Rev. 1 (2001). Do the Guidelines solve this problem? Or are they formalist as well? In particular, consider what distinguishes a patentable data structure from an unpatentable one under the Guidelines. Is it anything other than the language of the claims?

Take as an example claims to software on a floppy disk. Richard Stern argues that a *Beauregard*-style claim ought merely to affect who is a direct infringer, and not expand the sorts of subject matter covered by section 101. Thus, he claims, if an algorithm were unpatentable as a process or apparatus, it shouldn't become patentable simply by virtue of being placed on a floppy disk. Richard Stern, An Attempt to Rationalize Floppy Disk Claims, 17 J. Marshall J. Computer & Info. L. 183, 198 (1998). Are the Guidelines consistent with this approach?

2. Do the Guidelines' provisions on patentable subject matter affect the scope of the patents that result? One possible explanation for the formal distinctions drawn in the Guidelines is that they are designed to allow narrow patent claims while excluding broad ones. For example, a claim directed to a computer program itself is not statutory, but a claim for a program implemented on a particular medium is statutory. Does this imply that the claim is infringed only by the use of the same program *recorded on the same medium*?

3. Patent and copyright protection have coexisted uneasily for some time in the software arena. Do the Guidelines draw a line between material that is patentable and material that is copyrightable? In particular, is the fact that a particular program element receives copyright protection evidence that it is (or should be)

unpatentable? Can you think of a way to patent copyrighted material in a computer-based medium that would pass muster under the Guidelines?

4. While the PTO Guidelines for examiners are obviously important to the continued development of the law in this area, they cannot substitute for the judgment of the courts. If the Federal Circuit decides, for example, that "software on a floppy disk" is not within the ambit of 35 U.S.C. §101, the PTO does not have the power to issue such patents regardless of the Court decision. Similarly, the PTO cannot reject an application under section 101 if the courts have decided that it is patentable subject matter. Thus, while important, the Guidelines do not represent the final word on the section 101 issue. For an argument that the Guidelines accurately reflect the case law, see Ruben Bains, A Comparison of the PTO's Computer-Implemented Guidelines with the Current Case Law, 5 Tex. Intell. Prop. L.J. 27 (1996).

At the same time, the evidence is growing that the courts may not have the final say on section 101 either. With over 80,000 software or software-related patents in force in the United States and several thousand more being issued every year, the real world seems to have left the courts (and perhaps even the Guidelines) behind. Numerous issued patents cover pure data structures (see, e.g., U.S. Patent No. 5,488,717, U.S. Patent No. 5,414,701, methods for performing calculations in a data processor; U.S. Patent No. 5,386,375, data compression algorithms; U.S. Patent No. 5,051,745 and software-based encryption algorithms; U.S. Patent No. 5,530,752; and U.S. Patent No. 4,405,829), despite the apparent nonstatutory nature of such claims. The "cognitive dissonance" that results between what the law is and what the actual practice has been suggests either that the law can be expected to change or that a large number of issued patents will have to be held invalid. Although these disputes may seem metaphysical (why should it matter whether I can patent software on a floppy disk, or a process of running a program, as opposed to a computer programmed with the same software?), they have real-world import. Different parties will be liable for infringement depending on whether the claim is drafted as an article of manufacture (produced by the software vendor) or as a process or system claim (infringed only by the end user running the program on his computer). For a variety of economic reasons, software patent owners generally prefer to sue their competitors rather than their competitors' customers. Keith Witek offers an exhaustive guide to patenting computer programs and algorithms in a number of different forms, along with some analysis of the advantages and disadvantages of each. Keith E. Witek, Developing a Comprehensive Claim Drafting Strategy for U.S. Software Patents, 11 Berkeley Tech. L.J. 363 (1996).

PROBLEMS

Problem 3-1. Yoshimoto, a company that makes software for video games, seeks a patent on a new and nonobvious computer program. Yoshimoto claims the program "implemented in a read-only memory (ROM) readable by a computer." Is this claim patentable subject matter? How would this question be answered under (1) *Benson*? (2) *Diehr*? (3) The PTO's Proposed Guidelines?

> *Problem 3-2.* Lynn, a programmer who specializes in computer-assisted design tools, develops a new and more efficient way of cataloguing data in a computer representative of "virtual objects." The virtual objects are in turn computer graphics used to model real-world objects. She claims "a data structure resident in a computer-readable memory." The data structure is further described and defined in the claims, but the memory is not. Is Lynn's claim patentable under the PTO's Proposed Guidelines? Is there any form of software such a claim would not cover?
>
> What other types of legal protection might Lynn be able to obtain?

State Street Bank & Trust v. Signature Financial Services

United States Court of Appeals for the Federal Circuit
149 F.3d 1368 (Fed. Cir. 1998)

RICH, Circuit Judge.

Signature Financial Group, Inc. (Signature) appeals from the decision of the United States District Court for the District of Massachusetts granting a motion for summary judgment in favor of State Street Bank & Trust Co. (State Street), finding U.S. Patent No. 5,193,056 (the '056 patent) invalid on the ground that the claimed subject matter is not encompassed by 35 U.S.C. sec. 101 (1994). See State Street Bank & Trust Co. v. Signature Financial Group, Inc., 927 F. Supp. 502, 38 USPQ2d 1530 (D.Mass. 1996). We reverse and remand because we conclude that the patent claims are directed to statutory subject matter.

Background

Signature is the assignee of the '056 patent which is entitled "Data Processing System for Hub and Spoke Financial Services Configuration." The '056 patent issued to Signature on March 9, 1993, naming R. Todd Boes as the inventor. The '056 patent is generally directed to a data processing system (the system) for implementing an investment structure which was developed for use in Signature's business as an administrator and accounting agent for mutual funds. In essence, the system, identified by the proprietary name Hub and Spoke®, facilitates a structure whereby mutual funds (Spokes) pool their assets in an investment portfolio (Hub) organized as a partnership. This investment configuration provides the administrator of a mutual fund with the advantageous combination of economies of scale in administering investments coupled with the tax advantages of a partnership.

State Street and Signature are both in the business of acting as custodians and accounting agents for multi-tiered partnership fund financial services. State Street negotiated with Signature for a license to use its patented data processing system described and claimed in the '056 patent. When negotiations broke down, State Street brought a declaratory judgment action asserting invalidity, unenforceability, and noninfringement in Massachusetts district court, and then filed a motion for partial summary judgment of patent invalidity for failure to claim statutory subject matter under sec. 101. The motion was granted and this appeal followed.

Discussion

. . . The patented invention relates generally to a system that allows an administrator to monitor and record the financial information flow and make all calculations necessary for maintaining a partner fund financial services configuration. As previously mentioned, a partner fund financial services configuration essentially allows several mutual funds, or "Spokes," to pool their investment funds into a single portfolio, or "Hub," allowing for consolidation of, inter alia, the costs of administering the fund combined with the tax advantages of a partnership. In particular, this system provides means for a daily allocation of assets for two or more Spokes that are invested in the same Hub. The system determines the percentage share that each Spoke maintains in the Hub, while taking into consideration daily changes both in the value of the Hub's investment securities and in the concomitant amount of each Spoke's assets.

In determining daily changes, the system also allows for the allocation among the Spokes of the Hub's daily income, expenses, and net realized and unrealized gain or loss, calculating each day's total investments based on the concept of a book capital account. This enables the determination of a true asset value of each Spoke and accurate calculation of allocation ratios between or among the Spokes. The system additionally tracks all the relevant data determined on a daily basis for the Hub and each Spoke, so that aggregate year end income, expenses, and capital gain or loss can be determined for accounting and for tax purposes for the Hub and, as a result, for each publicly traded Spoke.

It is essential that these calculations are quickly and accurately performed. In large part this is required because each Spoke sells shares to the public and the price of those shares is substantially based on the Spoke's percentage interest in the portfolio. In some instances, a mutual fund administrator is required to calculate the value of the shares to the nearest penny within as little as an hour and a half after the market closes. Given the complexity of the calculations, a computer or equivalent device is a virtual necessity to perform the task. . . .

The district court began its analysis by construing the claims to be directed to a process, with each "means" clause merely representing a step in that process. However, "machine" claims having "means" clauses may only be reasonably viewed as process claims if there is no supporting structure in the written description that corresponds to the claimed "means" elements. See In re Alappat, 33 F.3d 1526, 1540-41, 31 USPQ2d 1545, 1554 (Fed.Cir. 1994) (in banc). This is not the case now before us.

When independent claim 1 is properly construed in accordance with section 112, para. 6, it is directed to a machine, as demonstrated below, where representative claim 1 is set forth, the subject matter in brackets stating the structure the written description discloses as corresponding to the respective "means" recited in the claims.

        1. A data processing system for managing a financial services configuration of a portfolio established as a partnership, each partner being one of a plurality of funds, comprising:

        (a) computer processor means [a personal computer including a CPU] for processing data;

        (b) storage means [a data disk] for storing data on a storage medium;

        (c) first means [an arithmetic logic circuit configured to prepare the data disk to magnetically store selected data] for initializing the storage medium;

        (d) second means [an arithmetic logic circuit configured to retrieve information from a specific file, calculate incremental increases or decreases based on specific input, allocate the results on a percentage basis, and store the output in a separate file] for processing data regarding assets in the portfolio and each of the funds from a previous day and data regarding increases or decreases in each of the funds, [sic, funds'] assets and for allocating the percentage share that each fund holds in the portfolio;

        (e) third means [an arithmetic logic circuit configured to retrieve information from a specific file, calculate incremental increases and decreases based on specific input, allocate the results on a percentage basis and store the output in a separate file] for processing data regarding daily incremental income, expenses, and net realized gain or loss for the portfolio and for allocating such data among each fund;

        (f) fourth means [an arithmetic logic circuit configured to retrieve information from a specific file, calculate incremental increases and decreases based on specific input, allocate the results on a percentage basis and store the output in a separate file] for processing data regarding daily net unrealized gain or loss for the portfolio and for allocating such data among each fund; and

        (g) fifth means [an arithmetic logic circuit configured to retrieve information from specific files, calculate that information on an aggregate basis and store the output in a separate file] for processing data regarding aggregate year-end income, expenses, and capital gain or loss for the portfolio and each of the funds.

    Each claim component, recited as a "means" plus its function, is to be read, of course, pursuant to sec. 112, para. 6, as inclusive of the "equivalents" of the structures disclosed in the written description portion of the specification. Thus, claim 1, properly construed, claims a machine, namely, a data processing system for managing a financial services configuration of a portfolio established as a partnership, which machine is made up of, at the very least, the specific structures disclosed in the written description and corresponding to the means-plus-function elements (a)-(g) recited in the claim. A "machine" is proper statutory subject matter under sec. 101. We note that, for the purposes of a sec. 101 analysis, it is of little relevance whether claim 1 is directed to a "machine" or a "process," as long as it falls within at least one of the four enumerated categories of patentable subject matter, "machine" and "process" being such categories.

    This does not end our analysis, however, because the court concluded that the claimed subject matter fell into one of two alternative judicially-created exceptions to statutory subject matter. The court refers to the first exception as the "mathematical algorithm" exception and the second exception as the "business method" exception. . . .

The repetitive use of the expansive term "any" in sec. 101 shows Congress's intent not to place any restrictions on the subject matter for which a patent may be obtained beyond those specifically recited in sec. 101. Indeed, the Supreme Court has acknowledged that Congress intended sec. 101 to extend to "anything under the sun that is made by man." Diamond v. Chakrabarty, 447 U.S. 303, 309, 100 S. Ct. 2204, 65 L. Ed.2d 144 (1980); see also Diamond v. Diehr, 450 U.S. 175, 182, 101 S. Ct. 1048, 67 L. Ed.2d 155 (1981). Thus, it is improper to read limitations into sec. 101 on the subject matter that may be patented where the legislative history indicates that Congress clearly did not intend such limitations. See *Chakrabarty*, 447 U.S. at 308, 100 S. Ct. 2204 ("We have also cautioned that courts 'should not read into the patent laws limitations and conditions which the legislature has not expressed.'" (citations omitted)).

The "Mathematical Algorithm" Exception

The Supreme Court has identified three categories of subject matter that are unpatentable, namely "laws of nature, natural phenomena, and abstract ideas." *Diehr*, 450 U.S. at 185, 101 S. Ct. 1048. Of particular relevance to this case, the Court has held that mathematical algorithms are not patentable subject matter to the extent that they are merely abstract ideas. See *Diehr*, 450 U.S. 175, 101 S. Ct. 1048, passim; Parker v. Flook, 437 U.S. 584, 98 S. Ct. 2522, 57 L. Ed.2d 451 (1978); Gottschalk v. Benson, 409 U.S. 63, 93 S. Ct. 253, 34 L. Ed.2d 273 (1972). In *Diehr*, the Court explained that certain types of mathematical subject matter, standing alone, represent nothing more than abstract ideas until reduced to some type of practical application, i.e., "a useful, concrete and tangible result." *Alappat*, 33 F.3d at 1544, 31 USPQ2d at 1557.[4]

Unpatentable mathematical algorithms are identifiable by showing they are merely abstract ideas constituting disembodied concepts or truths that are not "useful." From a practical standpoint, this means that to be patentable an algorithm must be applied in a "useful" way. In *Alappat*, we held that data, transformed by a machine through a series of mathematical calculations to produce a smooth waveform display on a rasterizer monitor, constituted a practical application of an abstract idea (a mathematical algorithm, formula, or calculation), because it produced "a useful, concrete and tangible result"—the smooth waveform.

Similarly, in Arrhythmia Research Technology Inc. v. Corazonix Corp., 958 F.2d 1053, 22 USPQ2d 1033 (Fed.Cir. 1992), we held that the transformation of electrocardiograph signals from a patient's heartbeat by a machine through a series of mathematical calculations constituted a practical application of an abstract idea (a mathematical algorithm, formula, or calculation), because it corresponded to a useful, concrete or tangible thing—the condition of a patient's heart.

---

4. This has come to be known as the mathematical algorithm exception. This designation has led to some confusion, especially given the Freeman-Walter-Abele analysis. By keeping in mind that the mathematical algorithm is unpatentable only to the extent that it represents an abstract idea, this confusion may be ameliorated.

Today, we hold that the transformation of data, representing discrete dollar amounts, by a machine through a series of mathematical calculations into a final share price, constitutes a practical application of a mathematical algorithm, formula, or calculation, because it produces "a useful, concrete and tangible result"— a final share price momentarily fixed for recording and reporting purposes and even accepted and relied upon by regulatory authorities and in subsequent trades.

The district court erred by applying the Freeman-Walter-Abele test to determine whether the claimed subject matter was an unpatentable abstract idea. . . .

After *Diehr* and *Chakrabarty*, the Freeman-Walter-Abele test has little, if any, applicability to determining the presence of statutory subject matter. As we pointed out in *Alappat*, 33 F.3d at 1543, 31 USPQ2d at 1557, application of the test could be misleading, because a process, machine, manufacture, or composition of matter employing a law of nature, natural phenomenon, or abstract idea is patentable subject matter even though a law of nature, natural phenomenon, or abstract idea would not, by itself, be entitled to such protection. The test determines the presence of, for example, an algorithm. Under *Benson*, this may have been a sufficient indicium of nonstatutory subject matter. However, after *Diehr* and *Alappat*, the mere fact that a claimed invention involves inputting numbers, calculating numbers, outputting numbers, and storing numbers, in and of itself, would not render it nonstatutory subject matter, unless, of course, its operation does not produce a "useful, concrete and tangible result." *Alappat*, 33 F.3d at 1544, 31 USPQ2d at 1557. . . .

The question of whether a claim encompasses statutory subject matter should not focus on which of the four categories of subject matter a claim is directed to— process, machine, manufacture, or composition of matter—but rather on the essential characteristics of the subject matter, in particular, its practical utility. Section 101 specifies that statutory subject matter must also satisfy the other "conditions and requirements" of Title 35, including novelty, nonobviousness, and adequacy of disclosure and notice. See In re Warmerdam, 33 F.3d 1354, 1359, 31 USPQ2d 1754, 1757-58 (Fed.Cir. 1994). For purpose of our analysis, as noted above, claim 1 is directed to a machine programmed with the Hub and Spoke software and admittedly produces a "useful, concrete, and tangible result." *Alappat*, 33 F.3d at 1544, 31 USPQ2d at 1557. This renders it statutory subject matter, even if the useful result is expressed in numbers, such as price, profit, percentage, cost, or loss.

COMMENTS AND QUESTIONS

1. The PTO revised its Examination Guidelines in late 1998 in response to the decision in *State Street* by adding several "training examples" dealing with business, artificial intelligence, and mathematical processing claims. The examples show a reluctance on the part of the PTO to abandon the physical transformation approach that characterized the case law through the mid-1990s. Why is there such a strong attachment to hardware aspects of computer programs? Is this somehow easier to square with the "traditional" subject matter of patents, such as machines?

≡ **AT&T Corp. v. Excel Communications, Inc.**
≡ *United States Court of Appeals for the Federal Circuit*
≡ *172 F.3d 1352 (Fed. Cir. 1999)*

PLAGER, Circuit Judge.

This case asks us once again to examine the scope of section 1 of the Patent Act, 35 U.S.C. §101 (1994). The United States District Court for the District of Delaware granted summary judgment to Excel Communications, Inc., Excel Communications Marketing, Inc., and Excel Telecommunications, Inc. (collectively "Excel"), holding U.S. Patent No. 5,333,184 (the '184 patent) invalid under §101 for failure to claim statutory subject matter. AT&T Corp. ("AT&T"), owner of the '184 patent, appeals. Because we find that the claimed subject matter is properly within the statutory scope of §101, we reverse the district court's judgment of invalidity on this ground and remand the case for further proceedings.

Background

A.

The '184 patent, entitled "Call Message Recording for Telephone Systems," issued on July 26, 1994. It describes a message record for long-distance telephone calls that is enhanced by adding a primary interexchange carrier ("PIC") indicator. The addition of the indicator aids long-distance carriers in providing differential billing treatment for subscribers, depending upon whether a subscriber calls someone with the same or a different long-distance carrier.

The invention claimed in the '184 patent is designed to operate in a telecommunications system with multiple long-distance service providers. The system contains local exchange carriers ("LECs") and long-distance service (interexchange) carriers ("IXCs"). The LECs provide local telephone service and access to IXCs. Each customer has an LEC for local service and selects an IXC, such as AT&T or Excel, to be its primary long-distance service (interexchange) carrier or PIC. IXCs may own their own facilities, as does AT&T. Others, like Excel, called "resellers" or "resale carriers," contract with facility-owners to route their subscribers' calls through the facility-owners' switches and transmission lines. Some IXCs, including MCI and U.S. Sprint, have a mix of their own lines and leased lines.

The system thus involves a three-step process when a caller makes a direct-dialed (1+) long-distance telephone call: (1) after the call is transmitted over the LEC's network to a switch, and the LEC identifies the caller's PIC, the LEC automatically routes the call to the facilities used by the caller's PIC; (2) the PIC's facilities carry the call to the LEC serving the call recipient; and (3) the call recipient's LEC delivers the call over its local network to the recipient's telephone.

When a caller makes a direct-dialed long-distance telephone call, a switch (which may be a switch in the interexchange network) monitors and records data related to the call, generating an "automatic message account" ("AMA") message record. This contemporaneous message record contains fields of information such as the originating and terminating telephone numbers, and the length of time of the call. These message records are then transmitted from the switch to a message accumulation system for processing and billing.

Because the message records are stored in electronic format, they can be transmitted from one computer system to another and reformatted to ease processing of the information. Thus the carrier's AMA message subsequently is translated into the industry-standard "exchange message interface," forwarded to a rating system, and ultimately forwarded to a billing system in which the data resides until processed to generate, typically, "hard copy" bills which are mailed to subscribers.

B.

The invention of the '184 patent calls for the addition of a data field into a standard message record to indicate whether a call involves a particular PIC (the "PIC indicator"). This PIC indicator can exist in several forms, such as a code which identifies the call recipient's PIC, a flag which shows that the recipient's PIC is or is not a particular IXC, or a flag that identifies the recipient's and the caller's PICs as the same IXC. The PIC indicator therefore enables IXCs to provide differential billing for calls on the basis of the identified PIC.

The application that issued as the '184 patent was filed in 1992. The U.S. Patent and Trademark Office ("PTO") initially rejected, for reasons unrelated to §101, all forty-one of the originally filed claims. Following amendment, the claims were issued in 1994 in their present form. The '184 patent contains six independent claims, five method claims and one apparatus claim, and additional dependent claims. The PTO granted the '184 patent without questioning whether the claims were directed to statutory subject matter under §101.

AT&T in 1996 asserted ten of the method claims against Excel in this infringement suit. The independent claims at issue (claims 1, 12, 18, and 40) include the step of "generating a message record for an interexchange call between an originating subscriber and a terminating subscriber," and the step of adding a PIC indicator to the message record. Independent claim 1, for example, adds a PIC indicator whose value depends upon the call recipient's PIC:

> A method for use in a telecommunications system in which interexchange calls initiated by each subscriber are automatically routed over the facilities of a particular one of a plurality of interexchange carriers associated with that subscriber, said method comprising the steps of:
>
> > *generating a message record for an interexchange call* between an originating subscriber and a terminating subscriber, and
> > *including, in said message record, a primary interexchange carrier (PIC) indicator* having a value which is *a function of whether or not the interexchange carrier associated with said terminating subscriber is a predetermined one* of said interexchange carriers.

(Emphasis added.)

The district court concluded that the method claims of the '184 patent implicitly recite a mathematical algorithm. The court was of the view that the only physical step in the claims involves data-gathering for the algorithm. Though the court recognized that the claims require the use of switches and computers, it nevertheless concluded that use of such facilities to perform a non-substantive change in the data's format could not serve to convert non-patentable subject matter into patentable subject matter. Thus the trial court, on summary judgment, held all of the method claims at issue invalid for failure to qualify as statutory subject matter.

Discussion

The Supreme Court has construed §101 broadly, noting that Congress intended statutory subject matter to "include anything under the sun that is made by man." See Diamond v. Chakrabarty, 447 U.S. 303, 309, 100 S. Ct. 2204, 65 L. Ed.2d 144 (1980) (quoting S.Rep. No. 82-1979, at 5 (1952); H.R.Rep. No. 82-1923, at 6 (1952)); see also Diamond v. Diehr, 450 U.S. 175, 182, 101 S. Ct. 1048, 67 L. Ed.2d 155 (1981). Despite this seemingly limitless expanse, the Court has specifically identified three categories of unpatentable subject matter: "laws of nature, natural phenomena, and abstract ideas." See *Diehr*, 450 U.S. at 185, 101 S. Ct. 1048.

In this case, the method claims at issue fall within the "process" category of the four enumerated categories of patentable subject matter in §101. The district court held that the claims at issue, though otherwise within the terms of §101, implicitly recite a mathematical algorithm and thus fall within the judicially created "mathematical algorithm" exception to statutory subject matter.

A mathematical formula alone, sometimes referred to as a mathematical algorithm, viewed in the abstract, is considered unpatentable subject matter. See Diamond v. Dichr, 450 U.S. 175, 101 S. Ct. 1048, 67 L. Ed.2d 155 (1981); Parker v. Flook, 437 U.S. 584, 98 S. Ct. 2522, 57 L. Ed.2d 451 (1978); Gottschalk v. Benson, 409 U.S. 63, 93 S. Ct. 253, 34 L. Ed.2d 273 (1972). Courts have used the terms "mathematical algorithm," "mathematical formula," and "mathematical equation," to describe types of nonstatutory mathematical subject matter without explaining whether the terms are interchangeable or different. Even assuming the words connote the same concept, there is considerable question as to exactly what the concept encompasses. See, e.g., *Diehr*, 450 U.S. at 186 n. 9, 101 S. Ct. 1048 ("The term 'algorithm' is subject to a variety of definitions . . . [Petitioner's] definition is significantly broader than the definition this Court employed in *Benson* and *Flook*."); *accord* In re Schrader, 22 F.3d 290, 293 n. 5, 30 USPQ2d 1455, 1457 n. 5 (Fed.Cir. 1994).

This court recently pointed out that any step-by-step process, be it electronic, chemical, or mechanical, involves an "algorithm" in the broad sense of the term. See State Street Bank & Trust Co. v. Signature Fin. Group, Inc., 149 F.3d 1368, 1374-75, 47 USPQ2d 1596, 1602 (Fed.Cir. 1998), *cert. denied*, 525 U.S. 1093, 119 S. Ct. 851, 142 L. Ed.2d 704 (1999). Because §101 includes processes as a category of patentable subject matter, the judicially-defined proscription against patenting of a "mathematical algorithm," to the extent such a proscription still exists, is narrowly limited to mathematical algorithms in the abstract. See *id.;* see also *Benson,* 409 U.S. at 65, 93 S. Ct. 253 (describing a mathematical algorithm as a "procedure for solving a given type of mathematical problem").

Since the process of manipulation of numbers is a fundamental part of computer technology, we have had to reexamine the rules that govern the patentability of such technology. The sea-changes in both law and technology stand as a testament to the ability of law to adapt to new and innovative concepts, while remaining true to basic principles. In an earlier era, the PTO published guidelines essentially rejecting the notion that computer programs were patentable. As the technology progressed, our predecessor court disagreed, and, overturning some of the earlier limiting principles regarding §101, announced more expansive principles formulated with computer technology in mind. In our recent decision in *State Street,* this court discarded the so-called "business method" exception and reassessed the "mathematical algorithm" exception, *see* 149 F.3d at 1373-77, 47 USPQ2d at 1600-04, both judicially-created "exceptions" to the statutory categories of §101. As this brief review suggests, this court (and its predecessor) has struggled to make our understanding of the scope of §101 responsive to the needs of the modern world.

The Supreme Court has supported and enhanced this effort. In *Diehr,* the Court expressly limited its two earlier decisions in *Flook* and *Benson* by emphasizing that these cases did no more than confirm the "long-established principle" that laws of nature, natural phenomena, and abstract ideas are excluded from patent protection.

[In the Federal Circuit,] [t]he *State Street* formulation, that a mathematical algorithm may be an integral part of patentable subject matter such as a machine or process if the claimed invention as a whole is applied in a "useful" manner, follows the approach taken by this court en banc in In re Alappat, 33 F.3d 1526 (Fed.Cir. 1994). In *Alappat,* we set out our understanding of the Supreme Court's limitations on the patentability of mathematical subject matter and concluded that:

> [The Court] never intended to create an overly broad, fourth category of [mathematical] subject matter excluded from §101. Rather, at the core of the Court's analysis . . . lies an attempt by the Court to explain a rather straightforward concept, namely, that certain types of mathematical subject matter, *standing alone,* represent nothing more than *abstract ideas until reduced to some type of practical application,* and thus that subject matter is not, in and of itself, entitled to patent protection.

Id. at 1543 (emphasis added). Thus, the *Alappat* inquiry simply requires an examination of the contested claims to see if the claimed subject matter as a whole is a disembodied mathematical concept representing nothing more than a "law of nature" or an "abstract idea," or if the mathematical concept has been reduced to some practical application rendering it "useful." *Id*. at 1544. In *Alappat,* we held that more than an abstract idea was claimed because the claimed invention as a whole was directed toward forming a specific machine that produced the useful, concrete, and tangible result of a smooth waveform display. *See id*. at 1544.

In both *Alappat* and *State Street,* the claim was for a machine that achieved certain results. In the case before us, because Excel does not own or operate the facilities over which its calls are placed, AT&T did not charge Excel with infringement of its apparatus claims, but limited its infringement charge to the specified method or process claims. Whether stated implicitly or explicitly, we consider the scope of §101 to be the same regardless of the form—machine or process—in which a particular claim is drafted. See, e.g., In re Alappat, 33 F.3d at 1581, 31

USPQ2d at 1589 (Rader, J., concurring) ("Judge Rich, with whom I fully concur, reads Alappat's application as claiming a machine. In fact, whether the invention is a process or a machine is irrelevant. The language of the Patent Act itself, as well as Supreme Court rulings, clarifies that Alappat's invention fits comfortably within 35 U.S.C. §101 whether viewed as a process or a machine."); *State Street,* 149 F.3d at 1372, 47 USPQ2d at 1600 ("[F]or the purposes of a §101 analysis, it is of little relevance whether claim 1 is directed to a 'machine' or a 'process,' . . . .").

C.

In light of this review of the current understanding of the "mathematical algorithm" exception, we turn now to the arguments of the parties in support of and in opposition to the trial court's judgment. We note that, at the time the trial court made its decision, that court did not have the benefit of this court's explication in *State Street* of the mathematical algorithm issue.

As previously explained, AT&T's claimed process employs subscribers' and call recipients' PICs as data, applies Boolean algebra to those data to determine the value of the PIC indicator, and applies that value through switching and recording mechanisms to create a signal useful for billing purposes. In *State Street,* we held that the processing system there was patentable subject matter because the system takes data representing discrete dollar amounts through a series of mathematical calculations to determine a final share price—a useful, concrete, and tangible result. *See* 149 F.3d at 1373.

In this case, Excel argues, correctly, that the PIC indicator value is derived using a simple mathematical principle (p and q). But that is not determinative because AT&T does not claim the Boolean principle as such or attempt to forestall its use in any other application. It is clear from the written description of the '184 patent that AT&T is only claiming a process that uses the Boolean principle in order to determine the value of the PIC indicator. The PIC indicator represents information about the call recipient's PIC, a useful, non-abstract result that facilitates differential billing of long-distance calls made by an IXC's subscriber. Because the claimed process applies the Boolean principle to produce a useful, concrete, tangible result without pre-empting other uses of the mathematical principle, on its face the claimed process comfortably falls within the scope of §101. See Arrhythmia Research Technology, Inc. v. Corazonix Corp., 958 F.2d 1053, 1060, 22 USPQ2d 1033, 1039 (Fed.Cir. 1992) ("That the product is numerical is not a criterion of whether the claim is directed to statutory subject matter.").

Excel argues that method claims containing mathematical algorithms are patentable subject matter only if there is a "physical transformation" or conversion of subject matter from one state into another. The physical transformation language appears in *Diehr,* see 450 U.S. at 184, 101 S. Ct. 1048 ("That respondents' claims involve the transformation of an article, in this case raw, uncured synthetic rubber, into a different state or thing cannot be disputed."), and has been echoed by this court in *Schrader,* 22 F.3d at 294, 30 USPQ2d at 1458 ("Therefore, we do not find in the claim any kind of data transformation.").

The notion of "physical transformation" can be misunderstood. In the first place, it is not an invariable requirement, but merely one example of how a mathematical algorithm may bring about a useful application. As the Supreme

Court itself noted, "when [a claimed invention] is performing a function which the patent laws were designed to protect (*e.g.*, transforming or reducing an article to a different state or thing), then the claim satisfies the requirements of §101." *Diehr*, 450 U.S. at 192, 101 S. Ct. 1048 (emphasis added). The "e.g." signal denotes an example, not an exclusive requirement.

This understanding of transformation is consistent with our earlier decision in *Arrhythmia*, 958 F.2d 1053 (Fed.Cir. 1992). Arrhythmia's process claims included various mathematical formulae to analyze electrocardiograph signals to determine a specified heart activity. See *id*. at 1059. The *Arrhythmia* court reasoned that the method claims qualified as statutory subject matter by noting that the steps transformed physical, electrical signals from one form into another form —a number representing a signal related to the patient's heart activity, a non-abstract output. See *id.*, 958 F.2d at 1059. The finding that the claimed process "transformed" data from one "form" to another simply confirmed that Arrhythmia's method claims satisfied §101 because the mathematical algorithm included within the process was applied to produce a number which had specific meaning— a useful, concrete, tangible result—not a mathematical abstraction. See *id*. at 1060.

Excel also contends that because the process claims at issue lack physical limitations set forth in the patent, the claims are not patentable subject matter. This argument reflects a misunderstanding of our case law. The cases cited by Excel for this proposition involved machine claims written in means-plus-function language. See, e.g., *State Street*, 149 F.3d at 1371, *Alappat*, 33 F.3d at 1541. Apparatus claims written in this manner require supporting structure in the written description that corresponds to the claimed "means" elements. See 35 U.S.C. §112, para. 6 (1994). Since the claims at issue in this case are directed to a process in the first instance, a structural inquiry is unnecessary.

The argument that physical limitations are necessary may also stem from the second part of the *Freeman-Walter-Abele* test,[1] an earlier test which has been used to identify claims thought to involve unpatentable mathematical algorithms. That second part was said to inquire "whether the claim is directed to a mathematical algorithm that is not applied to or limited by physical elements." *Arrhythmia*, 958 F.2d at 1058. Although our en banc *Alappat* decision called this test "not an improper analysis," we then pointed out that "the ultimate issue always has been whether the claim as a whole is drawn to statutory subject matter." 33 F.3d at 1543 n. 2. Furthermore, our recent *State Street* decision questioned the continuing viability of the *Freeman-Walter-Abele* test, noting that, "[a]fter *Diehr* and *Chakrabarty*, the *Freeman-Walter-Abele* test has little, if any, applicability to determining the presence of statutory subject matter." 149 F.3d at 1374. Whatever may be left of the earlier test, if anything, this type of physical limitations analysis seems of little value because "after *Diehr* and *Alappat*, the mere fact that a claimed invention involves inputting numbers, calculating numbers, outputting numbers, and storing numbers, in and of itself, would not render it nonstatutory subject matter, unless, of course, its operation does not produce a 'useful, concrete and tangible result.'" *Id*. at 1374 (quoting *Alappat*, 33 F.3d at 1544).

---

1. See In re Freeman, 573 F.2d 1237, 197 USPQ 464 (CCPA 1978), as modified by In re Walter, 618 F.2d 758, 205 USPQ 397(CCPA 1980), and In re Abele, 648 F.2d 902, 214 USPQ 682 (CCPA 1982).

D.

In his dissent in *Diehr,* Justice Stevens noted two concerns regarding the §101 issue, and to which, in his view, federal judges have a duty to respond:

First, the cases considering the patentability of program-related inventions do not establish rules that enable a conscientious patent lawyer to determine with a fair degree of accuracy which, if any, program-related inventions will be patentable. Second, the inclusion of the ambiguous concept of an "algorithm" within the "law of nature" category of unpatentable subject matter has given rise to the concern that almost any process might be so described and therefore held unpatentable.

Diehr, 450 U.S. at 219 (Stevens, J., dissenting).

Despite the almost twenty years since Justice Stevens wrote, these concerns remain important. His solution was to declare all computer-based programming unpatentable. That has not been the course the law has taken. Rather, it is now clear that computer-based programming constitutes patentable subject matter so long as the basic requirements of §101 are met. Justice Stevens's concerns can be addressed within that framework.

His first concern, that the rules are not sufficiently clear to enable reasonable prediction of outcomes, should be less of a concern today in light of the refocusing of the §101 issue that *Alappat* and *State Street* have provided. His second concern, that the ambiguous concept of "algorithm" could be used to make any process unpatentable, can be laid to rest once the focus is understood to be not on whether there is a mathematical algorithm at work, but on whether the algorithm-containing invention, as a whole, produces a tangible, useful, result.

In light of the above, and consistent with the clearer understanding that our more recent cases have provided, we conclude that the district court did not apply the proper analysis to the method claims at issue. Furthermore, had the court applied the proper analysis to the stated claims, the court would have concluded that all the claims asserted fall comfortably within the broad scope of patentable subject matter under §101. Accordingly, we hold as a matter of law that Excel was not entitled to the grant of summary judgment of invalidity of the '184 patent under §101.

Since the case must be returned to the trial court for further proceedings, and to avoid any possible misunderstandings as to the scope of our decision, we note that the ultimate validity of these claims depends upon their satisfying the other requirements for patentability such as those set forth in 35 U.S.C. §§102, 103, and 112. Thus, on remand, those questions, as well as any others the parties may properly raise, remain for disposition.

Reversed and Remanded.

COMMENTS AND QUESTIONS

1. The opinion cites older Supreme Court cases, some examined elsewhere in this chapter, while recognizing that much has changed in the world of software technology since these opinions were handed down in the period from 1970 to 1980. In a fast-changing area such as computer software patenting, should Supreme Court precedent have less force over time? In the wake of an opinion such as *AT&T,* should further inaction by the Supreme Court (or Congress) constitute acquiescence in the reinterpretation and refinement of its earlier rulings?

2. Cases such as *AT&T* and *State Street Bank*, later this section, go a long way toward eliminating the rule that computer programs (or "algorithms") "as such" may not be patented. But do they go all the way? The answer seems to be "perhaps not," especially in light of the fact that the older Supreme Court cases (such as *Gottschalk*, see below) have not been directly overruled. Consider for example a recent district court case, Electronic Planroom, Inc. v. McGraw-Hill Companies, Inc., 135 F. Supp.2d 805 (E.D.Mich. 2001). One issue in this case was whether defendant had infringed plaintiff's U.S. Patent 5,625,827 claiming a computer-aided design (CAD) software package for representing and manipulating construction blueprints. In the midst of a consideration of whether the patented invention was obvious or not (the court held that it was), the court addressed the subject matter patentability of the claimed invention under §101:

> [T]he '827 patent still might well run afoul of the longstanding patent-law principle that mathematical algorithms cannot be patented. See Gottschalk v. Benson, 409 U.S. 63, 71-72 (1972). As indicated earlier, the "how" of the calibration and measurement functions is the only new teaching disclosed in the '827 Patent—or, at least, in the claims at issue in this litigation—that was not suggested by [a prior art patent]. Thus, these claims assert patentable subject matter only if this new teaching qualifies for patent protection.
>
> There is reason to suspect that it might not. To be sure, the Federal Circuit has recently sought to narrowly circumscribe the "mathematical algorithm" exception to patentability. While acknowledging the still-controlling principle that "[a] mathematical formula alone, sometimes referred to as a mathematical algorithm, viewed in the abstract, is considered unpatentable subject matter," the Federal Circuit has held that this principle is "narrowly limited to mathematical algorithms in the abstract," and does not reach patents where the "claimed invention as a whole" produces a "useful, concrete, and tangible result." [citing *AT&T*, 172 F.3d at 1356-57]
>
> The claims at issue here might well fall within even this narrow rule. All that they teach, when viewed in light of the prior [art patent] is a method for calibrating a computer-based image to an underlying real-world coordinate system so that measurements can be made on the computer-based image and the results displayed in real-world dimensions. Stated differently, these claims disclose—albeit abstractly, and without stating any express formulas—a method for translating from computer-based to real-world dimensions. Plainly, this same methodology must be applied in a variety of fields (medical imaging and computer-aided design, to name but two), whenever one wishes to view a real-world object on a computer display and perform real-world measurements on the computer-based image. To award a patent on this method would raise precisely the concern cited by the Supreme Court in *Gottschalk*—namely, that "the patent would wholly pre-empt the mathematical formula," which "in practical effect would be a patent on the algorithm itself." *Gottschalk*, 409 U.S. at 72.

135 F. Supp.2d 805, 837-38. If an invention is useful in computer programming, shouldn't that meet the rather lax standard of *AT&T*?

PROBLEM

Problem 3-3. Safe Flight is an aircraft instrument company. It seeks to obtain a patent on avionic windshear equipment designed to give warnings to a plane's pilot on takeoff or landing when the plane encounters violent shifts in wind direction ("windshear"). This can result in disaster if the pilot cannot compensate quickly and properly for the changing conditions. Windshear is measured in Safe Flight's invention by means of an algorithm that compares the rate of change of the instantaneous airspeed (the speed of an aircraft measured against the surrounding air) with the change in groundspeed (the speed of an aircraft measured against the ground, which the patentee calls "horizontal inertial acceleration"). Safe Flight claims a "windshear measurement and control system" in an aircraft cockpit, which employs the algorithm to constantly recalculate windshear during landing and automatically generates a warning buzzer if windshear exceeds a certain threshold level.

Is Safe Flight's claim patentable subject matter under section 101? Should it be? Would it be patentable if it were not implemented in a computer?

2. Software as a "Method of Doing Business"

State Street Bank & Trust v. Signature Financial Services
United States Court of Appeals for the Federal Circuit
149 F.3d 1368 (Fed. Cir. 1998)

[The factual background of this case, and the court's decision on the mathematical algorithm exception, are reprinted above.]

The Business Method Exception

As an alternative ground for invalidating the '056 patent under sec. 101, the court relied on the judicially-created, so-called "business method" exception to statutory subject matter. We take this opportunity to lay this ill-conceived exception to rest. Since its inception, the "business method" exception has merely represented the application of some general, but no longer applicable legal principle, perhaps arising out of the "requirement for invention"—which was eliminated by sec. 103. Since the 1952 Patent Act, business methods have been, and should have been, subject to the same legal requirements for patentability as applied to any other process or method.[10]

---

10. As Judge Newman has previously stated,

[The business method exception] is . . . an unwarranted encumbrance to the definition of statutory subject matter in section 101, that [should] be discarded as error-prone, redundant, and obsolete. It merits retirement from the glossary of section 101. . . . All of the "doing business" cases could have been decided using the clearer concepts of Title 35. Patentability does not turn on whether the claimed method does "business" instead of something else, but on whether the method, viewed as a whole, meets the requirements of patentability as set forth in Sections 102, 103, and 112 of the Patent Act.

In re Schrader, 22 F.3d 290, 298, 30 USPQ2d 1455, 1462 (Fed.Cir. 1994) (Newman, J., dissenting).

The business method exception has never been invoked by this court, or the CCPA, to deem an invention unpatentable. Application of this particular exception has always been preceded by a ruling based on some clearer concept of Title 35 or, more commonly, application of the abstract idea exception based on finding a mathematical algorithm. Illustrative is the CCPA's analysis in In re Howard, 55 C.C.P.A. 1121, 394 F.2d 869, 157 USPQ 615 (CCPA 1968), wherein the court affirmed the Board of Appeals' rejection of the claims for lack of novelty and found it unnecessary to reach the Board's section 101 ground that a method of doing business is "inherently unpatentable." *Id*. at 872, 55 C.C.P.A. 1121, 394 F.2d 869, 157 USPQ at 617.[12]

Similarly, In re Schrader, 22 F.3d 290, 30 USPQ2d 1455 (Fed.Cir. 1994), while making reference to the business method exception, turned on the fact that the claims implicitly recited an abstract idea in the form of a mathematical algorithm and there was no "transformation or conversion of subject matter representative of or constituting physical activity or objects." 22 F.3d at 294, 30 USPQ2d at 1459 (emphasis omitted).

State Street argues that we acknowledged the validity of the business method exception in *Alappat* when we discussed *Maucorps* and *Meyer*:

> *Maucorps* dealt with a business methodology for deciding how salesmen should best handle respective customers and *Meyer* involved a "system" for aiding a neurologist in diagnosing patients. Clearly, neither of the alleged "inventions" in those cases falls within any sec. 101 category.

Alappat, 33 F.3d at 1541, 31 USPQ2d at 1555. However, closer scrutiny of these cases reveals that the claimed inventions in both *Maucorps* and *Meyer* were rejected as abstract ideas under the mathematical algorithm exception, not the business method exception. See In re Maucorps, 609 F.2d 481, 484, 203 USPQ 812, 816 (CCPA 1979); In re Meyer, 688 F.2d 789, 796, 215 USPQ 193, 199 (CCPA 1982).

Even the case frequently cited as establishing the business method exception to statutory subject matter, Hotel Security Checking Co. v. Lorraine Co., 160 F. 467 (2d Cir. 1908), did not rely on the exception to strike the patent. In that case, the patent was found invalid for lack of novelty and "invention," not because it was improper subject matter for a patent. The court stated "the fundamental principle of the system is as old as the art of bookkeeping, i.e., charging the goods of the employer to the agent who takes them." *Id*. at 469. "If at the time of [the patent] application, there had been no system of bookkeeping of any kind in restaurants, we would be confronted with the question whether a new and useful system of cash registering and account checking is such an art as is patentable under the statute." *Id*. at 472.

This case is no exception. The district court announced the precepts of the business method exception as set forth in several treatises, but noted as its primary

---

12. See also Dann v. Johnston, 425 U.S. 219, 96 S. Ct. 1393, 47 L. Ed.2d 692 (1976) (the Supreme Court declined to discuss the section 101 argument concerning the computerized financial record-keeping system, in view of the Court's holding of patent invalidity under section 103); In re Chatfield, 545 F.2d 152, 157, 191 USPQ 730, 735 (CCPA 1976); Ex parte Murray, 9 USPQ2d 1819, 1820 (Bd.Pat.App & Interf. 1988) ("[T]he claimed accounting method [requires] no more than the entering, sorting, debiting and totaling of expenditures as necessary preliminary steps to issuing an expense analysis statement. . . .") states grounds of obviousness or lack of novelty, not of nonstatutory subject matter. [sic].

reason for finding the patent invalid under the business method exception as follows:

> If Signature's invention were patentable, any financial institution desirous of implementing a multi-tiered funding complex modelled (sic) on a Hub and Spoke configuration would be required to seek Signature's permission before embarking on such a project. This is so because the '056 Patent is claimed [sic] sufficiently broadly to foreclose virtually any computer-implemented accounting method necessary to manage this type of financial structure.

927 F. Supp. 502, 516, 38 USPQ2d 1530, 1542. Whether the patent's claims are too broad to be patentable is not to be judged under §101, but rather under §§102, 103 and 112. Assuming the above statement to be correct, it has nothing to do with whether what is claimed is statutory subject matter.

. . . [T]he U.S. Patent and Trademark 1996 Examination Guidelines for Computer Related Inventions now read:

> Office personnel have had difficulty in properly treating claims directed to methods of doing business. Claims should not be categorized as methods of doing business. Instead such claims should be treated like any other process claims.

Examination Guidelines, 61 Fed.Reg. 7478, 7479 (1996). We agree that this is precisely the manner in which this type of claim should be treated. Whether the claims are directed to subject matter within sec. 101 should not turn on whether the claimed subject matter does "business" instead of something else.

Conclusion

The appealed decision is reversed and the case is remanded to the district court for further proceedings consistent with this opinion.

COMMENTS AND QUESTIONS

1. *State Street* is not the first case to permit a patent on a business method implemented in computer form. In Paine Webber Jackson & Curtis, Inc. v. Merrill Lynch, Pierce, Fenner & Smith, Inc., 564 F. Supp. 1358 (D. Del. 1983), the court permitted a similar program to be patented over the objection that it covered a business method. For criticism of the *Paine Webber* case, which the author says allowed the preemption of a broad program idea, see Comment, A Plea for Due Process: Defining the Proper Scope of Patent Protection for Computer Software, 85 Nw. U.L. Rev. 1103 (1991).

2. A number of patents on basic business methods in electronic commerce issued during the late 1990s. These included patents to PriceLine for its system of matching buyers and sellers online (U.S. Pat. No. 5,794,207), to Cybergold for the concept of paying customers to view online ads (U.S. Pat. No. 5,794,210), and to OpenMarket for its online auction system. Other recently issued electronic commerce patents include U.S. Patent No. 5,778,173 (for a method of performing secure purchases on the Web), U.S. Patent No. 5,778,067 (for Mondex's

electronic cash system), and U.S. Patent No. 5,768,385 (for "untraceable electronic cash," patented by Microsoft). Each of these patent applications was filed long before *State Street* was decided, but they are clearly part of a trend towards patenting the new models of electronic commerce.

3. Is the process of playing a musical instrument any less "technological" than the process of implementing a business plan? Does *State Street* suggest that other "inventions" that don't fit easily within traditional technological categories may nonetheless be patentable? Does *State Street* prove that the dissent in *Alappat* was right? For an argument that the door has now been opened to the patenting of all sorts of ideas in the "liberal professions," see John R. Thomas, The Patenting of the Liberal Professions, 40 B.C. L. Rev. 1139 (1999).

Should this expansion be troubling? Is there any reason to patent technological advances but not advances in the liberal arts or professions?

Note on *Musgrave* and the "Technological Arts"

Consider the following passage from Parker v. Flook:

> The rule that the discovery of a law of nature cannot be patented rests, not on the notion that natural phenomena are not processes, but rather on the more fundamental understanding that they are not the kind of "discoveries" that the statute was enacted to protect.

437 U.S. at 593.

Does it follow from this that computer programs, or at least some aspects of them, are not within the class of human "inventions?" An early version of this argument was made in the 1966 Presidential Commission Report on the patent system, entitled To Promote the Progress of Science and the Useful Arts . . . , and in the first set of Patent Office Guidelines on patenting computer programs, 33 Fed. Reg. 15,609 (1968). In one sense it is simply a restatement of the core of the "mental steps" doctrine as applied to software. But in In re Musgrave, 431 F.2d 882 (C.C.P.A. 1970), the CCPA had attempted to make it the cornerstone of patentability in this area. Near the end of the *Musgrave* opinion, which reversed the Patent Office Board of Appeals and upheld the patentability of a process for determining subsurface geological characteristics with computer assistance, the CCPA made the following statement:

> We cannot agree with the board that these claims (all the steps of which can be carried out by the disclosed apparatus) are directed to non-statutory processes merely because some or all the steps therein can also be carried out in or with the aid of the human mind or because it may be necessary for one performing the processes to think. All that is necessary, in our view, to make a sequence of operational steps a statutory "process" within 35 USC §101 is that it be in the technological arts so as to be in consonance with the Constitutional purpose to promote the progress of "useful arts." Const. Art. 1, sec. 8.

The effort to define software patentability according to whether a particular set of claims falls within the "technological arts" has its supporters, most notably Professor Donald Chisum, who wrote that *Musgrave* was "the highwater mark of rationality" in the software patent debate. Chisum, The Future of Software Protection: The Patentability of Algorithms, 47 U. Pitt. L. Rev. 959, 961 (1986). Even so, the technological arts argument was met with immediate skepticism in a concurring opinion by Judge Baldwin in *Musgrave*:

> It seems that whenever a court decides to go beyond what is necessary to decide the case before it, more problems are generated than are solved. I foresee quite a few with the majority's new holding.
>
> First and foremost will be the problem of interpreting the meaning of "technological arts". . . .
>
> Justifying the decision finding claims drawn entirely to purely mental processes to be statutory, the majority states that "[a] step requiring the exercise of subjective judgment without restriction might be objectionable as rendering a claim indefinite." It should not require much imagination to see the many problems sure to be involved in trying to decide whether a step requiring certain human judgment evaluations is definite or not.
>
> As one more example, suppose a claim happens to contain a sequence of operational steps which can reasonably be read to cover a process performable both within and without the technological arts? This is not too far fetched. Would such a claim be statutory? Would it comply with section 112 [on enablement]? We will have to face these problems some day.

415 F.2d at 893-94.

The problems identified by Judge Baldwin are largely the result of the ever-expanding applications of computer programs. One case that illustrates this well is In re Toma, 575 F.2d 872, 877 (C.C.P.A. 1978). Toma's claim was for an algorithm for a computerized natural language translation process. The Patent Office rejected the claim because it was for an algorithm under *Benson* and for a mental process, and because it made a contribution to the liberal, not the technological, arts. Toma's claim, however, was eventually ruled patentable by the CCPA.

Do recent developments suggest a need for some limitation on patentable subject matter based on a distinction between technological and liberal arts? If so, where should the court draw such a line? For a suggestion to demarcate patent and copyright along Cartesian lines of objective versus subjective problems, with implications for software patents, see Allen B. Wagner, Patenting Computer Science: Are Computer Instruction Writings Patentable?, 17 J. Marshall J. Computer & Info. L. 5 (1998).

State Street Bank is widely viewed as a seminal case. There is now a small mountain of commentary on the case, its holding, and particularly what it portends for the patent system. This note captures only a few of the highlights from this growing literature.

Most academics disagreed with the breadth of *State Street*. See, *e.g.*, Rochelle Cooper Dreyfuss, Are Business Method Patents Bad For Business? 16 Santa Clara Computer & High Tech. L.J. 263 (2000); Alan Durham, "Useful Arts" in the Information Age, 1999 B.Y.U. L. Rev. 1419; Leo Raskind, The State Street Bank Decision: The Bad Business of Unlimited Patent Protection for Methods of Doing Business, 10 Fordham Intell. Prop. Media & Ent. L.J. 61 (1999). Others foresaw a flood of new patent applications predicted to reveal latent structural weaknesses in the patent system. Mark D. Janis, Inter Partes Patent Reexamination, 10 Fordham Intell. Prop. Media & Ent. L.J. 481 (2000); Robert P. Merges, As Many as

Six Impossible Patents Before Breakfast: Property Rights for Business Concepts and Patent System Reform, 14 Berkeley Tech. L.J. 577 (1999).

Still others saw *State Street* as an opportunity to examine the foundations of patentable subject matter doctrine in the U.S. These scholars divide into two camps: (1) those who see *State Street* as wrong, and use it to define with greater precision inherent notions of traditional patentable inventions—i.e., "technology"; and (2) those who see *State Street* as a watershed in our expanding conception of what constitutes an economically valuable contribution.

The first group—the "hard technology" school—believes that "traditional" patentable subject matter can be defined and cordoned off from other subject matter such as business methods. Some simply assume this; for example, Professor Rochelle Dreyfuss of NYU Law School argues that:

> The costs of business method patents are very high. The benefits, at least the traditional benefits, are low. The ratio is terrible. The case for patents on business methods is simply not there, at least not in general. . . . State Street now provides the opportunity to tie up . . . knowledge for the future, to privatize it, and prevent it from leaking out to all users.

Dreyfuss, *supra*, 16 Santa Clara Computer & High Tech. L.J. at 276-277 (footnote omitted).

A recent article by John R. Thomas of Georgetown Law School takes a similar tack, but is much more explicit about how to divide patentable from unpatentable subject matter. The key for Thomas is that patents should protect only "technology." John R. Thomas, The Patenting of the Liberal Professions, 40 B.C. L. Rev. 1139 (1999). By clearly defining "technology," Thomas argues, we will have a defensible criterion by which to distinguish what is patentable from what is not. His definition is as follows:

> [T]echnological activities are concerned with the production or transformation of artifacts through the systematic manipulation of physical forces. Bounded by interaction with the external environment, technological activities expend resources and knowledge in order to fabricate or modify products, or to develop procedural systems for so doing. Furthermore, technology presents a form of rational and systematic knowledge, oriented towards efficiency and capable of being assessed through objective criteria.

Id., at 1142. The "hard technologists" can also point to comparative law sources for support: The European Patent Office has long relied on notions such as "industrial use" and "technical effect" to resolve various doctrinal issues. See Note, Brian P. Biddinger, Limiting the Business Method Patent: A Comparison and Proposed Alignment of European, Japanese and United States Patent Law, 69 Fordham L. Rev. 2523 (2001).

On the other side of the debate stands the "soft technology" school. These scholars observe that our economy is increasingly driven by "information." As more of the value in the economy is contributed by software, marketing schemes, and internet trade and communication, they argue that the patent system must adjust. The core of their critique of the "hard technology" school is this: Since patents were adopted in this country to cover the *most valuable* assets of the founding era, our era's patent system must be expanded to cover what is of value *today*. See, e.g., Richard S. Gruner, Intangible Inventions: Patentable Subject Matter for an Information Age, 35 Loy. L.A. L. Rev. 355 (2002). See also Note, Erik S. Maurer, An Economic Justification for a Broad Interpretation of Patentable Subject Matter 95 Nw. U. L. Rev. 1057, 1058 (2001) (arguing that the "wealth-generating characteristics of innovation fundamentally justify a broad interpretation of patentable subject matter").

Thus, one way to view the debate is to ask whether "technology"—the patentable category created, but of course in no way fixed at the nation's founding—is still of paramount importance to the economy, or is for other reasons still deserving of unique legal status. If technology really is special, then the "hard technologists" have a case. Perhaps it is special because it still has distinctive qualities that require property rights to call it forth in the socially optimal amount. Perhaps it is special because it is easier to define and delimit than other value-adding components of the economy. Or perhaps the critics are right—the era is over when plows, axes, guns, and harvesters (and their "hard technology" descendants) make a special contribution to the economy.

This debate is not purely esoteric. One recent case in the Patent Office, for example, explicitly relied on the notion of the "technological arts" in affirming a rejection of claims to a method of creating a chart to represent the value of an asset and plotting points on the chart. After pointing out that the claims were not limited to a computer environment—and hence would cover hand-drawn charts—the Board of Appeals and Interferences noted:

> The phrase "technological arts" has been created to offer another view of the term "useful arts." The Constitution of the United States authorizes and empowers the government to issue patents only for inventions which promote the progress [of science and] the useful arts. We find that the invention before us, as disclosed and claimed, does not promote the progress of science and the useful arts, and does not fall within the definition of technological arts. The abstract idea which forms the heart of the invention before us does not become a technological art merely by the recitation in the claim of "transforming physical media into a chart" [*sic*, drawing or creating a chart] and "physically plotting a point on said chart."

Ex parte Bowman, 61 U.S.P.Q.2d 1669, 1671 (Bd. Pat. App. & Interferences June 12, 2001). See also Ex parte Tsu-Chang Lee, 2000 WL 33741050 (Bd. Pat. App. & Interferences Nov. 30, 2000), at 4 ("From our review of the disclosed and claimed invention and the relevant citation by the examiner . . . we find that the claimed invention is directed to any and every process for evaluating and modifying distances between objects in circuit design using a programmed computer as described throughout the specification . . . [and] we find that this computer-based process has a practical application in the technological arts which produces a 'useful, concrete and tangible result' and is, therefore, directed to statutory subject matter.").

The second practical application of the debate over proper subject matter pertains to the "first inventor" defense of 35 U.S.C. §273. This section makes an exception to general U.S. law in permitting a first inventor who does not file an application to continue using technology claimed in another inventor's later patent application. Section 273(a)(3) limits the defense to inventions claiming a "method of doing or conducting business," so the definition of this category will have immediate practical impact. If the "hard technology" school succeeds in establishing a notion of "traditional" patentable subject matter, perhaps this can be used to define (negatively, as it were) what constitutes nontraditional "business methods."

B. EXAMINATION AND VALIDITY OF SOFTWARE PATENTS

Deciding whether (and under what circumstances) computer programs qualify as patentable subject matter is only the first hurdle in obtaining a software patent. A valid patent must pass four other tests in examination in the Patent Office: it must be useful (35 U.S.C. §101), novel (35 U.S.C. §102), nonobvious (35 U.S.C. §103), and clearly described in the patent application (35 U.S.C. §112 ¶1). Utility is not a particularly strict test; most computer programs that work will meet it easily. But each of the other steps in the patent examination process presents unique issues in the software context. With §101 issues mostly behind us, these will increasingly be the important issues in the future.

1. Novelty and Nonobviousness

Netscape Communications Corp. v. Konrad
United States Court of Appeals for the Federal Circuit
295 F.3d 1315 (Fed. Cir. 2002)

MAYER, Chief Judge.

Allan M. Konrad appeals from the judgment of the United States District Court for the Northern District of California granting Netscape Communications Corp., Microsoft Corp., and America Online, Inc. ("Netscape") summary judgment that U.S. Patent Nos. 5,544,320 (the "'320 patent"), 5,696,901 (the "'901 patent"), and 5,974,444 (the "'444 patent") are invalid under the public use and on-sale bars of 35 U.S.C. §102(b). Because we agree with the district court that Konrad has not raised a genuine issue as to any material fact pertaining to pre-critical date demonstrations, public uses by others, and his commercial offer to create the high energy physics remote database object, we affirm.

Background

Konrad is the owner of the '320, '901, and '444 patents, all directed to systems that allow a computer user to access and search a database residing on a remote computer. He began working as a staff scientist for the Lawrence Berkeley Laboratory in 1977, where he studied how an individual computer workstation user could obtain services from a remote computer. On September 26, 1990, while working with Cynthia Hertzer, a Lawrence Berkeley Laboratory staff assistant, Konrad successfully tested the remote database object system. The first prototype of this system was configured to access Lawrence Berkeley Laboratory's STAFF database from a remote workstation. The Lawrence Berkeley Laboratory STAFF database resided on an IBM mainframe computer on the Berkeley campus of the University of California. A local starter portion of the remote database object system prototype was created for installation on users' personal computers to allow the display of an icon by which the user could access the remote database. In 1991, Konrad and Hertzer adapted the Lawrence Berkeley Laboratory STAFF remote database object system prototype for the high energy physics data-base, maintained at the Stanford Linear Accelerator Center, which is a national laboratory operated by Stanford University. The high energy physics database was a compilation of abstracts and technical papers used as a research tool for physicists worldwide.

The '320 patent, Konrad's first issued patent, is a continuation of an application filed on January 8, 1993. The '901 patent is a continuation of the '444 patent application, which is a continuation of the '320 patent application. Thus, the earliest filing date that Konrad is entitled to is January 8, 1993, making the critical date for the public use and on-sale inquiry January 8, 1992.

[In an infringement dispute,] Netscape moved for partial summary judgment that prototypes of the invention were in public use or on-sale under 35 U.S.C. §102(b) based on Konrad's activities prior to January 8, 1992. The California district court entered partial summary judgment for Netscape concluding that: (1) Konrad's demonstration of the claimed invention to Shuli Roth and Dick Peters, University of California computing personnel, without any obligation of confidentiality was a public use; (2) his demonstration of the high energy physics remote database object to the Stanford Linear Accelerator Center in conjunction with the use of the remote database object by University Research Association Superconducting Super Collider Laboratory employees was a public use; and (3) his offer to create the high energy physics remote database object system for the University Research Association Superconducting Super Collider Laboratory in exchange for four months full-time employment or no more than $48,000, and his stipulation that the reduction to practice of the invention occurred prior to that event, satisfied the on-sale bar. Konrad stipulated that all of the claims of the patents in suit would be invalid if the court were to find that his activities qualified as prior art. In view of this stipulation, on June 18, 2001, the district court entered the parties' joint stipulation for final judgment on invalidity.

Discussion

Under 35 U.S.C. §102(b), "[a] person shall be entitled to a patent unless . . . the invention was in public use or on sale in this country, more than one year prior to the date of the application for patent in the United States. . . ." 35 U.S.C. §102(b) (2000). Whether a patent is invalid for a public use or sale is a question of law based on underlying facts. A conclusion that a section 102(b) bar invalidates a patent must be based on clear and convincing evidence.

I.

Public use includes "any use of [the claimed] invention by a person other than the inventor who is under no limitation, restriction or obligation of secrecy to the inventor." Petrolite Corp. v. Baker Hughes Inc., 96 F.3d 1423, 1425

(Fed.Cir. 1996) "The public use bar serves the policies of the patent system, for it encourages prompt filing of patent applications after inventions have been completed and publicly used, and sets an outer limit to the term of exclusivity." Allied Colloids v. Am. Cyanamid Co., 64 F.3d 1570, 1574 (Fed.Cir. 1995).

The law recognizes that an inventor may test his invention in public without incurring the public use bar. "Experimental use negates public use; when proved, it may show that particular acts, even if apparently public in a colloquial sense, do not constitute a public use within the meaning of section 102." Baxter Int'l, Inc. v. Cobe Labs., Inc., 88 F.3d 1054, 1059 (Fed.Cir. 1996). "The use of an invention by the inventor himself, or of any other person under his direction, by way of experiment, and in order to bring the invention to perfection, has never been regarded as such a use." City of Elizabeth v. Am. Nicholson Pavement Co., 97 U.S. 126, 134 (1877).

We look to the totality of the circumstances when evaluating whether there has been a public use within the meaning of section 102(b). The totality of the circumstances is considered in conjunction with the policies underlying the public use bar. The circumstances may include: the nature of the activity that occurred in public; the public access to and knowledge of the public use; whether there was any confidentiality obligation imposed on persons who observed the use; whether persons other than the inventor performed the testing; the number of tests; the length of the test period in relation to tests of similar devices; and whether the inventor received payment for the testing.

A.

Konrad argues that the district court erred in determining that his 1991 demonstration of the Lawrence Berkeley Laboratory STAFF remote database object to University of California computing personnel was an invalidating public use. He maintains that the invention disclosure he submitted to the Lawrence Berkeley Laboratory patent department in October of 1990, established an expectation of confidentiality from Roth and Peters. Netscape responds that the district court correctly determined that Konrad failed to establish a genuine issue of material fact that the demonstrated prototype was not in public use, and was prior art for the purpose of evaluating the validity of the patents in suit.

We agree with Netscape. Konrad did not show that Roth or Peters were ever made aware of any requirement of confidentiality or even apprised of the invention disclosure forms that he submitted to the Lawrence Berkeley Laboratory patent department. He also did not make any discernable effort to inform the 1991 demonstration attendees of the requirement of confidentiality, or otherwise indicate to them that they would owe him a duty of confidentiality.

"In some circumstances, . . . it would be significant that no pledge of confidentiality was obtained from the user." TP Labs., Inc. [v. Prof'l Positioners, Inc.], 724 F.2d [965 (Fed. Cir. 1984)] at 972. Lack of a confidentiality agreement is significant here because Roth and Peters were computer personnel who could easily demonstrate the invention to others.

Next, Konrad argues that the 1991 demonstration was not a public use because he did not disclose every limitation of his invention, particularly the starter client of the remote database object, to Roth and Peters. We are not persuaded. Section 102(b) may bar patentability by anticipation if the device used in public includes every limitation of the later claimed invention, or by obviousness if the differences between the claimed invention and the device used would have been obvious to one of ordinary skill in the art. See Lough v. Brunswick Corp., 86 F.3d 1113, 1122 n. 5 (Fed.Cir. 1996). Konrad testified that he demonstrated a remote object client and that the only difference between it and the remote database object was initialization by a starter client. He further testified that his use of a computer keyboard to initiate the remote database object could have been accomplished by clicking a mouse pointer on a starter client icon on a computer screen. Based on this testimony, the starter client is very similar to, if not the same as, software program icons created to quickly initiate a program. The difference between the claimed invention and the device used would have been obvious to persons of ordinary skill in the art.

Konrad also argues that the 1991 demonstration was an experimental use for the purpose of obtaining technical support to incorporate upgrades and make the invention run more smoothly. To establish that an otherwise public use does not run afoul of section 102(b), it must be shown that the activity was "substantially for purposes of experiment." Baker Oil Tools, Inc. [v. Geo Vann, Inc.,] 828 F.2d [1558 (Fed. Cir. 1987)], at 1564. Konrad presented no objective evidence to support experimental use. Indeed, his testimony leads to the opposite conclusion. He said that the purpose of the demonstration "was to convince the people in the Berkeley computer center VM systems group that there was a viable project." He added that he hoped showing them the remote database object would make them supportive of it. Konrad's demonstration was geared more toward making the remote database object more commercially attractive, with endorsements from outside technical people, than for experimental use purposes. The experimental use negation is unavailable to a patentee when the evidence presented does not establish that he was conducting a bona fide experiment. *TP Labs., Inc.,* 724 F.2d at 969. Furthermore, Konrad presented no objective evidence that he maintained any records of testing the remote database object. This failure weighs against him. *Allied Colloids,* 64 F.3d at 1576; *TP Labs., Inc.,* 724 F.2d at 972-73 (recognizing that whether records were kept of progress may indicate that an inventor was testing the device, not the market).

Konrad also argues that at all relevant times he took affirmative steps to maintain control of his invention and questions the substantiality of the evidence to the contrary. He asserts that Moleculon Research Corp. v. CBS, Inc., 793 F.2d 1261 (Fed.Cir. 1986), applies here. That case said that the display of a device to friends and colleagues of the inventor was subject to an implied restriction of confidentiality, and thus did not constitute a public use. However, that inventor always retained control over the use of the device as well as over the distribution of information concerning it. *Id.* at 1266. Here, Konrad testified that during 1991 he did not monitor tests of the remote database object, but that he would simply turn on the system and let people try it out. He further testified that he was aware that a workstation was made available to use the remote database object system, but was unaware of where it was located. There was no indication that he ever monitored this workstation's use or imposed a confidentiality agreement on those persons exercising the database.

B.

Konrad argues that the district court erred in determining that the demonstration of the high energy physics remote database object system to Stanford Linear Accelerator Center and use by University Research Association Superconducting Super Collider Laboratory employees were invalidating public uses under section 102(b). He contends that the Department of Energy owned all of the intellectual property rights to the invention, and that all Department of Energy laboratory employees were under an obligation of confidentiality to the government during all demonstrations and testing. To support this contention, Konrad relies on the testimony of Paul Martin concerning the invention disclosure rules of Lawrence Berkeley Laboratory, and the contract between Lawrence Berkeley Laboratory and the Department of Energy. Konrad also relies on the testimony of Louise Addis, a librarian at Stanford Linear Accelerator Center, to support his position that he maintained control over his invention through the use of passwords.

Konrad tries to cloak his failure to protect the confidentiality of his invention and maintain control of others use by arguing that because the Department of Energy was providing the funding for his project, it ultimately owned the invention; therefore, anyone working on the remote database object server was subject to Department of Energy confidentiality. This argument is without merit. Konrad is the inventor of the patents; the limitation, restriction, or obligation of secrecy of others using the invention is owed to him, not the persons or entities providing the funding. See Egbert v. Lippmann, 104 U.S. 333, 336, 26 L. Ed. 755 (1881). The onus is on him, as the inventor, to protect the confidentiality of his invention and its use by others before the critical date. The contract between Lawrence Berkeley Laboratory and the Department of Energy provides for the protection of government property, the University of California's duty to safeguard restricted data and provide written disclosures, and the government's right to duplicate and disclose the subject invention. Moreover, Konrad has not shown that this contract applied to the University Research Association Superconducting Super Collider Laboratory or Stanford Linear Accelerator Center employees.

Konrad says that the demonstration of the high energy physics remote database object system at the Stanford Linear Accelerator Center was not enabling because there was no evidence that the source code was delivered to the Superconducting Super Collider Laboratory before the critical date. However, it is the claims that define a patented invention. As we have already said, Konrad's failure to monitor the use of his remote database object system, and failure to impose confidentiality agreements on those that used it was enough to place the claimed features of the patents in the public's possession. Lockwood v. American Airlines, 107 F.3d 1565, 1570 (Fed.Cir. 1997). Konrad cannot negate this by evidence showing that other, unclaimed aspects, such as the source code, was not publicly available.

II.

The on-sale bar applies when the invention is the subject of a commercial offer for sale, and is ready for patenting before the critical date. Pfaff v. Wells Electronics, Inc., 525 U.S. 55, 67 (1998). The ready for patenting condition "may be satisfied in at least two ways: by proof of reduction to practice before the critical date; or by proof that prior to the critical date the inventor had prepared drawings or other descriptions of the invention that were sufficiently specific to enable a person skilled in the art to practice the invention." *Id.* at 67-68. The overriding concern of the on-sale bar is an inventor's attempt to commercialize his invention beyond the statutory term. STX, LLC v. Brine, Inc., 211 F.3d 588, 590 (Fed.Cir. 2000). When the asserted basis of invalidity is an on-sale bar, the court should determine "whether the subject of the barring activity met each of the limitations of the claim, and thus was an embodiment of the claimed invention." Scaltech Inc. v. Retec/Tetra, L.L.C., 178 F.3d 1378, 1383, 51 USPQ2d 1055, 1058 (Fed.Cir. 1999). "Only an offer which rises to the level of a commercial offer for sale, one which the other party could make into a binding contract by simple acceptance (assuming consideration), constitutes an offer for sale under [section] 102(b)." Group One, Ltd. v. Hallmark Cards, Inc., 254 F.3d 1041, 1048, 59 USPQ2d 1121, 1126 (Fed.Cir. 2001). To determine if the offer is sufficiently definite, one must examine the language of the proposal in accordance with the principles of general contract law. See *id.*

Konrad primarily argues that the court erroneously concluded that his offer to make the high energy physics remote database object for the University Research Association Superconducting Super Collider Laboratory in exchange for four months full time employment or no more than $48,000 constituted a commercial offer for sale. He contends that the memorandum purchase order memorializing the agreement is not a contract, but merely an accounting instrument used to track the transfer of research funds between two Department of Energy laboratories, and therefore did not involve the sale of a commercial embodiment of the invention.

Netscape responds that the memorandum purchase order is only one of the contemporaneous documents relied on by the district court in its analysis of whether Konrad's offer was within the purview of the on-sale bar of section 102(b). It contends that the memorandum purchase order is an offer to sell a working prototype of the remote database object to the Stanford Linear Accelerator Center and qualifies as such by listing the product to be purchased, the delivery date, and the price. The district court observed that Konrad had extended commercial offers for the sale of the remote database object prototype to the University Research Association Superconducting Super Collider Laboratory in September of 1991. The court also determined that he failed to establish a genuine issue of material fact that the commercial offer between Lawrence Berkeley Laboratory and University Research Association Superconducting Super Collider Laboratory involved two Department of Energy controlled entities.

The evidence on summary judgment evinces that the memorandum purchase order memorialized Konrad's proposal, which was accepted by Lawrence Berkeley Laboratory subject to revisions, to provide a working prototype of a remote database object configured to support the high energy physics database at Stanford Linear Accelerator Center for $48,000. But, we have held that a sale or offer to sell under section 102(b) must be between two separate entities. In re Caveney, 761 F.2d 671, 676, 226 USPQ 1, 4 (Fed.Cir. 1985). Where, as in this case, both parties to an alleged commercial offer for sale receive research funds from the same entity, it may be more difficult to determine whether the inventor is attempting to commercialize his invention. Accordingly, in such cases whether there is a bar depends on whether the seller so controls the purchaser that the invention remains out of the public's hands. Ferag v. Quipp, Inc., 45 F.3d 1562, 1567, 33 USPQ2d 1512, 1515 (Fed.Cir. 1995) (citing In re Caveney, 761 F.2d at 676, 226 USPQ at 4). All indications are that the Department of Energy funded specific projects of Lawrence Berkeley Laboratory, the Superconducting Super Collider Laboratory, and Stanford Linear Accelerator Center, but never exercised such control over them, as to render all part of the same entity. Therefore, the first condition of the on-sale bar is satisfied because this transaction constituted an offer from the University Research Association Superconducting Super Collider Laboratory for the sale of the remote database object prototype that was accepted by Lawrence Berkeley Laboratory.

The only remaining question is whether the invention was ready for patenting at the time of the offer for sale. Konrad admitted that the reduction to practice date was on or about September 26, 1990, before the critical date, and his disclosure of the remote database object to Roth and Peters in October of 1990 was sufficiently specific to enable them, as persons of ordinary skill in the art, to practice the invention. Therefore, all the claims of the '320, '901, and '444 patents are invalid under the on-sale bar of section 102(b).

Conclusion

Accordingly, the judgment of the United States District Court for the Northern District of California is affirmed.

COMMENTS AND QUESTIONS

1. Imagine a lawsuit between a patentee, call it Company A, and an accused infringer such as Netscape. What if Konrad's program had been asserted as prior art by Netscape in an effort to defeat the validity of the Company A patent? Would Netscape win? How easy would it be for Netscape to discover a third-party piece of software? See Section B.2, *infra*.

2. Under what circumstances can software that is publicly distributed only in object code form trigger the "on-sale" bar of 35 U.S.C. section 102(b)? Recall from Chapter 1 that software vendors can successfully maintain their programs as trade secrets under certain circumstances by distributing them only as object code, even though they are widely used. While one might argue that the patented invention was not disclosed to the public by such distribution, the Federal Circuit has foreclosed this defense. In In re Epstein, 32 F.3d 1559 (Fed. Cir. 1994), the court held that section 102(b) did not require that an invention be disclosed to trigger the bar—just that it be on sale. And as the Supreme Court made clear recently, an invention doesn't even have to be finished to be put on sale. See Pfaff v. Wells Electronics, 525 U.S. 55 (1998).

Even if the distribution of the product itself does not bar a patent more than one year afterwards, the dissemination of product marketing literature may do so if it discloses the advances claimed in the patent. See Constant v. Advanced Micro Devices, 848 F.2d 1560 (Fed. Cir. 1988).

Lockwood v. American Airlines, Inc.
United States Court of Appeals for the Federal Circuit
107 F.3d 1565 (Fed. Cir. 1997)

LOURIE, Circuit Judge.

Lawrence B. Lockwood appeals from the final judgment of the United States District Court for the Southern District of California, Lockwood v. American Airlines, Inc., No. 91-1640E (CM) (S.D.Cal. Dec. 19, 1995), granting summary judgment in favor of American Airlines, Inc. In that summary judgment, the court held that (1) U.S. Patent Re. 32,115, U.S. Patent 4,567,359, and U.S. Patent 5,309,355 were not infringed by American's SABREvision reservation system, and that (2) the '355 patent and the asserted claims of the '359 patent were invalid under 35 U.S.C. §102 and 35 U.S.C. §103, respectively. Lockwood v. American Airlines, Inc., 834 F. Supp. 1246, 28 USPQ2d 1114 (S.D.Cal. 1993), *req. for reconsideration denied*, 847 F. Supp. 777 (S.D.Cal. 1994) (holding the '115 and '359 patents not infringed); Lockwood v. American Airlines, Inc., 877 F. Supp. 500, 34 USPQ2d 1290 (S.D.Cal. 1994) (holding the asserted claims of the '355 patent invalid and not infringed); Lockwood v. American Airlines, Inc., 37 USPQ2d 1534, 1995 WL 822659 (S.D.Cal. 1995) (holding the '359 patent invalid). Because the district court correctly determined that there were no genuine issues of material fact in dispute and that American was entitled to judgment as a matter of law, we affirm.

Background

The pertinent facts are not in dispute. Lockwood owns the '115, '355, and '359 patents, all of which relate to automated interactive sales terminals that provide sales presentations to customers and allow the customers to order goods and services. Lockwood sued American asserting that American's SABREvision airline reservation system infringed all three patents. SABREvision is used by travel agents to access schedule and fare information, to book itineraries, and to retrieve photographs of places of interest, including hotels, restaurants, and cruises, for display to consumers. It improves upon American's SABRE reservation system, which originated in the 1960s and which cannot display photographs. . . .

The '359 patent discloses a system of multiple interactive self-service terminals that provide audio-visual sales presentations and dispense goods and services from multiple institutions. Claim 1, the only independent claim, reads in pertinent part:

> A system for automatically dispensing information, goods, and services for a plurality of institutions in a particular industry, comprising: . . .
> > at least one customer sales and information terminal . . .
> . . . said sales and information terminal including:
> > audio-visual means for interaction with a customer, comprising:
> > > means for storing a sequence of audio and video information to be selectively transmitted to a customer;
> > > means for transmitting a selected sequence of said stored information to the customer; customer operated input means for gathering information from a customer. . . .

The district court held that SABREvision did not infringe the '359 patent because it lacked the "audio-visual means" and "customer operated input means." The court also held the '359 patent invalid because it would have been obvious in light of the original SABRE system in combination with the self-service terminal disclosed in U.S. Patent 4,359,631, which issued in 1982 and was subsequently reissued as the '115 patent. . . .

Discussion . . .

A. *Validity*

The district court held that the asserted claims of the '359 patent would have been obvious in light of the prior art '631 patent and the original SABRE system. A determination of obviousness under 35 U.S.C. §103 is a legal conclusion involving factual inquiries. Uniroyal, Inc. v. Rudkin-Wiley Corp., 837 F.2d 1044, 1050, 5 USPQ2d 1434, 1438 (Fed.Cir. 1988). Lockwood argues that the subject matter of the '359 claims would not have been obvious and that the district court impermissibly drew adverse factual inferences in concluding that the patent was invalid. Lockwood first argues that the district court erred in concluding that the SABRE system qualified as prior art.

American submitted an affidavit averring that the SABRE system was introduced to the public in 1962, had over one thousand connected sales desks by 1965, and was connected to the reservation systems for most of the other airlines by 1970. Lockwood does not dispute these facts, but argues that because "critical aspects" of the SABRE system were not accessible to the public, it could not have been prior art. American's expert conceded that the essential algorithms of the SABRE software were proprietary and confidential and that those aspects of the system that were readily apparent to the public would not have been sufficient to enable one skilled in the art to duplicate the system. However, American responds that the public need not have access to the "inner workings" of a device for it to be considered "in public use" or "used by others" within the meaning of the statute.

We agree with American that those aspects of the original SABRE system relied on by the district court are prior art to the '359 patent. The district court held that SABRE, which made and confirmed reservations with multiple institutions (e.g., airlines, hotels, and car rental agencies), combined with the terminal of the '631 patent rendered the asserted claims of the '359 patent obvious. The terminal of the '631 patent admittedly lacked this "multiple institution" feature. It is undisputed, however, that the public was aware that SABRE possessed this capability and that the public had been using SABRE to make travel reservations from independent travel agencies prior to Lockwood's date of invention.

If a device was "known or used by others" in this country before the date of invention or if it was "in public use" in this country more than one year before the date of application, it qualifies as prior art. See 35 U.S.C. §102(a) and (b) (1994). Lockwood attempts to preclude summary judgment by pointing to record testimony that one skilled in the art would not be able to build and practice the claimed invention without access to the secret aspects of SABRE. However, it is the claims that define a patented invention. See Constant v. Advanced Micro-

Devices, Inc., 848 F.2d 1560, 1571, 7 USPQ2d 1057, 1064 (Fed.Cir. 1988). As we have concluded earlier in this opinion, American's public use of the high-level aspects of the SABRE system was enough to place the claimed features of the '359 patent in the public's possession. See In re Epstein, 32 F.3d 1559, 1567-68, 31 USPQ2d 1817, 1823 (Fed.Cir. 1994) ("Beyond this 'in public use or on sale' finding, there is no requirement for an enablement-type inquiry."). Lockwood cannot negate this by evidence showing that other, unclaimed aspects of the SABRE system were not publicly available. Moreover, the '359 patent itself does not disclose the level of detail that Lockwood would have us require of the prior art. For these reasons, Lockwood fails to show a genuine issue of material fact precluding summary judgment.

Lockwood further argues that even if the SABRE system is effective prior art, the combination of that system and the '631 patent would not have yielded the invention of the '359 patent. The terminal in the claims of the '359 patent includes a number of means-plus-function limitations, subject to 35 U.S.C. §112, ¶6, including "means for gathering information from a customer" and "means for storing a sequence of audio and video information to be selectively transmitted to a customer." Means-plus-function clauses are construed "as limited to the corresponding structure[s] disclosed in the specification and equivalents thereof." In re Donaldson Co., 16 F.3d 1189, 1195, 29 USPQ2d 1845, 1850 (Fed.Cir. 1994) (in banc); see 35 U.S.C. §112, ¶6 (1994). Lockwood argues that the structures disclosed in the '359 patent differ substantially from the terminal disclosed in the '631 patent and that, at the very least, his expert's declaration raised genuine issues of material fact sufficient to preclude summary judgment.

We do not agree. We believe that American has met its burden, even in light of the presumption of patent validity, to show that the means limitations relating to the terminal in the claims of the '359 patent appear in the '631 specification. Lockwood has failed to respond by setting forth specific facts that would raise a genuine issue for trial. Specifically, Lockwood has not alleged that the '631 disclosure lacks the structures disclosed in the '359 patent specification or their equivalents. As the district court noted, Lockwood's expert, Dr. Tuthill, relied on structures that are not mentioned in either the '631 or the '359 patents. For example, Tuthill states that the claimed invention differs from the '631 patent because the terminal described in the '631 patent uses a "backward-chaining" system to solve problems while the '359 patent uses a "forward-chaining" system. Yet neither the '359 nor the '631 patents mentions backward- or forward-chaining. Nor does the '359 specification describe any hardware or software structure as being limited to any particular problem-solving technique. In addition, Lockwood argues that the hardware and software disclosed in the two patents are not equivalent to each other. However, the '359 patent claims the hardware and software in broad terms, and the patents both describe similar computer controlled self-service terminals employing video disk players that store and retrieve audio-visual information. For example, with regard to the "means for controlling said storage and transmitting means," Lockwood's expert avers that the "structure described in the '359 patent which corresponds to this means is the processor unit and the application program which the processor executes." Yet, the only software descriptions in the '359 patent consist of high level exemplary functional flowcharts. Lockwood's arguments and his expert's statements are thus conclusory. They fail to identify which structures in the '359 patent are thought to be missing from the '631 patent disclosure. Accordingly, we agree with the district court that Lockwood's and his expert's declarations have not adequately responded to American's motion by raising genuine issues of material fact, and we therefore conclude that the district court properly held the asserted claims of the '359 patent to have been obvious as a matter of law. . . .

Affirmed.

COMMENTS AND QUESTIONS

1. The court holds that the SABRE system was "known or used by others" before the critical date of the '359 patent. But is affirmatively secret use sufficient to constitute prior art? Has the public really "known or used" the invention if they are prevented from seeing how it works or duplicating it? Does it matter whether American protected the SABRE system as a trade secret during the 1960s? In patent law, the answer appears to depend on whether the use was nominally open to the public, even if as a practical matter it was impossible for the public to find out about it. If it was open, it was in public use; if not, it does not constitute prior art. See, e.g., Rosaire v. National Lead Co., 218 F.2d 72 (5th Cir. 1955) (work done "openly" constituted prior art, even if it was done underground on private property); National Tractor Pullers Ass'n v. Watkins, 205 U.S.P.Q. 892 (N.D. Ill. 1980) (prior knowledge must be "reasonably accessible" to the public). For discussion of a related issue, "concealment" under 35 U.S.C. section 102(g), see the Note on §102(g), *infra*.

2. The court notes that Lockwood has not disclosed much more structural detail in his patent specification than the prior art '631 patent, and therefore cannot claim to have differentiated his invention from that prior patent. Does this holding improperly conflate the enablement requirement and the test for obviousness? Recent cases have begun to apply §103 to software inventions on a routine basis. See, e.g., Ex parte Huang, 2002 WL 1801547 (Bd. Pat. App & Interf. 2002) (reaffirming examiner's statements that algorithm claims are directed to statutory subject matter, and reversing the final rejection on obviousness grounds).

3. Is a design alternative that accomplishes the same goal as a prior program, but does so in a different way, necessarily obvious? Or should programmers be entitled to patent their new designs that accomplish well-known goals?

A related question is the relevance of how competitors in the industry have addressed the same problem. For example, it is not uncommon in the software industry for many companies to come up with the same invention at roughly the same time. See, e.g., John Kasdan, Obviousness and New Technologies (working paper 1999) (noting that in one software spreadsheet case, Refac Int'l v. Lotus Dev. Corp., 15 U.S.P.Q.2d 1747 (S.D.N.Y. 1990), every company in the industry had independently come to the same conclusion that the plaintiff patented). Should such simultaneous invention be evidence of obviousness? On this point, compare In re Merck & Co., 800 F.2d 1091, 1098 (Fed. Cir. 1986) (simultaneous invention can be evidence of obviousness), with Hybritech v. Monoclonal Antibodies, 802 F.2d 1367, n.2 (Fed. Cir. 1986) (simultaneous invention is not evidence of obviousness).

4. Some argue that prior art in this particular industry may be difficult or, in some cases, impossible to find because of the nature of the software business. As Julie Cohen explains:

> [I]n the field of computers and computer programs, much that qualifies as prior art lies outside the areas in which the PTO has traditionally looked—previously issued patents and previous scholarly publications. Many new developments in computer programming are not documented in scholarly publications at all. Some are simply incorporated into products and placed on the market; others are discussed only in textbooks or user manuals that are not available to examiners on line. In an area that relies so heavily on published, "official" prior art, a rejection based on "common industry knowledge" that does not appear in the scholarly literature is unlikely. Particularly where the examiner lacks a computer science background, highly relevant prior art may simply be missed. In the case of the multimedia data retrieval patent granted to Compton's New Media,[1] industry criticism prompted the PTO to reexamine the patent and ultimately to reject it because it did not represent a novel and nonobvious advance over existing technology. However, it would be inefficient, and probably impracticable, to reexamine every computer program-related patent, and the PTO is unlikely to do so.

Julie E. Cohen, Reverse Engineering and the Rise of Electronic Vigilantism: Intellectual Property Implications of "Lock-Out" Technologies, 68 S. Cal. L. Rev. 1091, 1179 (1995). The current PTO Examination Guidelines for Computer-Related Inventions direct that examiners must "conduct a thorough search of the prior art," but they give no indication of how to accomplish that task.

Do the problems discovering software prior art suggest that the Patent Office should be more cautious about granting inventions in this industry than in other technologies? If not, what should be done about this problem? For an ongoing critique of the quality of software patents, visit www.bustpatents.com, a Web site run by Greg Ahoronian, an outspoken critic of and consultant on software prior art issues.

Note on Obviousness and
Computer-Implemented Inventions

It is not enough that an applicant for a patent simply invent something new. To qualify for patent protection, the new invention must also show an "inventive leap" over the prior art—it must not be merely obvious to one skilled in the art. 35 U.S.C. §103. Application of the nonobviousness standard is never easy, because it requires examiners and courts to make a judgment call regarding what would have been considered obvious to scientists in the field at the time the invention was made. But as Professor Cohen points out, determining obviousness is

---

1. Compton's received a patent on an application filed in the late 1980s which purported to cover basic use of hypertext. When Compton's announced the existence of the patent at a computer trade show, and offered everyone in the multimedia industry a chance to license it, public outrage prompted the PTO to initiate a reexamination proceeding sua sponte. The PTO rejected the application after considering a number of prior art references submitted by third parties. [— EDS.]

particularly problematic in the case of inventions that use a computer to solve problems outside the field of programming itself:

> Intuitively, the most troubling aspect of many computer program-related patents is that they appear to reward the inventor for recognizing the obvious—that a given function may be performed more efficiently or more accurately if computerized—and using general purpose computer equipment and standard programming techniques to computerize it. Other computer program-related patents simply reward the programmer for developing otherwise unpatentable mathematical formulas. . . .
>
> In response to *Iwahashi*, Richard Stern, former chief of the Department of Justice's Intellectual Property Section, proposed reconceiving the standard for nonobviousness for computer program-related inventions. His solution, which may be termed the "innovative programmer" standard, adds a third step to the *Freeman-Walter-Abele* test. If a claimed invention recites a mathematical algorithm, but appears to be statutory subject matter when taken as a whole, the examiner must ask whether the claimed invention would have been obvious to "a person of ordinary skill . . . who: (a) knew the particular algorithm; (b) desired to accomplish the function or task to be performed; and (c) desired to do so with the aid of a computer. . . ." If not, it is nonobvious, and so patentable. By taking general purpose computer equipment and the mathematical algorithm as part of the prior art for purposes of assessing nonobviousness, the innovative programmer standard is intended to avoid [granting patents to the first person to implement a known physical process on a computer, regardless of how straightforward that implementation might be].

Cohen, *supra,* at 1170. *Accord* Vincent Chiappetta, Patentability of Computer Software Instruction as an "Article of Manufacture": Software as Such as the Right Stuff, 17 J. Marshall J. Computer & Info. L. 89, 169-70 (1998). Does the Stern-Cohen proposal make sense? Is it consistent with patent law outside the computer context, or would it require the creation of a new, higher standard of examination specific to computer-implemented inventions? See Mark A. Lemley & David W. O'Brien, Encouraging Software Reuse, 49 Stan. L. Rev. 255 (1997) (suggesting that patent law is too lenient to inventions of the form "*A*, a known entity, plus *B*, a known entity," and that this explains many of the bad software patents currently in force).

The first case involving the obviousness of a software-implemented invention is, perhaps surprisingly, a Supreme Court case from the 1970s. In Dann v. Johnston, 425 U.S. 219 (1976), the Court held a patent on a "machine system for automatic record-keeping of bank checks and deposits" invalid for obviousness. The Court took a rather broad view of obviousness in the computer industry, focusing on whether systems analogous to the patentee's had been implemented in computers before, rather than analyzing the precise differences between the patentee's program and the prior art programs. The clear implication of the opinion is that if a reasonably skilled programmer could produce a program analogous to the patented one, and if there was motivation in the prior art to do so, the patented program is obvious.

On the other hand, the Federal Circuit in In re Zurko, 111 F.3d 887 (Fed. Cir. 1997), held that a patented invention was nonobvious even though each of the elements of the invention could be found in the prior art where the prior art did not identify the problem to be solved. This offers another outlet for patentees: they can focus their invention on solving a previously unknown problem rather than on the particular elements of their solution.

2. Section 102(g), the Software Industry, and Prior User Rights

Section 102(g) of the Patent Act renders a patent invalid if the claimed invention was invented by someone else first. Subsection (g)(1) applies to interferences —priority contests between rival patentees/applicants for patent. Subsection (g)(2) is a general defense: It permits a patent examiner or one accused of infringement to prove that someone else in the U.S. invented the claimed invention before the patentee/applicant for patent's invention date. Section 102(g) reads (emphasis added):

> (g)(1) during the course of an interference . . . , another inventor involved therein establishes, to the extent permitted in section 104 . . . that before such person's invention thereof the invention was made by such other inventor and not abandoned, suppressed, or concealed, or (2) before such person's invention thereof, the invention was made in this country by another inventor *who had not abandoned, suppressed, or concealed it.* In determining priority of invention under this subsection, there shall be considered not only the respective dates of conception and reduction to practice of the invention, but also the reasonable diligence of one who was first to conceive and last to reduce to practice, from a time prior to conception by the other.

The phrase in §102(g)(2) that raised concerns for the software industry was "abandoned, suppressed, or concealed." The issue was whether computer software that was kept as a trade secret would be deemed "abandoned" under §102(g)(2). Trade secret protection has been important in the software industry, particularly during its formative years. As a consequence of section 102(g) and the growing importance of patents in this industry, some commentators expressed concern that software creators who keep their software as trade secrets could wind up having to license a later inventor of the same software, or even being forced to stop using their software altogether. See Albert C. Smith & Jared A. Slosberg, Beware! Trade Secret Software May Be Patented by a Later Inventor, 7 Computer Law. 15 (1990); Gates, Trade Secret Software: Is It Prior Art?, 6 Computer Law. 11 (1989). This results from the argument that exploiting an invention by treating it as a trade secret can amount to concealment under section 102(g). If so, the concealed invention cannot be offered as prior art to bar a different, later inventor from patenting the same invention!

In the era after *Benson*, this was not much of a threat because patents for software were generally not available. Now, however, software is clearly patentable, whether or not it is defined in physical terms. The result: Later inventors may possibly leapfrog over earlier inventors of the same software. This follows from section 102(g), which not only makes it impossible for the first inventor to obtain a patent because of their delay, but also (in (g)(2)) directs the Patent Office and courts to disregard the first inventor's secret use when evaluating the validity of the second inventor's patent. In short, the combination of the section 102(g) rule and the growing role of patents creates the possibility of a serious threat to established software vendors who have been relying on trade secret protection for a long time. In some such cases, the second inventor will have in effect barred the first inventor from using her own invention. This is so even if—indeed, *especially* if—the first inventor invented long before the second.

On the other hand, in those cases where the first inventor's actions are not deemed intentional, or her delay in filing for a patent is not deemed excessive, her invention will defeat the novelty of the second inventor's patent application due to section 102(g). Judge Learned Hand of the Second Circuit delivered an important opinion on the issue of prior invention in Gillman v. Stern, 114 F.2d 28 (2d Cir. 1940). The court held that a completed invention will be deemed abandoned, suppressed, or concealed if no steps are taken to make the invention publicly known within a reasonable time. The inventor in *Gillman* kept his invention completely secret from the outside world, which included his employees and his wife. The court held that such a secret invention could not be used as prior art against the patent of a subsequent inventor. An important point regarding *Gillman* is that the invention at issue was a pneumatic "puffing" machine used for quilting. Only the *output* of the machine—the products it produced—was offered for sale; the machine itself "was always kept as strictly secret as possible, consistently with its exploitation." 114 F.2d at 30. Thus, even though the quilting produced by the machine was publicly available, the machine itself was still deemed to have been concealed and hence could not be used as prior art to defeat the patentability of a later, independently developed version of the machine. See also Horwath v. Lee, 564 F.2d 948 (C.C.P.A. 1977) (the longer an inventor delays in filing application after reduction to practice, the greater are the equities that may be raised on behalf of one who made the same invention and promptly filed); Brokaw v. Vogel, 429 F.2d 476 (C.C.P.A. 1970) (five-year delay between reduction to practice and filing of patent application was too long).

If one were to analogize software object code to the quilting in *Gillman* and compare source code to the hidden-from-view quilting machine, this case could pose a serious threat to any seller of software who relies on source code trade secrecy for legal protection for an extended period of time.

Fortunately, the suggested rule in *Gillman* has not yet clearly prevailed. The Federal Circuit has held, for instance, that merely because research is secret does not mean it has necessarily been "abandoned, suppressed or concealed" under section 102(g). See E.I. du Pont de Nemours & Co. v. Phillips Petroleum Co., 849 F.2d 1430 (Fed. Cir.), *cert. denied*, 488 U.S. 986 (1988). Cf. Lockwood v. American Airlines, 107 F.3d 1565 (Fed. Cir. 1997) (secret computer program could be prior art under section 102(a) where it was "known or used by others," even though they could not see how it worked). Further, at least one court has concluded that an invention that was the subject of a secrecy order was not "concealed" within the meaning of section 102(g). Del Mar Engineering Labs v. United States, 524 F.2d 1178 (Ct. Cl. 1975). And an important recent case allows a patentee to avoid a charge of concealment despite a long delay as long as she resumes active pursuit of a patent before the second inventor's entry into the field. Paulik v. Rizkalla, 760 F.2d 1270, 226 U.S.P.Q. (BNA) 224 (Fed. Cir. 1985).

Despite the policy objective of encouraging early filing of patents, cases such as *Gillman* are troubling. To rule that secret use renders a prior invention "abandoned, suppressed or concealed" under section 102(g) is to punish those who elect to keep their inventions as trade secrets. Under *Gillman* and related cases, a later inventor who files a patent application can avoid the prior art effect of earlier secret uses by arguing that the earlier inventor abandoned, suppressed, or concealed the invention. This removes it from the definition of "prior art" under a section 102(g) and clears the way for the later inventor/patent applicant to obtain a patent. (Note that this assumes that the earlier use of the secret invention will not constitute section 102(a) "known or used by others" prior art; there is a strong possibility that section 102(a) would not defeat novelty, given the prevailing interpretation of knowledge or use as implying some degree of *public* knowledge or use.)

The rule proposed in *Gillman* is troubling because many industries rely heavily on trade secret protection to appropriate the value of their research and development. See, e.g., Levin et al., Appropriating the Returns from Industrial Research and Development, 1987 Brookings Papers Econ. Activity 783 (1987) (reporting results of extensive empirical survey of research and development personnel at U.S. corporations; many industries value trade secrets more highly than patents as appropriability mechanism, although nonlegal techniques such as lead time advantages were valued most highly in most industries). Also, although several cases have held that state trade secret law may co-exist with federal patent law, see, e.g., Kewanee Oil Co. v. Bicron Corp., 416 U.S. 470 (1974), section 102(g)'s implicit "punishment" for those who elect trade secret protection raises the question how far the patent statute can or should go in disfavoring state law forms of protection.

Note on Prior User Rights for Business Method Patents

Partly in response to concerns about secret prior art, Congress in 1999 passed the first "prior inventor defense"—i.e., prior user rights—statute in U.S. history. American Inventors Protection Act, Pub.L. 106-113, Div. B, §1000(a)(9) [Title IV, §4302(a)], Nov. 29, 1999, 113 Stat. 1536, 1501A-555, codified at 35 U.S.C. §273 (2002). (Other jurisdictions, particularly in Europe, have had such provisions for many years.) It is important in reading the statute that, despite its apparent application to all method claims, it is strictly limited to "*method[s] of doing or conducting business.*" 35 U.S,C. §273(a)(3).

The new section 273 reads in part (emphasis added):

§273. Defense to infringement based on earlier inventor
      (b) Defense to infringement—
         (1) In general.—*It shall be a defense* to an action for infringement under section 271 of this title with respect to any subject matter that would otherwise infringe one or more claims for a method in the patent being asserted against a person, *if such person had, acting in good faith, actually reduced the subject matter to practice at least 1 year before the effective filing date of such patent, and commercially used the subject matter before the effective filing date of such patent.*

These are significant restrictions, particularly the one-year earlier provision. In the fast-changing software industry, where many method-of-doing-business patents may have their greatest impact, any invention made in-house will not defeat patentability for another if it has been reduced to practice less than a year before the other's patent filing.

Another important issue in the statute is the definition of "commercial use," found in §273(a)(1):

    (a) Definitions.—For purposes of this section —
      (1) the terms "commercially used" and "commercial use" mean use of a method in the United States, so long as such use is in connection with an internal

commercial use or an actual arm's-length sale or other arm's-length commercial transfer of a useful end result, whether or not the subject matter at issue is accessible to or otherwise known to the public . . . .

The statute has other limitations as well:

§273(b)(3) Limitations and qualifications of defense.—The defense to infringement under this section is subject to the following:

(1) Patent. —A person may not assert the defense under this section unless the invention for which the defense is asserted is for a method.

(2) Derivation.—A person may not assert the defense under this section if the subject matter on which the defense is based was derived from the patentee or persons in privity with the patentee.

(3) Not a general license.—The defense asserted by a person under this section is not a general license under all claims of the patent at issue, but extends only to the specific subject matter claimed in the patent with respect to which the person can assert a defense under this chapter, except that the defense shall also extend to variations in the quantity or volume of use of the claimed subject matter, and to improvements in the claimed subject matter that do not infringe additional specifically claimed subject matter of the patent.

(4) Burden of proof.—A person asserting the defense under this section shall have the burden of establishing the defense by clear and convincing evidence.

(5) Abandonment of use.—A person who has abandoned commercial use of subject matter may not rely on activities performed before the date of such abandonment in establishing a defense under this section with respect to actions taken after the date of such abandonment.

(6) Personal defense.—The defense under this section may be asserted only by the person who performed the acts necessary to establish the defense and, except for any transfer to the patent owner, the right to assert the defense shall not be licensed or assigned or transferred to another person except as an ancillary and subordinate part of a good faith assignment or transfer for other reasons of the entire enterprise or line of business to which the defense relates.

(7) Limitation on sites.—A defense under this section, when acquired as part of a good faith assignment or transfer of an entire enterprise or line of business to which the defense relates, may only be asserted for uses at sites where the subject matter that would otherwise infringe one or more of the claims is in use before the later of the effective filing date of the patent or the date of the assignment or transfer of such enterprise or line of business.

(8) Unsuccessful assertion of defense.—If the defense under this section is pleaded by a person who is found to infringe the patent and who subsequently fails to demonstrate a reasonable basis for asserting the defense, the court shall find the case exceptional for the purpose of awarding attorney fees under section 285 of this title.

(9) Invalidity.—A patent shall not be deemed to be invalid under section 102 or 103 of this title solely because a defense is raised or established under this section.

COMMENTS AND QUESTIONS

1. By creating a prior inventor defense for business method patents, Congress implicitly ratified the issuance of these patents. Thus, despite the creation of a defense to infringement, there is much in the new §273 to cheer the holders of these patents.

2. Note §273(b)(9), which says that a successful assertion of this defense does not necessarily invalidate a patent under §§102 or 103. This suggests the possibility of a category of prior art that constitutes a defense for one party but not invalidating prior art for another. It also suggests that perhaps the drafters of the bill thought that not all internally developed methods that are commercially exploited constitute prior art under §102(g)(2)—i.e., maybe some software, for example, can be "commercially used" yet still be "abandoned, suppressed or concealed" under §102(g)(2). Good developments, or bad?

3. Enablement of Software Inventions

35 U.S.C. Section 112, ¶1

The specification shall contain a written description of the invention, and of the manner and process of making and using it, in such full, clear, concise and exact terms as to enable any person skilled in the art to which it pertains, or with which it is most nearly connected, to make and use the same, and shall set forth the best mode contemplated by the inventor of carrying out his invention.

One significant issue for software patents under section 112, the disclosure provision of the patent code, has been whether a patent applicant must deposit source code to meet the enablement (i.e., "how to make and use") requirement of section 112, ¶1. Two cases in particular have defined the terms of this debate.

In White Consolidated Industries v. Vega Servo-Control, Inc., 713 F.2d 788 (Fed. Cir. 1983), the Federal Circuit invalidated a patent for a machine tool control system that was run by a computer program. Part of the invention was a programming language translator designed to convert an input program into machine language, which the system could then execute. The patent specification identified an example of a translator program, the so-called "SPLIT" program, which was a trade secret of Sundstrand, a company that later became the plaintiff White Consolidated. When the application was filed, the SPLIT program was available exclusively from Sundstrand.

The defendant, Vega, asserted patent invalidity as a defense to the infringement claim. Specifically, Vega argued that the SPLIT program was the only suitable translator program, and merely identifying it was not sufficient to meet the standards of section 112. White claimed that widely available equivalent translators could also be used and that, in any event, the specification described the characteristics of the necessary translator program in terms that enabled a programmer of ordinary skill to create it from scratch.

The court held that the program translator was an integral part of the invention and that mere identification of it was not sufficient to discharge the applicant's duty under section 112. The court seemed concerned that maintaining the translator program as a trade secret would allow White to extend the patent beyond the 17-year term then specified in the patent code.

In Northern Telecom, Inc. v. Datapoint Corp., 908 F.2d 931 (Fed. Cir.), *cert. denied*, 498 U.S. 920 (1990), the Federal Circuit once again confronted the enablement requirement in the context of an invention containing a computer program. In *Northern Telecom*, the court reversed the district court's holding of invalidity on enablement grounds. Here the patent claimed an improved method of entering, verifying, and storing (or "batching") data with a special data entry terminal. The district court invalidated certain claims of the patent on the grounds that they were inadequately disclosed under section 112.

In a decision reversing this aspect of the district court's ruling, the Federal Circuit held that when claims pertain to a computer program that implements a claimed device or method, the enablement requirement varies according to the nature of the claimed invention as well as the role and complexity of the computer program needed to implement it. Under the facts in this case, the core of the claimed invention was the combination of components or steps, rather than the details of the program the applicant actually used. The court noted expert testimony that various programs could be used to implement the invention, and that it would be "relatively straightforward [in light of the specification] for a skilled computer programmer to design a program to carry out the claimed invention." *Id*. at 941-942. The court continued:

> The computer language is not a conjuration of some black art, it is simply a highly structured language. . . . [T]he conversion of a complete thought (as expressed in English and mathematics, i.e. the known input, the desired output, the mathematical expressions needed and the methods of using those expressions) into a language a machine understands is necessarily a mere clerical function to a skilled programmer.

Id.

The court refused to state categorically that source code would never have to be disclosed, however, especially in cases, such as *White*, where it was estimated that it would take two years for a skilled programmer to produce a working program of the type called for by the specification.

COMMENTS AND QUESTIONS

1. The rule that actual program code need not be disclosed in a patent specification is now well-accepted. See, e.g., *Ex Parte Lee*, 2000 WL 33741050 (Bd. Pat. App & Interf. Nov 30, 2000), at 3:

> The examiner maintains that the specification fails to disclose the program in some form and therefore, the claim is not supported by the specification. . . . [T]he examiner maintains that the skilled artisan would not only have to be skilled in multiple arts, but that a solution implementing multiple disciplines would require entirely too much experimentation to implement the claimed invention. We disagree with the examiner that the solution would require undue experimentation. Appellant argues . . . that the specification is enabling and that the actual computer program code is not necessary to enable the claimed invention. We agree with appellant.

2. Failure to disclose the specifics of a program that would take two years to re-create renders a patent invalid under section 112. What if the program were to take one year to re-create? How about six months? One month?

3. On the related issue of the scope of sofware patents drafted in "means plus function" format under 35 U.S.C. §112 ¶6, see *infra,* Section C, Note on the Optimal Breadth of Software Patents.

4. Best Mode and Software

Even where disclosure is adequate under the enablement standard, it can run into problems under the "best mode" aspect of section 112. An inventor runs afoul of the best mode requirement if she intentionally withholds from the patent specification information that discloses the best means of which she is aware for practicing her invention. Does the best mode requirement compel the disclosure of source code, on the theory that the actual way in which the programmer has implemented an invention must be the best way known to the inventor? Consider the following case.

≡
≡ *Fonar Corp. v. General Electric Co.*
≡ **United States Court of Appeals for the Federal Circuit**
≡ **107 F.3d 1543 (Fed. Cir. 1997)**

LOURIE, Circuit Judge. . . .

Background

The '966 patent concerns a technique for using a magnetic resonance imaging ("MRI") machine in order to obtain multiple image slices of a patient's body at different angles in a single scan, referred to as multi-angle oblique ("MAO") imaging. Prior art machines were able to obtain multiple parallel images along the same axis in a single scan, but they required multiple scans in order to obtain multiple images at varying angles. MAO resulted in shortened imaging times and hence allowed for the imaging of more patients per day. Claim 1 of the '966 patent recites this feature and reads in part:

> 1. A method for obtaining in the course of a single scan NMR [nuclear magnetic resonance] image data for a plurality of differently oriented selected planes in an object using nuclear magnetic resonance techniques, said method comprising the steps of:
> (a) positioning an object in a static homogeneous magnetic field;
> (b) determining first and second selected planes in said object for which NMR image data is to be obtained . . .
> (c) subjecting said object to a plurality of repetitions of a first repetition sequence composed of NMR excitation and magnetic gradient field pulses, each of said repetitions of said first repetition sequence including the steps of applying an excitation pulse and reading out of an NMR signal produced by said excitation pulse . . . said plurality of repetitions of said first repetition sequence being

carried out in a manner to encode spatial information into a first collection of said NMR signals, said first collection of NMR signals being representative of NMR image data for said first selected plane; and

(d) subjecting said object to a plurality of repetitions of a second repetition sequence composed of NMR excitation and magnetic field gradient pulses, each of said repetitions of said second repetition sequence including the steps of applying an excitation pulse and reading out of an NMR signal produced, by said excitation pulse . . . said plurality of repetitions of said second repetition sequence being carried out in a manner to encode spatial information into a second collection of NMR signals, said second collection of NMR signals being representative of NMR image data for said second selected plane;

said plurality of repetitions of said first and second repetition sequences each being carried out during the course of a single scan of said object and each being continued substantially throughout said single scan, the repetition time interval for repeating each of said first and second repetition sequences being substantially the same and said steps of applying an excitation pulse and reading out of an NMR signal for each repetition of said second repetition sequence being performed at a different time during said repetition time interval than each of said steps of applying an excitation pulse and reading out of an NMR signal for said first repetition sequence.

. . . Fonar sued GE for infringement of the two patents, asserting infringement of claims 1, 2, 4, 5, and 12 of the '966 patent and claims 1 and 2 of the '832 patent. A jury returned a verdict finding that the asserted claims were not invalid and were infringed. . . .

The court denied GE's motions for JMOL relating to its assertion of a violation of the best mode requirement and to damages for direct infringement of the '966 patent. The court concluded that the testimony of Fonar's witnesses provided substantial evidence to support the jury's finding that the patent satisfied the best mode requirement, and the court found that substantial evidence supported the jury's damages findings. The court summarily denied GE's motions for JMOL relating to the other issues now on appeal. The court awarded Fonar prejudgment interest and entered a final award against GE in the amount of $68,421,726.

GE now appeals to this court, arguing that the district court erred in its judgment concerning validity and infringement of the '966 patent. . . .

Discussion . . .

A. Best Mode of the '966 Patent

GE argues that the patent fails to disclose two software routines, the LGRAD and GETMAO programs, which the inventors testified were the best means they knew of to accomplish MAO imaging. GE also argues that a critical aspect of the invention, a gradient multiplier board ("GMB"), was not disclosed in sufficient detail to satisfy the best mode requirement. Furthermore, GE argues that the inventors failed to identify a new integrated circuit "chip" for implementing certain functions of the hardware.

Fonar responds that its disclosure was adequate to satisfy the best mode requirement, that the specification adequately describes the functions of the software, and that it is not necessary that the actual computer program be disclosed. According to Fonar, providing a description of the software's functions is what is important for a best mode disclosure, rather than actual source code, because the code was tailored to a specific hardware embodiment and it thus would not necessarily have worked with other hardware. Fonar also argues that the '966 specification adequately disclosed the GMB and the functions of the new "chip."

The patent statute requires that a patent specification "shall set forth the best mode contemplated by the inventor of carrying out his invention." 35 U.S.C. §112 (1994). Determining whether a patent satisfies the best mode requirement involves two factual inquiries. First, a fact-finder must determine whether at the time an applicant filed an application for a patent, he or she had a best mode of practicing the invention; this is a subjective determination. Second, if the inventor had a best mode of practicing the invention, the fact-finder must determine whether the best mode was disclosed in sufficient detail to allow one skilled in the art to practice it, which is an objective determination. United States Gypsum Co. v. National Gypsum Co., 74 F.3d 1209, 1212, 37 USPQ2d 1388, 1390 (Fed.Cir. 1996); Chemcast Corp. v. Arco Indus. Corp., 913 F.2d 923, 927-28, 16 USPQ2d 1033, 1036 (Fed.Cir. 1990).

We agree with Fonar that the jury's finding that the '966 patent satisfied the best mode requirement was supported by substantial evidence. There was evidence that the inventors had a best mode, and that the software, the GMB, and the "chip" were part of that best mode. However, with respect to the software routines, Fonar's witnesses testified that the '966 patent contained a sufficient description of the software's functions. Specifically, Robert Wolf, one of the inventors, testified as follows:

Q. From that written description, is there sufficient description to a software engineer, such as yourself, of what software needs to be written in order to perform the multi-angle oblique invention?

A. Yes. . . .

Q. In any event, the software, itself, as we see in the hundred pages of Exhibit 816, is not reproduced in its entirety in the patent. Is that right?

A. That's correct.

Q. Why is that?

A. For a few reasons. First of all, it's large as you can see. It's several hundred pages. It wouldn't help someone to have that software anyway because that software only works on a Fonar machine. What's much more important is to have a description of what the software has to do, and that is what you will find in the patent.

Fonar's witnesses further testified that providing the functions of the software was more important than providing the computer code. We agree.

As a general rule, where software constitutes part of a best mode of carrying out an invention, description of such a best mode is satisfied by a disclosure of the functions of the software. This is because, normally, writing code for such software is within the skill of the art, not requiring undue experimentation, once its functions have been disclosed. It is well established that what is within the skill of the art need not be disclosed to satisfy the best mode requirement as long as that mode is described. Stating the functions of the best mode software satisfies that description test. We have so held previously and we so hold today. See In re Hayes Microcomputer Prods., Inc. Patent Litigation, 982 F.2d 1527, 1537-38, 25 USPQ2d 1241, 1248-49 (Fed.Cir. 1992); In re Sherwood, 613 F.2d 809, 816-17, 204 USPQ 537, 544 (CCPA 1980). Thus, flow charts or source code listings are not a requirement for adequately disclosing the functions of software. See *Sherwood*, 613 F.2d at 816-17, 204 USPQ at 544. Here, substantial evidence supports a finding that the software functions were disclosed sufficiently to satisfy the best mode requirement. See *Hayes*, 982 F.2d at 1537, 25 USPQ2d at 1248-49 (stating that there was no best mode violation where the specification failed to disclose a firmware listing or flow charts, but did disclose sufficient detail to allow one skilled in the art to develop a firmware listing for implementing the invention).

A finding that the GMB was sufficiently disclosed to satisfy the best mode requirement was also supported by substantial evidence. Fonar's witness testified that the '966 patent provided a description of the function of the GMB with reference to the components within the dotted line in Figure 7 of the '966 patent, reproduced on p. 347.

David Hertz, one of the inventors, testified in particular that the patent provides a description of the functions required for one skilled in the art to build a GMB that will work with a general MRI system and that the GMB disclosed in the patent is the one built by Fonar. More importantly, he testified that the GMB used in the Fonar machine was not the only means to accomplish MAO imaging and that it was not necessarily the best way to do it for every machine. GE argues nonetheless that the '966 patent failed to disclose the use of comparators as part of the GMB, which it alleged were an essential element of the best mode. However, Hertz testified that if an MRI machine performing MAO imaging according to the '966 patent were to require a comparator as part of the GMB, a skilled engineer would know that a comparator should be used. He further testified that each MRI machine has its own set of requirements for the functionality of the GMB, which is why the '966 patent described in general terms how to build the invention. Hertz's testimony provides substantial evidence to support a finding that there was no best mode violation with respect to the GMB.

Substantial evidence also supports the finding that the functions of the new "chip" were disclosed sufficiently to satisfy the best mode requirement. The '966 patent schematically disclosed the functions of that "chip" in Figure 7 and provided a textual description of its functions. See '966 patent, col. 13, lines 41-64. Because adequate disclosure of the functions of the "chip" was in the specification, failure to specifically identify a particular manufacturer's "chip" was not fatal to satisfaction of the best mode requirement. Accordingly, the jury's finding that the '966 patent satisfied the best mode requirement was supported by substantial evidence, and the district court did not err in denying GE's motion for JMOL concerning that issue. . . .

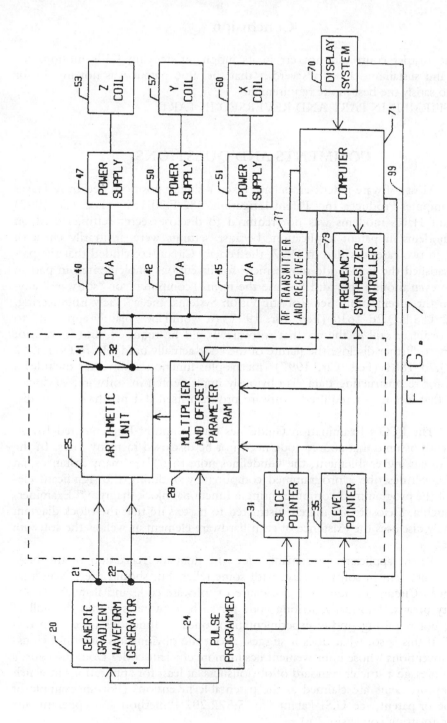

FIGURE 3-1
Figure 7 of the '966 patent.

Conclusion

The district court did not err in its judgment denying GE's motions for JMOL and sustaining the jury's verdict that the '966 patent was not invalid for failure to satisfy the best mode requirement. . . .

AFFIRMED IN PART AND REVERSED IN PART.

COMMENTS AND QUESTIONS

1. Most software patent cases have taken a similar position. See In re Hayes Microcomputer Products, Inc. Patent Litigation, 982 F.2d 1527 (Fed. Cir. 1992) (maker of Hayes modems was not required to disclose secret settings used on those modems in patent application, because settings were arbitrarily chosen). Indeed, in two cases decided in 1997, the Federal Circuit concluded that the patentees satisfied the best-mode requirement for inventions implemented in part in software even though they did not use the terms "computer" or "software" anywhere in the specification! See Robotic Vision Systems, Inc. v. View Engineering, Inc., 42 U.S.P.Q.2d 1619 (Fed. Cir. 1997) (it would be "plainly apparent" to one of ordinary skill in the art that software would be required, and it was not necessary to further disclose the nature of the code actually used); In re Dossel, 42 U.S.P.Q.2d 1881 (Fed. Cir. 1997) (means-plus-function claim that includes a "means for reconstructing data" is obviously implemented in software, so disclosure of that fact is not required; software program itself did not have to be disclosed).

2. The PTO's Examination Guidelines for Computer-Implemented Inventions clearly assume that source code need not be disclosed in many cases. In the section discussing enablement, the Guidelines note that "[i]n many instances, an applicant will describe a programmed computer by outlining the significant elements of the programmed computer using a functional block diagram." Examiners facing such a disclosure are merely instructed to make sure that the block diagram adequately discloses the existence of each hardware element as well as the software elements.

3. Patent applicants presumably view the dramatic relaxation of the best-mode requirement in software cases with some relief. But should they? Note that the Federal Circuit considers the disclosure of software code and flow charts unnecessary because "normally, writing code for such software is within the skill of the art, not requiring undue experimentation, once its functions have been disclosed." If this is so, what does it suggest about the obviousness or nonobviousness of inventions whose improvement lies in more efficient code? Does the court's opinion presage a stricter standard of obviousness, at least for applications in which code improvements are claimed as the patentable invention? (For an example of this type of patent, see U.S. Patent No. 5,572,207 ("method and apparatus for numeric-to-string conversion").)

4. For a recent summary of practitioner issues, see William F. Heinze, A Risk-Balancing Approach to Best Mode Disclosure in Software Patent Applications, 84 J. Pat. & Trademark Off. Soc'y 40 (2002).

C. INFRINGEMENT

=== *Alpex Computer Corporation v. Nintendo*
=== *Company Ltd.*
United States Court of Appeals for the Federal Circuit
102 F.3d 1214 (Fed. Cir. 1996)

ARCHER, Chief Judge.

Nintendo Company, Ltd. and Nintendo of America, Inc. (collectively Nintendo) appeal the January 6, 1995, judgment of the United States District Court for the Southern District of New York, Alpex Computer Corp. v. Nintendo Co., 1994 U.S. Dist. LEXIS 17515, 34 U.S.P.Q.2d (BNA) 1167 (S.D.N.Y. 1994), holding U.S. Patent No. 4,026,555 (the '555 patent), owned by Alpex Computer Corporation (Alpex), not invalid, willfully infringed, and awarding $253,641,445 in damages and interest. We affirm the judgment as to validity and reverse the judgment of infringement.

I.

This case deals with an invention within the art of video games. The video game industry began in the early 1970s and includes two branches, arcade video games and home video games. Arcade video games are large, expensive, coin-operated machines that are placed in high traffic areas such as amusement arcades. These machines are generally referred to as "dedicated" because they can play only one game. Home video games, in contrast, are small, relatively inexpensive devices that are easily connected to the antennae terminals of a standard television.

The Magnavox Odyssey was the first home video game. It too was a dedicated system playing only one game which was referred to as the "ball and paddle" because a dot of light bounced between two player-controlled vertical lines. In early 1974, the inventors of the patent in suit conceived of a new microprocessor-based home video game system that used modular plug-in units—replaceable, read-only memory, or ROM, cartridges—to permit home video systems to play multiple games, including games with rotating images. The '555 patent on this invention issued to Alpex on May 31, 1977. The patented invention was commercialized in systems by Atari, Mattel, and Coleco. In the early 1980s, Nintendo entered the home video game market with the Nintendo Entertainment System (NES). After the NES was featured at the 1985 Consumer Electronics Show, Alpex notified Nintendo of possible infringement of the '555 patent. Soon thereafter, in February 1986, Alpex filed suit against Nintendo for patent infringement. . . . Following a four-week liability trial, the jury returned a verdict for Alpex. . . . Nintendo now appeals the judgment as to validity, infringement, and damages, and Alpex cross-appeals the amount of damages.

II.

The '555 patent claims a keyboard-controlled apparatus for producing video signals by means of random access memory (RAM) with storage positions corresponding to each discrete position of the raster for a standard television receiver. Figure 2 of the '555 patent depicts the structure of the invention, as follows: The television raster comprises numerous discrete dots or bars, approximately 32,000, which the cathode ray beam illuminates on a standard cycle, which in turn creates the image on the television screen. The patented invention requires sufficient RAM to accommodate each of the approximately 32,000 memory positions needed to represent the raster image. Thus, the RAM holds at least one "bit" of data for each position in the memory "map" of the raster. Accordingly, this video display system is called "bit-mapping." The advantage of this system, as disclosed in the patent, is that it provides for the representation of every image within the raster RAM, or display RAM, and thereby provides greater control of the display for the manipulation of complex images and symbols. To achieve this flexibility, however, bit-mapping requires the construction of each image within the display RAM before display, a process that requires the microprocessor to erase and rewrite each image. Because the microprocessor must refresh the display RAM for each frame to show the movement of images, the operation of the system is slowed down.

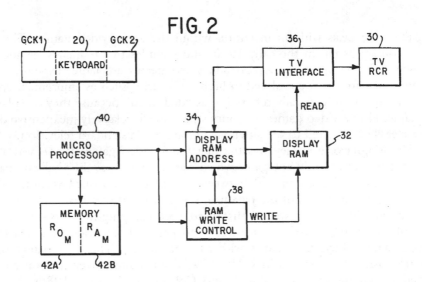

FIGURE 3-2
Figure 2 of the '555 patent.

The accused NES with its game cartridges is also an apparatus for producing video signals by means of storage positions corresponding to discrete positions of the raster for a standard television receiver. A trial exhibit illustrates the NES:

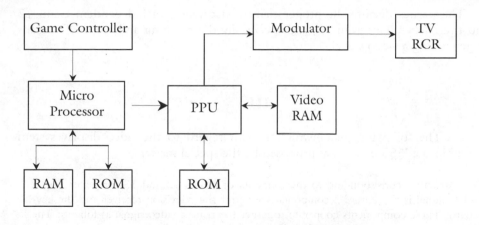

FIGURE 3-3
Illustration of structure of Nintendo device.

The video display system for the NES does not include RAM with storage positions corresponding to each discrete position of the raster. Instead, the NES utilizes a patented picture processing unit, or PPU, to perform the generation of images on the screen. The PPU receives pre-formed, horizontal slices of data and places each slice in one of eight shift registers, each of which can store a maximum of 8 pixels. These slices of data are then processed directly to the screen. The PPU repeats this process to assemble the initial image on the screen. Thereafter it repeats the process as necessary to form changes in images throughout the progression of the game. Nintendo refers to the PPU as an "on-the-fly" system. It is undisputed that the NES video display system, using shift registers to process slices of images (as opposed to entire screens), is a faster means of displaying movement of images on the video screen than the bit-mapping of the RAM based system of the '555 patent. The claims at issue are 12 and 13 of the '555 patent:

> 12. Apparatus for playing games by displaying and manipulating player and ball image devices on the screen of a display tube, comprising
> first means for generating a video signal representing a linear player image device aligned in a first direction,
> second means for generating a video signal representing a ball image device,
> manually operable game control means, and
> means responsive to said manually operable game control means for causing said first means to generate a video signal representing the player image device rotated so that it is aligned in a second direction different from said first direction.
> 13. Apparatus according to claim 12, wherein said means for causing includes programmed microprocessor means and a replaceable memory having program game instructions stored therein for controlling said microprocessor means, whereby different games may be played with said apparatus by replacing said replaceable memory.

The parties dispute the proper claim construction of independent claim 12 (and thus dependent claim 13) and specifically the meaning and scope of "means for generating a video signal."

III.

. . . The following jury instruction with regard to the video display system claimed in the '555 patent was proposed by the special master:

> The structure corresponding to the elements of claims 12 and 13 for generating a video signal is the Figure 2 components without the television receiver and the keyboard. These components cooperate together to create a video signal as follows: The linear player image device and the ball image device to be displayed on the video unit 30 are stored as data within ROM 42A. The "intelligence" of the system is provided by micro-processor 40. The operation of the micro-processor 40 is under the control of a program stored in ROM 42A. Micro-processor 40 causes this information in ROM 42A to be written into RAM 32 by using the write control circuit 38. RAM 32 has discrete storage positions which correspond to each of the bars or pixels of the TV screen. TV interface 36 causes display RAM address 34 to scan each of these storage positions in display RAM 32 to provide the video signal to the TV receiver 30.

Alternatively, the special master recommended leaving the issue of claim construction to the jury. The district court chose only to adopt the first sentence of the special master's recommended jury instruction, relegating the remainder of the claim construction issues to the jury. After the jury returned a verdict of infringement, Nintendo challenged on motion for JMOL the interpretation that the jury appeared to give the claim in reaching its verdict, but the district court denied Nintendo's motion. The court seemed to adopt the entirety of the claim interpretation of the special master in ruling on the JMOL motion and held that there was sufficient evidence to support the jury's presumed claim construction. Nintendo argues that, by denying its JMOL, the district court approved an erroneous claim construction, allowing claims for a RAM-based, bit-map video display system to read on a device that used a shift register-based, on-the-fly video display system. Nintendo argues that the '555 patent requires the use of a RAM memory map for all of the 32,000 pixels in the raster, whereas the NES uses shift registers that only provide for a maximum of 64 pixels. Because of this difference in structure, Nintendo contends that there can be neither literal infringement nor infringement under the doctrine of equivalents. Nintendo further contends that Alpex is barred from claiming that the NES infringes the '555 patent because during prosecution Alpex distinguished the invention of the '555 patent from a relevant prior art patent using shift registers.

In prosecuting its patent application before the Patent and Trademark Office (PTO), Alpex specifically distinguished the RAM-based, bit-map video display structure of the '555 patent from a prior art patent, Okuda, which claimed a shift register-based video display structure. Alpex explained to the PTO that, unlike Alpex's bit-map system, the Okuda video display system comprised an entirely different structure than the Alpex system. Specifically, Alpex noted that Okuda was unable to modify selectively a single pixel on the screen. Alpex explained:

Applicants' display system utilizes a random access memory (RAM) 32 which is under the control of a micro-processor 40. When the keyboard is operated, as explained in the specification, micro-processor 40 extracts an appropriate image device from the read-only memory (ROM) 42A and transfers this particular image device directly into the appropriate location within the RAM 32. The random access capability is important since this enables the selected image device to be located directly in any desired area of the RAM 32.

Okuda, in contrast, does not use a random access memory but, instead, employs a series of shift registers as his refresh memory 17 which corresponds to applicants' RAM 32. Because random access to the shift registers is not possible, Okuda is unable to selectively modify a single bit in the memory 17 but, instead, must operate on a line at a time to modify the stored display data. . . .

Okuda contemplates modification of one line of data at a time and there is no provision for modifying a single "dot." The random access techniques of applicants' invention enables any single point on the TV screen to be altered at will (under control of the micro-processor).

. . . Nintendo contends that the statements regarding the Okuda prior art patent were relevant and should have been considered for purposes of claim construction even though they may not give rise to prosecution history estoppel as to asserted claims 12 and 13. . . .

IV.

Prosecution history is relevant not only for purposes of prosecution history estoppel but also for construing the meaning and scope of the claims.

In this case, the Okuda patent is directly relevant to claim construction. The prosecution history of the '555 patent shows that the examiner rejected claim 1 of the application as being anticipated by Okuda. Claim 1 specified a series of limitations in means-plus-function format to a display control apparatus utilizing a RAM-based, bit-map system. Alpex distinguished Okuda before the PTO based on the structural difference of a RAM-based versus a shift register-based video display system: "Claim 1, as amended, now clearly distinguishes over Okuda. The claim requires a random access memory which, as indicated previously, is not disclosed in Okuda." . . .

The district court recognized that claims 12 and 13, and the specification of the '555 patent, call for the use of a RAM-based, bit-map video display system. Moreover, the statements made by Alpex during prosecution with regard to the Okuda prior art patent emphasize that Alpex claimed a video display system based on the use of RAM capable of modifying a single bit, or pixel, on the television receiver. These statements distinguish any video display system based on shift registers, as shift registers do not allow the selective modification of a single bit in memory, that is, a single pixel. It is undisputed that the NES utilized this type of video display system. Indeed, Alpex's own technical expert, Mr. Milner, testified that the NES utilized shift registers, not RAM. Further, Mr. Milner explained that the NES could not directly modify a single pixel. Thus, Mr. Milner's testimony confirms that random access capability is not possible by use of shift registers. In short, the structure and operation of the NES paralleled the structure and operation of the Okuda video display system.

Alpex attempts to distinguish Okuda from the NES because Okuda only allows the modification of horizontal lines on the raster, whereas the NES allows the modification of any 8-bit slice on the raster. This distinction, however, affects neither the structural similarities (both Okuda and the NES use shift registers) nor the pertinent functional similarities (both Okuda and the NES cannot modify a single pixel). Therefore, because Alpex admitted during prosecution that its claims do not cover a video display system based on shift registers as in Okuda, i.e., it argued that a system based on shift registers is not structurally or functionally equivalent to a RAM based system that can randomly access a single bit, Alpex's claims cannot now be construed to cover the NES, which possesses the same structural and functional traits as Okuda.

V.

On the jury verdict form, Interrogatory 1 asked the following: "Do you find that claims 12 and 13 require a structure that includes a display RAM which has discrete storage positions which correspond to each of the bars or pixels of the TV screen?" The jury answered this question in the affirmative. This response is consistent with and supported by the prosecution history of the '555 patent.

The jury then found that the accused products, the NES and most of its accompanying game cartridges, infringed claims 12 and 13 of the 555 patent, implicitly finding structural equivalence between a RAM-based, bit-map video display system and a shift register-based, NES system under §112, ¶6. The district court determined that these findings were supported by substantial evidence and denied the motion for JMOL. See Kearns v. Chrysler Corp., 32 F.3d 1541, 1547-48, 31 U.S.P.Q.2d (BNA) 1746, 1751 (Fed. Cir. 1994) (deeming reversal proper "only if the jury's factual findings, presumed or express, are not supported by substantial evidence or, if they are, that the legal conclusions implied from the jury's verdict cannot in law be supported by those findings"); Perkin-Elmer Corp. v. Computervision Corp., 732 F.2d 888, 893, 221 U.S.P.Q. (BNA) 669, 673 (Fed. Cir. 1984) ("Only when the court is convinced upon the record before the jury that reasonable persons would not have reached a verdict for the non-mover, should it grant the motion for [JMOL]."). We review the district court's JMOL ruling applying the same standard. Read Corp. v. Portec, Inc., 970 F.2d 816, 821, 23 U.S.P.Q.2d (BNA) 1426, 1431 (Fed. Cir. 1992).

The district court held that Nintendo had literally infringed claims 12 and 13 of the '555 patent based primarily on the testimony of Alpex's expert Mr. Milner that the distinction between a bit-map system and the NES "is insignificant and insufficient to defeat a claim of equivalence under section 112(6)." Accordingly, the district court concluded that the NES is not only a functional equivalent but also a structural equivalent to the bit-map structure. For the reasons stated above, however, the NES cannot infringe claims 12 and 13 of the '555 patent as equivalents under §112, ¶6, under a proper claim construction. . . .

Moreover, while Mr. Milner's testimony purports to be an analysis of the structure of the specification and the accused device, it actually provides no more than an analysis of functional equivalency. Mr. Milner described the shift registers of the NES as storing "just one little slice of an object" to be imaged; whereas he said the bit-map system "stores the whole screen." He concluded that displaying a slice of an object is equivalent to displaying the "whole screen." Specifically, Mr. Milner testified that "the reason they are equivalent is by storing one line at a time and using it over and over and over again very quickly you can do the same thing." Thus, Mr. Milner concluded that by repeating the NES process the entire screen will eventually be imaged as is done with the bit map system. This is a conclusion, however, of equivalency of function—both systems store data and will eventually display an image on the whole screen. Mr. Milner did not compare the structure of the NES with the bit map structure disclosed in the specification. Moreover, the bit map structure was clearly distinguished over a shift register structure during the prosecution of the '555 patent.

Because Alpex defined its claims during the prosecution of the '555 patent as not covering a system using shift registers and because the testimony relied on by Alpex to establish infringement under §112, ¶6, was based only on a functional, not a structural, analysis, we conclude the court erred in sustaining the jury verdict of literal infringement.

VI.

The district court also denied Nintendo's motion for JMOL on the issue of infringement under the doctrine of equivalents primarily based on its conclusion that the jury could reasonably have found infringement under §112, ¶6. The court reasoned that equivalence under the doctrine of equivalents is a slightly broader concept than equivalence under §112, ¶6, and that, as a result, its discussion of equivalence for literal infringement applied equally to infringement under the doctrine of equivalents.

While equivalency under the doctrine of equivalents and equivalency under §112, ¶6, both relate to insubstantial changes, each has a separate origin, purpose and application. Valmont Indus., Inc. v. Reinke Mfg. Co., 983 F.2d 1039, 1043-44, 25 U.S.P.Q.2d (BNA) 1451, 1454 (Fed. Cir. 1993). Under §112, the concern is whether the accused device, which performs the claimed function, has the same or an equivalent structure as the structure described in the specification corresponding to the claim's means. D.M.I. Inc. v. Deere & Co., 755 F.2d 1570, 1575, 225 U.S.P.Q. (BNA) 236, 239 (Fed. Cir. 1985). Under the doctrine of equivalents, on the other hand, the question is whether the accused device is only insubstantially different than the claimed device. Hilton Davis Chem. Co. v. Warner-Jenkinson Co., 62 F.3d 1512, 1517, 35 U.S.P.Q.2d (BNA) 1641, 1644-45 (Fed. Cir. 1995) (in banc), *cert. granted*, 116 S. Ct. 1014 (1996). The latter question often turns on whether the accused device performs substantially the same function in substantially the same way to achieve substantially the same result. See *id.* at 1518, 35 U.S.P.Q.2d (BNA) at 1645.

In this case, the court concluded, based on the testimony of Alpex's expert, Mr. Milner, that the jury's finding of infringement under the doctrine of equivalents was supported by substantial evidence. However, Mr. Milner's testimony that the claimed and accused devices were substantially the same in terms of function/way/result was merely conclusory as acknowledged by the district court. However, the court said that Mr. Milner's conclusory statements on function/

way/result, when considered with his testimony in relation to infringement under the §112, ¶6, were sufficient to establish infringement under the doctrine of equivalents.

As discussed earlier, however, Mr. Milner's testimony concerning §112, ¶6, only related to equivalence of the functional result. Neither he nor the court considered whether the accused device and the claimed device operated in substantially the same way. Indeed, in describing equivalency for §112, ¶6, purposes, Mr. Milner acknowledged that the accused and claimed devices do not operate in the same way. For example, Mr. Milner testified that the bit map system creates an image by copying the bit map (the entire stored image) into the display RAM and then reading out the entire image onto the full screen. On the other hand, he explained that the NES creates an image by taking a piece of the image, placing it in temporary storage, and then reading only that piece of the image onto the screen. According to Mr. Milner, by repeating this process "a little bit at a time" until the entire image is placed on the screen, the NES can achieve the same functional result as the bit-map system. This testimony does not support a conclusion that the claimed system and the NES operate in substantially the same way. . . .

AFFIRMED IN PART and REVERSED IN PART.

COMMENTS AND QUESTIONS

1. To similar effect as *Alpex* is Wiener v. NEC Electronics, Inc., 102 F.3d 534 (Fed. Cir. 1996). In that case, the Federal Circuit upheld the district court's finding of noninfringement under the doctrine of equivalents because there were substantial differences between the patent's requirement that a computer program "call on" columns of data one byte at a time and the defendant's product, where the columns alleged to be equivalent were not in the data matrix and therefore were not called upon to read data. The court rejected the "conclusory" declaration of plaintiff's expert that the two processes were identical. In General Electric v. Nintendo of America, 179 F.3d 1350 (Fed. Cir. 1999), the court held that Nintendo's video game systems did not infringe GE's television switch patents because the patents, written in means-plus-function format, did not disclose a function for the switches identical to Nintendo's function. And in Digital Biometrics, Inc. v. Identix, Inc., 149 F.3d 1335 (Fed. Cir. 1998), the court construed narrowly a patent claim to "image arrays" storing a two-dimensional slice of video data and that were merged into a "composite array" storing a fingerprint image. The court held that the defendant's systems, which constructed the composite array directly rather than by using two-dimensional slices, did not create "image arrays" within the meaning of the claims.

The trend in software infringement cases seems to be toward interpreting the claims narrowly. Does this make sense, in light of what we know about the validity of software patents? Or does it render software patents ineffective, particularly in view of the fast-changing nature of the technology?

2. One possible explanation for the narrow construction given software patents in infringement cases to date is that most of those patents have claim elements written in means-plus-function format. A large number of early software patent claims were drafted in means-plus-function language, largely in order to meet the "structure" requirements the courts have imposed on patentees under

section 101. How should the "corresponding structure or equivalents thereof" in the specification be interpreted for infringement purposes? Does *Alpex* provide guidance on this issue? In particular, suppose that a patentee, to fall within the dictates of section 101, claims a "means for processing data" of a particular type. In the specification, the patentee discloses the use of an IBM-compatible personal computer with a Pentium microprocessor. Is this claim infringed by a defendant who runs the same software on a 486 microprocessor? An Apple computer using a Motorola microprocessor? A Sun Microsystems SPARC workstation? A Cray supercomputer? See IGT v. Global Gaming Technology Inc., 42 U.S.P.Q.2d 1144 (D. Nev. 1997) (microprocessors in a computer game were equivalent to hardwired logic circuits disclosed in the patent, and therefore literally infringed under Section 112, ¶6).

3. Is a computer-implemented process "equivalent" to an older physical or analog process? The Federal Circuit has been struggling with this issue for some time. Compare Texas Instruments, Inc. v. International Trade Comm'n, 805 F.2d 1558 (Fed. Cir. 1986) (modern calculators did not infringe TI's original patent on the integrated circuit) with Hughes Aircraft Co. v. United States, 717 F.2d 1351 (Fed. Cir. 1983) (patent on means for controlling satellites from the ground via telemetry was infringed by use of on-board microprocessors to control satellites). For a case applying the doctrine of equivalents in a software context, see Safe Flight Instrument Corp. v. Sundstrand Data Control, Inc., 706 F. Supp. 1146 (D. Del. 1989).

4. The doctrine of equivalents, mentioned at the end of the *Alpex* opinion, was reaffirmed by the Supreme Court in two recent opinions: (1) Warner-Jenkinson Co. v. Hilton Davis Chemical Co., 520 U.S. 17 (1997) (authorizing an "insubstantial differences" test for infringement under the doctrine of equivalents); and (2) Festo Corp. v. Shoketsu Kinzoku Kogyo Kabushiki Co., Ltd., __ U.S. __, 122 S. Ct. 1831 (2002) (reiterating the presumption that claim amendments made during prosecution history give rise to prosecution history estoppel—announced in *Warner-Jenkinson*—and refining the test for application of the estoppel doctrine).

Note on the Optimal Breadth of Software Patents

The software industry is an interesting proving ground for theoretical issues regarding patent scope. Academics in the 1990s introduced the notion that the scope of a pioneer's patent could affect the incentives for third parties to create improvements on it. See, e.g., Suzanne Scotchmer, Standing on the Shoulders of Giants: Cumulative Research and the Patent Law, 5 J. Econ. Persp. 29, 29-31 (1991); Robert P. Merges & Richard R. Nelson, On the Complex Economics of Patent Scope, 90 Colum. L. Rev. 839 (1990). Because patents are now routine in the software industry, and because software generally improves so rapidly from one "generation" of product to the next, the allocation of incentives between successive generations of software developers is an important practical issue.

One scholarly team has argued that the patent scope literature has important lessons to teach courts as they are confronted with software patents. Julie E. Cohen and Mark A. Lemley, Patent Scope and Innovation in the Software Indus-

try, 89 Cal. L. Rev. 1 (2001). In keeping with certain precepts in the early literature, Cohen and Lemley argue that software patents ought to be applied narrowly:

> It is . . . important that not only established patent holders but also newcomers
> and small stakeholders have continued incentives to innovate. This is particularly so in
> an industry with many players and a constant supply of new entrants. The software in-
> dustry has precisely these characteristics. Indeed, because of the many generations of
> improvers who would have to bargain with an initial inventor, it may be unrealistic to
> think that most or even many efficient transactions will occur [with a single "pioneer"
> holder of a broad patent].
>
> More generally, the presumption that only pioneering improvers are worth pro-
> tecting is inappropriate for an industry characterized by networked, interdependent
> products . . . The resulting pattern of innovation by leaps and bounds (rather than in-
> cremental innovation) may actually decrease social welfare, both by reducing interop-
> erability among programs (and therefore foregoing the corresponding network
> benefits) and by rendering the resulting untested programs less reliable. If so, treating
> software patents as broad "prospects" will hinder progress.

89 Cal. L. Rev. 1, 53-54.

Cohen and Lemley then turn to an examination of how to apply their proposed policy within particular doctrinal areas. The authors argue in support of a
nascent trend in some early software patent cases where courts "have rejected arguments that read claim language written for one product generation at such a
high level of abstraction that it covers accused products from a different generation." 89 Cal. L. Rev. 1, 53. A case in point is Digital Biometrics, Inc. v. Identix,
Inc., 149 F.3d 1335 (Fed. Cir. 1998), in which the Federal Circuit construed
narrowly a patent claim to "image arrays" storing a two-dimensional slice of video
data, and which were merged into a "composite array" storing a fingerprint image.
The court held that the defendant's systems, which constructed the composite
array directly rather than by storing and then piecing together individual image
"slices", did not create "image arrays" within the meaning of the claims. See Figure 3-4, taken from the *Digital Biometrics* case, 149 F.3d at 1341. See also WMS
Gaming, Inc. v. International Game Technology, 184 F.3d 1339 (Fed. Cir. 1999)
(newer generation of computer-controlled slot machine did not infringe patent on
older generation employing less computer control).

For a contrary view of the *Digital Biometrics* case, see David C. Radulescu,
The Federal Circuit's Narrowing of the Literal Scope of Patent Claims by Focus-
sing on Embodiments Disclosed in the Specification, 82 J. Pat. & Trademark Off.
Soc'y 539, 548 (2000):

> Because the specification of the patent [in *Digital Biometrics*] did not disclose an em-
> bodiment of the invention other than one making use of a "digital" array, the other-
> wise broad and general term "array" was construed narrowly to be limited to cover
> only the specific type disclosed in the patent (i.e., "digital" arrays stored in memory).
> Indeed, the Court attempted to parse the specification of the patent on its own, with-
> out the assistance of extrinsic evidence such as expert testimony, to determine if it
> could glean an embodiment of the disclosed invention making use of a broader inter-
> pretation of the term "array." Because it could not do so based on the information
> within the four corners of the specification, the disputed term was narrowly construed.

In effect, the Court . . . required the patentee to expressly describe, in the body of the patent itself, the scope of the types of "arrays" his invention could employ. Accordingly, although the claims did not include an explicit limitation on the "array" type, what otherwise would have been considered to be broad and general language in the claims, was narrowly construed based on what was disclosed in the specification.

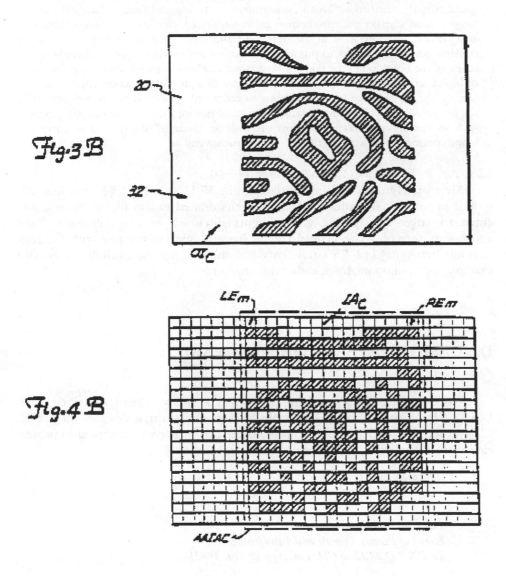

FIGURE 3-4
Digital Biometrics image arrrays.

Perhaps more significantly, as the following passage shows, Radulescu believes patent prosecutors can "draft around" at least some of the courts' attempts to limit patent scope by making detailed use of a patent's disclosure in interpreting its claims:

> [I]n what appears to be a growing number of cases decided by the Federal Circuit involving the drawing of the . . . line [between using the specification to construe claims, and improperly narrowing claims by "reading in" claim limitations from the specification], whether a "broad" construction was adopted over a "narrow" one hinged upon whether the specification either suggested, implied or otherwise hinted at a "broad" interpretation of the disputed claim term. Such an approach to claim construction would appear to put a burden on the patentee to expressly describe the scope of the invention in the body of the patent, rather than merely relying on the use of broad terminology in the claims. At the same time, it has a practical effect of narrowing the literal scope of patent claims to cover only disclosed "embodiments" of the invention. . . . [This article] suggests practical tips for drafting patent applications with an eye towards obtaining claims that will be "broadly" interpreted to cover a scope commensurate with the breadth of the true invention.

82 J. Pat. & Trademark Off. Soc'y 539, 539-540.

Means-plus-function claims, authorized in 35 U.S.C. §112 ¶6, are often employed in software inventions. Claim elements drafted in this format allow a patentee to cover the specific embodiments disclosed in a specification, "and equivalents thereof." The Federal Circuit has struggled in the past with the relationship between §112 ¶6 equivalents and the doctrine of equivalents. See for example the opinion in *Alpex*, earlier this chapter.

D. DESIGN PATENTS ON SOFTWARE

While the most common form of patent is a "utility" patent, described in 35 U.S.C. §101, patents are also available for certain industrial designs. 35 U.S.C. §171 et seq. Relatively recently, some software designers have attempted to protect elements of their user interface as design patents.

Ex Parte Donaldson
Board of Patent Appeals and Interferences
26 U.S.P.Q.2d 1250 (Bd. Pat. App. & Int. 1992)

MANBECK, Commissioner.

This is an appeal from the examiner's decision finally rejecting the sole claim in the application.

The subject matter on appeal is a design for an icon. The sole claim on appeal states:

> The ornamental design for a softkey display or the like, as shown and described.

The design as shown in the drawing figures is reproduced below [Figure 3-5]:

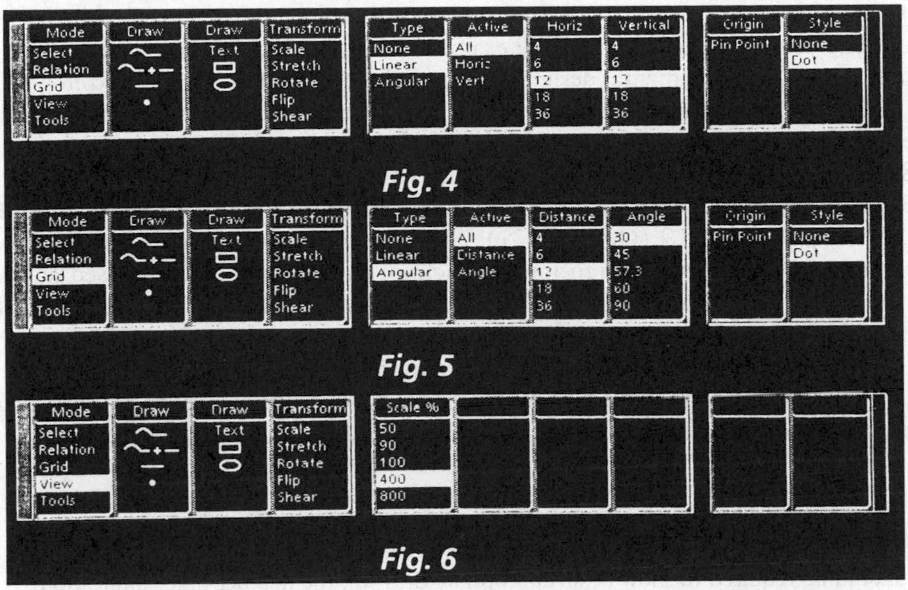

Mode	Draw	Draw	Transform	Type	Active	Horiz	Vertical	Origin	Style
Select	∿	Text	Scale	None	All	4	4	Pin Point	None
Relation	∿•—		Stretch	Linear	Horiz	6	6		Dot
Grid	—		Rotate	Angular	Vert	12	12		
View	•		Flip			18	18		
Tools			Shear			36	36		

Fig. 4

Mode	Draw	Draw	Transform	Type	Active	Distance	Angle	Origin	Style
Select	∿	Text	Scale	None	All	4	30	Pin Point	None
Relation	∿•—		Stretch	Linear	Distance	6	45		Dot
Grid	—		Rotate	Angular	Angle	12	57.3		
View	•		Flip			18	60		
Tools			Shear			36	90		

Fig. 5

Mode	Draw	Draw	Transform	Scale %
Select	∿	Text	Scale	50
Relation	∿•—		Stretch	90
Grid	—		Rotate	100
View	•		Flip	400
Tools			Shear	800

Fig. 6

FIGURE 3-5
Ornamental design for a Softkey display.

. . . The sole claim stands rejected as unpatentable under 35 U.S.C. §171. After careful consideration of appellant's arguments presented in the briefs and at oral hearing, we affirm the examiner's rejection.

Section 171 of Title 35 provides:

> Whoever invents any new, original and ornamental design for an article of manufacture may obtain a patent therefor, subject to the conditions and requirements of this title.

The examiner concluded that the claimed design was nonstatutory, finding that the design was not an "ornamental design for an article of manufacture. . . ." While the examiner set forth her reasoning in great detail, the thrust of her position is that the design, as claimed, is merely a picture or surface ornamentation per se rather than a design applied to an article. The examiner notes that the specification does not describe, claim or show the claimed design applied to any article of manufacture. Appellant argues that the

> claimed invention is an ornamental design for the display screen of a programmed computer system. A programmed computer system, comprising a processor, a display device and a program executing on the processor is an article of manufacture. The claimed design is surface ornamentation for a particular region of the display screen, and thus qualifies as statutory subject matter.

The examiner responded stating:

> The fact that a programmed computer system running the necessary software may be an article of manufacture, does not help appellant here. No programmed

computer system is either depicted or described. Section 1.152 [of 37 C.F.R.] is explicit in requiring that the article of manufacture be shown in the drawings.

The respective positions of the examiner and appellant require us to consider the meaning of "ornamental design for an article of manufacture" as used in §171.

The phrase "design for an article of manufacture" has long appeared in the design statutes. The language appears in Revised Statutes §4929, May 9, 1902, ch. 783, 32 Stat. 209; was reenacted in 35 U.S.C. §73 (1946) and again reenacted in 35 U.S.C. §171 (1952). The CCPA construed the phrase in In re Schnell, 46 F.2d 203, 8 USPQ 19 (CCPA 1931). The court noted that the language "new, original and ornamental design for an article of manufacture encompassed at least three kinds of designs: 1) a design for an ornament, impression, print or picture to be applied to an article of manufacture (surface ornamentation); 2) a design for the shape or configuration of an article of manufacture; and 3) a combination of the first two categories. 46 F.2d at 209, 8 USPQ at 26. With respect to the first category the court indicated the design statute required more than a mere picture.

> We think that Assistant Commissioner Clay was right in saying [in Ex parte Cady, 1916 Dec. Com'r. Pat. 57, 58] that the design must be shown not to be the mere invention of a picture, irrespective of its manner of use, but that the applicant should be required to show by an appropriate drawing the manner of its application.

46 F.2d at 209, 8 USPQ at 26. The Court went on to state:

> It is the application of the design to an article of manufacture that Congress wishes to promote, and an applicant has not reduced his invention to practice and has been of little help to the art if he does not teach the manner of applying his design.

46 F.2d at 209, 8 USPQ at 26.

The CCPA again interpreted the phrase in In re Zahn, 617 F.2d 261, 204 USPQ 988 (CCPA 1980). The issue in *Zahn* was whether or not §171 permitted claiming a design for a portion of an article of manufacture, a drill tool. The court noted that under §171 a design must be "embodied" in an article:

> Section 171 authorizes patents on ornamental designs *for* articles of manufacture. While the design must be *embodied* in some article, the statute is not limited to designs for complete articles, or "discrete" articles, and certainly not to articles separately sold. . . . Here the design is embodied in the shank portion of a drill and a drill is unquestionably an article of manufacture. It is applied design as distinguished from abstract design. (Emphasis original.)

617 F.2d at 268, 204 USPQ at 995.

These decisions indicate that a picture standing alone is not protectable by a design patent. The factor which distinguishes statutory design subject matter from mere pictures or surface ornamentation per se (i.e., abstract designs) is the embodiment of the design in an article of manufacture. In order to meet this threshold requirement of an applied design, we conclude that an applicant's specification must expressly disclose some article of manufacture ornamented by the design.

We find that appellant's claimed design, as disclosed in the application before us, is merely a picture. Appellant's specification does not show, describe or claim the design embodied in any article of manufacture. Only pictures of the icon are shown or described. The claimed subject matter, therefore, does not meet the requirements of 35 U.S.C. §171.

Appellant asserts that the design should be considered surface ornamentation upon the display screen of a computer system. We have no doubt that the claimed design, like all surface ornamentation-type designs, could be used to ornament a wide variety of articles, including computers. However, the phrase "design for an article of manufacture" in §171 requires more than a depiction of the surface ornamentation alone. It requires disclosure of the ornamentation applied to or embodied in an article of manufacture. More than an applicant's generalized intent to ornament some article is required. It is the application of the design to an article which separates mere pictures from a design protectable by a patent. Without express disclosure of an article, the design is not an applied design contemplated for protection under §171.

Consistent with §171, PTO regulations expressly require such disclosure. Thus, 37 CFR §1.153(a) states:

> (a) The title of the design must designate the particular article. No description, other than a reference to the drawing, is ordinarily required. The claim shall be in formal terms to the ornamental design for the article (specifying name) as shown, or as shown and described. . . .

37 CFR §1.152 states:

> The design must be represented by a drawing made in conformity with the rules laid down for drawings of mechanical inventions and must contain a sufficient number of views to constitute a *complete disclosure of the appearance of the article*. Appropriate surface shading must be used to show the character or contour of the surfaces represented. Broken lines may be used to show visible environmental structure, but may not be used to show hidden planes and surfaces which cannot be seen through opaque materials. (Emphasis added [by court].)

Appellant has not described, shown or claimed the design as surface ornamentation for a computer system. The word "icon" does not limit the design to use with a display screen of a computer or any other article of manufacture. Icons are and have been used with a variety of articles. As we stated above, appellant's design, as shown and described, is merely a picture which has not been disclosed applied to any article.

AFFIRMED 37 CFR §1.196(b).

COMMENTS AND QUESTIONS

1. In a companion case to *Donaldson*, the Board of Patent Applications and Interferences (BPAI) held that an applicant was not entitled to claim an icon on a computer screen as a design patent, for essentially the same reasons. Ex parte Strijland, 26 U.S.P.Q.2d 1259 (Bd. Pat. App. & Int. 1992). However, the Board suggested that if the patentee had claimed an "information icon for display screen of a programmed computer system," and submitted a drawing *of the entire computer system* showing the icon on the screen, the Board would have held the claim

to be patentable subject matter. Indeed, the Board even offered a proposed drawing (Figure 3-6) as an appendix to the opinion.

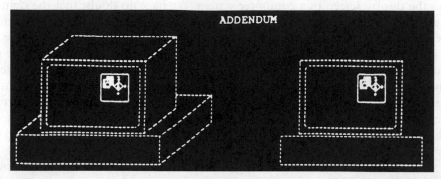

FIGURE 3-6
Proposed drawing of acceptable computer system.

Why does it matter how the design is described in the drawings?

2. In 1996, the PTO issued final guidelines governing the examination of design patent applications directed to computer icons. The guidelines follow the suggestion in *Strijland* that icons are patentable so long as they are shown on a computer screen, monitor, "or a portion thereof." The guidelines also suggest that computer-generated type fonts may be the subject of design patent protection. This is only the latest twist in a history of vacillations by the PTO over whether icons and other user interface elements should be entitled to design patents.

3. Design patents are not available for designs that are "dictated by functional considerations." See Power Controls Corp. v. Hybrinetics, Inc., 806 F.2d 234, 238 (Fed. Cir. 1986). To what extent does this limit the availability of design patent protection for the screen displays in *Donaldson*? For the icon in *Strijland*?

4. Design patents are in many respects more like trademarks than like utility patents. It is worth considering the extent to which design patent protection for computer icons overlaps with copyright and trademark protection. We consider trademark and trade dress protection in the next chapter.

4

Trademarks and Trade Dress

The computer industry relies not only on trade secrecy, copyrights, and patents, but also on trademark and trade dress protection. Some of the strongest brands in America are computer industry brands—IBM, Intel, and Microsoft—and many others are also household names. Even where products are technically interchangeable, campaigns like "Intel inside" have given consumers a preference for specific brands.

In part, the reliance of this industry on trademarks is due to network effects. Consumers place significant value on obtaining application programs that are compatible with popular operating systems and peripheral equipment that connects with their base computer systems. Equipment and software manufacturers, therefore, use trademarks as an important part of their overall strategy to protect and market their products. Trademarks can signal or suggest compatibility and can serve as guarantors that a product meets a certain standard. In this way, trademark protection can significantly enhance the protection for new technology. On the other hand, trademark protection can also potentially inhibit competition if it limits the ability of new entrants to inform consumers of the compatible attributes of their products. Similar problems exist with respect to trademark law and Internet domain names.[1]

In the United States, protection for trademarks and trade dress is provided by the Lanham Act, 15 U.S.C. §1051 et seq., and by state common law. Trademark law generally applies to computers and computer companies in the same way that it does to other industries. For instance, Apple Computer is entitled to prevent competitors from selling computers with names confusingly similar to Apple (such as Pineapple). Apple Computer v. Formula Int'l, 562 F. Supp. 775 (C.D. Cal. 1983). Intel was not entitled to protect its "386" name for microprocessors because the x86 designation has been generic in the industry for some time, at least among the computer industry professionals who buy such chips and resell them in computers. Intel v. Advanced Micro Devices, 756 F. Supp. 1292 (N.D. Cal.

---

1. Those problems are discussed in Chapter 10.

229

1991). In this chapter, though, we are not concerned with "ordinary" trademark issues that happen to come up in the computer context; rather, we focus on several circumstances in which the computer industry presents unique trademark issues.

We identify three such circumstances in the sections that follow. As you work through these cases and problems, assess the degree to which trademark law promotes (or retards) innovation in the computer industry, and consider whether that is even the goal of trademark law.

A. PROTECTING PROGRAMS THROUGH TRADEMARK

Note on Protection of Product Configurations

Trademarks are traditionally thought of as words or other written symbols or logos describing a product, service, or company. However, the Lanham Act also protects "trade dress"—a term that encompasses the total design of product packaging, including its shape and color. In a series of cases during the past decade, the Supreme Court has refined the scope of trade dress protection.

In Two Pesos, Inc. v. Taco Cabana, 505 U.S. 763 (1992), the Court recognized that the total design of the interior of a fast-food Mexican restaurant was entitled to Lanham Act protection. Courts have since struggled with determining the requirements for trade dress protection. In Wal-Mart Stores, Inc. v. Samara Brothers, Inc., 529 U.S. 205 (2000), the Court distinguished between two forms of trade dress: product packaging and product configuration. In an effort to constrain the expansion of trade dress protection, the Court held that the former obtains trade dress protection if it is inherently distinctive, whereas the latter garners such protection only upon establishing secondary meaning (even if it is inherently distinctive). More recently, the Court has held that a person asserting trade dress protection for a patented (whether in force or expired) product design or element bears a heavy burden in rebutting a presumption that the trade dress is functional and hence not protectable under trademark law. TrafFix Devices, Inc. v. Marketing Displays, Inc., 532 U.S. 23 (2001).

These considerations are relevant to the computer industry because some—and perhaps all—of the products capable of trademark protection in that industry qualify as product configurations and many have functional aspects. Certainly, the shape of a computer or monitor such as the iMac is a product configuration. Cf. Digital Computer Controls v. C. Itoh, 229 U.S.P.Q. 598 (D.N.J. 1985) (evaluating product configuration protection for the shape of a computer monitor). Arguably, so is the layout of icons and menus on a computer screen—though the "product" being shaped in the latter case is a bit more ephemeral. Cf. Ex parte Donaldson, 26 U.S.P.Q.2d 1250 (Bd. Pat. App. & Int. 1992) (reproduced in Chapter 3).

In previous chapters, we have discussed various means of protecting computer software and hardware against imitation by others. The following article suggests that trademark could also be used to protect the "look and feel" of computer software against imitation. As you review this excerpt, consider whether graphical user interfaces should be thought of as trade dress or as product configuration and, indeed, whether it makes sense to protect them under trademark law at all.

Lauren Fisher Kellner, Trade Dress Protection for Computer User Interface "Look and Feel"
61 U. Chi. L. Rev. 1011 (1994)

An employee on the way back to his office glances at the illuminated screen of a nearby computer. He sees the small trash can in the lower right corner; graphics of labeled folders, documents, and applications in the center; and a strip of words across the top of the screen. He immediately assumes that the computer is an Apple Macintosh. A spreadsheet programmer determines that an application program requires her to use a backslash to access multi-layered command menus and to strike the first letter of layered menu items in sequence in order to execute any series of commands. She knows the software must be Lotus 1-2-3.

Apple and Lotus realize that computer users rely on these elements to identify computer programs. Accordingly, both companies have invested time and money to build consumer recognition of their programs and have sought legal protection for their user interfaces. . . .

Both the academic literature and litigants' briefs have focused on copyright as a way to protect a developer's intellectual property rights in a software product's "look and feel." Trademark law, however, would be a better source of protection. Trademark law recognizes consumers' interests in identifying a product's source, and trade dress law, a subset of trademark law, protects a product's overall appearance to the purchasing public. While trade dress infringement claims have become more common in all product areas over the past few years, only a few attorneys have aggressively sought trade dress protection for the "look and feel" of user interfaces. . . .

The first requirement for trademark protection of any product feature or set of features is "distinctiveness"—the feature must be able to indicate the source of the product. . . .

Some user interfaces create an inherently distinctive visual impression. For example, Berkeley Systems's After Dark screen saver program features a stylized underwater scene: colorful fish, gurgling noises, and winged toasters. That visual display is unique and unusual enough to qualify as inherently distinctive. In general, then, program developers that create unique visual displays should be able to meet trademark law's distinctiveness requirement without showing secondary meaning. . . .

The trend toward standardization of user interfaces presents a potential obstacle to manufacturers' attempts to establish distinctiveness. Most user interfaces are unique when introduced. But microcomputer markets are moving toward "standard user interfaces" among programs in an attempt to reduce the time it takes to learn a new application. This "family look" promotes sales *within* product lines (among all programs designed to run on one type of computer) and *across* product lines (between programs designed for different computer systems) by increasing consumer confidence in and familiarity with standard techniques. Standardization may make it difficult, if not impossible, for a plaintiff to establish distinctiveness because "in markets with standard user interfaces, programs are *expected* to look and feel the same." [Gregory Wrenn, Federal Intellectual Property Protection for Computer Software Audiovisual Look and Feel: The Lanham, Copyright, and Patent Acts, 4 High Tech. L.J. 279, 284 (1989).]

. . . The likelihood of point-of-sale consumer confusion seems low because computers and software are typically sold in clearly marked packages. It is thus unlikely (though conceivable) that a purchaser intending to buy Lotus 1-2-3 would end up buying, say, VP-Planner instead.

In contrast, potential consumers of computer products may see a computer's user interface on co-workers' desks or in store windows and assume that they are viewing the Apple Macintosh or Lotus 1-2-3 interface. By the time they eventually discover that they were really viewing Microsoft Windows or VP-Planner, they may already have invested time and energy in researching and shopping for the wrong product. Microsoft Windows or VP-Planner retailers could then convince these potential consumers that the look-alike products are indistinguishable from the Macintosh or Lotus 1-2-3; they will have used Apple's or Lotus's reputation and customer recognition to lure customers into investigating and ultimately purchasing look-alike products. Trade dress law attempts to prevent precisely this kind of misappropriation of another product's good reputation.

COMMENTS AND QUESTIONS

1. "Distinctiveness" is a term of art that encompasses trademarks that are arbitrary, suggestive, or fanciful, or that are descriptive of the products they identify but have acquired "secondary meaning" in the minds of consumers as identifying a product from a particular source. Trademark protection does not extend to trademarks or trade dress that are merely descriptive of the things being identified. Further, in no case can a generic term or dress be protected. Kellner suggests that many user interfaces will be inherently distinctive because the way the interface works is unrelated to the nature of the functions performed. In practice, however, individual elements of the user interface may merely be descriptive of the functions performed. How would a court classify the "trash can" icon in the Macintosh graphical user interface (GUI), which serves to delete files? the Lotus 1-2-3 program's choice of the "D" key for delete, "F" for file, or "Q" for quit? the choice of the terms themselves? See Lotus v. Borland, discussed in Chapter 2. Note that these problems are not necessarily specific to computer icons; arguably, any trade dress or product configuration is hard to classify using guidelines designed for word marks. See Wal-Mart Stores, Inc. v. Samara Brothers, 529 U.S. 205 (2000).

Must these individual elements be distinctive in order to be protected, or is it sufficient that the interface *as a whole* is not "descriptive" of a computer operating system? Note the parallels here to the copyright case of Apple v. Microsoft, reprinted in Chapter 2. There, Apple argued for a wholistic "look and feel" approach to copyright infringement—an approach rejected by the court. Is there any reason to prefer such an approach in trademark law? Would *Apple* have been decided differently if Apple had alleged trademark rather than copyright infringement?

2. User interfaces may also run afoul of the "genericide" doctrine. If a particular interface has become the de facto standard in the industry, so people naturally use that interface for a certain type of program, the interface is likely to be generic and therefore unprotectable. A good example is the QWERTY keyboard, an "interface" that may have been arbitrary as a means of organizing letters when it was introduced but that has since become a universal keyboard standard. Because consumers do not associate the QWERTY keyboard with a particular maker, but rather with the general idea of a typewriter, that keyboard is generic and therefore incapable of trademark protection. The same fate may befall certain elements of graphical user interfaces, such as pull-down menus. Even if the use of pull-down menus once identified the computer as an Apple, their prevalence in numerous programs today suggests that Apple may no longer be able to claim to own them.

Does it make sense that the very success of a GUI should be its undoing from the standpoint of trademark law? Quite possibly. One effect of the genericness rule is to prevent a particular company from using trademark law to corner the market on an industry standard and thereby foreclose competition in the underlying products. We discuss this issue in more detail in the next Section.

3. Kellner acknowledges that consumers are unlikely to be confused between different GUIs at the point of sale. There is no question that Apple and Microsoft, for example, package their products very differently. Neither is attempting to trade on the business goodwill of the other. But she suggests that post-sale confusion is still possible—that is, that consumers will see one operating system in action, think it is the other, and proceed to buy the wrong computer. (The last step in this chain is critical, because the Lanham Act is concerned with the likelihood of confusion among *consumers* of the products at issue.)

Whether you think such post-sale confusion is likely depends in part on your assessment of the sophistication of the purchasing public. Several courts have found confusion unlikely in the computer context because the buyers were relatively sophisticated and they were purchasing "big ticket" items. See, e.g., Engineering Dynamics, Inc. v. Structural Software, Inc., 26 F.3d 1335, 1350 (5th Cir. 1994) (competing software programs did not create a likelihood of confusion among sophisticated users in a limited market; consumers pay little attention to trade dress in determining which product to purchase); Intel v. Advanced Micro Devices, 756 F. Supp. 1292 (N.D. Cal. 1991) (purchasers of Intel microprocessors were computer hardware manufacturers, not end users; hardware manufacturers were sophisticated enough to distinguish between Intel 386 and AMD 386 chips). In both cases, however, the consumers were not end users but sophisticated purchasers of computer equipment.

4. Before some of the Supreme Court's recent decisions curtailing the scope of trade dress protection, Tom Bell expressed concern that trade dress protection of virtual reality—from video game environments to distinctive Web sites—could result in excessive protection. See Tom W. Bell, Virtual Trade Dress: A Very Real Problem, 56 Md. L. Rev. 384 (1997). Does this seem likely?

5. Even if consumers are not confused, might programmers have a cause of action for trademark dilution, a theory that protects certain famous marks against any use in connection with other goods, even if consumers are not confused? See 15 U.S.C. §1125(c) (standards under new federal antidilution act). Can the Mac-

intosh GUI be said to be "famous"? If so, does the use of pull-down menus by other companies reduce the identification value of the Apple mark?

6. How does protecting GUIs under trademark law comport with the purposes of the Lanham Act? Does it overreach—and thus destroy useful competition in an attempt to prevent some relatively minor instances of consumer confusion? In this regard, it is worth noting that the use of trade dress law to protect user interfaces has so far been rare. In 1996, one commentator reported that only two decisions had considered the question of interface trade dress protection, and both had rejected the trade dress claim. See Lisa T. Oratz, User Interfaces: Copyrights vs. Trade Dress Protection, 13 Computer Law. 1, 3 (1996).

7. The most significant limitation on trade dress protection for computer programs is functionality. Trademark protection does not extend to any part of the dress that is functional. Since computer icons normally serve a purpose, application of functionality should significantly limit their protection. Further, since the goal of interface design is to simplify a consumer's interaction with the machine, certain types of user interface elements (say, those based on the principle "what you see is what you get") may inherently serve a useful function.

Recall that much of the debate over the appropriate scope of protection for GUIs in the copyright context had to do with whether elements of the interface were dictated by functional considerations. See Apple Computer v. Microsoft Corp., 35 F.3d 1435 (9th Cir. 1994). Isn't that debate likely to be replicated in the trademark context, with courts disagreeing over whether particular portions of the GUI are economically or aesthetically functional? If so, is there any advantage to seeking trademark rather than copyright protection?

One possible difference between trademark and copyright law may be the way in which functionality is tested. There is a debate in trademark law over whether the functionality of trade dress is to be tested by looking at the dress as a whole or by evaluating the purpose of individual elements. On this point, see Stormy Clime Ltd. v. Progroup, Inc., 809 F.2d 971 (2d Cir. 1987) (jacket contained a unique and protectable combination of functional elements). This debate, too, has its parallels in the copyright context, though it is all but resolved that copyright focuses on the individual elements rather than the program as a whole in determining functionality. Compare Computer Associates v. Altai, 982 F.2d 693 (2d Cir. 1992), and its progeny with Whelan Associates v. Jaslow Dental Laboratory, 797 F.2d 1222 (3d Cir. 1986).

An "element by element" approach to trademark functionality may be particularly appropriate in the software context, where alleged infringers take only a few key pieces of the plaintiff's trade dress (such as overlapping folders and pull-down menus from the Macintosh interface). If the elements taken are all functional, presumably no court would find trademark infringement even if the interface as a whole is protectable.[2]

Is there reason for trademark owners to prefer one of these approaches over the other? It is reasonable to assume that testing functionality as a whole will allow

---

2. In 1998, Congress codified functionality as a basis for refusing registration, as well as a ground for opposition and cancellation and a defense to incontestability. Functional marks may appear on the *Supplemental Register.* See Pub. L. 105-330, Title II, §201(a)(4), Title III, §301, 112 Stat. 3070, codified at 15 U.S.C. §§1052, 1064, 1091, 1115 (1998).

greater leeway for protecting partially functional trade dress, but the reverse may be true: If any part of the interface is functional, none of it is protectable.

8. Protecting software product configurations obviously overlaps not only with copyright law but also with design patent law, which now protects computer icons in certain circumstances. See A. Hugo Word, The New Guidelines on Protection of Computer-Generated Icons and Typeface, 24 AIPLA Q.J. 415 (1996). Should such overlap be permissible? Note that some courts are unwilling to permit product configurations that are the subject of a utility patent to be protected under trade dress law as well, perhaps out of a concern that the owner of the design will be able to extend protection beyond the term of the patent. See Vornado Air Circulation Systems v. Duracraft Corp., 58 F.3d 1498 (10th Cir. 1995). For a detailed discussion of this issue, see Jay Dratler, Jr., Trade Dress Protection for Product Configurations: Is There a Conflict with Patent Policy?, 24 AIPLA Q.J. 427 (1996); Michael S. Perez, Reconciling the Patent Act and the Lanham Act: Should Product Configurations Be Entitled to Trade Dress Protection After the Expiration of a Utility or Design Patent?, 4 Tex. Intell. Prop. L.J. 383 (1996).

9. America Online has obtained rights in the service mark "ONLINE TODAY" and successfully opposed another company from registering "ON-LINE TODAY" for an electronic publication. See On-Line Careline, Inc. v. America Online, Inc., 229 F.3d 1080 (Fed. Cir. 2000). On the other hand, "You Have Mail" was held generic. America Online, Inc. v. AT&T Corp., 243 F.3d 812 (4th Cir. 2001).

PROBLEMS

Problem 4-1. Apple's Macintosh graphical user interface has three main components that are copied by Kiwi Computer in its competing operating system. The three components are pull-down menus, in which the user commands are contained in a bar at the top of the screen that can be opened by clicking on the relevant command with a mouse and by dragging the mouse downward; a series of icons on the right-hand side of the screen to perform common commands or to open particular folders; and overlapping windows that show the most recently used document or program on top of other open applications.

Apple contends that none of these three components is functional and points to other ways in which Kiwi could have implemented a graphical user interface. For example, Apple argues that Kiwi could have used "pull-up" or "pull-across" menus, or an expandable list of commands controlled by the keyboard or by voice rather than by the mouse. Kiwi responds that it is easier and more logical for most computer users to drag the mouse downward than to push it up or across. Apple points to alternatives to its overlapping windows such as "tiled windows" that appear side by side; Kiwi responds that tiled windows are inefficient because they limit both the number of windows that can be open and the size of each open window.

Are Apple's design features functional? Does you answer depend on the legal standard you apply?

> *Problem 4-2.* Intel manufactures generations of microprocessor chips with identifying number sequences. For reference, these number sequences are shortened to the last three digits and are commonly referred to by computer users in this way (e.g., the 286, 287, 386, 387, 486, etc.). Advanced Micro Devices, a competing microprocessor manufacturer, refers to its comparable chips by the same number sequences. Has AMD infringed an Intel trademark?
>
> Intel refers to its latest generation of chip as the Pentium. From a trademark perspective, what are the advantages and disadvantages of this change-in-naming convention?

B. COMPATIBILITY AND STANDARDIZATION

A second way in which trademark law may operate to influence the market for computer products directly is in the areas of standardization and compatibility.[3] Because computer hardware and software are sold in complex markets with high network externalities both among and between products, there is tremendous value to be gained not only in identifying one's own product, but in describing for consumers how it interacts with other products on the market. For example, the sellers of applications programs want to be able to tell their customers whether or not their program will run with a particular operating system. Because identifying the operating system often involves the use of a competitor's trademark, however, trademark law stands as a potential barrier to this form of compatibility identification.

≡
≡
≡   *Creative Labs, Inc. v. Cyrix Corporation*
≡   United States District Court for the Northern District of California
≡   *42 U.S.P.Q.2d 1872 (N.D. Cal. 1997)*

WILKEN, District Judge.

Plaintiffs Creative Labs and Creative Technology (collectively "Creative") move for a preliminary injunction against Defendants Cyrix Corporation and Tiger Direct, Inc. ("Tiger") for copyright infringement and false advertising. Defendants oppose the motion. The matter was heard on May 2, 1997. On May 2, 1997, Creative also filed an ex parte application for an order to show cause re contempt. Having considered all of the papers filed by the parties and oral argument on the motion, the Court GRANTS the motion for a preliminary injunction and DENIES the ex parte application for an order to show cause.

---

3. We have already encountered standardization in the previous Section in the context of genericness.

Background

Plaintiff Creative is the maker of the Sound Blaster line of sound cards, devices that interact with computer hardware and software to create sound effects. Sound Blaster is currently the dominant sound card on the market. Defendant Cyrix has recently introduced a microprocessor, the Media GX, which is capable of producing audio effects without the assistance of a sound card. The audio component of the Media GX is referred to as XpressAUDIO.

Cyrix has advertised XpressAUDIO as "compatible with Sound Blaster" and as "fully compatible with Sound Blaster." Tiger, a computer manufacturer which plans to introduce a line of computers that use the Media GX, claims that its products feature "integrated SoundBlaster 16/Pro compatible audio." Compaq uses the Media GX in one of its computers, the Presario 2100, but does not advertise that the Presario 2100 is Sound Blaster compatible.

Creative tested the Media GX on a Presario 2100 computer to determine whether Cyrix's claims concerning XpressAUDIO's compatibility with Sound Blaster were accurate. In a study testing 200 computer games, Creative discovered that sixteen games, or 8% of the total tested, did not run properly on the Presario 2100. Creative also found that the Presario 2100 did not support two functions supported by Sound Blaster: Adaptive Delta Pulse Code Modulation ("ADPCM") and Musical Instrument Digital Interface ("MIDI").

Creative also learned that Cyrix was making some Creative Labs software programs available for copying by the public on Cyrix's website.

Creative filed suit against Cyrix for copyright infringement, 17 U.S.C. §510 et seq.; against Cyrix and Tiger for false advertising and trademark dilution, 15 U.S.C. §1125(a), (c); and against Cyrix, Tiger, and Compaq for trademark infringement, 15 U.S.C. §§1114(a), 1125(a), and unfair competition, Cal.Bus. & Prof.Code §17200 et seq. The Court granted Creative's application for a temporary restraining order against Cyrix and Tiger. Creative now seeks a preliminary injunction enjoining all Defendants from trademark infringement, Cyrix and Tiger from false advertising, and Cyrix from copyright violations. In this order, the Court considers only the claims concerning false advertising and copyright infringement.

Discussion . . .

B. *False Advertising*

Creative alleges that Cyrix and Tiger advertisements which assert that the XpressAUDIO system is "compatible" with Sound Blaster constitute false advertising in violation of Lanham Act §43(a), 15 U.S.C. §1125(a). The elements of a Lanham Act false advertising claim are:

> (1) a false statement of fact by the defendant in a commercial advertisement about its own or another's product; (2) the statement actually deceived or has the tendency to deceive a substantial segment of its audience; (3) the deception is material, in that it is likely to influence the purchasing decision; (4) the defendant caused its false statement to enter interstate commerce; and (5) the plaintiff has been or is

likely to be injured as a result of the false statement, either by direct diversion of sales from itself to defendant or by a lessening of the goodwill associated with its products.

Southland Sod Farms v. Stover Seed Co., 108 F.3d 1134, 1139 (9th Cir. 1997). Plaintiffs do not need to prove injury to be entitled to injunctive relief. *Id.* at 1145-46.

Plaintiffs seek to enjoin Cyrix and Tiger from advertising that their systems are Sound Blaster compatible. Cyrix and Tiger respond that XpressAUDIO is compatible with Sound Blaster. The dispute thus turns on the definition of the term "compatible." Creative maintains that competing computer products are compatible only if "the first product can be used in place of the second product without producing any difference in performance and that the first product has the same capabilities and functions as the second product." Creative supplied the declaration of an individual who works in the computer games industry asserting that the phrase "Sound Blaster compatible" indicates that the hardware "will properly play any software title that plays properly on a genuine Creative Labs Sound Blaster." Creative also refers to three dictionary definitions to support its interpretation. One provides that "[c]ompatibility means that the hardware ideally operates in all respects like the standard on which it is based." The second dictionary defines compatibility as, "[t]he capability of a peripheral [or] program . . . to function with or substitute for a given make and model of computer. . . . To be truly compatible, a program or device should operate on a given system without modification; all features should operate as intended, and a computer claiming to be compatible with another should run all the other computer's software without modification." By referring to a device for measuring how IBM-compatible personal computers are, however, the definition suggests that compatibility is not necessarily a matter of all or nothing. The third dictionary provides that compatibility is "[t]he extent to which a given piece of hardware or software conforms to an accepted standard. . . . This implies that the device will perform in every way just like the standard device." Cyrix cites a dictionary which defines the term "compatible" as describing a product which meets some, but not all, parts of a specification.

Princeton Graphics Operating, L.P. v. NEC Home Electronics (U.S.A.), Inc., 732 F. Supp. 1258 (S.D.N.Y. 1990), supports Creative's definition of compatibility. In *Princeton Graphics*, the court chose the more restrictive definition because of the importance of precise definitions in the computer industry. *Id.* at 1261. It also believed that it is appropriate to apply a more precise definition of compatibility when a well-known industry standard is being used. *Id.* at 1262 n. 9. The Court therefore finds that a product advertising itself as Sound Blaster compatible must support the same functions as Sound Blaster.

Creative argues that XpressAUDIO is not compatible with Sound Blaster because it does not support all games that can function with Sound Blaster. Creative relies on a study in which sixteen computer games, 8% of all games tested, did not function properly on a Presario 2100 computer. The study, however, does not establish that those failures were due to incompatibilities between XpressAUDIO and Sound Blaster. Cyrix counters that it did not encounter problems when running six of these games on a properly configured computer. *Id.* Cyrix's own study indicates a failure rate of approximately 2%. Even if the failure rate of games played on computers with XpressAUDIO is closer to 2% than 8%, the evidence indicates that some games that function with Sound Blaster do not function with Xpress-AUDIO.

Creative also argues that XpressAUDIO is not Sound Blaster compatible because it does not support two specific functions supported by Sound Blaster: ADPCM and MIDI. Cyrix concedes that XpressAUDIO does not support ADPCM, but it maintains that few games employ ADPCM, that those games are not currently being sold, and that ADPCM does not meet consumer expectations of sound quality. The lack of ADPCM support, while perhaps insufficient to establish lack of compatibility alone, supports such a finding.

Creative also maintains that XpressAUDIO does not support Sound Blaster's MIDI function. XpressAUDIO, however, does support MIDI. The MIDI function can be turned off by the computer manufacturer. Compaq has turned off the MIDI feature on the XpressAUDIO systems used in Presario 2100 computers. Cyrix has not advertised that Presario 2100s are Sound Blaster compatible.

Because some computer games that function with Sound Blaster do not function with XpressAUDIO, the Court finds that XpressAUDIO is probably not compatible with Sound Blaster. Cyrix and Tiger's claims that systems using XpressAUDIO are Sound Blaster compatible will probably mislead consumers who would interpret the claim of Sound Blaster compatibility to mean that any product that functions with Sound Blaster would also function with XpressAUDIO.

Because Creative has established the likelihood of consumer confusion, it has also established the possibility of irreparable harm. The Court also finds that injunctive relief would further the public's interest in being protected from false trade descriptions. See U-Haul Int'l, Inc. v. Jartran, Inc., 681 F.2d 1159, 1162 (9th Cir. 1982).

The Court therefore grants Creative's motion for a preliminary injunction enjoining Cyrix and Tiger from claiming that XpressAUDIO and computer systems using XpressAUDIO are Sound Blaster compatible. . . .

E. Temporary Restraining Order

The first part of the temporary restraining order signed March 28, 1997, was premised on the assumption that Cyrix motherboards or Media GX Architectural Systems caused computer systems to misidentify sound devices as Sound Blasters. The record no longer supports a finding that Cyrix hardware causes the misidentification. The portion of the temporary restraining order enjoining Cyrix and Tiger from selling hardware that causes computer systems to misidentify sound devices as Sound Blaster is therefore vacated.

Conclusion

For the foregoing reasons, Creative's motion for a preliminary injunction is GRANTED with regard to false advertising and copyright infringement.

1. Defendant Cyrix shall be and hereby is enjoined from distributing Creative's proprietary "applet" software; and

2. Defendants Cyrix Corporation and Tiger Direct, Inc. are hereby ordered to cease all advertising, promotional material, or packaging which claim that the

Media GX chip or microprocessor system, or the XpressAUDIO feature provided by the Media GX chip or microprocessor system, or any personal computer based on the Media GX chip or microprocessor system, including the "Tiger Gx86", is Sound Blaster compatible. Defendants Cyrix and Tiger may resume advertising XpressAUDIO or computer systems using XpressAUDIO as Sound Blaster compatible only if they render XpressAUDIO Sound Blaster compatible.

IT IS SO ORDERED.

COMMENTS AND QUESTIONS

1. In *Princeton Graphics*, cited in *Creative Labs*, Princeton, the maker of a monitor for IBM computers, sued NEC, a competing maker of monitors, because NEC had claimed its monitor was "compatible" with the new IBM video standard (a claim Princeton could not make for its own monitors). The court determined that the term "compatible" had a precise meaning specific to the computer industry, and that it required a high degree of interoperability:

> We find that within the "retail channel," the term "compatible" does not have the broad and flexible meaning as suggested by defendant when, as here, there is a possibility that a more precise definition may be applied.[8] Indeed, if there was one over-arching impression left on this court after the testimony given in this case it was that the computer industry is concerned with and depends upon accuracy. Thus, the testimony confirms our view that in an industry which depends upon accuracy, a lack of precision in the use of common terms, particularly in circumstances where those terms have the potential to be specific, would be an anomaly.
>
> . . . We therefore find that in light of the evidence the definition of "compatible" as understood in the "retail channel" of sophisticated users has a clear and definite meaning—i.e., when a clearly defined standard, like IBM's VGA standard, exists and is widely accepted within the industry, a "compatible" product must meet that standard or at least perform in a manner equivalent to the standard's requirements.[11]

Princeton Graphics Operating v. NEC Home Electronics USA, 732 F. Supp. 1258 (S.D.N.Y. 1990). The court went on to conclude that falsely advertising compati-

---

8. We make no finding as to the understanding of the term "compatible" in the broader consumer market.

11. We find that the dictionary and glossary definitions offered by defendant were of little probative value. Either the exhibit indicated only what the understanding might be within the general population and not the "retail channel," or the definition was worded in such a way to lend support to either party's position. The definitions set forth in the exhibits did little to indicate the common construction and understanding of the term within the "retail channel" when applied to concrete products.

Further, defendant offered articles published in trade magazines as evidence that "compatible" had a broad and flexible meaning within the "retail channel." However, the context of the use of "compatibility" varied in those articles. In certain articles "compatibility" was used in relation to "Super VGA" capability or in relation to a monochrome gas plasma video display's VGA capability. Thus, in those articles "compatibility" was being discussed in a different context than the instant situation. For example, testimony at trial indicated that "Super VGA" (800 x 600 resolution) is not an IBM standard. Accordingly, defendant's articles are not of great persuasive weight since we believe that a broader understanding of compatible is favored by the "retail channel" in the absence of a clear industry standard.

Moreover, although the articles were not offered for the truth of their contents, we note only one short article offered by defendant explicitly stated that the MultiSync was "fully compatible" with VGA, and that explicit representation was only contained in a caption to the article's accompanying illustration.

bility could affect market purchasing decisions, and therefore cause actionable injury:

> We believe that plaintiff has presented a reasonable basis for its belief it was likely that defendant's advertising caused it damage. First, it is logical to conclude that had consumers been faced with two monitor products in the spring and summer of 1987, neither of which claimed PS/2 compatibility, some might have chosen plaintiff's. It is also reasonable to assume that had there been no compatibility claim on the part of defendant in the spring of 1987, some consumers would have waited until the summer of 1987 to buy plaintiff's PS/2 compatible UltraSync. Accordingly, we conclude that plaintiff has standing to bring this action.[16]

Does holding NEC to such a high threshold for compatibility help or hurt consumers? On the one hand, preventing NEC from falsely claiming that it is fully compatible with IBM's VGA standard prevents consumers from buying the monitor under false pretenses. In this sense, defining compatibility strictly ensures that consumers will know what they are getting. On the other hand, this strict definition means that at that time, no one except IBM could claim that they made a VGA-compatible monitor. If consumers are unwilling to buy products unless they are advertised as compatible, the effect is to give IBM a monopoly on monitor sales associated with IBM computers. From a consumer standpoint, this may actually be less desirable. If a consumer is willing to settle for a cheaper, 95 percent compatible monitor, shouldn't they be allowed to do so?

Should NEC or Cyrix be allowed to advertise their "near-compatibility"? Under these decisions, how could they do so?

2. Both of the *Creative Labs* and *Princeton Graphics* cases arose under the false advertising provisions of section 43(a) of the Lanham Act. The Lanham Act's prohibition on false advertising operates in parallel to its protection of trademarks. (Because Princeton Graphics did not own the IBM or VGA trademarks, it had no right to bring a claim for trademark infringement.) Presumably IBM could have brought a similar case for false advertising. See Intel Corp. v. Advanced Micro Devices, Computer Indus. Lit. Rptr. 11730 (N.D. Cal. Aug. 27, 1990) (enjoining AMD from claiming that its products were compatible with Intel's 287 microprocessor).

3. In *Princeton Graphics*, the issue was whether NEC's monitor was in fact compatible with the VGA standard. Presumably Princeton would not have had a cause of action against NEC if its statements regarding compatibility were accurate. But would IBM have a cause of action for trademark infringement? After all, NEC is in some sense trading on the value of the IBM standard by associating its product with IBM in the minds of consumers.

The doctrine of non-trademark use provides that it is acceptable to use a party's trademark *to refer to that party's product*. The Lanham Act is concerned only with the appropriation of that trademark to refer to another product. See

---

16. Defendant asserts that since many customers in the "retail channel" research and test a monitor's capabilities before buying, even if defendant's claims were false it is unlikely that many in the "retail channel" were misled. Since the action has been bifurcated between liability and relief, during this liability phase plaintiff was not required to show proof of actual loss and to what extent any within the "retail channel" were actually influenced by defendant's claims to purchase MultiSync monitors. Thus, our conclusion that plaintiff has standing to bring this Lanham Act action does not imply that this court has reached any conclusion as to damages.

New Kids on the Block v. News America Publishing, 971 F.2d 302 (9th Cir. 1992). Just as it is allowable to identify a competitor's product accurately in a comparative advertisement, shouldn't it be allowable to make an accurate statement that your product works well with another product?

In a case parallel to *Creative Labs*, Creative claimed that Cyrix's advertisements constituted trademark infringement because they referred to Creative too often and might therefore create confusion as to sponsorship or affiliation in the minds of consumers. How should this argument be evaluated? If a consumer sees an NEC advertisement and assumes either (1) that IBM is selling the NEC monitor or (2) that IBM has endorsed or somehow approved the NEC monitor, the consumer's purchasing decision may be influenced. Confusion as to source and sponsorship are actionable under the Lanham Act. Companies such as IBM and Microsoft may try to prevent the use of their trademarks as compatibility identifiers, either because they are afraid of being associated with an inferior product or because restricting the use of the marks for compatibility purposes will boost their own sales of competing products.

Should trademark law prevent true statements concerning compatibility? The answer depends on the relative weight you place on competing policies. If you believe that a trademark confers strong property rights and that trademark owners are right to be concerned about free riders selling inferior goods on the basis of their compatibility, you might favor trademark protection in this context. On the other hand, if you believe that compatibility ought to be encouraged, you are likely to think consumers benefit from access to more accurate information about product alternatives.

4. *Standard-Setting Organizations.* The setting of industry standards, particularly where it is done by a group of industry representatives, may be protected as a collective or certification mark.[4] A certification mark is a mark used to designate goods that meet certain quality or accuracy standards. Rather than being reserved by a particular company, use of the certification mark is open to anyone who meets the standards set out by the owner of the mark. If VGA was protected by a certification mark, IBM could sue anyone who falsely claimed to meet the VGA compatibility standard, but it would have to permit use of its mark to identify goods that were, in fact, in compliance with the standard.

A number of companies have already established such certification standards. Examples include "SPARC" for computer equipment that meets standards set by Sun Microsystems, and "Windows—Ready to Run" for third-party programs that run on Microsoft's Windows operating system. See generally Mark A. Lemley, Intellectual Property Rights and Standard-Setting Organizations, 90 Calif. L. Rev. __ (forthcoming 2002); Mark F. Radcliffe, Trademarks in the Computer Industry: A New Role, 18:2 New Matter 1 (1993). Standards may also be set by third-party organizations, such as the Industrial Organization for Standardization (ISO) or the American National Standards Institute (ANSI). Companies who submit their product specifications as a standard to such groups generally give up control over the trademark to the standard-setting organization, which will permit anyone who meets the specification to use the mark.

---

4. 15 U.S.C. §1054 provides that certification marks may be registered under the same standards as a normal trademark.

Is the use of certification marks a reasonable compromise between the competing policies outlined above? Does it solve the problem of free riding?

5. *Java™*. In 1995, Sun Microsystems introduced Java™, an object-oriented programming language designed to allow software developers to distribute a single version of programming code capable of being run on many different operating system platforms and Web browsers. Sun initially applied to ISO to have Java designated a standard, while reserving the rights to the term "Java-compatible" to itself. Microsoft and other companies complained, suggesting that Sun was "trying to have their cake and eat it too." See Laurence Zuckerman, Sun Microsystems Rejects Suggestions That It Give Up Java, N.Y. Times, Sept. 23, 1997, at C7. In the end, Sun withdrew its application and has maintained JAVA as a proprietary, although essentially open, standard, subject to various contractual limitations. See David McGowan & Mark A. Lemley, Could Java Change Everything? The Competitive Propriety of a Proprietary Standard, 43 Antitrust Bull. 715 (1998).

PROBLEM

Problem 4-3. Microsoft Corporation uses the mark "Windows" for its graphical user interface computer operating system. It first introduced Microsoft Windows 1.0 in 1983. It filed for federal registration of the mark in 1990, which was initially rejected. After an appeal, the PTO ultimately dropped its opposition and registered the mark in 1995. Microsoft has continued to use the Windows mark for its family of graphical user interface operating system products.

In 2001, Michael Robertson founded Lindows.com, a company that sells a desktop computer operating system program called LindowsOS. LindowsOS is designed to run application programs written for both the Linux (open source) and Microsoft Windows operating systems.

Microsoft has filed a trademark infringement action alleging infringement and dilution of its federally registered mark by the use of Lindows.com and LindowsOS.

> A. What is Robertson's best argument for challenging the validity of the Windows mark? What is Microsoft's best rebuttal?
> B. What is your analysis of likelihood of confusion? Who should prevail?
> C. Who should prevail on the dilution claim?

Sun Microsystems, Inc. v. Microsoft Corp.
United States District Court for the Northern District of California
87 F. Supp.2d 992 (N.D. Cal. 2000)

WHYTE, District Judge. . . .

B. *The Compatibility Provisions of the TLDA*

Sun and Microsoft entered into a Technology Licensing and Distribution Agreement ("TLDA") on March 12, 1996. Pursuant to the TLDA, Sun granted to Microsoft a nonexclusive development license "under the Intellectual Property Rights of SUN to make, access, use, copy, view, display, modify, adapt, and create Derivative Works of the Technology in Source Code form for the purposes of developing, compiling to binary form and supporting Products." TLDA §2.1(a). Sun also granted Microsoft a limited distribution license to "make, use, import, reproduce, license, rent, lease, offer to sell, sell or otherwise distribute to end users as part of a Product or an upgrade to a Product, the Technology and Derivative Works thereof in binary form." TLDA §2.2(a)(iii). However, the TLDA also places compatibility requirements on Microsoft's commercially distributed implementations of the Java Technology. See TLDA §2.6(a)(vi) ("Licensee agrees that any new version of a Product that Licensee makes commercially available to the public after the most recent Compatibility Date shall only include the corresponding Compatible Implementation (subject to Licensee's right to exclude the Supplemental Java Classes pursuant to Section 2.7); provided, that any version of a Product which, as of such Compatibility Date, is being beta tested by third parties, shall be exempt from such requirement."). The TLDA also places similar compatibility obligations on any Java Compiler that Microsoft develops and distributes. See TLDA §2.6(b)(iv) ("any new version of a Product that includes the Java Language compilation function that Licensee makes commercially available to the public after the most recent Compatibility Date shall include a mode which a Tool Customer may use to permit such Product to pass the Java Language Test Suite that accompanied the Significant Upgrade.").

As to the Java Virtual Machine, section 2.6(a) sets forth a compliance validation scheme resulting in Microsoft's development and eventual delivery of a "Compatible Implementation." According to the TLDA, Sun may develop and deliver Upgrades to the Java Technology. See TLDA §2.6(a)(iii), 3.1. Sun may designate two such Upgrades per year as "Significant Upgrades" and, subject to the backwards compatibility obligations of section 2.6(a)(iii), require Microsoft to deliver a "Java Reference Implementation" that is compatible with the Significant Upgrade. TLDA §§2.6(a)(iv), 2.6(a)(v). Compatibility under the TLDA hinges on passing the test suite accompanying the Significant Upgrade. See TLDA §2.6(a)(iv) ("[Microsoft] shall deliver to SUN . . . an upgrade to the Java Reference Implementation (each, a 'Compatible Implementation' that passes the test suite that accompanied the Significant Upgrade.")). The TLDA marks the date that Microsoft delivers the Compatible Implementation in response to a Significant Upgrade as the "Compatibility Date." *Id.* Microsoft agreed to limit commercial distribution to Products including the Compatible Implementation corresponding to the most recent Compatibility Date. TLDA §2.6(a)(vi).

C. Sun's Theory of Unfair Competition

1. Distribution of Non-Compliant Java Technology

Sun bases its claim of unfair competition, in part, on Microsoft's allegedly illegal efforts to squash the competitive threat posed by Sun's Java Technology in order to maintain its monopoly in desktop operating systems. Sun labels Microsoft's allegedly anti-competitive conduct as an "embrace and extend" strategy. First, Microsoft "embraced" the Java Technology by licensing from Sun the right to use its Java Technology to develop and distribute compatible Products. Second, Microsoft "extended" the Java platform by developing strategic incompatibilities into its Java runtime and development tools products. According to Sun, these incompatibilities tied applications using Microsoft's Java development tools to Microsoft's virtual machine and the Windows platform. Third, Microsoft used its distribution channels to flood the market with its version of the Java Technology in an attempt to "hijack the Java Technology and transform it into a Microsoft proprietary programming and runtime environment."

According to Sun, Microsoft's strategic incompatibilities were designed to exploit its market power and the economic and technical constraints imposed on software developers. These strategic incompatibilities included unauthorized extensions to the java.* class libraries, which ensured that applications created with Microsoft's Java development tools were tied to its virtual machine and operating system. Second, Microsoft's refusal to implement JNI in its Java runtime or development tools products, says Sun, prevented developers from writing a Java/native application for all virtual machines running on a given platform. The exclusion of JNI, therefore, forced developers to write one Java/native application for Microsoft's virtual machine and another version for other implementations. Microsoft's use of its dominant market power in operating systems to flood the market with its Java runtime products, contends Sun, ensured that developers would write Java/native applications for Microsoft's implementation before any other. In addition, the cost of porting, says Sun, discouraged developers from also creating the same Java/native application for compliant Java implementations. Moreover, Microsoft's substitution of the RNI and J/Direct native method interfaces in place of Sun's JNI, according to Sun, ensured that developers wanting to develop hybrid Java/native applications that would run on Microsoft's virtual machine had no choice but to use Microsoft's Java development tools products.

Lastly, Sun contends that, in an effort to further fragment the Java programming environment, Microsoft extended the Java language to ensure that applications developed with its Java tools products were tied to Microsoft's implementation of the Java virtual machine. Microsoft's keyword extensions and compiler directives, says Sun, replaced the contractual lock-in Microsoft initially employed. Specifically, Microsoft once required certain licensees to exclusively distribute Microsoft's virtual machine and to use Microsoft's native code interfaces as the sole method of calling native code. Microsoft's exclusion of JNI and its Java language extensions embedded in its Java development tools products allegedly provided a technical lock-in that forced developers to use Microsoft's native code interfaces and distribute Microsoft's implementation of the Java virtual machine.

Sun also decries Microsoft's more recent efforts to license the technology embodying Microsoft's non-compliant language extensions to software developers, tools vendors, and entities in the business of cloning the Java technology. Beyond their distribution in Microsoft's own software products, Microsoft makes available its Windows-specific extensions to the Java Technology in a variety of ways. For example, it has paid Tower Technology Corporation ("Tower") to develop a modified version of IBM's Jikes Compiler that supports Microsoft's language extensions. The Tower agreement also allows Tower to incorporate Microsoft's language extensions into its "TowerJ high performance deployment system." According to Tower, neither the IBM's Jikes compiler nor its own technology incorporates any Sun copyrighted program code. Microsoft similarly paid Transvirtual Technologies, a "cloner" of the Java Technology, to include Microsoft's language extensions in its independently developed implementations. Microsoft also grants royalty-free licenses to its Developer Tools Interoperability Kit ("DTIK"), which assists tools vendors in the implementation and support of Microsoft's extensions. . . .

2. False and Misleading Advertising

Sun also claims that Microsoft has made certain misrepresentations about its software products and technologies relating to the Java Technology in an effort to confuse and induce developers to create applications using Microsoft's extended Java programming environment. In its May 12, 1998 motion, Sun alleged that Microsoft misleadingly advertised its implementation of the Java Technology as the "official reference implementation" for Win32-based systems. More recently, Microsoft has falsely promoted, says Sun, its @com compiler directive technology as complying with Sun's specifications for the Java Technology and being approved by Sun. . . .

II. Legal Standard for Preliminary Injunctive Relief

A plaintiff seeking preliminary injunctive relief must demonstrate "either a likelihood of success on the merits and the possibility of irreparable injury, or that serious questions going to the merits were raised and the balance of hardships tips sharply in its favor." Johnson Controls, Inc. v. Phoenix Control Systems, Inc., 886 F.2d 1173, 1174 (9th Cir. 1989). . . .

III. Analysis

A. *Irreparable Harm and Balance of Hardships*

In the present case, Sun has demonstrated a possibility of irreparable harm, if an injunction restraining Microsoft's distribution of non-compliant Java Technology is not issued. Microsoft's unauthorized distribution of incompatible implementations of Sun's Java Technology threatens to undermine Sun's goal of cross-platform and cross-implementation compatibility. The threatened fragmentation of the Java programming environment harms Sun's relationship with other licensees who have implemented Java virtual machines for Win32-based and other platforms. In addition, Microsoft's unparalleled market power and distribution channels relating to computer operating systems pose a significant risk that an incompatible and unauthorized version of the Java Technology will become the de facto standard. The court further finds that money damages are inadequate to compensate Sun for the harm resulting from Microsoft's distribution of software products incorporating non-compliant Java Technology as the harm to Sun's revenues and reputation is difficult to quantify.

In addition, the balance of hardships tips sharply in Sun's favor, since the potential harm to Sun outweighs the hardship advanced by Microsoft. The relief Sun seeks requires Microsoft to maintain the previously required, non-extended mode as the default setting in its Java compiler and to continue to warn developers that use of its language extensions results in program code that will run only on Microsoft's Java Virtual Machine. As to Microsoft's Java Virtual Machine, Sun's requested relief requires inclusion of JNI, Sun's native method interface. Such requested relief poses little, if any, harm to Microsoft. According to Microsoft, its Java software products comply with the now-vacated preliminary injunction of November 17, 1998. Microsoft submits that it has no plans "for the foreseeable future" to change its currently distributed implementations of the Java Technology. Microsoft's concern over the stigma associated with an injunction does not suffice to overcome the harm asserted by Sun. Sun identifies significant harm to it and to competition if its requested relief is not granted. As discussed below, for example, Microsoft's exclusion of JNI threatens injury to Sun and its licensees of the Java Technology, as well as competition in the market for Java development tools. In addition, Microsoft's extensions to the Java language and its false and misleading statements to the developer community similarly threaten[s] harm to Sun, independent software developers, and the public.

Lastly, the injunction Sun seeks does not appear to harm the public interest. Sun's requested injunction merely seeks to require Microsoft to continue to set the default setting on its Java compiler to the non-extended mode and to continue to warn developers that use of its language extensions results in program code that will run only on Microsoft's Java Virtual Machine. Such relief does not deprive the public of Microsoft's language extensions and compiler directives. In fact, Sun's requested injunction advances the public interest by ensuring that developers are adequately informed about the consequences of using Microsoft's added keywords and compiler directives. Moreover, the absence of an injunction requiring Microsoft's distributed software products to support Sun's JNI may harm software developers if Microsoft were to discontinue its inclusion and support for this native method interface in its Java Virtual Machine.

B. Unfair Competition—Likelihood of Success on the Merits

California law defines unfair competition as, in part, "any unlawful, unfair or fraudulent business act or practice." Cal. Bus. & Prof. Code §17200. In the past, California courts have construed section 17200 broadly to embrace "anything that can properly be called a business practice and at the same time is forbidden by law." See Rubin v. Green, 4 Cal.4th 1187, 1200, 17 Cal. Rptr.2d 828, 847 P.2d 1044 (1993) (quoting Barquis v. Merchants Collection Assn., 7 Cal.3d 94, 113, 101 Cal. Rptr. 745, 496 P.2d 817 (1972)). However, the California Supreme Court recently clarified what constitutes an "unfair" business act or practice in suits between competitors. See Cel-Tech Communications, Inc. v. Los Angeles Cellular Telephone Co., 20 Cal.4th 163, 178-87, 83 Cal. Rptr.2d 548, 973 P.2d 527 (1999). *Cel-Tech* requires

> [w]hen a plaintiff who claims to have suffered injury from a direct competitor's "unfair" act or practice invokes section 17200, the word "unfair" in that section means conduct that threatens an incipient violation of an antitrust law, or violates the policy or spirit of one of those laws because its effects are comparable to or the same as a violation of the law, or otherwise significantly threatens or harms competition.

Id. at 187, 83 Cal. Rptr.2d 548, 973 P.2d 527.

[F]or at least two reasons, the court believes *Cel-Tech* provides the standard to be applied to the alleged unfair business practices in this case with the exception of those dealing with Microsoft's allegedly false advertising.

First, the unfair practices alleged by Sun affect Sun as a direct competitor of Microsoft for the business of software developers for software development tools and, ultimately, consumers for operating systems or platforms. Second, *Cel-Tech* appears to distinguish the proof required in cases by a competitor alleging "unfair" anticompetitive business practices from claims by competitors or consumers for "fraudulent" or "unlawful" business practices or "unfair, deceptive, untrue or misleading advertising." *Cel-Tech*, 20 Cal.4th at 187 n. 12, 83 Cal. Rptr.2d 548, 973 P.2d 527. The claims by Sun, other than those dealing with advertising, fall into the first category which is covered by *Cel-Tech*. There has been no showing that Microsoft has engaged in any fraudulent business practice or scheme or that it violated some specific statutory proscription. Therefore, it seems appropriate to measure Microsoft's conduct against the *Cel-Tech* standard except with respect to Sun's misleading advertising claims.

In determining whether a challenged act or practice is unfair within the meaning of section 17200 of the California Business and Professions Code, *Cel-Tech* endorses looking at federal authorities interpreting the prohibition against "unfair methods of competition" in section 5 of the Federal Trade Commission Act. *Id.* at 186, 83 Cal. Rptr.2d 548, 973 P.2d 527. According to the Supreme Court, "the Federal Trade Commission Act was designed to supplement and bolster the Sherman Act and the Clayton Act . . . to stop in their incipiency acts and practices which, when full blown, would violate those Acts . . . as well as to condemn as 'unfair methods of competition' existing violations of them." F.T.C. v. Brown Shoe Co., 384 U.S. 316 (1966) (quoting F.T.C. v. Motion Picture Advertising Service Co., 344 U.S. 392 (1953)). Accordingly, "unfair methods of competition" under section 5 of the Federal Trade Commission Act covers business practices "which conflict with the basic policies of the Sherman and Clayton Acts even though such practices may not violate these laws." *Id.* at 1504; see also Atlantic Refining Co. v. F.T.C., 381 U.S. 357 (1965) (section 5 proscribes "conduct that runs counter to the policies declared in the Act.") (citations and internal quotations omitted). In addition, where the adverse effects on competition are clear, a "full-scale economic analysis of competitive effect" is not required. *Atlantic Refining,* 85 S. Ct. at 1507. Rather, it is enough that "the practice in question unfairly burden[s] competition for a not insignificant volume of commerce." F.T.C. v. Texaco, Inc., 393 U.S. 223 (1968).

1. Distribution of Non-Compliant Java Technology

Sun asserts that its claim of unfair competition supports an injunction prohibiting Microsoft from distributing non-compliant Java Technology that fails to support Sun's JNI and includes unauthorized language extensions. Specifically, Sun asserts that Microsoft's distribution of software products incorporating non-compliant versions of Sun's Java Technology as part of a scheme to "kill cross-platform Java by grow[ing] the polluted Java market" constitutes an "unfair" business practice.

Preliminarily, Sun has established a reasonable likelihood of success in demonstrating that Microsoft's distribution of non-compliant Java technology violates the compatibility provisions of the TLDA. See *Sun,* 21 F. Supp.2d at 1119-22, 1122-25; *Sun,* 188 F.3d at 1120 (holding that substantial evidence demonstrates that Microsoft violated the TLDA). In addition, Sun has also demonstrated reasonably likely success in establishing that Microsoft's alleged violations of the TLDA were committed as part of a concerted effort to devalue the cross-platform and cross-implementation promise of the Java Technology it licensed and, ultimately, to gain control of the Java programming environment. See Day 9/3/99 Decl. Ex. 6 ("get control of Java with Java support/tools"); Ex. 11 ("Eliminate/contain cross-platform Java by growing the polluted Java market."); Ex. 7 ("without something to pollute Java more to Windows (show new cool features that are only in Windows) we expose ourselves to more portable code on other platforms"). Moreover, Microsoft's ongoing use of compiler directives and keyword extensions indicates continuing harm to Sun. More importantly, however, Sun has raised a serious question on the merits of its claim for unfair competition arising out of Microsoft's distribution of non-compliant Java Technology. Specifically, Sun has raised a serious question as to whether the incompatibilities introduced by Microsoft into its commercially distributed versions of the Java Technology harm competition.

Sun has demonstrated that Microsoft introduced strategic incompatibilities in its implementations of the Java Technology and relied on its unparalleled market power and distribution channels in computer operating systems to unfairly impede competition in the Java development tools market. Without apparent technological or pro-competitive justification and in contravention of the TLDA, Microsoft excluded Sun's JNI native method interface from commercially distributed versions of its Java Virtual Machine implementation. In place of JNI, Microsoft created its own native method interfaces, such as RNI, Java/COM and J/Direct, which are supported by its Java development tools products. Furthermore, Microsoft's wide array of distribution channels and overwhelming market share in operating systems ensured that its Java Virtual Machine omitting JNI enjoyed a large installed base.

The exclusion of JNI and the ubiquitous distribution of Microsoft's non-compliant virtual machine achieved for Microsoft an unfair commercial advantage in the Java development tools market. Specifically, software developers are naturally motivated to create software applications for the operating system platform having the largest installed base—i.e., Microsoft's Windows operating system including its Java Virtual Machine implementation. Here, Microsoft's exclusion of JNI rendered competitive Java tools products incapable of creating hybrid Java/native applications that run on Microsoft's Java Virtual Machine. The economic and technological constraints resulting from Microsoft's exclusion of JNI, thus, compel software developers wishing to write hybrid Java/native applications for the Windows platform to use Microsoft's Java development tools. This also adversely affects the commercial viability of competitive Java runtime products, since the use of Microsoft's Java development tools results in Java/native applications that only run on Microsoft's virtual machine. Accordingly, Microsoft's Java tools products did not compete on their merits alone, but also possessed the added, unfair advantage of offering the only way of creating hybrid Java/native applications that run on Microsoft's non-compliant virtual machine.

2. Microsoft's Language Extensions and Its Current Licensing Practices

According to Sun, Microsoft's distribution of Java runtime and development tools products, which incorporate added keywords and compiler directives, constitutes unfair competition. Sun also contends that Microsoft has attempted to circumvent this court's order of November 17, 1998 by inducing third parties to distribute Microsoft's technology embodying its added keywords and compiler directives without the safeguards required by the November 17, 1998 Order. Sun seeks to reinstate the injunction to the extent it requires Microsoft's compiler to include certain safeguards designed to warn developers about the use of Microsoft's extensions. Sun reasons that Microsoft's licensing practices are acts of unfair competition, and, therefore, requests expansion of the injunction to force Microsoft to require licensees of its extended Java technologies to include the same safeguards.

Sun's present showing fails to establish reasonably likely success or a serious question going to the merits on its claim that Microsoft's distribution and licensing practices relating to its language extensions constitute "unfair" business practices under section 17200 of the California Business and Professions Code. Sun appears to complain that inducing others to distribute Windows-optimized, albeit non-compliant, software development tools that emulate Sun's Java Technology constitutes unfair competition. Sun offers no evidence that these agreements or Microsoft's independently developed language extensions implicate any Sun intellectual property right. Moreover, Sun's evidence merely indicates harm to its commercial interests, rather than harm to competition.

The cases upon which Sun relies are materially distinguishable and appear to be inapposite to Microsoft's distribution of extended Java programming tools and present licensing efforts. Unlike *Atlantic Refining, Texaco* and *Brown Shoe*, Sun submits insufficient evidence suggesting that Microsoft continues to use its economic power to coerce software developers or other relevant entities in a manner restricting competition in a relevant market. See *Atlantic Refining,* 85 S. Ct. at 1506-07 (proscribing use of dominant economic power over gas station retailers to coerce them into buying tires, batteries and accessories from one source); *Texaco,* 89 S. Ct. at 431-33 (same); *Brown Shoe,* 86 S. Ct. at 1503 (holding that FTC was within its power to declare as an unfair method of competition the payment of valuable consideration to shoe retailers to "secure a contractual promise . . . not [to] purchase conflicting lines of shoes."). Rather, Microsoft essentially altered the Java Technology to create a programming environment that enhances a software developer's ability to create Windows-specific applications using an extended form of the Java language. This modified Java programming environment competes directly with Sun's standard or "pure" Java programming environment. In contrast to the cases on which Sun relies, there is insufficient evidence to suggest that Microsoft continues to use its economic power to unfairly force software developers into buying its tools products to the exclusion of competitive tools products or using its development environment to the exclusion of Sun's standard Java programming environment.

Given Microsoft's inclusion and support of JNI, its Java runtime and tools products do not enjoy an unfair commercial advantage over competitive Java runtime and tools products. In addition, Microsoft's Java development tools products do not restrict the growth of Sun's standard Java programming environment, since software developers using Microsoft's Java tools products have the option to write software applications that are cross-platform compatible, cross-implementation compatible, or specific to Microsoft's virtual machine. Moreover, Microsoft's current licensing agreements do not appear to require exclusive distribution of Microsoft's virtual machine or exclusive use of Microsoft's native method interfaces. Accordingly, software developers will decide whether Microsoft's added keywords and compiler directives benefit them, taking into account the advantages and disadvantages of writing cross-platform, cross-implementation, or Microsoft-virtual-machine-specific applications. Sun cannot complain that it is "unfair" within the meaning of §17200 that, given the large installed base of Microsoft's operating system and virtual machine and the efficient methods of invoking native code, software developers may be naturally motivated to use Microsoft's extensions to the Java Technology when creating Windows-specific applications. Therefore, assuming that software developers are not mislead [*sic*] as to the consequences of using Microsoft's Windows-specific enhancements, it appears that whether Sun's standard Java programming environment succeeds in the market is largely up to the merits of Sun's technology, the range of functionality it offers, the software developers who use it to develop software applications, and, ultimately, consumers.

3. Microsoft's Representations Concerning Sun's Java Technology

According to Sun, as part of an effort to confuse and induce developers to use its non-conforming language extensions, Microsoft has falsely advertised that its implementation of the Java Technology is the "official reference implementation" for Win32-based systems and that its "@com" compiler directive is authorized by Sun and complies with the specifications for the Java Technology.

Here, Sun has raised a reasonable likelihood of success or, at a minimum, a serious question going to the merits on its claim that Microsoft's representations concerning Microsoft's implementation of Sun's Java Technology are false or misleading. Microsoft's representations are likely to confuse or mislead developers into thinking that (1) Sun approves of Microsoft's extended Java programming technology, (2) the such extended Java programming technology complies with Sun's specifications, and, therefore, (3) is a compatible addition to the standard Java programming and runtime environment. A developer who is mislead [*sic*] into using Microsoft's language extensions faces significant costs to port the application from the Windows-dependent environment to the standard Java runtime environment. Microsoft's white paper entitled "Integrating Java and COM" states that the class attributes created using the @com compiler directive "adhere to the Java specification, and are an approved method for adding functionality to Java classes." In addition, a second Microsoft white paper states that:

> According to the Java Virtual Machine Specification [published] by Addison Wesley, custom class attributes are the best way to extend Java functionality, and th[e] virtual machines ignore directives they don't understand.

These statements are misleading since they are likely to convey that Microsoft's @com compiler directive technology is "approved" by Sun. In a similar manner, Microsoft's previously-enjoined advertising of its implementation of the Java Technology as "official" falsely suggests that its extended Java programming environment possesses some form of endorsement or approval by Sun and, therefore, is also likely to confuse developers as to the compatibility of Microsoft's extensions to the Java Technology.

In addition, Sun has also shown reasonably likely success in establishing that Microsoft's @com compiler directive technology does not comply with Sun's specifications and that, therefore, Microsoft's statements to the contrary are false. Microsoft relies on section 4.7.1 of the Java Virtual Machine Specification to demonstrate the veracity of these statements. However, section 4.7.1 contains no indication that custom class attributes are the "best way" to extend Java functionality. Rather, that section indicates that additional attributes in class files are permitted, but must not affect the semantics of the class file. The example in the Java Virtual Machine Specification of a permissible added attribute underscores this caveat. Specifically, the Java Virtual Machine Specification states that "defining a new attribute to support vendor-specific debugging is permitted." A Java virtual machine that does not support this attribute can safely ignore it, since it does not affect the semantics of the class file. *Id.* ("Java virtual machine implementations are specifically prohibited from throwing an exception or otherwise refusing to use class files simply because of the presence of some new attribute."). See also *Sun,* 21 F. Supp. 2d at 1124. . . .

IV. Order

Since the court finds that Sun has at least raised serious questions going to the merits and that the balance of hardships tips sharply in its favor if Microsoft is not enjoined, a preliminary injunction is hereby issued against Microsoft, and its officers, agents, servants, employees, attorneys, and those in active concert or participation with them who receive actual notice of this order by personal service or otherwise, pending trial, from:

(A) Selling or distributing, directly or indirectly, any operating system or browser product containing or implementing, in whole or in part, Sun's Java Technology as that term is defined in the TLDA (i.e., the Java Runtime Interpreter, Java Classes, Supplemental Java Classes, Java Compiler, and all Upgrades), unless such product includes a Java runtime implementation which supports Sun's JNI in a manner which passes the compatibility test suite accompanying the latest version of the Java Technology contained in, implemented by, or emulated by such product;

(B) Selling or distributing, directly or indirectly, any software development tool or product containing or implementing Sun's Java Technology as that term is defined in the TLDA, including SDKJ 2.0, SDKJ 3.0 and VJ++ 6.0, unless such product: (1) includes a Java runtime implementation which supports Sun's JNI in a manner which passes the compatibility test suite accompanying the latest version of the Java Technology contained in, implemented by, or emulated by such product, (2) has the default mode in the compiler configured such that (a) Microsoft's keyword extensions and compiler directives are disabled and (b) wherein the compiler mode switch enables, rather than disables, such keyword extensions and compiler directives, and (3) includes a dialog box which appears when a user elects to use the extended mode of the compiler (either when the user accesses the compiler from a DOS command line or when the user checks a box provided during execution of the compiler software) and which warns the user that use of Microsoft's language extensions results in compiled code which may not comply with Sun's specifications for the Java Technology and will only run on Microsoft's virtual machine or other virtual machines that support the special Microsoft extensions (Microsoft's compiler directive and keyword technologies);

(C) Advertising any product that contains, implements or emulates the Java Technology as the "official" Java reference implementation; however, nothing in this order prevents Microsoft from making advertising claims with respect to the performance of its reference implementation; and

(D) Advertising, promoting, or otherwise publicly describing Microsoft's @com, @dll, @security compiler directives as complying with Sun's specifications for the Java Technology or as being approved by Sun.

Furthermore, Microsoft's development tools products shall include at least as much support for Sun's JNI as Microsoft's RNI, e.g. help files, header files, etc.

Nothing in this order requires Microsoft to recall any product. This order does not prevent any purchaser of Microsoft's products from continuing to use them. . . .

COMMENTS AND QUESTIONS

1. *Settlement.* In January 2001, before the case was fully litigated, Sun and Microsoft reached a settlement in which Microsoft agreed to pay Sun $20 million, to accept Sun's termination of the prior license agreement, and to a permanent injunction against unauthorized use of Sun's Java-compatible trademark. To pro-

tect developers and consumers using Microsoft's outdated version of Java technology, Sun agreed to grant Microsoft a seven-year limited license to continue to distribute its current version of the software provided that all future versions of such products pass Sun's compatibility tests. Beyond the seven-year period, Microsoft cannot distribute Java technology or use any of Sun's intellectual property. See Microsoft Agrees to Settlement That Protects Future Integrity of the Java™ Platform, http://java.sun.com/lawsuit/.

2. *Antitrust Enforcement.* The federal and state governments' antitrust lawsuit against Microsoft increasingly focused upon Microsoft's efforts to undermine the so-called "middleware" level of the software market: Netscape's Navigator browser and Sun's "write-once, run anywhere" Java programming environment. Both of these technologies opened up the microcomputer market to new competition beyond the control of Microsoft. Following the D.C. Circuit's determination that Microsoft had violated federal antitrust law in June 2001, Sun Microsystems filed its own antitrust lawsuit. See Sun Files Suit Against Microsoft for Antitrust Violations, 19 Computer and Internet Lawyer, No. 5, 34 (May 2002). Michael Morris, Senior Vice President and General Counsel of Sun, stated that:

> While this suit is based on the past actions of Microsoft, Sun also believes that Microsoft's continuing practices in the marketplace represent a threat to lawful competition and the millions of developers who depend on the existence of an open software industry. This behavior manifests Microsoft's goal to use its monopoly position to turn the Internet into its proprietary platform. What is at stake here is the future of an open software industry and an open Internet.

Id. In the lawsuit, Sun seeks to require Microsoft to distribute Sun's current binary implementation of the Java plug-in as part of Windows XP and Internet Explorer and stop distribution of Microsoft's Java Virtual Machine through separate downloads. Sun also seeks to require Microsoft to disclose and license proprietary interfaces, protocols, and formats and to unbundle tied products, such as Internet Explorer, IIS Web server, and the .Net framework. We will return to these issues in the antitrust chapter.

C. TRADEMARKS AS LOCKOUT DEVICES

Software developers have also sought to control a computer product market by incorporating trademarks into the product itself.

Sega Enterprises Ltd. v. Accolade, Inc.
United States Court of Appeals for the Ninth Circuit
977 F.2d 1510 (9th Cir. 1992)

REINHART, Circuit Judge.

[The factual background of this case is set out in Chapter 2, Section E. Briefly, Sega manufactures video games under the Genesis label and permits only authorized programmers to write Sega-compatible games. To prevent the use of unauthorized games, Sega incorporated a "lockout" program in its Genesis game box. Accolade reverse engineered the code of the box in order to find a way to defeat the lockout program and to make its games compatible.]

All of Accolade's Genesis-compatible games are packaged in a similar fashion. The front of the box displays Accolade's "Ballistic" trademark and states "for use with Sega Genesis and Mega Drive Systems." The back of the box contains the following statement: "Sega and Genesis are registered trademarks of Sega Enterprises, Ltd. Game 1991 Accolade, Inc. All rights reserved. Ballistic is a trademark of Accolade, Inc. Accolade, Inc. is not associated with Sega Enterprises, Ltd. All product and corporate names are trademarks and registered trademarks of their respective owners." . . .

IV. Trademark Issues

Ordinarily in a trademark case, a trademark holder contends that another party is misusing the holder's mark or is attempting to pass off goods or services as those of the trademark holder. The other party usually protests that the mark is not being misused, that there is no actual confusion, or that for some other reason no violation has occurred. This case is different. Here, both parties agree that there is a misuse of a trademark, both agree that there is unlawful mislabeling, and both agree that confusion may result. The issue, here, is—which party is primarily responsible? Which is the wrongdoer—the violator? Is it Sega, which has adopted a security system governing access to its Genesis III console that displays its trademark and message whenever the initialization code for the security system is utilized, even when the video game program was manufactured by a Sega competitor? Or is it Accolade, which, having discovered how to gain access to the Genesis III through the initialization code, uses that code even though doing so triggers the display of Sega's trademark and message in a manner that leads observers to believe that Sega manufactured the Accolade game cartridge? In other words, is Sega the injured party because its mark is wrongfully attached to an Accolade video game by Accolade? Or is Accolade wronged because its game is mislabeled as a Sega product by Sega? The facts are relatively straightforward and we have little difficulty answering the question.

Sega's trademark security system (TMSS) initialization code not only enables video game programs to operate on the Genesis III console, but also prompts a screen display of the SEGA trademark and message. As a result, Accolade's inclusion of the TMSS initialization code in its video game programs has an effect ultimately beneficial neither to Sega nor to Accolade. A Genesis III owner who purchases a video game made by Accolade sees Sega's trademark associated with Accolade's product each time he inserts the game cartridge into the console. Sega claims that Accolade's inclusion of the TMSS initialization code in its games constitutes trademark infringement and false designation of origin in violation of sections 32(1)(a) and 43(a) of the Lanham Trademark Act, 15 U.S.C. §§1114(1)(a), 1125(a), respectively. Accolade counterclaims that Sega's use of the TMSS to prompt a screen display of its trademark constitutes false designation of origin under Lanham Act section 43(a), 15 U.S.C. §1125(a).

Because the TMSS has the effect of regulating access to the Genesis III console, and because there is no indication in the record of any public or industry awareness of any feasible alternate method of gaining access to the Genesis III, we hold that Sega is primarily responsible for any resultant confusion. Thus, it has not demonstrated a likelihood of success on the merits of its Lanham Act claims. Accordingly, the preliminary injunction it obtained must be dissolved with respect to the trademark claim also. However, we decline to instruct the district court to grant Accolade's request for preliminary injunctive relief at this time. The decision whether to grant such relief requires the making of factual and equitable determinations in light of the legal conclusions we express here. Such determinations are best left in the first instance to the district court.

A. False Labeling

Section 32(1)(a) of the Lanham Act creates a cause of action for trademark infringement against any person who, without the consent of the trademark owner, "uses in commerce any reproduction . . . of a registered mark in connection with the sale, offering for sale, distribution, or advertising of any goods or services on or in connection with which such use is likely to cause confusion, or to cause mistake, or to deceive. . . ." 15 U.S.C. §1114(1)(a). Section 43(a) proscribes the use in commerce of a false designation of origin in connection with goods or services where such use is "likely to cause confusion, or . . . mistake." *Id*. §1125(a). Both Sega and Accolade agree that the screen display of the Sega trademark and message creates a likelihood of consumer confusion regarding the origin of Accolade's games. The question is: which party is legally responsible for that confusion? We disagree with the answer given by the district court.

The district court found that Accolade bore primary responsibility for any consumer confusion that resulted from the display of the false Sega Message. However, Accolade had no desire to cause the Sega Message to appear or otherwise to create any appearance of association between itself and Sega; in fact, it had precisely the opposite wish. It used the TMSS initialization code only because it wanted to gain access for its products to the Genesis III, and was aware of no other method for doing so. On the other hand, while it may not have been Sega's ultimate goal to mislabel Accolade's products, the record is clear that the false labeling was the result of a deliberate decision on the part of Sega to include in the Genesis III a device which would both limit general access and cause false labeling. The decision to use the SEGA trademark as an essential element of a functional device that regulates access and to cause the SEGA trademark and message to be displayed whenever that functional device was triggered compels us to place primary responsibility for consumer confusion squarely on Sega.

With respect to Accolade, we emphasize that the record clearly establishes that it had only one objective in this matter: to make its video game programs compatible with the Genesis III console. That objective was a legitimate and a lawful one. There is no evidence whatsoever that Accolade wished Sega's trademark to be displayed when Accolade's games were played on Sega's consoles. To the contrary, Accolade included disclaimers on its packaging materials which stated that "Accolade, Inc. is not associated with Sega Enterprises, Ltd." When questioned regarding the Sega Message and its potential effect on consumers, Alan Miller testified that Accolade does not welcome the association between its product and Sega and would gladly avoid that association if there were a way to do so. Miller testified that Accolade's engineers had not been able to discover any way to modify their game cartridges so that the games would operate on the Genesis III without prompting the screen display of the Sega Message.

In contrast, Sega officials testified that Sega incorporated the TMSS into the Genesis console, known in Asia as the Mega-Drive, in order to lay the groundwork for the trademark prosecution of software pirates who sell counterfeit cartridges in Taiwan and South Korea, as well as in the United States. Sega then marketed the redesigned console worldwide. Sega intended that when Sega game programs manufactured by a counterfeiter were played on its consoles, the Sega Message would be displayed, thereby establishing the legal basis for a claim of trademark infringement. However, as Sega certainly knew, the TMSS also had the potential to affect legitimate competitors adversely. First, Sega should have foreseen that a competitor might discover how to utilize the TMSS, and that when it did and included the initialization code in its cartridges, its video game programs would also end up being falsely labeled. Sega should also have known that the TMSS might discourage some competitors from manufacturing independently developed games for use with the Genesis III console, because they would not want to become the victims of such a labeling practice. Thus, in addition to laying the groundwork for lawsuits against pirates, Sega knowingly risked two significant consequences: the false labeling of some competitors' products and the discouraging of other competitors from manufacturing Genesis-compatible games. Under the Lanham Act, the former conduct, at least, is clearly unlawful.

"Trademark policies are designed '(1) to protect consumers from being misled . . . (2) to prevent an impairment of the value of the enterprise which owns the trademark; and (3) to achieve these ends in a manner consistent with the objectives of free competition.'" Anti-Monopoly, Inc. v. General Mills Fun Group, 611 F.2d 296, 300-01 (9th Cir. 1979) (quoting HMH Publishing Co. v. Brincat, 504 F.2d 713, 716 (9th Cir. 1974)). Sega violated the first and the third of these principles. "The trademark is misused if it serves to limit competition in the manufacture and sales of a product. That is the special province of the limited monopolies provided pursuant to the patent laws." *Id.* at 301 (citation omitted).

Sega makes much of the fact that it did not adopt the TMSS in order to wage war on Accolade in particular, but rather as a defensive measure against software counterfeiters. It is regrettable that Sega is troubled by software pirates who manufacture counterfeit products in other areas of the world where adequate copyright remedies are not available. However, under the Lanham Act, which governs the use of trademarks and other designations of origin in this country, it is the effect of the message display that matters. Whatever Sega's intent with respect to the TMSS, the device serves to limit competition in the market for Genesis-compatible games and to mislabel the products of competitors. Moreover, by seeking injunctive relief based on the mislabeling it has itself induced, Sega seeks once again to take advantage of its trademark to exclude its competitors from the market. The use of a mark for such purpose is inconsistent with the Lanham Act.

B. *Functionality*

Sega argues that even if the legal analysis we have enunciated is correct, the facts do not support its application to this case. Specifically, Sega contends that the TMSS does not prevent legitimate unlicensed competitors from developing and marketing Genesis III-compatible cartridges that do not trigger a display of the Sega trademark and message. In other words, Sega claims that Accolade could have "engineered around" the TMSS. Accolade strongly disagrees with Sega's factual assertions. It contends that the TMSS initialization sequence is a functional feature that must be included in a video game program by a manufacturer in order for the game to operate on the Genesis III. Sega's factual argument stands or falls on the Nagashima declaration and the accompanying modified game cartridges that Sega introduced at the hearing. Having carefully reviewed the declaration, we conclude that Sega has not met its burden of establishing nonfunctionality.

Based on the Nagashima declaration and on the modified cartridges, the district court concluded that the TMSS initialization sequence was not a necessary component of a Genesis-compatible game. The court found that Accolade could have created a game cartridge that lacked the TMSS initialization code but would still operate on the Genesis III, or could have programmed its games in such a way that the false Sega Message would not be displayed on the screen. The court further found that either modification could have been accomplished at minimal additional expense to Accolade. Accordingly, the court ruled that Accolade could not assert a functionality defense.

. . . Viewed in the correct light, the record before us supports only one conclusion: The TMSS initialization code is a functional feature of a Genesis-compatible game and Accolade may not be barred from using it.

"Functional features of a product are features 'which constitute the actual benefit that the consumer wishes to purchase, as distinguished from an assurance that a particular entity made, sponsored, or endorsed a product.'" Vuitton et Fils S.A. v. J. Young Enterprises, Inc., 644 F.2d 769, 774 (9th Cir. 1981) (quoting International Order of Job's Daughters v. Lindeburg & Co., 633 F.2d 912, 917 (9th Cir. 1980), *cert. denied*, 452 U.S. 941, 69 L. Ed. 2d 956, 101 S. Ct. 3086 (1981)). A product feature thus is functional "if it is essential to the use or purpose of the article or if it affects the cost or quality of the article." *Inwood Laboratories*, 456 U.S. at 850 n.10. The Lanham Act does not protect essentially functional or utilitarian product features because such protection would constitute a grant of a perpetual monopoly over features that could not be patented. Keene Corp. v. Paraflex Industries, Inc., 653 F.2d 822, 824 (3d Cir. 1981). Even when the allegedly functional product feature is a trademark, the trademark owner may not enjoy a monopoly over the functional use of the mark. *Job's Daughters*, 633 F.2d at 918-19.

In determining whether a product feature is functional, a court may consider a number of factors, including—but not limited to—"the availability of alternative designs; and whether a particular design results from a comparatively simple or cheap method of manufacture." Clamp Mfg. Co. v. Enco Mfg. Co., Inc., 870 F.2d 512, 516 (9th Cir.), *cert. denied*, 493 U.S. 872 (1989). The availability of alternative methods of manufacture must be more than merely theoretical or speculative, however. The court must find "that commercially feasible alternative configurations *exist*." *Id*. (emphasis added). Moreover, some cases have even suggested that in order to establish nonfunctionality the party with the burden must demonstrate that the product feature "'serves no purpose other than identification.'" *Keene Corp.*, 653 F.2d at 826 (quoting SK&F Co. v. Premo Pharmaceutical Laboratories, Inc., 625 F.2d 1055, 1063 (3d Cir. 1980)). With these principles in mind, we turn to the question whether the TMSS initialization code is a functional feature of a Genesis-compatible game.

It is indisputable that, in the case before us, part of "the actual benefit that the consumer wishes to purchase" is compatibility with the Genesis III console. The TMSS initialization code provides that compatibility. Sega argues that the modified cartridges that were introduced in the district court establish the actual existence of technically and commercially feasible alternative methods of gaining access to the Genesis III. The cartridges were prepared by Nagashima, an employee in Sega's Hardware Research and Development Department who was "familiar with the TMSS system." At most, the Nagashima affidavit establishes that an individual familiar with the operation of the TMSS can discover a way to engineer around it. It does not establish that a competitor with no knowledge of the workings of the TMSS could do so. Nor is there any evidence that there was any public or industry awareness of any alternate method for gaining access to the Genesis III. Evidence that an individual, even an independent expert, produced one or more cartridges is not sufficient proof that an alternate method exists. What is needed for proof of that fact is proof of the method itself. Here, such proof is totally lacking. What is also needed is proof that knowledge of the alternate method exists or is readily available to knowledgeable persons in the industry. That proof also is totally lacking here. Accordingly, the district court erred as a matter of law in concluding that the Nagashima declaration and the modified cartridges were sufficient to establish nonfunctionality.

Because the TMSS serves the function of regulating access to the Genesis III, and because a means of access to the Genesis III console without using the TMSS initialization code is not known to manufacturers of competing video game cartridges, there is an insufficient basis for a finding of nonfunctionality. Moreover, we note that the only evidence in the record (other than the Nagashima declaration) relating to Accolade's ability to gain access to the Genesis III through the use of any process other than the TMSS is the affidavit of Alan Miller. Miller stated that Accolade's software engineers—who, absent any evidence to the contrary, we presume to be reasonably competent representatives of their profession —have not been able to discover such a method. This evidence supports our conclusion that Sega has not met its burden of establishing nonfunctionality. . . .

In summary, because Sega did not produce sufficient evidence regarding the existence of a feasible alternative to the use of the TMSS initialization code, it did not carry its burden and its claim of nonfunctionality fails. Possibly, Sega will be able to meet its burden of proof at trial. We cannot say. However, we conclude that in light of the record before the district court, Sega was not entitled to preliminary injunctive relief under the Lanham Act.[11]

---

11. Sega contends that even if the TMSS code is functional, Accolade, as the copier, was obligated to take the most effective measures reasonably available to eliminate the consumer confusion that has arisen as a result of the association of Sega's trademark with Accolade's product. . . . When a product feature is both functional and source-identifying, the copier need only take reasonable measures to avoid consumer confusion. American Greetings Corp. v. Dan-Dee Imports, Inc., 807 F.2d 1136, 1141 (3d Cir. 1986); *Job's Daughters*, 633 F.2d at 919 (the degree of protection afforded a product feature that has both functional and source-identifying aspects depends on the characteristics of the use and on the copier's merchandising practices). Assuming arguendo that the rules applicable to copiers apply here, the measures adopted by Accolade satisfy a reasonableness standard. Accolade placed disclaimers on its packaging materials which stated that "Accolade, Inc. is not associated with Sega Enterprises, Ltd." While Accolade could have worded its disclaimer more strongly, the version that it chose would appear to be sufficient.

COMMENTS AND QUESTIONS

1. In considering Sega's claim of copyright infringement, the Ninth Circuit held that Accolade had a right to make intermediate and final copies of Sega's code to the extent necessary to its purpose of achieving compatibility. Does the court's trademark holding depend on this conclusion? If the court had decided that Accolade could not copy any Sega code or that there was no right to create compatible programs, would Accolade be guilty of trademark as well as copyright infringement? If not, why not?

2. Is there any merit to *Accolade*'s claim for trademark infringement? Surely Sega did not intend to identify Accolade's products as its own, since it did not intend Accolade to have access to its system at all. Can consumers really be said to be confused if they have bought their products from Accolade?

3. Has the Sega mark itself become functional? Has it done so in this particular context?

4. *Antitrust/Misuse/Unclean Hands.* While the courts have recognized the theoretical possibility of an antitrust misuse/unclean hands defense to trademark infringement, Carl Zeiss Stiftung v. V.E.B. Carl Zeiss, Jena, 298 F. Supp. 1309 (S.D.N.Y. 1969), *modified*, 433 F.2d 686 (2d Cir. 1970), *cert. denied*, 403 U.S. 905 (1971), Phi Delta Theta Fraternity v. J.A. Buchroeder & Co., 251 F. Supp. 968 (W.D.Mo. 1966), no reported decision has actually refused to enforce a trademark because it was used in violation of antitrust law. See Herbert Hovenkamp et al., IP and Antitrust §3.5 (2002).

5

Sui Generis Protection of Computer Technology

Previous chapters have explored the ways in which courts have applied existing laws to computer technology, particularly to computer software. As we have seen, the "fit" between existing law (which largely evolved to deal with the challenges of a manufacturing-based economy) and some aspects of computer technology, particularly computer software (which is arguably at the heart of an emerging information-based economy), has sometimes been difficult to achieve. No wonder, then, that the past several decades have witnessed numerous proposals to protect some aspects of computer technology with new forms of intellectual property law specially devised for them. This has included not only computer software and semiconductor chip designs, but also computer databases, computer-generated works, and digital audio recording devices.

These proposals have generally been grounded on a theory that existing law did not provide sufficient protection to provide incentives for necessary levels of investment in their development and distribution, or on a theory that it would unduly distort existing laws to apply them to provide appropriate incentives for such innovations. Such "sui generis" (of its own kind) proposals have generally been an amalgam of existing legal concepts drawn or adapted from copyright law or patent, along with some specially tailored rules aimed at addressing particular concerns of the industry sector. J.H. Reichman speaks of these sui generis proposals as "legal hybrids between the patent and copyright paradigms" and offers a thesis (discussed below) to explain why these regimes have proliferated in the past several decades. See J.H. Reichman, Legal Hybrids Between the Patent and Copyright Paradigms, 94 Colum. L. Rev. 2432 (1994).

In view of the pervasive orthodoxy of using copyright law to protect computer programs, it may come as a surprise to learn that in the 1970s and through the 1980s, many thought that computer programs should be protected by a sui generis regime. The World Intellectual Property Organization, for example, proposed a sui generis form of legal protection for computer programs in the 1970s. The principal rationale for these proposals for software protection arose from concerns that it would distort copyright principles to apply this law to protect such a highly utilitarian subject matter. See, e.g., Pamela Samuelson, CONTU Revisited: The Case Against Copyright Protection for Computer Programs in Machine-Readable Form, 1984 Duke L.J. 663 (1984). The lack of experience in the copyright field in protecting utilitarian subject matters also meant that it might lack workable doctrines with which to analyze infringement claims.

In the early 1980s, the Japanese Ministry for International Trade (MITI) proposed a sui generis form of legal protection for computer programs built on modified copyright principles. Early on, MITI recognized that computer programs would pose compatibility and standardization issues that a legal regime protecting software would need to address. MITI expressed concern about the market power that computer firms might attain if the law conferred on them exclusive rights that enabled them to block the development of compatible systems. See Dennis S. Karjala, Lessons From the Computer Software Protection Debate in Japan, 1984 Ariz. St. L. Rev. 53 (1984) (discussing the MITI proposal). Owing in substantial part to strong U.S. opposition to the MITI proposal—especially to its compulsory license provisions—the government of Japan decided to follow the U.S. lead and use copyright law to protect computer programs. *Id.*

Even in the late 1980s and into the very early 1990s, the European Union (EU) was seriously considering a sui generis form of legal protection for computer programs. When in 1991 the EU issued its directive on such programs, which adopted the copyright model (see Chapter 8), the sui generis debate on an international level was largely settled as a political matter. However, the decompilation and interoperability provisions of the European directive are arguably sui generis rules within the body of copyright law that respond to the same concerns as were raised by MITI about undue market power if copyright protection could be used to stop the development of interoperable programs. One way to think about the U.S. experience with software protection is to say that the United States has, more or less, developed a sui generis form of legal protection for computer software within the body of copyright law through a common law litigation process. The courts have addressed unprecedented issues, such as the decompilation, interoperability, look and feel, and related issues in computer program cases and have devised new tests of infringement.

Although it did not emerge as the favored means for protecting computer software, sui generis legislation has been adopted for some other computer-related products. One example is the Semiconductor Chip Protection Act of 1984 in the United States (and its counterpart laws in other countries) that protect the topography of integrated circuits. A second example is the sui generis legal regime that the EU adopted in 1996 to protect the contents of databases (distinct from copyright protection for the creative selection and arrangement of data). Similar sui generis legislation has been pending for four legislative sessions in the U.S. Congress. Proponents assert that the U.S. Supreme Court's repudiation of the "sweat of the brow" theory of originality in Feist Publications v. Rural Telephone Serv., 499 U.S. 340 (1991) opened up a "gap" in legal protection available to database developers that makes them vulnerable to market-destructive appropriations. Some, however, question the existence of such a gap or its extent. Also debated is whether an unfair competition approach, rather than an exclusive property rights approach, to legal protection should be used to fill any gap that might exist. A third example of computer-related sui generis legislation is the form the United

Kingdom adopted some years ago to protect computer-generated works (e.g., of music or pictorial images). All three of these legal regimes have been built primarily on modified copyright principles, although, as will become more evident below, the Semiconductor Chip Protection Act (SCPA) has some modified patent features as well.

But other legislation with a sui generis character has also been adopted in response to challenges arising from advances in computer-related technologies. This includes the Audio Home Recording Act of 1992 (requiring the installation of copy-control systems in digital audio recording devices) and the anti-circumvention provisions of the Digital Millennium Copyright Act of 1998 (see Chapter 10), which outlaws circumvention of technical measures used by copyright owners to protect access to their works and the manufacture or distribution of technologies primarily designed to bypass such technical measures. No underlying copyright infringement (e.g., illegal copying or public performance of a work) need occur to violate either of these laws.

Even though the political debate over sui generis protection for computer software has died down, questions continue to arise as to whether the law actually protects the "right" things about computer programs, just as questions continue to occur about whether the patent system can appropriately protect computer program inventions. This chapter includes some consideration of these issues and some proposals to protect software in part because they illustrate the difficulties that may arise when rules initially devised to create incentives for innovation in a manufacturing economy are applied to promote innovation in an information economy. As you review these materials, recall issues raised in previous chapters and consider whether patent and copyright laws can successfully be adapted to regulate the new information technology environment or whether new paradigms of intellectual property law need to be devised.

A. THE SEMICONDUCTOR CHIP PROTECTION ACT

United States firms were the initial world market leaders in the production of semiconductor chips. In the late 1970s, however, the U.S. semiconductor industry was in a serious slump, in part because of the rise of Asian competitors who were making substantial headway in the world market for semiconductor chips. One contributing cause of this slump, according to representatives of certain U.S. chip producers (Intel prominently among them), was that the law did not provide sufficient legal protection to the layout of integrated circuits on semiconductor chips. In one congressional hearing on this problem, Intel pointed out that it might need to invest tens of millions of dollars to develop a new family of chips. However, once these chips appeared in the open market, they could be quickly copied by a competitor with an investment of only about $50,000 of equipment. The disparity between the high cost of development and low cost of copying was, Intel officials reported, having a chilling effect on Intel's willingness to make such substantial investments. Moreover, Intel was not the only innovative U.S. chip producer being hurt by both offshore and domestic competitive copying.

Intel initially sought to deal with the gap-in-protection problem by claiming copyright protection in the layout of circuits on its semiconductors. It first registered copyright claims in drawings of its chip circuit layouts and then sought to register masks made from those drawings as derivative works of the drawings. The U.S. Copyright Office accepted registration of the drawings but refused the request to register the masks because of their utilitarian character (the masks were intended for use in the semiconductor chip manufacturing process). Intel then asked Congress to amend the copyright law to add semiconductor designs or mask works to the subject matter of copyright. In hearings on this legislation before Congress, Professor Arthur Miller, who had chaired the Commission on New Technological Uses of Copyright (CONTU) subcommittee responsible for recommending copyright protection for computer programs, argued that the same arguments that CONTU relied on to decide that copyright protection was appropriate for software applied to computer chips as well. Miller likened the design of semiconductor chips to Mondrian paintings. However, the Copyright Office and others raised objections to the use of copyright law as such to protect layout designs for circuits in semiconductors, saying that the "useful article" limitation on the scope of copyright protection for pictorial, sculptural, and graphic works was too fundamental to American copyright law. Representative Kastenmeier eventually introduced a sui generis bill for the legal protection of mask works (adapted from an industrial design bill that had nearly been made part of the Copyright Act of 1976). The legislative history and development of SCPA is described in Robert W. Kastenmeier & Michael J. Remington, The Semiconductor Chip Protection Act of 1984: A Swamp or Firm Ground?, 70 Minn. L. Rev. 417 (1985). The main provisions of SCPA are discussed in the case that follows.

Brooktree Corp. v. Advanced Micro Devices, Inc.
United States Court of Appeals for the Federal Circuit
977 F.2d 1555 (Fed. Cir. 1992)

NEWMAN, Circuit Judge.

Brooktree Corporation brought suit against Advanced Micro Devices, Inc. (herein AMD) for patent infringement, 35 U.S.C. §271, and infringement of mask work registrations, 17 U.S.C. §910, in connection with certain semiconductor chips used in color video displays. The United States District Court for the Southern District of California entered judgment that the patents were valid and infringed and that the registered mask works were infringed, assessing damages.

. . . [F]or issues of fact and law under the Semiconductor Chip Protection Act we apply the discernible law of the Ninth Circuit, in accordance with the principles set forth in Atari, Inc. v. JS & A Group, Inc., 747 F.2d 1422, 1438-40, 223 USPQ 1074, 1086-87 (Fed. Cir. 1984) (en banc) (applying copyright law of the circuit in which the case was tried, thus avoiding creating new opportunities for forum shopping). Judicial consideration of the Semiconductor Chip Protection Act has thus far been sparse, and we have given particular attention to the statute and its history, for the parties dispute significant aspects of statutory interpretation. . . .

I. Mask Works

The Semiconductor Chip Protection Act

The Semiconductor Chip Protection Act of 1984, Pub.L. 98-620, Title III, 98 Stat. 3347, codified at 17 U.S.C. §§901-914, arose from concerns that existing intellectual property laws did not provide adequate protection of proprietary rights in semiconductor chips that had been designed to perform a particular function. The Act, enacted after extensive congressional consideration and hearings over several years, adopted relevant aspects of existing intellectual property law, but for the most part created a new law, specifically adapted to the protection of design layouts of semiconductor chips.

Chip design layouts embody the selection and configuration of electrical components and connections in order to achieve the desired electronic functions. The electrical elements are configured in three dimensions, and are built up in layers by means of a series of "masks" whereby, using photographic depositing and etching techniques, layers of metallic, insulating, and semiconductor material are deposited in the desired pattern on a wafer of silicon. This set of masks is called a "mask work", and is part of the semiconductor chip product. The statute defines a mask work as:

> a series of related images, however fixed or encoded
> > (A) having or representing the predetermined, three dimensional pattern of metallic, insulating, or semiconductor material present or removed from the layers of a semiconductor chip product; and
> > (B) in which series the relation of the images to one another is that each image has the pattern of the surface of one form of a semiconductor chip product.

17 U.S.C. §901(a)(2). The semiconductor chip product in turn is defined as:

> the final or intermediate form of any product—
> > (A) having two or more layers of metallic, insulating, or semiconductor material, deposited or otherwise placed on, or etched away or otherwise removed from, a piece of semiconductor material in accordance with a predetermined pattern; and
> > (B) intended to perform electronic circuitry functions.

17 U.S.C. §901(a)(1).

The design of a satisfactory chip layout may require extensive effort and be extremely time consuming, particularly as new and improved electronic capabilities are sought to be created. A new semiconductor chip may incur large research and development costs, yet after the layout is imprinted in the mask work and the chip is available in commerce, it can be copied at a fraction of the cost to the originator. Thus there was concern that widespread copying of new chip layouts would have adverse effects on innovative advances in semiconductor technology, as stated in the Senate Report:

> In the semiconductor industry, innovation is indispensable; research breakthroughs are essential to the life and health of the industry. But research and innovation in the

design of semiconductor chips are threatened by the inadequacies of existing legal protection against piracy and unauthorized copying. This problem, which is so critical to this essential sector of the American economy, is addressed by the Semiconductor Chip Protection Act of 1984. . . .

The Semiconductor Chip Protection Act of 1984, . . . would prohibit "chip piracy"—the unauthorized copying and distribution of semiconductor chip products copied from the original creators of such works.

S.Rep. No. 425, 98th Cong., 2d Sess., 1 (1984) (hereinafter Senate Report).

In the evolution of the Semiconductor Chip Protection Act it was first proposed simply to amend the Copyright Act, 17 U.S.C. §101 et seq., to include semiconductor chip products and mask works as subject of copyright. See H.R. 1028, 98th Cong., 1st Sess. (1983). However, although some courts had interpreted copyright law as applicable to computer software imbedded in a semiconductor chip, see Apple Computer, Inc. v. Franklin Computer Corp., 714 F.2d 1240, 1249, 219 USPQ 113, 121 (3d Cir. 1983), *cert. dismissed*, 464 U.S. 1033, 104 S. Ct. 690, 79 L. Ed.2d 158 (1984), it was uncertain whether the copyright law could protect against copying of the pattern on the chip itself, if the pattern was deemed inseparable from the utilitarian function of the chip. Indeed, the Copyright Office had refused to register patterns on printed circuit boards and semiconductor chips because no separate artistic aspects had been demonstrated. Copyright Protection for Semiconductor Chips: Hearings on H.R. 1028 Before the Subcomm. on Courts, Civil Liberties, and the Administration of Justice of the House Comm. on the Judiciary, 98th Cong., 1st Sess., 77 (1983) (hereinafter 1983 House Hearings) (statement of Dorothy Schrader, Associate Register of Copyrights for Legal Affairs). Concern was also expressed that extension of the copyright law to accommodate the problems of mask works would distort certain settled copyright doctrines, such as fair use. 1983 House Hearings at 16-17 (statement of Jon A. Baumgarten, Copyright Counsel, Association of American Publishers, Inc.).

The patent system alone was deemed not to provide the desired scope of protection of mask works. Although electronic circuitry and electronic components are within the statutory subject matter of patentable invention, see 35 U.S.C. §101, and some original circuitry may be patentable if it also meets the requirements of the Patent Act, as is illustrated in this case, Congress sought more expeditious protection against copying of original circuit layouts, whether or not they met the criteria of patentable invention. Senate Report at 8.

The Semiconductor Chip Protection Act of 1984 was an innovative solution to this new problem of technology-based industry. While some copyright principles underlie the law, as do some attributes of patent law, the Act was uniquely adapted to semiconductor mask works, in order to achieve appropriate protection for original designs while meeting the competitive needs of the industry and serving the public interest.

The Semiconductor Chip Protection Act provides for the grant of certain exclusive rights to owners of registered mask works, including the exclusive right "to reproduce the mask work by optical, electronic, or any other means", and the exclusive right "to import or distribute a semiconductor chip product in which the mask work is embodied". 17 U.S.C. §905. Mask works that are not "original", or that consist of "designs that are staple, commonplace, or familiar in the semiconductor industry, or variations of such designs, combined in a way that, considered as a whole, is not original", are excluded from protection. 17 U.S.C. §902(b). Protection is also not extended to any "idea, procedure, process, system, method of operation, concept, principle, or discovery, regardless of the form in which it is described, explained, illustrated or embodied" in the mask work. 17 U.S.C. §902(c). The sponsors and supporters of this legislation foresaw that there would be areas of uncertainty in application of this new law to particular situations, and referred to "gray areas" wherein factual situations could arise that would not have easy answers. Those areas are emphasized by both parties in the assignments of error on this appeal.

Brooktree's Mask Work Registrations

Brooktree was granted mask work registration MW 2873 on August 6, 1987, and registration MW 3838 on July 6, 1988, for its chips identified as Bt451 and Bt458. These Brooktree chips embody a circuit design that combines the functions of a static random access memory (SRAM) and a digital to analog converter (DAC). This circuitry, sometimes referred to as RAMDAC, acts as a "color palette", producing the colors in color video displays having high speed and enhanced picture resolution. A Brooktree witness described these chips as a technological breakthrough, exceeding limits in speed and performance that had been believed impossible to exceed. Brooktree stated that a single Bt458 chip replaced a previously used set of 36 chips (an AMD product) and offered many advantages. A Brooktree witness testified that these chips were extremely successful commercially, and were soon incorporated into new designs for video display systems made by several large manufacturers.

A critical component of the Brooktree chips is the core cell, a ten-transistor SRAM cell which is repeated over six thousand times in an array covering about eighty percent of the chip area. Each core cell consists of ten transistors and metal conductors electrically connecting the transistors throughout the three dimensions of the multilayered cell. Brooktree charged that this core cell was copied by AMD, thus infringing Brooktree's mask work registrations.

AMD does not challenge the validity of these mask work registrations, or dispute Brooktree's position that its chips are protected under the Semiconductor Chip Protection Act. AMD does, however, assert that its accused chips are not infringements, for reasons we shall discuss.

Infringement

The Semiconductor Chip Protection Act defines an "infringing semiconductor chip product" as one which is "made, imported, or distributed in violation of the exclusive rights" of the mask work owner. 17 U.S.C. §901(a)(9). The text of the Semiconductor Chip Protection Act sets forth the subject matter of protection in terms of certain exclusive rights, including, *inter alia*, the exclusive right to "reproduce the mask work", 17 U.S.C. §905. This usage mirrors the words of the Copyright Act, which states the exclusive rights of copyright owners "to reproduce the copyrighted work". 17 U.S.C. §106. Although the Semiconductor Chip Protection Act does not use the word "copy" to describe infringement, the parallel language reflects the incorporation of the well-explicated copyright principle of substantial similarity into the Semiconductor Chip Protection Act, as discussed infra.

The jury instruction on the criteria for establishing infringement included the instruction that infringement requires substantial similarity to a material portion of the registered mask work:

> To establish infringement, Brooktree must show that A.M.D.'s mask works are substantially similar to a material portion of the mask works in Brooktree's chips covered by Brooktree's mask work registration. No hard and fast rule or percentage governs what constitutes a "substantial similarity." Substantial similarity may exist where an important part of the mask work is copied, even though the percentage of the entire chip which is copied may be relatively small. It is not required that A.M.D. make a copy of the entire mask work embodied in the Brooktree chip.

AMD states that it does not on appeal challenge this jury instruction. Instead, AMD argues that because the non-SRAM portion of its accused chip was not copied, the chips are not "substantially similar", whatever the materiality of the SRAM cell to the total mask work. It was undisputed that there was not duplication of the entire chip. AMD states that the Semiconductor Chip Protection Act requires copying of the entire chip, and therefore that it was entitled to judgment in its favor as a matter of law, or at least to a new trial on the issue.

The principle of substantial similarity recognizes that the existence of differences between an accused and copyrighted work may not negate infringement if a material portion of the copyrighted work is appropriated. Shaw v. Lindheim, 919 F.2d 1353, 1362, 15 USPQ2d 1516, 1523 (9th Cir. 1990). If the copied portion is qualitatively important, the finder of fact may properly find substantial similarity under copyright law, Baxter v. MCA, Inc., 812 F.2d 421, 425, 2 USPQ2d 1059, 1063 (9th Cir.), *cert. denied*, 484 U.S. 954, 108 S. Ct. 346, 98 L. Ed.2d 372 (1987), and under the Semiconductor Chip Protection Act.

Brooktree agrees that the SRAM portion of the accused chips covers only eighty percent of the chip area, and that the remaining circuitry was not copied by AMD. Infringement under the statute does not require that all parts of the accused chip be copied. The district court's explanation to the jury was in full accord with the statutory grant of exclusive rights to reproduce the mask work. The statutory interpretation now pressed by AMD, *viz.*, that the entire chip must have been copied, is unsupported. Indeed, the House Report states that it was contemplated that the cell layout alone could be misappropriated:

> Mask works sometimes contain substantial areas (of so-called "cells") whose layouts involve creativity and are commercially valuable. In appropriate fact settings, the misappropriation of such a cell—assuming it meets the original standards of this chapter —could be the basis for an infringement action under this chapter.

H.R.Rep. No. 781, 98th Cong., 2d Sess., 26, 27 (1984), reprinted in 1984 U.S. Code Cong. & Admin. News 5708, 5750, 5775, 5776 (hereinafter House Report) (footnote omitted). As explained in the Explanatory Memorandum—Mathias-Leahy Amendment to S. 1201, 130 Cong. Rec. S12,916 (daily ed. Oct. 3, 1984) (hereinafter Mathias-Leahy Memorandum), written to explain the House and Senate bills as they were enacted, *id.* at S12,923, the Congressional intention was to protect against "piecemeal copying" and "copying of a material portion" of a chip:

> . . . the amendment, like both bills, incorporates the familiar copyright principle of substantial similarity. Although as a practical matter, copying of an insubstantial portion of a chip and independent design of the remainder is not likely, copying of a material portion nevertheless constitutes infringement. This concept is particularly important in the semiconductor industry, where it may be economical, for example, to copy 75% of a mask work from one chip and combine that with 25% of another mask work, if the copies are transferable modules, such as units from a cell library.
>
> As the Senate report notes, no hard and fast percentages govern what constitutes a "substantial" copying because substantial similarity may exist where an important part of a mask work is copied even though the percentage copied may be relatively small. Nonetheless, mask work owners are protected not only from wholesale copying but also against piecemeal copying of substantial or material portions of one or more mask works.

Mathias-Leahy Memorandum at S12,917.

Whether an appropriation of a cell layout constitutes infringement in a particular case is for the trier of fact, and can not be decided as a matter of law. See *Sid & Marty Krofft Television Productions, Inc. v. McDonald's Corp.*, 562 F.2d 1157, 1164, 196 USPQ 97, 102-03 (9th Cir. 1977) (question of substantial similarity under copyright law is for the trier of fact). We shall discuss this question post, for it was litigated in the context of AMD's defense of reverse engineering.

The Reverse Engineering Defense

AMD's position at trial, and on appeal, was that its core cell was the product of reverse engineering of the Brooktree chip, and therefore does not constitute infringement under the Semiconductor Chip Protection Act. Reverse engineering is a statutory defense, included in the Act upon extensive congressional attention to the workings of the semiconductor chip industry.

The statute provides that it is not an infringement of a registered mask work for

> (1) a person to reproduce the mask work solely for the purpose of teaching, analyzing, or evaluating the concepts or techniques embodied in the mask work or the circuitry, logic flow, or organization of components used in the mask work; or
> (2) a person who performs the analysis or evaluation described in paragraph (1) to incorporate the results of such conduct in an original mask work which is made to be distributed.

17 U.S.C. §906(a). The statute thus provides that one engaged in reverse engineering shall not be liable for infringement when the end product is itself original. In performing reverse engineering a person may disassemble, study, and analyze an existing chip in order to understand it. This knowledge may be used to create an original chip having a different design layout, but which performs the same or equivalent function as the existing chip, without penalty or prohibition. Congress was told by industry representatives that reverse engineering was an accepted and

fair practice, and leads to improved chips having "form, fit, and function" compatibility with the existing chip, thereby serving competition while advancing the state of technology. Senate Report at 21.

Much attention was given by Congress and by witnesses to the question of how to determine whether a chip layout was born of legitimate reverse engineering or of copying. It was foreseen that there would be a "gray area" wherein the rights of the parties, on the facts of a particular chip design, would require resolution on a fact-dependent, case-by-case basis. The following colloquy illustrates concerns raised at the hearings:

> *Rep. Edwards*: . . . Is the chief reservation here the idea that reverse engineering, which all the witnesses agree is appropriate, might be confused with pirating and that any kind of reverse engineering might be interpreted under this law as pirating?
>
> *Mr. MacPherson* (of Fairchild Camera & Instrument Corp.): I think that's one of the very strong concerns that we have, yes. There is a very gray area here in the very nature of reverse engineering, which would leave an individual engaged in that practice uncertain what his ultimate rights would be should he use that particular result in another product.

Copyright Protection for Imprinted Design Patterns on Semiconductor Chips: Hearings Before the Subcomm. on Courts, Civil Liberties, and the Administration of Justice of the House Comm. on the Judiciary, 96th Cong., 1st Sess., 66 (1979).

This aspect was explored over the several years of legislative gestation. The reverse engineering procedure was described by witnesses, and distinguished in purpose and mechanism from the copying against which the Semiconductor Chip Protection Act was intended to guard. It was explained that a person engaged in reverse engineering seeks to understand the design of the original chip with the object of improving the circuitry, the chip layout, or both. The presence of innovation and improvement was stressed as the hallmark of an original layout. A witness explained the difference as determining "was anything innovative done in the process or was it simply a reproduction of what was already there?" The Semiconductor Chip Protection Act of 1983: Hearings on S. 1201 Before the Subcomm. on Patents, Copyrights, and Trademarks of the Senate Comm. on the Judiciary, 98th Cong., 1st Sess., 84 (1983) (testimony of Stanley C. Corwin). Another witness explained that reverse engineering generally produces a "paper trail" recording the engineer's efforts to understand the original chip and to design a different version after reverse engineering:

> Whenever there is a true case of reverse engineering, the second firm will have prepared a great deal of paper—logic and circuit diagrams, trial layouts, computer simulations of the chip, and the like; it will also have invested thousands of hours of work. All of these can be documented by reference to the firm's ordinary business records. A pirate has no such papers, for the pirate does none of this work. Therefore, whether there has been a true reverse engineering job or just a job of copying can be shown by looking at the defendant's records. The paper trail of a chip tells a discerning observer whether the chip is a copy or embodies the effort of reverse engineering.

Senate Report at 22 (quoting statement of Leslie L. Valdasz, Senior Vice President, Intel Corporation). The Committee reports and the statements of the Semiconductor Chip Protection Act's supporters show the belief that evidence of the presence or absence of such a paper trail would significantly reduce the gray area between legitimate and illegitimate behavior. See Mathias-Leahy Memorandum at S12,917; House Report at 21.

Senators Mathias and Leahy explained that §906(a) includes a provision

> to clarify the intent of both chambers that competitors are permitted not only to study the protected mask works, but also to use the results of that study to design, distribute and import semiconductor chip products embodying their own original mask works. . . .
>
> The end product of the reverse engineering process is not an infringement, and itself qualifies for protection under the Act, if it is an original mask work as contrasted with a substantial copy. If the resulting semiconductor chip product is not substantially identical to the original, and its design involved significant toil and investment, so that it is not mere plagiarism, it does not infringe the original chip, even if the layout of the two chips is, in substantial part, similar.

Mathias-Leahy Memorandum at S12,917.

In illuminating the meaning of "original" in the context of reverse engineering, Senators Mathias and Leahy distinguished between a substantial copy, on one hand, and the product of reverse engineering which might be similar to the original, but if not a substantial copy would not be an infringement. For the latter, the "paper trail" was expected to document efforts in "analyzing, or evaluating the concepts or techniques embodied in the mask work or the circuitry, logic flow, or organization of components used in the mask work", as the effort required would be reflected in the documents. *Id*.

AMD's defense was that its chips were independently designed after the Brooktree chips were subjected to reverse engineering to learn the Brooktree design. The question of whether AMD's activities were acceptable reverse engineering, or unacceptable copying, was explained to the jury as follows:

> Reverse engineering is permitted and is authorized by the Chip Protection Act. It is not infringement of an owner's exclusive right and protected mask work for another person, through reverse-engineering, to photograph and to study the mask work for the purpose of analyzing its circuitry—correction—the circuitry, logic flow and organization of the components used in the mask work and to incorporate such analysis into an original mask work.
>
> The end product of the reverse-engineering process may be an original mask work, and therefore not an infringing mask work, if the resulting semiconductor chip product is not substantially identical to the protected mask work and its design involved significant toil and investment so that it is not mere plagiarism.
>
> You should place great weight on the existence of reverse paperwork trail in determining whether the defendant's mask work is an original mask work from reverse-engineering.
>
> A.M.D. mask work constitutes an original mask work if A.M.D.'s mask work incorporates its own new design elements which offered improvements over or an alternative to Brooktree's mask work.

These instructions focus the jury on whether AMD produced an original mask work, as the statute requires. The instructions were not challenged by AMD on its motion for new trial or on appeal, and were adapted from AMD's proposed instructions. Brooktree calls the instructions "too lenient". Whether or not too lenient, they were not objected to by AMD at trial, and are not now criticized by AMD as incorrect. They are the law applied in this case. See Fed. R. Civ. P. 51; Herrington v. County of Sonoma, 834 F.2d 1488, 1500 n.12 (9th Cir. 1987), *cert. denied*, 489 U.S. 1090, 109 S. Ct. 1557, 103 L. Ed.2d 860 (1989) (failure to object to a jury instruction precludes appellate review).

The Trial

The factual premises of the issues of infringement and AMD's reverse engineering defense were extensively explored at trial, through examination and cross-examination of witnesses, exhibits, displays, and attorney argument. To summarize, AMD argued at trial, and repeats on this appeal, that it did not intend to copy Brooktree's layout, and did not do so. AMD pointed to its "paper trail" of its two and a half years of effort at a cost in excess of three million dollars. AMD stated that if its intent had been to copy the Brooktree layout, it would simply have directed duplication of the circuit layouts, requiring a matter of months, not years. AMD stressed differences between its chips and those of Brooktree, and pointed out its aversion to piracy. According to AMD, this case is not in the gray area where reasonable minds could differ over whether there was reverse engineering or copying. AMD argues that Congress could not have intended that mask work infringement be found in the circumstances of this case, and that this court should hold, as a matter of law, that AMD did not infringe Brooktree's mask work registrations.

Brooktree, on its part, argued that AMD's cell layout is not original, but was directly copied from Brooktree's SRAM core cell, and repeated 6,000 times. Brooktree stressed AMD's lengthy and expensive failures at designing a layout. Brooktree observed that AMD had incorrectly analyzed Brooktree's chip during its attempts at reverse engineering, and that throughout this entire period of attempted duplication of function, AMD was unable to come close to Brooktree's results. Brooktree pointed to the rapidity with which AMD changed to Brooktree's layout when the error in analysis was discovered, AMD immediately producing, without further experimentation, a substantially identical SRAM cell.

[The court proceeded to review the evidence at length.]

We conclude that there was a legally sufficient evidentiary basis whereby a reasonable jury could have found infringement of the mask work registrations.

The judgment is affirmed.

COMMENTS AND QUESTIONS

1. Review sections 905 and 906 of the SCPA. What exactly is illegal? Section 905 makes it illegal to reproduce a mask work, and *Brooktree* applies the copyright standard for reproduction: it is illegal to copy not only a whole work but even a significant part of the work. At the same time, section 906 provides that others may reverse engineer a mask work in order to "evaluate the concepts or techniques embodied in the mask work or the circuitry, logic flow or organiza-

tion of components used in the mask work" *and* that they may "incorporate the results of" this reverse engineering in their own chips.

But isn't that exactly what AMD did here? The court seems to hinge liability on AMD's adoption of Brooktree's 10-transistor design. But AMD learned of that design through reverse engineering, and it certainly represents the "circuitry, logic flow, or organization of components used" in Brooktree's chip. See Richard H. Stern, Determining Liability for Infringement of Mask Works Under the Semiconductor Chip Protection Act, 70 Minn. L. Rev. 271, 295 n.81 (1985) ("aspects of mask works that are dictated by chip function are not protected."). So why isn't AMD safe unless they physically duplicated the Brooktree chip for production? Notice that there is no derivative work right in section 905.

The statute clearly analogizes mask works to copyright law, both in prohibiting copying and in allowing reverse engineering. Section 906 seems to be suggesting that there is an "idea-expression dichotomy" in the SCPA, and that third parties are free to copy the unprotectable "idea" of a chip design. See Stern, supra, at 299-300. But how can we distinguish idea from expression in the context of semiconductor technology? Does *Brooktree* help draw a line? After *Brooktree*, what can AMD safely do with the chips it reverse engineers?

2. The court applies a "substantially identical" standard for determining infringement—tougher than the normal standard of "substantial similarity"—as long as the defendant can produce a paper trail establishing reverse engineering. Does this inappropriately burden the plaintiff in enforcing the SCPA? Alternatively, does it largely address the piracy concern that motivated the Act and ensure substantial lead-time advantages to registrants of mask works?

3. Some years ago Professor Raskind predicted that SCPA's reverse engineering provision would have "ramifications wider and deeper than than the Chip Act itself," perhaps reshaping the law's understanding about acts that should be considered fair use or unfair competition in the high technology field. See Leo J. Raskind, Reverse Engineering, Unfair Competition, and Fair Use, 70 Minn. L. Rev. 385 (1985). Think back to the Sega v. Accolade decision in Chapter 2 and consider what, if any, impact the SCPA provision might have had on the Ninth Circuit's ruling in that case. Would it affect your view to know that Sega argued in *Accolade* that the legislative history of SCPA supported its position that decompilation was not fair use? Some witnesses in congressional hearings on the chip protection legislation had expressed doubts about whether reverse engineering would be lawful under the fair use doctrine if semiconductor masks were added to the subject matter of copyright.

4. Although several aspects of SCPA are copyright-like (e.g., its originality requirement, its restatement of the idea/expression distinction, and the substantial similarity and substantial identity tests for infringement), other aspects of SCPA are more patent-like. The 10-year duration of protection, for example, is more patent-than copyright-like. SCPA also requires registration of mask works within two years of the first commercial exploitation of the mask work in order for SCPA rights to last up to 10 years. See 17 U.S.C. §908(a). The 10-year term of protection begins from the date of registration or first commercial use, whichever comes first. 17 U.S.C. §904(a). Registration is relatively straightforward and is modeled after copyright registration rather than the more detailed and time-consuming patent or trademark applications.

5.   One of the most remarkable aspects of SCPA has been the dearth of litigation. Indeed, *Brooktree* is the only reported case litigated under the Act. Given
that congressional testimony prior the SCPA's enactment indicated that there had
been rampant piracy, the paucity of litigation is surprising. A number of explanations have been offered for this discrepancy. First, it may be that most "piracy"
prior to the Act was due to uncertainty about the scope of mask work protection
under the copyright law. The SCPA clarified the law, according to this argument,
thereby leading firms to conform their behavior to the requirements of the Act. Is
this explanation persuasive? Based on *Brooktree*, is it fair to say that the scope of the
law is clear?

Ron Laurie, a leading computer law practitioner, has suggested an alternative
explanation—that the outright piracy alluded to during the hearings either did not
exist or has become technologically obsolete. Highly integrated modern mask
works cannot be quickly and accurately duplicated without using a fabrication
process virtually identical to the original manufacturer's. Because such processes are
highly proprietary, it is unlikely that pirates could have duplicated complex, high-
density chip designs without reverse engineering. Ronald S. Laurie, The First
Year's Experience Under the Chip Act or "Where Are the Pirates Now That We
Need Them?" 3 Computer Law. 11, 21 (Feb. 1986). In addition, the technologies of chip production have moved beyond the use of "masks," thereby rendering
the subject matter for protection under SCPA outmoded. Other nations have
characterized the subject matter of their laws as covering the layout or topography
of integrated circuits.

Commentators differ in their assessment of SCPA's success (or lack thereof).
Compare John Barton, Adapting the Intellectual Property System to New Tech-
nologies (viewing SCPA as a success) and Morton David Goldberg, Semiconduc-
tor Chip Protection As a Case Study (viewing SCPA as a failure) *in* Global
Dimensions of Intellectual Property Rights in Science and Technology (Mitchel B.
Wallerstein et al., eds., 1993).

6.   Congress decided to adopt a reciprocity rule for mask works produced by
foreign nationals. For reasons that will be explained in Chapter 8, this decision was
probably a strategic mistake. However, SCPA still provides that to have mask work
rights under SCPA, an owner of a mask work first commercially exploited in a
foreign country must be a "national, domiciliary, or sovereign authority of a foreign nation that is a party to a treaty affording protection to mask works to which
the U.S. is a party," §902(a)(1)(A), or the President must issue a proclamation
finding that the owner's country provides protection to owners of U.S. mask
works "on substantially the same basis as that on which the country extends protection to its own mask work owners and to mask works first commercially exploited in that country" and "on substantially the same basis as provided by the
SCPA," §902(a)(2). For further consideration of the international dimensions of
chip protection, see Chapter 8.

7.   Had CONTU been asked to consider whether semiconductor chip designs should be protected by copyright law, it might have said yes. See, e.g., Pamela Samuelson, Creating a New Kind of Intellectual Property Law: Applying the
Lessons of the Chip Law to Computer Programs, 70 Minn. L. Rev. 471 (1985)
(arguing that CONTU's rationale for advocating the use of copyright law to protect computer programs also applied to chip designs and, conversely, that the same

rationale Congress had for choosing to protect semiconductor chips with a sui generis form of legal protection also applied to computer programs).

PROBLEM

Problem 5-1. Amazingly Large-Scale Integrated Circuits, Inc. (ALSI) obtains a commercially sold version of a competitor's new semiconductor chip, which cost millions of dollars to design. ALSI engages in the process of reverse engineering the chip, peeling away its various layers and developing cross-section photographs and materials analyses. Based on this investigation, ALSI produces a layout diagram of the chip for around $30,000. Using a commercially available computer program that designs mask works automatically given a logic-level layout diagram, ALSI produces a chip with a mask different from its competitor's but with identical functionality and circuit design. The total cost to ALSI is about $65,000.

Has ALSI violated the SCPA? Would your answer be any different if the computer program produced masks virtually identical to the competitor's?

B.   SUI GENERIS PROTECTION FOR DATABASES

Advances in computer technology are largely responsible for the recent spate of sui generis proposals aimed at protecting the contents of databases. There are at least three reasons for this. One is that digital technologies make it so much easier and cheaper to appropriate information, regardless of whether it is in print form (e.g., by scanning) or in digital form (e.g., by stripping digitized information from a CD). Second, much of the value in databases lies not in the creativity of the compiler's selection and arrangement of the data, but rather in the data themselves. Especially when data are in electronic form, it is, moreover, very easy to reselect and rearrange the data in a manner so as to avert copyright liability, even though the appropriation may have competitively harmful consequences. Third, a large number of commercially valuable databases are products of automated data collection processes, are comprehensive in character and organized in a standard or functionally determined way, or require only modest and uncreative adjustments (e.g., correcting spelling or citations) to maintain. As a result, there may be insufficient originality in selection and arrangement of the data to support a claim of copyright. Although the legal protection of factual information has been a difficult area for copyright for many years, see, e.g., Jane C. Ginsburg, Creation and Commercial Value: Copyright Protection for Works of Information, 90 Colum. L. Rev. 1865 (1990), advances in computer technology have made the problem more acute.

The EU emphasized the vulnerability of databases to market-destructive appropriations when it proposed a new form of legal protection for databases. In fact, the first draft of the European Directive on the Legal Protection of Computer Databases would have provided a sui generis right to control the extraction and reuse of data from electronic databases. Partly because the drafters realized that digital technologies could be used to appropriate print as well as electronic information, subsequent drafts and the final directive confer this right on makers of all "databases," which are defined as "a collection of independent works, data or other materials arranged in a systematic or methodical way and individually accessible by electronic or other means." Chapter 8 discusses the European sui generis right in greater detail. For purposes of this chapter, however, readers should know that the U.S. Congress has considered adopting a similar, if not equivalent, law. Chances are that a sui generis law to protect compilations of information from market-destructive appropriations is likely to be enacted, although it may differ from the European Directive in some significant details. For a detailed discussion of the database proposals, their shortcomings, and the need for database protection, see Charles R. McManis, Database Protection in the Digital Information Age, 7 Roger Williams L. Rev. 7 (2001); J.H. Reichman & Pamela Samuelson, Intellectual Property Rights in Data?, 50 Vand. L. Rev. 51 (1997).

The debate over database protection raises a number of philosophical issues central to intellectual property protection for software. Deciding whether and how to protect computer databases requires that a legislature consider what protection already exists and how well the industry would perform without sui generis protection. If it decides to adopt a system of database protection, it then needs to consider how to provide incentives for investment while at the same time minimizing the damage that would be done to competition. To date, much of this discussion has been missing from the debate over database protection. The *Warren* case, below, illustrates the limitations on copyright protection for factual compilations in the post-*Feist* environment. Not surprisingly, publishers of factual works have been among the most ardent advocates of sui generis database protection legislation in the United States.

Warren Publishing, Inc. v. Microdos Data Corp.
United States Court of Appeals for the Eleventh Circuit
115 F.3d 1509 (11th Cir. 1997) (en banc)

BIRCH, Circuit Judge: . . .

Warren Publishing, Inc. ("Warren") compiles and publishes annually a printed directory called the Television & Cable Factbook ("Factbook"), which provides information on cable television systems throughout the United States. The Factbook contains two volumes, the "Station" volume and the "Cable and Services" volume. The focus of this case is the "Cable & Services" volume of the 1988 edition of the Factbook, and, in particular, the two sections of this volume entitled "Directory of Cable Systems" and "Group Ownership of Cable Systems in the United States." These sections are comprised of approximately 1,340 pages of factual data on 8,413 cable systems throughout the country and their owners.

The "Directory of Cable Systems" section contains extensive information on cable systems, including, inter alia, the name, address, and telephone number of the cable system operator, the number of subscribers, the channels offered, the price of service, and the types of equipment used. The entries in this section are arranged state by state in alphabetical order, and, within each state, all of the communities receiving cable television service are listed alphabetically. The "Group Ownership" section contains listings of selected information on "all persons or companies which have an interest in 2 or more systems or franchises." Factbook, Cable and Services Volume, at B-1301. The persons or entities listed in the group ownership section are known as multiple-system operators ("MSOs"), as contrasted with single-systems operators ("SSOs").

In the "Directory of Cable Systems" section, the factual data for each cable system is not printed under the name of each community that the cable system serves. The reason for this is that many communities are part of multiple-community cable systems, and it would be duplicative to list the same factual information under the individual community names for each community that comprises a multiple-community system. Therefore, a determination is made as to what community is the "principal" or "lead" (hereinafter "principal") community served by a particular cable system, and Warren prints the data only under the name of the principal community. Under the entries for the nonprincipal communities of a multiple-community cable system, there is a cross-reference to the principal community listing. Communities in north-central Georgia are cross-referenced to Atlanta in the 1988 Factbook: Alpharetta, Avondale Estates, Clarkston, College Park, Decatur, DeKalb County, East Point, Lithonia, Pine Lake, Sandy Springs, and Stone Mountain. In addition, Fulton County, although it has its own separate listing with factual data (since it is served by cable system different from that which serves Atlanta), also has a cross-reference that states "See also ATLANTA, GA." We infer from these listings that there are portions of Fulton County that are served by the cable system listed under the Fulton County heading, and that there are other portions of Fulton County served by the cable system listed under the Atlanta heading. The same holds true for DeKalb County, which is cross-referenced to both Atlanta and Chamblee, Georgia. We note that, in many cases, a cable system is a single-community system, and thus there is only one possible principal community.

Microdos Data Corp. and Robert Payne ("Microdos") also market a compilation of facts about cable systems. Robert Payne is the principal officer and shareholder of Microdos. Microdos's compilation comes in the form of a computer software package called "Cable Access." The Cable Access program, like the Factbook, provides detailed information on both SSOs and MSOs. The district court described the format of Cable Access as follows:

> The Cable Access software package is broken into three databases. The first database provides information on the individual cable systems. This database is referred to as "the system database." The second database provides information on multiple system operators and is simply referred to as "the MSO database." The third database is a historical database which provides selected information on the cable industry from 1965 to the present. . . .
>
> Defendant's Cable Access software package comes pre-sorted by state and city. The customer may rearrange the data in a format of its choosing. The customer may construct searches of the database's information on cable systems as required to fit its particular needs, as well as output the data to a hard copy in various formats, again to fit the specific needs of the customer.

There is no dispute that Warren's Factbook predates the Cable Access program. Warren has been publishing cable television information since 1948, whereas Microdos began marketing Cable Access in 1989. Shortly after Warren became aware of the existence of the Cable Access software, it notified Microdos that it believed that the Cable Access program infringed its copyright in the Factbook. In 1989, Microdos ceased marketing the original version of Cable Access, and, after some delay, began marketing a second version of Cable Access. Subsequently, a third and fourth version of Cable Access were marketed.

In July of 1990, Warren filed suit against Microdos, alleging copyright infringement and unfair competition. Warren alleged that all four versions of Cable Access infringed upon its compilation copyright in the 1988 Factbook. . . . Warren contended that Microdos infringed its compilation copyright in the Factbook in three areas: (1) the communities covered/principal community system, (2) the data fields, and (3) the data field entries. Following discovery, Warren and Microdos each moved for partial summary judgment on these three copyright infringement issues. With respect to the data fields issue, the district court found that Microdos had not infringed Warren's data field format. With respect to the data field entries issue, the district court found that these entries were uncopyrightable facts, and therefore Warren's "sweat of the brow" argument on this issue could not prevail in light of the Supreme Court's *Feist* decision. Accordingly, the district court entered partial summary judgment for Microdos on these two issues.

The district court, however, reached a different conclusion on the communities covered issue. It found that the principal community system utilized by Warren in presenting the data on cable systems in its Factbook was "sufficiently creative and original to be copyrightable." The district court then analyzed the selection of communities employed by Microdos and found it to be "substantially similar" to that of Warren. Based on this finding, and its conclusion that Microdos failed to prove that it obtained its information from a source independent of the Factbook, the district court denied Microdos's motion for summary judgment on the principal community system and granted Warren's cross-motion on that issue. The district court subsequently denied Microdos's motion for reconsideration of the order and granted Warren's motion for a "permanent" injunction. The court "enjoined [Microdos] from violating [Warren's] copyright of the Factbook through the use, copying, distribution or selling of any version of [Microdos's] Cable Access products." Microdos appeals the interlocutory order granting the injunction.

II. Discussion

Microdos argues that the district court improperly granted Warren's motion for an injunction based on an erroneous ruling of law. As a predicate for injunctive relief, the district court granted Warren's motion for partial summary judgment on the principal community system issue. Microdos contends that the district court erred, as a matter of law, in finding the principal community system protectable under copyright law.

A. *Review of Relevant Statutory Provisions and Case Law . . .*

The Supreme Court, in its most recent decision focusing on compilation copyrights, noted that "[t]he sine qua non of copyright is originality." *Feist*, 499

U.S. at 345. The Court emphasized that originality is a constitutional requirement, noting that the Constitution "authorizes Congress to 'secur[e] for limited
times to Authors . . . the exclusive Right to their respective Writings.'" *Id*. at 346
(quoting U.S. Const. art. I, §8, cl. 8). The Court also admonished that:

> Facts, whether alone or as part of a compilation, are not original and therefore
> may not be copyrighted. A factual compilation is eligible for copyright if it features an
> original selection or arrangement of facts, but the copyright is limited to the particular
> selection or arrangement. In no event may copyright extend to the facts themselves.

Id. at 350.

Thus, the compiler's choices as to selection, coordination, or arrangement are
the only portions of the compilation that arguably are even entitled to copyright
protection. As the *Feist* Court noted, these choices must be made "independently
by the compiler and entail a minimal degree of creativity" in order to be entitled to
compilation copyright protection. *Id*. at 348. The *Feist* Court further explained:

> This protection is subject to an important limitation. The mere fact that a work
> is copyrighted does not mean that every element of the work may be protected.
> Originality remains the sine qua non of copyright; accordingly, copyright protection
> may extend only to those components of a work that are original to the author.

Id. Given these limitations on the scope of copyright protection in a factual compilation, it is abundantly clear that "copyright in a factual compilation is thin." *Id*. at
349. Only when one copies the protected selection, coordination, or arrangement
in a factual compilation has one infringed the compilation copyright; copying of
the factual material contained in the compilation is not infringement.

B. The Principal Community System Employed by Warren

. . . The district court found that "Warren has developed a system for selecting communities which is original in the industry. This selection process represents
a part of the format of the compilation which *is* copyrightable" (emphasis added).
Since the district court concluded that Microdos had "substantially appropriated
the copyrightable selection of communities portion of the format of Warren's
Factbook," it held that "Microdos ha[d] infringed Warren's copyright in the Factbook." The district court was correct in employing "substantial similarity" analysis
once it concluded that Warren's system for selecting communities was copyrightable. Where it erred, however, was in concluding that Warren's system of selection
was copyrightable in the first place.

1. Warren's "System" of Selection

Section 102(b) of the Copyright Act specifically excludes "any idea, procedure, process, system, method of operation, concept, principle, or discovery" from
copyright protection "regardless of the form in which it is described, explained,
illustrated, or embodied in such work." 17 U.S.C. §102(b). Nonetheless, the
district court concluded that Warren's "system" of selecting communities was

original and entitled to copyright protection. This conclusion is contrary to the plain language of 17 U.S.C. §102(b), and is clearly incorrect. If Warren actually does employ a system to select the communities to be represented in the book, then section 102(b) of the Act bars the protection of such a system.

Even if we were to assume that the district court incorrectly denominated Warren's selection of communities as a "system," such an assumption would not validate the district court's finding of copyrightability. Warren contends that it has a unique method of choosing which communities to include in its directory, based on its "principal community" system. Warren defines a "cable system" as an entity offering subscribers in one or more communities the same cable services for the same price. As the district court found, "[t]he principal community, used to represent the entire cable system, is then selected by contacting the cable operator to determine which community is considered the lead community within the cable system. Other communities within the same cable system are then listed under the principal community, not independently." The Federal Communication Commission ("FCC"), unlike Warren, does not use a principal community system; rather, it lists individually every geographical community having cable service. As a result, if there are five communities served by one "cable system," Warren would list the system's data under the principal community name, and there would be cross-references under the listings of the names of the other four communities. The FCC, on the other hand, would list the data on all five communities separately.

At oral argument, Warren asserted, and the dissent agrees, that the district court was correct in finding that Warren is entitled to copyright protection in its "selection" of communities, which is based on its putatively unique definition of a cable system. The problem with this is that Warren does not undertake any "selection" in determining what communities to include in the Factbook. Warren claims that its system of listing communities does not include the entire universe of cable systems, and thus there is "selection" involved as to which communities they include in their Factbook. This assertion, however, is plainly wrong.

The district court found that the FCC, which attempts to list individually every community across the country with a cable system, had 724 communities listed for Illinois. Warren, it observed, listed 406 communities under its principal community concept. It did note that "[n]umerous additional communities were listed under the various principal communities," but stated that they were not separately listed. Given that Warren did not list all of the communities that the FCC did, the district court concluded that Warren did "select" which communities to include in the Factbook, and thus its selection was copyrightable. In an unintentionally prescient footnote, however, the district court noted that:

> This is not to say that the selection of cable systems would be copyrightable in all cases. Had Warren selected every cable system listed by the F.C.C., then there would not be sufficient originality in the "selection" to warrant copyrightability.

Yet, this is precisely what Warren did. The district court made the mistake of comparing the number of principal communities listed with the number of individual communities listed by the FCC. Given the way the principal community system works, however, that is like comparing apples to oranges. The proper method is to compare the 724 individual communities listed by the FCC for Illinois with the total number of communities listed by Warren for Illinois; in other words, include not only the principal communities listed, but also those that are listed and are cross-referenced to one of the 406 principal communities. Our count of the total number of communities listed for Illinois by Warren, both principal and nonprincipal, is approximately 1,000. Therefore, Warren seems to have included not only all that the FCC listed, but also some others that the FCC did not.

The Second Circuit has noted that "[s]election implies the exercise of judgment in choosing which facts from a given body of data to include in a compilation." Key Publications, Inc. v. Chinatown Today Publishing Enters., Inc., 945 F.2d 509, 513 (2d Cir. 1991). In *Key Publications*, the record indicated that the compilation copyright holder did not include the entire relevant universe in her directory; she testified that she chose to exclude certain businesses based on her belief that they would not remain open for very long. As the court noted, "[t]his testimony alone indicates thought and creativity in the selection of businesses included in the 1989-90 Key Directory." *Id*. Warren, to the contrary, has failed to make such a showing in this case. It did not exercise any creativity or judgment in "selecting" cable systems to include in its Factbook, but rather included the entire relevant universe known to it. The only decision that it made was that it would not list separately information for each community that was part of a multiple-community cable system; in other words, it decided to make the Factbook commercially useful. Therefore, it cannot prevail in its claim that it "selected" which communities to include in its Factbook. The district court erred in determining that Warren's system of selecting communities was copyrightable.

2. The Originality Requirement

Even were we to assume that the presentation of the selection of principal communities made by Warren was creative and original and therefore copyrightable, its claim that it is entitled to protection would nonetheless fail, because the selection is not its own, but rather that of the cable operators. The district court found that the principal community was "selected by contacting the cable operator to determine which community is considered the lead community within the cable system." As we observed in *BellSouth*, "these acts are not acts of authorship, but techniques for the discovery of facts." 999 F.2d at 1441.

In *BellSouth*, a case involving a "yellow pages" classified business directory, we held that Donnelley Information Publishing, Inc. ("Donnelley"), "[b]y copying the name, address, telephone number, business type, and unit of advertisement purchased for each listing in the BAPCO [BellSouth Advertising & Publishing Corporation] directory . . . copied no original element of selection, coordination or arrangement," and thus Donnelley was entitled to summary judgment on BAPCO's copyright infringement claim. *Id*. at 1446. The en banc court stated that "[w]hile BAPCO may select the headings that are offered to the subscriber, it is the subscriber who selects from those alternatives the headings under which the subscriber will appear in the directory. The headings that actually appear in the directory thus[] do not owe their origin to BAPCO. . . ." *Id*. at 1444. In this case, Warren employed a method similar to that of BAPCO in "selecting" the principal community heading under which to list the data for the multiple-community systems.

Lynn Levine, the Director of Market Research and Data Sales for Warren, stated in her deposition that Warren determines the names of the communities served by a cable system by contacting the operators of the cable systems and asking them which communities they serve. In addition, she stated that Warren, in gathering data for the Factbook, relied in "great part" on the questionnaire responses received from the various cable operators. *Id.* at 35. These acts are nothing more than techniques for the discovery of facts. Simply because Warren may have been the first to discover and report a certain fact on cable systems does not translate these acts of discovery into acts of creation entitled to copyright protection. See *Feist*, 499 U.S. at 347 (distinguishing creation from discovery). "Just as the Copyright Act does not protect 'industrious collection,' it affords no shelter to the resourceful, efficient, or creative collector." *BellSouth*, 999 F.2d at 1441.

The record indicates that it is the cable operators, not Warren, that determine, in the case of a multiple-community system, the community name under which to list the factual data for the entire cable system. Therefore, Warren cannot prevail in its claim that it undertakes original selection in employing the principal community concept. Rather, it has created an effective system for determining where the cable operators prefer to have the data listed. While Warren may have found an efficient method of gathering this information, it lacks originality, which is the sine qua non of copyright. See *Feist*, 499 U.S. at 345. Thus, the district court erred in finding that Warren's principal community "system" was sufficiently creative and original to be entitled to copyright protection. . . .

GODBOLD, Senior Circuit Judge, dissenting.

At the initial stage of choosing the facts that it wanted, Warren moved from idea to intellectual expression through selection. The selection of facts it wanted were not the facts that previously the industry had compiled in terms of community. Rather Warren chose to select and present facts that reflected the way the industry is currently actually operating. Its choice was reflected in functional service/operations/management terms. The building block, the data-reporting unit, for selection and presentation of industry data was the "cable system" as newly defined by Warren, "an entity composed as one or more communities that are offered the same service by the same cable system owner at the same price." Warren had . . . devised a framework for the data to be assembled and had formulated selective rules and categories. Reporting data by a functional unit was a new and original concept, and the implementing definition of "cable system" was new to the industry and crafted by Warren.

Next, it was necessary for Warren to define and identify the universe of raw data from which it would select and present information. It chose a universe composed of all geographic communities (in the state of Illinois, the representative state) having cable television service. This defined universe was itself new. It consisted of 1,000 plus geographic communities (1,017 by one count, 1,045 by another). It included cities, towns, and villages, and also included counties and townships, which historically were not usual franchise-granting units. The FCC maintained its own list of cable systems (as it defined them), composed of cities, towns and villages, that is, franchise-granting units. FCC's universe was 724 communities. Warren's functional/operational definition swept in non-franchising geographic areas receiving service. Its universe of raw data was thus new in concept and some 40% larger in number of communities than the FCC universe.

As its next step Warren identified and selected from its universe 406 data-reporting units in Illinois, each a "cable system" pursuant to its functional definition. Then, drawing from the 1,000 plus universe, Warren had to identify and properly locate within the proper unit of the 406 each geographic community enjoying cable service. More than half of the 406 Illinois cable operations turned out to be single-system operations (SSO's), that is, each served only a single community. A multiple community system (MSO) served more than one community. Each SSO, because of its singularity, fell within Warren's same operator/same service/same price definition of a cable system. The name under which its data was presented was necessarily that of the single community it served. Having located within the proper cable system (MSO or SSO) each community served, for MSO's Warren had to merge or combine the operating data for each community into one unitary body of operating data to be reported for the system. Data relating to each geographic community served was no longer independently listed community-by-community but instead was included in the unitary system data. The name of an individual (nonprincipal) geographic community whose service was operated and managed as part of a cable system appeared but without data and was cross-referenced to the system where its data was included in the unitary data. This referencing was necessary, of course, because data-reporting was unitary rather than individual.

As part of Warren's acts of selection it was necessary for it to choose a name by which each cable system would be listed and identified and under which the system data would be set out. For this purpose Warren elected to use a geographic name, and the type of geographic name it chose was that of the "lead" or "principal" geographic community within the system. Obviously, for an SSO the name of the single community served was selected. When these acts were concluded Warren's selection (406 units) consisted of 45% fewer data-reporting units than the FCC's listing of 724. . . .

Warren's selection entails more than the required degrees of originality and creativity. Warren saw the need, chose the facts it wanted to compile, chose how it wanted to arrange them in gathering points for data rather than by individualized presentations. It employed a new concept of gathering cable data into a smaller number of units and, for this purpose, it devised a new concept of a cable system as functionally defined and a new concept (and new title) of "principal community." It is sufficient if there is a "small spark of distinctiveness," but this is no small spark. It is a fundamental change in reporting data of a changing and developing industry. The fact that some of the data-reporting units were SSO's does not diminish the fact of Warren's acts of selection or of the originality and creativity of the selection, which required Warren to determine whether each of the 1,000 plus systems was a single community system (SSO) or part of a multiple community system (MSO) and to assemble and report system data accordingly.

COMMENTS AND QUESTIONS

1. Does the dissent's additional information about Warren's activities change your perception about whether the majority correctly ruled that there was insufficient originality in Warren's compilation?

2. Microdos would almost certainly have violated the sui generis right created by the European Directive if that law applied to its actions. Article 7 provides: "[T]he maker of a database which shows that there has been a qualitatively and/or quantitatively substantial investment in either the obtaining, verification, or presentation of the contents [of the database shall have the right] to prevent the extraction and/or reutilization of the whole or a substantial part, evaluated qualitatively and/or quantitatively, of the contents of the database." The Directive provides for very limited exceptions to the norm for private study, for teaching or research, and for administrative proceedings.

Consider how Microdos would fare under the various bills that have recently been considered in the U.S. Congress.

The principal norm of H.R. 354, as first introduced in the 106th Congress, was:

> Any person who extracts, or uses in commerce, all or a substantial part, measured either quantitatively or qualitatively, of a collection of information gathered, organized, or maintained by another person through the investment of substantial monetary or other resources, so as to cause harm to the actual or potential market of that other person, or a successor in interest of that other person, for a product or service that incorporates that collection of information and is offered or intended to be offered for sale or otherwise in commerce by that other person, or a successor in interest of that person, shall be liable to that person or successor in interest for the remedies set forth in section 1406.

Some months later, this norm changed under a substitute H.R. 354. It would outlaw making available to others or extracting to make available to others all or a substantial part of another's collection of information so as to cause material harm to the primary market or a related market of that person. H.R. 354 also provides for some exclusions from protection (principally for government information) and for some permitted acts (e.g., for news reporting, verification, and scientific or educational uses).

Consider also the principal norm of an alternative bill, H.R. 1858, that has been endorsed by a substantial number of high technology companies:

> It is unlawful for any person, by any means or instrumentality of interstate or foreign commerce or communications, to sell or distribute to the public a database that—
>
> > (1) is a duplicate of another database that was collected and organized by another person; and
> >
> > (2) is sold or distributed in commerce in competition with that other database.

Why would high technology firms prefer H.R. 1858 to either version of H.R. 354? Is it accurate to characterize any of these approaches as unfair competition-based, as contrasted with the exclusive property rights approach of the European Directive? What are the relevant pros and cons of an unfair competition versus an exclusive property rights approach? Which, if any, of the approaches should Congress adopt and why?

3. In view of the Court's insistence in *Feist* on the constitutional nature of the originality requirement, questions have arisen about what power the U.S. Congress has to adopt sui generis protection to unoriginal databases. See, e.g., Jane C. Ginsburg, No "Sweat"? Copyright and Other Protection of Works of In-

formation After Feist v. Rural Telephone, 92 Colum. L. Rev. 338, 348 (1992); Paul J. Heald & Suzanna Sherry, Implied Limits on the Legislative Power: The Intellectual Property Clause as an Absolute Constraint on Congress, 2000 Univ. of Illinois L. Rev. 1119 (suggesting that Congress could not protect databases under the Commerce Clause).

4. *State Misappropriation Law and Copyright Preemption.* Over the course of the past century, courts have vacillated in recognizing a cause of action against those who misappropriate value created by others in the absence of formal intellectual property protection. In a controversial case that gave rise to this equitable cause of action, the Supreme Court held that one news agency could be prohibited from copying and sending to its subscribers the news reports of another agency, notwithstanding the fact that the content of the news reports was not copyrighted. International News Service v. Associated Press, 248 U.S. 215 (1918). Subsequent lower federal court decisions construed this decision narrowly. Judge Learned Hand went so far as to say that "[w]hile it is of course true that the law ordinarily speaks in general terms, there are cases where the occasion is at once the justification for, and the limit of, what is decided. [INS v. AP] appears to us such an instance; we think that no more was covered than situations substantially similar to those then at bar." Cheney Bros. v. Doris Silk Corp., 35 F.2d 29 (2d Cir. 1929), *cert. denied,* 281 U.S. 728 (1930). Judge Hand went on to characterize the problems with the Court's decision as "insuperable," and to state that it "flagrantly conflict[ed]" with the federal statutory intellectual property laws.

The federal law of misappropriation came to an abrupt end in 1938 when the U.S. Supreme Court abolished the concept of federal common law in diversity of citizenship cases. Erie R. Co. v. Tompkins, 304 U.S. 64 (1938). The doctrine survived, however, through state common law. A number of states adopted, and in some cases expanded, the tort of misappropriation. A New York court, for example, characterized its state misappropriation law as "broad and flexible" and designed to address "business malpractices offensive to the ethics of . . . society." Metropolitan Opera Association v. Wagner-Nichols Recorder Corp., 10 N.Y.S.2d 483, 492 (Sup. Ct. 1950), *aff'd* 279 A.2d 632 (1951). The court there held that plaintiffs could obtain judicial relief where a defendant simply usurps, for commercial advantage, commercial value deriving from the plaintiff's efforts and expense.

In general, the tort of misappropriation requires proof of the following elements:

    i.   the plaintiff has made a substantial investment of time, effort, and money in creating the thing misappropriated, such that the court can characterize that "thing" as a kind of property right;

    ii.   the defendant has appropriated the "thing" at little or no cost, such that the court can characterize the defendant's actions as "reaping where it has not sown"; and

    iii.   the defendant's acts have injured the plaintiff, such as by a direct diversion of profits from the plaintiff to the defendant or a loss of royalties that the plaintiff charges to others to use the thing misappropriated.

McCarthy, Trademarks and Unfair Competition §10.51; United States Golf Association v. Arroyo Software, 40 U.S.P.Q.2d 1840 (Cal. Superior Ct. 1996), *aff'd* 69 Cal. App.4th 607 (1999).

The preemptive scope of federal patent and copyright law, however, limit the reach of state misappropriation doctrine. See 17 U.S.C. §301; NBA v. Motorola, 105 F.3d 841 (2d Cir. 1997). Courts have held that the scope of preemption under §301 extends not only to copyrightable works, but also to uncopyrightable works that are within the general scope of copyright (e.g., ideas, facts). In order to avoid copyright preemption, the Second Circuit has limited New York's "hot news" misappropriation doctrine to situations where:

> (i) a plaintiff generates or gathers information at a cost; (ii) the information is time sensitive; (iii) a defendant's use of the information constitutes free riding on the plaintiff's efforts; (iv) the defendant is in direct competition with a product or service offered by the plaintiffs; and (v) the ability of other parties to free-ride on the effort of the plaintiff or others would so reduce the incentive to produce the product or service that its existence or quality would be substantially threatened.

NBA v. Motorola, 105 F.3d 841, 852 (2d Cir. 1997). The limitation to situations of direct competition appears consistent with the unfair competition rather than the property rationale for database protection.

5. The ready appropriability of digital information may give rise to additional proposals for sui generis protection. Consider, for example, what courts will do if computer-generated works eventually become commercially valuable. In a pre-*Feist* era, it might have been possible to argue that copyright protection might extend to such works. See, e.g., Pamela Samuelson, Allocating Ownership Rights in Computer-Generated Works, 47 U. Pitt. L. Rev. 1185 (1986). Post-*Feist*, however, this seems unlikely.

Especially because of the vulnerability of personal information in digital networked environments, some economists have even proposed that legislatures create a sui generis property right in personal information as a way to protect privacy. See, e.g., Kenneth C. Laudon, Markets and Privacy, 39 Comm. ACM 92 (Sept. 1996). Would this be a good idea? Why or why not? For criticism of such property-based privacy rights, see Pamela Samuelson, Privacy as Intellectual Property? 52 Stan. L. Rev. 1125 (2000); Mark A. Lemley, Private Property, 52 Stan. L. Rev. 1545 (2000).

C. PROPOSALS FOR SUI GENERIS PROTECTION FOR SOFTWARE

A number of commentators have suggested that Congress should adopt for computer software a type of protection similar to the SCPA but tailored specifically to the needs of the computer software industry. These commentators normally call attention to three perceived problems with existing legal rules. First, they argue that the term of protection afforded the owners of copyrights (95 years for works for hire) and patents (20 years from the application date) is simply too long for the rapidly changing software industry. Some proposals are for patent-like protection but with a quicker application process and a term of five to seven years. Second, they argue that the overlapping protection now afforded computer software both confuses the market and distorts incentives to create and distribute software, because it is not always obvious what rights exist in a particular program. Sui generis protection is generally envisioned as a replacement for other forms of intellectual property protection. Finally, supporters of sui generis protection argue that none of the existing intellectual property regimes works particularly well in the software context. For instance, trade secrets law must stretch to protect mass-market software code, and cannot expect to protect screen displays at all. Copyright law protects only certain parts of computer programs—generally not the parts that the programmers generally consider most valuable. Patent protection is expensive and generally takes several years to get. Arguably, it provides too much protection once it has been acquired.

How to remedy these problems has been the subject of considerable academic debate. Consider the following views.

≡
≡ *Peter S. Menell, Tailoring Legal Protection*
≡ *for Computer Software*
≡ 39 Stan. L. Rev. 1329 (1987)

. . . B.   Tailoring Legal Protection
for Operating Systems

Part of the reason for copyright's inability to promote economic efficiency in the provision of computer products is that the public goods and network externality problems suggest conflicting modes of legal protection. Public goods problems are alleviated by expanding legal protection for intellectual work. External benefits from networks are promoted by facilitating access to a standard. Thus, the difficult policy question is how to promote standardization while at the same time encouraging continuing innovation (along the entire spectrum from software to hardware). By closely tailoring legal protection to reward desired innovation while permitting reasonable access to industry standards, it is possible to reach a satisfactory accommodation of these apparently conflicting objectives.

In theory, patent law is more appropriate than copyright for protecting the intellectual work contained in computer operating systems. A patent protects new and useful processes and machines. Given the interchangeability of hardware and software, it seems logical to protect computer operating systems and dedicated computers that embody a particular operating system with the same form of legal protection. Because patent law protects ideas, those who create patentable operating systems could be better assured of appropriating a substantial portion of the benefits of their efforts.

. . . [I]t is difficult to obtain patent protection for computer programs.[1] It should be pointed out, however, that although the scope of patent protection for computer software is uncertain, some of the recent cases that have upheld the pat-

---

1. [Keep in mind that this article was written in 1987.—Eds.]

entability of computer programs involved programs that manipulate the internal operations of a computer. Moreover, the importance of network externalities flowing from widespread access to a common mini- and microcomputer operating system suggests that legal protection should be hard to come by and relatively short in duration.

To encourage innovation in operating system technology, Congress should consider creating a hybrid form of patent protection specifically tailored to accommodate the market failures endemic to the provision of computer operating systems.[190] As with traditional patent law, the standard for protection should be novelty, nonobviousness, and usefulness; dominant firms (or anyone else) should not be able to "lock up" an industry standard simply by expressing it in a unique way.

To be feasible, the modified form of patent protection for computer operating systems should be based on a timely examination of patent applications. And given the rapid pace of technological change in the computer field and the interest in promoting access to industry standards, patent protection for operating systems should be shorter in duration than traditional patent protection.

In order to promote continued innovation in widely used operating systems, the operating system patent code should, like the Semiconductor Chip Protection Act, permit some limited form of reverse engineering. And like traditional patent law, the hybrid code should allow consumers to buy a ROM chip or other device containing a patented operating system and modify it for sale to a third person.

Because traditional patent law affords absolute protection, however, it would inhibit realization of network externalities from operating systems satisfying the above subject matter requirements. In order to facilitate realization of network externalities, therefore, the hybrid patent code should contain a flexible compulsory licensing provision. Such a provision would promote access to an industry standard while assuring rewards to the creator of an innovative and socially valuable operating system. It would also limit the ability of dominant firms in the industry to engage in anticompetitive practices.

The need for compulsory licensing as a means for promoting competition and rewarding innovation is brought into focus by the decision of the Ninth Circuit Court of Appeals in Digidyne Corp. v. Data General Corp. In *Data General*, the defendant (Data General), a manufacturer of computers, refused to license its RDOS operating system to firms using a central processing unit other than Data General's "NOVA" system. Recognizing the anticompetitive effects of this practice in a market with network externalities,[196] the Ninth Circuit held that Data Gen-

---

190. Congress has recently followed a sui generis approach in designing legal protection for semiconductor chips. . . . Other commentators have also urged Congress to create a hybrid form of legal protection for computer software. See Davidson, [Protecting Computer Software: A Comprehensive Analysis, 1983 Ariz. St. L.J. 611, 673-674]; Galbi, Proposal for New Legislation to Protect Computer Programming, 17 J. Copyright Soc'y 280 (1970); Karjala, [Lessons from the Computer Software Protection Debate in Japan, 1984 Ariz. St. L.J. 53, 63]; Samuelson, Creating a New Kind of Intellectual Property: Applying the Lessons of the Chip Law to Computer Programs, 70 Minn. L. Rev. 471, 507, 529-31 (1985); Stern, The Case of the Purloined Object Code: Can It Be Solved? (Part 2), Byte, Oct. 1982, at 210, 222.

196. The court accepted the plaintiffs' proof of market power on the basis of software "lock-in." Software lock-in occurs when a computer user develops or purchases application software designed to run on a particular operating system. This installed base locks the consumer into the hardware products of the owner of that operating system if competitors cannot gain access to the operating system and the costs of converting software to run on different operating systems are high. But see Helein, Software Lock-in and

eral's licensing practices were an unlawful tying arrangement that violated federal antitrust law.

In light of the strong network externalities flowing from compatibility, computer operating systems serve as "essential facilities" in computer hardware markets. Unless a firm can get onto the network, its products will be at a great disadvantage relative to those that can run the vast stock of application programs designed for the industry standard. The operating system royalty rate per use should be set so as to compensate true innovators for the cost of building a useful "highway" for the market plus a fair profit (adjusted for the risk of failure). For high volume products, these rates would probably be low. In the microcomputer market, for example, the rate would probably be less than one dollar for access to the major operating systems (assuming that the Apple and IBM operating systems merited hybrid patent protection at all).

A patent code for operating systems based on the above outline strikes a preferable balance of the conflicting policy concerns raised by computer operating systems. By providing solid protection for truly innovative and useful operating systems, the code would reward innovation in operating systems. The limits on this regime of protection—moderate duration, reverse engineering, adaptation— and the provision for compulsory licensing would promote access to operating systems that emerge as industry standards, wide diffusion of computer products, and innovation in hardware products. The code would also avoid wasteful expenditure of resources on efforts to emulate an industry standard.

The proposed operating system code would probably entail somewhat higher administrative costs than the current system. Patent examinations, though streamlined, would be significantly more expensive than the cost of copyright registration. Moreover, compulsory licensing proceedings, as well as the cost of monitoring use of protected operating systems, would add to the expense of the system. If the royalty rates were low (as the microcomputer example indicates), however, members of the industry could be expected to cooperate in ensuring that patent owners were properly compensated.

C. Tailoring Legal Protection for Application Programs

As with legal protection for operating systems, Congress should consider creating a special form of legal protection for application programs. Given the importance of improving existing programs as a primary mode of technological innovation and the presence of some network externalities, legal protection should be significantly shorter in duration than traditional copyright protection. The relatively short commercial life of most application programs indicates that legal protection should be correspondingly short.

The regime for protecting application programs should also allow for reverse engineering. In designing legal protection for semiconductor chips, Congress recognized the importance of reverse engineering in enabling researchers to advance a field in which innovations are cumulative. A limited reverse engineering

---

Antitrust Tying Arrangements: The Lessons of Data General, 5 Computer/L.J. 329, 337, 342-43 (1985) (suggesting that conversion costs might not be so high as to justify a finding of market power).

provision in the application software code would similarly promote the advancement of application software technology.

Congress should also consider the desirability of a limited form of compulsory licensing of application packages. In order to realize the benefits of network externalities and to promote creativity in the integration of software programs, it would seem worthwhile to allow limited access to application programs, particularly those that emerge as industry standards. This could be achieved without dulling primary creative incentives by delaying the availability of compulsory licensing for a limited period to allow the creator of the program to reap the rewards of commercial success.

COMMENTS AND QUESTIONS

1. How does the Menell proposal compare with how copyright and patent protection have evolved to protect computer software? Think back to the cases in Chapter 2 and consider whether the software developers involved in those cases would have proceeded differently with their legal protection strategies had Menell's proposal been adopted.

2. How would Menell protect screen displays (if at all)? Mathematical algorithms embodied in computer software? Computer languages? Source code? Object code? Would all of these parts of a computer program require a different statute to protect them? Or should protection be subsumed within a broader "software" framework?

3. Presumably Menell's proposal would replace patent and copyright law. Should it also replace trademark and trade secret law insofar as they apply directly to computer software?

4. Does Menell's suggestion of treating applications programs differently from operating systems make sense? Are the differences between the two types of programs—something he discusses in detail in the balance of his piece—sufficient to warrant different statutory treatment? To the extent that there are differences, such as the standardization problem with operating systems, are they appropriately addressed in other ways? Recall that the Third Circuit in the Apple v. Franklin case rejected the idea of distinguishing between operating system and application programs.

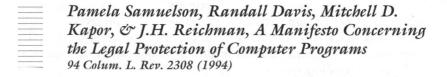

Pamela Samuelson, Randall Davis, Mitchell D. Kapor, & J.H. Reichman, A Manifesto Concerning the Legal Protection of Computer Programs
94 Colum. L. Rev. 2308 (1994)

1. Important Characteristics of Computer Programs

Computer programs have a number of important characteristics that have been difficult for legal commentators and decisionmakers to perceive. First, the primary source of value in a program is its behavior, not its text. Second, program text and behavior are independent in the sense that a functionally indistinguishable imitation can be written by a programmer who has never seen the text of the original program. Third, programs are, in fact, machines (entities that bring about useful behavior) that have been constructed in the medium of text (source and object code). The engineering designs embodied in programs could as easily be implemented in hardware as in software, and the user would be unable to distinguish between the two. Fourth, the industrial designs embodied in programs are typically incremental in character, the result of software engineering techniques and a large body of practical know-how. . . .

2.1.1 Programs Reveal a Substantial Amount of Their Know-How in Products Distributed in the Market

. . . Computer programs are an unusual kind of industrial product because the bulk of the know-how required to create them is accessible on or near the face of the product distributed in the marketplace. There are several reasons why this is so: (1) Software products need little specialized mass-production know-how; (2) they are particularly rich in design know-how; and (3) they are more susceptible in some respects to reverse engineering than traditional industrial products.

Software is easy to mass-produce because it is an information product. There is no steel to cut or bend, no wires to attach, and no parts to be cast in plastic or rubber. Mass production is as simple as loading copies onto floppy disks or tapes, a routine, inexpensive, and low-technology undertaking. Because there are no special processes required for mass production of the software products, there is no opportunity to accumulate specialized know-how about mass production. Lack of mass-production know-how matters because this is the kind of know-how that can most easily be kept out of the product, i.e., maintained as a trade secret. . . .

Software is, instead, rich in surface design know-how. This is particularly true for interactive software, i.e., programs that involve a great deal of hands-on usage. For such software, the metaphor or conception of the task is particularly important. . . .

Software is not only especially rich in design know-how; much of the value of software arises from it. . . .

The difficult task in creating interactive software, the innovations embodied in it, and the value of those innovations are typically found in conception and design: determining how to think about the task (e.g., the desktop metaphor), and then determining what capabilities the program should have (e.g., what can be done with documents, or folders). Determining the answers to these questions requires both informed insight and the time-consuming and expensive process of having real users test the software for extended periods. We can summarize by saying that interactive software is, by its nature, rich in design know-how.

Such know-how is, inescapably, present on the face of the product, and immediately evident on inspection. The hard-won insights and innovations embodied in surface design are prominently displayed by the program in operation; they are also explained in online help, and further detailed in the manual. Insights not readily explained by the tool or the manual will often become evident to a sophisticated user of the program who runs the program over a variety of examples. Since program innovation often lies in finding a way to make program behavior easier for people to use, the behavior and its insights must be evident to the user. . . .

We stress the triviality of some acquisitions of behavioral equivalence because this triviality can be the source of market-destructive effects. The particular means a firm uses to acquire behavioral equivalence is not important from a market-preservation standpoint. The crucial concern is whether it is trivially easy and quick to copy a software innovation that was very expensive to develop. If the disproportion in cost of copying and cost of innovation is substantial enough, it can destroy the innovator's opportunity to recoup its expenses, and consequently, can destroy incentives to invest in software innovation. . . .

2.2.3 Why Copyright Law Is Ill-Suited to Protecting Software Innovations

. . . Copyright law is mismatched to software, in part, because it does not focus on the principal source of value in a program (its useful behavior). As explained above, program text and behavior are largely independent, so that protecting program texts does not prevent second comers from copying valuable program behavior. The ability to copy valuable behavior legally would sharply reduce incentives for innovation, and thus thwart the policy behind legal protection. As we explain below, the right way out of this bind is not to conceive of behavior as a nonliteral element of the program's text, as some courts have done, but instead to regard it as the entity that an appropriate legal regime should protect.

Once one recognized that computer programs are machines whose medium of construction is text, it becomes obvious why copyright is an inappropriate vehicle for protecting most program behavior. Copyright law does not protect the behavior of physical machines (nor their internal constructions), no matter how much originality they may embody. Historically, innovations in the design of machine behavior have been left to the rigors of patent law. . . .

If the industrial designs of programs cannot generally be protected by patents because they do not meet the patent invention standard, but need some legal protection, one might ask whether copyright law could supply this protection. . . .

However, by enacting section 102(b), Congress intended to exclude industrial design elements of program—processes, procedures, systems and methods of operation—from the scope of copyright protection. . . .

This result does not change if one characterizes the abstract design of programs as an industrial compilation of applied know-how. Of course, copyright law has a long history of protecting compilations of information. It has, however, accorded either no or relatively thin protection to compilations of industrial or technological elements. Many industrial compilations (such as a combination of machine components) have been excluded from copyright protection because of their intrinsic utility. Others, such as those created when someone selects or arranges information in accordance with a method, system or other functionally determined design, are also unprotectable by copyright law. Even when copyright protection has been available for a work consisting largely of industrial information (such as a manual for operating a power plant), it has not protected the know-how, only the author's manner of describing the know-how. The commercially valuable aspects of industrial compilations of applied know-how have generally been protected by trade secret, not copyright.

[In the balance of the Manifesto, the authors propose a relatively brief period of anti-"cloning" protection in addition to the protection already provided by copyright law for program code and for expressive textual or pictorial material displayed on computer screens by the program code. While the authors regard patents as an inappropriate form of legal protection for software, they acknowledge that patent law is being used to protect software designs, and hope to provide an alternative protection mechanism that would permit firms to protect valuable functional designs without resort to the patent system.]

COMMENTS AND QUESTIONS

1. Mitchell D. Kapor, one of the co-authors of the Manifesto, was the founder and former CEO of Lotus Development Corp., as well as co-author of Lotus 1-2-3. The first of the Lotus "look and feel" lawsuits was initiated while Kapor was still with Lotus. Kapor's sponsorship of and participation in the Manifesto project was in part an attempt to grapple with how intellectual property law should deal with software innovations. The consensus among the co-authors of the Manifesto was that Paperback, Borland, Jaslow, and Microsoft had cloned industrial design and/or behavioral components of software products developed, respectively, by Lotus, Whelan, and Apple. Even though such cloning may have involved a competitively harmful trivial acquisition of equivalence, the Manifesto's authors would not have used copyright law to protect against such appropriations. They would, however, favor blocking clones for a period of years. See Manifesto, 94 Colum. L. Rev. at 2396-2399 (analyzing major cases).

2. A companion article to the Manifesto was J.H. Reichman, Legal Hybrids Between the Patent and Copyright Paradigms, 94 Colum. L. Rev. 2432, 2444 (1994). Reichman suggested that the problems experienced by software developers were symptomatic of a larger problem confronting advanced technology innovators generally:

> To avoid underinvestment in research and development of unpatentable innovation likely to ensure from a pervasive contraction of lead time in advanced technological sectors, the world's intellectual property system and the domestic competition laws with which it is allied have come under intense pressure to obtain artificial lead time through one legal device or another. . . . [G]overnments tend to respond by extending patent and copyright laws to protect subject matters for which these laws were not intended or by implementing legal hybrid [sui generis] regimes that grant exclusive property rights to new objects of protection that fall outside the classical legal framework. These ad hoc efforts to accommodate nontraditional forms of innovation have spawned a proliferation of restraints on trade that strain the international intellectual property system to the breaking point and weaken the competitive ethos from within.

Reichman explores at length the legal hybrid regimes built on modified copyright and modified copyright principles and suggests an alternative paradigm, built on modified trade secrecy principles, that would offer a short-term form of protection for industrial compilations of applied know-how.

In an earlier work, Reichman offered this explanation of the legal protection dilemma for high technology industries:

> The bulk of today's most valuable innovations flow from incremental improvements in applied scientific know-how. Traditionally, unpatentable industrial know-how remained exempt from free competition only so long as it was neither voluntarily disclosed nor reverse engineered. Because the task of reverse engineering took time and cost money, it endowed innovators with a period of natural lead time in which to secure a foothold in the market.
>
> In contrast, much of today's most advanced technology enjoys a less favorable competitive position than that of conventional machinery because of the unpatentable, intangible know-how responsible for its commercial value becomes embodied in products that are distributed on the open market. A product of the new technologies, such as a computer program, an integrated circuit design, or even a biogenetically altered organism may thus *bear its know-how on its face*, a condition that renders it as vulnerable to rapid appropriation by second-comers as any published literary or artistic work.
>
> From this perspective, a major problem with the kinds of innovative know-how underlying important new technologies is that they do not lend themselves to secrecy even when they represent the fruit of enormous investment in research and development. Because third parties can rapidly duplicate the embodied information and offer virtually the same products at lower prices than those of the originators, there is no secure interval of lead time in which to recuperate the originators' initial investment or their losses from unsuccessful essays, not to mention the goal of returning a profit.
>
> When innovators turn to the world's intellectual property system for relief, however, they find that its dominant paradigms are structured to protect "art" and "inventions." Present-day innovation fits imperfectly within either category. Viewed as industrial inventions, advances in the new technologies often appear too incremental and too small in scale to qualify as major breakthroughs under the "nonobviousness" or "inventive step" requirements of patent law. At the same time, these technologies serve impersonal, functional goals that make them alien to the spirit of laws devised to protect literary and artistic works. Today's most economically significant technologies are thus likely to be *intermediate technologies* that fall between the patent and copyright paradigms. . . .
>
> From a behavioral standpoint, investors in applied scientific know-how find the copyright paradigm attractive because of its inherent disposition to supply artificial lead time to all comers without regard to innovative merit and without requiring originators to preselect the products that are most worthy of protection.

J.H. Reichman, Design Protection and the New Technologies: The United States Experience in a Transnational Perspective, 1991 Indus. Prop. 220, 269, 271 (1991) (emphasis in original).

3. Some commentators on the Manifesto thought it might give too much reward to software developers. See Paul Goldstein, Comments on A Manifesto Concerning the Legal Protection of Computer Programs, 94 Colum. L. Rev. 2573, 2574-2575 (1994); Peter S. Menell, The Challenges of Reforming Intellectual Property Protection for Computer Software, 94 Colum. L. Rev. 2644, 2647 (1994). Other commentators questioned the timing of the Manifesto's call for new legislation. They pointed out that copyright law was providing a workable form of legal protection in the early 1990s and that drafting an entirely new statute would disturb this settling-in process. Further, the GATT agreement's Trade-Related Aspects of Intellectual Property (TRIPS) had just adopted copyright law as

the dominant mode of legal protection for software throughout the world, and changing the rules of the game now would be a difficult and time-consuming process. See Jane C. Ginsburg, Four Reasons and a Paradox: The Manifest Superiority of Copyright Over Sui Generis Protection of Computer Software, 94 Colum. L. Rev. 2559 (1994); Menell, supra, at 2651-2654.

4. What is the appropriate level of protection for computer programs? Is it consistent with efforts to reward every inventive, creative, or time-consuming aspect of program development? Or should the goal be something less than that? Most economists would suggest that intellectual property rights ought to extend no further than necessary to encourage optimal investment in research and development. But how much protection is "just enough"?

5. Menell proposed that a sui generis statute for software should replace copyright and patent law. The Manifesto proposes that an additional form of legal protection should be available to software developers. Both papers evaluate software from an economic standpoint. What accounts for their different conclusions?

6. A larger issue pertains to the appropriate level of generality of a software protection statute. On the one hand, more specific statutes are easier to tailor to the particular needs of an industry, and they afford the legislature the opportunity to clarify the law. On the other hand, it is hard to anticipate all possible circumstances in drafting legislation, and judicial flexibility may benefit litigants in the long run and guard against technological advances that render the statutes irrelevant. One commentator has argued against sui generis legislation on the following grounds:

Now is the time to begin considering copyright law for the 21st century. Technology will change current concepts and policies faster than in the past. . . . [N]ew information processing technology like databases, personal computer workstations and optical disks will radically change the form of information and scholarship. We will soon see new computerized tools for creating music, industrial designs, entertainment and a myriad of other activities much more quickly. The distinctions copyright pundits now cherish will blur.

We are at an intellectual property crossroads. One road is to man the bulwarks and preserve the traditional scope of copyright until new technology makes the contradictions in that approach all too apparent. Down that road lies repeated efforts to fine-tune the law with such sui generis experiments as the Semiconductor Chip Protection Act, until congressional delay and impatience pushes even the lawyers who benefit most from increased legislative complexity to yearn for a more comprehensive approach.

The other road is to allow copyright to evolve, as it has when faced with new technology in the past. Recent software cases and practice are showing us where that road leads: to a misappropriation law where we are more concerned with the ethics and behavior of infringers than the technical details of infringement. The standards for proper and improper behavior (if trends continue) will reflect and reinforce a current consensus among engineers and users, and the new system will be largely self-enforcing. The fair use idea will expand to allow more flexibility in using new technology for private purposes. One can hope a common law license will develop allowing flexible, self-executing price and scope of use arrangements.

Perhaps best of all, the method for analyzing infringement will be similar to the determination of misuse of information in a broad number of areas of law under the privacy rubric. This will reinforce the development of a lay understanding and appreciation of the boundaries of tortious activity in the information economy.

We are at a seminal moment in history, equivalent to the beginnings of the industrial age. If our law can share the same vision as our engineering, we can promote the immense potential wealth in the information age.

Duncan M. Davidson, Common Law, Uncommon Software, 47 U. Pitt. L. Rev. 1037, 1116-1117 (1986).

Davidson advocated a common law evolution of copyright law that would allow it to serve as a misappropriation law applicable equally well to computer programs, appropriations of contents of databases, semiconductor chip designs, DNA sequences, and readily copied chemical compounds. The competitive norm embodied in Davidson's view of copyright was that persons could reverse engineer and copy externally visible aspects of these works but would be penalized for going inside the "black box" to reverse engineer internal details that he thought should be protected against unauthorized access, use, or disclosure. In what ways has copyright evolved as Davidson recommended, and in what ways has it diverged from his expectations? How would the computer software industry have been affected if Davidson's approach had been adopted? Would the result have been better or worse, or just different?

7. Consider this further proposal by Davidson:

> The common law development of copyright into a misappropriation law can create in effect a "common law license" that would work like self-executing licenses; it would delineate certain acceptable and unacceptable manners of reverse engineering, publishing or otherwise using products that contain information. Misappropriation law would be based on an underlying limited use doctrine that would apply if (1) the source of information was the plaintiff's products, and (2) the information was used beyond the reasonable expectations of the relationship. The "license" would result from the expectations of the parties; these expectations could vary depending upon the rights granted by the software company [or other information provider].

47 U. Pitt. L. Rev. at 1112. We will shortly be considering the enforceability of shrinkwrap, click-through, and other mass-market licenses. Although the legal status of these licenses has evolved by a common law process, it has not been in the context of copyright law. When reading in Chapter 6 about the proposed Uniform Computer Information Transactions Act, consider whether Davidson may have been more prescient than you might at first have thought.

8. Lawrence Lessig has recently weighed in on the debate over the appropriate legal protection for expressive works in general and computer software in particular. See Lawrence Lessig, The Future of Ideas: The Fate of the Commons in a Connected World (2001). In order to reequilibrate copyright's public and private balance in the digital era, Lessig proposes the reinstitution of the copyright registration requirement and affording a five-year term of protection that is renewable for up to 15 terms for published works. Failure to renew results in a work falling into the public domain. *Id.* at 250-52. Due to the distinctive nature of software, Lessig would allow software copyrights to be renewed only once, thereby limiting protection to no more than a decade. *Id.* at 252-53. Furthermore, Lessig would condition software protection upon the authors' deposit in escrow of a source code version of the software program so that its inherent knowledge could be disclosed upon expiration of the copyright. Such a requirement would address the inherent secrecy afforded software by compilation in object code form. Lessig also

recommends that a moratorium be imposed on the enforceability of software and business method patents until their efficacy can be more systematically assessed. *Id.* at 259-61. At a minimum, he supports proposals such as those offered by Jeff Bezos and Tim O'Reilly to reduce the term of such patents to five or fewer years. Cf. Tim O'Reilly, Amazon's Patent Reform Proposal, http://www.oreilly.com /ask_tim/patent_reform_0300.html.

9. Legal academics and technologists are not the only people to have suggested that advances in information technologies may bring about the need for new intellectual property laws. See, e.g., Lester Thurow, Needed: A New System of Intellectual Property Rights, Harv. Bus. Rev. 95, 95 (Sept.-Oct. 1995) (expressing concern that inadequate legal protection will impede public disclosure of innovations in knowledge-intensive industries):

> Fundamental shifts in technology and in the economic landscape are rapidly making the current system of intellectual property rights unworkable and ineffective. Designed more than 100 years ago to meet the simpler needs of an industrial era, it is an undifferentiated, one-size-fits-all system. Although treating all advances in knowledge in the same way may have worked when most patents were granted for new mechanical devices, today's brainpower industries pose challenges that are far more complex.

In this essay, Thurow, like his MIT colleague, Nicholas Negroponte, expresses doubts about the viability of existing copyright law concepts as applied to digital information distributed via global networks. When reading Chapter 10's coverage on intellectual property issues in cyberspace, consider whether Thurow and Negroponte might be right.

6

Software Licensing

Typically, computer software vendors claim that their wares are licensed rather than sold. This arguably distinguishes software from most similar business or consumer goods, which are generally sold to customers, and even from much intellectual property (such as books, sound recordings, and patented devices), particular copies of which are sold to end users. Software licenses take a variety of forms—from complex agreements governing use and support obligations negotiated and signed by both parties to "shrinkwrap" licenses included with most mass-market software.

Licensing has been a fundamental paradigm of the distribution of computer software from the earliest days of the industry. Software developers have developed some innovative licensing schemes, often in response to customer demands: site licenses, network licenses, per-seat licenses, so-many-users-at-a-time licenses, and the like. Historically, most of these licenses were in effect leases of computer hardware, or "true" licenses of intellectual property rights (i.e., the right to make 500 copies of a program for use in a business). Negotiated licenses between software developers and their customers have generally presented many interesting *business* issues, but few novel legal challenges, except as regards warranty and performance issues.

As mass markets for software emerged, one might have expected licenses to wither away in favor of outright sales. Instead, software developers widely used shrinkwrap licenses in commercially distributing mass-market software products. The validity of these licenses, as a matter of both contract law and public policy (e.g., insofar as they purport to override rights otherwise made available by intellectual property law) is the subject of ongoing controversy. Similar licenses are becoming common in the distribution of digital information more generally, and here too the validity and scope of such licenses have been hotly contested. Legislation to validate mass-market licenses for computer information transactions is currently under consideration. Thus the licensing approach may become more important not just for software but for digital information more generally. Using licenses in place of sales may enable more flexibility and price discrimination but may also conflict with intellectual property law or policy.

This chapter addresses two issues critical to software licensing: (1) ownership rights in licensed software, and (2) the power of licenses to alter the legal rules that would otherwise apply to software. It is perhaps best to begin by noting that the entire concept of licensing software is a controversial one. Licensing is a paradigm that has traditionally been applied to intellectual property. By contrast, no one speaks of licensing tangible goods (such as books), even if those goods contain intellectual property within them. Similarly, David Nimmer has suggested that there is properly no licensing of tangible software merely because the computer program that is transferred contains intellectual property within it. David Nimmer et al., The Metamorphosis of Contract into Expand, 87 Cal. L. Rev. 17 (1999). By contrast, proponents of software licensing contend that software is not itself a product—that, like pure intellectual property licenses, "the license is the product." See Robert Gomulkiewicz, The License Is the Product: Comments on the Promise of Article 2B for Software and Information Licensing, 13 Berkeley Tech. L.J. 891 (1998). We discuss this debate in more detail below.

Information licensing takes many forms indeed. One useful typology is to break transactions down into basic types: negotiated and non-negotiated (or standard form) contracts. The former are the norm when complex one-of-a-kind information is being transferred for a very specific purpose. The latter are becoming more and more common in conjunction with numerous off-the-shelf types of consumer information products—from online newspaper subscriptions entered into over the Internet to the purchase of prepackaged software in a retail store. Although we touch on an important example of negotiated agreements at the end of this chapter, for the most part we will be discussing mass-market information transactions. This means that, in the main, we will be considering standard form contracts.[1] Issues such as how these contracts are entered into and whether they are binding on the parties and the like are discussed throughout this chapter.

A. LICENSE VERSUS SALE

Virtually all software vendors would like to license rather than sell their software, not only for the economic reasons we discuss below but because licensing may allow them to avoid the restraints and limitations intellectual property law imposes on them. This Section discusses the circumstances under which a software transaction constitutes a "license." In particular, it explores the extent to which the vendor can create a license by fiat—that is, by declaring that the transaction is in fact a license.

---

1. It is worth noting that mass-market transactions in software aren't necessarily sales to individual *consumers*, though many transactions do involve consumers. Small and even large businesses also buy mass-market software, and are therefore subject to the same license provisions. The draft Uniform Computer Information Transactions Act (UCITA) distinguishes in certain ways between the rules that apply to mass-market transactions and those that apply to consumer transactions. See infra.

Microsoft Corp. v. Harmony Computers & Electronics, Inc.
United States District Court for the Eastern District of New York
846 F. Supp. 208 (E.D.N.Y. 1994)

DEARIE, District Judge.

This is an action for copyright infringement, trademark infringement, and related statutory and common law claims. Plaintiff Microsoft Corporation, a developer, manufacturer, and marketer of computer software programs, seeks declaratory and injunctive relief and treble damages against Harmony Computers & Electronics Inc. ("Harmony") and its president, Stanley Furst (together the "defendants"), for allegedly selling, without license or authorization, copyrighted Microsoft MS-DOS and Microsoft Windows software programs and accompanying materials ("Microsoft Products" or "Products").

Background . . .

Plaintiff argues that because defendants are not licensed by Microsoft, they are not legitimately in possession of, and are not entitled to sell, any Microsoft Products, whether counterfeit or not. To the extent that defendants bought their Microsoft Products from legitimate Microsoft licensees, plaintiff argues that defendants violated Microsoft's licensing restrictions by distributing the Products "stand-alone," that is, by themselves rather than bundled with one of the personal computer systems manufactured by Microsoft licensees. Furthermore, plaintiff alleges, and defendants acknowledge, that defendants persisted in their sales of Microsoft Products despite being notified of the alleged illegality of their activity by plaintiff's cease and desist letters of April 19, June 16, July 14, and September 14, 1993. Plaintiff has advised the Court, by the declarations of Robert Wanezek, Program Manager of Microsoft's Replication Group, and of Lee Gates, its Software Design Test Engineer, that twenty-one pieces of the Products seized from defendants' premises were counterfeit.

Defendants do not contest that they sold Microsoft Products, or that they sold such Products stand-alone as well as loaded onto the hard disks of computers. Defendants argue, however, that because the Products they sold were purchased from Microsoft licensees, they are immune from liability for copyright infringement under the first sale doctrine. In response, plaintiff argues that the first sale doctrine does not apply to the present case because Microsoft never sells but rather only licenses its Products. Defendants also deny that any of the Microsoft Products that they sold were counterfeit. Alternatively, defendants argue, even if any of the Products were counterfeit, they bought them from Microsoft licensees under the good faith belief that the Products were genuine. . . .

Discussion . . .

B. Unauthorized Distribution

Defendants are not Microsoft licensees and therefore are not authorized to sell Microsoft Products. Barbara Schmidt, an accounting supervisor for Microsoft's domestic Original Equipment Manufacturer ("OEM") licensing, declares that defendant Harmony was never at any time a Microsoft licensee. Defendants do not contest this fact. Furthermore, although defendant Stanley Furst was a signatory to a license agreement dated December 2, 1993, between Microsoft and another one of Furst's companies, Everything Computers, Inc., Mr. Furst was not himself a Microsoft licensee. The license held by Everything Computers does not authorize defendants Harmony or Furst to distribute Microsoft Products.

Defendants sold Microsoft Products, as evidenced by the fact that private investigators hired by Microsoft successfully bought various Microsoft Products from defendants, that Harmony advertised the sale of MS-Dos 6.0, and that persons who had bought Microsoft Products from Harmony had called Microsoft's Piracy Hotline to question the legitimacy of their purchases. Defendants do not contest that they sold Microsoft Products, nor do they dispute that such activity would constitute copyright infringement absent the protection of the first sale doctrine. Because defendants are not authorized by Microsoft to distribute Microsoft Products, their distribution of those Products constitutes a prima facie case, that is, a likelihood of success on the merits of plaintiff's copyright infringement claim. Irreparable harm to plaintiff is therefore presumed.

Defendants argue that they in good faith believed that they were buying Products from authorized Microsoft licensees, and that their sales of the Products were therefore lawful. It is unlikely, in this case, that defendants were innocent infringers, as they were notified by Microsoft of the unlawfulness of their activities by letters dated April 19, June 16, July 14, and September 14, of 1993. Moreover, good faith is no defense against liability for copyright infringement. ISC-Bunker Ramo Corp. v. Altech, Inc., 765 F. Supp. 1310, 1331 (N.D.Ill. 1990) ("there is no such thing as a bona fide purchase for value in copyright law"). Accordingly, defendants' good faith defense must fail.

Finally, it is undisputed that any sale of counterfeit Microsoft Products by defendants would violate the federal copyright laws. Plaintiff has submitted the declarations of Robert L. Wanezek, Program Manager of Microsoft's Replication Group, and of Lee R. Gates, a Software Design Test Engineer for Microsoft, and samples of seized "counterfeit" Microsoft Products from defendants' premises, to support their claim that defendants sold counterfeit Products. Although defendants deny that any of the Products they sold were counterfeit, they provide no evidence to contradict plaintiff's sworn assertions. In the absence of an evidentiary hearing, and given that plaintiff is likely to succeed on the merits of its copyright infringement claim on the grounds that defendants were not licensees and therefore not authorized to distribute any Microsoft products, counterfeit or not, the Court declines at this juncture to make a finding as to the genuineness of the Microsoft Products sold by defendants.

III. First Sale Doctrine Does Not Apply

Defendants argue that even though they sold Microsoft Products without a license, they are immune under the first sale doctrine from liability for copyright infringement. Defendants fail to prove that the first sale doctrine applies because they do not trace their purchase of Microsoft Products to a "first sale" by Microsoft or any party authorized by Microsoft to sell the Products.

The first sale doctrine is codified at section 109(a) of title 17 of the United States Code, which provides that:

> (a) Notwithstanding the provisions of section 106(3), the owner of a particular copy . . . lawfully made under this title, or any person authorized by such owner, is entitled, without the authority of the copyright owner, to sell or otherwise dispose of the possession of that copy . . .

17 U.S.C. §109(a) (1977). This statute "restates and confirms the principle that, where the copyright owner has transferred ownership of a particular copy . . . of a work, the person to whom the copy . . . is transferred is entitled to dispose of it by sale . . . or any other means." Historical Note to 17 U.S.C. §109. In civil actions for copyright infringement, the defendant has the burden of proving that the particular pieces of the copyrighted work that he sold were lawfully made or acquired. See Historical Note to 17 U.S.C. §109, cited in American Int'l Pictures, Inc. v. Foreman, 576 F.2d 661, 663 n.1 (5th Cir. 1978).

Defendants argue that a "first sale" occurred when they bought their Microsoft Products from entities whom they believed to be authorized Microsoft licensees. Although a sale of a copyrighted work by a party authorized by the copyright holder may constitute a "first sale" for purposes of the first sale doctrine, see Burke & Van Heusen Inc. v. Arrow Drug, Inc., 233 F. Supp. 881, 884 (E.D.Pa. 1964), defendants have the burden of tracing the chain of title to show that their authority to sell Microsoft Products flows from the copyright holder. American Int'l Pictures, Inc., 576 F.2d at 664-65; Microsoft Corp. v. ATS Computers, Inc. et al., CV 93-1273, at 14 (S.D.Cal. 1993).

Defendants' only evidence of a chain of title for any of their Products is an invoice of their purchase of several pieces of Microsoft Products from an entity called Innovative Datronics Corp. The fact that defendants bought their Microsoft Products from another party does not by itself establish a first sale. "Even an unwitting purchaser who buys a copy in the secondary market can be held liable for infringement if the copy was not the subject of a first sale by the copyright holder. . . . [U]nless title to the copy passes through a first sale by the copyright holder, subsequent sales do not confer good title." *American Int'l Pictures, Inc.*, 576 F.2d at 664. See also Platt & Munk Co. v. Republic Graphics, Inc., 315 F.2d 847 (2d Cir. 1963) ("it has been held that sale of a book purchased from a merchant who bought it from an agent of the copyright proprietor, where the agent had been entrusted with possession of the book but not with actual authority to sell it, is infringement"). No evidence has been presented to show that Innovative Datronics or any party in the chain of title was a licensee of Microsoft and authorized to sell the product.

Defendants' failure to trace their Microsoft Products to a "first sale" by the copyright holder is aggravated by the fact that plaintiff has "established a course of conduct . . . consistent with an intention to retain all the rights associated with the grant of copyright" of the Microsoft Products. American Int'l Pictures, Inc., 576 F.2d at 665. Plaintiff's counsel declares that Microsoft only licenses and does not sell its Products. Entering a license agreement is not a "sale" for purposes of the first sale doctrine. *ISC-Bunker Ramo Corp.*, 756 F. Supp. at 1331. Moreover, the only chain of distribution that Microsoft authorizes is one in which all possessors of Microsoft Products have only a license to use, rather than actual ownership of the Products.

Defendants' failure to meet their burden of proving a chain of title distinguishes this case from *Burke* and precludes the applicability of the first sale doctrine to this case.

IV. Exceeding Scope of License Agreements

Plaintiff is likely to succeed on its claim that defendants are liable for copyright infringement for exceeding the scope of Microsoft's license agreements.

Plaintiff has traced a unit of MS-DOS 6.0 that Harmony had sold to plaintiff's undercover investigators, back to Amax Engineering, a Microsoft licensee that was authorized to distribute MS-DOS 6.0 exclusively with the sale of its personal computer systems. Plaintiff has also traced four of the MS-DOS 6.2 units seized from defendants' premises, back to Arche Technologies, a Microsoft licensee that was authorized to distribute MS-DOS and Windows only with its computer systems. The remainder of the Microsoft software seized from defendants' premises were not traceable to a specific licensee, but plaintiff's counsel affirms that none of the Products was authorized to be sold stand-alone.

To the extent that defendants bought their Microsoft Products from authorized Microsoft licensees, they were subject to the same licensing restrictions under which those licensees operated. See Major League Baseball Promotion v. Colour-Tex, 729 F. Supp. 1035, 1041, 1042 (D.N.J. 1990). Plaintiff's counsel have represented to the Court that every Microsoft license agreement contains the same licensing language, which provides in relevant part, that licensees:

> . . . shall distribute Product(s) only with [licensee's] Customer System(s) . . . for the particular Product(s) and only inside the Customer System package. [The licensee] shall provide a copy of the . . . Product with, and only with, each Customer System on which the corresponding Preinstalled Product Software is distributed.

(Microsoft License Agreement, P 5(a)(i)). This restriction requires that Microsoft Products only be sold together with a "Customer System," that is, a "single user computer system." (Microsoft License Agreement, P 1(c)), rather than on a stand-alone basis. Indeed, plaintiff's in-house counsel declares that "it is generally known in the computer software industry that except for upgrade products, Microsoft does not authorize anyone to distribute standalone MS-DOS product." Plaintiff explains that Products that are sold stand-alone or otherwise outside the scope of Microsoft's license agreements, though identical in exterior appearance to authorized Microsoft Products, do not come with the product support system, warranties, and assured compatibility with their personal computer systems that Microsoft provides for its legitimately distributed Products. Therefore, plaintiff argues, the sale of stand-alone Products irreparably harms Microsoft's goodwill and reputation as a reliable software producer. *Id.* . . .

≡ *Softman Products Company v. Adobe Systems Inc.*
United States District Court for the Central District of California
171 F. Supp. 2d 1075 (C.D. Cal. 2001)

PREGERSON, District Judge.

This matter comes before the Court on the counter-claimant Adobe's application for a preliminary injunction. After reviewing and considering the materials submitted by the parties, and hearing oral argument, the Court adopts the following order.

I. Background

The counter-claimant Adobe Systems Inc. ("Adobe") is a leading software development and publishing company. The counter-defendant SoftMan Products Company ("SoftMan") is a Los Angeles-based company that distributes computer software products primarily through its website, www.buycheapsoftware.com. Adobe alleges that since at least November 1997, SoftMan has distributed unauthorized Adobe software, including Adobe Educational software and unbundled Adobe "Collections." By distributing the individual pieces of Adobe Collections, Adobe contends that SoftMan is infringing Adobe's copyright in these products and violating the terms of Adobe's licenses. While SoftMan agrees that it is breaking apart various Adobe Collections and distributing the individual pieces of them as single products, SoftMan claims that it is entitled to distribute Adobe software in this manner. There is no direct contractual relationship between Adobe and SoftMan.

Adobe distributes its products through "licensing" agreements with distributors. Each piece of Adobe software is also accompanied by an End User License Agreement ("EULA"), which sets forth the terms of the license between Adobe and the end user for that specific Adobe product. The EULA is electronically recorded on the computer disk and customers are asked to agree to its terms when they attempt to install the software. . . .

III. Discussion . . .

A. *Copyright Infringement Claim*

Copyright infringement exists when any of the rights granted under 17 U.S.C. §106 are violated. *Buck v. Jewell-La Salle Realty*, 283 U.S. 191, 51 S. Ct. 410, 75 L. Ed. 971 (1931). Title 17 U.S.C. §106(3) grants a copyright holder the exclusive right to distribute, and to authorize distribution of, its copyrighted work. Adobe chooses to distribute copies of its products through licensing agreements with various distributors and dealers.[5] It is not disputed that SoftMan has no licensing agreement with Adobe.

---

5. These agreements are signed licenses between Adobe and the named distributor. Adobe's general distribution agreement provides in part: "Distributor acknowledges that the Software Products are to be licensed to End Users in accordance with the terms and conditions of the current End User License Agreement. . . . Distributor shall distribute the Software Products solely in the form and packaging in which they were obtained from Adobe." Adobe's Reseller Agreement states that: "Reseller acknowledges that the structure and organization of the Software is proprietary to Adobe and that Adobe retains exclusive ownership of the Software and the Trademarks."

Most computer program and database product copies are distributed with standard form terms in a document characterized as a "license". The standard terms purport, among other things: to specify permitted uses of a copy, e.g., consumer or personal versus commercial; to prohibit certain uses of a computer program copy, e.g., reverse engineering of the computer program code; to forbid any use that is not expressly authorized, e.g., commercial processing of third party data or business records; and to bar transfer of a copy and the "license" to another person.

In addition, each piece of Adobe software is accompanied by the EULA.[6] Once the products are distributed to the end-user, the EULA prohibits the individual distribution of software that was originally distributed as part of a Collection. Specifically, the Adobe EULA provides that the end user may "transfer all [his] rights to the Use of the Software to another person or legal entity provided that (a) [he] also transfer this Agreement, the Software and all other software or hardware bundled or pre-installed with the Software."

In this case, Adobe alleges that by distributing unbundled Collections, SoftMan has exceeded the scope of the EULA and has infringed Adobe's copyrights, specifically Adobe's §106 right to distribute and control distribution. SoftMan contends that the first sale doctrine allows for the resale of Adobe's Collection software.

(1) First Sale Doctrine

The "first sale" doctrine was first analyzed by the United States Supreme Court in Bobbs-Merrill Co. v. Straus, 210 U.S. 339, 28 S. Ct. 722, 52 L. Ed. 1086 (1908). The Court held that the exclusive right to "vend" under the copyright statute applied only to the first sale of the copyrighted work. The doctrine has been codified at 17 U.S.C. §109(a). It states in relevant part: "the owner of a particular copy . . . lawfully made under this title . . . is entitled, without the authority of the copyright owner, to sell or otherwise dispose of the possession of that copy." 17 U.S.C. §109(a). One significant effect of §109(a) is to limit the exclusive right to distribute copies to their first voluntary disposition, and thus negate copyright owner control over further or "downstream" transfer to a third party. Quality King Distrib. v. L'anza Research Int'l, Inc., 523 U.S. 135, 142-44, 118 S. Ct. 1125, 140 L. Ed.2d 254 (1998). (*See* Rice Decl. ¶11.) The first sale doctrine vests the copy owner with statutory privileges under the Act which operate as limits on the exclusive rights of the copyright owners.

Adobe argues that the first sale doctrine does not apply because Adobe does not sell or authorize any sale of its software. Adobe characterizes each transaction throughout the entire stream of commerce as a license. Adobe asserts that its license defines the relationship between Adobe and any third-party such that a breach of the license constitutes copyright infringement. This assertion is not accurate because copyright law in fact provides certain rights to owners of a particular copy. This grant of rights is independent from any purported grant of rights from Adobe. The Adobe license compels third-parties to relinquish rights that the third-parties enjoy under copyright law.

In short, the terms of the Adobe EULA at issue prohibit licensees from transferring or assigning any individual Adobe product that was originally distributed as

---

6. The EULA states in part: "The receiving party accepts the terms and conditions of this Agreement (EULA) and any other terms and conditions upon which [the end user] legally purchased a license to the Software." Adobe's EULA permits an end user, subject to certain restrictions, to transfer the software, media, and documentation to another end user. The restrictions relating to an end user's ability to transfer include that the EULA must also be transferred and that "[t]he Software and all other software or hardware bundled or pre-installed with the Software, including all copies, Updates, and prior verison, and all copies of font software converted into other formats."

part of a Collection unless it is transferred with all the software in the original Collection. This license provision conflicts with the first sale doctrine in copyright law, which gives the owner of a particular copy of a copyrighted work the right to dispose of that copy without the permission of the copyright owner.

(2) Sale v. License

(a) Historical Background

Historically, the purpose of "licensing" computer program copy use was to employ contract terms to augment trade secret protection in order to protect against unauthorized copying at a time when, first, the existence of a copyright in computer programs was doubtful, and, later, when the extent to which copyright provided protection was uncertain. Computer program copy use "licensing" continued after federal courts interpreted the Copyright Act to provide substantial protection for computer programs as literary works. In Step-Saver Data Systems, Inc. v. Wyse Technology, the Third Circuit examined the historical development of the use of licensing in the software industry and concluded that subsequent changes to the Copyright Act had rendered the need to characterize the transaction as a license "largely anachronistic." 939 F.2d 91, 96 n. 7 (3d Cir. 1991).

(b) Adobe Sells Its Software

A number of courts have held that the sale of software is the sale of a good within the meaning of Uniform Commercial Code. Advent Sys. Ltd. v. Unisys Corp., 925 F.2d 670, 676 (3d Cir. 1991); *Step-Saver*, 939 F.2d at 99-100; Downriver Internists v. Harris Corp., 929 F.2d 1147, 1150 (6th Cir. 1991). It is well-settled that in determining whether a transaction is a sale, a lease, or a license, courts look to the economic realities of the exchange. Microsoft Corp. v. DAK Indus., 66 F.3d 1091 (9th Cir. 1995); United States v. Wise, 550 F.2d 1180 (9th Cir. 1977). In *DAK*, Microsoft and DAK entered into a license agreement granting DAK certain nonexclusive license rights to Microsoft's computer software. The agreement provided that DAK would pay a royalty rate per copy of computer software that it distributed. Subsequently, DAK filed a petition for bankruptcy, and failed to pay the final two out of a total of five installments. Microsoft filed a motion for the payment of an administrative expense, claiming that it should be compensated for DAK's post-bankruptcy petition use of the license agreement. On appeal, the Ninth Circuit held that the economic realities of the agreement indicated that it was a sale, not a license to use. Thus, Microsoft simply held an unsecured claim and not an administrative expense. The court found that the agreement was best characterized as a lump sum sale of software units to DAK, rather than a grant of permission to use an intellectual property. The court in *DAK* noted:

> Because we look to the economic realities of the agreement, the fact that the agreement labels itself a "license" and calls the payments "royalties," both terms that arguably imply periodic payment for the use rather than sale of technology, does not control our analysis.

DAK, 66 F.3d at 1095, n. 2. Other courts have reached the same conclusion: software is sold and not licensed. See, e.g., RRX Indus., Inc. v. Lab-Con, Inc., 772 F.2d 543, 546 (9th Cir. 1985); Applied Info. Mgmt., Inc. v. Icart, 976 F. Supp. 149, 155 (E.D.N.Y. 1997) (finding that whether a transaction denominated a "license" was in fact a sale conveying ownership was a disputed question of fact); Novell, Inc. v. CPU Distrib., Inc., 2000 U.S. Dist. Lexis 9975 (S.D.Tex. 2000). In *Novell*, a software manufacturer was pursuing a discount retailer for copyright infringement. Like Adobe, CPU argued that it purchased the software from an authorized source and was entitled to resell it under the first sale doctrine. Novell claimed that it did not sell software but merely licensed it to distribution partners. The court held that these transactions constituted sales and not a license, and therefore that the first sale doctrine applied. 2000 U.S. Dist. Lexis 9975 at *18.

Adobe frames the issue as a dispute about the ownership of intellectual property. In fact, it is a dispute about the ownership of individual pieces of Adobe software. Section 202 of the Copyright Act recognizes a distinction between tangible property rights in copies of the work and intangible property rights in the creation itself. In this case, no claim is made that transfer of the copy involves transfer of the ownership of the intellectual property within. What is at stake here is the right of the purchaser to dispose of that purchaser's particular copy of the software.

The Court finds that the circumstances surrounding the transaction strongly suggests that the transaction is in fact a sale rather than a license. For example, the purchaser commonly obtains a single copy of the software, with documentation, for a single price, which the purchaser pays at the time of the transaction, and which constitutes the entire payment for the "license." The license runs for an indefinite term without provisions for renewal. In light of these indicia, many courts and commentators conclude that a "shrinkwrap license" transaction is a sale of goods rather than a license.

The reality of the business environment also suggests that Adobe sells its software to distributors. Adobe transfers large amounts of merchandise to distributors. The distributors pay full value for the merchandise and accept the risk that the software may be damaged or lost. The distributors also accept the risk that they will be unable to resell the product. The distributors then resell the product to other distributors in the secondary market. The secondary market and the ultimate consumer also pay full value for the product, and accept the risk that the product may be lost or damaged. This evidence suggests a transfer of title in the good. The transfer of a product for consideration with a transfer of title and risk of loss generally constitutes a sale. VWP of Am., Inc. v. United States, 175 F.3d 1327, 1338-39 (Fed.Cir. 1999). Professor Raymond Nimmer writes:

> Ownership of a copy should be determined based on the actual character, rather than the label, of the transaction by which the user obtained possession. Merely labeling a transaction as a lease or license does not control. If a transaction involves a single payment giving the buyer an unlimited period in which it has a right to possession, the transaction is a sale. In this situation, the buyer owns the copy regardless of the label the parties use for the contract. Course of dealing and trade usage may be relevant, since they establish the expectations and intent of the parties. The pertinent issue is whether, as in a lease, the user may be required to return the copy to the vendor after the expiration of a particular period. If not, the transaction conveyed not only possession, but also transferred ownership of the copy.

Raymond Nimmer, *The Law of Computer Technology* §1.18[1] p. 1-103 (1992). The Court agrees that a single payment for a perpetual transfer of possession is, in reality, a sale of personal property and therefore transfers ownership of that property, the copy of the software.

Other commentators have urged courts to look at the substance rather than the form of licensing agreements. See, e.g., David A. Rice, Licensing the Use of Computer Program Copies and the Copyright Act First Sale Doctrine, 30 Jurimetrics J. 157 (1990). In particular, the following factors require a finding that distributing software under licenses transfers individual copy ownership: temporally unlimited possession, absence of time limits on copy possession, pricing and payment schemes that are unitary not serial, licenses under which subsequent transfer is neither prohibited nor conditioned on obtaining the licensor's prior approval (only subject to a prohibition against rental and a requirement that any transfer be of the entity), and licenses under which the use restriction[']s principal purpose is to protect intangible copyrightable subject matter, and not to preserve property interests in individual program copies. *Id.* at 172.

Adobe relies primarily on two cases to support its proposition that software is licensed and not sold. In Microsoft Corp. v. Harmony Computers & Elecs., Inc., 846 F. Supp. 208, 212 (E.D.N.Y. 1994), the court assumed without analysis that the transaction was a license rather than a sale and held that distribution outside the scope of a license agreement constituted copyright infringement. The Court finds *Harmony's* facts to be distinguishable. In that case, the defendants were selling *counterfeit* Microsoft products. Here, Adobe does not allege that SoftMan sells counterfeit Adobe software.

Adobe also relies on Adobe Sys. Inc. v. One Stop Micro, Inc., 84 F. Supp.2d 1086, 1093 (N.D.Cal. 2000). The court held that One Stop's distribution of Educational versions of Adobe software to non-educational end users was outside the scope of Adobe's license and in violation of Adobe's exclusive right to distribute under §106(3). In *One Stop,* an unlicensed reseller admitted to adulterating the packaging for Adobe Educational software and transferring it as retail Adobe products for prices below the street price of the retail product. *Id.* The court further held that One Stop could not claim to have title for first sale purposes while the end user only obtained a license. The Court finds the facts of *One Stop* to be distinguishable from the instant case. In *One Stop,* the issue was peeling off and destroying the "Education version" stickers on software, as well as destroying bar code and serial numbers on the software, and then reselling it as commercial software. *Id.* at 1088. To the extent that the court in *One Stop* found that the transaction at issue was in fact a license, and not a sale, this Court simply declines to adopt that analysis. In *One Stop,* the court placed great weight on the declarations of Adobe's experts that licensing is the preferred method of distributing software. The Court understands fully why licensing has many advantages for software publishers. However, this preference does not alter the Court's analysis that the substance of the transaction at issue here is a sale and not a license.

(c) EULA Terms

Adobe argues that the EULA requires construction of the transaction as a license rather than a sale. The Court finds that SoftMan is not bound by the EULA because there was no assent to its terms.

i) Assent

Adobe contends that the EULA limits the consumer's ability to transfer the software after buying it. According to SoftMan, a hard copy of the EULA agreement is not enclosed with the individual Adobe software disk. Instead, consumers are asked to agree to its terms as part of the installation process.

Courts have required that assent to the formation of a contract be manifested in some way, by words or other conduct, if the contract is to be effective. E. Allan Farnsworth, Farnsworth on Contracts §3.1 (2d ed. 2000). As the court noted in *Specht v. Netscape Communications Corp.*, 150 F. Supp.2d 585 (S.D.N.Y. 2001): "The case law on software licensing has not eroded the importance of assent in contract formation. Mutual assent is the bedrock of any agreement to which the law will give force. Defendants' position, if accepted, would so expand the definition of assent as to render it meaningless." *Id*. at 596.

In the instant case, the Court finds that there is only assent on the part of the consumer, if at all, when the consumer loads the Adobe program and begins the installation process. It is undisputed that SoftMan has never attempted to load the software that it sells. Consequently, the Court finds that SoftMan is not subject to the Adobe EULA.

Adobe fails to offer a compelling rationale for how SoftMan becomes subject to Adobe's licenses if SoftMan never loads the software onto computers. Adobe claims that the EULA is enforceable against SoftMan because the boxes containing Adobe software (including Collections) clearly indicate that use is subject to the consumer's agreement to the terms contained in EULA inside. See, e.g., *ProCD*, 86 F.3d at 1451. Like the CD boxes in *ProCD*, Adobe's EULAs state that the product can be returned if the terms are not agreed to by the end user. The Adobe Collections boxes state: "NOTICE TO USERS: This product is offered subject to the license agreement included with the media." (Navarro Decl. at p. 2.) However, the existence of this notice on the box cannot bind SoftMan. Reading a notice on a box is not equivalent to the degree of assent that occurs when the software is loaded onto the computer and the consumer is asked to agree to the terms of the license.

Adobe further asserts that whether SoftMan is characterized as a distributor or reseller, SoftMan would be bound by the terms of these license agreements, which state that Adobe retains ownership of its software products, as well as the media upon which these software products are distributed. It is undisputed that SoftMan is not a signatory to any licensing agreements. Yet Adobe claims that although SoftMan has never signed an agreement with Adobe, the terms of Adobe's distribution agreements all apply to SoftMan.

In *One Stop*, the court stated that although One Stop was not a signatory to an Adobe licensing agreement, it was nevertheless subject to the restrictions of those agreements. 84 F. Supp.2d at 1092. The court found that by obtaining Adobe software from a party to an Adobe licensing agreement, One Stop was bound by any restrictions imposed by that agreement. *Id*. at 1093. In *Harmony*, the court found that "to the extent that defendants bought their Microsoft Products from authorized Microsoft licensees, they were subject to the same licensing restrictions under which those licensees operated." *Harmony*, 846 F. Supp. at 213. The Court declines to adopt the analysis of these cases.

The Court finds that Adobe's EULA cannot be valid without assent. Therefore, SoftMan is not bound by the EULA because it has never loaded the software, and therefore never assented to its terms of use.

ii) Shrinkwrap Licenses In General

Whether contracts such as Adobe's EULA, often referred to as "shrinkwrap" licenses, are valid is a much-disputed question. A number of courts that have addressed the validity of the shrinkwrap license have found them to be invalid, characterizing them as contracts of adhesion, unconscionable, and/or unacceptable pursuant to the Uniform Commercial Code. *Step-Saver*, 939 F.2d 91; *Vault Corp. v. Quaid Software Ltd.*, 847 F.2d 255 (5th Cir. 1988). These courts have refused to recognize a bargain in shrinkwrap license that is not signed by the party against whom it is enforced. In *Step-Saver*, the Third Circuit found that the terms of a contract were formed when the parties shipped, received and paid for the product. Therefore, the software shrinkwrap agreement constituted additional terms to the contract, and under Uniform Commercial Code §2-207 (governing commercial counter-offers), these terms were invalid without express assent by the purchaser. In contrast, other courts have determined that the shrinkwrap license is valid and enforceable. *ProCD*, 86 F.3d at 1453; *Harmony*, 846 F. Supp. at 212.

The Court finds it unnecessary to reach the question of the general validity of shrinkwrap licenses at this stage because the Court has determined that SoftMan is not bound by the EULA because there was no assent to its terms. . . .

(3) Copyright Infringement Conclusion

In short, the transfer of copies of Adobe software making up the distribution chain from Adobe to SoftMan are sales of the particular copies, but not of Adobe's intellectual rights in the computer program itself, which is protected by Adobe's copyright. SoftMan is an "owner" of the copy and is entitled to the use and enjoyment of the software, with the rights that are consistent with copyright law. The Court rejects Adobe's argument that the EULA gives to purchasers only a license to use the software. The Court finds that SoftMan has not assented to the EULA and therefore cannot be bound by its terms. Therefore, the Court finds that Adobe has not demonstrated a likelihood of success on the merits of its copyright infringement claim. . . .

(c) Public Interest

Traditionally, courts have looked to public policy considerations in determining whether to grant preliminary injunctive relief. Chalk v. United States Dist. Court, Cent. Dist. of Cal., 840 F.2d 701, 711 (9th Cir., 1988) ("We recognize that the public interest is one of the traditional equitable criteria which a court should consider in granting injunctive relief."). In this case, the Court finds that important public policy considerations weigh on each side.

The Court finds that the provisions contained in Adobe's EULA purport to diminish the rights of customers to use the software in ways ordinarily enjoyed by customers under copyright law. Therefore, these restrictions appear to be inconsistent with the balance of rights set forth in intellectual property law.[19] Commentators have noted that the arguments for enforcing this balance are particularly persuasive in the context of shrinkwrap licenses because the balance of rights in intellectual property law is already tilted heavily in favor of the intellectual property owner. "The only countervailing forces favoring users are those rights specifically granted to users by federal law. In this context more than any other, therefore, it is justifiable to fear that removing or eviscerating those user rights may bring the whole edifice crumbling down."[20]

This is an area fraught with conflicting policy considerations. Software publishers are desirous of augmenting the protections offered under copyright law. In this case, through the use of licensing, Adobe seeks a vast and seemingly unlimited power to control prices and all channels of distribution. On the other hand, in the absence of copyright law violations, the market can often best regulate prices and all subsequent transactions that occur after the first sale. Sound policy rationales support the analysis of those courts that have found shrinkwrap licenses to be unenforceable. A system of "licensing" which grants software publishers this degree of unchecked power to control the market deserves to be the object of careful scrutiny.

For the reasons stated above, the Court finds that this factor weighs in favor of the counter-defendants. . . .

IV. Conclusion

As set forth above, the Court finds that Adobe has not demonstrated a likelihood of success on the merits of its trademark or copyright claims. . . . The Court denies Adobe's application for a preliminary injunction. . . .

COMMENTS AND QUESTIONS

1. Is it possible to reconcile *Softman* and *Harmony?* What did Microsoft do that Adobe did not to characterize its transaction as a license?

2. Both cases point to significant legal reasons why a software vendor might prefer to characterize its transaction as a license rather than a sale. First, licensees may be able to avoid rules in the Uniform Commercial Code governing product warranties. Second, licensors retain certain rights under copyright law that sellers

---

19. Scholars have suggested that Congress contemplated that parties might attempt to contract out of a first sale right. "Congress was explicit in the context of section 109(a) that it intended for vendors who 'contract around' the first sale doctrine to be limited to contract remedies. The approach of shrinkwrap licenses—to attempt to extend vendor rights by contract while retaining the panoply of copyright remedies—was explicitly disavowed by the Committee Note." Mark A. Lemley, *Intellectual Property and Shrinkwrap Licenses,* 68 S. Cal. L. Rev. 1239, 1283 (1995) (citing H.R. Rep. 94-1476 (1976) (providing that the parties may contract around the first sale doctrine in 17 U.S.C. 109(a), but limiting the copyright owner to contract rather than copyright remedies if they do so)).

20. Lemley, Intellectual Property, at 1283.

do not. (We discuss below whether software vendors may use license provisions to *alter* substantive copyright law.) Note that these legal consequences are in addition to the economic reasons for licensing discussed in the next section.

On the other hand, a product licensed to a user with a "no resale" restriction would be expected to sell at a lower price than one sold without such a restriction. The obvious example here is a car lease versus an outright purchase. Do the transaction costs of such an arrangement make sense for a single copy of software? If it is impossible to enforce a "no resale" clause against the average individual, perhaps its only effective use would be against large-volume resellers. Does this affect your view about whether "no resale" clauses should be legally permitted?

3. The *Harmony* court certainly seems to be influenced by the fact that the defendants in that case were apparently counterfeiting Microsoft programs. But is the opinion limited to that circumstance, or does it extend further? In particular, what if Harmony had purchased copies of Microsoft programs only from legitimate end users, who had bought them along with computers they no longer wanted. Do the original end users have a right to dispose of their copies as they see fit? Does it depend on the terms of the license written by Microsoft? Who are the parties to that license agreement? Even without contractual "privity," a copyright owner may sue a secondary purchaser or sublicensee for copyright infringement. But would contractual restrictions apply to such a party—i.e., would there be a breach of contract cause of action as well? *Cf.* Robert P. Merges, *The End of Friction? Property Rights and Contract in the 'Newtonian' World of On-line Commerce,* 12 Berkeley Tech. L.J. 115, 118-121 (1997).

In the context of mass-market transactions for software, virtually all courts have looked to the totality of the circumstances surrounding the transaction in concluding that it was in fact a sale rather than a license. An instructive example is DSC Communications Corp. v. Pulse Communications, Inc., 170 F.3d 1354 (Fed. Cir. 1999). In that case, the court came to two different conclusions regarding the status of different copies of the same computer program. One of those copies was governed by a complex bargained license agreement. The court concluded that this program was licensed rather than sold:

> Not only do the agreements characterize the RBOCs as non-owners of copies of the software, but the restrictions imposed on the RBOCs' rights with respect to the software are consistent with that characterization. In particular, the licensing agreements severely limit the rights of the RBOCs with respect to the POTS-DI software in ways that are inconsistent with the rights normally enjoyed by owners of copies of software. . . .
>
> The fact that the right of possession is perpetual, or that the possessor's rights were obtained through a single payment, is certainly relevant to whether the possessor is an owner, but those factors are not necessarily dispositive if the possessor's right to use the software is heavily encumbered by other restrictions that are inconsistent with the status of owner.

By contrast, different copies of the same software obtained by resale from a previous buyer were sold rather than licensed, because they were purchased "on the open market" and "without restriction on their use." *Id.*

In a typical mass-market software transaction, there is no bargaining over license terms. The purchaser (licensee?) commonly obtains a single copy of the software, along with documentation, in a box that is picked up at a retail software store or shipped to the home after being ordered online. The box contains a single price, which the purchaser pays up front and which constitutes the entire payment for the "license." The purchaser pays sales tax on the "license." The license does not run for a definite term and need not be renewed, but it is perpetual unless terminated by the vendor (something that almost never occurs).

In light of these indicia, and because most purchasers think they are *buying* a physical copy of a program, almost all courts and commentators to have considered the issue have concluded that a shrinkwrap license transaction involving software is a sale of goods rather than a license, and is therefore covered by Article 2 of the current UCC. See, e.g., Step-Saver Data Sys. v. Wyse Technology, 939 F.2d 91 (3d Cir. 1991); Advent Sys. v. Unisys Corp., 925 F.2d 670 (3d Cir. 1991); Arizona Retail Sys. v. Software Link, Inc., 831 F. Supp. 759 (D. Ariz. 1993); Hospital Computer Sys. v. Staten Island Hosp., 788 F. Supp. 1351 (D.N.J. 1992); In re Amica, Inc., 135 B.R. 534 (Bankr. N.D. Ill. 1992); Neilson Bus. Equip. Center v. Italo Monteleone, 524 A.2d 1172 (Del. 1987); Photo Copy, Inc. v. Software, Inc., 510 So. 2d 1337 (La. Ct. App. 1987); USM Corp. v. Arthur Little Sys., 546 N.E.2d 888 (Mass. Ct. App. 1989); Drier Co. v. Unitronix Corp., 3 U.C.C. Rep. Serv. 2d 1728 (App. Div. N.J. 1987); Schroeders, Inc. v. Hogan Sys., 522 N.Y.S.2d 404 (Sup. Ct. 1987); Communications Groups, Inc. v. Warner Communications, 527 N.Y.S.2d 341 (Civ. Ct. 1988). Cf. ProCD, Inc. v. Zeidenberg, 86 F.3d 1447 (7th Cir. 1996) (concluding that a mass market transaction involving software was a "sale of goods" to which UCC Article 2 applied but nonetheless enforcing a "license agreement" under Article 2). The *ProCD* case is discussed in more detail below.

4. In an insightful article, David Nimmer has challenged the entire concept of a license of tangible goods, as opposed to a license of intellectual property. In Nimmer's view, there are two basic types of transactions involving software: (1) leases or other transactions in which title to the physical goods does not pass, and they are returned after a fixed term of periodic payments; and (2) sales of goods that happen to embody intellectual property. He faults *Harmony* for failing to establish what transfer mechanism was actually in use:

> Which circumstance actually obtained in Microsoft v. Harmony, the exemplar of the "licensing" paradigm? Sadly, the opinion fails to clarify the matter, and that inability to distinguish between differing paradigms is only too typical. Nonetheless, lack of clarity does not create a new "licensing" paradigm. Instead, if there were a bona fide *lease* of the physical goods, then one legal regime pertained; if Microsoft actually *sold* or otherwise permanently disposed of those physical goods, retaining full copyright ownership in itself, then another legal regime governed. Current copyright law does not recognize any regime of "licensing" that stands intermediate between those two possibilities.

David Nimmer et al., The Metamorphosis of Contract into Expand, 87 Cal. L. Rev. 17, 38 (1999). See also David A. Rice, Digital Information As Property and Product: U.C.C. Article 2B, 22 U. Dayton L. Rev. 621 (1997). It is worth noting that the "licensing" approach has been tried before, with sound recordings and with books around the beginning of the last century, but courts always rejected the idea that a good was being licensed rather than sold merely because it embodied intellectual property.

Software industry lawyers dispute this characterization, of course. They have argued that licenses are indeed a valid, albeit new, method of distribution. The primary argument seems to be one of *fait accompli*: because virtually all software vendors provide shrinkwrap licenses or the equivalent along with their software, refusing to enforce them would upset settled commercial expectations. See Robert W. Gomulkiewicz, The License Is the Product: Comments on the Promise of Article 2B for Software and Information Licensing, 13 Berkeley Tech. L.J. 891 (1998); Robert W. Gomulkiewicz & Mary Williamson, A Brief Defense of End-User Licensing Agreements, 19 Rutgers Computer & Tech. L.J. 335 (1996). It is certainly true that most software vendors expect their license agreements to be enforceable, despite early case law to the contrary. See Michael Rustad & Lori E. Eisenschmidt, The Commercial Law of Internet Security, 10 High Tech. L.J. 213 (1995) (reporting results of a survey of software company lawyers in which two-thirds thought shrinkwrap licenses were enforceable). Should this fact be used by courts to enforce the licenses? For a contrary argument, see Mark A. Lemley, The Law and Economics of Internet Norms, 73 Chi.-Kent L. Rev. 1257, 1273-74 (1999) (arguing that the assumptions of vendors regarding such licenses are at odds with the assumptions of consumers and that as a result there is no industry "norm" to which courts can reasonably defer). For a detailed analysis of the role of custom and trade usage in the software industry, see David McGowan, Legal Implications of Open Source Software, 2001 U. Ill. L. Rev. 241.

Note on the Uniform Computer Information Transactions Act

The legal distinction between a license and sale, and more general questions regarding the applicability of the UCC to transfers of software and other information-intensive assets, were some of the forces behind a move to draft a new law governing software transactions, the Uniform Computer Information Transactions Act (UCITA). UCITA is a giant statute—336 pages in draft with reporter's comments—that aims to fundamentally rewrite the law of contracts for software and information transactions. One aim of the proposal is to unify the law of software licensing in a comprehensive statute similar to the Uniform Commercial Code. Indeed, UCITA was originally drafted as a new article of the UCC, Article 2B.

UCITA has proven extraordinarily controversial. In 1999 the American Law Institute, one of the partners in the original Article 2B project, withdrew, dooming the project to revise the UCC. Instead, the National Conference of Commissioners on Uniform State Laws decided to promulgate the renamed UCITA as a free-standing statute. Nonetheless, UCITA has not been successful in the states. Only two states (Virginia and Maryland) have adopted UCITA in modified form, and several other states have adopted so-called "bomb shelter" statutes that preclude a court from applying UCITA to their residents.

There are several reasons why so many groups have opposed UCITA, but the consensus reason seems to be a perception that UCITA rewrites the law of software contracting in ways that favors vendors over purchasers. One significant change concerns the sale-license debate just discussed. UCITA defines a "license" as "a contract that authorizes access to, or use, distribution, performance, modification, or reproduction of, information or informational rights, but expressly limits the access or uses authorized or expressly grants fewer than all rights in the information, whether or not the transferee has title to a licensed copy." UCITA §102(41) (2001 "Final" Version). Under this definition, any transaction involving software or data other than an outright assignment of intellectual property is a license subject to UCITA, even if it involves the sale of a physical medium. UCITA would thus eliminate the "totality of the circumstances" test applied in *Softman* in favor of a bright-line rule: Information products can only be licensed, not sold.

Most commentators to consider the issue have argued that UCITA would in fact significantly change the rules governing transactions in software and digital information. Consider the following criticism, suggesting that UCITA "would remake the law of software and intellectual property licensing in a radical way":

> [UCITA] expands the scope and power of contracts in three ways. First, [UCITA] reverses the well-settled rule of existing law that whether a transaction is a sale, a lease, or a license can only be determined by looking at the economic realities of an exchange. Under [UCITA], a transaction is automatically a license unless it constitutes an assignment of the intellectual property right itself. And if it is a license, [UCITA] applies. [UCITA] thus creates a new meaning of "licensing" intellectual property rights, one unknown to copyright or patent law and one that encompasses transactions that intellectual property has always dealt with as sales.
>
> Second, [UCITA] redefines what constitutes a contract, abandoning the focus on offer and acceptance, and therefore on the agreement at the time the parties conclude a deal, in favor of a rule that the intellectual property owner's standard form terms will be enforced, even if they are contained in a "shrinkwrap" or "clickwrap" license that the buyer cannot see until the transaction has already occurred. In so doing, [UCITA] adopts a view that is decidedly in the minority among current courts, and that is dramatically to the benefit of the drafters of standard forms, who now do not even need a signature (or its electronic equivalent) in order to enforce their terms. Because of this shift, contracts under [UCITA] are really more akin to property rights: the contracts can be viewed as equitable servitudes that "run with" the goods in much the way some property owners once tried to impose restrictions on chattel. This shift is extremely important. The existing relationship between intellectual property and contract law is based on a conception of what constitutes an enforceable contract. [UCITA] changes that conception; as a result, it cannot help but change the relationship as well.
>
> Finally, [UCITA] makes virtually all of its default rules subject to change by "agreement of the parties". . . . And since [UCITA] makes it so easy to write and enforce the terms of a contract, a software vendor with a good lawyer can quite easily enforce virtually whatever terms it likes simply by putting them "conspicuously" in a multi-page document the user cannot even see (much less agree to) until after buying, installing, and beginning to run the software. There are only a few limitations on a software vendor's power to create whatever terms it likes. . . .

Mark A. Lemley, Beyond Preemption: The Law and Policy of Intellectual Property Licensing, 87 Cal. L. Rev. 111 (1999) (footnotes omitted). See also Jessica Litman, The Tales That Article 2B Tells, 13 Berkeley Tech. L.J. 931 (1998) (criticizing UCITA as "disingenuous" with respect to its characterization of existing law); David McGowan, Free Contracting, Fair Competition, and Article 2B: Some Reflections on Federal Competition Policy, Information Transactions, and "Aggressive Neutrality," 13 Berkeley Tech. L.J. 1173 (1998) (disputing UCITA's characterization of itself as "neutral" in relation to existing law).

Recall David Nimmer's challenge to the concept of a "licensing" paradigm. If he is correct that there is no such paradigm, is there any need for UCITA? Certainly the main purpose of UCITA seems to be to set up uniform rules for licensing software and digital information.

UCITA does other things as well, of course. It updates the basic rules of contract law for the world of electronic commerce—for example, by setting up rules for digital signatures and authentication. But similar rules were developed in the Uniform Electronic Transactions Act, which applies not just to transactions in information products but to all transactions that occur online.[2] And some commentators have questioned whether the rules UCITA would apply to electronic transactions are in fact the right ones. See A. Michael Froomkin, Article 2B as Legal Software for Electronic Contracting—Operating System or Trojan Horse?, 13 Berkeley Tech. L.J. 1023 (1998).

B. WHAT IS AT STAKE IN THE LICENSE VERSUS SALE DEBATE

Having introduced the debate over whether software is transferred subject to a license agreement, we pause to ask a more profit-minded question: what does a seller of information want its customers to agree to, and why? In other words, why does it matter whether software is licensed or sold?

The particular answers depend on the nature of the industry, the distribution mode, and the costs of providing the information. This last factor in turn has two components, production cost and transaction cost.

1. Bundling

In some industries, sellers can make more money by selling bundles of information instead of individual, discrete components of it. The economics of this are well explained in an excellent recent book about the new information economy. Carl Shapiro & Hal R. Varian, Information Rules (Harvard Bus. School Press, 1998). The basic idea is that in many cases there is less variation in how consumers value bundles of information than in how they value individual components. This derives, paradoxically, from the fact that individual consumers value individual components differently.

Take as an example an online service that reports snow, weather, and crowd information for ski resorts across the United States. The service sells for $100 per year. One user, Anita, lives in Boston and usually skis in New England; for her, the regional reports for Vermont and New Hampshire are worth $75 per year, and the reports for the western United States are worth only $25. Another subscriber, Bill, lives in San Francisco and usually skis in the California Sierras. For him, the Western ski reports are the valuable ones: he would be willing to pay up to $75 for

2. We discuss UETA in more detail in Chapter 14.

them. Because he occasionally skis in the East, the reports for New England are worth $25 to him.

If we make the simplifying (i.e., fantastical) assumption that Anita and Bill are the only consumers in the market, we can see that at $100 per year, the seller will sell subscriptions to both Anita and Bill and thereby earn revenues of $200. If the seller sold each regional service for $75, revenues would be only $150. (Neither Anita nor Bill would pay $75 for out-of-area information.) And if the seller sold regional service at a price Anita and Bill would be willing to pay—$25—it would still make only $100. It might also be more expensive to break the data down into regional reports, which would further eat into the seller's profit.

From an economic point of view, the ski report service is simply taking advantage of the variance or dispersion in individual buyers' valuation of the information. The revenue is higher in this case for a bundled product because consumers who value one component highly are likely to value another much less. If individuals who value one component very highly are more likely to value others highly, bundling would not work any better than selling individual components. One way to think about bundling is that different consumers may well have the same "average" valuation of each piece of information in the bundle but very different valuations of individual components. If high valuers of one component are likely to be low valuers of others, it behooves the seller to approximate this "average value" for a large number of consumers in pricing the bundle. See Yannis Bakos et al., Shared Information Goods, 42 J. Law & Econ. 199 (1999).

Bundling makes sense in the ski report example and, indeed, in many other examples. We can see this from the fact that bundling information is extremely common—everything from LEXIS law firm pricing to magazine subscriptions (which are really just bundles of individual stories, and meta-bundles of individual issues) bear this out. See Shapiro & Varian, Information Rules, supra.

From the point of view of legalities, the economic benefit of bundling explains a number of features of information licenses—for example (1) pay-up-front agreements; (2) subscription or multi-installment purchases; and, in some cases, (3) no ability to buy individual components. Unfortunately for producers, many forms of bundling violate the antitrust laws, an issue we shall return to in the next chapter.

2. Price Discrimination

In the ski report example above, the information seller was assumed not to know about the precise valuations of each user or—equivalently—was presumed not to be able to do anything about it. Perhaps, for example, the cost of selling personally tailored information services is too high—it is too expensive to tell the high valuers for each region from the low valuers. (What the seller really worries about is selling information regarding Sierra ski conditions to Bill for $25 when Bill would have been willing to pay $75.)

But what if the seller could determine this? In our example, it would not add anything: charging Anita $75 for the Eastern ski report and charging her $25 for the Western one while charging Bill the opposite would yield the same revenue as with bundling. But if we change the numbers slightly, things change. Assume Anita is a more avid skier, or Bill values ski report information less overall (e.g., because California ski conditions are less variable). To be specific, let's say Anita is willing to pay $90 for Eastern information, but Bill will pay only $75 for Western information.

Now, if only the information seller can determine that this is so, it can capture the extra $15 in valuation from Anita. To be precise, if the seller can *find out* this information for less than it's worth—for less than $15—it will do so. Assuming the information is accurate, the seller can raise its price *to Anita* and reap the rewards. If the seller prices Anita's total bundle at $115, she will still buy; and by keeping Bill's the same as it was ($100), the seller will now earn revenues of $215.

The principle here is known as *price discrimination*—charge the higher valuer more and the lower valuer less, in layman's terms. In technical terms, take as much of the consumer surplus as you can. (If Anita is willing to pay $90 for Eastern ski reports but the seller has set a uniform price of $75 per region, Anita would have $15 in consumer surplus: the difference between what she is willing to pay and what she in fact has to pay.)

If you want to price-discriminate, you need good information. If you raise the price of all regional reports to $90, Bill will no longer buy one—and you would lose money. (Anita's extra $15 will not offset the loss of Bill's $75.) In addition, you need something else: you need to be able to prevent one buyer from "buying low, selling high"—a process known as "arbitrage." The following excerpt describes this concept in more detail. (Note that the excerpt refers to a case called ProCD v. Zeidenberg, which the court viewed as an example of (attempted) arbitrage: the buyer of a set of CD-ROM directories made the public domain data in them available for free over the Internet in contravention of a licensing agreement contained on the product packaging. The case is excerpted and discussed in Section C of this chapter.)

Michael J. Meurer, Price Discrimination, Personal Use and Piracy: Copyright Protection of Digital Works
45 Buff. L. Rev. 845 (1997)

Effective price discrimination requires: (1) measurement of consumer preferences; (2) a means to stop arbitrage by favored consumers; and (3) market power. Are the conditions for price discrimination met in ProCD? . . . Judge Easterbrook explains that commercial buyers have higher valuations. Elsewhere in the opinion he explains that a term in the software license precludes consumer buyers from making commercial use of the product. Such a term limits arbitrage. One can only speculate about whether ProCD has sufficient market power to successfully discriminate. Judge Easterbrook comments that ProCD has rivals. Market power declines as the number of rivals increases. But a firm does not have to be a monopolist to price discriminate. Some measure of market power is provided by the copyright which protects the search engine used in the software and the high fixed cost of selecting and maintaining the database. Time will tell. Persistent discriminatory pricing suggests sufficient market power. . . .

Economists use a three-way classification scheme for price discrimination depending on how preferences are measured. In third degree price discrimination, price differentials are tied to a characteristic of a buyer that is correlated with the buyer's valuation. An example is a senior citizen who gets a discounted movie ticket. The seller observes the characteristic and infers that on average this type of buyer has a lower valuation. In second degree price discrimination, price differentials are tied to actions chosen by the buyer. The seller believes that certain actions reflect the preferences of a low valuation buyer and other actions reflect the preferences of a high valuation buyer. In the movie example, a Tuesday night discount illustrates second degree price discrimination. In first degree price discrimination, the seller knows or learns the exact valuation of all buyers. This, of course, is an idealized benchmark.

The distinction between second and third degree discrimination is important because second degree discrimination is usually more costly to implement. The greater cost arises from the need to get buyers to sort themselves in a manner that makes discrimination possible. Economists call this a sorting condition. The price and characteristics of the good intended for the low end of the market must not attract the high end, and the price and characteristics of the good intended for the high end must not attract the low end. The sorting condition imposes an implicit cost on the seller because it restricts the freedom of the seller to set efficient prices. With third degree price discrimination the seller can choose prices for the two classes of consumers independently. With second degree price discrimination the prices are linked. Economic theory shows that a monopoly seller should set the efficient price for the high valuation consumers and an inefficient price for the low valuation consumers. This inefficiency yields the implicit cost of sorting.

Second degree price discrimination is common in the software market. A simple method is to grant a site license. A site license authorizes a customer to install a certain number of copies of software on stand alone machines at a site, or allow a certain number of networked users to access the software on a server. By making licensing fees sensitive to the number of users at a site, the seller can profitably discriminate as long as the number of users has a positive correlation to value.

Software publishers also use product design to facilitate second degree price discrimination. Educational versions of software may sell for a fraction of the price of standard versions. Sellers disable some of the features in the standard version so the quality is reduced. A similar strategy is to include documentation and customer support with the standard version and not with the educational version. Buyers who prize quality must pay more for the standard version, and students who are less sensitive to quality buy the cheaper version. Sorting will not occur unless the discount is large enough to justify the quality reduction to the low valuation buyers. But the discount cannot be too large or both types of buyers will purchase the cheap version.

If it is feasible to check student IDs before selling a cheap version then third degree price discrimination is possible. Comparing optimal second and third degree discrimination: both lead to the same price for the expensive version, while third degree price discrimination leads to a lower price on the cheap version and higher profits to the seller. The important intuition behind the economic theory is that the sorting condition reduces the seller's freedom and less freedom means lower profit. This discussion shows that sellers prefer third degree discrimination. But in many markets sellers are forced to rely on second degree discrimination because they cannot condition sales terms on directly relevant buyer characteristics.

A more sophisticated version of second degree price discrimination requires metering. In some cases metering can approximate first degree price discrimination. A classic example is provided in the antitrust case International Business Machines v. United States. IBM tied the sales of its tabulator machines to purchases of punch cards that were used in the machines. The likely purpose of this tied sale was to implement price discrimination. Discrimination was accomplished by charging a relatively low price for the tabulators, and a price above the competitive price for the punch cards. The purchase of punch cards meters (or measures) the frequency of use of the tabulator. The effect of the tied sale is to charge a high price to those who use the machine frequently and a low price to infrequent users. IBM reasonably believed that frequent use was positively correlated with high valuation.

Suppliers can sometimes directly meter the use of their product. Photocopy machines have counters that record the number of copies that have been made. Lease agreements often charge rates that depend directly on measured usage. Digital technology will expand the use of direct metering. For example, rather than selling hard copies of encyclopedias at a fixed price, a digital publisher could offer access to a digital encyclopedia and charge based on usage. Frequent users pay more for access and infrequent users pay less. As long as use is linked to value, metering can implement price discrimination. . . .

Arbitrage is limited by many factors; I concentrate on the role of transaction costs, technology, and law because they are especially relevant to digital works. Even though arbitrage is feasible sometimes it does not happen because the transaction costs are too high. In the movie example, even if the ticket taker is not very vigilant arbitrage would be limited by the hassle of setting up a secondary market in movie tickets. Further, theaters would resist arbitrage by limiting ticket sales to a small number per customer. In a digital world where it may be possible to buy individual songs or newspaper articles or photographs for pennies, small scale arbitrage might be too costly and large scale arbitrage too easily detected to be feasible.

When quality differentials are the source of price discrimination, arbitrage may be blocked by technology. As described above, educational discounts accompany software that has limited features compared to the higher priced version. Arbitrage is only possible if an educational user can alter the software to add or restore the missing features at a cost less than the discriminatory price differential.

New digital distribution technologies promise to limit arbitrage opportunities for digital works. Many transactions involving copyrighted works are being converted from sales of goods to sales of services. Text published in encyclopedias or legal digests can be resold, but a subscription to a database cannot. Videotapes can be resold but video that is delivered over the Internet by streaming technology cannot. On the other hand, the transaction costs that block arbitrage will fall as digital commerce appears.

The possibility of contract or copyright lawsuits raises the barrier to arbitrage of copyrighted works. The link between the first sale doctrine and arbitrage is obvious. If favored buyers can purchase a work and then sell or lease it to disfavored buyers then price discrimination may be defeated. Contract restrictions on resale or other transfers deter arbitrage.

Contract terms can impede arbitrage in other ways. In *ProCD* a field of use restriction in the software contract did the job. Customers were sorted into the commercial and consumer categories and charged different prices. The favored consumer buyers were discouraged from making commercial use of the database by the threat of contract litigation. The tying contract in *IBM* was designed to prevent high valuation customers from buying low cost punch cards in the open market. Contracts often limit the modification of software or the movement (migration) of software from one platform to another. One purpose of this limitation is to reduce arbitrage possibilities. For example, an application program like a statistics package can be designed to run on a DOS or UNIX operating system. The UNIX buyers tend to have more powerful machines and higher valuations for the software. If the price charged for UNIX versions is higher, then UNIX buyers may want to purchase a DOS version and modify it to run on UNIX. This arbitrage can be deterred if the price differential is less than the cost of modification. But the seller might want a larger price differential which makes the contract limitation valuable.

COMMENTS AND QUESTIONS

Sometimes licensors of information might want users to copy and disseminate an informational work, either because this will lead to indirect revenues (e.g., the later sale of related items), or because it will cause the copied work to become a standard of one sort or another, leading to enhanced revenues later. Consider the following from Lisa N. Takeyama, The Welfare Implications of Unauthorized Reproduction of Intellectual Property in the Presence of Demand Network Externalities, 42 J. Ind. Econ. 155 (1994):

> [U]nauthorized reproduction of intellectual property in the presence of demand network externalities can not only induce greater firm profits relative to the case where there is no copying, it can lead to a Pareto improvement in social welfare. Ceteris paribus, when network externalities are present, firms have a greater incentive to expand output because marginal revenue is higher and/or they may wish to create preemptive installed bases. [U]nauthorized copying can [also] be a relatively efficient means of achieving this by allowing the firm, in effect, to "price discriminate" among different classes of consumers.

This latter argument is dependent on the presence of strong network effects, so that expanding market share (even at a price of 0) brings its own rewards: existing and future customers value the product more highly than they would if it had a small market share. On network effects, see Mark A. Lemley & David McGowan, Legal Implications of Network Economic Effects, 86 Cal. L. Rev. 479, 523-41 (1998); Michael L. Katz & Carl Shapiro, Network Externalities, Competition, and Compatibility, 75 Am. Econ. Rev. 424 (1985).

3. Control After Resale

Yet another economic motivation for vendors to license rather than sell their products is to enable them to retain control over those products after they have been delivered to customers. Both intellectual property and antitrust law draw a distinction between a vendor's control of its product before sale and attempts to control the product after it has been sold. Thus, copyright's "first sale" doctrine, 17 U.S.C. §109(a), provides that a copyright owner has no right to control the use or distribution of a particular copy of her work once it has been sold to another. The buyer can dispose of *that particular copy* as he wishes, at least so long as he does not violate another of the copyright owner's exclusive rights (e.g., by making additional copies or publicly performing the work). This means that a buyer is generally free to resell his copy of the work, to lend it to others, and in most cases even to rent it out for profit.[3] Similarly, patent law's "exhaustion" doctrine provides that the sale of a patented device to a customer carries with it an implied license to the customer allowing him to use or resell the device. Trademark law contains a similar exhaustion rule, which permits consumers, for example, to advertise and sell their used cars using the trademarked brand name. And antitrust law precludes certain efforts on the part of vendors to control the conditions under which a product may be resold—notably, efforts to set the resale price.

Why might a software vendor want to control the use or disposition of its product after it has been sold to a customer? A number of possible reasons come to mind. First, control over resale may be necessary to make a price discrimination scheme work. As noted above, price discrimination is possible only if the seller has some means to prevent arbitrage. If low-cost buyers could resell their products to high-cost buyers, they would swiftly undermine any such scheme for price discrimination. If the software vendor can control resale, either by precluding it entirely or by limiting the class of purchasers to whom a buyer can resell, the vendor may be able to prop up a price discrimination scheme.

Second, a software vendor may simply not be willing to sell to a particular class of purchasers at all, such as to its major competitor or to a company that it suspects might compete with it in a downstream market, or perhaps to a company that is suing it on an unrelated matter. Preventing the resale of software by a buyer, or conditioning resale on prior approval from the vendor, is a way to achieve these goals. (Whether software vendors *should* be able to achieve these goals is another matter. Certainly some restrictions that vendors periodically impose, such as a contract provision prohibiting the buyer from competing against the seller, are potentially anticompetitive, especially when the software vendor has market power.)

For a discussion of restrictions on transferability, both under current law and under the draft UCITA, see David A. Rice, License with Contract and Precedent: Publisher-Licensor Protection Consequences and the Rationale Offered for the Nontransferability of Licenses Under Article 2B, 13 Berkeley Tech. L.J. 1239 (1998). Among other things, Rice argues that the idea of nontransferability is inconsistent with general principles of contract and commercial law.

COMMENTS AND QUESTIONS

It is worth noting that most of these rationales are not limited to the software industry. Sellers of books, cars, and copy machines would doubtless like to be able

---

3. Section 109(c) of the Copyright Act creates an exception for computer software and music, which cannot be rented for profit. Other works in digital form, such as books, movies, and even video games, can be rented out by the owner of the copy without the permission of the copyright owner.

to bundle products, price-discriminate, and control the use of their products after a first sale. It is worth considering why all sorts of goods aren't licensed rather than sold. Is there something about the software industry that makes the license mechanism uniquely viable? Or should we expect to see a wide variety of manufacturers attempting to license their products in the future?

C. CONTRACT FORMATION, ENFORCEMENT, AND WARRANTIES

1. Contract Formation

a. Shrinkwrap Licenses

Step-Saver Data Systems v. Wyse Technology
United States Court of Appeals for the Third Circuit
939 F.2d 91 (3d Cir. 1991)

WISDOM, Circuit Judge.

The "Limited Use License Agreement" printed on a package containing a copy of a computer program raises the central issue in this appeal. The trial judge held that the terms of the Limited Use License Agreement governed the purchase of the package, and, therefore, granted the software producer, The Software Link, Inc. ("TSL"), a directed verdict on claims of breach of warranty brought by a disgruntled purchaser, Step-Saver Data Systems, Inc. We disagree with the district court's determination of the legal effect of the license, and reverse and remand the warranty claims for further consideration. . . .

I. Factual and Procedural Background

The growth in the variety of computer hardware and software has created a strong market for these products. It has also created a difficult choice for consumers, as they must somehow decide which of the many available products will best suit their needs. To assist consumers in this decision process, some companies will evaluate the needs of particular groups of potential computer users, compare those needs with the available technology, and develop a package of hardware and software to satisfy those needs. Beginning in 1981, Step-Saver performed this function as a value added retailer for International Business Machines (IBM) products. It would combine hardware and software to satisfy the word processing, data management, and communications needs for offices of physicians and lawyers. It originally marketed single computer systems, based primarily on the IBM personal computer. . . .

After evaluating the available technology, Step-Saver selected a program by TSL, entitled Multilink Advanced, as the operating system for the multi-user system. Step-Saver selected WY-60 terminals manufactured by Wyse, and used an

IBM AT as the main computer. For applications software, Step-Saver included in the package several off-the-shelf programs, designed to run under Microsoft's Disk Operating System ("MS-DOS"), as well as several programs written by Step-Saver. Step-Saver began marketing the system in November of 1986, and sold one hundred forty-two systems mostly to law and medical offices before terminating sales of the system in March of 1987. Almost immediately upon installation of the system, Step-Saver began to receive complaints from some of its customers.

Step-Saver, in addition to conducting its own investigation of the problems, referred these complaints to Wyse and TSL, and requested technical assistance in resolving the problems. After several preliminary attempts to address the problems, the three companies were unable to reach a satisfactory solution, and disputes developed among the three concerning responsibility for the problems. As a result, the problems were never solved. At least twelve of Step-Saver's customers filed suit against Step-Saver because of the problems with the multi-user system.

Once it became apparent that the three companies would not be able to resolve their dispute amicably, . . . Step-Saver then filed a . . . complaint alleging breach of warranties by both TSL and Wyse and intentional misrepresentations by TSL. The district court's actions during the resolution of this second complaint provide the foundation for this appeal.

On the first day of trial, the district court specifically agreed with the basic contention of TSL that the form language printed on each package containing the Multilink Advanced program ("the box-top license") was the complete and exclusive agreement between Step-Saver and TSL under §2-202 of the Uniform Commercial Code (UCC).[6] Based on §2-316 of the UCC, the district court held that the box-top license disclaimed all express and implied warranties otherwise made by TSL. . . .

The trial proceeded on Step Saver's breach of warranties claims against Wyse. At the conclusion of Wyse's evidence, the district judge denied Step-Saver's request for rebuttal testimony on the issue of the ordinary uses of the WY-60 terminal. The district court instructed the jury on the issues of express warranty and implied warranty of fitness for a particular purpose. Over Step-Saver's objection, the district court found insufficient evidence to support a finding that Wyse had breached its implied warranty of merchantability, and refused to instruct the jury on such warranty. The jury returned a verdict in favor of Wyse on the two warranty issues submitted.

Step-Saver appeals. . . .

II. The Effect of the Box-Top License

The relationship between Step-Saver and TSL began in the fall of 1984 when Step-Saver asked TSL for information on an early version of the Multilink program. TSL provided Step-Saver with a copy of the early program, known simply as Multilink, without charge to permit Step-Saver to test the program to see what it

---

6. All three parties agree that the terminals and the program are "goods" within the meaning of UCC §§2-102 & 2-105. Cf. Advent Sys. Ltd. v. Unisys Corp., 925 F.2d 670, 674-76 (3d Cir. 1991). . . .

could accomplish. Step-Saver performed some tests with the early program, but did not market a system based on it.

In the summer of 1985, Step-Saver noticed some advertisements in Byte magazine for a more powerful version of the Multilink program, known as Multilink Advanced. Step-Saver requested information from TSL concerning this new version of the program, and allegedly was assured by sales representatives that the new version was compatible with ninety percent of the programs available "off-the-shelf" for computers using MS-DOS. The sales representatives allegedly made a number of additional specific representations of fact concerning the capabilities of the Multilink Advanced program.

Based on these representations, Step-Saver obtained several copies of the Multilink Advanced program in the spring of 1986, and conducted tests with the program. After these tests, Step-Saver decided to market a multi-user system which used the Multilink Advanced program. From August of 1986 through March of 1987, Step-Saver purchased and resold 142 copies of the Multilink Advanced program. Step-Saver would typically purchase copies of the program in the following manner. First, Step-Saver would telephone TSL and place an order. (Step-Saver would typically order twenty copies of the program at a time.) TSL would accept the order and promise, while on the telephone, to ship the goods promptly. After the telephone order, Step-Saver would send a purchase order, detailing the items to be purchased, their price, and shipping and payment terms. TSL would ship the order promptly, along with an invoice. The invoice would contain terms essentially identical with those on Step-Saver's purchase order: price, quantity, and shipping and payment terms. No reference was made during the telephone calls, or on either the purchase orders or the invoices with regard to a disclaimer of any warranties.

Printed on the package of each copy of the program, however, would be a copy of the box-top license. The box-top license contains five terms relevant to this action:

> (1) The box-top license provides that the customer has not purchased the software itself, but has merely obtained a personal, non-transferable license to use the program.
> (2) The box-top license, in detail and at some length, disclaims all express and implied warranties except for a warranty that the disks contained in the box are free from defects.
> (3) The box-top license provides that the sole remedy available to a purchaser of the program is to return a defective disk for replacement; the license excludes any liability for damages, direct or consequential, caused by the use of the program.
> (4) The box-top license contains an integration clause, which provides that the box-top license is the final and complete expression of the terms of the parties's agreement.
> (5) The box-top license states: "Opening this package indicates your acceptance of these terms and conditions. If you do not agree with them, you should promptly return the package unopened to the person from whom you purchased it within fifteen days from date of purchase and your money will be refunded to you by that person."

The district court, without much discussion, held, as a matter of law, that the box-top license was the final and complete expression of the terms of the parties's agreement. . . .

Step-Saver contends that the contract for each copy of the program was formed when TSL agreed, on the telephone, to ship the copy at the agreed price. The box-top license, argues Step-Saver, was a material alteration to the parties's contract which did not become a part of the contract under UCC §2-207.[10] Alternatively, Step-Saver argues that the undisputed evidence establishes that the parties did not intend the box-top license as a final and complete expression of the terms of their agreement, and, therefore, the parol evidence rule of UCC §2-202 would not apply.[11]

TSL argues that the contract between TSL and Step-Saver did not come into existence until Step-Saver received the program, saw the terms of the license, and opened the program packaging. TSL contends that too many material terms were omitted from the telephone discussion for that discussion to establish a contract for the software. Second, TSL contends that its acceptance of Step-Saver's telephone offer was conditioned on Step-Saver's acceptance of the terms of the box-top license. Therefore, TSL argues, it did not accept Step-Saver's telephone offer, but made a counteroffer represented by the terms of the box-top license, which was accepted when Step-Saver opened each package. Third, TSL argues that, however the contract was formed, Step-Saver was aware of the warranty disclaimer, and that Step-Saver, by continuing to order and accept the product with knowledge of the disclaimer, assented to the disclaimer.

In analyzing these competing arguments, we first consider whether the license should be treated as an integrated writing under UCC §2-202, as a proposed modification under UCC §2-209, or as a written confirmation under UCC §2-207. Finding that UCC §2-207 best governs our resolution of the effect of the box-top license, we then consider whether, under UCC §2-207, the terms of the box-top license were incorporated into the parties's agreement.

---

10. Section 2-207 provides:

Additional Terms in Acceptance or Confirmation.

(1) A definite and seasonable expression of acceptance or a written confirmation which is sent within a reasonable time operates as an acceptance even though it states terms additional to or different from those offered or agreed upon, unless acceptance is expressly made conditional on assent to the additional or different terms.

(2) The additional terms are to be construed as proposals for addition to the contract. Between merchants such terms become part of the contract unless:

(a) the offer expressly limits acceptance to the terms of the offer;

(b) they materially alter it; or

(c) notification of objection to them has already been given or is given within a reasonable time after notice of them is received.

(3) Conduct by both parties which recognizes the existence of a contract is sufficient to establish a contract for sale although the writings of the parties do not otherwise establish a contract. In such case the terms of the particular contract consist of those terms on which the writings of the parties agree, together with any supplementary terms incorporated under any other provisions of the Act.

11. Two other issues were raised by Step-Saver. First, Step-Saver argued that the box-top disclaimer is either unconscionable or not in good faith. Second, Step-Saver argued that the warranty disclaimer was inconsistent with the express warranties made by TSL in the product specifications. Step-Saver argues that interpreting the form language of the license agreement to override the specific warranties contained in the product specification is unreasonable, citing Consolidated Data Terminals v. Applied Digital Data Sys., 708 F.2d 385 (9th Cir. 1983). See also Northern States Power Co. v. ITT Meyer Indus., 777 F.2d 405 (8th Cir. 1985). Because of our holding that the terms of the box-top license were not incorporated into the contract, we do not address these issues.

A. Does UCC §2-207 Govern the Analysis?

As a basic principle, we agree with Step-Saver that UCC §2-207 governs our analysis. We see no need to parse the parties's various actions to decide exactly when the parties formed a contract. TSL has shipped the product, and Step-Saver has accepted and paid for each copy of the program. The parties's performance demonstrates the existence of a contract. The dispute is, therefore, not over the existence of a contract, but the nature of its terms. When the parties's conduct establishes a contract, but the parties have failed to adopt expressly a particular writing as the terms of their agreement, and the writings exchanged by the parties do not agree, UCC §2-207 determines the terms of the contract.

As stated by the official comment to §2-207:

> 1. This section is intended to deal with two typical situations. The one is the written confirmation, where an agreement has been reached either orally or by informal correspondence between the parties and is followed by one or more of the parties sending formal memoranda embodying the terms so far as agreed upon and adding terms not discussed. . . .
>
> 2. Under this Article a proposed deal which in commercial understanding has in fact been closed is recognized as a contract. Therefore, any additional matter contained in the confirmation or in the acceptance falls within subsection (2) and must be regarded as a proposal for an added term unless the acceptance is made conditional on the acceptance of the additional or different terms.

Although UCC §2-202 permits the parties to reduce an oral agreement to writing, and UCC §2-209 permits the parties to modify an existing contract without additional consideration, a writing will be a final expression of, or a binding modification to, an earlier agreement only if the parties so intend. It is undisputed that Step-Saver never expressly agreed to the terms of the box-top license, either as a final expression of, or a modification to, the parties's agreement. In fact, Barry Greebel, the President of Step-Saver, testified without dispute that he objected to the terms of the box-top license as applied to Step-Saver. In the absence of evidence demonstrating an express intent to adopt a writing as a final expression of, or a modification to, an earlier agreement, we find UCC §2-207 to provide the appropriate legal rules for determining whether such an intent can be inferred from continuing with the contract after receiving a writing containing additional or different terms.

To understand why the terms of the license should be considered under §2-207 in this case, we review briefly the reasons behind §2-207. Under the common law of sales, and to some extent still for contracts outside the UCC, an acceptance that varied any term of the offer operated as a rejection of the offer, and simultaneously made a counteroffer. This common law formality was known as the mirror image rule, because the terms of the acceptance had to mirror the terms of the offer to be effective. If the offeror proceeded with the contract despite the differing terms of the supposed acceptance, he would, by his performance, constructively accept the terms of the "counteroffer", and be bound by its terms. As a result of these rules, the terms of the party who sent the last form, typically the seller, would become the terms of the parties's contract. This result was known as the "last shot rule".

The UCC, in §2-207, rejected this approach. Instead, it recognized that, while a party may desire the terms detailed in its form if a dispute, in fact, arises, most parties do not expect a dispute to arise when they first enter into a contract. As a result, most parties will proceed with the transaction even if they know that the terms of their form would not be enforced. The insight behind the rejection of the last shot rule is that it would be unfair to bind the buyer of goods to the standard terms of the seller, when neither party cared sufficiently to establish expressly the terms of their agreement, simply because the seller sent the last form. Thus, UCC §2-207 establishes a legal rule that proceeding with a contract after receiving a writing that purports to define the terms of the parties's contract is not sufficient to establish the party's consent to the terms of the writing to the extent that the terms of the writing either add to, or differ from, the terms detailed in the parties's earlier writings or discussions. In the absence of a party's express assent to the additional or different terms of the writing, section 2-207 provides a default rule that the parties intended, as the terms of their agreement, those terms to which both parties have agreed, along with any terms implied by the provisions of the UCC.

The reasons that led to the rejection of the last shot rule, and the adoption of section 2-207, apply fully in this case. TSL never mentioned during the parties's negotiations leading to the purchase of the programs, nor did it, at any time, obtain Step-Saver's express assent to, the terms of the box-top license. Instead, TSL contented itself with attaching the terms to the packaging of the software, even though those terms differed substantially from those previously discussed by the parties. Thus, the box-top license, in this case, is best seen as one more form in a battle of forms, and the question of whether Step-Saver has agreed to be bound by the terms of the box-top license is best resolved by applying the legal principles detailed in section 2-207.

B. Application of §2-207

TSL advances several reasons why the terms of the box-top license should be incorporated into the parties's agreement under a §2-207 analysis. First, TSL argues that the parties's contract was not formed until Step-Saver received the package, saw the terms of the box-top license, and opened the package, thereby consenting to the terms of the license. TSL argues that a contract defined without reference to the specific terms provided by the box-top license would necessarily fail for indefiniteness. Second, TSL argues that the box-top license was a conditional acceptance and counter-offer under §2-207(1). Third, TSL argues that Step-Saver, by continuing to order and use the product with notice of the terms of the box-top license, consented to the terms of the box-top license.

[The court held that the terms of the telephone agreement and purchase order were sufficiently definite to constitute a contract, and under UCC §2-204 the remaining terms (including warranty provisions) could be filled in with default rules provided in the UCC itself. Next, the court discusses TSL's argument that its acceptance of the order for goods was conditional upon the conditions of the box-top license:]

Using this test, it is apparent that the integration clause and the "consent by opening" language is not sufficient to render TSL's acceptance conditional. As other courts have recognized, this type of language provides no real indication that the party is willing to forego the transaction if the additional language is not included in the contract.

The second provision [providing for a refund if the buyer returns the software within 15 days] provides a more substantial indication that TSL was willing to forego the contract if the terms of the box-top license were not accepted by Step-Saver. On its face, the box-top license states that TSL will refund the purchase price if the purchaser does not agree to the terms of the license. Even with such a refund term, however, the offeree/counterofferor may be relying on the purchaser's investment in time and energy in reaching this point in the transaction to prevent the purchaser from returning the item. Because a purchaser has made a decision to buy a particular product and has actually obtained the product, the purchaser may use it despite the refund offer, regardless of the additional terms specified after the contract formed. But we need not decide whether such a refund offer could ever amount to a conditional acceptance; the undisputed evidence in this case demonstrates that the terms of the license were not sufficiently important that TSL would forego its sales to Step-Saver if TSL could not obtain Step-Saver's consent to those terms.

As discussed, Mr. Greebel testified that TSL assured him that the box-top license did not apply to Step-Saver, as Step-Saver was not the end user of the Multilink Advanced program. Supporting this testimony, TSL on two occasions asked Step-Saver to sign agreements that would put in formal terms the relationship between Step-Saver and TSL. Both proposed agreements contained warranty disclaimer and limitation of remedy terms similar to those contained in the box-top license. Step-Saver refused to sign the agreements; nevertheless, TSL continued to sell copies of Multilink Advanced to Step-Saver.

Additionally, TSL asks us to infer, based on the refund offer, that it was willing to forego its sales to Step-Saver unless Step-Saver agreed to the terms of the box-top license. Such an inference is inconsistent with the fact that both parties agree that the terms of the box-top license did not represent the parties's agreement with respect to Step-Saver's right to transfer the copies of the Multilink Advanced program. Although the box-top license prohibits the transfer, by Step-Saver, of its copies of the program, both parties agree that Step-Saver was entitled to transfer its copies to the purchasers of the Step-Saver multi-user system. Thus, TSL was willing to proceed with the transaction despite the fact that one of the terms of the box-top license was not included in the contract between TSL and Step-Saver. We see no basis in the terms of the box-top license for inferring that a reasonable offeror would understand from the refund offer that certain terms of the box-top license, such as the warranty disclaimers, were essential to TSL, while others such as the non-transferability provision were not.

Based on these facts, we conclude that TSL did not clearly express its unwillingness to proceed with the transactions unless its additional terms were incorporated into the parties's agreement. The box-top license did not, therefore, constitute a conditional acceptance under UCC §2-207(1).

3. Did the Parties's Course of Dealing Establish That the Parties Had Excluded Any Express or Implied Warranties Associated with the Software Program?

TSL argues that because Step-Saver placed its orders for copies of the Multilink Advanced program with notice of the terms of the box-top license, Step-Saver is bound by the terms of the box-top license. Essentially, TSL is arguing that, even if the terms of the box-top license would not become part of the contract if the case involved only a single transaction, the repeated expression of those terms by TSL eventually incorporates them within the contract. . . .

For two reasons, we hold that the repeated sending of a writing which contains certain standard terms, without any action with respect to the issues addressed by those terms, cannot constitute a course of dealing which would incorporate a term of the writing otherwise excluded under §2-207. First, the repeated exchange of forms by the parties only tells Step-Saver that TSL desires certain terms. Given TSL's failure to obtain Step-Saver's express assent to these terms before it will ship the program, Step-Saver can reasonably believe that, while TSL desires certain terms, it has agreed to do business on other terms—those terms expressly agreed upon by the parties. Thus, even though Step-Saver would not be surprised to learn that TSL desires the terms of the box-top license, Step-Saver might well be surprised to learn that the terms of the box-top license have been incorporated into the parties's agreement.

Second, the seller in these multiple transaction cases will typically have the opportunity to negotiate the precise terms of the parties's agreement, as TSL sought to do in this case. The seller's unwillingness or inability to obtain a negotiated agreement reflecting its terms strongly suggests that, while the seller would like a court to incorporate its terms if a dispute were to arise, those terms are not a part of the parties's commercial bargain. For these reasons, we are not convinced that TSL's unilateral act of repeatedly sending copies of the box-top license with its product can establish a course of dealing between TSL and Step-Saver that resulted in the adoption of the terms of the box-top license. . . .

4. Public Policy Concerns.

TSL has raised a number of public policy arguments focusing on the effect on the software industry of an adverse holding concerning the enforceability of the box-top license. We are not persuaded that requiring software companies to stand behind representations concerning their products will inevitably destroy the software industry. We emphasize, however, that we are following the well-established distinction between conspicuous disclaimers made available before the contract is formed and disclaimers made available only after the contract is formed.[45] When a

---

45. Compare Hill v. BASF Wyandotte Corp., 696 F.2d 287, 290-91 (4th Cir. 1982). In that case, a farmer purchased seventy-three five gallon cans of a herbicide from a retailer. Because the disclaimer was printed conspicuously on each can, the farmer had constructive knowledge of the terms of the disclaimer before the contract formed. As a result, when he selected each can of the herbicide from the shelf and purchased it, the law implies his assent to the terms of the disclaimer. See also Bowdoin v. Showell Growers, Inc., 817 F.2d 1543, 1545 (11th Cir. 1987) (disclaimers that were conspicuous before the contract for sale has formed are effective; post-sale disclaimers are ineffective); Monsanto Agricultural Prods. Co. v. Edenfield, 426 So. 2d at 575-76.

disclaimer is not expressed until after the contract is formed, UCC §2-207 governs the interpretation of the contract, and, between merchants, such disclaimers, to the extent they materially alter the parties's agreement, are not incorporated into the parties's agreement.

If TSL wants relief for its business operations from this well-established rule, their arguments are better addressed to a legislature than a court.

C. *The Terms of the Contract*

Under section 2-207, an additional term detailed in the box-top license will not be incorporated into the parties's contract if the term's addition to the contract would materially alter the parties's agreement. Step-Saver alleges that several representations made by TSL constitute express warranties, and that valid implied warranties were also a part of the parties's agreement. Because the district court considered the box-top license to exclude all of these warranties, the district court did not consider whether other factors may act to exclude these warranties. The existence and nature of the warranties is primarily a factual question that we leave for the district court, but assuming that these warranties were included within the parties's original agreement, we must conclude that adding the disclaimer of warranty and limitation of remedies provisions from the box-top license would, as a matter of law, substantially alter the distribution of risk between Step-Saver and TSL. Therefore, under UCC §2-207(2)(b), the disclaimer of warranty and limitation of remedies terms of the box-top license did not become a part of the parties's agreement.

Based on these considerations, we reverse the trial court's holding that the parties intended the box-top license to be a final and complete expression of the terms of their agreement. Despite the presence of an integration clause in the box-top license, the box-top license should have been treated as a written confirmation containing additional terms. Because the warranty disclaimer and limitation of remedies terms would materially alter the parties's agreement, these terms did not become a part of the parties's agreement. We remand for further consideration the express and implied warranty claims against TSL. . . .

ProCD, Inc. v. Zeidenberg
United States Court of Appeals for the Seventh Circuit
86 F.3d 1447 (7th Cir. 1996)

EASTERBROOK, Circuit Judge.

Must buyers of computer software obey the terms of shrinkwrap licenses? The district court held not, for two reasons: first, they are not contracts because the licenses are inside the box rather than printed on the outside; second, federal law forbids enforcement even if the licenses are contracts. 908 F. Supp. 640 (W.D. Wis. 1996). The parties and numerous amici curiae have briefed many other issues, but these are the only two that matter—and we disagree with the district judge's conclusion on each. Shrinkwrap licenses are enforceable unless their terms are objectionable on grounds applicable to contracts in general (for example, if they violate a rule of positive law, or if they are unconscionable). Because no one argues that the terms of the license at issue here are troublesome, we remand with instructions to enter judgment for the plaintiff.

I

ProCD, the plaintiff, has compiled information from more than 3,000 telephone directories into a computer database. We may assume that this database cannot be copyrighted, although it is more complex, contains more information (nine-digit zip codes and census industrial codes), is organized differently, and therefore is more original than the single alphabetical directory at issue in Feist Publications, Inc. v. Rural Telephone Service Co., 499 U.S. 340, 113 L. Ed. 2d 358, 111 S. Ct. 1282 (1991). See Paul J. Heald, The Vices of Originality, 1991 Sup. Ct. Rev. 143, 160-68. ProCD sells a version of the database, called Select-Phone (trademark), on CD-ROM discs. (CD-ROM means "compact disc—read only memory." The "shrinkwrap license" gets its name from the fact that retail software packages are covered in plastic or cellophane "shrinkwrap," and some vendors, though not ProCD, have written licenses that become effective as soon as the customer tears the wrapping from the package. Vendors prefer "end user license," but we use the more common term.) A proprietary method of compressing the data serves as effective encryption too. Customers decrypt and use the data with the aid of an application program that ProCD has written. This program, which is copyrighted, searches the database in response to users' criteria (such as "find all people named Tatum in Tennessee, plus all firms with 'Door Systems' in the corporate name"). The resulting lists (or, as ProCD prefers, "listings") can be read and manipulated by other software, such as word processing programs.

The database in SelectPhone™ cost more than $10 million to compile and is expensive to keep current. It is much more valuable to some users than to others. The combination of names, addresses, and SIC codes enables manufacturers to compile lists of potential customers. Manufacturers and retailers pay high prices to specialized information intermediaries for such mailing lists; ProCD offers a potentially cheaper alternative. People with nothing to sell could use the database as a substitute for calling long distance information, or as a way to look up old friends who have moved to unknown towns, or just as a[n] electronic substitute for the local phone book. ProCD decided to engage in price discrimination, selling its database to the general public for personal use at a low price (approximately $150 for the set of five discs) while selling information to the trade for a higher price. It has adopted some intermediate strategies too: access to the SelectPhone (trademark) database is available via the America Online service for the price America Online charges to its clients (approximately $3 per hour), but this service has been tailored to be useful only to the general public.

If ProCD had to recover all of its costs and make a profit by charging a single price—that is, if it could not charge more to commercial users than to the general public—it would have to raise the price substantially over $150. The ensuing reduction in sales would harm consumers who value the information at, say, $200. They get consumer surplus of $50 under the current arrangement but would cease to buy if the price rose substantially. If because of high elasticity of demand in the consumer segment of the market the only way to make a profit turned out to be a price attractive to commercial users alone, then all consumers would lose out—and so would the commercial clients, who would have to pay more for the listings because ProCD could not obtain any contribution toward costs from the consumer market.

To make price discrimination work, however, the seller must be able to control arbitrage. An air carrier sells tickets for less to vacationers than to business travelers, using advance purchase and Saturday-night-stay requirements to distinguish the categories. A producer of movies segments the market by time, releasing first to theaters, then to pay-per-view services, next to the videotape and laserdisc market, and finally to cable and commercial tv. Vendors of computer software have a harder task. Anyone can walk into a retail store and buy a box. Customers do not wear tags saying "commercial user" or "consumer user." Anyway, even a commercial-user-detector at the door would not work, because a consumer could buy the software and resell to a commercial user. That arbitrage would break down the price discrimination and drive up the minimum price at which ProCD would sell to anyone.

Instead of tinkering with the product and letting users sort themselves—for example, furnishing current data at a high price that would be attractive only to commercial customers, and two-year-old data at a low price—ProCD turned to the institution of contract. Every box containing its consumer product declares that the software comes with restrictions stated in an enclosed license. This license, which is encoded on the CD-ROM disks as well as printed in the manual, and which appears on a user's screen every time the software runs, limits use of the application program and listings to non-commercial purposes.

Matthew Zeidenberg bought a consumer package of SelectPhone (trademark) in 1994 from a retail outlet in Madison, Wisconsin, but decided to ignore the license. He formed Silken Mountain Web Services, Inc., to resell the information in the SelectPhone (trademark) database. The corporation makes the database available on the Internet to anyone willing to pay its price—which, needless to say, is less than ProCD charges its commercial customers. Zeidenberg has purchased two additional SelectPhone (trademark) packages, each with an updated version of the database, and made the latest information available over the World Wide Web, for a price, through his corporation. ProCD filed this suit seeking an injunction against further dissemination that exceeds the rights specified in the licenses (identical in each of the three packages Zeidenberg purchased). The district court held the licenses ineffectual because their terms do not appear on the outside of the packages. The court added that the second and third licenses stand no different from the first, even though they are identical, because they might have been different, and a purchaser does not agree to—and cannot be bound by—terms that were secret at the time of purchase. 908 F. Supp. at 654.

II

Following the district court, we treat the licenses as ordinary contracts accompanying the sale of products, and therefore as governed by the common law of contracts and the Uniform Commercial Code. Whether there are legal differences between "contracts" and "licenses" (which may matter under the copyright doctrine of first sale) is a subject for another day. See Microsoft Corp. v. Harmony Computers & Electronics, Inc., 846 F. Supp. 208 (E.D. N.Y. 1994). Zeidenberg does not argue that Silken Mountain Web Services is free of any restrictions that apply to Zeidenberg himself, because any effort to treat the two parties as distinct would put Silken Mountain behind the eight ball on ProCD's argument that copying the application program onto its hard disk violates the copyright laws. Zeidenberg does argue, and the district court held, that placing the package of software on the shelf is an "offer," which the customer "accepts" by paying the asking price and leaving the store with the goods. Peters v. State, 154 Wis. 111, 142 N.W. 181 (1913). In Wisconsin, as elsewhere, a contract includes only the terms on which the parties have agreed. One cannot agree to hidden terms, the judge concluded. So far, so good—but one of the terms to which Zeidenberg agreed by purchasing the software is that the transaction was subject to a license. Zeidenberg's position therefore must be that the printed terms on the outside of a box are the parties' contract—except for printed terms that refer to or incorporate other terms. But why would Wisconsin fetter the parties' choice in this way? Vendors can put the entire terms of a contract on the outside of a box only by using microscopic type, removing other information that buyers might find more useful (such as what the software does, and on which computers it works), or both. The "Read Me" file included with most software, describing system requirements and potential incompatibilities, may be equivalent to ten pages of type; warranties and license restrictions take still more space. Notice on the outside, terms on the inside, and a right to return the software for a refund if the terms are unacceptable (a right that the license expressly extends), may be a means of doing business valuable to buyers and sellers alike. See E. Allan Farnsworth, 1 Farnsworth on Contracts §2.6 (1990); Restatement (2d) of Contracts §211 comment a (1981) ("Standardization of agreements serves many of the same functions as standardization of goods and services; both are essential to a system of mass production and distribution. Scarce and costly time and skill can be devoted to a class of transactions rather than the details of individual transactions."). Doubtless a state could forbid the use of standard contracts in the software business, but we do not think that Wisconsin has done so.

Transactions in which the exchange of money precedes the communication of detailed terms are common. Consider the purchase of insurance. The buyer goes to an agent, who explains the essentials (amount of coverage, number of years) and remits the premium to the home office, which sends back a policy. On the district judge's understanding, the terms of the policy are irrelevant because the insured paid before receiving them. Yet the device of payment, often with a "binder" (so that the insurance takes effect immediately even though the home office reserves the right to withdraw coverage later), in advance of the policy, serves buyers' interests by accelerating effectiveness and reducing transactions costs. Or consider the purchase of an airline ticket. The traveler calls the carrier or an agent, is quoted a price, reserves a seat, pays, and gets a ticket, in that order. The ticket contains elaborate terms, which the traveler can reject by canceling the reservation. To use the ticket is to accept the terms, even terms that in retrospect are disadvantageous. See Carnival Cruise Lines, Inc. v. Shute, 499 U.S. 585, 113 L. Ed. 2d 622, 111 S. Ct. 1522 (1991); see also Vimar Seguros y Reaseguros, S.A. v. M/V Sky

Reefer, 132 L. Ed.2d 462, 115 S. Ct. 2322 (1995) (bills of lading). Just so with a ticket to a concert. The back of the ticket states that the patron promises not to record the concert; to attend is to agree. A theater that detects a violation will confiscate the tape and escort the violator to the exit. One could arrange things so that every concertgoer signs this promise before forking over money, but that cumbersome way of doing things not only would lengthen queues and raise prices but also would scotch the sale of tickets by phone or electronic data service.

Consumer goods work the same way. Someone who wants to buy a radio set visits a store, pays, and walks out with a box. Inside the box is a leaflet containing some terms, the most important of which usually is the warranty, read for the first time in the comfort of home. By Zeidenberg's lights, the warranty in the box is irrelevant; every consumer gets the standard warranty implied by the UCC in the event the contract is silent; yet so far as we are aware no state disregards warranties furnished with consumer products. Drugs come with a list of ingredients on the outside and an elaborate package insert on the inside. The package insert describes drug interactions, contraindications, and other vital information—but, if Zeidenberg is right, the purchaser need not read the package insert, because it is not part of the contract.

Next consider the software industry itself. Only a minority of sales take place over the counter, where there are boxes to peruse. A customer may place an order by phone in response to a line item in a catalog or a review in a magazine. Much software is ordered over the Internet by purchasers who have never seen a box. Increasingly software arrives by wire. There is no box; there is only a stream of electrons, a collection of information that includes data, an application program, instructions, many limitations ("MegaPixel 3.14159 cannot be used with Byte-Pusher 2.718"), and the terms of sale. The user purchases a serial number, which activates the software's features. On Zeidenberg's arguments, these unboxed sales are unfettered by terms—so the seller has made a broad warranty and must pay consequential damages for any shortfalls in performance, two "promises" that if taken seriously would drive prices through the ceiling or return transactions to the horse-and-buggy age.

According to the district court, the UCC does not countenance the sequence of money now, terms later. (Wisconsin's version of the UCC does not differ from the Official Version in any material respect, so we use the regular numbering system. Wis. Stat. §402.201 corresponds to UCC §2-201, and other citations are easy to derive.) One of the court's reasons—that by proposing as part of the draft Article 2B a new UCC §2-2203 that would explicitly validate standard-form user licenses, the American Law Institute and the National Conference of Commissioners on Uniform Laws have conceded the invalidity of shrinkwrap licenses under current law, see 908 F. Supp. at 655-66—depends on a faulty inference. To propose a change in a law's text is not necessarily to propose a change in the law's effect. New words may be designed to fortify the current rule with a more precise text that curtails uncertainty. To judge by the flux of law review articles discussing shrinkwrap licenses, uncertainty is much in need of reduction—although businesses seem to feel less uncertainty than do scholars, for only three cases (other than ours) touch on the subject, and none directly addresses it. See Step-Saver Data Systems, Inc. v. Wyse Technology, 939 F.2d 91 (3d Cir. 1991); Vault Corp. v. Quaid Software Ltd., 847 F.2d 255, 268-70 (5th Cir. 1988); Arizona Retail

Systems, Inc. v. Software Link, Inc., 831 F. Supp. 759 (D. Ariz. 1993). As their titles suggest, these are not consumer transactions. Step-Saver is a battle-of-the-forms case, in which the parties exchange incompatible forms and a court must decide which prevails. See Northrop Corp. v. Litronic Industries, 29 F.3d 1173 (7th Cir. 1994) (Illinois law); Douglas G. Baird & Robert Weisberg, Rules, Standards, and the Battle of the Forms: A Reassessment of §2-207, 68 Va. L. Rev. 1217, 1227-31 (1982). Our case has only one form; UCC §2-207 is irrelevant. *Vault* holds that Louisiana's special shrinkwrap-license statute is preempted by federal law, a question to which we return. And *Arizona Retail Systems* did not reach the question, because the court found that the buyer knew the terms of the license before purchasing the software.

What then does the current version of the UCC have to say? We think that the place to start is §2-204(1): "A contract for sale of goods may be made in any manner sufficient to show agreement, including conduct by both parties which recognizes the existence of such a contract." A vendor, as master of the offer, may invite acceptance by conduct, and may propose limitations on the kind of conduct that constitutes acceptance. A buyer may accept by performing the acts the vendor proposes to treat as acceptance. And that is what happened. ProCD proposed a contract that a buyer would accept by using the software after having an opportunity to read the license at leisure. This Zeidenberg did. He had no choice, because the software splashed the license on the screen and would not let him proceed without indicating acceptance. So although the district judge was right to say that a contract can be, and often is, formed simply by paying the price and walking out of the store, the UCC permits contracts to be formed in other ways. ProCD proposed such a different way, and without protest Zeidenberg agreed. Ours is not a case in which a consumer opens a package to find an insert saying "you owe us an extra $10,000" and the seller files suit to collect. Any buyer finding such a demand can prevent formation of the contract by returning the package, as can any consumer who concludes that the terms of the license make the software worth less than the purchase price. Nothing in the UCC requires a seller to maximize the buyer's net gains.

Section 2-606, which defines "acceptance of goods", reinforces this understanding. A buyer accepts goods under §2-606(1)(b) when, after an opportunity to inspect, he fails to make an effective rejection under §2-602(1). ProCD extended an opportunity to reject if a buyer should find the license terms unsatisfactory; Zeidenberg inspected the package, tried out the software, learned of the license, and did not reject the goods. We refer to §2-606 only to show that the opportunity to return goods can be important; acceptance of an offer differs from acceptance of goods after delivery, see Gillen v. Atalanta Systems, Inc., 997 F.2d 280, 284 n.1 (7th Cir. 1993); but the UCC consistently permits the parties to structure their relations so that the buyer has a chance to make a final decision after a detailed review.

Some portions of the UCC impose additional requirements on the way parties agree on terms. A disclaimer of the implied warranty of merchantability must be "conspicuous." UCC §2-316(2), incorporating UCC §1-201(10). Promises to make firm offers, or to negate oral modifications, must be "separately signed." UCC §§2-205, 2-209(2). These special provisos reinforce the impression that, so far as the UCC is concerned, other terms may be as inconspicuous as the forum-selection clause on the back of the cruise ship ticket in Carnival Lines. Zeidenberg has not located any Wisconsin case—for that matter, any case in any state—holding that under the UCC the ordinary terms found in shrinkwrap licenses require any special prominence, or otherwise are to be undercut rather than enforced. In the end, the terms of the license are conceptually identical to the contents of the package. Just as no court would dream of saying that SelectPhone (trademark) must contain 3,100 phone books rather than 3,000, or must have data no more than 30 days old, or must sell for $100 rather than $150—although any of these changes would be welcomed by the customer, if all other things were held constant—so, we believe, Wisconsin would not let the buyer pick and choose among terms. Terms of use are no less a part of "the product" than are the size of the database and the speed with which the software compiles listings. Competition among vendors, not judicial revision of a package's contents, is how consumers are protected in a market economy. Digital Equipment Corp. v. Uniq Digital Technologies, Inc., 73 F.3d 756 (7th Cir. 1996). ProCD has rivals, which may elect to compete by offering superior software, monthly updates, improved terms of use, lower price, or a better compromise among these elements. As we stressed above, adjusting terms in buyers' favor might help Matthew Zeidenberg today (he already has the software) but would lead to a response, such as a higher price, that might make consumers as a whole worse off. . . .

COMMENTS AND QUESTIONS

1. Courts are sharply split on the enforceability of shrinkwrap licenses. *ProCD* was the first court to enforce a shrinkwrap license; a number of courts before that time had refused to enforce them. See Step-Saver v. Wyse Technology, 939 F.3d 91 (3d Cir. 1991); Vault Corp. v. Quaid, Inc., 847 F.2d 255 (5th Cir. 1988); Arizona Retail Sys. v. Software Link, Inc., 831 F. Supp. 759 (D. Ariz. 1993); cf. Foresight Resource Corp. v. Pfortmiller, 719 F. Supp. 1006 (D. Kan. 1989) (dictum). Since *ProCD*, a majority of courts have enforced shrinkwrap licenses. See M.A. Mortenson Co. v. Timberline Software Corp., 998 P.2d 305 (Wash. 2000); Information Handling Servs. v. LRP, 2000 Copr. L. Decisions ¶28,177 (E.D. Pa. Sept. 20, 2000); Peerless Wall & Window Coverings v. Synchronics, 85 F. Supp. 2d 519 (W.D. Pa. 2000); Adobe v. One Stop Micro, 84 F. Supp. 2d 1086 (N.D. Cal. 2000).

A significant number of recent cases have refused to enforce shrinkwrap licenses, however. See Novell v. Network Trade Center, 25 F. Supp. 1218 (D. Utah 1997); Klocek v. Gateway, Inc., 104 F. Supp. 2d 1332 (D. Kan. 2000). Cf. Morgan Labs, Inc. v. Micro Data Base Sys., 41 U.S.P.Q.2d 1850 (N.D. Cal. 1997) (refusing to allow a shrinkwrap license to modify a prior signed contract). The reasoning of these cases differs. Some courts (*Arizona Retail*, for instance) follow the rationale of *Step-Saver*, holding that the shrinkwrap license should be treated as a "battle of the forms" under U.C.C. 2-207. Other courts (*Pfortmiller*, the district court in *Vault*) conclude that shrinkwrap licenses are unenforceable as "contracts of adhesion." And the Fifth Circuit in *Vault* relied on the federal intellectual property laws to preempt contrary provisions in shrinkwrap licenses. See *infra* section VI.D.

The contract of adhesion rationale is suspect. Under traditional doctrines of contract law, a "contract of adhesion" is a standardized contract prepared entirely by one party and, due to the disparity in bargaining power between the parties, is effectively offered on a "take it or leave it" basis. Contrary to the holding of the district court in *Vault*, contracts of adhesion are generally enforceable unless certain other factors (such as unconscionability) are present. According to the Restatement (Second) of Contracts, §211(3), "[w]here the other party has reason to believe that the party manifesting such assent would not do so if he knew that the writing contained a particular term, the term is not part of the agreement." Comment f states that "[r]eason to believe [that the adherent would not knowingly have signed] may be inferred from the fact that the term is bizarre or oppressive, from the fact that it eviscerates the nonstandard terms explicitly agreed to, or from the fact that it eliminates the dominant purpose of the transaction."

On the other hand, a shrinkwrap license is not an ordinary contract of adhesion. Unlike most form contracts, in this case the party bound by the contract does not even sign or otherwise manifest consent to the terms that bind her. Indeed, in many cases she may not even be aware of them.

2. UCITA would enforce shrinkwrap licenses, provided that there was in fact an opportunity for consumers who disagree with the terms of the license to obtain a full and effective refund. UCITA §208. UCITA would enforce any terms in a shrinkwrap license that were not unconscionable. In so doing, the drafters of UCITA expressly reject Restatement (2d) of Contracts §211. Dissatisfaction with the draft of these sections, particularly section 208, was strong in the academic community, certain industries, and among those interested in consumer rights:

> Shrinkwrap licenses represent a significant further step away from the basic idea of contract law, stretching even the concept of blanket assent beyond its limits. Here, there is no signed writing at all. Indeed, the "contract" to be enforced is only discovered by the purchaser after the actual commercial transaction has already taken place.[216] The "fiction" of blanket assent has given way to fantasy in the case of shrinkwrap licenses.
>
> Nor does the "notice assent" approach of most shrinkwrap licenses overcome this problem. In a typical mass-market software transaction, the consumer pays for software at the retail store and takes the box containing the software back to her home or office. Sometimes she will open the package relatively soon; in other circumstances, it could sit unopened for as long as a month.[217] When the box is opened, the user will encounter shrinkwrapped software. Assuming that she sees the license[218] and begins

---

216. Courts have been uniform in concluding that the commercially significant transaction that constitutes the basic "contract" is the exchange of money for software at the retail store, or (in the case of telephone orders) the telephonic agreement to exchange money for software.

217. For example, programs that are purchased as gifts are unlikely to be opened immediately. Nor are software programs that must be installed on a network likely to be opened immediately by busy system administrators.

As an interesting aside, the nontransferability provisions of most shrinkwrap licenses, if enforceable, make it a breach of contract to give computer programs or games as birthday or Christmas presents. While this particular restriction seems unlikely to be tested in court in the near future, it is evidence of just how removed shrinkwrap licenses are from commercial reality.

218. If our customer picks up the package the wrong way, she is unlikely to notice the license until after the package has been opened, and she has already "consented" to the terms of the license.

reading it before opening the package,[219] she will discover that she has in fact purchased only an option contract, and that she has (or once had) the "opportunity" to reject a new contract by returning the software to the store where she bought it (presumably at her own expense), and then relying on the timeliness of software vendors and the United States mail for her refund.

In these circumstances, it is simply unrealistic to believe that a failure to return the software for a refund constitutes any form of "agreement" to the terms of the form license. Even if we accept the notion of blanket assent uncritically, a significant portion of the consumers purchasing the software may be physically unable to return it for a refund. A second group may choose not to return the software because they believe the shrinkwrap license is unenforceable, a commonly held belief among software consumers and one with significant support in the current caselaw. A third group may choose not to return the software because it is simply too much effort, or because they need software right away and cannot afford to wait and select a different brand. A final group may object to particular terms in a license, but be unwilling to reject the software as a whole because of those objections.

The plight of this last group is particularly interesting. Shrinkwrap licenses purport to offer only a "yes or no" choice to consumers. [UCITA] ratifies this approach. This means that even where there is emphatically *not* a meeting of the minds on a particular term—for example, where a consumer expressly does not consent to that term —she may still be bound if she uses the software. At this point, we have come around 180 degrees from the doctrinal foundations of contract law. Contract law is based on agreement between the parties. Shrinkwrap licenses not only are not based on such agreement in any realistic sense, but may be enforceable even where it is utterly clear that they *do not* reflect agreement between the parties.

Mark A. Lemley, Intellectual Property and Shrinkwrap Licenses, 68 S. Cal. L. Rev. 1239 (1995) (footnotes omitted). See also Symposium: Intellectual Property and Contract Law in the Information Age: The Impact of Article 2B of the Uniform Commercial Code on the Future of Transactions in Information and Electronic Commerce, 13 Berkeley Tech. L.J. 809 (1998).

UCITA undoubtedly endorses the result in *ProCD*, though the current version of section 208 provides a rather more robust refund right than current shrinkwrap licenses seem to envision. On the refund right, see Jeffrey C. Selman & Christopher S. Chen, Steering the Titanic Clear of the Iceberg: Saving the Sale of Software From the Perils of Warranties, 31 U.S.F. L. Rev. 531 (1997). It is worth noting that recent public efforts actually to collect a refund from Microsoft as provided in the shrinkwrap license have proven difficult if not impossible.

Section 111 governs the conduct necessary to "manifest assent." Earlier drafts of Article 2B explicitly rejected the *Hill* result, providing that "mere retention of a record without objection is not a manifestation of assent." But the current version of UCITA removes this restriction and appears to endorse the result in *Hill*.

3. Why did shrinkwrap licenses develop in the software context? They were certainly a fixture of the mass-market software industry by the early 1980s. One answer may be that shrinkwrap licenses serve (or once served) as a declaration of the vendor's rights. Generally, proprietary rights provisions of shrinkwrap licenses

---

219. While the idea of "notice assent" is premised on the user's opportunity to reject the "bargain" by returning the software unopened, the user can learn of that option only if she actually reads the license before opening the package. In spite of this fact, the UCC draft provides that the shrinkwrap license is enforceable whether or not the user ever even learns of its existence by reading it. [UCITA draft §208.]

assert that the information contained in the accompanying computer software is confidential and proprietary to the vendor and may not be copied or disclosed without the vendor's permission. Software vendors who needed proof that they were not in fact disclosing their trade secrets by selling copies to whoever wanted them created the legal fiction that they were really licensing rather than selling their software. Because the "license" contained provisions that required customers to keep the software confidential, the trade secrets contained therein could be protected under decisions like *Data General.*

This rationale has much less force today, when it is clear that patent and copyright law are available to protect software sold on the mass market. Unlike trade secrets law, patent and copyright laws operate against the world and do not require proof of a confidential relationship (or, indeed, any relationship at all) between the parties.

4. Judge Easterbrook points out that certain contract terms have special contract formation procedures and requirements under the UCC. Finding none for shrinkwrap contracts, he reverts to the general formation procedure under Article 2. But is the Code section he relies on—section 2-204—the right one? Other courts have characterized shrinkwrap licenses under U.C.C. §2-207 (dealing with the battle of the forms) or U.C.C. §2-209 (dealing with modifications to an existing contract). The last provision seems particularly appropriate for a common class of shrinkwrap licenses that give no indication of the license terms until after the consumer has purchased the product and left the store.

Is *ProCD* such a case? The box containing the ProCD disks did not disclose the license terms but did at least indicate that there *were* additional terms contained in the box. Should this make a difference in deciding whether to enforce the terms?

5. In Judge Easterbrook's view, ProCD's business model relied heavily on the ability to price-discriminate between different classes of users.[4] Judge Easterbrook argues the benefits of this practice and of contracts to carry it out. Cf. Frank H. Easterbrook, Cyberspace and the Law of the Horse, 1996 U. Chi. Legal F. 205. Are there counterarguments or limits to the degree to which law ought to enable price discrimination? See the excerpt by Meurer in Section A, The Business Background, *supra.* And see generally, Wendy J. Gordon, Intellectual Property as Price Discrimination: Implications for Contract, 73 Chi.-Kent L. Rev. 1367 (1998).

b. *"Clickwrap" Licenses, Browsewrap Licenses, and Electronic Commerce*

The shrinkwrap license cases discussed so far have all been based on a rather traditional model of software distribution in which software is sold off the shelf in a storefront or delivered in a box via the mail. Increasingly, however, software is not distributed by these means at all. Rather, software (and other forms of digital

---

4. In fact, there was no evidence introduced in the case that indicated ProCD would be willing to authorize a use such as Zeidenberg's at any price. The price discrimination rationale is a construct based on Judge Easterbrook's assumption about what a rational actor might do.

information) is likely to be distributed over the Internet directly. This new distribution mechanism has a number of implications for the contract rules that govern the transactions.

Specht v. Netscape Communications Corp.
United States Court of Appeals for the Second Circuit
306 F.3d 17 (2d Cir. 2002)

SOTOMAYOR, Circuit Judge:

This is an appeal from a judgment of the Southern District of New York denying a motion by defendants-appellants Netscape Communications Corporation and its corporate parent, America Online, Inc. (collectively, "defendants" or "Netscape"), to compel arbitration and to stay court proceedings. In order to resolve the central question of arbitrability presented here, we must address issues of contract formation in cyberspace. Principally, we are asked to determine whether plaintiffs-appellees ("plaintiffs"), by acting upon defendants' invitation to download free software made available on defendants' webpage, agreed to be bound by the software's license terms (which included the arbitration clause at issue), even though plaintiffs could not have learned of the existence of those terms unless, prior to executing the download, they had scrolled down the webpage to a screen located below the download button. We agree with the district court that a reasonably prudent Internet user in circumstances such as these would not have known or learned of the existence of the license terms before responding to defendants' invitation to download the free software, and that defendants therefore did not provide reasonable notice of the license terms. In consequence, plaintiffs' bare act of downloading the software did not unambiguously manifest assent to the arbitration provision contained in the license terms. . . .

We therefore affirm the district court's denial of defendants' motion to compel arbitration and to stay court proceedings.

Background

I. Facts

In three related putative class actions, plaintiffs alleged that, unknown to them, their use of SmartDownload transmitted to defendants private information about plaintiffs' downloading of files from the Internet, thereby effecting an electronic surveillance of their online activities in violation of two federal statutes, the Electronic Communications Privacy Act, 18 U.S.C. §§2510 et seq., and the Computer Fraud and Abuse Act, 18 U.S.C. §1030.

Specifically, plaintiffs alleged that when they first used Netscape's Communicator—a software program that permits Internet browsing—the program created and stored on each of their computer hard drives a small text file known as a "cookie" that functioned "as a kind of electronic identification tag for future communications" between their computers and Netscape. Plaintiffs further alleged that when they installed SmartDownload—a separate software "plug-in" that served to enhance Communicator's browsing capabilities—SmartDownload created and stored on their computer hard drives another string of characters, known as a "Key," which similarly functioned as an identification tag in future communications with Netscape. According to the complaints in this case, each time a computer user employed Communicator to download a file from the Internet, SmartDownload "assume[d] from Communicator the task of downloading" the file and transmitted to Netscape the address of the file being downloaded together with the cookie created by Communicator and the Key created by Smart-Download. These processes, plaintiffs claim, constituted unlawful "eavesdropping" on users of Netscape's software products as well as on Internet websites from which users employing SmartDownload downloaded files.

In the time period relevant to this litigation, Netscape offered on its website various software programs, including Communicator and SmartDownload, which visitors to the site were invited to obtain free of charge. It is undisputed that five of the six named plaintiffs—Michael Fagan, John Gibson, Mark Gruber, Sean Kelly, and Sherry Weindorf—downloaded Communicator from the Netscape website. These plaintiffs acknowledge that when they proceeded to initiate installation of Communicator, they were automatically shown a scrollable text of that program's license agreement and were not permitted to complete the installation until they had clicked on a "Yes" button to indicate that they accepted all the license terms.[4] If a user attempted to install Communicator without clicking "Yes," the installation would be aborted. All five named user plaintiffs expressly agreed to Communicator's license terms by clicking "Yes." The Communicator license agreement that these plaintiffs saw made no mention of SmartDownload or other plug-in programs, and stated that "[t]hese terms apply to Netscape Communicator and Netscape Navigator" and that "all disputes relating to this Agreement (excepting any dispute relating to intellectual property rights)" are subject to "binding arbitration in Santa Clara County, California."

Although Communicator could be obtained independently of Smart-Download, all the named user plaintiffs, except Fagan, downloaded and installed Communicator in connection with downloading SmartDownload. Each of these plaintiffs allegedly arrived at a Netscape webpage captioned "SmartDownload Communicator" that urged them to "Download With Confidence Using Smart-Download!" At or near the bottom of the screen facing plaintiffs was the prompt "Start Download" and a tinted button labeled "Download." By clicking on the button, plaintiffs initiated the download of SmartDownload. Once that process was complete, SmartDownload, as its first plug-in task, permitted plaintiffs to

---

4. This kind of online software license agreement has come to be known as "clickwrap" (by analogy to "shrinkwrap," used in the licensing of tangible forms of software sold in packages) because it "presents the user with a message on his or her computer screen, requiring that the user manifest his or her assent to the terms of the license agreement by clicking on an icon. The product cannot be obtained or used unless and until the icon is clicked." *Specht,* 150 F. Supp.2d at 593-94 (footnote omitted). Just as breaking the shrinkwrap seal and using the enclosed computer program after encountering notice of the existence of governing license terms has been deemed by some courts to constitute assent to those terms in the context of tangible software, see, e.g., ProCD, Inc. v. Zeidenberg, 86 F.3d 1447, 1451 (7th Cir. 1996), so clicking on a webpage's clickwrap button after receiving notice of the existence of license terms has been held by some courts to manifest an Internet user's assent to terms governing the use of downloadable intangible software, see, e.g., Hotmail Corp. v. Van$ Money Pie Inc., 47 U.S.P.Q.2d 1020, 1025 (N.D.Cal. 1998).

proceed with downloading and installing Communicator, an operation that was accompanied by the clickwrap display of Communicator's license terms described above.

The signal difference between downloading Communicator and downloading SmartDownload was that no clickwrap presentation accompanied the latter operation. Instead, once plaintiffs Gibson, Gruber, Kelly, and Weindorf had clicked on the "Download" button located at or near the bottom of their screen, and the downloading of SmartDownload was complete, these plaintiffs encountered no further information about the plug-in program or the existence of license terms governing its use. The sole reference to SmartDownload's license terms on the "SmartDownload Communicator" webpage was located in text that would have become visible to plaintiffs only if they had scrolled down to the next screen.

Had plaintiffs scrolled down instead of acting on defendants' invitation to click on the "Download" button, they would have encountered the following invitation: "Please review and agree to the terms of the *Netscape SmartDownload software license agreement* before downloading and using the software." Plaintiffs Gibson, Gruber, Kelly, and Weindorf averred in their affidavits that they never saw this reference to the SmartDownload license agreement when they clicked on the "Download" button. They also testified during depositions that they saw no reference to license terms when they clicked to download SmartDownload, although under questioning by defendants' counsel, some plaintiffs added that they could not "remember" or be "sure" whether the screen shots of the SmartDownload page attached to their affidavits reflected precisely what they had seen on their computer screens when they downloaded SmartDownload.[10]

In sum, plaintiffs Gibson, Gruber, Kelly, and Weindorf allege that the process of obtaining SmartDownload contrasted sharply with that of obtaining Communicator. Having selected SmartDownload, they were required neither to express unambiguous assent to that program's license agreement nor even to view the license terms or become aware of their existence before proceeding with the invited download of the free plug-in program. Moreover, once these plaintiffs had initiated the download, the existence of SmartDownload's license terms was not mentioned while the software was running or at any later point in plaintiffs' experience of the product.

Even for a user who, unlike plaintiffs, did happen to scroll down past the download button, SmartDownload's license terms would not have been immediately displayed in the manner of Communicator's clickwrapped terms. Instead, if such a user had seen the notice of SmartDownload's terms and then clicked on the underlined invitation to review and agree to the terms, a hypertext link would have taken the user to a separate webpage entitled "License & Support Agreements." The first paragraph on this page read, in pertinent part:

> The use of each Netscape software product is governed by a license agreement. You must read and agree to the license agreement terms BEFORE acquiring a product.

10. In the screen shot of the SmartDownload webpage attached to Weindorf's affidavit, the reference to license terms is partially visible, though almost illegible, at the bottom of the screen. In the screen shots attached to the affidavits of Gibson, Gruber, and Kelly, the reference to license terms is not visible.

Please click on the appropriate link below to review the current license agreement for the product of interest to you before acquisition. For products available for download, you must read and agree to the license agreement terms BEFORE you install the software. If you do not agree to the license terms, do not download, install or use the software.

Below this paragraph appeared a list of license agreements, the first of which was "*License Agreement for Netscape Navigator and Netscape Communicator Product Family* (Netscape Navigator, Netscape Communicator and Netscape Smart-Download)." If the user clicked on that link, he or she would be taken to yet another webpage that contained the full text of a license agreement that was identical in every respect to the Communicator license agreement except that it stated that its "terms apply to Netscape Communicator, Netscape Navigator, and Netscape SmartDownload." The license agreement granted the user a nonexclusive license to use and reproduce the software, subject to certain terms:

BY CLICKING THE ACCEPTANCE BUTTON OR INSTALLING OR USING NETSCAPE COMMUNICATOR, NETSCAPE NAVIGATOR, OR NETSCAPE SMARTDOWNLOAD SOFTWARE (THE "PRODUCT"), THE INDIVIDUAL OR ENTITY LICENSING THE PRODUCT ("LICENSEE") IS CONSENTING TO BE BOUND BY AND IS BECOMING A PARTY TO THIS AGREEMENT. IF LICENSEE DOES NOT AGREE TO ALL OF THE TERMS OF THIS AGREEMENT, THE BUTTON INDICATING NON-ACCEPTANCE MUST BE SELECTED, AND LICENSEE MUST NOT INSTALL OR USE THE SOFTWARE.

Among the license terms was a provision requiring virtually all disputes relating to the agreement to be submitted to arbitration:

Unless otherwise agreed in writing, all disputes relating to this Agreement (excepting any dispute relating to intellectual property rights) shall be subject to final and binding arbitration in Santa Clara County, California, under the auspices of JAMS/EndDispute, with the losing party paying all costs of arbitration. . . .

II. *Proceedings Below*

In the district court, defendants moved to compel arbitration and to stay court proceedings pursuant to the Federal Arbitration Act ("FAA"), 9 U.S.C. §4, arguing that the disputes reflected in the complaints, like any other dispute relating to the SmartDownload license agreement, are subject to the arbitration clause contained in that agreement. Finding that Netscape's webpage, unlike typical examples of clickwrap, neither adequately alerted users to the existence of Smart-Download's license terms nor required users unambiguously to manifest assent to those terms as a condition of downloading the product, the court held that the user plaintiffs had not entered into the SmartDownload license agreement. *Specht*, 150 F. Supp.2d at 595-96.

[Defendants appealed]

Discussion . . .

III. Whether the User Plaintiffs Had Reasonable Notice of and Manifested Assent to the SmartDownload License Agreement

Whether governed by the common law or by Article 2 of the Uniform Commercial Code ("UCC"), a transaction, in order to be a contract, requires a manifestation of agreement between the parties. See Windsor Mills, Inc. v. Collins & Aikman Corp., 101 Cal. Rptr. 347, 350 (Cal. Ct. App. 1972) ("[C]onsent to, or acceptance of, the arbitration provision [is] necessary to create an agreement to arbitrate."); see also Cal. Com. Code §2204(1) ("A contract for sale of goods may be made in any manner sufficient to show agreement, including conduct by both parties which recognizes the existence of such a contract.").[13] Mutual manifestation of assent, whether by written or spoken word or by conduct, is the touchstone of contract. Binder v. Aetna Life Ins. Co., 89 Cal. Rptr.2d 540, 551 (Cal.Ct.App. 1999); cf. Restatement (Second) of Contracts §19(2) (1981) ("The conduct of a

---

13. The district court concluded that the SmartDownload transactions here should be governed by "California law as it relates to the sale of goods, including the Uniform Commercial Code in effect in California." *Specht*, 150 F. Supp.2d at 591. It is not obvious, however, that UCC Article 2 ("sales of goods") applies to the licensing of software that is downloadable from the Internet. Cf. Advent Sys. Ltd. v. Unisys Corp., 925 F.2d 670, 675 (3d Cir. 1991) ("The increasing frequency of computer products as subjects of commercial litigation has led to controversy over whether software is a 'good' or intellectual property. The [UCC] does not specifically mention software."); Lorin Brennan, Why Article 2 Cannot Apply to Software Transactions, PLI Patents, Copyrights, Trademarks, & Literary Property Course Handbook Series (Feb.-Mar.2001) (demonstrating the trend in case law away from application of UCC provisions to software sales and licensing and toward application of intellectual property principles). There is no doubt that a sale of tangible goods over the Internet is governed by Article 2 of the UCC. See, e.g., Butler v. Beer Across Am., 83 F. Supp.2d 1261, 1263-64 & n.6 (N.D.Ala. 2000) (applying Article 2 to an Internet sale of bottles of beer). Some courts have also applied Article 2, occasionally with misgivings, to sales of off-the-shelf software in tangible, packaged formats. See, e.g., ProCD, 86 F.3d at 1450 ("[W]e treat the [database] licenses as ordinary contracts accompanying the sale of products, and therefore as governed by the common law of contracts and the Uniform Commercial Code. Whether there are legal differences between 'contracts' and 'licenses' (which may matter under the copyright doctrine of first sale) is a subject for another day."); i.LAN Sys., Inc. v. NetScout Serv. Level Corp., 183 F. Supp.2d 328, 332 (D.Mass. 2002) (stating, in the context of a dispute between business parties, that "Article 2 technically does not, and certainly will not in the future, govern software licenses, but for the time being, the Court will assume that it does").

Downloadable software, however, is scarcely a "tangible" good, and, in part because software may be obtained, copied, or transferred effortlessly at the stroke of a computer key, licensing of such Internet products has assumed a vast importance in recent years. Recognizing that "a body of law based on images of the sale of manufactured goods ill fits licenses and other transactions in computer information," the National Conference of Commissioners on Uniform State Laws has promulgated the Uniform Computer Information Transactions Act ("UCITA"), a code resembling UCC Article 2 in many respects but drafted to reflect emergent practices in the sale and licensing of computer information. UCITA, prefatory note (rev. ed. Aug. 23, 2001) (available at www.ucitaonline.com/ucita.html). UCITA—originally intended as a new Article 2B to supplement Articles 2 and 2A of the UCC but later proposed as an independent code—has been adopted by two states, Maryland and Virginia. See Md. Code Ann. Com. Law §§22-101 *et seq.;* Va. Code Ann. §§59.1-501.1 *et seq.*

We need not decide today whether UCC Article 2 applies to Internet transactions in downloadable products. The district court's analysis and the parties' arguments on appeal show that, for present purposes, there is no essential difference between UCC Article 2 and the common law of contracts. We therefore apply the common law, with exceptions as noted.

party is not effective as a manifestation of his assent unless he intends to engage in the conduct and knows or has reason to know that the other party may infer from his conduct that he assents."). Although an onlooker observing the disputed transactions in this case would have seen each of the user plaintiffs click on the SmartDownload "Download" button, see Cedars Sinai Med. Ctr. v. Mid-West Nat'l Life Ins. Co., 118 F. Supp.2d 1002, 1008 (C.D.Cal. 2000) ("In California, a party's intent to contract is judged objectively, by the party's outward manifestation of consent."), a consumer's clicking on a download button does not communicate assent to contractual terms if the offer did not make clear to the consumer that clicking on the download button would signify assent to those terms, see *Windsor Mills,* 101 Cal. Rptr. at 351 ("[W]hen the offeree does not know that a proposal has been made to him this objective standard does not apply."). California's common law is clear that "an offeree, regardless of apparent manifestation of his consent, is not bound by inconspicuous contractual provisions of which he is unaware, contained in a document whose contractual nature is not obvious." *Id.;* see also Marin Storage & Trucking, Inc. v. Benco Contracting & Eng'g, Inc., 107 Cal. Rptr.2d 645, 651 (Cal.Ct.App. 2001) (same).

Arbitration agreements are no exception to the requirement of manifestation of assent. "This principle of knowing consent applies with particular force to provisions for arbitration." *Windsor Mills,* 101 Cal. Rptr. at 351. . . .

A. The Reasonably Prudent Offeree of Downloadable Software

Defendants argue that plaintiffs must be held to a standard of reasonable prudence and that, because notice of the existence of SmartDownload license terms was on the next scrollable screen, plaintiffs were on "inquiry notice" of those terms. We disagree with the proposition that a reasonably prudent offeree in plaintiffs' position would necessarily have known or learned of the existence of the SmartDownload license agreement prior to acting, so that plaintiffs may be held to have assented to that agreement with constructive notice of its terms. See Cal. Civ.Code §1589 ("A voluntary acceptance of the benefit of a transaction is equivalent to a consent to all the obligations arising from it, so far as the facts are known, or ought to be known, to the person accepting."). It is true that "[a] party cannot avoid the terms of a contract on the ground that he or she failed to read it before signing." *Marin Storage & Trucking,* 107 Cal. Rptr.2d at 651. But courts are quick to add: "An exception to this general rule exists when the writing does not appear to be a contract and the terms are not called to the attention of the recipient. In such a case, no contract is formed with respect to the undisclosed term." *Id.;* cf. Cory v. Golden State Bank, 157 Cal. Rptr. 538, 541 (Cal.Ct.App. 1979) ("[T]he provision in question is effectively hidden from the view of money order purchasers until after the transactions are completed. . . . Under these circumstances, it must be concluded that the Bank's money order purchasers are not chargeable with either actual or constructive notice of the service charge provision, and therefore cannot be deemed to have consented to the provision as part of their transaction with the Bank."). . . .

[R]eceipt of a physical document containing contract terms or notice thereof is frequently deemed, in the world of paper transactions, a sufficient circumstance to place the offeree on inquiry notice of those terms. "Every person who has actual notice of circumstances sufficient to put a prudent man upon inquiry as to a particular fact, has constructive notice of the fact itself in all cases in which, by prosecuting such inquiry, he might have learned such fact." Cal. Civ.Code §19. These principles apply equally to the emergent world of online product delivery, pop-up screens, hyperlinked pages, clickwrap licensing, scrollable documents, and urgent admonitions to "Download Now!". What plaintiffs saw when they were being invited by defendants to download this fast, free plug-in called SmartDownload was a screen containing praise for the product and, at the very bottom of the screen, a "Download" button. Defendants argue that under the principles set forth in the cases cited above, a "fair and prudent person using ordinary care" would have been on inquiry notice of SmartDownload's license terms. *Shacket,* 651 F. Supp. at 690.

We are not persuaded that a reasonably prudent offeree in these circumstances would have known of the existence of license terms. Plaintiffs were responding to an offer that did not carry an immediately visible notice of the existence of license terms or require unambiguous manifestation of assent to those terms. Thus, plaintiffs' "apparent manifestation of . . . consent" was to terms "contained in a document whose contractual nature [was] not obvious." *Windsor Mills,* 101 Cal. Rptr. at 351. Moreover, the fact that, given the position of the scroll bar on their computer screens, plaintiffs may have been aware that an unexplored portion of the Netscape webpage remained below the download button does not mean that they reasonably should have concluded that this portion contained a notice of license terms. In their deposition testimony, plaintiffs variously stated that they used the scroll bar "[o]nly if there is something that I feel I need to see that is on—that is off the page," or that the elevated position of the scroll bar suggested the presence of "mere [ ] formalities, standard lower banner links" or "that the page is bigger than what I can see." Plaintiffs testified, and defendants did not refute, that plaintiffs were in fact unaware that defendants intended to attach license terms to the use of SmartDownload.

We conclude that in circumstances such as these, where consumers are urged to download free software at the immediate click of a button, a reference to the existence of license terms on a submerged screen is not sufficient to place consumers on inquiry or constructive notice of those terms. The SmartDownload webpage screen was "printed in such a manner that it tended to conceal the fact that it was an express acceptance of [Netscape's] rules and regulations." *Larrus,* 266 P.2d at 147. Internet users may have, as defendants put it, "as much time as they need[ ]" to scroll through multiple screens on a webpage, but there is no reason to assume that viewers will scroll down to subsequent screens simply because screens are there. When products are "free" and users are invited to download them in the absence of reasonably conspicuous notice that they are about to bind themselves to contract terms, the transactional circumstances cannot be fully analogized to those in the paper world of arm's-length bargaining. In the next two sections, we discuss case law and other legal authorities that have addressed the circumstances of computer sales, software licensing, and online transacting. Those authorities tend strongly to support our conclusion that plaintiffs did not manifest assent to SmartDownload's license terms.

B. Shrinkwrap Licensing and Related Practices

Defendants cite certain well-known cases involving shrinkwrap licensing and related commercial practices in support of their contention that plaintiffs became bound by the SmartDownload license terms by virtue of inquiry notice. [The Court discusses *Hill*, *ProCD*, and *Mortenson*].

These cases do not help defendants. To the extent that they hold that the purchaser of a computer or tangible software is contractually bound after failing to object to printed license terms provided with the product, *Hill* and *Brower* do not differ markedly from the cases involving traditional paper contracting discussed in the previous section. Insofar as the purchaser in *ProCD* was confronted with conspicuous, mandatory license terms every time he ran the software on his computer, that case actually undermines defendants' contention that downloading in the absence of conspicuous terms is an act that binds plaintiffs to those terms. In *Mortenson,* the full text of license terms was printed on each sealed diskette envelope inside the software box, printed again on the inside cover of the user manual, and notice of the terms appeared on the computer screen every time the purchaser executed the program. *Mortenson,* 970 P.2d at 806. In sum, the foregoing cases are clearly distinguishable from the facts of the present action.

C. Online Transactions

Cases in which courts have found contracts arising from Internet use do not assist defendants, because in those circumstances there was much clearer notice than in the present case that a user's act would manifest assent to contract terms. [The court discussed several clickwrap license cases, and also referred to UCITA as a relevant statement of analogous rules].

After reviewing the California common law and other relevant legal authority, we conclude that under the circumstances here, plaintiffs' downloading of Smart-Download did not constitute acceptance of defendants' license terms. Reasonably conspicuous notice of the existence of contract terms and unambiguous manifestation of assent to those terms by consumers are essential if electronic bargaining is to have integrity and credibility. We hold that a reasonably prudent offeree in plaintiffs' position would not have known or learned, prior to acting on the invitation to download, of the reference to SmartDownload's license terms hidden below the "Download" button on the next screen. We affirm the district court's conclusion that the user plaintiffs, including Fagan, are not bound by the arbitration clause contained in those terms.

Conclusion

For the foregoing reasons, we affirm the district court's denial of defendants' motion to compel arbitration and to stay court proceedings.

COMMENTS AND QUESTIONS

1. Clickwrap and browsewrap licenses differ in significant respects from shrinkwrap licenses. First, bits sent over a modem seem less like traditional, tangible goods to which Article 2 has traditionally applied. This doesn't necessarily

mean that the information in question is licensed, of course. Software sold over the Internet is still distributed in the form of copies, at least in a copyright law sense; it's just that those copies are created at the buyer's site rather than being shipped there in physical form. Further, most of the indicia of sale in a mass-market transaction—the possession of one copy, with perpetual use rights in exchange for a single lump-sum payment—are still present in an online transaction. But even if the transaction looks more like a sale than a lease (or license), it is more and more difficult to apply Article 2 to such a deal, except perhaps by analogy.

Second, the nature of online sales gives vendors an opportunity to avoid the problems of shrinkwrap licenses entirely, by disclosing terms to buyers and obtaining an agreement to those terms before the purchase is completed. It is relatively common for Web sites to require agreement to certain terms and conditions by asking the user to click "OK" before proceeding. Such an agreement, entered into before the vendor sells the software or other information, is certainly a contract of adhesion. The buyer has no realistic choice other than to "take it or leave it." It is not a shrinkwrap license, however. The buyer has the opportunity to read and agree to the terms before she pays her money. It is not surprising, therefore, that such "clickwrap" licenses are easier to enforce than their shrinkwrap counterparts. See i.Lan Systems v. Netscout, 183 F. Supp. 328 (D. Mass. 2002); Caspi v. Microsoft Network LLC, 732 A.2d 528 (N.J. App. Div. 1999); Hotmail Corp. v. Van$ Money Pie, 47 U.S.P.Q.2d 1020 (N.D. Cal. 1998) (assuming such an agreement was enforceable, without discussing the issue).

2. Does the consumer really benefit from being able to see the terms in advance if they still have no choice regarding what those terms are? Is the real objection to shrinkwrap licenses their immutable monolithic character, and not how they are presented to the consumer? Cf. Robert P. Merges, Intellectual Property and the Costs of Commercial Exchange: A Review Essay, 93 Mich. L. Rev. 1570, 1612 (1995) (suggesting that shrinkwrap license terms should be preempted when there is sufficient uniformity in the industry that the terms in effect amount to "private legislation" by software vendors); Maureen O'Rourke, Drawing the Boundary Between Copyright and Contract: Copyright Preemption of Software License Terms, 45 Duke L.J. 479 (1995); Maureen A. O'Rourke, Copyright Preemption After the *ProCD* Case: A Market-Based Approach, 12 Berkeley Tech. L.J. 53 (1997).

3. Despite the obvious legal advantages to giving consumers terms to review and approve before entering into a contract, many Web sites (like the one in *Specht*) do not in fact require purchasers to read and agree to their terms. Not surprisingly, courts have generally refused to enforce such unilateral statements as contracts. In addition to *Specht* and the cases it discusses, see Ticketmaster Corp. v. Tickets.com, 2000 WL 525390 (C.D. Cal. March 27, 2000); Westcode, Inc. v. RBE Electronics, Inc., 2000 WL 124566 (E.D. Pa. Feb. 1, 2000). Can you think of any reason why they wouldn't do so? What does such a policy say about the importance of the terms to the vendor? To the transaction?

═══ ### Hill v. Gateway 2000, Inc.
═══ *United States Court of Appeals for the Seventh Circuit*
═══ *105 F.3d 1147 (7th Cir. 1997)*

EASTERBROOK, Circuit Judge.

A customer picks up the phone, orders a computer, and gives a credit card number. Presently a box arrives, containing the computer and a list of terms, said to govern unless the customer returns the computer within 30 days. Are these terms effective as the parties' contract, or is the contract term-free because the order-taker did not read any terms over the phone and elicit the customer's assent?

One of the terms in the box containing a Gateway 2000 system was an arbitration clause. Rich and Enza Hill, the customers, kept the computer more than 30 days before complaining about its components and performance. They filed suit in federal court arguing, among other things, that the product's shortcomings make Gateway a racketeer (mail and wire fraud are said to be the predicate offenses), leading to treble damages under RICO for the Hills and a class of all other purchasers. Gateway asked the district court to enforce the arbitration clause; the judge refused, writing that "[t]he present record is insufficient to support a finding of a valid arbitration agreement between the parties or that the plaintiffs were given adequate notice of the arbitration clause." Gateway took an immediate appeal, as is its right.

The Hills say that the arbitration clause did not stand out: they concede noticing the statement of terms but deny reading it closely enough to discover the agreement to arbitrate, and they ask us to conclude that they therefore may go to court. Yet an agreement to arbitrate must be enforced "save upon such grounds as exist at law or in equity for the revocation of any contract." 9 U.S.C. §2. Doctor's Associates, Inc. v. Casarotto, —U.S.—, 116 S. Ct. 1652, 134 L. Ed.2d 902 (1996), holds that this provision of the Federal Arbitration Act is inconsistent with any requirement that an arbitration clause be prominent. A contract need not be read to be effective; people who accept take the risk that the unread terms may in retrospect prove unwelcome. Carr v. CIGNA Securities, Inc., 95 F.3d 544, 547 (7th Cir. 1996); Chicago Pacific Corp. v. Canada Life Assurance Co., 850 F.2d 334 (7th Cir. 1988). Terms inside Gateway's box stand or fall together. If they constitute the parties' contract because the Hills had an opportunity to return the computer after reading them, then all must be enforced.

ProCD, Inc. v. Zeidenberg, 86 F.3d 1447 (7th Cir. 1996), holds that terms inside a box of software bind consumers who use the software after an opportunity to read the terms and to reject them by returning the product. Likewise, Carnival Cruise Lines, Inc. v. Shute, 499 U.S. 585, 111 S. Ct. 1522, 113 L. Ed.2d 622 (1991), enforces a forum-selection clause that was included among three pages of terms attached to a cruise ship ticket. *ProCD* and *Carnival Cruise Lines* exemplify the many commercial transactions in which people pay for products with terms to follow; *ProCD* discusses others. 86 F.3d at 1451-52. The district court concluded in *ProCD* that the contract is formed when the consumer pays for the software; as a result, the court held, only terms known to the consumer at that moment are part of the contract, and provisos inside the box do not count. Although this is one way a contract could be formed, it is not the only way: "A vendor, as master of the offer, may invite acceptance by conduct, and may propose limitations on the kind of conduct that constitutes acceptance. A buyer may accept by performing the acts the vendor proposes to treat as acceptance." *Id.* at 1452. Gateway shipped computers with the same sort of accept-or-return offer *ProCD* made to users of its software. *ProCD* relied on the Uniform Commercial Code rather than any peculiarities of Wisconsin law; both Illinois and South Dakota, the two states whose law might govern relations between Gateway and the Hills, have adopted the UCC; neither side has pointed us to any atypical doctrines in those states that might be pertinent; *ProCD* therefore applies to this dispute.

Plaintiffs ask us to limit *ProCD* to software, but where's the sense in that? *ProCD* is about the law of contract, not the law of software. Payment preceding the revelation of full terms is common for air transportation, insurance, and many other endeavors. Practical considerations support allowing vendors to enclose the full legal terms with their products. Cashiers cannot be expected to read legal documents to customers before ringing up sales. If the staff at the other end of the phone for direct-sales operations such as Gateway's had to read the four-page statement of terms before taking the buyer's credit card number, the droning voice would anesthetize rather than enlighten many potential buyers. Others would hang up in a rage over the waste of their time. And oral recitation would not avoid customers' assertions (whether true or feigned) that the clerk did not read term X to them, or that they did not remember or understand it. Writing provides benefits for both sides of commercial transactions. Customers as a group are better off when vendors skip costly and ineffectual steps such as telephonic recitation, and use instead a simple approve-or-return device. Competent adults are bound by such documents, read or unread. For what little it is worth, we add that the box from Gateway was crammed with software. The computer came with an operating system, without which it was useful only as a boat anchor. See Digital Equipment Corp. v. Uniq Digital Technologies, Inc., 73 F.3d 756, 761 (7th Cir. 1996). Gateway also included many application programs. So the Hills' effort to limit *ProCD* to software would not avail them factually, even if it were sound legally—which it is not.

For their second sally, the Hills contend that *ProCD* should be limited to executory contracts (to licenses in particular), and therefore does not apply because both parties' performance of this contract was complete when the box arrived at their home. This is legally and factually wrong: legally because the question at hand concerns the formation of the contract rather than its performance, and factually because both contracts were incompletely performed. *ProCD* did not depend on the fact that the seller characterized the transaction as a license rather than as a contract; we treated it as a contract for the sale of goods and reserved the question whether for other purposes a "license" characterization might be preferable. 86 F.3d at 1450. All debates about characterization to one side, the transaction in *ProCD* was no more executory than the one here: Zeidenberg paid for the software and walked out of the store with a box under his arm, so if arrival of the box with the product ends the time for revelation of contractual terms, then the time ended in *ProCD* before Zeidenberg opened the box. But of course *ProCD* had not completed performance with delivery of the box, and neither had Gateway. One element of the transaction was the warranty, which obliges sellers to fix defects in their products. The Hills have invoked Gateway's warranty and are not satisfied with its response, so they are not well positioned to say that Gateway's obligations were fulfilled when the motor carrier unloaded the box. What is more, both *ProCD* and Gateway promised to help customers to use their products. Long-term service and information obligations are common in the computer business, on both hardware and software sides. Gateway offers "lifetime service" and has a round-the-clock telephone hotline to fulfil this promise. Some vendors spend more money helping customers use their products than on developing and manufacturing them. The document in Gateway's box includes promises of future performance that some consumers value highly; these promises bind Gateway just as the arbitration clause binds the Hills.

Next the Hills insist that *ProCD* is irrelevant because Zeidenberg was a "merchant" and they are not. Section 2-207(2) of the UCC, the infamous battle-of-the-forms section, states that "additional terms [following acceptance of an offer] are to be construed as proposals for addition to a contract. Between merchants such terms become part of the contract unless . . .". Plaintiffs tell us that *ProCD* came out as it did only because Zeidenberg was a "merchant" and the terms inside *ProCD*'s box were not excluded by the "unless" clause. This argument pays scant attention to the opinion in *ProCD*, which concluded that, when there is only one form, "§2-207 is irrelevant." 86 F.3d at 1452. The question in *ProCD* was not whether terms were added to a contract after its formation, but how and when the contract was formed—in particular, whether a vendor may propose that a contract of sale be formed, not in the store (or over the phone) with the payment of money or a general "send me the product," but after the customer has had a chance to inspect both the item and the terms. *ProCD* answers "yes," for merchants and consumers alike. Yet again, for what little it is worth we observe that the Hills misunderstand the setting of *ProCD*. A "merchant" under the UCC "means a person who deals in goods of the kind or otherwise by his occupation holds himself out as having knowledge or skill peculiar to the practices or goods involved in the transaction", §2-104(1). Zeidenberg bought the product at a retail store, an uncommon place for merchants to acquire inventory. His corporation put *ProCD*'s database on the Internet for anyone to browse, which led to the litigation but did not make Zeidenberg a software merchant.

At oral argument the Hills propounded still another distinction: the box containing *ProCD*'s software displayed a notice that additional terms were within, while the box containing Gateway's computer did not. The difference is functional, not legal. Consumers browsing the aisles of a store can look at the box, and if they are unwilling to deal with the prospect of additional terms can leave the box alone, avoiding the transactions costs of returning the package after reviewing its contents. Gateway's box, by contrast, is just a shipping carton; it is not on display anywhere. Its function is to protect the product during transit, and the information on its sides is for the use of handlers rather than would-be purchasers.

Perhaps the Hills would have had a better argument if they were first alerted to the bundling of hardware and legal-ware after opening the box and wanted to return the computer in order to avoid disagreeable terms, but were dissuaded by the expense of shipping. What the remedy would be in such a case—could it exceed the shipping charges?—is an interesting question, but one that need not detain us because the Hills knew before they ordered the computer that the carton would include some important terms, and they did not seek to discover these in advance. Gateway's ads state that their products come with limited warranties and lifetime support. How limited was the warranty—30 days, with service contingent on shipping the computer back, or five years, with free onsite service? What sort of support was offered? Shoppers have three principal ways to discover these things. First, they can ask the vendor to send a copy before deciding whether to buy. The Magnuson-Moss Warranty Act requires firms to distribute their warranty terms on request, 15 U.S.C. §2302(b)(1)(A); the Hills do not contend that Gateway would have refused to enclose the remaining terms too. Concealment would be bad for business, scaring some customers away and leading to excess returns from others. Second, shoppers can consult public sources (computer magazines, the Web sites of vendors) that may contain this information. Third, they may inspect the documents after the product's delivery. Like Zeidenberg, the Hills took the third option. By keeping the computer beyond 30 days, the Hills accepted Gateway's offer, including the arbitration clause.

The Hills' remaining arguments, including a contention that the arbitration clause is unenforceable as part of a scheme to defraud, do not require more than a citation to Prima Paint Corp. v. Flood & Conklin Mfg. Co., 388 U.S. 395, 87 S. Ct. 1801, 18 L. Ed.2d 1270 (1967). Whatever may be said pro and con about the cost and efficacy of arbitration (which the Hills disparage) is for Congress and the contracting parties to consider. Claims based on RICO are no less arbitrable than those founded on the contract or the law of torts. Shearson/American Express, Inc. v. McMahon, 482 U.S. 220, 238-42, 107 S. Ct. 2332, 2343-46, 96 L. Ed.2d 185 (1987). The decision of the district court is vacated, and this case is remanded with instructions to compel the Hills to submit their dispute to arbitration.

COMMENTS AND QUESTIONS

1. Does it really comport with traditional principles of offer and acceptance to conclude that contract terms can always be added after the fact? Would *Hill* come out differently if the piece of paper included in the box was a demand for an additional $1,000? A contract term providing that the computer could not be used for more than 30 days? A provision that there were no warranties at all associated with the computer? If these terms were added after the fact, most courts (perhaps even *Hill*) would doubtless invalidate them. So why does it permit the term at issue here? Is it because it considers the term unimportant—at least in the sense that the deal wouldn't have foundered on it? Cf. Brower v. Gateway 2000, 676 N.Y.S.2d 579 (Sup. Ct. App. Div. 1998) (concluding in accordance with *Hill* that the arbitration term formed part of the contract, but going on to conclude that the term itself was substantively unconscionable). If the term isn't critical to the deal, why enforce it at all? Article 2 is full of default rules that the law will supply where the parties haven't bothered to agree about the issue. Realistically, isn't that exactly what happened here?

2. *Hill* seems to expand *ProCD* significantly. First, it is clear that the rule of *ProCD* is not limited to software—or even to "licenses." Any transaction can presumably be altered after the fact by the provision of additional terms. After *Hill*, one can readily imagine sales of standard goods and even services being made subject to these additional contract terms. Further, *Hill* dispenses with the *ProCD* requirement of at least some manifestation of assent to the terms—satisfied in the classic shrinkwrap case by tearing open the package after being offered an option to return it. Where is the "assent" here? Keeping the computer? Does silence really imply consent in this context, even when it might actually mean that the buyer never discovered the terms (or for that matter, didn't open the box in time)? Finally, the apparent requirement in *ProCD* that notice of additional terms be given before sale (in that case, on the outside of the box) disappears without discussion in *Hill*.

One way to approach this question is to ask whether the rule in *Hill* treats the parties neutrally. Suppose a consumer mails additional terms to sellers after she buys a product and in that term sheet announces that a failure to object to those terms (and to come to her house to refund her money and take back the software) implies assent. Would Judge Easterbrook enforce such a "contract"? After *Hill*, is there any legitimate reason not to?

PROBLEMS

Problem 6-1. Megaware, a major vendor of over-the-counter applications software, desires to characterize its transactions with consumers as sales rather than licenses. Megaware places its software in a box on store shelves. Conspicuous on the front of the box is a statement "THIS SOFTWARE IS FOR LICENSE, NOT FOR SALE." Megaware enforces a company policy that software stores refuse to release its software to a customer unless they sign a preprinted form "License Agreement" that Megaware has provided. Stores keep the forms behind their counter, and present them to customers at the point of sale. All other economic aspects of the transaction remain the same, however: the customer pays one price in exchange for perpetual rights to use one copy of the software, which they physically take with them.

Has Megaware sold, leased, or licensed its software? Does it matter whether the market for Megaware's software is composed of individual consumers or of businesses?

Problem 6-2. Terrell, an individual, buys a computer game from her local Brainiac Software outlet. The game is manufactured by Genesis Systems. Genesis has included inside the box a shrinkwrap license agreement. When Terrell returns home from the Brainiac store and opens her software, she discovers and reads the agreement, which contains terms that differ from those the UCC would otherwise imply. She nonetheless loads the game into her computer and plays it. The next day, she mails a postcard to Genesis that reads as follows:

> To whom it may concern: Thank you for your offer of additional terms to our recent contract. However, I must decline your offer. If you wish to cancel the contract, you may do so by appearing at my residence within the next 10 days to refund my money and collect your computer disk.

What terms govern the transaction under U.C.C. §2-207? Under UCITA?

---

2. Extra-Legal Enforcement: Self-Help and the Like

If a shrinkwrap, clickwrap, or browsewrap license does not create an enforceable contract, the rights of the parties will be a function of the default rules contained in the UCC or in the common law of contracts. Even if such a license forms a binding contract, though, it does not necessarily follow that every term in the license will be enforced. Terms that violate some public policy may be stricken from a contract. For example, in America Online v. Superior Court, 90 Cal. App. 4th 1, 108 Cal. Rptr. 2d 699 (2001), the court refused to enforce choice of forum and choice of law clauses in AOL subscriber agreements because they would unfairly disadvantage plaintiff consumers, denying them their rights under California law. *Accord* Williams v. America Online, 43 UCC Rep. Serv. 2d 1101 (Mass. Super. Ct. Feb. 8, 2001). As courts tend increasingly to enforce software licenses, the enforceability of particular terms takes on added significance. See Ryan J. Casamiquela, Contractual Assent and Enforceability in Cyberspace, 17 Berkeley Tech. L.J. 475 (2002) (concluding that clickwrap licenses are likely to be enforceable, but that particular terms may not be). In this section and the next, we consider two common but controversial types of contract provisions.

American Computer Trust Leasing v. Jack Farrell Implement Co.
United States District Court for the District of Minnesota
763 F. Supp. 1473 (D. Minn. 1991)

DOTY, J.

[This case arose out of the following facts: Plaintiff American Computer Trust Leasing (ACTL), a computer hardware leasing firm affiliated with a software firm called Automatic Data Processing, Inc. (ADP), brought suit against defendants Boerboom International, Inc. (Boerboom) and Jack Farrell Implement Co. (Farrell) to collect payments for computer hardware leased from ACTL. Defendants were agricultural equipment dealers who leased hardware and licensed software designed by ADP especially for farm equipment dealerships. Boerboom and Farrell each claimed that their obligation should be excused because the hardware did not work properly. The defendants also brought various counterclaims against plaintiffs ACTL and ADP, Navistar International Transportation Corporation (formerly International Harvester) (IH) and J.I. Case Company (Case), including a claim their computer software was wrongfully deactivated under the provisions of various state and federal statutes. The following excerpt is from the district court opinion granting plaintiffs' motion for summary judgment and dismissing the counterclaims. This opinion was in turn affirmed and remanded in part. See 967 F.2d 1208 (8th Cir. 1992).]

It is undisputed that ADP did deactivate Farrell's software. The deactivation occurred, however, as a result of Farrell's nonpayment under the terms of the software license agreement. Both Boerboom and Farrell signed agreements providing that the licenses granted by ADP for software could be canceled upon the client's default. Moreover, the software license agreements expressly provided that ADP retain full ownership of the software used by Boerboom and Farrell. Both Boerboom and Farrell stopped paying the software license fees due under the software license agreements. Steven Farrell testified that Farrell was aware of the fact that software services would be discontinued if payments were not made. After Farrell's account had fallen significantly past due, ADP notified Farrell on June 30, 1987 that it would terminate all processing and support services on July 8, 1987 if payment was not received by that date. On July 8, 1987, ADP deactivated Farrell's software as previously warned. After Farrell discovered that its software had been shut off for nonpayment, Farrell paid the amounts past due on its account and ADP promptly reactivated the software. At that point, ADP contends that Farrell disconnected its modem so that ADP could no longer access the system for service and support. Farrell made no further payments to ADP although ADP contends that Farrell continued to use ADP software and hardware.

The software deactivation claims do not support a RICO violation because the federal and state extortion statutes cited by the defendants do not apply to those claims based on the foregoing facts. The defendants assert that the software deactivation constitutes "extortion" in violation of Minn.Stat. §§609.27, 609.275 and 18 U.S.C. §§875, 1951. Violation of 18 U.S.C. §875 is not a racketeering activity listed under §1961(1) and thus cannot support the RICO claims. As discussed above, ADP suspended the defendants' use of its software because Boerboom requested deactivation when it changed to another type of computer system and because Farrell stopped paying ADP the license fees due under its software license agreement. ADP had a legal right to deactivate the defendants' software pursuant to the contracts and the extortion statutes do not apply. The federal statute defines extortion as the "obtaining of property from another, without his consent, induced by wrongful use of actual or threatened force, violence, or fear, or under color of official right." 18 U.S.C. §1951(b)(2). The Minnesota statute similarly requires "unlawful" activities. Minn.Stat. §609.27. Because ADP's deactivation was not unlawful or wrongful but merely an exercise of its rights under the software license agreement, its deactivation does not violate either extortion statute and thus is not a racketeering activity.

COMMENTS AND QUESTIONS

1. Software vendors whose customers default on lease payments or other obligations related to the software are in a difficult position. Unlike real property, it is not easy to repossess intellectual property. Even if the software vendor is entitled to the return of its computer disks, copies of its program may remain resident in off-site backup tapes, on floppy disks, on hard drives, or in a computer network. If the vendor's goal is to prevent the defaulting party from making any use of the software, it may be put to the time-consuming and ultimately impossible task of policing the computer systems of another company.

Some software vendors have tried to get around this problem by disabling the software of a nonpaying user. The simplest method of attack is the brute-force method—the software vendor simply enters the company (physically or virtually) and disables the software. A more sophisticated vendor might plant "logic bombs" in its software before ever releasing it. The programmer may, for example, embed in the code a "refresher" lock that will shut down the program automatically if the programmer doesn't supply the proper key every so often (say, every six months). If the company stops payment, the vendor doesn't have to do anything—the software will simply stop working at some point.

2. The acceptability of self-help deactivation of a user's computer or program is hotly disputed. Notwithstanding the *Farrell* case above, courts have gener-

ally not been sympathetic to software vendors who apply such self-help remedies. In one case, a vendor who went to a customer site under the pretext of providing software maintenance and modified the program to shut down at a specific time was arrested and charged with computer tampering, a felony in New York! See Lance Rose, Next Time, Use a Collection Agency, Wired, May 1994, at 2. Virginia has a similar statute. Va. Code §18.2-152.7:1. Civil remedies are sometimes also available to the user whose software is affected. See Clayton X-Ray Co. v. Professional Systems Corp., 812 S.W.2d 565 (Mo. Ct. App. 1991) (finding software vendor liable for conversion and awarding punitive damages).

Even the pre-programmed logic bombs do not fare well in court, although their use may not be criminal. See Franks & Sons, Inc. v. Information Solutions, Inc., 1989 Computer Indus. Lit. Rptr. 8927 (N.D. Okla. Dec. 8, 1988) (enjoining the use of logic bomb); Werner, Zaroff, Slotnick, Stern & Askenazy v. Lewis, 588 N.Y.S.2d 960 (Civ. Ct. 1992) (awarding damages in the amount necessary to fix the software after the bomb "exploded," plus punitive damages).

3. Should the permissibility of self-help depend on whether the limitations are inherent in the device, or whether they are activated by the seller during a dispute? Whether the seller is in the right—that is, the seller turns out to have just cause to terminate the contract?

For a suggestion that lawfulness of logic bombs should depend on whether they were disclosed to the user at the time the original transaction occurred, see Esther C. Roditti, Is Self-Help a Lawful Contractual Remedy?, 21 Rutgers Computer & Tech. L.J. 431 (1995).

4. An increasing number of software vendors do not sell or license copies of their programs at all. Rather, they retain control over the programs, which customers access remotely when they want to use them. This "applications software provider" (or ASP) model can cause some problems for customers, who must wait to access the program each time they want to use it, and who face the prospect of losing access to their data if the ASP goes out of business or its server goes down. But the ASP model does give software vendors much more control over the uses that are made of its software. The ASP can monitor and charge for multiple uses by a single corporation, for example. And ASPs have an automatic form of "self-help": they can simply deny a customer access to their server in case of a dispute between the two. While refusing access may breach the ASP license agreement, it doesn't subject the ASP to tort or criminal liability, because the ASP doesn't need access to the customer's computer in order to block access.

5. The drafters of UCITA have struggled with the problem of self-help. The current draft permits a licensor to use self-help to regain control of copies of a program or prevent the licensee from continuing to use the program, but only if self-help can be exercised without a breach of the peace, without personal injury, and without physical damage to other information or property. UCITA §815(b). Section 815(e) precludes self-help if the information licensed is inextricably mingled with data the licensor doesn't own. But section 815(b) would appear to permit self-help that results in the destruction of the licensee's own data, so long as there is not "physical damage" to computers.

The most likely form of self-help in the computer context—shutting down access by electronic means—is further governed by UCITA §816. That section precludes electronic self-help altogether in mass market transactions. UCITA

§816(b). In other transactions, the parties can agree to the use of electronic self-help if they separately assent to the term, and if the licensor provides notice before exercising the self-help right. UCITA §816(c)-(d). In the case of electronic self-help, the licensee has a right to recover for its losses due to the use of self-help. UCITA §816(e)-(f).

For criticism of UCITA's rules allowing electronic self-help measures, see Julie E. Cohen, Copyright and the Jurisprudence of Self-Help, 13 Berkeley Tech. L.J. 1089 (1998) (arguing that the provisions of proposed UCITA authorize an unprecedented degree of intrusion into private homes and offices, that they lack a sound theoretical basis, and that their adoption would threaten constitutionally mandated limits on copyright protection; and concluding that the law should afford *users* of digital works rights of electronic self-help where necessary to preserve the copyright balance). See also Gary J. Edwards, Comment, Self-Help Repossession of Software: Should Repossession Be Available in Article 2B of the UCC?, 58 U. Pitt. L. Rev. 763 (1997) (arguing that "the law of computer software transactions should not recognize any form of electronic repossession. Other remedies, such as injunctive relief, are easily obtainable and are much more capable of protecting the interests of all parties to the dispute. The unilateral decision on the part of the software vendor to deprive the purchaser of access to the system should not be supported."). Are these criticisms fair? Does the current draft of UCITA provide licensors with any more rights than existing law?

6. For a broad-based defense of self-help and private ordering in general, see David Friedman, In Defense of Private Orderings: Comments on Julie Cohen's "Copyright and the Jurisprudence of Self-Help," 13 Berkeley Tech. L.J. 1151 (1998).

Is "private ordering" really what is at stake here? Or should the law place limits on what a software vendor can do even if the contract does provide for it? In this regard, note two things about the UCITA self-help rules: (1) the "contract" that authorizes them can be a shrinkwrap license or even the sort of "after the fact" terms permitted in *Hill*; and (2) section 816 clearly contemplates that self-help will be allowed even though it involves a "breach of the peace."

7. UCITA permits some (but not all) forms of self-help to occur "without judicial process." Why? Would a rule that required some judicial process, akin to that required for repossession of physical items, impose an unfair burden on software vendors?

3. Warranties and Disclaimers

Neilson Business Equipment Center, Inc. v. Monteleone

Supreme Court of Delaware
524 A.2d 1172 (Del. 1987)

MOORE, J.

Following a nonjury trial in the Superior Court, defendant Neilson Business Equipment Center, Inc. (Neilson), appeals a judgment awarding plaintiff, Dr. Italo V. Monteleone, P.A., damages of $34,983.42 for breaches of the warranties of merchantability and fitness arising from a lease contract for computer hardware, software and related services. The trial court found that the objects of the lease constituted "goods" under the Uniform Commercial Code and granted relief under the Code's implied warranties of merchantability and fitness. 6 Del.C. §§2-314(1) and 2-315.

Neilson's primary contentions are that the trial court erred (1) in classifying the computer software and related technical services as goods, and (2) in applying the Uniform Commercial Code's warranties to this transaction. Thus, we address for the first time the issue of computer software (programs) being treated as "goods" under the Code.

Both parties concede error in the computation of damages. We find that the classification of the contract as one involving "goods" is supported by substantial evidence. Accordingly, we affirm the judgment relating to breaches of the implied warranties of merchantability and fitness, but reverse and remand for a recomputation of damages.

I.

Dr. Monteleone is a neurologist. In March, 1982, his office began investigating various computer information systems, since record keeping was entirely manual. The doctor gave Toni Reed, his bookkeeper and office manager, complete authority to acquire a suitable computer system. However, Ms. Reed had no prior experience in buying computer technology.

She initially considered four possible computer dealers, including Neilson. An advertisement in the local telephone directory listed Neilson as a dealer in microcomputers. Ultimately, Ms. Reed chose Neilson, in part because she had previously purchased an office photocopier from the defendant with satisfactory results.

After an initial meeting at Neilson's office, the company sent two representatives to study Dr. Monteleone's manual billing system. The parties ultimately signed a lease/purchase option agreement covering hardware equipment and software. As part of the agreement, Neilson agreed to customize the computer system to meet Dr. Monteleone's needs. The purchase price was $18,995, but Dr. Monteleone chose to lease the equipment in order to obtain favorable cash flow and tax benefits. The total of all lease payments amounted to $32,800.80. Dr. Monteleone retained an option to purchase the system at the end of the lease at fair market value, not exceeding 10% of the original purchase price. In addition to the lease, the parties executed a separate maintenance agreement valued at $2,182.00. To facilitate the transaction, Neilson sold the equipment and software to Tri-Continental Leasing Corporation, who in turn leased the items to Dr. Monteleone.

Although Neilson did not design the software, it renamed the program it had acquired elsewhere the "Neilson Medical Office Management System." However, Neilson did alter the program at various times in an attempt to make it meet the doctor's needs.

The computer was delivered in July, 1982, and problems immediately developed. For example, the system printed a separate bill for each treatment rather than one bill encompassing the doctor's services to a patient for a specific period; the bills and medical insurance forms were not compatible with Dr. Monteleone's records; patient information was not as detailed as required; and incorrect balances appeared in the accounts receivable register. Attempts to modify the system failed, and in August, 1982, Neilson hired a program consultant to solve the problems.

In February, 1983, Dr. Monteleone notified Neilson that the lease was terminated for cause. Thereafter, plaintiff stopped using the computer, although in March, 1983, Neilson's program consultant successfully effected some modifications. In June, 1983, Neilson took possession of the system pursuant to an agreement which allowed Neilson to try and resell it. While in possession of the computer, Neilson modified the billing program and returned the system to Dr. Monteleone's office. The doctor never used the machine after its return, but continued timely lease payments under the contract.

The Superior Court ruled that the transaction involved goods and applied the warranty provisions of the Uniform Commercial Code. The trial court found that Neilson had breached the implied warranties of merchantability and fitness for a particular purpose, and awarded Dr. Monteleone damages totaling $34,983.42, with interest from March 11, 1983.

II.

[The court characterized the transaction as predominantly for the sale of goods, and so applied the UCC.]

Every contract of sale entered into by a merchant includes an implied warranty that the goods sold be "merchantable." The computer system, to be merchantable, must have been capable of passing without objection in the trade under the contract description, and be fit for the ordinary purposes for which it was intended. 6 Del.C. §2-314(1) and (2). There is no dispute that the computer system failed in that regard. In general, the computer system did not meet Dr. Monteleone's expressed record and bookkeeping needs, even though Neilson's sales representatives informed Ms. Reed that the system would do so. The trial court correctly found that plaintiff had established all the elements necessary to prove a breach of the warranty of merchantability, namely: (1) that a merchant sold the goods; (2) that such goods were not "merchantable" at the time of sale; (3) that plaintiff was damaged; (4) that the damage was caused by the breach of the warranty of merchantability; and (5) that the seller had notice of the damage. See F.E. Myers Co. v. Pipe Maintenance Servs., Inc., 599 F. Supp. 697, 703 (D. Del. 1984).

An implied warranty of fitness for a particular purpose arises when a seller, at the time of contracting, has reason to know a particular purpose of the buyer's for which the goods are required, and has reason to know that the buyer is relying on the seller's skill or judgment to select or furnish suitable goods. 6 Del.C. §2-315. The buyer need not provide the seller with actual knowledge of the particular purpose for which the goods are intended or of his reliance on the seller's skill and judgment, if the circumstances are such that the seller has reason to perceive the purpose intended or that reliance exists. See J. White and R. Summers, Uniform Commercial Code, Section 9-9 (2d ed. 1980).

Here, Neilson knew that Dr. Monteleone, through his assistant, Ms. Reed, sought a computer system to meet specific information processing needs. Neilson admits that it was responsible for selecting the proper equipment, and also agreed to customize the software so that the computer system would be compatible with Dr. Monteleone's manual records. There could hardly be a clearer case where a buyer relies on the professional expertise of the seller than that presented here. Dr. Monteleone needed a system that would perform specific functions, and relied on Neilson's professional expertise and experience in the computer and information processing field to develop and deliver a satisfactory computer system. Neilson clearly had reason to know of Monteleone's reliance on the company's expertise and breached the warranty of fitness for a particular purpose. Its liability is established under the Uniform Commercial Code.

COMMENTS AND QUESTIONS

1. Most provisions of the Uniform Commercial Code can be disclaimed or altered by contracting parties. Why should warranty terms be any different? What if two business parties agree that warranties are not appropriate in a particular situation (say, because the software is in an early stage of development and the customer wants to be able to use it before it is fully tested)? Should they be prevented from agreeing otherwise? See Scott v. Bell Atlantic Corp., 726 N.Y.S.2d 60 (App. Div. 2001) (conspicuous disclaimer of warranty in contract enforceable even though plaintiff did not read it).

2. What does a warranty on software cover? Is it limited to the price of the software, or is the vendor liable for lost data as a result of system crashes? For clients lost as a result of the failure to get a bid in on time, again traceable to software glitches? For consequential damages, including loss of life, in cases where the software runs a mission-critical system (a nuclear power plant, say, or an air traffic control center)?

3. Commentators regularly observe that software consumers are forced to put up with design defects and substandard performance that would be unthinkable in most other industries. See, e.g., Cem Kaner, Bad Software (1998). Why is this? For an argument that implied warranties have proven inadequate to assure performance in the software industry because they are universally disclaimed, see Peter A. Alces, W(h)ither Warranty: The B(l)oom of Products Liability Theory in Cases of Deficient Software Design, 87 Cal. L. Rev. 271 (1999). Alces criticizes draft UCITA for making it even easier to disclaim all warranties in software, and suggests that the appropriate solution may be to apply principles of products liability to computer programs.

Some software industry lawyers, by contrast, fear that warranties will destroy the software industry. See, e.g., Jeffrey C. Selman & Christopher S. Chen, Steering the Titanic Clear of the Iceberg: Saving the Sale of Software From the Perils of Warranties, 31 U.S.F. L. Rev. 531 (1997). Others have suggested compromises designed to create an implied warranty of merchantability that the software industry at least can live with. See Robert W. Gomulkiewicz, The Implied Warranty of Merchantability in Software Contracts: A Warranty No One Dares to Give and How to Change That, 16 J. Marshall J. Computer & Info. L. 393 (1998).

4. Should digital information be treated differently from software for warranty purposes? UCITA takes the position that it cannot impose any warranties regarding the accuracy of the information provided for fear of running afoul of the

First Amendment. UCITA §404, Reporter's Note 3.b. ("Published informational content is the subject matter of general commerce in ideas, political, economic, entertainment or the like, whose distribution entails fundamental public policy interests in supporting distribution and not chilling this process through liability risks."). Some (but not all) cases have indeed taken that position, drawing from the libel cases a restrictive view of when speakers can be liable for making false statements of fact. See Daniel v. Dow Jones & Co., 520 N.Y.S.2d 334 (N.Y. City Ct. 1987).

On the other hand, courts regularly enforce contracts that restrict the free speech rights of parties to the contract. See Cohen v. Cowles Media, 501 U.S. 663 (1991). And courts in the trademark and false advertising contexts have no difficulty in imposing liability on those who make misleading statements, even if they do it unintentionally.

Should the law distinguish between liability for factual misstatements, which the First Amendment may protect, and liability for a database containing software flaws that crash someone's system?

D. THE CONTRACT-INTELLECTUAL PROPERTY BOUNDARY

In the case that follows, the software vendor attempted to circumvent copyright and trade secrets law by requiring the "licensee" to agree not to reverse engineer the computer program. Consider whether and under what circumstances vendors should be able to "contract around" intellectual property law.

Vault Corp. v. Quaid Software Ltd.
United States Court of Appeals for the Fifth Circuit
847 F.2d 255 (5th Cir. 1988)

REAVLEY, Circuit Judge: . . .

I

Vault produces computer diskettes under the registered trademark "PROLOK" which are designed to prevent the unauthorized duplication of programs placed on them by software computer companies, Vault's customers. Floppy diskettes serve as a medium upon which computer companies place their software programs. To use a program, a purchase loads the diskette into the disk drive of a computer, thereby allowing the computer to read the program into its memory. The purchaser can then remove the diskette from the disk drive and operate the program from the computer's memory. This process is repeated each time a program is used.

The protective device placed on a PROLOK diskette by Vault is comprised of two parts: a "fingerprint" and a software program ("Vault's program").[1] The "fingerprint" is a small mark physically placed on the magnetic surface of each PROLOK diskette which contains certain information that cannot be altered or erased. Vault's program is a set of instructions to the computer which interact with the "fingerprint" to prevent the computer from operating the program recorded on a PROLOK diskette (by one of Vault's customers) unless the computer verifies that the original PROLOK diskette, as identified by the "fingerprint", is in the computer's disk drive. While a purchaser can copy a PROLOK protected program onto another diskette, the computer will not read the program into its memory from the copy unless the original PROLOK diskette is also in one of the computer's disk drives. The fact that a fully functional copy of a program cannot be made from a PROLOK diskette prevents purchasers from buying a single program and making unauthorized copies for distribution to others.

Vault produced PROLOK in three stages. The original commercial versions, designated as versions 1.01, 1.02, 1.03, 1.04 and 1.06 ("version 1.0") were produced in 1983. Vault then incorporated improvements into the system and produced version 1.07 in 1984. The third major revision occurred in August and September of 1985 and was designated as versions 2.0 and 2.01 ("version 2.0"). Each version of PROLOK has been copyrighted and Vault includes a license agreement with every PROLOK package that specifically prohibits the copying, modification, translation, decompilation or disassembly of Vault's program.[2] Be-

---

1. A PROLOK diskette contains two programs, the program placed on the diskette by a software company (e.g., word processing) and the program placed on the diskette by Vault which interacts with the "fingerprint" to prevent the unauthorized duplication of the software company's program. We use the term "software program" or "program" to refer to the program placed on the diskette by Vault's customers (a computer company) and "Vault's program" to refer to the program placed on the diskette by Vault as part of the protective device. We collectively refer to the "fingerprint" and Vault's program as the "protective device."

2. The license agreement refers to the program placed on the diskette by Vault, not the software program placed on the diskette by Vault's customers.... The companies that place their software programs on PROLOK diskettes, not Vault, own the copyright to their programs and may include a license agreement covering their programs in the package for sale to the public.

Vault's license agreement reads:

IMPORTANT! VAULT IS PROVIDING THE ENCLOSED MATERIALS TO YOU ON THE EXPRESS CONDITION THAT YOU ASSENT TO THE SOFTWARE LICENSE. BY USING ANY OF THE ENCLOSED DISKETTE(S), YOU AGREE TO THE FOLLOWING PROVISIONS. IF YOU DO NOT AGREE WITH THESE LICENSE PROVISIONS, RETURN THESE MATERIALS TO YOUR DEALER, IN ORIGINAL PACKAGING WITHIN 3 DAYS FROM RECEIPT, FOR A REFUND.

1. This copy of the PROLOK Software Protection System and this PROLOK Software Protection Diskette (the "Licensed Software") are licensed to you, the end-user, for your own internal use. Title to the Licensed Software and all copyrights and proprietary rights in the Licensed Software shall remain with VAULT. You may not transfer, sublicense, rent, lease, convey, copy, modify, translate, convert to another programming language, decompile or disassemble the Licensed Software for any purpose without VAULT's prior written consent.

2. THE LICENSED SOFTWARE IS PROVIDED "AS-IS". VAULT DISCLAIMS ALL WARRANTIES AND REPRESENTATIONS OF ANY KIND WITH REGARD TO THE LICENSED SOFTWARE, INCLUDING THE IMPLIED WARRANTIES OF MERCHANTABILITY AND FITNESS FOR A PARTICULAR PURPOSE. UNDER NO CIRCUMSTANCES WILL VAULT BE LIABLE FOR ANY CONSEQUENTIAL, INCIDENTAL, SPECIAL OR EXEMPLARY DAMAGES EVEN IF VAULT IS APPRISED OF THE LIKELIHOOD OF SUCH DAMAGES OCCURRING. SOME STATES DO NOT ALLOW THE LIMITATION OR EXCLUSION OF LIABILITY FOR INCIDENTAL OR CONSEQUENTIAL DAMAGES, SO THE ABOVE LIMITATION OR EXCLUSION MAY NOT APPLY TO YOU.

ginning with version 2.0 in September 1985, Vault's license agreement continued a choice of law clause adopting Louisiana law.[3]

Quaid's product, a diskette called "CopyWrite," contains a feature called "RAMKEY" which unlocks the PROLOK protective device and facilitates the creation of a fully functional copy of a program placed on a PROLOK diskette. The process is performed simply by copying the contents of the PROLOK diskette onto the CopyWrite diskette [which] can then be used to run the software program without the original PROLOK diskette in a computer disk drive. RAMKEY interacts with Vault's program to make it appear to the computer that the CopyWrite diskette contains the "fingerprint," thereby making the computer function as if the original PROLOK diskette is in its disk drive. A copy of a program placed on a CopyWrite diskette can be used without the original, and an unlimited number of fully functional copies can be made in this manner from the program originally placed on the PROLOK diskette.

Quaid first developed RAMKEY in September 1983 in response to PROLOK version 1.0. In order to develop this version of RAMKEY, Quaid copied Vault's program into the memory of its computer and analyzed the manner in which the program operated. When Vault developed version 1.07, Quaid adapted RAMKEY in 1984 to defeat this new version. The adapted version of RAMKEY contained a sequence of approximately 30 characters found in Vault's program and was discontinued in July 1984. Quaid then developed the current version of RAMKEY which also operates to defeat PROLOK version 1.07, but does not contain the sequence of characters used in the discontinued version. Quaid has not yet modified RAMKEY to defeat PROLOK version 2.0, and has agreed not to modify RAMKEY pending the outcome of this suit. Robert McQuaid, the sole owner of Quaid, testified in his deposition that while a CopyWrite diskette can be used to duplicate programs placed on all diskettes, whether copy-protected or not, the only purpose served by RAMKEY is to facilitate the duplication of programs placed on copy-protected diskettes. He also stated that without the RAMKEY feature, CopyWrite would have no commercial value.

II

Vault brought this action against Quaid seeking preliminary and permanent injunctions to prevent Quaid from advertising and selling RAMKEY, an order impounding all of Quaid's copies of CopyWrite which contain the RAMKEY feature, and monetary damages in the amount of $100,000,000. Vault asserted three copyright infringement claims. . . . Vault also asserted two claims based on Louisiana law, contending that Quaid breached its license agreement by decompiling or disassembling Vault's program in violation of the Louisiana Software License Enforcement Act, La.Rev.Stat.Ann. §51:1961 et seq. (West 1987), and that Quaid

---

3. The license agreement included the following language beginning with version 2.0:

To the extent the laws of the United States of America are not applicable, this license agreement shall be governed by the laws of the State of Louisiana.

misappropriated Vault's program in violation of the Louisiana Uniform Trade Secrets Act, La.Rev.Stat.Ann. §51:1431 et seq. (West 1987).

[The court concluded that Quaid's reverse engineering did not violate the Copyright Act.]

IV. Vault's Louisiana Claims

Seeking preliminary and permanent injunctions and damages, Vault's original complaint alleged that Quaid breached its license agreement by decompiling or disassembling Vault's program in violation of the Louisiana Software License Enforcement Act (the "License Act"), La.Rev.Stat.Ann. §51:1961 et seq. (West 1987), and that Quaid misappropriated Vault's program in violation of the Louisiana Uniform Trade Secrets Act, La.Rev.Stat.Ann. §51:1431 et seq. (West 1987). On appeal, Vault abandons its misappropriation claim,[26] and, with respect to its breach of license claim, Vault only seeks an injunction to prevent Quaid from decompiling or disassembling PROLOK version 2.0.

Louisiana's License Act permits a software producer to impose a number of contractual terms upon software purchasers provided that the terms are set forth in a license agreement which comports with La.Rev.Stat.Ann. §§51:1963 & 1965, and that this license agreement accompanies the producer's software. Enforceable terms include the prohibition of: (1) any copying of the program for any purpose; and (2) modifying and/or adapting the program in any way, including adaptation by reverse engineering, decompilation or disassembly. La.Rev.Stat.Ann. §51:1964.[28] The terms "reverse engineering, decompiling or disassembling" are defined as "any

---

26. While the district court held that the Louisiana Uniform Trade Secrets Act, La.Rev.Stat.Ann. §51:1431 et seq., was not preempted by the Copyright Act, the court held that the process of ascertaining information by "reverse engineering," used by Quaid to analyze the operation of Vault's program, did not constitute a violation of the Louisiana Trade Secrets Act. *Vault*, 655 F. Supp. at 761. This holding is not challenged on appeal.

28. Section 51:1964 reads, in full:

Terms of which shall be deemed to have been accepted under R.S. 51:1963, if included in an accompanying license agreement which conforms to the provisions of R.S. 51:1965, may include any or all of the following:

(1) Provisions for the retention by the licensor of title to the copy of the computer software.

(2) If title to the copy of computer software has been retained by the licensor, provisions for the prohibition of any copying of the copy of computer software for any purpose and/or limitations on the purposes for which copies of the computer software can be made and/or limitations on the number of copies of the computer software which can be made.

(3) If title to the copy of computer software has been retained by the licensor, provisions for the prohibition or limitation of rights to modify and/or adapt the copy of the computer software in any way, including without limitation prohibitions on translating, reverse engineering, decompiling, disassembling, and/or creating derivative works based on the computer software.

(4) If title to the copy of computer software has been retained by the licensor, provisions for prohibitions on further transfer, assignment, rental, sale, or other disposition of that copy or any other copies made from that copy of the computer software, provided that terms which prohibit the transfer of a copy of computer software in connection with the sale or transfer by operation of law of all or substantially all of the operating assets of a licensee's business shall to that extent only not be deemed to have been accepted under R.S. 51:1963.

(5) Provisions for the automatic termination without notice of the license agreement if any provisions of the license agreement are breached by the licensee.

process by which computer software is converted from one form to another form which is more readily understandable to human beings, including without limitation any decoding or decrypting of any computer program which has been encoded or encrypted in any manner." La.Rev.Stat.Ann. §51:1962(3).

Vault's license agreement, which accompanies PROLOK version 2.0 and comports with the requirements of La.Rev.Stat.Ann. §§51:1963 & 1965, provides that "[y]ou may not . . . copy, modify, translate, convert to another programming language, decompile or disassemble" Vault's program. Vault asserts that these prohibitions are enforceable under Louisiana's License Act, and specifically seeks an injunction to prevent Quaid from decompiling or disassembling Vault's program.

The district court held that Vault's license agreement was "a contract of adhesion which could only be enforceable if the [Louisiana License Act] is a valid and enforceable statute." *Vault*, 655 F. Supp. at 761. The court noted numerous conflicts between Louisiana's License Act and the Copyright Act, including: (1) while the License Act authorizes a total prohibition on copying, the Copyright Act allows archival copies and copies made as an essential step in the utilization of a computer program, 17 U.S.C. §117; (2) while the License Act authorizes a perpetual bar against copying, the Copyright Act grants protection against unauthorized copying only for the life of the author plus fifty years, 17 U.S.C. §302(a); and (3) while the License Act places no restrictions on programs which may be protected, under the Copyright Act, only "original works of authorship" can be protected, 17 U.S.C. §102. *Vault*, 655 F. Supp. at 762-63. The court concluded that, because Louisiana's License Act "touched upon the area" of federal copyright law, its provisions were preempted and Vault's license agreement was unenforceable. *Id*. at 763.

In Sears, Roebuck & Co. v. Stiffel Co., 376 U.S. 225, 84 S. Ct. 784, 11 L. Ed.2d 661 (1964), the Supreme Court held that "[w]hen state law touches upon the area of [patent or copyright statutes], it is 'familiar doctrine' that the federal policy 'may not be set at naught, or its benefits denied' by the state law." *Id*. at 229, 84 S. Ct. at 787 (quoting Sola Elec. Co. v. Jefferson Elec. Co., 317 U.S. 173, 176, 63 S. Ct. 172, 173, 87 L. Ed. 165 (1942)). See Compco Corp. v. Day-Brite Lighting, Inc., 376 U.S. 234, 84 S. Ct. 779, 11 L. Ed.2d 669 (1964); see also Mitchell v. Penton/Indus. Publishing Co., 486 F. Supp. 22 (N.D. Ohio 1979) (holding that common law unfair competition claim preempted by the Copyright Act); Triangle Publications, Inc. v. Sports Eye, Inc., 415 F. Supp. 682, 686-87 (E.D.Penn. 1976) (holding that state regulation of unfair competition preempted as to matters falling within broad confines of the Copyright Act). Section 117 of the Copyright Act permits an owner of a computer program to make an adaptation of that program provided that the adaptation is either "created as an essential step in the utilization of the computer program in conjunction with a machine," §117(1), or "is for archival purpose only," §117(2). The provision in Louisiana's License Act, which permits a software producer to prohibit the adaptation of its licensed computer program by decompilation or disassembly, conflicts with the rights of computer program owners under §117 and clearly "touches upon an area" of federal copyright law. For this reason, and the reasons set forth by the district court, we hold that at least this provision of Louisiana's License Act is preempted by federal law, and thus that the restriction in Vault's license agreement against decompilation or disassembly is unenforceable. . . .

Shrinkwrap Agreements enforceable

≡
ProCD, Inc. v. Zeidenberg
United States Court of Appeals for the Seventh Circuit
86 F.3d 1447 (7th Cir. 1996)

[The facts of this case are reprinted *supra,* section VI.C.1.a.]

Shrinkwrap Licenses

III

[The district court held that, even if Wisconsin treats shrinkwrap licenses as contracts, §301(a) of the Copyright Act, 17 U.S.C. §301(a), prevents their enforcement.] 908 F. Supp. at 656-59. The relevant part of §301(a) preempts any "legal or equitable rights [under state law] that are equivalent to any of the exclusive rights within the general scope of copyright as specified by section 106 in works of authorship that are fixed in a tangible medium of expression and come within the subject matter of copyright as specified by sections 102 and 103". ProCD's software and data are "fixed in a tangible medium of expression", and the district judge held that they are "within the subject matter of copyright". The latter conclusion is plainly right for the copyrighted application program, and the judge thought that the data likewise are "within the subject matter of copyright" even if, after *Feist,* they are not sufficiently original to be copyrighted. 908 F. Supp. at 656-57. Baltimore Orioles, Inc. v. Major League Baseball Players Ass'n, 805 F.2d 663, 676 (7th Cir. 1986), supports that conclusion, with which commentators agree. E.g., Paul Goldstein, III Copyright §15.2.3 (2d ed. 1996); Melville B. Nimmer & David Nimmer, Nimmer on Copyright §101[B] (1995); William F. Patry, II Copyright Law and Practice 1108-09 (1994). [One function of §301(a) is to prevent states from giving special protection to works of authorship that Congress has decided should be in the public domain, which it can accomplish only if "subject matter of copyright" includes all works of a type covered by sections 102 and 103, even if federal law does not afford protection to them.] Cf. Bonito Boats, Inc. v. Thunder Craft Boats, Inc., 489 U.S. 141, 103 L. Ed. 2d 118, 109 S. Ct. 971 (1989) (same principle under patent laws).

But are rights created by contract "equivalent to any of the exclusive rights within the general scope of copyright"? Three courts of appeals have answered "no." National Car Rental Systems, Inc. v. Computer Associates International, Inc., 991 F.2d 426, 433 (8th Cir. 1993); Taquino v. Teledyne Monarch Rubber, 893 F.2d 1488, 1501 (5th Cir. 1990); Acorn Structures, Inc. v. Swantz, 846 F.2d 923, 926 (4th Cir. 1988). The district court disagreed with these decisions, 908 F. Supp. at 658, but we think them sound. Rights "equivalent to any of the exclusive rights within the general scope of copyright" are rights established by law—rights that restrict the options of persons who are strangers to the author. Copyright law forbids duplication, public performance, and so on, unless the person wishing to copy or perform the work gets permission; silence means a ban on copying. A copyright is a right against the world. Contracts, by contrast, generally affect only their parties; strangers may do as they please, so contracts do not create "exclusive rights." Someone who found a copy of SelectPhone (trademark) on the street would not be affected by the shrinkwrap license—though the federal copyright laws of their own force would limit the finder's ability to copy or transmit the application program.

Think for a moment about trade secrets. One common trade secret is a customer list. After *Feist*, a simple alphabetical list of a firm's customers, with address and telephone numbers, could not be protected by copyright. Yet Kewanee Oil Co. v. Bicron Corp., 416 U.S. 470, 40 L. Ed. 2d 315, 94 S. Ct. 1879 (1974), holds that contracts about trade secrets may be enforced—precisely because they do not affect strangers' ability to discover and use the information independently. If the amendment of §301(a) in 1976 overruled *Kewanee* and abolished consensual protection of those trade secrets that cannot be copyrighted, no one has noticed—though abolition is a logical consequence of the district court's approach. Think, too, about everyday transactions in intellectual property. A customer visits a video store and rents a copy of Night of the Lepus. The customer's contract with the store limits use of the tape to home viewing and requires its return in two days. May the customer keep the tape, on the ground that §301(a) makes the promise unenforceable?

A law student uses the LEXIS database, containing public-domain documents, under a contract limiting the results to educational endeavors; may the student resell his access to this database to a law firm from which LEXIS seeks to collect a much higher hourly rate? Suppose ProCD hires a firm to scour the nation for telephone directories, promising to pay $100 for each that ProCD does not already have. The firm locates 100 new directories, which it sends to ProCD with an invoice for $10,000. ProCD incorporates the directories into its database; does it have to pay the bill? Surely yes; Aronson v. Quick Point Pencil Co., 440 U.S. 257, 59 L. Ed.2d 296, 99 S. Ct. 1096 (1979), holds that promises to pay for intellectual property may be enforced even though federal law (in *Aronson*, the patent law) offers no protection against third-party uses of that property. See also Kennedy v. Wright, 851 F.2d 963 (7th Cir. 1988). But these illustrations are what our case is about. ProCD offers software and data for two prices: one for personal use, a higher price for commercial use. Zeidenberg wants to use the data without paying the seller's price; if the law student and Quick Point Pencil Co. could not do that, neither can Zeidenberg.

Although Congress possesses power to preempt even the enforcement of contracts about intellectual property—or railroads, on which see Norfolk & Western Ry. v. Train Dispatchers, 499 U.S. 117, 111 S. Ct. 1156, 113 L. Ed.2d 95 (1991)—courts usually read preemption clauses to leave private contracts unaffected. American Airlines, Inc. v. Wolens, 130 L. Ed. 2d 715, 115 S. Ct. 817 (1995), provides a nice illustration. A federal statute preempts any state "law, rule, regulation, standard, or other provision . . . relating to rates, routes, or services of any air carrier." 49 U.S.C. App. §1305(a)(1). Does such a law preempt the law of contracts—so that, for example, an air carrier need not honor a quoted price (or a contract to reduce the price by the value of frequent flyer miles)? The Court allowed that it is possible to read the statute that broadly but thought such an interpretation would make little sense. Terms and conditions offered by contract reflect private ordering, essential to the efficient functioning of markets. 115 S. Ct. at 824-25. Although some principles that carry the name of contract law are designed to defeat rather than implement consensual transactions, *id.* at 826 n.8, the rules that respect private choice are not preempted by a clause such as §1305(a)(1). Section 301(a) plays a role similar to §1301(a)(1): it prevents states from substituting their own regulatory systems for those of the national government. Just as §301(a) does not itself interfere with private transactions in intellectual property, so it does not prevent states from respecting those transactions. Like the Supreme Court in *Wolens*, we think it prudent to refrain from adopting a rule that anything with the label "contract" is necessarily outside the preemption clause: the variations and possibilities are too numerous to foresee. *National Car Rental* likewise recognizes the possibility that some applications of the law of contract could interfere with the attainment of national objectives and therefore come within the domain of §301(a). But general enforcement of shrinkwrap licenses of the kind before us does not create such interference.

Aronson emphasized that enforcement of the contract between Aronson and Quick Point Pencil Company would not withdraw any information from the public domain. That is equally true of the contract between ProCD and Zeidenberg. Everyone remains free to copy and disseminate all 3,000 telephone books that have been incorporated into ProCD's database. Anyone can add sic codes and zip codes. ProCD's rivals have done so. Enforcement of the shrinkwrap license may even make information more readily available, by reducing the price ProCD charges to consumer buyers. To the extent licenses facilitate distribution of object code while concealing the source code (the point of a clause forbidding disassembly), they serve the same procompetitive functions as does the law of trade secrets. Rockwell Graphic Systems, Inc. v. DEV Industries, Inc., 925 F.2d 174, 180 (7th Cir. 1991). Licenses may have other benefits for consumers: many licenses permit users to make extra copies, to use the software on multiple computers, even to incorporate the software into the user's products. But whether a particular license is generous or restrictive, a simple two-party contract is not "equivalent to any of the exclusive rights within the general scope of copyright" and therefore may be enforced.

REVERSED AND REMANDED.

COMMENTS AND QUESTIONS

1. Even if the Louisiana License Act is preempted by federal law, could state contract law (or the UCC) provide that agreements prohibiting reverse engineering will be enforced under state contract law? Would contract law as a whole be preempted in that case, on the grounds that it conflicts with the right to reverse engineer computer programs generally thought to exist in the Copyright Act? More likely, federal law would simply preclude the state from using its judicial power to enforce this contract term. On this point, compare Meehan v. PPG Indus., 802 F.2d 881, 886 (7th Cir. 1986), and Boggild v. Kenner Prods., 776 F.2d 1315 (6th Cir. 1985) (both finding illegal agreements to extend the term of patented or copyrighted products) with Aronson v. Quick Point Pencil Co., 440 U.S. 257 (1979) (contract could require the payment of royalties on an invention in the public domain).

2. Section 301 is designed to prevent states from passing or enforcing laws "equivalent" to copyright. Whether a particular law is equivalent to copyright can be difficult to determine, however. Courts generally do not ask whether a body of law as a whole (contract or trade secrets, say) is equivalent to copyright. Rather, the question is whether the application of a state law to a particular factual circumstance would create a state-law right equivalent to copyright. Even *ProCD*, which

takes a fairly categorical approach to section 301 preemption, is careful to note that it is not holding that section 301 will never preempt contract terms.

Nonetheless, Judge Easterbrook sees a categorical difference between enforcement of contract law and enforcement of other state laws. The court reasoned:

> Rights 'equivalent to any of the exclusive rights within the general scope of copyright' are rights established *by law*—rights that restrict the options of persons who are strangers to the author. Copyright law forbids duplication, public performance, and so on, unless the person wishing to copy or perform the work gets permission; silence means a ban on copying. A copyright is a right against the world. Contracts, by contrast, generally affect only their parties; strangers may do as they please, so contracts do not create "exclusive rights." Someone who found a copy of [the plaintiff's software product] on the street would not be affected by the shrinkwrap license * * *

Is this distinction between judicial enforcement of contracts and other state laws persuasive? Commentators have been skeptical. Radin and Wagner point out that the Legal Realist movement in the last century exploded the myth that contracts are purely "private" creatures; they depend on the legal system for their enforcement. Margaret Jane Radin & R. Polk Wagner, The Myth of Private Ordering: Rediscovering Legal Realism in Cyberspace, 73 Chi.-Kent L. Rev. 1295 (1998). And Lemley observes that "even truly 'private' contracts affect third parties who haven't agreed to the contract terms. Many contracts have significant negative externalities." Mark A. Lemley, Beyond Preemption: The Law and Policy of Intellectual Property Licensing, 87 Calif. L. Rev. 111 (1999).

It is interesting to note that, whatever the validity of the general distinction, the court in *ProCD* applied it to validate a "shrinkwrap license," a peculiar form of contract drafted by the creator of the product and that purports to bind to its terms anyone who uses the product. While it is technically true in such a case that only "parties" to the contract are bound by it, anyone who has access to the product will automatically become such a party. Shrinkwrap licenses look less like contracts in the pure sense, and more like examples of private legislation. As Lemley argues:

> [T]he viability of the distinction between private contracts and public legislation is diminishing day by day. One of the main changes [*ProCD* and its progeny] would make in current law would be to render enforceable contract "terms" to which the parties did not agree in the classic sense, and indeed of which one party may be entirely unaware. [They] would also enable the enforcement of such contract terms "downstream"—that is, against whomever later acquires the software—despite the fact that a first sale under both patent and copyright law would free the purchaser from upstream contractual restrictions. Technology facilitates this change by allowing a vendor to interpose contract terms even in a downstream transaction that would not ordinarily be thought to demonstrate privity between the "contracting" parties.

Id.

3. Does copyright preemption of state contract law depend on the remedy asserted for breach of contract? Should federal law be more concerned if a party seeks by contract to bring the weapons of copyright law to bear? For example, the House Committee Notes to section 109(a) of the Copyright Act (the "first sale" doctrine) provide that a contract limiting a user's first sale rights may be enforce-

able by an action for breach of contract, but do not give rise to an action for copyright infringement. Contract remedies are ordinarily limited to expectation damages, rather than the consequential damages, statutory damages, attorneys' fees, and injunctions available under the copyright law. But suppose a license agreement provided that *resale* of a copyrighted work—permissible under copyright law—voids the entire license, rendering the reseller liable for copyright infringement. Should such a contract be preempted by copyright law? If not, is there anything left in practice of the first sale doctrine?

Some courts have held that breach of a license agreement can itself violate the intellectual property laws. In Microsoft Corp. v. Harmony Computers, discussed supra, the court held:

> Third, if defendants purchased their Products from Microsoft licensees who were acting outside the scope of their licenses by selling the Products stand-alone, any distribution of the Products by defendants, whether within the scope of plaintiff's license agreement or not, would constitute copyright infringement. Microsoft Corp. v. ATS Computers, Inc. et al., CV 93-1273 (S.D.Cal. 1993); Major League Baseball Promotion v. Colour-Tex, 729 F. Supp. 1035, 1041 (D.N.J. 1990) ("A licensee who has failed to satisfy a condition of the license or has materially breached the licensing contract has no rights to give a sublicensee under which the sublicensee can take cover in a copyright infringement case, and therefore, both the licensee and the sublicensee can be held liable for acting without authorization and thereby infringing the licensor's copyright.").
>
> Finally, plaintiff's claim that defendants exceeded the scope of its license agreements states a claim for copyright infringement rather than breach of contract. Not being parties to any license agreement with Microsoft, defendants are "complete strangers" to Microsoft, and their violations of the licensing restrictions must of necessity be seen as claims arising under the copyright laws rather than the law of contracts. See Marshall v. New Kids on the Block Partnership, 780 F. Supp. 1005, 1008 (S.D.N.Y. 1991). Even if defendants were seen as parties to Microsoft's license agreements, their undisputed distribution of Products outside the scope of the license agreements puts them in the same position as an infringer having no contractual relationship with the copyright holder and again makes them "strangers" to Microsoft. *Id.* at 1009; Kanakos v. MX Trading Corp., 1981 WL 1377, *2 (S.D.N.Y. Sept. 16, 1981). Accordingly, plaintiff's allegation that defendants exceeded the scope of the license agreement states a claim for copyright infringement.

Does this result make sense? Does it affect your view of whether federal law should preempt contract terms? Should the outcome turn on the nature of the breach—in particular, on whether the licensee was doing something that would have been illegal but for the license, or whether he was doing something (like reverse engineering) that he would otherwise have had a right to do? See Tom W. Bell, Escape from Copyright: Market Success vs. Statutory Failure in the Protection of Expressive Works, 69 U. Cin. L. Rev. 741 (2001) (arguing that copyright owners should have to elect copyright remedies within copyright's limits or contract remedies if they go beyond copyright's limits).

4. After *ProCD*, is there any set of circumstances in which section 301 will preempt a contract? Suppose that a contract provided that the buyer of a book could not make fair use of the book. Should such a contract term be enforced? Would section 301 stand in the way? Cf. Wright v. Warner Books, 953 F.2d 731, 741 (2d Cir. 1991) (suggesting that a contract forbidding fair use would conflict

with copyright policy). Should the context of the contract (whether it was a shrinkwrap, whether the product was widely sold, whether the buyer was a consumer) matter? See Dennis S. Karjala, Federal Preemption of Shrinkwrap and On-Line Licenses, 22 U. Dayton L. Rev. 511 (1997).

Note on Supremacy Clause Preemption

Section 301 is not all there is to copyright preemption. Congress enacted section 301 because it intended to "preempt the field" of copyright law, precluding states from passing laws that mimicked the federal statute. But even where Congress has not preempted the field, state statutes will still be preempted if they conflict with the specific mandate of federal law or if they stand as an obstacle to the purposes of a federal statute. In copyright law, such "conflicts" or "Supremacy Clause" preemption obviously occurs when a state law prevents the enforcement of a federal copyright. For example, if the state of California were to pass a law stating that the Copyright Act did not apply to citizens of California, the law would arguably survive section 301 preemption, since it contains an "extra element" (citizenship) and does not create a right equivalent to copyright. But it would surely be struck down by the courts as an interference with the federal scheme.

Not all interferences are so straightforward. In ASCAP v. Pataki, 930 F. Supp. 873 (S.D.N.Y. 1996), the court invalidated a state statute regulating the activities of performing rights societies such as ASCAP and BMI. The state statute required (among other things) that such groups provide owners of establishments performing music with written notice of an investigation within 72 hours after it is initiated, thus making it difficult for ASCAP and others to conduct "undercover" investigations for violations of the copyright laws. The court's opinion addressed only the issue of "conflict preemption, which occurs either where compliance with both federal and state regulations is a physical impossibility, or where state law stands as an obstacle to the accomplishment and execution of the full purposes and objectives of Congress." *Id.* The court found that the state statutory provisions "hinder the realization of the federal copyright scheme" for several reasons: the statute made it more difficult for copyright owners to enforce their rights; it effectively established a "statute of limitations" on copyright investigations that was shorter than the federal statute; and it gave copyright defendants a counterclaim that they could use to offset copyright damages. See also College Entrance Examination Board v. Pataki, 889 F. Supp. 554 (N.D.N.Y. 1995) (state law requiring disclosure of standardized test questions and answers preempted by Copyright Act because it conflicted with the rights of copyright owners to restrict distribution of copyrighted material).

Because the Copyright Act is an attempt by Congress to balance the interests of creators and users of intellectual property, state laws that give *too much* protection to copyrighted works may also interfere with the objectives of Congress. See, e.g., United States ex rel. Berge v. Trustees of the University of Alabama, 104 F.3d 1453 (4th Cir. 1997) ("the shadow actually cast by the Act's preemption is notably broader than the wing of its protection"). As the Supreme Court explained in Goldstein v. California, 412 U.S. 546 (1973), the question is whether Congress intended to place a particular work or use in the public domain:

At any time Congress determines that a particular category of "writing" is worthy of national protection and the incidental expenses of federal administration, federal copyright protection may be authorized. Where the need for free and unrestricted distribution of a writing is thought to be required by the national interest, the Copyright Clause and the Commerce Clause would allow Congress to eschew all protection. In such cases, a conflict would develop if a State attempted to protect that which Congress intended to be free from restraint or to free that which Congress had protected. However, where Congress determines that neither federal protection nor freedom from restraint is required by the national interest, it is at liberty to stay its hand entirely. Since state protection would not then conflict with federal action, total relinquishment of the States' power to grant copyright protection cannot be inferred.

Although *Goldstein* was decided before the enactment of section 301, conflict preemption is still a significant part of copyright law. A number of cases have in fact preempted contract terms that conflict with federal patent and copyright policy. For example, contract terms that purport to extend a patent or copyright beyond its expiration have repeatedly been held unenforceable. Other courts have held that contracts that purport to protect uncopyrightable elements of a work are preempted by the Copyright Act. See, e.g., Selby v. New Line Cinema, 96 F. Supp. 2d 1053 (C.D. Cal. 2000). One decision also preempts a claim for breach of implied contract, on the theory that the "implied contract" for idea protection violated the federal policy in favor of protecting only expression in a copyrighted work. Endemol Entertainment v. Twentieth Television Inc., 48 U.S.P.Q.2d 1524 (C.D. Cal. 1998). On the distinction between "conflicts preemption" and copyright field preemption in the contract area, see David Nimmer et al., The Metamorphosis of Contract into Expand, 87 Calif. L. Rev. 17 (1999); Apik Minassian, Comment, The Death of Copyright: Enforceability of Shrinkwrap Licensing Agreements, 45 UCLA L. Rev. 569, 570 (1998) (arguing in favor of "a case-by-case, fact-specific approach to each shrinkwrap agreement to determine whether the license creates contractual rights that are equivalent to the exclusive rights of copyright law, and thus whether it implicates federal copyright preemption issues").

COMMENTS AND QUESTIONS

1. Is *ProCD* in fact a case of conflict between copyright and contract? The stage for such a conflict is set by the Supreme Court decision in *Feist*, which held that the telephone white pages at issue in *ProCD* were constitutionally ineligible for copyright protection. Does the fact that ProCD's shrinkwrap license gives, if anything, even greater protection than copyright would, suggest there is a conflict here? In ProCD v. Zeidenberg, 908 F. Supp. 640 (W.D. Wisc. 1996), the district court reasoned in dictum that state contract law could not be used to prevent the copying of telephone white pages, which the Supreme Court had determined in *Feist* were uncopyrightable. The district court applied a constitutional copyright preemption analysis similar to the patent analysis undertaken in *Bonito Boats*. The Seventh Circuit reversed the district court's decision, concluding that under section 301 of the Copyright Act state contract law could not be preempted in this case. ProCD v. Zeidenberg, 86 F.3d 1447 (7th Cir. 1996). Judge Easterbrook's opinion did not mention Supremacy Clause preemption at all, even though the

issue was briefed and was necessary to the decision, leaving the issue in some doubt. See also Bowers v. Baystate Technologies, 302 F.3d 1334 (Fed. Cir. 2002) (following *ProCD* in concluding that section 301 does not preempt shrinkwrap license terms, and also failing to consider Supremacy Clause preemption). The one court actually to address a similar issue, Vault Inc. v. Quaid Corp., 847 F.2d 255 (5th Cir. 1988), concluded that a state statute permitting enforcement of shrink-wrap licenses was invalid under the Supremacy Clause.

If the federal copyright scheme intends unoriginal works such as the telephone white pages to be in the public domain, is there any way to prevent the sort of use Zeidenberg made of this data? States presumably would lack the power to do so. There is some question whether Congress could avoid the constitutional limitation of originality in the Copyright Clause by enacting protection for databases under the Commerce Clause. In United States v. Moghadam, 175 F.3d 1269 (11th Cir. 1999), the court concluded that Congress could protect unfixed works under the Commerce Clause because it perceived no conflict between the anti-bootlegging statute at issue there and the policies of copyright law. But a Congressional effort to overrule *Feist* might be more problematic. See Paul J. Heald & Suzanna Sherry, Implied Limits on the Legislative Power: The Intellectual Property Clause as an Absolute Constraint on Congress, 2000 U. Ill. L. Rev. 1119.

E. OPEN SOURCE LICENSING

Since the early days of computer programming, it has been customary among some developers of computer programs to publish source code versions of their programs and otherwise make their programs freely available to others. Richard Stallman is a technologist associated with the Massachusetts Institute of Technology and key contributor to a set of computer programs that emulate the functionality of AT&T's UNIX operating system. Stallman is known not only for his work on these programs, known as GNU (GNU is a recursive signifier that GNU is Not Unix), but also for an innovative approach to licensing software (which Stallman called "copyleft") that is embodied in the widely used GNU General Public License (GPL) excerpted below. Stallman recognized that dedicating a program to the public domain would not necessarily ensure that the program would remain freely available, because anyone can make a proprietary derivative work of a truly public domain program. Stallman and fellow researchers sought to preserve certain freedoms in respect of programs they developed, such as freedom to publish source code versions, freedom to distribute the program widely, and freedom to modify the program. To ensure that these freedoms were preserved in successive generations of the program, the GPL invokes copyright protection in the program and conditions licensing the copyright on subsequent users' agreement to use the same license terms in any subsequent distribution of the program or in any derivative work thereof. Stallman and fellow researchers established the Free Software Foundation to promote the development of "free software" and use of the GPL by other software developers. Stallman means for the "free" in "free software" to express liberties in the sense of "free speech," not in the sense of "free beer." The

GPL does not forbid commercialization of software, just the imposition of certain restrictions on what Stallman regards as important programming freedoms.

The open source movement grew out of the free software movement and shares many values and concepts of the free software movement, although open source developers tend to have a more accepting attitude toward developers of proprietary software. A good resource on the open source movement is Open Sources: Voices from the Open Source Revolution (Chris DiBona, Sam Ockman, and Mark Stone, eds., 1999), available at http://www.oreilly.com/catalog/opensources/book/. In recent years, open source development of computer programs has become increasingly common and widely used—even at companies, such as IBM, Hewlett-Packard, and Sun Microsystems, that commercially distribute proprietary software. Some open source development firms, such as VA Linux and RedHat Software, are publicly traded companies. However, many participants in open source development projects are volunteers. One of the most widely known open source projects is the UNIX kernel work alike, coordinated by Finnish programmer Linus Torvalds and widely known as Linux (although to give credit where it is due, the system should be known as GNU/Linux). Because GNU/Linux and many other open source programs use the GPL, it is worthwhile to study this license.

GNU GENERAL PUBLIC LICENSE
Version 2, June 1991
Copyright (C) 1989, 1991 Free Software Foundation, Inc.
59 Temple Place, Suite 330, Boston, MA 02111-1307 USA
Everyone is permitted to copy and distribute verbatim copies
of this license document, but changing it is not allowed.

GNU GENERAL PUBLIC LICENSE
TERMS AND CONDITIONS FOR COPYING, DISTRIBUTION AND MODIFICATION

0. This License applies to any program or other work which contains a notice placed by the copyright holder saying it may be distributed under the terms of this General Public License. The "Program", below, refers to any such program or work, and a "work based on the Program" means either the Program or any derivative work under copyright law: that is to say, a work containing the Program or a portion of it, either verbatim or with modifications and/or translated into another language. (Hereinafter, translation is included without limitation in the term "modification".) Each licensee is addressed as "you".

Activities other than copying, distribution and modification are not covered by this License; they are outside its scope. The act of running the Program is not restricted, and the output from the Program is covered only if its contents constitute a work based on the Program (independent of having been made by running the Program). Whether that is true depends on what the Program does.

1. You may copy and distribute verbatim copies of the Program's source code as you receive it, in any medium, provided that you conspicuously and appropriately publish on each copy an appropriate copyright notice and disclaimer of warranty; keep intact all the notices that refer to this License and to the ab-

sence of any warranty; and give any other recipients of the Program a copy of this License along with the Program.

You may charge a fee for the physical act of transferring a copy, and you may at your option offer warranty protection in exchange for a fee.

2. You may modify your copy or copies of the Program or any portion of it, thus forming a work based on the Program, and copy and distribute such modifications or work under the terms of Section 1 above, provided that you also meet all of these conditions:

a) You must cause the modified files to carry prominent notices stating that you changed the files and the date of any change.

b) You must cause any work that you distribute or publish, that in whole or in part contains or is derived from the Program or any part thereof, to be licensed as a whole at no charge to all third parties under the terms of this License.

c) If the modified program normally reads commands interactively when run, you must cause it, when started running for such interactive use in the most ordinary way, to print or display an announcement including an appropriate copyright notice and a notice that there is no warranty (or else, saying that you provide a warranty) and that users may redistribute the program under these conditions, and telling the user how to view a copy of this License. (Exception: if the Program itself is interactive but does not normally print such an announcement, your work based on the Program is not required to print an announcement.)

These requirements apply to the modified work as a whole. If identifiable sections of that work are not derived from the Program, and can be reasonably considered independent and separate works in themselves, then this License, and its terms, do not apply to those sections when you distribute them as separate works. But when you distribute the same sections as part of a whole which is a work based on the Program, the distribution of the whole must be on the terms of this License, whose permissions for other licensees extend to the entire whole, and thus to each and every part regardless of who wrote it.

Thus, it is not the intent of this section to claim rights or contest your rights to work written entirely by you; rather, the intent is to exercise the right to control the distribution of derivative or collective works based on the Program.

In addition, mere aggregation of another work not based on the Program with the Program (or with a work based on the Program) on a volume of a storage or distribution medium does not bring the other work under the scope of this License.

3. You may copy and distribute the Program (or a work based on it, under Section 2) in object code or executable form under the terms of Sections 1 and 2 above provided that you also do one of the following:

a) Accompany it with the complete corresponding machine-readable source code, which must be distributed under the terms of Sections 1 and 2 above on a medium customarily used for software interchange; or,

b) Accompany it with a written offer, valid for at least three years, to give any third party, for a charge no more than your cost of physically performing source distribution, a complete machine-readable copy of the corresponding source code, to be distributed under the terms of Sections 1 and 2 above on a medium customarily used for software interchange; or,

c) Accompany it with the information you received as to the offer to distribute corresponding source code. (This alternative is allowed only for noncommercial distribution and only if you received the program in object code or executable form with such an offer, in accord with Subsection b above.)

The source code for a work means the preferred form of the work for making modifications to it. For an executable work, complete source code means all the source code for all modules it contains, plus any associated interface definition files, plus the scripts used to control compilation and installation of the executable. However, as a special exception, the source code distributed need not include anything that is normally distributed (in either source or binary form) with the major components (compiler, kernel, and so on) of the operating system on which the executable runs, unless that component itself accompanies the executable.

If distribution of executable or object code is made by offering access to copy from a designated place, then offering equivalent access to copy the source code from the same place counts as distribution of the source code, even though third parties are not compelled to copy the source along with the object code.

4. You may not copy, modify, sublicense, or distribute the Program except as expressly provided under this License. Any attempt otherwise to copy, modify, sublicense or distribute the Program is void, and will automatically terminate your rights under this License. However, parties who have received copies, or rights, from you under this License will not have their licenses terminated so long as such parties remain in full compliance.

5. You are not required to accept this License, since you have not signed it. However, nothing else grants you permission to modify or distribute the Program or its derivative works. These actions are prohibited by law if you do not accept this License. Therefore, by modifying or distributing the Program (or any work based on the Program), you indicate your acceptance of this License to do so, and all its terms and conditions for copying, distributing or modifying the Program or works based on it.

6. Each time you redistribute the Program (or any work based on the Program), the recipient automatically receives a license from the original licensor to copy, distribute or modify the Program subject to these terms and conditions. You may not impose any further restrictions on the recipients' exercise of the rights granted herein. You are not responsible for enforcing compliance by third parties to this License.

7. If, as a consequence of a court judgment or allegation of patent infringement or for any other reason (not limited to patent issues), conditions are imposed on you (whether by court order, agreement or otherwise) that contradict the conditions of this License, they do not excuse you from the conditions of this License. If you cannot distribute so as to satisfy simultaneously your obligations under this License and any other pertinent obligations, then as a consequence you may not distribute the Program at all. For example, if a patent license would not permit royalty-free redistribution of the Program by all those who receive copies directly or indirectly through you, then the only way you

E. Open Source Licensing ≡ 379

could satisfy both it and this License would be to refrain entirely from distribution of the Program.

If any portion of this section is held invalid or unenforceable under any particular circumstance, the balance of the section is intended to apply and the section as a whole is intended to apply in other circumstances.

It is not the purpose of this section to induce you to infringe any patents or other property right claims or to contest validity of any such claims; this section has the sole purpose of protecting the integrity of the free software distribution system, which is implemented by public license practices. Many people have made generous contributions to the wide range of software distributed through that system in reliance on consistent application of that system; it is up to the author/donor to decide if he or she is willing to distribute software through any other system and a licensee cannot impose that choice.

This section is intended to make thoroughly clear what is believed to be a consequence of the rest of this License.

8. If the distribution and/or use of the Program is restricted in certain countries either by patents or by copyrighted interfaces, the original copyright holder who places the Program under this License may add an explicit geographical distribution limitation excluding those countries, so that distribution is permitted only in or among countries not thus excluded. In such case, this License incorporates the limitation as if written in the body of this License.

9. The Free Software Foundation may publish revised and/or new versions of the General Public License from time to time. Such new versions will be similar in spirit to the present version, but may differ in detail to address new problems or concerns.

Each version is given a distinguishing version number. If the Program specifies a version number of this License which applies to it and "any later version", you have the option of following the terms and conditions either of that version or of any later version published by the Free Software Foundation. If the Program does not specify a version number of this License, you may choose any version ever published by the Free Software Foundation.

10. If you wish to incorporate parts of the Program into other free programs whose distribution conditions are different, write to the author to ask for permission. For software which is copyrighted by the Free Software Foundation, write to the Free Software Foundation; we sometimes make exceptions for this. Our decision will be guided by the two goals of preserving the free status of all derivatives of our free software and of promoting the sharing and reuse of software generally.

NO WARRANTY

11. BECAUSE THE PROGRAM IS LICENSED FREE OF CHARGE, THERE IS NO WARRANTY FOR THE PROGRAM, TO THE EXTENT PERMITTED BY APPLICABLE LAW. EXCEPT WHEN OTHERWISE STATED IN WRITING THE COPYRIGHT HOLDERS AND/OR OTHER PARTIES PROVIDE THE PROGRAM "AS IS" WITHOUT WARRANTY OF ANY KIND, EITHER EXPRESSED OR IMPLIED, INCLUDING, BUT NOT LIMITED TO, THE IMPLIED WARRANTIES OF MERCHANTABILITY AND FITNESS FOR A PARTICULAR PURPOSE. THE ENTIRE

RISK AS TO THE QUALITY AND PERFORMANCE OF THE PROGRAM IS WITH YOU. SHOULD THE PROGRAM PROVE DEFECTIVE, YOU ASSUME THE COST OF ALL NECESSARY SERVICING, REPAIR OR CORRECTION.

12. IN NO EVENT UNLESS REQUIRED BY APPLICABLE LAW OR AGREED TO IN WRITING WILL ANY COPYRIGHT HOLDER, OR ANY OTHER PARTY WHO MAY MODIFY AND/OR REDISTRIBUTE THE PROGRAM AS PERMITTED ABOVE, BE LIABLE TO YOU FOR DAMAGES, INCLUDING ANY GENERAL, SPECIAL, INCIDENTAL OR CONSEQUENTIAL DAMAGES ARISING OUT OF THE USE OR IN-ABILITY TO USE THE PROGRAM (INCLUDING BUT NOT LIMITED TO LOSS OF DATA OR DATA BEING RENDERED INACCURATE OR LOSSES SUSTAINED BY YOU OR THIRD PARTIES OR A FAILURE OF THE PROGRAM TO OPERATE WITH ANY OTHER PROGRAMS), EVEN IF SUCH HOLDER OR OTHER PARTY HAS BEEN ADVISED OF THE POSSIBILITY OF SUCH DAMAGES.

END OF TERMS AND CONDITIONS

How to Apply These Terms to Your New Programs

If you develop a new program, and you want it to be of the greatest possible use to the public, the best way to achieve this is to make it free software which everyone can redistribute and change under these terms.

To do so, attach the following notices to the program. It is safest to attach them to the start of each source file to most effectively convey the exclusion of warranty; and each file should have at least the "copyright" line and a pointer to where the full notice is found.

> <one line to give the program's name and a brief idea of what it does.>
> Copyright (C) <year> <name of author>
>
> This program is free software; you can redistribute it and/or modify it under the terms of the GNU General Public License as published by the Free Software Foundation; either version 2 of the License, or (at your option) any later version.
>
> This program is distributed in the hope that it will be useful, but WITHOUT ANY WARRANTY; without even the implied warranty of MERCHANTABILITY or FITNESS FOR A PARTICULAR PURPOSE. See the GNU General Public License for more details.
>
> You should have received a copy of the GNU General Public License along with this program; if not, write to the Free Software Foundation, Inc., 59 Temple Place, Suite 330, Boston, MA 02111-1307 USA . . .

This General Public License does not permit incorporating your program into proprietary programs. If your program is a subroutine library, you may consider it more useful to permit linking proprietary applications with the library. If this is what you want to do, use the GNU Library General Public License instead of this License.

COMMENTS AND QUESTIONS

1. Many of the same issues posed earlier in this chapter about the enforceability of shrinkwrap and other mass-market licenses apply to the GPL and other open source licenses. The GPL assumes that the first developer of GPL software can bind all subsequent users of the software to the terms of the GPL, even those with whom the developer has never had any dealings. Under what theory or theories might such a developer be able to bind subsequent users to GPL terms? The GPL also assumes that downstream users and modifiers of GPL software will also be bound by subsequent versions of the GPL, should it be revised. Under what theory or theories might this be possible? See Christian H. Nadan, Open Source Licensing: Virus or Virtue?, 10 Tex. Intell. Prop. L.J. 349 (2002); Margaret Jane Radin, Humans, Computers, and Binding Commitment, 75 Ind. L.J. 1125 (2000); Ira Heffan, Copyleft: Licensing Collaborative Works, 49 Stan. L. Rev. 1487 (1997).

2. Some legal questions about the GPL and other open source licenses are more specific to these licenses. For example, the GPL and many open source licenses disclaim all warranties for the software. Do you agree with open source developers that the law should allow them to disclaim all liability for errors? A licensing lawyer for Microsoft has argued that Microsoft and other developers of software need the same freedom from warranty liability. See Robert Gomulkiewicz, How Copyleft Uses License Rights To Succeed in the Open Source Revolution and the Implications for Article 2B, 36 Houston L. Rev. 179 (1999). What if any reasons might there be to distinguish between warranty disclaimers by GPL developers and those by Microsoft Corp.?

3. Microsoft officials have sometimes been very critical of open source initiatives and in particular of the GPL. See Prepared Text of Remarks by Craig Mundie, Microsoft Senior Vice President, The Commercial Software Model, The New York University Stern School of Business, May 3, 2001 *http://www.microsoft. com/presspass/exec/craig/05-03sharedsource.asp*. Among other things, Mundie states: "The GPL mandates that any software that incorporates source code already licensed under the GPL will itself become subject to the GPL. When the resulting software product is distributed, its creator must make the entire source code base freely available to everyone, at no additional charge. This viral aspect of the GPL poses a threat to the intellectual property of any organization making use of it. It also fundamentally undermines the independent commercial software sector because it effectively makes it impossible to distribute software on a basis where recipients pay for the product rather than just the cost of distribution." Do you agree?

4. Several legal commentators have explored a range of interesting implications of open source development of computer programs. See, e.g., Yochai Benkler, Coase's Penguin, or Linux and the Nature of the Firm, 112 Yale L.J. (forthcoming 2002); David McGowan, Legal Implications of Open Source Software, 2001 U. Ill. L. Rev. 241 (2001); Stephen McJohn, The Paradoxes of Free

Software, 9 Geo. Mason L. Rev. 25 (2000); Lawrence Lessig, The Limits in Open Code: Regulatory Standards and the Future of the Net, 14 Berkeley Technology L.J. 759 (1999).

5. The Open Source Initiative is a nonprofit organization that maintains a website that provides access to many resources about open source software, including examples of different kinds of open source licenses. The website can be found at http://www.opensource.org.

6. Does it make sense to use the GPL to provide open source-like protection to other works of authorship, such as text documents, images, music, or motion pictures? Why or why not? For an example of an open source license applied to audio, look at the Open Audio License which is available at http://eff.org/IP/Open_licenses/eff_oal.html. For an open source license applicable to content in any medium, see the Open Content License at http://opencontent.org/opl.shtml. For a list of open source-like licenses, see http://eff.org/IP/Open_licenses/open_alternatives.html. Creative Commons is an organization working to develop licensing models and machine-executable licenses to enable those who wish to share their works with others. Its website is at http://www.creativecommons.org. How does Creative Commons resemble and differ from open source and GPL licensing models?

7. A group of bioinformatics researchers has called for adoption of a requirement that all publicly funded research should be released on an open source basis. Their petition is available at http://www.openinformatics.org and is discussed at http://www.oreilly.net/pub/a/network/2002/01/12/openinf.html. What are the pros and cons of such a proposal?

F. SOFTWARE CONSULTING AGREEMENTS

The emphasis on mass-market licensing and the issues it presents sometimes obscure an important fact: more than one-third of all software industry revenues in the United States come from custom, as opposed to off-the-shelf, software. The legal issues surrounding creation of custom software are very different from those involved in the prepackaged software market. Of paramount importance are:

- The status of the software engineer(s) who write the code—that is, employee or consultant;
- The understanding regarding reuse of the code; and
- Agreement regarding which party will maintain the software, and who is permitted to adapt and modify it.

1. Employee or Consultant?

Aymes v. Bonelli, 980 F.2d 857 (2d Cir. 1992) [In this typical case, a computer programmer named Aymes was paid to write software by Island, Inc., a company that installed swimming pools. After a dispute regarding payment and reuse of the programs Aymes had written—in particular a program called

"CSALIB"—Aymes registered the copyright to the programs. This lawsuit followed. Island won below when the trial court determined that (a) there was no written agreement between the parties on which to base a determination of ownership; and (b) Aymes was an employee under the many-factored test laid down by the Supreme Court in CCNV v. Reid, 490 U.S. 730 (1989), thus rendering CSALIB a work for hire under the Copyright Act and making Island the owner of the work.]

A review of this analysis shows that the significant factors supporting Island's contention that Aymes was an employee include Island's right to control the means of CSALIB's creation and Island's right to assign other projects. The significant factors supporting Aymes's argument that he was an independent contractor include: the level of skill needed to create CSALIB; the decision of Island not to offer him benefits; and his payment of his own social security taxes. The other factors were either indeterminate, because they were evenly balanced between the parties, or of marginal significance, because they were inapplicable to these facts.

Examining the factors for each side in terms of their importance, we conclude that the only major factor strongly supporting Island is that it directed the creation of the program. Island did reserve the right to assign Aymes other projects, which is a major factor, but under these facts this was not necessarily inconsistent with an independent contractor relationship. Supporting Aymes's argument that he was an independent contractor, however, are several important factors—his skill, and the tax and benefit factors—that outweigh the elements supporting Island. The other factors outlined in *Reid* are either indeterminate or of negligible importance, and cannot outweigh the significance we attach to Island's choice to treat Aymes as an independent contractor when it was to Island's financial benefit. Now that this treatment is no longer to Island's benefit, the company must still adhere to the choice it made.

Note that the court's conclusion—that Aymes was an independent contractor—means that Aymes owns the copyright in the work. Absent an assignment agreement or even a written license, he, not the company, owns the right to make future copies and adaptations of the work regardless of how much the company paid him to write it.

COMMENTS AND QUESTIONS

1. The Copyright Act defines "work for hire" as follows:

A "work made for hire" is—
    (1) a work prepared by an employee within the scope of his or her employment; or
    (2) a work specially ordered or commissioned for use as a contribution to a collective work, as part of a motion picture or other audiovisual work, as a translation, as a supplementary work, as a compilation, as an instructional text, as a test, as answer material for a test, or as an atlas, if the parties expressly agree in a written instrument signed by them that the work shall be considered a work made for hire. . . .

17 U.S.C. §101 (1998).

2. In addition to *Aymes*, see Maclean Assocs. v. Wm. M. Merver-Meidinger-Hansen, Inc., 952 F.2d 769 (3d Cir. 1991), where a dispute erupted over personnel management software written for the defendant by ex-employee Barry MacLean:

> We believe that consideration of the nine factors the Supreme Court listed in *Reid* could bring a rational jury to conclude that Mr. MacLean was not an actual servant of Mercer when JEMSystem was created. Mr. MacLean says he wrote the JEMSystem software after he left Mercer and continued in a consulting relationship with it on the NYSE project. His task of writing sophisticated computer software required skill and creativity. Mr. MacLean worked with his own software on his own computer at his own facility to complete Mercer's obligation under its contract with NYSE. Although Mr. MacLean was a principal of Mercer for almost five years, the duration of his relationship as a consultant for Mercer on the NYSE project was fairly short. Mercer did not have the right to assign additional projects to Mr. MacLean. Mr. MacLean had absolute discretion over when and how long to work. Mercer paid Mr. MacLean for the delivery of his services as a consultant, instead of paying him a regular periodic salary. It is obvious that Mercer's regular business is compensation consulting. It was not a part of Mercer's regular business at the relevant time to provide software for its clients' use on personal computers; instead, prior to Mr. MacLean's creation of the JEMSystem software, Mercer took raw data its clients provided and produced for its clients computerized reports that evaluated and synthesized the data. Mercer did not pay any payroll or social security taxes on behalf of Mr. MacLean after he ceased to be one of Mercer's principals, nor did it thereafter provide him with workers' compensation coverage or contribute to unemployment insurance or workers' compensation funds. It is not known how Mercer treated its payments to Mr. MacLean for its own corporate tax purposes.

3. In the case of some types of copyrightable works, a written agreement prepared at the outset of the project can take care of all potential ownership claims, regardless of whether the work is prepared by an employee. See 17 U.S.C. §201(b) (1998). In other cases, employment status determines initial ownership: *Aymes* is an example. It is important to recognize that work-for-hire status only governs the initial ownership, however; technically, it defines who is the "author" of a work. Regardless of initial ownership, copyright in all works can be assigned. An agreement to assign a work before it is created is also fully enforceable. Hence work-for-hire issues are important as a practical matter only when the parties fail to specify ownership allocation in advance. This happens surprisingly often in the software world, however.

The impact of failing to obtain an assignment is fairly dramatic: a company that hires a consultant to write a program for the company's use and that pays the consultant for the program may end up not owning the program. Not only may the consultant resell the same program to a competitor, but the purchasing company's own ability to use the software may be put in jeopardy. It is critical, therefore, that the parties agree up front who will own what rights in the software to be created.

A surprisingly large number of contracts to write software or design Web sites lack any agreement as to ownership. As a result, the courts have been forced to determine whether the person hired to write the program was an employee who created the work for hire. Compare Favela v. Fritz Cos., 1994 Copr. L. Decs. ¶27,276 (C.D. Cal. 1993) (software program created by an employee of a temp agency was a work made for hire) with Kirk v. Harter, 188 F.3d 1005 (8th Cir. 1999) (contractor who wrote computer program for company was independent contractor who retained copyright in program; company had only an implied license to use the program). Cf. Holtzbrinck Publishing Holdings v. Vyne Communications, 2000 Copr. L. Decs. ¶28,081 (S.D.N.Y. 2000) (factual issues concerning ownership of the *Scientific American* Web site precluded summary judgment). Obviously, the easiest way to avoid this problem is to specify ownership of the works in question up front and in writing.

2. Rights to Re-Use Software

Even when it is clear that a consultant owns her work product, the parties can of course apportion use rights any number of ways by assignment or license. It is important to note that assignment is different from even a very broad license. An assignment conveys title, which can be thought of as the right to decide what to do with a work under all sorts of contingencies that the parties could not have even thought of when the agreement was signed. This can have very important practical ramifications, which by their nature are difficult to foresee.

Beyond that of ownership, the important threshold questions for the parties are (1) whether and to what extent each can re-use the work that is the subject of the contract; (2) whether and to what extent each or both can modify or adapt it; and (3) whether and to what extent the parties can resell the work, as originally created or in modified form.

Agreements on these terms take many forms, but some common ones include:

- The consultant owns the work outright, and the customer can only use it as originally delivered in its original form;
- The consultant owns the work, but the customer can reuse it and resell it in original or modified form, perhaps subject to limitations (no resale before a certain date; no resale to competitors of the consultant, etc.);
- The customer owns the work, but the consultant has the right to reuse it in meeting the needs of other customers, perhaps subject to a time limitation and/or a prohibition on reusing it in projects of the customer's direct competitors; or
- Both the customer and the consultant retain rights to use and license the work for their own purposes.

See generally Raymond Ocampo, Jr., Drafting and Negotiating Software Consulting Agreements (Glasser Legal Works, 1996 & Supp.).

7

Antitrust in the Computer Industry

Antitrust has recently taken on great prominence in the computer industry, to an extent not seen since the 1970s, when government and private cases against dominant computer manufacturer IBM captured the attention of the world. In the 1990s, it was a new market (software) and a new dominant player (Microsoft) that were the focus of antitrust scrutiny. Nonetheless, the multifarious cases against Microsoft are only a small part of the antitrust picture in the computer industry. There are a number of important issues relating to the interaction between antitrust and intellectual property law, for example. In addition, the confusing and fast-changing structure of the industry poses particular challenges for the sometimes-ponderous machinery of antitrust law. In this chapter, we approach all of these issues, paying particular attention to how antitrust rules interact with intellectual property and licensing in the computer context.

A. PRINCIPLES OF ANTITRUST LAW[1]

1. The Scope of Antitrust Law

Antitrust law protects competition and the competitive process by preventing certain types of conduct that threaten a free market. For example, antitrust prohibits competitors from agreeing on the price they will charge. It prohibits certain predatory practices designed to exclude competitors from the market, and it places certain limits on the behavior of firms with market power.

Competition is good for a variety of reasons. Basic economics tells us that competing firms produce more and price lower than monopolists. Monopolists

---

1. This Section is provided for the benefit of those students who have not previously been exposed to antitrust law. Students with prior antitrust background may wish to begin with Section B.

not only take money away from consumers by raising prices, but they impose a "deadweight loss" on society by reducing their output below the level that consumers would be willing to purchase at a competitive price. A monopoly has other problems as well: it inherently reduces consumer choice, and it provides fewer incentives to innovate than do competitive firms.

The first U.S. antitrust law was passed in 1890. The Sherman Act, as the statute is called, was a reaction to populist pressure on Congress to do something about the trusts that had come to dominate the American business landscape. The Sherman Act granted broad powers to government to break up trusts and other conspiracies in restraint of trade. The Sherman Act, which is still in force today, provides in part:

> Section 1 [15 U.S.C. §1]. Every contract, combination in the form of trust or otherwise, or conspiracy, in restraint of trade or commerce among the several States, or with a foreign nation, is declared to be illegal. . . .
> Section 2 [15 U.S.C. §2]. Every person who shall monopolize, or attempt to monopolize, or combine or conspire with any other person or persons, to monopolize any part of the trade or commerce among the several States, or with foreign nations, shall be deemed guilty of a felony. . . .

By their terms, these laws are broad indeed. In some sense, *every* contract necessarily restrains trade, because it forecloses options that were once open. Under the literal terms of section 1, employment contracts and sales contracts might be considered antitrust violations.

In practice, courts quickly gave the Sherman Act a more restrictive interpretation. The Supreme Court read section 1 as prohibiting only *unreasonable* restraints of trade. Much antitrust jurisprudence in the last century has attempted to distinguish reasonable from unreasonable restraints of trade.

The courts also limited the reach of section 2 to ensure that successful businesses would not be punished because of their success. Because the antitrust laws provide for felony criminal punishments, private treble damage actions and injunctions, and plaintiffs' attorneys' fees, the possibility of overdeterring legitimate business conduct is a real concern. To avoid this problem, the courts have distinguished between possessing a monopoly and actively acquiring or maintaining a monopoly through anticompetitive conduct. Section 2 prohibits only the latter.

Congress has never amended the core provisions of the Sherman Act. In 1914, however, in response to what it perceived as lax judicial enforcement of the antitrust laws, Congress passed the Clayton Act. The Clayton Act contains a number of specific provisions that serve to clarify the Sherman Act. For example, section 3 of the Clayton Act enumerates and prohibits certain types of agreements that are also included within the general scope of section 1.

The Clayton Act was amended in 1950 to prohibit certain types of mergers. Section 7 of the Act prohibits mergers and acquisitions (of a corporation, stock, or assets) where "the effect of such acquisition may be substantially to lessen competition or to tend to create a monopoly" in "any line of commerce . . . in any section of the country." Thus the antitrust laws prevent businesses from acting anticompetitively in three basic ways.

Monopolization.   It is not illegal to have a monopoly. However, monopolists and firms gaining market power need to be very careful about their behavior.

A monopolist violates section 2 if it has "market power" (defined as the power to raise prices or exclude competition in a relevant market) and engages in anticompetitive conduct designed to maintain or extend that power. Over time, the courts have identified a number of anticompetitive practices (and the circumstances in which they are actionable). We will discuss several in this chapter. A company may also be guilty of "attempted monopolization" if it intends to monopolize a market, engages in anticompetitive conduct, and has a "dangerous probability of successful monopolization." See, e.g., Spectrum Sports v. McQuillen, 506 U.S. 447 (1993).

To find that a defendant has monopolized a market, the court must first decide what the relevant market is. Specifically, the court must identify a product or set of products and a geographic region within which most consumers make their purchases. Controlling such a market will allow a monopolist to raise prices without losing customers to competitors from outside the market. The definition of a relevant market and the analysis of power in that market are both extremely complex questions, and a good deal of legal and economic work has gone into the attempt to define exactly what market power is. For a more detailed discussion of this issue, see U.S. Department of Justice and Federal Trade Commission, Revised Merger Guidelines §1 (April 2, 1992).

Agreements. Courts have identified two basic types of agreements that may be in restraint of trade—agreements among competitors (called "horizontal restraints") and agreements between buyers and sellers (called "vertical restraints").[2] Vertical restraints are generally less threatening to competition than horizontal restraints. With the exception of vertical price-fixing, they are generally judged under the rule of reason, under which the courts balance the anticompetitive harms of a restraint against its procompetitive benefits. Only those restraints that produce harms significantly in excess of benefits to competition are deemed unreasonable.

Horizontal restraints are more troubling because they may allow the participants to create a cartel, which can then behave anticompetitively, much as a monopolist would. At first, most agreements between competitors were deemed illegal per se, without any necessity for a weighing of harms and benefits to competition. Today, the Supreme Court has retreated from that position, recognizing that certain agreements among competitors may be efficient and procompetitive. Many horizontal restraints are now judged under the rule of reason. Only certain forms of "naked" agreements to fix prices or divide territories remain illegal per se.

Mergers. Section 7 of the Clayton Act is intended to catch monopolies "in their incipiency." Because of this, the standard for proving the existence of market power is significantly lower in the case of a merger than in a section 2 monopolization claim. If a merger would substantially lessen competition in a relevant market, the courts may prohibit it. As with most other areas of antitrust law, however, courts are usually willing to consider a merger's potential benefits to competition in deciding whether it should be prevented.

---

2. Actually, the term "vertical restraints" refers to a whole class of transactions between companies in a vertical relationship in the chain of distribution, including dealers, franchisors, distributors, resellers, etc.

Most merger enforcement takes place at the Antitrust Division of the U.S. Department of Justice and at the Federal Trade Commission (FTC). The Hart-Scott-Rodino Act of 1976 requires companies to file a statement with the Antitrust Division and the FTC and to seek approval for mergers over a certain size. If the Division or the FTC feels that a merger will restrain competition, it can challenge the merger in court before the merger takes place. 15 U.S.C. §7A.

Note on Antitrust Theory

The antitrust laws clearly reflect some congressional judgment that "big is bad." But *why* it is bad has been the subject of almost continuous debate since the enactment of the antitrust laws. At least three different rationales have been advanced to explain the antitrust laws. The first view may be called the "populist" view of antitrust. Populists take the position that big is *intrinsically* bad. It may be bad for a variety of reasons: it concentrates wealth; it reduces product diversity; or it concentrates political power, for example. But regardless of the reason, populists would use the antitrust laws as a weapon against all monopolies and against oligopolies as well. Populists can find substantial support for their position in the legislative history of the Sherman Act and in the political climate in the late nineteenth century. For an elaboration of the populist view, see Walter Adams, The Bigness Complex: Industry, Labor and Government in the American Economy (1986); Victor H. Kramer, The Supreme Court and Tying Arrangements: Antitrust as History, 69 Minn. L. Rev. 1013 (1985).

In the second view, antitrust is designed to protect small businesses from being driven out of the market. This view is related to the populist view, as both are likely to vigorously oppose monopolies and growing concentration in an industry, but these views differ in the perception of the instrumental value served by preventing monopoly. Advocates of this latter view tend to view antitrust as an unfair-competition statute, and to apply the antitrust laws to a number of practices that are bad for competitors but good for competition. For example, small-business advocates are likely to be skeptical of price cuts by large national companies, which they fear will "squeeze out" local independents. The legislative history of the Clayton Act and subsequent antitrust laws lends some support to this view.

A third theory of the antitrust laws—and the theory that clearly dominates modern antitrust analysis—is the "economic" or "social welfare" model. This approach sees the purpose of the antitrust laws as promoting social welfare by ensuring that markets work freely and without interference. Antitrust law is aimed at practices that corrupt the market or usurp its function. On this view, antitrust is particularly concerned with preventing horizontal restraints of trade. While there is relatively little in the history of the antitrust laws that suggests Congress was primarily concerned with economics,[3] this approach has gained great currency with courts and scholars in the last 25 years. See, e.g., Robert H. Bork, The Antitrust Paradox: A Policy at War with Itself (1978); Richard Posner, Antitrust Law: An Economic Perspective (2d ed. 2001). Most antitrust experts now use economic

---

3. But cf. F.M. Scherer, Efficiency, Fairness, and the Early Contributions of Economists to the Antitrust Debate, 29 Washburn L. J. 243, 250-251 (1990) (arguing that the views of mainstream economists in 1890 were consistent with the goals of the Sherman Act).

effects as the basis for their analysis, although they continue to disagree vigorously over how those effects are to be analyzed.

2. Intellectual Property and Antitrust Law

Intellectual property law grants certain exclusive rights to the creators, inventors, or discoverers of certain intangible but valuable assets. In previous chapters, we have discussed the nature of these rights at length. There is substantial disagreement as to whether intellectual property rights are "property" in the ordinary sense of the term. But whatever they are, intellectual property rights give their owners the right to exclude others from using or copying their inventions or creations.

Traditionally, the conventional wisdom has been that the antitrust laws and the intellectual property laws are in conflict. See, e.g., Stephen Calkins, Patent Law: The Impact of the 1988 Patent Misuse Reform Act and Noerr-Pennington Doctrine on Misuse Defenses and Antitrust Counterclaims, 38 Drake L. Rev. 175, 176 n.1 (1989) (noting this historic belief). Baldly stated, the conflict is said to arise because the intellectual property laws grant "monopolies" to inventors, while the goal of the antitrust laws is to prevent or restrict monopoly.

However, scholars have increasingly taken the position that the two laws are not in conflict at all. Rather, they are complementary efforts to promote an efficient marketplace and long-run, dynamic competition through innovation. Professor Goldstein was an early proponent of the idea that the intellectual property laws were designed to promote competition. See Paul Goldstein, The Competitive Mandate: From Sears to Lear, 59 Cal. L. Rev. 971 (1971). He was soon joined by others, including Ward Bowman, Jr., Patent and Antitrust Law: A Legal and Economic Appraisal (1973). These critics argue that both intellectual property and antitrust law serve the broader goal of productive efficiency, intellectual property by encouraging innovation and antitrust by encouraging efficient allocation of existing resources. How the two laws should interact is a function of which goal—innovation or allocative efficiency—will best promote social welfare in any given case. See generally Michael Carrier, Unraveling the Patent-Antitrust Paradox, 150 U. Pa. L. Rev. 761 (2002).

In the first half of the twentieth century, Joseph Schumpeter advanced the classic incentive theory that underlies much of intellectual property. In his view, competition will lead to a focus on short-run marginal cost, to the exclusion of (long-run efficient) capital investments in research and development. In the absence of intellectual property protection, the result of competition is insufficient innovation. If that is true (and we have certainly assumed that it is for much of this book), what does it say about the wisdom of applying the antitrust laws to intellectual property? Is it a good idea to enforce competition in the computer industry? Or should the goal of antitrust law be modified somehow in this context?

Recent advances in economic thought have complicated the innovation story. In particular, a significant paper by Richard Levin and others forcefully demonstrates that different industries depend on different types of appropriability mechanisms. Richard Levin et al., Appropriating the Returns from Industrial Research and Development, 3 Brookings Papers on Economic Activity 783 (1987). The fact that appropriability varies from industry to industry significantly complicates the simple economic model of patents that Bowman sets forth. Further, recent work by David Teece and others suggests that firms within an industry will adapt strategically to the appropriability environment of that industry by taking advantage of what David Teece calls "co-specific assets." David J. Teece, Profiting from Technological Innovation: Implications for Integration, Collaboration, Licensing and Public Policy, 15 Res. Pol'y 285 (1986). And important work by Ken Arrow suggests that in many cases competition, not monopoly, is the best spur to innovation. See Kenneth J. Arrow, Economic Welfare and the Allocation of Resources for Invention, in The Rate and Direction of Inventive Activity: Economic and Social Factors 609 (Richard R. Nelson ed., 1962). The upshot of this recent work is that the economic model of patent incentives is substantially more complicated than it appeared to be in an earlier generation.

This new literature has particular application to the computer industry, where people frequently argue that innovation in software, for example, will be stifled if the innovators are not allowed to build on the work that went before them. We have discussed this argument before, calling it the "on the shoulders of giants" (OTSOG) principle. In copyright law, the argument is used to justify narrowing the scope of protection copyright affords to computer software. Does the same argument suggest a more active role for antitrust law in this industry?

Professor Bowman's conclusion that the patent laws and the antitrust laws do not have conflicting purposes can be misleading. Bowman is best understood as saying that both patent law and antitrust law are tools to be used in promoting wealth maximization. They are designed to be used together to achieve a certain result. However, they strive toward that result in ways that are often in tension. Antitrust law seeks to maximize wealth by preventing monopoly, while patent law may in some cases encourage monopoly.

It is too facile to say that the patent laws give a monopoly to the patentee. Most patents cover a product or products that are only a small subset of a *product market.* It is therefore possible to have a perfectly competitive industry composed of patent holders if each holds a patent on one of several possible products in a market. Only where an innovation creates an entirely new market, or represents a quantum advance in an old one, is the patent likely to confer an economic monopoly directly.

There is room, therefore, for the patent and antitrust laws to coexist in the service of long-run dynamic efficiencies. In this scheme, patents constitute an exception to the reach of the antitrust laws, and antitrust constrains what a patentee can do with its patent. Efficient wealth maximization requires that a line be drawn between conduct that is permissible and that which is impermissible. Drawing that line in the particular context of the computer industry is a major subject of this chapter.

B. MONOPOLIZATION

1. Defining the Market

The first step in any antitrust inquiry is to define the relevant product and geographic markets. Monopolization does not occur in a vacuum. To be liable, an antitrust defendant must have monopolized *something, somewhere.* Market definition and market power analysis are well developed in antitrust law; thus we will not repeat the general issues here.

There are, however, some market definition issues that are specific to the computer industry. The first of these results from the importance of intellectual property to computer law. Antitrust courts have entertained a long-standing presumption that intellectual property rights confer market power. The Supreme Court has reasoned that, because a patent confers the right to exclude competitors *from practicing the patented invention,* it must confer monopoly power over that invention. Thus the Supreme Court has on several occasions presumed market power from the existence of patents or copyrights. E.g., Jefferson Parish Hospital District v. Hyde, 466 U.S. 2 (1984); United States v. Loew's, Inc., 371 U.S. 38 (1962). In the computer industry, the key case embodying this presumption is Digidyne Corp. v. Data General Corp., 734 F.2d 1336 (9th Cir. 1984). There, the court held that because Data General's operating system was copyrighted and therefore could not be copied without permission, it was a unique good that must be evaluated in a market by itself.

This presumption that intellectual property rights confer market power has little basis in fact. Patents grant the right to exclude in a tightly defined technological domain. In most cases, this does not translate into what an economist would call a "monopoly," because the technological domain is rarely co-extensive with an economic product market. For example, consider a typical mechanical patent—say, on a new type of muffler for lawn mowers. This typical patent does not confer the right to exclude others from making lawn mowers, of course; nor even from making most types of mufflers for lawn mowers. Only the new muffler is covered. Whether one considers the market for lawn mowers, for lawn mower components, or even for lawn mower mufflers, this patent does not confer a monopoly. *Only* in the very limited market defined by this new type of muffler and its close technological substitutes does the patent holder have exclusionary power—that is, a "monopoly."[4] Most patents are like that. Occasionally, however, a patent (and, even more rarely, a copyright) is granted on a "pioneering" or "basic" invention—for example, the lightbulb, or the laser, or the communication satellite, or recombinant DNA techniques. In these rare instances, the patent may confer exlusionary power over an entire market, and hence qualify as a true economic monopoly.

Commentators have been virtually unanimous in their criticism of the market power presumption. See, e.g., Philip Areeda & Louis Kaplow, Antitrust Analysis 441 (1987); Herbert Hovenkamp, Economics and Federal Antitrust Law §8.3, at 219 (1985); William Montgomery, Note, The Presumption of Economic Power for Patented and Copyrighted Products in Tying Arrangements, 85 Colum. L. Rev. 1140, 1156 (1985). Perhaps in response to this criticism, some courts have rejected the market power presumption in recent years. See Abbott Labs. v. Brennan, 952 F.2d 1346, 1354-1355 (Fed. Cir. 1991); A.I. Root Co. v. Computer/Dynamics, Inc., 806 F.2d 673 (6th Cir. 1986); 3 P.M., Inc. v. Basic Four

---

4. It is sometimes asserted that a patent is merely a property right, as opposed to a monopoly, and that the exclusionary power of a patent should not be deemed any more forceful than property rights in one's house. This is misleading, however, because unlike a house or any piece of tangible (real or personal) property, a patent grants its owner the right to exclude others from doing certain things with their own physical property.

Corp., 591 F. Supp. 1350 (E.D. Mich. 1984). Moreover, the new U.S. Department of Justice Antitrust Guidelines for the Licensing and Acquisition of Intellectual Property (Intellectual Property Guidelines) specifically reject the market power presumption:

> Market power is the ability profitably to maintain prices above, or output below, competitive levels for a significant period of time. The Agencies will not presume that a patent, copyright or trade secret necessarily confers market power upon its owner. Although the intellectual property right confers the power to exclude with respect to the *specific* product, process, or work in question, there will often be sufficient actual or potential close substitutes for such product, process or work to prevent the exercise of market power.

Intellectual Property Guidelines §2.2 (1995). Legislation has periodically been introduced in Congress to abolish the market power presumption. See, e.g., H.R. 401, 105th Cong., 1st Sess. (1997).

The economic literature on the market power issue is complex. See, e.g., David J. Teece et al., Assessing Market Power in Regimes of Rapid Technological Change, 2 Indus. & Corp. Change 3, 7 (1993) ("The more innovative the new product or process, the greater the conventional market power will appear, because price changes will have little or no influence on demand for a truly innovative product."); *id.* at 29 (proposing to measure market power by performance attributes, not price changes). See also Kenneth Burchfiel, Patent Misuse and Antitrust Reform: "Blessed Be the Tie," 4 Harv J.L. & Tech. 1 (1991) (suggesting simpler tests for determining market power, including: (1) whether a royalty was paid by licensees; (2) whether accused infringers chose to keep infringing during litigation; (3) the profit derived from the patented product); Jesse Markham, Concentration: A Stimulus or Retardant to Innovation?, in Industrial Concentration: The New Learning 247 (Harvey Goldschmid et al. eds., 1974) (summarizing empirical tests of the Schumpeterian hypothesis).

The Antitrust Division takes the position that markets may need to be defined differently in the intellectual property context. In addition to evaluating the effect of intellectual property rights on markets for goods, the Division has defined two additional types of markets:

3.2.2 Technology Markets

Technology markets consist of intellectual property that is licensed (the "licensed technology") and its close substitutes—that is, the technologies or goods that are close enough substitutes significantly to constrain the exercise of market power with respect to the intellectual property that is licensed.[19] When rights to intellectual property are marketed separately from the products in which they are used, the Agencies may rely on technology markets to analyze the competitive effects of a licensing arrangement.

---

19. For example, the owner of a process for producing a particular good may be constrained in its conduct with respect to that process not only by other processes for making that good, but also by other goods that compete with the downstream good and by the processes used to produce those other goods.

To identify a technology's close substitutes and thus to delineate the relevant technology market, the Agencies will, if the data permit, identify the smallest group of technologies and goods over which a hypothetical monopolist of those technologies and goods likely would exercise market power—for example, by imposing a small but significant and nontransitory price increase. The Agencies recognize that technology often is licensed in ways that are not readily quantifiable in monetary terms. In such circumstances, the Agencies will delineate the relevant market by identifying other technologies and goods which buyers would substitute at a cost comparable to that of using the licensed technology.

In assessing the competitive significance of current and likely potential participants in a technology market, the Agencies will take into account all relevant evidence. When market share data are available and accurately reflect the competitive significance of market participants, the Agencies will include market share data in this assessment. The Agencies also will seek evidence of buyers' and market participants' assessments of the competitive significance of technology market participants. . . . When market share data or other indicia of market power are not available, and it appears that competing technologies are comparably efficient, the Agencies will assign each technology the same market share. For new technologies, the Agencies generally will use the best available information to estimate market acceptance over a two-year period, beginning with commercial introduction.

3.2.3 Research and Development: Innovation Markets

. . . A licensing arrangement may have competitive effects on innovation that cannot be adequately addressed through the analysis of goods or technology markets. For example, the arrangement may affect the development of goods that do not yet exist. Alternatively, the arrangement may affect the development of new or improved goods or processes in geographic markets where there is not actual or likely potential competition in the relevant goods.

An innovation market consists of the research and development directed to particular new or improved goods or processes, and the close substitutes for that research and development. The close substitutes are research and development efforts, technologies, and goods that significantly constrain the exercise of market power with respect to the relevant research and development, for example by limiting the ability and incentive of a hypothetical monopolist to retard the pace of research and development. The Agencies will delineate an innovation market only when the capabilities to engage in the relevant research and development can be associated with specialized assets or characteristics of specific firms.

In assessing the competitive significance of current and likely potential participants in an innovation market, the Agencies will take into account all relevant evidence. When market share data are available and accurately reflect the competitive significance of market participants, the Agencies will include market share data in this assessment. The Agencies also will seek evidence of buyers' and market participants' assessments of the competitive significance of innovation market participants. . . . The Agencies may base the market shares of participants in an innovation market on their shares of identifiable assets or characteristics upon which innovation depends, on shares of research and development expenditures, or on shares of a related product. When entities have comparable capabilities and incentives to pursue research and development that is a close substitute for the research and development activities of the parties to a licensing arrangement, the Agencies may assign equal market shares to such entities.

Intellectual Property Guidelines §§3.2.2, 3.2.3.

COMMENTS AND QUESTIONS

1. Does defining separate technology and innovation markets make sense? Another way of approaching this question is to ask whether these market definitions capture any anticompetitive conduct that could not be challenged under a traditional product market definition. One possible answer is that alleging a market for innovation allows the Division to challenge mergers or anticompetitive conduct earlier than they could in product markets, as the Division need not wait until an actual product market is affected. Whether this is good or bad depends on your confidence in the ability of the courts to define innovation markets and assess anticompetitive effects accurately.

But it is also possible that technology and innovation markets allow the antitrust laws to reach conduct that could not be attacked under traditional product market definitions. For example, a dominant company in a product market may be able to merge with or drive out a competitor whose current market share is insignificant but who has the best technology and is therefore well placed to challenge the dominant firm. If nothing else, technology markets may make market power analysis more forward-looking by requiring the parties to focus on likely future market power rather than just current market shares. At the same time, technology and innovation markets may be used by the government to attack mergers that do not present product market overlaps at all.

Finally, technology markets may sometimes have the opposite effect: they could require the courts to consider as potential future competitors firms that do not now compete with the antitrust defendant. For an argument in favor of such "dynamic" market power analysis, see David Teece et al., Assessing Market Power in Regimes of Rapid Technological Change, 2 Indus. & Corp. Change 439 (1993).

2. How can we define a market for "research and development" (R&D)? The Guidelines suggest several possible ways of determining market shares, including arbitrarily assigning each participant an equal share. Is this reasonable? Is R&D expenditure a fair measure? One problem with the Guidelines' suggestion that innovation monopolists can "profitably retard or restrict innovation" is that it assumes a fairly static model of monopoly. Monopolists who cut back on R&D may reap the rewards in the short term but are likely to be left behind as new companies enter the market for R&D. Can an argument be made the other way—that the real danger is that a dominant firm will extend its product monopoly by spending excessively on research and development?

Market definition issues in the computer industry are complicated not only by the existence of intellectual property rights and the dynamic nature of market power, but also by the rather heavy interdependence of products in the industry. Defining a market may require consideration of upstream and downstream as well as horizontally competitive products. Further, the market may be constrained to some extent by compatibility requirements. Consider the following case.

Allen-Myland, Inc. v. International Business Machines Corp.
United States Court of Appeals for the Third Circuit
33 F.3d 194 (3d Cir. 1994)

NYGAARD, Circuit Judge.

Allen-Myland, Inc. ("AMI") appeals from the district court's judgment in favor of IBM in this intricate antitrust tying case. We conclude that the district court erred and will vacate its judgment and remand the cause for further proceedings.

I. Facts and Procedure

A. *Mainframes and Upgrades . . .*

IBM is the world's largest manufacturer of large-scale mainframe computers. These machines have the capacity to process millions of records at a time and manage a tremendous volume of information, making modern operations possible for large corporations, public utilities and government agencies. Without them, business would soon slow or halt. Mainframes are physically large machines, generally occupying significant floor space and requiring a full-time staff to keep them in operation. Needless to say, they are quite expensive, with prices commonly in excess of $1 million.

Mainframes are available in a wide range of computing capacities, to fit the needs of each individual customer. One common measure of capacity is computing speed, measured in millions of instructions per second ("MIPS"). IBM mainframes may also be upgraded, as its customers' computing needs change over time, in what is known as a MIPS upgrade.

Many IBM mainframes are not purchased outright from IBM by their end users, but are instead leased through third-party leasing companies such as CMI and Comdisco. A mainframe will typically be leased to several end users during its life cycle, and then when obsolete will be scrapped. Often, when the lease term expires and the mainframe returns to the lessor, the computer will need to be reconfigured to meet the needs of the next lessee.

Companies like AMI found a profitable market reconfiguring mainframe computers such as the IBM 303X series. Lessors could not afford to have their machines idle and generating no revenue while waiting for a reconfiguration, yet IBM often took months to install an upgrade. AMI, on the other hand, would turn the job around in a matter of only a few days. Either AMI or the leasing company would buy the required parts outright from IBM for inventory on what were known as SWRPQ terms, meaning that IBM installation was not included. It would then install the parts in the user's computer, set up the appropriate software and test the system. Old parts could often then be used on another computer. Because the 303X series of computers was based on "MST" circuit board technology, which required significant technical skill and time to reconfigure, AMI was in a position to add considerable value in terms of its labor. As a result, AMI grew into a company with $50 million in annual revenue.

In 1980, however, IBM introduced its next generation of mainframe computers, the 308X series, which caused a major erosion in AMI's reconfiguration business. . . .

In marketing its 308X series, IBM used a policy known as net pricing. Under this policy, IBM installation labor was bundled in with the price of the parts for TCM-based MIPS upgrades; SWRPQ pricing was either eliminated or was priced prohibitively high. In addition, any old TCMs recovered from a mainframe during reconfiguration became IBM's property. As a result, customers desiring non-IBM installation of upgrades were required to pay IBM's labor charge anyway. And because the net pricing policy limited the supply of the TCMs on the open market, acquiring parts from sources other than IBM became impractical. . . .

The district court found that IBM's net pricing structure did not constitute a per se section 1 violation, for two reasons: first, that IBM's share of the relevant market was not high enough to impose per se liability; and second, that net pricing did not foreclose AMI from a "viable business opportunity." The court also found that net pricing did not violate section 1 under a rule of reason analysis because sufficient procompetitive reasons existed for it. . . .

III. Scope of the Relevant Market

A. Introduction

AMI asserts that the tying product is the "large-scale mainframe computer," defined as computers that are "among the largest in memory capacity, the fastest in computing speed, and the most expensive of computers available." *Allen-Myland*, 693 F. Supp. at 270-71. Alternatively, it sets forth two submarkets consisting of the parts and services required for the conversion and upgrade of either IBM mainframes or all manufacturers' mainframes. AMI defines the tied product as the labor required to install upgrades.

The district court found AMI's proposed market definition and submarkets to be too narrow. When the court broadened the market to include various substitutes that it believed shared cross-elasticity of demand with large-scale mainframes, IBM's market share dropped from as high as 79% to under 34.4%, too low to impose per se liability. See *Jefferson Parish*, 466 U.S. at 26-27, 104 S. Ct. at 1566 (30% market share insufficient); Times-Picayune Publishing Co. v. United States, 345 U.S. 594, 611-12, 73 S. Ct. 872, 882, 97 L. Ed. 1277 (1953) (33-40% market share insufficient). The court stated:

> Standing alone, AMI's market share evidence tends to show that IBM enjoys substantial economic power. However, AMI's definitions of large scale mainframes and the relevant market are flawed in several respects and tend to overstate IBM's market share and power.

Allen-Myland, 693 F. Supp. at 271. The district court defined the relevant market to include not only large-scale mainframes, but also added upgrades to large-scale mainframes, leased and smaller capacity computers, peripheral products and software, "box swaps," and upgrades using customer-provided parts to the relevant market. . . .

B. Leasing Companies

The district court first added leasing companies into AMI's proposed market definition. It reasoned as follows: Leasing companies, such as Comdisco and CMI, purchase computer equipment from manufacturers and lease it to users. From a consumer's standpoint, they are an alternative source of computer equipment. They compete with IBM. Leasing companies own approximately 40 percent of all large scale mainframe computers, as defined by AMI. Prof. Levin testified that IBM's share of the market would be reduced by an amount he was unable to determine if leasing companies were taken into account in AMI's market definition. If leasing company transactions involving computers comparable and in many cases identical to the large scale mainframes marketed by IBM are included in the relevant market, and the market is measured on a "transaction basis," IBM's share of the market, according to Prof. Almarin Phillips, who testified for IBM as an expert economist, drops to 34.4 percent. Prof. Phillips testified that such a share would not reflect "overwhelming" activity in the market on IBM's part. *Allen-Myland*, 693 F. Supp. at 273-74 (footnote and record citations omitted). We cannot affirm the district court's finding that leasing companies form a part of the relevant market.

. . . [W]e think that the opinion reveals an analytical flaw. Leasing companies lease both new and used computers. They purchase new mainframes from IBM and lease them to end users; when the lease term is up, if the mainframe is not obsolete and can be leased again, the leasing company will place it with another end user. In addition, leasing companies deal in both IBM and non-IBM computers. There are important legal and competitive distinctions between the various types of equipment in which the leasing companies deal, so they cannot be lumped together.

New computers are, of course, already in the relevant market as defined by AMI. It was therefore incorrect to add them in again when end users lease new computers rather than purchase them outright. In this situation, leasing companies provide nothing more than an alternate way of financing a new computer, but do nothing to increase the supply of new machines. See Transamerica Computer Co. v. IBM Corp. (In re IBM Peripheral EDP Devices Antitrust Litig.), 481 F. Supp. 965, 979 (N.D. Cal. 1979), *aff'd*, 698 F.2d 1377 (9th Cir.), *cert. denied*, 464 U.S. 955, 104 S. Ct. 370, 78 L. Ed. 2d 329 (1983). They do not increase the number of new mainframes, as leasing companies still must purchase them from their manufacturers. Thus, to the extent that IBM had the power to set prices, that power would not be diminished, or at most would only be slightly diminished, by its sales to leasing companies rather than end users. Since these purchases are already in the relevant market, it was double counting to also include them as part of the leasing market. Cf. *id*.

With respect to leases of used computers, there is a significant difference whether those machines were made by IBM or by some other manufacturer. Where used IBM computers are leased, we think that United States v. Aluminum Co. of America ("Alcoa"), 148 F.2d 416 (2d Cir. 1945) is apposite. There, Alcoa controlled 90 percent of the market for virgin aluminum ingot. It sought to reduce its market share for antitrust purposes by arguing that secondary ingot derived from scrap competed with virgin ingot for sales. The court held that because all secondary ingot was ultimately derived from virgin ingot, Alcoa, by properly exercising its power over the supply of virgin, could indirectly control the supply of secondary as well. *Id.* at 425.

Alcoa's analysis is persuasive. Indeed, we think the case is even stronger here for excluding the secondary market. Refined aluminum can be melted down and reused repeatedly, and in any event, products made with it may last for decades before they are scrapped and the aluminum is recycled. It therefore may have been quite difficult for Alcoa to estimate future supply and demand for aluminum ingot over a long period of time with sufficient accuracy to maximize its profits by manipulating the supply of virgin ingot it produced. See 2 Phillip Areeda & Donald F. Turner, Antitrust Law ¶530c (1978).

Computers, however, have considerably more limited lives than aluminum ingot. Technology and price/performance ratios have been advancing so rapidly in the computer industry that used machines cannot be re-leased indefinitely. Accordingly, a powerful manufacturer like IBM was in a position to maximize its profits by carefully controlling the number of mainframes that would later appear on the used leasing market. This is particularly true when, as here, that control was enhanced by IBM's policy of recapturing old parts that could otherwise have been used to extend the useful service lives of existing used mainframes by allowing them to be upgraded and placed with new customers. We therefore conclude that the district court erred when it added leases of used IBM mainframes into the relevant market.

On the other hand, to the extent that leasing companies deal in used, non-IBM mainframes that have not already been counted in the sales market, these machines belong in the relevant market for large-scale mainframe computers. Unlike IBM, there is no allegation that the manufacturers of these computers possess the market power to control prices, much less that they would do so in concert with IBM. When these computers are placed in service by leasing companies, they provide an alternative that limits IBM's power in the market.

Accordingly, we conclude that the district court erred when it included all leasing company transactions in the relevant market. On remand, the court should include only leases of used, non-IBM mainframes and determine the extent to which those leases reduce IBM's market share.

C. *Box Swaps*

The district court also added "box swaps"—replacing an existing computer with a more powerful, new or used computer—into the relevant market, although it did not calculate the degree to which these box swaps eroded IBM's market share.

The analytical problem with this finding is similar to the error with respect to leasing companies. To the extent that a box swap involves purchasing a new IBM or a new or used non-IBM mainframe computer, it constitutes double counting to add box swaps to the market because those sales are already included in the market definition. On the other hand, if a used IBM computer is used in the swap, then to include that machine in the market is incorrect under *Alcoa* for the same reason it was error to include them in the leasing market.

D.   Used Parts Upgrades

Including "used parts upgrades" in the relevant market was also error. A used parts upgrade is an upgrade performed with parts obtained from another computer, either one belonging to the organization needing the upgrade or one belonging to a leasing company. See *Allen-Myland*, 693 F. Supp. at 277.

The district court correctly recognized that the viability of used parts upgrades could be limited by the scarcity of the necessary parts. It then relied on the many memory and channel upgrades and downgrades that had been performed with used parts not acquired from IBM. The record indicates, however, that most memory and channel upgrade parts are not based on TCM technology and were thus not subject to IBM's net pricing and parts recapture policies. The parts required for MIPS upgrades, however, were mostly TCM-based and subject to net pricing and recapture. Thus, that other non-net priced parts were readily available does not support the implicit conclusion that there was no scarcity of MIPS upgrade parts.

Even if used parts were available to perform MIPS upgrades, the record does not suggest any manufacturer of those parts other than IBM. Hence, the reasoning of Alcoa is as controlling here as it was for used IBM computers. . . .

E.   Smaller Capacity Computers

The district court considered AMI's proposed market definition to be too narrow because it failed to include "smaller capacity computers"—computers below the size and sophistication of a large-scale mainframe that nevertheless would be reasonable substitutes, either singly or in combination. See *Allen-Myland*, 693 F. Supp. at 274-75. AMI argues that it was error for the district court to include these smaller machines because there was not sufficient evidence of substitutability between these two types of computers. The district court rejected AMI's argument, citing evidence that smaller computers had effectively displaced mainframes in certain applications and noting a trend toward the replacement of large, centralized systems with "distributed" systems consisting of greater numbers of smaller capacity computers. *Id.*

AMI argues on appeal that this reasoning was flawed because it failed to consider the rapid development of technology over the life cycle of a typical computer. It agrees that some installations that initially required older generation mainframes might be satisfied with "smaller" machines when it came time to replace their mainframes, because the smaller machines would by then have all the power of the earlier mainframes. Nevertheless, AMI contends, the fact that some users of older mainframe computers might switch to smaller capacity machines proves nothing about whether those smaller machines effectively compete against IBM's current, more powerful mainframes, which are the focus of this litigation. AMI's argument is sound, but unavailing. There was testimony admitted at trial indicating that at least one smaller capacity computer, the Hewlett-Packard HP 3000 series, competed against the IBM 308X series "in many applications." The district court was entitled to, and did, credit this evidence. *Allen-Myland*, 693 F. Supp. at 275.

The amici argue that the district court failed to consider the problem of "lock-in." Although mainframes and smaller capacity computers may be substitutable when a new computer application is being developed or when an existing application is no longer useful and must be rewritten anyway, they argue that there are significant switching costs that prevent this from happening in the short run. For example, to "port" an existing application from a mainframe to a smaller computer, the applications software may have to be rewritten, the data files may have to be converted to new formats, and personnel may have to be extensively trained on the new system. The costs of doing so and the delay involved could well cause the computer user to remain with a mainframe-based system rather than convert to a smaller computer; indeed, one court has noted that, for compatibility reasons, over 80 percent of users remain loyal to the manufacturer of their original systems. See *Transamerica*, 481 F. Supp. at 980 & n.32.

. . . [T]his remains an issue of fact for the district court to resolve in the first instance. . . .

F. Peripheral Devices and Software

AMI also argues that the district court erred when it added peripheral devices and software into the relevant market. The court found that these items, which provide data input, storage and output capabilities and direct the computer in its processing of information, "provided significant and reasonable alternatives to a wide variety of upgrades and modifications of large scale mainframes." *Allen-Myland*, 693 F. Supp. at 276.

Similar or substitute products are those that "have the ability—actual or potential—to take significant amounts of business away from each other." Smith-Kline Corp. v. Eli Lilly & Co., 575 F.2d 1056, 1063 (3d Cir.), *cert. denied*, 439 U.S. 838, 99 S. Ct. 123, 58 L. Ed. 2d 134 (1978). Thus, the relevant product market "is composed of products that have reasonable interchangeability for the purposes for which they are produced—price, use and qualities considered." *Id.* at 1062-63 (quoting United States v. E.I. du Pont de Nemours & Co., 351 U.S. 377, 404, 76 S. Ct. 994, 1012, 100 L. Ed. 1264 (1956) (The Cellophane Case)); Tunis Bros. Co. v. Ford Motor Co., 952 F.2d 715, 722 (3d Cir. 1991), *cert. denied*, 120 L. Ed. 2d 903, 112 S. Ct. 3034 (1992).

"Interchangeability" implies that one product is roughly equivalent to another for the use to which it is put; while there might be some degree of preference for the one over the other, either would work effectively. A person needing transportation to work could accordingly buy a Ford or a Chevrolet automobile, or could elect to ride a horse or bicycle, assuming those options were feasible. The key test for determining whether one product is a substitute for another is whether there is a cross-elasticity of demand between them: in other words, whether the demand for the second good would respond to changes in the price of the first. *Tunis Bros.*, 952 F.2d at 722.

In the six years since the district court issued its opinion, the personal computer has consolidated its position in modern life, and what once seemed mired in impenetrable technical jargon is now within the vocabulary of the general public.

Moreover, technology changes rapidly and if one has an older computer and wishes to use the latest software applications, one often must either upgrade the central processor—the equivalent of a MIPS upgrade—or buy a new computer. Increasing the size of the disk drive, buying more memory or installing the latest version of the operating system may help in some cases but in many others will be ineffective. It thus may be argued that the same situation obtains in the case of larger computers; that is, peripherals and software are complementary goods but are not substitutes for mainframe computers.

The issue, nevertheless, remains a factual one for the district court to resolve. Here, if peripherals and software are reasonable substitutes for mainframes, we should expect to see an increased demand for them as the price of mainframes rises, but the district court cited no evidence of this type. Instead, it relied on the fact that IBM considers peripheral products and software when pricing its computer systems. *Allen-Myland*, 693 F. Supp. at 276. Pricing a large mainframe system on the basis of peripherals included with it against competitive offerings by other manufacturers, however, is simply not evidence that peripherals and mainframes are substitutes for one another.

The district court relied even more heavily on several anecdotes in which large mainframe users had upgraded memory, disks, software or other peripherals rather than perform a MIPS upgrade. *Id*. at 276-77. This testimony fell into two categories. First, some users testified that it was possible to delay a MIPS upgrade for a while by upgrading peripherals or software: akin perhaps to saying that installing new brakes may delay the necessity of purchasing a new car, but it is not sufficient evidence on which to conclude that the products are reasonably interchangeable in use. See Kaiser Aluminum & Chemical Corp. v. Federal Trade Comm'n, 652 F.2d 1324, 1331-32 (7th Cir. 1981) ("specialties," which delayed the necessity of replacing refractory bricks in furnaces, did not belong in the same relevant market).

Second, there was testimony to the effect that there are many ways to enhance the performance of a computer system, including MIPS upgrades and peripheral/software upgrades. Although it is doubtless true that improvements to peripherals or software will improve a computer's performance somewhat under certain circumstances, we find no evidence on how much or under what conditions improvement could be expected. There was thus no evidence from which to conclude whether peripheral and software upgrades were reasonably interchangeable with either a MIPS upgrade or a different mainframe computer in enough cases that those alternate upgrades could properly be termed substitutes. Nor was there evidence that, because of a price change in mainframes, there was a greater or lesser demand for peripheral/software upgrades. In sum, the evidence was insufficient to support the wholesale inclusion of peripherals and software into the relevant market for large-scale mainframes.

We emphasize, however, that we are not holding that peripheral and software must be excluded from the relevant market, only that, upon review, the evidence cited in the district court's opinion is insufficient to warrant including them. On remand, the district court will of course determine whether there is some degree of interchangeability or other evidence of cross-elasticity of demand. If there is, then the court is free to adjust IBM's share of the market by its best estimate of the true competition from peripherals and software. . . .

VI. Conclusion

We will accordingly vacate the district court's judgment in favor of IBM and remand for further proceedings consistent with this opinion.

Telex Corp. v. IBM Corp., 510 F.2d 894 (10th Cir. 1975): In 1975, IBM was the largest manufacturer of computer hardware. IBM sold both computers themselves and "peripheral devices" which could be plugged into IBM computers. Telex, which also made peripheral devices designed to be plugged into IBM computers, charged that IBM had monopolized the market for "IBM plug-compatible peripheral products." IBM contended that the market was "electronic data processing systems," and that it had no power in that market. The definition of the relevant market in which Telex and IBM competed was central to the case. The district court agreed with Telex, but the court of appeals reversed. It reasoned that peripheral devices which were not "IBM-compatible" were nonetheless "reasonably interchangeable" with IBM products because these devices could easily be modified for use with an IBM computer "by the use of interfaces designed for this purpose." Further, the court held that these competing products were part of a larger relevant market for computer *systems*, in which IBM competed with numerous other companies. This competition constrained any power IBM might have in the separate market for compatible peripherals.

COMMENTS AND QUESTIONS

Doesn't the relevant market in these cases depend on which consumers you consider, and when you consider them? It is surely true, as *Telex* suggests, that new computer purchasers look for entire systems of compatible products, and perhaps the competition of DEC, Wang, and others for computer systems prevented IBM from exercising market power over those consumers. However, once a consumer has purchased a computer, he may be significantly more limited in the peripheral devices he can buy to work with that computer. Should antitrust protect consumers from companies who would monopolize these "aftermarkets"? We will return to this issue in detail when we consider tying arrangements below.

PROBLEM

Problem 7-1. Two companies (*A* and *B*) agree to cross-license future patents relating to the development of a new system for modeling data structures in 3-D terms, in combination with a virtual reality device. Innovation in the development of the model requires the capability to interoperate with an advanced virtual reality helmet patented by a third party (*C*), which so far has been freely licensed to interested software developers. Aspects of the licensing arrangement between *A* and *B* raise the possibility that competition in research and development of this and related modeling programs will be lessened. Both *A* and *B* estimate that they are approximately two years away from marketing any software. The Antitrust Division is considering whether to define an innovation market in which to evaluate the competitive effects of the arrangement. What factors should it take into account in making this decision?

2. Anticompetitive Conduct

It is not enough to define a market and determine that an intellectual property owner is a monopolist, for monopoly alone is not illegal. Rather, it must be combined with some form of anticompetitive conduct. Assuming that the intellectual property owner has market power in a particular case, what conduct will suffice? It is in this context that the conflict between intellectual property and the antitrust laws arises most starkly.

Certainly, antitrust law must make some accommodation for monopolies that result from intellectual property if those intellectual property rights are to have any meaning. In particular, it is evident that merely possessing and enforcing a patent, copyright, trademark, or trade secret against competitors ought not violate the antitrust laws. See, e.g., Corsearch v. Thomson & Thomson, 792 F. Supp. 305 (S.D.N.Y. 1992) (owner of copyright in a computer database did not violate the antitrust laws by denying a competitor access to that database; a copyright owner has the right to limit or terminate the use of its intellectual property as it deems appropriate).

If we start from the proposition that it cannot be illegal to possess a patent (or other intellectual property right), what role remains for antitrust law? Several types of factual situations may still present antitrust problems. First, the patentee may have acquired his patent illegally (for example, through fraud). Second, a patentee may use his patent to acquire or maintain power beyond that granted by the intellectual property right itself. In both situations, antitrust courts are properly concerned with the effects that anticompetitive use of the intellectual property right may have.

a. Enforcing Intellectual Property Rights

Walker Process Equipment, Inc. v. Food Machinery & Chemical Corp.
Supreme Court of the United States
382 U.S. 172 (1965)

MR. JUSTICE CLARK delivered the opinion of the Court.

The question before us is whether the maintenance and enforcement of a patent obtained by fraud on the Patent Office may be the basis of an action under §2 of the Sherman Act . . . [Food Machinery sued Walker for patent infringement, and Walker counterclaimed for violations of the antitrust laws.] Walker then amended its counterclaim to charge that Food Machinery had "illegally monopolized interstate and foreign commerce by fraudulently and in bad faith obtaining and maintaining . . . its patent . . . well knowing that it had no basis for . . . a patent." It alleged fraud on the basis that Food Machinery had sworn before the Patent Office that it neither knew nor believed that its invention had been in public use in the United States for more than one year prior to filing its patent application when, in fact, Food Machinery was a party to prior use within such time.

[The District Court dismissed Walker's counterclaim, and the Court of Appeals affirmed.] . . .

. . . The gist of Walker's claim is that since Food Machinery obtained its patent by fraud it cannot enjoy the limited exception to the prohibitions of §2 of the Sherman Act, but must answer under that section and §4 of the Clayton Act in treble damages to those injured by any monopolistic action taken under the fraudulent patent claim. Nor can the interest in protecting patentees from "innumerable vexatious suits" be used to frustrate the assertion of rights conferred by the antitrust laws. It must be remembered that we deal only with a special class of patents, i.e. those procured by intentional fraud.

Under the decisions of this Court a person sued for infringement may challenge the validity of the patent on various grounds, including fraudulent procurement. In fact, one need not await the filing of a threatened suit by the patentee; the validity of the patent may be tested under the Declaratory Judgment Act. . . . At the same time, we have recognized that an injured party may attack the misuse of patent rights. To permit recovery of treble damages for the fraudulent procurement of the patent coupled with violations of §2 accords with these long-recognized procedures. It would also promote the purposes so well expressed in Precision Instrument [Mfg. Co. v. Automotive Maintenance Machinery, 324 U.S. 806 (1945)] at 816:

> A patent by its very nature is affected with a public interest. . . . [It] is an exception to the general rule against monopolies and to the right to access to a free and open market. The far-reaching social and economic consequences of a patent, therefore, give the public a paramount interest in seeing that patent monopolies spring from backgrounds free from fraud or other inequitable conduct and that such monopolies are kept within their legitimate scope.

III.

Walker's counterclaim alleged that Food Machinery obtained the patent by knowingly and willfully misrepresenting facts to the Patent Office. Proof of this assertion would be sufficient to strip Food Machinery of its exemption from the antitrust laws. By the same token, Food Machinery's good faith would furnish a complete defense. This includes an honest mistake as to the effect of prior installation upon patentability—so-called "technical fraud."

To establish monopolization or attempt to monopolize a part of trade or commerce under §2 of the Sherman Act, it would then be necessary to appraise the exclusionary power of the illegal patent claim in terms of the relevant market for the product involved. Without a definition of that market there is no way to measure Food Machinery's ability to lessen or destroy competition. It may be that the device—knee-action swing diffusers—used in sewage treatment systems does not comprise a relevant market. There may be effective substitutes for the device which do not infringe the patent. This is a matter of proof, as is the amount of damages suffered by Walker.

[The Court remanded the case with instructions to consider the antitrust claim on its merits.]

Remanded

COMMENTS AND QUESTIONS

1. The Supreme Court's decision in *Walker Process* has given rise to a whole series of antitrust claims (such as Brunswick Corp. v. Riegel Textile Corp., 752 F.2d 261 (7th Cir. 1984)) that are based on fraudulent procurement of a patent. Indeed, these antitrust suits have come to be referred to as "*Walker Process* claims."

However, the idea that fraudulent procurement of a patent itself violates the antitrust laws is highly misleading. As the last section of the Court's opinion makes clear, the only effect of the defendant's fraud was that it lost the protection of the patent laws. The Court still required that Walker prove all the substantive elements of a section 2 violation (market power, anticompetitive conduct, and—for attempt claims—intent to monopolize). Indeed, Justice Harlan concurred precisely in order to emphasize that point:

Must prove §2 Elements

> We hold today that a treble-damage action for monopolization . . . may be maintained under §4 of the Clayton Act if two conditions are satisfied: (1) the relevant patent is shown to have been produced by knowing and willful fraud . . . ; and (2) all the elements otherwise necesary to establish a §2 monopolization charge are proved. Conversely, such a private cause of action would *not* be made out if the plaintiff . . . failed to prove the elements of a §2 charge even though he has established actual fraud in the procurement of the patent and the defendant's knowledge of that fraud.

Patent Faud
⊕
§2 Elements
=
Treble Damages

382 U.S. at 179. Thus, *Walker Process* is limited to removing the cloak of protection afforded by patent law to patents themselves where the patent in question was obtained by fraud.

2. Even if a patent is lawfully acquired, using it as an anticompetitive weapon might violate the antitrust laws. After all, baseless infringement suits on a valid patent are just as troubling as infringement suits on a baseless patent. Several courts have held that "anticompetitive litigation," standing alone, can suffice to violate the antitrust laws. See, e.g., Handgards, Inc. v. Ethicon, Inc., 601 F.2d 986, 996 (9th Cir. 1979); CVD, Inc. v. Raytheon Co., 769 F.2d 842, 851 (1st Cir. 1985). Still other courts have held that baseless litigation may constitute anticompetitive conduct sufficient to satisfy one element of the monopolization test. See Daralyn Durie & Mark A. Lemley, The Antitrust Liability of Labor Unions for Anticompetitive Litigation, 80 Cal. L. Rev. 757, 778 n.128 (1992) (collecting cases).

3. There is a significant limitation on antitrust claims or counterclaims that are based on the filing of an infringement suit. That limitation is the antitrust petitioning immunity doctrine. Before considering the merits of an antitrust counterclaim, courts must first decide whether the patentee is immune from antitrust liability under the *Noerr-Pennington* doctrine, a doctrine that protects antitrust defendants from liability for petitioning the government. The Supreme Court

Antitrust Petitioning Immunity Doctrine

has consistently held that filing a lawsuit or an action before an administrative agency is "petitioning" and therefore is presumptively entitled to immunity from antitrust suit.

There is an exception to antitrust immunity for sham litigation, however. If a patent or copyright infringement lawsuit is a sham, rather than a "genuine effort . . . to influence" the court, it is not entitled to antitrust immunity, and the counterclaim will be evaluated on the merits. Allied Tube & Conduit Corp. v. Indian Head, Inc., 486 U.S. 492 (1988). Not surprisingly, there has been heated debate over the precise scope of the "sham" exception. The Supreme Court visited this issue in the 1993 case of Professional Real Estate Investors v. Columbia Pictures, Inc., 508 U.S. 49 (1993), in which Columbia Pictures had brought a copyright infringement suit against PREI based on PREI's performance of copyrighted movies in guests' hotel rooms. PREI counterclaimed on the grounds that Columbia had conspired to monopolize the market and restrain trade. Columbia lost its copyright case on summary judgment, but the district court held that PREI was not entitled to pursue its antitrust claim because Columbia's copyright suit, though unsuccessful, was not a sham.

The Supreme Court affirmed the application of antitrust immunity to PREI's counterclaim. In doing so, it set out a new two-part test to determine whether a lawsuit is a sham. "First, the lawsuit must be objectively baseless in the sense that no reasonable litigant could realistically expect success on the merits." *Id*. at 60. Second, "the court should focus on whether the baseless lawsuit conceals an attempt to interfere directly with the business relationships of a competitor through the use of governmental *process*—as opposed to the *outcome* of that process—as an anticompetitive weapon." *Id*. at 60-61 (emphasis in original). These are commonly referred to as the "objectively baseless" and "subjectively baseless" tests, respectively. Only if the suit is a sham under this definition will the court proceed to consider the substantive elements of an antitrust violation. *Id*. The effect of this new test is to make it extremely difficult to prevail in an antitrust counterclaim based on wrongful enforcement of an intellectual property right.

b. Exclusionary Practices

≡ **United States v. Microsoft Corporation**
≡ *United States District Court for the District of Columbia*
≡ *159 F.R.D. 318 (D.D.C. 1995), rev'd, 56 F.3d 1448 (D.C. Cir. 1995)*

SPORKIN, District Judge:

The issue before this Court is whether the entry of a proposed antitrust consent decree between Microsoft Corporation and the United States is in "the public interest." Microsoft is the world's largest developer of computer software. On July 15, 1994, the Government filed a complaint charging Microsoft with violating Sections 1 and 2 of the Sherman Anti-Trust Act. 15 U.S.C. §§1-7 (1973). On the same day the parties filed a proposed consent judgment.

I. Background

The Government filed the complaint and proposed judgment after a four-year investigation of Microsoft. The Federal Trade Commission ("FTC") initiated the investigation in 1990. According to Microsoft, but not confirmed by the Government, the FTC considered a wide range of practices including: (1) that Microsoft gave its developers of applications software information about its operating systems software before providing it to other applications developers; (2) that Microsoft announced that it was developing a non-existent version of operating software to dissuade Original Equipment Manufacturers ("OEMs") from leasing a competitor's operating system; (3) that Microsoft required OEMs that licensed its operating system software also to license Microsoft applications; and (4) that Microsoft licensed its operating systems to OEMs on a per processor basis. Microsoft asserts that before the FTC investigation was completed, it was expanded to include every aspect of Microsoft's business.

There was never a majority vote among the FTC commissioners to file an administrative complaint against Microsoft. In late 1993, after a 2-2 deadlock by the commissioners, no administrative action was filed, and the FTC suspended its investigation of Microsoft.

Following the suspension of the FTC investigation, Assistant Attorney General Bingaman, the head of the Antitrust Division of the Department of Justice, decided to revive the investigation. In June, 1994 Microsoft and the Department of Justice initiated settlement negotiations. Approximately a month later the parties came to agreement and filed a proposed judgment with the Court.

II. The Complaint

The complaint charges that Microsoft violated Sections 1 and 2 of the Sherman Anti-Trust Act. 15 U.S.C. §§1-7. The primary allegations in the complaint concern licensing agreements between Microsoft and OEMs of personal computers ("PCs"). The complaint also addresses provisions of non-disclosure agreements ("NDAs") between Microsoft and other developers of applications software, known as independent software developers ("ISVs"). The complaint narrowly tailors the relevant product market to the market for certain operating systems software for x86 microprocessors. The geographic market is not limited. . . .

Microsoft has a monopoly on the market for PC operating systems. Microsoft's share of the operating systems market identified in the complaint is consistently well above 70%. According to Microsoft's 1993 Annual Report, as of June 30, 1993, 120 million PCs ran on Microsoft's MS-DOS. Microsoft also developed and sells Windows, a sophisticated operating system that runs on top of MS-DOS or a similar operating system. Windows allows a PC user to run more than one application at a time and shift between them. Windows is known as a "graphical user interface." Approximately 50 million PCs now use Windows. Microsoft generally does not sell its operating systems directly to consumers. Instead, it licenses its operating systems to OEMs for inclusion in the PCs they make.

Microsoft, the Justice Department, and a number of competitors who oppose the entry of the decree all agree that it is very difficult to enter the operating systems market. There are two main reasons for this, each of which reinforces the other. First, consumers do not want to buy PCs with an operating system that does not already have a large installed base because of their concern that there will not be a wide range of applications software available for that operating system. The second, complementary reason why there are large barriers to entry into the operating systems market is that ISVs do not want to spend time and money developing applications for operating systems that do not have a large installed base. They perceive that demand for that software will be low. As a result, OEMs have little incentive to license an operating system that does not have a large installed base and include it in their PCs.

In addition to these "natural" barriers to entry the complaint identifies Microsoft's use of per processor licenses and long term commitments as "exclusionary and anti-competitive contract terms to maintain its monopoly." A per processor license means that Microsoft licenses an operating system to an OEM which pays a royalty to Microsoft for each PC sold regardless of whether a Microsoft operating system is included in that PC. In other words, under a per processor license, if an OEM sells some PCs with a competitor's operating system installed (e.g., IBM'S OS/2), and others with MS-DOS installed, the OEM would pay Microsoft royalties for all PCs sold. In effect, the OEM pays twice every time it sells a PC with a non-Microsoft operating system—once to the company that licensed the operating system to the OEM and once to Microsoft. The complaint charges that per processor licenses discourage OEMs from licensing competing operating systems and/or cause OEMs to raise the price for PCs with a competing operating system to recoup the fee paid to Microsoft.

The complaint further alleges that Microsoft's use of long-term licensing agreements with or without minimum commitments, and the rolling over of unused commitments unreasonably extended some licensing agreements with Microsoft. These practices allegedly foreclosed OEMs from licensing operating systems from Microsoft's competitors.

The other anticompetitive practice cited in the complaint is the structure of Microsoft's non-disclosure agreements ("NDAs") with ISVs during the development of its new Windows operating system. ISVs work with Microsoft during the development and testing of new operating systems so they can produce applications that run with that operating system and release them around the time the operating system is released. This collaboration benefits Microsoft in two ways. First, Microsoft receives input from the ISVs on how to improve the operating system. Second, a new operating system is more attractive to consumers if there are compatible applications programs immediately available. In order to protect confidential information about its new software, Microsoft requires ISVs to sign NDAs in order to obtain product information.

The complaint alleges that the recent NDAs Microsoft has executed with ISVs are overly restrictive and anti-competitive. The Government alleges that the NDAs not only legitimately protect against the disclosure of confidential information to competing developers of operating systems but also discourage ISVs from developing their own competing operating systems and/or from developing applications for competing operating systems.

In sum, the Government alleges that the practices outlined above deprive competitors of substantial opportunities to license their operating systems to OEMs, preventing them from developing a large installed base. This discourages both ISVs from designing software for competing operating systems and consumers from buying PCs with these competing operating systems. These practices also harm consumers by limiting the variety of available operating systems and raising the prices for non-Microsoft operating systems. . . .

III. The Proposed Decree

The proposed decree negotiated and entered into by the parties is significantly and substantially narrower than the requests contained in the prayer for relief in the complaint. The consent decree limits certain of Microsoft's contract and NDA practices. The prohibitions concern licensing agreements and NDAs for certain operating systems software; operating systems software for workstations are not covered. The decree does not address any of Microsoft's applications software.

The decree enjoins Microsoft from entering into any licensing agreement longer than one year, though OEMs may at their discretion include in the licensing agreement a one year option to renew. Microsoft can impose no penalty or charge on an OEM for its choice not to renew the licensing agreement, nor can it require an OEM to commit not to license a competitor's operating system.

Microsoft may only license the operating systems covered by the decree on a per copy basis, with one exception.[11] Microsoft cannot include minimum commitments in its covered licensing agreements. The agreements cannot be structured so that the OEM pays royalties for including MS-DOS in a fixed number of PCs, whether or not the OEM actually sells that number of PCs with a Microsoft operating system included.

The decree restricts the scope of the NDAs that Microsoft may negotiate with ISVs. Microsoft cannot enter into an NDA whose duration extends beyond, (i) commercial release of the operating system, (ii) an earlier public disclosure by Microsoft, or (iii) one year from the date of the disclosure of information covered by the NDA to a person subject to the NDA, whichever comes first. The decree also prohibits the use of NDAs that would prevent persons covered by that NDA from developing applications for competing operating systems unless the application entailed use of proprietary Microsoft information.

The decree explicitly states that it does not constitute "any evidence or admission by any party with respect to any issue of fact or law." Indeed, Microsoft has denied in its submissions to the Court that any of the allegations set forth in the complaint constitute violations of the antitrust laws. . . .

---

11. This exception allows for certain Per System Licenses. A per system license means a license for a particular system or model. The decree allows OEMs to designate identical machines containing different operating systems as distinct systems. This is intended to prevent OEMs from paying royalties to Microsoft for all the computers of a certain system even if some do not include a Microsoft operating system.

(margin handwritten notes: Consent Decree: Not in Public Interest)

V.

B. Public Interest Determination

The Court cannot find the proposed decree to be in the public interest for four reasons. First, the Government has declined to provide the Court with the information it needs to make a proper public interest determination. Second, the scope of the decree is too narrow. Third, the parties have been unable and unwilling adequately to address certain anticompetitive practices, which Microsoft states it will continue to employ in the future and with respect to which the decree is silent. Thus, the decree does not constitute an effective antitrust remedy. Fourth, the Court is not satisfied that the enforcement and compliance mechanisms in the decree are satisfactory. . . .

V.B.2. Scope of the Decree

(margin handwritten note: Too narrow in scope)

The Court finds the decree on its face to be too narrow. Its coverage is restricted to PCs with x86 or Intel x86 compatible microprocessors. The decree covers only MS-DOS and Windows and its predecessor and successor products. Neither party has even addressed the Court's concern that the decree be expanded to cover all of Microsoft's commercially marketed operating systems. Given the pace of technological change, the decree must anticipate covering operating systems developed for new microprocessors.[25] In addition, taking into account Microsoft's penchant for narrowly defining the antitrust laws, the Court fears there may be endless debate as to whether a new operating system is covered by the decree.

V.B.3. Ineffective Remedy

(margin handwritten note: Not open market)

The Court cannot find the proposed decree to be in the public interest because it does not find that the decree will "effectively pry open to competition a market that has been closed by defendant['s] illegal restraints." *AT&T*, 552 F. Supp. at 150. During the period in which this matter was before the Court the Government did little to show that the decree would meet this test beyond telling the Court that it had labored hard, that the decree was good, and that it should be approved. At the eleventh hour, only after the Court again requested information to allay its concerns, did the Government finally produce an affidavit from Nobel Laureate economist, Professor Kenneth Arrow.

The affidavit made three main points: 1) that the market is an increasing returns market with large barriers to entry; 2) that the violations set forth in the complaint contributed in some part to Microsoft's monopoly position; and 3) that the decree will eliminate "artificial barriers that Microsoft had erected to prevent or slow the entry of competing suppliers of operating system software products."

The Court does not doubt the Government's position that the practices alleged in the complaint are artificial barriers. Nor does it doubt that the decree does

---

25. It is difficult to imagine in this dynamic area that by the end of the period (7 years) the decree will be in effect, there will not be wholesale change with respect to microprocessors and operating systems.

address those practices. But what the Government fails to show is that the proposed decree will open the market and remedy the unfair advantage Microsoft gained in the market through its anticompetitive practices.

Professor Arrow's affidavit states that the operating systems market is an increasing returns market. In layman's terms that means that once a company has a monopoly position, it is extremely hard to dislodge it. Professor Arrow and the Government also concur that part of Microsoft's monopoly position is attributable to the artificial barriers it erected. Professor Arrow only argues that the decree prospectively removes these artificial barriers. He does not explain how the decree remedies the monopolist position Microsoft has achieved through alleged illegal means in an increasing returns market. If it is concededly difficult to open up an increasing returns market to competition once a company has obtained a monopoly position, the Government has not shown how prospectively prohibiting violative conduct that contributed to defendant's achieving its monopoly position will serve to return the market to where it should have been absent its anticompetitive practices. Simply telling a defendant to go forth and sin no more does little or nothing to address the unfair advantage it has already gained. In short, given the Government's expert's own analysis of this market, the decree is "too little, too late."

The proposed decree without going further, is not in the public interest because it does not meet the test of an effective antitrust remedy. The decree deals with licensing and nondisclosure practices that the Government found to be anticompetitive and detrimental to a free and open market. What the decree does not address are a number of other anticompetitive practices that from time to time Microsoft has been accused of engaging in by others in the industry. Since a Court cannot shut its eyes to the obvious, it has asked the parties to discuss these widespread public allegations. The Government has refused, and Microsoft has claimed that the accusations are false.

The accusations range from charges that Microsoft engages in the practice of vaporware i.e., the public announcement of a computer product before it is ready for market for the sole purpose of causing consumers not to purchase a competitor's product that has been developed and is either currently available for sale or momentarily about to enter the market. Other allegations include charges that Microsoft uses its dominant position in operating systems to give it an undue advantage in developing applications software and that it manipulates its operating systems so competitors' applications software are inoperable or more difficult for the consumers to utilize effectively.

Throughout these proceedings, this Court has expressed repeated concern about these allegations, in part, because it is concerned that if they are true and defendant continues to engage in them, it will continue to hold and possibly expand its monopoly position, even if it ceases the practices alleged in the complaint.

The Court has been particularly concerned about the accusations of "vaporware." Microsoft has a dominant position in the operating systems market, from which the Government's expert concedes it would be very hard to dislodge it. Given this fact, Microsoft could unfairly hold onto this position with aggressive preannouncements of new products in the face of the introduction of possibly superior competitive products. In other words, all participants concede that consumers and OEMs will be reluctant to shift to a new operating system, even a superior one, because it will mean not only giving up on both its old operating systems and applications, but also risking the possibility that there will not be adequate applications to run on the superior product. If this is true, Microsoft can hold onto its market share gained allegedly illegally, even with the introduction of a competitor's operating system superior to its own. By telling the public, "we have developed a product that we are about to introduce into the market (when such is not the case) that is just as good and is compatible with all your old applications," Microsoft can discourage consumers and OEMs from considering switching to the new product. It is for this reason that courts may consider practices outside the complaint. See *AT&T*, 552 F. Supp. at 150.

. . . [The court admitted two Microsoft documents submitted by an amicus curiae.] Both of these documents are internal Microsoft records. They are part of two Microsoft employee evaluation forms. In the first, the Microsoft employee writes that during the past six months he engaged in the following beneficial activities for Microsoft, "QB3 preannounce to hold off Turbo buyers."

The second document is even more specific. In a self-evaluation, a Microsoft employee wrote, "I developed a rollout plan for QuickC and CS that focused on minimizing Borland's first mover advantage by preannouncing with an aggressive communications campaign." These documents indicate that the highest officials of the company knew of the practices that were utilized to impact adversely on the market plans of a competitor. Whether the documents are actionable or not, certainly at a minimum they require explanation from the parties. No satisfactory explanation has been given.

Although Microsoft acknowledges the authenticity of the documents, it denies they describe the practice of vaporware and indeed, states that the practice that is described is a perfectly legitimate competitive practice. When pressed as to why the practices described in the documents were not vaporware, counsel for Microsoft stated he would limit "vaporware" to those instances where no product at all exists at the time of the so-called "preannouncement." According to counsel, it does not even matter that the date for introduction of the preannounced product is not met. Counsel further advised the Court that he would advise his client to continue to engage in the described practices. . . .

This Court cannot ignore the obvious. Here is the dominant firm in the software industry admitting it "preannounces" products to freeze the current software market and thereby defeat the marketing plans of competitors that have products ready for market. Microsoft admits that the preannouncement is solely for the purpose of having an adverse impact on a competitor's product. Its counsel states it has advised its client that the practice is perfectly legal and it may continue the practice. This practice of an alleged monopolist would seem to contribute to the acquisition, maintenance, or exercise of market share.

The Government has pressed for the adoption of its decree on the grounds that it will open up competition. Given the Government's desire to open up competition why does it not want to take on the vaporware issue?

When the Court gave Microsoft the opportunity to disavow this practice by an undertaking it declined to do so. What is more, the Government told the Court that if it conditioned its approval on Microsoft's undertaking no longer to engage in the practice, the Government would withdraw its approval of the decree even if Microsoft agreed to the undertaking.

The Court cannot sign off on a decree knowing that the defendant intends to continue to engage in an anticompetitive practice without the Government providing a full explanation as to its "no action" stance. It would almost be the equivalent of a Court accepting a probationary plea from a defendant who has told the Court he will go out and again engage in inappropriate conduct.

V.B.4. Compliance

The only change in the decree that the Government stated it would accept is the Court's suggestion that Microsoft establish an internal mechanism to monitor the decree. This too Microsoft has declined even to consider. Microsoft's position is that its 50 or so in-house lawyers, along with its outside retained counsel, are sufficient to monitor the decree. This is the same group that has advised its client that "product preannouncements" to impede competition is proper behavior.

[handwritten: No internal monitoring mechanism]

This Court finds itself in a position similar to that of Judge Greene in *AT&T*, who refused to approve the decree without modification because of his concern as to its compliance and enforcement. *AT&T*, 552 F. Supp. at 214-17.

Based on Microsoft's counsel's representations to this Court, the Court is concerned about the question of compliance. This concern is heightened because even though the Company on prior occasions has publicly stated it does not and will not abuse its dominant position in the operating systems market vis-a-vis its development of application products, it has refused to give the Court the same assurance. Without a compliance mechanism, the Court cannot make the public interest finding. This is particularly so because Microsoft denies that the conduct charged in the Government's complaint to which it has consented, violates the antitrust laws.

[handwritten: Compliance]

This is clearly the kind of case that Congress had in mind when it passed the Tunney Act. Microsoft is a company that has a monopolist position in a field that is central to this country's well being, not only for the balance of this century, but also for the 21st Century. The Court is certainly mindful of the heroic efforts of the Antitrust Division to negotiate the decree. There is no doubt its task was formidable. Here is a company that is so feared by its competitors that they believe they will be retaliated against if they disclose their identity even in an open proceeding before a U.S. District Court Judge.

The picture that emerges from these proceedings is that the U.S. Government is either incapable or unwilling to deal effectively with a potential threat to this nation's economic well being. How else can the four year deadlocked investigation conducted by the FTC be explained. What is more, the Justice Department, although it labored hard in its follow up investigation, likewise was unable to come up with a meaningful result.

It is clear to this Court that if it signs the decree presented to it, the message will be that Microsoft is so powerful that neither the market nor the Government is capable of dealing with all of its monopolistic practices. The attitude of Microsoft confirms these observations. While it has denied publicly that it engages in anticompetitive practices, it refuses to give the Court in any respect the same assurance.[36] It has refused to take even a small step to meet any of the reasonable concerns that have been raised by the Court. . . .

---

36. Microsoft has stated to the Press over the years that there is a "Chinese Wall" between its operating systems and applications divisions. In Microsoft's submission to the Court, it maintains that there is no such separation and that one is not necessary.

Microsoft has done extremely well in its business in a relatively short period of time, which is a tribute both to its talented personnel and to this nation's great ethic that affords every citizen the ability to rise to the top. Microsoft, a rather new corporation, may not have matured to the position where it understands how it should act with respect to the public interest and the ethics of the market place. In this technological age, this nation's cutting edge companies must guard against being captured by their own technology and becoming robotized. . . .

[Judge Sporkin refused to accept the proposed consent decree between the Antitrust Division and Microsoft.]

United States v. Microsoft Corp., 253 F.3d 34 (D.C. Cir. 2001) (en banc): The government filed suit against Microsoft again in 1998, challenging a variety of conduct related to the Windows 98 operating system. The district court found Microsoft to have engaged in a wide variety of anticompetitive conduct, a finding affirmed in most respects by the D.C. Circuit. Among the most significant issues were those related to Microsoft's efforts to maintain its operating system monopoly by bundling new features into Windows 98.

The D.C. Circuit adopted the government's theory that defensive leveraging violated section 2 by helping Microsoft maintain its existing monopoly in the operating system market. The defensive leveraging allegations in that case focused on Microsoft's conduct related to Java. Java is a computing language developed by Sun Microsystems that is intended to permit software to run on multiple platforms. As a result, software code does not need to be rewritten for each operating system on which the program is intended to run—"write once, run anywhere" is Sun's campaign slogan to software producers. Microsoft immediately perceived Java as a significant competitive hazard because it threatened to increase compatibility between Windows and non-Windows operating systems, thus forcing Windows to compete on price and features rather than attracting customers by means of its large installed base alone.

Under license with Sun, Microsoft developed its own version of Java, which ran faster than Sun's Java but was incompatible with non-Windows systems. At the same time Microsoft entered into agreements with software developers under which the latter received preferred access and support in exchange for their promise to use the Microsoft version rather than the Sun version of Java. Microsoft also gave software developers a set of "development tools" for making their software access Java, but deceptively failed to tell them that if they used these tools, their software would run only on the Microsoft version of Java. "As a result, even Java "developers who were opting for [operating system] portability over performance . . . unwittingly [wrote] Java applications that [ran] only on Windows." Further:

> Microsoft documents confirm that Microsoft intended to deceive Java developers, and predicted that the effect of its actions would be to generate Windows-dependent Java applications that their developers believed would be cross-platform; these documents also indicate that Microsoft's ultimate objective was to thwart Java's threat to Microsoft's monopoly in the market for operating systems.

Id. at 56. The court then concluded:

> Microsoft's conduct related to its Java developer tools served to protect its monopoly of the operating system in a manner not attributable either to the superiority of the operating system or to the acumen of its makers, and therefore was anticompetitive. Unsurprisingly, Microsoft offers no procompetitive explanation for its campaign to deceive developers. Accordingly, we conclude this conduct is exclusionary, in violation of §2 of the Sherman Act.

Id. Interestingly, the court rejected the government's more traditional claim that Microsoft was leveraging its monopoly into the Internet browser market, concluding that the government had failed to define such a market and prove harm in that market with sufficient specificity.

The D.C. Circuit also held that Microsoft's commingling of browser and operating system code, and its efforts to prevent OEMs and users from separating the two, violated section 2 of the Sherman Act. As the D.C. Circuit noted:

> Technologically binding IE to Windows, the District Court found, both prevented OEMs from pre-installing other browsers and deterred consumers from using them. In particular, having the IE software code as an irremovable part of Windows meant that pre-installing a second browser would "increase an OEM's product testing costs," because an OEM must test and train its support staff to answer calls related to every software product preinstalled on the machine; moreover, pre-installing a browser in addition to IE would to many OEMs be "a questionable use of the scarce and valuable space on a PC's hard drive."

The district court had found that three different "technological shackles" effectively bound IE to the Windows system:

> [e]xcluding IE from the "Add/Remove Programs" utility; designing Windows so as in certain circumstances to override the user's choice of a default browser other than IE; and commingling code related to browsing and other code in the same files, so that any attempt to delete the files containing IE would, at the same time, cripple the operating system.

Before proceeding, the court gave this warning:

> As a general rule, courts are properly very skeptical about claims that competition has been harmed by a dominant firm's product design changes. . . . In a competitive market, firms routinely innovate in the hope of appealing to consumers, sometimes in the process making their products incompatible with those of rivals; the imposition of liability when a monopolist does the same thing will inevitably deter a certain amount of innovation. This is all the more true in a market, such as this one, in which the product itself is rapidly changing. Judicial deference to product innovation, however, does not mean that a monopolist's product design decisions are per se lawful.

The court found that all three of the challenged practices were prima facie anticompetitive. For two of the three—excluding IE from the add/remove utility and commingling the code—it had offered no business justification. For the third—causing Windows to override the users selection of Netscape as the default browsers in certain invocations—the court found that Microsoft offered as a valid justification that this feature limited conflict when the user was attempting to use certain subfeatures that existed only on IE, not on Netscape. Further, the override affected only a few of the numerous ways in which Windows permitted the browser to be launched. Since the government had not rebutted these claims, this particular practice was found not to be unlawful.

Transamerica Computer Co. v. IBM Corp., 481 F. Supp. 965 (N.D. Cal. 1979), *aff'd*, 698 F.2d 1377 (9th Cir. 1983): IBM, which at that time held a dominant position in the mainframe and minicomputer markets, was accused of "predatory design changes." In particular, Transamerica (a maker of IBM-compatible peripheral devices) claimed that IBM frequently changed the design specifications of its peripheral interfaces, solely in order to make competing products obsolete and extend its own power into the market for peripherals. The court held that IBM was not liable for monopolizing the market, even though it acknowledged that IBM's "predominant intent . . . was undoubtedly to preclude or delay PCM competition and gain a competitive advantage." The court reasoned:

> It is not difficult to imagine situations where a monopolist could utilize the design of its own product to maintain market control or to gain a competitive advantage. For instance, the PCMs were only able to offer IBM's customers an alternative because they had duplicated the interface, the electrical connection between the IBM System/360 CPU and the IBM peripheral (or peripheral subsystem). Had IBM responded to the PCMs' inroads on its assumed monopoly by changing the System/360 interfaces with such frequency that PCMs would have been unable to attach and unable to economically adapt their peripherals to the ever-changing interface designs, and, if those interface changes had no purpose and effect other than the preclusion of PCM competition, this Court would not hesitate to find that such conduct was predatory. Or, if a monopolist frequently changed the teleprocessing interface by which its computers communicate with remote terminals in such a way that its terminals would continue to function while others would fail, and, if the only purpose and effect of the change was to gain a competitive advantage in the terminal market (where the monopolist lacked monopoly power), that use of monopoly power would be condemned.
>
> It is more difficult to formulate a legal standard for design conduct than it is to imagine clearly illegal situations. Any such standard must properly balance a concern for the preservation of desirable incentives with the need to prevent monopolization by technology. Like pricing, equipment design can have procompetitive as well as anticompetitive aspects. Truly new and innovative products are to be encouraged, and are an important part of the competitive process. For this reason, the acquisition or maintenance of monopoly power as a result of a superior product does not violate the Sherman Act. One court has even suggested that where there is a valid engineering dispute over a product's superiority the inquiry should end; the product is innovative and the design is legal. That view, probably the result of a concern for the creativity that has characterized the history of computers, is overprotective. It ignores the possibility that a superior product might be used as a vehicle for tying sales of other products, and would pronounce products superior even where the predominant evidence indicated they were not.
>
> Another approach would be to examine the designers' intent. If a technological design were chosen for an illegal purpose (such as to effectuate a tie) and if that purpose was fulfilled, it would be illegal. If that standard were to apply only where the intent was solely an illegal one, creativity would not be stifled. But usually many results are intended, and if only one, even the predominating, intent is illegal, and thus pun-

ished, legitimate incentives will be imperiled. Discerning corporate intent is seldom easy, and, in any event, the law against monopolization is much more concerned with the effect of conduct rather than with its purpose. . . .

Large firms attempting to conform their conduct to Transamerica's proposed rule would have a difficult time indeed. Any successful action they might take to win sales necessarily tends to improve or preserve their market position. Disappointed competitors, if they can conceive of some alternative price, product, modification or practice they would have preferred, would be encouraged to bring suit. Even if the large firm recognizes and tries to resolve the problem, it cannot assure its safety. One alternative might exclude or restrict one set of potential plaintiffs, while another set would be affected by the other alternative. Management's safest course might be to do nothing, but that, of course, would violate their duty to shareholders, and would do nothing to benefit a healthy, innovative and competitive market.

It is an unwise policy for the law to coddle competitors, especially if the protection comes at the expense of destroying a larger firm's incentive to compete. Even companies that choose to enter dominated markets must be prepared to face competition on the merits. Where a monopolist chooses an alternative that does not unreasonably restrict competition, the law is not offended. It is the choice of an unreasonable alternative, not the failure to choose the least restrictive alternative, that leads to liability.

IBM did not lie dead in the water when faced with competition. It took action. And the action it took may have caused some competitors to suffer more than other actions would have. But the action IBM took, under the circumstances in which it acted, did not unreasonably restrict competition, and thus, did not violate the law.

COMMENTS AND QUESTIONS

1. Judge Sporkin's decision in United States v. Microsoft Corp. was reversed by the D.C. Circuit on appeal. United States v. Microsoft Corp., 56 F.3d 1448 (D.C. Cir. 1995). The Court of Appeals held that Judge Sporkin simply lacked the power under the Tunney Act, 15 U.S.C. §16(e), to expand his inquiry beyond the bounds of the complaint filed by the government. Thus, the Court of Appeals did not address the "vaporware" issue on the merits; it simply reversed on the grounds that the agreement between the United States and Microsoft *on the issues alleged in the complaint* was consonant with the public interest. The Court of Appeals also took the unusual step of ordering that the case be reassigned to another judge on remand.

2. Judge Sporkin in *Microsoft* expressed concern that the Antitrust Division has not taken sufficient steps to ensure compliance with the consent decree. What additional steps would appropriately protect the public? In particular, consider Judge Sporkin's proposed prohibition on "vaporware," which he notes includes preannouncements as well as announcements concerning nonexistent products. How can the Justice Department ensure that Microsoft does not engage in vaporware announcements? Would government scrutiny of all Microsoft product announcements be too invasive a remedy?

For a discussion of the vaporware issue, see Stephan M. Levy, Should "Vaporware" Be an Antitrust Concern?, 42 Antitrust Bull. 33 (1997); Robert Prentice, Vaporware: Imaginary High-Tech Products and Real Antitrust Liability in a Post-Chicago World, 57 Ohio St. L.J. 1163 (1996).

3. Not all courts have agreed with *Transamerica* that product design changes cannot be predatory. An interesting development in the patent context is C.R. Bard v. M3 Systems, 157 F.3d 1340 (Fed. Cir. 1998), where the Federal Circuit (over a vigorous dissent by Judge Newman) held that deliberate acts to create incompatibility between a patented system and a competitor's product could be the sort of predatory conduct that was actionable under the antitrust laws.

c. Unilateral Refusals to Deal

Data General Corp. v. Grumman Systems Support Corp.
United States Court of Appeals for the First Circuit
36 F.3d 1147 (1st Cir. 1994)

STAHL, Circuit Judge.

While this case raises numerous issues touching on copyright law, Grumman's most intriguing argument—presented below as both a defense and a counterclaim—is that DG illegally maintained its monopoly in the market for service of DG computers by unilaterally refusing to license ADEX to Grumman and other competitors. The antitrust claims are intriguing because they present a curious conflict, namely, whether (and to what extent) the antitrust laws, in the absence of any statutory exemption, must tolerate short-term harm to the competitive process when such harm is caused by the otherwise lawful exercise of an economically potent "monopoly" in a copyrighted work.

After a careful analysis, we affirm [a jury verdict for Data General on the question of copyright infringement] on all but one relatively minor issue concerning the calculation of damages.

I. Background

DG and Grumman are competitors in the market for service of computers manufactured by DG, and the present litigation stems from the evolving nature of their competitive relationship. DG not only designs and manufactures computers, but also offers a line of products and services for the maintenance and repair of DG computers. Although DG has no more than a 5% share of the highly competitive "primary market" for mini-computers, DG occupies approximately 90% of the "aftermarket" for service of DG computers. As a group, various "third party maintainers" ("TPMs") earn roughly 7% of the service revenues; Grumman is the leading TPM with approximately 3% of the available service business. The remaining equipment owners (typically large companies in the high technology industry) generally maintain their own computers and peripherals, although they occasionally need outside service on a "time and materials" basis. . . .

From 1976 until some point in the mid-1980s, DG affirmatively encouraged the growth of TPMs with relatively liberal policies concerning TPM access to service tools. DG sold or licensed diagnostics directly to TPMs, and allowed TPMs to use diagnostics sold or licensed to DG equipment owners. DG did not restrict access by TPMs to spare parts manufactured by DG or other manufacturers. DG allowed (or at least tolerated) requests by TPMs for DG's repair depot to fix malfunctioning circuit boards, the heart of a computer's central processing unit ("CPU"). DG sold at least some schematics and other documentation to TPMs. DG also sold TPMs engineering change order kits. And finally, DG training classes were open to TPM field engineers. Grumman suggests that DG's liberal policies were beneficial to DG because increased capacity (and perhaps competition) in the service aftermarket would be a selling point for DG equipment.

3. Increased Restrictions

In the mid-1980s, DG altered its strategy. With the goal of maximizing revenues from its service business, DG began to refuse to provide many service tools directly to TPMs. DG would not allow TPMs to use the DG repair depot, nor would it permit TPMs to purchase schematics, documentation, "change order" kits, or certain spare parts. DG no longer allowed TPM technicians to attend DG training classes. Finally, DG developed and severely restricted the licensing of ADEX, a new software diagnostic for its MV computers. The MV series was at once DG's most advanced computer hardware and an increasingly important source of sales and service revenue for DG.

A number of items unavailable to TPMs directly from DG were either available to all equipment owners (even customers of TPMs) from DG, or were available to TPMs from sources other than DG. For example, DG depot service, change order kits, and at least some documentation were available to all equipment owners. There is also evidence that Grumman had its own repair depot and that Grumman could make use of repair depots run by other service organizations (sometimes called "fourth party maintainers"). Likewise, there is evidence that TPMs could purchase at least some spare parts from sources other than DG.

The situation was different with respect to ADEX. DG service technicians would use ADEX [a computer diagnostic program developed by Data General] in performing service for DG equipment owners. DG would also license ADEX for the exclusive use of the in-house technicians of equipment owners who perform most of their own service. However, DG would not license ADEX to its own service customers or to the customers of TPMs. Nor was ADEX available to TPMs from sources other than DG. At least two other diagnostics designed to service DG's MV computers may have become available as early as 1989, but no fully functional substitute was available when this case was tried in 1992.

Grumman found various ways to skirt DG's ADEX restrictions. Some former DG employees, in violation of their employment agreements, brought copies of ADEX when they joined Grumman. In addition, DG field engineers often stored copies of ADEX at the work sites of their service customers, who were bound to preserve the confidentiality of any DG proprietary information in their possession. Although DG service customers had an obligation to return copies of ADEX to DG should they cancel their service agreement and switch to a TPM, few customers did so. It is essentially undisputed that Grumman technicians used and duplicated copies of ADEX left behind by DG field engineers. There is also uncontroverted evidence that Grumman actually acquired copies of ADEX in this manner in order to maintain libraries of diagnostics so that Grumman technicians could freely duplicate and use any copy of ADEX to service any of Grumman's customers with DG's MV computers.

C. The Present Litigation

In 1988, DG filed suit against Grumman in the United States District Court for the District of Massachusetts. . . . In one count, DG alleged that Grumman's use and duplication of ADEX infringed DG's ADEX copyrights, and requested [i]njunctive relief, 17 U.S.C. §502 (1988), as well as actual damages and profits, 17 U.S.C. §504(b) (1988). In another count, DG alleged that Grumman had violated Massachusetts trade secrets law by misappropriating copies of ADEX in violation of confidentiality agreements binding on former DG employees and DG service customers. . . .

b. Antitrust Defenses

Grumman claimed that DG could not maintain its infringement action because DG had used its ADEX copyrights to violate Sections 1 and 2 of the Sherman Antitrust Act, 15 U.S.C. §§1 and 2 (1988 & Supp. IV 1992). Specifically, Grumman charged that DG misused its copyrights by (1) tying the availability of ADEX to a consumer's agreement either to purchase DG support services (a "positive tie") or not to purchase support services from TPMs (a "negative tie"), and (2) willfully maintaining its monopoly in the support services aftermarket by imposing the alleged tie-in and refusing to deal with TPMs. . . .

In rejecting Grumman's motion for reconsideration of the grant of summary judgment on the monopolization claim, the district court also directly addressed Grumman's contention that DG's refusal to license ADEX to TPMs constitutes exclusionary conduct. The court stated that DG's refusal to license ADEX to TPMs was not exclusionary because "DG offers to the public a license to use MV/ADEX on any computer owned by the customer," and therefore DG "'did not withhold from one member of the public a service offered to the rest[.]'" *Grumman III*, slip op. at 5 (citing Olympia Equip. Leasing Co. v. Western Union Tel. Co., 797 F.2d 370, 377 (7th Cir. 1986), *cert. denied*, 480 U.S. 934, 94 L. Ed. 2d 765, 107 S. Ct. 1574 (1987)). . . .

III. . . .

B. Grumman's Antitrust Counterclaims . . .

2. Monopolization . . .

a. Unilateral Refusals to Deal

Because a monopolization claim does not require proof of concerted activity, even the unilateral actions of a monopolist can constitute exclusionary conduct. See 15 U.S.C. §2 (referring to "every person who shall monopolize . . . or combine or conspire with any other person . . . to monopolize") (emphasis added); Moore v. Jas. H. Matthews & Co., 473 F.2d 328, 332 (9th Cir. 1973) (observing that "section 2 is not limited to concerted activity"). Thus, a monopolist's unilateral refusal to deal with its competitors (as long as the refusal harms the competitive process) may constitute prima facie evidence of exclusionary conduct in the context of a Section 2 claim. See *Kodak*, 112 S. Ct. at 2091 n.32 (citing Aspen Skiing Co. v. Aspen Highlands Skiing Corp., 472 U.S. 585, 602-05, 86 L. Ed.2d 467, 105 S. Ct. 2847 (1985)). A monopolist may nevertheless rebut such evidence by establishing a valid business justification for its conduct. See *Kodak*, 112 S. Ct. at 2091 n. 32 (suggesting that monopolist may rebut an inference of exclusionary conduct by establishing "legitimate competitive reasons for the refusal"); *Aspen Skiing*, 472 U.S. at 608 (suggesting that sufficient evidence of harm to consumers and competitors triggers further inquiry as to whether the monopolist has "persuaded the jury that its [harmful] conduct was justified by [a] normal business purpose"). In general, a business justification is valid if it relates directly or indirectly to the enhancement of consumer welfare. Thus, pursuit of efficiency and quality control might be legitimate competitive reasons for an otherwise exclusionary refusal to deal, while the desire to maintain a monopoly market share or thwart the entry of competitors would not. See *Kodak*, 112 S. Ct. at 2091 (discussing the validity and sufficiency of various business justifications); *Aspen Skiing*, 472 U.S. at 608-11 (same); see generally 7 Areeda & Turner ¶1504, at 377-83; 9 Areeda & Turner ¶¶1713, 1716-17, at 148-61, 185-239. In essence, a unilateral refusal to deal is prima facie exclusionary if there is evidence of harm to the competitive process; a valid business justification requires proof of countervailing benefits to the competitive process.

[margin note: Business Justification]

[margin note: Rule/Test]

Despite the theoretical possibility, there have been relatively few cases in which a unilateral refusal to deal has formed the basis of a successful Section 2 claim. Several of the cases commonly cited for a supposed duty to deal were actually cases of joint conduct in which some competitors joined to frustrate others. See Associated Press v. United States, 326 U.S. 1, 89 L. Ed. 2013, 65 S. Ct. 1416 (1945); United States v. Terminal R.R. Ass'n, 224 U.S. 383, 56 L. Ed. 810, 32 S. Ct. 507 (1912). Prior to *Aspen Skiing*, the case that probably came closest to condemning a true unilateral refusal to deal was Otter Tail Power Co. v. United States, 410 U.S. 366, 35 L. Ed. 2d 359, 93 S. Ct. 1022 (1973), which condemned the refusal of a wholesale power supplier either to sell wholesale power to municipal systems or to "wheel power" when Otter Tail's retail franchises expired and local municipalities sought to supplant Otter Tail's local distributors. The case not only involved a capital-intensive public utility facility—which could not effectively be duplicated and occupied a distinct separate market—but the Supreme Court laid considerable emphasis on "supported" findings in the district court "that Otter Tail's refusals to sell at wholesale or to wheel were solely to prevent municipal power systems from eroding its monopolistic position." 410 U.S. at 378.

[margin note: Otter TRAIL]

In *Aspen Skiing*, the Court criticized a monopolist's unilateral refusal to deal in a very different situation, casting serious doubt on the proposition that the Court has adopted any single rule or formula for determining when a unilateral refusal to deal is unlawful. In that case, an "all-Aspen" ski ticket—valid at any mountain in Aspen—had been developed and jointly marketed when the three (later four) ski areas in Aspen were owned by independent entities. 472 U.S. at 589. Some time after Aspen Skiing Company ("Ski Co.") came into control of

[margin note: Aspen]

three of the four ski areas, Ski Co. refused to continue a joint agreement with Aspen Highlands Skiing Corp. ("Highlands"), the owner of the fourth area. *Id.* at 592-93. Although there was no "essential facility" involved, the Court found that it was exclusionary for Ski Co., as a monopolist, to refuse to continue a presumably efficient "pattern of distribution that had originated in a competitive market and had persisted for several years." *Id.* at 603.

It is not entirely clear whether the Court in *Aspen Skiing* merely intended to create a category of refusal-to-deal cases different from the essential facilities category or whether the Court was inviting the application of more general principles of antitrust analysis to unilateral refusals to deal. We follow the parties' lead in assuming that Grumman need not tailor its argument to a preexisting "category" of unilateral refusals to deal.

b. Unilateral Refusals to License

[handwritten: Presumption Test]

DG attempts to undermine Grumman's monopolization claim by proposing a powerful irrebuttable presumption⎣a unilateral refusal to license a copyright can never constitute exclusionary conduct.⎤We agree that some type of presumption is in order, but reach that conclusion only after an exhaustive inquiry touching on the general character of presumptions, the role of market analysis in the copyright context, existing responses to the tension between the antitrust and patent laws, the nature of the rights extended by the copyright laws, and our duty to harmonize two conflicting statutes.

(1)   The Propriety of a Presumption

We begin our analysis with two observations. First, DG's rule of law could be characterized as either an empirical assumption or a policy preference. For example, if we were convinced that refusals to license a copyright always have a net positive effect on the competitive process, we might adopt a presumption to this effect in order to preclude wasteful litigation about a known fact. On the other hand, if we were convinced that the rights enumerated in the Copyright Act should take precedence over the responsibilities set forth in the Sherman Act, regardless of the realities of the market, we might adopt a blanket rule of preference. DG's argument contains elements of both archetypal categories of presumptions.

Second, we note that the phrase "competitive process" may need some refinement in order to evaluate either an empirical assumption or a policy presumption concerning the desirability of unilateral refusals to license a copyright. *[handwritten circled: Antitrust law]* generally seeks to punish and prevent harm to consumers in particular markets, with a focus on relatively specific time periods. See, e.g., *Jefferson Parish*, 466 U.S. at 18 (holding that "any inquiry into the validity of a tying arrangement must focus on the market or markets in which the two products are sold, for that is where the anticompetitive forcing has its impact"). Thus, in determining whether conduct is exclusionary in the context of a monopolization claim, we ordinarily focus on harm to the competitive process in the relevant market and time period. *[handwritten: Harm to Comp Process in A Market During A Time Period]* See generally 3 Areeda & Turner ¶¶517-28, at 346-88, ¶¶533-36, at 406-431. Confining the competitive process in this way assists courts in deciding particular disputes based primarily on case-specific adjudicative facts rather than generally-applicable "legislative" facts or assumptions. The use and protection of copyrights also affects the "competitive process," but it may not be appropriate to judge the effect of the use of a copyright by looking only at one market or one time period.

We now consider what appears to be an empirical proclamation from DG: "The refusal to make one's innovation available to rivals . . . is pro-competitive conduct." As support, DG cites *Grinnell*, 384 U.S. at 570-71, in which the Court held that willful maintenance of monopoly does not include "growth or development as a consequence of a superior product." It is not the superiority of a work that allows the author to exclude others, however, but rather the limited monopoly granted by copyright law. Moreover, one reason why the Copyright Act fosters investment and innovation is that it may allow the author to earn monopoly profits by licensing the copyright to others or reserving the copyright for the author's exclusive use. See Sony Corp. of Am. v. Universal City Studios, Inc., 464 U.S. 417, 429, 78 L. Ed.2d 574, 104 S. Ct. 774 (1984) (explaining that the limited copyright monopoly "is intended to motivate the creative activity of authors and inventors by the provision of a special reward"). Thus, at least in a particular market and for a particular period of time, the Copyright Act tolerates behavior that may harm both consumers and competitors. Cf. SCM Corp. v. Xerox Corp., 645 F.2d 1195, 1203 (2d Cir. 1981) ("The primary purpose of the antitrust laws—to preserve competition—can be frustrated, albeit temporarily, by a holder's exercise of the patent's inherent exclusionary power during its term."), *cert. denied*, 455 U.S. 1016, 72 L. Ed.2d 132, 102 S. Ct. 1708 (1982).

DG does not in fact argue that consumers are better off in the short term because of the inability of TPMs to license ADEX. Instead, DG suggests that allowing copyright owners to exclude others from the use of their works creates incentives which ultimately work to the benefit of consumers in the DG service aftermarket as well as to the benefit of consumers generally. In other words, DG seeks to justify any immediate harm to consumers by pointing to countervailing long-term benefits. Certainly, a monopolist's refusal to license others to use a commercially successful patented idea is likely to have more profound anti-competitive consequences than a refusal to allow others to duplicate the copyrighted expression of an unpatented idea (although such differences may become less pronounced if copyright law becomes increasingly protective of intellectual property such as computer software). But by no means is a monopolist's refusal to license a copyright entirely "pro-competitive" within the ordinary economic framework of the Sherman Act. Accordingly, it may be inappropriate to adopt an empirical assumption that simply ignores harm to the competitive process caused by a monopolist's unilateral refusal to license a copyright. Even if it is clear that exclusive use of a copyright can have anti-competitive consequences, some type of presumption may nevertheless be appropriate as a matter of either antitrust law or copyright law.

(2) Antitrust Law and the Accommodation of Patent Rights

Antitrust law is somewhat instructive. Although creation and protection of original works of authorship may be a national pastime, the Sherman Act does not explicitly exempt such activity from antitrust scrutiny and courts should be wary of creating implied exemptions. See Square D Co. v. Niagara Frontier Tariff Bureau, Inc., 476 U.S. 409, 421, 90 L. Ed.2d 413, 106 S. Ct. 1922 (1986) ("Exemptions from the antitrust laws are strictly construed and strongly disfavored."); cf. Flood v. Kuhn, 407 U.S. 258, 32 L. Ed.2d 728, 92 S. Ct. 2099 (1972) (holding that the longstanding judicially created exemption of professional baseball from the Sherman Act is an established "aberration" in which Congress has acquiesced). The Supreme Court has suggested that an otherwise reasonable yet anti-competitive use of a copyright should not "be deemed a per se violation of the Sherman Act," Broadcast Music, Inc. v. CBS, Inc., 441 U.S. 1, 19, 60 L. Ed.2d 1, 99 S. Ct. 1551 (1979), but a monopolistic refusal to license might still violate the rule of reason, see Rural Tel. Serv. Co. v. Feist Publications, Inc., 957 F.2d 765, 767-69 (10th Cir.) (analyzing reasonableness of monopolist's unilateral refusal to license copyrighted telephone listings to a competing distributor of telephone directories), *cert. denied*, 121 L. Ed.2d 429, 113 S. Ct. 490 (1992).[63] Should an antitrust plaintiff be allowed to demonstrate the anti-competitive effects of a monopolist's unilateral refusal to grant a copyright license? Would the monopolist then have to justify its refusal to license by introducing evidence that the protection of the copyright laws enabled the author to create a work which advances consumer welfare?

The courts appear to have partly settled an analogous conflict between the patent laws and the antitrust laws, treating the former as creating an implied limited exception to the latter. In Simpson v. Union Oil Co., 377 U.S. 13, 24, 12 L. Ed.2d 98, 84 S. Ct. 1051 (1964), the Supreme Court stated that "the patent laws which give a 17-year monopoly on 'making, using, or selling the invention' are in pari materia with the antitrust laws and modify them pro tanto." Similarly, we have suggested that the exercise of patent rights is a "legitimate means" by which a firm may maintain its monopoly power. *Barry Wright*, 724 F.2d at 230. Other courts have specifically held that a monopolist's unilateral refusal to license a patent is ordinarily not properly viewed as exclusionary conduct. See *Miller Insituform*, 830 F.2d at 609 ("A patent holder who lawfully acquires a patent cannot be held liable under Section 2 of the Sherman Act for maintaining the monopoly power he lawfully acquired by refusing to license the patent to others."); *Westinghouse*, 648 F.2d at 647 (finding no antitrust violation because "*Westinghouse* has done no more than to license some of its patents and refuse to license others"); *SCM Corp.*,

63. It is in any event well settled that concerted and contractual behavior that threatens competition is not immune from antitrust inquiry simply because it involves the exercise of copyright privileges. See, e.g., *Kodak*, 112 S. Ct. at 2089 n.29 ("The Court has held many times that power gained through some natural and legal advantage such as a patent, copyright, or business acumen can give rise to liability if 'a seller exploits his dominant position in one market to expand his empire into the next.'") (quoting Times-Picayune Publishing Co. v. United States, 345 U.S. 594, 611, 97 L. Ed. 1277, 73 S. Ct. 872 (1953) (tying case)); United States v. Paramount Pictures, Inc., 334 U.S. 131, 143, 92 L. Ed. 1260, 68 S. Ct. 915 (1948) (holding that horizontal conspiracy to engage in price-fixing in copyright licenses is illegal per se); *id.* at 159 (holding that block-booking of motion pictures—"a refusal to license one or more copyrights unless another copyright is accepted"—is an illegal tying arrangement); Straus v. American Publishers' Ass'n, 231 U.S. 222, 234, 58 L. Ed. 192, 34 S. Ct. 84 (1913) ("No more than the patent statute was the copyright act intended to authorize agreements in unlawful restraint of trade. . . ."); Digidyne Corp. v. Data General Corp., 734 F.2d 1336 (9th Cir. 1984) (affirming finding of illegal tie between copyrighted software and computer hardware), *cert. denied*, 473 U.S. 908, 87 L. Ed.2d 657, 105 S. Ct. 3534 (1985); cf. Miller Insituform, Inc. v. Insituform of N. Am., Inc., 830 F.2d 606, 608-09 & n.4 (6th Cir. 1987) (describing ways in which patent holder may violate the antitrust laws), *cert. denied*, 484 U.S. 1064, 98 L. Ed.2d 988, 108 S. Ct. 1023 (1988); United States v. Westinghouse Elec. Corp., 648 F.2d 642, 646-47 (9th Cir. 1981) (same).

645 F.2d at 1206 (holding that "where a patent has been lawfully acquired, subsequent conduct permissible under the patent laws cannot trigger any liability under the antitrust laws"); see also 3 Areeda & Turner ¶704, at 114 ("The patent is itself a government grant of monopoly and is therefore an exception to usual antitrust rules."). This exception is inoperable if the patent was unlawfully "acquired." *SCM Corp.*, 645 F.2d at 1208-09 (analyzing legality of Xerox's acquisition of plain-paper copier patent); see generally 3 Areeda & Turner ¶¶705-707, at 117-45 (discussing effect of patent acquisition, internal development of patents, and improprieties in patent procurement on applicability of antitrust laws).

The "patent exception" is largely a means of resolving conflicting rights and responsibilities, i.e., a policy presumption. See, e.g., *Miller Insituform*, 830 F.2d at 609 (declaring summarily that "there is no adverse effect on competition since, as a patent monopolist, [the patent holder] had [the] exclusive right to manufacture, use, and sell his invention"). At the same time, the exception is grounded in an empirical assumption that exposing patent activity to wider antitrust scrutiny would weaken the incentives underlying the patent system, thereby depriving consumers of beneficial products. See, e.g., *SCM Corp.*, 645 F.2d at 1209 (holding that imposition of antitrust liability for an arguably unreasonable refusal to license a lawfully acquired patent "would severely trample upon the incentives provided by our patent laws and thus undermine the entire patent system").

(3) Copyright Law

Copyright law provides further guidance. The Copyright Act expressly grants to a copyright owner the exclusive right to distribute the protected work by "transfer of ownership, or by rental, lease, or lending." 17 U.S.C. §106. Consequently, "the owner of the copyright, if [it] pleases, may refrain from vending or licensing and content [itself] with simply exercising the right to exclude others from using [its] property." Fox Film Corp. v. Doyal, 286 U.S. 123, 127, 76 L. Ed. 1010, 52 S. Ct. 546 (1932). See also Stewart v. Abend, 495 U.S. 207, 229, 109 L. Ed.2d 184, 110 S. Ct. 1750 (1990). We may also venture to infer that, in passing the Copyright Act, Congress itself made an empirical assumption that allowing copyright holders to collect license fees and exclude others from using their works creates a system of incentives that promotes consumer welfare in the long term by encouraging investment in the creation of desirable artistic and functional works of expression. See Feist Publications, Inc. v. Rural Tel. Serv. Co., 499 U.S. 340, 111 S. Ct. 1282, 1290, 113 L. Ed.2d 358 (1991) ("The primary objective of a copyright is not to reward the labor of authors, but 'to promote the Progress of Science and useful Arts.'") (quoting U.S. Const. art. I. §8, cl. 8); *Sony Corp.*, 464 U.S. at 429 (discussing goals and incentives of copyright protection); Twentieth Century Music Corp. v. Aiken, 422 U.S. 151, 156, 45 L. Ed.2d 84, 95 S. Ct. 2040 (1975) ("The immediate effect of our copyright law is to secure a fair return for an 'author's' creative labor. But the ultimate aim is, by this incentive, to stimulate artistic creativity for the general public good."). We cannot require antitrust defendants to prove and reprove the merits of this legislative assumption in every case where a refusal to license a copyrighted work comes under attack. Nevertheless, although "nothing in the copyright statutes would prevent an author from hoarding all of his works during the term of the copyright," *Stewart*, 495 U.S. at 228-29, the Copyright Act does not explicitly purport to limit the scope of the

Sherman Act. And, if the Copyright Act is silent on the subject generally, the silence is particularly acute in cases where a monopolist harms consumers in the monopolized market by refusing to license a copyrighted work to competitors.

We acknowledge that Congress has not been entirely silent on the relationship between antitrust and intellectual property laws. Congress amended the patent laws in 1988 to provide that "no patent owner otherwise entitled to relief for infringement . . . of a patent shall be denied relief or deemed guilty of misuse or illegal extension of the patent right by reason of [the patent owner's] refusal to license or use any rights to the patent." 35 U.S.C. §271(d) (1988). Section 271(d) clearly prevents an infringer from using a patent misuse defense when the patent owner has unilaterally refused a license, and may even herald the prohibition of all antitrust claims and counterclaims premised on a refusal to license a patent. See Stephen Calkins, Patent Law: The Impact of the 1988 Patent Misuse Reform Act and Noerr-Pennington Doctrine on Misuse Defenses and Antitrust Counterclaims, 38 Drake L. Rev. 192-97 (1988-89). Nevertheless, while Section 271(d) is indicative of congressional "policy" on the need for antitrust law to accommodate intellectual property law, Congress did not similarly amend the Copyright Act.

(4) Harmonizing the Sherman Act and the Copyright Act

Since neither the Sherman Act nor the Copyright Act works a partial repeal of the other, and since implied repeals are disfavored, e.g., Watt v. Alaska, 451 U.S. 259, 267, 68 L. Ed.2d 80, 101 S. Ct. 1673 (1981), we must harmonize the two as best we can, *id.*, mindful of the legislative and judicial approaches to similar conflicts created by the patent laws. We must not lose sight of the need to preserve the economic incentives fueled by the Copyright Act, but neither may we ignore the tension between the two very different policies embodied in the Copyright Act and the Sherman Act, both designed ultimately to improve the welfare of consumers in our free market system. Drawing on our discussion above, we hold that while exclusionary conduct can include a monopolist's unilateral refusal to license a copyright, an author's desire to exclude others from use of its copyrighted work is a presumptively valid business justification for any immediate harm to consumers.[64]

c. DG's Refusal to License ADEX to non-CMOs

Having arrived at the applicable legal standards, we may resolve Grumman's principal allegation of exclusionary conduct. Although there may be a genuine factual dispute about the effect on DG equipment owners of DG's refusal to license ADEX to TPMs, DG's desire to exercise its rights under the Copyright Act is a presumptively valid business justification. . . .

Grumman attempts to analogize this case to *Aspen Skiing* by focusing on the fact that DG once encouraged firms to enter the DG service aftermarket by allowing liberal access to service tools, but no longer does so. The analytical framework of *Aspen Skiing* cannot function in these circumstances, however, because we are unable to view DG's market practices in both competitive and noncompetitive

---

64. Wary of undermining the Sherman Act, however, we do not hold that an antitrust plaintiff can never rebut this presumption, for there may be rare cases in which imposing antitrust liability is unlikely to frustrate the objectives of the Copyright Act.

conditions. While TPMs have made inroads in the market for service of DG computers, DG has always been a monopolist in that market, and competitive conditions have never prevailed. Therefore, it would not be "appropriate to infer" from DG's change of heart that its former policies "satisfy consumer demand in free competitive markets." *Aspen Skiing*, 472 U.S. at 603.

[handwritten margin note: Change of Heart]

Nor does it appear that Grumman would be able at trial to overcome the presumption on any other theory. There is no evidence that DG acquired its ADEX copyrights in any unlawful manner; indeed, the record suggests that DG developed all its software internally. Cf. 3 Areeda & Turner ¶706, at 127-28 (arguing that although an internally developed patent may be as exclusionary as one acquired from outside a firm, labelling the former as exclusionary would "discourage progressiveness by monopolists"). And, while there is evidence that DG knew that developing a "proprietary position" in the area of diagnostic software would help to maintain its monopoly in the aftermarket for service of DG computers, there is also evidence that DG set out to create a state-of-the-art diagnostic that would help to improve the quality of DG service. Cf. *id.* ¶706, at 128-29 (suggesting that "nearly all commercial research rests on a mixture of motivations" and that a search for an overriding "antisocial" motivation would be unilluminating). In fact, there is clearly some evidence that ADEX is a significant benefit to owners of DG's MV computers. ADEX is a better product than any other diagnostic for MV computers. The use of ADEX appears to have increased the efficiency and reduced the cost of service because technicians can locate problems more quickly and, through the use of the software's "remote assistance" capability, can arrive at customer sites having determined ahead of time what replacement parts are necessary. In addition to the possibility of lower prices occasioned by such gains in efficiency, ADEX also promises to lower prices through gains in effectiveness. For example, customers may save the cost of replacing expensive hardware components because the use of advanced diagnostics increases the possibility that technicians can locate a problem and repair the component.

COMMENTS AND QUESTIONS

Consider the court's conclusion that a refusal to license a copyrighted work is a presumptively valid business justification. How does this square with the rationales behind the copyright law? Is it inconsistent with the ultimate goal of copyright —to promote the *dissemination* of works of authorship to the general public?

Note on a Monopolist's Duty to Disclose

Antitrust law sometimes imposes burdens on monopolists that it does not impose on ordinary competitors. One of the most contentious issues in antitrust law is the duty of monopolists to give competitors access to their facilities. In limited circumstances, courts have been willing to require monopolists to provide such access on nondiscriminatory terms. For example, the Supreme Court has held that a group of railroads that together owned the central railroad switching yard in St. Louis, Missouri, could not deny access to that yard to nonmembers. United States v. Terminal Ry., 212 U.S. 1 (1912). *Terminal Railway* reasoned that because it was the only rail yard serving St. Louis and because of the importance of the city as a hub, the rail yard was an "essential facility" from which its owners could not exclude others to the detriment of competition. A more recent case held that the owner of ski resorts with local market power could not discontinue a multi-area ski lift ticket it had shared with a smaller competitor in the absence of a legitimate business justification, even though the Court was unwilling to describe the lift ticket as an "essential facility." Aspen Skiing Co. v. Aspen Highlands Skiing Corp., 472 U.S. 585 (1985).

With these limited exceptions, however, the general rule is that businesses—even monopolists—do not have to give their competitors access to their facilities. In Berkey Photo, Inc. v. Eastman Kodak Co., 603 F.2d 263 (2d Cir. 1979), the court rejected Berkey's argument that Kodak owed it a duty to predisclose its forthcoming products so Berkey could prepare compatible products. The court recognized that Kodak's size and advance knowledge of its own plans gave it an advantage over Berkey. But, the court said,

> a large firm does not violate section 2 simply by reaping the competitive rewards attributable to its efficient size, nor does an integrated business offend the Sherman Act whenever one of its departments benefits from association with a division possessing a monopoly in its own market. So long as we allow a firm to compete in several fields, we must expect it to seek the competitive advantages of its broad-based activity. . . .
>
> Berkey postulates that Kodak had a duty to disclose limited types of information to certain competitors under specific circumstances. But it is difficult to comprehend how a major corporation, accustomed though it is to making business decisions with antitrust considerations in mind, could possess the omniscience to anticipate all the instances in which a jury might one day in the future retrospectively conclude that predisclosure was warranted. And it is equally difficult to discern workable guidelines that a court might set forth to aid the firm's decision. For example, how detailed must the information conveyed be? And how far must research have progressed before it is "ripe" for disclosure? These inherent uncertainties would have an inevitable chilling effect on innovation. They go far, we believe, towards explaining why no court has ever imposed the duty Berkey seeks to create here.

Id.

The already difficult line between these two strands of cases is further complicated when the subject matter at issue is intellectual property. An intellectual property right is an exclusive right. It would be stripped of much of its value if antitrust law were to compel intellectual property owners to share it with their competitors. But there may be circumstances in which access to a patent or copyright has become an "essential facility" for competitors in the same or in a downstream market. In those circumstances, courts must face a direct conflict between the rights granted by intellectual property law and the prohibitions of antitrust law. Cf. David Scheffman, The Application of Raising Rivals' Costs Theory to Antitrust, 37 Antitrust Bull. 187 (1992) (suggesting that raising the cost of a key input to a rival creates a problem similar to the problem of denying access to an essential facility).

This problem has arisen on several different occasions in the computer industry. In each case, the issue is one of standardization. One company's system (protected by intellectual property rights) has become the de facto standard for an entire industry. Is the company entitled therefore to control the entire industry? To date, courts have not answered this question. Instead, they have dealt with these problems as problems of copyright law, and have not considered antitrust issues at all. See, e.g., Apple Computer v. Franklin Computer, 714 F.2d 1240 (3d Cir. 1983) (Franklin had no right to create programs compatible with the Apple II operating system that would justify access to Apple's operating system code); Sega v. Accolade, 977 F.2d 1510 (9th Cir. 1992) (Accolade had right under copyright fair use doctrine to reverse engineer Sega's copyrighted code in order to create games that would work on Sega's video game system). Cf. DSC Communications v. DGI Technologies, 81 F.3d 597 (5th Cir. 1996) (attempt to use copyright to prevent a competitor's access to microcode was copyright misuse). Issues of standardization and the role of monopolists with intellectual property will recur—in the computer industry and elsewhere.

COMMENTS AND QUESTIONS

1. As we shall see in the next section, antitrust law normally is intensely skeptical of agreements and exchanges of information between competitors. The plaintiff in *Berkey Photo* seems to be asking that the court *require* that competitors share information about their new product specifications. Shouldn't the court be concerned about helping facilitate a cartel between the parties in an "essential facilities" case?

2. Some recent cases have cast doubt on the strength of the presumption that an intellectual property owner is always justified in unilaterally refusing to license its patents. In Kodak v. Image Technical Services, Inc., 125 F.3d 1195 (9th Cir. 1997), the court faced an appeal from a jury verdict that Kodak had tied the purchase of replacement parts for its copiers to the purchase of service from Kodak in an effort to drive independent service organizations out of business. (A prior Supreme Court ruling on the legal theory of this case is discussed in the section on tying, *infra*). One of Kodak's arguments on appeal was that because some of its spare parts were patented, it was free to refuse to license those patents to anyone it chose. The Ninth Circuit rejected that argument, reasoning that the "refusal to license" asserted in that case was really a part of an unlawful tying arrangement and that Kodak asserted its patents as a pretext. This result is perfectly consistent with the existing case law on patents and tying arrangements. Indeed, the court applied the *Data General* presumption: it simply concluded that the presumption was rebutted in this case. Strong language in the opinion suggests, however, that the Ninth Circuit is skeptical about the ability of patent owners to refuse to license under all conditions.

The Federal Circuit dealt with the legality of unilateral refusals to license patent rights in two cases at the tail end of the twentieth century. The two decisions are somewhat at odds in their holdings. The first case is Intergraph v. Intel, 195 F.3d 1346 (Fed. Cir. 1999). Intergraph alleged that Intel's failure to continue to supply it with access to proprietary information, chips, and technical support constituted a refusal to deal that violated section 2. The court rejected this claim. It began by observing that

it is well established that in the absence of any purpose to create or maintain a monopoly, the Sherman act does not restrict the long-recognized right of a trader or manufacturer engaged in an entirely private business, freely to exercise his own independent discretion as to parties with whom he will deal.

Id. at 1358. The court acknowledged that refusals to deal "may raise antitrust concerns when the refusal is directed against competition and the purpose is to create, maintain, or enlarge a monopoly." *Id.* Nonetheless, it found no section 2 violation based on Intel's refusal to deal, both because it concluded that Intel and Intergraph did not compete at all, and because it saw the fact that Intergraph had sued Intel as a valid reason for Intel to cease giving Intergraph preferential treatment. The court made no specific reference to Intel's patents as a factor in this decision, despite the district court's determination that Intel had used its patents to restrain trade, and that its patent rights did not immunize it from antitrust liability. See Intergraph Corp. v. Intel Corp., 3 F. Supp.2d 1255, 1279 (N.D. Ala. 1998).

Only three months later, the Federal Circuit took a very different approach to unilateral refusals to license intellectual property in In re Independent Service Organizations Antitrust Litigation, 203 F.3d 1322 (Fed. Cir. 2000) (herein *Xerox*). In that case, a group of independent service organizations (ISOs) that provided service for Xerox copiers sued Xerox for violating the antitrust laws because Xerox refused to sell parts to them or their customers. Xerox designed its policy so that it sold parts only to end users who serviced the machines themselves or to end users who hired Xerox to perform service. The effect of the Xerox policy was to drive the ISOs out of the business of servicing Xerox copiers and to reserve that business exclusively to Xerox.

Xerox counterclaimed for patent and copyright infringement, arguing that it had patents on a number of its parts and copyrights on its service drawings that the ISOs had infringed. Xerox also argued that it could not be held liable for violating the antitrust laws if all it did was unilaterally refuse to sell patented or copyrighted products to the ISOs, regardless of the purpose or effect of that refusal.

The Federal Circuit agreed with Xerox. The court asserted that there was "no reported case in which a court has imposed antitrust liability for a unilateral refusal to sell or license a patent." *Id.* at 1326. The court held that a patentee's right to refuse to license its intellectual property right was limited only in certain circumstances: where the patent was obtained through fraud, where a lawsuit to enforce the patent was a sham, or where the patent holder uses his "statutory right to refuse to sell patented parts to gain a monopoly in a market *beyond the scope of the patent.*" *Id.* at 1327.

In the case before it, the court held that Xerox had not sought to extend its patents beyond the scope of the statutory grant. It noted that patents themselves could cover more than one market, and it held without explanation that Xerox's parts patents entitled it to control the market for service of Xerox copiers as well. And it refused to inquire into Xerox's motivation for refusing to license its parts patents. Thus, the Federal Circuit created a per se rule of legality, in accord with earlier statements from both the Second and Sixth Circuits.[5]

---

5. See Miller Insituform Inc. v. Insituform of North Am., 830 F.2d 606, 609 (6th Cir. 1987) ("A patent holder who lawfully acquires a patent cannot be held liable under Section 2 of the Sherman Act for maintaining the monopoly power he lawfully acquired by refusing to license the patent to others."); SCM Corp. v. Xerox Corp., 645 F.2d 1195, 1206 (2d Cir. 1981) ("where a patent has been lawfully acquired,

The *Xerox* court also considered Xerox's refusal to license its copyrights. In doing so, it applied Tenth Circuit law. In the absence of any precedent from the Tenth Circuit, the court adopted the First Circuit's approach in *Data General* and rejected the Ninth Circuit's approach in *Image Technical*.

If Intel's chip architecture is really an "essential facility," does Intel have a similar obligation to provide this information to its competitors in the microprocessor business? What does this case suggest about Microsoft's power to deny competitors access to the APIs of its Windows operating system? Cf. Aldridge v. Microsoft Corp., 995 F. Supp. 728 (S.D. Tex. 1998) (holding that Microsoft's Windows 95 operating system was potentially subject to an "essential facilities" claim but that the portions at issue in this case were not in fact essential facilities).

3. For an argument that intellectual property owners should not be compelled to license their rights to competitors even in a network market, see David McGowan, Networks and Intention in Antitrust and Intellectual Property, 24 J. Corp. L. 485 (1999); David McGowan, Regulating Competition in the Information Age: Computer Software as an Essential Facility Under the Sherman Act, 18 Hastings Comm. & Ent. L.J. 771 (1996).

C. AGREEMENTS TO RESTRAIN TRADE

1. Vertical Restraints

a. *Tying Arrangements*

In a tying arrangement, the seller forces the buyer to buy a product he does not want (the tied product) in order to get a product he does want (the tying product). According to traditional tying theory, sellers with market power in the tying product can leverage that monopoly into the tied product by forcing captive buyers to buy the tied product exclusively from them. Whether this strategy is economically viable has been the subject of heated debate, as we discuss below. Tying arrangements, like joint ventures, have proven difficult to pigeonhole for antitrust purposes. They have been attacked under section 1 of the Sherman Act as involving a conspiracy,[6] under section 2 of the Sherman Act as involving monopolization of the tied product market, and under section 3 of the Clayton Act as requiring an exclusive dealing arrangement.

Tying is one of the theories most commonly asserted against intellectual property owners. A common antitrust complaint is that a patentee, who has some power in the (patented) tying product by virtue of her intellectual property right, is requiring buyers to purchase unpatented tied products as well. In the computer industry, in which components that interoperate (work together) play a fundamental role, the claim is often somewhat more subtle—that an intellectual property

---

subsequent conduct permissible under the patent laws cannot trigger any liability under the antitrust laws.").

6. The presumed "conspiracy" here is between the coercing seller and the coerced buyer. This is hardly the sort of collusion one normally thinks of as subject to section 1. But see Perma-Life Mufflers v. International Parts Corp., 392 U.S. 134 (1968) (defendant may be guilty of conspiracy with plaintiff he coerces under section 1).

owner has tied some desirable part of the system to the purchase of the entire system.

An important 1992 Supreme Court case (not directly involving intellectual property) held that such a tying claim could be evaluated in the relevant antitrust "aftermarket" for parts or service for a single brand of photocopier, because consumers were "locked in" to that copier once they had purchased it. Eastman Kodak Co. v. Image Technical Servs., Inc., 504 U.S. 451 (1992). That case has obvious importance for the computer industry, in which consumer lock-in plays a major role.

Virtual Maintenance, Inc. v. Prime Computer, Inc.
United States Court of Appeals for the Sixth Circuit
11 F.3d 660 (6th Cir. 1993)

SUHRHEINRICH, Circuit Judge. . . .

I.

. . . Defendant Prime Computer, Inc. ("Prime") manufactures and markets computer systems, and provides maintenance services for those systems. Of significance to this lawsuit is one of its hardware lines, the "50 Series" minicomputer, and one of its applications software products, the so-called Computer-Aided Design/Computer-Aided Manufacturing system ("CAD/CAM"), which can be used with the 50 Series minicomputers.

Ford Motor Company ("Ford") created and owns a CAD/CAM software design program for use in designing automobiles. Ford's CAD/CAM program is called Product Design Graphic System ("PDGS"). Ford frequently revises the software program, and requires the automotive design companies with which it does business to use the most recent version of Ford's PDGS in order to facilitate the transmission of design specifications through CAD/CAM software.

Ford licenses defendant Prime as the exclusive distributor of Ford's version of PDGS under a year-to-year contract. Ford's version of PDGS runs only in Prime's 50 Series minicomputers, but can be translated to other systems at a higher cost.

Prime also distributes software support (i.e., revisions, modifications, updates, and support services) for PDGS software. Prime offers this software support to Ford's design companies as part of a package that includes hardware maintenance on the Prime 50 Series minicomputers. PDGS revisions may be purchased separately from the hardware maintenance, but only at a prohibitive expense. In contrast, the general contract to purchase PDGS does not contain a hardware maintenance requirement.

Plaintiff Virtual Maintenance, Inc. ("Virtual") brought this antitrust action after unsuccessfully attempting to enter into hardware maintenance contracts with owners of Prime 50 Series computers. Virtual contended that Prime's package constituted an illegal tying arrangement in violation of §1 of the Sherman Act, 15 U.S.C. §1, by conditioning the purchase of software support required by Ford to hardware maintenance from Prime (the tying product). . . .

II. . . .

B. . . .

2.

Under Virtual's first per se claim, the district court defined the relevant market as "the sale of software revisions and support for the CAD/CAM industry in general." We found no error in the legal adequacy of the district court's definition, but concluded that Prime possessed at most an 11% share of the market, which is insufficient as a matter of law to confer market power. *Virtual I*, 957 at 1325 (citing *Jefferson Parish Hosp. Dist. No. 2* in *Hyde*, 466 U.S. 2, 26, 80 L. Ed.2d 2, 104 S. Ct. 1551 (1984) (30% market share does not confer market power); A.I. Root v. Computer/Dynamics, Inc., 806 F.2d 673, 675 (6th Cir. 1986) (2-4% market share is insufficient); Grappone, Inc. v. Subaru of New England, Inc., 858 F.2d 792, 796 (1st Cir. 1985) (5% market share insufficient)). We find nothing in *Eastman Kodak* which requires us to alter this analysis. We therefore hold that a per se tying violation could not be established under Virtual's first per se theory because Prime lacks market power in the general CAD/CAM product market, for the reasons stated here and in section II.B.1. of our decision in *Virtual I*.

3.

Our ruling regarding Virtual's second per se claim requires much closer scrutiny. The other market that Virtual urged was defined as "the sale of software revisions and support of software necessary to do business with Ford Motor Company." *Virtual I*, 957 F.2d at 1325. Prime argued that this instruction defined the tying product market too narrowly as a matter of law, and we agreed. We found that market definition defective as a matter of law because it was "based solely on one customer's requirements," which "this court has held . . . does not create a separate product market." *Id.* at 1327 (citing International Logistics Group, Ltd. v. Chrysler Corp., 884 F.2d 904, 908 (6th Cir. 1989), *cert. denied*, 494 U.S. 1066, 108 L. Ed.2d 784, 110 S. Ct. 1783 (1990); Dunn & Mavis, Inc. v. Nu-Car Driveaway, Inc., 691 F.2d 241 (6th Cir. 1982)).

In response to Virtual's contention that Ford is not the only customer of Prime's products, but that all of Ford's design suppliers made up the customer market for "Ford-required CAD/CAM," we stated:

> Virtual seeks to distinguish these cases by pointing out that Ford is not the only customer of Prime's products; rather, all of Ford's design suppliers make up the customer market for "Ford-required CAD/CAM." This ignores the fact that Ford requires its suppliers to purchase the software updates for Ford's benefit. Ford is ultimately the single consumer of its specialized design software because Ford's requirements define the demand for the software and the updates. But defining the market by Ford's requirements creates the appearance of market power based only upon the demand side of the market. Defining a market, or "submarket," on the basis of demand considerations alone is erroneous because such an approach fails to consider the supply side of the market. Philip E. Areeda & Herbert Hovenkamp, Antitrust Law, ¶518.1g at 471 & n.26 (Supp. 1990) (citing United States v. Central State

Bank, 817 F.2d 22 (6th Cir. 1987)). The relevant product market cannot be determined without considering the cross-elasticity of supply.

957 F.2d at 1327.

Virtual countered that Prime has no supply side competition because of its exclusive license for PDGS. We rejected this argument as "confusing the tying product (software support for PDGS) with the interbrand market relevant for antitrust analysis," *id.*, and ruled that "the relevant tying market is comprised of all CAD/CAM software reasonably interchangeable with PDGS." *Id.* Critical to this analysis was the view that PDGS software support is an intrabrand "submarket":

> Prime has market power in the trivial sense that no one else makes PDGS. But true market power—power sufficient to change and sustain anticompetitive prices— cannot be inferred from this because were Prime to charge exorbitant prices for its software support, its customers would simply switch to some other manufacturer of PDGS-type software. Prime's lack of market power over the general market for CAD/CAM software thus prevents Prime from controlling the "submarket" for PDGS software.

957 F.2d at 1327-28. Upon refusing to view Ford-required PDGS software support as a separate tying product market, we rejected Virtual's lock-in and switching costs arguments as a matter of law:

> Virtual responds that Ford and its design suppliers cannot switch to a new supplier of software support because they are "locked-in" to Prime as the sole supplier due to their substantial investments in Prime 50 Series computers and other hardware. While Ford might believe it is "locked-in," this is due in large part to its own decision to purchase Prime's software and invest in Prime's computer systems. But a customer's initial purchase of a particular manufacturer's product does not justify a limited market definition. Defining the market by customer demand after the customer has chosen a single supplier fails to take into account that the supplier (here Prime) must compete with other similar suppliers to be designated the sole source in the first place.

Id. at 1328 (citation omitted).

Under *Eastman Kodak*, our rejection of Virtual's second per se claim based on a tying product of Ford-required software support was misguided. That Ford had many competitors to choose from when it made its initial decision to grant the exclusive license to Prime cannot, after *Eastman Kodak*, preclude as a matter of law Virtual's proposed theory of market power because it ignores information costs. It follows that our rejection of Virtual's "lock-in" argument, on the basis of an interbrand competitive market in the initial purchase of Prime's software package and Prime 50 Series minicomputers, was also in error.

Eastman Kodak also requires us to rethink our characterization of the tying product market here as merely the preference of one customer. Unlike *Eastman Kodak*, the initial decision to purchase Prime equipment and software was made by a single consumer, Ford. However, by shifting the focus to the derivative aftermarket of software support, there is not a single consumer, but numerous automotive design companies doing business with Ford. In contrast with *International Logistics*, 894 F.2d at 904, which involved vertical nonprice restraints unilaterally imposed by defendant Chrysler upon its distributors, the automotive design companies in the present case are independent companies, not a part of Ford. Unlike *Dunn & Mavis*, 691 F.2d 241, where it was held that an agreement between a single seller of transportation services and a single automobile manufacturer was not an illegal "group boycott," the present case does not involve merely an arrangement between a single consumer and a single supplier. Thus, the market in this case is not defined by Ford, as a customer of Prime, but by Ford's requirements that affect the choice of Prime's other customers, Ford suppliers.

The similarities between this case and *Eastman Kodak* are apparent. As in *Eastman Kodak*, the alleged tie is not between equipment and parts, where interbrand competition would defeat market power and a per se tying claim. Rather, the alleged tie is in the derivative aftermarkets. Like Kodak, Prime is able to exercise control over the sale of software support because of its exclusive distribution license from Ford, and Ford's requirement that its automotive design suppliers use the most current version of Prime's software support. Thus, it can be argued that Prime enjoys a significant advantage in the Ford-required software support market by virtue of Ford's license and the requirement Ford places on the automotive design companies to use the most current version of PDGS. In other words, there is evidence to make the argument that Prime's tying arrangement bears that "essential characteristic" of an illegal tying arrangement, the ability to exploit control over the tying product to force the buyer to purchase an unwanted tied product. *Jefferson Parish*, 466 U.S. at 12. . . .

Virtual offered expert testimony concerning lock-in and switching costs. Virtual's industry experts testified that customers were "locked-in" to the hardware maintenance by the substantial cost incurred for hardware, maintenance, and training, most of which would be substantially worthless if the customer switched to another manufacturer's system. A Ford employee, called by Prime, testified that Ford itself felt "locked-in" to Prime, stating that Ford could not change from Prime's computer system and remain economically viable in the automotive industry. Virtual's expert also opined that Prime could substantially raise its maintenance prices before customers would abandon their investment.

Finally, Virtual made a showing that a "not insubstantial" amount of commerce was affected in that it stood to lose significant profits over a five-year period. Thus, under *Eastman Kodak*, we conclude that Virtual's second definition of tying product market was not improper.

COMMENTS AND QUESTIONS

1. Is market power required for an antitrust plaintiff to prevail on a tying claim? Historically, the answer has been no—tying two products together was illegal per se. In 1984, the Supreme Court addressed this issue in Jefferson Parish Hospital v. Hyde, 466 U.S. 2 (1984). In that case, the majority voted to maintain the per se rule in tying cases, but they did require some showing of a market effect. The result is a curious "per se" rule in which liability is not automatic, but depends on proof of market power. Four concurring justices would have required proof that the antitrust defendant had market power in the tying product, as well as there being a dangerous possibility of obtaining market power in the tied product.

2. Does *Virtual Maintenance* interpret *Kodak* correctly? Is an aftermarket for a single product *always* the correct market for antitrust purposes? If not, how can courts distinguish between single-firm monopolists and intrabrand competitors?

3. In the wake of *Kodak*, a number of similar cases were reopened in the computer industry. See Virtual Maintenance, Inc. v. Prime Computer, Inc., 957 F.2d 1318 (6th Cir. 1992), *vacated and remanded*, 113 S. Ct. 314 (1992), *on remand*, 995 F.2d 1324 (6th Cir. 1993) (the latter opinion was reproduced above); Datagate, Inc. v. Hewlett-Packard Co., 941 F.2d 864 (9th Cir. 1991), *cert. denied*, 503 U.S. 984 (1992). It also spurred a host of new cases. A large number of these post-*Kodak* cases turn on whether the plaintiff can characterize the tied product as having a genuinely separate product market. See, e.g., Tricom Inc. v. Electronic Data Systems, 902 F. Supp. 741 (E.D. Mich. 1995) (conditioning of a software lease agreement on the purchase of CPU time from the software dealer was actionable tying arrangement).

Many of these recent cases have limited the applicability of *Kodak* in the computer industry. For example, in Digital Equipment Corp. v. Uniq Digital Technologies, 73 F.3d 756 (7th Cir. 1996), the Seventh Circuit held that DEC was not liable for tying sales of its mid-range computers to its operating system because it lacked power in the market for mid-range computers. The court distinguished *Kodak*, calling the Supreme Court's conclusions an "assumption" rather than a holding and noting that in any event *Kodak* applied only to ties between two different aftermarkets. Two other cases have found sufficient market power but failed to find evidence that consumers were actually coerced to purchase the tied product. See Amerinet, Inc. v. Xerox Corp., 972 F.2d 1483 (8th Cir. 1992); Service & Training, Inc. v. Data General Corp., 963 F.2d 680 (4th Cir. 1992).

An example of such a limiting approach is Advanced Computer Services v. MAI Systems, 845 F. Supp. 356 (E.D. Va. 1994). MAI Systems attempted for several years to prevent independent computer repair services from servicing its computers. In 1993, MAI convinced the Ninth Circuit that independent repairers were engaged in copyright infringement, as they necessarily made a copy of the operating system when they started the computer in an attempt to repair it. MAI v. Peak Computing, 991 F.2d 511 (9th Cir. 1993). After this decision, a number of computer repairers filed an antitrust claim against MAI, alleging that MAI was tying the sale of its operating system to the sale of repair service. The District Court granted summary judgment for MAI on the antitrust claim, reasoning that there was no separate market for MAI's operating system and that MAI lacked market power in the broader market for minicomputer operating systems.

What exactly would it mean to tie service to the initial product? What would be wrong with such an agreement? In SMS Systems Maintenance Services, Inc. v. Digital Equipment Corp., 188 F.3d 11 (1st Cir. 1999), the plaintiff claimed that DEC had entered into an unlawful tying arrangement by offering a three-year warranty with its computers. SMS reasoned that with a long-term warranty, buyers would have no incentive to use independent service organizations. The court rejected this claim because DEC did not have market power in the market for computers, and (unlike in *Kodak*) consumers could find out up front that their computer purchase came with a warranty. Further, the court argued that the warranty was generally of benefit to consumers: "a warranty has obvious virtue as a tool of competition. . . . [P]eople ordinarily associate warranties with consumer welfare and highly competitive markets."

4. Both *Kodak* and *Virtual Maintenance* are part of a raging debate on the role of tying claims in antitrust law. On the one hand, the *Kodak* court's analysis of the combined problems of imperfect information and consumer lock-in suggests serious imperfections in the market, which Kodak apparently was able to exploit. As one commentator has noted, this is the key to the *Kodak* decision. Richard Stern, Anti-trust Enforcement in the United States: Eastman Kodak Revives Tie-in Claims, 14 Eur. Intell. Prop. Rev. 369 (1992). The dissent attempts to refute these arguments but ultimately falls back on its assumption that "rational" consumers (that is, those with perfect information and who are not already locked in) will make the right choice. On the other hand, the dissent is surely correct in stating that allowing antitrust to correct this market imperfection will dramatically expand the scope of antitrust law.

Is there a real danger that power in a computer equipment market could profitably be leveraged into aftermarkets—or, alternatively, markets for complementary goods, such as operating system programs? Economists have debated the validity of "leveraging" theory for some time. Both Judge Bork and Judge Posner have advanced the idea that leveraging is economically irrational. See Robert Bork, The Antitrust Paradox: A Policy at War with Itself (1978):

> The fallacy of the cases on tying arrangements may be shown through a hypothetical example based on the facts of *International Salt*. Suppose that a food canner is just willing to pay $100 for a one-year lease of a salt-dispensing machine. How is it possible for the lessor of the machine to make him pay $100 and, in addition, require him to take all his salt from the lessor? If the requirement is necessary, the lessee is giving up something he values. If the lessor has charged the full value of the machine, he cannot then charge still more in the form of coercion to take what amounts to a requirements contract for salt. That is double counting of monopoly power. The tying arrangement, whatever else it may accomplish, is obviously not a means of gaining two monopoly profits from a single monopoly.
>
> The argument is identical with respect to reciprocity. In *Consolidated Foods* the Supreme Court struck down Consolidated's acquisition of Gentry, a small manufacturer of dehydrated onion and garlic, on the theory that Consolidated, a large food processor, might condition its purchases from food suppliers upon their willingness to purchase from Gentry. There is, however, no way in which that practice could be anticompetitive. Suppose that both Consolidated and Gentry buy and sell in fully competitive markets. Consolidated will then have no market power with which to force its suppliers to purchase from Gentry. The suppliers can turn to other customers. Suppose, however, that all markets involved display large elements of market power. Consolidated, before its acquisition of Gentry, may be presumed to have negotiated the best price it could from its suppliers. The acquisition of Gentry does not alter Consolidated's purchasing power, but the attempt after the acquisition to force Gentry's onions and garlic on suppliers as a condition of continued purchases by Consolidated is merely a way of demanding a still lower price from the suppliers. If the tactic works, Consolidated merely learns that it was paying too high a price to begin with: it would be better off renegotiating prices than cramming unwanted onions and garlic down its suppliers' throats. Nor is the theory improved by assuming that Consolidated understands all this and agrees to pay suppliers more in return for purchases from Gentry as a tactic of monopolizing the onion market. Rival sellers in Gentry's market can respond in a variety of ways, the most obvious being a price cut that just matches the price increase laid out by Consolidated. In that kind of price war, Consolidated has no advantages.

But perhaps the most concise devastation of the law's tie-in theory was provoked by the Supreme Court's 1962 *Loew's* decision. Distributors of pre-1948 copyrighted motion-picture feature films for television exhibition engaged in the practice of block booking their films to television stations. The stations had to take entire groups of films and could not pick and choose particular films from the proffered packages. The Court majority held, of course, that the practice violated Section 1 of the Sherman Act. The opinion's economic analysis of block booking was confined to a recitation of Justice Frankfurter's by then clearly indefensible dictum on the purpose of tying arrangements.

The inadequacy of the Supreme Court's theory of tying was well stated by George Stigler in a critique of the *Loew's* opinion:

> Consider the following simple example. One film, Justice Goldberg cited "Gone with the Wind," is worth $10,000 to the buyer, while a second film, the Justice cited "Getting Gertie's Garter," is worthless to him. The seller could sell the one for $10,000 and throw away the second, for no matter what its cost, bygones are forever bygones. Instead the seller compels the buyer to take both. But surely he can obtain no more than $10,000, since by hypothesis this is the value of both films to the buyer. Why not, in short, use his monopoly power directly on the desirable film? It seems no more sensible, on this logic, to blockbook the two films than it would be to compel the exhibitor to buy "Gone with the Wind" and seven Ouija boards, again for $10,000.

To these queries the law has no answers. Indeed, it has so far successfully managed to ignore the existence of the queries.

Id. at 372-374; *accord* Richard Posner, Antitrust Law (1976); cf. Melissa Hamilton, Software Tying Arrangements Under the Antitrust Laws: A More Flexible Approach, 71 Denv. U. L. Rev. 607 (1994) (making the rather different argument that tying is efficient in the software context because it allows programmers to continue to upgrade their products). The logic of Judge Bork's argument is appealing. But is it correct? Louis Kaplow has offered a powerful critique of the Bork-Posner theory. Louis Kaplow, Extension of Monopoly Power Through Leverage, 85 Colum. L. Rev. 515 (1985). There, he argues that

> There are a number of deficiencies in the analysis of recent commentators who have attempted to proclaim the death of leverage theory. The basic mistake in their central thesis is that antitrust law should be indifferent to the exploitation of monopoly power because extant power is a fixed sum and thus will result in the same damage regardless of how it is deployed. Although of some superficial appeal, it can readily be demonstrated that their analysis is strongly counterintuitive. Consider the case of a terrorist on the loose with one stick of dynamite. The fixed sum thesis posits that since the power is fixed — that is, the terrorist has one and only one dynamite stick — we should be indifferent to where the dynamite is placed. It is all too obvious, however, that the potential damage resulting from power in this context, as well as in virtually any other we can imagine, is overwhelmingly dependent upon how it may be used. . . .
>
> The position of these commentators [Bork, Posner, others] can be given more meaning only by developing it more extensively. The most reasonable interpretation, I believe, is that their two categories represent an implicit attempt to distinguish between short-run and long-run phenomena — or, to use more technical language, between static and dynamic models. Profit-maximizing practices are meant to refer roughly to those actions that can have fairly direct and immediate effects, while monopoly extension refers to behavior designed to have implications on the magnitude of profits and welfare loss in the future. The prototypical example of a profit maximiza-

tion device is a pricing decision by a firm with market power, a decision which can be implemented rather quickly. By contrast, practices designed to affect the market share and elasticity of market demand might be labelled monopoly extension devices. These practices do not increase short-run profits, and might even decrease them. The firm's motivation is to change the structural conditions it faces in the future in order that it may receive greater profits in the future.

Id. at 516, 523-524. Professor Kaplow goes on to point out a number of reasons why leveraging may be possible in the real world. His reasons include the dynamic nature of markets in which firms may give up short-run profits in order to maximize long-run gains and inherent imperfections in markets that may allow monopolists to gain limited power in new markets through leveraging. See also George Stigler, United States v. Loew's, Inc.: A Note on Block Booking, 1963 Sup. Ct. Rev. 152 (explaining price discrimination potential inherent in tying).

PROBLEMS

Problem 7-2. Intelligent Co. is the world's largest manufacturer of computer microprocessors, the semiconductor chips that power computers. Intelligent sells 78 percent of the 25 million personal computer microprocessors sold every year and 42 percent of the 4 million workstation and mid-range computer microprocessors. Intelligent carefully protects the design of its microprocessors, going to extreme measures to prevent employees from removing any data about its designs or manufacturing processes from the company's high-security facilities. Intelligent also has a number of patents related to its semiconductor manufacturing. Many of these patents govern the process by which its chips are made, but one Intelligent patent (as well as a number of mask work registrations) governs the layout of the current chip itself (called the 586 chip). Intelligent is in the process of designing a new and faster chip called the 686 but has not yet received any patent or SCPA protection for that chip.

Charybdis is a competing maker of computer microprocessors that sells a much smaller share (8 percent) of personal computer microprocessors each year. Charybdis does not sell microprocessors for other types of computers. Charybdis has filed an antitrust suit against Intelligent. In discovery, the following facts have come out:

- Intelligent comes out with new generations of microprocessors approximately every two years. For several months after it releases a new generation of chips, its competitors are unable to produce an equivalent chip. During this period, Intelligent faces competition only from the older generation of chips.
- The length of time it takes Charybdis to produce an equivalent chip is a function of Intelligent's intellectual property rights in its chips. If Charybdis were permitted to copy the design directly without risk of patent infringement, it could produce an equivalent chip in a much shorter period of time.
- Virtually all software vendors design their operating systems and applications programs to work with the Intelligent chip architecture.

Thus, if another company wants to sell chips that will run these programs, it must design its chips to be compatible with Intelligent's. Only one company (Starfruit) uses a different architecture for PC microprocessors. It has only a 4 percent share of the PC microprocessors sold, and it writes its own software.

- The prices of Intelligent's chips drop by approximately 30 percent the day that Charybdis or another competitor first comes out with a similar chip.

- When Intelligent releases a new generation of chip, the chips are in great demand. Because Intelligent cannot produce them fast enough during the initial month of release, it has developed a system to "ration" demand for its new chips. Under its "preferred customer" policy, Intelligent will sell its new chips first to its good customers— defined as those who bought its last generation of chips and did not buy a competitor's chips.

- Intelligent has on occasion licensed its proprietary microprocessor design know-how to other competitors, though never to Charybdis. These licensing agreements require the competitors to give Intelligent the exclusive rights to any changes or improvements they make to the licensed technology, and require the competitors to sell only to a specified set of customers at a specified price.

Based on this evidence, Charybdis seeks a court order requiring Intelligent to make its microprocessor design technology available on "reasonable, nondiscriminatory terms" without the restrictions in Intelligent's current licenses. It also seeks an order ending Intelligent's "Preferred Customer" program. How should the court rule?

Problem 7-3. Nintendo of America sells the Nintendo Entertainment System (NES), one of the most popular videogame "boxes" on the market. Nintendo's box was particularly successful in the late 1980s, when its market share was over 80 percent. (The development by competitors of new, more technologically sophisticated games has reduced Nintendo's share of the market to around 45 percent today.)

Nintendo's box allows its owner to play a variety of video games by purchasing game cartridges that are plugged into the box. Nintendo does not directly require that its consumers buy games made or licensed by Nintendo. However, Nintendo has included in its box a lockout device that prevents non-Nintendo games from working on the NES box. As a result, owners of Nintendo boxes know that they must buy only Nintendo or Nintendo-licensed games.

Atari Games Corp., which makes games for a box that competes with Nintendo's, sued Nintendo, alleging that Nintendo was tying the sale of NES boxes to the sale of its game cartridges. How should this suit be resolved?

Note on Tying and Product Integration

In a much-reported decision, United States v. Microsoft Corp., 147 F.3d 935 (D.C. Cir. 1998), the D.C. Circuit considered the legality of Microsoft's bundling its Internet Explorer browser into its Windows 95 operating system. The fundamental facts of the case were that Microsoft had originally sold Windows 95 and Internet Explorer separately but proceeded through various upgrades to link the two more closely together and to sell Windows 95 only in conjunction with Internet Explorer (though not vice versa). The Justice Department charged that this violated a 1994 consent decree. For purposes of interpreting that consent decree, the key question was whether the two bundled programs constituted a permissible "integrated product." The district court issued an injunction precluding Microsoft from offering Windows 95 only on the condition that the user also take Internet Explorer.

The D.C. Circuit reversed. The majority held that Microsoft's actions did not violate the consent decree. Two of the judges went beyond that question, however, and, in far-reaching dicta, addressed the propriety of a tying theory:

> The point of the test is twofold and may be illustrated by its application to the paradigm case of the Novell complaint and the subsequent release of Windows 95. First, "integration" suggests a degree of unity, something beyond merely placing disks in the same box. If an OEM or end user (referred to generally as "the purchaser") could buy separate products and combine them himself to produce the "integrated product," then the integration looks like a sham. If Microsoft had simply placed the disks for Windows 3.11 and MS-DOS in one package and covered it with a single license agreement, it would have offered purchasers nothing they could not get by buying the separate products and combining them on their own.[11]
>
> Windows 95, by contrast, unites the two functionalities in a way that purchasers could not; it is not simply a graphical user interface running on top of MS-DOS. Windows 95 is integrated in the sense that the two functionalities — DOS and graphical interface — do not exist separately: the code that is required to produce one also produces the other. Of course one can imagine that code being sold on two different disks, one containing all the code necessary for an operating system, the other with all the code necessary for a graphical interface. But as the code in the two would largely overlap, it would be odd to speak of either containing a discrete functionality. Rather, each would represent a disabled version of Windows 95. The customer could then "repair" each by installing them both on a single computer, but in such a case it would not be meaningful to speak of the customer "combining" two products. Windows 95 is an example of what Professor Areeda calls "physical or technological interlinkage that the customer cannot perform." X Areeda, Antitrust Law §1746b at 227, 228 (1996).
>
> So the combination offered by the manufacturer must be different from what the purchaser could create from the separate products on his own. The second point is that it must also be better in some respect; there should be some technological value to integration. Manufacturers can stick products together in ways that purchasers

---

11. The same analysis would apply to peripherals. If, for example, Microsoft tried to bundle its mouse with the operating system, it would have to show that the mouse/operating system package worked better if combined by Microsoft than it would if combined by OEMs. This is quite different from showing that the mouse works better with the operating system than other mice do. See X Areeda, Elhauge & Hovenkamp, Antitrust Law ¶1746b. Problems seem unlikely to arise with peripherals, because their physical existence makes it easier to identify the act of combination. It seems unlikely that a plausible claim could be made that a mouse and an operating system were integrated in the sense that neither could be said to exist separately. An operating system used with a different mouse does not seem like a different product. But Windows 95 without IE's code will not boot, and adding a rival browser will not fix this. If the add/remove utility is run to hide the IE 4 technologies, Windows 95 reverts to an earlier version, OEM service release ("OSR") 2.0.

cannot without the link serving any purpose but an anticompetitive one. The concept of integration should exclude a case where the manufacturer has done nothing more than to metaphorically "bolt" two products together, as would be true if Windows 95 were artificially rigged to crash if IEXPLORE.EXE were deleted. Cf. ILC Peripherals Leasing Corp. v. International Business Machines Corp., 448 F. Supp. 228, 233 (N.D.Cal. 1978) ("If IBM had simply bolted a disk pack or data module into a drive and sold the two items as a unit for a single price, the 'aggregation' would clearly have been an illegal tying arrangement.") *aff'd per curiam sub nom.* Memorex Corp. v. International Business Machines Corp., 636 F.2d 1188 (9th Cir. 1980); X Areeda, Elhauge & Hovenkamp, Antitrust Law ¶1746 at 227 (discussing literal bolting). Thus if there is no suggestion that the product is superior to the purchaser's combination in some respect, it cannot be deemed integrated.[12]

It might seem difficult to put the two elements discussed above together. If purchasers cannot combine the two functionalities to make Windows 95, it might seem that there is nothing to test Windows 95 against in search of the required superiority. But purchasers can combine the functionalities in their stand-alone incarnations. They can install MS-DOS and Windows 3.11. The test for the integration of Windows 95 then comes down to the question of whether its integrated design offers benefits when compared to a purchaser's combination of corresponding stand-alone functionalities. The decree's evident embrace of Windows 95 as a permissible single product can be taken as manifesting the parties' agreement that it met this test.

The short answer is thus that integration may be considered genuine if it is beneficial when compared to a purchaser combination. But we do not propose that in making this inquiry the court should embark on product design assessment. In antitrust law, from which this whole proceeding springs, the courts have recognized the limits of their institutional competence and have on that ground rejected theories of "technological tying." A court's evaluation of a claim of integration must be narrow and deferential. As the Fifth Circuit put it, "[S]uch a violation must be limited to those instances where the technological factor tying the hardware to the software has been designed for the purpose of tying the products, rather than to achieve some technologically beneficial result. Any other conclusion would enmesh the courts in a technical inquiry into the justifiability of product innovations." Response of Carolina, Inc. v. Leasco Response, Inc., 537 F.2d 1307, 1330 (5th Cir. 1976). . . .

We emphasize that this analysis does not require a court to find that an integrated product is superior to its stand-alone rivals. See ILC Peripherals Leasing Corp. v. International Business Machines Corp., 458 F. Supp. 423, 439 (N.D.Cal. 1978) ("Where there is a difference of opinion as to the advantages of two alternatives which can both be defended from an engineering standpoint, the court will not allow itself to be enmeshed 'in a technical inquiry into the justifiability of product innovations.'") (quoting *Leasco,* 537 F.2d at 1330), *aff'd per curiam sub nom.* Memorex Corp. v. IBM Corp., 636 F.2d 1188 (9th Cir. 1980). We do not read §IV(E)(i) to "put[] judges and juries in the unwelcome position of designing computers." IX Areeda, Antitrust Law ¶1700j at 15 (1991). The question is not whether the integration is a net plus but merely whether there is a plausible claim that it brings some advantage. Whether or not this is the appropriate test for antitrust law generally, we believe it is the only sensible reading of §IV(E)(i).

Judge Wald dissented from this opinion. She suggested a somewhat less deferential interpretation of the consent decree—and of tying law generally:

---

12. Thus of course we agree with the separate opinion that "commingling of code . . . alone is not sufficient evidence of true integration." Commingling for an anticompetitive purpose (or for no purpose at all) is what we refer to as "bolting."

I think the prohibition [in the consent decree on tying] and the proviso [allowing integrated products] could reasonably be construed to state that Microsoft may offer an "integrated" product to OEMs under one license only if the integrated product achieves synergies great enough to justify Microsoft's extension of its monopoly to an otherwise distinct market.

Id. at 957-958. Judge Wald would balance the productive efficiencies against the harm to competition in determining whether an antitrust violation had occurred.

The D.C. Circuit revisited the issue three years later in the Windows 98 antitrust case. United States v. Microsoft, 253 F.3d 34 (D.C. Cir. 2001). In *Microsoft*, the D.C. Circuit treated Microsoft's efforts to bundle the browser into the operating system under both tying and monopolization law. Interestingly, it reached different results in those two analyses. Most of what was alleged to be unlawful tying was independently condemned as monopolization under section 2, without any finding of tying law's "separate products"—an approach advocated by Areeda & Hovenkamp, Antitrust Law ¶777 (2d ed.), when the defendant is a monopolist in the "tying product." In the section 2 finding, the court specifically rejected the approach it had taken in the Windows 95 case just cited. The court did hold that the rule of reason, not the per se rule, was appropriate for the limited case of technological ties involving computer operating systems. However, the fact that the court found section 2 liability for bundling made most of its subsequent tying discussion superfluous on the basic question of the legality or illegality of specific practices. Indeed, the government abandoned its tying claims on remand, since it had won essentially the same arguments in the monopolization context.

COMMENTS AND QUESTIONS

1. Is the deference shown by the majority in *Microsoft* appropriate? Under Judge Williams's opinion, how likely is it that any "integrated" product will ever be held to be a tie? Does the *Microsoft* opinion have implications beyond the integration of software products—to cover the synergistic combination of any kind of products?

On the other hand, surely there is some value to embedding Internet Explorer in Windows 95 to make it easier for novice computer users to access the Internet without having to obtain separate software to do so. Is this valuable enough to outweigh the elimination of competition in the browser market that will almost certainly result from Microsoft's bundling?

2. The pros and cons of browser bundling are discussed in Mark A. Lemley & David McGowan, Could Java Change Everything? The Competitive Propriety of a Proprietary Standard, 43 Antitrust Bull. 715 (1998); Dan Gifford, Java and Microsoft: How Will the Antitrust Story Unfold?, 44 Vill. L. Rev. 501 (1999).

For an argument that Microsoft's conduct should not be evaluated under tying law at all, but rather as an instance of monopolization, see Thomas A. Piraino Jr., An Antitrust Remedy for Monopoly Leveraging by Electronic Networks, 93 Nw. U. L. Rev. 1 (1998) (arguing that Microsoft is improperly using an essential facility to leverage its monopoly power). Piraino points out that Microsoft cannot evade his approach simply by integrating the two products. The D.C. Circuit's 2001 opinion adopted precisely this approach.

3. The *Microsoft* case offers some interesting thoughts on the role of intellectual property law in justifying licensing restrictions. In United States v. Microsoft Corp., 253 F.3d 34 (D.C. Cir. 2001), the case brought against Windows 98, Microsoft defended its allegedly anticompetitive licensing restrictions in part on the ground that its license terms "merely highlight and expressly state the rights that Microsoft already enjoys under federal copyright law" and therefore could not violate the antitrust laws. The court resoundingly rejected this argument, noting that the copyright laws did not give Microsoft unlimited power over its software. It wrote:

> Microsoft argues that the license restrictions are legally justified because, in imposing them, Microsoft is simply "exercising its rights as the holder of valid copyrights."
> Microsoft's primary copyright argument borders upon the frivolous. The company claims an absolute and unfettered right to use its intellectual property as it wishes: "[I]f intellectual property rights have been lawfully acquired," it says, then "their subsequent exercise cannot give rise to antitrust liability." That is no more correct than the proposition that use of one's personal property, such as a baseball bat, cannot give rise to tort liability. As the Federal Circuit succinctly stated: "Intellectual property rights do not confer a privilege to violate the antitrust laws." In re Indep. Serv. Orgs. Antitrust Litig., 203 F.3d 1322, 1325 (Fed. Cir. 2000).

Id. at 62-63. Is this approach consistent with the general principles of antitrust and intellectual property law we have discussed so far?

Note on "Open Access" to the Internet

The Internet was designed using simple, nonproprietary protocols that would transport any data formatted in the right way. Telecommunications companies provide the traditional physical infrastructure of the Internet—the wires—but they are "common carriers" who cannot discriminate among content. The result is what computer scientists have called "end-to-end" architecture: the Internet itself remains a simple transport protocol, and any complexity introduced by software resides at the "ends" of the network. And because the owners of the infrastructure did not also provide Internet content or services, competitive markets for Internet service, Internet software, and content have flourished.

The development of broadband Internet access has changed the picture somewhat. Although one form of broadband access—DSL—is provided by telecommunications companies subject to the same common carrier requirement, most broadband access is provided through cable modems by cable television companies, which are under no such requirement. The largest of these cable companies—AT&T and AOL Time Warner—have purchased Internet service providers and in 1999 and 2000 began requiring that cable modem customers use their in-house Internet service providers to access the Internet.

Critics have charged that the effort by cable broadband providers to bundle ISP services with the physical transport of data is a tying arrangement that poses anticompetitive risks to innovation in the ISP service market. Lemley and Lessig point to several such concerns:

The first risk is the cost of losing ISP competition. The benefits of this competition in the Internet's history should not be underestimated. The ISP market has historically been extraordinarily competitive. This competition has driven providers to expand capacity and to lower prices. Also, it has driven providers to give highly effective customer support. This extraordinary build-out of capacity has not been encouraged through the promise of monopoly protection. Rather, the competitive market has provided a sufficient incentive, and the market has responded.

The loss of ISP competition means more than the loss of the attractive, low-cost services we see today. One should not think of ISPs as providing a fixed and immutable set of services. Right now, ISPs typically provide customer support as well as an Internet protocol (IP) address that channels the customer's data. Competition among ISPs focuses on access speed and content. AOL, for example, is both an access provider and content provider. Mindspring, on the other hand, simply provides access. In the future, however, ISPs could be potential vertical competitors to access providers who could provide competitive packages of content, differently optimized caching servers, different mixes of customer support, or advanced Internet services. ISP competition would provide a constant pressure on access providers to optimize access.

The second risk is that legacy monopolies will improperly affect the architecture of the Internet in an effort to protect their own turf. Broadband Internet service is a potential competitor to traditional cable video services. Traditional cable providers might well view this competition as a long-term threat to their business models and might not want to adapt to that competitive threat. By gaining control over the network architecture, however, cable providers are in a position to affect the development of the architecture so as to minimize the threat of broadband to their own video market. For example, a broadband cable provider that has control over the ISPs its customers use might be expected to restrict customers' access to streaming video from competitive content sources, in order to preserve its market of traditional cable video. AT&T has announced just such a policy. When asked whether users of the AT&T/MediaOne network would be permitted to stream video from competing providers across their network, Internet Services President Daniel Somers reportedly said that AT&T did not spend $56 billion to get into the cable business "to have the blood sucked out of our vein."

Even absent a deliberate intent to restrict some forms of innovation, giving the owners of the pipes control over the nature of the network will inherently skew innovation in the network. As Bar and Sandvig observe, "those who control communication networks tend to design communication platforms which support the patterns of interaction that further their interest [and that] reflect their own history and technical expertise." The old Bell System did not design a packet-switched alternative to the telephone system, because it simply did not think in those terms. Similarly, cable companies should be expected to design the systems they control in ways that are consistent with their experience and their interests. But in doing so, they will disadvantage other approaches, even if they do not intend to do so.

The third risk of giving control of the network to a strategic actor is the threat to innovation. Innovators are less likely to invest in a market in which a powerful actor has the power to behave strategically against it.

One example of this cost to innovation is the uncertainty created for future applications of broadband technology. One specific set of applications put in jeopardy are those that count on the Internet being always on. Applications are being developed, for example, that would allow the Internet to monitor home security or the health of an at-risk resident. These applications would depend upon constant Internet access. Whether as a software designer it makes sense to develop these applications depends in part upon the likelihood that they could be deployed in broadband cable contexts. Under the e2e design of the Internet, this would not be a question. The network would carry everything; the choice about use would be made by the user. But under the design proposed by the cable industry, AT&T and Time Warner affiliates would have the power to decide whether these particular services would be "permitted" on the cable broadband network. AT&T has already exercised this power to discriminate against some services.[45] They have given no guarantee of nondiscrimination in the future. Thus if cable companies decided that certain services would not be permitted, the return to an innovator would be reduced by the proportion of the residential broadband market controlled by cable companies.

The point is not that cable companies would necessarily discriminate against any particular technology. Rather, the point is that the possibility of discrimination increases the risk an innovator faces when deciding whether to design for the Internet. Innovators are likely to be cautious about how they spend their research efforts if they know that one company has the power to control whether that innovation will ever be deployed.[46] The increasing risk is a cost to innovation, and this cost should be expected to reduce innovation.

Mark A. Lemley & Lawrence Lessig, The End of End-to-End: Preserving the Architecture of the Internet in the Broadband Era, 48 UCLA L. Rev. 925, 943-46 (2001). Lemley and Lessig argue that cable broadband providers should not be permitted to compel users to choose a particular ISP. See also Daniel L. Rubinfeld & Hal J. Singer, Open Access to Broadband Networks: A Case Study of the AOL/Time Warner Merger, 16 Berkeley Tech. L.J. 631 (2001); Jim Chen, The Authority to Regulate Broadband Internet Access Over Cable, 16 Berkeley Tech. L.J. 677 (2001).

By contrast, those who would permit cable companies to bundle ISP service with data transmission offer a variety of justifications for such conduct. Some argue that antitrust law need not intervene because cable companies will have an economic incentive to open access to ISPs on their own. James B. Speta, Handicapping the Race for the Last Mile?: A Critique of Open Access Rules for Broadband Platforms, 17 Yale J. Reg. 39 (2000). Others argue that the presence of DSL will keep the broadband market competitive, preserving some market for independent ISPs and precluding cable companies from raising prices or reducing output. Christopher Yoo, Vertical Integration and Media Regulation in the New Economy, 19 Yale J. Reg. 171 (2002). Both of these arguments presuppose that bundling by cable companies will not generate supracompetitive profits. Still others argue that cable companies should be permitted to bundle ISP service precisely in order to generate such supracompetitive profits, since those profits are needed to provide the incentives for cable companies to expand their networks. Howard She-

45. For example, @Home's policy limits the amount of video its consumers can download, limits total upstream traffic, precludes running a server of any sort, and prevents the use of corporate local area networks over the cable connection. See, e.g., Francois Bar et al., Defending the Internet Revolution in the Broadband Era: When Doing Nothing Is Doing Harm, http://brie.berkeley.edu/~briewww/pubs/wp/wp137.html. (listing @Home's policies). These policies are presumably driven by bandwidth limitations.

46. Cf. Mark A. Lemley, The Economics of Improvement in Intellectual Property Law, 75 Tex. L. Rev. 989, 1048-65 (1997) (noting that giving one company the power to centrally coordinate improvements on an existing product is likely to reduce innovation in those improvements).

In economic terms, a potential innovator of a product that must interoperate with a bottleneck monopolist faces reduced incentive to innovate compared to an innovator facing a competitive industry. This is true because the innovator's only option in the bottleneck setting is to sell out to the monopolist, who in this case will act as a monopsonist in the market for the innovation. It is well established that monopsonists purchase products at artificially low prices. See Herbert Hovenkamp, Federal Antitrust Policy: The Law of Competition and Its Practice 14 (1994).

lanski, The Speed Gap: Broadband Infrastructure and Electronic Commerce, 14 Berkeley Tech. L.J. 721 (1999).

Does the bundling of Internet services by cable companies pose a competitive threat that antitrust law should address? Does your answer depend on whether you believe cable companies have significant power in the broadband Internet market, either nationally or in particular regions? On the size of the cable company imposing the restriction? The Federal Trade Commission in 2001 approved the AOL/Time Warner merger subject to the requirement that the merged company open access to its broadband cable services to a minimum number of ISPs.

Does it make sense to impose different requirements on broadband cable and telephone companies? Advocates of open access argue that there is no reason for differential treatment. But those who would permit bundling—including the Federal Communications Commission—have responded by proposing to eliminate the common carrier requirement for broadband telephone lines. This would also eliminate the difference in treatment.

b. Licensing Restrictions

One of the most difficult antitrust issues surrounding intellectual property rights concerns the limitations placed on the licensing of intellectual property. Intellectual property owners may wish to license their rights to others for a number of reasons: they may be ill-equipped to make the protected product; they may want a revenue stream without having to invest in producing and selling the product; they may wish to reserve one geographic or product market to themselves while allowing others to exploit the intellectual property right elsewhere; or they may simply feel that broad dissemination of their product will redound to their benefit —for example, because there is value in having their product become an industry standard. Economic theory encourages licensing because it allows the market to transfer the intellectual property right to the most productive user of that right.

There is no antitrust problem with licensing per se. Indeed, the Antitrust Division's Intellectual Property Guidelines take the position that licensing is essentially procompetitive:

> Intellectual property typically is one component among many in a production process and derives value from its combination with complementary factors. Complementary factors of production include manufacturing and distribution facilities, workforces, and other items of intellectual property. The owner of intellectual property has to arrange for its combination with other necessary factors to realize its commercial value. Often, the owner finds it most efficient to contract with others for these factors, to sell rights to the intellectual property, or to enter into a joint venture arrangement for its development, rather than supplying these complementary factors itself.
>
> Licensing, cross-licensing, or otherwise transferring intellectual property (hereinafter "licensing") can facilitate integration of the licensed property with complementary factors of production. This integration can lead to more efficient exploitation of the intellectual property, benefiting consumers through the reduction of costs and the introduction of new products. Such arrangements increase the value of intellectual property to consumers and to the developers of the technology. By potentially increasing the expected returns from intellectual property, licensing also can increase the incentive for its creation and thus promote greater investment in research and development. . . .

Field-of-use, territorial and other limitations on intellectual property licenses may serve procompetitive ends by allowing the licensor to exploit its property as efficiently and effectively as possible. These various forms of exclusivity can be used to give a licensee an incentive to invest in the commercialization and distribution of products embodying the licensed intellectual property and to develop additional applications for the licensed property. The restrictions may do so, for example, by protecting the licensee against free-riding on the licensee's investments by other licensees or by the licensor. They may also promote the licensor's incentive to license, for example, by protecting the licensor from competition in the licensor's own technology in a market niche that it prefers to keep to itself. These benefits of licensing restrictions apply to patent, copyright, and trade secret licenses, and to know-how agreements.

Intellectual Property Guidelines §2.3. For many of these reasons, the Division's prior set of Guidelines governing intellectual property licensing (promulgated by the Reagan Administration in 1988 and contained in the International Guidelines) took a very "hands off" approach to intellectual property licensing transactions. That has changed with the current Guidelines, however. While the new Guidelines recognize the procompetitive benefits of licensing, they also identify some licensing arrangements that are cause for antitrust concerns:

[A]ntitrust concerns may arise when [a] licensing arrangement harms competition among entities that would have been actual or likely potential competitors in a relevant market in the absence of a license (entities in a "horizontal relationship"). A restraint in a licensing arrangement may harm such competition, for example, if it facilitates market division or price fixing. In addition, license restrictions with respect to one market may harm such competition in another market by anticompetitively foreclosing access to, or significantly raising the price of, an important input, or by facilitating coordination to increase price or reduce output.

Id., §3.1.

COMMENTS AND QUESTIONS

1. Consider the Division's new policy statement—that they are concerned about agreements that reduce competition that would have existed but for the license. On the one hand, this policy can be (and has been) criticized as being too aggressive. By declaring that intellectual property is like any other form of property, the Guidelines narrowly circumscribe the terms of licensing agreements. The effect may be to prevent some efficient licensing agreements from being signed, even though the procompetitive effects of the agreement would outweigh its negative effects on preexisting competition.

On the other hand, perhaps the policy can be criticized from the other side for not being aggressive enough. Why should the antitrust laws be concerned only with protecting competition that would have existed absent the license? If licensing is favored because it is procompetitive, doesn't antitrust law have some obligation to see that those procompetitive benefits that result from the license itself are not lost because of restrictive license provisions?

One way of resolving this debate is to distinguish between the effects inherent to the license, and the effects that result from restrictive provisions ancillary to the license. For example, an agreement to license a patent may promote competition in the market for the patented product, but the agreement may also contain a term dividing geographic territories or setting resale prices. To the extent that these restrictive terms can be severed from the balance of the license, antitrust law may be able to challenge them without threatening the license itself.

2. The Guidelines also establish that most licensing agreements will be treated under the rule of reason, rather than under the per se rule. Does this help to alleviate any concern that the Guidelines are too restrictive in their treatment of intellectual property licensing?

Note on Intellectual Property and Exclusive Dealing

Section 3 of the Clayton Act prohibits some "exclusive dealing arrangements" under the rule of reason. "Exclusive dealing" refers to agreements that prevent the agreeing party from buying or selling the goods of a competitor. For example, a company with a significant share of the market may attempt to drive its competitors out of business by requiring that all its customers buy exclusively from the company. If the customers consider the exclusive dealer to be their most important source of supply, they will likely agree to purchase all their goods from that dealer. The result may be that the dealer expands its market power into an actual monopoly.

On the other hand, exclusive dealing arrangements may have procompetitive justifications. Agreements to buy everything you need from (or sell everything you produce to) one source may significantly reduce transaction costs and may allow smaller companies to take advantage of discounts resulting from economies-of-scale purchasing. They also permit a company to insure itself against the vagaries of the market. The problem for antitrust law is to distinguish exclusive dealing arrangements that restrict competition from those that merely serve to make business transactions easier. To draw this line, antitrust requires some showing of market power to make out a Clayton Act section 3 violation.

Intellectual property licenses often contain exclusivity provisions. Such provisions can bind either the licensor or the licensee (or conceivably both). The licensor might agree to grant an exclusive license for his patent that gives only the licensee the right to work the patent. The licensor cannot license anyone else to work the patent and in some circumstances gives up the right to work it himself. On the other end, a patent license may bind the licensee not to use or sell products other than the patentee's product. In either case, the contract expressly requires that one party deal exclusively with the other. The Antitrust Division's Intellectual Property Guidelines take the position that exclusive licenses do not raise antitrust concerns unless the parties to the agreement (or other potential licensees) would have been actual or potential competitors absent the exclusivity provision. See Intellectual Property Guidelines §4.3.2.

Exclusive dealing practices need not be express. Certain types of licensing provisions have the practical effect of coercing the licensee into using only the licensor's product. One example is a type of nonmetered royalty. In a recent complaint, the Antitrust Division charged that Microsoft had dominated the market for installed computer operating systems by requiring that computer manufacturers pay royalties to Microsoft on each computer they shipped, regardless of whether the computer had a Microsoft operating system installed. Because the manufacturers had to pay for Microsoft's operating system anyway, they were extremely unlikely to install a competitor's operating system, because if they did they would have had to pay twice for an operating system. United States v. Microsoft Corp., 159 F.R.D. 318 (D.D.C. 1995). When Microsoft settled the Division's complaint, it agreed to stop the use of nonmetered royalties.

COMMENTS AND QUESTIONS

1. Several companies have alleged that after they asserted their intellectual property rights against Intel—either by filing suit or by entering into license negotiations—Intel threatened to cut them off from the supply of its crucial technology unless they dropped their suits. In effect, the allegation is that Intel is using its power in the market for microprocessors to obtain royalty-free licenses to everyone else's intellectual property. Is this a reciprocal tying arrangement of a sort between Intel's technology and the intellectual property asserted against it? Is it an exclusive dealing arrangement? If so, does it violate the antitrust laws? See Intergraph Corp. v. Intel Corp., 195 F.3d 1346 (Fed. Cir. 1999); In re Intel Corp., FTC No. 9288 (complaint filed June 8, 1998).

Intel and the FTC entered into a consent decree in 1999. Under that decree, Intel agreed not to terminate its supply of chips or information to a buyer merely because that buyer sued it for intellectual property infringement. Intel retained the right to terminate supply for a number of legitimate business reasons, however. Further, the consent decree provided that Intel could cut off any purchaser who sued it for infringement if that purchaser sought to enjoin the sale of Intel's core products. In essence, therefore, Intel has retained the power to demand a compulsory license of intellectual property rights from the companies with which it does business.

Is the consent decree an appropriate compromise between the positions of the parties? Is it likely to have procompetitive effects?

PROBLEM

Problem 7-4. Assume that Microsoft owns a registered trademark for Windows to identify its graphical user interface on a computer operating system. Microsoft agrees to license the Windows trademark to certain companies that wish to indicate that their applications programs are "Windows-compatible." However, assume that Microsoft requires as a condition of the license that the companies sell only applications programs that run exclusively on Microsoft Windows operating systems. Has Microsoft violated the antitrust laws? What role should market power play in the analysis? Does the Windows trademark itself confer market power?

Note on Other Common Licensing Restrictions

Besides exclusivity, a number of other common features of intellectual property licenses raise potential antitrust issues. We consider several here.

Grantback Clauses. Intellectual property owners sometimes require as a condition of the license that the licensee "grant back" to the licensor the rights to use any improvements the licensee makes in the technology. Some grantback clauses simply require that the licensee agree not to sue the licensor for infringing on any improvement patents that result from the licensee's work. Others are more strict, however; they require the assignment or exclusive license of the rights to any improvement.

One reason licensors use grantback clauses is obvious: they don't want to lose the right to practice their invention or be held "hostage" by their licensees. By retaining the right to use any improvements the licensee makes, the original intellectual property owner can ensure that she stays current in her technology. Grantback clauses may also help to avoid the "blocking patents" problem by ensuring that the senior intellectual property owner always has the dominant right.

The precise nature of the grantback clause may differ from case to case. Some patentees require that their licensee *assign* any improvement patents back to the licensee. In this instance, the grantback clause avoids the blocking-patents problem entirely, because the original patentee ends up owning both the original and the improvement patents. By contrast, if the original patentee requires only that the improver license back the right to use the improvement, the grantback clause looks more like an ex ante cross-licensing solution to a prospective blocking-patents problem.

On the other hand, grantback clauses may be used to stifle innovation. Grantbacks allow a dominant industry player to license her intellectual property freely, without worrying that her licensees may develop an improved process for manufacturing her product and therefore compete with her. Indeed, such licenses may be an effective way of *preventing* serious competition, because they allow the dominant player to "capture" potential competitors and take advantage of their ideas. Further, because licensees no longer have the exclusive (or perhaps any) right to their improvements, they may be less willing to invest in research and development of such improvements.

Most grantback clauses have survived antitrust scrutiny. (A notable exception is United Shoe Machinery Co. v. United States, 258 U.S. 451 (1922).) The Antitrust Division's current Intellectual Property Guidelines, however, provide that "[i]n deciding whether to challenge a grantback, the Department will consider the extent to which, as compared with no license at all, the license with the grantback provision may diminish total research and development investment or lessen competition in innovation or technology markets." Intellectual Property Guidelines, §5.6. Nonexclusive grantbacks are less likely to pose an antitrust problem than exclusive ones, because the licensee in a nonexclusive arrangement still retains some control over its improvement. See John Barton, Patents and Antitrust: A Rethinking in Light of Patent Breadth and Sequential Innovation, 65 Antitrust L.J. 449, 461-462 (1997) (endorsing the Division's case-by-case approach).

Is this the right comparison to make? Does it suggest that the Division will treat patent grantbacks differently from copyright grantbacks (because of the difference between the blocking-patents rule and the rule in copyright)?[7]

Field-of-Use Restrictions. Alluded to earlier, field-of-use restrictions in intellectual property licenses grant licensees the right to work a patent in only a limited area. The area may be limited either geographically or by product market. Such restrictions may enable a patentee to exploit his technology efficiently in several markets while maintaining the exclusivity granted him by the patent laws. But field-of-use restrictions may also be an efficient means of enforcing a territorial market division agreement between horizontal competitors. Horizontal market division can have the effect of creating mini-monopolies in what would otherwise be a competitive market. If the patent licensed is a sham or is only a minor part of the business of the licensor and licensee, it is possible that the patent license is really a "front" for a market division scheme. Territorial market division is normally illegal per se under the rule of United States v. Topco Associates, 405 U.S. 596 (1972). However, the scope of that rule is limited in the patent area by 35 U.S.C. §261, which explicitly permits geographic field-of-use restrictions in patent licenses.

Are there legitimate reasons for some field-of-use restrictions that inhere in the nature of the intellectual property laws? Consider, for example, an geographic market division scheme that granted each licensee an exclusive territory in a different country. Because of the national nature of patents, this means that each licensee received the exclusive right to work the patent (although not the exclusive worldwide right to sell the technology). Is there anything wrong with such a scheme? See United States v. Westinghouse, 471 F. Supp. 532, *aff'd*, 648 F.2d 642 (9th Cir. 1981) (approving such an arrangement).

Extension of Patent or Copyright Term. This is primarily an issue in patent law, because patents have shorter terms than copyrights. A license may seek to extend the exclusive rights of the patent laws beyond the 20-year patent term, either by compelling the continued payment of royalties or by imposing collateral obligations (such as exclusive dealing arrangements or grantback clauses) that do not terminate when the patent expires.

Whether extensions of the patent term by contract should be of concern to anyone but the contracting parties themselves has been a matter of some debate. Compare Robert Merges, Reflections on Current Legislation Affecting Patent Misuse, 70 J. Pat. & Trademark Off. Soc'y 793, 801-802 (1988) (patent term extensions are anticompetitive) with Mark Lemley, Comment, The Economic Irrationality of the Patent Misuse Doctrine, 78 Cal. L. Rev. 1599, 1630 (1990) (agreements to extend patent term are not anticompetitive). In some sense, the issue here is one we have been considering repeatedly throughout this book — the right of private parties to change the scope of the intellectual property laws by contract.

In another sense, however, these issues have a different spin on them in the antitrust context. To the extent that patent term extensions reduce competition by

---

7. On this difference, see Mark A. Lemley, The Economics of Improvement in Intellectual Property Law, 75 Tex. L. Rev. 989 (1997).

removing the incentive for licensees to compete directly with the patentee after the patent expires, it is consumers and society who suffer the consequences. Cf. Lasercomb America v. Reynolds, 911 F.2d 970 (4th Cir. 1990) (invalidating 99-year software license under copyright misuse doctrine).

2.   Horizontal Restraints

Cartels—loosely defined as agreements among competitors to restrict output and raise prices—are illegal under section 1 of the Sherman Act, 15 U.S.C. §1. When competitors have agreed to set prices or output levels or divide markets, the Sherman Act may be violated without regard to proof of market power or effect. This is the "per se" rule. However, the courts have been backing away from the per se rule in a number of situations involving horizontal agreements between competitors, particularly where the agreement arguably serves some procompetitive purpose, such as in the cases discussed below.

One example of such an arguably procompetitive arrangement is the "patent pool" under which competitors cross-license their patents. An argument can be made that patent pooling is more desirable than controls on the licensing of a single patent. The argument focuses on the problem of blocking patents. Where one company patents an original invention and a second company (presumably but not necessarily a licensee) patents an improvement on that invention, the law leaves the two companies in a rather peculiar situation. In order to make the most efficient use of the invention, each company wants to use both the original invention and its improvement. Alone, however, neither company can do so without infringing the other's patent. One obvious solution to the blocking-patents problem is for the companies to cross-license their patents, which allows both companies to use the invention efficiently and thereby benefit society and preserve some measure of competition.

The problem of blocking patents is common in the patent-antitrust literature. See Robert P. Merges, Intellectual Property Rights and Bargaining Breakdown: The Case of Blocking Patents, 62 Tenn. L. Rev. 75 (1994). Blocking patents can take one of two forms. First, two or more companies may have valid patents on different steps of a process in which each step is necessary to make the end product. This can be thought of as "pure" technical necessity. Without cross-licensing, neither company would be able to produce the product at all. The case against applying antitrust law is fairly clear: preventing patent pooling will reduce rather than increase market participation. In this circumstance, at least some courts have been willing to permit pools of blocking patents. For example, in Carpet Seaming Tape Licensing Corp. v. Best Seam, Inc., 616 F.2d 1133 (9th Cir. 1980), *cert. denied*, 464 U.S. 818 (1983), the court held:

> A well-recognized legitimate purpose for a pooling agreement is exchange of blocking patents. The trial court . . . demonstrates a misunderstanding as to the nature of the relationship which can give rise to a blocking situation. The trial judge found that the Winkler and Clymin patents did not block the Burgess patents, but ignored the possibility that the Burgess patents may well have blocked the Winkler and Clymin patents despite well-established law that patents on basic processes and products may block patents on improvements to those products and processes. As the Supreme Court stated in Standard Oil Co. v. United States, 283 U.S. at 172, n.5:

This is often the case where patents covering improvements of a basic process, owned by one manufacturer, are granted to another. A patent may be rendered quite useless, or 'blocked,' by another unexpired patent which covers a vitally related feature of the manufacturing process. Unless some agreement can be reached, the parties are hampered and exposed to litigation. And, frequently, the cost of litigation to a patentee is greater than the value of a patent for a minor improvement. . . .

The economics underlying this attitude toward the accumulation of improvement patents is ably and succinctly stated by Professor Ward S. Bowman:

"If . . . one patent was subservient to the other, and improvement patent unusable without infringing the basic patent, then combining or pooling them eliminates no user alternative. In terms of possible trade restraint, this case is indistinguishable from a vertical merger. The two patents combined . . . could not restrict output or raise price any more than if the two were exploited separately." W. Bowman, Patent and Antitrust Law at 201 (1973).

Id. at 1142. See also Clorox Co. v. Sterling Winthrop, 932 F. Supp. 469 (E.D.N.Y. 1996) (agreement settling trademark dispute over the terms "Lysol" and "Pine-Sol" by limiting the product markets in which each could sell was not anticompetitive because owner of Pine-Sol can compete with Lysol using other marks).

A more common problem involves a number of patents whose validity is open to question. This may be thought of as practical technical necessity. Rather than entering into prohibitively expensive and protracted litigation over the validity of their respective patents, can firms in this situation settle their differences by pooling their patents (at least one of which is presumably valid)? Standard Oil Co. v. United States, 283 U.S. 163 (1931), seems to suggest that such an agreement would be treated under the rule of reason. Of course, that does not mean that the agreement will always be upheld. If the companies with blocking patents together comprise only a small part of the industry, their agreement would presumably survive rule-of-reason scrutiny. But if the new technology encompassed by the patents dominates a market, even the *Standard Oil* rule presents an antitrust problem. Is this a desirable outcome?

On the one hand, allowing the agreement would get the product to market more quickly and inexpensively. Further, because each firm in our hypothetical holds an arguably valid patent, one firm (the firm whose patent is upheld) is likely to end up with a monopoly in the product anyway. On the other hand, allowing competitors to resolve their differences by cross-licensing their patents could foreclose any incentive for those firms to compete in the future. Instead of a monopoly patent holder being faced with several competitors trying to unseat it, the patent cartel would face no foreseeable competition. See John Barton, Patents and Antitrust: A Rethinking in Light of Patent Breadth and Sequential Innovation, 65 Antitrust L.J. 449, 462-465 (1997). Whether you believe the rule of reason or outright legality should govern this situation depends on your assessment of the relative costs of each approach.

Does it matter for antitrust analysis whether the parties to the pool are in the same market? Is the existence of the pool presumptive evidence that they are? Market definition problems have plagued patent-pooling cases. See Roger B. Andewelt, Analysis of Patent Pools Under the Antitrust Laws, 53 Antitrust L.J. 611 (1984).

Can a similar argument be made for copyright "pools"? Consider the following case.

a. Industry Standardization

Broadcast Music, Inc. v. Columbia Broadcasting System, Inc.
Supreme Court of the United States
441 U.S. 1 (1978)

MR. JUSTICE WHITE delivered the opinion of the Court.

This case involves an action under the antitrust and copyright laws brought by respondent Columbia Broadcasting System, Inc. (CBS), against petitioners, American Society of Composers, Authors and Publishers (ASCAP) and Broadcast Music, Inc. (BMI), and their members and affiliates. The basic question presented is whether the issuance by ASCAP and BMI to CBS of blanket licenses to copyrighted musical compositions at fees negotiated by them is price fixing *per se* unlawful under the antitrust laws. . . .

BMI, a nonprofit corporation owned by members of the broadcasting industry, was organized in 1939, is affiliated with or represents some 10,000 publishing companies and 20,000 authors and composers, and operates in much the same manner as ASCAP. Almost every domestic copyrighted composition is in the repertory either of ASCAP, with a total of three million compositions, or of BMI, with one million.

Both organizations operate primarily through blanket licenses, which give the licensees the right to perform any and all of the compositions owned by the members or affiliates as often as the licensees desire for a stated term. Fees for blanket licenses are ordinarily a percentage of total revenues or a flat dollar amount, and do not directly depend on the amount or type of music used. Radio and television broadcasters are the largest users of music, and almost all of them hold blanket licenses from both ASCAP and BMI. Until this litigation, CBS held blanket licenses from both organizations for its television network on a continuous basis since the late 1940's and had never attempted to secure any other form of license from either ASCAP or any of its members. *Id.*, at 752-754.

The complaint filed by CBS charged various violations of the Sherman Act and the copyright laws. CBS argued that ASCAP and BMI are unlawful monopolies and that the blanket license is illegal price fixing, an unlawful tying arrangement, a concerted refusal to deal, and a misuse of copyrights. The District Court, though denying summary judgment to certain defendants, ruled that the practice did not fall within the *per se* rule. 337 F. Supp. 394, 398 (SDNY 1972). After an 8-week trial, limited to the issue of liability, the court dismissed the complaint, rejecting again the claim that the blanket license was price fixing and a *per se* violation of §1 of the Sherman Act, and holding that since direct negotiation with individual copyright owners is available and feasible there is no undue restraint of trade, illegal tying, misuse of copyrights, or monopolization. 400 F. Supp., at 781-783.

[The Court of Appeals reversed, holding that the agreement was *per se* illegal.]

A

As a preliminary matter, we are mindful that the Court of Appeals' holding would appear to be quite difficult to contain. If, as the court held, there is a *per se* antitrust violation whenever ASCAP issues a blanket license to a television network for a single fee, why would it not also be automatically illegal for ASCAP to negotiate and issue blanket licenses to individual radio or television stations or to other users who perform copyrighted music for profit? Likewise, if the present network licenses issued through ASCAP on behalf of its members are *per se* violations, why would it not be equally illegal for the members to authorize ASCAP to issue licenses establishing various categories of uses that a network might have for copyrighted music and setting a standard fee for each described use?

Although the Court of Appeals apparently thought the blanket license could be saved in some or even many applications, it seems to us that the *per se* rule does not accommodate itself to such flexibility and that the observations of the Court of Appeals with respect to remedy tend to impeach the *per se* basis for the holding of liability.

CBS would prefer that ASCAP be authorized, indeed directed, to make all its compositions available at standard per-use rates within negotiated categories of use. 400 F. Supp., at 747 n. 7.[28] But if this in itself or in conjunction with blanket licensing constitutes illegal price fixing by copyright owners, CBS urges that an injunction issue forbidding ASCAP to issue any blanket license or to negotiate any fee except on behalf of an individual member for the use of his own copyrighted work or works.[29] Thus, we are called upon to determine that blanket licensing is unlawful across the board. We are quite sure, however, that the *per se* rule does not require any such holding.

B

In the first place, the line of commerce allegedly being restrained, the performing rights to copyrighted music, exists at all only because of the copyright laws. Those who would use copyrighted music in public performances must secure consent from the copyright owner or be liable at least for the statutory damages for each infringement and, if the conduct is willful and for the purpose of financial gain, to criminal penalties. Furthermore, nothing in the Copyright Act of 1976 indicates in the slightest that Congress intended to weaken the rights of copyright owners to control the public performance of musical compositions. Quite the contrary is true. Although the copyright laws confer no rights on copyright owners to fix prices among themselves or otherwise to violate the antitrust laws, we would not expect that any market arrangements reasonably necessary to effectuate the rights that are granted would be deemed a *per se* violation of the Sherman Act. Otherwise, the commerce anticipated by the Copyright Act and protected against

---

28. Surely, if ASCAP abandoned the issuance of all licenses and confined its activities to policing the market and suing infringers, it could hardly be said that member copyright owners would be in violation of the antitrust laws by not having a common agent issue per-use licenses. Under the copyright laws, those who publicly perform copyrighted music have the burden of obtaining prior consent. Cf. Zenith Radio Corp. v. Hazeltine Research, Inc., 395 U.S., at 139-140.

29. In its complaint, CBS alleged that it would be "wholly impracticable" for it to obtain individual licenses directly from the composers and publishing houses, but it now says that it would be willing to do exactly that if ASCAP were enjoined from granting blanket licenses to CBS or its competitors in the network television business.

restraint by the Sherman Act would not exist at all or would exist only as a pale reminder of what Congress envisioned.[32]

C

More generally, in characterizing this conduct under the *per se* rule, our inquiry must focus on whether the effect and, here because it tends to show effect, see United States v. United States Gypsum Co., 438 U.S. 422, 436 n. 13 (1978), the purpose of the practice are to threaten the proper operation of our predominantly free-market economy—that is, whether the practice facially appears to be one that would always or almost always tend to restrict competition and decrease output, and in what portion of the market, or instead one designed to "increase economic efficiency and render markets more, rather than less, competitive." *Id.*, at 441 n. 16; see National Society of Professional Engineers v. United States, 435 U.S., at 688; Continental T.V., Inc. v. GTE Sylvania Inc., 433 U.S., at 50 n. 16; Northern Pac. R. Co. v. United States, 356 U.S., at 4.

The blanket license, as we see it, is not a "naked restrain[t] of trade with no purpose except stifling of competition," White Motor Co. v. United States, 372 U.S. 253, 263 (1963), but rather accompanies the integration of sales, monitoring, and enforcement against unauthorized copyright use. See L. Sullivan, Handbook of the Law of Antitrust §59, p. 154 (1977). As we have already indicated, ASCAP and the blanket license developed together out of the practical situation in the marketplace: thousands of users, thousands of copyright owners, and millions of compositions. Most users want unplanned, rapid, and indemnified access to any and all of the repertory of compositions, and the owners want a reliable method of collecting for the use of their copyrights. Individual sales transactions in this industry are quite expensive, as would be individual monitoring and enforcement, especially in light of the resources of single composers. Indeed, as both the Court of Appeals and CBS recognize, the costs are prohibitive for licenses with individual radio stations, nightclubs, and restaurants, 562 F.2d, at 140 n. 26, and it was in that milieu that the blanket license arose.

A middleman with a blanket license was an obvious necessity if the thousands of individual negotiations, a virtual impossibility, were to be avoided. Also, individual fees for the use of individual compositions would presuppose an intricate schedule of fees and uses, as well as a difficult and expensive reporting problem for the user and policing task for the copyright owner. Historically, the market for public-performance rights organized itself largely around the single-fee blanket license, which gave unlimited access to the repertory and reliable protection against infringement. When ASCAP's major and user-created competitor, BMI, came on the scene, it also turned to the blanket license.

---

32. Cf. Silver v. New York Stock Exchange, 373 U.S. 341 (1963).

Because a musical composition can be "consumed" by many different people at the same time and without the creator's knowledge, the "owner" has no real way to demand reimbursement for the use of his property except through the copyright laws and an effective way to enforce those legal rights. See Twentieth Century Music Corp. v. Aiken, 422 U.S. 151, 162 (1975). It takes an organization of rather large size to monitor most or all uses and to deal with users on behalf of the composers. Moreover, it is inefficient to have too many such organizations duplicating each other's monitoring of use.

With the advent of radio and television networks, market conditions changed, and the necessity for and advantages of a blanket license for those users may be far less obvious than is the case when the potential users are individual television or radio stations, or the thousands of other individuals and organizations performing copyrighted compositions in public. But even for television network licenses, ASCAP reduces costs absolutely by creating a blanket license that is sold only a few, instead of thousands, of times, and that obviates the need for closely monitoring the networks to see that they do not use more than they pay for. ASCAP also provides the necessary resources for blanket sales and enforcement, resources unavailable to the vast majority of composers and publishing houses. Moreover, a bulk license of some type is a necessary consequence of the integration necessary to achieve these efficiencies, and a necessary consequence of an aggregate license is that its price must be established.

MR. JUSTICE STEVENS, dissenting.

The Court holds that ASCAP's blanket license is not a species of price fixing categorically forbidden by the Sherman Act. I agree with that holding. The Court remands the cases to the Court of Appeals, leaving open the question whether the blanket license as employed by ASCAP and BMI is unlawful under a rule-of-reason inquiry. I think that question is properly before us now and should be answered affirmatively. . . .

COMMENTS AND QUESTIONS

1. There is no "technical necessity" for the copyright collective in *Broadcast Music*. It is certainly possible in theory to require each copyright holder to offer licenses independently and to punish cooperation in the market for copyright licenses in the same way section 1 punishes other cooperation among competitors. But the result would be that most licenses currently offered would not be available because of prohibitive transaction costs. "Economic necessity" therefore requires that we exempt such sales from the per se rule. The Court concludes that the rule of reason applies, and remands the case.

The transactions-cost rationale seems to require that copyright collectives have a certain degree of market power. After all, if the industry were composed of thousands of small "collectives," transactions costs would still be a significant barrier to copyright licenses. In fact, the "efficient scale" of a copyright collective would seem to be the entire industry. Given this fact, should antitrust courts be less or more concerned about the market power of copyright collectives?

2. The Court reasons that since the market in question was created by the copyright laws in the first place, it ought to be protected from per se antitrust scrutiny. But is it fair to say that ASCAP and BMI created the market? Certainly, they facilitate the granting of copyright permissions, although they do so at the expense of competition among copyright owners in the sale of permissions. It may be that, absent large organizations such as BMI that have significant bargaining power, most musicians would trade away any performance right royalty in exchange for the public exposure that comes from having their songs played on the radio. If this is true, BMI skews the ordinary market distribution in favor of copyright owners, with the result that radio stations pay a higher price. Indeed, the Supreme Court

has previously condemned similar copyright "aggregation" arrangements under the per se rule. See United States v. Loew's, Inc., 371 U.S. 38 (1962) ("block-booking" of movies in theatres illegal).

There are two possible responses to this argument. First, the transactions-cost problem discussed above may be so great that absent a copyright collective, artists and broadcasters might never connect at all. As a result, broadcasters would be unable to play songs by artists who would like to have their songs played. Second, BMI may actually restore equity to the bargaining situation by providing counter-vailing power to match the power of the broadcasters, and individual copyright owners might feel they have no choice but to give up their royalties. They are likely to be in a much better bargaining position as part of a large collective organization.

3. Can an analogous argument be made in favor of patent-pooling on the grounds that it reduces transactions costs? Consider the following excerpt:

Patent pools arise because it makes sense for firms in industries characterized by crossing and conflicting IPRs [intellectual property rights] to "institutionalize" technology exchange. In many cases, pools are creatures of necessity. For example, where different firms hold patents on the basic building blocks of the industry's products, they will have to cross-license to produce at all. This was the case, for example, with the aircraft industry in the early days of the twentieth century, and with sewing machines. Even where no single patent or set of patents is essential, however, firms in an industry often find that they engage in such frequent negotiations that a regularized institution with formal rules, or even general guidelines, is helpful in reducing transaction costs. An example of a pool such as this is the one formed by the early shoe machinery industry. The economic literature on institutions explains this quite well; to use one popular metaphor, the "repeat-play" nature of an institution makes it easier to reach agreement on any particular issue, because disparities tend to balance out over many transactions. . . .

All patent pools share one fundamental characteristic: they provide a regularized transactional mechanism in place of the statutory property rule baseline which requires an individual bargain for each transaction. But my review of particular pools shows that this general structure has encompassed a diversity of organizational forms. . . .

Many patent pools are in essence contracts. Firms agree to consolidate patents and license them collectively. The royalties from licensing the patents, and sometimes from sales of products made by one or more parties to the pooling agreement, are divided according to a contractual formula. . . . In this simple example, the contract integrated numerous transactions that would otherwise have been negotiated separately. And, most importantly for present purposes, it translated the contribution of each major patent holder into a precise percentage of the royalty stream.

Robert P. Merges, Contracting into Liability Rules: Intellectual Property Rights and Collective Rights Organizations, 84 Cal. L. Rev. 1293, 1341-1342 (1996).

The music industry is not the only one to have developed collectives of copyright owners. In the publishing industry, an organization called the Copyright Clearance Center (CCC) has taken a leading role in granting permissions and collecting fees from people who photocopy pages out of books or periodicals. The CCC's standard fee for photocopying permissions is fairly high—a standard fee is 25 cents per page. (The royalty for copying a 200-page book at this rate would be $50. This price does not include any reproduction cost.) While the CCC is in much the same situation as BMI or ASCAP, the people with whom it is bargaining (individuals, corporations, and universities) are generally smaller than broadcasters and have less bargaining power. Does this fact make CCC's existence as the dominant publishing collective troublesome from an antitrust perspective? See Merges, supra; Stanley M. Besen et al., An Economic Analysis of Copyright Collectives, 78 Va. L. Rev. 383 (1992) (copyright collectives lower transactions costs and are therefore generally procompetitive).

Note on Standards, Interoperability, and Standard-Setting Organizations

A significant portion of the intellectual property debate in the computer industry centers around the idea of interoperability or compatibility. A strong argument can be made that the efficient use of computers requires that they be able to "talk to" each other, so that work on one machine can be shared with other users. This argument is even stronger in the case of computer networks and the Internet, where the very existence of the network requires that computers be able to communicate in a standardized format.

How is this to be accomplished? If consumers are to be able to translate their word processing documents from one word processing program to another, someone who knows the nature of one system must write a compatibility component into the other system. Compatibility (particularly one-way compatibility—my system will run your documents, whether or not your system runs mine) does not require that the two programs be developed together or that two competitors work together. It does require that the party making the compatible product have the opportunity to reverse engineer the other product or otherwise have access to the applications programming interfaces (APIs). We have seen significant debate in the case law concerning the propriety of reverse engineering copyrighted software.

But reverse engineering has its problems. As we noted in the introductory chapter, it is an imperfect and time-consuming process. It also requires access to the competitor's product, something that may not be available until after the product is sold commercially. If reverse engineers must wait until a product reaches the shelves and then spend six months taking it apart in order to produce a compatible product, their new product may have only a short shelf life before a new revision of the original product renders the compatible software obsolete.

There is a better way. If the procompatibility programmers have advanced access to the new program—or, better yet, if the necessary compatibility components have been published—it is cheaper and easier to make compatible products, and society benefits. But such standardization requires cooperation among competitors,[8] and such cooperation makes antitrust lawyers very nervous. There is a fine line between wanting to encourage the efficient production of software—which may mean the use of compatibility and interface standards—and wanting to deter cartels that limit innovation. For this reason, the antitrust status of standard-setting groups in the computer industry remains uncertain today.

---

8. An alternative to direct cooperation is for a standard to be published under an open-source license. Such an open-source standard can be modified by anyone. It may not produce an agreed-upon standard, however.

At the same time, there is reason to be concerned about *not* allowing such groups to function. There is a natural tendency for the computer industry to coalesce around certain devices as industry standards. If those standards are not set by industry agreement, one company's product may become the de facto standard. If that product is difficult to reverse engineer, or if strong intellectual property protection prevents the development of compatible products, the standard-setter will become a monopolist. De facto standards controlled by a single company can be very hard to change, and they may continue to dominate an industry due to inertia long after they are technically obsolete.

In industries characterized by large standardization externalities—that is, where the market naturally tends toward a single product or type of product—group standard-setting organizations can serve valuable procompetitive purposes. They may allow a number of companies to make and sell competing products that are compatible with each other, thus allowing for more flexible use of the products by consumers and preventing one firm from dominating the market with a de facto standard. See Mark A. Lemley, Antitrust and the Internet Standardization Problem, 28 Conn. L. Rev. 1041 (1996).

Unfortunately, standard-setting organizations are sometimes subject to "capture" by a particular participant. In several recent cases, antitrust plaintiffs have alleged that defendants persuaded a standard-setting organization to adopt their proposed standard by misrepresenting its status as intellectual property. This misrepresentation sometimes takes the form of an omission (failing to assert ownership in the standard publicly until after it is adopted), and sometimes the form of an affirmative falsehood (signing a statement indicating that the party has no intellectual property rights in the proposed standard). For a detailed discussion of antitrust law in this context, see Herbert Hovenkamp et al., IP and Antitrust §35.5b (2001).

One example of such a claim is the *Dell* case. In 1992, the Video Electronics [*Dell*] Standards Association (VESA) adopted a computer hardware standard called the VL-Bus standard, which governs the transmission of information between a computer's CPU and its peripheral devices. In re Dell Computer Corp., No. 931-0097 (F.T.C. 1995). Each of the members voting to adopt the standard, including Dell Computer Corporation, was required by VESA rules to affirm that they did not own any patent rights that covered the VL-Bus standard. Dell's representative did in fact make such a statement. Nonetheless, Dell had obtained a patent covering the standard and asserted it against other VESA members using the VL-Bus standard eight months later, after the VL-Bus standard had been widely adopted in the marketplace. By working to adopt as a group standard a technology Dell allegedly knew was proprietary,[9] the FTC argued that Dell could obtain the help of its competitors in establishing a standard that it would ultimately be able to control. Dell and the FTC ultimately entered into a consent decree in which Dell agreed not to assert its intellectual property rights in the VL-Bus.

The most likely avenue of antitrust attack against efforts to control the standard-setting process by failure to disclose an intellectual property right is not section 1 but an [attempted monopolization claim under section 2 of the Sherman [§2] Act] Attempted monopolization has three elements: a specific intent to monopo- [*Elements*]

---

9. Whether Dell in fact knew this is a matter of some dispute. In her dissent to the Commission's proposed consent decree, Commissioner Azcuenaga claimed that there was "no evidence to support such a finding of intentional conduct." *Dell Computer* (Azcuenaga, Comm., dissenting).

lize, anticompetitive conduct in furtherance of that intent, and a dangerous probability of successful monopolization. Spectrum Sports v. McQuillen, 506 U.S. 447 (1993). Even a full-blown monopolization claim requires proof of conduct "willfully intended" to further the acquisition or maintenance of monopoly power. United States v. Grinnell Corp., 384 U.S. 563 (1966). As a result, market power, anticompetitive conduct, and intent will all have to be proven to make out an antitrust violation. [Although an accidental failure to disclose the existence of a patent might have anticompetitive consequences, that sort of mistake is not the kind of conduct that should be punished as an antitrust violation.]

Misrepresentations can constitute anticompetitive conduct in appropriate circumstances, though by no means do all or even most misrepresentations by a competitor raise antitrust concerns. [In the standard-setting context, the theory is that the patentee has manipulated the standard-setting process in a way that helps it achieve market power.] Not only does the capturing party end up with exclusive control over the market standard, converting a group standard-setting process into a de facto one, but the capturing party can use the group standard to achieve a dominant position it could not have attained in an open standards competition. Had Dell announced up front that the standard it was backing was proprietary, it is unlikely that VESA would have chosen that standard. At the very least, the standard would have faced stiffer competition than it did. Put more formally, the competitive risk is that the misrepresentation will cause a standard-setting organization to adopt a standard it otherwise would have rejected, and that the adoption of that standard will in turn confer on the defendant market power it would not otherwise have obtained. This is a rather long chain of inferences, and each step in the chain should be elaborated.

First, [an antitrust plaintiff must establish that the standard-setting organization adopted the standard in question and would not have done so but for the misrepresentation or omission.] The failure to disclose the existence of a patent to a standard-setting organization will not affect the competitive marketplace if the standard-setting organization would have approved the standard even if it had known about the patent. Some standard-setting organizations have no policy with respect to intellectual property ownership in the standards they promulgate. Misrepresentation before such a standard-setting organization should not raise competitive concerns, even if it violates some other duty, because the misrepresentation did not cause the adoption of the standard and therefore presumably did not contribute to or create market power.

A separate issue is raised by different standard-setting organizations that, notwithstanding their stated policy, have a history of promulgating standards even when they are aware that the proposer owns intellectual property rights in the standard. In that case, the misrepresentation has not necessarily caused the adoption of the standard. Given the standard-setting organization's willingness to consider proprietary standards, it is possible that they would have adopted the proposed standard even if they knew about the patent rights. Nonetheless, in such a case it is possible that the standard-setting organization would have decided differently had they been aware of the patent. Thus, the first step in the causation chain requires factual inquiry in such a case.

Second, the standard-setting organization's decision to adopt the standard must in turn <u>influence the market</u>. Not all or even most standards adopted through a standard-setting organization control their relevant markets. See Hovenkamp et al. §35.4a2. Only in a limited number of cases will a standard achieve market dominance (or the "dangerous probability" of successful monopolization needed to sustain an attempted monopolization claim under section 2 of the Sherman Act). Efforts to capture an industry standard in any given case would constitute anticompetitive conduct precisely in the situation where those efforts are likely to threaten monopolization—that is, where the standard being set is one that will likely dominate the industry. Market power may be the necessary result of patent enforcement in some cases—those few cases in which the patent actually confers an economic monopoly—while in others the patent owner's control over the market stems from a failure of information in the market, a failure that the patent owner herself has induced. Market control is most likely when the standard-setting organization members collectively have a dominant share of the market, past standards the standard-setting organization has promulgated have dominated the market, standard setting is exclusive (that is, only one standard can be selected), and the intellectual property owner is unwilling to license the undisclosed patent on reasonable and nondiscriminatory terms. In the absence of some these conditions, even if the patentee's nondisclosure convinces the standard-setting organization to accept the proposed standard, the promulgation of that standard is less likely to affect competition.

Even if the standard does achieve market power, that power must be attributable at least in substantial part to the actions of the standard setting organization. If a standard would have become dominant anyway in a de facto standards competition, its adoption by the standard-setting organization (and thus the patentee's misrepresentation) has not caused the market dominance. For example, if the patent is one that actually confers an economic monopoly because of the absence of feasible noninfringing alternatives, it is the patent itself—not the patentee's failure to disclose it to the standard-setting organization—that restricts competition in the market.

Finally, assuming that both market power (or a dangerous probability of its acquisition) and anticompetitive conduct helping to acquire or maintain that power can be proven, an antitrust plaintiff must prove that the defendant's failure to disclose relevant intellectual property rights was intentional and not an oversight. An actual intent to monopolize is difficult to prove. In some cases it can be inferred from conduct. In many standard-setting cases, such an inference will be easy to draw. In many cases of misrepresentations concerning intellectual property, an inference might be drawn from facts suggesting that knowledge was likely (for instance, where the inventor of the patent is also the person signing a statement to the standard-setting organization, as has happened in several recent cases). A court should not be too quick to draw an inference of intent, however, because in many cases, deciding whether a patent covers a particular standard will require an individual to construe the meaning of the patent claims. Patent claim construction is a complex and uncertain legal inquiry, and courts should be hesitant to impute knowledge of a patent's scope if there is evidence that the defendant believed in good faith that the patent would not cover the standard.[10]

---

10. Cf. Mitek Surgical Prods. v. Arthrex, Inc., 230 F.3d 1383 (Fed. Cir. 2000) (suit not objectively baseless where alternative patent claim constructions were both plausible). This will of necessity be a very limited number of cases. By hypothesis, the defendant is now asserting in litigation that the patent *does* cover the standard. Thus, only where the defendant can prove that it legitimately believed one thing, but now legitimately believes the opposite, will this issue be relevant.

Procompetitive

Of course, not all patents covering standards will necessarily be anticompetitive. While one approach to standards is to require them to be intellectual property-free (the Internet Engineering Task Force's approach, at least until recently), intellectual property can coexist with procompetitive standard-setting. For example, ANSI and other groups do not require that an intellectual property owner give up any claim to a standard but merely that they license their intellectual property rights on a reasonable basis. Other examples of reasonable and even procompetitive uses of intellectual property in the standard-setting context are possible. It is only in that subset of cases where the patent is used as a competitive weapon that concerns about market control are implicated.[11]

PROBLEM

Problem 7-5. The Graphics Interchange Format, or GIF, is a tool used to exchange images between computers on the Internet. While it is not the only format by which pictures can be exchanged, it is the most popular. The GIF format has been publicly available without restriction since the mid-1980s, and has been incorporated into many of the most popular Net-surfing programs (such as the Mosaic Web-browsing program).

In late 1994, Unisys Corp. asserted for the first time that it had a patent that covered GIF technology. It immediately began to approach commercial Internet providers, seeking to obtain royalties for their continuing use of its patented technology. The Unisys announcement (and its subsequent license with CompuServe Inc.) created a firestorm of controversy, with many Internet users accusing Unisys of deliberately waiting until GIF was adopted as an industry standard before asserting its patent rights.

Has Unisys violated the antitrust laws? If so, how? Does it matter whether Unisys deliberately waited to enforce its patent until GIF had achieved a dominant position in the industry?

---

11. In rare cases, a rule *precluding* patents on standards might be found to be anticompetitive. In In re American Soc'y of Sanitary Eng., 106 F.T.C. 324, 328-329 (1985), the FTC alleged that a standard-setting organization could not refuse to consider revising its standards to include a new product solely on the grounds that that product was patented. The case was settled by consent decree. It is significant that the standard in question was inclusive rather than exclusive, so allowing the complainant's product to be included would not have restricted the rights of other members to make use of other technology covered by the standard. Nonetheless, the case should serve as a caution for rules such as Internet Engineering Task Force's (IETF's) requiring participants to relinquish their intellectual property rights.

8

International Protection for Computer Technology

Because the market for computer technology is worldwide, the need for legal protection on an international scale is evident. Protecting computer technology in the international marketplace is complicated in part because of differences among national legal rules, traditions, procedures, and institutional frameworks. However, countries generally have the same basic types of legal protection for computer technology as those types discussed in earlier chapters. International treaties provide significant procedural and substantive protections to distributors of computer technology who do business in other lands.[1] In general, these treaties obligate member states to protect the innovations of foreign nationals on a "national treatment" basis—that is, they oblige countries not to discriminate against innovations originating in fellow treaty member states. This principle is fulfilled by a commitment to provide at least as much protection to the innovations of foreign nationals as local laws provide to the country's own nationals.

An especially significant development in international protection of computer technology occurred in 1994 when the Agreement on Trade-Related Aspects of Intellectual Property Rights (TRIPS) became an annex to the agreement establishing the World Trade Organization (WTO). TRIPS, like other international treaties, relies on national treatment and nondiscrimination principles to ensure that innovations, including computer technology, receive adequate protection in member state nations.[2] However, TRIPS also establishes detailed minimum standards for seven

---

1. The Berne Convention for the Protection of Literary and Artistic Works, Sept. 9, 1886, as last revised at Paris on July 24, 1971, 828 U.N.T.S. 221, and the Paris Convention for the Protection of Industrial Property, Mar. 20, 1883, as revised at Stockholm on July 14, 1967, 21 U.S.T. 1583, have historically been the two principal international intellectual property treaties. Other multilateral treaties include the International Convention for the Protection of Performers, Producers of Phonograms, and Broadcasting Organizations (often referred to as the Rome Convention); the Universal Copyright Convention; the Patent Cooperation Treaty; and the Treaty on Intellectual Property in Respect of Integrated Circuits. There are, in addition, numerous bilateral or regional treaties with provisions on intellectual property rights. See, e.g., the North American Free Trade Agreement and the European Patent Convention.

2. Articles 3-4, TRIPS Agreement.

467

intellectual property regimes, five of which may be relied upon by U.S. software developers (i.e., copyright, patent, trade secrecy, trademark, and semiconductor chip design).[3] TRIPS not only requires WTO members to have substantive laws that meet the minimum standards of protection that TRIPS sets forth; it also requires that a generous array of remedies be available for infringement of intellectual property rights.[4] Furthermore, TRIPS commits WTO member states to adequate enforcement of intellectual property rights and remedies.[5] TRIPS thus offers international distributors of computer technology reason to be confident that their legal rights will be respected in WTO countries.

The TRIPS Agreement establishes a dispute resolution system by which one WTO member state may make a formal complaint against another member state about the inadequacy of intellectual property protection available to the complainant's nationals in that other state. These complaints, it should be noted, can only be made by one WTO member state against another, not by private parties. In general, it will take more than one erroneous ruling in a jurisdiction before a viable complaint can be made that a country is in violation of its TRIPS obligations. Moreover, a formal complaint will not lead to immediate litigation. The Dispute Settlement Body first attempts to help resolve disputes between countries informally, via mediation and consultations. However, if a dispute cannot be resolved informally, the Dispute Settlement Body will, at the request of one of the parties, empanel a tribunal of experts to consider a formal complaint and to make a determination that, for example, state X violated this or that provision of the TRIPS Agreement and that state Y's nationals suffered this or that harm. If a WTO panel determines that a complaint has merit, it can authorize the imposition of trade sanctions against products of the offending nation until that nation adapts its practices to conform to TRIPS requirements. An appeal process exists for WTO panel determinations, but once a determination has been affirmed on appeal, it is a final ruling with which the member state must comply. Compliance is ensured by sanctions, which may gradually extend to products not involved in the original dispute —products whose export is sufficiently important to the offending nation that it will want to comply with the ruling to have the sanctions lifted. In all cases, the goal of the dispute resolution process is to bring states into compliance with TRIPS norms, not to punish them for past transgressions. See Rochelle C. Dreyfuss & Andreas F. Lowenfeld, Two Achievements of the Uruguay Round: Putting TRIPS and Dispute Settlement Together, 37 Va. Int'l L. Rev. 275 (1997).

This chapter, for the most part, parallels the structure of earlier chapters and provides representative cases, laws, regulations, and guidelines that indicate the nature and degree of protection available under various national laws for computer technology. It also describes major intellectual property treaties affecting international transactions in computer technology. Finally, it provides guidance on extraterritoriality issues of concern to computer hardware and software developers and their lawyers.

---

3. The principal way TRIPS establishes these minimum standards is by requiring members to comply with specified provisions of the Berne Convention, the Paris Convention, the Rome Convention, and the Treaty on Intellectual Property in Respect of Integrated Circuits. See arts. 2 and 9(1) of the TRIPS Agreement. Other substantive minima are set forth in arts. 9(2)-40.

4. See arts. 42-46.

5. See arts. 41 (generally), 61 (criminal measures). See also arts. 42-43, 47, 49-50 (procedural requirements). TRIPS also contains provisions aimed at establishing effective border measures to control trafficking in pirated goods. Arts. 51-60.

A. TRADE SECRECY

Given the well-established nature of trade secrecy law in the United States, it may come as a surprise to learn that the legal concept of trade secrecy is far from universally accepted in the international community. Some countries have U.S.-style trade secrecy laws, but some do not.[6] In countries that do not have U.S.-style trade secrecy laws, it will generally be possible to get a similar degree of protection by other means. It is common in other countries, for example, to protect commercially valuable secrets through license restrictions on use or disclosure of the information. Even where a licensing agreement is not explicit about the need to keep certain secret information confidential, courts in many jurisdictions may use implied contract theory to find that the parties to a contract intended that certain information not be disclosed. Many countries also have rules against disclosure of confidential information, including information of the sort that in the U.S. would be protected as a trade secret. Breaches of fiduciary duty may be, in an appropriate case, yet another way to protect what U.S. firms will consider to be trade secrets. Hence, the substance of U.S.-style trade secrecy protection can generally be achieved outside the U.S. by reliance on other legal theories.

≡≡≡ *Northern Office Micro Computers (Pty)*
≡≡≡ *Ltd. v. Rosenstein*
≡≡≡ **Cape Provincial Division, South Africa**
≡≡≡ *1981 (4) S.A. 123(C)*

MARAIS, A.J.
[A former employee had developed a suite of programs during the course of employment. Under South African copyright law, he was the owner of the copyright in these programs. After determining that computer programs could be protected by South African copyright law and that the respondent, a former part-time employee of one of the applicants, was the owner of a valid copyright in the program at issue, the court turned to the main issue raised by the applicants.] . . .

May the Employer Prevent the Employee from Exploiting the Copyright?

At the outset, it is necessary to emphasize two things. Firstly, applicants' case is not based upon any claim to copyright in the programmes. Their case is based solely upon the threatened exploitation by respondent of their trade secrets. Secondly, the mere fact that a particular computer programme may qualify for copyright protection, does not mean that the programme is also a trade secret. Whether

---

6. Prior to the 1990 amendments to the Japanese Unfair Competition Act, Japan, for example, had no trade secrecy law as such and provided little protection by other means. See, e.g., Jay Dratler, Jr., Trade Secrets in the United States and Japan: A Comparison and Prognosis, 14 Yale J. Int'l L. 68 (1989). However, Japan now has a formal trade secrecy law. See Trade Secret Act, An Amendment of the Unfair Competition Prevention Act (118th Diet, 66th Act, 1990).

it is a trade secret, depends upon different considerations and is another enquiry altogether. If the result of such an enquiry is that the programme is found to be a trade secret, I fail to see how the fact that copyright in it vests in an employee, gives him the right to disregard the obligation which the common law imposes upon him to respect his employer's trade secrets. Section 41 (3) of the Copyright Act provides that nothing in the Act shall affect the operation of any rule of equity relating to breaches of trust or confidence. While it is so that this provision cannot be read as introducing in South African law principles of the English common law which do not exist here (Dun and Bradstreet (Pty) Ltd v SA Merchants Combined Credit Bureau Cape (Pty) Ltd 1968 (1) SA 209 (C) at 215), it is plainly intended to have some effect in South Africa. If it does not save the express or implied rights of employers to have their employees respect their trade secrets, it is difficult to conceive of any field of application which it might have.

But, even if sec. 41(3) had not existed, I would have been of the same opinion. It would be contrary to well-known principles of statutory construction to read the Copyright Act as abolishing, or derogating from, the common law rights of an employer unless express language, or the clearest of necessary implications, compelled such a reading. In my view, the mere fact that copyright is vested in an employee in certain circumstances does not mean that, even if the subject of the copyright is confidential and a trade secret, the employee may divulge it to whom he pleases. I do not think that the adoption of this view emasculates or nullifies the employee's copyright. He will still have *locus standi* to *protect* his copyright against infringement by third parties. Indeed, he will even be able to protect it against infringement by his employer, to the extent that the employer's use of it goes beyond what was expressly, or impliedly, authorised by the contract of employment. It is true that he will be hampered in his *exploitation* of the copyright if he has to respect his employer's trade secret, but I do not think the Legislature intended otherwise. To make copyright protection available to an employee is one thing. To strip an employer of his common law right to have his trade secrets respected is another. And, of course, if the subject of the copyright is not a trade secret, the employee is free to exploit it.

If I am right in so thinking, it follows that, if the suite of programmes in issue is a trade secret, it is no answer to the claim for an interdict for respondent to say that he is vested with the copyright. The critical question then is whether the applicants have established that the suite of programmes is indeed a trade secret and, if so, to what extent respondent should be restricted in dealing with it. That computer programmes may qualify for the protection which the common law accords to confidential matter and trade secrets seems to me to be plain. In his work Computer Law (1978) Tapper says this of computer programmes in the context of trade secrets and confidentiality:

> So far no reported cases on this topic in the United Kingdom have concerned computer programmes, but here too there can be no reasonable doubt that in principle such programmes are eligible for this sort of protection as soon as they have progressed beyond being merely a general idea and have been transmitted into a set of instructions.

(At 30.) I agree with this view of the matter, provided, of course, that the programme is not commonplace.

The dividing line between the use by an employee of his own skill, knowledge and experience, and the use by him of his employer's trade secrets is notoriously difficult to draw. An employer's trade secret may be no more than the result of the application by an employee of his own skill, knowledge and experience. But, if the employee was engaged to evolve the secret, it remains the employer's trade secret for all that. The employee may not simply copy it if, by copy, one means that literally. For example, if he has conducted a confidential market survey for his erstwhile employer to establish what demand, if any, exists in a particular area for a particular type of product, he cannot simply copy the survey and hand it to his new employer. But *non constat* that the employee may never again set out to establish the market demand for that particular type of product in the same area. Generally speaking, he cannot be prevented from using his own skill and experience to attain a particular result, merely because it is a result which he has achieved before for a previous employer. I say, generally speaking, because one can conceive of cases where the result sought to be achieved is so elusive that only a solution of the kind which legend has it prompted Archimedes to say "Eureka" will do, and the employee has been engaged specifically to find it. In such a case, it may well be that the employee who has evolved the solution may have to refrain from solving it in the same way for a future employer.

What have we here? The respondent is qualified in a particular technology, namely computer programming. He has learnt a computer language which is the *lingua franca* of the Datapac computers. It is not suggested by the applicants that the language of the Datapac computer is a trade secret. While in applicants' employ, respondent worked upon a particular project, namely the development of a suite of programmes which provide an accounting and administrative system for doctors and dentists. The object of the computer programme was to provide them with "a speedy, accurate and comprehensive source of information . . . relating to all aspects of their financial affairs".

The use of computer technology to achieve this purpose can hardly be described as inspired. This is the kind of thing which computers are vaunted to be able to do. Their field of application is virtually limitless. Programmes can be devised to cater for the needs of almost anybody, from banks, building societies and insurance companies to engineers, astronomers, and mariners. All this is common knowledge. That being so, I am unable to see that the *concept* of a computer programme of this kind for doctors and dentists is confidential to the applicants and so, a trade secret. Particularly when it is not disputed that some of applicants' competitors are already marketing, or have advertised their intention of marketing, computer programmes for doctors and dentists. (Applicants stress that the other systems are different, but the remarks which I have made are confined to the broad *concept* of a computer programme attuned to the needs of doctors and dentists.)

To pass from the general to the particular. What is there in this particular suite of programmes which gives it a quality of such confidentiality that respondent should be restrained

from communicating all computer language instructions relating exclusively to the accounting and administrative requirements of doctors and dentists, whether in writing or otherwise, embodied in the suite of programmes designed by respondent for the purposes of producing an accounting system for doctors and dentists irrespective of the nature or type of computer in conjunction with which such instruction may be used?

In my view, the evidence before me does not enable me to conclude that what has gone into the development of this suite of programmes is of so confidential a character that respondent should be restrained in either of these ways. I emphasize that I am not here referring to the copying of the suite of programmes. That respondent plainly cannot do. It is common cause that much work, skill and time is needed to produce a suite of programmes of this kind. If respondent were permitted simply to copy it, he would be unfairly nullifying the advantage of the "long start" over anyone else to which applicants are entitled. To that limited extent, the suite of programmes is, in my opinion, a trade secret.

But it does not follow from this that respondent may not again apply his mind to the development of a suite of programmes to cater for the accounting and financial needs of doctors and dentists, or that, if he does, he must wipe clean from the slate of his memory (as if that were possible) any recollection he may have of the things which it seemed to him were appropriate for inclusion in such a suite of programmes, or of appropriate formulae, or the like. To accept the contrary view would halter respondent's use of his own training, skill and experience to an unacceptable degree. This remains so whether he is restrained permanently, or for a limited period of two years such as Mr. Dison suggested. As CROSS J said in Printers and Finishers Ltd v Holloway (1964) 3 All ER 731 at 736F:

> The law will defeat its own object if it seeks to enforce in this field standards which would be rejected by the ordinary man.

. . . But, as I have said, I think that applicants are entitled to have respondent restrained from copying, or permitting to be copied, the suite of programmes, or any part of it. They are entitled to have respondent restrained from making use of, or permitting anyone to make use of, any existing copy of the whole, or any part, of the suite of programmes. In saying this, I include, within the concept of copying, translating the programmes into any other computer language.

COMMENTS AND QUESTIONS

1.   Why does the employee own the copyright in the program? He was hired to write it, and paid to write it. Contrast the U.S. rule, under which employees acting within the scope of their employment in creating copyrighted works do not own the works. Perhaps the South African rule reflects a more continental treatment of copyrighted works (including computer programs) as extensions of the "author's" personality.

On the other hand, it is worth noting that an independent contractor under U.S. law would still retain the copyright in a computer program written under contract for a company. Perhaps it is U.S. law that is inconsistent on this ownership issue.

2.   If the court is correct in concluding that Rosenstein owns the copyright in his program, why should it come to a different result regarding ownership of the trade secret? What is the practical outcome of this case? Who—if anyone—is entitled to use the program? To make additional copies? To sell the program to another company?

3.   How would the rule in *Northern Office* apply across international borders? Rosenstein's copyright is presumably protected under the Berne Convention in most countries in the world. Is Northern Office entitled to a worldwide injunction against his use of trade secrets abroad? Does it matter whether there is a similar international treaty guaranteeing trade secret rights? (There was no such agreement until 1994, when the TRIPS Agreement was adopted by most countries in the world. TRIPS includes sections establishing minimum substantive requirements for legal protection of confidential information in member states. See *infra*.)

4.   The *Northern Office* court suggests that while Rosenstein can't copy his own program without misappropriating a trade secret, there is nothing to prevent him from using his own knowledge and skill to write another program. Compare this case with the U.S. decision in *Rivendell*, discussed in Chapter 1. Would U.S. courts be so lenient to a trade secret defendant?

≡
≡
≡   *Computer Workshops Ltd. v. Banner Capital*
≡   *Market Brokers Ltd.*
≡   *Ontario High Court of Justice*
≡   *64 O.R. (2d) 266, 21 C.P.R.3d 116 [1988]*

CRAIG J.:

This an action for damages resulting from an alleged breach of contract by the defendants. The plaintiff company, having its office located in Toronto, is engaged in the sale of microcomputers and related accessories. The defendants Banner Capital Market Brokers Ltd. (Banner) and Shorcan International Brokers Limited (Shorcan) are bond brokers also having their offices located in Toronto. They are related corporations sharing common offices and having interlocking officers and directors.

Pursuant to the terms of an agreement between the plaintiff and the defendants, the plaintiff was to provide to the defendant 100 Toshiba T-300 microcomputers and accessories; also the plaintiff was to provide assistance in the adaptation of the appropriate software programs and in the installation of the hardware system. The defendants terminated the contract with the plaintiff at a time when 75 of the microcomputers had not yet been delivered.

The defendants allege breach of an implied term of the contract that the plaintiff:

(a)   would keep confidential the knowledge it obtained of the defendants' business and of the system and would not reveal such knowledge to third parties or potential competitors, and

(b)   would not attempt to sell the system or a comparable system to any competitor or potential competitor of the defendants.

Apart from the contractual relationship, the defendants further allege breach of:

(c)   a relationship of confidentiality between the parties;

(d)   infringement of copyright held by the defendants in the relevant software programs, and

(e)   breach of a fiduciary relationship between the plaintiff and the defendants.

The ultimate issue in this case is whether the plaintiff is entitled to damages for breach of contract (wrongful termination of contract by the defendants).

The defendants submit that they were entitled to terminate the contract based upon allegations (a), (b), (c), (d) and (e) above; alternatively that they were entitled to terminate for breach of implied term alone because it was a breach of serious and major importance which was coupled with a breach of confidence, infringement of copyright and breach of fiduciary relationship or some of them.

. . . The plaintiff and the defendants entered into an agreement for the purchase and installation of 20 Toshiba T-100 microcomputers and accessories. In addition, the plaintiff was to provide assistance in adapting and developing the software programs. Morrison converted his software program for use on the Toshiba T-100. Upon testing the Toshiba T-100 did not meet Banner's requirements. It did not have the necessary communication ability; it was too slow; the "flashing" did not perform properly and there were other difficulties. One Wilfred Steimle, an independent consultant, was retained by the plaintiff to assist Morrison in making the required adjustments of the software programs to conform with the Toshiba T-100s and to arrange for the necessary configuration of the hardware. In this capacity Steimle acquired an intimate and detailed knowledge of the Shorcan system and proposed Banner system. On March 6, 1984, because the T-100s did not meet the defendant's requirements the plaintiff and the defendants agreed to the cancellation of the purchase of the T-100s and accessories; also that the defendants would purchase from the plaintiff 100 T-300 microcomputers and accessories. It was understood that the plaintiff would continue to provide assistance in the adaptation of Morrison's software programs and configuration of the hardware system. The plaintiff agreed to and did provide to the defendants a full credit on the return of the Toshiba T-100 microcomputers and accessories.

The configuration consisted of a host computer—with input terminals at the Banner office connected by wires to a modem. The modem was connected to a "bridge" which splits the signal into a certain number of identical amplified signals for transmission over dedicated data or phase lines to the exchange and then from the exchange to the customers' sites where it is connected to another modem which converts the analog signal back to a digital signal that is fed into the computers.

All of the above-mentioned equipment could be purchased "off the shelf", but I accept the evidence of Steimle that a "bridge" was designed for use in electrical alarm systems. Morrison and Steimle testified that they were not aware that a "bridge" had ever been used before in this particular application, and this evidence was not denied. This configuration was therefore unique in that sense. Also it resulted in a very substantial saving in costs because up until that time a separate modem for each customer would have been required at the Banner offices.

I find that the Banner system was unique in that the hardware configuration with the bridge had not been in place up to that time; the software had been written specifically and adapted for that application; it employed the use of colour (flashing) display screens at customer sites. I accept Steimle's evidence that to create a similar system "from scratch" would require six to nine months and the assistance from a person such as Morrison who was knowledgeable in the bond brokerage industry, at a cost of [Canadian] $50 per hour.

This was a commercial transaction between the plaintiff and the defendants, but upon my findings of fact and reasons to follow it is my view that the plaintiff stood in a fiduciary relationship to the defendants; the defendants through Morrison sought out the plaintiff and gave it confidential information. Because the defendants reposed trust and confidence in the plaintiff, the latter was not entitled to derive any profit or advantage, other than that which arose out of the contract, except with the knowledge and consent of the defendants.

In argument counsel for the plaintiff admitted (for the first time) that in order to give business efficacy to the contract between the plaintiff and the defendants it may be necessary to imply a term that the plaintiff would not sell a system similar to Banner to someone else. He submitted that the evidence did not go beyond an attempt to sell on the part of the plaintiff, and that an *attempt* to sell a similar system would not constitute breach of the implied term.

The information given to the plaintiff by the defendants (including Steimle) had the necessary quality of confidence (the uniqueness or novelty of the configuration and the copyright in the software). Steimle was an independent contractor, but for the purpose of performing the plaintiff's contract with the defendants he was the plaintiff's agent up until he "abandoned ship" on or about March 30, 1984. This is not to say that some aspects of the Banner system were not public property or publicly known. Applying the language of *Saltman* the defendants used their available brain power "to produce a result which can only be produced by someone who goes through the same process." The configuration of the hardware was simple but it was entitled to protection along with the software. If Crook wanted to devise his own system there could be no objection. What he was not entitled to was a copy of the Banner system. At least six months were required to develop the software and these programs had been carefully protected by Morrison. In my opinion, the Banner system as a unit was clearly confidential information. The plaintiff and/or Crook were entitled to compete but what happened was a classic case of wrongfully using the defendants' confidential information as a spring-board for activities detrimental or potentially detrimental to the defendants.

I find as fact that on March 28, 1984, the plaintiff formed an intention to duplicate and agreed to duplicate the Banner system for another customer (the defendants' competitor). The fact that there might be cosmetic changes is irrelevant. Having done that the plaintiff was in breach of the implied term of its contract with the defendants, and in breach of confidence and fiduciary duty. Whether there was only an attempted rather than an actual infringement of copyright is not material to the result in the circumstances of the case.

The plaintiff submits that Steimle acted without authority and unethically herein in making various disclosures to the defendants. If there is any substance to that allegation it is not relevant to the result in this action. Also any rights the plaintiff may have in relation to Steimle are not impaired by the judgment in this action.

Was the Breach of Implied Term of Such Major Importance That the Defendants Are Discharged from Liability?

As of March 28, 1984, the plaintiff and Denda intended to sell the Banner system to a competitor through Crook as a middleman. Cosmetic changes only were contemplated. On March 30th, Banner gave notice to the plaintiff that his proposed conduct was "unethical" and a "breach of Banner's copyright and proprietary rights, as well as breach of your obligation to Banner". On April 5th, and without notifying the defendants, Denda in his personal capacity entered into a contract with TEO to collect a commission for business generated through the Investment Dealers Association and/or Crook. On April 6th, the defendants again wrote to the plaintiff and Denda requiring the support of the plaintiff and Denda for the protection of the Banner system, and advising them of the importance of keeping the system confidential. On April 11, 1984 (and again without disclosing that he personally had contracted with TEO on April 5th), Denda made a counter-proposal on behalf of the plaintiff only. The defendants had become aware of the contract between Denda and TEO. On April 12th they wrote to both Denda and the plaintiff terminating their contract because of "misconduct and breaches of contract."

I find that there was a repudiation or breach of contract by the plaintiff of the implied term of the contract in circumstances where, on the part of the plaintiff, there was a breach of confidence, a breach of fiduciary duty and an infringement or attempted infringement of copyright. The implied term of the contract was of the utmost importance to the defendants. As stated by Morrison, it could be a matter of "life and death" for the defendants. It can also be said that it was a breach going to the root of the contract. The time for final performance by the plaintiff had not yet arrived (delivery of the 75 T-300 Toshiba computers). As indicated earlier, repudiation may occur before the time for final performance has arrived (anticipatory breach). For the reasons stated above the defendants were entitled to terminate the contract with the plaintiff on and after March 28, 1984. Nothing happened between that date and April 12, 1984 (the date of termination), that would preclude the defendants from exercising the right to terminate. In my opinion the defendants acted very reasonably in writing the above-mentioned letters of April 3rd and April 6th, expressing their urgent concerns and imposing certain requirements for the continuation of the contract and relationship. Denda himself was not a party to the contract but he was the sole directing mind of the plaintiff company and in the circumstance he himself stood in the same position to the defendants as the plaintiff.

COMMENTS AND QUESTIONS

What exactly did the defendants take in this case? The court suggests that the defendants may not use the plaintiff's proprietary program as a "springboard" to develop their own. Does this comport with the South African rule discussed above? With the U.S. case law?

Note on TRIPS and Trade Secret Protection

The prospects for improved legal protection for trade secrets in the international arena have increased considerably since adoption of the TRIPS Agreement. It includes a provision requiring WTO member states to provide adequate protection for undisclosed information. Article 39(2) of TRIPS sets forth the following obligations regarding undisclosed information protection:

1. In the course of ensuring effective protection against unfair competition as provided in Article 10bis of the Paris Convention (1967), Members shall protect undisclosed information in accordance with paragraph 2 and data submitted to governments or governmental agencies in accordance with paragraph 3.

2. Natural and legal persons shall have the possibility of preventing information lawfully within their control from being disclosed to, acquired by, or used by others without their consent in a manner contrary to honest commercial practices[10] so long as such information: (a) is secret in the sense that it is not, as a body or in the precise configuration and assembly of its components, generally known among or readily accessible to persons within the circles that normally deal with the kind of information in question; (b) has commercial value because it is secret; and (c) has been subject to reasonable steps under the circumstances, by the person lawfully in control of the information, to keep it secret.

3. Members, when requiring, as a condition of approving the marketing of pharmaceutical or of agricultural chemical products which utilize new chemical entities, the submission of undisclosed test or other data, the origination of which involves a considerable effort, shall protect such data against unfair commercial use. In addition, Members shall protect such data against disclosure, except where necessary to protect the public, or unless steps are taken to ensure that the data are protected against unfair commercial use.

The North American Free Trade Agreement (NAFTA), to which the United States, Canada, and Mexico are signatories, has a more explicit and detailed set of provisions binding its members to protect trade secrets. Article 1711(1) resembles Article 39(2) of the TRIPS Agreement, except that the NAFTA provision refers to protection of trade secrets as such, not just to protection of undisclosed information. It also regards trade secrecy protection to be available to information with potential, as well as actual, commercial value because it is unknown. Unlike the TRIPS provision, the NAFTA trade secrecy provision does not define "honest commercial practices." Neither agreement makes any explicit reference to reverse engineering as a legitimate way to obtain secret information.

Another noteworthy provision for computer technology is Article 1711(2), which permits NAFTA members to require in their national laws that "a trade secret must be evidenced in documents, electronic or magnetic means, optical discs, microfilms, films or other similar instruments." NAFTA members may not, however, under Article 1711(3) and (4), limit the duration of trade secrecy protection or discourage the voluntary licensing of trade secrets by the imposition of "excessive or discriminatory conditions on such licenses or conditions that dilute the value of the trade secrets."

---

10. For the purposes of this provision, 'a manner contrary to honest commercial practices' shall mean at least practices such as breach of contract, breach of confidence and inducement to breach, and includes the acquisition of undisclosed information by third parties who knew, or were grossly negligent in failing to know, that such practices were involved in the acquisition.

COMMENTS AND QUESTIONS

1. What does the silence of NAFTA and TRIPS on the question of reverse engineering suggest for the legality of the U.S. reverse engineering exception? Is the exception permissible? Mandatory? Perhaps it could be inferred from language in TRIPS Article 39(2), which would punish only conduct that is "contrary to honest commercial practices." It is, however, worth noting that the new U.S. Economic Espionage Act, 18 U.S.C. §§1831 et seq., does not appear to permit reverse engineering either.

2. Does a trade secret exist in intangible form? Consider DSC v. Brown, a recent U.S. case in which an employer sued an employee who came up with a potentially valuable new idea and refused to disclose it to the company. United States trade secret law has no great difficulty in concluding that Brown had violated his obligation to the company in this situation, assuming the information really is the sort of thing DSC would have a claim to own. But because Brown never wrote the secret down, it is not clear that the case would produce the same result under TRIPS.

B. COPYRIGHT

Today copyright protection for computer programs is universally accepted in the international community, especially after incorporation of this rule in Article 10 of the TRIPS Agreement. This is noteworthy in part because some early legal decisions in the United States and elsewhere questioned the availability of copyright protection for computer programs. See, for example, the Australian case, Apple Computer Inc. v. Computer Edge Pty Ltd., 50 A.L.R. 581 (1983) (no breach of copyright because computer programs were not, under then existing copyright law, protectable "literary works"). During the late 1980s and into the early 1990s, largely at the urging of the U.S. Trade Representative, a trend emerged internationally toward using copyright as the principal form of legal protection for source and object code forms of computer programs. In the early 1980s, however, no clear consensus existed on this subject.

Some countries, notably Brazil, adopted a sui generis form of protection for computer programs. Others, including Japan and the European Economic Community (now the European Union), were considering a sui generis form of protection for programs. Indeed, the World Intellectual Property Organization (WIPO) was among the organizations to propose sui generis legislation for computer programs. By the late 1980s, however, WIPO had backed away from its own proposal and came to favor the copyright approach. Even within nations that did protect programs by means of copyright law, there were variations. France, for example, initially decided to place computer programs (a form, perhaps, of industrial literature) in the same legal category as works of industrial art. Among the implications of this designation was a more limited duration of copyright protection for programs. One notable German case seemed to require almost a patent-like level of creativity before a programmer's work product could qualify for copyright protection.

The decision of the European Commission in 1989 to adopt copyright protection for computer programs turned the international tide in favor of copyright.

However, it was not until the 1994 TRIPS Agreement that there was an international treaty explicitly requiring countries to use copyright protection for computer programs. Article 10(1) of the TRIPS Agreement states simply that "[c]omputer programs, whether in source or object code, shall be protected as literary works under the Berne Convention (1971)." A very similar provision appears in Article 4 of the WIPO Copyright Treaty concluded in December 1996: "Computer programs are protected as literary works within the meaning of Article 2 of the Berne Convention [which defines the term 'literary work']. Such protection applies to computer programs, whatever may be the mode or form of their expression."

Even with this harmonization, variations in national laws continue to exist on basic issues regarding computer programs. Some writings may be "computer programs" under European Union (EU) law that would not be classified as such under U.S. law. In the EU, the term "computer program" includes "preparatory design materials," such as flowcharts. Flowcharts do not qualify as "computer programs" under U.S. law, although they may be protectable as pictorial, sculptural, or graphic works. Because of concerns that any specific definition might become technologically outmoded, the EU Directive does not define the term "computer program"; it protects computer programs regardless of their form. United States law, by contrast, defines this term as "a set of statements or instructions to be used, directly or indirectly, to bring about a certain result." 17 U.S.C. §101. Although Japanese copyright law defines "computer program" in a manner similar to U.S. law, Japanese authorities have expressed doubt that microcode programs fall within their statutory definition of "computer program."

While the TRIPS and WIPO Treaty provisions unquestionably require countries to protect the source and object code forms of programs from exact duplication, it is less clear whether these provisions require member or signatory countries to protect the nonliteral elements of programs, such as their structure, sequence, and organization or user interfaces. See, e.g., Charles R. McManis, Taking Trips on the Information Superhighway: International Intellectual Property Protection and Emerging Computer Protection, 41 Vill. L. Rev. 207, 232-251 (1996) (asserting TRIPS does not require copyright to protect structure); Eric Smith, Worldwide Copyright Protection Under the TRIPS Agreement, 29 Vand. J. Trans'l L. 559, 576-577 (1996) (anticipating a successful challenge before the WTO to jurisdictions not protecting structural elements of programs). Both TRIPS and the WIPO Copyright Treaty provide some guidance on scope of protection issues as regards computer programs. Article 9(2) of the TRIPS Agreement states: "Copyright protection shall extend to expressions and not to ideas, procedures, methods of operation, or mathematical concepts as such." The WIPO Copyright Treaty adopted two years later contains a virtually identical rule. Interestingly, this was the first explicit manifestation of the idea-expression distinction in a Berne Convention-related agreement.

Many national laws also contain provisions providing some guidance on scope of protection issues. Article 1(2) of the European Directive on the Legal Protection of Computer Programs states: "Protection in accordance with this Directive shall apply to the expression in any form of a computer program. Ideas and principles which underlie any element of a program, including those that underlie its interfaces, are not protected by copyright under this Directive." The Recitals of the Directive also indicate that "in accordance with this principle of copyright, to the extent that logic, algorithms, and programming languages comprise ideas and principles, those ideas and principles are not protected under this Directive." Recitals do not have the same authority as the black-letter provision of a Directive, but they provide some guidance about the intended interpretation to be given to any provision to which the Recital pertains.

Perhaps the most elaborate statutory statement on scope of protection issues can be found in Article 7 of China's regulations for the protection of computer software. It states that "[t]he protection provided to software under these regulations cannot be expanded to encompass the ideas, concepts, discoveries, principles, algorithms, processing methods and operations used in the development of software." In addition, Article 31 states that "[r]esulting similarities between software developed and software already in existence does not constitute a violation of the copyright of existing software in the following situations: (1) Because it is necessary for the execution of national policies, laws, and rules and regulations; (2) Because it is necessary for the setting of technical standards; (3) Because of the limited categories of forms of expression."

In keeping with their obligations under the Berne Convention (which establishes minimum standards for national copyright laws), most countries provide the owners of copyrights in computer programs with exclusive rights to reproduce the software, to make derivative works or adaptations of the software, and to control distribution of copies. Article 9(1) of the TRIPS Agreement incorporates the pertinent exclusive rights provisions of the Berne Convention and establishes them as minimum standards for the national laws of WTO members.

COMMENTS AND QUESTIONS

1. How similar or different would you expect interpretations to be of the exclusion from protection provisions found in both the TRIPS agreement and the WIPO Copyright Treaty? What significance should be attached to the "as such" language in the exclusion (i.e., that copyright shall not extend to ideas, etc. "as such")? Does this imply that ideas, processes, and the like *may* be protected by copyright under some circumstances? How do these provisions compare with those in the European Directive and the Chinese software regulations?

2. How would you predict U.S. courts would treat program elements "necessary for the setting of technical standards," which are excluded from protection under Chinese law?

Further detail about copyright protection for computer programs under national laws outside the United States is presented in the subsections that follow. The first concerns copyright protection in Japan, the second considers the same legal protection in Europe, and the third provides a look at Australian software copyright law.

1. Copyright Protection for Computer Programs in Japan

Japan is one of the principal markets for computer software. Although there has sometimes been tension between the United States and Japan over the adequacy of legal protection of computer programs under Japanese law, these tensions are in abeyance. While Japanese copyright law clearly protects the source and object code forms of programs, it is somewhat unclear to what extent copyright protection is available for nonliteral elements of computer programs. This is mainly because Japanese law limits the scope of copyright protection in programs to a considerable degree. Article 10(3) of Japan's copyright law states that copyright protection for computer programs "shall not extend to any programming language, rule or algorithm used for making such work." This provision defines these terms as follows: "(i) 'programming language' means letters and other symbols as well as their systems for use as a means of expressing a program; (ii) 'rule' means a special rule on how to use in a particular program a programming language mentioned in the preceding item; (iii) 'algorithm' means methods of combining, in a program, instructions given to a computer." For further discussion of this provision of Japanese law and its implications for the scope of copyright protection in Japan, see Dennis S. Karjala, The Protection of Operating Software Under Japanese Law, 12 E.I.P.R. 359 (1988).

There has been relatively little litigation in Japan interpreting copyright law as applied to computer programs. ICM Corp. v. Met's, Inc.[7] is one of the few reported cases with an appellate ruling. This decision is discussed at length in the excerpt that appears below.

Dennis S. Karjala, *Programs and Data Files Under Japanese Law*
[1993] Eur. Intell. Prop. Rev.

Facts of the Case and the Lower Court Decision

The petitioners in *ICM* held the copyright in a utility program called 'EO System', written in assembly language, that worked in conjunction with the MS-DOS operating system to help users in the hard disk installation and file management of some 81 selected application programs. EO System comprised a number of programs, including a main driver program written in assembly language called 'MENU.EXE' as well as the software at issue in the case, called 'IBF Files'.

IBF Files was a collection of 81 distinguishable pieces (files), one for each of the application programs that EO System was designed to install and manage. Each of the files included in IBF Files had the same overall format or structure and carried information or commands enabling MENU.EXE to carry out the function of installing the particular application program represented by that file. For example, there was an ID Line permitting MENU.EXE to recognise the file as one belonging to EO System, a Title Line identifying the application program covered by the file, a Command Line containing the command used to start the application program and allowing MENU.EXE to create an automatically executable batch file for

---

7. Toyko Dist. Ct. (Civ. Div. No. 29) Decision of 27 Feb. 1991, Heisei 1 (yo) no. 2577, *aff'd*, Tokyo High Court Decision of 31 March 1992. Karjala's article relies on an unpublished English translation of the ICM decision by Edward G. Durney.

that purpose with the correct parameters, a Message Line that would appear verbatim on the screen instructing the user to insert the application program floppy disk, and an Installation Sequence Line telling MENU.EXE the order in which to install application program files.

The respondents in the action offered a similar utility system covering, among others, some 42 of the 81 application programs handled by the petitioners' EO System. The respondents' main driver program was called 'MFD.EXE', written in the 'C' language, and the functional equivalent of IBF Files in the respondents' system was called 'HCA Files'. Although the petitioners argued that the respondents' overall system had the same functional objectives and similar operating characteristics as EO System, with almost identical program file composition and structure, their formal claim was only that HCA Files was copied from IBF Files, based on an asserted near one-to-one correspondence between the two works.

The issue of whether the IBF Files constituted programs was argued in the district court, but the judge elected not to decide it. Rather, based on the assumption that they did constitute programs, the Court denied relief on the ground that they nevertheless failed to qualify for copyright protection under the JCL because they lacked the statutorily required creativity.

The district court first determined that the overall structure of the individual IBF Files was unprotected because (1) it comprised a format or grammar excluded from protection by the 'programming languages' limitation of the JCL, and because (2) the format of the IBF Files was constrained by MENU.EXE. The Court next found that the content of the individual IBF Files also lacked creativity because such content was largely constrained either by MENU.EXE (such as the ID Line) or the application program (such as the Title Line) for each file, so there was no room for choice. The Court found some slight degree of freedom available in choosing the installation sequence of files from the application program being installed and in the message on the Installation Message Line, but concluded that the range of selection was too small to permit a finding of statutory creativity. Moreover, while admitting that there was some freedom of choice in determining which and how many application programs EO System should cover, the Court concluded that such a choice amounted to no more than an idea, and ideas cannot supply the expressive creativity required by the statute.

The Tokyo High Court Decision

The High Court opinion addresses the threshold issue whether IBF Files was [sic], in fact, a program within statutory definition. (Given its negative resolution of that question, the Court did not address any further issues.) Quite properly, the Court began with the statutory definition itself:

> "Program" means a combination of instructions causing a computer to function so as to achieve a certain result.

The decision focuses strongly on the word 'instructions' in this definition in formulating its test for what constitutes a computer program:

> [A] program under the Copyright Law must be a set of instructions for a computer that cause the computer to effect a specific process. . . .

Therefore, even where something is recorded electromagnetically in a storage medium as an electronic file that can be read by a computer, it is not a program if it does not carry out the above function.

In processing a program on a computer, one effects a specific process through calls on given programs in the system, and for this purpose, in addition to the program, data giving processing information are necessary, but for reasons of efficiency data are often kept in files separate from the main program. In these circumstances, the data file is read by the program and processed by the computer, but it cannot be said to include sets of instructions for the computer, and therefore it is not a program under the Copyright Law. Of course, when different files are used, the processing result will be different, but that follows from the differences in the data content stored in the files. Clearly we cannot say that the data give instructions to the computer. *Similarly, where data are described by specific symbols or letters ('symbols, etc.') that are defined by the program itself, we might concede that the program will read those symbols, etc., and effect the process contained in their meaning. But even so, this amounts to nothing more than the program's effecting a specific process upon reading the symbols, etc., as data, and we cannot say that the symbols, etc., are instructions for the computer. Therefore, the data contained in the symbols, etc., cannot be said to constitute a program under the Copyright Law* (emphasis added).

In applying its distinction between data files and program files to the IBF Files at issue in the case, the Court first rejected the appellants' (petitioners') argument that the individual IBF Files were batch files, apparently on the superficial ground that they did not employ the '.BAT' extension used by MS-DOS for batch files.

The Court next looked to the content of the individual IBF Files and concluded that they contained nothing more than installation information (name of the application software to be installed, device drivers, and so on) that was simply read by MENU.EXE as data. As a factual matter, it accepted the lower court determination that the role of IBF Files was over once it was read by MENU.EXE. It rejected, as 'clear', that the IBF Files were not ultimately converted into machine language effecting instructions to the computer.

The Court even applies this to the 'COPY', '!' and '?' symbols mutually employed by IBF Files and MENU.EXE:

> The 'COPY' used by IBF Files employs identical characters as the MS-DOS command 'COPY', but those characters are simply defined by the MENU.EXE program. They are character information read by the MENU.EXE program not a command causing a computer to operate. The symbols '!', '?', etc., are similar. They are simply defined by the MENU.EXE program and are nothing more than symbols that can be understood solely by that program.
>
> . . . [E]ven if we concede that, when a program processes data, the program processing will vary depending on the content of the symbols, etc., that is something that is determined by the program itself. The symbols, etc., and combinations do not function as commands; it is simply a question of the method of entering data defined by the program. The commands that appellants assert are uniquely valid for functioning with EO System, too, are simply entered according to the demands of the MENU.EXE program and are nothing more than symbols, etc., to be read as data by it. In other words, program means the descriptive expression based on combinations of instructions to cause a computer to function so as to achieve a particular result. The descriptive content of IBF Files is similar to the descriptive format of the MS-DOS start command, or 'DEVICE=' setting, or 'COPY' command, but in EO System they are no more than

data. They do not cause a computer to function, so they do not have the characteristics of a program.

. . . Conclusion

The Tokyo High Court in the *ICM* case appears to have arrived at the correct result on the facts but on erroneous reasoning. Its conclusion that data files are not protected as computer programs, while technically finding justification in the specific language of the JCL, leaves such files vulnerable to slavish electronic copying as databases that show no creativity in selection or arrangement. A better approach may be to treat data files as potentially protected elements of programs but to ensure that protection is limited to unfair extraction of their content and does not extend to functional, efficient, standard or obvious aspects of their formats or to aspects in which industry or user standardisation is desirable.

COMMENTS AND QUESTIONS

1. How would the *ICM* case have been decided under U.S. copyright law? How would the analysis in an American court decision have differed from that of the Tokyo High Court?

2. How similar or different is the Japanese scope of protection provision from section 102(b) of U.S. copyright law, from the European Directive's provision, and from the Chinese scope of protection rule? Is it consistent with Article 9(2) of the TRIPS Agreement?

3. One of the stress points between the United States and Japan has concerned the decompilation of computer programs. When Japan proposed adoption of an explicit decompilation privilege in its copyright law (akin to that adopted in Europe, on which more below), some U.S. officials objected strenuously. Japanese officials eventually decided not to move forward with this initiative, but some commentators nevertheless believe that decompilation for purposes of interoperability is lawful in Japan. For a historical overview of divergent viewpoints on this issue, see Jonathan Band and Masanobu Katoh, Interfaces on Trial: Intellectual Property and Interoperability in the Global Software Industry (1995).

2. The European Union and Its Member States

The market for computer technology in Europe is strong, and, as one might expect, the legal protection environment is also strong. The most important development in European copyright law as applied to computer programs has undoubtedly been the adoption of the Council Directive on the Legal Protection of Computer Programs, 91/250, 1991 O.J. (L122) 42. Several provisions of this Directive appear below. However, even before the Directive took effect, courts in Europe found little difficulty in applying copyright protection to computer programs. It is difficult, in view of the paucity of European case law, to state with a great deal of confidence how broad or narrow copyright protection for computer programs is likely to be in Europe. There, as here, commentators disagree on some important scope of protection issues. However, the *Ibcos* case, which arose under U.K. copyright law prior to the U.K.'s implementation of the European Directive, provides a glimpse of a different approach to applying copyright law to computer programs than that which currently prevails in the United States.

IBCOS Computers Ltd. v. Barclay's Mercantile Highland Finance Ltd.
Chancery Division, United Kingdom
[1994] F.S.R. 275

[A programmer named Poole developed a suite of programs for license to an agricultural business owned by Clayton. Poole and Clayton formed a company, PK Ltd., to further develop and market this suite of programs under the name ADS. When Poole left this firm, Clayton insisted on Poole's agreement that the firm owned the copyright in ADS and further insisted on a restrictive covenant limiting Poole's ability to sell a similar comprehensive set of programs or be employed by another company intending to develop such software for two years. Poole developed a competing program, Unicorn, in his spare time and, after the expiration of the two-year restriction, undertook to distribute Unicorn through Highland. Ibcos, the successor to PK Ltd.'s interest in the software, sued Poole and Highland for copyright infringement.]

Was There Copying?

For infringement there must be copying. Whether there was or not is a question of fact. To prove copying the plaintiff can normally do no more than point to bits of his work and the defendant's work which are the same and prove an opportunity of access to his work. If the resemblance is sufficiently great then the court will draw an inference of copying. It may then be possible for the defendant to rebut the inference—to explain the similarities in some other way. For instance, he may be able to show both parties derived the similar bits from some third party or material in the public domain. Or he may be able to show that the similarity arises out of a functional necessity—that anyone doing this particular job would be likely to come up with similar bits. So much is common ground between the parties. The concept of sufficient similarities shifting the onus onto the defendant to prove non-copying is well recognised in copyright law. . . .

It should be noted that at this stage (namely "Was there copying?") both the important and the unimportant bits of the works being compared count. Indeed it is often identity of trivial matter which traps a copyist. As Hoffmann J observed in Billhofer Maschinenfabrik GmbH v Dixon & Co Ltd ([1990] FSR 105 at 123.):

> It is the resemblances in inessentials, the small, redundant, even mistaken elements of the copyright work which carry the greatest weight. This is because they are least likely to have been the result of independent design.

What then is the position here? Is there an inference of copying? I have no doubt that there is. It is overwhelming. There are bits of ADS in Unicorn which cannot really be explained in any other way. It would be burdensome in this judgment to set out all the similarities which raise the inference. They were all well identified in Mr Turner's report for the plaintiffs before the trial began. I find it surprising that the defendant's experts did not seem to have addressed or faced up to these resemblances. Only at moments in the witness box did Mr Kenny (the better of the defendants' experts) seem to recognise that there were real difficulties in the way of a case of independent design.

I must set out some of the key items.

(a) Common Spelling Mistakes

Computer programs are inherently less tolerant of spelling mistakes than ordinary literary works. Normally only in comments can they appear without affecting the working of the program. And comments are apt to be short and limited in number, so there is limited material in which misspellings can occur. However in both ADS and Unicorn there are significant spelling mistakes in the comments. The words of particular interest are, "Alpfa," "PIONT," "Didgit," "NUMREIC," "detached," "Channal" and "Shedule." I have set out the words as they are used, namely where capitals are used and where lower case are used. These words appear in identical comments in both programs. To be more precise they appear in different programs within each suite of programs. Moreover each of those words is correctly spelt in a number of different places in other parts of each program, as Mr Howe's search program was able to reveal with ease.

I am quite incapable of believing that this is all due to coincidence or due to the fact that Mr Poole has difficulty in spelling (which seems to be the case). If the latter was the explanation then why are the words spelt correctly many times in other places? And why are the errors always in the same place? It will be recalled that if there is disk-to-disk copying then this kind of thing will be copied accurately. Only disk-to-disk copying from ADS can explain the identity of these misspelled words.

(b) Headings

Then there are the identical comment headings. A document called X11 conveniently shows a series of headings in comments which are the same in an important program of ADS (SKPER, for manufacturers' prices of spare parts) and the corresponding program in Unicorn (PAMUPP). For instance the word FORD is presented in a comment in both programs with 23 hyphens to the left and 30 to the right. Likewise the words INTERNATIONAL HARVESTER are presented with 21 hyphens to the left and 13 to the right. An explanation for this was suggested by counsel for Mr Poole in his re-examination. The idea was that a line of 60 hyphens was copied into a fresh line and then the name of the part manufacturer was typed over some of the hyphens. Mr Poole seemed keen to accept this explanation. It will not wash. First that does not explain the identical positioning of the manufacturers' names (no less than six in identical not quite alphabetical order).

Secondly, the last two manufacturers have a missing hyphen at the end in both sets of programs which cannot be explained by sticking down 60 hyphens and overtyping. Thirdly, Mr Poole's evidence was that he added the manufacturers to Unicorn as and when he needed. However at the time when the plaintiffs obtained a copy of Unicorn pursuant to the 1989 delivery-up order he had not got customers who were dealers with some of the manufacturers to be found in PAMUPP.

I was also unhappy about his explanation of how he got any of the information as to manufacturers' price tape formats. It seemed to me that after the event a story was being concocted.

It is not only in this pair of programs where there are headings that are the same. For example in one place in another ADS program there is a heading, "**DEFFERED ENTRY**" which occurs also in the Unicorn program. Here it is not so much the misspelling which matters (for it seems Mr Poole regularly misspells "defer") as the surrounding **'s. This is atypical of the headings in either program. . . .

(e) Redundant and Unexplained Code in Both Programs

It is not only comments, labels and names which are involved in identity. There are bits of ADS and Unicorn in the program code which were also identical. These too would be copied by disk-to-disk copying. It would technically not matter if they were redundant codes or if they had a purpose in ADS and were redundant in Unicorn. But their presence would betray copying. The difficulty from Mr Poole's point of view is that those portions of code are in Unicorn at all. For if he was genuinely writing it from scratch one would not expect redundant code at all. That is the sort of thing that arises when a program is first written and then modified as time goes on. One would certainly not at all expect identical pieces of redundant code in Unicorn and ADS or bits of redundant code in Unicorn which had a function in ADS. Yet that is what we find here.

(f) Other Matter

One could go on with this list of detailed similarities. . . .

The upshot of all this is that the similarities between the two programs can only have resulted from disk to disk copying. The statistical chance of these resemblances occurring twice in the two programs must be infinitesimal. I say this bearing well in mind that many many lines in the two suites of programs are not the same. I am not prepared to accept that there was a fluke upon a fluke upon a fluke to the nth power. Nor can I understand why the defendants' experts did not see these details as overwhelming indicia of copying. They seem not to have focused on this aspect of the case at all. . . .

There is a danger in jumping from a conclusion that there was copying to a conclusion that a substantial part of a work has been taken. It is all too easy to say that a defendant who has lied about copying must have taken a lot. Of course it is likely in most cases that this is so. But the court must always go on to look at the further question of whether a substantial part was copied. In relation to conventional kinds of work this it can do reasonably readily. Even in the case of technical drawings it is possible to examine the parties' drawings to see whether a substantial part of the plaintiff's work is to be found in the defendant's. A good example of the right way to go about the problem is the *Billhofer* case. Even though there was copying (betrayed by the inessential details) there was no taking of sufficient visual features of the copyright drawing. In a computer program case, however, the court cannot so readily assess the question of substantial part unaided by expert evidence. I believe I should therefore be largely guided by such evidence. . . .

It is of course possible for two programs to be similar as a result of mere style. Such was the case of a minor program within Unicorn written not by Mr Poole but by one Joy Masters who had learned programming with Mr Poole at Supaflo many years earlier. In the case of Mr Poole's programs however the question is not whether the similarities could have arisen by reason of style and programming habits, but did they? Mr Poole was capable of producing something like Unicorn independently (though probably not in the time-frame within which it was done). He is manifestly good at programming. His skill in producing both ADS and Unicorn shows this. Unicorn is undoubtedly to the user a much friendlier program than ADS was at the time (it has now been much enhanced I understand). It has got convenient cursor movements, colour, error correction and so on, all absent from ADS as I was shown. Users doubtless think of the programs as very different because they present differently. Indeed Mr Dance, a customer, told me that was so in his case. But I think Mr Poole was taking short-cuts by starting with ADS and making considerable additions and modifications. Unicorn is a major enhancement of ADS, not a wholly independent creation. Given his failure to be "frank and candid" I think the proper inference is that the similarities identified by Mr Turner and not explained by independent evidence are due to copying. That is the guide by which I think it right to judge the question of whether a substantial part was taken. I turn to Mr Turner's similarities.

"Substantial Part": Program Structure

Under the head "program structure" Mr Turner has identified individual programs in each package which correspond. The correspondence is very close, though there are some cases where an individual Unicorn program corresponds to two or three ADS programs. Now is the compilation of ADS programs a copyright work in itself? True it is that most if not all of the functions achieved by these programs would have to be implemented by an independent programmer. But it by no means follows that he would achieve those functions by the same set of programs. As Mr Turner observes:

> The architect and designer of a software package has considerable freedom to decide how such functionality [ie of the program at system module level] is to be implemented.

I think that the putting together of the various programs in ADS, by a kind of organic growth over the years, did result in a copyright work. I of course bear in mind that within the set are some self evident programs (eg open printer) but the putting together of the whole package involved considerable skill and labour.

Was that copyright infringed? I think it was. It is true that in some cases several ADS programs have been combined into one (explicable by the improvements in hardware which make this possible) and that Unicorn has added to it many further programs which have no ADS equivalent as is shown by a list made by Mr Poole's solicitor. But I think Mr Poole took as his starting point the ADS set and that set remains substantially in Unicorn.

I should mention another level at which Mr Turner considered similarities, namely that of "design feature." He pointed out that both programs had the following identities:

— nine levels of security;
— a unique ability to create different invoice types (Mr Kenny suggested this was not unique but I was not convinced he understood what was being talked about);
— an internal sales system within the ordinary sales ledger package;
— month end sales audit combined with VAT;
— 22 character parts description;
— use of 3 separate programs for the stock ordering facility;
— 12 labour rates;
— 5 levels of sub-totalling;
— audit report by posting in identical form;
— automatic check on depreciation;
— holiday stamp facility (wholly inappropriate for an agricultural dealer. It was only in ADS as a historical accident).

Now these matters may well have arisen as a result of copying. I rather think they were. I found, for instance, Mr Poole's explanation of why there was a holiday stamp feature in Unicorn unconvincing. He said that he felt he had to have the facility as a sales point against ADS. But since no customer could conceivably want this it is a rotten sales point. One might as well put in a cube root facility. But I do not regard these matters as themselves constituting a copyright compilation. They are features of the package of interest to the customers and no more. We are here at a level of generality where there is little of the programmer's skill, labour and judgment. Even if the set were copyright, the mere taking of those functions would not be an infringement—it would be the taking of a mere general idea or scheme. . . .

Unicorn 2

This is a further revision of Unicorn issued in 1993. Many of the literal similarities which were present in Unicorn have disappeared. There has been a considerable cleaning up of comments. Mr Turner in an un-crossexamined further report concluded:

> In this brief examination into whether the literal similarities between the ADS and Unicorn software packages identified in [his earlier report] also exist in [Unicorn 2] no clear pattern has emerged. At one extreme many similarities no longer exist and original work has obviously been done to create an alternative solution. At the other, some similarities still exist intact, and no attempt has been made to create an alternative, original solution. Between the two extremes I have found a complete spectrum of cases including many instances of minimal cosmetic changes.

Plainly Unicorn 2 was made starting from Unicorn.

Mr Turner has considered whether the literal similarities in his 49 examples are present still in Unicorn 2 and has concluded that many are not. I do not have much detail on the evidence and in the circumstances I find myself in considerable difficulty in deciding one way or the other whether what remains in Unicorn is or is not a substantial part of an ADS copyright work. I do not propose to find infringement of matter I have been unable to consider in detail. However where Mr Turner has given unchallenged evidence that there has been virtually no change, or that changes were merely cosmetic, I accept that evidence. On that basis I hold that the following programs of Unicorn 2 infringe: TAX, MESS, NOMCBS, DATST, PRINT, PAMUPP, ASSAPM, PAYDIN, CUSCSH, PAYNAL, NAREC.

The overall structure remains virtually unchanged. Mr Turner says so. The copyright in ADS as a whole is likewise infringed.

COMMENTS AND QUESTIONS

1. The facts of *Ibcos* overwhelmingly suggest copyright infringement. In dictum, however, the court went on to sketch a vision of U.K. copyright law that is fundamentally different from the U.S. approach. In the excerpt that follows, the court suggests some truly radical differences between U.S. and U.K. law:

> It was sometimes suggested in a general sort of way that because a particular program had a function, and especially if that function could only be achieved in one or a limited number of ways, there could be no copyright in it. The extreme form of this idea is expressed by Judge Baker in the *Total* case. He said:
>
>> Secondly, stemming from the principle that copyright does not exist in ideas but in the expression of them is the line of authorities commencing with Kenrick v Lawrence that if there is only one way of expressing an idea that way is not the subject of copyright.
>
> That statement is in error in two ways. First, *Kenrick* (the case about a drawing of a hand showing voters which way to vote on a voting slip) did not decide that if there is only one way of expressing an idea no copyright can subsist in it. What was held was that there was no copyright infringement in taking the idea of using a picture of a hand showing how to vote. Accordingly a different picture embodying the same idea was not a taking of a substantial part of the copyright work. In that sense only the principle that there is no copyright in an idea applied.
>
> Secondly there is, I think, danger in the proposition that, "If there is only one way of expressing an idea that way is not the subject of copyright." As Lord Hailsham observed in LB Plastics v Swish ([1979] RPC 551):
>
>> But of course as the late Professor Joad used to observe it all depends on what you mean by "ideas." What the respondents in fact copied from the appellants was no mere general idea.
>
> It is of course true that copyright cannot protect any sort of general principle, such as the principle of drawing a hand to show how to vote, but it can protect a detailed literary or artistic expression. Thus in the case of an exhaust pipe it was said that the copyright was protecting the engineering principles which went into its design. Nevertheless there was copyright in the drawing and the copying of the drawing (via the medium of an exhaust pipe made from it) amounted to an infringement. This was so even though there was also a copying of the engineering principles that went into the original design. Thus Oliver LJ said in British Leyland v Armstrong ([1986] RPC 279 at 296):

> What the plaintiffs seek to protect is not the idea of an exhaust system, but their monopoly in the drawings of this particular exhaust system, the salient feature of which is the flow-line into which months of research have gone, and for the embodiment of which the drawings, taken together, form a complete set of working instructions.

The question in every case is no doubt, whether a given three-dimensional object "reproduces" the substance of the two-dimensional drawing or drawings, but I can see nothing in the Act which justifies a distinction being drawn, so far as the ambit of "reproduction" is concerned, between drawings which are purely functional, and drawings which have some aesthetic appeal. I can find no context at all for giving the word some different and more extended or restricted meaning according to the intention of the author, or the emotional response of the beholder.

To my mind that passage is inconsistent with Judge Baker's statement, which was not supported by any counsel before me. The true position is that where an "idea" is sufficiently general, then even if an original work embodies it, the mere taking of that idea will not infringe. But if the "idea" is detailed, then there may be infringement. It is a question of degree. The same applies whether the work is functional or not, and whether visual or literary.

It should be noted that the aphorism "there is no copyright in an idea" is likely to lead to confusion of thought. Sometimes it is applied to the question of subsistence of copyright (is there a "work" and if there is, is it "original"?). Sometimes it is applied to the different question of infringement (has a substantial part been taken?). That is not to say that the expression has no use: for instance if all a defendant has done is to copy a general idea then it does not matter whether there is copyright in the plaintiff's work, or whether the plaintiff owns that copyright.

In this context there was some appeal to United States cases on copyright. The fact is that United States copyright law is not the same as ours, particularly in the area of copyright works concerned with functionality and of compilations. The Americans (many would say sensibly) never developed copyright so that functional things like exhaust pipes could not be copied. This is partly due to their statute, which is different from our Act.

Moreover United States case law has, ever since Baker v Selden, been extremely careful to keep copyright out of the functional field, either by saying there is no copyright in, or that copyright cannot be infringed by taking, the functional. In *Baker* a design of ledger sheets which had a particular function was refused copyright. I doubt that would have happened here.

2.   Does the court's distinction between U.S. and U.K. law make sense? Does it explain the radically different vision of copyright law that the court articulates in *Ibcos*? Or has the *Ibcos* court arguably fallen into the same trap as the Third Circuit in Whelan v. Jaslow, in defining copyrightable expression in computer programs in an overbroad and simplistic way simply because the defendant in that case was so obviously guilty?

3.   Consider the implications of a copyright regime like the one the court describes. Copyright could presumably protect all sorts of machines and devices, whether functional or not, by the simple expedient of preventing the copying or use of plans or diagrams of the devices. Wouldn't the result be tremendous overlap between copyright and patent law? Is there anything wrong with such overlap? Have the devices set up in U.S. law to channel protection between copyright and patent worked very well? It should be noted that the U.K. eventually amended its copyright law to overturn the *British Leyland* decision to which Judge Jacob referred in *Ibcos*. However, as with U.S. copyright law, the new English copyright law limits the scope of copyright in drawings of functional designs; that is, copyrighted

drawings cannot be infringed by manufacturing the functional design depicted in the drawing. What implications might this change in English law have for computer programs that, after all, are classified as "literary works"?

4. In contrast to *Ibcos* is Judge Ferris's decision in John Richardson Computers Ltd. v. Flanders, [1993] F.S.R. 497, another pre-Directive U.K. decision. Although finding infringement based on the copying of some details of a computer program in that case, Judge Ferris took note of the Second Circuit decision in Computer Associates, Inc. v. Altai, Inc. and announced that he found nothing in English law that conflicted with the analytic approach of *Altai*. Further, he stated:

> But at the stage at which the substantiality of any copying falls to be assessed in an English case the question which has to be answered, in relation to the originality of the plaintiff's program and the separation of an idea from its expression, is essentially the same question as the United States court was addressing in *Computer Associates*. In my judgment it would be right to adopt a similar approach in England.

In *Ibcos*, Judge Jacobs took issue with Judge Ferris's conclusion, saying:

> For myself I do not find the route of going via United States case law particularly helpful. As I have said, United Kingdom copyright cannot prevent the copying of a mere general idea but can protect the copying of a detailed "idea." It is a question of degree where a good guide is the notion of overborrowing of the skill, labour and judgment which went into the copyright work. Going via the complication of the concept of a "core of protectable expression" merely complicates the matter so far as our law is concerned. It is likely to lead to overcitation of United States authority based on a statute different from ours. In the end the matter must be left to the value judgment of the court.

5. The defendant's explanation for many of the similarities between the two programs was that they resulted from his particular programming style. In light of the details in this case, the argument doesn't seem all that convincing. But it raises a more general issue: to what extent should programmers be able to take their skills, experience, and style to another company? A programmer who writes a program for one company and is then hired to write a similar program for a different company arguably couldn't start from scratch even if she wanted to. Her new program will necessarily look a bit like the old—presumably not at the level of shared typographical errors, but perhaps in sharing structure and even the odd line of code. Is this "copying"? If so, does the law effectively preclude programmers from pursuing their livelihood once they leave their employer?

6. Consider whether the European Directive on the Legal Protection of Computer Programs, which follows, would change the analysis in *Ibcos*. See generally Pamela Samuelson, Comparing U.S. and E.C. Copyright Protection for Computer Programs: Are They More Different Than They Seem?, 13 J. Law & Comm. 279 (1994).

EC Council Directive on the Legal Protection of Computer Programs
E.C. 91/250, 1991 O.J. (L 122) 42

The Council of the European Communities, having regard to the treaty establishing the European Economic Community and in particular article 100a thereof, having regard to the proposal from the Commission, in cooperation with the European Parliament, having regard to the opinion of the economic and social committee,

whereas computer programs are at present not clearly protected in all member states by existing legislation and such protection, where it exists, has different attributes;

whereas the development of computer programs requires the investment of considerable human, technical and financial resources while computer programs can be copied at a fraction of the cost needed to develop them independently;

whereas computer programs are playing an increasingly important role in a broad range of industries and computer program technology can accordingly be considered as being of fundamental importance for the community's industrial development;

whereas certain differences in the legal protection of computer programs offered by the laws of the member states have direct and negative effects on the functioning of the common market as regards computer programs and such differences could well become greater as member states introduce new legislation on this subject;

whereas existing differences having such effects need to be removed and new ones prevented from arising, while differences not adversely affecting the functioning of the common market to a substantial degree need not be removed or prevented from arising;

whereas the community's legal framework on the protection of computer programs can accordingly in the first instance be limited to establishing that member states should accord protection to computer programs under copyright law as literary works and, further, to establishing who and what should be protected, the exclusive rights on which protected persons should be able to rely in order to authorize or prohibit certain acts and for how long the protection should apply;

whereas, for the purpose of this directive, the term 'computer program' shall include programs in any form, including those which are incorporated into hardware;

whereas this term also includes preparatory design work leading to the development of a computer program provided that the nature of the preparatory work is such that a computer program can result from it at a later stage;

whereas, in respect of the criteria to be applied in determining whether or not a computer program is an original work, no tests as to the qualitative or aesthetic merits of the program should be applied;

whereas the community is fully committed to the promotion of international standardization;

whereas the function of a computer program is to communicate and work together with other components of a computer system and with users and, for this purpose, a logical and, where appropriate, physical interconnection and interaction is required to permit all elements of software and hardware to work with other software and hardware and with users in all the ways in which they are intended to function;

whereas the parts of the program which provide for such interconnection and interaction between elements of software and hardware are generally known as 'interfaces';

whereas this functional interconnection and interaction is generally known as 'interoperability';

whereas such interoperability can be defined as the ability to exchange information and mutually to use the information which has been exchanged;

whereas, for the avoidance of doubt, it has to be made clear that only the expression of a computer program is protected and that ideas and principles which underlie any element of a program, including those which underlie its interfaces, are not protected by copyright under this directive;

whereas, in accordance with this principle of copyright, to the extent that logic, algorithms and programming languages comprise ideas and principles, those ideas and principles are not protected under this directive;

whereas, in accordance with the legislation and jurisprudence of the member states and the international copyright conventions, the expression of those ideas and principles is to be protected by copyright; . . .

whereas the provisions of this directive are without prejudice to the application of the competition rules under articles 85 and 86 of the treaty if a dominant supplier refuses to make information available which is necessary for interoperability as defined in this directive; whereas the provisions of this directive should be without prejudice to specific requirements of community law already enacted in respect of the publication of interfaces in the telecommunications sector or Council decisions relating to standardization in the field of information technology and telecommunication;

whereas this directive does not affect derogations provided for under national legislation in accordance with the Berne Convention on points not covered by this directive,

has adopted this directive:

Article 1   Object of Protection

1. In accordance with the provisions of this directive, member states shall protect computer programs, by copyright, as literary works within the meaning of the Berne Convention for the Protection of Literary and Artistic Works. For the purposes of this directive, the term 'computer programs' shall include their preparatory design material.

2. Protection in accordance with this directive shall apply to the expression in any form of a computer program. Ideas and principles which underlie any element of a computer program, including those which underlie its interfaces, are not protected by copyright under this directive.

3. A computer program shall be protected if it is original in the sense that it is the author's own intellectual creation. No other criteria shall be applied to determine its eligibility for protection.

Article 2   Authorship of Computer Programs

1. The author of a computer program shall be the natural person or group of natural persons who has created the program or, where the legislation of the member state permits, the legal person designated as the rightholder by

that legislation. Where collective works are recognized by the legislation of a member state, the person considered by the legislation of the member state to have created the work shall be deemed to be its author.

2. In respect of a computer program created by a group of natural persons jointly, the exclusive rights shall be owned jointly.

3. Where a computer program is created by an employee in the execution of his duties or following the instructions given by his employer, the employer exclusively shall be entitled to exercise all economic rights in the program so created, unless otherwise provided by contract.

Article 3 Beneficiaries of Protection

1. Protection shall be granted to all natural or legal persons eligible under national copyright legislation as applied to literary works.

Article 4 Restricted Acts

1. Subject to the provisions of articles 5 and 6, the exclusive rights of the rightholder within the meaning of article 2, shall include the right to do or to authorize:

(a) the permanent or temporary reproduction of a computer program by any means and in any form, in part or in whole. Insofar as loading, displaying, running, transmission or storage of the computer program necessitate such reproduction, such acts shall be subject to authorization by the rightholder;

(b) the translation, adaptation, arrangement and any other alteration of a computer program and the reproduction of the results thereof, without prejudice to the rights of the person who alters the program;

(c) any form of distribution to the public, including the rental, of the original computer program or of copies thereof.

2. The first sale in the community of a copy of a program by the rightholder or with his consent shall exhaust the distribution right within the community of that copy, with the exception of the right to control further rental of the program or a copy thereof.

Article 5 Exceptions to the Restricted Acts

1. In the absence of specific contractual provisions, the acts referred to in article 4 (a) and (b) shall not require authorization by the rightholder where they are necessary for the use of the computer program by the lawful acquirer in accordance with its intended purpose, including for error correction.

2. The making of a back-up copy by a person having a right to use the computer program may not be prevented by contract insofar as it is necessary for that use.

3. The person having a right to use a copy of a computer program shall be entitled, without the authorization of the rightholder, to observe, study or test the functioning of the program in order to determine the ideas and principles which underlie any element of the program if he does so while performing any of the acts of loading, displaying, running, transmitting or storing the program which he is entitled to do.

Article 6   Decompilation

1. The authorization of the rightholder shall not be required where re-production of the code and translation of its form within the meaning of article 4 (a) and (b) are indispensable to obtain the information necessary to achieve the interoperability of an independently created computer program with other programs, provided that the following conditions are met:

(a) these acts are performed by the licensee or by another person having a right to use a copy of a program, or on their behalf by a person authorized to do so;

(b) the information necessary to achieve interoperability has not previously been readily available to the persons referred to in subparagraph (a); and

(c) these acts are confined to the parts of the original program which are necessary to achieve interoperability.

2. The provisions of paragraph 1 shall not permit the information obtained through its application:

(a) to be used for goals other than to achieve the interoperability of the independently created computer program;

(b) to be given to others, except when necessary for the interoperability of the independently created computer program; or

(c) to be used for the development, production or marketing of a computer program substantially similar in its expression, or for any other act which infringes copyright.

Article 7   Special Measures of Protection

1. Without prejudice to the provisions of articles 4, 5 and 6, member states shall provide, in accordance with their national legislation, appropriate remedies against a person committing any of the acts listed in subparagraphs (a), (b) and (c) below:

(a) any act of putting into circulation a copy of a computer program knowing, or having reason to believe, that it is an infringing copy;

(b) the possession, for commercial purposes, of a copy of a computer program knowing, or having reason to believe, that it is an infringing copy;

(c) any act of putting into circulation, or the possession for commercial purposes of, any means the sole intended purpose of which is to facilitate the unauthorized removal or circumvention of any technical device which may have been applied to protect a computer program.

2. Any infringing copy of a computer program shall be liable to seizure in accordance with the legislation of the member state concerned.

3. Member states may provide for the seizure of any means referred to in paragraph 1 (c).

Article 8   Term of Protection

1. Protection shall be granted for the life of the author and for fifty years after his death or after the death of the last surviving author; where the computer program is an anonymous or pseudonymous work, or where a legal person is designated as the author by national legislation in accordance with article 2 (1), the

term of protection shall be fifty years from the time that the computer program is first lawfully made available to the public. The term of protection shall be deemed to begin on the first of January of the year following the abovementioned events.

2. Member states which already have a term of protection longer than that provided for in paragraph 1 are allowed to maintain their present term until such time as the term of protection for copyright works is harmonized by community law in a more general way.

Article 9   Continued Application of Other Legal Provisions

1. The provisions of this directive shall be without prejudice to any other legal provisions such as those concerning patent rights, trade-marks, unfair competition, trade secrets, protection of semi-conductor products or the law of contract. Any contractual provisions contrary to article 6 or to the exceptions provided for in article 5 (2) and (3) shall be null and void.

2. The provisions of this directive shall apply also to programs created before 1 January 1993 without prejudice to any acts concluded and rights acquired before that date.

COMMENTS AND QUESTIONS

1. The European Directive is far more explicit about some copyright issues in relation to computer programs than is U.S. copyright law. Do these more explicit provisions favor software developers?

2. What implications should one draw about whether the structure, sequence, and organization of a computer program is protected by copyright from the Directive's characterization of computer programs as "literary works"? What implications might there be for user interface similarities or for "look and feel"?

3. How would you predict ICM v. Met's would be decided under the Directive or under *Ibcos*?

4. Some European countries do not have "work made for hire" rules in their copyright laws; they require instead a transfer-of-rights agreement with employees. How does the Directive deal with this matter?

5. Notice the difference between the European Directive and U.S. law in terms of the exclusive rights conferred on authors. Does the absence of a public performance or display right have any significance?

6. Compare Article 5's "Exceptions to the Restricted Acts" provision with 17 U.S.C. section 117. How are they similar or different?

7. How does the decompilation privilege under Article 6 compare with the U.S. ruling in Sega Enterprises v. Altai? It may be worth knowing that the European Council adopted the Directive and its decompilation privilege before there had been a definitive ruling in the United States on the decompilation issue.

8. The Directive's decompilation privilege under Article 6 is nonwaivable by contract. How does this compare to U.S. law?

9. Continental European law provides protection for the moral rights of authors as well as their economic interests. Notice that the Directive is totally silent on the issue of moral rights. Given the utilitarian nature of computer programs and

given that the texts of computer programs are generally not widely distributed, one might wonder whether authors of computer programs do or should have moral rights to stop customers from modifying their programs. At least one European case has applied moral rights law to programs. See Bodin v. AGOSAP (D. Ct. Paris, France, Jan. 20, 1993) (author of computer program retained moral right of integrity in program; modifying the source code to allow the program to run on a different operating system violated the author's moral rights). Japan, by contrast, has limited moral rights in computer programs in recognition that situations may arise in which users may need to modify computer programs to fix coding errors, make adjustments in its functioning, and the like.

3. Copyright in Computer Programs in Australia

Data Access Corporation v. Powerflex Services Pty Ltd.
High Court of Australia
[1999] H.C.A. 49

. . . Data Access owns the copyright in a system of computer programs which is known as "Dataflex".

. . . It is a system which allows a programmer or developer to develop customised database applications or databases.

The Dataflex system incorporates:

- a program development system, which provides the means to write, edit, compile and run programs under development;
- a computer programming language known as the "Dataflex language", which is an application development language in which the source code for all Dataflex programs is written or generated;
- a compiler program which translates the Dataflex source code programs written in the Dataflex language by using the program development system, into an internal format which is then able to be run by the runtime program; and
- a runtime program, which is the executable program required to run the compiled application programs developed using the program development system.

Mr Cory Casanave, Executive Vice-President of Data Access, gave evidence as to the nature of the language used in computer programs. He said:

A computer language defines the names of each word in the language and the rules governing the use of each word (syntax). Each word in a computer language is an instruction to the computer to invoke lower level proccesses, the word chosen to invoke those processes is generally chosen to suggest the nature of the process that will be invoked.

A computer language is comprised of a set of reserved words which are used in accordance with the rules of syntax governing their use. A computer language syntax, like the syntax of a human language, comprises the rules by which the words can be combined to form statements which are correct for the language. For each command or function there is a specific syntax which describes how arguments may be applied to the command. Arguments can be likened to a noun phrase, they describe what the command will act on. Various documents also refer to 'functions' as well as commands. Functions are a type of command which perform a computation and return a result.

Two hundred and fifty-four words of the Dataflex language are listed in the Dataflex encyclopedia. However, 29 of those words, which express commands for developing graphics, are not used at all in the PFXplus language. Of the other 225, 192 are used in the PFXplus language in a way which eventually causes the computer to perform the same function as those words perform in the Dataflex language.

At first instance, the reasons of Jenkinson J suggest that he considered that copyright subsisted in each of these 192 common words and that the use of them in PFXplus infringed Data Access' copyright in them. However, the orders made by his Honour restrain the use of only 169 of the common words, three of which are "Macros". It may be that, after judgment but before the orders were made, Data Access conceded that the remaining 23 words (which include words such as "SHOW" and "ENTRY") were not protected by copyright. Perhaps a concession was made during argument and, in a complex case, overlooked when the reasons for judgment were being prepared. But whatever the reason for not dealing with these 23 words, the issue of copyright in this Court is confined to the 169 words the subject of the order made by his Honour.

We will deal with the three "Macros" separately from the remaining 166 common words which can conveniently be called the "Reserved Words". Of these Reserved Words, at least 55 are unique to the Dataflex program. But many are ordinary English words—such as "BOX", "CHART", and "RETAIN". Others are a combination of two English words such as "PAGEBREAK". Some are not only common English words but are used in most, if not all, computer programs. Examples are "DIRECTORY" and "SAVE".

The PFXplus System

Some years ago, the third respondent, Dr David Bennett ("Dr Bennett"), became familiar with the Dataflex system. He decided to create and market an application development system which would be compatible with the Dataflex language and the Dataflex database file structure so that persons who were familiar with the Dataflex system would be able to use his new product.

The Full Court of the Federal Court found the following facts to be common ground between the parties to the appeal:

- by a process of reverse engineering and study of both the documentation and operation of the Dataflex system, Dr Bennett created a system of computer programs, which was originally known as "Powerflex", but is now known as "PFXplus", intending that the system would be compatible with the Dataflex system, i.e. that certain commands and "reserved words" (including the Macros) used as commands in the Dataflex system would operate in like manner in the PFXplus system;

- the source code in which the Dataflex system is written is quite different from the source code in which the PFXplus system is written; and
- there is not necessarily any similarity between the object code used in the Dataflex system and that used in the PFXplus system.

PFXplus achieved Dr Bennett's aim of being highly compatible with Dataflex. Dr Bennett and his wife subsequently incorporated a company, the second respondent, to sell PFXplus.

The Issues

The only allegations of copyright infringement that are now in issue are the claims that by publishing PFXplus the respondents have infringed the copyright which Data Access has in:

A. The Reserved Words.
B. The Macros.
C. The Dataflex Huffman compression table, to which reference will later be made.

A. *The Reserved Words*

The appellant contends:

1. Copyright subsists in each of the Reserved Words because each is a "computer program" within the definition in §10(1) of the Act.

2. Copyright subsists in the collocation of the Reserved Words comprising the Dataflex language because this collocation is a "computer program".

3. Alternatively to 2, even if the collocation of Reserved Words is not itself a literary work, it nevertheless forms a substantial part of a literary work (the Dataflex system) so that copying of it is an infringement of the appellant's copyright in the Dataflex system.

4. Copyright subsists in the table or compilation of Reserved Words in the Dataflex User's Guide on the footing that it is a literary work within par (a) of the definition in §10(1) of the Act.

We turn to consider each of these contentions.

1. Is Each of the Reserved Words a "Computer Program" within the Meaning of §10(1) of the Act?

The appellant contends that each of the Reserved Words is itself a "computer program" within the meaning of the definition in §10(1) of the Act. In order to determine the validity of the appellant's submissions, it is convenient to divide the definition of "computer program" into its component parts.

The definition of "computer program" requires that each Reserved Word be:

(i) "an expression,"

(ii) "in any language, code or notation,"

(iii) "of a set of instructions (whether with or without related information)"

(iv) "intended, either directly or after either or both of the following:

(a) conversion to another language, code or notation;

(b) reproduction in a different material form; to cause"

(v) "a device having digital information processing capabilities to perform a particular function."

Each of the first four of these elements qualifies what follows and the scope of the definition is marked out by the requirement of an intention that the device be caused "to perform a particular function". In form, the definition of a computer program seems to have more in common with the subject matter of a patent than a copyright. Inventions when formulated as a manner of new manufacture traditionally fell within the province of patent law, with the scope of the monopoly protection being fixed by the terms of a public document, the patent specification. In Australia claims to computer programs which are novel, not obvious and otherwise satisfy the Patents Act 1990 (Cth) and which have the effect of controlling computers to operate in a particular way, have been held to be proper subject matter for letters patent, as "achieving an end result which is an artificially created state of affairs of utility in the field of economic endeavour", within the meaning of National Research Development Corporation v Commissioner of Patents.

The amendment of the definition of "literary work" in §10(1) of the Act to include as item (b) "a computer program or compilation of computer programs" obviously marked a significant departure from what previously had been the understanding of what was required for subsistence of copyright in an original literary work. It is true that copyright may subsist in a literary work which is related to the exercise of mechanical functions. A set of written instructions for the assembly and operation of a domestic appliance is an example. However, it is not to the point in copyright law that, if followed, the instructions do not cause the appliance to function. The protection of the function performed by the appliance will be for the patent law, including the law as to inutility. This is what was indicated by Bradley J in a passage in Baker v Selden which was repeated by Brennan J in *Computer Edge*. Bradley J said that no one would contend that the exclusive right to the manner of manufacture described in a treatise would be given by the subsistence of copyright in that work, and continued:

> The copyright of the book, if not pirated from other works, would be valid without regard to the novelty, or want of novelty, of its subject-matter. . . . To give to the author of the book an exclusive property in the art described therein, when no examination of its novelty has ever been officially made, would be a surprise and a fraud upon the public. That is the province of letters-patent, not of copyright.

Further, the requirement in copyright law that a work be "original" is to be distinguished from the requirements that an alleged invention be novel and that it not be obvious. The question for copyright law is whether "the work emanates from the person claiming to be its author, in the sense that he has originated it or brought it into existence and has not copied it from another". If so, the work does not lack originality because of the anterior independent work of another, although, in such circumstances, an invention might lack novelty.

Finally, to say that the copyright law does not protect function and extends only to the expression of systems or methods does not deny that a work may serve utilitarian rather than aesthetic ends. A map and a recipe book are obvious examples.

There is, with respect, some oversimplification of these principles in the following statement by Dawson J in Autodesk Inc v Dyason ("*Autodesk No 1*"):

> [W]hen the expression of an idea is inseparable from its function, it forms part of the idea and is not entitled to the protection of copyright.

The 1984 amendment departed from traditional principles by identifying for copyright purposes a species of literary work, the very subsistence of which requires an expression of a set of instructions intended to cause a device to perform a particular function. The difficulties which arise from accommodating computer technology protection to principles of copyright law have been remarked upon but the Act now expressly requires such an accommodation.

In the present case, no question arises with respect to the relationship between the Act and the protection given to the designers of computer chips by the Circuit Layouts Act 1989 (Cth). The first issue in the appeal turns solely on the application of the definition of "computer program" in §10(1) of the Act.

The appellant submits that each Reserved Word meets each component of the definition of "computer program". The appellant contends:

> (i) A Reserved Word itself is identified as being the relevant "expression" for the purposes of the definition. The term "expression" is used in the definition to preserve the distinction between the set of instructions and the manner in which the set is expressed in a particular programming language. The choice of expressions for words and commands in a language is determined by the author of the language.
>
> (ii) Each Reserved Word is in a code or notation, the relevant code or notation being the Dataflex language.
>
> (iii) Each Reserved Word expresses a set of instructions, that set being either the underlying set of instructions in source code, or the meaning and syntax of the word or command in question.
>
> (iv) and (v) Each Reserved Word is in a high level language, and each is intended, after conversion into a lower level language by a compiler and runtime program, to cause a computer (which is a device having digital information processing capabilities) to perform a particular function.

In our opinion, none of the Reserved Words satisfies the statutory definition. Each Reserved Word is undoubtedly in "code or notation"—the Dataflex language. It follows that whether a Reserved Word is a "computer program" within the meaning of the definition depends on whether it is an "expression . . . of a set of instructions . . . intended . . . to cause a device having digital information processing capabilities to perform a particular function". However, each of the Reserved Words is a single word; none is a set of instructions in the Dataflex language. Further, none of the Reserved Words intends to express, directly or indirectly, an algorithmic or logical relationship between the function desired to be performed and the physical capabilities of the "device having digital information processing capabilities".

We turn to explain these conclusions.

The Findings in the Courts Below

The trial judge held that each Reserved Word was itself a computer program. Jenkinson J said:

> Each of the words of the DataFlex language found also in the PFXplus language is in my opinion an expression of a set of instructions intended to cause a device having digital information processing capabilities to perform a particular function. The circumstance that the expression of those instructions in source code is different is in my opinion immaterial. At the level of abstraction under consideration the objective similarity is complete: the set of instructions intended to cause the performance of the particular function is expressed, at that level where the "language, code or notation" is based upon concatenations of letters of the alphabet, by the same concatenation of letters in each language. If at that level some of the concatenations constitute or resemble words of the English language descriptive or suggestive of the functions to be performed, that may facilitate the use of the computer program by those who understand English. But each concatenation of letters is nonetheless an expression of a set of instructions intended to cause the device to perform a particular function, in my opinion, and therefore a "computer program" within the meaning of that expression in the Copyright Act.

The Full Court came to the opposite conclusion. It said:

> Each of the words in the so-called Dataflex language is but a cipher. The underlying program is the set of instructions which directs the computer what to do when that cipher is in fact used, for example by being typed on to the screen. It is not to the point that the cipher bears some resemblance to an ordinary English word. The cipher or command is not an expression of the set of instructions, although it appears in that set of instructions. It is the trigger for the set of instructions to be given effect to by the computer.
>
> It may not be inaccurate to describe each of the commands as itself an instruction. It is likewise not necessarily inaccurate to talk of each of those words as representing the set of instructions in the sense that the use of one of them triggers the instructions contained in the computer program to be acted upon. But it is in our view not accurate to refer to each of the words as being an expression of the set of instructions. The set of instructions is expressed in the source code which is the computer program and, at least at a higher level, includes the particular word which is a command. The computer program will also in other forms exist in lower level language, ultimately through to an object code in nonvisible form. Each of these representations will fall within the definition of "computer program". In each of them, in some language, code or notation, the word said to be part of the computer language will be able to be found.
>
> The passage earlier quoted from the judgment of Gaudron J in *Autodesk*, placing as it does emphasis upon the requirement that it is the set of instructions in their entirety which is the computer program, also points to the conclusion that the individual words of command are not, themselves, computer programs within the definition. . . .

The Relevant "Set of Instructions" Executed by a Computer . . . .

It is impossible to overemphasise the importance of the fact that a computer has no "intelligence" to execute instructions over and beyond the simple logical functions which are hard wired into its circuits. In order for the simple logical functions of a computer to translate into a useful result, it is necessary to express complex problems in terms of a sequence of a large number of these simple operations. A "set of instructions" will not cause a computer to execute a particular function unless that set of instructions can be ultimately expressed in terms of a sequence of the logical operations which are hard wired into the computer. No doubt it is very rare to express a complex computer program in terms of the simple logical operations which are hard wired into a computer. That is because the process of writing programs becomes practically unmanageable unless the "set of instructions" is perceived at a high level of abstraction. Such a level of abstraction is required in order to express what are millions of simple logical operations in terms of a manageable number of more complex instructions which themselves are reducible to these simple logical operations. . . .

No doubt, at the highest level of abstraction, the word "PRINT" is an expression of an instruction which is intended to cause a device having digital information processing capabilities to perform a particular function. Thus, at the highest level of abstraction, each of the Reserved Words in Dataflex may likewise be regarded as an expression of an instruction which is intended to cause a device having digital information processing capabilities to perform a particular function.

However, the appellant must show that each Reserved Word is an "expression, in any language, code or notation, of a set of instructions . . . intended, either directly or after . . . conversion to another language, code or notation . . . to cause a device having digital information processing capabilities to perform a particular function".

In order to overcome the difficulty that a Reserved Word is only one instruction in the Dataflex language, the appellant made two related arguments:

- first, that after "conversion to another language, code or notation" (i.e. source code), each Reserved Word is a "set of instructions" in source code and each Reserved Word is therefore the expression, in the Dataflex language, of this underlying set of instructions; and
- second, that each Reserved Word is an expression, in the Dataflex language, of, as the appellant put it, "the meaning and syntax of the word or command in question".

In relation to the first argument, it is true that after a Reserved Word is converted to source code, there is a "set of instructions" in source code.

The question then arises as to the level of abstraction (or in other words, the level of language) at which the appellant must show that the Reserved Word meets the definition of a computer program.

Two Competing Interpretations of "Computer Program"

In our view, there are two competing interpretations of the definition of "computer program" in §10(1) of the Act. The two competing interpretations arise from the effect of the words "in any language, code or notation" and the words "either directly or after . . . conversion to another language, code or notation" in the definition.

On one view, the effect of these words is that, if an item written in language *A* is not an "expression . . . of a set of instructions . . . intended . . . to cause a device having digital information processing capabilities to perform a particular function" in language *A*, but after conversion to language *B* is such an expression of a set of instructions in language *B*, the statutory requirements are met in respect of the expression in both language *A* and language *B*. Thus, the item would be regarded as a "computer program" in both language *A* and language *B*, even though it is only an "expression . . . of a set of instructions . . . intended . . . to cause a device having digital information processing capabilities to perform a particular function" in language *B*.

The second, opposing view is that the requirement that there be an "expression . . . of a set of instructions . . . intended . . . to cause a device having digital information processing capabilities to perform a particular function" is a requirement that must be applied to each new language in which the item may be expressed in order for the item to be a "computer program" in that language. On this view, if an item is not an "expression . . . of a set of instructions . . . intended . . . to cause a device having digital information processing capabilities to perform a particular function" in language *A*, its expression in language *A* is not a computer program, even if, after conversion to language *B*, the item meets the criteria of an "expression . . . of a set of instructions . . . intended . . . to cause a device having digital information processing capabilities to perform a particular function" in language *B*.

On the second view, the question whether an item is an "expression . . . of a set of instructions . . . intended . . . to cause a device having digital information processing capabilities to perform a particular function" must be determined separately for each language in which that item is expressed. The fact that an item meets the criteria of an "expression . . . of a set of instructions . . . intended . . . to cause a device having digital information processing capabilities to perform a particular function" in one language does not automatically mean that the item will meet that criteria in any other language in which that item may be expressed.

In our opinion, the second view is the preferable one. The definition of "computer program" begins with the words "an expression, in any language, code or notation". The phrase relates to a singular expression (the word "an" is used) and the words "any language" envisage that the expression will be in a particular language, whatever that language might be. However, the "expression" must be of a "set of instructions" which has a particular intention.

The meaning of the phrase "expression . . . of a set of instructions" was referred to in the Explanatory Memorandum to the Copyright Amendment Bill 1984:

> The phrase "expression . . . of a set of instructions" is intended to make clear that it is not an abstract idea, algorithm or mathematical principle which is protected but rather a particular expression of that abstraction. The word "set" indicates that the instructions are related to one another rather than being a mere collection.

It is the particular selection, ordering, combination and arrangement of instructions within a computer program which provide its expression. A computer program in a particular language may be relatively inefficient because it uses many instructions to achieve the function that a single instruction could achieve. A computer program in a particular language may also operate relatively inefficiently because of the way it is structured, in terms of the ordering of the instructions and the sequence in which they are executed. Considerations of efficiency are largely a function of the particular language which is used. It is the skill of the programmer in a particular language which determines the expression of the program in that language.

The Explanatory Memorandum states that it is a "particular expression" of an abstract idea which is protected. As a particular expression is a function of the language of the expression, whether a word or words is or are a relevant expression of a set of instructions needs to be asked separately for each language in which there is purportedly a set of instructions.

For an item to be a computer program, it must not only be an "expression . . . of a set of instructions", but the expression of that set of instructions must also be designed to achieve a particular purpose. That is to say, it must be "intended . . . to cause a device having digital information processing capabilities to perform a particular function". The emphasis on a singular function in the phrase "a particular function" indicates that it is necessary to identify precisely the relevant function.

As we have already indicated, the only operations which a computer is physically capable of performing are those logic operations which are hard wired into its circuits. This physical limitation manifests itself at every level of computer programming, at different levels of abstraction. At the lowest level, when programming in object code, the limitation is perhaps most evident. That is because the computer program is written in terms which are closely related to physical events within the processor and memory of the computer. In higher level languages, the physical limitations of the computer manifest themselves to a programmer in a more subtle way. In the particular language in which a programmer is working, there is a limited set of commands which can be used. Each of these commands has its own syntactical and grammatical rules which must be followed in order for the command to be successfully recognised by the compiler program which converts the commands into object code. This is because each command in the high level language is nothing more than a "pre-packaged set" of sequences of the logic operations which the computer is capable of performing. The compiler program, upon reading a command, merely opens the pre-packaged set and launches the corresponding logic operations which the computer is capable of performing. If a set of instructions in a high level language is intended to cause a computer to perform a particular function, it is an expression which intends to express an algorithmic or logical relationship between the desired function and the physical capabilities of the computer, albeit indirectly. Owing to programming errors, or what are commonly called "bugs", it may not actually do so. The presence of "bugs" in a computer program, however, does not disentitle it to copyright protection, because as the Explanatory Memorandum stated:

> The phrase "intended . . . to cause" is used in preference to words such as "capable . . . of causing" to cover the situation where the program, as written, may not operate for technical reasons such as the presence of a programming error.

It is the ability to express in a computer language an algorithmic or logical relationship between an identifiable function which is desired to be performed and the physical capabilities of the computer, which is the true skill of the programmer. This remains true even if the programmer is working via the medium of a high level language and is unaware of the physical capabilities of the computer. It is the expression of this skill which is intended to be protected by the Act.

In our opinion, the foregoing conclusion also explains the reference in the definition of "computer program" to "a set of instructions (whether with or without any related information)". The Explanatory Memorandum stated:

> The phrase "whether with or without related information" is intended to make clear that the protected program may include material other than instructions for the computer (such as information for programmers or users of the program, or data to be used in connection with the execution of the program).

The distinction between "data" or "related information" on the one hand and "instructions for the computer" on the other indicates that Parliament has conceived of a "set of instructions" that are truly "instructions for the computer" in the sense that they are referable to the computer's physical capabilities. The inclusion in the definition of "computer program" of the words "(whether with or without related information)", in parenthesis, effected the legislative intent that the inclusion of "related information" within the "expression . . . of a set of instructions" would not take that expression outside the definition. "Data" or "related information" is that part of the computer program which is not in any sense referable to the computer's physical capabilities. The examples given in the Explanatory Memorandum indicate that it may be a wide category. It is unnecessary to consider what may constitute "information" which is not "related information", a matter removed from the task of construing the phrase "set of instructions".

In our opinion, whether what is claimed to be a "computer program" is an "expression . . . of a set of instructions . . . intended . . . to cause a device having digital information processing capabilities to perform a particular function" must be answered separately for each language in which the item in question is said to be a computer program.

Moreover, something is not a "computer program" within the meaning of the definition in §10(1) unless it intends to express, either directly or indirectly, an algorithmic or logical relationship between the function desired to be performed and the physical capabilities of the "device having digital information processing capabilities". Thus, in the sense employed by the definition, a program in object code causes a device to perform a particular function "directly" when executed. A program in source code does so "after . . . conversion to another language, code or notation".

Some support, by way of analogy, may be derived from considering the position in the United States. In Baystate Technologies Inc v Bentley Systems Inc, it was held that whilst the computer program comprising "CADKEY" was protected, the particular "data structures" with which the case was concerned "[did] not bring about any result on their own", so that they were protected, if at all, only as part of the whole computer program. This was because, as was later expressed in the judgment: "a computer cannot read data structures and perform any function".

Once these principles are applied to each Reserved Word in the Dataflex language, it is clear that they are not "computer programs". Each Reserved Word comprises but a single instruction in that language. Each Reserved Word, considered alone, is not a "set of instructions" in that language. It is not a "computer program" expressed in the Dataflex language.

Meaning and Syntax

There remains to be addressed the further argument of the appellant that the relevant set of instructions at the level of the Dataflex language is the "meaning and syntax of the word or command in question". In response to questions from members of this Court during the argument of the appeal, counsel for the appellant was asked on a number of occasions to identify the relevant "set of instructions". His answer was that it was the "meaning and syntax of the word or command in question".

However, the function which will be executed by a particular Reserved Word depends entirely on the source code underlying the Reserved Word. Thus, its "meaning" depends on the source code underlying it. This is also the case with the "syntax". There are, of course, grammatical and syntactical rules for the use of the Reserved Words. These rules would be written in the source code underlying the Dataflex commands. Equivalent rules would be written in the source code underlying the PFXplus commands. The meaning of the Reserved Words, and the grammatical and syntactical rules for their use, are not an "expression" until they are reduced to the underlying source code. However, the appellant does not, and could not, contend that Dr Bennett's source code expression of the meaning of commands or of the grammatical and syntactical rules in PFXplus is a reproduction of the source code expression of those meanings or rules in the Dataflex language. There was a finding that the source code of PFXplus was dissimilar to the source code of Dataflex.

Furthermore, as the Full Court of the Federal Court pointed out:

> It goes without saying that, but for ease of usage, the precise words used in a particular computer language are irrelevant. A particular program could use the letters "XZB", or any other combination of letters or symbols, so that when the computer was confronted with those letters it would perform a particular set of instructions, for example, displaying a particular item in a particular database. The use of a string of letters forming an English word such as "display" will, however, more easily be recalled and reproduced by the user than will a meaningless combination to that user.

Thus, from the computer's perspective, any of the Reserved Words in the Dataflex language could have been replaced with any other word or string of characters. If it had, the same function would have been performed provided the necessary modifications were made to the compiler and runtime programs. In our opinion, this shows that the particular characters of a Reserved Word in the Dataflex language, considered alone, do not intend to express a logical or algorithmic relationship between the function it intends to cause the computer to perform and the physical capabilities of the computer.

It is true that, from the user's perspective, the particular words chosen allow for ease of use. No doubt this explains the focus in the appellant's submissions on the "meaning" of a Reserved Word. However, ease of use is an intended function which the author of the Reserved Words had in relation to the user. It is not an intended function which the author of the Reserved Words had in relation to the computer. The definition of a computer program requires that the intention be in relation to the performance of a particular function by the computer.

It is true that in any high level language, the particular commands might be replaced with any other string of characters and necessary modifications made to the compiler program. But that does not mean that nothing expressed in a high level language could ever be a computer program. Once more than one instruction is expressed in a high level language with the intention that the expression will, after conversion to object code, cause a computer to perform a particular function, there will ordinarily be a computer program for the purposes of the Act. The choice and interrelationship of the particular instructions used and their sequence and structure will ordinarily constitute the expression of a logical or algorithmic relationship between the function intended to be performed and the physical capabilities of the computer.

The conclusion that the Reserved Words themselves are not a computer program in Dataflex does not mean that their expression in source code and object code is not a computer program. As the Full Court stated, correctly in our view:

> [I]t is in our view not accurate to refer to each of the words as being an expression of the set of instructions. The set of instructions is expressed in the source code which is the computer program and, at least at a higher level, includes the particular word which is a command. The computer program will also in other forms exist in lower level language, ultimately through to an object code in non-visible form. Each of these representations will fall within the definition of a "computer program". In each of them, in some language, code or notation, the word said to be part of the computer language will be able to be found.

However, the appellant does not contend that the source code in PFXplus underlying any of the 166 commands in question is an infringement of the source code underlying the corresponding commands in Dataflex. That being so, the claim that each Reserved Word is a computer program fails.

2. Is the Collocation of the Reserved Words a Computer Program?

Furthermore, the collocation of the Reserved Words is not a "computer program". Although the Reserved Words together form "an expression . . . of a set of instructions", their simple listing together, without more, does not cause a computer to perform any identifiable function. There is no interrelationship of the instructions with one another which is an expression of a logical or algorithmic relationship between an identifiable function and the physical capabilities of the computer via the medium of the Dataflex language.

It is no answer that there is a set of instructions with a single identifiable function in that it provides a programmer with the vocabulary to enable him or her to program in the Dataflex language. As in the case of each individual Reserved Word, this is a function which the author of the Reserved Words intended them to perform in relation to the user, not in relation to the computer. As we have indicated, the definition of a "computer program" requires that the set of instructions be intended to cause the computer to perform a particular function.

3. Does the Collocation of the Reserved Words Form a Substantial Part of a Literary Work (the Dataflex System)?

The Dataflex system is a computer program. Hence it is a literary work for the purpose of the Act. The appellant contends that the collocation of Reserved Words, even if it is not itself a literary work, constitutes a substantial part of the Dataflex system. Section 14(1)(b) of the Act provides that in the Act "a reference to a reproduction . . . of a work shall be read as including a reference to a reproduction . . . of a substantial part of the work". A copyright owner's exclusive right to reproduce a work is therefore infringed if another person reproduces a "substantial part" of the work.

In *Autodesk No 1*, this Court held that it was not necessary that the reproduction of a substantial part of a computer program should itself be a computer program. Relying on that reasoning, the appellant contends that its copyright is infringed because the collocation of Reserved Words is a substantial part of the Dataflex system.

Substantiality

The question whether something is a substantial part of a computer program created difficulty in *Autodesk No 1* and *Autodesk No 2*. In *Autodesk No 1*, in the course of determining whether the 127-bit series embedded in the EPROM in Dyason's Auto Key lock infringed the copyright in Autodesk's Widget C, Dawson J, with whom the other members of the Court agreed, said:

> For Widget *C* is a computer program and a substantial, indeed essential, part of that program is the look-up table by reference to which Widget *C* processes the information which it receives from the AutoCAD lock. . . . In effect, both Widget *C* and the Auto Key lock contain the same look-up table.
> . . . Whilst the 127-bit look-up table does not of itself constitute a computer program within the meaning of the definition—it does not by itself amount to a set of instructions—it is a substantial part of Widget *C* and its reproduction in the Auto Key lock is a reproduction of a substantial part of that program.

In *Autodesk No 2*, when discussing whether the 127-bit series embedded in the EPROM constituted a reproduction of a substantial part of Widget *C*, Brennan J said:

> A further submission is that the look-up table is not a substantial part of the relevant computer program. The bytes contained in the look-up table are but a minute fraction of the bytes in the whole of the Widget *C* program. Nevertheless, the series of digits in the look-up table is both original and critical to the set of instructions designed to cause the computer to run the AutoCAD application. When the running of the Auto-CAD application is the purpose of the set of instructions expressed in that program, it would be difficult, if not impossible, to contend that the look-up table is not a substantial part of that program.

Gaudron J said:

The only other matter on which the respondents rely is the question whether the look-up table can be said to be a substantial part of Widget *C*. In truth, the table was the linchpin of the program, to borrow an expression from a different technology. It was the critical part of the instructions in that the other parts depended on and were made by reference to it. Whatever may be the situation in cases in which information plays a less significant role, given that the look-up table was crucial to Widget *C* and given that copyright protection extends to information as well as the commands involved in a set of instructions of the kind constituting a computer program as defined in §10 of the Act, there is, in my view, simply no basis for an argument that the look-up table was not a substantial part of Widget *C*.

The above passages in the various judgments in the two *Autodesk* cases relied on the "essentiality" or "criticality" of the look-up table to determine its substantiality. The reasoning appears to come close to a "but for" analysis, i.e. but for the look-up table, the AutoCAD program would not execute and therefore the look-up table was a "substantial part" of the program. To some degree the course taken in the above passages may reflect the statement by Dawson J that, although the 127-bit look-up table did not itself constitute a computer program within the meaning of the definition because it did not by itself amount to a set of instructions, so that no reliance was placed upon it as a literary work in itself, "there can be no doubt about the originality of authorship of the look-up table expressed as it is in Widget *C*". This may have suggested that what was "original" ought itself to be protected.

However, as Mr Prescott QC has said:

In general, a computer program—any computer program—will not work if even one digit therein is altered or corrupted. It is therefore "essential". But it would be a startling conclusion to hold that not even a single number from a computer program may be copied. If one digit will not infringe, why should 127? Only if it takes substantially more skill and labour to create the 127. But it does not.

In Cantor Fitzgerald International v Tradition (UK) Ltd, Pumfrey J, sitting in the English Patents Court, observed of the reasoning in *Autodesk No 1* that it "would result in any part of any computer program being substantial since without any part the program would not work, or at best not work as desired".

In *Autodesk No 2*, Mason CJ, who dissented, took a different view of the substantiality issue. His Honour thought that the judgment in *Autodesk No 1* should be re-opened in order to hear the respondent's argument as to whether the look-up table was a substantial part of Widget *C*. Mason CJ said:

It is clear that the phrase "substantial part" refers to the quality of what is taken rather than the quantity. In Ladbroke (Football) Ltd v William Hill (Football) Ltd, Lord Pearce stated:

Whether a part is substantial must be decided by its quality rather than its quantity. The reproduction of a part which by itself has no originality will not normally be a substantial part of the copyright and therefore will not be protected. For that which would not attract copyright except by reason of its collocation will, when robbed of that collocation, not be a substantial part of the copyright and therefore the courts will not hold its reproduction to be an infringement. It is this, I think, which is meant by one or two judicial observations that "there is no copyright" in some unoriginal part of a whole that is copyright.

As this statement makes clear, in determining whether the quality of what is taken makes it a "substantial part" of the copyright work, it is important to inquire into the importance which the taken portion bears in relation to the work as a whole: is it an "essential" or "material" part of the work?

In this case, it is argued by the appellants that such an inquiry compels an affirmative answer as the look-up table is essential to the operation of the AutoCAD locking mechanism. Such an argument, however, misconceives the true nature of the inquiry and seeks to re-introduce by another avenue an emphasis upon the copyright work's function. True it is that the look-up table is essential to the functioning of the Auto-CAD lock. However, in the context of copyright law, where emphasis is to be placed upon the "originality" of the work's expression, the essential or material features of a work should be ascertained by considering the originality of the part allegedly taken. This is particularly important in the case of functional works, such as a computer program, or any works which do not attract protection as ends in themselves (e.g., novels, films, dramatic works) but as means to an end (e.g., compilations, tables, logos and devices).

There is great force in the criticism that the "but for" essentiality test which is effectively invoked by the majority in *Autodesk No 2* is not practicable as a test for determining whether something which appears in a computer program is a substantial part of it. For that reason, we prefer Mason CJ's opinion that, in determining whether something is a reproduction of a substantial part of a computer program, the "essential or material features of [the computer program] should be ascertained by considering the originality of the part allegedly taken".

In order for an item in a particular language to be a computer program, it must intend to express, either directly or indirectly, an algorithmic or logical relationship between the function desired to be performed and the physical capabilities of the "device having digital information processing capabilities". It follows that the originality of what was allegedly taken from a computer program must be assessed with respect to the originality with which it expresses that algorithmic or logical relationship or part thereof. The structure of what was allegedly taken, its choice of commands, and its combination and sequencing of commands, when compared, at the same level of abstraction, with the original, would all be relevant to this inquiry.

That being so, a person who does no more than reproduce those parts of a program which are "data" or "related information" and which are irrelevant to its structure, choice of commands and combination and sequencing of commands will be unlikely to have reproduced a substantial part of the computer program. We say "unlikely" and not "impossible" because it is conceivable that the data, considered alone, could be sufficiently original to be a substantial part of the computer program.

It follows that we are unable to agree with the approach to determining "substantiality" which the majority took in *Autodesk No 1* and *Autodesk No 2*. Because of the importance of the question, we think that the Court should re-open the question of what constitutes a substantial part of a computer program. To depart from the reasoning in the *Autodesk* cases does not necessarily mean that the outcomes in those cases were wrong. In our view, the look-up table in Widget *C* was merely data and was not capable of being a substantial part of the AutoCAD program unless the data itself had its own inherent originality. However, re-opening the reasoning in the *Autodesk* cases does not require the Court to express a view on whether the look-up table in that case had its own inherent originality.

Substantiality and the Collocation of the Reserved Words

As they appear in the source code of the Dataflex system, the Reserved Words are irrelevant to the structure, choice of commands and combination and sequencing of the commands in source code. They are merely literal strings which, from the computer's perspective, could be replaced by any other literal string. Accordingly, they are not a substantial part of the Dataflex program as it appears in source code unless they have their own inherent originality.

The evidence is that at least 55 of the Reserved Words are unique to the Dataflex program. When looking at the list of the Reserved Words in respect of which the respondent was held at first instance to be infringing copyright, it can be seen that many of the words are ordinary English words which are suggestive of the function they perform, such as "BOX"; "CHART"; "CHECK"; "CLEAR"; "INDICATOR"; "INSERT"; "LOOP"; "NAME"; "PAD"; "PALETTE"; "PLOT"; "POINTS"; "REQUIRED"; "RETAIN"; "SELECTION"; "STATUS"; "TOTAL" and "UNLOCK".

Others are concatenations of two or more English words which together suggest the function performed, such as "AUTOFIND"; AUTOPAGE"; "AUTORETURN"; "BACKFIELD"; "PAGEBREAK"; "PAGECHECK"; "PAGECOUNT"; "SAVE_GRAPHIC"; "SET_LINE_STYLE"; "SKIPFOUND" and "WINDOWINDEX".

Still other Reserved Words are single words which are in common use in other computer languages such as "DIRECTORY" and "SAVE", or concatenations of other words which are common computer terms such as "FILELIST", "MAKE_FILE", "RUNPROGRAM", and "SAVERECORD". As the Full Court pointed out, even those Reserved Words which are more removed from English usage than the examples above, such as "ENTAGAIN", "KEYPROC", and "MOVEINT", have a function which can be guessed from the English association.

In our opinion, even when the Reserved Words are considered as a collocation, they do not possess sufficient originality as data to constitute a substantial part of the computer program which is the Dataflex system.

4. Does Copyright Subsist in the Table or Compilation of the Reserved Words in the Dataflex User's Guide?

The Reserved Words are contained in the Dataflex User's Guide. The appellant did not submit that any of the Reserved Words themselves were traditional literary works protected by copyright, no doubt because they would face significant hurdles in the form of originality and substantiality. Given that the Reserved Words are arranged in alphabetical order in the Dataflex User's Guide, very little skill or labour was involved in compiling the Reserved Words in the form in which they appear in the User's Guide over and above the sum of the skill and labour involved in devising each individual Reserved Word. As the Full Court said:

> This is not a case where disconnected words are used in a particular order so that the order becomes the linchpin for copyright.

Furthermore, as we have already said, each of the Reserved Words is suggestive of the function it performs. In many cases, it is an ordinary English word, or a concatenation of two or more ordinary English words.

Even if the skill and labour involved in devising each individual Reserved Word is combined and consideration given to the total skill and labour, there may still be a real question as to whether there is sufficient originality for copyright to subsist in the combination. This is so even allowing for the inclusion in the definition of par (b) of "literary work" of a "compilation of computer programs".

The totality of the Reserved Words cannot be protected as a "compilation" within the definition because it requires a "compilation of computer programs" and the Reserved Words are not themselves programs. This does not necessarily preclude them together from protection as constituting a single program, but the set of instructions said to constitute such a program would still require identification. For the reasons leading to the conclusion that each of the Reserved Words does not constitute programs, a collection thereof does not constitute a program. The English letters which make them up are never at any stage executed by the computer. They are not instructions. They never cause a computer to perform a function. Their totality might be considered a "set", but of labels or data, rather than of instructions as required by the definition.

In any event, even if copyright does subsist in the table or compilation of the Reserved Words, we do not think that the respondents have infringed this copyright. The Reserved Words appear in the PFXplus source code program not as an alphabetical list, but as literal strings to which certain commands are assigned.

B. The Macros

The appellant also contends that copyright subsists in what are referred to as "Macros". It contends that each of these commands is a "computer program" within the statutory definition and that Dr Bennett made an adaptation of the Dataflex Macro commands. Consequently, it submits that Dr Bennett infringed the appellant's copyright in them.

Three particular commands in the Dataflex language, "REPORT", "ENTERGROUP" and "ENTER", are described as "Macros" because they cause the performance of a more complex function than any of the other Reserved Words. Executing a Macro command causes a sequence of other functions to be executed, so that the overall effect of performing a more complex function is achieved.

Are the Macros Computer Programs in Dataflex?

It follows from the nature of a "computer program" as defined in §10(1) of the Act that the words assigned to the Macros, comprising as they do one instruction in the Dataflex language, cannot qualify as a "computer program". However, the underlying source code of each Macro may qualify as a "computer program". In practice, the source code underlying each Macro is a small fragment of the source code of the overall Dataflex computer program (the relevant portion was said by the Full Court of the Federal Court to be some 229 lines).

The Full Court said that the question of whether a component part of a computer program is itself a computer program for the purposes of the Act is a question of fact. However, the Full Court went on to say that "[i]f a particular set of instructions is functionally separate from the entirety of the program, then . . . there is no difficulty in treating that set of instructions as being a literary work separate from the balance of the program". Although it did not expressly say so, the Full Court must have considered that the particular set of instructions comprising each Macro was not functionally separate from the remainder of the Dataflex compiler program. This is because it said that "the relevant program to be considered here would not be that small fragment of program which causes the macro command to perform its function (some 229 lines), but the Dataflex compiler program itself".

The Full Court stated no statutory basis for taking a "functionally separate" approach. If there is a statutory basis it must be found in the words of the definition "intended . . . to cause a device having digital information processing capabilities to perform a particular function". If the segment of the larger program in question can be said to have a function which is not merely one of the functions in the set of functions performed by the larger program, but is a separate and distinct particular function, it may be that this segment can be properly viewed as a computer program in and of itself. The *Autodesk* example given by the Full Court would illustrate that kind of distinction. The lock program in Widget *C* had a function (to prevent use of the software unless the correct key was inserted) which was not merely one of the functions in the set of functions performed by the computer aided design program which was AutoCAD.

The Full Court appears to have concluded in this case that as a matter of fact the function performed by the segment of the Dataflex source code which underlies each Macro is merely one of the functions performed by the larger program, and therefore that segment is not a computer program in and of itself. We need not consider that conclusion because even if it is not right and the segment of source code which underlies each Macro is a computer program, there was no reproduction and no adaptation of those works.

Reproduction or Adaptation of the Macros?

The learned trial judge found strong objective similarity between the underlying source code of the PFXplus Macros and the underlying source code of the Dataflex Macros. Jenkinson J did not find that Dr Bennett had reproduced the Dataflex Macros, but instead found that Dr Bennett had "made an adaptation of the expression in I-Code of each of the three sets of instructions". The finding of no reproduction was not challenged; the appellant contended that there was an adaptation.

The meaning of "adaptation" in relation to computer programs, as set out in §10(1) of the Act, is "a version of the work (whether or not in the language, code or notation in which the work was originally expressed) not being a reproduction of the work". In examining the meaning of the word "version", the Full Court referred to the meanings of the word "version" given by the Macquarie Dictionary "2. a translation. 3. a particular form or variant of anything".

The Full Court also quoted the following passages from the Explanatory Memorandum:

11. Copyright in literary works includes exclusive rights to reproduce or adapt such works and computer programs will be treated as literary works. However, the present definition of adaptation in relation to literary works only includes translation, conversion between dramatic and non-dramatic forms, and conversion to a pictorial form.

12. Of these, only translation is likely to be relevant to adaptation of programs and there are legal doubts as to whether this refers only to translations between human languages.

13. The new definition is intended to cover translation either way between the various so-called "high-level programming languages" in which the programs may be written by humans (often called "source code") and languages, codes or notations which actually control computer operations (often called "machine code" or "object code"). Thus "adaptation" is intended, for example, to cover the compilation of a FORTRAN program to produce machine code which will directly control the operation of a computer. Languages, etc of intermediate level would also be covered.

14. It is also possible for a program to be converted from object code into source code, or between different languages of similar level. In some circumstances this process will result largely in a substantial reproduction of the original program. In other cases, however, such as compilation followed by de-compilation, the differences may be so substantial that one cannot speak of a reproduction although the final product is clearly derived from the original. The new definition of adaptation is intended to cover such situations.

The Full Court said:

The evidence is clear that while Dr D Bennett carefully studied the Dataflex program so as to ensure that the PFXplus commands in question performed the same functions as the Dataflex commands, the expression of the source program as written by him was an original expression, albeit having much which was objectively similar to the expression of the source code in the Dataflex program. But it is clear that the process involved no translation from one form or language to another, nor did it involve the kind of process referred to in par 14 of the Explanatory Memorandum involving compilation followed by decompilation, or vice versa. In our view, a process of devising a source code to perform the same function as is performed in some other source code expressed in original language does not involve creating a version of the original source code.

Thus, the Full Court was of the opinion that there needed to be "translation from one form or language to another", or, alternatively, "the kind of process referred to in par 14 of the Explanatory Memorandum involving compilation followed by decompilation, or vice versa" in order for there to be a "version" within the meaning of the statute.

In response to this reasoning, the appellant contends that while the word "version" includes these two processes, it is not limited to these two processes. Furthermore, the appellant argues that the statutory context does not support the approach of the Full Court. It points out that where, in the course of the amendments to the Act that included the definition of "adaptation", Parliament wished to refer to conversion of a program from one language, code or notation to another, it used the word "conversion". The definition of "computer program" contains one example. Furthermore, so the appellant submits, the word "version" is ordinarily used in a much looser sense than that adopted by the Full Court. Ordinarily, it refers to the substance of the work but not the form. Examples are rendering a novel into a play or vice versa or turning a story into a series of pictures.

Paragraph 12 of the Explanatory Memorandum states that "only translation is likely to be relevant to adaptation of programs". This indicates that Parliament did not intend the word "version" to cover situations where, although the functionality of a computer program was copied, original code has been written to perform that function. The focus on translation indicates that Parliament was concerned to ensure that the different languages in which a computer program may be expressed did not provide a means by which copying could occur and infringement be avoided on the ground that the expression in the new language was not a "reproduction".

The use of the words "derived from the original" in par 14 of the Explanatory Memorandum also indicates that the focus is on copying. In accordance with the fundamental principle that copyright protects expression and not ideas, this must relate to the copying of the code (the "expression . . . of a set of instructions"), rather than a copying of the idea or function underlying the code.

There was no adaptation of the Macros.

C. *The Dataflex Huffman Compression Table*

The respondents seek special leave to cross-appeal against the Full Court's finding that they infringed the copyright which the appellant held in the Huffman compression table embedded in the Dataflex program.

Usually, in storing data, all of the 256 characters which a computer recognises are stored in memory as bit strings which are eight bits in length. Huffman compression is a method of reducing the amount of memory space consumed by data files. It stores characters in a data file as bit strings which have a length which relates to the character's frequency of occurrence in the data file. If a character occurs frequently in the data file, it is stored as a bit string of shorter length than a character which occurs infrequently in a data file. . . .

The Huffman algorithm, when expressed in source code, analyses a data file to determine the relative frequency of the occurrence of characters, and then assigns a bit string of appropriate length to each character, depending on its frequency of occurrence. There is no allegation in this case that Dr Bennett copied the source code of the Huffman algorithm from the Dataflex program. Dr Bennett states that he obtained "freely distributable" source code for this purpose.

In about 1992, Mr Cory Casanave created the "standard" or "default" Dataflex Huffman compression table by writing a program which applied the Huffman algorithm to a database file known as SERIAL.DAT. There is also provision in the Dataflex program for users to create their own custom Huffman compression tables. This enables the user to compress the data in his or her files with reference to the frequency of occurrence of characters in the actual file to be compressed, rather than with reference to the frequency of occurrence of characters in the file SERIAL.DAT. It appears that SERIAL.DAT simply served the purpose of being a representative sample of data which would suffice for standard compressions. If the user wanted the greater efficiency which would flow from the compression table actually being derived from the data in the file to be compressed, custom compression could be used.

Dr Bennett wished PFXplus to be able to compress and decompress Dataflex files, and vice versa, when standard compression was used. Consequently, he needed to be able to replicate precisely the default Huffman compression table used in Dataflex. Dr Bennett did not have access to the file SERIAL.DAT. For that reason, he could not replicate the Huffman table simply by applying the Huffman algorithm to that file. His evidence is that he refrained from "decompiling or looking inside the Dataflex runtime", and instead carried out the following process:

> The process I eventually devised was as follows. First I obtained a program which would dump out the contents of a file in bits, rather than the more usual hex dump.
>
> I then wrote a small Dataflex program which would create an empty database file using Standard compression, and would then add 256 records to the file. The records had the following appearance:
>
> AEAEAEAEAEAEAEA!AEAEAEAEAEAEAEAAEA
> AEAEAEAEAEAEAEA@AEAEAEAEAEAEAEAAEA
> AEAEAEAEAEAEAEA#AEAEAEAEAEAEAEAAEA
> AEAEAEAEAEAEAEA$AEAEAEAEAEAEAEAAEA
> AEAEAEAEAEAEAEA%AEAEAEAEAEAEAEAAEA
> and so on, for a total of 256 records.
>
> The position in the middle could be occupied by one of 256 possible characters, and the program cycled through all 256 possibilities. I knew that the pattern of AE repeated would create a distinctive and reproducible bit pattern in the Huffman encoding, to act as a background. It would then be possible to make out the single changed character, standing out in relief against the background.
>
> I ran the program, dumped the output to a file using the bit dump program, and printed out the result. I then marked out the 256 bit strings by pencil. . . . I found that they did indeed stand out well against the background. This process took just a few hours.

By this process, Dr Bennett deduced the bit string for each of the 256 characters as it appeared in the standard Dataflex compression table. This enabled him to create an identical table for use in PFXplus. . . .

In our opinion, the Dataflex Huffman table is a table expressed in figures and symbols, and falls squarely within the statutory definition of a "literary work". The reference in the Explanatory Memorandum to "data . . . stored in a computer as a table" clearly describes the Dataflex Huffman table. The Dataflex Huffman table is similar to the look-up table in Widget *C* which, in *Autodesk No 1,* Dawson J considered was a "literary work" within the meaning of the above definition. His Honour thought this was so even though no reliance was placed on that point by *Autodesk.*

For copyright to subsist in the standard Dataflex Huffman table, it must be an "original literary . . . work". As we have indicated, the requirement that a work be "original" in copyright law is a requirement that "the work emanates from the person claiming to be its author, in the sense that he has originated it or brought it into existence and has not copied it from another". At first instance, Jenkinson J found that "[t]he use of the Huffman system to produce a compression table requires the employment of substantial skill and judgment and a very great deal of hard work". The Full Court agreed with this finding.

The skill and judgment employed by Dataflex was perhaps more directed to writing the program setting out the Huffman algorithm and applying this program to a representative sample of data than to composing the bit strings in the Huffman table. Nevertheless, the standard Dataflex Huffman table emanates from Dataflex as a result of substantial skill and judgment. That being so, the Full Court was correct in holding that the standard Dataflex Huffman table constituted an original literary work.

In addition, in our opinion the Full Court was correct in holding that the process undertaken by Dr Bennett constituted a "reproduction" of the standard Dataflex Huffman table. The fact that Dr Bennett used an ingenious method of determining the bit string assigned to each character does not make the output of such a process any less a "reproduction" than if Dr Bennett had sat down with a print-out of the table and copy-typed it into the PFXplus program.

The finding that the respondents infringed the appellant's copyright in the Huffman table embedded in the Dataflex program may well have considerable practical consequences. Not only may the finding affect the relations between the parties to these proceedings, it may also have wider ramifications for anyone who seeks to produce a computer program that is compatible with a program produced by others. These are, however, matters that can be resolved only by the legislature reconsidering and, if it thinks it necessary or desirable, rewriting the whole of the provisions that deal with copyright in computer programs.

COMMENTS AND QUESTIONS

1.   Consider how differently the court in *Powerflex* deals with the command language and macro issues than did the First Circuit in the Lotus v. Borland case in Chapter 2. Which decision is more persuasive?

2.   The High Court's *Powerflex* decision calls into question the reasoning of Autodesk Inc. v. Dyason (1992), 173 C.L.R. 330, 176 C.L.R. 300, an earlier Australian software copyright case that had a substantial influence on the lower court's decision in *Powerflex*. The *Autodesk* court had determined that a "look-up table," though not itself a computer program, was a "substantial part" of a computer program such that reproduction of this table was an infringement of the copyright of the computer program of which it was a part. How significant is this critique of *Autodesk* for other software copyright issues arising in Australia or elsewhere?

4.   Copyright in Computer Programs in Canada

In Delrina Corp. v. Triolet Systems Inc., [2002] O.A.C. TBEd. MR.003, the Ontario Court of Appeals addressed the scope of protection for non-literal elements of computer programs. The lower court quoted at length from Computer Associates v. Altai, essentially adopting its abstraction-filtration-comparison standard. On appeal, the plaintiff argued that this approach conflicted with Canadian copyright principles, which call for assessing copyrightability based upon the work as a whole and judging infringement on whether the defendant has copied a substantial part of the whole. Canadian courts follow the standard set forth in Ladbroke (Football) Ltd. v. William Hill (Football), Ltd., [1964] 1 All E.R. 465 (H.L.), in which the British House of Lords stated:

> Did the appellants reproduce a substantial part of it? Whether a part is substantial must be decided by its quality rather than its quantity. *The reproduction of a part which by itself has no originality will not normally be a substantial part of the copyright and therefore will not be protected. For that which would not attract copyright except by reason of its collocation will, when robbed of that collocation, not be a substantial part of the copyright and therefore the courts will not hold its reproduction to be an infringement.* It is this, I think, which is meant by one or two judicial observations that "there is no copyright" in some unoriginal part of a whole that is copyright. They afford no justification, in my view, for holding that one starts the inquiry as to whether copyright exists by dissecting the compilation into component parts instead of starting it by regarding the compilation as a whole and seeing whether the whole has copyright. *It is when one is debating whether the part reproduced is substantial that one considers the pirated portion on its own.*

See *Delrina* ¶24 (citing *Ladbroke* at 481; emphasis added by Ontario Court of Appeals).

Although recognizing that Canadian copyright law does not break down a work into constituent parts and assess each part's copyrightability separately, the Court of Appeals nonetheless articulated a test that would appear to achieve the same results as the *Altai* standard. Under the *Delrina* standard, the court first asks whether the plaintiff's work is copyrighted—whether it is fixed, original, and a work of the type defined in the Copyright Act). If so, the court then considers whether the defendant's work is a "substantial" copy of the plaintiff's. In determining substantiality, the court disregards copied elements of the work lacking originality, dictated by functional considerations, or otherwise not protectable by copyright (e.g., because they constitute an idea). In essence, the court filters and compares the works simultaneously. Thus, the Canadian standard requires that the court analyze only those elements that are common to both works. The net result, however, would appear to be identical to *Altai*. See Wendy Gross and Andrew Bernstein, The Same, Only Different: The Status of the Abstraction-Filtration-Comparison Test in Ontario (Delrina v. Triolet).

Does this approach offer analytical or practical advantages to the *Altai* formulation? Disadvanatges?

C. PATENTS

Patents are widely used to protect computer hardware throughout the world and are increasingly being used to protect software-related inventions. According to one source, "[m]ore than 70 of the 176 countries in the world that grant patents permit the patenting of software related inventions, at least to some degree."[8] This report suggests that there has been a worldwide trend toward greater protection of software by patents. This trend has accelerated since the TRIPS Agreement,[9] even though there is no express mention of computer software in the patent provisions of TRIPS.

The TRIPS Agreement incorporates many provisions of the Paris Convention by reference and transforms them into minimum standards of patent protection for member states of the WTO. In addition, the TRIPS Agreement contains a number of other patent substantive minima. For example, Article 27(1) of TRIPS states that "patents shall be available for any inventions, whether products or processes, in all fields of technology, provided that they are new, involve an inventive step, and are capable of industrial application." Those who favor patent protection for program-related inventions may perceive in this provision a requirement that WTO member nations must grant patent protection to program inventions. After all, computer programs would seem to be part of a "field of technology." However, only a minority of patent-granting states presently provide patent protection to program-related inventions, and those that do have varying standards for what program-related inventions are patentable. Because of this, it is far from clear that TRIPS mandates patent protection for such inventions. Two prominent academic commentators, one a specialist in international trade and the other a specialist in intellectual property, have expressed doubts that a WTO panel would find a violation of TRIPS in a member state's denial of patent protection to software-related inventions. See Rochelle C. Dreyfuss & Andreas Lowenfeld, Two Achievements of the Uruguay Round: Putting TRIPS and Dispute Settlement Together, 37 Va. J. Int'l L. 275 (1997). Over time, if patents for program-related inventions become more widely accepted and international consensus arises, TRIPS may eventually encompass an obligation to make patent protection for program-related inventions available. However, this may not occur soon.

Among those countries and regions that do protect computer program-related inventions, there are varying standards and tests for patentability. The Taiwanese Patent Office, for example, has adopted an approach consistent with the rule in the United States in the 1980s: hardware inventions that utilize software may be patented, but pure software inventions may not be. In Japan, mathematical algorithms, such as the Karmarkar linear programming algorithm that received patent protection in the United States, have been denied patent protection, even when the claims have been limited to certain industrial applications. Relatively common in the international community has been a requirement that a software-related invention represent a "technical solution" to an industrial problem or achieve "a technical effect" —for example, by enabling faster operations in a computer or more efficient execution of a chemical process. The Japanese Patent Office (JPO) has issued new guidelines concerning computer-related inventions, however, and its attitude may be changing.

Typical of the intermediate approach is the policy and practice of the European Patent Office (EPO). The EPO, it should be noted, is constrained to a signifi-

8. Fenwick & West LLP, 1999 Update: International Legal Protection for Software at 18. The Fenwick & West annual update, which includes a chart identifying the countries that offer patent protection to program-related inventions, can be found on the Web at <http://www.softwareprotection .com>.

9. *Id.*

cant degree by the European Patent Convention (EPC), which established the Office and under which the Office operates. The EPC mirrors the national laws of a number of European nations in its exclusion of computer programs from patent protection. Because several of the EPC exclusions may affect program-related inventions, it is worth reviewing both what is and is not patentable under the EPC. Article 52 of that treaty provides as follows:

> (1) European patents shall be granted for any inventions which are susceptible of industrial application, which are new and which involve an inventive step.
> (2) The following in particular shall not be regarded as inventions within the meaning of paragraph 1:
>   (a) discoveries, scientific theories, and mathematical methods;
>   (b) aesthetic creations;
>   (c) schemes, rules and methods for performing mental acts, playing games or doing business, and programs for computers;
>   (d) presentations of information.

This does not, however, mean that computer program-related inventions can never be patented in Europe. If patent applications are drawn with some care, program inventors can often obtain significant protection from the EPO.

The EPO Guidelines on the patentability of computer program-related inventions set forth the following criteria:

(1) A computer-related "invention" is a patentable invention if the real contribution which the alleged invention, when considered as a whole, adds to the known art is of a technical character;

(2) The "invention" issue is separate and distinct from the issues of novelty, inventiveness, and industrial applicability;

(3) A computer program (i.e., a list of instructions for a computer per se) is excluded from patentability. This ban must be seen as extending to computer instructions recorded on an ordinary computer disk, loaded on to an ordinary computer, or implemented through physical alteration of the circuitry of a computer;

(4) Nonetheless, an alleged invention featuring a program and which represents a technical process (e.g., a program-controlled manufacturing process) or which has a technical effect (e.g., a program which increases the working memory of a computer) must be seen as making a technical contribution and patentable.

Although the legal force of the Guidelines has been eroded by some recent decisions of the EPO, and the EPO's more recent interpretation of the EPC rules has brought the EPO closer to the U.S. and Japanese standards for software-related patents, a review of some of the older cases provides a better understanding of the evolution of the law on these matters in the EU. Application of the EPC rules was at issue in the case that follows.

IBM/Text Processing
European Patent Office, Technical Board of Appeal 3.5.1
T65/86 (1989)

Claim 1 is worded as follows:

1. A method for automatically detecting and correcting contextual homophone errors in a text document, in a text processing system comprising a processor (11) with a memory (23) and a process execution unit (24), a keyboard (10) with graphic symbol keys and control keys including a display cursor control key and a data enter key, said keyboard being connected to the input (21) of said processor (11) for entering data into a keystroke queue portion (26) of said memory (23), a text buffer portion (27) of said memory (23) being connected to said keystroke queue portion (26) for receiving data therefrom, and a display refresh buffer (12) connected to the output (23) of said processor (11) for controlling the generation of characters on a screen (40) of a display device (14) said method being *characterised in that* it includes the steps of:

a) defining sets of homophones and storing, under control of said execution unit (24), said sets of homophones in a portion (31) of said memory (23);

b) defining contextual characteristics for each said homophones and storing, under control of said execution unit (24), said characteristics in a portion (32) of said memory (23);

c) storing in a portion (34) of said memory (23) a set of data segments related to each homophone;

d) entering from said keyboard (10) a text document into said text buffer portion (27) and said display refresh buffer (12) for displaying by said display device (14);

e) controlling said execution unit (24) of said processor (11) to scan word-by-word the contents of said display refresh buffer (12) and to compare each scanned word to the said sets of homophones stored in said memory portion (31), in order to determine whether homophones are present in said display refresh buffer (12);

f) controlling said execution unit (24) to compare the data segments surrounding each homophone found in step (e) to the defined contextual characteristics stored in portion (32) for the homophone;

g) highlighting on said display device (14) each homophone whose surrounding data segments do not compare with said defined contextual characteristics;

h) controlling said executive unit (24) to access those sets of data segments stored in said memory portion (34), and related to said highlighted homophones, and to cause said display device (14) to display said sets of data segments;

i) moving said display cursor, through actuation of said cursor control key, underneath a data segment selected among the displayed set of data segments related to an highlighted homophone;

j) actuating said data enter key on the keyboard (10) to cause said cursored data segment to be substituted for the highlighted homophone in the said text document.

Claims 2 to 5 are dependent on Claim 1.

Reasons for the Decision

2. As can be seen from the opening words of Claim 1, the claim is directed to a method for automatically detecting and correcting contextual homophone errors in a text document. A 'contextual homophone error' occurs when one of a number of confusable words, such as 'affect' and 'effect' for example, has been used in an inappropriate context. In the opinion of the Board, a contextual homophone error is a purely linguistic error and has no technical significance at all.

3. Claim 1 goes on to specify that the method is carried out in a text process-ing system comprising a processor with a memory and a process execution unit, a keyboard with graphic symbol keys and control keys including a display cursor con-trol key and a data enter key, said keyboard being connected to the input of said processor for entering data into a keystroke queue portion of said memory, a text buffer portion of said memory being connected to said keystroke queue portion for receiving portion data therefrom, and display refresh buffer connected to the out-put of said processor for controlling the generation of characters on a screen of a display device. The appellant does not dispute the fact that the above mentioned hardware is conventional.

4. In step (a) of Claim 1, namely 'defining sets of homophones and storing, under control or said execution unit (24), said sets of homophones in a portion (31) of said memory (23);' information required solely for linguistic purposes is entered and stored in a manner which is conventional from a technical point of view.

5. In step (b) of Claim 1, namely 'defining contextual characteristics for each said homophone and storing, under control of said execution unit (24), said characteristics in a portion (32) of said memory (23);' information required solely for linguistic purposes is entered and stored in a manner which is conventional from a technical point of view.

6. In step (c) of Claim 1, namely 'storing a portion (34) of said memory (23) a set of data segments related to each homophone,' information required solely for linguistic purposes is entered and stored in a manner which is conventional from a technical point of view.

7. In step (d) of Claim 1, namely 'entering, from said keyboard (10) a text document into said text buffer portion (27) and said display refresh buffer (12) for displaying by said display device (14);' information required solely for linguistic purposes is entered and stored in a manner which is conventional from a technical point of view.

8. In step (e) of Claim 1, namely 'controlling said execution unit (24) of said processor (11) to scan word-by-word the contents of said display refresh buffer (12) and to compare each scanned word to the sets of homophones stored in said mem-ory portion (31), in order to determine whether homophones are present in said

display refresh buffer (12);' data are compared in a manner which is conventional from a technical point of view for the sole purpose of determining whether the data in the display refresh buffer meet certain purely linguistic criteria.

9. In step (f) of Claim 1, namely 'controlling the execution unit (24) to compare the data segments surrounding each homophone found in step (c) to defined contextual characteristics stored in portion (32) for the homophone;' data are compared in a manner which is conventional from a technical point of view for the sole purpose of determining whether the data in the display refresh buffer meet certain purely linguistic criteria.

10. In step (g) of Claim 1, namely 'highlighting on said display device (14) each homophone whose surrounding data segments do not compare with said define contextual characteristics;' the outcome of the comparisons performed in step (f) is displayed to the operator in manner which is conventional from a technical point of view. The information displayed is required solely for linguistic purposes, namely to indicate to the operator those of the detected homophones which are suspected of being incorrectly used.

11. In step (h) of Claim 1, namely 'controlling said execution unit (24) to access those sets of data segments stored in said memory portion (34), and related to said highlighted homophones, and to cause the display device (14) to display said sets of data segments;' information which is required solely for linguistic purposes, namely to assist the operator in selecting a homophonic for inclusion in the text, is retrieved and displayed in a manner which is conventional from a technical point of view.

12. In step (i) of Claim 1, namely 'moving said display cursor through actuation of said cursor control key, underneath a data segment selected among the displayed set of data segments related to a highlighted homophone;' the actual selection is made by the operator using only his skill and judgment. The selection of one of several displayed options by positioning the cursor under it is conventional from a technical point of view.

13. In step (j) of Claim 1, namely 'actuating said data entry key on the keyboard (10) to cause said cursored data segment to be substituted for the highlighted homophone in the said text document,' one item of data having only linguistic significance is replaced by another item of data having only linguistic significance. This is done in a manner which is conventional from a technical point of view.

14. It seems to the Board that a person who wishes to detect and correct homophone errors in a text document, doing everything by himself with pencil and paper, would have to proceed in a similar way and follow the same sequence of steps (a) to (j) as described in Claim 1, but without using the technical facilities described there he would:

(A) define sets of homophones and either hold them in his head or write them down;

(B) define contextual characteristics for each of said homophones and either hold them in his head or write them down;

(C) ascertain possible replacement words and their correct meanings and usage for each of said homophones and either hold them in his head or write them down;

(D) take up a text document to be checked and

(E)   scan it word by word, comparing each scanned word with the sets of homophones defined in step (A) to determine whether any homophones are present in the text document;

(F)   compare the words surrounding each homophone found in step (E) with the contextual characteristics defined in step (B) for that homophone;

(G)   mark on the text document each homophone whose surrounding words do not satisfy said defined contextual characteristics;

(H)   consider the possible word(s) and their correct meanings and usage for each of said marked homophones;

(I)   choose a replacement word and

(J)   substitute the chosen word for the marked word in the text document.

15.   Processing in this way, the said person would only use his skill and judgment and would consequently perform purely mental acts within the meaning of Article 52(2)(c) EPC. The schemes, rules and methods, that is, the steps as enumerated under the foregoing items (A) and (J), for performing these mental acts are not inventions within the meaning of Article 52 (1) EPC.

16.   The Board recognises that the use of technical means for carrying out a method, partly or entirely without human intervention, which method, if performed by a human being, would require him to perform mental acts, *may*, having regard to Article 52(3) EPC, render such a method a technical process or method and therefore an invention within the meaning of Article 52(1) EPC, that is, one which is not excluded from patentability under Article 52(2) (c) EPC. This is because paragraph 3 of Article 52 EPC makes it clear that patentability is excluded only to the extent to which the patent application relates to excluded subject-matter or activities as such. In the opinion of the Board, while it follows that the EPC does not prohibit the patenting of inventions consisting of a mix of excluded and non-excluded features (in conformity with T26/86 (J) EPO, 1988, 19) it does not necessarily follow that all such mixes are patentable. Since patentability is excluded only to the extent to which the patent application relates to excluded subject-matter or activities as such, it appears to be the intention of the EPC to permit patenting in those cases in which the invention involves some contribution to the art in a field not excluded from patentability. In other words, inventions involving such a contribution must be considered to constitute inventions within the meaning of paragraph 1 of Article 52 EPC.

17.   In the opinion of the Board, paragraph 1 of Article 52 EPC, as qualified by paragraphs 2 and 3 of that Article, states in effect that European patents shall be granted for any inventions (except those excluded by virtue of paragraphs 2 and 3 of Article 52 EPC) which are susceptible of industrial application, which are new and which involve an inventive step.

18.   The method claimed in Claim 1 of the present application does not appear to involve an inventive step. Once the step of the method for performing the mental acts in question (enumerated under the foregoing item 14) have been defined, the implementation of the technical means to be used in those steps, at least at the level of generality specified in Claim 1, involves no more than the straightforward application of conventional techniques of entering, storing, retrieving and comparing data, displaying, highlighting and selecting options from a menu, and must therefore be considered to be obvious to a person skilled in the technical art.

19. Although a computer program is not expressly recited in Claim 1, it is clear to a reader skilled in the art that the claim covers the case in which a computer program is used and, indeed, in the only embodiment disclosed in the application the text processing system is controlled by a set of programs and data stored in the memory.

20. The overall effect of the method claimed in Claim 1 is that signals representing one linguistic expression in the text document are replaced with signals representing another linguistic expression. These signals are not different from a technical point of view. They differ only in that they represent different linguistic expressions, which are purely abstract expressions without any technical significance. The overall effect of the method is thus not technical.

21. The present case is therefore distinguishable from the previous Decisions T208/84* (VICOM, OJ EPO, 1987, 14) and T26/86† (X-ray apparatus, OJ EPO, 1988, 19). In T208/84* the claimed method is patentable, even though it could be carried out by known hardware suitably programmed, because it makes a contribution in a field not excluded namely a more efficient restoration or enhancement of the technical quality of an image. Similarly, in T26/86† the claimed apparatus is patentable, even though the X-ray apparatus without the computer program was known, because it makes a contribution in a field not excluded from patentability, namely controlling the X-ray tubes so that optimum exposure is obtained with adequate protection against overloading of the X-ray tubes.

22. In the opinion of the Board, the method according to Claim 1 of the present application does not contribute to the art anything involving an inventive step within the meaning of Article 56 EPC in a field not excluded from patentability by Article 52(2)(c) EPC.

23. It follows that Claim 1 cannot be accepted. The same applies to the dependent Claims 2 to 5, which concern further details of steps (b), (c) and (h), according to which only conventional operations are performed on non-technical data. These claims do not include anything which could involve an inventive step in a field not excluded from patentability by Article 52(2)(c) EPC.

24. As far as the disclosed embodiment is concerned, some of its hardware is explicitly acknowledged to be conventional. Near the bottom of page 4, it says: 'The microprocessor may be an IBM Series 1, INTEL model 8086, or any of the functionally equivalent, currently available microprocessors.' On page 5, line 14, it says: 'The printer may be any suitable printer known in the art.' The description of the remaining hardware is not very detailed and does not mention any feature which is not conventional, it being assumed in the application that a person skilled in the art would know of suitable devices which may be used. The manner in which the hardware devices are interconnected is indicated only in a very general way. The required functions and interactions are achieved by means of programs and data stored in the memory.

25. While it cannot be denied that there is an interaction between the programs and the hardware, since the programs without the hardware or the hardware without the programs could do nothing, but together they make it possible to perform the method claimed in Claim 1, this fact alone cannot confer patentability on either the method or the apparatus. Since the only conceivable use for a computer program is the running of it on a computer, the exclusion from patentability of programs for computers would be effectively undermined if it could be circumvented by including in the claim a reference to conventional hardware features, such

as a processor, memory, keyboard and display, which, in practice, are indispensable if the program is to be used at all. In the opinion of the Board, in such cases patentability must depend on whether the operations performed involve an inventive step in a field not excluded from patentability by Article 52(2) EPC.

26. In the present case, all the operations performed are conventional from a technical point of view and amount to no more than the processing of abstract data, for a non-technical purpose, by means of computer programs running on conventional hardware. The Board has found nothing in the claims, description and drawings of the present application which could be regarded as making a contribution to the art in a field which is not excluded from patentability by Article 52(2)(c) EPC.

In the opinion of the Board, therefore, the present application must be refused.

COMMENTS AND QUESTIONS

1. How plausible is it that someone using pen and paper—or her memory—would solve the problem in the same way? Is it really logical to talk about the algorithms at issue here as "mental steps"? If the goal is to prevent a patent that could be infringed by thinking "patented thoughts," this invention seems fairly low-risk.

2. Suppose IBM had built a machine to do the same thing. Is there any question that such a machine *would* be patentable subject matter? Is the EPC simply adopting metaphysical distinctions that once burdened U.S. law?

3. Is IBM entitled to *any* form of intellectual property protection for its invention? Would a broad interpretation of copyright law allow it to recoup its investment? If so, is copyright a better vehicle than patent for protecting this sort of creativity? Cf. Pamela Samuelson et al., A Legal Manifesto Concerning the Protection of Computer Programs, 94 Colum. L. Rev. 2308 (1994) (suggesting "gap-filling" protection between patent and copyright).

As you read the case that follows and compare it to the previous case, keep in mind the evolution of software-related patents in the United States, discussed in Chapter 3.

≣
≣ *Petterson/Queuing System*
≣ **European Patent Office, Technical Board of Appeal 3.4.1**
≣ **T1002/92 (1994)**

I. The respondent is proprietor of European patent No. 0 086 199. Claim 1 as granted reads as follows:

1. System for determining the queue sequence for serving customers at a plurality of service points comprising a turn-number allocating unit (4) for allocating a turn-number to every customer desiring to be served, a plurality of terminals (31, 32, 33, 34), one for each service point, and an information unit (2) receiving signals identifying the particular turn-number to be served and the particular free service point for indicat-

ing them to the customers, *characterised in that* the system comprises a selection unit (5) associated with the turn-number allocating unit (4) in a turn-number device (1), enabling customers to select a desired service point among said plurality of service points, computing means (6) for memorising the sequence of allocated turn-numbers with the selected desired service points, for receiving from the plurality of terminals (31, 32, 33, 34) signals identifying a particular service point which is free for serving a customer, for deciding which particular turn-number is to be served at the particular free service point and for feeding-out signals identifying this particular turn-number and the particular free service point to the information unit (2), the particular turn-number to be served being the next in turn in the memorised sequence of allocated turn-numbers for which no desired service point is selected or for which the selected desired service point is the particular free service point.

. . . The appellant (opponent) requested that the decision under appeal be set aside and that the European patent No. 0 086 199 be revoked. The respondent (patentee) requested that the appeal be dismissed and that the patent be maintained as granted.

Reasons for the Decision

1. Relationship between Article 52 EPC and Article 56 EPC

. . . [T]he appellant submitted in the Grounds of Appeal that the subject-matter of Claim 1 is a scheme, rule or method of doing business within the meaning of Article 52(2)(c) EPC, because the apparatus features of the claim are in very general terms corresponding to the steps of a method, which would be unpatentable, and such apparatus does not contribute anything more to the art than the method.

The submission was further developed during the oral hearing, when it was emphasised that the only feature in Claim 1 which was not disclosed in the Malmö [reference] prior to use was that set out in the last lines of the claim (column 7, lines 41 to 46), and that the feature was not a technical feature, so that the claimed subject-matter did not involve 'some contribution to the art in a field not excluded from patentability'.

In the Board's view, these submissions result from a misinterpretation of the relationship between Articles 52 and 56 EPC. In a case such as the present, a first question to be considered is whether the appellant is correct in his contention that the subject-matter of Claim 1 does not constitute an 'invention' within the meaning of Article 52(1) EPC. If, contrary to the appellant's contention, such subject-matter is not excluded from being patentable under Article 52 EPC, a further and separate question, also raised by the appellant, is whether the claimed subject-matter involves an inventive step.

2. Articles 52(2)(c) and (3) EPC

Article 52(2) EPC excludes patentability under the EPC for certain categories of 'subject-matter or activities as such', which are set out in sub-paragraphs (a) to

(d) of Article 52(2) EPC. A common characteristic of such excluded categories is that their subject-matter is abstract in nature. In the present case the appellant has submitted that the apparatus system claimed in Claim 1 constitutes in effect a scheme, rule or method for doing business, which is one of the excluded categories. The Board does not accept this submission. The claimed apparatus is clearly technical in nature, and has practical application to the service of 'customers'. The fact that one such practical application of such apparatus concerns the service of customers of 'a business equipment' does not mean that the claimed subject-matter must be equated with a method of doing business, as such.

Thus in the Board's judgment the claimed subject matter is not excluded from patentability under Article 52(2) and (3) EPC. This conclusion is also supported by the following detailed considerations.

2.2 The wording of Claim 1 leaves no doubt that protection is sought for a 'system which is capable to determine the queue sequence of customers', and thus for a three-dimensional object with the aforementioned capacities. Claim 1 explicitly indicates that this system comprises: 'a turn-number allocation unit, a selection unit, terminals, an information unit and computing means'. Hence, the wording employed in the claim defines a technical item with at least five constructional components, which item clearly belongs to the category of an apparatus. Each of the five components is characterised in terms of its functions. In the present case, such a broad claiming is justified on the basis of the disclosed embodiments and examples. As generally recognised, a characterisation of an apparatus component by its function does not *per se* transform the corresponding claim feature into a measure which a user will exercise onto this apparatus component.

2.3 Among the functions indicated in Claim 1, there is a first group which can be exclusively interpreted as apparatus properties inherent to the corresponding system component. This first group consists of the following functions: 'Allocating a turn-number to every customer desiring to be served' is a property of the 'turn-number allocating unit'. 'Receiving signals identifying the particular turn-number to be served and the free service point for indicating them to the customers' is an attribute of the 'information unit'. 'Enabling customers to select a desired service point among said plurality of service points' is a function of the 'selection unit'. 'Memorising the sequence of allocated turn-numbers with the selected desired service point' is a hardware property of the 'computing means'. 'Receiving from the plurality of terminals signals identifying a particular service point which is free for serving a customer' specifies the circuit interconnection between terminal outputs and the input of the computing means. 'Feeding out signals identifying the particular turn-number and the particular free service point to the information unit' characterises the circuit interconnection between the output of the computing means and the input of the information unit. The above-mentioned functions do not correspond technically to the steps of a method, and therefore the true nature of the subject-matter of Claim 1 when considered as a whole cannot be interpreted as a method for doing business as such.

2.4 There remains only one more function in Claim 1. It describes the basic working principle of the claimed computing means: 'deciding which particular turn-number is to be served at the particular free service point' according to the rule: 'the particular turn-number to be served being the next in turn in the memorised sequence of allocated turn-numbers for which no desired service point is selected or (next in turn) for which the selected desired service point is the particular free service point'. In the Board's view only this functional term in Claim 1 is of an ambiguous nature in that it is a step of a method for doing business which may be performed by a mental act as well as a hardware capacity of the computing means, which allows the achievement of the intended technical result by the claimed subject-matter without human intervention. The activation of the selection unit by a customer and that of a terminal by a person attending the terminal are not to be considered as human interventions in a method of doing business, but as manual inputs of control data and trigger signals into a technical system. Taking Claim 1 as a whole, it is clear to the skilled reader that the above functional term is not an independent constituent underlying the entire claim, which can be examined on its own merits as an intellectual concept. The wording of Claim 1 links this functional term logically with the remaining technical features of the claim in an inseparable way, in that it is indispensable for achieving the intended technical result disclosed in the description column 1, lines 37 to 45. Hence, within the overall teaching of Claim 1, the nature of the above functional term is limited to a hardware property. Claim 1 excludes, in the Board's opinion, any interpretation of the above functional term as a step of an unpatentable method for doing business, and only allows the understanding of this functional term as a computer program according to which the claimed hardware operates.

2.5 Any interpretation of the above functional term as a step of an unpatentable method contradicts the integral technical information which the skilled reader derives from the total claim wording and would be the result of an interpretation of claim features in isolation from the remaining wording of the claim. In the Board's view, such an interpretation out of its context disregards the explicitly claimed technical co-operation between the claimed features, changes the disclosed nature of a particular feature and is therefore not justified.

2.6 As results from the above analysis, Claim 1 is directed to an apparatus which comprises, *inter alia*, computer hardware operating according to a particular computer program. The program-determined output signal of the hardware is used for an automatic control of the operation of another system component (information unit) and thus solves a problem which is completely of a technical nature. In such a case—according to the case law established by the Boards of Appeal—a mix of technical and non-technical elements shall not be excluded from patentability under Article 52(2) and (3) EPC. For this reason Claim 1 is allowed.

2.7 During the proceedings before the Opposition Division, the opponent relied on the fact that, in response to an opposition against the Swedish priority application in Sweden on the ground that the subject-matter was not patentable, the Swedish Patent Office rejected the application. In appeal proceedings, the Swedish Court of Patent Appeals also rejected the application. In a further appeal, the Swedish Supreme Administrative Court also rejected the application. The claims of the Swedish application were essentially in respect of the same subject-matter as the claims of the patent in suit. The ground of rejection of the Swedish application essentially corresponded to the ground of objection under Article 52(2) and (3) EPC against the patent in suit.

Although this history of the corresponding Swedish application was not specifically relied on by the opponent during the proceedings before the Board of Appeal, nevertheless in deference to the views expressed in support of the rejection of the Swedish application by the Swedish Patent Office, the Court of Patent Appeals and the Supreme Administrative Court, and in view of the object of harmonising patent protection within the Contracting States which underlies the EPC, the Board makes the following observations.

2.8 The Board notes that both the Swedish Patent Office and the Court of Patent Appeal regarded the subject-matter of the Swedish application as constituting a solution to a problem which was not of a technical nature, and therefore unpatentable. Although the supreme Administrative Court confirmed the rejection of the application, its judgment included a dissenting opinion.

Since the issue of these decisions in Sweden between 1983 and 1987, the case law of the Boards of Appeal concerning the interpretation of Article 52 EPC has been developed, and has been matched by corresponding development of the law in Sweden, as shown in the judgment of the Supreme Administrative Court issued on 13 June 1990 in a case concerning an application by N.V. Philips Glocilampenfabricken. This judgment indicates that earlier Swedish case law, at the time of the above-identified decisions on the corresponding Swedish application, had deviated from the EPO case law.

Having regard to what is now established case law within the Boards of Appeal, and for the reasons set out in detail above, the Board does not agree with the reasoning which led to the rejection of the corresponding Swedish application.

COMMENTS AND QUESTIONS

1. Can this decision be reconciled with the previous one? What explains why this application receives a patent, but the IBM application didn't?

2. Why does it matter under the EPC whether an object is "three-dimensional"? Is it less likely to involve mathematics or mental steps if it is built in three dimensions? The formalism of this distinction is reminiscent of the U.S. rules for design patents, which grant protection to computer icons only if the entire computer is drawn, rather than merely the icon itself.

3. Are the EPC rules any less subject to evasion by artful drafting of patent claims than were the U.S. rules set out in Diamond v. Diehr?

Recent decisions of the EPO have continued the evolution of European computer patents toward greater harmony with the current U.S. model. Two of the most important of these decisions are discussed in the following excerpt.

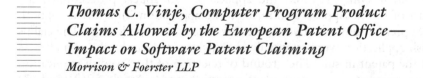

Thomas C. Vinje, Computer Program Product Claims Allowed by the European Patent Office— Impact on Software Patent Claiming
Morrison & Foerster LLP

The Board of Appeal of the European Patent Office (EPO) recently rendered two important decisions relating to the patentability of software inventions in Europe. Both cases relate to patent applications filed by IBM Corporation. In these cases, the Board of Appeal decided in favor of computer program product claims (similar to those allowed in In re Beauregard, 53 F. 3d 1583 (Fed. Cir. 1995)). These decisions nullify, and reverse, a passage in the Guidelines for Examination in the European Patent Office, where it is stated that a computer program claimed by itself or as a record on a carrier is not patentable irrespective of its contents.

Under the reasoning of the Board, a computer program claimed by itself is not excluded from patentability if the program, when running on a computer or loaded into a computer, brings about, or is capable of bringing about, a technical effect which goes beyond the "normal" physical interactions between the program (software) and the computer (hardware) on which it is run. In addition, the Board said that it does not make any difference whether a computer program is claimed by itself or as a record on a carrier.

These decisions offer significant new patent protection for software, especially for a software-implemented invention which is supplied or downloaded over the Internet.

Background of the EPO Statutes on Computer Software

A threshold condition for patentability in the EPO is that the claimed invention must make a *technical* contribution to the prior art. Rules 27 and 29 EPC. In addition, Article 52 on "patentable Inventions" states in part that (1) "European patents shall be granted for any inventions which are susceptible of *industrial* application . . ."; (2) "The following in particular shall not be regarded as inventions within the meaning of paragraph (1): . . . (c) schemes, rules and methods for performing mental acts, playing games or doing business, and *programs for computers;*" (3) "The provisions of paragraph 2 shall exclude patentability . . . *only* to the extent to which . . . [a] European patent relates to such subject matter or activities *as such.*" In the past these restrictions on *"computer programs as such"* have been the basis for the EPO refusal to grant claims to a computer program product on a computer-readable medium or on a carrier wave. Guidelines for examination in the European Patent Office C-IV, 2.3 indicate that "[a] computer program claimed by itself or as a record on a carrier, is not patentable irrespective of its content." These two IBM case decisions, however, allowed such claims.

Subject Matter in the IBM Cases

In one case, T 0935/97-3.5.1, the invention relates to detecting where a second window in a computer display overlies part of a first window, obscuring information in a portion of the first window. The invention in this circumstance detects the overlay and causes the information obscured by the second window to be displayed in another portion of the first window not obscured by the second window by moving the obscured data to a portion of the first window not covered by the second window.

In the other case, T 1173/97-3.5.1, the invention relates to resource recovery in a computer system, including implementing a commit procedure for a work request; in the event that the commit procedure fails, notifying an application that it may continue; and, while the application continues to run, resynchronizing the incomplete commit procedure.

The Decisions in the Examination Division

In both cases, the Examination Division accepted system and method claims directed to the invention but rejected computer program product and element claims.

In T 0935/97, the Examiners allowed claims 1-6 directed to method and apparatus claims, indicating that the requirements of the European Patent Convention, and in particular those of novelty and inventive step, were fulfilled. Claims 7-10 were rejected as computer program code stored on a computer-readable medium. The Examiners concluded that "the subject matter claimed was distinguished from the prior art only by the information pattern represented by the stored program code. Therefore," the Examiners reasoned, "the problem solved would merely be how to store the particular computer program on a data carrier; this problem was well known in the prior art, so was its solution. Neither would this problem be a technical problem nor would any technical effects be achieved by its solution, since a computer program stored on a data carrier in the form of bits and bytes would still be nothing more than a computer program as such which was explicitly excluded from patentability by Article 52 (2) and (3) EPC."

Under similar reasoning, in case T 1173/97, the Examination Division allowed method and apparatus claims 1-19 and rejected claims 20 and 21 related to computer program products stored in computer-readable memory.

The Board of Appeal Decisions

In these decisions, the Board noted that, in the context of the interpretation of the EPC, the *technical character* of an invention is an essential requirement for patentability, referring to Rules 27 and 29 EPC.

Construing the phrase "as such" in 52(3), the Board considered that the exclusions from patentability of programs for computers *as such* in Article 52(2) and (3) EPC mean that programs are considered to be mere abstract creations, lacking in technical character, which necessarily follows if they are "not to be regarded as inventions." The Board concluded that it follows from this logic that *programs for computers must be considered as patentable inventions when they do have technical character.*

The Board spent some time discussing the *technical character* of programs for computers and indicated that the normal physical modifications of the hardware (e.g., the generation of electric currents) deriving from the execution of the instructions given by programs for computers *cannot per se* constitute the technical character required for avoiding the exclusion of those programs. However, technical character can be found in *further technical effects* deriving from the execution (by the hardware) of the instructions given by a computer program. Apparently, such a *further technical effect* could have the necessary technical character where, for example, it causes the software to solve a technical problem (see, for example, the VICOM decision T 208/84, OJ 1987, 14), or where technical considerations are involved to arrive at the invention (see, for example, the SOHEI decision T 769/92, OJ 1995, 525).

As to computer program product claims, the Board said the central question is what "*further technical effect*" can lead to this subject matter not being excluded under Article 52(2) and (3) EPC. Where a computer program product produces such a further technical effect when run on a computer, the Board described such a computer program product as having the potential to produce such a further technical effect. Accordingly, in a case where a specific computer program product, when run on a computer, brings about such a further technical effect, the Board could see no good reason to distinguish between a direct technical effect and an indirect technical effect.

Using a line of reasoning similar to the VICOM decision, the Board found that it would be illogical to grant a patent for a method, and an apparatus adapted for carrying out the same method, but not for the computer program, which comprises all the features enabling the implementation of the method and which, when loaded in a computer, is indeed able to carry out that method.

Accordingly, the Board stated that "a computer program claimed by itself is not excluded from patentability if the program, when running on a computer or loaded into a computer, brings about, or is capable of bringing about, a technical effect which goes beyond the 'normal' physical interactions between the program (software) and the computer (hardware) on which it is run." Also, referring to the findings in the BBC decision T 163/85, OJ 1990, 379, where it was held that a television signal was patentable, the Board concluded that it did not make any difference whether a computer program product is claimed by itself or as a record on a carrier.

As an interesting side note, IBM argued to the Board that a narrower interpretation of the "computer program as such" language would "accord with the TRIPS Agreement, especially Article 27," which says, "Patents shall be available for any inventions, whether products or processes, in all fields of technology." The Board noted pointedly that TRIPS is not directly applicable to the EPC, and that although TRIPS is binding on many of the EPC member states, not all of its members are so bound. Nevertheless, the Board recognized that cognizance of TRIPS and an interpretation of the EPC which is compatible with it is not inappropriate.

Conclusion

The Board of Appeal in these rulings has taken a giant step in bringing the treatment of computer program product claims in the European Patent Office in harmony with the treatment provided in the United States and Japan. Practitioners in the United States filing computer software applications must continue to be aware of the "technical effect" requirements of the EPO but should consider including computer program product claims in EPO filings, including, where appropriate, claims to a computer program product on a carrier wave, for example for a software-implemented invention supplied via the Internet.

COMMENTS AND QUESTIONS

1. In response to IBM's argument in the IBM/Data Processing case that Article 52(2) and (3) of the EPC violated Article 27(1) the TRIPS Agreement (which requires patents to be available "for any inventions, whether products or processes, in all fields of technology"), the Board stated: "[A]lthough TRIPS may not be

applied directly to the EPC, the Board thinks it appropriate to take it into consideration, since it is aimed at setting common standards and principles concerning the availability, scope, and use of trade-related intellectual property rights, and therefore of patent rights." Do you expect other legal decision-makers will be as responsive to arguments about the interpretation of their laws in light of TRIPS? Why or why not?

2. The European Commission has recently prepared a draft directive designed to harmonize national laws on the patentability of computer programs. In addition, the Commission has proposed a modification to Article 52 of the European Patent Convention to omit computer programs from the list of nonpatentable inventions. The Commission's report steadfastly rejected the patentability of business methods and other nontechnical inventions, however, placing it at odds with the rule in the United States in light of *State Street*.

Note on the Japanese Patent Office Guidelines

Those seeking patent protection in Japan should refer to two sets of guidelines to judge whether computer-related inventions will be ruled patentable there and how best to claim such inventions. The Implementing Guidelines for Examination of Industrially Applicable Inventions defines what is and is not statutory subject matter under Japanese patent law. The Implementing Guidelines for Inventions in Specific Fields, Chapter 1 of which concerns computer software-related inventions, explains best practices for those drafting claims for software-related inventions. These guidelines may be found on the Web at <http://www.jpo-miti.go.jp>. Also on this Web site is the classification system that the JPO has devised for searching software technologies, in cooperation with the EPO and the U.S. PTO.

The Industrially Applicable Invention Guidelines begin by observing that section 29(1) of the Patent Law of Japan provides that "[a]ny person who has made an industrially applicable invention may obtain a patent therefor." This provision is understood in Japan to require both that the subject matter of the patent be a "statutory invention" and that it be "industrially applicable." The Guidelines set forth interpretations of both concepts. Its definition of "statutory invention," drawn from section 2(1) of the Patent Law of Japan, is "a highly advanced creation of technical ideas utilizing natural laws." To clarify the meaning of this definition, section 1 of the Guidelines identifies eight categories of "nonstatutory inventions." In addition to excluding natural laws as such and mere discoveries, the Guidelines exclude "laws or the like other than natural laws, and an invention in which solely such laws are utilized." The Guidelines explain: "If a claimed invention is any laws [sic] other than natural laws (economic laws, for example), arbitrary arrangements, mathematical methods or mental activities, or utilizes only these laws, the invention is not considered statutory." Nor are mere "presentations of information," a category that expressly includes computer program listings—that is, "representations of program codes by means of printing them on paper, displaying them on a screen, etc." When a technical feature resides in a presentation of information, however, that technical feature can be a statutory invention. The JPO Guidelines give as an example "[a] plastic card on which information is recorded with characters, letters, and figures embossed on it . . . [where] this card enables one to copy the information by affixing the card on a paper, and in this sense [a] technical feature resides in the presentation of information." Section 2 of the Industrial Application Guidelines articulates the standard for "industrial applicability." In general, an invention that doesn't fall within one of the specific exclusions in the Guidelines will be considered an industrially applicable invention. Methods of calculating numbers, of drawing geometric shapes, and of playing games are among the examples given in the Guidelines of inventions that are not industrially applicable.

The JPO Guidelines on Software-Related Inventions offer many helpful examples of successful and unsuccessful ways to claim such inventions, as well as information about the criteria that Japanese patent examiners will use to determine whether the application has complied with the "inventive step" requirement. In addition to permitting program-related inventions to be claimed as processes, the JPO Guidelines, as of April 1997, contemplate that claims can be made in the form "A computer-readable storage medium having a program recorded thereon, where the program is to make the computer execute procedure A, procedure B, procedure C, etc. . . . or where the program is to make the computer operate as (the combination of) means A, means B, means C." It also advises against claims for a program, data signals, or a data structure, none of which adequately identifies the category of invention for which the patent is sought. Even if a computer program solution utilizes natural laws, "when it is no more than the 'mere processing of information by using a computer,' 'mere recording of a program or data on a storage medium,' or 'mere processing of information by using a computer and mere recording of a program or data on a storage medium,' the claimed invention is deemed as nonstatutory." Very important under the JPO Guidelines is how the claims "suggest, directly or indirectly, how the hardware resources of the computer is [sic] utilized in the processing." Unless this is done, the claim will be considered nonstatutory. The Guidelines give an example of two claims which have in common the calculation of the sum of natural numbers from 'n' to 'n+k' with the use of a computer. The claim that made specific references to the role played by specific hardware resources in carrying out this function is considered statutory. By contrast, the claim for an apparatus to calculate such a sum without reference to these resources is deemed nonstatutory because it is a "mere processing of information by using a computer."

In the past, the United States and Japan have been at odds about procedural issues, and have had as well substantively different conceptions of the patentability of software-related inventions. The main concerns of U.S. officials about the Japanese patent system, according to a Letter of Agreement between the United States and Japan, dated August 16, 1994, was "the inability to make English-language filings in Japan that are followed up with Japanese translations; the long delays in the examination of patent application in the JPO; the pre-grant opposition system and the practice of addressing oppositions seriatim rather than at the same time; the narrow grant of patent claims; the availability of dependent patent compulsory licenses; and the lack of a full 12-month grace period. The U.S. representatives also raised concerns about delays in court cases in Japan and the absence of a mechanism to protect confidential information in court proceedings." The JPO responded to these concerns by committing itself to introduce legislation by April 1995 that would end pre-grant opposition and promote consolidation of oppositions. It established a target date of January 1996 to establish a procedure whereby applicants can request that their applications be fully processed within 36 months. And by July 1995, it undertook to restrict considerably the grant of compulsory

1995, it undertook to restrict considerably the grant of compulsory licenses for dependent inventions.[10]

Note on International Patent Treaties and Substantive Harmonization

When one seeks patent protection for computer-related inventions outside the United States, it is important to understand that other nations have significantly different rules, some of which are substantive, and some of which are procedural, for their patent systems. The U.S. patent system is, in fact, the exception rather than the rule in its adherence, for example, to a "first inventor" rather than a "first to file" rule to qualify for patent protection. In addition, outside the United States it is common for national patent laws to have absolute novelty rules (that is, the claimed invention must absolutely be new to the art, not merely new in the sense that it has not been described in a printed publication or other patent) and to require publication of the patent application within 18 months of filing in that country. This obviously affects the ability of patent applicants to claim trade secrecy protection for an innovation for which a patent might be sought.

Over time, it is likely that there will be additional harmonization in the patent area and more cooperation among patent-granting countries so that an inventor need not file individual patent applications in all countries of the world at the same time. A significant regional development that enables inventors to use one application to get patent protection in many countries is the EPC that established the EPO. Under the EPC, inventors can choose to file one application and designate in which of the 20 participating countries it wishes to have patent protection. EPO patents are valid in those countries designated in the EPO application as long as there has been a subsequent perfection of the patent in each such country. There is, however, no pan-European enforcement mechanism. Enforcement of the patent must be done in national courts under the national law of that state. Alternatively, an inventor may file applications in individual European countries. This may be advantageous, for example, where the national law of an EPO member state has a broader view of the patentability of program-related inventions than the EPO itself has. Apart from regional treaties, such as EPC, there are several treaties affecting patent protection on an international scale. These treaties are critical to the effective international exploitation of a patented invention, as will be discussed below.

Coordinating International Prosecution

Patent lawyers face two problems in coordinating the prosecution of a series of national patents. First, a common priority date must be obtained to ensure that protection will be uniform and unaffected by prior art published (or otherwise having an effective date) before one or more of the national patent applications. Also, a common date will ensure that prosecution of a patent in country *A* does not some-

10. By contrast, the United States still has not complied with *its* obligations under the executive agreement, because Congress has been unwilling to join the rest of the world in permitting patent applications to be published 18 months after filing.

how compromise the patentability of the invention in country *B*. Second, the patent lawyer has to deal with the logistics of international protection; she must oversee multiple filings in diverse languages in numerous countries. The wide variations in national practices and the high cost of conducting a large-scale application barrage make this one of the more challenging professional tasks in patent law.

Fortunately, two international agreements make these tasks a bit more tolerable. The first is the Paris Convention, whose primary function is to guarantee a uniform worldwide priority date across all member countries. An applicant may file in any member country of the Convention up to one year after an initial (typically home-country) filing without losing the priority date of the initial filing. (This treatment is provided under U.S. law in 35 U.S.C. section 119.) The second is the Patent Cooperation Treaty (PCT), which streamlines the filing of multiple national patent applications. Each agreement in its own way is an indispensable tool of the patent trade. Although detailed discussions of the agreements would take up too much room to fit in this volume, a few words about the essential features of each is in order.

a) The Paris Convention

The Paris Convention was signed in 1883, a product of the first true internationalization wave in the field of patent law. Paris Convention for the Protection of Industrial Property, as last revised, July 14, 1967, 21 U.S.T. 1583, T.I.A.S. No. 6295, 828 U.N.T.S. 305 (last revision, sometimes referred to as the Stockholm revision, entered into force April 26, 1970). Its primary function is to define a common priority date so that one may file an application in one member state and have the benefit of that same filing date when filing later in another member state. One purpose of this is to prevent interlopers from copying patents applied for or issued in one state and claiming them as their own in another before the legitimate owner has time to file in the other country.

The key provision in the Convention as regards priority is Article 4. The relevant portions read as follows:

Article 4

A(1)   Any person who has duly filed an application for a patent, or for the registration of a utility model, or of an industrial design, or of a trademark, in one of the countries of the Union, or his successor in title, shall enjoy, for the purpose of filing in the other countries, a right of priority in the periods hereinafter fixed.

A(2)   Any filing that is equivalent to a regular national filing under the domestic legislation of any country of the Union or under bilateral or multilateral treaties concluded between countries of the Union shall be recognized as giving rise to the right of priority.

A(3)   By a regular national filing is meant any filing that is adequate to establish the date on which the application was filed in the country concerned, whatever may be the subsequent fate of the application.

B.   Consequently, any subsequent filing in any of the other countries of the Union before the expiration of the periods referred to above shall not be invalidated by reason of any acts accomplished in the interval, in particular, another filing, the publication or exploitation of the invention, the putting on sale of copies of the design, or the use of the mark, and such acts cannot give rise to any third-party right or any right of personal possession. Rights acquired by third parties before the date of the first application that serves as the basis for the right of priority are reserved in accordance with the domestic legislation of each country of the Union.

C(1)   The periods of priority referred to above shall be twelve months for patents and utility models, and six months for industrial designs and trademarks.

Thus, filing in one country that is a signatory to the Paris Convention gives an applicant some breathing room—12 months in which to prepare to file in other signatory nations. The filing of an application for a patent in Canada on May 15, 1997, for example, will enable the inventor to have until May 15, 1998, to file patent applications for the same invention in other Paris Union states, such as Japan and Australia. If the inventor filed an application for a patent on this invention in Japan on April 10, 1998, Japan would consider the date of filing to be May 15, 1997, because of the earlier filing in a Paris Union jurisdiction (namely, Canada). This is especially important for those firms operating in the international environment, given the first-to-file and absolute novelty rules of most patent systems.

b)   The Patent Cooperation Treaty

The Patent Cooperation Treaty (PCT) was signed in 1970 and opened for signature June 19, 1970, 28 U.S.T. 7645, T.I.A.S. No. 8733 (entered into force Jan. 24, 1978). Its major purpose is to streamline the early prosecution stages of patent applications filed in numerous countries. It is often described as a clearinghouse for international patent applications. As a practical matter, its major advantage is that it gives an inventor (and her patent lawyer) more time, a precious commodity in the prosecution of an application destined for many countries. The signatories to the PCT have agreed to permit an applicant to wait for up to 30 months after the initial filing of a patent application in one country to begin the in-depth prosecution of the application in other countries. This allows the inventor more time, compared to non-PCT prosecution, in which to test the product, decide which countries' protection is worthwhile, and pay the patent office filing fees in the various countries.

There are two main parts of the PCT. Chapter 1 provides that an applicant who files in a national patent office may elect within 12 months to add a PCT filing. The PCT filing is simply an additional filing in any national patent office designated in the PCT. In this case, the applicant has up to 20 months from the initial filing to request that the PCT preliminary prosecution procedure be initiated. At that time, the applicant must also select the PCT member nations that the applicant wishes to be covered under the PCT filing. Note that Chapter 1 preserves the applicant's priority date (in PCT member countries), without having to begin active prosecution, for eight months longer than the simple Paris Convention priority period.

Chapter 2 of the PCT extends the election period to 30 months. To qualify under Chapter 2, the applicant must make her PCT filing at most five months after the first national filing. Chapter 2 gives an inventor 18 extra months, compared to the Paris Convention, to select countries for coverage and to initiate multiple national prosecutions. In other words, so-called Chapter 2 PCT filings give the inventor up to 30 months to make his or her national elections.

The extra time is a substantial advantage. Besides simply delaying the expenditure of filing and examination fees, the PCT allows an inventor a significant extra period to assess the technical merits and commercial potential of the invention. This extra time helps the inventor save wasted filing fees for inventions that fail to blossom; for those that show great promise, the various patent applications that grow out of the PCT filing can be tailored to reflect the commercially significant embodiments that have emerged from the extensive testing.

D. SEMICONDUCTOR CHIP DESIGN PROTECTION

The market in semiconductors is, of course, as global as the market for computer technology generally. Outside the United States, makers of semiconductors can rely on patent, trade secrecy (or confidential information), and licensing laws for some of the legal protection they need, just as in the United States. Many countries also have industrial design laws that can be used to protect semiconductor chip designs or sui generis laws akin to the U.S. Semiconductor Chip Protection Act of 1984. There is, in addition, an international treaty specifically relating to semiconductor chip designs. A diplomatic conference hosted by the World Intellectual Property Organization produced the Treaty on Intellectual Property in Respect of Integrated Circuits (widely known as the Washington Convention).[11] Because some provisions of this Convention were unacceptable to the United States, it did not join this Convention. However, the United States successfully pushed for stronger international protection of semiconductor chip designs in the negotiations leading up to the successful conclusion of the TRIPS Agreement. As a result, minimum standards for international protection of semiconductor chip designs—or in the parlance of TRIPS, the layout-designs of integrated circuits—is now assured by Articles 35-38 of TRIPS.[12]

The main obligation is found in Article 35, which obliges WTO member states to provide protection to the layout designs of integrated circuits and incorporates by reference several provisions of the Washington Convention. Article 3 establishes important scope of protection rules that go beyond the protections of the Washington Convention. Article 36 makes it illegal to perform any of the following acts without authority of the rights holder: "importing, selling, or otherwise distributing for commercial purposes a protected layout-design, an integrated circuit in which a protected layout-design is incorporated, or an article incorporating such an integrated circuit only in so far as it continues to contain an unlawfully reproduced layout-design." Article 37 limits liability for violations of Article 36 when the person in violation neither knew nor had reason to know of the infringing acts of its supplier. Article 38 provides for a 10-year minimum term of protection for layout-

---

11. For a discussion of other national semiconductor chip laws, the Washington Convention, and the reasons it has been perceived to be deficient, see Carl A. Kukkonen III, The Need to Abolish Registration for Integrated Circuit Topographies Under TRIPS, 38 IDEA: J. L. & Tech. 105 (1997).

12. Very similar provisions may be found in Article 1710 of NAFTA.

designs of integrated circuits. The tangibility of semiconductors and devices in which they may be embedded will allow U.S. firms to look to border control measures to control trafficking in illegal chips. The TRIPS Agreement obligates WTO member states to institute border control measures to stop the flow of counterfeit products, including semiconductors.[13]

In view of these TRIPS obligations, computer lawyers are today unlikely to encounter significant difficulties in asserting legal protection of U.S. semiconductor designs distributed in the international market. Nevertheless, it is worth knowing something about the checkered history of international protection of semiconductor chip designs. When the U.S. Congress adopted a sui generis form of legal protection in the Semiconductor Chip Protection Act of 1984, 17 U.S.C. §901, et seq., it chose to accord protection to semiconductor chips manufactured by non-U.S. firms only if the countries of origin of these firms had been certified by the U.S. Secretary of Commerce as having a form of protection "equivalent" to the U.S. chip law. That is, the United States adopted a reciprocity-based, rather than a national treatment-based, approach to protecting the mask works of foreign nationals.[14]

The reciprocity provision of the U.S. semiconductor law may have been a tactical success, in that many nations thereafter adopted similar laws to protect mask works (that is, stencils used in the manufacturing process) or layout designs for integrated circuits,[15] but in retrospect it was a strategic mistake. The reciprocity provision of the U.S. chip law created considerable resentment in the international community as a kind of power play by the United States. This contributed to a lack of consensus and cooperation that in turn caused the Washington Convention, eventually negotiated in 1989, to be so unsatisfactory that none of the major semiconductor producing nations are even signatories of this treaty.[16]

The United States would likely have been better off in the long run had it worked more closely and cooperatively with the international community to build support for universal recognition of the need for legal protection for chip layouts. It might, for example, have promoted the idea that the unfair competition provisions of the Paris Convention (e.g., Article 10bis) already provided a basis for international legal protection for semiconductor designs. Or it might have worked with countries having industrial design laws to persuade them to protect chip layouts under these laws. This would have avoided establishing a precedent in the international community for using reciprocity rules in new legislation affecting high technology industries. The U.S. expenditure of political capital to adopt an international mask work protection system is particularly remarkable given that these laws, including the U.S. statute, are virtually never used.

---

13. See TRIPS, arts. 51-60. It should be noted that use of unilateral sanctions against another country for violation of TRIPS norms is itself a violation of TRIPS. One consequence of this is that the United States is not as free in the post-TRIPS environment to use special 301 sanctions as it was in the pre-TRIPS environment. See Charles R. McManis, Taking TRIPS on the Information Superhighway: International Intellectual Property Protection and Emerging Computer Technology, 41 Vill. L. Rev. 207 (1996).

14. See 17 U.S.C. §914 (setting forth procedures).

15. See Andrew Christie, Integrated Circuits and Their Contents: International Protection (1995).

16. See, e.g., Morton David Goldberg, Semiconductor Chip Protection as a Case Study, in Global Dimensions of Intellectual Property Rights in Science and Technology 329, 335 (Mitchel B. Wallerstein, et al., eds., 1993) (observing that the WIPO-negotiated treaty on semiconductor chips was so weak that leading chip-producing nations would not sign it).

The United States found itself on the unwelcome receiving end of a reciprocity rule when a 1996 European Directive established a new form of legal protection for the contents of databases on a reciprocity basis. This Directive essentially requires member states of the EU to deny protection to the contents of U.S. databases in Europe unless the United States has adopted a law that the Europeans deem equivalent to their law. We discuss this Directive in further detail in the next subsection.

E. DATABASE PROTECTION

The principal form of legal protection available to databases in the international arena is found in the law of copyright. Article 10(2) the TRIPS Agreement binds member states of the WTO to protect databases by copyright law. It provides that "[c]ompilations of data or other material, whether in machine readable or other form, which by reason of the selection or arrangement of their contents constitute intellectual creations shall be protected as such. Such protection, which shall not extend to the data or material itself, shall be without prejudice to any copyright subsisting in the data or material itself." The 1996 WIPO Copyright Treaty contains a very similar provision.[17]

A noteworthy feature of these treaty provisions is that they adopt an "intellectual creation" standard for copyright protection of databases. There has been a longstanding divide between two alternative conceptions of the basis for copyright protection: a creativity-based standard of originality, and a reward-based standard that protects the "sweat of the brow." The U.S. Supreme Court's decision in Feist Publications v. Rural Telephone Service came down strongly in favor of requiring creativity, not simply labor, as a condition for protection. *Feist* contributed to an erosion in the international community of "sweat of the brow" copyrights. In 1997, for example, the Canadian Federal Court of Appeals in Tele-Direct (Publications), Inc. v. American Business Information, Inc., interpreted its copyright law as imposing a *Feist*-like creativity standard of originality for data compilations. The U.K., the jurisdiction that originated "sweat of the brow" copyrights for data collections, has seemingly capitulated to the creativity-based originality standard, at least for data collections developed after the effective date of the European Directive on the legal protection of databases that harmonizes EU member states' copyright laws to an intellectual creation standard for databases.[18] Indeed, after TRIPS it is not entirely clear that a member state would even be *permitted* to protect unoriginal data compilations under copyright on a "sweat of the brow" or "industrious compilation" basis. On the one hand, Article 1(1) allows member states to adopt more extensive protection than the minima established by TRIPS. On the other hand, Article 10(2) indicates that the copyright protection it contemplates for databases cannot extend to the data in the database.

17. See art. 5.
18. See European Parliament and Council Directive 96/9/EC of 11 March 1996 on the Legal Protection of Databases, 1996 O.J. (L 77) 20.

Several other aspects of the European Database Directive merit attention. The Directive defines the term "database" in Article 1 as "a collection of independent works, data or other materials arranged in a systematic or methodical way and individually accessible by electronic or other means." This provision may allow a wider array of databases to be protected under European copyright law than under U.S. copyright law. Systematic and methodical arrangements of data might be excluded from copyright protection under U.S. law by virtue of section 102(b)'s exclusion of systems, procedures, methods of operation, and the like, and the Baker v. Selden tradition of denying copyright protection to systematically arranged data.

Article 5 of the European Database Directive grants to authors of original databases a set of five exclusive rights to carry out or authorize:

    (a)   temporary or permanent reproduction by any means and in any form, in whole or in part;

    (b)   translation, adaptation, arrangement, and any other alteration; any form of distribution to the public of the database or copies thereof . . . ;

    (c)   any communication, display, or performance to the public;

    (d)   any reproduction, distribution, communication, display or performance to the public of the results of the acts referred to in (b).

While the database Directive is independent of copyright protection, the list of rights given to database owners is remarkably similar to the rights granted by the U.S. Copyright Act.

Article 5 also indicates that "[t]he first sale in the Community of a copy of the database by the rightsholder or with his consent shall exhaust the right to control resale of that copy within the Community."[19]

In addition to its provisions harmonizing the law of copyright as applied to databases, the European Database Directive also establishes a sui generis form of legal protection for the contents of databases in the EU. Prior to the Directive, some Nordic countries had adopted laws that protected the makers of certain uncreative data compilations, such as catalogs, against directly competitive appropriations. Other countries have used unfair competition law to protect data collections from market-destructive appropriations. Both to harmonize national laws within the EU and to promote a higher level of investment within the EU in database development, the European Commission and Council decided that this new sui generis law was necessary and desirable.

The key provision of the sui generis part of the European Database Directive is Article 7(1):

---

19. Article 6 enables, but does not require, EU member states to adopt the following exceptions to or limitations on the exclusive rights granted under Article 5:

    (a) in the case of reproduction for private purposes of a non-electronic database;

    (b) where there is use for the sole purpose of illustration for teaching or scientific research, as long as the source is indicated and to the extent justified by the non-commercial purpose to be achieved;

    (c) where there is use for the purpose of public security or for the purpose of an administrative or judicial procedure;

    (d) where other exceptions to copyright which are traditionally authorized under national law are involved, without prejudice to points (a), (b), and (c).

Member states shall provide for a right for the maker of a database which shows that there has been a qualitatively or quantitatively substantial investment in either the obtaining, verification or presentation of the contents to prevent extraction and/or reutilization of the whole or a substantial part, evaluated qualitatively and/or quantitatively, of the contents of that database.

The Directive establishes a 15-year duration of protection for database contents. A substantial change in the contents of the database, whether by reason of deletions, additions, or alterations, can give rise to a new term of rights if a qualitatively or quantitatively substantial new investment was made to bring them about. The principal public policy limitation on the scope of the sui generis right is the nonwaivable right of lawful users of a database to take "insubstantial" parts of that database. Unfortunately, there is little guidance from the Commission about how to measure the substantiality or insubstantiality of a taking. As a result, the reach of the E.C. Database Directive will be defined significantly by court decisions. The following excerpt reviews the first wave of such decisions.

═══ *Xuqiong (Joanna) Wu, E.C. Database Directive,*
═══ 17 Berkeley Tech. L.J. 571, 578-86 (2002)

. . .

C.   The Courts' Responses

Since its enactment, courts in various Member States have handed down more than two dozen decisions under the E.C. Directive. Most of the cases concerned database makers in France, Germany, and The Netherlands, while two involved United Kingdom databases. Commentators also noted that more than half of these cases were about "synthetic data," which, unlike discovered, existing facts, could not have been independently generated by those other than the database maker. Simply put, only the database creators could have generated the contents of these databases.

1.   Database Protection

The E.C. Directive provides a two-pronged test to determine whether a database is eligible for protection. First, a database can qualify for protection if it contains information arranged in a qualifying way, e.g., a systematic collection of individually accessible data. Second, the database must be created through a substantial investment. The first part of the qualifying test is "extremely elastic." For example, factual data—including information about the times and places of horse races and telephone directories—can qualify as core information in protectible databases. Further, even information in the public domain such as laws and regulations can become contents of a protectible database. Courts have formulated different factors in determining what constitutes a substantial investment in the creation of a database, and thus qualifies for the sui generis protection under the E.C. Directive. Under one relatively consistent test that may represent a quantitative evaluation dictated by the E.C. Directive, the court looks at the investment itself in monetary terms. For example, the costs of collecting, verifying and maintaining the data in an electronic telephone directory can qualify as "substantial investment," if the court finds them substantial. Similarly, the costs or investment in hiring someone else to create the database can amount to "substantial investment." Some courts seem to base their quantitative evaluation on the amount of labor involved in collecting and compiling the data. For example, a British trial court held that controlling, verifying and maintaining horseracing information—a four to five-month annual process of compiling, granting and publishing the fixture list for horse racing and maintaining and constantly updating a computer database—was a substantial investment. Moreover, a German court held that converting classified advertisements from a newspaper into digital form and the amount of labor in selecting, updating and verifying the ads qualified for substantial investment.

A second judicial test measures substantiality of investment in making a database by inferring "investment by examining the face of the database." Such an evaluation can be either quantitative or qualitative, and, therefore, this test appears to be almost as elastic as the test for qualifying ways of arranging data. For example, a German court held that a catalogue of 251 alphabetically ordered links to sites on parenting-related subjects constituted a protectible database, finding substantial investment in "compiling, researching, and up-dating" the list. An "effort [to put] [sic] 'frames' around another provider's Web pages was not 'substantial,'" although a similar web site containing a collection of web pages was held to be a database within the meaning of the E.C. Directive. To the German court, designing a way to display data on a web site is relevant to determining the substantiality of efforts in making the web site, a potentially protectible collection of data under the Directive. The absolute amount of data also matters to another German court: "a single promoter's concert schedule was [therefore] 'insubstantial,' although the combined schedule of 400 such promoters would not be." Finally, merely reproducing data weighs against a finding of "substantial investment." A French court found no substantial investment in making a database of advertised calls for tender in the field of public procurement, because such a maker merely reproduced calls received from the advertisers.

Despite the broad scope of protection of databases under the E.C. Directive, several Dutch courts have tried to limit the database right by creating a "spin-off" doctrine when finding against substantial investment in creating a database. For example, because the headlines were a spin-off of newspaper publishing, a court found no substantial investment in creating a web site of automatic hyperlinks (in the form of headlines) to newspaper articles. Another appellate court, also applying the spin-off doctrine, held that a collection of real estate objects on a web site did not qualify for the sui generis database right, because individual real estate brokers in the plaintiff organization had designed it for use in an internal network. Further, broadcasters' program listings were also the products of a spin-off activity, reflecting no substantial investment in their making. However, in other cases, several Dutch courts have rejected the defendants' argument that the database in question was a mere spin-off of plaintiffs' core activities. For example, two different courts held that telephone subscriber listings and online telephone directories were not mere spin-off products of the plaintiff company's core activity of providing telephone services.

In sum, the E.C. Directive does not provide a clear guideline for determining whether a database qualifies for the sui generis right. The ambiguity inherent in the word "substantial" makes it difficult for courts in different Member States to interpret the Directive in a consistent manner. A British appellate court, deciding to refer its case to the European Court of Justice ("ECJ") said, "we cannot say that we can resolve the [Directive's interpretation] issues with complete confidence nor that there is no scope for any reasonable doubt, still less that the matter is equally obvious to the courts of other Member States." The ECJ will likely be called upon to formulate a consistent test for: (1) interpreting the Directive; (2) determining how much or what kind of time, money, efforts, etc., spent in making a database constitute "substantial investment;" and (3) determining whether any factors limiting the scope of the database right, e.g., the Dutch spin-off doctrine, are feasible.

2. Prohibited Extraction and/or Re-utilization

After determining whether a collection of data conforms to the E.C. Directive's definition of "database," and qualifies for the sui generis right based on substantial investment expended in making it, a court must then assesses whether another party infringed the database right. The Directive defines infringement of protectible databases as the unauthorized substantial "extraction" and/or "re-utilization," or the "repeated and systematic extraction" of insubstantial parts, "evaluated quantitatively and qualitatively." However, courts have not established a definitive test for database infringement. A court may measure the substantiality of extraction and/or re-utilization by looking at the data's value to an infringer, and a few pieces of data of great value to an infringer would be "substantial." According to a British trial court, to determine the substantiality of unauthorized extraction, the extracted data's value to an infringer must be appraised both quantitatively and qualitatively. Courts may also look at the infringer's acts or the infringing activities from a database maker's perspective when making this determination. For example, a German court found substantial extraction because the alleged infringer copied 239 of the 251 links, including the same grammatical errors, in the catalogue of alphabetically ordered links to parenting-related subjects. Therefore, either extracting and re-utilizing core information of great value to an infringer or verbatim copying a substantial part of content from a protectible database can amount to substantial extraction and/or re-utilization prohibited by the E.C. Directive.

Further, two German courts have held that "[t]he use of [a] search engine amounted to repeated and systematic extraction of insubstantial parts of the database that unreasonably damaged the lawful interests of the owner of the database right." In both of these German cases, the search engine systematically bypassed advertisements on the originating web sites and sent extracted information directly to end users and therefore affected the database owners' commercial interests. Similarly, a Dutch court also found "a dedicated search engine" infringed an online telephone directory owner's database right, because it provided its users the extracted data without referring them to the original directory.

In sum, the E.C. Directive does not provide definitive guidelines for determining what constitutes prohibited extraction and re-utilization. The courts have yet to reach a consensus on whether the substantiality of prohibited extraction and/or re-utilization depends on the objective amount of extracted contents or the subjective value of the extracted contents to an alleged infringer or both. As for "repeated and systematic extraction of insubstantial parts," the three decisions on search engines are illustrative of potential judicial treatment, but cannot reflect whether the courts in different Member States would adopt a similar test.

3. Effect of Competition Rules

The E.C. Directive provides that, "in the interests of competition, protection by the sui generis right must not be afforded in such a way as to facilitate abuses of a dominant position." As indicated by several cases discussed below, national courts of Member States are willing to apply the Community or national competition rules in deciding cases involving alleged database right infringement. The famous "Magill" decision exemplifies the Community competition rule that prohibits abuse of a dominant position.

Courts in different Member States have attempted to apply the E.C. Directive in conjunction with the Community or their respective national competition rules. At least three Dutch courts found for the alleged infringers, because the database owners, while not eligible for the sui generis right for lack of substantial investment in creating the databases in question, abused their dominant positions by refusing to license under reasonable terms. In contrast, a French court held for the plaintiff under both the E.C. Directive and the competition rule, because the plaintiff's electronic telephone subscriber directory qualified for the database right and because the plaintiff was willing to license the information for a reasonable fee, and, therefore, did not display anti-competitive behavior.

Other courts have also applied the competition rule by focusing on the alleged infringers' conducts, regardless of whether the databases at issue qualify for protection under the E.C. Directive. For example, the German Supreme Court upheld a plaintiff's database right in its subscriber telephone directories, and additionally considered the defendant's unfair competition behavior of scanning and subsequently publishing the plaintiff's data on a CD-ROM. Further, a French court, without any explicit determination of a database right, found no copyright infringement in the defendant's copying of the contents of agreements in the plaintiff's collection of over 400 collective bargaining agreements. But the court held that the defendant's parasitic behavior amounted to unfair competition. Therefore, unfair competition principles can strengthen database protection, even in the absence of a clear database right.

Although the cases discussed above indicate that national courts in the Community have attempted to reconcile the E.C. Directive and competition rules, the courts have yet to decide upon a potential situation where a database owner, eligible for the sui generis right, abuses its dominant position. For example, whose side would the French court take, had France Telecom displayed anti-competitive behavior by refusing to license under a reasonable fee? It remains uncertain whether competition rules would undercut database right, as the E.C. Directive permits. Perhaps the Office of Fair Trading in the United Kingdom is the first to address such uncertainty: preliminary inquiries, following a complaint by William Hill Organization Ltd., indicated that the British Horseracing Board might have abused its dominant position by setting excessive and discriminatory pricing and restrictive licensing terms. So far, unfair competition principles have strengthened database protection. But applying national unfair competition rules that are not uniform throughout the Community in the database context may defeat an important goal that the E.C. Directive intended to achieve—a Community-wide harmonized level of database protection.

4. *Current Problems Facing Courts*

The decisions discussed above reflect the difficulties that courts are facing in interpreting the E.C. Directive. They further highlight the uncertainties that the E.U. will face in attempting to harmonize the level of database protection among its Member States through the new legal regime of database protection.

First, the E.C. Directive does not offer courts much help in defining the key concepts of the sui generis database right. Because the E.C. Directive defines the database concept and the scope of protection so broadly, courts have not been able to apply consistent tests. As noted by the British appellate court, the ECJ would have to resolve these uncertainties, if and when cases reach this highest-level court.

Second, the inconsistency displayed by the courts' interpretation of the E.C. Directive suggests that this new law has not reached its first goal of harmonizing database protection in Europe. For example, a spin-off database, not granted protection by some Dutch courts, may qualify for the sui generis protection in the United Kingdom or Germany.

Third, the courts have yet to reconcile the potential tension between the competition rules and the new database right. Whether the Commission will reconsider a compulsory license requirement in amending the E.C. Directive to avoid such a situation remains an open question. Applying national unfair competition rules would further undermine the effort to harmonize the level of database protection in different Member States.

Finally, a recent empirical study has also indicated that the E.C. Directive is yet to reach its goal of promoting and sustaining the growth of the database industry in the Community. Despite that only database makers in the E.U. qualify for the strong property-like right in database contents, the E.C. Directive has not generated enough incentive for U.S. database companies to move to Europe. The E.C. Directive, therefore, has yet to reach its original goals of granting uniform protection of databases among the Member States and of providing sufficient, sustained incentives to invest in the database industry in Europe.

COMMENTS AND QUESTIONS

1. The European Database Directive, which creates a new intellectual property right, should not be confused with the roughly contemporaneous European Data Protection Directive. The latter provides individuals with substantial protections against the gathering and use of personal data by governments and corporations. For a general discussion of the European Data Protection Directive, see Paul M. Schwartz & Joel R. Reidenberg, Data Privacy Law (1997); Peter P. Swire & Robert E. Litan, None of Your Business: World Data Flows, Electronic Commerce, and the European Privacy Directive (1998).

2.   The European Database Directive seems to adopt a copyright-like model for protection. Are the rights it grants equivalent to copyright? If so, why not protect databases under copyright law? Does the answer lie in the limitations imposed by the Berne Convention and the TRIPS Agreement, which seem to contemplate some minimum creativity standard for copyright protection? Is the European Database Directive nothing more than an end run around the limitations of international copyright law? How is it different from an unfair competition-based model for database protection? Which approach is better and why?

3.   The European Directive on the Legal Protection of Databases is not self-executing. It must be implemented in national laws, and member nations of the EU have significant leeway in adopting implementation legislation, especially as to remedies for violation of the sui generis extraction right.

4.   By including a reciprocity provision in the database Directive, the European Commission very clearly intended to encourage the international community to adopt an equivalent form of legal protection for the contents of databases. United States database companies have understandably been nervous about the vulnerability of their data to depredations in Europe since the database Directive became effective in January 1998. However, a variety of legal protection mechanisms, including copyright, contract, and unfair competition law, should generally suffice to provide meaningful protection to U.S. database firms operating in Europe. Some commentators, notably Professor Charles McManis, have argued that the EU would be vulnerable to a challenge that the reciprocity provision of its database Directive violates the national treatment norm of the TRIPS Agreement. See Charles R. McManis, Taking TRIPS on the Information Superhighway: International Intellectual Property Protection and Emerging Computer Technology, 41 Vill. L. Rev. 207, 258-262 (1996). The United States is among the nations that have considered adopting some new form of legal protection for the contents of databases. However, this legislation has been controversial in the United States, and, to date, Congress has not enacted such a law.

5.   *Effects upon Research.* Scholars assessing the effects of the E.C. Directive have raised concerns about the potential adverse effects on particular areas of research, such as biotechnology. One group of researchers note that

> Companies worry about committing hundreds of millions of dollars to a project if there is the slightest chance that the underlying data could belong to someone else. For this reason, some companies warn employees never to acquire data by surfing the Web. Until recently, this kind of rule worked surprisingly well. However, pose-genome science is changing. In order to make progress, scientists will have to combine data from dozens of academic and commercial sources. Under these circumstances, discovery could soon be limited to the pace at which lawyers write contracts.

Stephen M. Maurer et al., Europe's Database Experiment, 294 Science 789 (2001).

6.   *Database Protection as a Basis for Limiting Deep Linking.* As we will see at various points in this book, Web publishers have sought to limit access to their Web sites in various ways in order to appropriate a return on their investment. Among the theories put forth in the United States have been unfair competition, copyright infringement, breach of contract (based on terms of use posted on Web sites and browsewrap and clickwrap agreements), trespass to chattels, and computer fraud and abuse. We explore each of these theories elsewhere in this book.

As noted above, the Database Directive has been invoked as another hook to hold deep linking unlawful. Although some European scholars had assumed that courts would not find liability in the act of linking to Web sites without permission because publishing a Web site arguably implies a license to link, Stephan Bechtold, Der Schutz des Anbieters von Information, Urheberrecht und Gewerblicher Rechtsschutz im Internet (1997); Zeitschrift fuer Urheber- und Medienrecht, at 432; U. Loewenheim & F. Koch, Praxis des Online Rechts (1998) Wiley-VCH, Weinhein, at 306; J. Weinknecht, Urheberrecht im Internet, courts have recognized database protection as the possible basis of claims against deep linking. Algemeen Dagblad a.o. v. Eureka—President District Court of Rotterdam, 22 August 2000 (accepting the legal argument, but rejecting the claim on factual grounds—the list of headlines maintained by plaintiff newspaper did not constitute a database since the newspapers had made no "substantial investment" in money or effort in developing the list of headlines); Stepstone v. Ofir—Landgericht Cologne, 28 O 692/00, 28 February 2002 (holding that online job advertisements of Norwegian-based recruitment company were protected as database and granting injunction against Danish-based competitor's deep links to ads); Baumarket.de—Oberlandgericht Düsseldorf, 29 June 1999 (holding that collection of web pages containing advertisements and information on building construction and do-it-yourself products constituted database, but plaintiff failed to show substantial investment by not bearing commercial risk since ads were published on the Web site on commission).

Two recent cases, in particular, have generated controversy and stimulated debate around the scope of the Directive. In Denmark a newsfeed Web site's deep linking to individual articles on commercial newspaper sites has been held to have violated newspapers' rights under the Danish implementation of the Directive, even though the links were removed within weeks. Danish Newspaper Publishers' Association v. Newsbooster.com ApS, Den. Fogedret, 5 July 2002. The court said that the newspaper sites' collections of articles were databases protected under the directive, since they were the result of "structured systems or methods" and Internet users are able to access them by various means. The court then determined that Newsbooster bots' repeated scouring of the plaintiffs' web sites in order to compile lists of headlines and links constituted "repeated and systematic extraction and/or re-utilization of insubstantial parts of the contents of the database implying acts which conflict with a normal exploitation of the database." See E.C. Directive, at art. 7(5). Newsbooster's publisher has said that he is waiting for other Danish or international technology companies to intervene before taking the case brought by the Danish Newspaper Publishers' Association to the higher court in Copenhagen. In a German case filed against news headline aggregator Newsclub.de by the newspaper Mainpost for deep linking to the newspaper's articles, the plaintiff also argues that the newspaper constitutes a database and that the Directive has been violated. Presse Zeitungsverlagsgesellschaft mbH & Co. v. Christian Kohlschütter—Oberlandesgericht Munich, 15 July 2002. Munich's upper court ruled against Newsclub in a provisional order that is likely to be affirmed in the hearings ahead. With a similar case before the German federal court after the search engine Paperboy.de won a verdict from the highest court in Cologne, Newsclub's publisher has said that he will take his case to federal court if the provisional order is not reversed. This case is particularly significant because the issue contested is the Directive itself, as opposed to the law of an individual country.

Newsbooster's CEO Anders Lautrup-Larsen has criticized the "isolating technology" for which the Danish Newspaper Publishers' Association argues. "The Internet consists of links[;] without the links there will only be stand-alone clones of information and services. Saying that other sites can't link to your site is like being a member of a community and asking people not to talk to you." http://www.wired.com/news/politics/0,1283,51887-2,00.html. What is the proper balance between commerce and community?

7. Should the United States adopt a database law? Should Europe abandon its regime?

F. TRADEMARK PROTECTION

Trademark law provides additional protection to computer technology firms operating in the global market. As with other laws discussed earlier in this chapter, there are some differences between U.S. and other national laws concerning trademark protection. Some of those differences are in substantive rules (for example, the extent to which trade dress protection is available at all or available through trademark law), but many are of a procedural nature. Managing trademark rights in an international marketplace can be challenging. Although counterfeiting of products and of trademarks has been a substantial problem in some parts of the world market, the TRIPS Agreement's trademark provisions and border measures offer new measures to combat this kind of activity. However, attaining and maintaining trademark protection in the international arena is challenging because this law is less harmonized in some key respects than would be optimal, and because the United States has yet to join one of the international treaties that would ease the need for multiple registrations for trademark protection.

1. United States Trademarks Abroad: The Failure (So Far) of Internationalization

Despite the obvious desirability of international trademark registration, the United States did not join an international convention that goes beyond the rather minimal protections afforded by the Paris Convention until 2002.

The U.S. recently adhered to the Madrid Protocol (MP), a corollary to the broader Madrid Trademark Agreement (MTA). The MP considerably softens some of the harsher impacts of the MTA, especially on the United States.[20] Specifically, the MP (1) allows for filing in English or French in the U.S. PTO or any other member country trademark office; (2) allows the filing of an international application based not only on a "basic" (home-country) registration, but also on a basic *application*—a substantial advantage given the relatively stringent prosecution standards in the United States, which can lead to long gaps between applications and registrations, especially now in light of intent-to-use registrations under the

---

20. Technically, members of the MP join the Madrid Union without signing the MTA. See MTA art. 1, 828 U.N.T.S. at 391 (states adhering to the Madrid Agreement "constitute a Special Union for the international registration of marks," known as the "Madrid Union."); Madrid Agreement Protocol, art. 1, at 9 (states adhering to the Madrid Agreement Protocol are also members of the Madrid Union).

Lanham Act; and (3) substantially lessens the impact of the "central attack" provision (under which a trademark invalidated in its home country is invalid everywhere) by allowing an international registrant to convert a successfully attacked registration into a bundle of individual national registrations if the attack occurs during the first five years of the international registration.[21]

Although some problems remain,[22] the MP is a substantial step toward international harmonization. Indeed, some degree of harmonization would seem to be incumbent, if only to keep up with trading partners. In Europe, for example, 1995 saw the advent of the Community Trademark Convention (CTC), a treaty providing for a single community trade mark (CTM) based on a single European trademark registration.[23] If further proof were needed, the CTC shows convincingly that the logic of trademark harmonization is compelling in this era of global trade and instantaneous communication.

2. Foreign Trademarks in the United States: Limited Internationalization

Even before U.S. adherence to an international trademark treaty, certain provisions of U.S. law made some concessions to the need for foreign trademark owners

---

21. MP art. 9, at 43-45.

22. See, e.g., Allan Zelnick, The Madrid Protocol—Some Reflections, 82 Trademark Rep. 651 (1992). Zelnick argues that U.S. companies might still prefer to pursue foreign trademark rights by filing individual foreign applications, because of the liberality of most foreign trademark systems regarding the classes of goods that can be identified with the mark in the application. (In many countries, a trademark application can specify *all* classes of goods—giving applicants substantially broader rights than under U.S. law.) According to Zelnick,

> [I]t seems likely that on the whole, most American trademark owners who file abroad today are unlikely to make use of the Madrid Protocol. The reason for this conclusion is that under our practice the specification of goods or services that will appear in the domestic application, on which the international application will be based, must be narrowly drawn to the specific goods or services in respect of which the mark shall have been used in interstate or foreign commerce of the United States (in the case of applications based on use) or restricted to the particular items or services identified by their common trade names in respect of which the applicant shall have a bona fide intention to use the mark. Since the international application under the Madrid Protocol will have the same specification of goods or services as the United States application upon which it is based, we will have, in effect, transferred our domestic practice in this regard to United States trademark owners' international filings.

Id. at 652.

23. Council Regulation (EC) no. 40/94 of 20 December 1993 on the Community Trademark, O.J. L 11/1. The CTM regulation built on a 1980 Directive that substantially harmonized the national trademark laws of the EC member states. Primary features of the recently added CTM are:

- Trademarks with renewable 10-year term, to be registered in the new European Trademark Office in Alicante, Spain;
- Marks valid in all member states but invalid everywhere if revoked;
- Substantive requirements for registration and grounds for opposition that would largely be familiar to American trademark practitioners—e.g., registration of nondistinctive marks upon proof of secondary meaning for limited class of goods or services, etc.
- The working languages are German, English, Spanish, French, and Italian. Applications can be filed in any Community language and are translated (for free); opposition proceedings are only conducted in one of the official languages, however, which must be selected at the time of filing.

See Eric P. Raciti, The Harmonization of Trademarks in the European Community: The Harmonization Directive and the Community Trademark, 78 J. Pat. & Trademark Off. Soc'y 51 (1996).

to register their marks in the United States. Primarily, section 44 of the Lanham Act allows foreign trademark owners to register their marks in the United States. In particular, section 44 reads:

(b) Rights of foreign owner of trademark. Any person whose country of origin is a party to any convention or treaty relating to trademarks, trade or commercial names, or the repression of unfair competition, to which the United States is also a party, or extends reciprocal rights to nationals of the United States by law, shall be entitled to the benefits of this section under the conditions expressed herein to the extent necessary to give effect to any provision of such convention, treaty, or reciprocal law, in addition to the rights to which any owner of a mark is otherwise entitled by this Act.

(c) Registration of mark in country of origin. No registration of a mark in the United States by a person described in subsection (b) of this section shall be granted until such mark has been registered in the country of origin of the applicant, unless the applicant alleges use in commerce. For the purposes of this section, the country of origin of the applicant is the country in which he has a bona fide and effective industrial or commercial establishment, or if he has not such an establishment the country in which he is domiciled, or if he has not a domicile in any of the countries described in subsection (b) of this section, the country of which he is a national.

(d) Effect of foreign application. An application for registration of a mark under sections 1051, 1053, 1054, 1091 or 1126(e) of this Act filed by a person described in subsection (b) shall be accorded the same force and effect as would be accorded to the same application if filed in the United States on the same date on which the application was first filed in such foreign country: *Provided*, that—

(1) the application in the United States is filed within 6 months from the date on which the application was first filed in the foreign country;

(2) the application conforms as nearly as practicable to the requirements of this Act, including a statement that the applicant has a bona fide intention to use the mark in commerce.

(3) the rights acquired by third parties before the date of the filing of the first application in the foreign country shall in no way be affected by a registration obtained on an application filed under this subsection (d);

(4) nothing in this subsection (d) shall entitle the owner of a registration granted under this section to sue for acts committed prior to the date on which his mark was registered in this country unless the registration is based on use in commerce.

Lanham Act §44, 15 U.S.C. §1126.

While section 44(d)(2) requires a statement of bona fide intent to use,[24] no subsequent proof of actual use in commerce in the United States is required. This allows foreign trademark owners to register their marks in the United States on

---

24. This provision was added in 1988 (effective 1989) in response to the decision of the Trademark Trial and Appeal Board's decision in Crocker National Bank v. Canadian Imperial Bank of Commerce, 223 U.S.P.Q. (BNA) 909 (T.T.A.B. 1984), which held valid a trademark registration application filed by a Canadian bank despite the absence of an allegation of use anywhere in the world.

terms slightly more favorable than those extended to domestic applicants under the Lanham Act.

3. "Gray-Market" Goods

United States law prohibits the importation of any goods bearing a registered U.S. trademark without the consent of the domestic trademark owner, even if the goods are genuine and even if they are imported by a licensed manufacturer (or the original trademark owner itself). 19 U.S.C. §1526. The so-called "gray-market" or "parallel imports" problem is a troubling one for courts and commentators alike. The Supreme Court has described the problem as follows:

> The gray market arises in any of three general contexts. The prototypical gray-market victim (case 1) is a domestic firm that purchases from an independent foreign firm the rights to register and use the latter's trademark as a United States trademark and to sell its foreign-manufactured products here. Especially where the foreign firm has already registered the trademark in the United States or where the product has already earned a reputation for quality, the right to use that trademark can be very valuable. If the foreign manufacturer could import the trademarked goods and distribute them here, despite having sold the trademark to a domestic firm, the domestic firm would be forced into sharp intrabrand competition involving the very trademark it purchased. Similar intrabrand competition could arise if the foreign manufacturer markets its wares outside the United States, as is often the case, and a third party who purchases them abroad could legally import them. In either event, the parallel importation, if permitted to proceed, would create a gray market that could jeopardize the trademark holder's investment.
>
> The second context (case 2) is a situation in which a domestic firm registers the United States trademark for goods that are manufactured abroad by an affiliated manufacturer. In its most common variation (case 2a), a foreign firm wishes to control distribution of its wares in this country by incorporating a subsidiary here. The subsidiary then registers under its own name (or the manufacturer assigns to the subsidiary's name) a United States trademark that is identical to its parent's foreign trademark. The parallel importation by a third party who buys the goods abroad (or conceivably even by the affiliated foreign manufacturer itself) creates a gray market. Two other variations on this theme occur when an American-based firm establishes abroad a manufacturing subsidiary corporation (case 2b) or its own unincorporated manufacturing division (case 2c) to produce its United States trademarked goods, and then imports them for domestic distribution. If the trademark holder or its foreign subsidiary sells the trademarked goods abroad, the parallel importation of the goods competes on the gray market with the holder's domestic sales.
>
> In the third context (case 3), the domestic holder of a United States trademark authorizes an independent foreign manufacturer to use it. Usually the holder sells to the foreign manufacturer an exclusive right to use the trademark in a particular foreign location, but conditions the right on the foreign manufacturer's promise not to import its trademarked goods into the United States. Once again, if the foreign manufacturer or a third party imports into the United States, the foreign-manufactured goods will compete on the gray market with the holder's domestic goods.

K-Mart Corp. v. Cartier, Inc., 486 U.S. 281, 286-87 (1988).

What is wrong with importing gray-market goods? In this case, unlike the typical trademark dispute, there is no question that the goods are genuine and are being sold as precisely what they are. Further, there is no question that they originated with the trademark owner (at least at some point). If a gray-market transaction occurred entirely within the United States, would it constitute trademark infringement? If not, is there any reason to treat importation differently?

One obvious rationale for prohibiting gray-market imports is that the U.S. trademark owner is losing the benefit of what she thought was an exclusive right to sell the trademarked goods in the United States. But does she really have such an exclusive right? Certainly, the right to use the "Ford" trademark on cars in the United States does not prevent bona fide purchasers of Ford cars from identifying them as such upon resale. And even if the U.S. trademark owner did obtain the exclusive rights to the first sale of goods in the United States, isn't the problem here really one of breach of contract?

Section 1526, which regulates gray-market goods, may violate Article 2 of the Paris Convention because it treats U.S. trademark holders differently from foreign trademark holders, and U.S. infringers differently from foreign infringers. See Raimund Steiner & Robert Sabath, Intellectual Property and Trade Law Approaches to Gray Market Importation, and the Restructuring of Transnational Entities to Permit Blockage of Gray Goods in the United States, 15 Wm. Mitchell L. Rev. 433, 441 (1989) (after *K-Mart,* to obtain benefits of section 526 of Tariff Act of 1930 and Lanham Act, companies must separate ownership of foreign and domestic trademarks); see generally Note, The Use of Copyright Law to Block the Importation of Gray-Market Goods: The Black and White of It All, 23 Loy. L.A. L. Rev. 645 (1990).

There is a debate in the economics literature about the wisdom of permitting gray-market imports. The argument generally runs along these lines: Those favoring restrictions on the gray market cite the importance of encouraging investments in brand quality by retailers, coupled with differing international product quality standards. In essence, the argument is that retailers will not engage in optimal expenditures to promote the product (advertising, clean showrooms, knowledgeable sales staff, etc.) if gray-market imports will undercut the retailers' prices. On the opposite side, those who support the gray market say it undercuts blatant price discrimination. See Robert J. Staaf, International Price Discrimination and the Gray Market, 4 Intellectual Prop. J. 301 (1989) (gray market presents an opportunity for arbitrage, allowing competitors to circumvent attempted price discrimination and therefore benefiting consumers).

The following case from the U.K. illustrates gray-market goods issues that sometimes arise in the context of computer software products.

Microsoft Corp. v. Computer Future Distribution Ltd.
United Kingdom Chancery Division
[1998] E.T.M.R. 597

RIMER J:

[Computer Future Distribution (CFD) lawfully acquired copies of Academic Edition (AE)-packaged Microsoft (MS) software from unnamed North American distributors. It then removed the outer packaging, which contained notices of restrictions on resale of the software outside North America and certificates of authentication (COA). CFD repackaged this software (correctly identifying Microsoft as its source) and then commercially distributed the software to various customers in the U.K. without inclusion of the end user license agreement (EULA) that Microsoft routinely includes in its packaged software. MS sued CFD for trademark infringement, passing off, and copyright infringement. When MS moved for summary judgment on all three counts, CFD argued that MS's sale of the software in North America exhausted its rights to control redistribution of the software in the U.K.]

Mr Baldwin submits that CFD's activities . . . constitute an infringement of Microsoft's registered trade marks. The action is governed by the Trade Marks Act 1994, which was passed to implement Council Directive 89/104/EEC, and which must be construed so as to give effect to the Directive. It is an infringement to use in the course of trade, without the consent of the proprietor, a sign identical to the registered trade mark in relation to goods identical to those for which it is registered: see ss.9 and 10 of the Act. In this case, CFD has used a sign identical to Microsoft's registered trade marks in relation to identical goods. Mr Baldwin submits that there has been no consent to CFD's acts.

An exhaustion defence is provided by s.12 of the Act, implementing Art.7 of the Directive. Mr Baldwin's position is that that cannot avail CFD since the relevant goods have not been marketed in the EEA by Microsoft or with its consent, but only in North America whence they have been imported. He claims that Microsoft's rights in respect of trade mark infringement are preserved in relation to goods marketed by or with its consent outside the EEA and he says that that is the position in relation to the supply of goods which are the subject of this action. He does not, however, ask the court to determine that particular point on this application. That is because the Austrian Supreme Court has recently referred the effect of Art. 7 to the ECJ: Silhouette v Hartlauer [1997] ETMR 219. Mr Baldwin concedes that, until that reference has been decided, the possibility of an international exhaustion defence based on the marketing of the goods in North America cannot be excluded.

He submits further, however, that even if an international exhaustion defence is available under s.12, it can anyway be of no assistance to CFD. That is because Art. 7(2) of the Directive and s.12(2) of the 1994 Act recognise that, even if the goods were put on the market by or with the consent of the trade mark owner, such owner's rights will not be exhausted if there are legitimate reasons for him to oppose further dealing in the goods. Section 12(2) provides that:

> Subsection (1) does not apply where there exist legitimate reasons for the proprietor to oppose further dealings in the goods (in particular, where the condition of the goods has been changed or impaired after they have been put on the market).

Mr Baldwin submits that in this case Microsoft has legitimate reasons for opposing the manner in which CFD has been dealing with the brown box software, the licence packs and the family bundles.

As to the brown box software, it appears plain that the whole, or at least the main, point of removing Microsoft's original outer packaging, and in supplying the software in brown boxes, was to conceal from purchasers the fact that the product was originally destined exclusively for the North American market or intended solely for North American academic users. All this was made clear on the removed packaging, but is not apparent from the plain brown box.

The effect of the removal of the outer packaging was to enable the software to be sold to non-North American users who would or might buy in ignorance that the product was designed and intended exclusively for the North American market and who would or might find that they had no money back guarantee or guarantee of support. In addition, it would enable software products intended by Microsoft exclusively for North American academic users, and originally sold by it at the generous concessionary AE price, instead to find their way into the hands of ordinary users and at an increased price. Further, the removal of Microsoft's outer packaging results in an inferior looking product, with resultant damage to Microsoft's goodwill. Microsoft asserts that purchasers cannot be sure who has packaged the product which is being sold, they cannot be sure that the contents of the brown box have not been altered or tampered with since it left Microsoft's control, and the removal of the COA contained on the outer packaging removes part of the evidence of the authenticity of the product. The removal of the outer packaging also opens up the scope for splitting up the products in a way which Microsoft does not permit, for example by extracting the EULAs and providing them to users of other software as a purported licence.

Mr Baldwin makes like points in relation to CFD's practice of stripping out EULAs so as to create a market in bogus licences. The particular examples complained of and proved are CFD's supply of the licence pack to Option Technology and the 40 EULAs to Sussex Training. The product sold to Option Technology suffers from being an incomplete package presented as emanating from Microsoft; and that supplied to Sussex Training looks shoddy, containing nothing to attribute the re-packaging to CFD. The sale of such separate EULAs, unattached to particular software items, is without Microsoft's licence and its availability facilitates and encourages the use of unlicensed copies of Microsoft's software.

As for the family bundles, they are supplied in a form which falls short of including an EULA and a COA for each item of software supplied, whereas authentic family bundles do or should include an EULA and a COA for each item. This results in surplus EULAs and COAs being available for use in conferring spurious authenticity on other items of software. The purchaser is deprived of an indication that the goods are genuine Microsoft products and Microsoft is deprived of the opportunity of discovering whether the product is counterfeit. The packaging gives no indication of who is responsible for it and no notice of the re-packaging is given to Microsoft.

Mr Baldwin submits that all this means that, in relation to each of the items within the three classes of goods in question, Microsoft's trade marks are diminished as an indication of authenticity and quality. He submits that it follows that 'there exist legitimate reasons' within the meaning of s.12(2) for Microsoft's opposition to such dealings. If so, then, whatever the result of the reference in the Silhouette case, there will be no exhaustion defence available to CFD under s.12.

In considering the application of s.12(2) to this case, Mr Baldwin referred me in particular to the decision of the ECJ in Bristol-Myers Squibb v Paranova (1996) 34 BMLR 59, [1997] FSR 102. That case was concerned, inter alia, with the extent to which the trade mark owner could object to the repackaging and sale of imported pharmaceutical products to which the trade mark had been affixed. The case depended on Art. 7(2) of the Directive, to which s.12(2) gives effect. The court said that:

39.   Article 7(2) of the Directive provides that the owner of a trade mark may oppose the further commercialisation of products where there is a legitimate reason for doing so, especially where the condition of the products has been changed or impaired since they were put on the market. The use of the word "especially" shows that the case envisaged is given only as an example.

40.   Article 7 of the Directive, like Article 36 of the Treaty, is intended to reconcile the fundamental interest in protecting trade mark rights with the fundamental interest in the free movement of goods within the common market, so that those two provisions, which pursue the same result, must be interpreted in the same way. . . .

47.   In answering the question whether a trade mark owner's exclusive rights include the power to oppose the use of the trade mark by a third party after the product has been repackaged, account must be taken of the essential function of the trade mark, which is to guarantee to the consumer or end user the identity of the trade-marked product's origin by enabling him to distinguish it without any risk of confusion from products of different origin. That guarantee of origin means that the consumer or end user can be certain that a trade-marked product offered to him has not been subject at a previous stage of marketing to interference by a third person, without the authorisation of the trade mark owner, in such a way as to affect the original condition of the product (*Hoffmann-La Roche*, paragraph 7; *Pfizer*, paragraph 8).

48.   Therefore the right conferred upon the trade mark owner to oppose any use of the trade mark which is liable to impair the guarantee of origin so understood forms part of the specific subject-matter of the trade mark right, the protection of which may justify derogation from the fundamental principle of free movement of goods (*Hoffmann-La Roche*, paragraph 7; *Pfizer*, paragraph 9). . . .

58.   In the light of the arguments of the plaintiffs in the main actions, it should be clarified at the outset that the concept of adverse effects on the original condition of the product refers to the condition of the product inside the packaging.

59.   The trade mark owner may therefore oppose any repackaging involving a risk of the product inside the package being exposed to tampering or to influences affecting its original condition. To determine whether that applies account must be taken, as the Court held in paragraph 10 of the *Hoffmann-La Roche* judgment, of the nature of the product and the method of repackaging.

60.   As regards pharmaceutical products, it follows from the same paragraph in *Hoffmann-La Roche* that repackaging must be regarded as having been carried out in circumstances not capable of affecting the original condition of the product where, for example, the trade mark owner has placed the product on the market in double packaging and the repackaging affects only the external layer, leaving the inner packaging intact, or where the repackaging is carried out under the supervision of a public authority in order to ensure that the product remains intact. . . .

67.   If the repackaging is carried out in conditions which cannot affect the original condition of the product inside the packaging, the essential function of the trade mark as a guarantee of origin is safeguarded. Thus, the consumer or end user is not misled as to the origin of the products, and does, in fact, receive products manufactured under the sole supervision of the trade mark owner.

68.   Whilst, in these circumstances, the conclusion that the trade mark owner may not rely on his rights as owner in order to oppose the marketing under his trade mark of products repackaged by an importer is essential in order to ensure the free movement of goods, it does, nevertheless, confer on the importer certain rights which, in normal circumstances, are reserved for the trade mark owner himself.

69.   In the interests of the owner as proprietor of the trade mark, and to protect him against any misuse, those rights must therefore, as the Court held in *Hoffmann-La Roche*, be recognised only in so far as the importer complies with a number of other requirements.

70.   Since it is in the trade mark owner's interest that the consumer or end user should not be led to believe that the owner is responsible for the repackaging, an indication must be given on the packaging of who repackaged the product. . . .

75.   Even if the person who carried out the repackaging is indicated on the packaging of the product, there remains the possibility that the reputation of the trade mark, and thus of its owner, may nevertheless suffer from an inappropriate presentation of the repackaged product. In such a case, the trade mark owner has a legitimate interest, related to the specific subject-matter of the trade mark right, in being able to oppose the marketing of the product. In assessing whether the presentation of the repackaged product is liable to damage the reputation of the trade mark, account must be taken of the nature of the product and the market for which it is intended. . . .

78.   Finally, as the Court pointed out in *Hoffmann-La Roche*, the trade mark owner must be given advance notice of the repackaged product being put on sale. The owner may also require the importer to supply him with a specimen of the repackaged product before it goes on sale, to enable him to check that the repackaging is not carried out in such a way as directly or indirectly to affect the original condition of the product and that the presentation after repackaging is not likely to damage the reputation of the trade mark. Similarly, such a requirement affords the trade mark owner a better possibility of protecting himself against counterfeiting.

The essence of Mr Wilson's argument for CFD was that all that had been done to Microsoft's original packaging was that, in creating the brown box format, the goods had been de-labelled, not re-labelled or repackaged, which he submitted was not, or was arguably not, an activity involving any relevant alteration to the condition of the goods after they had been put onto the market by Microsoft. The customer would still be getting genuine, unaltered, Microsoft software in sealed jewel cases bearing Microsoft's trade marks, and he submitted that the reference to 'goods' in s.12(2) was to the contents of Microsoft's packaging, not to the packaging itself, a proposition supported by para 58 of the judgment in the *Bristol-Myers* case. Moreover, he said that CFD dealt only with OEMs, so that the appearance of the packages they were supplying was of less importance than if they were dealing with end users direct. He did not submit that these points were necessarily a complete answer to the case based on trade mark infringement, but he did submit that the question of whether Microsoft had 'legitimate reasons' to oppose CFD's dealings in the goods was a matter giving rise to a triable issue deserving full investigation and in respect of which CFD was entitled to leave to defend.

I feel unable to accept Mr Wilson's argument. I do not find the decision in the *Bristol-Myers* case of direct assistance in this case, since the circumstances there were rather different. I am inclined to agree with Mr Wilson that this case is not strictly about the repackaging of Microsoft's product. It is rather about the deliberate destruction of a material part of the packaging which Microsoft has applied to its products, the object of such exercise being to conceal from the purchaser features about the product which Microsoft had intentionally spelt out on the destroyed packaging, namely that the enclosed product was either designed and intended solely for the North American market or for North American academic users at the concessionary price. Products supplied by Microsoft for retail distribution in North America are only licensed for use by an end user if the first end user purchases in North America. Likewise, products supplied by Microsoft for retail distribution to academic users in North America are only licensed for use if the first end user is an academic who purchases in North America. The purpose of the destruction of Microsoft's outer packaging was to facilitate sales of the software which Microsoft had not authorised. CFD's dealings in supplying the licence packs and family bundles were similarly unauthorised by Microsoft.

I agree with Mr Wilson that marketing the products in plain brown boxes was not an exercise which was likely to have any adverse effects on the condition of the software itself. On the other hand, Microsoft does not sell its software separately, since it is a feature of its operations that a particular item of software must be accompanied by a related EULA. One possible effect of the marketing of the products in the brown boxes was the increased risk that there would be an intermediate splitting up of software and EULAs. Microsoft claims that this is what CFD did when selling MLP12 to Technology plc. CFD denies that, and I do not consider that I can resolve that factual dispute on this application. However, the point is that the brown box trade facilitated the tampering with the contents of the original product in this way. Further, I do not accept that CFD dealt only with OEMs. Mr Stuart's evidence is to the effect that his supply of EULAs to Option Technologies derived from software packages returned to CFD by dissatisfied purchasers, by which I interpret him to mean end users.

I have come to the conclusion that CFD's contention that Microsoft can have no legitimate reasons for opposing CFD's manner of trading is one that does not give rise to a triable issue. I accept Mr Baldwin's submission that Microsoft has established trade mark infringement by CFD with regard to all six heads of complaint. . . .

[Microsoft also prevailed on the passing off and copyright infringement counts. The latter was based on the theory that CFD did not have authority to license use of the software because Microsoft had not consented to this.]

G. CONTRACTS AND LICENSING

Computer software is often distributed in the world market in packages containing shrinkwrap licenses, such as those discussed in Chapter 6. Although individually negotiated license agreements are generally enforceable in the international arena, national laws differ considerably as to whether or under what circumstances mass-market shrinkwrap licenses are enforceable, as the excerpts below explain:

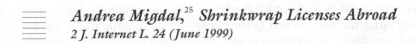

Andrea Migdal,[25] *Shrinkwrap Licenses Abroad*
2 J. Internet L. 24 (June 1999)

Questions Regarding Enforceability

The problem of finding an "offer and acceptance" of shrinkwrap licenses has resulted in judicial uncertainty as to their enforceability, both at home and abroad.

---

25. Andrea Migdal is a partner in the Intellectual Property and Technology Group of Gray Cary Ware & Freidenrich in San Diego, CA.

Until recently, courts in the United States refused to enforce shrinkwraps. However, in 1996, the Seventh Circuit upheld the provisions of a shrinkwrap license in the case of ProCD, Inc. v. Zeidenberg, departing from previous court decisions and creating a split in judicial precedent. Since *ProCD*, most US courts have upheld shrinkwrap licenses. Shrinkwraps are more likely to be upheld if the consumer has the opportunity to read the license requirements and, if the consumer disagrees with the terms of the license, is afforded the opportunity to return the software for a refund.

Similarly, the laws of foreign countries have swung back and forth and are unclear and incomplete in many instances as to the enforceability of shrinkwraps. Some nations expressly forbid the use of shrinkwraps; others allow them without limitation. Many other countries tread the middle ground by allowing the use of shrinkwraps subject to limitations.

This article provides a brief overview of the positions of selected foreign countries on the enforceability of shrinkwrap licenses. As will be noted in the information provided below, in many countries there has been neither a definitive court ruling on the enforceability of shrinkwraps nor legislation in favor of prohibiting shrinkwraps. Accordingly, conclusions reached regarding the enforceability of shrinkwraps in many countries is based on (1) analogy to the treatment of other consumer terms or (2) consumer acceptance.

Fairness to Consumers Governs Shrinkwrap Enforcement

The countries noted below are divided roughly into two groups. The first consists of countries that appear to have either an extremely general policy or no articulated policy at all toward shrinkwraps. The second includes countries that appear to have developed at least a modest set of enforcement standards to govern shrinkwraps.

A number of countries generally enforce shrinkwrap licenses. These countries include Argentina (preliminary measures granted in favor of shrinkwraps), Belgium (shrinkwraps upheld when general conditions of validity are met), Egypt (shrinkwraps enforced without specific requirements), Hong Kong (shrinkwraps upheld when they are reasonable and for which reasonable consideration has been given), and Malaysia (shrinkwraps upheld, though courts would defer to US or UK judicial decisions).

In contrast, there is a view among foreign counsel in a number of countries that shrinkwraps would not be enforced if the terms were actually tested by a consumer. These countries include Finland (shrinkwraps are commonly used, but are probably not enforceable), Italy (enforcement would probably not be possible unless shrinkwraps became an industry standard), Norway, Poland, Singapore, South Africa, Taiwan, and Venezuela.

In general, the extent of shrinkwrap enforcement is limited by a concern for fairness to consumers. Nations that have developed enforcement standards for shrinkwraps often restrict enforcement to prevent the same abuses sought to be prevented by the contracts doctrine of "unconscionability." Thus, not surprisingly, limitations on shrinkwraps are usually imposed in two ways. The first is by prohibiting "surprise" to the consumer by making sure shrinkwrap terms are visible and understandable to purchasers prior to purchase (procedural unconscionability). The second is by invalidating shrinkwrap terms that are grossly unfair or illegal (substantive unconscionability).

Other Countries Enforce Shrinkwraps Subject to Limitations

A handful of countries enforce shrinkwrap licenses subject to articulated limitations. Various limitations are aimed at preventing surprise to the consumer. For example, many countries require the shrinkwrap to be in the purchaser's native language (e.g., Colombia, Denmark, France, Germany, Japan, and Italy). Other countries require clear and visible presentation of the license terms on the exterior of the packaging (e.g., Australia, Denmark, the Dominican Republic, France, Germany, Italy, Japan, and the United Kingdom).

Other limitations aim less at preventing surprise than at preventing substantive unfairness. For example, many countries prohibit shrinkwrap terms that are unduly burdensome or illegal. These countries include Austria (shrinkwraps are subject to certain restrictions under the Austrian Consumer Protection Law), Brazil (shrinkwraps must not violate "mandatory legal provisions"), Colombia (limits enforcement of shrinkwrap terms, requiring the payment of royalties), France (declares invalid severe limitations on reverse engineering and consumer remedies against the manufacturer), Germany (declares invalid severe limitations on consumer remedies and the purchaser's right to use the product), Italy (declares invalid severe limitations on consumer remedies and transferability), Israel (shrinkwraps are subject to the Standard Contracts Act of 1982, which invalidates depriving or restricting conditions), Japan (courts protect consumer remedies), and the United Kingdom (encroachment on European Community law is suspect; some limitations on consumer remedies and reverse engineering are invalid).

Conclusion

The use of shrinkwraps, though widespread as a business practice, is not universally and definitively recognized as a valid contract. Further, the wide variety of loosely articulated enforcement standards has created a potential maze for software manufacturers attempting to maximize the use of shrinkwraps internationally. However, even where no precedent or laws governing enforceability exist, shrinkwrap licenses can be useful to the licensor, at least as a potential deterrent to widespread copying, reverse engineering, and related licensing concerns. A licensor can also create the conditions for more likely enforcement of its shrinkwrap license by:

- providing a clear opportunity for the consumer to accept the license (e.g., "click here to accept and install");
- avoiding overly onerous terms, which might be voided as an adhesion contract or against public policy; and
- "localizing" licenses through translation and attention to other consumer law provisions.

≣ *Imprimatur, Report on Formation and Validity of*
On-Line Contracts in the European Union
Institute for Information Law, U. Amsterdam, June 1998

. . . Under British law the legal qualification of a shrinkwrap license is complex. First there is the doctrine of "privity of contract." This prescribes a direct contractual connection between parties. In the software business there is no such direct connection between producer and user. Software is sold through retailers. Secondly, according to the doctrine of "consideration" in order to achieve a binding license between producer and user, consideration has to be given for such a contract. It is doubtful whether merely breaking a cellophane seal can be said to amount to consideration. Judges confronted with a shrinkwrap case, will have to apply these doctrines, but may also want to give effect to a shrinkwrap license. To reconcile these interests is a dilemma under British law.

In December 1995 the first British judgment on the enforceability of shrinkwrap licences was passed: Beta v. Adobe. The facts of this case brought before a Scottish court are the following. Adobe placed an order with retailer Beta for the supply of software produced by Informix. Beta delivered the software package to user Adobe. Adobe ultimately did not want the software, and relying on the producer's shrinkwrap provisions including the right to return the software, tried to return the package. But Beta refused it and later sued Adobe for payment of the invoiced price. Beta contended that the purchaser had made an unconditional order. The supply had been made and so the price was due. Adobe's position was that the shrinkwrap terms were incorporated into the contract at point of sale. The court gave judgement to Adobe. It did give effect to the shrinkwrap license by applying the Scottish doctrine of *ius quaesitum tertio*. This doctrine allows a party to a bilateral contract (i.e. Beta) to create contractual rights for the benefit of a third party (i.e. the producer). This implies the third party is able to enforce these rights directly against the end user. . . .

Netherlands

Only one decision dealing with the enforceability of a shrinkwrap license has been reported. It is a judgment by the Amsterdam court of first instance of May 24, 1995 in the case of Coss Holland B.V. v. TM Data Nederland B.V. The facts of this case are the following. Distributor TM Data supplied software, produced by Raima, to user Coss. According to TM Data, the text of Raima's shrinkwrap license terms were enclosed in the packing of the software. Coss denied the terms were present in the packing. When the computer program turned out not to function properly and attempts to repair it failed, Coss claimed damages from TM Data. TM Data refused to pay damages contending that TM Data was not a party to the shrinkwrap license, the license being concluded between Raima and Coss. The court rejected this defence. It held a licence agreement cannot be formed by simply opening the packing of software. A license agreement can only be concluded validly if a user is aware that by opening a packing he becomes party to a license agreement. Moreover the contents of the license terms will have to be clear to the user beforehand.

From this judgement one can conclude that under Dutch law shrinkwrap licenses may be enforceable provided that users are aware of the use of such licenses and know the contents of the license terms before the agreement is formed. Dutch commentators opine that a user has to be familiar with the contents of the license terms before or at the moment the license agreement is formed.

Conclusion

. . . From case law it becomes clear that the enforceability of shrinkwrap licenses will be determined by the following factors:

- the awareness of the user of the existence of a shrinkwrap license: is a user aware that the product he ordered is subject to a shrinkwrap license? If so is he aware that by opening the product's packing he agrees to the license terms?
- the user's familiarity with the contents of the license terms. The license terms have to be available.
- the moment upon which the user was informed about the terms.

COMMENTS AND QUESTIONS

1. The Scottish case cited by the Imprimatur Report involved an attempt by the recipient of a shrinkwrap license to enforce terms that were favorable to the purchaser. This reverses the normal model. Should this matter in determining the enforceability of the shrinkwrap license? Can a user turn the document drafted by the licensor into a binding contract by adopting it? If so, what, if any, support does this provide for efforts by licensors to enforce shrinkwrap licenses?

2. Most shrinkwrap licenses contain provisions purporting to determine both the forum in which disputes may be litigated and the law that will apply to those disputes. If these provisions are enforceable in most countries, they will significantly skew the resolution of software disputes, probably toward certain states in the United States.

3. Software vendors in the United States have been pushing for the adoption of the Uniform Computer Information Transactions Act, which would govern transactions involving computer software and digital information. This model law is discussed in detail in Chapter 6. There is no similar statute in the works in the rest of the world that would validate shrinkwrap licenses or enact many of the other provisions that benefit software vendors.

4. For a discussion of the status of contract law in Japan, see, e.g., Tsuneo Matsumoto, Article 2B and Mass Market License Contracts: A Japanese Perspective, 13 Berkeley Tech. L.J. 1283 (1998).

H. ANTITRUST AND COMPETITION POLICY

Approximately 60 countries in the world have antitrust-like laws. These countries typically use the term "competition law" to describe their body of law that performs the functions that antitrust law serves in the United States. Many of these competition laws are relatively new (i.e., less than 10 years old) and less fully developed than U.S. antitrust law. In general, computer technology firms are free to exercise their intellectual property rights in the international marketplace in a manner that will best serve the firm's interests. There are, however, several areas where competition policy issues tend to arise in regulation of the computer technology marketplace.

One prominent example was an action that the Competition Directorate of the European Commission took against IBM Corporation in the 1980s because IBM's alterations to program interfaces were perceived to have harmed competition in the market for peripheral devices. This case was settled with IBM's agreement to disclose changes in its interfaces. The Commission's experience in the IBM case contributed to the Commission's subsequent insistence that the European Council's Directive on the Legal Protection of Computer Programs include three competition-enhancing rules: (1) a rule that interfaces necessary for achieving interoperability of computer programs should not be protected by copyright law; (2) a rule that decompilation of computer program code should be permissible when necessary to achieve interoperability; and (3) a rule that contract terms aiming to override the decompilation privilege would be null and void.

Similar considerations led the European Commission to make the right of lawful users of a database to extract and reuse under the new sui generis right in the contents of databases nonwaivable by contract. Concerns about potential abuses of dominant firms in the database industry nearly led the Commission to adopt a compulsory license scheme for sole source and government databases in the sui generis database law. However, the *Magill* decision (below) apparently persuaded the Commission that competition policy could adequately address abuses of dominant positions in the database market. The Commission is sufficiently concerned about the potential for abuse by database providers that it intends to review and periodically report on licensing practices in this field. However, the *Magill* decision will apply more generally to the licensing of intellectual property rights in the EU.

Radio Telefis Eireann (RTE) and Independent Television Publications Ltd. (ITP) v. Commission of the European Communities
Court of Justice of the European Communities
1995 E.C.J. CELEX LEXIS 3670, [1995] E.C.R. I-743,
[1995] 4 C.M.L.R. 718

. . . 6   According to the judgments of the Court of First Instance, most households in Ireland and 30% to 40% of households in Northern Ireland can receive television programmes broadcast by RTE, ITV and BBC.

7   At the material time, no comprehensive weekly television guide was available on the market in Ireland or in Northern Ireland. Each television station published a television guide covering exclusively its own programmes and claimed, under Irish and United Kingdom legislation, copyright protection for its own weekly programme listings in order to prevent their reproduction by third parties. . . .

9   ITP, RTE and BBC practised the following policy with regard to the dissemination of programme listings. They provided their programme schedules free of charge, on request, to daily and periodical newspapers, accompanied by a licence for which no charge was made, setting out the conditions under which that information could be reproduced. Daily listings and, if the following day was a public holiday, the listings for two days, could thus be published in the press, subject to certain conditions relating to the format of publication. Publication of "highlights" of the week was also authorized. ITP, RTE and the BBC ensured strict compliance with the licence conditions by instituting legal proceedings, where necessary, against publications which failed to comply with them.

10   Magill TV Guide Ltd ("Magill") attempted to publish a comprehensive weekly television guide but was prevented from doing so by the appellants and the BBC, which obtained injunctions prohibiting publication of weekly television listings.

11   Magill lodged a complaint with the Commission on 4 April 1986 under Article 3 of Regulation No 17 of the Council of 6 February 1962, the First Regulation implementing Articles 85 and 86 of the Treaty (OJ, English Special Edition 1959-1962, p. 87) ("Regulation No 17") seeking a declaration that the appellants and the BBC were abusing their dominant position by refusing to grant licences for the publication of their respective weekly listings. The Commission decided to initiate a proceeding, at the end of which it adopted Decision 89/205/EEC of 21 December 1988 relating to a proceeding under Article 86 of the EEC Treaty (IV/31.851. Magill TV Guide/ITP, BBC and RTE) (OJ 1989 L 78, p. 43) ("the decision"), which was the subject-matter of the proceedings before the Court of First Instance.

12   In that decision the Commission found that there had been a breach of Article 86 of the EEC Treaty and ordered the three organizations to put an end to that breach, in particular "by supplying . . . third parties on request and on a non-discriminatory basis with their individual advance weekly programme listings and by permitting reproduction of those listings by such parties". It was also provided that, if the three organizations chose to grant reproduction licences, any royalties requested should be reasonable. . . .

24   So far as the existence of a dominant position is concerned, the Court of First Instance held that "ITP enjoyed, as a consequence of its copyright in ITV and Channel 4 programme listings, which had been transferred to it by the television companies broadcasting on those channels, the exclusive right to reproduce and market those listings. It was thus able, at the material time, to secure a monopoly over the publication of its weekly listings in the TV Times, a magazine specializing in the programmes of ITV and Channel 4". Consequently, in the opinion of the Court of First Instance, "the applicant clearly held at that time a dominant position both on the market represented by its weekly listings and on the market for the magazines in which they were published in Ireland and Northern Ireland. Third parties such as Magill who wished to publish a general television magazine were in a situation of economic dependence on the applicant, which was thus in a position to hinder the emergence of any effective competition on the market for information on its weekly programmes" (*ITP* judgment, paragraph 49). With regard to RTE, the Court of First Instance reached the same conclusion in nearly identical terms (*RTE* judgment, paragraph 63).

25   So far as the existence of an abuse of that dominant position was concerned, the Court of First Instance considered that it was necessary to interpret Article 86 in the light of copyright in programme listings. It pointed out that, in the absence of harmonization of national rules or Community standardization, determination of the conditions and procedures under which copyright was protected was a matter for national rules (*ITP* judgment, paragraphs 50 and 51). The relationship between national intellectual property rights and the general rules of Community law was governed expressly by Article 36 of the EEC Treaty, which provided for the possibility of derogating from the rules relating to the free movement of goods on grounds of the protection of industrial or commercial property, subject to the conditions set out in the second sentence of Article 36. Article 36 thus emphasized that the reconciliation between the requirements of the free movement of goods and the respect to which intellectual property rights were entitled had to be achieved in such a way as to protect the legitimate exercise of such rights, which alone was justified within the meaning of that article, and to preclude any improper exercise thereof likely to create artificial partitions within the market or pervert the rules governing competition within the Community. The Court of First Instance took the view that the exercise of intellectual property rights conferred by national legislation had consequently to be restricted as far as was necessary for that reconciliation (*ITP* judgment, paragraph 52).

26   The Court of First Instance found, in the light of the case-law of the Court of Justice, that it followed from Article 36 of the Treaty that only those restrictions on freedom of competition, free movement of goods or freedom to provide services which were inherent in the protection of the actual substance of the intellectual property right were permitted in Community law. It based its view in particular on the judgment of the Court of Justice in Case 78/70 Deutsche Grammophon v Metro 1971 ECR 487, paragraph 11, in which the Court of Justice held that, although it permitted prohibitions or restrictions on the free movement of products which were justified for the purpose of protecting industrial and commercial property, Article 36 only admitted derogations from that freedom to the extent to which they were justified for the purpose of safeguarding rights which constituted the specific subject-matter of such property (*ITP* judgment, paragraph 54).

27   The Court of First Instance then observed that in principle the protection of the specific subject-matter of a copyright entitled the copyright-holder to reserve the exclusive right to reproduce the protected work (*ITP* judgment, paragraph 55).

28   However, the Court of First Instance took the view that, while it was plain that the exercise of the exclusive right to reproduce a protected work was not in itself an abuse, that did not apply when, in the light of the details of each individual case, it was apparent that that right was being exercised in such ways and circumstances as in fact to pursue an aim manifestly contrary to the objectives of Article 86. In that event, the Court of First Instance continued, the copyright was no longer being exercised in a manner which corresponded to its essential function, within the meaning of Article 36 of the Treaty, which was to protect the moral rights in the work and ensure a reward for the creative effort, while respecting the aims of, in particular, Article 86. From this the Court of First Instance concluded that the primacy of Community law, particularly as regards principles as fundamental as those of the free movement of goods and freedom of competition, prevailed over any use of a rule of national intellectual property law in a manner contrary to those principles (*ITP* judgment, paragraph 56).

29   In the present case, the Court of First Instance noted that the applicants, by reserving the exclusive right to publish their weekly television programme listings, were preventing the emergence on the market of a new product, namely a general television magazine likely to compete with their own magazines. The applicants were thus using their copyright in the programme listings produced as part of the activity of broadcasting in order to secure a monopoly in the derivative market of weekly television guides in Ireland and Northern Ireland. The Court of First Instance also regarded it as significant in that regard that the applicants had authorized, free of charge, the publication of their daily listings and highlights of their weekly programmes in the press in both Ireland and the United Kingdom.

30   The Court of First Instance accordingly took the view that conduct of that type . . . characterized by preventing the production and marketing of a new product, for which there was potential consumer demand, on the ancillary market of weekly television guides and thereby excluding all competition from that market solely in order to secure the applicants' respective monopolies clearly went beyond what was necessary to fulfil the essential function of the copyright as permitted in Community law. The applicants' refusal to authorize third parties to publish their weekly listings was, in this case, the Court of First Instance ruled, arbitrary in so far as it was not justified by the requirements peculiar to the activity of publishing television magazines. It was thus possible for the applicants to adapt to the conditions of a television magazine market which was open to competition in order to ensure the commercial viability of their weekly publications. The applicants' conduct could not, in those circumstances, be covered in Community law by the protection conferred by their copyright in the programme listings (*ITP* judgment, paragraph 58). . . .

32   The Court of First Instance accordingly dismissed the plea in law based on breach of Article 86.

33   RTE, supported by IPO, relies on the judgment in Case 238/87 Volvo v Veng 1988 ECR 6211 in arguing that the exercise by an owner of intellectual property rights of his exclusive rights, in particular his refusal to grant a licence, cannot in itself be regarded as an abuse of a dominant position.

34   According to RTE, ITP and IPO, one of the essential rights of the owner of a copyright, without which that right would be deprived of its substance, is the exclusive right of reproduction. That right, which has not been placed in question by the Treaty rules, entitles its holder to be rewarded by the exclusive sale of the products incorporating the protected work and to prevent competition by a third party in respect of those products.

35   ITP denies that the exercise of the exclusive right of reproduction is itself an abuse where it is in pursuit of an aim manifestly contrary to the objectives of Article 86 (*ITP* judgment, paragraph 56) since copyright owners ordinarily and naturally exercise their copyright in order to restrict competition with their own product by other products made using their copyright material, even on a derived market. That, it continues, is the essence of copyright.

36   IPO considers that copyright is by nature beneficial for competition, pointing out that it attributes exclusive proprietorial rights only to a particular expression of an idea or concept, not to the concept or idea itself.

37   RTE and IPO point out that, in the absence of Community harmonization, the scope of national copyright laws can be defined only by the legislature of each Member State. The definition of that scope cannot be altered by a measure

adopted in implementation of Article 86, but only by specific Community legislation.

38   Moreover, according to RTE, the right of first marketing has been considered in the case-law of the Court of Justice as the specific subject-matter of all industrial property rights.

39   RTE contends that the owner of an intellectual property right is under no obligation to offer justification for his refusal to grant a licence, contrary to the view taken by the Court of First Instance. ITP adds that this view of the Court of First Instance is not supported by the case-law of the Court of Justice and that, due to the imprecision of the criteria used, it undermines legal certainty for copyright owners.

40   According to RTE and IPO, a refusal, by the owner of a right, to grant a licence forms part of the specific subject-matter of his exclusive right. RTE considers that this would constitute an abuse only in very particular circumstances and IPO adds that the use of an intellectual property right is justified if it is within the scope of the specific subject-matter of the right in question.

41   IPO and RTE criticize the approach, adopted by the Court of First Instance and the Commission in this case, of seeing copyright as a mere combination of the right of attribution of authorship and the right to compensation for exploitation. IPO claims that this is in marked contrast not only to the laws of the various Member States but also to the Berne Convention and would represent a significant diminution of the protection afforded by copyright. ITP adds that this view overlooks the right of exclusive reproduction and distinguishes between the protection of moral rights and the protection of commercial rights with the result that assignees of the creator, such as ITP, cannot avail themselves of moral rights, which are inalienable, and will therefore be unable to exercise the right of exclusive reproduction.

42   RTE submits that consumer demand cannot justify application of Article 86 to the present cases and that it is for the national legislature alone to remedy such a situation, as has been done in the United Kingdom. ITP adds that it is ordinarily the case that a copyright owner who sells his own product made from his copyright material deprives consumers of the opportunity of obtaining it elsewhere.

43   Next, according to IPO, there is no presumption that the holder of an intellectual property right is in a dominant position within the meaning of Article 86 (judgments in Case 40/70 *Sirena v EDA and Others* 1971 ECR 69 and Case 78/70 *Deutsche Grammophon*, cited above). Relying in particular on the judgment in Case 322/81 *Michelin v Commission* 1983 ECR 3461, IPO takes the view that a dominant position presupposes a position of economic strength and for that reason it calls in question the analysis of the Court of First Instance that the appellants were dominant merely because they held copyrights without reference to any analysis whatever of economic power in the marketplace.

44   IPO also criticizes the Commission for having failed to apply the criterion of dominant position based on economic power and having taken the view that the appellants and the BBC held a factual monopoly. In doing so, the Commission takes the view that a factual monopoly is likely to arise wherever there exists a primary market and a secondary market and a third party wishes to avail itself of the products or services on the primary market in order to carry on business on the secondary market. According to IPO, the Commission considers that such a situa-

tion will result in a position of economic dependence which is characteristic of the existence of a dominant position.

45   IPO criticizes this conception in so far as it artificially links economic dependence with the intention of a third party, who would always have the possibility of undertaking some other economic venture. For IPO, the concept of "factual monopoly" appears to be an artificial construct whereby the Commission seeks to justify the use of competition law in order to change the specific subject-matter of copyright.

(a)   Existence of a Dominant Position

46   So far as dominant position is concerned, it is to be remembered at the outset that mere ownership of an intellectual property right cannot confer such a position.

47   However, the basic information as to the channel, day, time and title of programmes is the necessary result of programming by television stations, which are thus the only source of such information for an undertaking, like Magill, which wishes to publish it together with commentaries or pictures. By force of circumstance, RTE and ITP, as the agent of ITV, enjoy, along with the BBC, a de facto monopoly over the information used to compile listings for the television programmes received in most households in Ireland and 30% to 40% of households in Northern Ireland. The appellants are thus in a position to prevent effective competition on the market in weekly television magazines. The Court of First Instance was therefore right in confirming the Commission's assessment that the appellants occupied a dominant position (see the judgment in Case 322/81 *Michelin*, cited above, paragraph 30).

(b)   Existence of Abuse

48   With regard to the issue of abuse, the arguments of the appellants and IPO wrongly presuppose that where the conduct of an undertaking in a dominant position consists of the exercise of a right classified by national law as "copyright", such conduct can never be reviewed in relation to Article 86 of the Treaty.

49   Admittedly, in the absence of Community standardization or harmonization of laws, determination of the conditions and procedures for granting protection of an intellectual property right is a matter for national rules. Further, the exclusive right of reproduction forms part of the author's rights, so that refusal to grant a licence, even if it is the act of an undertaking holding a dominant position, cannot in itself constitute abuse of a dominant position (judgment in Case 238/87 *Volvo*, cited above, paragraphs 7 and 8).

50   However, it is also clear from that judgment (paragraph 9) that the exercise of an exclusive right by the proprietor may, in exceptional circumstances, involve abusive conduct.

51   In the present case, the conduct objected to is the appellants' reliance on copyright conferred by national legislation so as to prevent Magill or any other undertaking having the same intention from publishing on a weekly basis informa-

tion (channel, day, time and title of programmes) together with commentaries and pictures obtained independently of the appellants.

52   Among the circumstances taken into account by the Court of First Instance in concluding that such conduct was abusive was, first, the fact that there was, according to the findings of the Court of First Instance, no actual or potential substitute for a weekly television guide offering information on the programmes for the week ahead. On this point, the Court of First Instance confirmed the Commission's finding that the complete lists of programmes for a 24-hour period and for a 48-hour period at weekends and before public holidays published in certain daily and Sunday newspapers, and the television sections of certain magazines covering, in addition, "highlights" of the week's programmes, were only to a limited extent substitutable for advance information to viewers on all the week's programmes. Only weekly television guides containing comprehensive listings for the week ahead would enable users to decide in advance which programmes they wished to follow and arrange their leisure activities for the week accordingly. The Court of First Instance also established that there was a specific, constant and regular potential demand on the part of consumers (see the *RTE* judgment, paragraph 62, and the *ITP* judgment, paragraph 48).

53   Thus the appellants, who were, by force of circumstance, the only sources of the basic information on programme scheduling which is the indispensable raw material for compiling a weekly television guide, gave viewers wishing to obtain information on the choice of programmes for the week ahead no choice but to buy the weekly guides for each station and draw from each of them the information they needed to make comparisons.

54   The appellants' refusal to provide basic information by relying on national copyright provisions thus prevented the appearance of a new product, a comprehensive weekly guide to television programmes, which the appellants did not offer and for which there was a potential consumer demand. Such refusal constitutes an abuse under heading (b) of the second paragraph of Article 86 of the Treaty.

55   Second, there was no justification for such refusal either in the activity of television broadcasting or in that of publishing television magazines (*RTE* judgment, paragraph 73, and *ITP* judgment, paragraph 58).

56   Third, and finally, as the Court of First Instance also held, the appellants, by their conduct, reserved to themselves the secondary market of weekly television guides by excluding all competition on that market (see the judgment in *Joined Cases* 6/73 and 7/73 Commercial Solvents v Commission 1974 ECR 223, paragraph 25) since they denied access to the basic information which is the raw material indispensable for the compilation of such a guide.

57   In the light of all those circumstances, the Court of First Instance did not err in law in holding that the appellants' conduct was an abuse of a dominant position within the meaning of Article 86 of the Treaty. . . .

91   In the present case, after finding that the refusal to provide undertakings such as Magill with the basic information contained in television programme listings was an abuse of a dominant position, the Commission was entitled under Article 3, in order to ensure that its decision was effective, to require the appellants to provide that information. As the Court of First Instance rightly found, the imposition of that obligation with the possibility of making authorization of publication dependent on certain conditions, including payment of royalties was the only way of bringing the infringement to an end.

COMMENTS AND QUESTIONS

1. Prior to adoption of the European Directive on the Legal Protection of Databases, U.K. copyright law allowed compilers of factual data to obtain copyright protection for their compilations on a "sweat of the brow" theory. Although the EU Directive now harmonizes European copyright law on an "intellectual creation" standard of originality, it "grandfathered" in copyright protection for compilations protected by national law prior to the effective date of the directive.

2. How would U.S. courts deal with the same issue as in *Magill*? In particular, it is interesting to contrast *Magill* with the Microsoft cases and the cases regarding mandatory disclosure of interfaces. Does *Magill* suggest that Microsoft might be forced to publish its APIs in a European court?

3. The *Magill* decision has been criticized in Europe for applying competition law too broadly. See, e.g., Per Jebsen & Robert Stevens, Assumptions, Goals, and Dominant Undertakings: The Regulation of Competition Under Article 86 of the European Union, 64 Antitrust L.J. 443, 461 (1996).

> "In that case, the primacy of Community Law, particularly as regards principles as fundamental as those of the free movement of goods and freedom of competition, prevails over any use of a rule of national intellectual property in a manner contrary to these principles." . . . With these words the CFI in *Radio Telefis Eireann* struck fear into the hearts of all businesses operating in sectors where intellectual property is of great significance. . . . The decision in *Radio Telefis Eireann*—undermining much of the assumed strength of intellectual property—is an appropriate place to begin our analysis of Article 86.

Seemingly consistent with *Magill*, however, is Article 8(2) of the TRIPS Agreement, which states that "[a]ppropriate measures . . . may be needed to prevent the abuse of intellectual property rights by rightsholders or the resort to practices which unreasonably restrain trade or adversely affect the international transfer of technology."

Most cases since *Magill* reinforce the propositions that *Magill* presented unusual facts, and that refusals to license intellectual property trigger Article 82 (formerly Article 86) scrutiny only in "exceptional circumstances." The *IMS Health* litigation may signal a new direction. IMS Health, in cooperation with German pharmaceutical companies, devised a scheme for tracking pharmaceutical sales data in Germany. The scheme is known as the "1860-brick structure" because it divides Germany into 1,860 geographic territories ("bricks"), allowing sales data to be broken down into small segments without necessarily identifying particular buyers. In 2000, IMS Health sued in Frankfurt District Court (*Landgericht*), alleging that two competitors, NDC and AzyX Geopharma, were infringing IMS's copyright in the 1860-brick structure. NDC (and eventually AzyX) requested that IMS grant a license under the brick structure copyright pending resolution of the copyright dispute, but IMS did not grant a license. NDC thereafter complained to the European Commission, alleging that IMS's refusal to license its copyright in the 1860-brick structure violated Article 82.

The Commission imposed interim measures in the form of a requirement that IMS grant a royalty-bearing license under the 1860-brick structure to NDC and AzyX, extending until the Commission rendered a final decision in the matter.

NDC Health/IMS Health: Interim Measures, Case COMP D3/38.044 (July 3, 2001), http://europa.eu.int/comm/competition/antitrust/cases/decisions/38044/en.pdf. Reviewing the Article 82 abuse cases, the Commission set out a three-part standard for evaluating Article 82 abuse "in cases relating to the exercise of a property right," particularly those which arguably involved exploitation of "essential facilities," defined as follows:

- the refusal of access to the facility is likely to eliminate all competition in the relevant market;
- such refusal is not capable of being objectively justified; and
- the facility itself is indispensable to carrying on business, inasmuch as there is no actual or potential substitute in existence for that facility.

The Commission concluded that the standard was satisfied here, even given the "exceptional circumstances" limitation enunciated in *Magill*. According to the Commission,

> [a] dominant company has negotiated over a long period with its customer industry so as to produce a structure on which the industry is now very highly dependent, to the extent that they consider it a de facto industry standard, and which a national court has now found is the dominant company's intellectual property. This dominant company now refuses to license this structure to competitors, so that no competing products based on this structure can be produced.

Putting it another way, the Commission concluded that the 1860-brick structure constituted an "indispensable input." That is, in *Magill*, "the basic information about TV programmes was considered to be an indispensable input to allow an undertaking to compete in a downstream market (that for television listings magazines)," and, similarly, in *IMS*, "the use of the 1860-brick structure is an indispensable input to allow undertakings to compete in the market for regional sales data services in Germany."

IMS appealed to the CFI, which issued an interim order, later confirmed after a hearing, suspending the duty to license pending resolution of the appeal. See Case T-184/01R1 (Oct. 26, 2001). For a detailed discussion, see Herbert Hovenkamp et al., IP and Antitrust §45.5b3. For commentary criticizing the interim measures decision as an objectionable extension of *Magill*, see Valentine Korah, The Interface Between Intellectual Property and Antitrust: The European Experience, 69 Antitrust L.J. 801, 828-30 (2001).

4. Both U.S. and EU law regulate competition matters by announcing broad principles against anticompetitive activity and leaving the specific application of these principles to the courts (and in the EU, the Commission) on a case-by-case basis. Article 81(1) (formerly 85(1)) of the Treaty Establishing the European Community, for example, outlaws all agreements that "have as their object or effect the prevention, restriction or distortion of competition within the common market," in particular those that:

(a) directly or indirectly fix purchase or selling prices or any other trading conditions;

(b)   limit or control production, markets, technical development, or investment;

(c)   share markets or sources of supply;

(d)   apply dissimilar conditions to equivalent transactions with other trading parties, thereby placing them at a competitive disadvantage;

(e)   make the conclusion of contracts subject to acceptance by the other parties of supplementary obligations which, by their nature or according to commercial usage, have no connection with the subject of such contracts.

Article 82 defines "an abuse of a dominant position" as those acts, done by a monopolist, that Article 81(1) (formerly 85(1)) (a), (b), (d), and (e) make illegal when done by combination among firms.

It is noteworthy that the EU, like the United States, recognizes the need for a flexible approach to certain practices that would be considered anticompetitive in an industrial economy but that may be necessary to the efficient exploitation of intellectual property rights. In Europe, this recognition comes in the form of block exemptions for many intellectual property licensing practices. See, e.g., Jiamming Shen, Block Exemption for Technology Licensing Agreements Under Commission Regulation (EC) No. 240/96, 20 B.C. Int'l & Comp. L. Rev. 251 (1997). European block exemptions are not found in the Treaty Establishing the European Community; they are implemented separately in the form of EC regulations.

5.   United States antitrust authorities have recognized that the global nature of the computer industry is a challenge for antitrust enforcers. Joel Klein of the U.S. Antitrust Division explained the U.S. strategy for applying antitrust to the global computer industry in this way:

> To seek effective antitrust enforcement in global industries, we in the Department of Justice have developed three approaches. First, we rely on coordinated enforcement actions, in which we pursue parallel investigations of particular practices with other national competition authorities through shared information and cooperation. Second, we invoke positive comity, a doctrine in which one enforcement agency requests enforcement action by another country where the latter may be better able to challenge or curb the anticompetitive activities in question. Finally, we directly apply our laws to conduct occurring in whole or in part in other jurisdictions where the effects of such conduct may be felt in the United States.

Joel Klein & Preeta Bansal, International Antitrust Enforcement in the Computer Industry, 41 Vill. L. Rev. 173 (1996) (giving examples of each strategy). See also U.S. Dep't of Justice & Fed. Trade Comm'n, Antitrust Enforcement Guidelines for International Operations (Apr. 1995).

6.   The lack of uniformity in competition policies around the world has alarmed some commentators, who suggest that, in a global market, companies should have to adhere to a single standard of conduct worldwide. For a discussion of the lack of uniformity among national antitrust laws, reasons for this diversity, and an explanation about why it may be difficult to get a WTO agreement on competition policy, see Eleanor M. Fox, Trade, Competition, and Intellectual Property —TRIPS and Its Antitrust Counterparts, 29 Vand. J. Transnat'l L. 481, 494 (1996). On the problems with achieving international cooperation in applying anti-

trust principles, see Andrew T. Guzman, Is International Antitrust Possible?, 73 N.Y.U. L. Rev. 1501 (1998).

The problems with lack of antitrust uniformity are exacerbated by the growing tendency of the United States and some other countries to apply their laws extraterritorially. The United States, for example, has applied its criminal statute to a price-fixing agreement that occurred entirely within Japan because the consequences of the agreement could be felt in the United States. See, e.g., United States v. Nippon Paper, 109 F.3d 1 (1st Cir. 1997), *cert. denied*, 118 S. Ct. 685 (1998).

This extraterritoriality problem is a single instance of a much larger problem in international law, one that affects intellectual property rules as well. We discuss the question of extraterritorial effect in more detail in the next section.

I. EXTRATERRITORIALITY

Given the complexity of dealing with the many substantive, procedural, and remedial differences in the laws and legal systems of other nations, some companies may heartily wish to bring an action in U.S. courts to get remedies for infringements, even though some or all of the acts have occurred outside the United States. United States courts have generally been reluctant to accept cases involving extraterritorial infringement. However, a predicate act in the United States that relates to activities outside the United States may provide a basis for U.S. courts to exercise jurisdiction.

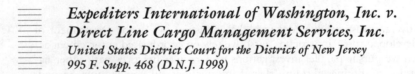

Expediters International of Washington, Inc. v. Direct Line Cargo Management Services, Inc.
United States District Court for the District of New Jersey
995 F. Supp. 468 (D.N.J. 1998)

This matter involves the alleged wrongful use of a computer software program. Plaintiff Expediters International ("EI") claims that a Taiwan company, Direct Line Cargo Management Services, Inc. ("CMS-Taiwan"), became affiliated with it and assigned to it the rights of an allegedly copyrighted software program. Prior to EI's affiliation with CMS-Taiwan, CMS-Taiwan was associated with the New Jersey defendant, Direct Line Cargo Management Services, Inc., ("DLCMS-USA"), and a group of affiliated Asian companies. During its association with the defendant, CMS-Taiwan issued a license to the defendant and its affiliates which permitted the companies to make limited use of the software. When CMS-Taiwan became associated with the plaintiff, however, this license expired. This lawsuit arises from the defendant's and its affiliates' alleged wrongful use of the software subsequent to the expiration of the license.

a. Extraterritoriality

The defendant urges the Court to grant its motion because the Asian companies allegedly copied the Software overseas, beyond the jurisdiction of the United

States Copyright Act. DLCMS-USA argues that the mere authorization of these infringing acts abroad is not sufficient to establish primary liability so as to bring the plaintiff's action within the jurisdiction of this Court. It also argues that, even if the Court were to attach primary liability to the mere act of authorizing infringement, there is no evidence that the defendant, in fact, authorized the Asian affiliates to copy the Software.

Section 501 of the Copyright Act states that "[a]nyone who violates any of the exclusive rights of the copyright owner as provided by sections 106 through 118 . . . is an infringer of the copyright. . . ." 17 U.S.C. §501(a). According to Section 106 of this act:

> [T]he owner of a copyright . . . has the exclusive rights to do and to authorize any of the following:
> > (1) to reproduce the copyrighted work in copies or phonorecords;
> > (2) to prepare derivative works based upon the copyrighted work;
> > (3) to distribute copies . . . of the copyrighted work to the public by sale or other transfer of ownership, or by rental, lease or lending. . . .

17 U.S.C. §106 (1996).

There is a division among courts as to whether a claim for infringement can be brought under the Copyright Act when the alleged infringing conduct consists solely of the authorization within the United States of acts that occur entirely abroad. For example, the Ninth Circuit has held that such authorization, by itself, cannot support a United States infringement claim. See Subafilms, Ltd. v. MGM-Pathe Communications Co., 24 F.3d 1088 (9th Cir. 1994). In contrast, a district court in the Sixth Circuit has held that, by authorizing the release of copyrighted music recordings overseas, a United States entity commits primary infringement that is actionable under Section 106. See Curb v. MCA Records, Inc., 898 F. Supp. 586 (M.D.Tenn. 1995).

In *Subafilms,* the plaintiffs alleged that Warner Brothers violated its copyright in the Beatles's movie, "Yellow Submarine," by authorizing distributors to release video versions of the movie abroad. 24 F.3d 1088. The Court tied the authorization right in Section 106 solely to a claim of contributory infringement; it reasoned that a defendant in the United States could not be liable based on its authorization of infringing acts, where the overseas entity who actually copied the materials was not subject to United States Copyright Law. See *id.* at 1094. The Court noted that "to hold otherwise would produce the untenable anomaly, inconsistent with the general principles of third party liability, that a party could be held liable as an infringer for violating the 'authorization' right when the party that it authorized could not be considered an infringer under the Copyright Act." *Id.*

While the defendant urges the Court to apply Subafilms' interpretation of Section 106, the Court departs from the Ninth Circuit's interpretation and adopts the holding set forth in Curb v. MCA Records, Inc., 898 F. Supp. 586. In *Curb,* the defendant counterclaimed that a music company violated its licensing agreement by authorizing infringing acts abroad. See *id.* The Court denied the plaintiff's summary judgment motion, finding that there was a genuine issue of material fact as to whether the plaintiff engaged in primary infringement by merely authorizing the release of copyrighted sound recordings overseas. See *id.* The court held that authorizing infringing acts may constitute primary infringement in light of both the language and legislative history[13] of the Statute. See *id.* at 595-96. Furthermore, it reasoned that imposing direct liability for authorizing infringement more closely serves the underlying policies of the Copyright Act in this modern era. See *id.* at 595. Specifically, the Court noted:

> [P]iracy has changed since the Barbary days. Today, the raider need not grab the bounty with his own hands; he need only transmit his go-ahead by wire or telefax to start the presses in a distant land. Subafilms ignores this economic reality, and the economic incentives underpinning the Copyright clause designed to encourage creation of new works, and transforms infringement of the authorization right into a requirement of domestic presence by a primary infringer. Under this view, a phone call to Nebraska results in liability; the same phone call to France results in riches. In a global marketplace, it is literally a distinction without a difference.

Id.

This Court agrees with *Curb*'s literal interpretation of Section 106, which clearly lends "the owner of a copyright . . . the exclusive rights to do and to authorize" the reproduction and distribution of copyrighted materials. 17 U.S.C. §106. Furthermore, the Court appreciates the policy observations set forth in *Curb*, which appear more closely adapted to our modern age of telefaxes, Internet communication, and electronic mail systems. The purpose behind the Copyright Act is to protect a copyright owner's right to be free from infringement in the United States. To allow an entity to curtail this right by merely directing its foreign agent to do its "dirty work" would be to hinder the deterrent effect of the statute and to thwart its underlying purpose. Because it is more closely aligned with the language, legislative history, and purpose of the statute, the Court adopts the *Curb* interpretation of Section 106 and finds that the mere authorization of infringing acts abroad constitutes direct infringement and is actionable under United States Copyright Law.

Having made this determination, the Court considers whether a reasonable jury could conclude that DLCMS-USA, in fact, authorized the Asian companies' actions. In light of DLCMS-USA's arguable motive and ability to control its affiliates, the Court cannot foreclose this possibility. A jury might reasonably infer that the defendant had a motive for authorizing the infringing acts, since the affiliates' use of the Software enabled the defendant to receive manifests and billing information to facilitate its consolidation ventures. McKenzie himself indicated that the Software was extremely valuable to the companies' business.[14] In its Answer to the Complaint, DLCMS-USA asserts as an affirmative defense that it signed the License Agreement limiting its use of the Software because it was under duress. Furthermore, during oral argument, defense counsel admitted that DLCMS-USA continued to use the Software after November 15, 1993 at the insistence of its customers. Finally, the fact that the defendant negotiated to use the Software during a transi-

---

13. The legislative history of Section 106 reveals: "Use of the phrase 'to authorize' is intended to avoid any questions as to the liability of contributory infringers. For example, a person who lawfully acquires an authorized copy of a motion picture would be an infringer if he or she engages in the business of renting it to others for purposes of unauthorized public performance." H.R.Rep. No. 1476, 94th Cong., 2d Sess. 61, reprinted in 1976 U.S.C.C.A.N. 5659, 5674, cited in *Curb*, 898 F. Supp. at 595.

14. McKenzie declared that he signed the June 1993 Agreement to permit DLCMS-USA's continued use of the Software; "if I refused to sign this document, DLCMS-Taiwan . . . would immediately withdraw from the DLCMS family and withhold further support of the computer systems. Such action would completely disrupt, if not completely destroy, the company."

tion period suggests that the defendant continued to need the Software, even after the license had expired.

In addition to motive, a jury might reasonably infer that the defendant had the ability to authorize the alleged infringing acts, owing to its close interaction with the affiliates. To prove this point, EI calls attention to the joint business dealings, the mutual agency agreements, and the shared profits, leadership, and ownership among the Asian companies and the defendant. Furthermore, it points to the defendant's own characterization of itself and its Asian affiliates as a "family of companies."

In light of the defendant's possible motive and power to authorize its affiliates to use the Software, the Court cannot, as a matter of law, find that the defendant did not direct its affiliates' actions. For this reason, the Court rejects the defendant's extraterritoriality argument.

COMMENTS AND QUESTIONS

1. Even when predicate acts in the United States permit the exercise of federal jurisdiction, U.S. courts will sometimes decide to dismiss infringement cases on forum non conveniens grounds. Two factors are relevant to this determination: (1) whether an adequate alternative forum exists, and (2) whether the balance of public and private interests warrants dismissal. See, e.g., Creative Technology, Ltd. v. Aztech System Pte, Ltd., 61 F.3d 696 (9th Cir. 1995) (dismissing an infringement claim brought by one Singapore company against another Singapore company, even though much of the allegedly infringing activity had taken place in the United States). Although Judge Ferguson's vigorous dissent in *Creative Technology* criticized the majority's conclusion on the adequacy of the Singaporean courts as an alternative forum, a Singaporean court later ruled in favor of Creative Technology in a decision that granted it stronger copyright protection than would have applied in the United States. See, e.g., Jonathan Band & Taro Isshiki, Interoperability in the Pacific Rim: Reversal of Fortunes in Singapore and Australia, 9 J. Proprietary Rts. 2 (July 1997) (disassembly held not to be fair dealing under Singapore's copyright law).

2. For a detailed discussion of extraterritoriality issues of U.S. intellectual property laws, see Curtis A. Bradley, Territorial Intellectual Property Rights in an Age of Globalism, 37 Va. J. Int'l L. 505 (1997) (arguing for a more unified and narrower approach to judging extraterritoriality issues in patent, copyright, and trademark cases); Jane C. Ginsburg, Extraterritoriality and Multiterritoriality in Copyright Infringement, 37 Va. J. Int'l L. 587 (1997) (distinguishing between multiterritorial claims and extraterritorial claims; arguing that U.S. courts ought to be more willing to adjudicate multiterritorial cases and apply the laws of other jurisdictions to acts occurring outside the territorial bounds of the United States).

3. Different intellectual property statutes have different extraterritoriality rules. By and large, intellectual property statutes are supposed to be territorial in nature. Thus it is clear that the patent laws do not have extraterritorial effect. If you want a patent to cover competitor conduct in England, for example, you must get a U.K. patent. While there are certain rules designed to stop the *importation* of infringing products (and products made abroad by infringing processes), the law itself does not reach conduct that occurs outside the United States.

By contrast, courts are much more willing to apply the trademark laws extra-territorially. See, e.g., Playboy Enterprises, Inc. v. Chuckleberry Pub'g, Inc., 939 F. Supp. 1032 (S.D.N.Y. 1996) (enjoining Italian-based "Playmen" Web site from offering products and services in English on an Italian server upon contempt motion deriving from earlier ruling that "Playmen" magazine was a trademark infringement under U.S. law, even though not under Italian law). Copyright occupies a middle position, and as the *Expediters* case indicates, the precedent on this issue is conflicting. Certain language from the Supreme Court's recent decision in Quality King v. L'Anza, 118 S. Ct. 1125 (1998), suggests that the copyright laws do not have extraterritorial effect, at least based on the "authorization" theory adopted in *Expediters.*

4.   The broad historical trend of international intellectual property law has been toward substantive harmonization. International treaties such as the Berne and Paris Conventions have established substantive rules for protection. They have also endorsed the principle of national treatment, discussed *supra,* under which an author's copyright is protected in a foreign country by application of foreign laws. Further, GATT TRIPS created the WTO, a new multilateral enforcement mechanism for resolving trade disputes, including disputes over intellectual property protection.

Does the existence of these substantive and procedural rules for resolving international intellectual property disputes militate against the extraterritorial effect of any one country's laws?

5.   How does the remedy for intellectual property infringement affect the extraterritoriality question? In an important software copyright case, Computer Associates v. Altai, discussed *supra,* the Second Circuit held that Altai's program did not infringe CA's copyright. As the trial was commencing in the United States, CA filed essentially the same suit against Altai in Bobigny, France. The trial court in France decided that, as a matter of French law, Altai did not violate CA's copyrights, and CA decided to appeal this ruling. The U.S. Second Circuit's copyright decision was handed down before the French case went to appeal, and Altai sought to enjoin the French appeal by alleging that the issue had already been finally adjudicated in a U.S. court. The Second Circuit, however, refused to bar the French suit, 126 F.3d 365 (2d Cir. 1997). In theory, at least, CA is now free to sue Altai in every country in which it sells its software. No matter how many times it loses, CA can always sue again elsewhere and relitigate the same case.

Suppose that CA wins one of these suits. To what remedies is it entitled? If the Second Circuit was right to conclude that a French copyright action is different from a U.S. copyright action, does it follow that the remedies in *either* action cannot extend beyond the national borders? Surely simple fairness requires such an outcome, else defendants could never win a case. But do copyright plaintiffs really benefit from a rule that requires them to go to court in every country in the world to get effective worldwide relief?

II

INTERNET LAW

Computer software was the first digital information product to challenge traditional legal categories and to require an adaptation of the law so that appropriate results could be achieved. Chapters 1 through 4 provide the results of this adaptation. It should be noted, however, that it took several decades before the contentious issues of software protection became relatively settled in the United States and the rest of the world. Later arising but nonetheless significant challenges to protection regimes have occurred as to semiconductor chip designs and computer databases. As Chapter 5 has shown, new legislation has been devised to meet the needs of these industries.

It should have been apparent that the ease with which digital information could be copied and redistributed, especially when made available in networked environments, would pose other challenges as well. As more information has become available in digital form, new copyright issues have arisen, and the law of copyright had to be adapted once again to answer new questions that the Internet posed. The challenges posed by digital information do not, however, pertain only to intellectual property law. Privacy is a big problem on the Internet in part because of the ease with which digital technologies can be used to collect and process personal data. Cryptography has become a major area for policy because digital implementations of this technology can protect digital information against abusive uses (such as copyright infringement or privacy invasions), overcoming in part some of the vulnerabilities that digital information would otherwise be subject to owing to the ease of duplication and dissemination. Yet cryptography can also be used to hide abusive activities, and this complicates the policy landscape, which might otherwise place great importance on enabling widespread adoption of strong encryption tools.

Scholars have debated whether "Internet law" is a coherent new discipline. Judge Easterbrook has argued that there is nothing new to Internet law, just the application of existing legal rules to somewhat new facts. Hon. Frank Easterbrook, Cyberspace and the "Law of the Horse," 1996 U. Chi. L. F. 207. By contrast,

Lessig points to some of the ways that the Internet differs from technologies that came before. Lawrence Lessig, The Law of the Horse: What Cyberlaw Might Teach, 113 Harv. L. Rev. 501 (1999). In particular, Lessig points to the malleability of the "physical" structure of the Internet, which permits lawmakers and indeed computer scientists to build freedom—or regulation—into the design of the Internet itself. See also Lawrence Lessig, Code and Other Laws of Cyberspace (1999). Both sides have a point. It is probably fair to say that there is no "law of the Internet" in any consistent sense; we have instead a series of laws designed to regulate different aspects of behavior on the Internet. At the same time, Judge Easterbrook's conclusion that there is nothing new here seems too facile. Changes in technology fundamentally reshape the landscape in which the law operates, with the result that rote application of legal rules to new circumstances is not always a good idea.

Part II will explore how the law is responding to the wider challenges posed by digital information in the global digital network environment (known today as the Internet). Given the state of flux in Internet law and the constant stream of developments that are yielding new Internet law questions, it may seem premature to include in this book a separate part on Internet law. However, the law on some key issues is relatively settled; where it is not yet settled, disputes over activities occurring in cyberspace present questions that the law will have to address. Students may benefit from exposure to the constantly evolving nature of the law of cyberspace. Some examples of how judges are grappling with these contentious issues may be useful even if the appellate courts or legislatures ultimately adopt different answers. There are, of course, some questions and legal developments in Internet law that are not dealt with in this book. New developments are especially likely in the law governing electronic commerce. Nonetheless, Part II provides a foundation concerning the law of the Internet at the end of the millennium.

9

Jurisdiction and Choice of Law

Jurisdiction—broadly conceived—pervades much of Internet law. For example, in judging whether information posted on the Internet is "harmful" to minors, courts have to decide what the relevant community is in applying contemporary community standards to the posting. When U.S.-based firms collect information online about individual users, they may need to be concerned about whether they comply with privacy laws in other countries. Posting an encryption computer program on the Internet may be an "export" of the technology that could run afoul of U.S. export control laws. Someone physically located outside the United States might let loose a virus program that causes computer networks in the United States to be disrupted.

For the purposes of this chapter, however, jurisdiction is more narrowly conceived as the power of courts to adjudicate disputes involving nonresident defendants based on information posted on the Internet. If a person or firm maintains a systematic or continuous presence in a state (for example, by regularly doing business there), courts may exercise general jurisdiction over that person or firm. If no such continuous or systematic presence exists, courts may exercise specific jurisdiction over a nonresident defendant when the nonresident's acts in the state (e.g., committing a tort there or doing business with state residents) give rise to the claim made against that defendant. State long-arm statutes identify under what circumstances courts may exercise personal jurisdiction over nonresident defendants. As the cases below make clear, the due process clauses of the U.S. Constitution limit the reach of state long-arm statutes. In addition, this chapter will consider the enforceability in U.S. courts of judgments entered against U.S. defendants in other jurisdictions as to matters where U.S. law and the law of the nation at issue may differ. One of the advantages of the Internet is the way it compresses or obscures distance and makes things appear to be close even though they are far away. What is an advantage in technology can be a problem for the law, however. If people act "on the Internet," where are they? What law applies to their conduct, and where can they be sued? Many courts have struggled with these questions.

A. PERSONAL JURISDICTION FOR ONLINE ACTIVITIES

Cybersell, Inc. v. Cybersell, Inc.
United States Court of Appeals for the Ninth Circuit
130 F.3d 414 (9th Cir. 1997)

RYMER, Circuit Judge.

We are asked to hold that the allegedly infringing use of a service mark in a home page on the World Wide Web suffices for personal jurisdiction in the state where the holder of the mark has its principal place of business. Cybersell, Inc., an Arizona corporation that advertises for commercial services over the Internet, claims that Cybersell, Inc., a Florida corporation that offers web page construction services over the Internet, infringed its federally registered mark and should be amenable to suit in Arizona because cyberspace is without borders and a web site which advertises a product or service is necessarily intended for use on a world wide basis. The district court disagreed, and so do we. Instead, applying our normal "minimum contacts" analysis, we conclude that it would not comport with "traditional notions of fair play and substantial justice," Core-Vent Corp. v. Nobel Indus. AB, 11 F.3d 1482, 1485 (9th Cir. 1993) (quoting International Shoe Co. v. Washington, 326 U.S. 310, 316, 66 S. Ct. 154, 158, 90 L. Ed. 95 (1945)), for Arizona to exercise personal jurisdiction over an allegedly infringing Florida web site advertiser who has no contacts with Arizona other than maintaining a home page that is accessible to Arizonans, and everyone else, over the Internet. We therefore affirm.

I

Cybersell, Inc. is an Arizona corporation, which we will refer to as Cybersell AZ. It was incorporated in May 1994 to provide Internet and web advertising and marketing services, including consulting. The principals of Cybersell AZ are Laurence Canter and Martha Siegel, known among web users for first "spamming" the Internet. Mainstream print media carried the story of Canter and Siegel and their various efforts to commercialize the web.

On August 8, 1994, Cybersell AZ filed an application to register the name "Cybersell" as a service mark. The application was approved and the grant was published on October 30, 1995. Cybersell AZ operated a web site using the mark from August 1994 through February 1995. The site was then taken down for reconstruction.

Meanwhile, in the summer of 1995, Matt Certo and his father, Dr. Samuel C. Certo, both Florida residents, formed Cybersell, Inc., a Florida corporation (Cybersell FL), with its principal place of business in Orlando. Matt was a business school student at Rollins College, where his father was a professor; Matt was particularly interested in the Internet, and their company was to provide business consulting services for strategic management and marketing on the web. At the time the Certos chose the name "Cybersell" for their venture, Cybersell AZ had no home page on the web nor had the PTO granted their application for the service mark.

As part of their marketing effort, the Certos created a web page at *http://www.cybsell.com/cybsell/index.htm*. The home page has a logo at the top with "CyberSell" over a depiction of the planet earth, with the caption underneath "Professional Services for the World Wide Web" and a local (area code 407) phone number. It proclaims in large letters "Welcome to CyberSell!" A hypertext link allows the browser to introduce himself, and invites a company not on the web—but interested in getting on the web—to "Email us to find out how!"

Canter found the Cybersell FL web page and sent an e-mail on November 27, 1995 notifying Dr. Certo that "Cybersell" is a service mark of Cybersell AZ. Trying to disassociate themselves from the Canters, the Certos changed the name of Cybersell FL to WebHorizons, Inc. on December 27 (later it was changed again to WebSolvers, Inc.) and by January 4, 1996, they had replaced the CyberSell logo at the top of their web page with WebHorizons, Inc. The WebHorizons page still said "Welcome to CyberSell!"

II

The general principles that apply to the exercise of personal jurisdiction are well known. As there is no federal statute governing personal jurisdiction in this case, the law of Arizona applies. Under Rule 4.2(a) of the Arizona Rules of Civil Procedure, an Arizona court

> may exercise personal jurisdiction over parties, whether found within or outside the state, to the maximum extent permitted by the Constitution of this state and the Constitution of the United States.

The Arizona Supreme Court has stated that under Rule 4.2(a), "Arizona will exert personal jurisdiction over a nonresident litigant to the maximum extent allowed by the federal constitution." Uberti v. Leonardo, 181 Ariz. 565, 569, 892 P.2d 1354, 1358, *cert. denied*, 516 U.S. 906, 116 S. Ct. 273, 133 L. Ed.2d 194 (1995). Thus, Cybersell FL may be subject to personal jurisdiction in Arizona so long as doing so comports with due process.

A court may assert either specific or general jurisdiction over a defendant. See Helicopteros Nacionales de Colombia, S.A. v. Hall, 466 U.S. 408, 414, 104 S. Ct. 1868, 1872, 80 L. Ed.2d 404 (1984). Cybersell AZ concedes that general jurisdiction over Cybersell FL doesn't exist in Arizona, so the only issue in this case is whether specific jurisdiction is available.

We use a three-part test to determine whether a district court may exercise specific jurisdiction over a nonresident defendant:

> (1) The nonresident defendant must do some act or consummate some transaction with the forum or perform some act by which he purposefully avails himself of the privilege of conducting activities in the forum, thereby invoking the benefits and protections[;] (2)[t]he claim must be one which arises out of or results from the defendant's forum-related activities[; and] (3)[e]xercise of jurisdiction must be reasonable.

Ballard v. Savage, 65 F.3d 1495, 1498 (9th Cir. 1995) (citations omitted).

Arguments (margin annotation)

Cybersell AZ argues that the test is met because trademark infringement occurs when the passing off of the mark occurs, which in this case, it submits, happened when the name "Cybersell" was used on the Internet in connection with advertising. Cybersell FL, on the other hand, contends that a party should not be subject to nationwide, or perhaps worldwide, jurisdiction simply for using the Internet.

A

Purposeful Availment (margin annotation)

Since the jurisdictional facts are not in dispute, we turn to the first requirement, which is the most critical. As the Supreme Court emphasized in Hanson v. Denckla, "it is essential in each case that there be some act by which the defendant purposefully avails itself of the privilege of conducting activities within the forum State, thus invoking the benefits and protections of its laws." 357 U.S. 235, 253, 78 S. Ct. 1228, 1239, 2 L. Ed.2d 1283 (1958). We recently explained in *Ballard* that

> the "purposeful availment" requirement is satisfied if the defendant has taken deliberate action within the forum state or if he has created continuing obligations to forum residents. "It is not required that a defendant be physically present within, or have physical contacts with, the forum, provided that his efforts 'are purposefully directed' toward forum residents."

Ballard, 65 F.3d at 1498 (citations omitted).

We have not yet considered when personal jurisdiction may be exercised in the context of cyberspace, but the Second and Sixth Circuits have had occasion to decide whether personal jurisdiction was properly exercised over defendants involved in transmissions over the Internet, see CompuServe, Inc. v. Patterson, 89 F.3d 1257 (6th Cir. 1996); Bensusan Restaurant Corp. v. King, 937 F. Supp. 295 (S.D.N.Y. 1996), *aff'd*, 126 F.3d 25 (2d Cir. 1997), as have a number of district courts. Because this is a matter of first impression for us, we have looked to all of these cases for guidance. Not surprisingly, they reflect a broad spectrum of Internet use on the one hand, and contacts with the forum on the other. As *CompuServe* and *Bensusan* seem to represent opposite ends of the spectrum, we start with them.[4]

CompuServe (margin annotation)

CompuServe is a computer information service headquartered in Columbus, Ohio, that contracts with individual subscribers to provide access to computing and information services via the Internet. It also operates as an electronic conduit to provide computer software products to its subscribers. Computer software generated and distributed in this way is often referred to as "shareware." Patterson is a Texas resident who subscribed to CompuServe and placed items of "shareware" on the CompuServe system pursuant to a "Shareware Registration Agreement" with CompuServe which provided, among other things, that it was "to be governed by and construed in accordance with" Ohio law. During the course of this relation-

---

4. Since *Bensusan* was decided on the basis of New York's long-arm statute (which requires presence in the forum and is therefore more stringent than due process), its holding is not instructive, but the district court's analysis is. The district court dismissed for lack of personal jurisdiction under the long-arm statute as well as on due process grounds, while the Second Circuit affirmed on the statute and did not discuss the constitutional issue.

ship, Patterson electronically transmitted thirty-two master software files to CompuServe, which CompuServe stored and displayed to its subscribers. Sales were made in Ohio and elsewhere, and funds were transmitted through CompuServe in Ohio to Patterson in Texas. In effect, Patterson used CompuServe as a distribution center to market his software. When Patterson threatened litigation over allegedly infringing CompuServe software, CompuServe filed suit in Ohio seeking a declaratory judgment of noninfringement. The court found that Patterson's relationship with CompuServe as a software provider and marketer was a crucial indicator that Patterson had knowingly reached out to CompuServe's Ohio home and benefitted from CompuServe's handling of his software and fees. Because Patterson had chosen to transmit his product from Texas to CompuServe's system in Ohio, and that system provided access to his software to others to whom he advertised and sold his product, the court concluded that Patterson purposefully availed himself of the privilege of doing business in Ohio.

By contrast, the defendant in *Bensusan* owned a small jazz club known as "The Bluc Note" in Columbia, Missouri. He created a general access web page that contained information about the club in Missouri as well as a calendar of events and ticketing information. Tickets were not available through the web site, however. To order tickets, web browsers had to use the names and addresses of ticket outlets in Columbia or a telephone number for charge-by-phone ticket orders, which were available for pick-up on the night of the show at the Blue Note box office in Columbia. Bensusan was a New York corporation that owned "The Blue Note," a popular jazz club in the heart of Greenwich Village. Bensusan owned the rights to the "The Blue Note" mark. Bensusan sued King for trademark infringement in New York. The district court distinguished King's passive web page, which just posted information, from the defendant's use of the Internet in CompuServe by observing that whereas the Texas Internet user specifically targeted Ohio by subscribing to the service, entering into an agreement to sell his software over the Internet, advertising through the service, and sending his software to the service in Ohio,

> King has done nothing to purposefully avail himself of the benefits of New York. King, like numerous others, simply created a Web site and permitted anyone who could find it to access it. Creating a site, like placing a product into the stream of commerce, may be felt nationwide—or even worldwide—but, without more, it is not an act purposefully directed toward the forum state.

Bensusan, 937 F. Supp. at 301 (citing the plurality opinion in Asahi Metal Indus. Co. v. Superior Court, 480 U.S. 102, 112, 107 S. Ct. 1026, 1032, 94 L. Ed.2d 92 (1992)). Given these facts, the court reasoned that the argument that the defendant "should have foreseen that users could access the site in New York and be confused as to the relationship of the two Blue Note clubs is insufficient to satisfy due process." *Id*. at 301.

"Interactive" web sites present somewhat different issues. Unlike passive sites such as the defendant's in *Bensusan*, users can exchange information with the host computer when the site is interactive. Courts that have addressed interactive sites have looked to the "level of interactivity and commercial nature of the exchange of information that occurs on the Web site" to determine if sufficient contacts exist to warrant the exercise of jurisdiction. See, e.g., Zippo Mfg. Co. v. Zippo Dot Com,

Inc., 952 F. Supp. 1119, 1124 (W.D.Pa. 1997) (finding purposeful availment based on Dot Com's interactive web site and contracts with 3000 individuals and seven Internet access providers in Pennsylvania allowing them to download the electronic messages that form the basis of the suit); Maritz, Inc. v. Cybergold, Inc., 947 F. Supp. 1328, 1332-33 (E.D.Mo.) (browsers were encouraged to add their address to a mailing list that basically subscribed the user to the service), *reconsideration denied*, 947 F. Supp. 1338 (1996).

Cybersell AZ points to several district court decisions which it contends have held that the mere advertisement or solicitation for sale of goods and services on the Internet gives rise to specific jurisdiction in the plaintiff's forum. However, so far as we are aware, no court has ever held that an Internet advertisement alone is sufficient to subject the advertiser to jurisdiction in the plaintiff's home state. See, e.g., Smith v. Hobby Lobby Stores, 968 F. Supp. 1356 (W.D.Ark. 1997) (no jurisdiction over Hong Kong defendant who advertised in trade journal posted on the Internet without sale of goods or services in Arkansas). Rather, in each, there has been "something more" to indicate that the defendant purposefully (albeit electronically) directed his activity in a substantial way to the forum state.

Inset Systems, Inc. v. Instruction Set, Inc., 937 F. Supp. 161 (D.Conn. 1996), is the case most favorable to Cybersell AZ's position. Inset developed and marketed computer software throughout the world; Instruction Set, Inc. (ISI) provided computer technology and support. Inset owned the federal trademark "INSET"; but ISI obtained "INSET.COM" as its Internet domain address for advertising its goods and services. ISI also used the telephone number "1-800-US-INSET." Inset learned of ISI's domain address when it tried to get the same address, and filed suit for trademark infringement in Connecticut. The court reasoned that ISI had purposefully availed itself of doing business in Connecticut because it directed its advertising activities via the Internet and its toll-free number toward the state of Connecticut (and all states); Internet sites and toll-free numbers are designed to communicate with people and their businesses in every state; an Internet advertisement could reach as many as 10,000 Internet users within Connecticut alone; and once posted on the Internet, an advertisement is continuously available to any Internet user.

Cybersell AZ further points to the court's statement in EDIAS Software International, L.L.C. v. BASIS International Ltd., 947 F. Supp. 413 (D.Ariz. 1996), that a defendant "should not be permitted to take advantage of modern technology through an Internet Web page and forum and simultaneously escape traditional notions of jurisdiction." *Id.* at 420. In that case, EDIAS (an Arizona company) alleged that BASIS (a New Mexico company) sent advertising and defamatory statements over the Internet through e-mail, its web page, and forums. However, the court did not rest its minimum contacts analysis on use of the Internet alone; in addition to the Internet, BASIS had a contract with EDIAS, it made sales to EDIAS and other Arizona customers, and its employees had visited Arizona during the course of the business relationship with EDIAS.

Some courts have also given weight to the number of "hits" received by a web page from residents in the forum state, and to other evidence that Internet activity was directed at, or bore fruit in, the forum state. See, e.g., Heroes, Inc. v. Heroes Found., 958 F. Supp. 1 (D.D.C. 1996) (web page that solicited contributions and provided toll-free telephone number along with the defendant's use on the web page of the allegedly infringing trademark and logo, along with other contacts, provided sustained contact with the District), amended by No. Civ.A. 96-1260(TAF) (1997); Pres-Kap, Inc. v. System One, Direct Access, Inc., 636 So.2d 1351 (Fla. Dist. Ct. App. 1994) (declining jurisdiction where defendant consumer subscribed to plaintiff's travel reservation system but was solicited and serviced instate by the supplier's local representative).

In sum, the common thread, well stated by the district court in *Zippo*, is that "the likelihood that personal jurisdiction can be constitutionally exercised is directly proportionate to the nature and quality of commercial activity that an entity conducts over the Internet." *Zippo*, 952 F. Supp. at 1124.

B

Here, Cybersell FL has conducted no commercial activity over the Internet in Arizona. All that it did was post an essentially passive home page on the web, using the name "CyberSell," which Cybersell AZ was in the process of registering as a federal service mark. While there is no question that anyone, anywhere could access that home page and thereby learn about the services offered, we cannot see how from that fact alone it can be inferred that Cybersell FL deliberately directed its merchandising efforts toward Arizona residents.

Cybersell FL did nothing to encourage people in Arizona to access its site, and there is no evidence that any part of its business (let alone a continuous part of its business) was sought or achieved in Arizona. To the contrary, it appears to be an operation where business was primarily generated by the personal contacts of one of its founders. While those contacts are not entirely local, they aren't in Arizona either. No Arizonan except for Cybersell AZ "hit" Cybersell FL's web site. There is no evidence that any Arizona resident signed up for Cybersell FL's web construction services. It entered into no contracts in Arizona, made no sales in Arizona, received no telephone calls from Arizona, earned no income from Arizona, and sent no messages over the Internet to Arizona. The only message it received over the Internet from Arizona was from Cybersell AZ. Cybersell FL did not have an "800" number, let alone a toll-free number that also used the "Cybersell" name. The interactivity of its web page is limited to receiving the browser's name and address and an indication of interest—signing up for the service is not an option, nor did anyone from Arizona do so. No money changed hands on the Internet from (or through) Arizona. In short, Cybersell FL has done no act and has consummated no transaction, nor has it performed any act by which it purposefully availed itself of the privilege of conducting activities, in Arizona, thereby invoking the benefits and protections of Arizona law.

We therefore hold that Cybersell FL's contacts are insufficient to establish "purposeful availment." Cybersell AZ has thus failed to satisfy the first prong of our three-part test for specific jurisdiction. We decline to go further solely on the footing that Cybersell AZ has alleged trademark infringement over the Internet by Cybersell FL's use of the registered name "Cybersell" on an essentially passive web page advertisement. Otherwise, every complaint arising out of alleged trademark infringement on the Internet would automatically result in personal jurisdiction wherever the plaintiff's principal place of business is located. That would not comport with traditional notions of what qualifies as purposeful activity invoking the benefits and protections of the forum state. See Peterson v. Kennedy, 771 F.2d

1244, 1262 (9th Cir. 1985) (series of phone calls and letters to California physician regarding plaintiff's injuries insufficient to satisfy first prong of test).

III

Effects Test

Cybersell AZ also invokes the "effects" test employed in Calder v. Jones, 465 U.S. 783, 104 S. Ct. 1482, 79 L. Ed.2d 804 (1984), and Core-Vent Corp. v. Nobel Industries, 11 F.3d 1482 (9th Cir. 1993), with respect to intentional torts directed to the plaintiff, causing injury where the plaintiff lives. However, we don't see this as a *Calder* case. Because Shirley Jones was who she was (a famous entertainer who lived and worked in California) and was libeled by a story in the National Enquirer, which was published in Florida but had a nationwide circulation with a large audience in California, the Court could easily hold that California was the "focal point both of the story and of the harm suffered" and so jurisdiction in California based on the "effects" of the defendants' Florida conduct was proper. *Calder*, 465 U.S. at 789, 104 S. Ct. at 1486. There is nothing comparable about Cybersell FL's web page. Nor does the "effects" test apply with the same force to Cybersell AZ as it would to an individual, because a corporation "does not suffer harm in a particular geographic location in the same sense that an individual does." *Core-Vent*, 11 F.3d at 1486. Cybersell FL's web page simply was not aimed intentionally at Arizona knowing that harm was likely to be caused there to Cybersell AZ.[6]

IV

We conclude that the essentially passive nature of Cybersell FL's activity in posting a home page on the World Wide Web that allegedly used the service mark of Cybersell AZ does not qualify as purposeful activity invoking the benefits and protections of Arizona. As it engaged in no commercial activity and had no other contacts via the Internet or otherwise in Arizona, Cybersell FL lacks sufficient minimum contacts with Arizona for personal jurisdiction to be asserted over it there. Accordingly, its motion to dismiss for lack of personal jurisdiction was properly granted.

AFFIRMED.

COMMENTS AND QUESTIONS

1. Some scholars have questioned whether existing jurisdictional law can solve the problems of jurisdiction in cyberspace. In particular, two scholars, David

---

6. Likewise unpersuasive is Cybersell AZ's reliance on Panavision International v. Toeppen, 938 F. Supp. 616 (C.D.Cal. 1996), where the court found the "purposeful availment" prong satisfied by the effects felt in California, the home state of Panavision, from Toeppen's alleged out-of-state scheme to register domain names using the trademarks of California companies, including Panavision, for the purpose of extorting fees from them. Again, there is nothing analogous about Cybersell FL's conduct.

Johnson and David Post, have argued in a number of articles that cyberspace should be its own jurisdiction, with its own courts (or "virtual magistrates") to resolve disputes that occur entirely online. For their arguments, see David R. Johnson & David Post, Law and Borders—The Rise of Law in Cyberspace, 48 Stan. L. Rev. 1367 (1996); David R. Johnson & David G. Post, And How Shall the Net Be Governed?: A Meditation on the Relative Virtues of Decentralized, Emergent Law, in Coordinating the Internet (Brian Kahin & James Keller eds., MIT Press, 1997). But see Lawrence Lessig, The Zones of Cyberspace, 48 Stan. L. Rev. 1403 (1996) (challenging the Johnson-Post model).

2. There are numerous cases involving the Internet and personal jurisdiction, many involving trademark disputes. Since 1996, there have been literally hundreds of articles written about the problem of jurisdiction on the Internet. Among the better treatments of the problem are Dan L. Burk, Jurisdiction in a World Without Borders, 1 Va. J.L. & Tech. (1996), http://www.student.virginia.edu/~vjolt/vol1/BURK.htm; Katherine Sheehan, Predicting the Future: Personal Jurisdiction for the 21st Century, 66 U. Cin. L. Rev. 385 (1998); Dan Burk, Federalism in Cyberspace, 28 Conn. L. Rev. 1095 (1996); Ira S. Nathenson, Showdown at the Domain Name Corral: Property Rights and Personal Jurisdiction Over Squatters, Poachers and Other Parasites, 58 U. Pitt. L. Rev. 911 (1997); Allan R. Stein, The Unexceptional Problem of Jurisidiction in Cyberspace, 32 International Lawyer 1167 (1998); Jack Goldsmith, Against Cyberanarchy, 65 U. Chi. L. Rev. 1199 (1998); Jeremy Gilman, Personal Jurisdiction and the Internet: Traditional Jurisprudence for a New Medium, 56 Bus. Law. 395 (2000); Allan R. Stein, Frontiers of Jurisdiction: From Isolation to Connectedness, 2001 U. Chi. Legal F. 373 (2001); Michael Geist, Is There a There There? Toward Greater Certainty for Internet Jurisdiction, 16 Berkeley Tech. L.J. 1345 (2001).

Generally, global "solutions" to the jurisdictional problem tend to resolve themselves in one of three ways:

(1) First, the defendant might be amenable to suit everywhere the Web page can be seen (essentially, this is everywhere in the world). *Inset Systems* took this approach to some extent. See also Maritz v. Cybergold, 947 F. Supp. 1328 (E.D. Mo. 1996) (a desire to transmit information everywhere in the world confers jurisdiction everywhere in the world). This assures the plaintiff a reasonable choice of forum but places an enormous burden on potential defendants, and may reduce online speech to the "least common denominator" acceptable to all jurisdictions worldwide.

(2) Second, the defendant might be amenable to suit only in its home forum (whether that "forum" is a physical state or an Internet locale, as Johnson and Post suggest). This relieves the burden on the defendant but imposes a corresponding burden on remote plaintiffs. It may also encourage the development of "data havens" that promise virtual immunity from trademark, copyright, or defamation laws to their residents.

(3) Finally, courts might attempt a rough compromise by applying traditional jurisdictional principles to determine on a case-by-case basis how fair the exercise of jurisdiction would be. *Cybersell* takes this approach. This last approach may produce the most reasonable results across a wide range of cases, though it is worth noting that it sacrifices a great deal of certainty and may produce a lot of litigation over jurisdictional issues.

3.   Efforts to take this middle road require courts to distinguish between cases in which a Web site should confer jurisdiction and cases where it shouldn't. On what basis should courts make this distinction? One possible factor (used in *Cybersell*) is how often people visit the Web site. A second possible factor, raised in many other cases, is the existence of other contacts with the forum, such as sales into the jurisdiction or telephone orders. Finally, some decisions (including the one below) have suggested that the extent of the interactive or passive nature of the Web page should be relevant to the jurisdictional question.

≡≡≡ ***Zippo Manufacturing Co. v. Zippo Dot Com, Inc.***
≡≡≡ *United States District Court for the Western District of Pennsylvania*
≡≡≡ *952 F. Supp. 1119 (W.D. Pa. 1997)*

McLaughlin, District Judge.

This is an Internet domain name dispute. At this stage of the controversy, we must decide the Constitutionally permissible reach of Pennsylvania's Long Arm Statute, 42 Pa.C.S.A. §5322, through cyberspace. Plaintiff Zippo Manufacturing Corporation ("Manufacturing") has filed a five count complaint against Zippo Dot Com, Inc. ("Dot Com") alleging trademark dilution, infringement, and false designation under the Federal Trademark Act, 15 U.S.C. §§1051-1127. In addition, the Complaint alleges causes of action based on state law trademark dilution under 54 Pa.C.S.A. §1124, and seeks equitable accounting and imposition of a constructive trust. Dot Com has moved to dismiss for lack of personal jurisdiction and improper venue pursuant to Fed.R.Civ.P. 12(b)(2) and (3) or, in the alternative, to transfer the case pursuant to 28 U.S.C. §1406(a). For the reasons set forth below, Defendant's motion is denied.

I.   Background

The facts relevant to this motion are as follows. Manufacturing is a Pennsylvania corporation with its principal place of business in Bradford, Pennsylvania. Manufacturing makes, among other things, well known "Zippo" tobacco lighters. Dot Com is a California corporation with its principal place of business in Sunnyvale, California. Dot Com operates an Internet Web site and an Internet news service and has obtained the exclusive right to use the domain names "zippo.com", "zippo.net" and "zipponews.com" on the Internet.

Dot Com's Web site contains information about the company, advertisements and an application for its Internet news service. The news service itself consists of three levels of membership—public/free, "Original" and "Super." Each successive level offers access to a greater number of Internet newsgroups. A customer who wants to subscribe to either the "Original" or "Super" level of service, fills out an on-line application that asks for a variety of information including the person's name and address. Payment is made by credit card over the Internet or the telephone. The application is then processed and the subscriber is assigned a password which permits the subscriber to view and/or download Internet newsgroup messages that are stored on the Defendant's server in California.

[handwritten margin notes: "Zippo Man. Penn."; "Zippo.net Cal."; "Zippo.net Cal."; "Membership Susbcrip."]

Dot Com's contacts with Pennsylvania have occurred almost exclusively over the Internet. Dot Com's offices, employees and Internet servers are located in California. Dot Com maintains no offices, employees or agents in Pennsylvania. Dot Com's advertising for its service to Pennsylvania residents involves posting information about its service on its Web page, which is accessible to Pennsylvania residents via the Internet. Defendant has approximately 140,000 paying subscribers worldwide. [Approximately two percent (3,000) of those subscribers are Pennsylvania residents.] These subscribers have contracted to receive Dot Com's service by visiting its Web site and filling out the application [Additionally, Dot Com has entered into agreements with seven Internet access providers in Pennsylvania to permit their subscribers to access Dot Com's news service.] Two of these providers are located in the Western District of Pennsylvania.

The basis of the trademark claims is Dot Com's use of the word "Zippo" in the domain names it holds, in numerous locations in its Web site and in the heading of Internet newsgroup messages that have been posted by Dot Com subscribers. When an Internet user views or downloads a newsgroup message posted by a Dot Com subscriber, the word "Zippo" appears in the "Message-Id" and "Organization" sections of the heading. The news message itself, containing text and/or pictures, follows. Manufacturing points out that some of the messages contain adult oriented, sexually explicit subject matter. . . .

III. Discussion

A. Personal Jurisdiction

1. The Traditional Framework

Our authority to exercise personal jurisdiction in this case is conferred by state law. Fed.R.Civ.P. 4(e); *Mellon*, 960 F.2d at 1221. The extent to which we may exercise that authority is governed by the Due Process Clause of the Fourteenth Amendment to the Federal Constitution. Kulko v. Superior Court of California, 436 U.S. 84, 91, 98 S. Ct. 1690, 1696, 56 L. Ed.2d 132 (1978).

Pennsylvania's long arm jurisdiction statute is codified at 42 Pa.C.S.A. §5322(a). The portion of the statute authorizing us to exercise jurisdiction here permits the exercise of jurisdiction over non-resident defendants upon:

(2) Contracting to supply services or things in this Commonwealth.

42 Pa.C.S.A. §5322(a). It is undisputed that Dot Com contracted to supply Internet news services to approximately 3,000 Pennsylvania residents and also entered into agreements with seven Internet access providers in Pennsylvania. Moreover, even if Dot Com's conduct did not satisfy a specific provision of the statute, we would nevertheless be authorized to exercise jurisdiction to the "fullest extent allowed under the Constitution of the United States." 42 Pa.C.S.A. §5322(b).

The Constitutional limitations on the exercise of personal jurisdiction differ depending upon whether a court seeks to exercise general or specific jurisdiction over a non-resident defendant. *Mellon*, 960 F.2d at 1221. General jurisdiction permits a court to exercise personal jurisdiction over a non-resident defendant for non-forum related activities when the defendant has engaged in "systematic and continuous" activities in the forum state. Helicopteros Nacionales de Colombia, S.A. v. Hall, 466 U.S. 408, 414-16, 104 S. Ct. 1868, 1872-73, 80 L. Ed.2d 404 (1984). In the absence of general jurisdiction, specific jurisdiction permits a court to exercise personal jurisdiction over a non-resident defendant for forum-related activities where the "relationship between the defendant and the forum falls within the 'minimum contacts' framework" of International Shoe Co. v. Washington, 326 U.S. 310, 66 S. Ct. 154, 90 L. Ed. 95 (1945) and its progeny. *Mellon*, 960 F.2d at 1221. Manufacturing does not contend that we should exercise general personal jurisdiction over Dot Com. Manufacturing concedes that if personal jurisdiction exists in this case, it must be specific.

A three-pronged test has emerged for determining whether the exercise of specific personal jurisdiction over a non-resident defendant is appropriate: (1) the defendant must have sufficient "minimum contacts" with the forum state, (2) the claim asserted against the defendant must arise out of those contacts, and (3) the exercise of jurisdiction must be reasonable. *Id*. The "Constitutional touchstone" of the minimum contacts analysis is embodied in the first prong, "whether the defendant purposefully established" contacts with the forum state. Burger King Corp. v. Rudzewicz, 471 U.S. 462, 475, 105 S. Ct. 2174, 2183-84, 85 L. Ed.2d 528 (1985) (citing International Shoe Co. v. Washington, 326 U.S. 310, 319, 66 S. Ct. 154, 159-60, 90 L. Ed. 95 (1945)). Defendants who "'reach out beyond one state' and create continuing relationships and obligations with the citizens of another state are subject to regulation and sanctions in the other State for consequences of their actions." *Id*. (citing Travelers Health Assn. v. Virginia, 339 U.S. 643, 647, 70 S. Ct. 927, 929, 94 L. Ed. 1154 (1950)). "[T]he foreseeability that is critical to the due process analysis is . . . that the defendant's conduct and connection with the forum State are such that he should reasonably expect to be haled into court there." World-Wide Volkswagen Corp. v. Woodson, 444 U.S. 286, 297, 100 S. Ct. 559, 567, 62 L. Ed.2d 490 (1980). This protects defendants from being forced to answer for their actions in a foreign jurisdiction based on "random, fortuitous or attenuated" contacts. Keeton v. Hustler Magazine, Inc., 465 U.S. 770, 774, 104 S. Ct. 1473, 1478, 79 L. Ed.2d 790 (1984). "Jurisdiction is proper, however, where contacts proximately result from actions by the defendant himself that create a 'substantial connection' with the forum State." *Burger King*, 471 U.S. at 475, 105 S. Ct. at 2183-84 (citing McGee v. International Life Insurance Co., 355 U.S. 220, 223, 78 S. Ct. 199, 201, 2 L. Ed.2d 223 (1957)).

The "reasonableness" prong exists to protect defendants against unfairly inconvenient litigation. *World-Wide Volkswagen*, 444 U.S. at 292, 100 S. Ct. at 564-65. Under this prong, the exercise of jurisdiction will be reasonable if it does not offend "traditional notions of fair play and substantial justice." *International Shoe*, 326 U.S. at 316, 66 S. Ct. at 158. When determining the reasonableness of a particular forum, the court must consider the burden on the defendant in light of other factors including: "the forum state's interest in adjudicating the dispute; the plaintiff's interest in obtaining convenient and effective relief, at least when that interest is not adequately protected by the plaintiff's right to choose the forum; the interstate judicial system's interest in obtaining the most efficient resolution of controversies; and the shared interest of the several states in furthering fundamental substantive social policies." *World-Wide Volkswagen*, 444 U.S. at 292, 100 S. Ct. at 564 (internal citations omitted).

2. The Internet and Jurisdiction

In Hanson v. Denckla, the Supreme Court noted that "[a]s technological progress has increased the flow of commerce between States, the need for jurisdiction has undergone a similar increase." Hanson v. Denckla, 357 U.S. 235, 250-51, 78 S. Ct. 1228, 1237-39, 2 L. Ed.2d 1283 (1958). Twenty seven years later, the Court observed that jurisdiction could not be avoided "merely because the defendant did not physically enter the forum state." *Burger King*, 471 U.S. at 476, 105 S. Ct. at 2184. The Court observed that:

> [I]t is an inescapable fact of modern commercial life that a substantial amount of commercial business is transacted solely by mail and wire communications across state lines, thus obviating the need for physical presence within a State in which business is conducted.

Id.

Enter the Internet, a global "'super-network' of over 15,000 computer networks used by over 30 million individuals, corporations, organizations, and educational institutions worldwide." Panavision Intern., L.P. v. Toeppen, 938 F. Supp. 616 (C.D.Cal. 1996) (citing American Civil Liberties Union v. Reno, 929 F. Supp. 824, 830-48 (E.D.Pa. 1996)). "In recent years, businesses have begun to use the Internet to provide information and products to consumers and other businesses." *Id.* The Internet makes it possible to conduct business throughout the world entirely from a desktop. With this global revolution looming on the horizon, the development of the law concerning the permissible scope of personal jurisdiction based on Internet use is in its infant stages. The cases are scant. Nevertheless, our review of the available cases and materials reveals that the likelihood that personal jurisdiction can be constitutionally exercised is directly proportionate to the nature and quality of commercial activity that an entity conducts over the Internet. This sliding scale is consistent with well developed personal jurisdiction principles. At one end of the spectrum are situations where a defendant clearly does business over the Internet. If the defendant enters into contracts with residents of a foreign jurisdiction that involve the knowing and repeated transmission of computer files over the Internet, personal jurisdiction is proper. E.g. CompuServe, Inc. v. Patterson, 89 F.3d 1257 (6th Cir. 1996). At the opposite end are situations where a defendant has simply posted information on an Internet Web site which is accessible to users in foreign jurisdictions. A passive Web site that does little more than make information available to those who are interested in it is not grounds for the exercise personal jurisdiction. E.g. Bensusan Restaurant Corp. v. King, 937 F. Supp. 295 (S.D.N.Y. 1996). The middle ground is occupied by interactive Web sites where a user can exchange information with the host computer. In these cases, the exercise of jurisdiction is determined by examining the level of interactivity and commercial nature of the exchange of information that occurs on the Web site. E.g. Maritz, Inc. v. Cybergold, Inc., 947 F. Supp. 1328 (E.D.Mo. 1996). . . .

Inset Systems, Inc. v. Instruction Set, 937 F. Supp. 161 (D.Conn. 1996) represents the outer limits of the exercise of personal jurisdiction based on the Internet. In *Inset Systems*, a Connecticut corporation sued a Massachusetts corporation in the District of Connecticut for trademark infringement based on the use of an Internet domain name. *Inset Systems*, 937 F. Supp. at 162. The defendant's contacts with

Connecticut consisted of posting a Web site that was accessible to approximately 10,000 Connecticut residents and maintaining a toll free number. *Id.* at 165. The court exercised personal jurisdiction, reasoning that advertising on the Internet constituted the purposeful doing of business in Connecticut because "unlike television and radio advertising, the advertisement is available continuously to any Internet user." *Id.* at 165.

Bensusan Restaurant Corp. v. King, 937 F. Supp. 295 (S.D.N.Y. 1996) reached a different conclusion based on a similar Web site. In *Bensusan*, the operator of a New York jazz club sued the operator of a Missouri jazz club for trademark infringement. *Bensusan*, 937 F. Supp. at 297. The Internet Web site at issue contained general information about the defendant's club, a calendar of events and ticket information. *Id.* However, the site was not interactive. *Id.* If a user wanted to go to the club, she would have to call or visit a ticket outlet and then pick up tickets at the club on the night of the show. *Id.* The court refused to exercise jurisdiction based on the Web site alone, reasoning that it did not rise to the level of purposeful availment of that jurisdiction's laws. The court distinguished the case from *CompuServe, supra,* where the user had "'reached out' from Texas to Ohio and 'originated and maintained' contacts with Ohio." *Id.* at 301. . . .

3. Application to this Case

First, we note that this is not an Internet advertising case in the line of *Inset Systems* and *Bensusan*, supra. Dot Com has not just posted information on a Web site that is accessible to Pennsylvania residents who are connected to the Internet. This is not even an interactivity case in the line of *Maritz*, supra. Dot Com has done more than create an interactive Web site through which it exchanges information with Pennsylvania residents in hopes of using that information for commercial gain later. We are not being asked to determine whether Dot Com's Web site alone constitutes the purposeful availment of doing business in Pennsylvania. This is a "doing business over the Internet" case in the line of *CompuServe*, supra. We are being asked to determine whether Dot Com's conducting of electronic commerce with Pennsylvania residents constitutes the purposeful availment of doing business in Pennsylvania. We conclude that it does. Dot Com has contracted with approximately 3,000 individuals and seven Internet access providers in Pennsylvania. The intended object of these transactions has been the downloading of the electronic messages that form the basis of this suit in Pennsylvania.

We find Dot Com's efforts to characterize its conduct as falling short of purposeful availment of doing business in Pennsylvania wholly unpersuasive. At oral argument, Defendant repeatedly characterized its actions as merely "operating a Web site" or "advertising." Dot Com also cites to a number of cases from this Circuit which, it claims, stand for the proposition that merely advertising in a forum, without more, is not a sufficient minimal contact. This argument is misplaced. Dot Com has done more than advertise on the Internet in Pennsylvania. Defendant has sold passwords to approximately 3,000 subscribers in Pennsylvania and entered into seven contracts with Internet access providers to furnish its services to their customers in Pennsylvania.

Dot Com also contends that its contacts with Pennsylvania residents are "fortuitous" within the meaning of *World-Wide Volkswagen*, 444 U.S. 286, 100 S. Ct.

559 (1980). [Defendant argues that it has not "actively" solicited business in Pennsylvania and that any business it conducts with Pennsylvania residents has resulted from contacts that were initiated by Pennsylvanians who visited the Defendant's Web site.] The fact that Dot Com's services have been consumed in Pennsylvania is not "fortuitous" within the meaning of *World-Wide Volkswagen*. In *World-Wide Volkswagen*, a couple that had purchased a vehicle in New York, while they were New York residents, were injured while driving that vehicle through Oklahoma and brought suit in an Oklahoma state court. *World-Wide Volkswagen*, 444 U.S. at 288, 100 S. Ct. at 562-63. The manufacturer did not sell its vehicles in Oklahoma and had not made an effort to establish business relationships in Oklahoma. *Id*. at 295, 100 S. Ct. at 566. The Supreme Court characterized the manufacturer's ties with Oklahoma as fortuitous because they resulted entirely out of the fact that the plaintiffs had driven their car into that state. *Id*.

Here, Dot Com argues that its contacts with Pennsylvania residents are fortuitous because Pennsylvanians happened to find its Web site or heard about its news service elsewhere and decided to subscribe. This argument misconstrues the concept of fortuitous contacts embodied in *World-Wide Volkswagen*. Dot Com's contacts with Pennsylvania would be fortuitous within the meaning of *World-Wide Volkswagen* if it had no Pennsylvania subscribers and an Ohio subscriber forwarded a copy of a file he obtained from Dot Com to a friend in Pennsylvania or an Ohio subscriber brought his computer along on a trip to Pennsylvania and used it to access Dot Com's service. That is not the situation here. Dot Com repeatedly and consciously chose to process Pennsylvania residents' applications and to assign them passwords. Dot Com knew that the result of these contracts would be the transmission of electronic messages into Pennsylvania. The transmission of these files was entirely within its control. Dot Com cannot maintain that these contracts are "fortuitous" or "coincidental" within the meaning of *World-Wide Volkswagen*. When a defendant makes a conscious choice to conduct business with the residents of a forum state, "it has clear notice that it is subject to suit there." *World-Wide Volkswagen*, 444 U.S. at 297, 100 S. Ct. at 567. Dot Com was under no obligation to sell its services to Pennsylvania residents. It freely chose to do so, presumably in order to profit from those transactions. If a corporation determines that the risk of being subject to personal jurisdiction in a particular forum is too great, it can choose to sever its connection to the state. *Id*. If Dot Com had not wanted to be amenable to jurisdiction in Pennsylvania, the solution would have been simple—it could have chosen not to sell its services to Pennsylvania residents.

Next, Dot Com argues that its forum-related activities are not numerous or significant enough to create a "substantial connection" with Pennsylvania. Defendant points to the fact that only two percent of its subscribers are Pennsylvania residents. However, the Supreme Court has made clear that even a single contact can be sufficient. *McGee*, 355 U.S. at 223, 78 S. Ct. at 201. The test has always focused on the "nature and quality" of the contacts with the forum and not the quantity of those contacts. *International Shoe*, 326 U.S. at 320, 66 S. Ct. at 160. The Sixth Circuit also rejected a similar argument in *CompuServe* when it wrote that the contacts were "deliberate and repeated even if they yielded little revenue." *CompuServe*, 89 F.3d at 1265.

We also conclude that the cause of action arises out of Dot Com's forum-related conduct in this case. The Third Circuit has stated that "a cause of action for trademark infringement occurs where the passing off occurs." Cottman Transmission Systems Inc. v. Martino, 36 F.3d 291, 294 (citing Tefal, S.A. v. Products Int'l Co., 529 F.2d 495, 496 n. 1 (3d Cir. 1976); Indianapolis Colts v. Metro. Baltimore Football, 34 F.3d 410 (7th Cir. 1994). In *Tefal*, the maker and distributor of T-Fal cookware sued a partnership of California corporations in the District of New Jersey for trademark infringement. *Tefal*, 529 F.2d at 496. The defendants objected to venue in New Jersey, arguing that the contested trademark accounted for only about five percent of national sales. *Id.* On appeal, the Third Circuit concluded that since substantial sales of the product bearing the allegedly infringing mark took place in New Jersey, the cause of action arose in New Jersey and venue was proper. *Tefal*, 529 F.2d at 496-97.

In *Indianapolis Colts*, also case cited by the Third Circuit in *Cottman*, an Indiana National Football League franchise sued a Maryland Canadian Football League franchise in the Southern District of Indiana, alleging trademark infringement. *Indianapolis Colts*, 34 F.3d at 411. On appeal, the Seventh Circuit held that personal jurisdiction was appropriate in Indiana because trademark infringement is a tort-like injury and a substantial amount of the injury from the alleged infringement was likely to occur in Indiana. *Id.* at 412.

In the instant case, both a significant amount of the alleged infringement and dilution, and resulting injury have occurred in Pennsylvania. The object of Dot Com's contracts with Pennsylvania residents is the transmission of the messages that Plaintiff claims dilute and infringe upon its trademark. When these messages are transmitted into Pennsylvania and viewed by Pennsylvania residents on their computers, there can be no question that the alleged infringement and dilution occur in Pennsylvania. Moreover, since Manufacturing is a Pennsylvania corporation, a substantial amount of the injury from the alleged wrongdoing is likely to occur in Pennsylvania. Thus, we conclude that the cause of action arises out of Dot Com's forum-related activities under the authority of both *Tefal* and *Indianapolis Colts*, supra.

Finally, Dot Com argues that the exercise of jurisdiction would be unreasonable in this case. We disagree. There can be no question that Pennsylvania has a strong interest in adjudicating disputes involving the alleged infringement of trademarks owned by resident corporations. We must also give due regard to the Plaintiff's choice to seek relief in Pennsylvania. *Kulko*, 436 U.S. at 92, 98 S. Ct. at 1696-97. These concerns outweigh the burden created by forcing the Defendant to defend the suit in Pennsylvania, especially when Dot Com consciously chose to conduct business in Pennsylvania, pursuing profits from the actions that are now in question. The Due Process Clause is not a "territorial shield to interstate obligations that have been voluntarily assumed." *Burger King*, 471 U.S. at 474, 105 S. Ct. at 2183. . . .

COMMENTS AND QUESTIONS

1. Does it make sense to treat electronic commerce sites differently from "passive" Web pages? Is it the act of sale into a jurisdiction or the offer for sale that makes an electronic commerce site liable for suit in that jurisdiction?

One implication of the "offer for sale" approach would seem to be that if you offer products for sale over the Internet, you are subject to suit *everywhere in the world.* Does this result make sense? Is there a way to limit jurisdiction while still holding ecommerce sites liable for suit in jurisdictions in which their products or conduct actually cause injury?

Of course, as with virtually all discussions of Internet jurisdiction, we are talking about specific rather than general jurisdiction here. That is, each of these disputes is about amenability to suits arising out of the plaintiff's interaction with the Web site. A court recently confirmed that *general* jurisdiction—jurisdiction over all types of claims, whether or not related to the forum contacts—cannot be conferred by the mere accessibility of a Web site, regardless of how interactive it is. See Coastal Video Comm. Corp. v. The Staywell Corp., 59 F. Supp.2d 562 (E.D. Va. 1999).

2. If a site does not itself sell products, should it automatically be considered passive? Many business models on the Internet today involve giving away useful information or services and funding the site with some other revenue source (such as advertising). Is a search engine interactive or passive within the meaning of the jurisdiction cases?

3. The case-by-case approach has drawn the adherence of a number of courts. Most courts to consider the question have concluded that passive Web pages alone are not enough for jurisdiction. In addition to *Cybersell,* see Bensusan Restaurant Corp. v. King, 937 F. Supp. 295 (S.D.N.Y. 1996); CD Solutions v. Tooker, 965 F. Supp. 17 (N.D. Tex. 1997); Rannoch Inc. v. Rannoch Corp., 52 F. Supp. 2d 681 (E.D. Va. 1999); Millennium Ents. v. Millennium Music, 33 F. Supp. 2d 907 (D.Or. 1999) (defining "passive" to include a Web page that was itself interactive but that could not be used to conduct commerce). By contrast, courts that found the presence of other "plus factors"—non-Internet advertising activities in the jurisdiction, for example, or sales or business relationships within the jurisdiction—are more likely to find personal jurisdiction. In addition to *Zippo,* see Heroes, Inc. v. Heroes Found., 958 F. Supp. 1 (D.D.C. 1996); Digital Equip. Corp. v. Altavista Tech., 960 F. Supp. 456 (D.Mass. 1997).

4. Although *Zippo* continues to be widely cited and influential, some commentators have voiced objections to it. See, e.g., Michael Geist, Is There a There There? Toward Greater Certainty for Internet Jurisdiction, 16 Berkeley Tech. L. J. 1345, 1378-81 (2001):

> One of the primary reasons for the early widespread support for the *Zippo* test was the desire for increased legal certainty for Internet jurisdiction issues. While the test may not have been perfect, supporters felt it offered a clear standard that would allow businesses to conduct effective legal risk analysis and make rational choices with regard to their approach to the Internet.
>
> In the final analysis, however, the *Zippo* test simply does not deliver the desired effect. First, the majority of websites are neither entirely passive nor completely active. Accordingly, they fall into the "middle zone" that requires courts to gauge all relevant evidence and determine whether the site is "more passive" or "more active." With many sites falling into this middle zone, their legal advisors are frequently unable to provide a firm opinion on how any given court might judge the interactivity of the website.
>
> Second, distinguishing between passive and active sites is complicated by the fact that some sites may not be quite what they seem. For example, sites that feature content best characterized as passive may actually be using cookies or other data collection technologies behind the scenes unbeknownst to the individual user. Given the value of

personal data, its collection is properly characterized as active, regardless of whether it occurs transparently or surreptitiously. Similarly, sites such as online chatrooms may appear to be active, yet courts have consistently characterized such sites as passive.

Third, it is important to note that the standards for what constitutes an active or passive website are constantly shifting. When the test was developed in 1997, an active website might have featured little more than an email link and some basic correspondence functionality. Today, sites with that level of interactivity would likely be viewed as passive, since the entire spectrum of passive versus active has shifted upward with improved technology. In fact, it can be credibly argued that owners of websites must constantly re-evaluate their positions on the passive versus active spectrum as web technology changes.

Fourth, the *Zippo* test is ineffective even if the standards for passive and active sites remain constant. With the expense of creating a sophisticated website now easily in excess of $100,000, few organizations will invest in a website without anticipating earning potential. Since revenue is typically the hallmark of active websites, most new sites are likely to feature interactivity, and therefore be categorized as active sites. From a jurisdictional perspective, this produces an effect similar to that found in the *Inset* line of cases—any court anywhere can assert jurisdiction over a website because virtually all sites will meet the *Zippo* standard. . . .

The *Zippo* experience suggests that the new test should remain technology neutral so as to: a) remain relevant despite ever-changing web technologies, b) create incentives that at a minimum do not discourage online interactivity, and c) provide sufficient certainty so that the legal risk of operating online can be effectively assessed in advance.

The solution submitted here is to move toward a targeting-based analysis. Unlike the *Zippo* approach, a targeting analysis would seek to identify the intentions of the parties and to assess the steps taken to either enter or avoid a particular jurisdiction. Targeting would also lessen the reliance on effects-based analyses, the source of considerable uncertainty because Internet-based activities can ordinarily be said to cause effects in most jurisdictions.

5. The Fourth Circuit Court of Appeals appears to have adopted *Zippo* but also adapted it in a manner consistent with the targeting approach that Geist endorses.

ALS Scan, Inc. v. Digital Service Consultants, Inc.
United States Court of Appeals for the Fourth Circuit
293 F.3d 707 (4th Cir. 2002)

NIEMEYER, Circuit Judge:

The question presented in this appeal is whether a Georgia-based Internet Service Provider subjected itself to personal jurisdiction in Maryland by enabling a website owner to publish photographs on the Internet, in violation of a Maryland corporation's copyrights. Adapting the traditional due process principles used to determine a State's authority to exercise personal jurisdiction over out-of-state persons to the Internet context, we hold that in the circumstances of this case, a Maryland court cannot constitutionally exercise jurisdiction over the Georgia Internet Service Provider. Accordingly, we affirm the district court's order dismissing the complaint against the Internet Service Provider for lack of personal jurisdiction.

I

ALS Scan, Inc., a Maryland corporation with its place of business in Columbia, Maryland, commenced this action for copyright infringement against Digital Service Consultants, Inc. ("Digital"), and Digital's customers, Robert Wilkins and Alternative Products, Inc. (collectively, "Alternative Products"). ALS Scan, which creates and markets adult photographs of female models for distribution over the Internet, claims that Alternative Products appropriated copies of hundreds of ALS Scan's copyrighted photographs and placed them on its websites, *www.abpefarc.net* and *www.abpeuarc.com*, thereby gaining revenue from them through membership fees and advertising. ALS Scan further alleges that Digital, as the Internet Service Provider ("ISP") for Alternative Products, "enabled" Alternative Products to publish ALS Scan's copyrighted photographs on the Internet by providing Alternative Products with the bandwidth service needed to maintain its websites. ALS Scan thus alleges that all of the defendants have infringed and are infringing its copyrights within Maryland and elsewhere by selling, publishing, and displaying its copyrighted photographs.

Digital filed a motion to dismiss the complaint against it under Federal Rule of Civil Procedure 12(b)(2), asserting that the district court lacked personal jurisdiction over it. In support of its motion, Digital provided affidavits demonstrating that Digital is a Georgia corporation with its only place of business in Atlanta. Digital asserts that it is an ISP which provided bandwidth service to Alternative Products as a customer but that it is not affiliated in any way with Alternative Products except through an arms-length customer relationship. In addition, Digital states that it did not select the infringing photographs for publication; it did not have knowledge that they were posted on Alternative Products' website; and it received no income from Alternative Products' subscribers. Digital acknowledges that it does maintain its own website, *www.dscga.com*, but asserts that its website "contains no means for any person to enter into a contract with, transfer funds to, or otherwise transact business with, Digital."

Digital also states that, other than through the Internet, it has no contacts with the State of Maryland. It avers that it conducts no business and has no offices in Maryland; that it has no contracts with any persons or entities in Maryland; that it derives no income from any clients or business in Maryland; that it does not advertise in Maryland (other than through its website); and that it owns no property in Maryland.

In a responding affidavit, ALS Scan asserts that copies of its copyrighted photographs have appeared on Alternative Products' two websites, *www.abpefarc.net* and *www.abpeuarc.com*. It also alleges that one of its employees in Maryland purchased an "on-line" membership to *www.abpefarc.net*, using a credit card, and, by obtaining that membership, the employee received a "user name" and a "password" to access the website. That website, it asserts, displayed ALS Scan's copyrighted photographs, allegedly in violation of the Copyright Act.

The district court granted Digital's motion to dismiss for lack of personal jurisdiction. The court found that it had neither specific nor general jurisdiction over Digital because "Digital does not engage in any continuous and systematic activities within Maryland, and there is no evidence that [ALS Scan's] claim arises out of any contacts which Digital may have with Maryland."

From the district court's ruling, ALS Scan filed this interlocutory appeal.

II

. . . Although the courts have recognized that the standards used to determine the proper exercise of personal jurisdiction may evolve as technological progress occurs, it nonetheless has remained clear that technology cannot eviscerate the constitutional limits on a State's power to exercise jurisdiction over a defendant. In *Hanson v. Denckla*, 357 U.S. 235, 2 L. Ed.2d 1283, 78 S. Ct. 1228 (1958), the Court explored the problem of reconciling technological advances with the limits of personal jurisdiction and stated:

> As technological progress has increased the flow of commerce between States, the need for jurisdiction over nonresidents has undergone a similar increase. At the same time, progress in communications and transportation has made the defense of a suit in a foreign tribunal less burdensome. In response to these changes, the requirements for personal jurisdiction over nonresidents have evolved from the rigid rule of *Pennoyer v. Neff* to the flexible standard of *International Shoe Co. v. State of Washington*. But it is a mistake to assume that this trend heralds the eventual demise of all restrictions on the personal jurisdiction of state courts. Those restrictions are more than a guarantee of immunity from inconvenient or distant litigation. They are a consequence of territorial limitations on the power of the respective States. However minimal the burden of defending in a foreign tribunal, a defendant may not be called upon to do so unless he has had the "minimal contacts" with that State that are a prerequisite to its exercise of power over him.

Id. at 250-51 (internal citations omitted); see also *McGee v. Int'l Life Ins. Co.*, 355 U.S. 220, 222, 2 L. Ed.2d 223, 78 S. Ct. 199 (1957) (noting that the trend toward expanding the permissible scope of personal jurisdiction is, in part, "attributable to the fundamental transformation of our national economy over the years"). The Court has thus mandated that limits on the states' power to exercise personal jurisdiction over nonresidents must be maintained, despite the growing ease with which business is conducted across state lines. . . .

III

In this case, ALS Scan argues that Digital's activity in enabling Alternative Products' publication of the infringing photographs on the Internet, thereby causing ALS Scan injury in Maryland, forms a proper basis for the district court's specific jurisdiction over Digital. The question thus becomes whether a person electronically transmitting or enabling the transmission of information via the Internet to Maryland, causing injury there, subjects the person to the jurisdiction of a court in Maryland, a question of first impression in the Fourth Circuit. . . .

In view of the traditional relationship among the States and their relationship to a national government with its nationwide judicial authority, it would be difficult to accept a structural arrangement in which each State has unlimited judicial power over every citizen in each other State who uses the Internet. That thought certainly would have been considered outrageous in the past when interconnections were made only by telephones. See, e.g., *Stover*, 84 F.3d at 137 (finding a defendant's "occasional telephonic requests for information from Maryland-based investigation services" to be insufficient to subject the defendant to personal jurisdiction in a

Maryland court). But now, even though the medium is still often a telephone wire, the breadth and frequency of electronic contacts through computers has resulted in billions of interstate connections and millions of interstate transactions entered into solely through the vehicle of the Internet. The convergence of commerce and technology thus tends to push the analysis to include a "stream-of-commerce" concept, under which each person who puts an article into commerce is held to anticipate suit in any jurisdiction where the stream takes the article. But the "stream-of-commerce" concept, although considered, has never been adopted by the Supreme Court as the controlling principle for defining the reach of a State's judicial power. See generally Asahi Metal Indus. Co. v. Superior Court of Cal., 480 U.S. 102, 94 L. Ed.2d 92, 107 S. Ct. 1026 (1987).

Until the due process concepts of personal jurisdiction are reconceived and rearticulated by the Supreme Court in light of advances in technology, we must develop, under existing principles, the more limited circumstances when it can be deemed that an out-of-state citizen, through electronic contacts, has conceptually "entered" the State via the Internet for jurisdictional purposes. Such principles are necessary to recognize that a State does have limited judicial authority over out-of-state persons who use the Internet to contact persons within the State. Drawing on the requirements for establishing specific jurisdiction, see *Helicopteros*, 466 U.S. at 414 & n.8, which requires *purposeful* conduct directed at the State and that the plaintiff's claims arise from the purposeful conduct, we adopt today the model developed in Zippo Manufacturing Co. v. Zippo Dot Com, Inc., 952 F. Supp. 1119 (W.D.Pa. 1997).

In *Zippo*, the court concluded that "the likelihood that personal jurisdiction can be constitutionally exercised is directly proportionate to the nature and quality of commercial activity that an entity conducts over the Internet." 952 F. Supp. at 1124. Recognizing a "sliding scale" for defining when electronic contacts with a State are sufficient, the court elaborated:

> At one end of the spectrum are situations where a defendant clearly does business over the Internet. If the defendant enters into contracts with residents of a foreign jurisdiction that involve the knowing and repeated transmission of computer files over the Internet, personal jurisdiction is proper. At the opposite end are situations where a defendant has simply posted information on an Internet Web site which is accessible to users in foreign jurisdictions. A passive Web site that does little more than make information available to those who are interested in it is not grounds for the exercise [of] personal jurisdiction. The middle ground is occupied by interactive Web sites where a user can exchange information with the host computer. In these cases, the exercise of jurisdiction is determined by examining the level of interactivity and commercial nature of the exchange of information that occurs on the Web site.

Id. (internal citations omitted); *accord* Soma Med. Int'l v. Standard Chartered Bank, 196 F.3d 1292, 1297 (10th Cir. 1999) (citing the *Zippo* standard for "passive" Web sites and thus finding a corporation's Web site an insufficient basis for an exercise of personal jurisdiction); Mink v. AAAA Dev. LLC, 190 F.3d 333, 336 (5th Cir. 1999) (applying *Zippo*'s sliding scale test to the case before it); Cybersell, Inc. v. Cybersell, Inc., 130 F.3d 414, 418 (9th Cir. 1997) (quoting *Zippo* for the proposition that "courts that have addressed interactive sites have looked to the 'level of interactivity and commercial nature of the exchange of information that occurs on the Web site' to determine if sufficient contacts exist to warrant the exercise of jurisdiction").

Thus, adopting and adapting the *Zippo* model, we conclude that a State may, consistent with due process, exercise judicial power over a person outside of the State when that person (1) directs electronic activity into the State, (2) with the manifested intent of engaging in business or other interactions within the State, and (3) that activity creates, in a person within the State, a potential cause of action cognizable in the State's courts. Under this standard, a person who simply places information on the Internet does not subject himself to jurisdiction in each State into which the electronic signal is transmitted and received. Such passive Internet activity does not generally include directing electronic activity into the State with the manifested intent of engaging business or other interactions in the State thus creating in a person within the State a potential cause of action cognizable in courts located in the State.

This standard for reconciling contacts through electronic media with standard due process principles is not dissimilar to that applied by the Supreme Court in Calder v. Jones, 465 U.S. 783, 79 L. Ed.2d 804, 104 S. Ct. 1482 (1984). In *Calder*, the Court held that a California court could constitutionally exercise personal jurisdiction over a Florida citizen whose only material contact with California was to write a libelous story in Florida, directed at a California citizen, for a publication circulated in California, knowing that the "injury would be felt by [the Californian] in the State in which she lives and works." *Id*. at 789-90. Analogously, under the standard we adopt and apply today, specific jurisdiction in the Internet context may be based only on an out-of-state person's Internet activity directed at Maryland and causing injury that gives rise to a potential claim cognizable in Maryland.

Applying this standard to the present case, we conclude that Digital's activity was, at most, passive and therefore does not subject it to the judicial power of a Maryland court even though electronic signals from Digital's facility were concededly received in Maryland. Digital functioned from Georgia as an ISP, and in that role provided bandwidth to Alternative Products, also located in Georgia, to enable Alternative Products to create a website and send information over the Internet. It did not select or knowingly transmit infringing photographs specifically to Maryland with the intent of engaging in business or any other transaction in Maryland. Rather, its role as an ISP was at most passive. Surely, it cannot be said that Digital "purposefully availed" itself of the privilege of conducting business or other transactions in Maryland. See *ESAB Group*, 126 F.3d at 623 (quoting *Hanson*, 357 U.S. at 253).

Indeed, the only *direct* contact that Digital had with Maryland was through the general publication of its website on the Internet. But that website is unrelated to ALS Scan's claim in this case because Digital's website was not involved in the publication of any infringing photographs. See *Christian Science Bd.*, 259 F.3d at 216.

Thus, under the standard articulated in this case, Digital did not direct its electronic activity specifically at any target in Maryland; it did not manifest an intent to engage in a business or some other interaction in Maryland; and none of its conduct in enabling a website created a cause of action in Maryland, although on this last point, facts would have to be developed about whether Digital continued to enable the website after receiving notice. See ALS Scan, Inc. v. RemarQ Communities, Inc., 239 F.3d 619, 620 (4th Cir. 2001). This factual issue, however, need not be resolved because Digital's conduct does not satisfy the first two prongs of the test.

Accordingly, we agree with the district court that Digital's contacts in Maryland do not justify a Maryland court's exercise of specific jurisdiction over Digital.

COMMENTS AND QUESTIONS

1. To what extent does *ALS Scan* adopt *Zippo*? Does it really adapt *Zippo* or has the court provided an alternative test for Internet jurisdiction cases? Which approach—*Zippo* or *ALS Scan*—is most consistent with the Supreme Court standards in the constitutional due process cases?

2. Would the Fourth Circuit have reached the same conclusion if the alleged infringer (also based in Georgia) had moved to dismiss for lack of personal jurisdiction?

≡ *GTE New Media Services Inc. v. Bellsouth Corp.*
   United States Court of Appeals for the D.C. Circuit
   199 F.3d 1343 (D.C. Cir. 2000)

EDWARDS, J.

The relevant facts are relatively simple. GTE alleges that in July 1997, five regional Bell operating companies (Ameritech Corp., Bell Atlantic, BellSouth, SBC Corp., US West) and their relevant subsidiaries conspired to capture, control, and dominate the Internet business directories' market. See GTE New Media Servs. Inc. v. Ameritech Corp., 21 F. Supp. 2d 27. After the alleged conspirators held meetings in California, Colorado, Georgia, and Michigan, they agreed to provide jointly a coded map of the United States that would allow users of their Internet Yellow Pages to access particular states and particular businesses. Each of the regional Bell operating companies would provide exclusive service to a particular region, and the other companies apparently agreed not to compete with the designated exclusive server in its given region. The regions designated to each regional Bell operating company corresponded to the region to which the company provided telecommunications service. The regional Bell operating companies' next step was to obtain exclusive links for their map on well-known Internet browser sites run by Netscape Communications Corp. ("Netscape") and Yahoo, Inc! ("Yahoo"), to ensure that users of these popular sites would be specifically directed to the operating companies' Internet Yellow Pages.

Before the alleged conspiracy, GTE had a non-exclusive contract with Netscape, pursuant to which Netscape offered a choice of Internet business directories on its site, including GTE's SuperPages. When users accessed the "Yellow Pages" option on Netscape's toolbar, they had access to GTE's website. GTE asserts, however, that Netscape terminated this arrangement on July 18, 1997, by removing its links to GTE's SuperPages, including hyperlinks on Yahoo.

On October 6, 1997, GTE filed its complaint against the five regional Bell operating companies, Netscape, and Yahoo, claiming, among other things, violations of Sections 1 and 2 of the Sherman Antitrust Act. Several defendants (i.e., Bell South, SBC Corp. and US West, excepting US West Dex, Inc.) moved to dismiss the complaint for lack of personal jurisdiction; two (i.e., BellSouth and SBC Corp.) also argued that venue was improper in the District of Columbia. On September

28, 1998, the District Court denied both motions to dismiss, finding that (1) the court had personal jurisdiction under section 13-423(a)(4) of the D.C. long-arm statute, because GTE had sufficiently alleged a tortious injury in the District caused by the defendants' acts outside of the District; and (2) because venue is proper under 28 U.S.C. §1391 wherever a party is subject to personal jurisdiction, the finding of personal jurisdiction also resolved the venue question. On March 29, 1999, however, the District Court certified an order for interlocutory appeal and ordered a stay of proceedings. The District Court noted that, although it had found that the defendants operated an interactive website that supported a finding of personal jurisdiction,

> the instant case differs from any other reported case . . . in that it involves an interactive website *with no other contacts with the District of Columbia*. All of the interactive website cases reviewed by this court involved defendants with at least some physical contact with the forum. While this court has concluded that the quality and nature of the [operating companies'] website favors the exercise of personal jurisdiction in the District of Columbia, certainly a substantial ground for difference of opinion concerning the ruling exists.

GTE New Media Servs. Inc., Order Certifying for Interlocutory Appeal the Court's Ruling that Personal Jurisdiction Exists and Staying Proceedings at 3, (emphasis added). On April 8, 1999, the defendants filed a petition for permission to appeal. This court entered an order granting permission to appeal on May 28, 1999.

A. The District of Columbia Long-Arm Statute and the Due Process Clause of the U.S. Constitution

To establish personal jurisdiction over a non-resident, a court must engage in a two-part inquiry: A court must first examine whether jurisdiction is applicable under the state's long-arm statute and then determine whether a finding of jurisdiction satisfies the constitutional requirements of due process. *See United States v. Ferrara*, 311 U.S. App. D.C. 421, 54 F.3d 825, 828 (D.C. Cir. 1995).

The District's long-arm statute provides, in relevant part, that

> [a] District of Columbia court may exercise personal jurisdiction over a person, who acts directly or by an agent, as to a claim for relief arising from the person's—
> (1) transacting any business in the District of Columbia;
> . . . (4) causing tortious injury in the District of Columbia by an act or omission outside the District of Columbia if he [i] regularly does or solicits business, [ii] engages in any other persistent course of conduct, or [iii] derives substantial revenue from goods used or consumed, or services rendered, in the District of Columbia.

D.C. Code Ann. §13-423(a) (1981). A plaintiff seeking to establish jurisdiction over a non-resident under the foregoing provisions of the long-arm statute must demonstrate, pursuant to section (a)(1), that the plaintiff transacted business in the District, or show, pursuant to section (a)(4), that the plaintiff caused a tortious injury in the District, the injury was caused by the defendant's act or omission outside of the District, and the defendant had one of the three enumerated contacts with the District. Section (a)(1)'s "transacting any business" clause generally has

been interpreted to be coextensive with the Constitution's due process requirements and thus to merge into a single inquiry. *See Ferrara*, 54 F.3d at 828. Section
(a)(4) has been construed more narrowly, however. *See Crane v. Carr*, 259 U.S.
App. D.C. 229, 814 F.2d 758, 762 (D.C. Cir. 1987) ("The drafters of this provision apparently intended that the (a)(4) subsection would not occupy all of the
constitutionally available space. . . . This court has explicitly noted, moreover, that
(a)(4) of the D.C. long-arm statute may indeed stop short of the outer limit of the
constitutional space.").

Even when the literal terms of the long-arm statute have been satisfied, a
plaintiff must still show that the exercise of personal jurisdiction is within the permissible bounds of the Due Process Clause. In other words, a plaintiff must show
"minimum contacts" between the defendant and the forum establishing that "the
maintenance of the suit does not offend traditional notions of fair play and substantial justice." *International Shoe Co. v. Washington*, 326 U.S. 310, 316, 90 L. Ed.
95, 66 S. Ct. 154 (1945) (internal quotation marks omitted). Under the "minimum contracts" standard, courts must insure that "the defendant's conduct and
connection with the forum State are such that he should reasonably anticipate being haled into court there." *World-Wide Volkswagen Corp. v. Woodson*, 444 U.S.
286, 297, 62 L. Ed.2d 490, 100 S. Ct. 559 (1980). . . .

The District Court in this case asserted personal jurisdiction, pursuant to D.C.
Code Ann. §13-423(a)(4), on the ground that the defendants allegedly caused
tortious injury in the District by an act outside the District followed by a persistent
course of conduct in the District. Under this theory of jurisdiction, it does not
matter that the defendants have no demonstrated physical contacts in the District.
Rather, it is enough, according to the District Court, that the defendants entered
into an agreement outside of the District with an eye toward attracting Internet
users in the District to their websites (instead of to GTE's SuperPages) and thereby
draw advertisers away from GTE. The District Court found that, on these asserted
facts alone, the defendants foreseeably caused tortious injury to GTE's business in
this forum. See *Ameritech Corp.*, Mem. Op. at 10, *reprinted in* J.A. 190. The defendants' course of conduct was seen to be "persistent" by the District Court, because their websites are "highly interactive" with District users and significantly
commercial in both quality and nature. *Id.* at 11-12, *reprinted* at J.A. 191-92. We
disagree with this line of reasoning.

There is no evidence in this record to support the claim that the defendants
"secured advertising revenue by increasing the user traffic on their websites." *Id.* at
13. At best, GTE has provided only conclusory statements and intimations to but-
tress its assertion that it lost advertising revenues as a result of the defendants' actions. These are not enough. *Cf.* First Chicago Int'l v. United Exchange Co., 267
U.S. App. D.C. 27, 836 F.2d 1375, 1378-79 (D.C. Cir. 1988) ("Conclusory
statements . . . '[do] not constitute the *prima facie* showing necessary to carry the
burden of establishing personal jurisdiction.' . . . The 'bare allegation' of conspiracy
or agency is insufficient to establish personal jurisdiction." (citation omitted)). We
will neither assume nor infer that the alleged conspiracy had *substantial effects* of
the sort alleged by GTE, because to do so would be to assume or infer the answer
to the very question that is before us.

Furthermore, it is difficult to understand, at least on the present record, what
tortious injury has been suffered by GTE *in the District*. GTE claims that it has lost
advertising revenues by virtue of the defendants' allegedly unlawful conspiracy.

However, nothing has been offered to indicate that these advertising revenues were lost in the District, either by lost sales or lost revenue collections.

Additionally, personal jurisdiction surely cannot be based solely on the ability of District residents to access the defendants' websites, for this does not by itself show any persistent course of conduct by the defendants in the District. Access to a website reflects nothing more than a telephone call by a District resident to the defendants' computer servers, all of which apparently are operated outside of the District. And, as this court has held, mere receipt of telephone calls outside the District does not constitute persistent conduct "in the District" within the meaning of the long-arm statute. See Tavoulareas v. Comnas, 232 U.S. App. D.C. 17, 720 F.2d 192, 194 (D.C. Cir. 1983).

Finally, GTE appears to suggest that, when a District resident accesses the defendants' Yellow Pages websites, the defendants are somehow "transacting business" in the District. This is a far-fetched claim on this record. Access to an Internet Yellow Page site is akin to searching a telephone book—the consumer pays nothing to use the search tool, and any resulting business transaction is between the consumer and a business found in the Yellow Pages, not between the consumer and the provider of the Yellow Pages. In short, there is nothing here to indicate that District residents actually engage in any business transactions with the defendants.

When stripped to its core, GTE's theory of jurisdiction rests on the claim that, because the defendants have acted to maximize usage of their websites in the District, mere accessibility of the defendants' websites establishes the necessary "minimum contacts" with this forum. This theory simply cannot hold water. Indeed, under this view, personal jurisdiction in Internet-related cases would almost always be found in any forum in the country. We do not believe that the advent of advanced technology, say, as with the Internet, should vitiate long-held and inviolate principles of federal court jurisdiction. The Due Process Clause exists, in part, to give "a degree of predictability to the legal system that allows potential defendants to structure their primary conduct with some minimum assurance as to where that conduct will and will not render them liable to suit." *World-Wide Volkswagen Corp.*, 444 U.S. at 297. In the context of the Internet, GTE's expansive theory of personal jurisdiction would shred these constitutional assurances out of practical existence. Our sister circuits have not accepted such an approach, and neither shall we.

COMMENTS AND QUESTIONS

1. The defendants in the *GTE New Media* case relied heavily on *Zippo* in arguing that personal jurisdiction was proper in the District of Columbia because of the interactivity of the defendants' websites. Did the D.C. Circuit Court of Appeals in this case repudiate *Zippo* or just come to a different conclusion in applying the test? Consider the D.C. Circuit opinion in Gorman v. Ameritrade Hold Corp., 293 F.3d 502 (D.C. Cir. 2002) which invoked *Zippo* as precedent for finding general jurisdiction over defendants in a breach of contract case because of the many D.C.-based clients.

2. The plaintiffs in both the *ALS Scan* and *GTE New Media* cases requested the right to conduct discovery on jurisdiction issues in the event that the court found the plaintiff's evidence to be insufficient for exercise of personal jurisdiction.

This was granted in the *GTE New Media* case, but not in the *ALS Scan* case. What criteria should courts use to decide when to allow jurisdictional discovery? What facts should such discovery aim to uncover?

3. Where in the physical world does injury take place for Internet-based activities? Does it depend on the sort of injury alleged?

B. JURISDICTION IN INTENTIONAL TORT CASES

≣≣≣ **Bochan v. LaFontaine**
United States District Court for the Eastern District of Virginia
68 F. Supp.2d 692 (E.D. Va. 1999)

ELLIS, J.

I.

Plaintiff, a devotee of John F. Kennedy (JFK) conspiracy theories, is the district manager of a group of theaters in Northern Virginia. Journalists Ray and Mary La Fontaine are Texas residents who wrote a book on the JFK assassination entitled *Oswald Talked: The New Evidence in the JFK Assassination.* Defendant Robert Harris, who is yet another JFK conspiracy devote [*sic*], is a resident of Albuquerque, New Mexico, where he owns Computer Works, a New Mexico-based computer systems business.

Plaintiff purchased the La Fontaines' book at Borders Bookstore in Fairfax, Va. sometime after it was published in 1996. He became a vocal critic of the book, often expressing his criticisms via the Internet, specifically by posting his critiques to the interactive newsgroup alt.conspiracy.jfk. These postings provoked defendants to post responses to the newsgroup, which responsive postings are the alleged defamations in this action.

The principal precipitating event occurred on October 12, 1998, when plaintiff posted a message to the La Fontaines that contained the following quote from the acknowledgments of the La Fontaines' book: "'We thank Charlotte and Eugenia for putting up with weird parents.'" The next day, Ray La Fontaine responded from Dallas, Texas, by posting a message to alt.conspiracy.jfk. This October 13, 1998 posting was labeled "The scum posts of Bochan," and stated, "I know you like kids, Bochan, but I suggest you limit your interest to trolling in alt.sex.fetish.tinygirls and leave our children out of it." La Fontaine then went on in this posting to provide "for anyone interested" what La Fontaine claimed was Bochan's October 1997 author profile with Deja News, an Internet discussion network. This author profile, as provided by Bochan, listed 238 articles, allegedly posted by Bochan, identifying the individual newsgroups to which each article was posted. The majority of the articles were listed as posted to various conspiracy theory sites, but according to La Fontaine's version of the author profile, Bochan also posted articles to three apparently pornographic sites: alt.sex.fetish.tinygirls, alt.sex.pictures.male, and alt.sex.snuff.cannibalism. La Fontaine followed the alleged profile with the following additional editorial comment directed to Bochan: "How come you only posted once to alt.sex.fetish.tinygirls and alt.sex.pictures.male, Bochan? Did you get lucky the first time around?"

AOL is located in Herndon, Virginia; Earthlink.net is located in Pasadena, California. The La Fontaines' AOL account is an auxiliary service that the La Fontaines used to screen responses to their posts; the AOL account does not provide access to the Internet, but instead specifically requires that the subscriber provide its own access to the Internet through another Internet service provider, such as Earthlink.net.

The matter did not end with Ray La Fontaine's seemingly unsavory posting. On October 14, 1998, Mary La Fontaine posted a message on alt.conspiracy.jfk to a friend of Bochan's, which defended the La Fontaines' actions in posting the alleged profile from Deja News. In this posting, Mary La Fontaine asserted that her husband had downloaded the profile directly from Deja News, and that she and her husband had decided to "reveal the truth" about the 1997 profile, then roughly a year old, because of the "not-so veiled attempt at intimidation" contained in the reference to the La Fontaines' children in Bochan's October 12, 1998 posting. Not content simply to defend the La Fontaine Deja News profile posting, Mary La Fontaine went on to suggest that Bochan's friend would be derelict as a mother were she to allow her children to associate with Bochan.

Harris also entered the fray on October 14, 1998, stating, in a posting to alt.conspiracy.jfk, that although Harris's children were grown, he could imagine how the La Fontaines must feel to have a "sicko" like plaintiff making "not very subtle references" to their children, and further, expressing the hope that Bochan's "tastes run more to sex.pictures.male than to tinygirls." On October 17, 1998, Harris posted another message to alt.conspiracy.jfk which called alt.sex.fetish.tinygirls "Bochan's newsgroup."

On the basis of these postings, Bochan sues both the La Fontaines and Harris in the Eastern District of Virginia for defamation and for intentional infliction of emotional distress, alleging that all defendants have publicly accused him of being a pedophile. At the threshold, defendants assert a lack of personal jurisdiction. In support of this contention, the La Fontaines state that they i) have not been in Virginia since 1993, when they drove from National Airport to the District of Columbia, ii) have not participated in any book promotions in Virginia, iii) receive no royalties from Virginia sales as they do not directly sell their book in Virginia, nor do they directly receive royalties on books sold by others in Virginia, but rather receive royalties on the total books sold by their publisher to national chains, and iv) have never derived any revenue that they are aware of from Virginia. Moreover, they note as significant that they i) do not have their own website, ii) do not conduct commercial activity over the Internet, and iii) made the allegedly defamatory postings by accessing the Internet through a California-based Internet service provider.

Harris, in support of his personal jurisdiction defense, states that he i) has never conducted any business in Virginia, ii) has only visited Virginia once, in 1994, to attend a Washington, D.C. conference and visit some historic sites in Virginia, iii) did not use any Virginia-based company in posting the allegedly defamatory comments, but instead used either California or New Mexico-based Internet service providers, and iv) did not direct his Internet postings to any Virginia resident. He further notes as significant that i) his website specifically states that Computer

Works sells computers only in New Mexico, and ii) Computer Works has never sold any computers or computer products to anyone in Virginia.

Bochan responds that the La Fontaines posted the allegedly defamatory messages using an account with AOL, a Virginia-based company, and moreover, that the La Fontaines have advertised, promoted and sold their book in Virginia. As to Harris, Bochan notes i) that the website for his business, Computer Works, is interactive, contains contact information and advertisements, and is accessible to Virginia residents 24 hours a day, and ii) that Harris has advertised specific computers in a variety of newsgroups, suggesting that he would take credit cards over the Internet, and that there were no geographical limitations on buyers. Bochan moreover states that all defendants knew that he resides and works in Virginia, and that the reputational harm, as well as the emotional distress, would be suffered in Virginia.

II. . . .

Bochan contends that jurisdiction exists over all defendants on the basis of two separate prongs of Virginia's long arm statute, Va. Code §8.01-328.1(A)(3), and §8.01-328.1(A)(4). Under §8.01-328.1(A)(3), a court may exercise personal jurisdiction over a defendant who causes "tortious injury by an act or omission in this Commonwealth." See Va. Code §8.01-328.1(A)(3). Under §8.01-328.1(A)(4), a court may exercise personal jurisdiction over a defendant who causes "tortious injury in this Commonwealth by an act or omission outside this Commonwealth" if that defendant i) regularly does or solicits business in Virginia, ii) engages in any other persistent course of conduct in Virginia, or iii) derives substantial revenue from goods used or consumed or services rendered, in Virginia. See Va. Code §8.01-328.1(A)(4). As defendants contend that neither prong of the long-arm reaches them, each defendant's contacts with the forum must be analyzed in turn under the relevant prongs of the long-arm.

A. The La Fontaine Defendants

Analysis properly begins with the question whether the La Fontaines' conduct fits within the reach of §8.01-328.1(A)(3). Put more concretely, the question is whether the La Fontaines committed a tort (i.e., libel) in Virginia by posting certain messages to an Internet newsgroup via AOL and Earthlink.net. This, as it happens, is a novel question in Virginia and there do not appear to be any decisions from other jurisdictions that are factually identical. There are, however, factually analogous cases that shed some light on how the Supreme Court of Virginia would analyze this issue. In Krantz v. Air Line Pilots Association, Int'l, 427 S.E.2d 326, 245 Va. 202 (1993), the defendant airline pilot posted a message from New York to ACCESS, a computer bulletin board physically located in Virginia. This message called for other pilots to pass the word that plaintiff was a "scab," apparently in an attempt to sabotage plaintiff's prospective employment at another airline. The Supreme Court of Virginia concluded that defendant's use of a bulletin board based in a Virginia facility satisfied §8.01-328.1(A)(3). In reaching this conclusion, the court stated that "without the use of ACCESS, a Virginia facility, [defendant] could not have obtained those recruits, and there would have been no interference with [plaintiff's] prospective contract, the third required element for a prima facie showing of this sort." See *Krantz*, 427 S.E.2d at 328.

Several federal district courts have applied the principles enunciated in *Krantz* to cases alleging Internet torts. In Telco Communications v. An Apple a Day, 977 F. Supp. 404 (E.D. Va. 1997), the court, in dicta, concluded that jurisdiction existed under §8.01-328.1(A)(3) on the ground that "but for the Internet service providers [AOL] and users present in Virginia, the alleged tort of defamation would not have occurred in Virginia." Thus, the court concluded that those defendants fell "under the jurisdictional net cast by *Krantz*." In contrast, the court in Mitchell v. McGowan, Civ. No. 98-1026- A, 1998 U.S. Dist. LEXIS 18587 (E.D. Va. September 18, 1998) (unpublished disposition), concluded that the defendant "appears to escape [the 'net' cast by *Krantz*] because the computer bulletin board he accessed is based in Texas," noting that this distinction, though rather "fine," was dispositive. Thus, since *Krantz* courts have focused in large measure on the location of the Internet service provider or the server on which the bulletin board is stored and the role played by this service or hardware in facilitating the alleged tort.

Under this analysis, a prima facie showing of a sufficient act by the La Fontaines in Virginia follows from their use of the AOL account, a Virginia-based service, to publish the allegedly defamatory statements. According to Bochan's expert, because the postings were accomplished through defendant's AOL account, they were transmitted first to AOL's USENET server hardware, located in Loudon County, Virginia. There, the message was apparently both stored temporarily and transmitted to other USENET servers around the world. Thus, as to the La Fontaines, because publication is a required element of defamation, and a prima facie showing has been made that the use of USENET server in Virginia was integral to that publication, there is a sufficient act in Virginia to satisfy §8.01-328.1(A)(3).

B. Defendant Harris

Because Harris did not use an AOL account after accessing the Internet, or use any Virginia-based service, but instead used only the Internet service providers Earthlink, located in California, or High Fiber, located in New Mexico, there is nothing in the record to suggest that Harris committed any tortious act in Virginia within the meaning of §8.01-328.1(A)(3).[26] Therefore, personal jurisdiction over

26. Bochan's contention to the contrary is that jurisdiction under §8.01-328.1(A)(3) exists because the messages were downloaded in Virginia, and therefore publication, the last act necessary for libel, occurred in Virginia. Rejecting essentially similar contentions, federal courts in non-Internet contexts have uniformly held that defamatory statements generated outside a forum state and transmitted by telephone or mail to the forum are not "acts" in the forum as required by §8.01-328.1(A)(3) or other similar long-arm statutes. See *Krantz*, 427 S.E.2d at 328 (citing Davis v. Costa-Gavras, 580 F. Supp. 1082, 1087 (S.D.N.Y. 1984); St. Clair v. Righter, 250 F. Supp. 148, 150-51 (W.D. Va. 1966), *disapproved on other grounds*, Beaty v. M.S. Steel Co., 401 F.2d 157 (4th Cir. 1968); Weller v. Cromwell Oil Co., 504 F.2d 927, 931 (6th Cir. 1974); Margoles v. Johns, 157 U.S. App. D.C. 209, 483 F.2d 1212 (D.C. Cir. 1973)); see also Booth v. Leaf, 40 F.3d 1243, 1994 WL 620651 (4th Cir. 1994) (unpublished disposition) ("§8.01-328.1(A)(3) does not grant jurisdiction over a person who wrote and mailed an allegedly defamatory letter outside Virginia."). The Supreme Court of Virginia has not addressed this point, specifically noting in *Krantz* that it was not called upon to do so because there it addressed "a communication that alone was not a tortious act." See *Krantz*, 427 S.E.2d at 328. Here, however, the communication at issue is the tortious act. In the absence of controlling Supreme Court of Virginia precedent to the contrary, and given the statute's clear distinction between the location of the act and

Harris, if it exists at all, must be based on §8.01-328.1(A)(4). In this regard, because there is no dispute that the alleged injury occurred in Virginia, the question is whether Harris regularly does or solicits business in Virginia or engages in any persistent course of conduct in Virginia.

Courts determining personal jurisdiction primarily on the basis of Internet activity generally focus on "the nature and quality of activity that a defendant conducts over the Internet." A judicial consensus has generally emerged that personal jurisdiction exists when Internet activities involve the conduct of business over the Internet, including on-line contracting with residents of the jurisdiction or other kinds of substantial commercial interactivity. Federal courts in Virginia in particular have generally found that Internet advertising accessible to Virginia residents 24 hours a day constitutes solicitation of business in Virginia sufficient to satisfy the requirements of §8.01-328.1(A)(4). Thus, in *Telco,* the district court, addressing §8.01-328.1(A)(4), found that jurisdiction existed over defendants who had issued press releases on the Internet that allegedly caused the plaintiffs' stock prices to fall. In that case, the district court concluded that defendants were conducting business over the Internet because they were advertising their firm and soliciting investment banking assistance when they posted the press releases. See Telco, 977 F. Supp. at 406. The court's reasoning was that "because [defendants] conducted their advertising and soliciting over the Internet, which could be accessed by a Virginia resident 24 hours a day" the defendants conducted their business "regularly" under the terms of the long-arm statute sufficient to satisfy 8.01-328.1(A)(4). *Id.* at 407.

Here, Harris, as the owner of Computer Works, has solicited business in Virginia by promoting and advertising his computer hardware company on the Internet through its website, accessible to Virginia Internet users 24 hours a day. This website is interactive in several ways, although no sales are concluded through it.[31] Moreover, even if the website contains sufficient geographic limitations to diminish its jurisdictional significance outside those geographic areas, Harris's own advertisements of specific computers on Internet newsgroups include his name, company and telephone numbers so that he can be contacted, and state that there are no surcharges for Visa or Mastercard, occasionally specifically request reply by email, and in no way appear to place geographical limits on buyers.[32] Under these circum-

---

the injury, the approach that has generally been followed by the federal courts will be followed here, as well. This approach is particularly sensible in the Internet context given the distinction between i) downloading a defamatory statement in Virginia that was posted by the tortfeasor to a server located outside Virginia, and ii) downloading a defamatory statement posted to a server in Virginia. For the purposes of §8.01-328.1(A)(3) it does not matter where the defamatory message was downloaded or read. Moreover, any suggestion by Bochan that because Harris was a part of "the events" leading to the lawsuit in some broad sense, Harris is tied to the La Fontaines and thus is necessarily subject to jurisdiction under §8.01-328.1(A)(3), is also unavailing. See Keeton v. Hustler Magazine, Inc., 465 U.S. 770, 781 n.13, 79 L. Ed.2d 790, 104 S. Ct. 1473 (1984) ("Each defendant's contacts with the forum State must be assessed individually.").

31 Though defendant does not conduct sales on his website, the website is sufficiently interactive to factor significantly in the jurisdictional analysis. See Blumenthal v. Drudge, 992 F. Supp. 44, 56 (D.D.C. 1998) ("Under the analysis adopted by these courts, the exercise of personal jurisdiction is contingent upon the website involving more than just the maintenance of a home page; it must allow browsers to interact directly with the website on some level."); Zippo Mfg. Co. v. Zippo Dot Com, 952 F. Supp. at 1124 ("[A] passive Web site that does little more than make information available to those who are interested in it is not grounds for the exercise of personal jurisdiction.").

32. It is not material that Harris's solicitations have yielded no sales in Virginia. The statutory language of §8.01-328.1(A)(4) does not require successful solicitation of business; the statute on its face, by asserting jurisdiction over those who regularly "do or solicit" business in Virginia, contemplates jurisdiction over individuals both who do business and those who merely solicit it. Moreover, there is no

stances, Harris sufficiently advertises and solicits business within Virginia to find personal jurisdiction within the meaning of §8.01-328.1(A)(4) of the Virginia long-arm.

III.

Given that §8.01-328.1(A)(3) reaches the La Fontaines and that §8.01-328.1(A)(4) reaches Harris, the next question is whether these reaches exceed the constitutional grasp of the provisions. In this regard, the Due Process Clause requires that no defendant shall be haled into court unless defendant has "certain minimum contacts [with the state] . . . such that the maintenance of the suit does not offend traditional notions of fair play and substantial justice." International Shoe Co. v. Washington, 326 U.S. 310, 316, 90 L. Ed. 95, 66 S. Ct. 154 (1945). And the constitutional analysis, unlike the statutory analysis, is virtually identical with respect to both the La Fontaines and Harris. The statements made by all defendants posted on the Internet concerned the presumably local activities of an individual each knew was a Virginia citizen. Bochan, and several of his Virginia friends, accessed the postings in Virginia, and the reputational harm resulting from defendants' actions and allegations of pedophilia and sexual deviancy, if any, has been primarily suffered in Virginia, where Bochan lives and works. Under these circumstances, because the predominant "effects" of the La Fontaines' and Harris's conduct are in Virginia, these defendants could reasonably foresee being haled into court in this jurisdiction. See Calder v. Jones, 465 U.S. 783, 789-90, 79 L. Ed.2d 804, 104 S. Ct. 1482 (1984) (holding that California court's assertion of personal jurisdiction over Florida-based reporters did not violate due process when allegedly defamatory article that was the basis of the suit focused on the California activities of California residents); First American First, Inc. v. National Ass'n of Bank Women, 802 F.2d 1511, 1517 (4th Cir. 1986) (concluding that Virginia court's exercise of jurisdiction did not violate Constitution when defendant knew or should have known that its alleged defamation would inflict the greatest injury upon plaintiff in Virginia, the state where he lived and conducted his business); *Telco,* 977 F. Supp. at 407 (noting that assertion of jurisdiction was supported by the fact that the effect of the challenged communication would be felt in Virginia). Thus, the constitutional prong of the inquiry is satisfied as to all defendants.

COMMENTS AND QUESTIONS

1. Is the *Bochan* case consistent with the Fourth Circuit Court of Appeals' decision in the *ALS Scan* case? Is it consistent with the *GTE New Media* decision? A case factually similar to *Bochan* that reached a different legal conclusion is Griffis v. Luban, 646 N.W.2d 527 (Minn. 2002). The Minnesota Supreme Court decided that Griffis could not execute a default judgment of $25,000 for defamation

---

reason in principle to require that such solicitations yield actual sales, as the fortuitous fact that no Virginia resident has responded to the solicitations does not alter the fact that the offers were apparently open to Virginia residents, and indeed, to anyone without geographical restrictions. Nor is it significant that the suit does not arise out of Harris's solicitations.

obtained in an Alabama court for Luban's posting on a USENET newsgroup that questioned Griffis's expertise as an Egyptologist because it was not persuaded that anyone in Alabama knew about Luban's postings other than Griffis. The Minnesota Supreme Court ruled that residents of Minnesota are not subject to jurisdiction as defendants in other states under Calder v. Jones, 465 U.S. 783 (1984) unless: (1) the person committed an intentional tort; (2) the plaintiff felt the brunt of the harm caused by that tort in the forum such that the forum state was the focal point of the plaintiff's injury; and (3) the defendant expressly aimed the tortious conduct at the forum such that the forum state was the focal point of the tortious activity. How would the court in *Bochan* have ruled on jurisdiction if it had followed this test?

2. The *Bochan* decision considers the location of AOL servers as an important factor in deciding whether personal jurisdiction existed in this case. Does the act of publication of an Internet posting take place at the ISP's server?

3. What would the court have done if the La Fontaines were ignorant about where Bochan lived?

4. Did the court find general or specific jurisdiction over Harris?

5. Should it matter what the defendant is accused of doing? Some courts have said yes. For example, in Panavision Int'l v. Toeppen, 141 F.3d 1316 (9th Cir. 1998), discussed in Chapter 10 in the Section on trademarks, defendant Toeppen was an Illinois resident who had registered the trademark "panavision" as an Internet domain name. Despite the fact that the registration did not take place in California, the court held that jurisdiction there was proper. It relied in part on the fact that Toeppen had knowingly registered a California corporation's mark as a domain name *in order to sell it to a California corporation* and therefore had purposefully "directed" his injurious activities into the forum in a way that had effects there.[1] A similar line of cases exists in the defamation context, where an intentional act of defamation against a person is held to be directed against that person, thereby conferring jurisdiction in that person's state of residence. See Calder v. Jones, 465 U.S. 783 (1984).

How far does this logic extend? Is trademark infringement always "directed" toward whatever jurisdiction the plaintiff resides in? How about copyright infringement? Does it matter whether the plaintiff alleges that the defendant's conduct was intentional? Whether they can prove it? Suppose that the defendant did not even *know* what state the plaintiff lived in. How can defamation be "directed toward" the state in that case? For a particularly expansive application of this principle, see Minnesota v. Granite Gate Resorts, 568 N.W.2d 715 (Minn. Ct. App. 1997).

6. In a novel approach to the jurisdiction question, Porsche recently brought an in rem action in Virginia (the home of Network Solutions (NSI), which registers most U.S. domain names) against a variety of domain names that it felt infringed its trademarks. Porsche argued that it need not prove personal jurisdiction over the variety of cybersquatters that had registered the domain names because the action was against the "property" itself, and the property was located in NSI's computers in Virginia. See Porsche Cars N. Am., Inc. v. Porsch.com, 51 F. Supp.2d 707 (E.D.Va. 1999). While Porsche's appeal from the dismissal order was pending,

---

1. By contrast, had Toeppen merely registered the mark without offering to sell it, jurisdiction apparently would not have been proper.

Congress enacted the Anticybersquatting Consumer Protection Act (ACPA or "the anticybersquatting statute"), authorizing in rem actions against domain names in certain circumstances. Pub. L. No. 106-113, 113 Stat. 1501, 1501A-545 (1999), codified in relevant part at 15 U.S.C.A. §1125(d) (2). The Fourth Circuit vacated the district court's order dismissing the case and remanded for consideration of the ACPA, without reaching the question of whether there was a basis for in rem jurisdiction for Porsche's trademark-dilution claims. See Porsche Cars N. Am., Inc.v. Allporsche.com, 2000 WL 742185 (4th Cir. June 9, 2000). Porsche then amended its complaint, adding anticybersquatting claims under 15 U.S.C.A. §1125(d)(1) and reiterating its trademark dilution claims. Under the ACPA in rem provision, plaintiffs can assert in rem jurisdiction over a domain name if unable to assert personal jurisdiction over the defendants, for example, if there is an inadequacy of personal jurisdiction over a foreign resident or if the defendant cannot be located after due diligence because the defendant filed false or outdated contact information. The Fourth Circuit affirmed the trial court's ruling that in rem jurisdiction is not available for trademark dilution claims, but ruled in Porsche's favor as to exercise of in rem jurisdiction under ACPA in spite of a constitutional challenge based on prior Supreme Court case law indicating that in rem jurisdiction is only constitutionally permissible where in personam jurisdiction can be asserted. See Porsche Cars North America, Inc. v. Porsch.com, 2002 WL 1941442 (4th Cir., Aug. 23, 2002). See also Harrods Limited v. Sixty Internet Domain Names, 2002 WL 1941428 (4th Cir., Aug. 23, 2002); Caesars World, Inc. v. Caesars-Palace.com, 112 F. Supp.2d 502 (E.D. Vir. 2000); Heathmount A.E. Corp. v. Technodome.com, 106 F. Supp.2d 860 (E.D.Vir. 2000); Broadbridge Media, LLC v. Hypercd.com, 106 F. Supp.2d 505 (S.D.N.Y. 2000); Alitalia-Linee Aeree Italiane v. Casinoalitalia.com, 128 F. Supp.2d 340 (E.D.Vir. 2001). For further discussion of the in rem provisions of the ACPA, see Andrew J. Grotto, Due Process and in Rem Jurisdiction Under the Anti-Cybersquatting Consumer Protection Act, 2 Columbia Sci. & Tech. L. Rev. 1 (2001); Xuan-Thao N. Nguyen, Blame It on the Cybersquatters: How Congress Partially Ends the Circus Among the Circuits with the Anti-Cybersquatting Consumer Protection Act, 32 Loyola U. of Chicago L.J. 777 (2001); Suzanna Sherry, Haste Makes Waste: Congress and the Common Law in Cyberspace, 55 Vanderbilt L. Rev. 309 (2002); David F. Fanning, Quasi In Rem on the Cyberseas, 76 Chicago-Kent L. Rev. 1887 (2001).

C. INTERNATIONAL JURISDICTION

The problem of Internet jurisdiction is not just confined to the United States. A number of cases have considered the related problem of international jurisdiction. In one trademark case, Playboy Enterprises v. Chuckleberry Publishing, 939 F. Supp. 1032 (S.D.N.Y. 1996), the court held that an Italian Web site allegedly infringing Playboy's trademark was subject to jurisdiction in New York (though in that case jurisdiction was largely based on a prior case between the parties). This case raises the spectre not only of being haled into court anywhere in the world to answer for the contents of your Web page, but also the even more troubling problem of conforming your conduct to different substantive laws in different jurisdictions. Chuckleberry's site was legal under Italian trademark laws, because the Italian courts had ruled that its "Playmen" mark did not infringe "Playboy." But U.S. courts had held the opposite, and the court concluded that Chuckleberry was bound by the prior U.S. rulings. Cases like *Inset Systems*, cited in *Cybersell*, are even more troubling because they suggest that anyone who puts up a Web page can be sued anywhere in the world.

Solving the problem of international jurisdiction and conflicting legal rules may require, at a minimum, harmonizing the substantive laws governing the Internet on a worldwide basis. See David W. Maher, Trademark Law on the Internet— Will It Scale? The Challenge to Develop International Trademark Law, 16 J. Marshall J. Computer & Info. L. 3 (1997).

Harmonization has proven difficult enough even in relatively uncontroversial areas like trademark law, however. It may well be impossible to harmonize laws where there is less agreement on principles among nations—laws relating to free speech, for example. And even if that problem is solved, courts will have to do something about an individual's risk of being sued in remote jurisdictions if they are to avoid chilling speech on the Internet. The prospect of being subject to litigation in a number of different countries is likely to be extremely daunting to individuals and even small and medium-sized businesses. While the law has faced this problem before, in the past companies subject to worldwide jurisdiction were almost all large, sophisticated entities with offices and lawyers in many parts of the world. What is different about the Internet is precisely its ability to make anyone who can afford a computer an international publisher. Unfortunately, the responsibilities that traditionally come with that international status—like amenability to suit— carry a large price tag.

Yahoo!, Inc. v. la Ligue Contre le Racisme et l'antisemitisme
U.S. District Court for the Northern District of California
169 F. Supp.2d 1181 (N.D.Cal. 2001)

[handwritten: D: LICRA L'Union (France) P: Yahoo Del. /Cal.]

FOGEL, J.

Defendants La Ligue Contre le Racisme et l'Antisemitisme ("LICRA") and L'Union des Etudiants Juifs de France, citizens of France, are non-profit organizations dedicated to eliminating anti-Semitism. Plaintiff Yahoo!, Inc. ("Yahoo!") is a corporation organized under the laws of Delaware with its principal place of business in Santa Clara, California. Yahoo! is an Internet service provider that operates various Internet websites and services that any computer user can access at the Uniform Resource Locator ("URL") *http://www.yahoo.com*. Yahoo! services ending in the suffix, ".*com*," without an associated country code as a prefix or extension (collectively, "Yahoo!'s U.S. Services") use the English language and target users who are residents of, utilize servers based in and operate under the laws of the United States. Yahoo! subsidiary corporations operate regional Yahoo! sites and services in twenty other nations, including, for example, Yahoo! France, Yahoo! India, and Yahoo! Spain. Each of these regional web sites contains the host nation's unique two-letter code as either a prefix or a suffix in its URL (e.g., Yahoo! France is found at *http://www.yahoo.fr* and Yahoo! Korea at *http://www.yahoo.kr*). Yahoo!'s regional sites use the local region's primary language, target the local citizenry, and operate under local laws.

Yahoo! provides a variety of means by which people from all over the world can communicate and interact with one another over the Internet. Examples include an Internet search engine, e-mail, an automated auction site, personal web page hostings, shopping services, chat rooms, and a listing of clubs that individuals can create or join. Any computer user with Internet access is able to post materials on many of these Yahoo! sites, which in turn are instantly accessible by anyone who logs on to Yahoo!'s Internet sites. As relevant here, Yahoo!'s auction site allows anyone to post an item for sale and solicit bids from any computer user from around the globe. Yahoo! records when a posting is made and after the requisite time period lapses sends an e-mail notification to the highest bidder and seller with their respective contact information. Yahoo! is never a party to a transaction, and the buyer and seller are responsible for arranging privately for payment and shipment of goods. Yahoo! monitors the transaction through limited regulation by prohibiting particular items from being sold (such as stolen goods, body parts, prescription and illegal drugs, weapons, and goods violating U.S. copyright laws or the Iranian and Cuban embargos) and by providing a rating system through which buyers and sellers have their transactional behavior evaluated for the benefit of future consumers. Yahoo! informs auction sellers that they must comply with Yahoo!'s policies and may not offer items to buyers in jurisdictions in which the sale of such item violates the jurisdiction's applicable laws. Yahoo! does not actively regulate the content of each posting, and individuals are able to post, and have in fact posted, highly offensive matter, including Nazi-related propaganda and Third Reich memorabilia, on Yahoo!'s auction sites.

On or about April 5, 2000, LICRA sent a "cease and desist" letter to Yahoo!'s Santa Clara headquarters informing Yahoo! that the sale of Nazi and Third Reich related goods through its auction services violates French law. LICRA threatened to take legal action unless Yahoo! took steps to prevent such sales within eight days. Defendants subsequently utilized the United States Marshal's Office to serve Yahoo! with process in California and filed a civil complaint against Yahoo! in the Tribunal de Grande Instance de Paris (the "French Court").

The French Court found that approximately 1,000 Nazi and Third Reich related objects, including Adolf Hitler's *Mein Kampf, The Protocol of the Elders of Zion* (an infamous anti-Semitic report produced by the Czarist secret police in the early 1900's), and purported "evidence" that the gas chambers of the Holocaust did not exist were being offered for sale on Yahoo.com's auction site. Because any French citizen is able to access these materials on Yahoo.com directly or through a link on Yahoo.fr, the French Court concluded that the Yahoo.com auction site violates Section R645-1 of the French Criminal Code, which prohibits exhibition of Nazi propaganda and artifacts for sale. On May 20, 2000, the French Court entered an order requiring Yahoo! to (1) eliminate French citizens' access to any material on the Yahoo.com auction site that offers for sale any Nazi objects, relics, insignia, emblems, and flags; (2) eliminate French citizens' access to web pages on Yahoo.com displaying text, extracts, or quotations from *Mein Kampf* and *Protocol of the Elders of Zion*; (3) post a warning to French citizens on Yahoo.fr that any search through Yahoo.com may lead to sites containing material prohibited by Section R645-1 of the French Criminal Code, and that such viewing of the prohibited material may result in legal action against the Internet user; (4) remove from all browser directories accessible in the French Republic index headings entitled "negationists" and from all hypertext links the equation of "negationists" under the heading "Holocaust." The order subjects Yahoo! to a penalty of 100,000 Euros for each day that it fails to comply with the order. The order concludes:

> We order the Company YAHOO! Inc. to take all necessary measures to dissuade and render impossible any access via Yahoo.com to the Nazi artifact auction service and to any other site or service that may be construed as constituting an apology for Nazism or a contesting of Nazi crimes.

High Court of Paris, May 22, 2000, Interim Court Order No. 00/05308, 00/05309 (translation attested accurate by Isabelle Camus, February 16, 2001). The French Court set a return date in July 2000 for Yahoo! to demonstrate its compliance with the order.

Yahoo! asked the French Court to reconsider the terms of the order, claiming that although it easily could post the required warning on Yahoo.fr, compliance with the order's requirements with respect to Yahoo.com was technologically impossible. The French Court sought expert opinion on the matter and on November 20, 2000 "reaffirmed" its order of May 22. The French Court ordered Yahoo! to comply with the May 22 order within three (3) months or face a penalty of 100,000 Francs (approximately U.S. $13,300) for each day of non-compliance. The French Court also provided that penalties assessed against Yahoo! Inc. may not be collected from Yahoo! France. Defendants again utilized the United States Marshal's Office to serve Yahoo! in California with the French Order.

Yahoo! subsequently posted the required warning and prohibited postings in violation of Section R645-1 of the French Criminal Code from appearing on Yahoo.fr. Yahoo! also amended the auction policy of Yahoo.com to prohibit individuals from auctioning:

> Any item that promotes, glorifies, or is directly associated with groups or individuals known principally for hateful or violent positions or acts, such as Nazis or the Ku Klux Klan. Official government-issue stamps and coins are not prohibited under this policy. Expressive media, such as books and films, may be subject to more permissive standards as determined by Yahoo! in its sole discretion.

Yahoo Auction Guidelines (visited Oct. 23, 2001) <http://user.auctions.Yahoo.com/html/guidelines.html>. Notwithstanding these actions, the Yahoo.com auction site still offers certain items for sale (such as stamps, coins, and a copy of *Mein Kampf*) which appear to violate the French Order. While Yahoo! has removed the *Protocol of the Elders of Zion* from its auction site, it has not prevented access to numerous other sites which reasonably "may be construed as constituting an apology for Nazism or a contesting of Nazi crimes."

Yahoo! claims that because it lacks the technology to block French citizens from accessing the Yahoo.com auction site to view materials which violate the French Order or from accessing other Nazi-based content of websites on Yahoo.com, it cannot comply with the French order without banning Nazi-related material from Yahoo.com altogether. Yahoo! contends that such a ban would infringe impermissibly upon its rights under the First Amendment to the United States Constitution. Accordingly, Yahoo! filed a complaint in this Court seeking a declaratory judgment that the French Court's orders are neither cognizable nor enforceable under the laws of the United States.

Defendants immediately moved to dismiss on the basis that this Court lacks personal jurisdiction over them. That motion was denied. Defendants' request that the Court certify its jurisdictional determination for interlocutory appeal was denied without prejudice pending the outcome of Yahoo!'s motion for summary judgment.

II. Overview

As this Court and others have observed, the instant case presents novel and important issues arising from the global reach of the Internet. Indeed, the specific facts of this case implicate issues of policy, politics, and culture that are beyond the purview of one nation's judiciary. Thus it is critical that the Court define at the outset what is and is not at stake in the present proceeding.

This case is *not* about the moral acceptability of promoting the symbols or propaganda of Nazism. Most would agree that such acts are profoundly offensive. By any reasonable standard of morality, the Nazis were responsible for one of the worst displays of inhumanity in recorded history. This Court is acutely mindful of the emotional pain reminders of the Nazi era cause to Holocaust survivors and deeply respectful of the motivations of the French Republic in enacting the underlying statutes and of the defendant organizations in seeking relief under those statutes. Vigilance is the key to preventing atrocities such as the Holocaust from occurring again.

Nor is this case about the right of France or any other nation to determine its own law and social policies. A basic function of a sovereign state is to determine by law what forms of speech and conduct are acceptable within its borders. In this instance, as a nation whose citizens suffered the effects of Nazism in ways that are incomprehensible to most Americans, France clearly has the right to enact and enforce laws such as those relied upon by the French Court here.

What *is* at issue here is whether it is consistent with the Constitution and laws of the United States for another nation to regulate speech by a United States resident within the United States on the basis that such speech can be accessed by Internet users in that nation. In a world in which ideas and information transcend borders and the Internet in particular renders the physical distance between speaker and audience virtually meaningless, the implications of this question go far beyond the facts of this case. The modern world is home to widely varied cultures with radically divergent value systems. There is little doubt that Internet users in the United States routinely engage in speech that violates, for example, China's laws against religious expression, the laws of various nations against advocacy of gender equality or homosexuality, or even the United Kingdom's restrictions on freedom of the press. If the government or another party in one of these sovereign nations were to seek enforcement of such laws against Yahoo! or another U.S.-based Internet service provider, what principles should guide the court's analysis?

The Court has stated that it must and will decide this case in accordance with the Constitution and laws of the United States. It recognizes that in so doing, it necessarily adopts certain value judgments embedded in those enactments, including the fundamental judgment expressed in the First Amendment that it is preferable to permit the non-violent expression of offensive viewpoints rather than to impose viewpoint-based governmental regulation upon speech. The government and people of France have made a different judgment based upon their own experience. In undertaking its inquiry as to the proper application of the laws of the United States, the Court intends no disrespect for that judgment or for the experience that has informed it. . . .

IV. Legal Issues

A. *Actual Controversy*

. . . The threshold question in any declaratory action [] is whether "there is a substantial controversy, between parties having adverse legal interests, of sufficient immediacy and reality to warrant the issuance of a declaratory judgment." Maryland Cas. Co. v. Pacific Coal & Oil Co., 312 U.S. 270, 273, 85 L. Ed. 826, 61 S. Ct. 510 (1941); National Basketball Ass'n v. SDC Basketball Club, Inc., 815 F.2d 562, 565 (9th Cir. 1987). The "mere possibility, even probability, that a person may in the future be adversely affected by official acts not yet threatened does not create an 'actual controversy' which is a prerequisite created by the clear language of the [Declaratory Judgment Act]. . . ." Garcia v. Brownell, 236 F.2d 356, 358 (9th Cir. 1956) *cert. denied,* 362 U.S. 963, 4 L. Ed. 2d 878, 80 S. Ct. 880 (1960). The party invoking federal jurisdiction bears the burden of showing that it faces an immediate or actual injury. Rincon Band of Mission Indians v. County of San Diego, 495 F.2d 1, 5 (9th Cir. 1974), *cert. denied,* 419 U.S. 1008, 42 L. Ed.2d 283, 95 S. Ct. 328 (1974).

1. Status of the French Order

Defendants contend that the "actual controversy" requirement is not met in the instant case. They point out that Yahoo! appealed the French Court's initial order of May 22, 2000, and that a successful appeal would nullify the order of November 20, 2000 that "reaffirmed" the May 22 order. They argue that even if the May 22 order is upheld on appeal, the French court may find that Yahoo! has substantially complied with the order. Alternatively, they assert that they themselves may elect not to initiate the complex process the French Court would use to fix an actual penalty, and that until that process is completed, there is no order that could be enforced against Yahoo! in the United States. Finally, Defendants offer declarations to the effect that they view Yahoo!'s revised policies with respect to its auction site and removal of *Protocol of the Elders of Zion* from its host sites as substantial compliance with the French order and that accordingly they have no present intention of taking legal action against Yahoo! in the United States.

While these points are facially appealing and suggest a way for the Court to avoid deciding the sensitive and controversial issues presented herein, the facts in the record do not support Defendants' position. First, there are no relevant appellate proceedings presently pending in France. In its order of November 20, 2000, the French Court determined that Yahoo! is technologically and legally capable of complying with the May 22 order and that Yahoo! is subject to a fine of approximately $13,000 for each day of non-compliance. That order was not appealed, and the record indicates that Yahoo! withdrew its appeal of the May 22 order on May 28, 2001 (Supp. Dec. of Mary Catherine Wirth, Exhibit A, Aug. 19, 2001).

Second, the fact that any penalty against Yahoo! is provisional and would require further legal proceedings in France prior to any enforcement action in the United States does not mean that Yahoo! does not face a present and ongoing threat from the existing French order. At oral argument, Defendants did not dispute that if the penalty enforcement process were initiated, the French Court could assess penalties retroactively for the entire period of Yahoo!'s non-compliance. Despite their declarations to the effect that they are satisfied with Yahoo!'s efforts to comply with the French order, Defendants have not taken steps available to them under French law to seek withdrawal of the order or to petition the French court to absolve Yahoo! from any penalty. See Societe de Conditionnement en Aluminium v. Hunter Engineering Co., Inc., 655 F.2d 938, 945 (9th Cir. 1981) ("It is not relevant that Hunter attempted to withdraw its 'threat' after the filing of this lawsuit. We do think it relevant, in the light of the circumstances, that Hunter has not indicated that it will not sue SCAL for infringement or in any other manner agree to a non-adversary position with respect to the patent.").

Third, it is by no means clear that Yahoo! can rely upon the assessment in Defendants' declarations that it is in "substantial compliance" with the French order. The French Court has not made such a finding, nor have Defendants requested or stipulated that such a finding be made. As set forth earlier, Yahoo.com continues to offer at least some Third Reich memorabilia as well as *Mein Kampf* on its auction site and permits access to numerous web pages with Nazi-related and anti-Semitic content. The fact that the Yahoo! does not know whether its efforts to date have met the French Court's mandate is the precise harm against which the Declaratory Judgment Act is designed to protect.

> The Declaratory Judgment Act was designed to relieve potential defendants from the Damoclean threat of impending litigation which a harassing adversary might brandish, while initiating suit at his leisure or never. The Act permits parties so situated to forestall the accrual of potential damages by suing for a declaratory judgment, once the adverse positions have crystallized and the conflict of interests is real and immediate.

Japan Gas Lighter Ass'n. v. Ronson Corp., 257 F. Supp. 219, 237 (D.N.J. 1966).

2. Real and Immediate Threat

The French order prohibits the sale or display of items based on their association with a particular political organization and bans the display of websites based on the authors' viewpoint with respect to the Holocaust and anti-Semitism. A United States court constitutionally could not make such an order. Shelley v. Kraemer, 334 U.S. 1, 92 L. Ed. 1161, 68 S. Ct. 836 (1948). The First Amendment does not permit the government to engage in viewpoint-based regulation of speech absent a compelling governmental interest, such as averting a clear and present danger of imminent violence. R.A.V. v. City of St. Paul, 505 U.S. 377, 120 L. Ed.2d 305, 112 S. Ct. 2538 (1992); Simon & Schuster, Inc. v. Members of New York State Crime Victims Board, 502 U.S. 105, 116 L. Ed.2d 476, 112 S. Ct. 501 (1991); Boos v. Barry, 485 U.S. 312, 99 L. Ed.2d 333, 108 S. Ct. 1157 (1988);

Police Dept. v. Mosley, 408 U.S. 92, 33 L. Ed.2d 212, 92 S. Ct. 2286 (1972); Brandenburg v. Ohio, 395 U.S. 444, 23 L. Ed.2d 430, 89 S. Ct. 1827 (1969); Kingsley Int'l Pictures Corp. v. Regents, 360 U.S. 684, 3 L. Ed.2d 1512, 79 S. Ct. 1362 (1959). In addition, the French Court's mandate that Yahoo! "take all necessary measures to dissuade and render impossible any access via Yahoo.com to the Nazi artifact auction service and to any other site or service that may be construed as constituting an apology for Nazism or a contesting of Nazi crimes" is far too general and imprecise to survive the strict scrutiny required by the First Amendment. The phrase, "and any other site or service that *may be construed* as an apology for Nazism or a contesting of Nazi crimes" fails to provide Yahoo! with a sufficiently definite warning as to what is proscribed. See, e.g., Coates v. City of Cincinnati, 402 U.S. 611, 29 L. Ed.2d 214, 91 S. Ct. 1686 (1971). Phrases such as "all necessary measures" and "render impossible" instruct Yahoo! to undertake efforts that will impermissibly chill and perhaps even censor protected speech. See Board of Airport Commissioners v. Jews for Jesus, 482 U.S. 569, 96 L. Ed.2d 500, 107 S. Ct. 2568 (1987); Gooding v. Wilson, 405 U.S. 518, 31 L. Ed.2d 408, 92 S. Ct. 1103 (1972). "The loss of First Amendment freedoms, for even minimal periods of time, unquestionably constitutes irreparable injury." Elrod v. Burns, 427 U.S. 347, 373, 49 L. Ed.2d 547, 96 S. Ct. 2673 (1976) citing New York Times Co. v. United States, 403 U.S. 713, 29 L. Ed.2d 822, 91 S. Ct. 2140 (1971).

Rather than argue directly that the French order somehow could be enforced in the United States in a manner consistent with the First Amendment, Defendants argue instead that at present there is no real or immediate threat to Yahoo!'s First Amendment rights because the French order cannot be enforced at all until after the cumbersome process of petitioning the French court to fix a penalty has been completed. They analogize this case to Int'l Soc. for Krishna Consciousness of California, Inc. v. City of Los Angeles, 611 F. Supp. 315, 319-20 (C.D.Cal. 1984), in which the City of Los Angeles sought a declaratory judgment that a resolution limiting speech activities adopted by its Board of Airport Examiners was constitutional. The district court concluded that the action was unripe because the resolution could not take effect without ratification by the City Council, which had not yet occurred. The cases, however, are distinguishable. While Defendants present evidence that further procedural steps in France are required before an actual penalty can be fixed, there is no dispute that the French order is valid under French law and that the French Court may fix a penalty retroactive to the date of the order. The essence of the holding in the *Krishna Consciousness* case is that the subject resolution had no legal effect at all.

Defendants also claim that there is no real or immediate threat to Yahoo! because they do not presently intend to seek enforcement of the French order in the United States. In Salvation Army v. Department of Community Affairs of the State of New Jersey, 919 F.2d 183 (3rd Cir. 1990), a religious group that operated a family center for disadvantaged persons claimed a state statute regulating boarding houses violated its right to the free exercise of religion. After the group brought suit, the state authorities agreed outside of the judicial proceedings to exempt the group from some of the provisions. The district court then granted summary judgment and dismissed the action. On appeal, the group claimed it still faced uncertainty with respect to future enforcement of the statute because the exemptions were not legally binding and the regulations in their entirety impermissibly intruded upon its First Amendment rights. The Court of Appeals for the Third Circuit agreed with the trial court that there was no immediate threat to the group because the state had provided an express assurance that it would not enforce any of the waived provisions, no criminal penalties could be imposed under the statute unless additional steps were taken by the state, the state could not impose fines without giving notice and opportunity to comply, and there was no evidence that the group's First Amendment rights actually would be affected by the threat of future law suits.

Salvation Army is distinguishable from this case in several significant respects. First, the New Jersey statute's penalties were "enforceable by the defendants only prospectively. . ." *Salvation Army,* 919 F.2d at 192. The French order permits *retroactive* penalties. Second, while the exemptions granted to the Salvation Army allowed it to maintain the status quo, the French order had the immediate effect of inducing Yahoo! to implement new restrictive policies on its auction site. Third, while the perceived threat to the Salvation Army was the potential withdrawal of the exemptions in the future, the provisions of the French order that require Yahoo! to regulate the content of its websites on Yahoo.com never have been waived, suspended or stayed and apparently remain in full force and effect. Under these circumstances, Defendants' assurances that they do not intend to enforce the order at the present time do not remove the threat that they may yet seek sanctions against Yahoo!'s *present and ongoing* conduct. See Abbott Labs. v. Gardner, 387 U.S. 136, 154, 18 L. Ed.2d 681, 87 S. Ct. 1507 (1969) ("There is no question in the present case that petitioners have sufficient standing as plaintiffs: the regulation is directed at them in particular; it requires them to make significant changes in their everyday business practices; if they fail to observe the Commissioner's rule they are quite clearly exposed to the imposition of strong sanctions."); Reno v. Catholic Soc. Servs., Inc., 509 U.S. 43, 57, 125 L. Ed.2d 38, 113 S. Ct. 2485 (1993) (construing *Abbott Laboratories* to mean that if "promulgation of the challenged regulations present[s] plaintiffs with the immediate dilemma to choose between complying with newly imposed, disadvantageous restrictions and risking serious penalties for violation," the controversy is ripe).

3. Abstention

Defendants next argue that this Court should abstain from deciding the instant case because Yahoo! simply is unhappy with the outcome of the French litigation and is trying to obtain a more favorable result here. Indeed, abstention is an appropriate remedy for international forum-shopping. In Supermicro Computer, Inc. v. Digitechnic, S.A., 145 F. Supp.2d 1147 (N.D.Cal. 2001), a California manufacturer was sued by a corporate customer in France for selling a defective product. The California company sought a declaratory judgment in the United States that its products were not defective, that the French customer's misuse of the product caused the product to fail, and that if the California company was at fault, only limited legal remedies were available. The court concluded that the purpose of the action for declaratory relief was to avoid an unfavorable result in the French courts. It noted that the action was not filed until a year after the French proceedings began, that the French proceedings were still ongoing, and that the French defendants had no intent to sue in the United States. It concluded that the declaratory relief action clearly was "litigation involving the same parties and the same disputed transaction." *Id.,* at 1152.

In the present case, the French court has determined that Yahoo!'s auction site and website hostings on Yahoo.com violate French law. Nothing in Yahoo!'s suit for declaratory relief in this Court appears to be an attempt to relitigate or disturb the French court's application of French law or its orders with respect to Yahoo!'s conduct in France. Rather, the purpose of the present action is to determine whether a United States court may enforce the French order without running afoul of the First Amendment. The actions involve distinct legal issues, and as this Court concluded in its jurisdictional order, a United States court is best situated to determine the application of the United States Constitution to the facts presented. No basis for abstention has been established.

4. Comity

No legal judgment has any effect, of its own force, beyond the limits of the sovereignty from which its authority is derived. 28 U.S.C. §1738. However, the United States Constitution and implementing legislation require that full faith and credit be given to judgments of sister states, territories, and possessions of the United States. U.S. Const. art. IV, §1, cl. 1; 28 U.S.C. §1738. The extent to which the United States, or any state, honors the judicial decrees of foreign nations is a matter of choice, governed by "the comity of nations." Hilton v. Guyot, 159 U.S. 113, 163, 40 L. Ed. 95, 16 S. Ct. 139 (1895). Comity "is neither a matter of absolute obligation, on the one hand, nor of mere courtesy and good will, upon the other." *Hilton,* 159 U.S. at 163-64 (1895). United States courts generally recognize foreign judgments and decrees unless enforcement would be prejudicial or contrary to the country's interests. Somportex Ltd. v. Philadelphia Chewing Gum Corp., 453 F.2d 435, 440 (3d Cir. 1971) *cert. denied,* 405 U.S. 1017, 31 L. Ed. 2d 479, 92 S. Ct. 1294 (1972); Laker Airways v. Sabena Belgian World Airlines, 235 U.S. App. D.C. 207, 731 F.2d 909, 931 (D.C. Cir. 1984) ("[The court] is not required to give effect to foreign judicial proceedings grounded on policies which do violence to its own fundamental interests."); Tahan v. Hodgson, 213 U.S. App. D.C. 306, 662 F.2d 862, 864 (D.C. Cir. 1981) ("Requirements for enforcement of a foreign judgment expressed in *Hilton* are that . . . the original claim not violate American public policy . . . that it not be repugnant to fundamental notions of what is decent and just in the State where enforcement is sought.").

As discussed previously, the French order's content and viewpoint-based regulation of the web pages and auction site on Yahoo.com, while entitled to great deference as an articulation of French law, clearly would be inconsistent with the First Amendment if mandated by a court in the United States. What makes this case uniquely challenging is that the Internet in effect allows one to speak in more than one place at the same time. Although France has the sovereign right to regulate what speech is permissible in France, this Court may not enforce a foreign order that violates the protections of the United States Constitution by chilling protected speech that occurs simultaneously within our borders. See, e.g., Matusevitch v. Telnikoff, 877 F. Supp. 1, 4 (D.D.C. 1995) (declining to enforce British libel judgment because British libel standards "deprive the plaintiff of his constitutional rights"); Bachchan v. India Abroad Publications, Inc., 154 Misc.2d 228, 585 N.Y.S.2d 661 (Sup.Ct. 1992) (declining to enforce a British libel judgment because of its "chilling effect" on the First Amendment); see also, Abdullah v. Sheridan Square Press, Inc., No. 93 Civ. 2515, 1994 WL 419847 (S.D.N.Y. May 4, 1994) (dismissing a libel claim brought under English law because "establishment of a claim for libel under the British law of defamation would be antithetical to the First Amendment protection accorded to the defendants."). The reason for limiting comity in this area is sound. "The protection to free speech and the press embodied in [the First] amendment would be seriously jeopardized by the entry of foreign [ ] judgments granted pursuant to standards deemed appropriate in [another country] but considered antithetical to the protections afforded the press by the U.S. Constitution." *Bachchan*, 585 N.Y.S.2d at 665. Absent a body of law that establishes international standards with respect to speech on the Internet and an appropriate treaty or legislation addressing enforcement of such standards to speech originating within the United States, the principle of comity is outweighed by the Court's obligation to uphold the First Amendment.

COMMENTS AND QUESTIONS

1. LICRA has appealed the District Court decision in favor of Yahoo! to the Ninth Circuit Court of Appeals. The appellate court decision in this case will be posted on the Software and Internet Law casebook website when it becomes available.

2. Some commentators perceive the French court's ruling in *LICRA v. Yahoo!* as a sign of the maturation of Internet and as a pro-democracy ruling because it requires companies to take responsibility for compliance with national law. See, e.g., Joel R. Reidenberg, Yahoo and Democracy on the Internet, 42 Jurimetrics J. 261 (2002). Shouldn't France be able to hold Yahoo! responsible for breach of democratically adopted French rules? Can it do so if a fine levied in France can't be enforced in U.S. courts?

3. The more general problem of how laws of different nations with different local values should respond to disputes involving Internet-based activities is given thoughtful treatment in National Research Council, Global Networks and Local Values: A Comparative Look at Germany and the United States (2002). For a discussion of different legal approaches to addressing this problem and some of the larger social policy questions they raise, see Paul Schiff Berman, The Globalization of Jurisdiction, 151 U. Pa. L. Rev. (forthcoming 2002). See also Graeme B. Dinwoodie, A New Copyright Order: Why National Courts Should Create Global Norms, 149 U. Penn. L. Rev. 469 (2000); Asaad Siddiqi, Welcome to the City of Bytes? An Assessment of the International Application of Jurisdiction over Internet Activities—Including a Critique of Suggested Approaches, 14 N.Y. Int'l. L. Rev. 43 (2001).

4. International negotiations are ongoing to develop an international treaty —to be known as the Hague Convention on International Jurisdiction and Foreign Judgments in Civil and Commercial Matters—to harmonize jurisdictional rules as to cross-border disputes, even where national laws themselves may not be harmonized. Information about this project is available at http://www.hcch.net/e/workprog/jdgm.html. This treaty, if adopted, would have major implications for civil disputes involving Internet-based activities.

D. CHOICE OF LAW

Choice of law is a neglected cousin to personal jurisdiction in Internet cases. Strictly speaking, determining where a defendant can be sued only settles where the case will take place—it does not settle the separate question of what jurisdiction's *legal rules* apply to the transaction. (As a practical matter, it may be that courts are inclined to favor applying the law of their own jurisdiction in close cases, since that is the law with which they are most familiar.)

Jurisprudence regarding choice of law has a long history, and we will not recapitulate it here. While courts historically inquired into the location of the contract (in contract cases) or the wrong (in tort cases), in modern times the choice of law inquiry in most jurisdictions has devolved into a multifactor test of general applicability. This test seeks to determine the jurisdiction with the most significant relationship to the transaction or injury in question, and to apply the law of that jurisdiction. See Restatement (Second) of Conflict of Laws §§148(2), 188(2). These factors may include the location of the plaintiff and defendant, the place where each of the acts relevant to the claim took place (i.e., where the contract was negotiated, where it was to be performed, where fraudulent representations were made, where a defamation was published, and so on).

On the Internet, it is likely that many of these locations will diverge between plaintiff and defendant. For example, where is an electronic contract formed—at the promisor's computer, or the promisee's? The logical answer would seem to be "both," but that is not terribly helpful in selecting one particular body of law to apply. One commentator has suggested that choice of law, like jurisdiction, will answer these questions differently for different causes of action. Thus,

> [plaintiff's] domicile will likely govern defamation actions arising in the [Internet]. Invasion of privacy claims, like defamation claims, are centered where the plaintiff lives and conducts his or her affairs, because that is where the privacy interest exists. The same result is appropriate for intellectual property actions unless the party arguing for the choice of different law can show that adversely affected markets are located elsewhere.

Henry H. Perritt Jr., Jurisdiction in Cyberspace, 41 Vill. L. Rev. 1 (1996). It is reasonable to predict that courts will generally apply well-worn rules of choice of law in Internet cases but will face new challenges in deciding *how* those rules apply to the Internet.

While courts have necessarily addressed choice of law questions in Internet cases, they have frequently done so *sub rosa*, assuming or concluding without much analysis that a particular law applied. For discussion and criticism of these cases, see Christopher P. Beall, The Scientological Defenestration of Choice-of-Law Doctrines for Publication Torts on the Internet, 15 J. Marshall J. Computer & Info. L. 361 (1997).

For further discussion of choice of law issues, particularly in the international context, see Andrew T. Guzman, Choice of Law: New Foundations, 90 Georgetown L. J. 883 (2002); William Patry, Choice of Law and International Copyright, 48 American J. of Comparative Law 383 (2000). Kai Burmeister, Jurisdiction,

Choice of Law, Copyright, and the Internet: Protection Against Framing in an International Setting, 9 Fordham Intell. Prop., Media & Ent. L.J. 625 (1999); John Rothchild, Protecting the Digital Consumer: The Limits of Cyberspace Utopianism, 74 Ind. L.J. 893, 918 (1999); Peter P. Swire, Of Elephants, Mice and Privacy: International Choice of Law and the Internet, 32 Int'l Law. 991 (1998); Matthew R. Burnstein, Conflicts on the Net: Choice of Law in Transnational Cyberspace, 29 Vand. J. Transnat'l L. 75 (1996).

10

Intellectual Property in Cyberspace

A. TRADEMARK LAW

In this section, we consider a number of issues of trademark law that have been litigated in the context of the Internet. We begin with a problem specific to the structure of the Internet itself, and that has generated abundant litigation: how domain names are treated under trademark law. We then consider a number of other trademark-related issues raised by the Internet.

1. Domain Names and Cybersquatting

Since the early days of the Internet, people have communicated with each other using domain names, mnemonic devices that map to a particular Internet Protocol address. Individuals, organizations, and companies have registered domain names that correspond to their names, to their trademarks, or to their products. Thus, Microsoft can be found at www.microsoft.com. Internet domain names are registered on a first-come, first-serve basis by a variety of registrars for a low price (roughly $35 per mark per year).

In the mid-1990s, a number of individuals registered domain names that corresponded to the name or trademark of someone else, often a large corporation. Many of these individuals registered the domain name not in order to use it themselves, but in order to sell the valuable domain name to the trademark owner for a price well in excess of $35. This practice is known as "cybersquatting." Others registered generic terms like business.com and resold them for a substantial profit. Still others may register a company's name for legitimate reasons: to criticize the company or to advertise the availability of that company's products at a Web site.

Trademark owners have been trying for years to stop cybersquatting. Existing trademark law has not adapted terribly well to cybersquatting, and in recent years trademark owners have turned to new statutes and rules to help them in their fight. Courts have struggled to stop cybersquatting without punishing legitimate uses of domain names. In this section, we consider Internet domain name cases decided under four different legal regimes.

a. Trademark Infringement and Dilution

The easiest case for application of trademark law to domain names is the registration of one company's trademark as a domain name by a direct competitor. For instance, an early case (resolved out of court) involved the Princeton Review, which registered kaplan.com and put information comparing the two education services companies at the site. Consumers who went to kaplan.com expecting to find information from Kaplan, Inc. were confused, not only by Princeton Review's use of the domain name but also by the Web site itself. This seems a straightforward case of trademark infringement: One company was using the domain name to falsely suggest an association with the other. The rule in these cases is straightforward: The trademark owner wins. Numerous cases have established liability for using another's trademark as a domain name. See, e.g., Comp Examiner Agency v. Juris, Inc., 1996 U.S. Dist. LEXIS 20259 (C.D. Cal. April 25, 1996) (injunction vs. direct competitor); Actmedia, Inc. v. Active Media Int'l, 1996 U.S. Dist. LEXIS 20814 (N.D. Ill. July 17, 1996) (same); Lozano Enters. v. La Opinion Pub. Co., 44 U.S.P.Q.2d 1764 (C.D. Cal. 1997) (same); Cardservice Int'l v. McGee, 950 F. Supp. 737 (E.D. Va. 1997) (same).

Not all domain name trademark cases involve cybersquatting, however. Sometimes two legitimate trademark owners with the same name dispute who should own a domain name. These problems often arise because trademarks that are widely separated in geographic or product space are thrown together on the Internet, which is worldwide and cuts across product lines. For example, *roadrunner* is the name of a bird, a computer company, a moving and storage company, and a Warner Brothers cartoon character. In the real world, all of these uses can coexist, because the products are so different that no one would be likely to confuse them. But on the Internet, only one company can register "roadrunner.com."

Courts faced with disputes of this sort have a number of choices, but none seem especially satisfactory. First, they could uphold the "first-come, first-served" approach to registration. Whoever wins the "race" to the registrar gets the name, and everyone else loses. This result is certainly easy to administer; indeed, the courts need not get involved at all. It may end up increasing consumer confusion, however, especially where the larger of two coexisting companies loses the race.

Second, courts (or registrars) might try to decide which claimant to a name was the "best" or most famous. This may produce the fairest result in the final analysis, but only if there is some way to make that determination. Network Solutions, Inc.'s old policy of placing domain names "on hold" if a registered trademark owner complains led to some problems here, particularly when both the registrant and the complainant had legitimate claims to the name. See Giacalone v. Network Solutions, 1996 U.S. Dist. LEXIS 20807 (N.D. Cal. June 14, 1996) (preliminary injunction against NSI placing a registered domain name on hold at the request of a trademark owner).

Finally, courts might force the competing applicants to coexist—either by choosing similar names ("road-runner.com" versus "roadrunner.com"), or by sharing a welcome page. The parties in Mattel v. Hasbro (C.D. Cal. 1997) chose the latter option. Hasbro owned the trademark rights to the game "Scrabble" in North America, and Mattel owned the rights elsewhere. The parties settled a trademark dispute by agreeing to create a joint page at scrabble.com that linked to both of their respective sites.

Whichever of these choices is most logical, it seems unlikely that trademark law or dilution will provide a cause of action against a legitimate user of a domain name. In Hasbro Inc. v. Clue Computing Inc., 232 F.3d 1 (1st Cir. 2000), the court refused to find trademark infringement or dilution by Clue Computing, which had registered the name *clue.com*, in a suit by the maker of the board game Clue. Even if the game Clue is famous, the court reasoned, it may be forced to coexist with other trademarks, and a legitimate trademark owner has not diluted the mark by using its own mark as a domain name.

In short, trademark infringement and dilution claims fit uneasily with many sorts of trademark disputes. Nonetheless, trademark owners frequently brought such claims, especially before 1999 when Congress acted specifically to deal with cybersquatting. The result were cases that stretched the boundaries of trademark infringement.

Panavision International, L.P. v. Toeppen
United States Court of Appeals for the Ninth Circuit
141 F.3d 1316 (9th Cir. 1998)

DAVID R. THOMPSON, Circuit Judge:

This case presents two novel issues. We are asked to apply existing rules of personal jurisdiction to conduct that occurred, in part, in "cyberspace." In addition, we are asked to interpret the Federal Trademark Dilution Act as it applies to the Internet. [The discussion of personal jurisdiction is omitted.]

Panavision accuses Dennis Toeppen of being a "cyber pirate" who steals valuable trademarks and establishes domain names on the Internet using these trademarks to sell the domain names to the rightful trademark owners. . . .

We conclude Panavision was entitled to summary judgment under the federal and state dilution statutes. Toeppen made commercial use of Panavision's trademarks and his conduct diluted those marks.

I Background

The Internet is a worldwide network of computers that enables various individuals and organizations to share information. The Internet allows computer users to access millions of web sites and web pages. A web page is a computer data file that can include names, words, messages, pictures, sounds, and links to other information.

Every web page has its own web site, which is its address, similar to a telephone number or street address. Every web site on the Internet has an identifier called a "domain name." The domain name often consists of a person's name or a company's name or trademark. For example, Pepsi has a web page with a web site domain name consisting of the company name, Pepsi, and .com, the "top level" domain designation: Pepsi.com.

The Internet is divided into several "top level" domains: .edu for education; .org for organizations; .gov for government entities; .net for networks; and .com for "commercial" which functions as the catchall domain for Internet users.

Domain names with the .com designation must be registered on the Internet with Network Solutions, Inc. ("NSI"). NSI registers names on a first-come, first-served basis for a $100 registration fee. NSI does not make a determination about a registrant's right to use a domain name. However, NSI does require an applicant to represent and warrant as an express condition of registering a domain name that (1) the applicant's statements are true and the applicant has the right to use the requested domain name; (2) the "use or registration of the domain name . . . does not interfere with or infringe the rights of any third party in any jurisdiction with respect to trademark, service mark, trade name, company name or any other intellectual property right"; and (3) the applicant is not seeking to use the domain name for any unlawful purpose, including unfair competition.

A domain name is the simplest way of locating a web site. If a computer user does not know a domain name, she can use an Internet "search engine." To do this, the user types in a key word search, and the search will locate all of the web sites containing the key word. Such key word searches can yield hundreds of web sites. To make it easier to find their web sites, individuals and companies prefer to have a recognizable domain name.

Panavision holds registered trademarks to the names "Panavision" and "Panaflex" in connection with motion picture camera equipment. Panavision promotes its trademarks through motion picture and television credits and other media advertising.

In December 1995, Panavision attempted to register a web site on the Internet with the domain name Panavision.com. It could not do that, however, because Toeppen had already established a web site using Panavision's trademark as his domain name. Toeppen's web page for this site displayed photographs of the City of Pana, Illinois.

On December 20, 1995, Panavision's counsel sent a letter from California to Toeppen in Illinois informing him that Panavision held a trademark in the name Panavision and telling him to stop using that trademark and the domain name Panavision.com. Toeppen responded by mail to Panavision in California, stating he had the right to use the name Panavision.com on the Internet as his domain name. Toeppen stated:

> If your attorney has advised you otherwise, he is trying to screw you. He wants to blaze new trails in the legal frontier at your expense. Why do you want to fund your attorney's purchase of a new boat (or whatever) when you can facilitate the acquisition of 'PanaVision.com' cheaply and simply instead?

Toeppen then offered to "settle the matter" if Panavision would pay him $13,000 in exchange for the domain name. Additionally, Toeppen stated that if Panavision agreed to his offer, he would not "acquire any other Internet addresses which are alleged by Panavision Corporation to be its property."

After Panavision refused Toeppen's demand, he registered Panavision's other trademark with NSI as the domain name Panaflex.com. Toeppen's web page for Panaflex.com simply displays the word "Hello."

Toeppen has registered domain names for various other companies including Delta Airlines, Neiman Marcus, Eddie Bauer, Lufthansa, and over 100 other marks. Toeppen has attempted to "sell" domain names for other trademarks such as inter-matic.com to Intermatic, Inc. for $10,000 and americanstandard.com to American Standard, Inc. for $15,000.

Panavision filed this action against Toeppen in the District Court for the Central District of California. Panavision alleged claims for dilution of its trademark under the Federal Trademark Dilution Act of 1995, 15 U.S.C. §1125(c), and under the California Anti-dilution statute, California Business and Professions Code §14330. Panavision alleged that Toeppen was in the business of stealing trademarks, registering them as domain names on the Internet and then selling the domain names to the rightful trademark owners. The district court determined it had personal jurisdiction over Toeppen, and granted summary judgment in favor of Panavision on both its federal and state dilution claims. This appeal followed.

II   Discussion . . .

B.   *Trademark Dilution Claims*

The Federal Trademark Dilution Act provides:

> The owner of a famous mark shall be entitled . . . to an injunction against another person's commercial use in commerce of a mark or trade name, if such use begins after the mark has become famous and causes dilution of the distinctive quality of the mark. . . .

15 U.S.C. §1125(c).

The California Anti-dilution statute is similar. See Cal. Bus. & Prof. Code §14330. It prohibits dilution of "the distinctive quality" of a mark regardless of competition or the likelihood of confusion. The protection extends only to strong and well recognized marks. Panavision's state law dilution claim is subject to the same analysis as its federal claim.

In order to prove a violation of the Federal Trademark Dilution Act, a plaintiff must show that (1) the mark is famous; (2) the defendant is making a commercial use of the mark in commerce; (3) the defendant's use began after the mark became famous; and (4) the defendant's use of the mark dilutes the quality of the mark by diminishing the capacity of the mark to identify and distinguish goods and services. 15 U.S.C. §1125(c).

Toeppen does not challenge the district court's determination that Panavision's trademark is famous, that his alleged use began after the mark became famous, or that the use was in commerce. Toeppen challenges the district court's determination that he made "commercial use" of the mark and that this use caused "dilution" in the quality of the mark.

1. Commercial Use

Toeppen argues that his use of Panavision's trademarks simply as his domain names cannot constitute a commercial use under the Act. Case law supports this argument. See Panavision International, L.P. v. Toeppen, 945 F. Supp. 1296, 1303 (C.D.Cal. 1996) ("Registration of a trade[mark] as a domain name, without more, is not a commercial use of the trademark and therefore is not within the prohibitions of the Act."); Academy of Motion Picture Arts & Sciences v. Network Solutions, Inc., 989 F. Supp. 1276, 1997 WL 810472 (C.D.Cal. Dec. 22, 1997) (the mere registration of a domain name does not constitute a commercial use); Lockheed Martin Corp. v. Network Solutions, Inc., 985 F. Supp. 949 (C.D.Cal. 1997) (NSI's acceptance of a domain name for registration is not a commercial use within the meaning of the Trademark Dilution Act).

Developing this argument, Toeppen contends that a domain name is simply an address used to locate a web page. He asserts that entering a domain name on a computer allows a user to access a web page, but a domain name is not associated with information on a web page. If a user were to type Panavision.com as a domain name, the computer screen would display Toeppen's web page with aerial views of Pana, Illinois. The screen would not provide any information about "Panavision," other than a "location window" which displays the domain name. Toeppen argues that a user who types in Panavision.com, but who sees no reference to the plaintiff Panavision on Toeppen's web page, is not likely to conclude the web page is related in any way to the plaintiff, Panavision.

Toeppen's argument misstates his use of the Panavision mark. His use is not as benign as he suggests. Toeppen's "business" is to register trademarks as domain names and then sell them to the rightful trademark owners. He "act[s] as a 'spoiler,' preventing Panavision and others from doing business on the Internet under their trademarked names unless they pay his fee." *Panavision*, 938 F. Supp. at 621. This is a commercial use. See Intermatic Inc. v. Toeppen, 947 F. Supp. 1227, 1230 (N.D.Ill. 1996) (stating that "[o]ne of Toeppen's business objectives is to profit by the resale or licensing of these domain names, presumably to the entities who conduct business under these names.").

As the district court found, Toeppen traded on the value of Panavision's marks. So long as he held the Internet registrations, he curtailed Panavision's exploitation of the value of its trademarks on the Internet, a value which Toeppen then used when he attempted to sell the Panavision.com domain name to Panavision.

In a nearly identical case involving Toeppen and Intermatic Inc., a federal district court in Illinois held that Toeppen's conduct violated the Federal Trademark Dilution Act. Intermatic, 947 F. Supp. at 1241. There, Intermatic sued Toeppen for registering its trademark on the Internet as Toeppen's domain name, intermatic.com. It was "conceded that one of Toeppen's intended uses for registering the Intermatic mark was to eventually sell it back to Intermatic or to some other party." *Id.* at 1239. The court found that "Toeppen's intention to arbitrage the 'intermatic.com' domain name constitute[d] a commercial use." *Id.* See also Teletech Customer Care Management, Inc. v. Tele-Tech Co., 977 F. Supp. 1407 (C.D.Cal. 1997) (granting a preliminary injunction under the Trademark Dilution Act for use of a trademark as a domain name).

Toeppen's reliance on Holiday Inns, Inc. v. 800 Reservation, Inc., 86 F.3d 619 (6th Cir. 1996), *cert. denied*, —U.S.—, 117 S. Ct. 770, 136 L. Ed.2d 715 (1997) is misplaced. In *Holiday Inns*, the Sixth Circuit held that a company's use of the most commonly misdialed number for Holiday Inns' 1-800 reservation number was not trademark infringement.

Holiday Inns is distinguishable. There, the defendant did not use Holiday Inns' trademark. Rather, the defendant selected the most commonly misdialed telephone number for Holiday Inns and attempted to capitalize on consumer confusion.

A telephone number, moreover, is distinguishable from a domain name because a domain name is associated with a word or phrase. A domain name is similar to a "vanity number" that identifies its source. Using Holiday Inns as an example, when a customer dials the vanity number "1-800-Holiday," she expects to contact Holiday Inns because the number is associated with that company's trademark. A user would have the same expectation typing the domain name HolidayInns.com. The user would expect to retrieve Holiday Inns' web page.

Toeppen made a commercial use of Panavision's trademarks. It does not matter that he did not attach the marks to a product. Toeppen's commercial use was his attempt to sell the trademarks themselves.[5] Under the Federal Trademark Dilution Act and the California Anti-dilution statute, this was sufficient commercial use.

2. Dilution

"Dilution" is defined as "the lessening of the capacity of a famous mark to identify and distinguish goods or services, regardless of the presence or absence of (1) competition between the owner of the famous mark and other parties, or (2) likelihood of confusion, mistake or deception." 15 U.S.C. §1127.

Trademark dilution on the Internet was a matter of Congressional concern. Senator Patrick Leahy (D-Vt.) stated:

> [I]t is my hope that this anti-dilution statute can help stem the use of deceptive Internet addresses taken by those who are choosing marks that are associated with the products and reputations of others.

141 Cong. Rec. §19312-01 (daily ed. Dec. 29, 1995) (statement of Sen. Leahy). See also Teletech Customer Care Management, Inc. v. Tele-Tech Co., Inc., 977 F. Supp. 1407, 1413 (C.D.Cal. 1997).

---

5. See Boston Pro. Hockey Assoc., Inc. v. Dallas Cap & Emblem Mfg., Inc., 510 F.2d 1004 (1975), which involved the sale of National Hockey League logos. The defendant was selling the logos themselves, unattached to a product (such as a hat or sweatshirt). The court stated: "The difficulty with this case stems from the fact that a reproduction of the trademark itself is being sold, unattached to any other goods or services." *Id*. at 1010. The court concluded that trademark law should protect the trademark itself. "Although our decision here may slightly tilt the trademark laws from the purpose of protecting the public to the protection of the business interests of plaintiffs, we think that the two become . . . intermeshed. . . ." *Id*. at 1011. "Whereas traditional trademark law sought primarily to protect consumers, dilution laws place more emphasis on protecting the investment of the trademark owners." *Panavision*, 945 F. Supp. at 1301.

To find dilution, a court need not rely on the traditional definitions such as "blurring" and "tarnishment." Indeed, in concluding that Toeppen's use of Panavision's trademarks diluted the marks, the district court noted that Toeppen's conduct varied from the two standard dilution theories of blurring and tarnishment. *Panavision*, 945 F. Supp. at 1304. The court found that Toeppen's conduct diminished "the capacity of the Panavision marks to identify and distinguish Panavision's goods and services on the Internet." *Id.* See also *Intermatic*, 947 F. Supp. at 1240 (Toeppen's registration of the domain name, "lessens the capacity of Intermatic to identify and distinguish its goods and services by means of the Internet.").

This view is also supported by *Teletech*. There, TeleTech Customer Care Management Inc. ("TCCM"), sought a preliminary injunction against Tele-Tech Company for use of TCCM's registered service mark, "TeleTech," as an Internet domain name. *Teletech*, 977 F. Supp. at 1410. The district court issued an injunction, finding that TCCM had demonstrated a likelihood of success on the merits on its trademark dilution claim. *Id.* at 1412. The court found that TCCM had invested great resources in promoting its servicemark and Teletech's registration of the domain name teletech.com on the Internet would most likely dilute TCCM's mark. *Id.* at 1413.

Toeppen argues he is not diluting the capacity of the Panavision marks to identify goods or services. He contends that even though Panavision cannot use Panavision.com and Panaflex.com as its domain name addresses, it can still promote its goods and services on the Internet simply by using some other "address" and then creating its own web page using its trademarks.

We reject Toeppen's premise that a domain name is nothing more than an address. A significant purpose of a domain name is to identify the entity that owns the web site. "A customer who is unsure about a company's domain name will often guess that the domain name is also the company's name." Cardservice Int'l v. McGee, 950 F. Supp. 737, 741 (E.D.Va. 1997). "[A] domain name mirroring a corporate name may be a valuable corporate asset, as it facilitates communication with a customer base." MTV Networks, Inc. v. Curry, 867 F. Supp. 202, 203-204 n. 2 (S.D.N.Y. 1994).

Using a company's name or trademark as a domain name is also the easiest way to locate that company's web site. Use of a "search engine" can turn up hundreds of web sites, and there is nothing equivalent to a phone book or directory assistance for the Internet. See *Cardservice*, 950 F. Supp. at 741.

Moreover, potential customers of Panavision will be discouraged if they cannot find its web page by typing in "Panavision.com," but instead are forced to wade through hundreds of web sites. This dilutes the value of Panavision's trademark. We echo the words of Judge Lechner, quoting Judge Wood: "Prospective users of plaintiff's services who mistakenly access defendant's web site may fail to continue to search for plaintiff's own home page, due to anger, frustration or the belief that plaintiff's home page does not exist." Jews for Jesus v. Brodsky, 993 F. Supp. 282, 306-07 (D.N.J. 1998) (Lechner, J., quoting Wood, J. in Planned Parenthood v. Bucci, 1997 WL 133313 at *4); see also *Teletech*, 977 F. Supp. at 1410 (finding that use of a search engine can generate as many as 800 to 1000 matches and it is "likely to deter web browsers from searching for Plaintiff's particular web site").

Toeppen's use of Panavision.com also puts Panavision's name and reputation at his mercy. See *Intermatic*, 947 F. Supp. at 1240 ("If Toeppen were allowed to use 'intermatic.com,' Intermatic's name and reputation would be at Toeppen's mercy and could be associated with an unimaginable amount of messages on Toeppen's web page.").

We conclude that Toeppen's registration of Panavision's trademarks as his domain names on the Internet diluted those marks within the meaning of the Federal Trademark Dilution Act, 15 U.S.C. §1125(c), and the California Anti-dilution statute, Cal.Bus. & Prof.Code §14330.

III Conclusion

Toeppen engaged in a scheme to register Panavision's trademarks as his domain names on the Internet and then to extort money from Panavision by trading on the value of those names. Toeppen's actions were aimed at Panavision in California and the brunt of the harm was felt in California. The district court properly exercised personal jurisdiction over Toeppen.

We also affirm the district court's summary judgment in favor of Panavision under the Federal Trademark Dilution Act, 15 U.S.C. §1125(c), and the California Anti-dilution statute, Cal.Bus. & Prof.Code §14330. Toeppen made commercial use of Panavision's trademarks and his conduct diluted those marks.

AFFIRMED.

COMMENTS AND QUESTIONS

1. From a policy perspective, punishing cybersquatters like Toeppen seems unobjectionable. But consider how well it really comports with trademark doctrine. Were consumers "confused" by Toeppen's use of the panavision.com domain? Perhaps initially—they might have gone to www.panavision.com expecting to find the Web site for the corporation. But any such confusion surely would have been quickly dispelled, since Toeppen's site had nothing to do with Panavision's business. The obvious alternative theory is dilution, but dilution requires the "commercial use in commerce" of a diluting mark by the defendant. 15 U.S.C. §1125(c). Has Toeppen really engaged in "commercial use" of the Panavision mark? What if he did not wish to sell it to Panavision at all, but simply wanted it for his own private use, or to deprive Panavision of the ability to use the mark? Cf. Juno Online Servs. v. Juno Lighting, 979 F. Supp. 684 (N.D. Ill. 1997) (suggesting that mere registration of a domain name without using it could not be trademark infringement; defendant in that case had a legitimate claim to the mark, however). Alternatively, suppose he devoted the site to a political diatribe against Panavision's employment practices. It is hard to see how this would constitute dilution in the traditional sense. See also 15 U.S.C. §1125(c), which exempts from dilution any "noncommercial use" of the mark.

Is there a way Toeppen could be said to cause consumer confusion? If so, how? The *Panavision* court, like many cybersquatting cases, grounded its rationale on dilution. Does this mean that only famous marks are entitled to protection against cybersquatters? In particular, consider the following case.

Avery Dennison Corporation v. Sumpton
United States Court of Appeals for the Ninth Circuit
51 U.S.P.Q.2d 1801 (9th Cir. 1999)

TROTT, Circuit Judge:

Jerry Sumpton and Freeview Listings Ltd. (together, "Appellants") appeal an injunction in favor of Avery Dennison Corp., entered after summary judgment for Avery Dennison on its claims of trademark dilution under the Federal Trademark Dilution Act of 1995 and the California dilution statute, Cal. Bus. & Prof. Code §14330 (West 1987). The district court published an opinion, 999 F. Supp. 1337 (C.D.Cal. 1998), holding that Appellants' maintenance of domain name registrations for avery.net and dennison.net diluted two of Avery Dennison's separate trademarks, "Avery" and "Dennison." . . . The district court then entered an injunction ordering Appellants to transfer the domain-name registrations to Avery Dennison in exchange for $300 each.

We have jurisdiction under 28 U.S.C. §1291 (1994). Because Avery Dennison failed to create a genuine issue of fact on required elements of the dilution cause of action, we reverse and remand with instructions to enter summary judgment for Appellants and to consider Appellants' request for attorneys' fees in light of this decision. . . .

II Facts

Sumpton is the president of Freeview, an Internet e-mail provider doing business as "Mailbank." Mailbank offers "vanity" e-mail addresses to users for an initial fee of $19.95 and $4.95 per year thereafter, and has registered thousands of domain-name combinations for this purpose. Most SLDs that Mailbank has registered are common surnames, although some represent hobbies, careers, pets, sports interests, favorite music, and the like. One category of SLDs is titled "Rude" and includes lewd SLDs, and another category, titled "Business," includes some common trademark SLDs. Mailbank's TLDs consist mainly of .net and .org, but some registered domain name combinations, including most in the "Business" and "Rude" categories, use the TLD .com. Mailbank's surname archives include the domain-name combinations avery.net and dennison.net.

Avery Dennison sells office products and industrial fasteners under the registered trademarks "Avery" and "Dennison," respectively. "Avery" has been in continuous use since the 1930s and registered since 1963, and "Dennison" has been in continuous use since the late 1800s and registered since 1908. Avery Dennison spends more than $5 million per year advertising its products, including those marketed under the separate "Avery" and "Dennison" trademarks, and the company boasts in the neighborhood of $3 billion in sales of all of its trademarks annually. No evidence indicates what percentage of these dollar figures apply to the "Avery" or "Dennison" trademarks. Avery Dennison maintains a commercial presence on the Internet, marketing its products at avery.com and averydennison.com, and maintaining registrations for several other domain-name combinations, all using the TLD .com.

Avery Dennison sued Appellants, alleging trademark dilution under the Federal Trademark Dilution Act and California Business and Professional Code

§14330. Avery Dennison also sued NSI, alleging contributory dilution and contributory infringement. The district court granted summary judgment to NSI on Avery Dennison's claims. The district court then concluded as a matter of law that the disputed trademarks were famous and denied summary judgment to Appellants and granted summary judgment to Avery Dennison on its dilution claims, entering an injunction requiring Appellants to transfer the registrations to Avery Dennison. 983 F. Supp. at 1342. . . .

V   Dilution Protection

We now turn to the dilution causes of action at issue in this case, brought under the Federal Trademark Dilution Act and California Business and Professional Code §14330.

In *Panavision*, we held that both the Federal Trademark Dilution Act and §14330 were implicated when the defendant registered domain-name combinations using famous trademarks and sought to sell the registrations to the trademark owners. 141 F.3d at 1318, 1327. Three differences made *Panavision* easier than the instant case. First, the defendant did not mount a challenge on the famousness prong of the dilution tests. *Panavision*, 141 F.3d at 1324. Second, the *Panavision* defendant did not challenge the factual assertion that he sought to profit by arbitrage with famous trademarks. *Id.* at 1324-25. Third, the diluting registrations in *Panavision* both involved the TLD .com. In the instant case, by contrast, Appellants contest Avery Dennison's claim of famousness, Appellants contend that the nature of their business makes the trademark status of "Avery" and "Dennison" irrelevant, and the complained-of registrations involve the TLD .net.

A   Famousness

The district court considered evidence submitted by Avery Dennison regarding marketing efforts and consumer association with its marks and concluded as a matter of law that "Avery" and "Dennison" were famous marks entitled to dilution protection. 999 F. Supp. at 1339. We hold that Avery Dennison failed to create a genuine issue of fact on the famousness element of both dilution statutes.

Dilution is a cause of action invented and reserved for a select class of marks—those marks with such powerful consumer associations that even non-competing uses can impinge on their value. See generally Frank L. Schechter, The Rational Basis for Trademark Protection, 40 Harv. L. Rev. 813 (1927) (proposing a cause of action for dilution); Krafte-Jacobs, supra, at 689-91. Dilution causes of action, much more so than infringement and unfair competition laws, tread very close to granting "rights in gross" in a trademark. See 3 McCarthy, supra, §24:108. In the infringement and unfair competition scenario, where the less famous a trademark, the less the chance that consumers will be confused as to origin, see AMF Inc. v. Sleekcraft Boats, 599 F.2d 341, 349 (9th Cir. 1979), a carefully-crafted balance exists between protecting a trademark and permitting non-infringing uses. In the dilution context, likelihood of confusion is irrelevant. See 15 U.S.C. §1127; Cal. Bus. & Prof.Code §14330; *Panavision*, 141 F.3d at 1326. If dilution protection were accorded to trademarks based only on a showing of inherent or acquired distinctiveness, we would upset the balance in favor of over-protecting trademarks, at the expense of potential non-infringing uses. See *Fruit of the Loom*, 994 F.2d at 1363 ("[The plaintiff] would sweep clean the many business uses of this quotidian word.").

We view the famousness prong of both dilution analyses as reinstating the balance—by carefully limiting the class of trademarks eligible for dilution protection, Congress and state legislatures granted the most potent form of trademark protection in a manner designed to minimize undue impact on other uses. See San Francisco Arts & Athletics, Inc. v. United States Olympic Comm., 483 U.S. 522, 564 n.25 (1987) (Brennan, J., dissenting) (citing 2 J. McCarthy, Trademarks & Unfair Competition §24:16, at 229 (2d ed. 1984)) (discussing limits on the dilution doctrine that help prevent overprotection of trademarks).

Therefore, to meet the "famousness" element of protection under the dilution statutes, " 'a mark [must] be truly prominent and renowned.'" I.P. Lund Trading ApS v. Kohler Co., 163 F.3d 27, 46 (1st Cir. 1998) (quoting 3 McCarthy, supra, §24.91). In a 1987 report, which recommended an amendment to the Lanham Act to provide a federal dilution cause of action, the Trademark Review Commission of the United States Trademark Association emphasized the narrow reach of a dilution cause of action: "We believe that a limited category of trademarks, those which are truly famous and registered, are deserving of national protection from dilution." Trademark Review Commission, Report & Recommendations, 77 Trademark Rep. 375, 455 (Sept.-Oct. 1987).

The Federal Trademark Dilution Act lists eight non-exclusive considerations for the famousness inquiry, 15 U.S.C. §1125(c)(1)(A)-(H), which are equally relevant to a famousness determination under Business and Professional Code §14330, see *Panavision*, 141 F.3d at 1324 ("Panavision's state law dilution claim is subject to the same analysis as its federal claim."). These are:

(A)   the degree of inherent or acquired distinctiveness of the mark;
(B)   the duration and extent of use of the mark in connection with the goods or services with which the mark is used;
(C)   the duration and extent of advertising and publicity of the mark;
(D)   the geographical extent of the trading area in which the mark is used;
(E)   the channels of trade for the goods or services with which the mark is used;
(F)   the degree of recognition of the mark in the trading areas and channels of trade used by the mark's owner and the person against whom the injunction is sought;
(G)   the nature and extent of use of the same or similar marks by third parties; and
(H)   whether the mark was registered . . . on the principal register.

15 U.S.C. §1125(c)(1).

We note the overlap between the statutory famousness considerations and the factors relevant to establishing acquired distinctiveness, which is attained "when the purchasing public associates the [mark] with a single producer or source rather than just the product itself." First Brands Corp. v. Fred Meyer, Inc., 809 F.2d 1378, 1383 (9th Cir. 1987). Proof of acquired distinctiveness is a difficult empirical inquiry which a factfinder must undertake, Taco Cabana Int'l, Inc. v. Two Pesos,

Inc., 932 F.2d 1113, 1119- 20 & n.7 (5th Cir. 1991), *aff'd*, 505 U.S. 763 (1992), considering factors including:

> [1] whether actual purchasers . . . associate the [mark] with [the plaintiff]; [2] the degree and manner of [the plaintiff's] advertising; [3] the length and manner of [the plaintiff's] use of the [mark]; and [4] whether [the plaintiff's] use of the [mark] has been exclusive.

Clamp Mfg. Co. v. Enco Mfg. Co., 870 F.2d 512, 517 (9th Cir. 1989). Furthermore, registration on the principal register creates a presumption of distinctiveness —in the case of a surname trademark, acquired distinctiveness. 15 U.S.C. §1057(b) (1994); Americana Trading Inc. v. Russ Berrie & Co., 966 F.2d 1284, 1287 (9th Cir. 1992) ("[R]egistration carries a presumption of secondary meaning.").

However, the Federal Trademark Dilution Act and Business and Professional Code §14330 apply "only to those marks which are both truly distinctive and famous, and therefore most likely to be adversely affected by dilution." S.Rep. No. 100-515, at 42. The Trademark Review Commission stated that "a higher standard must be employed to gauge the fame of a trademark eligible for this extraordinary remedy." 77 Trademark Rep. at 461. Thus, "[t]o be capable of being diluted, a mark must have a degree of distinctiveness and 'strength' beyond that needed to serve as a trademark." 3 McCarthy, supra, §24:109; see also Krafte-Jacobs, supra, at 690 ("If all marks are distinctive, and a showing of distinctiveness meets the element of fame, what marks would be outside the protection of the FTDA? [T]he FTDA does not indicate that any particular degree of distinctiveness should end the inquiry." (interpreting the Federal Trademark Dilution Act)). We have previously held likewise under California Business and Professional Code §14330. Accuride Int'l, Inc. v. Accuride Corp., 871 F.2d 1531, 1539 (9th Cir. 1989) (requiring more than mere distinctiveness).

Applying the famousness factors from the Federal Trademark Dilution Act to the facts of the case at bench, we conclude that Avery Dennison likely establishes acquired distinctiveness in the "Avery" and "Dennison" trademarks, but goes no further. Because the Federal Trademark Dilution Act requires a showing greater than distinctiveness to meet the threshold element of fame, as a matter of law Avery Dennison has failed to fulfill this burden.

1 Distinctiveness

We begin with the first factor in the statutory list: "inherent or acquired distinctiveness." §1125(c)(1)(A). No dispute exists that "Avery" and "Dennison" are common surnames—according to evidence presented by Appellants, respectively the 775th and 1768th most common in the United States. A long-standing principle of trademark law is the right of a person to use his or her own name in connection with a business. See Howe Scale Co. v. Wyckoff, Seamans & Benedict, 198 U.S. 118, 140 (1905). This principle was incorporated into the Lanham Act, which states that a mark that is "primarily merely a surname" is not protectable unless it acquires secondary meaning. 15 U.S.C. §1052(e)(4), (f) (1994); Abraham Zion Corp. v. Lebow, 761 F.2d 93, 104 (2d Cir. 1985); see L.E. Waterman Co. v. Modern Pen Co., 235 U.S. 88, 94 (1914) (pre-Lanham Act case stating that protection from confusion is available to the holder of a surname trademark that has acquired public recognition); Horlick's Malted Milk Corp. v. Horluck's, Inc., 59 F.2d 13, 15 (9th Cir. 1932) (pre-Lanham Act case limiting the defendant's right to use his surname as a trademark where the name had acquired public recognition from the efforts of a competitor). Avery Dennison cannot claim that "Avery" and "Dennison" are inherently distinctive, but must demonstrate acquired distinctiveness through secondary meaning.

The drafters of the Federal Trademark Dilution Act continued the concern for surnames when adding protection against trademark dilution to the federal scheme. On early consideration of the Act, the report from the Senate Judiciary Committee emphasized: "[T]he committee intended to give special protection to an individual's ability to use his or her own name in good faith." S.Rep. No. 100-515, at 43 (1988). The Federal Trademark Dilution Act imports, at a minimum, the threshold secondary-meaning requirement for registration of a surname trademark.

Avery Dennison maintains registrations of both "Avery" and "Dennison" on the principal register, prima facie evidence that these marks have achieved the secondary meaning required for protection from infringement and unfair competition. See Americana Trading, 966 F.2d at 1287. We reject Appellants' argument that the distinctiveness required for famousness under the Federal Trademark Dilution Act is inherent, not merely acquired distinctiveness. See 15 U.S.C. §1125(c)(1)(A) (referring to "inherent or acquired distinctiveness"). However, because famousness requires a showing greater than mere distinctiveness, the presumptive secondary meaning associated with "Avery" and "Dennison" fails to persuade us that the famousness prong is met in this case.

2 Overlapping Channels of Trade

We next consider the fifth and sixth factors of the statutory inquiry: the channels of trade for the plaintiff's goods and the degree of recognition of the mark in the trading areas and channels of trade used by plaintiff and defendant. §1125(c)(1)(E), (F). The drafters of the Federal Trademark Dilution Act broke from the Trademark Review Commission's recommendation that only marks "which have become famous throughout a substantial part of the United States" could qualify for protection. Report & Recommendation, 77 Trademark Rep. at 456. Instead, fame in a localized trading area may meet the threshold element under the Act if plaintiff's trading area includes the trading area of the defendant. S.Rep. No. 100-515, at 43; Washington Speakers Bureau, Inc. v. Leading Auths., Inc., 33 F. Supp.2d 488, 503-04 (E.D.Va. 1999) (citing *I.P. Lund*, 163 F.3d at 46; Teletech Customer Care Mgt., Inc. v. TeleTech Co., 977 F. Supp. 1407, 1413 (C.D.Cal. 1997)). The rule is likewise for specialized market segments: specialized fame can be adequate only if the "diluting uses are directed narrowly at the same market segment." *Washington Speakers*, 33 F. Supp.2d at 503. No evidence on the record supports Avery Dennison's position on these two prongs of the famousness inquiry.

In *Teletech*, fame in a narrow market segment was present when the plaintiff showed "that the Teletech Companies may be the largest provider of primarily inbound integrated telephone and Internet customer care nationwide." 977 F. Supp. at 1409. The defendant was "a contractor providing engineering and installation services to the telecommunications industry," and maintained the domain-name combination, teletech.com. *Id.* at 1409-10. The court held that the showing on the threshold element under the Federal Trademark Dilution Act was adequate to qualify for a preliminary injunction. *Id.* at 1413. In *Washington Speakers,* both the plaintiff and defendant were in the business of scheduling speaking engagements for well-known lecturers. 33 F. Supp.2d at 490, 503 & n.31 (citing cases). In the instant case, by contrast, Appellants' sought-after customer base is Internet users who desire vanity e-mail addresses, and Avery Dennison's customer base includes purchasers of office products and industrial fasteners. No evidence demonstrates that Avery Dennison possesses any degree of recognition among Internet users or that Appellants direct their e-mail services at Avery Dennison's customer base.

3   Use of the Marks by Third Parties

The seventh factor, "the nature and extent of use of the same . . . marks by third parties," §1125(c)(1)(G), undercuts the district court's conclusion as well. All relevant evidence on the record tends to establish that both "Avery" and "Dennison" are commonly used as trademarks, both on and off of the Internet, by parties other than Avery Dennison. This evidence is relevant because, when "a mark is in widespread use, it may not be famous for the goods or services of one business." Report & Recommendation, 77 Trademark Rep. at 461; see *Accuride*, 871 F.2d at 1539 (affirming the district court's holding that widespread use of elements of a trademark helped to defeat a dilution claim).

The record includes copies of five trademark registrations for "Avery" and "Averys," a computer printout of a list of several businesses with "Avery" in their names who market products on the Internet, and a list of business names including "Avery," which, according to a declaration submitted by NSI, is a representative sample of over 800 such businesses. The record also contains a computer printout of a list of several businesses with "Dennison" in their names which market products on the Internet and a list of business names including "Dennison," a representative sample of over 200 such businesses. Such widespread use of "Avery" and "Dennison" makes it unlikely that either can be considered a famous mark eligible for the dilution cause of action.

4   Other Famousness Factors

Avery Dennison argues that evidence of extensive advertising and sales, international operations, and consumer awareness suffices to establish fame. We agree that the remaining four statutory factors in the famousness inquiry likely support Avery Dennison's position. Both "Avery" and "Dennison" have been used as trademarks for large fractions of a century and registered for decades. Avery Dennison expends substantial sums annually advertising each mark, with some presumable degree of success due to Avery Dennison's significant annual volume of sales. In addition, Avery Dennison markets its goods internationally. See 15 U.S.C. §1125(c)(1)(B)-(D), (G). However, we disagree that Avery Dennison's showing establishes fame.

Avery Dennison submitted three market research studies regarding perceptions of the "Avery" and "Avery Dennison" brands. Discussion groups through which one study was conducted were formed "using Avery client lists," and produced the conclusion that the "Avery" name has "positive associations . . . among current customers." Surveyed persons in the other two studies were mostly "users and purchasers of office products" and "[o]ffice supply consumers." The one consumer group that did not necessarily include office supply purchasers for businesses was still required to be "somewhat" or "very" familiar with Avery products in order to be counted.

Avery Dennison's marketing reports are comparable to a survey we discussed in Anti-Monopoly, Inc. v. General Mills Fun Group, Inc., 684 F.2d 1316 (9th Cir. 1981), proving only the near tautology that consumers already acquainted with Avery and Avery Dennison products are familiar with Avery Dennison. See *id.* at 1323-24. The marketing reports add nothing to the discussion of whether consumers in general have any brand association with "Avery" and "Avery Dennison," and no evidence of product awareness relates specifically to the "Dennison" trademark. Although proper consumer surveys might be highly relevant to a showing of fame, we reject any reliance on the flawed reports submitted by Avery Dennison.

Finally, Avery Dennison—like any company marketing on the Internet—markets its products worldwide. See 15 U.S.C. §1125(c)(1)(D). By itself, this factor carries no weight; worldwide use of a non-famous mark does not establish fame. Because famousness requires more than mere distinctiveness, and Avery Dennison's showing goes no further than establishing secondary meaning, we hold that Avery Dennison has not met its burden to create a genuine issue of fact that its marks are famous. Avery Dennison's failure to fulfill its burden on this required element of both dilution causes of action mandates summary judgment for Appellants.

5 Likelihood of Confusion Remains Irrelevant

We recognize that our discussion of the breadth of fame and overlapping market segments begins to sound like a likelihood of confusion analysis, and we agree with Avery Dennison that likelihood of confusion should not be considered under either the Federal Trademark Dilution Act or Business and Professional Code §14330. However, as we discuss above, the famousness element of the dilution causes of action serves the same general purpose as the likelihood of confusion element of an infringement or unfair competition analysis—preventing the trademark scheme from granting excessively broad protection at the expense of legitimate uses. See *Fruit of the Loom*, 994 F.2d at 1363 ("Whittling away will not occur unless there is at least some subliminal connection in a buyer's mind between the two parties' uses of their marks."). The close parallels between the two analyses are therefore not surprising; nor do they cause us concern.

B Commercial Use

Addressing the second element of a cause of action under the Federal Trademark Dilution Act, the district court held that Appellants' registration of avery.net and dennison.net constituted commercial use. 999 F. Supp. at 1339-40. We disagree.

Commercial use under the Federal Trademark Dilution Act requires the defendant to be using the trademark as a trademark, capitalizing on its trademark status. See *Panavision*, 141 F.3d at 1325. Courts have phrased this requirement in various ways. In a classic "cybersquatter" case, one court referenced the defendants "intention to arbitrage" the registration which included the plaintiff's trademark. *Intermatic*, 947 F. Supp. at 1239. Another court, whose decision we affirmed, noted that the defendant "traded on the value of marks as marks." Panavision Int'l, L.P. v. Toeppen, 945 F. Supp. 1296, 1303 (C.D.Cal. 1996), *aff'd*, 141 F.3d 1316 (9th Cir. 1998). In our *Panavision* decision, we considered the defendant's "attempt to sell the trademarks themselves." 141 F.3d at 1325.

All evidence in the record indicates that Appellants register common surnames in domain-name combinations and license e-mail addresses using those surnames, with the consequent intent to capitalize on the surname status of "Avery" and "Dennison." Appellants do not use trademarks qua trademarks as required by the caselaw to establish commercial use. Rather, Appellants use words that happen to be trademarks for their non-trademark value. The district court erred in holding that Appellants' use of avery.net and dennison.net constituted commercial use under the Federal Trademark Dilution Act, and this essential element of the dilution causes of action likewise mandates summary judgment for Appellants.

C Dilution

The district court then considered the dilution requirement under both statutes, holding that Appellants' use of avery.net and dennison.net caused dilution, or a likelihood of dilution, of "Avery" and "Dennison." 999 F. Supp. at 1340-41. We hold that genuine issues of fact on this element of the causes of action should have precluded summary judgment for Avery Dennison.

Two theories of dilution are implicated in this case. First, Avery Dennison argues that Appellants' conduct is the cybersquatting dilution that we recognized in *Panavision*. See 141 F.3d at 1326-27. Second, Avery Dennison argues that Appellants' conduct in housing the avery.net and dennison.net domain names in the same database as various lewd SLDs causes tarnishment of the "Avery" and "Dennison" marks.

1 Cybersquatting

Cybersquatting dilution is the diminishment of "'the capacity of the [plaintiff's] marks to identify and distinguish the [plaintiff's] goods and services on the Internet.'" *Panavision*, 141 F.3d at 1326 (quoting the *Panavision* district court, 945 F. Supp. at 1304). We recognized that this can occur if potential customers cannot find a web page at trademark.com. *Id.* at 1327; see also *Brookfield*, 174 F.3d at 1045 ("The Web surfer who assumes that "'X'.com" will always correspond to the web site of company *X* or trademark *X* will, however, sometimes be misled."). Dilution occurs because " '[p]rospective users of plaintiff's services . . . may fail to continue to search for plaintiff's own home page, due to anger, frustration or the belief that plaintiff's home page does not exist.'" *Panavision*, 141 F.3d at 1327 (quoting Jews for Jesus v. Brodsky, 993 F. Supp. 282, 306-07 (D.N.J. 1998)).

In the instant case, Appellants registered the TLD .net, rather than .com, with the SLDs avery and dennison. As we recognized in *Panavision*, .net applies to networks and .com applies to commercial entities. 141 F.3d at 1318. Evidence on the record supports this distinction, and courts applying the dilution cause of action to domain-name registrations have universally considered trademark.com registrations. See Brown, Note, *supra,* at 251-54 (discussing cases); *id.* at 262-63 (addressing the .com versus .net distinction). Although evidence on the record also demonstrates that the .com and .net distinction is illusory, a factfinder could infer that dilution does not occur with a trademark.net registration. This genuine issue of fact on the question of cybersquatting dilution should have prevented summary judgment for Avery Dennison.

2   Tarnishment

Tarnishment occurs when a defendant's use of a mark similar to a plaintiff's presents a danger that consumers will form unfavorable associations with the mark. See Hasbro, Inc. v. Internet Ent. Group, Ltd., 40 U.S.P.Q.2d 1479, 1480 (W.D.Wash. 1996) (candyland.com as a domain-name combination for a sexually explicit web site diluted plaintiff's trademark, "Candyland," for a children's game); 3 McCarthy, supra, §24:104. The district court did not reach Avery Dennison's claims regarding tarnishment.

Avery Dennison offers, as an alternative ground for affirming the district court, the fact that Appellants house avery.net and dennison.net at the same web site as lewd domain-name registrations. However, the evidence likewise indicates that to move from avery.net or dennison.net to a lewd SLD requires "linking" through the Mailbank home page, which might remove any association with the "Avery" and "Dennison" trademarks that the Internet user might have had. See *Fruit of the Loom,* 994 F.2d at 1363 (requiring some connection between the two parties' uses of their marks). Whether Appellants' use of the registrations presents a danger of tarnishment is an issue of fact that could not be decided on summary judgment. . . .

VII   Conclusion

We reverse the district court's summary judgment in favor of Avery Dennison and remand with instructions to enter summary judgment for Sumpton and Freeview. We also remand Appellants' request for attorneys' fees for a determination by the district court. Finally, we deny Avery Dennison's motion to strike portions of Appellants' brief, and we deny Appellants' request for judicial notice.

REVERSED and REMANDED.

COMMENTS AND QUESTIONS

1.   Is the court's distinction between cybersquatting and what Sumpton is doing persuasive? Is the difference simply the intent of the parties?

2.   Suppose that Sumpton had registered "averydennison.com" and offered to sell it to the company. Clearly, in that case he would be a cybersquatter, just as

Toeppen was. But under the rationale of the Ninth Circuit's decision, would Avery-Dennison have a cause of action against him? If so, for what?

A case presenting just such a problem is Archdiocese of St. Louis v. Internet Entertainment Group, 34 F. Supp.2d 1145 (E.D. Mo. 1999). There, a well-known Internet pornographer registered "papalvisit.com" and "papalvisit1999.com" in advance of the Pope's visit to the United States. The site contained information about the Pope's visit, but also contained links to the defendant's porn sites. The district court held that the use of these names diluted the trademarks of the Catholic church. It seems quite implausible, however, that the church's unregistered mark "Papal Visit 1999," of recent and only casual usage, was really famous. Rather, the court seemed to be reacting to the defendant's intent to mislead those coming to the site.

3. One possible point of distinction between Toeppen and Sumpton is that Sumpton is not using the term in question *as a trademark*. *Avery-Dennison* is a difficult case, because Sumpton *is* selling the domain names for profit. But there is a distinction in trademark law between using a mark to identify goods or services and merely using the mark (for example, on T-shirts, or in a newspaper article). The domain name cases blur that line, in part because use of domain names is exclusive —that is, if I register a mark, you can't register the same mark. Still, it is important to distinguish different uses of the mark in question.

Some uses may not be commercial at all, rendering trademark law inapplicable. For example, in one widely reported dispute, a 12-year-old boy with the nickname "Pokey" registered pokey.org for his personal Web site. The company that owned the "Gumby" and "Pokey" trademarks threatened to sue but backed down in the face of adverse publicity. But if they had sued, they could not have proven trademark infringement or dilution. Do you see why?

Should the noncommercial nature of a defendant's use of a domain name always mean that trademark law does not apply? Consider the following case.

Planned Parenthood Federation of America, Inc. v. Bucci
United States District Court for the Southern District of New York
42 U.S.P.Q.2d 1430 (S.D.N.Y. 1997)

KIMBA M. WOOD, District Judge.

Plaintiff Planned Parenthood Federation of America, Inc. ("Planned Parenthood") has moved to preliminarily enjoin defendant Richard Bucci ("Bucci"), doing business as Catholic Radio, from using the domain name "plannedparenthood.com," and from identifying his web site on the Internet under the name "www.plannedparenthood.com." The Court held a hearing on February 20, 1997 and February 21, 1997, and now issues the preliminary injunction sought by Planned Parenthood.

I. Undisputed Facts

The parties do not dispute the following facts. Plaintiff Planned Parenthood, founded in 1922, is a non-profit, reproductive health care organization that has used its present name since 1942. Plaintiff registered the stylized service mark "Planned Parenthood" on the Principal Register of the United States Patent and Trademark Office on June 28, 1955, and registered the block service mark "Planned Parenthood" on the Principal Register of the United States Patent and Trademark Office on September 9, 1975. Plaintiff's 146 separately incorporated affiliates, in 48 states and the District of Columbia, are licensed to use the mark "Planned Parenthood." Plaintiff expends a considerable sum of money in promoting and advertising its services. The mark "Planned Parenthood" is strong and incontestable.

Plaintiff operates a web site at "www.ppfa.org," using the domain name "ppfa.org." Plaintiff's home page offers Internet users resources regarding sexual and reproductive health, contraception and family planning, pregnancy, sexually transmitted diseases, and abortion, as well as providing links to other relevant web sites. In addition, plaintiff's home page offers Internet users suggestions on how to get involved with plaintiff's mission and solicits contributions.[2]

Defendant Bucci is the host of "Catholic Radio," a daily radio program broadcast on the WVOA radio station in Syracuse, New York. Bucci is an active participant in the anti-abortion movement. Bucci operates web sites at "www.catholicradio.com" and at "lambsofchrist.com." On August 28, 1996, Bucci registered the domain name "plannedparenthood.com" with Network Solutions, Inc. ("NSI"), a corporation that administers the assignment of domain names on the Internet. After registering the domain name, Bucci set up a web site and home page on the Internet at the address "www.plannedparenthood.com."

Internet users who type in the address "www.plannedparenthood. com," or who use a search engine such as Yahoo or Lycos to find web sites containing the term "planned parenthood," can reach Bucci's web site and home page. Once a user accesses Bucci's home page, she sees on the computer screen the words "Welcome to the PLANNED PARENTHOOD HOME PAGE!" These words appear on the screen first, because the text of a home page downloads from top to bottom. Once the whole home page has loaded, the user sees a scanned image of the cover of a book entitled The Cost of Abortion, by Lawrence Roberge ("Roberge"), under which appear several links: "Foreword," "Afterword," "About the Author," "Book Review," and "Biography."

After clicking on a link, the user accesses text related to that link. By clicking on "Foreword" or "Afterword," the Internet user simply accesses the foreword or afterword of the book The Cost of Abortion. That text eventually reveals that The Cost of Abortion is an anti-abortion book. The text entitled "About the Author" contains the curriculum vitae of author Roberge. It also notes that "Mr. Roberge is available for interview and speaking engagements," and provides his telephone number. The "Book Review" link brings the Internet user to a selection of quotations by various people endorsing The Cost of Abortion. Those quotations include exhortations to read the book and obtain the book. "Biography" offers more information about Roberge's background.

---

2. Plaintiff's Houston affiliate owns the domain name "plannedparenthood.org," and is in the process of transferring that domain name to plaintiff.

II. Disputed Facts

The parties dispute defendant's motive in choosing plaintiff's mark as his domain name. Plaintiff alleges that defendant used plaintiff's mark with the "specific intent to damage Planned Parenthood's reputation and to confuse unwitting users of the Internet." Discussing the difference between the domain name at issue here and defendant's other web sites, defendant's counsel states that "[t]he WWWPLANNNEDPARENTHOOD.COM [sic] website . . . enables Defendant's message to reach a broader audience." Defendant's counsel made the following statement to the Court regarding defendant's use of plaintiff's mark to designate his web site:

> My belief is that it was intended to reach people who would be sympathetic to the proabortion position. . . . [I]t is an effort to get the . . . political and social message to people we might not have been otherwise able to reach. I think it's analogous to putting an advertisement in the New York Times rather than The National Review. You are more likely to get people who are sympathetic to the proabortion position, and that's who you want to reach. I believe that is exactly what Mr. Bucci did when he selected Planned Parenthood.

. . . Defendant's counsel also admitted that Bucci was trying to reach Internet users who thought, in accessing his web site, that they would be getting information from plaintiff.

Defendant stated that his motive in using plaintiff's mark as his domain name was "to reach, primarily, Catholics that are disobedient to the natural law." *Id.* at 21. In an affidavit submitted to the Court, defendant stated that he wanted his "anti-abortion message to reach as many people as possible, and particularly the people who do not think that abortion has an inimical effect on society." Defendant conceded that he was aware that by using plaintiff's mark to identify his web site, he was likely to draw in Internet users who are "pro-abortion." Defendant demonstrated full knowledge of plaintiff's name and activities, and admitted to an understanding that using plaintiff's mark as his domain name would attract "pro-abortion" Internet users to his web site because of their misapprehension as to the site's origin. I therefore now make the factual finding that defendant's motive in choosing plaintiff's mark as his domain name was, at least in part, to attract to his home page Internet users who sought plaintiff's home page.

III. Analysis . . .

B. *Whether the Lanham Act Is Applicable*

Defendant argues that his use of plaintiff's mark cannot be reached under the Lanham Act because it is non-commercial speech. Planned Parenthood has brought suit under §§1114, 1125(a), and 1125(c) of the Lanham Act, Title 15, United States Code. Section 1114 of the Lanham Act forbids a party to "use in commerce any reproduction, counterfeit, copy, or colorable imitation of a registered mark in connection with the sale, offering for sale, distribution, or advertising of any goods or services on or in connection with which such use is likely to cause confusion, or to cause mistake, or to deceive." An injunction under §1125(c) is proper to stop "commercial use in commerce of a mark or trade name" if that use causes dilution of a famous mark. Finally, with respect to §1125(a), defendant may be liable if he has used the plaintiff's mark "in commerce" in a way that either "is likely to cause confusion, or to cause mistake, or to deceive as to the affiliation, connection, or association of such person with another person, or as to the origin, sponsorship, or approval of his or her goods, services, or commercial activities by another person," §1125(a)(1)(A), or "in commercial advertising or promotion, misrepresents the nature, characteristics, qualities, or geographic origin of his or her or another person's goods, services, or commercial activities," §1125(a)(1)(B). Section 1125(c)(4)(B) specifically exempts from the scope of all provisions of §1125 the "noncommercial use of a mark."

As a preliminary matter, I note that although the parties agreed at a hearing before me on February 21, 1997 that defendant's use of plaintiff's mark is "in commerce" within the meaning of the Lanham Act, defendant now argues that his activities are not subject to the Lanham Act because they are not "in commerce." I find this argument meritless. The "use in commerce" requirement of the Lanham Act is a jurisdictional predicate to any law passed by Congress. It is well settled that the scope of "in commerce" as a jurisdictional predicate of the Lanham Act is broad and has a sweeping reach. Steele v. Bulova Watch Co., 344 U.S. 280, 283, 73 S. Ct. 252, 97 L. Ed. 319 (1952). The activity involved in this action meets the "in commerce" standard for two reasons. First, defendant's actions affect plaintiff's ability to offer plaintiff's services, which, as health and information services offered in forty-eight states and over the Internet, are surely "in commerce." Thus, even assuming, arguendo, that defendant's activities are not in interstate commerce for Lanham Act purposes, the effect of those activities on plaintiff's interstate commerce activities would place defendant within the reach of the Lanham Act. See Franchised Stores of New York. Inc. v. Winter, 394 F.2d 664, 669 (2d Cir. 1968). Second, Internet users constitute a national, even international, audience, who must use interstate telephone lines to access defendant's web site on the Internet. The nature of the Internet indicates that establishing a typical home page on the Internet, for access to all users, would satisfy the Lanham Act's "in commerce" requirement. See Intermatic v. Toeppen, 947 F. Supp. 1227, 1239 (N.D.Ill. 1996), quoting 1 Gilson, Trademark Protection and Practice, §5.11(2), p. 5-234 ("there is little question that the 'in commerce' requirement would be met in a typical Internet message"). Therefore, I conclude that defendant's actions are "in commerce" within the meaning of that term for jurisdictional purposes. I now turn to the specific language of each provision of the Lanham Act under which plaintiff has brought suit.

1. Section 1114

Notwithstanding its jurisdictional "in commerce" requirement, Section 1114 contains no commercial activity requirement; rather, it prohibits any person from, without consent of the registrant of a mark, using the mark "in connection with the sale, offering for sale, distribution, or advertising of any good or services on or in connection with which such use is likely to cause confusion, or to cause mistake, or to deceive." The question the Court must decide, then, is whether defendant's use of plaintiff's mark is properly viewed as in connection with the distribution or advertising of goods or services.

Defendant's use of plaintiff's mark satisfies the requirement of §1114 in a variety of ways. First, defendant has stated that he chose to place materials about The Cost of Abortion on the "www.plannedparenthood.com" web site because he wanted to help Roberge "plug" his book. In addition, defendant agreed that he, by this activity, was helping the author sell his book. Although defendant receives no money from any sales of the book that result from its exposure on his home page, there is no personal profit requirement in §1114. The materials on the home page, which are similar to a publisher's publicity kit, certainly relate to the advertisement and distribution of The Cost of Abortion.

Second, defendant's home page is merely one portion of his, and Catholic Radio's, broader effort to educate Catholics about the anti-abortion movement. With respect to that effort, defendant solicits funds and encourages supporters to join him in his protest activities. Much like plaintiff, defendant has a practical as well as a political motive. While plaintiff seeks to make available what it terms "reproductive services," including, inter alia, birth control and abortion services, defendant offers informational services for use in convincing people that certain activities, including the use of plaintiff's services, are morally wrong. In this way, defendant offers his own set of services, and his use of plaintiff's mark is in connection with the distribution of those services over the Internet. See MGM-Pathe Communications v. Pink Panther Patrol, 774 F. Supp. 869 (S.D.N.Y. 1991) (holding that a group formed to offer the free service of protecting gay individuals from assault was subject to §1114).

In addition, defendant's use of plaintiff's mark is "in connection with the distribution of services" because it is likely to prevent some Internet users from reaching plaintiff's own Internet web site. Prospective users of plaintiff's services who mistakenly access defendant's web site may fail to continue to search for plaintiff's own home page, due to anger, frustration, or the belief that plaintiff's home page does not exist. One witness explained, "We didn't resume the search [for plaintiff's web site] after [finding defendant's web site] because . . . we were pretty much thrown off track." Therefore, defendant's action in appropriating plaintiff's mark has a connection to plaintiff's distribution of its services. For these reasons, §1114 is applicable to defendant's use of plaintiff's mark.

2. Section 1125(c)

Section 1125(c), the Lanham Act's anti-dilution provision, provides that the owner of a famous mark is entitled to an injunction against another person's "commercial use in commerce of a mark or trade name, if such use begins after the mark has become famous and causes dilution of the distinctive quality of the mark." The provision has no requirement that there be advertising or a sale of goods or services. Defendant argues that his use is not "commercial" within the meaning of §1125(c). I hold, however, that defendant's use of plaintiff's mark is "commercial" for three reasons: (1) defendant is engaged in the promotion of a book, (2) defendant is, in essence, a non-profit political activist who solicits funds for his activities, and (3) defendant's actions are designed to, and do, harm plaintiff commercially.

First, as discussed above, defendant's home page is a showcase for The Cost of Abortion, offering excerpts of the book, information about the author (specifically including how to contact the author for speaking engagements), and endorsements of the book (including statements such as "I want to see this book in the hands of EVERY Catholic priest and Protestant minister in the country"). This showcase is surely commercial in nature, despite the fact that defendant derives no monetary gain from these activities. Although defendant does not seek a profit from his actions, §1125(c) carries no "for-profit" requirement. Therefore, defendant's use of plaintiff's mark to further his self-styled effort to "plug" The Cost of Abortion falls within the purview of the commercial use requirement of §1125(c).

Second, defendant's use of plaintiff's mark to identify his web site is one part of defendant's sustained effort, through his radio show and other means, to achieve his end of persuading the public to eschew birth control and abortion. Defendant is a vocal supporter of the anti-abortion movement. Defendant also opposes the use of contraceptives. Through his radio program, he seeks to educate his listeners about the teachings of the Catholic church, specifically trying to discourage his audience from using birth control and obtaining abortions. In this connection, defendant is a vocal critic of plaintiff and plaintiff's activities.

In *MGM-Pathe*, 774 F. Supp. 869, Judge Leval considered whether a non-profit group that uses another's trademark in support of its own non-profit aims is subject to the Lanham Act. Specifically, he examined whether a group whose aim was to provide protection to the gay community and to educate the general public about violence against that community could appropriate a part of the name of a movie produced by plaintiff ("Pink Panther"). After finding that there was a likelihood of confusion, Judge Leval concluded that defendant's goal of political activism did not confer immunity from the Lanham Act, noting that "[t]he seriousness and virtue of a cause do not confer any right to the use of the trademark of another." Defendant attempts to distinguish *MGM-Pathe* from the case now before the Court on the ground that defendant in this action has used plaintiff's mark in an effort to criticize plaintiff, while the *MGM-Pathe* defendants had no intent to criticize the Pink Panther movies. The Court finds this distinction unhelpful. The mere fact that defendant seeks to criticize plaintiff cannot automatically immunize a use that is otherwise prohibited by the Lanham Act.

Additionally, defendant has testified that he solicits contributions on his "Catholic Radio" radio show and has solicited contributions on the air in connection with the instant lawsuit. Defendant's ownership of the domain name "plannedparenthood.com" is part and parcel of Catholic Radio's broader efforts in the anti-abortion movement. Specifically, defendant has told his radio listeners that "Catholic Radio owns the name 'Planned Parenthood.'" Courts have found that fund-raising activities may bring a defendant's actions within the scope of the Lanham Act. See Cancer Research Institute. Inc. v. Cancer Research Society, Inc., 694 F. Supp. 1051 (S.D.N.Y. 1988) (enjoining defendant from using plaintiff's name for soliciting funds for cancer research), Girls Club of Am., Inc. v. Boys Clubs of Am., Inc., 683 F. Supp. 50, 53 (S.D.N.Y.), *aff'd*, 859 F.2d 148 (2d Cir. 1988) (enjoining defendant from adding plaintiff's name to its own for broad range of non-profit activities including fundraising); Brach van Houten Holding v. Save Brach's Coalition, 856 F. Supp. 472 (N.D.Ill. 1994) (enjoining defendant from use of plaintiff's name in soliciting funds); American Diabetic Assoc. v. National Diabetic Assoc., 533 F. Supp. 16, 20 (E.D.Pa. 1981) (enjoining defendant from use of similar name in relation to its non-profit fund-raising). I find that defendant's use of plaintiff's mark is sufficiently tied to defendant's fund-raising efforts for the use to be deemed "commercial" within the meaning of §1125(c).

Finally, defendant's use is commercial because of its effect on plaintiff's activities. First, defendant has appropriated plaintiff's mark in order to reach an audience of Internet users who want to reach plaintiff's services and viewpoint, intercepting them and misleading them in an attempt to offer his own political message. Second, defendant's appropriation not only provides Internet users with competing and directly opposing information, but also prevents those users from reaching plaintiff and its services and message. In that way, defendant's use is classically competitive: he has taken plaintiff's mark as his own in order to purvey his Internet services—his web site—to an audience intending to access plaintiff's services. . . .

3. Section 1125(a)(1)(A)

In relevant part, §1125(a)(1)(A) prohibits a person from using in commerce any term or false designation of origin which "is likely to cause confusion . . . as to the affiliation, connection, or association of such person with another person, or as to the origin, sponsorship, or approval of his or her goods, services, or commercial activities by another person." Section 1125(a)(1) is also limited by §1125(c)(4)(B), which states that "noncommercial use of a mark" is not actionable under the Lanham Act.

Here, as discussed above, defendant offers informational services relating to the anti-abortion and anti-birth control movement, specifically providing his audience with relevant literature and the means to contact Roberge. In addition, defendant's solicitation of funds in relation to his anti-abortion efforts are commercial in nature. Therefore, because defendant's labelling of his web site with plaintiff's mark relates to the "origin, sponsorship, or approval" by plaintiff of defendant's web site, I find that §1125(a)(1)(A) may govern defendant's actions in this case. . . .

I therefore determine that §1114, §1125(c), and §1125(a)(1)(a) of the Lanham Act are applicable here. I turn now to whether defendant's use of plaintiff's mark results in a likelihood of confusion.

C. The Likelihood of Confusion

1. The Polaroid Factors

The Second Circuit set out the factors a court must consider in determining the likelihood of consumer confusion in Polaroid Corp. v. Polarad Elecs. Corp., 287 F.2d 492, 495 (2d Cir. 1961). Those factors include: the strength of plaintiff's mark, the degree of similarity between the two marks, the competitive proximity of the products or services, the likelihood that the plaintiff will bridge the gap between the two markets, the existence of actual confusion, the defendant's good faith in adopting the mark, the quality of the defendant's product, and the sophistication of the purchasers.

a. The Strength of the Mark

The strength of plaintiffs' mark is conceded by defendant, which is reasonable in light of plaintiffs' trademark registration of the mark and plaintiffs' continued use of the mark for over 50 years. The strength of plaintiffs' mark weighs in favor of likelihood of confusion.

b. The Degree of Similarity Between the Marks

The two marks, "Planned Parenthood" and "plannedparenthood. com" are nearly identical; the only distinctions are the latter's lack of initial capitalization, the lack of a space between words, and the ".com" that is necessary to designate a domain name. The degree of similarity between defendant's domain name and the domain name owned by plaintiff's affiliate, Planned Parenthood of Houston, "plannedparenthood.org," is even stronger. Plaintiff was originally under the impression that according to Internet usage, it could operate using only a ".org" designation. Currently, however, NSI allows non-profit corporations, as well as for-profit businesses and individuals, to use the ".com" designation. The ".com" designation is commonly used by businesses. The degree of similarity between the marks thus increases the likelihood of confusion among Internet users.

c. The Competitive Proximity of the Products or Services

The web sites of plaintiff and defendant are both located on the World Wide Web. Therefore, defendant's web site at "www.plannedparenthood. com" is close in proximity to plaintiff's own web site, "www.ppfa.org." Both sites compete for the same audience—namely, Internet users who are searching for a web site that uses plaintiff's mark as its address. The degree of competitive proximity, therefore, increases the likelihood of confusion among Internet users.

d. The Likelihood that Plaintiff Will Bridge the Gap Between the Markets

Because plaintiff's web site and defendant's web site are both on the Internet, the parties are vying for users in the same "market." Where the market for competing goods or services is the same, there is no need to consider whether plaintiff will bridge the gap between the markets. Paddington Corp. v. Attiki Importers & Distributors, Inc., 996 F.2d 577, 586 (2d Cir. 1993). I therefore do not consider this factor in determining the likelihood of confusion.

e. The Existence of Actual Confusion

Plaintiff has produced testimony demonstrating that actual confusion has occurred among Internet users. The confusion has occurred both in a user who attempted to go directly to "www.plannedparenthood.com," thinking that it was likely to be plaintiff's web address, and in a user who used a search engine to find web sites containing, or designated by, plaintiff's mark.

This specific testimony exemplifies the likelihood of confusion due to the nature of domain names and home page addresses. First, because ".com" is a popular designation for Internet domain names, an Internet user is likely to assume that ".com" after a corporation's name will bring her to that corporation's home page, if one exists. Second, an Internet user cannot immediately determine the content of a home page maintained by the owner of a particular domain name or located at a specific address. Only after a user has seen or entered "plannedparenthood.com" can she access the web site; such access occurs after at least a temporary delay. In addition, there is a delay while the home page "loads" into the computer. Because the words on the top of the page load first, the user is first greeted solely with the "Welcome to the Planned Parenthood Home Page!" It is highly likely that an Internet user will still believe that she has found plaintiff's web site at that point.

Even when the picture of The Cost of Abortion finally does appear on the screen, the user is unlikely to know that she is not at plaintiff's home page. The book's ambiguous title "The Cost of Abortion," alone, cannot disabuse every Internet user of the notion that she has found plaintiff's home page. The Internet user must actually click on a link to read excerpts from the book, biographical information about the author, or book endorsements. Only in the course of reading those items can the user determine that she has not reached plaintiff's home page. Depending on which link the user has chosen to access, there may be an additional delay before the user can grasp that plaintiff is not the true provider of the home page. This lengthy delay between attempting to access plaintiff's home page and learning that one has failed to do so increases the likelihood of consumer confusion.

f. The Defendant's Good Faith in Adopting the Mark

Defendant's testimony, and his counsel's admission at the hearing before this Court on the temporary restraining order, show that defendant chose his domain name and home page name with full knowledge and intent that some Internet users seeking to find plaintiff's home page would instead encounter his. However, defendant may have acted under the good faith assumption that his actions were protected by the First Amendment. I need not conclude that defendant acted in bad faith to conclude that there is a likelihood of confusion, and I therefore make no such finding at this time.

g. The Quality of Defendant's Product

A comparison of the quality of plaintiff's and defendant's products—their web sites—is irrelevant; the Court cannot compare the two web sites in terms of superior or inferior quality. However, I note that the two products are vastly different and convey quite divergent messages. Plaintiff's web site offers educational resources, suggests ways to get involved in plaintiff's activities, to join plaintiff in its advocacy mission, and to contribute to plaintiff, and offers links to plaintiff's local affiliates, related organizations, and job listings. In sum, plaintiff's web site provides Internet users with an array of information and services related to Planned Parenthood's mission of providing reproductive choice for women. Defendant's home page bearing plaintiff's mark offers users information, including an advertisement for a book, and ways to contact a vocal anti-abortion advocate. Any ensuing confusion resulting from defendant's use of plaintiff's mark as his domain name and home page address is likely to be destructive to the image that plaintiff, the senior user of the mark, has established. See *MGM-Pathe*, 774 F. Supp. at 876.

h. The Sophistication of the Purchasers

Plaintiff argues that its primary purchasers are low income, relatively unsophisticated women. I note that those with access to the Internet may not be coextensive with the segment of the population to whom plaintiff normally offers its services; those with Internet access may be more sophisticated. However, testimony has shown that even sophisticated Internet users were confused by defendant's web site. Although the sophisticated Internet user may discover, after reading the text of one of the links on defendant's home page, that she has not reached plaintiff's web site, some users may not be so immediately perspicacious. Because the sophistication of the user is no guarantee, here, that the consumer will not be confused, I find that this factor is of limited value in determining whether the consumer is likely to be confused.

In sum, I find that the bulk of the Polaroid factors demonstrate that there is a significant likelihood of confusion that warrants the granting of a preliminary injunction.

D. *Defendant's Additional Defenses*

Defendant also argues that his use of plaintiff's mark is protected from injunction because (1) it is a parody, and (2) it is protected speech under the First Amendment. I consider these arguments in turn.

1. The Parody Exception

Defendant argues that his use of the "planned parenthood" mark is not likely to confuse because it is similar to a parody. A parody "depends on a lack of confusion to make its point," and "'must convey two simultaneous—and contradictory —messages: that it is the original, but also that it is not the original and is instead a parody.'" Hormel Food Corp. v. Jim Henson Productions, Inc., 73 F.3d 497, 503 (2d Cir. 1996) (internal citations omitted). Here, an Internet user may either find the defendant's web site through a search engine or may simply enter the words "planned parenthood" in the expectation that she will find the plaintiff's web site. Seeing or typing the "planned parenthood" mark and accessing the web site are two separate and nonsimultaneous activities. Furthermore, the greeting "Welcome to the Planned Parenthood Home Page!" does not immediately contradict an Internet user's assumption that she has accessed the plaintiff's home page. Only when an Internet user actually "clicks" on one of the topics and accesses commentary on The Cost of Abortion does she encounter defendant's message.

I am not persuaded by defendant's argument that the message of the home page provides an ironic and contrasting allusion to plaintiff, nor do I find convincing his argument that the banner heading of the home page is sarcastic. Similarly, I do not conclude that defendant's use of the term "planned parenthood" in the context described above is intended not to confuse the user into an association with plaintiff, but rather "to reference Plaintiff as the 'enemy.'" Because defendant's use of "planned parenthood" does not convey the simultaneous message that the home page and web site are those of plaintiff and those of defendant, defendant's argument that his use of the mark is a parody fails. Thus, the Polaroid factors must govern the issue of whether there is a likelihood of confusion. Here, I have found that the Polaroid factors demonstrate that there is a likelihood of confusion that arises from defendant's use of the domain name "plannedparenthood.com," the home page address "www.plannedparenthood.com," and the banner at the top of the home page stating, "Welcome to the Planned Parenthood Home Page!"

2. The First Amendment Exception

Defendant also argues that his use of the "planned parenthood" mark is protected by the First Amendment. As defendant argues, trademark infringement law does not curtail or prohibit the exercise of the First Amendment right to free speech. I note that plaintiff has not sought, in any way, to restrain defendant from speech that criticizes Planned Parenthood or its mission, or that discusses defendant's beliefs regarding reproduction, family, and religion. The sole purpose of the Court's inquiry has been to determine whether the use of the "planned parenthood" mark as defendant's domain name and home page address constitutes an infringement of plaintiff's trademark. Defendant's use of another entity's mark is entitled to First Amendment protection when his use of that mark is part of a communicative message, not when it is used to identify the source of a product. Yankee Publishing. Inc. v. News America Publishing, Inc., 809 F. Supp. 267, 275 (S.D.N.Y. 1992). By using the mark as a domain name and home page address and by welcoming Internet users to the home page with the message "Welcome to the Planned Parenthood Home Page!" defendant identifies the web site and home page as being the product, or forum, of plaintiff. I therefore determine that, because defendant's use of the term "planned parenthood" is not part of a communicative message, his infringement on plaintiff's mark is not protected by the First Amendment.

Defendant argues that his use of the "Planned Parenthood" name for his web site is entitled to First Amendment protection, relying primarily on the holding of *Yankee Publishing*, 809 F. Supp. at 275. In that case, Judge Leval noted that the First Amendment can protect unauthorized use of a trademark when such use is part of an expression of a communicative message: "the Second Circuit has construed the Lanham Act narrowly when the unauthorized use of the trademark is for the purpose of a communicative message, rather than identification of product origin." *Id.* Defendant argues that his use of the "Planned Parenthood" name for his web site is a communicative message.

However, *Yankee Publishing* carefully draws a distinction between communicative messages and product labels or identifications:

When another's trademark . . . is used without permission for the purpose of source identification, the trademark law generally prevails over the First Amendment. Free speech rights do not extend to labelling or advertising products in a manner that conflicts with the trademark rights of others.

Id. at 276. Defendant offers no argument in his papers as to why the Court should determine that defendant's use of "plannedparenthood.com" is a communicative message rather than a source identifier. His use of "plannedparenthood.com" as a domain name to identify his web site is on its face more analogous to source identification than to a communicative message; in essence, the name identifies the web site, which contains defendant's home page. The statement that greets Internet users who access defendant's web site, "Welcome to the Planned Parenthood Home Page," is also more analogous to an identifier than to a communication. For those reasons, defendant's use of the trademarked term "planned parenthood" is not part of a communicative message, but rather, serves to identify a product or item, defendant's web site and home page, as originating from Planned Parenthood.

Defendant's use of plaintiff's mark is not protected as a title under Rogers v. Grimaldi, 875 F.2d 994, 998 (2d Cir. 1989). There, the Court of Appeals determined that the title of the film "Ginger and Fred" was not a misleading infringement, despite the fact that the film was not about Ginger Rogers and Fred Astaire, because of the artistic implications of a title. The Court of Appeals noted that "[f]ilmmakers and authors frequently rely on word-play, ambiguity, irony, and allusion in titling their works." *Id.* The Court of Appeals found that the use of a title such as the one at issue in *Rogers* was acceptable "unless the title has no artistic relevance to the underlying work"; even when the title has artistic relevance, it may not be used to "explicitly mislead[ ] [the consumer] as to the source or content of the work." *Id.* Here, even treating defendant's domain name and home page address as titles, rather than as source identifiers, I find that the title "plannedparenthood.com" has no artistic implications, and that the title is being used to attract some consumers by misleading them as to the web site's source or content. Given defendant's testimony indicating that he knew, and intended, that his use of the domain name "plannedparenthood.com" would cause some "pro-abortion" Internet users to access his web site, he cannot demonstrate that his use of "planned parenthood" is entitled to First Amendment protection.

Because defendant's use of plaintiff's mark is subject to the Lanham Act, because the Polaroid factors demonstrate that there is a likelihood of confusion arising from defendant's use of plaintiff's mark, and because defendant has not raised a defense that protects his use of the mark, plaintiff has met its burden of demonstrating that a preliminary injunction against defendant's use of plaintiff's mark is warranted. *Hasbro*, 858 F.2d at 73.

E. *Whether a Disclaimer Will Cure the Confusion*

Defendant argues that a disclaimer, rather than an injunction, is the appropriate remedy here. I disagree. Due to the nature of Internet use, defendant's appropriation of plaintiff's mark as a domain name and home page address cannot adequately be remedied by a disclaimer. Defendant's domain name and home page address are external labels that, on their face, cause confusion among Internet users and may cause Internet users who seek plaintiff's web site to expend time and energy accessing defendant's web site. Therefore, I determine that a disclaimer on defendant's home page would not be sufficient to dispel the confusion induced by his home page address and domain name. . . .

COMMENTS AND QUESTIONS

1. The district court's opinion was affirmed without opinion by the Second Circuit. 152 F.3d 920 (2d Cir. 1998). For a similar result, see Jews for Jesus v. Brodsky, 46 U.S.P.Q.2d 1652 (D.N.J. 1998) (enjoining the use of the jewsforjesus.com domain name by a Jewish group opposed to Jews for Jesus), *aff'd without opinion*, 159 F.3d 1351 (3d Cir. 1998). But cf. Playboy Enter. Inc. v. Universal Tel-A-Talk, 48 U.S.P.Q.2d 1779 (E.D. Pa. 1998) (use of the Playboy term as a link to Playboy's Web site was not trademark infringement or counterfeiting).

2. Does it make sense to use the traditional analysis of likelihood of confusion here? What exactly is Bucci selling? In what way are the goods or services similar to those of Planned Parenthood?

3. Why was Bucci's use "commercial use in commerce," as the federal dilution statute requires? Was it because he promoted someone else's book on the site? What if he hadn't done so? Isn't it rather more plausible that this Web page was using the Planned Parenthood name for political purposes, not as a trademark to sell goods or services? If so, should this affect the court's analysis? For an argument that courts are distorting trademark principles in this and related cases in order to reach what appears to be a just result, see Mark A. Lemley, The Modern Lanham Act and the Death of Common Sense, 108 Yale L.J. 1687 (1999).

If the court determined that the speech in question was political, not commercial, presumably the trademark laws would not apply. But does that mean that Bucci would avoid liability altogether? Arguably, his use of plannedparenthood.com and his title "Welcome to the Planned Parenthood Home Page" are false statements of fact, and therefore unprotectable under First Amendment principles.

For a political speech dispute that seems more like a parody, compare www.gwbush.com (a parody site not authorized by the George Bush presidential campaign) with the real site (www.georgewbush.com).

4. The court in *Bucci* concluded that the defendant registered the plannedparenthood.com name in order to confuse visitors to the site. The content of the site itself was strong evidence of this confusion, since the Web page Bucci put up pretended to be the official Planned Parenthood page. But suppose that Bucci had just registered the domain name, and had not put up a confusingly similar page. Should the court reach the same result? Consider the following case.

≡ *People for the Ethical Treatment of Animals v. Doughney*
United States Court of Appeals for the Fourth Circuit
≡ *263 F.3d 359 (4th Cir. 2001)*

GREGORY, Circuit Judge:

People for the Ethical Treatment of Animals ("PETA") sued Michael Doughney ("Doughney") after he registered the domain name peta.org and created a website called "People Eating Tasty Animals." PETA alleged claims of service mark infringement under 15 U.S.C. §1114 and Virginia common law, unfair competition under 15 U.S.C. §1125(a) and Virginia common law, and service mark dilution and cybersquatting under 15 U.S.C. §1123(c). Doughney appeals the district court's decision granting PETA's motion for summary judgment and PETA cross-appeals the district court's denial of its motion for attorney's fees and costs. Finding no error, we affirm.

I.

PETA is an animal rights organization with more than 600,000 members worldwide. PETA "is dedicated to promoting and heightening public awareness of animal protection issues and it opposes the exploitation of animals for food, clothing, entertainment and vivisection."

Doughney is a former internet executive who has registered many domain names since 1995. For example, Doughney registered domain names such as dubyadot.com, dubyadot.net, deathbush.com, RandallTerry.org (Not Randall Terry for Congress), bwtel.com (Baltimore-Washington Telephone Company), pmrc.org ("People's Manic Repressive Church"), and ex-cult.org (Ex-Cult Archive). At the time the district court issued its summary judgment ruling, Doughney owned 50-60 domain names.

Doughney registered the domain name peta.org in 1995 with Network Solutions, Inc. ("NSI"). When registering the domain name, Doughney represented to NSI that the registration did "not interfere with or infringe upon the rights of any third party," and that a "non-profit educational organization" called "People Eating Tasty Animals" was registering the domain name. Doughney made these representations to NSI despite knowing that no corporation, partnership, organization or entity of any kind existed or traded under that name. Moreover, Doughney was familiar with PETA and its beliefs and had been for at least 15 years before registering the domain name.

After registering the peta.org domain name, Doughney used it to create a website purportedly on behalf of "People Eating Tasty Animals." Doughney claims he created the website as a parody of PETA. A viewer accessing the website would see the title "People Eating Tasty Animals" in large, bold type. Under the title, the viewer would see a statement that the website was a "resource for those who enjoy eating meat, wearing fur and leather, hunting, and the fruits of scientific research." The website contained links to various meat, fur, leather, hunting, animal research, and other organizations, all of which held views generally antithetical to PETA's views. Another statement on the website asked the viewer whether he/she was "Feeling lost? Offended? Perhaps you should, like, *exit immediately.*" The phrase "*exit immediately* " contained a hyperlink to PETA's official website.

Doughney's website appeared at "www.peta.org" for only six months in 1995-96. In 1996, PETA asked Doughney to voluntarily transfer the peta.org domain name to PETA because PETA owned the "PETA" mark ("the Mark"), which it registered in 1992. See U.S. Trademark Registration No. 1705,510. When Doughney refused to transfer the domain name to PETA, PETA complained to NSI, whose rules then required it to place the domain name on "hold" pending resolution of Doughney's dispute with PETA. Consequently, Doughney moved the web-

website to www.mtd.com/tasty and added a disclaimer stating that "People Eating Tasty Animals is in no way connected with, or endorsed by, People for the Ethical Treatment of Animals."

In response to Doughney's domain name dispute with PETA, *The Chronicle of Philanthropy* quoted Doughney as stating that, "[i]f they [PETA] want one of my domains, they should make me an offer." Non-Profit Groups Upset by Unauthorized Use of Their Names on the Internet, The Chronicle of Philanthropy, Nov. 14, 1996. Doughney does not dispute making this statement. Additionally, Doughney posted the following message on his website on May 12, 1996:

> "PeTa" has no legal grounds whatsoever to make even the slightest demands of me regarding this domain name registration. If they disagree, they can sue me. And if they don't, well, perhaps they can behave like the polite ladies and gentlemen that they evidently aren't and negotiate a settlement with me. . . . Otherwise, "PeTa" can wait until the significance and value of a domain name drops to nearly nothing, which is inevitable as each new web search engine comes on-line, because that's how long it's going to take for this dispute to play out.

PETA sued Doughney in 1999, asserting claims for service mark infringement, unfair competition, dilution and cybersquatting. . . .

II. . . .

A. *Trademark Infringement/Unfair Competition*

There is no dispute here that PETA owns the "PETA" Mark, that Doughney used it, and that Doughney used the Mark "in commerce." Doughney disputes the district court's findings that he used the Mark in connection with goods or services and that he used it in a manner engendering a likelihood of confusion.

1.

To use PETA's Mark "in connection with" goods or services, Doughney need not have actually sold or advertised goods or services on the www.peta.org website. Rather, Doughney need only have prevented users from obtaining or using PETA's goods or services, or need only have connected the website to other's goods or services.

While sparse, existing caselaw on infringement and unfair competition in the Internet context clearly weighs in favor of this conclusion. For example, in OBH, Inc. v. Spotlight Magazine, Inc., the plaintiffs owned the "The Buffalo News" registered trademark used by the newspaper of the same name. 86 F. Supp.2d 176 (W.D.N.Y. 2000). The defendants registered the domain name thebuffalonews. com and created a website parodying The Buffalo News and providing a public forum for criticism of the newspaper. *Id*. at 182. The site contained hyperlinks to other local news sources and a site owned by the defendants that advertised Buffalo-area apartments for rent. *Id*. at 183.

The court held that the defendants used the mark "in connection with" goods or services because the defendants' website was "likely to prevent or hinder Internet users from accessing plaintiffs' services on plaintiffs' own web site." *Id.*

> Prospective users of plaintiffs' services who mistakenly access defendants' web site may fail to continue to search for plaintiffs' web site due to confusion or frustration. Such users, who are presumably looking for the news services provided by the plaintiffs on their web site, may instead opt to select one of the several other news-related hyperlinks contained in defendants' web site. These news-related hyperlinks will directly link the user to other news-related web sites that are in direct competition with plaintiffs in providing news-related services over the Internet. Thus, defendants' action in appropriating plaintiff's mark has a connection to plaintiffs' distribution of its services.

Id. Moreover, the court explained that defendants' use of the plaintiffs' mark was in connection with goods or services because it contained a link to the defendants' apartment-guide website. *Id.*

[The court also relied on *Bucci.*]

The same reasoning applies here. As the district court explained, Doughney's use of PETA's Mark in the domain name of his website

> is likely to prevent Internet users from reaching [PETA's] own Internet web site. The prospective users of [PETA's] services who mistakenly access Defendant's web site may fail to continue to search for [PETA's] own home page, due to anger, frustration, or the belief that [PETA's] home page does not exist.

Doughney, 113 F. Supp.2d at 919 (quoting *Bucci,* 42 U.S.P.Q.2d at 1435). Moreover, Doughney's web site provides links to more than 30 commercial operations offering goods and services. By providing links to these commercial operations, Doughney's use of PETA's Mark is "in connection with" the sale of goods or services.

2.

The unauthorized use of a trademark infringes the trademark holder's rights if it is likely to confuse an "ordinary consumer" as to the source or sponsorship of the goods. Anheuser-Busch, Inc. v. L & L Wings, Inc., 962 F.2d 316, 318 (4th Cir. 1992) (citing 2 J. McCarthy, Trademarks and Unfair Competition §23:28 (2d ed. 1984)). To determine whether a likelihood of confusion exists, a court should not consider "how closely a fragment of a given use duplicates the trademark," but must instead consider "whether the use in its entirety creates a likelihood of confusion." *Id.* at 319.

Doughney does not dispute that the peta.org domain name engenders a likelihood of confusion between his web site and PETA. Doughney claims, though, that the inquiry should not end with his domain name. Rather, he urges the Court to consider his website in conjunction with the domain name because, together, they purportedly parody PETA and, thus, do not cause a likelihood of confusion.

A "parody" is defined as a "simple form of entertainment conveyed by juxtaposing the irreverent representation of the trademark with the idealized image created by the mark's owner." L.L. Bean, Inc. v. Drake Publishers, Inc., 811 F.2d 26, 34 (1st Cir. 1987). A parody must "convey two simultaneous—and contradictory—messages: that it is the original, but also that it is *not* the original and is instead a parody." Cliffs Notes, Inc. v. Bantam Doubleday Dell Publ. Group, Inc., 886 F.2d 490, 494 (2d Cir. 1989) (emphasis in original). To the extent that an alleged parody conveys only the first message, "it is not only a poor parody but also vulnerable under trademark law, since the customer will be confused." *Id.* While a parody necessarily must engender some initial confusion, an effective parody will diminish the risk of consumer confusion "by conveying [only] just enough of the original design to allow the consumer to appreciate the point of parody." Jordache Enterprises, Inc. v. Hogg Wyld, Ltd., 828 F.2d 1482, 1486 (10th Cir. 1987).

Looking at Doughney's domain name alone, there is no suggestion of a parody. The domain name peta.org simply copies PETA's Mark, conveying the message that it is related to PETA. The domain name does not convey the second, contradictory message needed to establish a parody—a message that the domain name is not related to PETA, but that it is a parody of PETA.

Doughney claims that this second message can be found in the content of his website. Indeed, the website's content makes it clear that it is not related to PETA. However, this second message is not conveyed *simultaneously* with the first message, as required to be considered a parody. The domain name conveys the first message; the second message is conveyed only when the viewer reads the content of the website. As the district court explained, "an internet user would not realize that they were not on an official PETA web site until after they had used PETA's Mark to access the web page 'www.peta.org.'" *Doughney,* 113 F. Supp.2d at 921. Thus, the messages are not conveyed simultaneously and do not constitute a parody. See also Morrison & Foerster LLP v. Wick, 94 F. Supp.2d 1125 (D.Co. 2000) (defendant's use of plaintiffs' mark in domain name "does not convey two simultaneous and contradictory messages" because "[o]nly by reading through the content of the sites could the user discover that the domain names are an attempt at parody"); *Bucci,* 42 U.S.P.Q.2d at 1435 (rejecting parody defense because "[s]eeing or typing the 'planned parenthood' mark and accessing the web site are two separate and nonsimultaneous activities"). The district court properly rejected Doughney's parody defense and found that Doughney's use of the peta.org domain name engenders a likelihood of confusion. Accordingly, Doughney failed to raise a genuine issue of material fact regarding PETA's infringement and unfair competition claims. . . .

COMMENTS AND QUESTIONS

1. Can you think of any use of a domain name that would not qualify as a "commercial use" under *PETA?*

A number of early domain name cases involved suits by both sides against Network Solutions, Inc. (NSI), for its role in domain name registration. Irate trademark owners sued NSI for allowing cybersquatters to register their marks, and demanding that the domain name be handed over to them. When NSI started putting domain names on hold, domain name owners not only sued the trademark owner who requested the hold, but in many cases also sued NSI for interfering with their rights. The courts have unanimously ruled that NSI's domain name registration policies do not themselves implicate the trademark laws. Lockheed Martin Corp. v. Network Solutions, Inc., 194 F.3d 980 (9th Cir. 1999); Lockheed Martin Corp. v. Network Solutions Inc., 141 F. Supp.2d 648 (N.D. Tex. 2001); Academy of Motion Picture Arts & Sciences v. Network Solutions, Inc., 989 F. Supp. 1276 (C.D. Cal. 1997). In each case, the court concluded that the mere act by NSI of registering a domain name by placing the entry on the DNS server database was not "use" necessary for a violation of the Lanham Act. The court opined in *Lockheed* that "The solution to the current difficulties faced by trademark owners on the Internet lies in . . . technical innovation, not in attempts to assert trademark rights over legitimate non-trademark uses of this important new means of communication." *Id.*

Is Judge Pregerson correct that accepting a domain name registration that infringes a trademark is a "legitimate non-trademark use"? Is this case distinguishable from *PETA*?

2. Once a visitor arrives at peta.org, the court acknowledges that no reasonable consumer would confuse "People Eating Tasty Animals" with "People for the Ethical Treatment of Animals." The court nonetheless finds Doughney liable for creating a brief moment of confusion, during the time in which the visitor clicks on the peta.org name but before the page opens. How has PETA been harmed by this moment of confusion? Is it likely that those intending to visit the PETA site will choose instead to stay at Doughney's site, depriving PETA of visitors?

For a discussion of more typical cases of "initial interest confusion," in which consumers are lured to a competitor's site and might decide to stay there, see section 2 below. Most initial interest confusion cases limit the doctrine to circumstances in which the two parties are direct competitors. See, e.g., Chatam Int'l v. Bodum, Inc., 157 F. Supp.2d 549 (E.D. Pa. 2001), *aff'd* 40 Fed. Appx. 685 (3d Cir. 2002). Is this the right rule?

3. The First Amendment permits parodies of trademarks, so long as they are not confusing. How can Doughney parody the PETA mark after this decision? The court suggests that the domain name itself must somehow convey both that it is the PETA mark and that it is instead a parody. Can a domain name do this? How?

If Doughney had chosen a different name that did not make reference to PETA, but still sought to draw people who searched for PETA to his site, would he still violate the law? For discussion of the use of metatags to draw visitors to a site, see section b below.

b. Anticybersquatting Consumer Protection Act

Trademark infringement and dilution are not well suited to preventing cybersquatting. While some uses of a domain name are infringing, most are not. Dilution reaches classic cases of cybersquatting—the registration of a domain name corresponding to someone else's trademark in order to extort money from the trademark owner—but only in the small number of cases in which the trademark in question is famous. This led to two problems. First, some instances of cybersquatting can't be punished under existing trademark laws. Second, courts sometimes stretched the requirements of the law in order to stop cybersquatting. For instance, many courts ignored or reduced the requirement of fame in order to apply dilution law against clear cases of cybersquatting.

In 1999, Congress sought to address both of these problems by passing a law directed specifically at cybersquatting. The Anticybersquatting Consumer Protection Act makes it illegal to register or use a domain name that corresponds to a trademark where the domain name registrant has no legitimate interest in using the name and acts in bad faith to deprive the trademark owner of the use of the name. 15 U.S.C. §1125(d). Since the end of 1999, dozens of cases have been decided under the ACPA. The critical parts of the statute are the definitions of bad faith and legitimate interest, which are discussed in the cases that follow.

≡ *Shields v. Zuccarini*
≡ *United States Court of Appeals for the Third Circuit*
≡ *254 F.3d 476 (3d Cir. 2001)*

ALDISERT, Circuit Judge.

John Zuccarini appeals from the district court's grant of summary judgment and award of statutory damages and attorneys' fees in favor of Joseph Shields under the new Anticybersquatting Consumer Protection Act ("ACPA" or "Act"). In this case of first impression in this court interpreting the ACPA, we must decide whether the district court erred in determining that registering domain names that are intentional misspellings of distinctive or famous names constitutes unlawful conduct under the Act. We must decide also whether the district court abused its discretion by assessing statutory damages of $10,000 per domain name. Finally, we must decide whether the court erred in awarding attorneys' fees in favor of Shields based on its determination that this case qualified as an "exceptional" case under the ACPA. We affirm the judgment of the district court. . . .

I.

Shields, a graphic artist from Alto, Michigan, creates, exhibits and markets cartoons under the names "Joe Cartoon" and "The Joe Cartoon Co." His creations include the popular "Frog Blender," "Micro-Gerbil" and "Live and Let Dive" animations. Shields licenses his cartoons to others for display on T-shirts, coffee mugs and other items, many of which are sold at gift stores across the country. He has marketed his cartoons under the "Joe Cartoon" label for the past fifteen years.

On June 12, 1997, Shields registered the domain name joecartoon.com, and he has operated it as a web site ever since. Visitors to the site can download his animations and purchase Joe Cartoon merchandise. Since April 1998, when it won "shock site of the day" from Macromedia, Joe Cartoon's web traffic has increased exponentially, now averaging over 700,000 visits per month.

In November 1999, Zuccarini, an Andalusia, Pennsylvania "wholesaler" of Internet domain names, registered five world wide web variations on Shields's site: joescartoon.com, joecarton.com, joescartons.com, joescartoons.com and cartoon-joe.com. Zuccarini's sites featured advertisements for other sites and for credit card companies. Visitors were trapped or "mousetrapped" in the sites, which, in the jargon of the computer world, means that they were unable to exit without clicking on a succession of advertisements. Zuccarini received between ten and twenty-five cents from the advertisers for every click.

In December 1999, Shields sent "cease and desist" letters to Zuccarini regarding the infringing domain names. Zuccarini did not respond to the letters. Immediately after Shields filed this suit, Zuccarini changed the five sites to "political protest" pages and posted the following message on them:

> This is a page of POLITICAL PROTEST
> —Against the web site joecartoon.com—
> joecartoon.com is a web site that depicts the mutilation and killing of animals in a shockwave based cartoon format—many children are inticed [*sic*] to the web site, not knowing what is really there and then encouraged to join in the mutilation and killing through use of the shockwave cartoon presented to them.
> —Against the domain name policys [*sic*] of ICANN—
> —Against the Cyberpiracy Consumer Protection Act—
> As the owner of this domain name, I am being sued by joecartoon.com for $100,000 so he can use this domain to direct more kids to a web site that not only desensitizes children to killing animals, but makes it seem like great fun and games.
> I will under no circumstances hand this domain name over to him so he can do that.
> I hope that ICANN and Network Solutions will not assist him to attaining this goal.
> —Thank You—

Shields v. Zuccarini, 89 F. Supp.2d 634, 635-636 (E.D. Pa. 2000).

Shields's Complaint invoked the ACPA . . .

On March 22, 2000, the court entered a preliminary injunction in favor of Shields, which required Zuccarini to transfer the infringing domain names to Shields and to refrain from "using or abetting the use of" the infringing domain names or any other domain names substantially similar to Shields's marks. . . .

On July 18, 2000, the district court entered an Order and Judgment awarding statutory damages in the amount of $10,000 for each infringing domain name and attorneys' fees and costs in the amount of $39,109.46. . . .

III.

On November 29, 1999, the ACPA became law, making it illegal for a person to register or to use with the "bad faith" intent to profit from an Internet domain name that is "identical or confusingly similar" to the distinctive or famous trademark or Internet domain name of another person or company. See 15 U.S.C. §1125(d) (Supp. 2000). The Act was intended to prevent "cybersquatting," an expression that has come to mean the bad faith, abusive registration and use of the distinctive trademarks of others as Internet domain names, with the intent to profit from the goodwill associated with those trademarks. See S.Rep. No. 106-140 (1999), 1999 WL 594571, at *11-18. Under the ACPA, successful plaintiffs may recover statutory damages in an amount to be assessed by the district court in its discretion, from $1,000 to $100,000 per domain name. See 15 U.S.C. §1117(d) (Supp. 2000). In addition, successful plaintiffs may recover attorneys' fees in "exceptional" cases. See *id.* at §1117(a). . . .

A.

To succeed on his ACPA claim, Shields was required to prove that (1) "Joe Cartoon" is a distinctive or famous mark entitled to protection; (2) Zuccarini's domain names are "identical or confusingly similar to" Shields's mark; and (3) Zuccarini registered the domain names with the bad faith intent to profit from them. See 15 U.S.C. §1125(d)(1)(A); cf. Sporty's Farm L.L.C. v. Sportsman's Market Inc., 202 F.3d 489, 497-499 (2d Cir. 2000).[3]

1.

Under §1125(d)(1)(A)(ii)(I) and (II), the district court first had to determine if "Joe Cartoon" is a "distinctive" or "famous" mark and, therefore, is entitled to protection under the Act. The following factors may be considered when making this inquiry:

> (A) the degree of inherent or acquired distinctiveness of the mark; (B) the duration and extent of use of the mark in connection with the goods or services with which the mark is used; (C) the duration and extent of advertising and publicity of the mark; (D) the geographical extent of the trading area in which the mark is used; (E) the channels of trade for the goods or services with which the mark is used; (F) the degree of recognition of the mark in the trading areas and channels of trade used by the marks' owner and the person against whom the injunction is sought; (G) the nature and extent of use of the same or similar marks by third parties.

15 U.S.C. §1125(c)(1).

Shields runs the only "Joe Cartoon" operation in the nation and has done so for the past fifteen years. This suggests both the inherent and acquired distinctiveness of the "Joe Cartoon" name. In addition to using the "Joe Cartoon" name for fifteen years, Shields has used the domain name joecartoon.com as a web site since June 1997 to display his animations and sell products featuring his drawings. The longevity of his use suggests that "Joe Cartoon" has acquired some fame in the marketplace. The New York Times ran a page one story that quoted Shields and cited Joe Cartoon. *See* Andrew Pollack, Show Business Embraces the Web, But Cautiously, N.Y. Times, Nov. 9, 1999, at A1.

Joe Cartoon T-shirts have been sold across the country since at least the early 1990s, and its products appear on the web site of at least one nationally known retail chain, Spencer Gifts. Shields has advertised in an online humor magazine with a circulation of about 1.4 million. The Joe Cartoon web site receives in excess of

---

3. Section 1125(d)(1)(A) of the Act provides in relevant part:

A person shall be liable in a civil action by the owner of a mark . . . if, without regard to the goods or services of the parties, that person

(i) has a bad faith intent to profit from that mark, including a personal name which is protected as a mark under this section; and

(ii) registers, traffics in, or uses a domain name that—

(I) in the case of a mark that is distinctive at the time of registration of the domain name, is identical or confusingly similar to that mark;

(II) in the case of a famous mark that is famous at the time of registration of the domain name, is identical or confusingly similar to or dilutive of that mark.

700,000 visits per month, bringing it wide publicity. According to Shields, word-of-mouth also generates considerable interest in the Joe Cartoon site. Shields trades nationwide in both real and virtual markets. The web site gives Joe Cartoon a global reach. Shields's cartoons and merchandise are marketed on the Internet, in gift shops and at tourist venues. The Joe Cartoon mark has won a huge following because of the work of Shields. In light of the above, we conclude that "Joe Cartoon" is distinctive, and, with 700,000 hits a month, the web site "joecartoon. com" qualifies as being famous. Therefore, the trademark and domain name are protected under the ACPA.

2.

Under the Act, the next inquiry is whether Zuccarini's domain names are "identical or confusingly similar" to Shields's mark. The domain names—joescartoon.com, joecarton.com, joescartons.com, joescartoons.com and cartoonjoe.com —closely resemble "joecartoon.com," with a few additional or deleted letters, or, in the last domain name, by rearranging the order of the words. To divert Internet traffic to his sites, Zuccarini admits that he registers domain names, including the five at issue here, because they are likely misspellings of famous marks or personal names.[4] The strong similarity between these domain names and joecartoon.com persuades us that they are "confusingly similar." Shields also produced evidence of Internet users who were actually confused by Zuccarini's sites. See, e.g., Pltf's Exh. 22, at [4] (copy of an email stating, "I tried to look up you[r] website yesterday afternoon and a protest page came up. Will I have trouble entering the site at times because of this?").

On appeal, Zuccarini argues that registering domain names that are intentional misspellings of distinctive or famous names (or "typosquatting," his term for this kind of conduct) is not actionable under the ACPA. Zuccarini contends that the Act is intended to prevent "cybersquatting," which he defines as registering someone's famous name and trying to sell the domain name to them or registering it to prevent the famous person from using it themselves. This argument ignores the plain language of the statute and its stated purpose as discussed in the legislative history.

The statute covers the registration of domain names that are "identical" to distinctive or famous marks, but it also covers domain names that are "confusingly similar" to distinctive or famous marks. See 15 U.S.C. §1125(d)(1)(A)(ii)(I), (II). A reasonable interpretation of conduct covered by the phrase "confusingly similar" is the intentional registration of domain names that are misspellings of distinctive or famous names, causing an Internet user who makes a slight spelling or typing error to reach an unintended site. The ACPA's legislative history contemplates such situations:

> [C]ybersquatters often register well-known marks to prey on consumer confusion by misusing the domain name to divert customers from the mark owner's site to the cybersquatter's own site, many of which are pornography sites that derive advertising

---

4. Zuccarini testified that he was amazed to learn that "people mistype [domain names] as often as they do," and thus variants on likely search names would result in many unintended visitors to his sites. *Shields*, 89 F. Supp.2d at 640.

revenue based on the number of visits, or "hits," the site receives. For example, the Committee was informed of a parent whose child *mistakenly typed in the domain name for 'dosney.com,' expecting to access the family-oriented content of the Walt Disney home page, only to end up staring at a screen of hardcore pornography because a cybersquatter had registered that domain name in anticipation that consumers would make that exact mistake.*

S. Rep. No. 106-140 (1999), 1999 WL 594571, at *15 (emphasis added).

Although Zuccarini's sites did not involve pornography, his intent was the same as that mentioned in the legislative history above—to register a domain name in anticipation that consumers would make a mistake, thereby increasing the number of hits his site would receive, and, consequently, the number of advertising dollars he would gain. We conclude that Zuccarini's conduct here is a classic example of a specific practice the ACPA was designed to prohibit. The district court properly found that the domain names he registered were "confusingly similar."

3.

The final inquiry under the ACPA is whether Zuccarini acted with a bad faith intent to profit from Shields's distinctive and famous mark or whether his conduct falls under the safe harbor provision of the Act. Section 1125(d)(1)(B)(i) provides a non-exhaustive list of nine factors for us to consider when making this determination:

(I) the trademark or other intellectual property rights of the person, if any, in the domain name; (II) the extent to which the domain name consists of the legal name of the person or a name that is otherwise commonly used to identify that person; (III) the person's prior use, if any, of the domain name in connection with the bona fide offering of any goods or services; (IV) the person's bona fide noncommercial or fair use of the mark in a site accessible under the domain name; (V) the person's intent to divert consumers from the mark owner's online location to a site accessible under the domain name that could harm the goodwill represented by the mark, either for commercial gain or with the intent to tarnish or disparage the mark, by creating a likelihood of confusion as to the source, sponsorship, affiliation, or endorsement of the site; (VI) the person's offer to transfer, sell, or otherwise assign the domain name to the mark owner or any third party for financial gain without having used, or having an intent to use, the domain name in the bona fide offering of any goods or services, or the person's prior conduct indicating a pattern of such conduct; (VII) the person's provision of material and misleading false contact information when applying for the registration of the domain name, the person's intentional failure to maintain accurate contact information, or the person's prior conduct indicating a pattern of such conduct; (VIII) the person's registration or acquisition of multiple domain names which the person knows are identical or confusingly similar to marks of others that are distinctive at the time of registration of such domain names, or dilutive of famous marks of others that are famous at the time of registration of such domain names, without regard to the goods or services of the parties; and (IX) the extent to which the mark incorporated in the person's domain name registration is or is not distinctive and famous within the meaning of subsection (c)(1) of this section.

Zuccarini's conduct satisfies a number of these factors. Zuccarini has never used the infringing domain names as trademarks or service marks; thus, he has no intellectual property rights in these domain names. See *id*. at (B)(i)(I). The domain names do not contain any variation of the legal name of Zuccarini, nor any other name commonly used to identify him. See *id*. at (B)(i)(II). Zuccarini has never used the infringing domain names in connection with the bona fide offering of goods or services. See *id*. at (B)(i)(III). He does not use these domain names for a noncommercial or "fair use" purpose. See *id*. at (B)(i)(IV). He deliberately maintains these domain names to divert consumers from Shields's web site. In so doing, he harms the goodwill associated with the mark. He does this either for commercial gain, or with the intent to tarnish or disparage Shields's mark by creating a likelihood of confusion. See *id*. at (B)(i)(V). He has knowingly registered thousands of Internet domain names that are identical to, or confusingly similar to, the distinctive marks of others, without the permission of the mark holders to do so. See *id*. at (B)(i)(VIII). We have already established that Shields's mark is distinctive and famous. See *id*. at (B)(i)(IX).

Zuccarini argues that his web sites were protected by the First Amendment because he was using them as self-described "protest pages." Therefore, he contends, his use falls under the safe harbor provision of §1125(d)(1)(B)(ii), which states that "[b]ad faith intent . . . shall not be found in any case in which the court determines that the person believed and had reasonable grounds to believe that the use of the domain name was a fair use or otherwise lawful." The district court rejected this argument based on its conclusion that Zuccarini's claim of good faith and fair use was a "spurious explanation cooked up purely for this suit." *Shields*, 89 F. Supp.2d at 640. We agree.

Zuccarini used his "Joe Cartoon" web sites for purely commercial purposes before Shields filed this action. Zuccarini was on notice that his use of the domain names was considered unlawful when he received the cease and desist letters from Shields in December 1999. Zuccarini continued to use the infringing domain names for commercial purposes until Shields filed this lawsuit. Zuccarini testified that he put up the protest pages at 3:00 A.M. on February 1, 2000, just hours after being served with Shields's Complaint. Thus, by his own admission, Zuccarini submits that his alleged "fair use" of the offending domain names for "political protest" began only after Shields brought this action alleging a violation of the ACPA. We are aware of no authority providing that a defendant's "fair use" of a distinctive or famous mark only after the filing of a complaint alleging infringement can absolve that defendant of liability for his earlier unlawful activities. Indeed, were there such authority we think it would be contrary to the orderly enforcement of the trademark and copyright laws.

We conclude that the district court properly rejected Zuccarini's argument that his web sites were protected under the safe harbor provision. There was sufficient evidence for the district court to find that Zuccarini acted with a bad faith intent to profit when he registered and used the five domain names at issue here. . . .

IV.

The Act provides for statutory damages for a violation of §1125(d)(1) "in the amount of not less than $1,000 and not more than $100,000 per domain name, as the court considers just." 15 U.S.C. §1117(d). Zuccarini argues that §1117(d) does not apply to him because he registered the offending domain names before the ACPA became law. The district court held that Zuccarini's continued use of the domain names after November 29, 1999 subjects him to the statute's proscriptions and remedies. We agree with the teachings of Virtual Works, Inc. v. Volkswagen of America, Inc., 238 F.3d 264, 268 (4th Cir. 2001) ("A person who unlawfully registers, traffics in, or uses a domain name after the ACPA's date of enactment, November 29, 1999, can be liable for monetary damages . . . .") (emphasis added); and E. & J. Gallo Winery v. Spider Webs Ltd., 129 F. Supp.2d 1033, 1047-1048 (S.D.Tex. 2001) (holding that defendant who registered domain name in bad faith could be held liable for statutory damages even though registration was prior to enactment of the ACPA when defendant continued to use web site after the enactment of the Act).

In the alternative, Zuccarini argues that he only used the web site for sixty days after the passage of the ACPA and prior to this lawsuit being filed. He implies that, because he only used the web site for a short period of time, the district court's assessment of statutory damages was punitive in nature. Under the statute, the court has the discretion to award statutory damages that it "considers just" within a range from $1,000 to $100,000 per infringing domain name. See 15 U.S.C. §1117(d). There is nothing in the statute that requires that the court consider the duration of the infringement when calculating statutory damages. We conclude that the district court properly exercised its discretion in awarding $10,000 for each infringing domain name. . . .

The judgment and the award of statutory damages and attorneys' fees will be affirmed.

≡ *People for the Ethical Treatment of Animals v. Doughney*
United States Court of Appeals for the Fourth Circuit
263 F.3d 359 (4th Cir. 2001)

GREGORY, Circuit Judge:

[The facts of this case are reprinted in section a, above.]

B. Anticybersquatting Consumer Protection Act

The district court found Doughney liable under the Anticybersquatting Consumer Protection Act ("ACPA"), 15 U.S.C. §1125(d)(1)(A). To establish an ACPA violation, PETA was required to (1) prove that Doughney had a bad faith intent to profit from using the peta.org domain name, and (2) that the peta.org domain name is identical or confusingly similar to, or dilutive of, the distinctive and famous PETA Mark. 15 U.S.C. §1125(d)(1)(A).

Doughney makes several arguments relating to the district court's ACPA holding: (1) that PETA did not plead an ACPA claim, but raised it for the first time in its motion for summary judgment; (2) that the ACPA, which became effective in 1999, cannot be applied retroactively to events that occurred in 1995 and 1996;

(3) that Doughney did not seek to financially profit from his use of PETA's Mark; and (4) that Doughney acted in good faith.

None of Doughney's arguments are availing . . . we reject Doughney's first contention.

Doughney's second argument—that the ACPA may not be applied retroactively—also is unavailing. The ACPA expressly states that it "shall apply to all domain names registered before, on, or after the date of the enactment of this Act[.]" Pub.L. No. 106-113, §3010, 113 Stat. 1536. See also Sporty's Farm L.L.C. v. Sportsman's Market, Inc., 202 F.3d 489, 496 (2d Cir. 2000) (same). Moreover, while the ACPA precludes the imposition of *damages* in cases in which domain names were registered, trafficked, or used before its enactment, Pub.L. No. 106-113, §3010, 113 Stat. 1536 ("damages under subsection (a) or (d) of section 35 of the Trademark Act of 1946 (15 U.S.C. 1117), . . . shall not be available with respect to the registration, trafficking, or use of a domain name that occurs before the date of the enactment of this Act"), it does not preclude the imposition of *equitable remedies*. See also Virtual Works, Inc. v. Volkswagen of America, Inc., 238 F.3d 264, 268 (4th Cir. 2001). Here, the district court did not award PETA damages (nor did PETA request damages), but ordered Doughney to relinquish the domain name, transfer its registration to PETA, and limit his use of domain names to those that do not use PETA's Mark. *Doughney,* 113 F. Supp.2d at 922. Thus, the district court properly applied the ACPA to this case.

Doughney's third argument—that he did not seek to financially profit from registering a domain name using PETA's Mark—also offers him no relief. It is undisputed that Doughney made statements to the press and on his website recommending that PETA attempt to "settle" with him and "make him an offer." The undisputed evidence belies Doughney's argument.

Doughney's fourth argument—that he did not act in bad faith—also is unavailing. [The court recited the statutory factors listed in *Shields.*] In addition to listing these nine factors, the ACPA contains a safe harbor provision stating that bad faith intent "shall not be found in any case in which the court determines that the person believed and had reasonable grounds to believe that the use of the domain name was fair use or otherwise lawful." 15 U.S.C. §1225(d)(1)(B)(ii).

The district court reviewed the factors listed in the statute and properly concluded that Doughney (I) had no intellectual property right in peta.org; (II) peta.org is not Doughney's name or a name otherwise used to identify Doughney; (III) Doughney had no prior use of peta.org in connection with the bona fide offering of any goods or services; (IV) Doughney used the PETA Mark in a commercial manner; (V) Doughney "clearly intended to confuse, mislead and divert internet users into accessing his web site which contained information antithetical and therefore harmful to the goodwill represented by the PETA Mark"; (VI) Doughney made statements on his web site and in the press recommending that PETA attempt to "settle" with him and "make him an offer"; (VII) Doughney made false statements when registering the domain name; and (VIII) Doughney registered other domain names that are identical or similar to the marks or names of other famous people and organizations. *People for the Ethical Treatment of Animals,* 113 F. Supp.2d at 920.

Doughney claims that the district court's later ruling denying PETA's motion for attorney fees triggers application of the ACPA's safe harbor provision. In that ruling, the district court stated that

Doughney registered the domain name because he thought that he had a legitimate First Amendment right to express himself this way. The Court must consider Doughney's state of mind at the time he took the actions in question. Doughney thought he was within his First Amendment rights to create a parody of the plaintiff's organization.

People for the Ethical Treatment of Animals, Inc. v. Doughney, Civil Action No. 99-1336-A, Order at 4 (E.D.Va. Aug. 31, 2000). With its attorney's fee ruling, the district court did not find that Doughney "had reasonable grounds to believe" that his use of PETA's Mark was lawful. It held only that Doughney *thought it* to be lawful.

Moreover, a defendant "who acts even partially in bad faith in registering a domain name is not, as a matter of law, entitled to benefit from [the ACPA's] safe harbor provision." *Virtual Works, Inc.*, 238 F.3d at 270. Doughney knowingly provided false information to NSI upon registering the domain name, knew he was registering a domain name identical to PETA's Mark, and clearly intended to confuse Internet users into accessing his website, instead of PETA's official website. Considering the evidence of Doughney's bad faith, the safe harbor provision can provide him no relief.

IV.

For the foregoing reasons, the judgment of the district court is affirmed.

COMMENTS AND QUESTIONS

1. Does the ACPA do away with the requirement of proving infringement or dilution? The statute applies only to domain names that are confusingly similar to ordinary trademarks, or that are likely to dilute a famous trademark. This is because the trademark owner must demonstrate that they are entitled to control the domain name in question. But the infringement and dilution inquiries under the ACPA focus on the domain name itself, not how it is used. Does the fact that the ACPA imposes this requirement limit its effectiveness?

2. Is it fair to apply the ACPA retroactively as *Shields* does, to anyone who registered a domain name before the effective date of the act but who continues to use the name after 1999? What is the point of making injunctive relief retroactive and damages prospective if continued use of an existing domain name can justify a "prospective" claim for damages?

3. What constitutes a legitimate interest in a domain name? Consider the following possible uses:

- The defendant has its own trademark that corresponds to the domain name. Identical trademarks often coexist in different industries. Consider Delta, a well-known trademark for an airline, but also for other companies that provide faucets, power tools, dental insurance, and even telecommunications. If more than one company has a legitimate claim to a trademark, any of those companies can register the domain name. The ACPA does not require that the domain name be assigned to the "best" or largest trademark owner. Nonetheless, some courts have ruled for plaintiffs in cases in which they apparently concluded that a defendant's bad faith outweighed its legitimate rights in the name. For example, in Virtual Works, Inc. v. Volkswagen of America, 238 F.3d 264 (4th Cir. 2001), the court found Virtual Works (a legitimate trademark owner in its own right) to have violated the ACPA by registering vw.net. It concluded that Virtual's knowledge of likely confusion with Volkswagen's mark, and its discussion of the possibility of selling the domain name to Volkswagen, meant that it did not have a legitimate interest in the name despite its corporate name. Why does bad faith matter under the statute if the defendant is in fact a legitimate trademark owner?

- The defendant is a legal reseller of the plaintiff's product. A number of independent businesses sell trademarked products. They may be retailers who sell consumer products, independent service organizations who service or resell used cars, or the like. Can a company that services Porsches register "porsche-service.com"? See General Motors v. E-Publications, Inc., 2001 WL 1798648 (E.D. Mich. 2001) (legitimate parts seller can't refer to "gm" in a domain name); Toma's LLC v. Florida Hi Performance, AF 00968 (eResolution Sept. 10, 2001) (collecting decisions on both sides of the issue, and ruling that advertising lawful resale is a legitimate use of a domain name).

- The defendant wants to criticize or make fun of the plaintiff. A number of cybersquatting cases involve suits against disaffected customers who set up criticism sites. For example, it is relatively common for an irate consumer to register [company name]sucks.com. It seems ludicrous to think that consumers viewing the site would be confused into thinking that it was owned or sponsored by the company. Nonetheless, while some cases have held that "sucks" sites are noninfringing, other decisions have granted the trademark owner the right to prevent the registration of such sites. Compare Ohio Art Co. v. Watts, No. 98 CV 7338, slip op. at 4 (N.D. Ohio June 23, 1998); BellSouth Corp. v. Internet Classified of Ohio, 1997 WL 33107251, No. 1:96-CV-0769-CC, slip op. at 29-30 (N.D. Ga. Nov. 12, 1997) (both finding infringement from the use of a "sucks" domain name) with Bally Total Fitness v. Faber, 29 F. Supp.2d 1161 (C.D. Cal. 1998) (Web page that used "ballysucks" in the URL was not dilution). Cf. Other defendants use the plaintiff's trademark in order to make fun of it. Consider the *PETA* case, above.

Should a bona fide desire to criticize a trademark owner be a legitimate reason to register a domain name? Should it matter whether the name consists merely of the trademark itself, or whether it contains an appendage like "sucks.com" that makes it unlikely anyone could confuse the site with the official trademark owner's site? If trademark owners can prevent the use of their mark in criticism, how can anyone criticize or make fun of the mark or its owner?

Some claims of legitimate interest are clearly pretextual. For example, the registrant of oxforduniversity.com attempted to demonstrate a legitimate interest in the mark by changing his name to Oxford University. It didn't work. See University of Oxford v. Seagle, No. D2001-7046 (WIPO Aug. 14, 2001).

4. If a domain name is confusingly similar to a trademark, and the registrant has no legitimate interest in using the name, shouldn't that be enough? Why require proof that the defendant registered the domain name in bad faith? The answer seems to be that the ACPA is not intended to allocate all domain names to the

proper owner. Rather, it is designed to single out a smaller class of cases in which the defendant's registration is clearly problematic.

How should a court decide whether a defendant has acted in bad faith? The statute provides a number of factors for the court to consider. Those factors are based on the characteristics of traditional "serial cybersquatters," many of whom have registered hundreds of different trademarks as domain names. Congress concluded that the registration of many different names, the use of false contact information, and demands for payment from trademark owners were all evidence of classic cybersquatting of the sort that the act was intended to prevent.

Was Doughney acting in bad faith? Suppose that he had come to you in 1998, before the ACPA was even adopted, to ask whether it was legal to register peta.org in order to parody PETA. Would you have told him he had a legitimate argument?

5. A variant on cybersquatting is "typosquatting." Typosquatters register common misspellings or variants on trademarked terms, hoping to draw consumers who type the wrong domain name into the URL. Should typosquatting be treated just like any other form of cybersquatting, because typosquatters can divert consumers away from their intended destination? Or is typosquatting different because the typosquatter is not creating confusion, but rather merely capitalizing on preexisting confusion? Courts have generally treated typosquatters just as they have cybersquatters. *Shields* is an obvious example.

6. The ACPA is designed to protect trademarks against cybersquatters. But cybersquatters have also registered domain names that correspond to terms other than trademarks. In particular, cybersquatters have registered the names of various celebrities, such as Julia Roberts. Does the ACPA protect celebrities, just as it does trademark owners? Generally speaking, the answer is no. Personal names are generally not trademarks, and so not entitled to protection. There are exceptions, however—some celebrities, like O. J. Simpson, have registered their names as trademarks, and they are entitled to the same protection as any corporate trademark owner under the statute. 15 U.S.C. §1125(d)(1)(A). And some Uniform Dispute Resolution Procedure (UDRP; see *infra* Section c) decisions have ordered the transfer of personal names, despite the absence of any authorization to do so in the UDRP. See Roberts v. Boyd, No. D2000-0210 (WIPO May 29, 2000) (ordering transfer of juliaroberts.com). But see Turner v. Fahmi, No. D2002-0251 (WIPO July 4, 2002) (refusing to transfer tedturner.com); Springsteen v. Burgar, No. D2000-1532 (WIPO Jan. 25, 2001) (refusing to transfer brucespringsteen.com) .

7. Cybersquatting is an international phenomenon, and one of the problems trademark owners face is how to find cybersquatters in order to sue them. The ACPA includes two ways for plaintiffs to get jurisdiction over cybersquatters. First, a trademark owner who finds a cybersquatter in the United States can sue him in any district with which the cybersquatter has minimum contacts. Second, the ACPA provides that if a trademark owner cannot find the cybersquatter, it can obtain in rem jurisdiction in the jurisdiction where the domain name "resides" by publishing legal notice of the suit and then filing suit "against" the domain name itself. 15 U.S.C. §1125(d)(2).

In rem jurisdiction has traditionally been used against real property, which of course doesn't move. But a number of courts have held that domain names themselves aren't property. See, e.g., Network Solutions, Inc. v. Umbro Int'l, 529 S.E.2d 80 (Va. 2000). Is proceeding in rem against an intangible thing like a domain name consistent with due process? Or is it fundamentally unfair to the owner of the domain name, who is likely to receive no notice of the suit and be unable to defend the domain name? See Harrod's Ltd. v. Sixty Internet Domain Names, 302 F.3d 214 (4th Cir. 2002); Porsche Cars North America v. Porsche.net, 302 F.3d 248 (4th Cir. 2002) (both upholding the constitutionality of the ACPA in rem provisions on the basis that domain names are property).

8. Because the ACPA—like other trademark doctrines—is designed to protect trademark owners, it does not create rights in generic terms. Nonetheless, generic domain names were very popular at the end of the twentieth century, and—because a domain name is necessarily exclusive in the sense that an ordinary trademark isn't—names like pets.com and toys.com gained widespread recognition. Some courts have given protection to generic domain names on a theory of unfair competition. Cf. E-Cards v. King, No. C-99-3726 SC (N.D. Cal. Dec. 13, 1999) (denying preliminary injunction to E-Cards in suit against ecards.com; the plaintiff later won a jury verdict at trial). Interestingly, a German court has held that the very act of registering a generic domain name constitutes unfair competition, on the theory that the name will give the registrant an unfair advantage over those who cannot use the name.

c. The Uniform Dispute Resolution Process

Congress and the courts were not the only ones concerned with cybersquatting. In the latter half of the 1990s, Network Solutions Inc., the company that registered domain names in the global top-level domains (gTLDs), faced a series of lawsuits by trademark owners that sought to hold NSI liable for permitting cybersquatters to register their trademarks as domain names. To solve this problem, NSI drafted a series of dispute resolution policies to help it determine when to turn a domain name over to a trademark owner or to put the name "on hold." NSI's policies have generally provided that domain name registrants agreed to arbitrate disputes with NSI. They have not, however, mandated arbitration between trademark owners and domain name registrants.

When the Internet Corporation for Assigned Names and Numbers (ICANN) was formed in 1999, it sought to deal with the problem of cybersquatting in a comprehensive way outside the judicial system. ICANN established a compulsory private dispute resolution process for dealing with cases of cybersquatting and required all Internet registrars to require their customers to subscribe to the process. Under this process, known as the Uniform Dispute Resolution Procedure (UDRP), a trademark owner can file a complaint online with an approved dispute resolution provider for a small fee. The domain name owner is notified and has a short time to file a responsive pleading. Then the dispute panelist or panelists rule on the case. Unlike arbitration or other forms of private dispute resolution, there is no evidence, no oral presentation, and very little in the way of due process. However, the panelist's powers are limited to deciding whether or not to transfer the domain name in question to the complainant. If the loser objects to the decision, they have ten days to file suit in court challenging the result.

The UDRP is international in scope. The substantive rules governing UDRP cases do not rely expressly on any nation's trademark law. Rather, they are designed to cover only true cases of cybersquatting, leaving doubtful cases for resolution by the courts. The standard for proving cybersquatting under the UDRP is quite similar to the standard under the ACPA:

This Paragraph sets forth the type of disputes for which you are required to submit to a mandatory administrative proceeding. These proceedings will be conducted before one of the administrative-dispute-resolution service providers listed at www.icann.org/udrp/approved-providers.htm (each, a "Provider").

a. Applicable Disputes. You are required to submit to a mandatory administrative proceeding in the event that a third party (a "complainant") asserts to the applicable Provider, in compliance with the Rules of Procedure, that

(i) your domain name is identical or confusingly similar to a trademark or service mark in which the complainant has rights; and

(ii) you have no rights or legitimate interests in respect of the domain name; and

(iii) your domain name has been registered and is being used in bad faith.

In the administrative proceeding, the complainant must prove that each of these three elements are present.

b. Evidence of Registration and Use in Bad Faith. For the purposes of Paragraph 4(a)(iii), the following circumstances, in particular but without limitation, if found by the Panel to be present, shall be evidence of the registration and use of a domain name in bad faith:

(i) circumstances indicating that you have registered or you have acquired the domain name primarily for the purpose of selling, renting, or otherwise transferring the domain name registration to the complainant who is the owner of the trademark or service mark or to a competitor of that complainant, for valuable consideration in excess of your documented out-of-pocket costs directly related to the domain name; or

(ii) you have registered the domain name in order to prevent the owner of the trademark or service mark from reflecting the mark in a corresponding domain name, provided that you have engaged in a pattern of such conduct; or

(iii) you have registered the domain name primarily for the purpose of disrupting the business of a competitor; or

(iv) by using the domain name, you have intentionally attempted to attract, for commercial gain, Internet users to your web site or other on-line location, by creating a likelihood of confusion with the complainant's mark as to the source, sponsorship, affiliation, or endorsement of your web site or location or of a product or service on your web site or location.

c. How to Demonstrate Your Rights to and Legitimate Interests in the Domain Name in Responding to a Complaint. When you receive a complaint, you should refer to Paragraph 5 of the Rules of Procedure in determining how your response should be prepared. Any of the following circumstances, in particular but without limitation, if found by the Panel to be proved based on its evaluation of all evidence presented, shall demonstrate your rights or legitimate interests to the domain name for purposes of Paragraph 4(a)(ii):

(i) before any notice to you of the dispute, your use of, or demonstrable preparations to use, the domain name or a name corresponding to the domain name in connection with a bona fide offering of goods or services; or

(ii) you (as an individual, business, or other organization) have been commonly known by the domain name, even if you have acquired no trademark or service mark rights; or

(iii) you are making a legitimate noncommercial or fair use of the domain name, without intent for commercial gain to misleadingly divert consumers or to tarnish the trademark or service mark at issue.

The fast and cheap nature of the UDRP—and arguably the pro-trademark slant of its decisions—have attracted hordes of trademark owners. The UDRP went into effect at the end of 1999, around the same time as the ACPA. But while the ACPA had produced just over 50 reported decisions by the middle of 2002, there were UDRP decisions in cases involving over 7000 domain names. The overwhelming majority of those panel decisions (around 80 percent) ruled for the trademark owner.

Individual UDRP decisions have garnered their share of controversy. Those controversies have centered on each of the four basic elements of a UDRP claim:

- *A legitimate trademark right.* Ordinarily this is not a problem; almost all of the complainants in UDRP proceedings are trademark owners. But sometimes a complainant will not have a trademark in the name it seeks to control. When that happens, the proper result under the UDRP is to dismiss the case. But panelists and even courts have been persuaded to grant the complainant rights in words that it simply doesn't own as a trademark. For example, panelists have transferred the domain name barcelona.com to the city of Barcelona, Spain, despite the absence of a trademark in the name, Excelentisimo Ayuntamiento de Barcelona v. Barcelona.com Inc., No. D2000-0505 (WIPO Aug. 5, 2000); transferred the common French term merci.com to a company that claimed to own it as a trademark, August Storck KG v. Unimetal Sanayi ve Tic A.S., No. D2001-1125 (WIPO November 23, 2001); and transferred paint.biz to a company that claims to own a trademark in the word "paint," Valspar Sourcing, Inc. v. TIGRE, FA0204000112596 (NAF June 4, 2002). Cf. Archdiocese of St. Louis v. Internet Entertainment Group, 34 F. Supp.2d 1145 (E.D. Mo. 1999) (concluding that "Papal Visit 1999" was a famous trademark entitled to dilution protection). By contrast, other panels have refused to transfer generic terms on the ground that they were not trademarks. For example, one panel refused to transfer the munich.biz domain name on the grounds that the city did not own the exclusive right to its name. Landeshauptstadt Muenchen v Beanmills, Inc., Case No. DBIZ2002-00147 (WIPO July 1, 2002). See also X/Open Company Limited v. Expeditious Investments, Case No. D2002-0294 (WIPO 2002) (refusing to transfer unix.com; a different panel decided the opposite way in a case involving unix.net).
- *An identical or confusingly similar domain name.* Trademark owners are entitled to prevent the registration only of names that are identical to or confusingly similar to their trademarks. But some panelists have ordered the transfer of domain names that clearly fail to meet this standard. For example, a majority of the cases involving domains of the type [trademark]sucks.com have been transferred to the trademark owner (7 out of 9 at this writing), even though no rational consumer would think that Wal-Mart sponsored the domain name "walmartsucks.com". And one panelist even held that the trade-

mark "Tata," the name of a large Indian conglomerate, was infringed by the domain name "bodacioustatas.com." Tata Sons Limited v. D & V Enterprises, Case No. D2000-0479 (WIPO Aug. 18, 2000).

- *Absence of a legitimate right.* Cybersquatting under the UDRP requires proof that the domain name registrant lacks any legitimate right to use the domain name. Trademark owners cannot use the UDRP to oust other trademark owners from the use of a mark; if both have a legitimate claim to use the name in commerce, the UDRP will not step in to decide who is "best" entitled to use the mark. But other claims to legitimate use are more controversial. Several panelists have considered whether a legitimate dealer in the plaintiff's products is entitled to use the plaintiff's trademark to advertise the presence of those products. See Toma's LLC v. Florida Hi-Performance, AF 0968 (eRes Sept. 10, 2001):

> Florida appears to be using Toma's trademarked domain name to sell Toma's products. The question is whether this is a legitimate use.
>
> A number of prior panel decisions have considered whether a distributor of a trademark owner's goods who uses the trademark as its domain name has made a bona fide use of the trademark. Unfortunately, the decisions are not in agreement. Compare Kabushiki Kaisha Toshiba v. Distribution Purchasing and Logistics Corp., WIPO D2000-0464 (July 27, 2000); Hydraroll Ltd. v. Morgan Corp., NAF FA2000094108 (April 14, 2000); Mariah Boats, Inc. v. Shoreline Marina, NAF FA4000094392 (May 5, 2000) (all concluding that a distributor has no right to use the trademark of the distributed goods as a domain name) *with* Freni Brembo S.p.A. v. Webs We Weave, WIPO D2000-1717 (March 19, 2001); K&N Engineering v. Kinnor Servs., WIPO D2000-1077 (January 19, 2001); Weber-Stephen Prods. v. Armitage Hardware, WIPO D2000-0187 (May 11, 2000); Koninklijke Philips Electronics v. Cun Siang Wang, WIPO D2000-1778 (March 15, 2001); Hewlett-Packard Co. v. Napier, NAF FA3000094368 (April 28, 2000) (all concluding that a distributor *is* entitled to use the trademark of the distributed goods as a domain name). See also *Philips, supra* (noting three additional decisions on each side of the issue).
>
> It is clear as a matter of trademark law that the purchaser of bona fide goods is entitled to resell those goods, and to truthfully advertise the goods bearing the trademark. Once the goods are sold into commerce, a trademark owner's rights in those goods are exhausted. See *Philips, supra* (citing authority).[3] Were it not so, distributors could not advertise their goods, car owners could not advertise their used cars, and so on. Since Toma's has not alleged that the "Fake Bake" goods sold on Florida's Web page are counterfeit or altered in any way, Florida is free to truthfully advertise that it is selling those products by using the trademark "Fake Bake." See generally Prestonettes, Inc. v. Coty, 264 U.S. 359, 368 (1924) ("When the mark is used in a way that does not deceive the public we see no such sanctity in the word as to prevent its being used to tell the truth.").
>
> Here, though, Florida has done somewhat more than truthfully advertise the availability of bona fide "Fake Bake" products on its Web site. By using the domain name "fakebake.com," Toma's alleges that Florida has confused consumers into thinking that Toma's runs or sponsors the Web page. Toma's is particularly concerned about this because Florida also sells competing products on its page. Whether this exceeds Florida's rights as a reseller of legitimate goods is a difficult

---

3. The "gray market" importation of bona fide goods from another country presents a more contentious issue, but there is no evidence of importation here.

question under trademark law. In *Mariah Boats, supra,* the panel concluded that because Shoreline sold both Mariah's boats and other, competing boats, its use of the domain name mariahboats.net was likely to confuse consumers. By contrast, in both *Freni Brembo, supra* and *Weber-Stephens, supra,* the panels concluded that such a use was legitimate notwithstanding the fact that the respondent also sold other goods on its site. And in *Philips,* the panel concluded as follows:

> The Panel accepts that it is possible for a trader in branded goods to adver-
> tise and sell goods under the brand without using a domain name incorpo-
> rating the brand name. Nevertheless such a domain name is of considerable
> assistance to a business selling the branded goods. The Panel considers that
> a person can have a legitimate interest in using a particular domain name
> even if it is not an essential requirement for him to do so.

Whether a bona fide reseller of trademarked goods is always entitled to use a do-main name incorporating the trademark is an unsettled legal question. It depends in part on the detailed factual circumstances of the case—how the name is being used, what evidence of confusion there is, whether there is an agreement between the parties, and so on. None of that evidence has been presented to me in this case, other than Toma's allegation (unsupported by evidence) that consumers are being confused. Such a case is not appropriate for resolution under the UDRP, which was designed to deal only with a narrow class of abusive registrations by cy-bersquatters. The difficult and uncertain allocation of rights in this case should be decided by a court, not by a UDRP panel. *Accord Freni-Brembo; Weber-Stephen.* Thus, I cannot conclude that Florida's use here was necessarily illegitimate.

Compare Educational Testing Service v. TOEFL USA, Case No. D2002-0380 (WIPO July 11, 2002) (ordering transfer of toeflusa.com, a domain name owned by TOEFL USA as a trademark for services related to the TOEFL test).

As a general matter in trademark law, "nominative" or nontrademark use —the use of the plaintiff's mark to refer to the plaintiff's own products—is not infringement. But in the context of domain names, the defendant's registration of the plaintiff's mark as a domain name may be more likely to confuse con-sumers into thinking that the defendant is the actual source of the product. This depends on the nature of the name, though. A domain name like micro-soft.com might suggest to consumers that the owner is Microsoft, not just an authorized dealer. By contrast, a name like porscheservice.com is more likely to accurately convey that the owner services Porsches, not that the owner is Por-sche itself. But see Academy of Motion Picture Arts and Sciences v. Khan, FA0109000100142 (NAF Nov. 14, 2001) (ordering cancellation of the do-main name oscarbetexchange.com for an online service in which people could bet on the outcome of the Oscars). Some trademark owners have even sued "fan sites" that register domain names in order to praise their subject.

Other disputed issues of legitimate use involve noncommercial uses of a name. For instance, a personal name or nickname may be a legitimate reason to register a domain name. An infamous case in this regard involves pokey.org, in which a 12-year-old nicknamed "Pokey" was threatened with suit by the own-ers of the "Gumby and Pokey" marks. See also Strick Corp. v. Strickland, No. FA # 94801 (NAF July 3, 2000) (refusing to transfer strick.com, owned by an individual whose nickname was "Strick"). Proof of a legitimate nickname presumably provides a legitimate reason to register a domain name.[1] At the same time, nickname arguments are particularly susceptible to abuse. For example, one panelist held that the registrant of the domain oxforduniversity.com could not show a legitimate interest in the mark by changing his legal name to Oxford University. See University of Oxford v. Seagle, No. D2001-7046 (WIPO Aug. 14, 2001).

A final category of possible legitimate interests involves criticism of the trademark owner. Frustrated customers and others who want to criticize a company naturally want to post their criticisms at a domain name that includes the trademark of the company in question. Where the domain name in question is one—like walmartsucks.com—that is unlikely to confuse consumers, the defendant clearly has a legitimate interest in using the mark. The question is more difficult if the critic registers only the trademark—say, walmart.com. Consumers may well be confused, at least initially, if walmart.com isn't run by Wal-Mart. See *Doughney, supra*. But even if the use will draw customers to the site because they are confused, arguably the critic has a legitimate interest in registering the domain name in order to attract the attention of those consumers. See Northland Ins. Co. v. Blaylock, 115 F. Supp.2d 1108 (D. Minn. 2000) (registration of company's trademark as a domain name in order to criticize the company was not infringing).

- *Bad faith.* Like the ACPA, the UDRP identifies a number of factors evidentiary of bad faith. Registration of multiple names, demanding money to relinquish them, and providing false address information are all considered evidence of bad faith. Some panelists have gone farther, however, holding that a desire to criticize a trademark owner can itself be evidence of bad faith. See Reg Vardy Plc v. Wilkinson, Case No. D2001-0593 (WIPO July 3, 2001). This seems particularly perverse, given the discussion above of criticism as a legitimate reason to register a domain name. Compare Savannah College of Art & Design v. Houeix, No. CPR 0206 (CPR Feb. 19, 2002) (former employee could register scad.info in order to criticize the College).

  On the other hand, at least one panelist has held that the mere registration of domain names does not constitute bad faith, leaving open the possibility that cybersquatters who do not ask for money may be entitled to keep the domain names they have registered even if they cannot show any legitimate interest in the name. See Ingram Micro v. Ingredients Among Modern Microwaves, No. D2002-0301 (WIPO May 15, 2002). But see Telstra Corporation Limited v. Nuclear Marshmallows, Case No. D2000-0003 (WIPO Feb. 18, 2000) (finding bad faith absent any "positive action" by registrant).

UDRP decisions have been roundly criticized as unduly favorable to trademark owners. See, e.g., Michael Geist, Fair.com?: An Examination of the Allegations of Systematic Unfairness in the ICANN UDRP, 27 Brook. J. Int'l. L. 903 (2002); Elizabeth G. Thornburg, Fast, Cheap and Out of Control: Lessons From the ICANN Dispute Resolution Process, 6 J. Sm. & Emerging Bus. L. 191 (2002).

---

1. It does not necessarily provide the registrant with the right to compete. For example, someone with the last name McDonald will be prevented from opening a hamburger stand using the name "McDonald's," because of the likelihood that consumers will be confused. See E. & J. Gallo Winery v. Gallo Cattle Co., 967 F.2d 1280 (9th Cir. 1992) (brother of Ernest & Julio Gallo could not use Gallo name to sell meat, because of the possibility of confusion).

These critics focus both on the outcomes of the cases, which overwhelmingly order transfers of domain names, and on deficiencies in the process by which the cases are decided. Because only the trademark owner gets to choose which dispute resolution company will decide the case, dispute resolution providers seem to compete for the approval of trademark owners. Eresolution, the one company whose decisions were roughly evenly divided between trademark owners and registrants, went out of business because trademark owners sent their work to NAF and WIPO instead. NAF and WIPO seem to assign cases to favored panelists, rather than randomly distributing them among eligible panelists. And NAF in particular has advertised its pro-trademark decisions in an effort to drum up more business.

Other concerns center on the short deadlines and the sketchy nature of the process required. Registrants have only a short time to respond to a UDRP complaint, and if they lose have only ten days to go to court to stop the transfer of their domain name. Many registrants are not represented by counsel, and so may have difficulty understanding the process and their obligations. As a result, a large percentage of registrants fail to answer a complaint, and relatively few registrants challenge the transfer of their domain names in court.

Froomkin has proposed a series of procedural reforms to improve the UDRP. A. Michael Froomkin, ICANN's "Uniform Dispute Resolution Policy": Causes and (Partial) Cures, 67 Brook. L. Rev. 605 (2002). Among other things, Froomkin suggests procedures for removing biased arbitrators; the creation of a substantive doctrine of "reverse domain name hijacking," in which domain name owners who are subject to abusive claims could recover money; and making it easier for respondents to meet the deadlines for filing a response and selecting an arbitration panel. Others have argued that an administrative appeal process would be a good idea. And it also seems reasonable to allow registrants to respond online, as eresolution once did.

Because of the limits of the UDRP, courts to consider the issue have unanimously concluded that it is not "arbitration" subject to judicial deference under the Federal Arbitration Act. Rather, UDRP decisions are reviewed de novo in the courts. See, e.g., Sallen v. Corinthians Licenciamentos Ltd., 273 F.3d 14 (1st Cir. 2001); Parisi v. Netlearning, Inc., 139 F. Supp.2d 745 (E.D. Va. 2001).

In 2001, ICANN permitted the creation of several new gTLDs, including .biz. The creation of these new gTLDs created new opportunities for cybersquatters. To deal with this problem, ICANN created a new dispute resolution process (called STOP) that included a "sunrise" registration period. Under this process, trademark owners get a chance to register their marks in the .biz domain before the registration is opened up to other registrants. Because some registrants falsely claimed to be trademark owners in order to take advantage of the sunrise process, a number of trademark owners have filed claims under the new STOP process. While the dispute resolution process is similar to the UDRP, it is not identical—and as a result the domain name dispute resolution procedure is no longer truly uniform.

2. Other Uses of Trademarks

While domain names have captured much of the public and judicial attention in Internet trademark law, there are a number of other Internet practices that present interesting trademark questions. In this section, we explore several such issues.

a. Metatagging

Brookfield Communications, Inc. v. West Coast Entertainment Corporation
United States Court of Appeals for the Ninth Circuit
174 F.3d 1036 (9th Cir. 1999)

O'SCANNLAIN, Circuit Judge:

We must venture into cyberspace to determine whether federal trademark and unfair competition laws prohibit a video rental store chain from using an entertainment-industry information provider's trademark in the domain name of its web site and in its web site's metatags.

I

Brookfield Communications, Inc. ("Brookfield") appeals the district court's denial of its motion for a preliminary injunction prohibiting West Coast Entertainment Corporation ("West Coast") from using in commerce terms confusingly similar to Brookfield's trademark, "MovieBuff." Brookfield gathers and sells information about the entertainment industry. Founded in 1987 for the purpose of creating and marketing software and services for professionals in the entertainment industry, Brookfield initially offered software applications featuring information such as recent film submissions, industry credits, professional contacts, and future projects. These offerings targeted major Hollywood film studios, independent production companies, agents, actors, directors, and producers.

Brookfield expanded into the broader consumer market with computer software featuring a searchable database containing entertainment-industry related information marketed under the "MovieBuff" mark around December 1993. Brookfield's "MovieBuff" software now targets smaller companies and individual consumers who are not interested in purchasing Brookfield's professional level alternative, The Studio System, and includes comprehensive, searchable, entertainment-industry databases and related software applications containing information such as movie credits, box office receipts, films in development, film release schedules, entertainment news, and listings of executives, agents, actors, and directors. This "MovieBuff" software comes in three versions—(1) the MovieBuff Pro Bundle, (2) the MovieBuff Pro, and (3) MovieBuff—and is sold through various retail stores, such as Borders, Virgin Megastores, Nobody Beats the Wiz, The Writer's Computer Store, Book City, and Samuel French Bookstores.

Sometime in 1996, Brookfield attempted to register the World Wide Web ("the Web") domain name "moviebuff.com" with Network Solutions, Inc. ("Network Solutions"), but was informed that the requested domain name had already been registered by West Coast. Brookfield subsequently registered "brookfield-comm.com" in May 1996 and "moviebuffonline .com" in September 1996. Sometime in 1996 or 1997, Brookfield began using its web sites to sell its "MovieBuff" computer software and to offer an Internet-based searchable database marketed under the "MovieBuff" mark. Brookfield sells its "MovieBuff" computer software through its "brookfieldcomm.com" and "moviebuffonline.com" web sites and offers subscribers online access to the MovieBuff database itself at its "inhollywood.com" web site.

On August 19, 1997, Brookfield applied to the Patent and Trademark Office (PTO) for federal registration of "MovieBuff" as a mark to designate both goods and services. Its trademark application describes its product as "computer software providing data and information in the field of the motion picture and television industries." Its service mark application describes its service as "providing multiple-user access to an on-line network database offering data and information in the field of the motion picture and television industries." Both federal trademark registrations issued on September 29, 1998. Brookfield had previously obtained a California state trademark registration for the mark "MovieBuff" covering "computer software" in 1994.

In October 1998, Brookfield learned that West Coast—one of the nation's largest video rental store chains with over 500 stores—intended to launch a web site at "moviebuff.com" containing, inter alia, a searchable entertainment database similar to "MovieBuff." West Coast had registered "moviebuff.com" with Network Solutions on February 6, 1996 and claims that it chose the domain name because the term "Movie Buff" is part of its service mark, "The Movie Buff's Movie Store," on which a federal registration issued in 1991 covering "retail store services featuring video cassettes and video game cartridges" and "rental of video cassettes and video game cartridges." West Coast notes further that, since at least 1988, it has also used various phrases including the term "Movie Buff" to promote goods and services available at its video stores in Massachusetts, including "The Movie Buff's Gift Guide"; "The Movie Buff's Gift Store"; "Calling All Movie Buffs!"; "Good News Movie Buffs!"; "Movie Buffs, Show Your Stuff!"; "the Perfect Stocking Stuffer for the Movie Buff!"; "A Movie Buff's Top Ten"; "The Movie Buff Discovery Program"; "Movie Buff Picks"; "Movie Buff Series"; "Movie Buff Selection Program"; and "Movie Buff Film Series." . . .

In its first amended complaint filed on November 18, 1998, Brookfield alleged principally that West Coast's proposed offering of online services at "moviebuff.com" would constitute trademark infringement and unfair competition in violation of sections 32 and 43(a) of the Lanham Act, 15 U.S.C. §§1114, 1125(a). Soon thereafter, Brookfield applied ex parte for a temporary restraining order ("TRO") enjoining West Coast "[f]rom using . . . in any manner . . . the mark MOVIEBUFF, or any other term or terms likely to cause confusion therewith, including moviebuff.com, as West Coast's domain name, . . . as the name of West Coast's website service, in buried code or metatags on their home page or web pages, or in connection with the retrieval of data or information on other goods or services."

On November 27, West Coast filed an opposition brief in which it argued first that Brookfield could not prevent West Coast from using "moviebuff.com" in commerce because West Coast was the senior user. West Coast claimed that it was the first user of "MovieBuff" because it had used its federally registered trademark, "The Movie Buff's Movie Store," since 1986 in advertisements, promotions, and letterhead in connection with retail services featuring videocassettes and video game cartridges. Alternatively, West Coast claimed seniority on the basis that it had garnered common-law rights in the domain name by using "moviebuff.com" before Brookfield began offering its "MovieBuff" Internet-based searchable database on the Web. In addition to asserting seniority, West Coast contended that its planned use of "moviebuff.com" would not cause a likelihood of confusion with Brookfield's trademark "MovieBuff" and thus would not violate the Lanham Act. . . .

II . . .

Using a Web browser, such as Netscape's Navigator or Microsoft's Internet Explorer, a cyber "surfer" may navigate the Web—searching for, communicating with, and retrieving information from various web sites. See *Microsoft*, 147 F.3d at 939-40, 950. A specific web site is most easily located by using its domain name. See *Panavision*, 141 F.3d at 1327. Upon entering a domain name into the web browser, the corresponding web site will quickly appear on the computer screen. Sometimes, however, a Web surfer will not know the domain name of the site he is looking for, whereupon he has two principal options: trying to guess the domain name or seeking the assistance of an Internet "search engine."

Oftentimes, an Internet user will begin by hazarding a guess at the domain name, especially if there is an obvious domain name to try. Web users often assume, as a rule of thumb, that the domain name of a particular company will be the company name followed by ".com." See *id.;* Playboy Enterprises v. Universal Tel-A-Talk, Inc., No. 96-6961, 1998 WL 767440, at *2 (E.D.Pa. Nov.3, 1998); Cardservice Int'l, Inc. v. McGee, 950 F. Supp. 737, 741 (E.D.Va. 1997), *aff'd by*, 129 F.3d 1258 (4th Cir. 1997). For example, one looking for Kraft Foods, Inc. might try "kraftfoods.com," and indeed this web site contains information on Kraft's many food products. Sometimes, a trademark is better known than the company itself, in which case a Web surfer may assume that the domain address will be " 'trademark'.com." See *Panavision*, 141 F.3d at 1327; Beverly v. Network Solutions, Inc., No. 98-0337, 1998 WL 320829, at *1 (N.D.Cal. June 12, 1998) ("Companies attempt to make the search for their web site as easy as possible. They do so by using a corporate name, trademark or service mark as their web site address."). One interested in today's news would do well visiting "usatoday.com," which features, as one would expect, breaking stories from Gannett's USA Today. Guessing domain names, however, is not a risk-free activity. The Web surfer who assumes that " 'X'.com" will always correspond to the web site of company X or trademark X will, however, sometimes be misled. One looking for the latest information on Panavision, International, L.P., would sensibly try "panavision.com." Until recently, that Web surfer would have instead found a web site owned by Dennis Toeppen featuring photographs of the City of Pana, Illinois. . . .

A Web surfer's second option when he does not know the domain name is to utilize an Internet search engine, such as Yahoo, Altavista, or Lycos. See ACLU v. Reno, 31 F. Supp.2d 473, 484 (E.D.Pa. 1999); Washington Speakers Bureau, Inc. v. Leading Authorities, Inc., 33 F. Supp.2d 488, 499 (E.D.Va. 1999). When a keyword is entered, the search engine processes it through a self-created index of web sites to generate a (sometimes long) list relating to the entered keyword. Each search engine uses its own algorithm to arrange indexed materials in sequence, so the list of web sites that any particular set of keywords will bring up may differ depending on the search engine used. See Niton Corp. v. Radiation Monitoring Devices, Inc., 27 F. Supp.2d 102, 104 (D.Mass. 1998); Intermatic Inc. v. Toeppen, 947 F. Supp. 1227, 1231-32 (N.D.Ill. 1996); Shea v. Reno, 930 F. Supp. 916,

929 (S.D.N.Y. 1996), *aff'd*, 521 U.S. 1113, 117 S. Ct. 2501, 138 L. Ed.2d 1006 (1997). Search engines look for keywords in places such as domain names, actual text on the web page, and metatags. Metatags are HTML code intended to describe the contents of the web site. There are different types of metatags, but those of principal concern to us are the "description" and "keyword" metatags. The description metatags are intended to describe the web site; the keyword metatags, at least in theory, contain keywords relating to the contents of the web site. The more often a term appears in the metatags and in the text of the web page, the more likely it is that the web page will be "hit" in a search for that keyword and the higher on the list of "hits" the web page will appear. See *Niton*, 27 F. Supp.2d at 104.

With this basic understanding of the Internet and the Web, we may now analyze the legal issues before us. . . .

[The court concluded that Brookfield was the senior user of the mark, because West Coast's prior use of "The Movie Buff's Movie Store" was too dissimilar to "moviebuff.com" to allow it to trace priority to the use of that phrase.]

V

Establishing seniority, however, is only half the battle. Brookfield must also show that the public is likely to be somehow confused about the source or sponsorship of West Coast's "moviebuff.com" web site—and somehow to associate that site with Brookfield. [The court went on to enjoin West Coast's use of moviebuff.com after concluding that it was likely to cause confusion with Brookfield's "Movie Buff" mark.]

B

So far we have considered only West Coast's use of the domain name "moviebuff.com." Because Brookfield requested that we also preliminarily enjoin West Coast from using marks confusingly similar to "MovieBuff" in metatags and buried code, we must also decide whether West Coast can, consistently with the trademark and unfair competition laws, use "MovieBuff" or "moviebuff.com" in its HTML code.[23]

At first glance, our resolution of the infringement issues in the domain name context would appear to dictate a similar conclusion of likelihood of confusion with respect to West Coast's use of "moviebuff.com" in its metatags. Indeed, all eight likelihood of confusion factors outlined in Part V-A—with the possible exception of purchaser care, which we discuss below—apply here as they did in our analysis of domain names; we are, after all, dealing with the same marks, the same products and services, the same consumers, etc. Disposing of the issue so readily, however,

---

23. As we explained in Part II, metatags are HTML code not visible to Web users but used by search engines in determining which sites correspond to the keywords entered by a Web user. Although Brookfield never explained what it meant by "buried code," the leading trademark treatise explains that "buried code" is another term for the HTML code that is used by search engines but that is not visible to users. See 3 McCarthy, *supra*, at §25:69 n. 1. We will use the term metatags as encompassing HTML code generally.

would ignore the fact that the likelihood of confusion in the domain name context resulted largely from the associational confusion between West Coast's domain name "moviebuff.com" and Brookfield's trademark "MovieBuff." The question in the metatags context is quite different. Here, we must determine whether West Coast can use "MovieBuff" or "moviebuff.com" in the metatags of its web site at "westcoastvideo.com" or at any other domain address other than "moviebuff.com" (which we have determined that West Coast may not use).

Although entering "MovieBuff" into a search engine is likely to bring up a list including "westcoastvideo.com" if West Coast has included that term in its metatags, the resulting confusion is not as great as where West Coast uses the "moviebuff.com" domain name. First, when the user inputs "MovieBuff" into an Internet search engine, the list produced by the search engine is likely to include both West Coast's and Brookfield's web sites. Thus, in scanning such list, the Web user will often be able to find the particular web site he is seeking. Moreover, even if the Web user chooses the web site belonging to West Coast, he will see that the domain name of the web site he selected is "westcoastvideo.com." Since there is no confusion resulting from the domain address, and since West Coast's initial web page prominently displays its own name, it is difficult to say that a consumer is likely to be confused about whose site he has reached or to think that Brookfield somehow sponsors West Coast's web site.

Nevertheless, West Coast's use of "moviebuff.com" in metatags will still result in what is known as initial interest confusion. Web surfers looking for Brookfield's "MovieBuff" products who are taken by a search engine to "westcoastvideo.com" will find a database similar enough to "MovieBuff" such that a sizeable number of consumers who were originally looking for Brookfield's product will simply decide to utilize West Coast's offerings instead. Although there is no source confusion in the sense that consumers know they are patronizing West Coast rather than Brookfield, there is nevertheless initial interest confusion in the sense that, by using "moviebuff.com" or "MovieBuff" to divert people looking for "MovieBuff" to its web site, West Coast improperly benefits from the goodwill that Brookfield developed in its mark. Recently in *Dr. Seuss*, we explicitly recognized that the use of another's trademark in a manner calculated "to capture initial consumer attention, even though no actual sale is finally completed as a result of the confusion, may be still an infringement." *Dr. Seuss*, 109 F.3d at 1405 (citing Mobil Oil Corp. v. Pegasus Petroleum Corp., 818 F.2d 254, 257-58 (2d Cir. 1987)).[24]

The *Dr. Seuss* court, in recognizing that the diversion of consumers' initial interest is a form of confusion against which the Lanham Act protects, relied upon *Mobil Oil*. In that case, Mobil Oil Corporation ("Mobil") asserted a federal trademark infringement claim against Pegasus Petroleum, alleging that Pegasus Petroleum's use of "Pegasus" was likely to cause confusion with Mobil's trademark, a flying horse symbol in the form of the Greek mythological Pegasus. Mobil established that "potential purchasers would be misled into an initial interest in Pegasus Petroleum" because they thought that Pegasus Petroleum was associated with Mo-

---

24. The *Dr. Seuss* court discussed initial interest confusion within its purchaser care analysis. As a district court within our circuit recognized in a recent case involving a claim of trademark infringement via metatags usage, "[t]his case . . . is not a standard trademark case and does not lend itself to the systematic application of the eight factors." Playboy Enters. v. Welles, 7 F. Supp.2d 1098 (S.D.Cal. 1998). Because we agree that the traditional eight-factor test is not well-suited for analyzing the metatags issue, we do not attempt to fit our discussion into one of the *Sleekcraft* factors.

bil. *Id.* at 260. But these potential customers would generally learn that Pegasus Petroleum was unrelated to Mobil well before any actual sale was consummated. See *id.* Nevertheless, the Second Circuit held that "[s]uch initial confusion works a sufficient trademark injury." *Id.*

Mobil Oil relied upon its earlier opinion in Grotrian, Helfferich, Schulz, Th. Steinweg Nachf. v. Steinway & Sons, 523 F.2d 1331, 1341-42 (2d Cir. 1975). Analyzing the plaintiff's claim that the defendant, through its use of the "Grotrian-Steinweg" mark, attracted people really interested in plaintiff's "Steinway" pianos, the Second Circuit explained:

> We decline to hold, however, that actual or potential confusion at the time of purchase necessarily must be demonstrated to establish trademark infringement under the circumstances of this case.
> The issue here is not the possibility that a purchaser would buy a Grotrian-Steinweg thinking it was actually a Steinway or that Grotrian had some connection with Steinway and Sons. The harm to Steinway, rather, is the likelihood that a consumer, hearing the "Grotrian-Steinweg" name and thinking it had some connection with "Steinway," would consider it on that basis. The "Grotrian-Steinweg" name therefore would attract potential customers based on the reputation built up by Steinway in this country for many years.

Grotrian, 523 F.2d at 1342.

Both *Dr. Seuss* and the Second Circuit hold that initial interest confusion is actionable under the Lanham Act, which holdings are bolstered by the decisions of many other courts which have similarly recognized that the federal trademark and unfair competition laws do protect against this form of consumer confusion. See *Green Prods.*, 992 F. Supp. 1070, 1076 (N.D.Iowa 1997) ("In essence, ICBP is capitalizing on the strong similarity between Green Products' trademark and ICBP's domain name to lure customers onto its web page."); Securacomm Consulting, Inc. v. Securacom Inc., 984 F. Supp. 286, 298 (D.N.J. 1997) ("'Infringement can be based upon confusion that creates initial customer interest, even though no actual sale is finally completed as a result of the confusion.'") (citing 3 McCarthy §23:6), *rev'd on other grounds*, 166 F.3d 182, 186 (3d Cir. 1999) ("In this appeal, [appellant] does not challenge the district court's finding of infringement or order of injunctive relief."); Kompan A.S. v. Park Structures, Inc., 890 F. Supp. 1167, 1180 (N.D. N.Y. 1995) ("Kompan argues correctly that it can prevail by showing that confusion between the Kompan and Karavan lines and names will mistakenly lead the consumer to believe there is some connection between the two and therefore develop an interest in the Karavan line that it would not otherwise have had."); Blockbuster Entertainment Group v. Laylco, Inc., 869 F. Supp. 505, 513 (E.D.Mich. 1994) ("Because the names are so similar and the products sold are identical, some unwitting customers might enter a Video Busters store thinking it is somehow connected to Blockbuster. Those customers probably will realize shortly that Video Busters is not related to Blockbuster, but under [Ferrari S.P.A. Esercizio v. Roberts, 944 F.2d 1235 (6th Cir. 1991)] and *Grotrian* that is irrelevant."); Jordache Enters., Inc. v. Levi Strauss & Co., 841 F. Supp. 506, 514-15 (S.D.N.Y. 1993) ("Types of confusion that constitute trademark infringement include where . . . potential consumers initially are attracted to the junior user's mark by virtue of its similarity to the senior user's mark, even though these consumers are not actually confused at the time of purchase."); Sara Lee Corp. v. Kayser-Roth

Corp., No. 92-00460, 1992 WL 436279, at *24 (W.D.N.C. Dec. 1, 1992) ("That situation offers an opportunity for sale not otherwise available by enabling defendant to interest prospective customers by confusion with the plaintiff's product."); Television Enter. Network, Inc. v. Entertainment Network, Inc., 630 F. Supp. 244, 247 (D.N.J. 1986) ("Even if the confusion is cured at some intermediate point before the deal is completed, the initial confusion may be damaging and wrongful."); Koppers Co. v. Krupp-Koppers GmbH, 517 F. Supp. 836, 844 (W.D.Pa. 1981) ("[S]ecuring the initial business contact by the defendant because of an assumed association between the parties is wrongful even though the mistake is later rectified."). See also Forum Corp. of North America v. Forum, Ltd., 903 F.2d 434, 442 n. 2 (7th Cir. 1990) ("We point out that the fact that confusion as to the source of a product or service is eventually dispelled does not eliminate the trademark infringement which has already occurred."). But see Astra Pharm. Prods., Inc. v. Beckman Instruments, Inc., 718 F.2d 1201, 1206-08 (1st Cir. 1983) (suggesting that only confusion that affects "the ultimate decision of a purchaser whether to buy a particular product" is actionable); Teletech Customer Care Mgmt. (Cal.), Inc. v. Tele-Tech Co., 977 F. Supp. 1407, 1410, 1414 (C.D.Cal. 1997) (finding likelihood of initial interest confusion but concluding that such "brief confusion is not cognizable under the trademark laws").

Using another's trademark in one's metatags is much like posting a sign with another's trademark in front of one's store. Suppose West Coast's competitor (let's call it "Blockbuster") puts up a billboard on a highway reading—"West Coast Video: 2 miles ahead at Exit 7"—where West Coast is really located at Exit 8 but Blockbuster is located at Exit 7. Customers looking for West Coast's store will pull off at Exit 7 and drive around looking for it. Unable to locate West Coast, but seeing the Blockbuster store right by the highway entrance, they may simply rent there. Even consumers who prefer West Coast may find it not worth the trouble to continue searching for West Coast since there is a Blockbuster right there. Customers are not confused in the narrow sense: they are fully aware that they are purchasing from Blockbuster and they have no reason to believe that Blockbuster is related to, or in any way sponsored by, West Coast. Nevertheless, the fact that there is only initial consumer confusion does not alter the fact that Blockbuster would be misappropriating West Coast's acquired goodwill. See *Blockbuster*, 869 F. Supp. at 513 (finding trademark infringement where the defendant, a video rental store, attracted customers' initial interest by using a sign confusingly [similar] to its competitor's even though confusion would end long before the point of sale or rental); see also *Dr. Seuss*, 109 F.3d at 1405; *Mobil Oil*, 818 F.2d at 260; *Green Prods.*, 992 F. Supp. at 1076.

The few courts to consider whether the use of another's trademark in one's metatags constitutes trademark infringement have ruled in the affirmative. For example, in a case in which Playboy Enterprises, Inc. ("Playboy") sued AsiaFocus International, Inc. ("AsiaFocus") for trademark infringement resulting from Asia-Focus's use of the federally registered trademarks "Playboy" and "Playmate" in its HTML code, a district court granted judgment in Playboy's favor, reasoning that AsiaFocus intentionally misled viewers into believing that its Web site was connected with, or sponsored by, Playboy. See Playboy Enters. v. Asiafocus Int'l, Inc., No. CIV.A. 97-734-A, 1998 WL 724000, at *3, *6-*7 (E.D.Va. Apr.10, 1998).

In a similar case also involving Playboy, a district court in California concluded that Playboy had established a likelihood of success on the merits of its claim that defendants' repeated use of "Playboy" within "machine readable code in Defendants' Internet Web pages, so that the PLAYBOY trademark [was] accessible to individuals or Internet search engines which attempt[ed] to access Plaintiff under Plaintiff's PLAYBOY registered trademark" constituted trademark infringement. See Playboy Enters. v. Calvin Designer Label, 985 F. Supp. 1220, 1221 (N.D.Cal. 1997). The court accordingly enjoined the defendants from using Playboy's marks in buried code or metatags. See *id.* at 1221-22.

In a metatags case with an interesting twist, a district court in Massachusetts also enjoined the use of metatags in a manner that resulted in initial interest confusion. See *Niton*, 27 F. Supp.2d at 102-05. In that case, the defendant Radiation Monitoring Devices ("RMD") did not simply use Niton Corporation's ("Niton") trademark in its metatags. Instead, RMD's web site directly copied Niton's web site's metatags and HTML code. As a result, whenever a search performed on an Internet search engine listed Niton's web site, it also listed RMD's site. Although the opinion did not speak in terms of initial consumer confusion, the court made clear that its issuance of preliminary injunctive relief was based on the fact that RMD was purposefully diverting people looking for Niton to its web site. See *id.* at 104-05.

Consistently with *Dr. Seuss*, the Second Circuit, and the cases which have addressed trademark infringement through metatags use, we conclude that the Lanham Act bars West Coast from including in its metatags any term confusingly similar with Brookfield's mark. West Coast argues that our holding conflicts with *Holiday Inns*, in which the Sixth Circuit held that there was no trademark infringement where an alleged infringer merely took advantage of a situation in which confusion was likely to exist and did not affirmatively act to create consumer confusion. See *Holiday Inns*, 86 F.3d at 622 (holding that the use of "1-800-405-4329" —which is equivalent to "1-800-H[zero]LIDAY"—did not infringe Holiday Inn's trademark, "1-800-HOLIDAY"). Unlike the defendant in *Holiday Inns*, however, West Coast was not a passive figure; instead, it acted affirmatively in placing Brookfield's trademark in the metatags of its web site, thereby creating the initial interest confusion. Accordingly, our conclusion comports with *Holiday Inns*.

C

Contrary to West Coast's contentions, we are not in any way restricting West Coast's right to use terms in a manner which would constitute fair use under the Lanham Act. See New Kids on the Block v. News America Pub., Inc., 971 F.2d 302, 306-09 (9th Cir. 1992); see also August Storck K.G. v. Nabisco, Inc., 59 F.3d 616, 617-18 (7th Cir. 1995). It is well established that the Lanham Act does not prevent one from using a competitor's mark truthfully to identify the competitor's goods, see, e.g., Smith v. Chanel, Inc., 402 F.2d 562, 563 (9th Cir. 1968) (stating that a copyist may use the originator's mark to identify the product that it has copied), or in comparative advertisements, see *New Kids on the Block*, 971 F.2d at 306-09. This fair use doctrine applies in cyberspace as it does in the real world. See Radio Channel Networks, Inc. v. Broadcast.Com, Inc., No. 98 Civ. 4799, 1999 WL 124455, at *5-*6 (S.D.N.Y. Mar.8, 1999); Bally Total Fitness Holding Corp. v. Faber, 29 F. Supp.2d 1161 (C.D.Cal. 1998); *Welles*, 7 F. Supp.2d at 1103-04; Patmont Motor Werks, Inc. v. Gateway Marine, Inc., No. 96-2703, 1997 WL

811770, at *3-*4 & n. 6 (N.D.Cal. Dec.18, 1997); see also *Universal Tel-A-Talk*, 1998 WL 767440, at *9.

In *Welles*, the case most on point, Playboy sought to enjoin former Playmate of the Year Terri Welles ("Welles") from using "Playmate" or "Playboy" on her web site featuring photographs of herself. See 7 F. Supp.2d at 1100. Welles's web site advertised the fact that she was a former Playmate of the Year, but minimized the use of Playboy's marks; it also contained numerous disclaimers stating that her site was neither endorsed by nor affiliated with Playboy. The district court found that Welles was using "Playboy" and "Playmate" not as trademarks, but rather as descriptive terms fairly and accurately describing her web page, and that her use of "Playboy" and "Playmate" in her web site's metatags was a permissible, good faith attempt to index the content of her web site. It accordingly concluded that her use was permissible under the trademark laws. See *id.* at 1103-04.

We agree that West Coast can legitimately use an appropriate descriptive term in its metatags. But "MovieBuff" is not such a descriptive term. Even though it differs from "Movie Buff" by only a single space, that difference is pivotal. The term "Movie Buff" is a descriptive term, which is routinely used in the English language to describe a movie devotee. "MovieBuff" is not. The term "MovieBuff" is not in the dictionary. See Merriam-Webster's Collegiate Dictionary 762 (10th ed. 1998); American Heritage College Dictionary 893 (3d ed. 1997); Webster's New World College Dictionary 889 (3d ed. 1997); Webster's Third New Int'l Dictionary 1480 (unabridged 1993). Nor has that term been used in any published federal or state court opinion. In light of the fact that it is not a word in the English language, when the term "MovieBuff" is employed, it is used to refer to Brookfield's products and services, rather than to mean "motion picture enthusiast." The proper term for the "motion picture enthusiast" is "Movie Buff," which West Coast certainly can use. It cannot, however, omit the space.

Moreover, West Coast is not absolutely barred from using the term "Movie-Buff." As we explained above, that term can be legitimately used to describe Brookfield's product. For example, its web page might well include an advertisement banner such as "Why pay for MovieBuff when you can get the same thing here for FREE?" which clearly employs "MovieBuff" to refer to Brookfield's products. West Coast, however, presently uses Brookfield's trademark not to reference Brookfield's products, but instead to describe its own product (in the case of the domain name) and to attract people to its web site in the case of the metatags. That is not fair use. . . .

VII

As we have seen, registration of a domain name for a Web site does not trump long-established principles of trademark law. When a firm uses a competitor's trademark in the domain name of its web site, users are likely to be confused as to its source or sponsorship. Similarly, using a competitor's trademark in the metatags of such web site is likely to cause what we have described as initial interest confusion. These forms of confusion are exactly what the trademark laws are designed to prevent.

Accordingly, we reverse and remand this case to the district court with instructions to enter a preliminary injunction in favor of Brookfield in accordance with this opinion.

≡≡≡ *Playboy Enterprises, Inc. v. Welles*
United States Court of Appeals for the Ninth Circuit
279 F.3d 796 (9th Cir. 2002)

T.G. NELSON, Circuit Judge.

Playboy Enterprises, Inc. (PEI), appeals the district court's grant of summary judgment as to its claims of trademark infringement, unfair competition, and breach of contract against Terri Welles; Terri Welles, Inc.; Pippi, Inc.; and Welles' current and former "webmasters," Steven Huntington and Michael Mihalko. We have jurisdiction pursuant to 28 U.S.C. §1291, and we affirm in part and reverse in part. . . .

I. Background

Terri Welles was on the cover of Playboy in 1981 and was chosen to be the Playboy Playmate of the Year for 1981. Her use of the title "Playboy Playmate of the Year 1981," and her use of other trademarked terms on her website are at issue in this suit. During the relevant time period, Welles' website offered information about and free photos of Welles, advertised photos for sale, advertised memberships in her photo club, and promoted her services as a spokesperson. A biographical section described Welles' selection as Playmate of the Year in 1981 and her years modeling for PEI. After the lawsuit began, Welles included discussions of the suit and criticism of PEI on her website and included a note disclaiming any association with PEI.

PEI complains of four different uses of its trademarked terms on Welles' website: (1) the terms "Playboy" and "Playmate" in the metatags of the website; (2) the phrase "Playmate of the Year 1981" on the masthead of the website; (3) the phrases "Playboy Playmate of the Year 1981" and "Playmate of the Year 1981" on various banner ads, which may be transferred to other websites; and (4) the repeated use of the abbreviation "PMOY '81" as the watermark on the pages of the website.[3] PEI claimed that these uses of its marks constituted trademark infringement, dilution, false designation of origin, and unfair competition. The district court granted defendants' motion for summary judgment. PEI appeals the grant of summary judgment on its infringement and dilution claims. We affirm in part and reverse in part. . . .

---

3. PEI claims that "PMOY" is an unregistered trademark of PEI, standing for "Playmate of the Year."

III. Discussion

A. *Trademark Infringement*

Except for the use of PEI's protected terms in the wallpaper of Welles' website, we conclude that Welles' uses of PEI's trademarks are permissible, nominative uses. They imply no current sponsorship or endorsement by PEI. Instead, they serve to identify Welles as a past PEI "Playmate of the Year."

We articulated the test for a permissible, nominative use in New Kids On The Block v. New America Publishing, Inc. The band, New Kids On The Block, claimed trademark infringement arising from the use of their trademarked name by several newspapers. The newspapers had conducted polls asking which member of the band New Kids On The Block was the best and most popular. The papers' use of the trademarked term did not fall within the traditional fair use doctrine. Unlike a traditional fair use scenario, the defendant newspaper was using the trademarked term to describe not its own product, but the plaintiff's. Thus, the factors used to evaluate fair use were inapplicable. The use was nonetheless permissible, we concluded, based on its nominative nature.

We adopted the following test for nominative use:

> First, the product or service in question must be one not readily identifiable without use of the trademark; second, only so much of the mark or marks may be used as is reasonably necessary to identify the product or service; and third, the user must do nothing that would, in conjunction with the mark, suggest sponsorship or endorsement by the trademark holder.

We noted in *New Kids* that a nominative use may also be a commercial one.

In cases in which the defendant raises a nominative use defense, the above three-factor test should be applied instead of the test for likelihood of confusion set forth in *Sleekcraft*. The three-factor test better evaluates the likelihood of confusion in nominative use cases. When a defendant uses a trademark nominally, the trademark will be identical to the plaintiff's mark, at least in terms of the words in question. Thus, application of the *Sleekcraft* test, which focuses on the similarity of the mark used by the plaintiff and the defendant, would lead to the incorrect conclusion that virtually all nominative uses are confusing. The three-factor test—with its requirements that the defendant use marks only when no descriptive substitute exists, use no more of the mark than necessary, and do nothing to suggest sponsorship or endorsement by the mark holder—better addresses concerns regarding the likelihood of confusion in nominative use cases.

We group the uses of PEI's trademarked terms into three for the purpose of applying the test for nominative use. First, we analyze Welles' use of the terms in headlines and banner advertisements. We conclude that those uses are clearly nominative. Second, we analyze the use of the terms in the metatags for Welles' website, which we conclude are nominative as well. Finally, we analyze the terms as used in the wall-paper of the website. We conclude that this use is not nominative and remand for a determination of whether it infringes on a PEI trademark.

1. Headlines and Banner Advertisements.

To satisfy the first part of the test for nominative use, "the product or service in question must be one not readily identifiable without use of the trademark[.]" This situation arises "when a trademark also describes a person, a place or an attribute of a product" and there is no descriptive substitute for the trademark. In such a circumstance, allowing the trademark holder exclusive rights would allow the language to "be depleted in much the same way as if generic words were protectable." In *New Kids,* we gave the example of the trademarked term, "Chicago Bulls." We explained that "one might refer to the 'two-time world champions' or 'the professional basketball team from Chicago,' but it's far simpler (and more likely to be understood) to refer to the Chicago Bulls." Moreover, such a use of the trademark would "not imply sponsorship or endorsement of the product because the mark is used only to describe the thing, rather than to identify its source." Thus, we concluded, such uses must be excepted from trademark infringement law.

The district court properly identified Welles' situation as one which must also be excepted. No descriptive substitute exists for PEI's trademarks in this context. The court explained:

> [T]here is no other way that Ms. Welles can identify or describe herself and her services without venturing into absurd descriptive phrases. To describe herself as the "nude model selected by Mr. Hefner's magazine as its number-one prototypical woman for the year 1981" would be impractical as well as ineffectual in identifying Terri Welles to the public.

We agree. Just as the newspapers in *New Kids* could only identify the band clearly by using its trademarked name, so can Welles only identify herself clearly by using PEI's trademarked title.

The second part of the nominative use test requires that "only so much of the mark or marks may be used as is reasonably necessary to identify the product or service[.]" *New Kids* provided the following examples to explain this element: "[A] soft drink competitor would be entitled to compare its product to Coca-Cola or Coke, but would not be entitled to use Coca-Cola's distinctive lettering." Similarly, in a past case, an auto shop was allowed to use the trademarked term "Volkswagen" on a sign describing the cars it repaired, in part because the shop "did not use Volkswagen's distinctive lettering style or color scheme, nor did he display the encircled 'VW' emblem." Welles' banner advertisements and headlines satisfy this element because they use only the trademarked words, not the font or symbols associated with the trademarks.

The third element requires that the user do "nothing that would, in conjunction with the mark, suggest sponsorship or endorsement by the trademark holder." As to this element, we conclude that aside from the wallpaper, which we address separately, Welles does nothing in conjunction with her use of the marks to suggest sponsorship or endorsement by PEI. The marks are clearly used to describe the title she received from PEI in 1981, a title that helps describe who she is. It would be unreasonable to assume that the Chicago Bulls sponsored a website of Michael Jordan's simply because his name appeared with the appellation "former Chicago Bull." Similarly, in this case, it would be unreasonable to assume that PEI currently sponsors or endorses someone who describes herself as a "Playboy Playmate of the

Year in 1981." The designation of the year, in our case, serves the same function as the "former" in our example. It shows that any sponsorship or endorsement occurred in the past.

In addition to doing nothing in conjunction with her use of the marks to suggest sponsorship or endorsement by PEI, Welles affirmatively disavows any sponsorship or endorsement. Her site contains a clear statement disclaiming any connection to PEI. Moreover, the text of the site describes her ongoing legal battles with the company.[26]

For the foregoing reasons, we conclude that Welles' use of PEI's marks in her headlines and banner advertisements is a nominative use excepted from the law of trademark infringement.

2. Metatags

Welles includes the terms "playboy" and "playmate" in her metatags. . . . Because Welles' metatags do not repeat the terms extensively, her site will not be at the top of the list of search results. Applying the three-factor test for nominative use, we conclude that the use of the trademarked terms in Welles' metatags is nominative.

As we discussed above with regard to the headlines and banner advertisements, Welles has no practical way of describing herself without using trademarked terms. In the context of metatags, we conclude that she has no practical way of identifying the content of her website without referring to PEI's trademarks.

A large portion of Welles' website discusses her association with Playboy over the years. Thus, the trademarked terms accurately describe the contents of Welles' website, in addition to describing Welles. Forcing Welles and others to use absurd turns of phrase in their metatags, such as those necessary to identify Welles, would be particularly damaging in the internet search context. Searchers would have a much more difficult time locating relevant websites if they could do so only by correctly guessing the long phrases necessary to substitute for trademarks. We can hardly expect someone searching for Welles' site to imagine the same phrase proposed by the district court to describe Welles without referring to Playboy—"the nude model selected by Mr. Hefner's organization. . . ." Yet if someone could not remember her name, that is what they would have to do. Similarly, someone searching for critiques of Playboy on the internet would have a difficult time if internet sites could not list the object of their critique in their metatags.

There is simply no descriptive substitute for the trademarks used in Welles' metatags. Precluding their use would have the unwanted effect of hindering the free flow of information on the internet, something which is certainly not a goal of trademark law. Accordingly, the use of trademarked terms in the metatags meets the first part of the test for nominative use.

We conclude that the metatags satisfy the second and third elements of the test as well. The metatags use only so much of the marks as reasonably necessary

---

26. By noting Welles' affirmative actions, we do not mean to imply that affirmative actions of this type are necessary to establish nominative use. *New Kids* sets forth no such requirement, and we do not impose one here.

and nothing is done in conjunction with them to suggest sponsorship or endorsement by the trademark holder. We note that our decision might differ if the metatags listed the trademarked term so repeatedly that Welles' site would regularly appear above PEI's in searches for one of the trademarked terms.

3. Wallpaper/Watermark.

The background, or wallpaper, of Welles' site consists of the repeated abbreviation "PMOY '81," which stands for "Playmate of the Year 1981." Welles' name or likeness does not appear before or after "PMOY '81." The pattern created by the repeated abbreviation appears as the background of the various pages of the website. Accepting, for the purposes of this appeal, that the abbreviation "PMOY" is indeed entitled to protection, we conclude that the repeated, stylized use of this abbreviation fails the nominative use test.

The repeated depiction of "PMOY '81" is not necessary to describe Welles. "Playboy Playmate of the Year 1981" is quite adequate. Moreover, the term does not even appear to describe Welles—her name or likeness do not appear before or after each "PMOY '81." Because the use of the abbreviation fails the first prong of the nominative use test, we need not apply the next two prongs of the test.

Because the defense of nominative use fails here, and we have already determined that the doctrine of fair use does not apply, we remand to the district court. The court must determine whether trademark law protects the abbreviation "PMOY," as used in the wallpaper.

B. Trademark Dilution

The district court granted summary judgment to Welles as to PEI's claim of trademark dilution. We affirm on the ground that all of Welles' uses of PEI's marks, with the exception of the use in the wallpaper which we address separately, are proper, nominative uses. We hold that nominative uses, by definition, do not dilute the trademarks.

[The court reviewed the Federal Trademark Dilution Act and the purpose of the statute.]

Uses that do not create an improper association between a mark and a new product but merely identify the trademark holder's products should be excepted from the reach of the anti-dilution statute. Such uses cause no harm. The anti-dilution statute recognizes this principle and specifically excepts users of a trademark who compare their product in "commercial advertising or promotion to identify the competing goods or services of the owner of the famous mark."

For the same reason uses in comparative advertising are excepted from antidilution law, we conclude that nominative uses are also excepted. A nominative use, by definition, refers to the trademark holder's product. It does not create an improper association in consumers' minds between a new product and the trademark holder's mark.

When Welles refers to her title, she is in effect referring to a product of PEI's. She does not dilute the title by truthfully identifying herself as its one-time recipient any more than Michael Jordan would dilute the name "Chicago Bulls" by referring to himself as a former member of that team, or the two-time winner of an Academy Award would dilute the award by referring to him or herself as a "two-time Academy Award winner." Awards are not diminished or diluted by the fact that they have been awarded in the past. Similarly, they are not diminished or diluted when past recipients truthfully identify themselves as such. It is in the nature of honors and awards to be identified with the people who receive them. Of course, the conferrer of such honors and awards is free to limit the honoree's use of the title or references to the award by contract. So long as a use is nominative, however, trademark law is unavailing.

The one exception to the above analysis in this case is Welles' use of the abbreviation "PMOY" on her wallpaper. Because we determined that this use is not nominative, it is not excepted from the anti-dilution provisions. Thus, we reverse as to this issue and remand for further proceedings. We note that if the district court determines that "PMOY" is not entitled to trademark protection, PEI's claim for dilution must fail. The trademarked term, "Playmate of the Year" is not identical or nearly identical to the term "PMOY." Therefore, use of the term "PMOY" cannot, as a matter of law, dilute the trademark "Playmate of the Year.". . .

COMMENTS AND QUESTIONS

1. Is initial interest confusion really the sort of thing trademark law should be concerned with? All the metatag cases seem to assume that consumers will not be confused at the time they make any purchase decisions—that is, that any confusion will be dispelled once they actually reach the site using the metatags. If that is true, what harm has been done? Does it matter what the Web site does or sells—that is, whether it is selling products in the real world, or whether its real "product" is consumer attention?

One possible harm, cited in *Brookfield*, is the "diversion" of consumer interest to the metatagging site. But this assumes that consumers will believe that all of the search engine results they get are necessarily relevant. If consumers understand the misuse of metatags and know to ignore irrelevant-looking sites in their search engine results, they may not be drawn in by the misuse of metatags.

A trademark owner might still be harmed in this instance, however, because the search process will have gotten more complex. For example, a search for "Playboy" on a major search engine is likely to pull up thousands of hits, most of which are not official pages of Playboy Magazine. Does a trademark owner have a right to a "clean" search result—that is, one in which only relevant sites appear?

2. A number of district court cases have held that the use of a competitor's trademark in your metatags is illegal. See, e.g., Playboy Ents. v. AsiaFocus Int'l, 1998 WL 724000 (1998); Playboy Ents. v. Calvin Designer Label, 985 F. Supp. 1218 (N.D. Cal. 1997). But a more difficult issue is posed when the site using the trademark in a metatag is not in fact a competitor. For example, in Oppedahl & Larson v. Advanced Concepts, No. 97CV1592 (D. Colo., filed July 24, 1997), the

law firm of Oppedahl & Larson challenged the use of its name in a metatag by a site that provided totally different products. Is there consumer confusion here? Alternatively, can a trademark owner maintain a cause of action for dilution via meta-tagging?

3. The *Welles* decision points up an important limit on the theory of initial interest confusion. While most metatagging cases involve Web sites with no legitimate right to use the mark in question, there are a number of circumstances in which a Web page might legitimately use another company's trademark. It might appear in a resumé, for example (essentially what was at issue in *Welles*), in an article about the trademark owner on a news site, or in comparative advertising by a competitor ("four out of five doctors prefer Brand X to Brand Y"). If a Web site is making legitimate use of a trademark, should it also be able to put that mark in its metatags?

4. For a good discussion of metatag trademark issues, see Maureen A. O'Rourke, Defining the Limits of Free-Riding in Cyberspace: Trademark Liability for Metatagging, 33 Gonzaga L. Rev. 277 (1998); Katherine E. Gasparek, Comment, Applying the Fair Use Defense in Traditional Trademark Infringement and Dilution Cases to Internet Meta Tagging or Linking Cases, 7 Geo. Mason L. Rev. 787 (1999); Ira S. Nathenson, Internet Infoglut and Invisible Ink: Spamdexing Search Engines with Meta Tags, 12 Harv. J. L. & Tech. 43 (1998); Bryce J. Maynard, The Initial Interest Confusion Doctrine and Trademark Infringement on the Internet, 57 Wash. & Lee L. Rev. 1303 (2000).

5. Most court decisions have generally followed the Ninth Circuit approach, punishing the use of metatags to confuse consumers but permitting the use of a metatag where the defendant has a legitimate claim to use or make reference to the trademark. But see Eli Lilly & Co. v. Natural Answers, 86 F. Supp.2d 834, 846 (S.D. Ind. 2000) (questioning whether the use of a trademark in a metatag can ever be fair).

6. In Ford Motor Co. v. 2600 Enterprises, 177 F. Supp.2d 661 (E.D. Mich. 2001), the court refused to apply trademark law to prevent linking, even in circumstances where it might cause confusion. Corley, the defendant in this case, registered the trademark "fuckgeneralmotors.com" and redirected visitors to the site automatically to the Ford site. Ford complained that visitors would assume it had sponsored the site. But the court held that Ford could not state a trademark infringement claim, both because it could not point to any commercial use of the mark and because it could not show that a mere link could dilute the distinctive significance of the Ford mark.

7. More recent cases have expanded the doctrine of initial interest confusion beyond the context of metatags. In J. K. Harris & Co. v. Kassel, 62 U.S.P.Q.2d 1926 (N.D. Cal. 2002), the court held that the defendant had infringed the plaintiff's trademark by organizing its Web site in such a way that Internet searches for the plaintiff's name brought up defendant's site before plaintiff's. The case is analytically similar to the metatag cases, in that it involves efforts to manipulate search engine results and also involves legitimate uses of the plaintiff's name, but the court's opinion focuses on the excessive nature of those uses in finding liability.

The section that follows considers other ways that companies might manipulate search engine results.

b. Keyword Buys

Playboy Enterprises, Inc. v. Excite, Inc.
United States District Court for the Central District of California
55 F. Supp.2d 1070 (C.D. Cal. 1999)

STOTLER, District J. . . .

II. Factual Background

Defendants operate search engines on the Internet. When a person searches for a particular topic in either search engine, the search engine compiles a list of sites matching or related to the user's search terms, and then posts the list of sites, known as "search results."

Defendants sell advertising space on the search result pages. Known as "banner ads," the advertisements are commonly found at the top of the screen. The ads themselves are often animated and whimsical, and designed to entice the Internet user to "click here." If the user does click on the ad, she is transported to the web site of the advertiser.

As with other media, advertisers seek to maximize the efficacy of their ads by targeting consumers matching a certain demographic profile. Savvy web site operators accommodate the advertisers by "keying" ads to search terms entered by users. That is, instead of posting ads in a random rotation, defendants program their servers to link a pre-selected set of banner ads to certain "key" search terms. Defendants market this context-sensitive advertising ability as a value-added service and charge a premium.

Defendants key various adult entertainment ads to a group of over 450 terms related to adult entertainment, including the terms "playboy" and "playmate." Plaintiff contends that inclusion of those terms violates plaintiff's trademarks rights in those words.

III. Parties' Contentions

Plaintiff has a trademark on "Playboy®" and "Playmate®." Plaintiff contends that defendants are infringing and diluting its trademarks (1) by marketing and selling the group of over 450 words, including "playboy" and "playmate," to advertisers, (2) by programming the banner ads to run in response to the search terms "playboy" and "playmate" (i.e., "keying"), and (3) by actually displaying the banner ad on the search results page. As a result, plaintiff contends, Internet users are diverted from plaintiff's official web site and web sites sponsored or approved by plaintiff, which generally will be listed as search results, to other adult entertainment web sites. Plaintiff further argues that defendants intend to divert the users to the non-PEI sites. Plaintiff does not contend, however, that defendants infringe or dilute the marks when defendants' search engines generate a list of Web sites related to "playboy" or "playmate."

Defendants respond that while plaintiff may have a trademark on "Playboy®" and "Playmate®," defendants do not actually "use" the trademarks qua trademarks. Moreover, even if defendants do use the trademarks, defendants argue that a trademark does not confer an absolute property right on all uses of the protected terms, and that defendants' use of the terms is permitted. Finally, defendants dispute that they have any intent to divert users from clicking on search results (such as PEI's sites) to clicking on banner ads.

IV. Discussion . . .

C. *Trademark Use*

Integral to plaintiff's success on the merits of its case, on either the infringement or dilution theory, is a showing that defendants use plaintiff's trademarks in commerce. Plaintiff does not so show. Rather, plaintiff can only contend that the use of the words "playboy" and "playmate," as keywords or search terms, is equivalent to the use of the trademarks "Playboy®" and "Playmate®." However, it is undisputed that an Internet user cannot conduct a search using the trademark form of the words, i.e., Playboy® and Playmate®. Rather, the user enters the generic word "playboy" or "playmate." It is also undisputed that the words "playboy" and "playmate" are English words in their own right, and that there exist other trademarks on the words wholly unrelated to PEI. Thus, whether the user is looking for goods and services covered by PEI's trademarks or something altogether unrelated to PEI is anybody's guess. Plaintiff guesses that most users searching the Web for "playboy" and "playmate" are indeed looking for PEI sites, goods and services. Based on that theory, plaintiff argues that since defendants also speculate that users searching for "playboy" and "playmate" are looking for things related to Playboy® and Playmate®, defendants use the trademarks when they key competing adult entertainment goods and services to the generic "playboy" and "playmate."

Plaintiff has not shown that defendants use the terms in their trademark form, i.e., Playboy® and Playmate®, when marketing to advertisers or in the algorithm that effectuates the keying of the ads to the keywords. Thus, plaintiff's argument that defendants "use" plaintiff's trademarks falls short.

D. *Trademark Infringement and Dilution*

Even if use of the generic "playboy" and "playmate" were construed to be use of the trademark terms Playboy® and Playmate®, plaintiff still must show that the use violates trademark law. Plaintiff has asserted two theories, trademark infringement and trademark dilution.

1. Infringement

"The core element of trademark infringement is the likelihood of confusion, i.e., whether the similarity of the marks is likely to confuse customers about the source of the products." Official Airline Guides, Inc. v. Goss, 6 F.3d 1385, 1391 (9th Cir. 1993). Assuming arguendo that defendants' use of "playboy" and "playmate" is use of plaintiff's marks, plaintiff must still show that confusion is likely to result from that use. Plaintiff has not so shown.

Rather, plaintiff relies on the recent case from the Court of Appeals for the Ninth Circuit, Brookfield Communications, Inc. v. West Coast Entertainment Corp., —F.3d—, 1999 WL 232014, *22-*24 (9th Cir. 1999), for the proposition that defendants cause "initial interest confusion" by the use of the words "playboy" and "playmate." Initial interest confusion, as coined by the Ninth Circuit, is a brand of confusion particularly applicable to the Internet. Generally speaking, initial interest confusion may result when a user conducts a search using a trademark term and the results of the search include web sites not sponsored by the holder of the trademark search term, but rather of competitors. *Id.* The Ninth Circuit reasoned that the user may be diverted to an unsponsored site, and only realize that she has been diverted upon arriving at the competitor's site. Once there, however, even though the user knows she is not in the site initially sought, she may stay. In that way, the competitor has captured the trademark holder's potential visitors or customers. *Id.*

Brookfield is distinguishable from this case, and where applicable, supportive of defendants' position.

First, the trademark at issue in *Brookfield* was not an English word in its own right. In *Brookfield*, the Court compared Brookfield's trademark "MovieBuff" with competitor West Coast's use of the domain name "moviebuff.com," and found them to be "essentially identical" despite the differences in capitalization, which the Court considered "inconsequential in light of the fact that Web addresses are not caps-sensitive. . . ." *Id.* at *14. However, the Court held that West Coast could use the term "Movie Buff" (or, presumably, "movie buff") with the space, as such is the "proper term for the 'motion picture enthusiast'. . . . It cannot, however, omit the space." *Id.* at 26. On the other hand, "[i]n light of the fact that it is not a word in the English language, when the term 'MovieBuff' is employed, it is used to refer to Brookfield's products and services, rather than to mean 'motion picture enthusiast.'" *Id.* at *26.

As English words, "playboy" and "playmate" cannot be said to suggest sponsorship or endorsement of either the web sites that appear as search results (as in *Brookfield*) or the banner ads that adorn the search results page. Although the trademark terms and the English language words are undisputedly identical, which, presumably, leads plaintiff to believe that the use of the English words is akin to use of the trademarks, the holder of a trademark may not remove a word from the English language merely by acquiring trademark rights in it. *Id.*

Second, the use by defendant of plaintiff's trademark in *Brookfield* was more suspect because the parties compete in the same market—as online providers of film industry information. See *id.*, at *16-*17 ("[n]ot only are they not non-competitors, the competitive proximity of their products is actually quite high"). The Ninth Circuit analogized the capture of unsuspecting Internet users by a competitor to highways and billboards. . . .

Here, the analogy is quite unlike that of a devious placement of a road sign bearing false information. This case presents a scenario more akin to a driver pulling off the freeway in response to a sign that reads "Fast Food Burgers" to find a well-known fast food burger restaurant, next to which stands a billboard that reads: "Better Burgers: 1 Block Further." The driver, previously enticed by the prospect of a burger from the well-known restaurant, now decides she wants to explore other burger options. Assuming that the same entity owns the land on which both the burger restaurant and the competitor's billboard stand, should that entity be liable to the burger restaurant for diverting the driver? That is the rule PEI contends the Court should adopt.

2. Dilution

Trademark dilution is defined as "the lessening of the capacity of a famous mark to identify and distinguish goods or services." 15 U.S.C. §1127. However, dilution is "not intended to serve as a mere fallback protection for trademark owners unable to prove trademark infringement." I.P. Lund Trading ApS v. Kohler Co., 163 F.3d 27, 48 (1st Cir. 1998).

To establish dilution, plaintiff must show that "(1) [defendants have] made use of a junior mark sufficiently similar to the famous mark to evoke in a relevant universe of consumers a mental association of the two that (2) has caused (3) actual economic harm to the famous mark's economic value by lessening its former selling power as an advertising agent for its goods and services." Ringling Bros.-Barnum & Bailey Combined Shows, Inc. v. Utah Div'n of Travel Dept., 170 F.3d 449, 459 (4th Cir. 1999). Dilution generally occurs through the blurring of a famous mark or tarnishment of the mark, but is not limited to these categories. See Panavision Int'l, L.P. v. Toeppen, 141 F.3d 1316, 1326 (9th Cir. 1998). Plaintiff has not shown blurring of its marks, which would occur if defendants used the marks to identify defendants' goods or services. *Id.* at 1326 n. 7. First, as discussed supra, plaintiff has not shown that defendant uses its marks Playboy® and Playmate®. Further, plaintiff has not presented any evidence that defendants' use of the words "playboy" and "playmate" causes any severance of the association between plaintiff and its marks Playboy® and Playmate®, much less in the minds of Internet users.

Plaintiff has also failed to show tarnishment, which occurs when a famous mark is associated improperly with an inferior or offensive product or service. *Id.* at 1326 n. 7. Plaintiff contends that because the content of the banner ads is more sexually explicit tha[n] PEI's content, PEI's marks are being tarnished. Again, plaintiff's argument is based on the incorrect assumption that defendants use plaintiff's marks, rather than the generic words "playboy" and "playmate." But even if the defendants could be said to use plaintiff's marks, plaintiff would still be required to show that associating marks admittedly famous for adult entertainment with other purveyors of adult entertainment somehow harms plaintiff's marks. Whether PEI is a cut above the rest, as it contends, is undercut by the fact that PEI's marks are associated with other purveyors of adult entertainment in other marketing channels, as defendants' exhibits graphically establish. Adoption of plaintiff's tarnishment would secure near-monopoly control of the placement of plaintiff's marks and the associated goods and services on the Internet, where, arguably, "placement" is a nebulous concept. A greater showing of harm is required.

V. Conclusion

Accordingly, and for the foregoing reasons, the plaintiff's motion is denied. . . .

COMMENTS AND QUESTIONS

1. Are you persuaded that Web users searching for "playboy" are often searching not for sites related to plaintiff's trademark but for sites using the term in its generic sense?

2. Keyword buys affect the advertising that appears alongside search results in a search engine. Are consumers likely to confuse ads with search results? When you see ads on a search result page, do you assume that they are somehow related to or sponsored by the owner of the trademark you have searched for? If not, how exactly has Playboy been injured by the keyword buy?

The court in Nissan Motor v. Nissan Computer, 204 F.R.D. 460 (C.D. Cal. 2001), followed *Excite* in holding that purchasing Internet search terms that corresponded to the plaintiff's domain name could not constitute a state law tort.

3. A variety of other conduct may be alleged to suggest a connection or affiliation between one Web site and another. Trademark cases have been litigated over links from one page to another, "frames" that display two pages in proximity to each other, and the use of logos to identify a link. Because these cases generally also involve copyright questions, we defer discussion of them until the next Section.

B. COPYRIGHT LAW

1. Direct Infringement

Kelly v. Arriba Soft Corp.
United States Court of Appeals for the Ninth Circuit
280 F.3d 934 (9th Cir. 2002)

T.G. NELSON, Circuit Judge:

This case involves the application of copyright law to the vast world of the internet and internet search engines. The plaintiff, Leslie Kelly, is a professional photographer who has copyrighted many of his images of the American West. Some of these images are located on Kelly's web site or other web sites with which Kelly has a license agreement. The defendant, Arriba Soft Corp., operates an internet search engine that displays its results in the form of small pictures rather than the more usual form of text. Arriba obtained its database of pictures by copying images from other web sites. By clicking on one of these small pictures, called "thumbnails," the user can then view a large version of that same picture within the context of the Arriba web page.

When Kelly discovered that his photographs were part of Arriba's search engine database, he brought a claim against Arriba for copyright infringement. The district court found that Kelly had established a prima facie case of copyright infringement based on Arriba's unauthorized reproduction and display of Kelly's works, but that this reproduction and display constituted a non-infringing "fair use" under Section 107 of the Copyright Act. Kelly appeals that decision, and we affirm in part and reverse in part. The creation and use of the thumbnails in the search engine is a fair use, but the display of the larger image is a violation of Kelly's exclusive right to publicly display his works. We remand with instructions to determine damages and the need for an injunction.

I.

The search engine at issue in this case is unconventional in that it displays the results of a user's query as "thumbnail" images. When a user wants to search the internet for information on a certain topic, he or she types a search term into a search engine, which then produces a list of web sites that have information relating to the search term. Normally, the list of results is in text format. The Arriba search engine, however, produces its list of results as small pictures.

To provide this functionality, Arriba developed a computer program that "crawls" the web looking for images to index. This crawler downloads full-sized copies of the images onto Arriba's server. The program then uses these copies to generate smaller, lower-resolution thumbnails of the images. Once the thumbnails are created, the program deletes the full-sized originals from the server. Although a user could copy these thumbnails to his computer or disk, he cannot increase the resolution of the thumbnail; any enlargement would result in a loss of clarity of the image.

The second component of the Arriba program occurs when the user double-clicks on the thumbnail. From January 1999 to June 1999, clicking on the thumbnail produced the "Images Attributes" page. This page contained the original full-sized image imported directly from the originating web site, along with text describing the size of the image, a link to the originating web site, the Arriba banner, and Arriba advertising. The process of importing an image from another web site is called inline linking. The image imported from another web site is displayed as though it is part of the current web page, surrounded by the current web page's text and advertising. As a result, although the image in Arriba's Image Attributes page was directly from the originating web site, and not copied onto Arriba's site, the user typically would not realize that the image actually resided on another web site.

From July 1999 until sometime after August 2000, the results page contained thumbnails accompanied by two links: "Source" and "Details." The "Details" link produced a screen similar to the Images Attributes page but with a thumbnail rather than the full-sized image. Alternatively, by clicking on the "Source" link or the thumbnail from the results page, the site produced two new windows on top of the Arriba page. The window in the forefront contained the full-sized image, imported directly from the originating web site. Underneath that was another window displaying the originating web page. This technique is known as framing. The image from a second web site is viewed within a frame that is pulled into the primary site's web page.

In January 1999, Arriba's crawler visited web sites that contained Kelly's photographs. The crawler copied thirty-five of Kelly's images to the Arriba database. Kelly had never given permission to Arriba to copy his images and objected when he found out that Arriba was using them. Arriba deleted the thumbnails of images that came from Kelly's own web sites and placed those sites on a list of sites that it would not crawl in the future. Several months later, Arriba received Kelly's complaint of copyright infringement, which identified other images of his that came from third-party web sites. Arriba subsequently deleted those thumbnails and placed those third-party sites on a list of sites that it would not crawl in the future.

The district court granted summary judgment in favor of Arriba. Although the court found that Kelly had established a prima facie case of infringement based on Arriba's reproduction and display of Kelly's photographs, the court ruled that such actions by Arriba constituted fair use. The court determined that two of the fair use factors weighed heavily in Arriba's favor. Specifically, the court found that the character and purpose of Arriba's use was significantly transformative and the use did not harm the market for or value of Kelly's works. Kelly now appeals this decision. . . .

This case involves two distinct actions by Arriba that warrant analysis. The first action consists of the reproduction of Kelly's images to create the thumbnails and the use of those thumbnails in Arriba's search engine. The second action involves the display of Kelly's images through the inline linking and framing processes when the user clicks on the thumbnails. Because these actions are distinct types of potential infringement, we will analyze them separately.

A.

An owner of a copyright has the exclusive right to reproduce, distribute, and publicly display copies of the work. To establish a claim of copyright infringement by reproduction, the plaintiff must show ownership of the copyright and copying by the defendant. As to the thumbnails, there is no dispute that Kelly owned the copyright to the images and that Arriba copied those images. Therefore, Kelly established a prima facie case of copyright infringement.

A claim of copyright infringement is subject to certain statutory exceptions, including the fair use exception. This exception "permits courts to avoid rigid application of the copyright statute when, on occasion, it would stifle the very creativity which that law is designed to foster." The statute sets out four factors to consider in determining whether the use in a particular case is a fair use. We must balance these factors, in light of the objectives of copyright law, rather than view them as definitive or determinative tests. We now turn to the four fair use factors.

1. Purpose and Character of the Use.

The Supreme Court has rejected the proposition that a commercial use of the copyrighted material ends the inquiry under this factor. Instead,

> the central purpose of this investigation is to see . . . whether the new work merely supersede[s] the objects of the original creation, or instead adds something new, with a further purpose or different character, altering the first with new expression, meaning, or message; it asks, in other words, whether and to what extent the new work is transformative.

[Campbell v. Acuff-Rose Music, Inc., 510 U.S. 569, 579 (1994)] The more transformative the new work, the less important the other factors, including commercialism, become.

There is no dispute that Arriba operates its web site for commercial purposes and that Kelly's images were part of Arriba's search engine database. As the district court found, while such use of Kelly's images was commercial, it was more incidental and less exploitative in nature than more traditional types of commercial use. Arriba was neither using Kelly's images to directly promote its web site nor trying to profit by selling Kelly's images. Instead, Kelly's images were among thousands of images in Arriba's search engine database. Because the use of Kelly's images was not highly exploitative, the commercial nature of the use only slightly weighs against a finding of fair use.

The second part of the inquiry as to this factor involves the transformative nature of the use. We must determine if Arriba's use of the images merely superseded the object of the originals or instead added a further purpose or different character. We find that Arriba's use of Kelly's images for its thumbnails was transformative.

Despite the fact that Arriba made exact replications of Kelly's images, the thumbnails were much smaller, lower-resolution images that served an entirely different function than Kelly's original images. Kelly's images are artistic works used for illustrative purposes. His images are used to portray scenes from the American West in an esthetic manner. Arriba's use of Kelly's images in the thumbnails is unrelated to any esthetic purpose. Arriba's search engine functions as a tool to help index and improve access to images on the internet and their related web sites. In fact, users are unlikely to enlarge the thumbnails and use them for artistic purposes because the thumbnails are of much lower resolution than the originals; any enlargement results in a significant loss of clarity of the image, making them inappropriate as display material.

Kelly asserts that because Arriba reproduced his exact images and added nothing to them, Arriba's use cannot be transformative. It is true that courts have been reluctant to find fair use when an original work is merely retransmitted in a different medium. Those cases are inapposite, however, because the resulting use of the copyrighted work in those cases was the same as the original use. For instance, reproducing music CD's into computer MP3 format does not change the fact that both formats are used for entertainment purposes. Likewise, reproducing news footage into a different format does not change the ultimate purpose of informing the public about current affairs. . . .

This case involves more than merely a retransmission of Kelly's images in a different medium. Arriba's use of the images serves a different function than Kelly's use—improving access to information on the internet versus artistic expression. Furthermore, it would be unlikely that anyone would use Arriba's thumbnails for illustrative or esthetic purposes because enlarging them sacrifices their clarity. Because Arriba's use is not superseding Kelly's use but, rather, has created a different purpose for the images, Arriba's use is transformative.

Comparing this case to two recent cases in the Ninth and First Circuits reemphasizes the functionality distinction. In Worldwide Church of God v. Philadelphia Church of God, we held that copying a religious book to create a new book for use by a different church was not transformative. The second church's use of the book merely superseded the object of the original book, which was to serve religious practice and education. The court noted that "where the use is for the same intrinsic purpose as [the copyright holder's] . . . such use seriously weakens a claimed fair use."

On the other hand, in Nunez v. Caribbean International News Corp., the First Circuit found that copying a photograph that was intended to be used in a modeling portfolio and using it instead in a news article was a transformative use. By putting a copy of the photograph in the newspaper, the work was transformed into news, creating a new meaning or purpose for the work. The use of Kelly's images in Arriba's search engine is more analogous to the situation in Nunez because Arriba has created a new purpose for the images and is not simply superseding Kelly's purpose.

The Copyright Act was intended to promote creativity, thereby benefitting the artist and the public alike. To preserve the potential future use of artistic works for purposes of teaching, research, criticism, and news reporting, Congress made the fair use exception. Arriba's use of Kelly's images promotes the goals of the Copyright Act and the fair use exception. The thumbnails do not stifle artistic creativity because they are not used for illustrative or artistic purposes and therefore do not supplant the need for the originals. In addition, they benefit the public by enhancing information gathering techniques on the internet.

In Sony Computer Entertainment America, Inc. v. Bleem, we held that when Bleem copied "screen shots" from Sony computer games and used them in its own advertising, it was a fair use. In finding that the first factor weighed in favor of Bleem, we noted that "comparative advertising redounds greatly to the purchasing public's benefit with very little corresponding loss to the integrity of Sony's copyrighted material." Similarly, this first factor weighs in favor of Arriba due to the public benefit of the search engine and the minimal loss of integrity to Kelly's images.

2. Nature of the Copyrighted Work.

"Works that are creative in nature are closer to the core of intended copyright protection than are more fact-based works." Photographs used for illustrative purposes, such as Kelly's, are generally creative in nature. The fact that a work is published or unpublished also is a critical element of its nature. Published works are more likely to qualify as fair use because the first appearance of the artist's expression has already occurred. Kelly's images appeared on the internet before Arriba used them in its search image. When considering both of these elements, we find that this factor only slightly weighs in favor of Kelly.

3. Amount and Substantiality of Portion Used.

"While wholesale copying does not preclude fair use per se, copying an entire work militates against a finding of fair use." However, the extent of permissible copying varies with the purpose and character of the use. If the secondary user only copies as much as is necessary for his or her intended use, then this factor will not weigh against him or her.

This factor will neither weigh for nor against either party because, although Arriba did copy each of Kelly's images as a whole, it was reasonable to do so in light of Arriba's use of the images. It was necessary for Arriba to copy the entire image to allow users to recognize the image and decide whether to pursue more information about the image or the originating web site. If Arriba only copied part of the image, it would be more difficult to identify it, thereby reducing the usefulness of the visual search engine.

4. Effect of the Use upon the Potential Market for or Value of the Copyrighted Work.

This last factor requires courts to consider "not only the extent of market harm caused by the particular actions of the alleged infringer, but also 'whether unrestricted and widespread conduct of the sort engaged in by the defendant . . . would result in a substantially adverse impact on the potential market for the original.'" A transformative work is less likely to have an adverse impact on the market of the original than a work that merely supersedes the copyrighted work.

Kelly's images are related to several potential markets. One purpose of the photographs is to attract internet users to his web site, where he sells advertising space as well as books and travel packages. In addition, Kelly could sell or license his photographs to other web sites or to a stock photo database, which then could offer the images to its customers.

Arriba's use of Kelly's images in its thumbnails does not harm the market for Kelly's images or the value of his images. By showing the thumbnails on its results page when users entered terms related to Kelly's images, the search engine would guide users to Kelly's web site rather than away from it. Even if users were more interested in the image itself rather than the information on the web page, they would still have to go to Kelly's site to see the full-sized image. The thumbnails would not be a substitute for the full-sized images because when the thumbnails are enlarged, they lose their clarity. If a user wanted to view or download a quality image, he or she would have to visit Kelly's web site. This would [ ] hold true whether the thumbnails are solely in Arriba's database or are more widespread and found in other search engine databases.

Arriba's use of Kelly's images also would not harm Kelly's ability to sell or license his full-sized images. Arriba does not sell or license its thumbnails to other parties. Anyone who downloaded the thumbnails would not be successful selling the full-sized images because of the low-resolution of the thumbnails. There would be no way to view, create, or sell a clear, full-sized image without going to Kelly's web sites. Therefore, Arriba's creation and use of the thumbnails does not harm the market for or value of Kelly's images. This factor weighs in favor of Arriba.

Having considered the four fair use factors and found that two weigh in favor of Arriba, one is neutral, and one weighs slightly in favor of Kelly, we conclude that Arriba's use of Kelly's images as thumbnails in its search engine is a fair use.

B.

The second part of our analysis concerns Arriba's inline linking to and framing of Kelly's full-sized images. This use of Kelly's images does not entail copying them but, rather, importing them directly from Kelly's web site. Therefore, it cannot be copyright infringement based on the reproduction of copyrighted works as in the previous discussion. Instead, this use of Kelly's images infringes upon Kelly's exclusive right to "display the copyrighted work publicly."

1. Public Display Right.

In order for Kelly to prevail, Arriba must have displayed Kelly's work without his permission and made that display available to the public. The Copyright Act defines "display" as showing a copy of a work. This would seem to preclude Kelly from arguing that showing his original images was an infringement. However, the Act defines a copy as a material object in which a work is fixed, including the material object in which the work is first fixed. The legislative history of the Act makes clear that "since 'copies' are defined as including the material object 'in which the work is first fixed,' the right of public display applies to original works of art as well as to reproductions of them." By inline linking and framing Kelly's images, Arriba is showing Kelly's original works without his permission.

The legislative history goes on to state that "'display' would include the projection of an image on a screen or other surface by any method, the transmission of an image by electronic or other means, and the showing of an image on a cathode ray tube, or similar viewing apparatus connected with any sort of information storage and retrieval system." This language indicates that showing Kelly's images on a computer screen would constitute a display.

The Act's definition of the term "publicly" encompasses a transmission of a display of a work to the public "by means of any device or process, whether the members of the public capable of receiving the performance or display receive it in the same place or in separate places and at the same time or at different times." A display is public even if there is no proof that any of the potential recipients was operating his receiving apparatus at the time of the transmission. By making Kelly's images available on its web site, Arriba is allowing public access to those images. The ability to view those images is unrestricted to anyone with a computer and internet access.

The legislative history emphasizes the broad nature of the display right, stating that "each and every method by which the images or sounds comprising a performance or display are picked up and conveyed is a 'transmission,' and if the transmission reaches the public in [any] form, the case comes within the scope of [the public performance and display rights] of section 106." Looking strictly at the language of the Act and its legislative history, it appears that when Arriba imports Kelly's images into its own web page, Arriba is infringing upon Kelly's public display right. The limited case law in this area supports this conclusion.

No cases have addressed the issue of whether inline linking or framing violates a copyright owner's public display rights. However, in Playboy Enterprises, Inc. v. Webbworld, Inc., the court found that the owner of an internet site infringed a magazine publisher's copyrights by displaying copyrighted images on its web site. The defendant, Webbworld, downloaded material from certain newsgroups, discarded the text and retained the images, and made those images available to its internet subscribers. Playboy owned copyrights to many of the images Webbworld retained and displayed. The court found that Webbworld violated Playboy's exclusive right to display its copyrighted works, noting that allowing subscribers to view copyrighted works on their computer monitors while online was a display. The court also discounted the fact that no image existed until the subscriber downloaded it. The image existed in digital form, which made it available for decoding as an image file by the subscriber, who could view the images merely by visiting the Webbworld site.

Although Arriba does not download Kelly's images to its own server but, rather, imports them directly from other web sites, the situation is analogous to *Webbworld*. By allowing the public to view Kelly's copyrighted works while visiting Arriba's web site, Arriba created a public display of Kelly's works. Arriba argues that Kelly offered no proof that anyone ever saw his images and, therefore, there can be no display. We dispose of this argument, as did the court in *Webbworld*, because Arriba made the images available to any viewer that merely visited Arriba's site. Allowing this capability is enough to establish an infringement; the fact that no one saw the images goes to the issue of damages, not liability.

In a similar case, Playboy Enterprises, Inc. v. Russ Hardenburgh, Inc., the court held that the owner of an electronic bulletin board system infringed Playboy's copyrights by displaying copyrighted images on its system. The bulletin board is a central system that stores information, giving home computer users the opportunity to submit information to the system (upload) or retrieve information from the system (download). In this case, the defendant encouraged its subscribers to upload adult photographs, screened all submitted images, and moved some of the images into files from which general subscribers could download them. Because these actions resulted in subscribers being able to download copyrighted images, it violated Playboy's right of public display. Again, the court noted that adopting a policy that allowed the defendants to place images in files available to subscribers entailed a display. This conclusion indicates that it was irrelevant whether anyone actually saw the images.

Both of these cases highlighted the fact that the defendants took an active role in creating the display of the copyrighted images. The reason for this emphasis is that several other cases held that operators of bulletin board systems and internet access providers were not liable for copyright infringement. These cases distinguished direct infringement from contributory infringement and held that where the defendants did not take any affirmative action that resulted in copying copyrighted works, but only maintained a system that acted as a passive conduit for third parties' copies, they were not liable for direct infringement.

The courts in *Webbworld* and *Hardenburgh* specifically noted that the defendants did more than act as mere providers of access or passive conduits. In *Webbworld*, the web site sold images after actively trolling the internet for them and deciding which images to provide to subscribers. The court stated that "Webbworld exercised total dominion over the content of its site and the product it offered its clientele." Likewise, in *Hardenburgh*, the court found that by encouraging subscribers to upload images and then screening those images and selecting ones to make available for downloading, the defendants were more than passive conduits.

Like the defendants in *Webbworld* and *Hardenburgh*, Arriba is directly liable for infringement. Arriba actively participated in displaying Kelly's images by trolling the web, finding Kelly's images, and then having its program inline link and frame those images within its own web site. Without this program, users would not have been able to view Kelly's images within the context of Arriba's site. Arriba acted as more than a passive conduit of the images by establishing a direct link to the copyrighted images. Therefore, Arriba is liable for publicly displaying Kelly's copyrighted images without his permission.

2. Fair Use of Full-sized Images.

The last issue we must address is whether Arriba's display of Kelly's full-sized images was a fair use. Although Arriba did not address the use of the full-sized images in its fair use argument, the district court considered such use in its analysis, and we will consider Arriba's fair use defense here.

Once again, to decide whom the first factor, the purpose and character of the use, favors, we must determine whether Arriba's use of Kelly's images was transformative. Unlike the use of the images for the thumbnails, displaying Kelly's full-sized images does not enhance Arriba's search engine. The images do not act as a means to access other information on the internet but, rather, are likely the end product themselves. Although users of the search engine could link from the full-sized image to Kelly's web site, any user who is solely searching for images would not need to do so. Because the full-sized images on Arriba's site act primarily as illustrations or artistic expression and the search engine would function the same without them, they do not have a purpose different from Kelly's use of them.

Not only is the purpose the same, but Arriba did not add new expression to the images to make them transformative. Placing the images in a "frame" or locating them near text that specifies the size and originating web site is not enough to create new expression or meaning for the images. In sum, Arriba's full-sized images superseded the object of Kelly's images. Because Arriba has not changed the purpose or character of the use of the images, the first factor favors Kelly.

The analysis of the second factor, the nature of the copyrighted work, is the same as in the previous fair use discussion because Kelly's images are still the copyrighted images at issue. Therefore, as before, this factor slightly weighs in favor of Kelly.

The third fair use factor turns on the amount of the work displayed and the reasonableness of this amount in light of the purpose for the display. Arriba displayed the full images, which cuts against a finding of fair use. And while it was necessary to provide whole images to suit Arriba's purpose of giving users access to the full-sized images without having to go to another site, such a purpose is not legitimate, as we noted above. Therefore, it was not reasonable to copy the full-sized display. The third factor favors Kelly.

The fourth factor often depends upon how transformative the new use is compared to the original use. A work that is very transformative will often be in a different market from the original work and therefore is less likely to cause harm to the original work's market. Works that are not transformative, however, have the same purpose as the original work and will often have a negative effect on the original work's market.

As discussed in the previous fair use analysis, Kelly's markets for his images include using them to attract advertisers and buyers to his web site, and selling or licensing the images to other web sites or stock photo databases. By giving users access to Kelly's full-sized images on its own web site, Arriba harms all of Kelly's markets. Users will no longer have to go to Kelly's web site to see the full-sized images, thereby deterring people from visiting his web site. In addition, users would be able to download the full-sized images from Arriba's site and then sell or license those images themselves, reducing Kelly's opportunity to sell or license his own images. If the display of Kelly's images became widespread across other web sites, it would reduce the number of visitors to Kelly's web site even further and increase the chance of others exploiting his images. These actions would result in substantial adverse effects to the potential markets for Kelly's original works. For this reason, the fourth factor weighs heavily in favor of Kelly.

In conclusion, all of the fair use factors weigh in favor of Kelly. Therefore, the doctrine of fair use does not sanction Arriba's display of Kelly's images through the inline linking or framing processes that puts [*sic*] Kelly's original images within the context of Arriba's web site.

COMMENTS AND QUESTIONS

1. Sorceron, the current owner of Arriba Soft (now called Ditto.com), asked the Ninth Circuit Court of Appeals to rehear this case en banc, a request that was still pending at this writing. The Electronic Frontier Foundation filed an amicus curiae brief in support of the petition for rehearing en banc which criticizes the *Kelly* decision, saying that "it goes astray by failing to realize what is being transmitted and by whom. A proper understanding of the technology involved in Ditto's activities makes it clear that at all times it is Kelly who is transmitting his works to end-users, and thus Kelly who is publicly displaying his own images. Ditto's only transmission is a URL, an address for the location on Kelly's website where the image may be found by an interested viewer." Do you agree? Did the Ninth Circuit reach the right result in its public display discussion?

2. Most legal commentators on linking have thought it should not give rise to copyright liability. See, e.g., Maureen A. O'Rourke, Fencing Cyberspace: Drawing Borders in a Virtual World, 81 Minn. L. Rev. 609 (1998); Edward A. Cavazos & Coe F. Miles, Copyright on the WWW: Linking and Liability, 4 Rich. J. L. & Tech. no. 2 (http://www.richmond.edu/~jolt/v4i2/cavazos.html); David Hayes, Advanced Copyright Issues on the Internet, 7 Texas Intell. Prop. L.J. 1 (1998); Mark A. Lemley, The Law and Economics of Internet Norms, 73 Chi.-Kent L. Rev. 1257 (1998). But see Walter A. Effross, Withdrawal of the Reference: Rights, Rules, and Remedies for Unwelcomed Web-Linking, 49 S.C. L. Rev. 651, 692-93 (1998) (seeming to accept the premise that companies ought to be entitled to prevent unauthorized links to their sites). The caselaw on linking, however, is more mixed than the law review literature. See Ticketmaster, Inc. v. Tickets.com, Copy. L. Rep. (CCH) P28,146 (C.D. Cal. 2000) (deep linking held not to be copyright infringement nor unfair competition); Intellectual Reserve, Inc. v. Utah House Light Ministry, 75 F. Supp.2d 1290 (D. Utah 1999) (preliminary injunction against linking to allegedly infringing copies of church handbook on Internet); Universal City Studios, Inc. v. Reimerdes, 111 F. Supp.2d 294 (S.D.N.Y. 2000) (injunction against links to sites where circumvention software DeCSS was posted).

Objections to liability for linking take two major forms. First, as a legal matter, a Web site that includes an HREF link has not copied anything. Rather, it has pointed the user to a page, and the user may go there and make a copy. If anyone is copying the page, therefore, it is the end user. But Web site owners generally want to encourage end users to visit their sites, even if they object to the particular links that bring them there. So they are unlikely to sue the end users directly. And without proof that the end user is directly infringing, the linking page cannot be liable for contributing to that infringement.

Second, commentators (and some courts) point to the devastating consequences liability for linking would have on the nature of the Internet, which is built on the idea of links. The one U.S. court to address the issue of liability for linking was Bernstein v. J.C. Penney, Inc., 50 U.S.P.Q.2d 1063 (C.D. Cal. 1998). The court rejected the claim. It wrote:

> Plaintiff Gary Bernstein sued Elizabeth Arden Co. and Parfums International, Ltd. (collectively "Arden") for copyright infringement based on multiple linking on the Internet. Plaintiff alleges that Arden and JC Penney were liable because Arden's Passion perfume was promoted on a JC Penney website that was "hyperlinked" to a website operated by the Internet Movie Database ("IMDB") that in turn linked to several other websites, one of which—the Swedish University Network ("SUNET")—contained infringing copies of two of plaintiff's photographs of the actress Elizabeth Taylor, the spokesperson for Arden's perfume.
>
> The parent of Arden, Conopco, moved to dismiss the complaint on the ground that it fails to state a claim upon which relief can be granted. Fed. R. Civ. Pro. 12(b)(6).
>
> Arden contends plaintiff's theory of infringement by multiple linking would have a devastating impact on the Internet and argues the claim should be dismissed for three reasons: (1) a company whose product is merely displayed on another entity's website cannot be held liable for any infringement by the author of that website; (2) linking cannot constitute direct infringement because the computer server of the linking website does not copy or otherwise process the content of the linked-to site; and (3) multiple linking cannot constitute contributory infringement because (a) Internet users viewing of the material at issue is not infringing and thus there was no direct infringement in the United States to which Arden could contribute, see Religious Tech. Center v. Netcom On-Line Comm. Servs., 907 F. Supp. 1361, 1378 n.25 (N.D.Cal. 1995); (b) linking "is capable of substantial noninfringing uses" and thus cannot support a claim for contributory infringement, Sony Corp. v. Universal City Studios, 464 U.S. 417, 442 (1984); and (c) the Court cannot infer from the facts alleged that Arden knew the photos had been posted to SUNET and multiple linking does not constitute substantial participation in any infringement where the linking website does not mention the fact that Internet users could, by following the links, find infringing material on another website. Cf. Sega Enterprises, Ltd. v. MAPHIA, 948 F. Supp. 923 (N.D.Cal. 1996). [The court accepted this argument and dismissed the case without leave to amend].

For an argument that linking should be fair use, see Pamela Samuelson, Fair Use for Computer Programs and Other Copyrightable Works in Digital Form: The Implications of *Sony, Galoob* and *Sega,* 1 J. Intell. Prop. L. 49, 112-116 (1993).

3. Should the same arguments protect efforts to "frame" another's site, as in the *Total News* case? As a technical matter, the code that appears on the framer's site is virtually identical to the code that appears on the linker's site. The only difference is a default instruction to the user's browser to display the two pages side by side, or one in a "frame" around the other. From a copyright perspective, it is hard to see how this changes the result. Indeed, the one U.S. case to have ruled on framing refused to enjoin it pending trial. See Futuredontics v. Applied Anagramics, 152 F.3d 925 (9th Cir. 1998) (unpublished).

Is there reason to be more concerned about framing than about linking? If so, is the concern a copyright concern? Is it a trademark concern—that unsuspecting Internet users will think the two sites are the same, or at least that they are related? Or is there some other theory (misappropriation, say, or unfair competition) that should apply here? Bruce Keller discusses the misappropriation theory in Bruce P. Keller, Condemned to Repeat the Past: The Reemergence of Misappropriation and Other Common Law Theories of Protection for Intellectual Property, 11 Harv. J. L. & Tech. 401 (1997).

4. Should the ability of Web sites to block or deflect unwanted links have any bearing on the legal status of those links?

5. Linking is not the only Internet-based activity as to which there has been a lively legal debate about digital copyright issues. A report issued by the Clinton Administration's Working Group on Intellectual Property Rights of the Information Infrastructure Task Force, entitled "Intellectual Property Rights and the National Information Infrastructure" (Sept. 1995), relied upon the *MAI* decision (discussed in Chapter 2) as precedent for its assertion that copyright owners have the right to control all temporary as well as permanent copies of digital works in computer memory. Other commentators have questioned this conclusion, concluding it would give rise to too much liability. Mark Lemley explored some implications of this issue:

> Resolution of these debates will affect the number of copies made in routine Net transactions, and may also affect who is liable for making those copies. But it should be clear that under any definition, most activities on the Net involve the making of one or more permanent copies that unquestionably implicate §106(1). Sending electronic mail to someone makes at least one copy of the message sent—the copy that resides in semipermanent memory in the recipient computer. Because many computer users regularly back up their systems, another semipermanent copy of the e-mail may be created on tape or floppy disk. Still other copies may be made if the recipient forwards the message to another, stores it in a computer file, or prints a hard copy. Similarly, posting material on a Web page involves making a long-term copy of it on the Web server, and transmitting still other copies to whomever accesses the page. Those who access the page may in turn make permanent or semipermanent copies of the Web page, either by storing or printing the material, forwarding it to another, or by "caching" the page automatically for a certain period of time.
>
> If one accepts the argument that RAM copies are actionable under §106(1), the number of copies made in even the most routine Net transactions increases dramatically. Obviously, each act of uploading or downloading makes a RAM copy in the recipient's computer, but that is only the beginning. When a picture is downloaded from a Web site, the modem at each end will buffer each byte, as will the router, the receiving computer, the Web browser, the video decompression chip, and the video display board. Those seven copies will be made on each such transaction. Further, since most Internet transmissions do not travel directly between sender and receiver, more copies will be made of the individual packets at each node they pass through on their way to the end point.
>
> Finally, consider who is responsible for making these copies. Some are generated by the computer where the message originates, and might therefore be within the control of the individual sending the message (or creating the Web site). But others are made automatically by the recipient's computer, meaning that under the rationale of *MAI* coupled with *Playboy* [*v. Frena*] even innocently receiving an e-mail message may well infringe the copyright in that message. For similar reasons, anyone who browses

the Net and unintentionally runs across infringing material is making infringing copies under this rationale. This includes not only the millions of casual Web browsers, but all the major search engine companies, which use "spiders" to crawl the Internet cataloguing Web sites and making RAM copies in the process. Further, intermediaries are also generating RAM copies and therefore infringing copyright under *MAI*. Intermediaries potentially held liable include not only the Internet service providers playing host to the message originator (for example, Netcom in the *RTC* case) but also every node on every intermediate network that routes one or more of the packets toward its destination, since those routers also buffer the packets they forward. It may be impossible to tell who made copies of which e-mails without conducting a packet routing analysis for each message. And for certain Net functions (notably Usenet and IRC), even the host of the network is a concept that cannot be clearly defined. As Judge Whyte warned in *RTC*, taking the RAM copying and direct infringement theories seriously

would also result in liability for every single Usenet server in the worldwide link of computers transmitting [each] message to every other computer. These parties, who are liable under plaintiff's theory, do no more than operate or implement a system that is essential if Usenet messages are to be widely distributed.

There is nothing in the nature of the Net that suggests the copyright laws will not apply to conduct occurring there. Rather, the problem seems to be how to cabin the definition of copying within reasonable bounds. See Mark A. Lemley, Dealing With Overlapping Copyrights on the Internet, 22 U. Dayton L. Rev. 547 (1997). Lemley goes on to point out that transmission or downloading of material over the Internet not only makes a copy, but is potentially also a public distribution, a public performance, and a public display.

The fact that everything is a copy on the Internet has two important implications. First, it can expand the set of activities that copyright owners get to control. Jessica Litman has argued that copyright owners may obtain what she terms "the exclusive right to read" in cyberspace. See Jessica Litman, The Exclusive Right to Read, 13 Cardozo Arts & Ent. L.J. 29 (1994). She points out that in real space, a customer who buys a book can read the book as many times as he wants, can lend or sell it to others, and can dispose of it as he chooses. By contrast, each new visit to a Web site to read a book—or for that matter, each time the consumer opens a computer file to read the book—is a separate copy over which the copyright owner has control. Litman worries that copyright owners may use that control to price-discriminate or at least to monitor what users are doing in the online environment. See also Julie E. Cohen, A Right to Read Anonymously: A Closer Look at "Copyright Management" in Cyberspace, 28 Conn. L. Rev. 981 (1996); Julie S. Cohen, Copyright and the Perfect Curve, 53 Vand. L. Rev. 1799 (2000).

Second, if everything a user can do on the Internet involves making a copy, every user is a potential infringer. If a user has made a copy of a copyrighted work, he is presumptively liable for infringement. Unless users generally have some sort of defense to copyright infringement, the entire operation of the Internet would seem to be illegal.

One possible defense is to claim an "implied license," an argument which has some plausibility. Companies presumably put information on their Web sites because they want people to be able to access that information. In so doing, they might be said to have granted an implied license to download that information. Cf. Effects, Inc. v. Cohen, 908 F.2d 555 (9th Cir. 1990) (discussing implied copyright licenses). But an implied license relies on the desire of the copyright owner to have the information downloaded. Implied licenses can be expressly disclaimed, which would leave copying illegal. Even if an implied license does exist, its scope may be unclear. Finally, and most significantly, implied license will protect only those who download information from the copyright owner itself or a legitimate licensee. A user who unwittingly stumbles across an infringing page and downloads it will be unable to rely on an implied license defense.

An alternative defense is fair use. Some people place strong reliance on the defense of fair use in the context of computer networks. They argue or assume that even if multiple copies, distributions, and performances occur in the everyday course of running a network, those uses will likely be deemed fair, exempting from liability those who make the copies. It is undoubtedly true that some of the copies at issue here, such as the copies made by routers passing through Internet message packets, ought to be deemed fair use. Nonetheless, exclusive reliance on fair use to justify the very existence of the Net seems unwise. First, it is a defense, and the Supreme Court has made quite clear that defendants face a strong evidentiary burden in demonstrating entitlement. Second, the fair use analysis is extremely fact-specific, which means both that it is hard to predict in advance and that it will be expensive to prove. Finally, courts periodically hold or suggest that exact copying of entire works for commercial purposes is unfair regardless of the circumstances. This is an approach that should worry commercial Internet service providers—and perhaps others as well. See Lemley, Overlapping Copyrights, at 566-67.

Finally, it may be that, as a practical matter, even if what individual users are doing is illegal, no one will bother to sue. The harm caused by an individual browsing the Internet may not be great enough—or the potential damages large enough—to justify an infringement suit. This arguably explains the paucity of Internet copyright decisions to date.

The issue of whether copyright owners should have the exclusive right to control all temporary as well as permanent copies of digital works in the random access memory of computers was hotly debated at the diplomatic conference in Geneva that led to the adoption of the World Intellectual Property Organization Copyright Treaty concluded in December 1996. The draft treaty included such a provision, but after it became clear there was no consensus on the issue, it was dropped from the text of the treaty. For a discussion of this and other controversial issues debated at this diplomatic conference, see Pamela Samuelson, The U.S. Digital Agenda at WIPO, 37 Va. J. Int'l L. 369 (1997). The European Union directive for implementation of the WIPO Copyright Treaty accords copyright owners the right to control temporary copies of works in digital form. See Directive 2001/29/EC of the European Parliament and of the Council of 22 May 2001 on the harmonization of certain aspects of copyright and related rights in the information society, Official Journal L 167, 22/06/2001, available at http://europa.eu.int/eur-lex/.

6. Not all Internet copyright issues originate online. One recent set of disputes has pitted authors against publishers who make back issues available online, either over the Web or in proprietary databases. The U.S. Supreme Court held in New York Times Co. v. Tasini, 120 S. Ct. 2381 (2001) that a license to publish a copyrighted work that was silent on the issue of electronic rights did not give the publisher a right to make the print work available online. (Presumably, contracts signed in the future will treat the issue of electronic rights expressly.) See also Random House, Inc. v. Rosetta Books, LLC, 283 F.3d 490 (2d Cir. 2002) (denying

Random House's motion for preliminary injunction to stop Rosetta from electronic publication of works previously published by Random House, because authors had licensed Random House the right to publish the works as "books," but the court was unconvinced this right extended to e-books that the authors had separately licensed to Rosetta); Greenberg v. National Geographic Society, 244 F.3d 1267 (11th Cir. 2001) (National Geographic did not have the right to republish photos from its magazines as part of a CD-ROM collection without new permission from the photographers).

2. Liability of Internet Service and Access Providers

Most of the early Internet copyright disputes came up in the context of the liability not of those who posted or downloaded infringing material, but of the ISPs or other intermediaries who passed it on. The reason for this is simple: ISPs had deeper pockets than most individual defendants.

The law of ISP liability was significantly changed in 1998, when Congress passed the Digital Millennium Copyright Act, discussed in detail below. The case that follows is still important, however, not only because it sets out the rules that apply to non-ISPs, but because it frames the debate over liability for serving as an intermediary.

Religious Technology Center v. Netcom On-Line Communication Services, Inc.
United States District Court for the Northern District of California
907 F. Supp. 1361 (N.D. Cal. 1995)

RONALD M. WHYTE, United States District Judge.

This case concerns an issue of first impression regarding intellectual property rights in cyberspace. Specifically, this order addresses whether the operator of a computer bulletin board service ("BBS"), and the large Internet access provider that allows that BBS to reach the Internet, should be liable for copyright infringement committed by a subscriber of the BBS.

Plaintiffs Religious Technology Center ("RTC") and Bridge Publications, Inc. ("BPI") hold copyrights in the unpublished and published works of L. Ron Hubbard, the late founder of the Church of Scientology ("the Church"). Defendant Dennis Erlich ("Erlich") is a former minister of Scientology turned vocal critic of the Church, whose pulpit is now the Usenet newsgroup alt.religion.scientology ("a.r.s."), an on-line forum for discussion and criticism of Scientology. Plaintiffs maintain that Erlich infringed their copyrights when he posted portions of their works on a.r.s. Erlich gained his access to the Internet through defendant Thomas Klemesrud's ("Klemesrud's") BBS "support.com." Klemesrud is the operator of the BBS, which is run out of his home and has approximately 500 paying users. Klemesrud's BBS is not directly linked to the Internet, but gains its connection through the facilities of defendant Netcom On-Line Communications, Inc. ("Netcom"), one of the largest providers of Internet access in the United States.

After failing to convince Erlich to stop his postings, plaintiffs contacted defendants Klemesrud and Netcom. Klemesrud responded to plaintiffs' demands that Erlich be kept off his system by asking plaintiffs to prove that they owned the copyrights to the works posted by Erlich. However, plaintiffs refused Klemesrud's request as unreasonable. Netcom similarly refused plaintiffs' request that Erlich not be allowed to gain access to the Internet through its system. Netcom contended that it would be impossible to prescreen Erlich's postings and that to kick Erlich off the Internet meant kicking off the hundreds of users of Klemesrud's BBS. Consequently, plaintiffs named Klemesrud and Netcom in their suit against Erlich, although only on the copyright infringement claims.

I.   Netcom's Motion for Summary Judgment of Noninfringement . . .

B.   *Copyright Infringement . . .*

1.   Direct Infringement

Infringement consists of the unauthorized exercise of one of the exclusive rights of the copyright holder delineated in section 106. 17 U.S.C. §501. Direct infringement does not require intent or any particular state of mind, although willfulness is relevant to the award of statutory damages. 17 U.S.C. §504(c). . . .

a.   Undisputed Facts

The parties do not dispute the basic processes that occur when Erlich posts his allegedly infringing messages to a.r.s. Erlich connects to Klemesrud's BBS using a telephone and a modem. Erlich then transmits his messages to Klemesrud's computer, where they are automatically briefly stored. According to a prearranged pattern established by Netcom's software, Erlich's initial act of posting a message to the Usenet results in the automatic copying of Erlich's message from Klemesrud's computer onto Netcom's computer and onto other computers on the Usenet. In order to ease transmission and for the convenience of Usenet users, Usenet servers maintain postings from newsgroups for a short period of time—eleven days for Netcom's system and three days for Klemesrud's system. Once on Netcom's computers, messages are available to Netcom's customers and Usenet neighbors, who may then download the messages to their own computers. Netcom's local server makes available its postings to a group of Usenet servers, which do the same for other servers until all Usenet sites worldwide have obtained access to the postings, which takes a matter of hours.

Unlike some other large on-line service providers, such as CompuServe, America Online, and Prodigy, Netcom does not create or control the content of the information available to its subscribers. It also does not monitor messages as they are posted. It has, however, suspended the accounts of subscribers who violated its terms and conditions, such as where they had commercial software in their posted files. Netcom admits that, although not currently configured to do this, it may be possible to reprogram its system to screen postings containing particular words or coming from particular individuals. Netcom, however, took no action after it was told by plaintiffs that Erlich had posted messages through Netcom's system that violated plaintiffs' copyrights, instead claiming that it could not shut out Erlich without shutting out all of the users of Klemesrud's BBS.

b.   Creation of Fixed Copies

The Ninth Circuit addressed the question of what constitutes infringement in the context of storage of digital information in a computer's random access memory ("RAM"). MAI Systems Corp. v. Peak Computer, Inc., 991 F.2d 511, 518 (9th Cir. 1993). In *MAI*, the Ninth Circuit upheld a finding of copyright infringement where a repair person, who was not authorized to use the computer owner's licensed operating system software, turned on the computer, thus loading the operating system into RAM for long enough to check an "error log." *Id.* at 518-19. Copyright protection subsists in original works of authorship "fixed in any tangible medium of expression, now known or later developed, from which they can be perceived, reproduced, or otherwise communicated, either directly or with the aid of a machine or device." 17 U.S.C. §102. A work is "fixed" when its "embodiment in a copy . . . is sufficiently permanent or stable to permit it to be perceived, reproduced, or otherwise communicated for a period of more than transitory duration." *Id.* §101. *MAI* established that the loading of data from a storage device into RAM constitutes copying because that data stays in RAM long enough for it to be perceived. *MAI Systems*, 991 F.2d at 518.

In the present case, there is no question after *MAI* that "copies" were created, as Erlich's act of sending a message to a.r.s. caused reproductions of portions of plaintiffs' works on both Klemesrud's and Netcom's storage devices. Even though the messages remained on their systems for at most eleven days, they were sufficiently "fixed" to constitute recognizable copies under the Copyright Act. See Information Infrastructure Task Force, Intellectual Property and the National Information Infrastructure: The Report of the Working Group on Intellectual Property Rights 66 (1995) ("IITF Report").

c.   Is Netcom Directly Liable for Making the Copies?

Accepting that copies were made, Netcom argues that Erlich, and not Netcom, is directly liable for the copying. *MAI* did not address the question raised in this case: whether possessors of computers are liable for incidental copies automatically made on their computers using their software as part of a process initiated by a third party. Netcom correctly distinguishes *MAI* on the ground that Netcom did not take any affirmative action that directly resulted in copying plaintiffs' works other than by installing and maintaining a system whereby software automatically forwards messages received from subscribers onto the Usenet, and temporarily stores copies on its system. Netcom's actions, to the extent that they created a copy of plaintiffs' works, are necessary to having a working system for transmitting Usenet postings to and from the Internet. Unlike the defendants in *MAI*, neither Netcom nor Klemesrud initiated the copying. The defendants in *MAI* turned on their customers' computers thereby creating temporary copies of the operating system, whereas Netcom's and Klemesrud's systems can operate without any human intervention. Thus, unlike *MAI*, the mere fact that Netcom's system incidentally makes temporary copies of plaintiffs' works does not mean Netcom has caused the copying. The court believes that Netcom's act of designing or implementing a system that automatically and uniformly creates temporary copies of all data sent through it is not unlike that of the owner of a copying machine who lets the public make copies with it.[12] Although some of the people using the machine may directly infringe copyrights, courts analyze the machine owner's liability under the rubric of contributory infringement, not direct infringement. See, e.g., RCA Records v. All-Fast Systems, Inc., 594 F. Supp. 335 (S.D.N.Y. 1984); 3 Melville B. Nimmer & David Nimmer, Nimmer on Copyright §12.04[A][2][b], at 12-78 to -79 (1995) ("Nimmer on Copyright"); *Elkin-Koren*, supra, at 363 (arguing that "contributory infringement is more appropriate for dealing with BBS liability, first, because it focuses attention on the BBS-users relationship and the way imposing liability on BBS operators may shape this relationship, and second because it better addresses the complexity of the relationship between BBS operators and subscribers"). Plaintiffs' theory would create many separate acts of infringement and, carried to its natural extreme, would lead to unreasonable liability. It is not difficult to conclude that Erlich infringes by copying a protected work onto his computer and by posting a message to a newsgroup. However, plaintiffs' theory further implicates a Usenet server that carries Erlich's message to other servers regardless of whether that server acts without any human intervention beyond the initial setting up of the system. It would also result in liability for every single Usenet server in the worldwide link of computers transmitting Erlich's message to every other computer. These parties, who are liable under plaintiffs' theory, do no more than operate or implement a

---

12. Netcom compares itself to a common carrier that merely acts as a passive conduit for information. In a sense, a Usenet server that forwards all messages acts like a common carrier, passively retransmitting every message that gets sent through it. Netcom would seem no more liable than the phone company for carrying an infringing facsimile transmission or storing an infringing audio recording on its voice mail. As Netcom's counsel argued, holding such a server liable would be like holding the owner of the highway, or at least the operator of a toll booth, liable for the criminal activities that occur on its roads. Since other similar carriers of information are not liable for infringement, there is some basis for exempting Internet access providers from liability for infringement by their users. The IITF Report concluded that "if an entity provided only the wires and conduit—such as the telephone company, it would have a good argument for an exemption if it was truly in the same position as a common carrier and could not control who or what was on its system." IITF Report at 122. Here, perhaps, the analogy is not completely appropriate as Netcom does more than just "provide the wire and conduits." Further, Internet providers are not natural monopolies that are bound to carry all the traffic that one wishes to pass through them, as with the usual common carrier. See *id.* at 122 n.392 (citing Federal Communications Commission v. Midwest Video Corp., 440 U.S. 689, 701, 59 L. Ed. 2d 692, 99 S. Ct. 1435 (1979)). Section 111 of the Copyright Act codifies the exemption for passive carriers who are otherwise liable for a secondary transmission. 3 Melville B. Nimmer & David Nimmer, Nimmer on Copyright §12.04[B][3], at 12-99 (1995). However, the carrier must not have any direct or indirect control over the content or selection of the primary transmission. *Id.*; 17 U.S.C. §111(a)(3). Cf. infra part I.B.3.a. In any event, common carriers are granted statutory exemptions for liability that might otherwise exist. Here, Netcom does not fall under this statutory exemption, and thus faces the usual strict liability scheme that exists for copyright. Whether a new exemption should be carved out for online service providers is to be resolved by Congress, not the courts. Compare Comment, "Online Service Providers and Copyright Law: The Need for Change," 1 Syracuse J. Legis. & Pol'y 197, 202 (1995) (citing recommendations of online service providers for amending the Copyright Act to create liability only where a "provider has actual knowledge that a work that is being or has been transmitted onto, or stored on, its system is infringing, and has the 'ability and authority' to stop the transmission, and has, after a reasonable amount of time, allowed the infringing activity to continue") with IITF Report at 122 (recommending that Congress not exempt service providers from strict liability for direct infringements).

system that is essential if Usenet messages are to be widely distributed. There is no need to construe the Act to make all of these parties infringers. Although copyright is a strict liability statute, there should still be some element of volition or causation which is lacking where a defendant's system is merely used to create a copy by a third party.

Plaintiffs point out that the infringing copies resided for eleven days on Netcom's computer and were sent out from it onto the "Information Superhighway." However, under plaintiffs' theory, any storage of a copy that occurs in the process of sending a message to the Usenet is an infringement. While it is possible that less "damage" would have been done if Netcom had heeded plaintiffs' warnings and acted to prevent Erlich's message from being forwarded, this is not relevant to its direct liability for copying. The same argument is true of Klemesrud and any Usenet server. Whether a defendant makes a direct copy that constitutes infringement cannot depend on whether it received a warning to delete the message. See D.C. Comics, Inc. v. Mini Gift, 912 F.2d 29, 35 (2d Cir. 1990). This distinction may be relevant to contributory infringement, however, where knowledge is an element. See infra part I.B.2.a.

The court will now consider two district court opinions that have addressed the liability of BBS operators for infringing files uploaded by subscribers.

d. Playboy Case

Playboy Enterprises, Inc. v. Frena involved a suit against the operator of a small BBS whose system contained files of erotic pictures. 839 F. Supp. 1552, 1554 (M.D. Fla. 1993). A subscriber of the defendant's BBS had uploaded files containing digitized pictures copied from the plaintiff's copyrighted magazine, which files remained on the BBS for other subscribers to download. *Id.* The court did not conclude, as plaintiffs suggest in this case, that the BBS is itself liable for the unauthorized reproduction of plaintiffs' work; instead, the court concluded that the BBS operator was liable for violating the plaintiff's right to publicly distribute and display copies of its work. *Id.* at 1556-57.

In support of their argument that Netcom is directly liable for copying plaintiffs' works, plaintiffs cite to the court's conclusion that "there is no dispute that [the BBS operator] supplied a product containing unauthorized copies of a copyrighted work. It does not matter that [the BBS operator] claims he did not make the copies himself." *Id.* at 1556. It is clear from the context of this discussion that the Playboy court was looking only at the exclusive right to distribute copies to the public, where liability exists regardless of whether the defendant makes copies. Here, however, plaintiffs do not argue that Netcom is liable for its public distribution of copies. Instead, they claim that Netcom is liable because its computers in fact made copies. Therefore, the above-quoted language has no bearing on the issue of direct liability for unauthorized reproductions. Notwithstanding *Playboy's* holding that a BBS operator may be directly liable for distributing or displaying to the public copies of protected works, this court holds that the storage on a defendant's system of infringing copies and retransmission to other servers is not a direct infringement by the BBS operator of the exclusive right to reproduce the work where such copies are uploaded by an infringing user. *Playboy* does not hold otherwise.

e. *Sega* Case

A court in this district addressed the issue of whether a BBS operator is liable for copyright infringement where it solicited subscribers to upload files containing copyrighted materials to the BBS that were available for others to download. Sega Enterprises Ltd. v. MAPHIA, 857 F. Supp. 679, 683 (N.D. Cal. 1994). The defendant's "MAPHIA" BBS contained copies of plaintiff Sega's video game programs that were uploaded by users. *Id.* at 683. The defendant solicited the uploading of such programs and received consideration for the right to download files. *Id.* Access was given for a fee or to those purchasing the defendant's hardware device that allowed Sega video game cartridges to be copied. *Id.* at 683-84. The court granted a preliminary injunction against the defendant, finding that plaintiffs had shown a prima facie case of direct and contributory infringement. *Id.* at 687. The court found that copies were made by unknown users of the BBS when files were uploaded and downloaded. *Id.* Further, the court found that the defendant's knowledge of the infringing activities, encouragement, direction and provision of the facilities through his operation of the BBS constituted contributory infringement, even though the defendant did not know exactly when files were uploaded or downloaded. *Id.* at 686-87.

This court is not convinced that *Sega* provides support for a finding of direct infringement where copies are made on a defendant's BBS by users who upload files. Although there is some language in *Sega* regarding direct infringement, it is entirely conclusory:

> Sega has established a prima facie case of direct copyright infringement under 17 U.S.C. §501. Sega has established that unauthorized copies of its games are made when such games are uploaded to the MAPHIA bulletin board, here with the knowledge of Defendant Scherman. These games are thereby placed on the storage media of the electronic bulletin board by unknown users.

Id. at 686. The court's reference to the "knowledge of Defendant" indicates that the court was focusing on contributory infringement, as knowledge is not an element of direct infringement. Perhaps, *Sega*'s references to direct infringement and that "copies . . . are made" are to the direct liability of the "unknown users," as there can be no contributory infringement by a defendant without direct infringement by another. See 3 Nimmer on Copyright §12.04[A][3][a], at 12-89. Thus, the court finds that neither *Playboy* nor *Sega* requires finding Netcom liable for direct infringement of plaintiffs' exclusive right to reproduce their works.[17]

f. Public Distribution and Display?

Plaintiffs allege that Netcom is directly liable for making copies of their works. They also allege that Netcom violated their exclusive rights to publicly display cop-

---

17. To the extent that *Sega* holds that BBS operators are directly liable for copyright infringement when users upload infringing works to their systems, this court respectfully disagrees with the court's holding for the reasons discussed above. Further, such a holding was dicta, as there was evidence that the defendant knew of the infringing uploads by users and, in fact, actively encouraged such activity, thus supporting the contributory infringement theory. *Id.* at 683.

ies of their works. There are no allegations that Netcom violated plaintiffs' exclusive right to publicly distribute their works. However, in their discussion of direct infringement, plaintiffs insist that Netcom is liable for "maintaining copies of [Erlich's] messages on its server for eleven days for access by its subscribers and 'USENET neighbors'" and they compare this case to the *Playboy* case, which discussed the right of public distribution. Plaintiffs also argued this theory of infringement at oral argument. Because this could be an attempt to argue that Netcom has infringed plaintiffs' rights of public distribution and display, the court will address these arguments.

Playboy concluded that the defendant infringed the plaintiff's exclusive rights to publicly distribute and display copies of its works. 839 F. Supp. at 1556-57. The court is not entirely convinced that the mere possession of a digital copy on a BBS that is accessible to some members of the public constitutes direct infringement by the BBS operator. Such a holding suffers from the same problem of causation as the reproduction argument. Only the subscriber should be liable for causing the distribution of plaintiffs' work, as the contributing actions of the BBS provider are automatic and indiscriminate. Erlich could have posted his messages through countless access providers and the outcome would be the same: anyone with access to Usenet newsgroups would be able to read his messages. There is no logical reason to draw a line around Netcom and Klemesrud and say that they are uniquely responsible for distributing Erlich's messages. Netcom is not even the first link in the chain of distribution—Erlich had no direct relationship with Netcom but dealt solely with Klemesrud's BBS, which used Netcom to gain its Internet access. Every Usenet server has a role in the distribution, so plaintiffs' argument would create unreasonable liability. Where the BBS merely stores and passes along all messages sent by its subscribers and others, the BBS should not be seen as causing these works to be publicly distributed or displayed.

Even accepting the *Playboy* court's holding, the case is factually distinguishable. Unlike the BBS in that case, Netcom does not maintain an archive of files for its users. Thus, it cannot be said to be "supplying a product." In contrast to some of its larger competitors, Netcom does not create or control the content of the information available to its subscribers; it merely provides access to the Internet, whose content is controlled by no single entity. Although the Internet consists of many different computers networked together, some of which may contain infringing files, it does not make sense to hold the operator of each computer liable as an infringer merely because his or her computer is linked to a computer with an infringing file. It would be especially inappropriate to hold liable a service that acts more like a conduit, in other words, one that does not itself keep an archive of files for more than a short duration. Finding such a service liable would involve an unreasonably broad construction of public distribution and display rights. No purpose would be served by holding liable those who have no ability to control the information to which their subscribers have access, even though they might be in some sense helping to achieve the Internet's automatic "public distribution" and the users' "public" display of files.

g. Conclusion

The court is not persuaded by plaintiffs' argument that Netcom is directly liable for the copies that are made and stored on its computer. Where the infringing subscriber is clearly directly liable for the same act, it does not make sense to adopt a rule that could lead to the liability of countless parties whose role in the infringement is nothing more than setting up and operating a system that is necessary for the functioning of the Internet. Such a result is unnecessary as there is already a party directly liable for causing the copies to be made. Plaintiffs occasionally claim that they only seek to hold liable a party that refuses to delete infringing files after they have been warned. However, such liability cannot be based on a theory of direct infringement, where knowledge is irrelevant. The court does not find workable a theory of infringement that would hold the entire Internet liable for activities that cannot reasonably be deterred. Billions of bits of data flow through the Internet and are necessarily stored on servers throughout the network and it is thus practically impossible to screen out infringing bits from noninfringing bits. Because the court cannot see any meaningful distinction (without regard to knowledge) between what Netcom did and what every other Usenet server does, the court finds that Netcom cannot be held liable for direct infringement. Cf. IITF Report at 69 (noting uncertainty regarding whether BBS operator should be directly liable for reproduction or distribution of files uploaded by a subscriber).

[The court also rejected plaintiff's claim for vicarious infringement, but found that factual issues precluded summary judgment on the contributory infringement claim.]

COMMENTS AND QUESTIONS

1. The *Netcom* ruling against direct liability of Internet service providers for copyright infringement initiated by users of their systems came at a critical juncture in the national debate on these issues. The Clinton Administration's Report of the Working Group on Intellectual Property Rights of the Information Infrastructure Task Force entitled "Intellectual Property Rights and the National Information Infrastructure" (Sept. 1995) had taken the position that Internet service providers were and should be strictly liable for all user infringements on account of the copying and distribution their computers did in facilitation of user activities. This report relied heavily on the *Playboy v. Frena* and *Sega v. MAPHIA* decisions in support of this conclusion. Most commentators, however, criticized this conclusion. See, e.g., 3 Nimmer on Copyright §12.04[A][2][b], at 12-78 to 12-79 (1995); Henry H. Perritt Jr., Law and the Information Superhighway 430 (1996); Lance Rose, Netlaw 91-92 (1995); Edward A. Cavazos & G. Chin Chao, System Operator Liability for a User's Copyright Infringement, 4 Tex. Intell. Prop. L.J. 13 (1995); Niva Elkin-Koren, Copyright Law and Social Dialogue on the Information Superhighway: The Case Against Copyright Liability of Bulletin Board Operators, 13 Cardozo Arts & Ent. L.J. 346, 390 (1995).

Since *Netcom*, most courts to consider the issue have rejected the *Frena* approach in favor of *Netcom*'s. The court in Sega v. MAPHIA reversed itself, issuing a permanent injunction based solely on a finding of inducement and contributory, rather than direct, infringement. Sega of America v. MAPHIA, 948 F. Supp. 923 (C.D. Cal. 1996). See also Marobie-FL Inc. v. National Ass'n of Fire Equipment Distributors, 983 F. Supp. 1167 (N.D. Ill. 1997) (following *Netcom*).

On the other hand, district courts in two cases involving copyrighted Playboy images have found direct infringement, even in circumstances where the defendant's role in providing the infringing material was less than clear. See Playboy Ents., Inc. v. Webbworld, 991 F. Supp. 543 (N.D. Tex. 1997); Playboy Ents., Inc. v. Hardenburgh, 982 F. Supp. 503 (N.D. Ohio 1997). For an excellent treatment of the problems of indirect and contributory infringement in the Internet context, see Elkin-Koren, supra at 345.

The liability of intermediaries, such as Internet access or service providers, was also debated at the diplomatic conference leading up to adoption of the WIPO Copyright Treaty. An agreed upon statement of interpretation to the WIPO Copyright Treaty says that merely providing services for transmission of digital works should not be construed as a communication to the public. Thus, the *Netcom* decision's conclusion about direct infringement liability of Internet access providers has become an international norm

2. The *Netcom* court notes that the holding in Playboy v. Frena was based on liability for distribution and public display, while the RTC claimed that Netcom had engaged in reproduction. What difference (if any) does this make? On the interaction between the various rights in section 106 in the context of the Internet, see Mark A. Lemley, Dealing with Overlapping Copyrights on the Internet, 22 U. Dayton L. Rev. 547 (1997); Jessica Litman, The Exclusive Right to Read, 13 Cardozo Arts & Ent. L.J. 29 (1994). Lemley argues that on the Internet, a single act (say, posting material on a Web page for download) may constitute reproduction, derivation, distribution, performance, display, *and* importation. The fact that the exclusive rights of copyright overlap on the Internet has some troubling consequences. In particular, it means that assignments and licenses of part, rather than all, of a copyright may be ineffective on the Internet and indeed may leave *no* party with the right to post material on the Web. It also means that certain specific copyright defenses, such as the "first sale" doctrine, are rendered ineffective on the Internet because they only apply to one of the exclusive rights, rather than all of them.

Is this a problem with copyright on the Internet? If so, what should be done about it?

3. How does the *Netcom* decision comport with the policies underlying the Copyright Act? On the one hand, it seems grossly unfair to hold Netcom liable for Internet postings that as a practical matter it could never effectively screen for copyright infringement. The case for shielding other parties from liability for direct infringement—such as those who own the routers through which the message passes —is even stronger. On the other hand, the practical effect of the court's holding may be that many copyright owners are unable to recoup their losses from infringement, because the individual who posts the infringing material is either unreachable by court, impecunious, or anonymous.

Which of these competing concerns is stronger? Is your answer affected by the possibility that ISPs could insure against liability? See I. Trotter Hardy, The Proper Legal Regime for Cyberspace, 55 U. Pitt. L. Rev. 993 (1994). Does the objection to holding Netcom liable reflect a more general objection to copyright's rather harsh rule of strict liability for direct infringement?

4. After rejecting RTC's direct liability theory, the court in *Netcom* went on to consider whether to grant Netcom's motion for summary judgment on RTC's

vicarious or contributory infringement claims. The court granted summary judgment in favor of Netcom on the vicarious liability claim because, although there was a genuine dispute as to whether Netcom could supervise and control user postings, Netcom derived no direct financial benefit from user infringements. Suppose that Netcom charged its subscribers per posting they made or per bit they downloaded. Would that make a difference? Should it?

More significant than the *Netcom* ruling on vicarious infringement was the court's analysis of the contributory infringement claim. The court decided that there was a genuine dispute as to whether Netcom knew or should have known about Erlich's infringements at least after receiving a letter from RTC's lawyers. The court observed:

> Netcom argues that its knowledge after receiving notice of Erlich's alleged infringing activities was too equivocal given the difficulty in assessing whether registrations are valid and whether use is fair. Although a mere unsupported allegation of infringement by a copyright owner may not automatically put a defendant on notice of infringing activity, Netcom's position that liability must be unequivocal is unsupportable. . . . Where a BBS operator cannot reasonably verify a claim of infringement, either because of a possible fair use defense, the lack of copyright notices on the copies, or the copyright holder's failure to provide the necessary documentation to show that there is a likely infringement, the operator's lack of knowledge will be found reasonable and there will be no liability for contributory infringement for allowing the continued distribution of the works on its system.

The court went on to say that if RTC could prove that Netcom knew or should have known of Erlich's infringement after receiving the letter from RTC's counsel, "Netcom will be liable for contributory infringement since its failure to simply cancel Erlich's infringing message and thereby stop an infringing copy from being distributed worldwide constitutes substantial participation in Erlich's public distribution of the message."

5. The *Netcom* decision was influential in Congress as well as in subsequent cases. Judge Whyte's conclusion that Internet service providers should not be liable for transmitting and routing infringing materials through their systems became the basis of one of four "safe harbor" provisions in the Digital Millennium Copyright Act in 1998. See 17 U.S.C. §512(a). His conclusion that ISPs should have a responsibility to investigate and take down infringing materials after receiving adequate notice from copyright owners about infringements became a basis for three other safe harbor provisions: §512(b) for the intermediate or temporary storage of material for purposes of system caching, §512(c) for storage of information on behalf of users on the ISPs' servers, and §512(d) for information-locating tools, such as search engines, that might provide links to infringing materials on other servers. ISPs have no liability for these activities as long as they have no actual knowledge of the infringing materials, are not aware of facts and circumstances from which infringement would be apparent, and upon learning of infringements, take expeditious action to remove or disable infringing materials from their servers. Section 512(c)(3) specifies the information that must be included in a communication to an ISP about allegedly infringing materials in order to be effective notice to trigger the duty to investigate. "Notice and take down" rules have also been adopted in other jurisdictions, notably the European Union.

The DMCA safe harbor provisions do not apply automatically. To qualify for them, an ISP must meet three general threshold conditions: (i) adopt, implement, and inform its subscribers of its policy for providing for termination of users who are repeat copyright infringers, 17 U.S.C. §512(i)(1)(A); (ii) adopt standard technical measures used by copyright owners to identify and protect copyrighted works, 17 U.S.C. §512(i)(1)(B); and (iii) designate an agent to receive notification of claimed infringement from copyright owners and register that agent with the Copyright Office. ISPs satisfying these and other specific safe harbor requirements will be relieved of liability for damages and for most equitable relief.

6.   DMCA safe harbor provisions have not resolved all disputes between copyright owners and ISPs without litigation. One contentious issue has been the adequacy of the copyright owner's notice to ISPs about infringing materials. See, e.g., ALS Scan, Inc. v. RemarQ Communities, Inc., 239 F.3d 619 (4th Cir. 2001) (rejecting arguments about inadequacy of notice); Arista Records, Inc. v. MP3Board, Inc., 2002 U.S. Dist. LEXIS 16165 (S.D.N.Y. 2002) (finding some notices ineffective and others effective). However, many ISPs have prevailed using DMCA safe harbor defenses. See, e.g., Ellison v. Robertson, 189 F. Supp.2d 1051 (C.D. Cal. 2002) (granting summary judgment to AOL under the DMCA safe harbor for intermediate and transient storage of materials in the course of transmission even though the complaining author's novel was available on AOL servers for two weeks and the author's agent had notified AOL and asked it to take the material down); Arista Records, Inc. v. MP3Board, Inc., 2002 U.S. Dist. LEXIS 16165 (S.D.N.Y. 2002) (denying cross motions for summary judgment on safe harbor defense raised by search engine); Hendrickson v. eBay, Inc., 165 F. Supp.2d 1082 (C.D. Cal. 2001) (online auction site qualified for DMCA safe harbor as to listings of allegedly infringing copies of movies). See also Stoner v. eBay, Inc., 56 U.S.P.Q.2d (BNA) 1852 (Calif. Super. Ct. 2000) (online auction site was immune under the Communications Decency Act, 47 U.S.C. sec. 230, for its customers' sales of "bootleg" sound recordings through its service).

7.   In the case we discuss below, Napster moved for partial summary judgment on grounds that it qualified for the §512(a) transmission and routing safe harbors. The court accepted Napster's claim that four of the five elements of a §512(a) defense were met because Napster did not initiate the transmissions alleged to be infringing, the transmission was carried out through an automatic technical process without selection of material by it, Napster did not select the recipients of the material, and the material was transmitted without modification of its contents. Yet, the judge denied the motion because Napster did not "transmit, route, or provide connections *through* its systems" within the meaning of §512(a) and therefore did fall within the scope of the transmission safe harbor. The trial judge also questioned whether Napster had established compliance with the threshold requirements of adopting and implementing a termination policy for repeat infringers. See A&M Records v. Napster, 2000 WL 573136 (N.D. Cal. 2000). On appeal, the Ninth Circuit questioned the district court's determination that the DMCA safe harbor could not shelter Napster from indirect liability, but inexplicably postponed resolution of that issue until trial. See 239 F.3d at 1025. Should the court have addressed the issue? Would this have provided a viable means for enabling Napster to operate?

3. Contributory and Vicarious Liability for Copyright Infringement

≡ *A&M Records, Inc. v. Napster, Inc.*
≡ United States Court of Appeals for the Ninth Circuit
≡ *239 F.3d 1004 (9th Cir. 2001)*

BEEZER, Circuit Judge . . .

In 1987, the Moving Picture Experts Group set a standard file format for the storage of audio recordings in a digital format called MPEG-3, abbreviated as "MP3." Digital MP3 files are created through a process colloquially called "ripping." Ripping software allows a computer owner to copy an audio compact disk ("audio CD") directly onto a computer's hard drive by compressing the audio information on the CD into the MP3 format. The MP3's compressed format allows for rapid transmission of digital audio files from one computer to another by electronic mail or any other file transfer protocol.

Napster facilitates the transmission of MP3 files between and among its users. Through a process commonly called "peer-to-peer" file sharing, Napster allows its users to: (1) make MP3 music files stored on individual computer hard drives available for copying by other Napster users; (2) search for MP3 music files stored on other users' computers; and (3) transfer exact copies of the contents of other users' MP3 files from one computer to another via the Internet. These functions are made possible by Napster's MusicShare software, available free of charge from Napster's Internet site, and Napster's network servers and server-side software. Napster provides technical support for the indexing and searching of MP3 files, as well as for its other functions, including a "chat room," where users can meet to discuss music, and a directory where participating artists can provide information about their music.

A. Accessing the System

In order to copy MP3 files through the Napster system, a user must first access Napster's Internet site and download the MusicShare software to his individual computer. See http://www.Napster.com. Once the software is installed, the user can access the Napster system. A first-time user is required to register with the Napster system by creating a "user name" and password.

B. Listing Available Files

If a registered user wants to list available files stored in his computer's hard drive on Napster for others to access, he must first create a "user library" directory on his computer's hard drive. The user then saves his MP3 files in the library directory, using self-designated file names. He next must log into the Napster system using his user name and password. His MusicShare software then searches his user library and verifies that the available files are properly formatted. If in the correct MP3 format, the names of the MP3 files will be uploaded from the user's computer to the Napster servers. The content of the MP3 files remains stored in the user's computer.

Once uploaded to the Napster servers, the user's MP3 file names are stored in a server-side "library" under the user's name and become part of a "collective directory" of files available for transfer during the time the user is logged onto the Napster system. The collective directory is fluid; it tracks users who are connected in real time, displaying only file names that are immediately accessible.

C. Searching for Available Files

Napster allows a user to locate other users' MP3 files in two ways: through Napster's search function and through its "hotlist" function.

Software located on the Napster servers maintains a "search index" of Napster's collective directory. To search the files available from Napster users currently connected to the network servers, the individual user accesses a form in the Music-Share software stored in his computer and enters either the name of a song or an artist as the object of the search. The form is then transmitted to a Napster server and automatically compared to the MP3 file names listed in the server's search index. Napster's server compiles a list of all MP3 file names pulled from the search index which include the same search terms entered on the search form and transmits the list to the searching user. The Napster server does not search the contents of any MP3 file; rather, the search is limited to "a text search of the file names indexed in a particular cluster. Those file names may contain typographical errors or otherwise inaccurate descriptions of the content of the files since they are designated by other users." *Napster,* 114 F. Supp.2d at 906.

To use the "hotlist" function, the Napster user creates a list of other users' names from whom he has obtained MP3 files in the past. When logged onto Napster's servers, the system alerts the user if any user on his list (a "hotlisted user") is also logged onto the system. If so, the user can access an index of all MP3 file names in a particular hotlisted user's library and request a file in the library by selecting the file name. The contents of the hotlisted user's MP3 file are not stored on the Napster system.

D. Transferring Copies of an MP3 File

To transfer a copy of the contents of a requested MP3 file, the Napster server software obtains the Internet address of the requesting user and the Internet address of the "host user" (the user with the available files). See generally Brookfield Communications, Inc. v. West Coast Entm't Corp., 174 F.3d 1036, 1044 (9th Cir. 1999) (describing, in detail, the structure of the Internet). The Napster servers then communicate the host user's Internet address to the requesting user. The requesting user's computer uses this information to establish a connection with the host user and downloads a copy of the contents of the MP3 file from one computer to the other over the Internet, "peer-to-peer." A downloaded MP3 file can be played directly from the user's hard drive using Napster's Music-Share program or other software. The file may also be transferred back onto an audio CD if the user has access to equipment designed for that purpose. In both cases, the quality of the original sound recording is slightly diminished by transfer to the MP3 format.

This architecture is described in some detail to promote an understanding of transmission mechanics as opposed to the content of the transmissions. The content is the subject of our copyright infringement analysis. . . .

III

Plaintiffs claim Napster users are engaged in the wholesale reproduction and distribution of copyrighted works, all constituting direct infringement. The district court agreed. We note that the district court's conclusion that plaintiffs have presented a prima facie case of direct infringement by Napster users is not presently appealed by Napster. We only need briefly address the threshold requirements.

A. Infringement

Plaintiffs must satisfy two requirements to present a prima facie case of direct infringement: (1) they must show ownership of the allegedly infringed material and (2) they must demonstrate that the alleged infringers violate at least one exclusive right granted to copyright holders under 17 U.S.C. §106. See 17 U.S.C. §501(a) (infringement occurs when alleged infringer engages in activity listed in §106). Plaintiffs have sufficiently demonstrated ownership. The record supports the district court's determination that "as much as eighty-seven percent of the files available on Napster may be copyrighted and more than seventy percent may be owned or administered by plaintiffs." *Napster,* 114 F. Supp.2d at 911.

The district court further determined that plaintiffs' exclusive rights under §106 were violated: "here the evidence establishes that a majority of Napster users use the service to download and upload copyrighted music. . . . And by doing that, it constitutes—the uses constitute direct infringement of plaintiffs' musical compositions, recordings." A&M Records, Inc. v. Napster, Inc., Nos. 99-5183, 00-0074, 2000 WL 1009483, at *1 (N. D. Cal. July 26, 2000) (transcript of proceedings). The district court also noted that "it is pretty much acknowledged . . . by Napster that this is infringement." Id. We agree that plaintiffs have shown that Napster users infringe at least two of the copyright holders' exclusive rights: the rights of reproduction, §106(1); and distribution, 4229 §106(3). Napster users who upload file names to the search index for others to copy violate plaintiffs' distribution rights. Napster users who download files containing copyrighted music violate plaintiffs' reproduction rights.

Napster asserts an affirmative defense to the charge that its users directly infringe plaintiffs' copyrighted musical compositions and sound recordings.

B. Fair Use

Napster contends that its users do not directly infringe plaintiffs' copyrights because the users are engaged in fair use of the material. See 17 U.S.C. §107 ("The fair use of a copyrighted work . . . is not an infringement of copyright."). Napster identifies three specific alleged fair uses: sampling, where users make temporary copies of a work before purchasing; space-shifting, where users access a sound recording through the Napster system that they already own in audio CD format; and permissive distribution of recordings by both new and established artists.

The district court considered factors listed in 17 U.S.C. §107, which guide a court's fair use determination. These factors are: (1) the purpose and character of the use; (2) the nature of the copyrighted work; (3) the "amount and substantiality of the portion used" in relation to the work as a whole; and (4) the effect of the use upon the potential market for the work or the value of the work. See 17 U.S.C. §107. The district court first conducted a general analysis of Napster system uses under §107, and then applied its reasoning to the alleged fair uses identified by Napster. The district court concluded that Napster users are not fair users. We agree. We first address the court's overall fair use analysis.

1. Purpose and Character of the Use

This factor focuses on whether the new work merely replaces the object of the original creation or instead adds a further purpose or different character. In other words, this factor asks "whether and to what extent the new work is 'transformative.'" See Campbell v. Acuff-Rose Music, Inc., 510 U.S. 569, 579, 127 L. Ed.2d 500, 114 S. Ct. 1164 (1994).

The district court first concluded that downloading MP3 files does not transform the copyrighted work. Napster, 114 F. Supp.2d at 912. This conclusion is supportable. Courts have been reluctant to find fair use when an original work is merely retransmitted in a different medium. See, e.g., Infinity Broadcast Corp. v. Kirkwood, 150 F.3d 104, 108 (2d Cir. 1994) (concluding that retransmission of radio broadcast over telephone lines is not transformative); UMG Recordings, Inc. v. MP3. com, Inc., 92 F. Supp.2d 349, 351 (S.D.N.Y.) (finding that reproduction of audio CD into MP3 format does not "transform" the work), *certification denied*, 2000 U.S. Dist. LEXIS 7439, 2000 WL 710056 (S.D.N.Y. June 1, 2000) ("Defendant's copyright infringement was clear, and the mere fact that it was clothed in the exotic webbing of the Internet does not disguise its illegality.").

This "purpose and character" element also requires the district court to determine whether the allegedly infringing use is commercial or noncommercial. See Campbell, 510 U.S. at 584-85. A commercial use weighs against a finding of fair use but is not conclusive on the issue. *Id*. The district court determined that Napster users engage in commercial use of the copyrighted materials largely because (1) "a host user sending a file cannot be said to engage in a personal use when distributing that file to an anonymous requester" and (2) "Napster users get for free something they would ordinarily have to buy." Napster, 114 F. Supp.2d at 912. The district court's findings are not clearly erroneous.

Direct economic benefit is not required to demonstrate a commercial use. Rather, repeated and exploitative copying of copyrighted works, even if the copies are not offered for sale, may constitute a commercial use. See Worldwide Church of God v. Philadelphia Church of God, 227 F.3d 1110, 1118 (9th Cir. 2000) (stating that church that copied religious text for its members "unquestionably profited" from the unauthorized "distribution and use of [the text] without having to account to the copyright holder"); American Geophysical Union v. Texaco, Inc., 60

F.3d 913, 922 (2d Cir. 1994) (finding that researchers at for-profit laboratory gained indirect economic advantage by photocopying copyrighted scholarly articles). In the record before us, commercial use is demonstrated by a showing that repeated and exploitative unauthorized copies of copyrighted works were made to save the expense of purchasing authorized copies. See *Worldwide Church,* 227 F.3d at 1117-18; Sega Enters. Ltd. v. MAPHIA, 857 F. Supp. 679, 687 (N.D. Cal. 1994) (finding commercial use when individuals downloaded copies of video games "to avoid having to buy video game cartridges"); see also *American Geophysical,* 60 F.3d at 922. Plaintiffs made such a showing before the district court.

We also note that the definition of a financially motivated transaction for the purposes of criminal copyright actions includes trading infringing copies of a work for other items, "including the receipt of other copyrighted works." See No Electronic Theft Act ("NET Act"), Pub. L. No. 105-147, 18 U.S.C. §101 (defining "Financial Gain").

2. The Nature of the Use

Works that are creative in nature are "closer to the core of intended copyright protection" than are more fact-based works. See Campbell, 510 U.S. at 586. The district court determined that plaintiffs' "copyrighted musical compositions and sound recordings are creative in nature . . . which cuts against a finding of fair use under the second factor." *Napster,* 114 F. Supp. 2d at 913. We find no error in the district court's conclusion.

3. The Portion Used

"While 'wholesale copying does not preclude fair use per se, 'copying an entire work 'militates against a finding of fair use.'" *Worldwide Church,* 227 F.3d at 1118 (quoting Hustler Magazine, Inc. v. Moral Majority, Inc., 796 F.2d 1148, 1155 (9th Cir. 1986)). The district court determined that Napster users engage in "wholesale copying" of copyrighted work because file transfer necessarily "involves copying the entirety of the copyrighted work." *Napster,* 114 F. Supp.2d at 913. We agree. We note, however, that under certain circumstances, a court will conclude that a use is fair even when the protected work is copied in its entirety. See, e.g., Sony Corp. v. Universal City Studios, Inc., 464 U.S. 417, 449-50, 78 L. Ed. 2d 574, 104 S. Ct. 774 (1984) (acknowledging that fair use of time-shifting necessarily involved making a full copy of a protected work).

4. Effect of Use on Market

"Fair use, when properly applied, is limited to copying by others which does not materially impair the marketability of the work which is copied." Harper & Row Publishers, Inc. v. Nation Enters., 471 U.S. 539, 566-67, 85 L. Ed.2d 588, 105 S. Ct. 2218 (1985). "The importance of this [fourth] factor will vary, not only with the amount of harm, but also with the relative strength of the showing on the other factors." Campbell, 510 U.S. at 591 n.21. The proof required to demonstrate present or future market harm varies with the purpose and character of the use:

A challenge to a noncommercial use of a copyrighted work requires proof either that the particular use is harmful, or that if it should become wide-spread, it would adversely affect the potential market for the copyrighted work. . . . *If the intended use is for commercial gain, that likelihood* [of market harm] *may be presumed. But if it is for a noncommercial purpose, the likelihood must be demonstrated.*

Sony, 464 U.S. at 451 (emphases added).

Addressing this factor, the district court concluded that Napster harms the market in "at least" two ways: It reduces audio CD sales among college students and it "raises barriers to plaintiffs' entry into the market for the digital downloading of music." *Napster*, 114 F. Supp.2d at 913. The district court relied on evidence plaintiffs submitted to show that Napster use harms the market for their copyrighted musical compositions and sound recordings. In a separate memorandum and order regarding the parties' objections to the expert reports, the district court examined each report, finding some more appropriate and probative than others. Notably, plaintiffs' expert, Dr. E. Deborah Jay, conducted a survey (the "Jay Report") using a random sample of college and university students to track their reasons for using Napster and the impact Napster had on their music purchases. *Id.* at *2. The court recognized that the Jay Report focused on just one segment of the Napster user population and found "evidence of lost sales attributable to college use to be probative of irreparable harm for purposes of the preliminary injunction motion." 114 F. Supp.2d at 923, *Id.* at *3.

Plaintiffs also offered a study conducted by Michael Fine, Chief Executive Officer of Soundscan, (the "Fine Report") to determine the effect of online sharing of MP3 files in order to show irreparable harm. Fine found that online file sharing had resulted in a loss of "album" sales within college markets. After reviewing defendant's objections to the Fine Report and expressing some concerns regarding the methodology and findings, the district court refused to exclude the Fine Report insofar as plaintiffs offered it to show irreparable harm.

Plaintiffs' expert Dr. David J. Teece studied several issues ("Teece Report"), including whether plaintiffs had suffered or were likely to suffer harm in their existing and planned businesses due to Napster use. *Id.* Napster objected that the report had not undergone peer review. The district court noted that such reports generally are not subject to such scrutiny and overruled defendant's objections. *Id.*

As for defendant's experts, plaintiffs objected to the report of Dr. Peter S. Fader, in which the expert concluded that Napster is beneficial to the music industry because MP3 music file-sharing stimulates more audio CD sales than it displaces. The district court found problems in Dr. Fader's minimal role in overseeing the administration of the survey and the lack of objective data in his report. The court decided the generality of the report rendered it "of dubious reliability and value." The court did not exclude the report, however, but chose "not to rely on Fader's findings in determining the issues of fair use and irreparable harm." 114 F. Supp.2d at 912, *Id.* at *8.

The district court cited both the Jay and Fine Reports in support of its finding that Napster use harms the market for plaintiffs' copyrighted musical compositions and sound recordings by reducing CD sales among college students. The district court cited the Teece Report to show the harm Napster use caused in raising barriers to plaintiffs' entry into the market for digital downloading of music. *Napster*, 114 F. Supp.2d at 910. The district court's careful consideration of defendant's objections to these reports and decision to rely on the reports for specific issues demonstrates a proper exercise of discretion in addition to a correct application of the fair use doctrine. Defendant has failed to show any basis for disturbing the district court's findings.

We, therefore, conclude that the district court made sound findings related to Napster's deleterious effect on the present and future digital download market. Moreover, lack of harm to an established market cannot deprive the copyright holder of the right to develop alternative markets for the works. See L.A. Times v. Free Republic, 2000 U.S. Dist. LEXIS 5669, 54 U.S.P.Q.2D (BNA) 1453, 1469-71 (C.D. Cal. 2000) (stating that online market for plaintiff newspapers' articles was harmed because plaintiffs demonstrated that "[defendants] are attempting to exploit the market for viewing their articles online"); see also *UMG Recordings*, 92 F. Supp.2d at 352 ("Any allegedly positive impact of defendant's activities on plaintiffs' prior market in no way frees defendant to usurp a further market that directly derives from reproduction of the plaintiffs' copyrighted works."). Here, similar to *L.A. Times* and *UMG Recordings*, the record supports the district court's finding that the "record company plaintiffs have already expended considerable funds and effort to commence Internet sales and licensing for digital downloads." 114 F. Supp.2d at 915. Having digital downloads available for free on the Napster system necessarily harms the copyright holders' attempts to charge for the same downloads.

Judge Patel did not abuse her discretion in reaching the above fair use conclusions, nor were the findings of fact with respect to fair use considerations clearly erroneous. We next address Napster's identified uses of sampling and space-shifting.

5. Identified Uses

Napster maintains that its identified uses of sampling and space-shifting were wrongly excluded as fair uses by the district court.

a. Sampling

Napster contends that its users download MP3 files to "sample" the music in order to decide whether to purchase the recording. Napster argues that the district court: (1) erred in concluding that sampling is a commercial use because it conflated a noncommercial use with a personal use; (2) erred in determining that sampling adversely affects the market for plaintiffs' copyrighted music, a requirement if the use is non-commercial; and (3) erroneously concluded that sampling is not a fair use because it determined that samplers may also engage in other infringing activity.

The district court determined that sampling remains a commercial use even if some users eventually purchase the music. We find no error in the district court's determination. Plaintiffs have established that they are likely to succeed in proving that even authorized temporary downloading of individual songs for sampling purposes is commercial in nature. See *Napster*, 114 F. Supp.2d at 913. The record supports a finding that free promotional downloads are highly regulated by the record company plaintiffs and that the companies collect royalties for song samples available on retail Internet sites. *Id.* Evidence relied on by the district court demonstrates that the free downloads provided by the record companies consist of thirty-to-sixty second samples or are full songs programmed to "time out," that is, exist only for a short time on the downloader's computer. *Id*. at 913-14. In comparison, Napster users download a full, free and permanent copy of the recording. *Id*. at 914-15. The determination by the district court as to the commercial purpose and character of sampling is not clearly erroneous.

The district court further found that both the market for audio CDs and market for online distribution are adversely affected by Napster's service. As stated in our discussion of the district court's general fair use analysis: The court did not abuse its discretion when it found that, overall, Napster has an adverse impact on the audio CD and digital download markets. Contrary to Napster's assertion that the district court failed to specifically address the market impact of sampling, the district court determined that "even if the type of sampling supposedly done on Napster were a non-commercial use, plaintiffs have demonstrated a substantial likelihood that it would adversely affect the potential market for their copyrighted works if it became widespread." *Napster*, 114 F. Supp.2d at 914. The record supports the district court's preliminary determinations that: (1) the more music that sampling users download, the less likely they are to eventually purchase the recordings on audio CD; and (2) even if the audio CD market is not harmed, Napster has adverse effects on the developing digital download market.

Napster further argues that the district court erred in rejecting its evidence that the users' downloading of "samples" increases or tends to increase audio CD sales. The district court, however, correctly noted that "any potential enhancement of plaintiffs' sales . . . would not tip the fair use analysis conclusively in favor of defendant." *Id*. at 914. We agree that increased sales of copyrighted material attributable to unauthorized use should not deprive the copyright holder of the right to license the material. See *Campbell*, 510 U.S. at 591 n.21 ("Even favorable evidence, without more, is no guarantee of fairness. Judge Leval gives the example of the film producer's appropriation of a composer's previously unknown song that turns the song into a commercial success; the boon to the song does not make the film's simple copying fair"). Nor does positive impact in one market, here the audio CD market, deprive the copyright holder of the right to develop identified alternative markets, here the digital download market.

We find no error in the district court's factual findings or abuse of discretion in the court's conclusion that plaintiffs will likely prevail in establishing that sampling does not constitute a fair use.

b.   Space-Shifting

Napster also maintains that space-shifting is a fair use. Space-shifting occurs when a Napster user downloads MP3 music files in order to listen to music he already owns on audio CD. See 114 F. Supp.2d at 915-16. Napster asserts that we have already held that space-shifting of musical compositions and sound recordings is a fair use. See Recording Indus. Ass'n of Am. v. Diamond Multimedia Sys., Inc., 180 F.3d 1072, 1079 (9th Cir. 1999) ("Rio [a portable MP3 player] merely makes copies in order to render portable, or 'space-shift,' those files that already reside on a user's hard drive. . . . Such copying is a paradigmatic noncommercial personal use."). See also generally *Sony*, 464 U.S. at 423 (holding that "time-shifting," where a video tape recorder owner records a television show for later viewing, is a fair use).

We conclude that the district court did not err when it refused to apply the "shifting" analyses of *Sony* and *Diamond*. Both *Diamond* and *Sony* are inapposite because the methods of shifting in these cases did not also simultaneously involve distribution of the copyrighted material to the general public; the time or space-shifting of copyrighted material exposed the material only to the original user. In *Diamond*, for example, the copyrighted music was transferred from the user's computer hard drive to the user's portable MP3 player. So too Sony, where "the majority of VCR purchasers . . . did not distribute taped television broadcasts, but merely enjoyed them at home." *Napster*, 114 F. Supp.2d at 913. Conversely, it is obvious that once a user lists a copy of music he already owns on the Napster system in order to access the music from another location, the song becomes "available to millions of other individuals," not just the original CD owner. See *UMG Recordings*, 92 F. Supp.2d at 351-52 (finding spaceshifting of MP3 files not a fair use even when previous ownership is demonstrated before a download is allowed); cf. Religious Tech. Ctr. v. Lerma, 1996 U.S. Dist. LEXIS 15454, No. 95-1107 A, 1996 WL 633131, at *6 (E. D. Va. Oct. 4, 1996) (suggesting that storing copyrighted material on computer disk for later review is not a fair use).

c. Other Uses

Permissive reproduction by either independent or established artists is the final fair use claim made by Napster. The district court noted that plaintiffs did not seek to enjoin this and any other noninfringing use of the Napster system, including: chat rooms, message boards and Napster's New Artist Program. *Napster*, 114 F. Supp.2d at 917. Plaintiffs do not challenge these uses on appeal.

We find no error in the district court's determination that plaintiffs will likely succeed in establishing that Napster users do not have a fair use defense. Accordingly, we next address whether Napster is secondarily liable for the direct infringement under two doctrines of copyright law: contributory copyright infringement and vicarious copyright infringement.

IV

We first address plaintiffs' claim that Napster is liable for contributory copyright infringement. Traditionally, "one who, with knowledge of the infringing activity, induces, causes or materially contributes to the infringing conduct of another, may be held liable as a 'contributory' infringer." Gershwin Publ'g Corp. v. Columbia Artists Mgmt., Inc., 443 F.2d 1159, 1162 (2d Cir. 1971); see also Fonovisa, Inc. v. Cherry Auction, Inc., 76 F.3d 259, 264 (9th Cir. 1996). Put differently, liability exists if the defendant engages in "personal conduct that encourages or assists the infringement." Matthew Bender & Co. v. West Publ'g Co., 158 F.3d 693, 706 (2d Cir. 1998).

The district court determined that plaintiffs in all likelihood would establish Napster's liability as a contributory infringer. The district court did not err; Napster, by its conduct, knowingly encourages and assists the infringement of plaintiffs' copyrights.

A. Knowledge

Contributory liability requires that the secondary infringer "know or have reason to know" of direct infringement. Cable/ Home Communication Corp. Network Prods., Inc., 902 F.2d 829, 845 & 846 n. 29 (11th Cir. 1990). The district court found that Napster had both actual and constructive knowledge that its users exchanged copyrighted music. The district court also concluded that the law does not require knowledge of "specific acts of infringement" and rejected Napster's contention that because the company cannot distinguish infringing from noninfringing files, it does not "know" of the direct infringement. 114 F. Supp.2d at 917.

It is apparent from the record that Napster has knowledge, both actual and constructive,[5] of direct infringement. Napster claims that it is nevertheless protected from contributory liability by the teaching of Sony Corp. v. Universal City Studios, Inc., 464 U.S. 417, 78 L. Ed. 2d 574, 104 S. Ct. 774 (1984). We disagree. We observe that Napster's actual, specific knowledge of direct infringement renders *Sony's* holding of limited assistance to Napster. We are compelled to make a clear distinction between the architecture of the Napster system and Napster's conduct in relation to the operational capacity of the system.

The *Sony* Court refused to hold the manufacturer and retailers of video tape recorders liable for contributory infringement despite evidence that such machines could be and were used to infringe plaintiffs' copyrighted television shows. *Sony* stated that if liability "is to be imposed on petitioners in this case, it must rest on the fact that they have sold equipment with constructive knowledge of the fact that their customers may use that equipment to make unauthorized copies of copyrighted material." *Id*. at 439 (emphasis added). The *Sony* Court declined to impute the requisite level of knowledge where the defendants made and sold equipment capable of both infringing and "substantial noninfringing uses." *Id*. at 442 (adopting a modified "staple article of commerce" doctrine from patent law).

We are bound to follow *Sony,* and will not impute the requisite level of knowledge to Napster merely because peer-to-peer file sharing technology may be used to infringe plaintiffs' copyrights. See 464 U.S. at 436 (rejecting argument that merely supplying the "'means' to accomplish an infringing activity" leads to imposition of liability). We depart from the reasoning of the district court that Napster failed to demonstrate that its system is capable of commercially significant noninfringing uses. The district court improperly confined the use analysis to current uses, ignoring the system's capabilities. See generally *Sony,* 464 U.S. at 442-43 (framing inquiry as whether the video tape recorder is *"capable* of commercially significant noninfringing uses") (emphasis added). Consequently, the district court placed undue weight on the proportion of current infringing use as compared to current and future noninfringing use. See generally Vault Corp. v. Quaid Software Ltd., 847 F.2d 255, 264-67 (5th Cir. 1997) (single noninfringing use implicated *Sony*).

---

5. The district court found actual knowledge because: (1) a document authored by Napster cofounder Sean Parker mentioned "the need to remain ignorant of users' real names and IP addresses 'since they are exchanging pirated music'"; and (2) the Recording Industry Association of America ("RIAA") informed Napster of more than 12,000 infringing files, some of which are still available. 114 F. Supp.2d at 918. The district court found constructive knowledge because: (a) Napster executives have recording industry experience; (b) they have enforced intellectual property rights in other instances; (c) Napster executives have downloaded copyrighted songs from the system; and (d) they have promoted the site with "screen shots listing infringing files." *Id*. at 919.

Nonetheless, whether we might arrive at a different result is not the issue here. See Sports Form, Inc. v. United Press Int'l, Inc., 686 F.2d 750, 752 (9th Cir. 1982). The instant appeal occurs at an early point in the proceedings and "the fully developed factual record may be materially different from that initially before the district court. . . ." *Id.* at 753. Regardless of the number of Napster's infringing versus noninfringing uses, the evidentiary record here supported the district court's finding that plaintiffs would likely prevail in establishing that Napster knew or had reason to know of its users' infringement of plaintiffs' copyrights.

This analysis is similar to that of Religious Technology Center v. Netcom On-Line Communication Services, Inc., which suggests that in an online context, evidence of actual knowledge of specific acts of infringement is required to hold a computer system operator liable for contributory copyright infringement. 907 F. Supp. at 1371. Netcom considered the potential contributory copyright liability of a computer bulletin board operator whose system supported the posting of infringing material. *Id.* at 1374. The court, in denying Netcom's motion for summary judgment of noninfringement and plaintiff's motion for judgment on the pleadings, found that a disputed issue of fact existed as to whether the operator had sufficient knowledge of infringing activity. *Id.* at 1374-75.

The court determined that for the operator to have sufficient knowledge, the copyright holder must "provide the necessary documentation to show there is likely infringement." 907 F. Supp. at 1374. If such documentation was provided, the court reasoned that Netcom would be liable for contributory infringement because its failure to remove the material "and thereby stop an infringing copy from being distributed worldwide constitutes substantial participation" in distribution of copyrighted material. *Id.*

We agree that if a computer system operator learns of specific infringing material available on his system and fails to purge such material from the system, the operator knows of and contributes to direct infringement. Conversely, absent any specific information which identifies infringing activity, a computer system operator cannot be liable for contributory infringement merely because the structure of the system allows for the exchange of copyrighted material. To enjoin simply because a computer network allows for infringing use would, in our opinion, violate *Sony* and potentially restrict activity unrelated to infringing use.

We nevertheless conclude that sufficient knowledge exists to impose contributory liability when linked to demonstrated infringing use of the Napster system. The record supports the district court's finding that Napster has actual knowledge that specific infringing material is available using its system, that it could block access to the system by suppliers of the infringing material, and that it failed to remove the material.

B. Material Contribution

Under the facts as found by the district court, Napster materially contributes to the infringing activity. Relying on *Fonovisa,* the district court concluded that "without the support services defendant provides, Napster users could not find and download the music they want with the ease of which defendant boasts." *Napster,* 114 F. Supp.2d at 919-20 ("Napster is an integrated service designed to enable users to locate and download MP3 music files."). We agree that Napster provides "the site and facilities" for direct infringement. See *Fonovisa*, 76 F.3d at 264; cf. *Netcom*, 907 F. Supp. at 1372 ("Netcom will be liable for contributory infringement since its failure to cancel [a user's] infringing message and thereby stop an infringing copy from being distributed world-wide constitutes substantial participation."). The district court correctly applied the reasoning in *Fonovisa*, and properly found that Napster materially contributes to direct infringement. . . .

V

We turn to the question whether Napster engages in vicarious copyright infringement. Vicarious copyright liability is an "outgrowth" of *respondeat superior*. *Fonovisa*, 76 F.3d at 262. In the context of copyright law, vicarious liability extends beyond an employer/employee relationship to cases in which a defendant "has the right and ability to supervise the infringing activity and also has a direct financial interest in such activities." *Id.* (quoting Gershwin, 443 F.2d at 1162).

Before moving into this discussion, we note that *Sony*'s "staple article of commerce" analysis has no application to Napster's potential liability for vicarious copyright infringement. See *Sony*, 464 U.S. at 434-435; see generally 3 Melville B. Nimmer & David Nimmer, Nimmer on Copyright §§12.04[A][2] & [A][2][b] (2000) (confining *Sony* to contributory infringement analysis: "Contributory infringement itself is of two types—personal conduct that forms part of or furthers the infringement and contribution of machinery or goods that provide the means to infringe"). The issues of Sony's liability under the "doctrines of 'direct infringement' and 'vicarious liability'" were not before the Supreme Court, although the Court recognized that the "lines between direct infringement, contributory infringement, and vicarious liability are not clearly drawn." *Id.* at 435 n. 17. Consequently, when the *Sony* Court used the term "vicarious liability," it did so broadly and outside of a technical analysis of the doctrine of vicarious copyright infringement. *Id.* at 435 ("Vicarious liability is imposed in virtually all areas of the law, and the concept of contributory infringement is merely a species of the broader problem of identifying the circumstances in which it is just to hold one individual accountable for the actions of another.").

A. Financial Benefit

The district court determined that plaintiffs had demonstrated they would likely succeed in establishing that Napster has a direct financial interest in the infringing activity. *Napster*, 114 F. Supp.2d at 921-22. We agree. Financial benefit exists where the availability of infringing material "acts as a 'draw' for customers." *Fonovisa*, 76 F.3d at 263-64 (stating that financial benefit may be shown "where infringing performances enhance the attractiveness of a venue"). Ample evidence supports the district court's finding that Napster's future revenue is directly dependent upon "increases in user-base." More users register with the Napster system as the "quality and quantity of available music increases." 114 F. Supp.2d at 902. We conclude that the district court did not err in determining that Napster financially benefits from the availability of protected works on its system.

B. Supervision

The district court determined that Napster has the right and ability to supervise its users' conduct. *Napster*, 114 F. Supp.2d at 920-21 (finding that Napster's representations to the court regarding "its improved methods of blocking users about whom rights holders complain . . . is tantamount to an admission that defendant can, and sometimes does, police its service"). We agree in part.

The ability to block infringers' access to a particular environment for any reason whatsoever is evidence of the right and ability to supervise. See *Fonovisa*, 76 F.3d at 262 ("Cherry Auction had the right to terminate vendors for any reason whatsoever and through that right had the ability to control the activities of vendors on the premises"). Here, plaintiffs have demonstrated that Napster retains the right to control access to its system. Napster has an express reservation of rights policy, stating on its website that it expressly reserves the "right to refuse service and terminate accounts in [its] discretion, including, but not limited to, if Napster believes that user conduct violates applicable law . . . or for any reason in Napster's sole discretion, with or without cause."

To escape imposition of vicarious liability, the reserved right to police must be exercised to its fullest extent. Turning a blind eye to detectable acts of infringement for the sake of profit gives rise to liability. See, e.g., *Fonovisa*, 76 F.3d at 261 ("There is no dispute for the purposes of this appeal that Cherry Auction and its operators were aware that vendors in their swap meets were selling counterfeit recordings.").

The district court correctly determined that Napster had the right and ability to police its system and failed to exercise that right to prevent the exchange of copyrighted material. The district court, however, failed to recognize that the boundaries of the premises that Napster "controls and patrols" are limited. Put differently, Napster's reserved "right and ability" to police is cabined by the system's current architecture. As shown by the record, the Napster system does not "read" the content of indexed files, other than to check that they are in the proper MP3 format.

Napster, however, has the ability to locate infringing material listed on its search indices, and the right to terminate users' access to the system. The file name indices, therefore, are within the "premises" that Napster has the ability to police. We recognize that the files are user-named and may not match copyrighted material exactly (for example, the artist or song could be spelled wrong). For Napster to function effectively, however, file names must reasonably or roughly correspond to the material contained in the files, otherwise no user could ever locate any desired music. As a practical matter, Napster, its users and the record company plaintiffs have equal access to infringing material by employing Napster's "search function."

Our review of the record requires us to accept the district court's conclusion that plaintiffs have demonstrated a likelihood of success on the merits of the vicarious copyright infringement claim. Napster's failure to police the system's "premises," combined with a showing that Napster financially benefits from the continuing availability of infringing files on its system, leads to the imposition of vicarious liability. . . .

VIII

The district court correctly recognized that a preliminary injunction against Napster's participation in copyright infringement is not only warranted but required. We believe, however, that the scope of the injunction needs modification in light of our opinion. . . .

The preliminary injunction which we stayed is overbroad because it places on Napster the entire burden of ensuring that no "copying, downloading, uploading, transmitting, or distributing" of plaintiffs' works occur on the system. As stated, we place the burden on plaintiffs to provide notice to Napster of copyrighted works and files containing such works available on the Napster system before Napster has the duty to disable access to the offending content. Napster, however, also bears the burden of policing the system within the limits of the system. Here, we recognize that this is not an exact science in that the files are user named. In crafting the injunction on remand, the district court should recognize that Napster's system does not currently appear to allow Napster access to users' MP3 files. . . .

COMMENTS AND QUESTIONS

1. On remand, Judge Patel issued a modified preliminary injunction. She directed the plaintiffs to provide more complete notice to Napster as to specific copyrighted recordings claimed to be infringing, including the title and file name on Napster's system. The court recognized the difficulty of identifying all infringing files given the transitory nature of the Napster system, but said that this did not relieve Napster of its duty to take reasonable steps to ascertain the presence of infringing files. Judge Patel expressed willingness to hold hearings if disputes about the injunction arose or to appoint an independent third party as a technical expert to assist in dispute resolution. The Ninth Circuit affirmed the modified injunction. See A&M Records, Inc. v. Napster, Inc., 2001 U.S. Dist. LEXIS 2186 (N.D. Cal. 2001), aff'd, 284 F.3d 1091 (9th Cir. 2002). Later, Napster persuaded Judge Patel to grant discovery on Napster's copyright misuse defense that alleged that the major labels' joint venture arrangements for online distribution of music were anticompetitive. See A&M Records, Inc. v. Napster, Inc., 61 U.S.P.Q.2d (BNA) 1877 (N.D. Cal. 2002). Since that time, Napster has gone into bankruptcy, and it is unclear whether the litigation in this case will proceed any further.

2. Some economists have been skeptical of the recording industry's claims that Napster harmed markets for CDs. See, e.g., Stan Liebowitz, Policing Pirates in the Networked Age, Cato Institute (2002), http://www.cato.org/pubs/pas/pa-438es.html. See also Richard J. Gilbert and Michael L. Katz, When Good Value Chains Go Bad: The Economics of Indirect Liability for Copyright Infringement, 52 Hastings L.J. 961 (2001); Raymond Shih Ray Ku, The Creative Destruction of Copyright: Napster and the New Economics of Digital Technology, 69 U. Chi. L. Rev. 263 (2002). However, legal commentators have generally been supportive of the Ninth Circuit's analysis. See, e.g., Stacey L. Dogan, Is Napster a VCR? The Implications of *Sony* for Napster and Other Internet Technologies, 52 Hastings L.J. 939 (2001).

One civil liberties lawyer who is critical of the Ninth Circuit's analysis nevertheless offers this advice to developers of peer-to-peer (P2P) technologies: "In the wake of the Napster decision, it appears that copyright law has foisted a binary choice on P2P developers: either build a system that allows for thorough monitoring and control over user activities, or build one that makes such monitoring and control completely impossible." Fred von Lohmann, Peer-to-Peer File Sharing and Copyright Law After *Napster* (2001), available at http://www.eff.org/IP/P2P/Napster/20010227_p2p_copyright_white_paper.html. Von Lohmann also considers, among other things, whether P2P developers should develop stand-alone software rather than ongoing services, whether functions should be disaggregated, whether they should use open source licenses, and other issues that may bear on the potential liability of peer-to-peer developers.

3. Several developers of peer-to-peer file-sharing technologies have become defendants in lawsuits similar to *Napster*. For example, major recording firms sued Aimster (later renamed Madster) because its software allowed users of AOL's instant messaging software to share music files. A trial court issued a preliminary injunction to stop its operation because the primary use of Aimster was, in its view, to distribute illegal copies of music. In re Aimster Litigation, 2002 WL 31006142 (N.D. Ill. 2002). The court distinguished Sony of Am. v. Universal City Studios, 464 U.S. 417 (1984) on the ground that the principal use of the Betamax machine was for fair use time-shifting purposes and that case did not involve distribution of copies. Yet another such lawsuit is that one brought by Metro-Goldwyn-Mayer Studios and other major motion picture and recording industry firms against Grokster, Ltd. and three other firms over their peer-to-peer file-sharing networks.

The main differences between Napster, on the one hand, and Morpheus, Kazaa, and Grokster, the three file-sharing networks now being sued, on the other hand, are (1) that Napster maintained central directories of the files on users' computers, and (2) that the Morpheus network can be used to share any type of file, not just music files. Like most of the file-sharing companies that emerged in Napster's wake, these three do not have central directories. As a result, they argue that they have no way to monitor or control what their users do. How much difference should this make? Should developers have a responsibility to build monitoring technologies into their systems? Should it matter that many of the files traded on the Morpheus network are not owned by the content industries, either because they are songs by independent bands or because they are documents or images rather than music or movies? For a discussion of legal implications of other peer-to-peer technologies, such as gnutella and freenet, which have a more distributed character, see, e.g., Mathias Strasser, Beyond Napster: How the Law Might Respond to Changing Internet Architecture, 28 No. Ky. L. Rev. 660 (2001).

4. Members of Congress, along with representatives of the recording and motion picture industry, have become frustrated because lawsuits against developers of peer-to-peer networks have not stopped digital infringement. Several prominent Senators and Representatives wrote on July 25, 2002, to urge the Attorney General to bring criminal charges of copyright infringement under the No Electronic Theft Act against individuals who intentionally allow mass copying of copyrighted works from their computers over peer-to-peer networks, as well as to prosecute operators of peer-to-peer systems who intentionally facilitate online copyright infringement. The No Electronic Theft Act makes copyright infringement a felony if it is done

willfully and if the aggregate loss to the copyright owner over a 180-day period exceeds $1000. See 17 U.S.C. §506(a)(2).

Representatives Berman and Coble have also proposed legislation, HR 5211, the Peer to Peer Piracy Prevention Act, 107th Cong., 2d Sess. (2002) to enable copyright owners to engage legally in computer hacking to sabotage peer-to-peer file-trading networks if they think their rights are being infringed. This bill would create a new Section 514(a) of the Copyright Act: "Notwithstanding any State or Federal statute or other law . . . , a copyright owner shall not be liable in any criminal or civil action for disabling, interfering with, blocking, diverting, or otherwise impairing the unauthorized distribution, display, performance, or reproduction of his or her copyrighted work on a publicly accessible peer-to-peer file trading network, if such impairment does not, without authorization, alter, delete, or otherwise impair the integrity of any computer file or data residing on the computer of a file trader."

Will criminal prosecutions against file sharers and granting immunity to the recording industry for using technical self-help succeed as strategies for solving the problems posed by peer-to-peer networking software? What other measures should be considered?

5. Napster was not the only Internet startup firm with an innovative business model for delivery of music online that incurred the wrath of major American recording industry companies. First introduced in October 1997, MP3.com quickly gained great popularity as a portal for recording artists to make available their songs for downloading and general information about the music industry. Its high traffic rate enabled the site to earn substantial advertising revenues from banner advertisements and attract substantial venture capital. In order to expand its operations and open up new revenue sources, MP3.com launched its "MyMP3.com" service in January 2000. This service enabled subscribers to develop a virtual online music locker from which they could access sound recordings from any Internet portal through a password-protected user interface. The service was premised on the idea that the fair use doctrine authorizes consumers to "space shift" music that they have lawfully acquired.

MP3.com purchased and uploaded thousands of CDs onto its servers. Subscribers to MyMP3.com service could demonstrate that they lawfully acquired particular CDs, either by purchasing the CD online through a cooperating online retailer (the "Instant Listening Service") or by loading a CD that the subscriber owned into his or her computer CD-ROM Drive (the "Beam-it Service"). Software on the computer could verify the presence of the particular CD. Once "ownership" was verified, MyMP3.com provided access to the copy of the CD stored on MP3.com's server. Thus, subscribers did not in fact access their own copy but rather MP3.com's copy. The notion of an actual private locker was metaphorical. In fact, subscribers had differential access to the same "locker," MP3.com's servers.

The major American record labels and music publishers sued MP3.com soon after the launch of MyMP3.com and moved for summary judgment on the ground that MP3.com's initial copying of CDs onto its server and its distribution of such music to its subscribers over the Internet infringed their copyrights. MP3.com defended both activities as falling within fair use. In UMG Recordings, Inc. v. MP3.com, Inc., 92 F. Supp.2d 359 (S.D.N.Y. 2000), the court found the service to be commercial in purpose and nontransformative in character, rejecting

MP3.com's argument that "space shifting" of a copyrighted work transforms it in legally cognizable ways. The court applied a more literal test: whether the defendant added "new aesthetics, new insights and understandings" to the sound recordings. The second and third fair use factors—the nature of the copyrighted work and the amount taken—clearly favored the plaintiffs. MP3.com relied principally upon the fourth factor—the effect upon the potential market for or value of the work—arguing that its service promotes sales of CDs by providing a means to make them more readily available. The court concluded, however, that this service interfered with the copyright owners' ability to develop their own online distribution channels.[2] Do you agree with Judge Rakoff's statement that "[t]he complex marvels of cyberspatial communication may create difficult legal issues; but not in this case"? How would you respond to his assessment of the fair use factors?

6. The *Napster* case illustrates that copying of digital music is very easy and cheap even for the technologically unsophisticated. The problems posed by digital copying are, however, hardly new. The recording industry recognized the potential of digital technologies to undermine control over digital music many years ago. When the consumer electronics industry was about to introduce digital audio taping (DAT) technologies into the market in the late 1980s, the recording industry went to Congress, first to ask for a moratorium on introduction of consumer-grade DAT equipment in the U.S. market, and then to ask Congress to enact legislation to require makers of consumer-grade DAT machines to install in them "serial copy management system" (SCMS) chips to control digital copying and to make it illegal to remove or bypass SCMS chips. This led to enactment of the Audio Home Recording Rights Act of 1992, codified at 17 U.S.C. §§1001-1010. SCMS chips enable users to make first-generation personal use copies of DAT recordings, but disable second-generation copies from being the perfect copies of perfect copies that digital technology would otherwise produce. AHRA requires manufacturers and importers of digital audio recording equipment and blank tapes, disks, or other storage media to pay a percentage of their prices into a royalty pool, to be distributed to owners of musical compositions (one-third) and sound recordings (two-thirds) based on prior year sales and air time in order to compensate copyright owners for personal use copies made with DAT machines. See 17 U.S.C. §§1003-1007. Section 1008 of AHRA immunizes consumers from infringement liability for the noncommercial use of analog or qualifying digital devices for making copies. Violations of the AHRA are not copyright violations. Rather, the AHRA contains its own enforcement, remedy, and dispute resolution provisions.

In the late 1990s, when Diamond Multimedia Systems was about to introduce a new portable music player allowing users to play about an hour's worth of digital music in MP3 format downloaded from their computer hard drives, the Recording Industry Association of America sought to enjoin this product from the market on the ground that it violated the AHRA because it did not contain an SCMS chip.

---

2. MP3.com subsequently settled the case with four out of the five major record labels for approximately $80 million. After the court assessed liability to Universal Music Group (UMG) at $25,000 per CD copied, the parties settled for another $53.4 million. MP3.com faced further exposure to independent record labels and music publishers. The various legal problems and licensing complexities eventually led MP3.com to abandon its efforts to establish a broad-based "music locker" service, limiting this venture to the files voluntarily loaded onto its website by independent artists and a few smaller record labels. In a somewhat surprising shift in direction, Vivendi Universal, UMG's parent corporation, acquired MP3.com in April 2001. See Brad King, MP3.com Goes Universal, Wired News (May 21, 2001).

The Ninth Circuit Court of Appeals decided that the Rio player was not a "digital audio recording device" within the meaning of AHRA, pointing out that RIAA's interpretation of AHRA would undermine the legislative compromise that excluded general purpose computers from the scope of the law. See Recording Industry Ass'n of Am. v. Diamond Multimedia Systems, Inc., 180 F.3d 1072 (9th Cir. 1999). As will become apparent in the next section, the recording industry, along with other major copyright industry sectors, are hoping that new technologies will provide new and more reliable protections to their works in digital form.

4. The Digital Millennium Copyright Act's Anticircumvention Rules

In the last days of the 1998 congressional session, Congress passed sweeping changes to the Copyright Act designed specifically to address a variety of Internet-related copyright issues. The Act was nominally intended to bring U.S. law into compliance with the 1996 WIPO treaties on copyright and the Internet, but in fact it went well beyond what those treaties required. The DMCA changed Internet copyright law in three significant ways. One of those, the safe harbor for ISPs, is discussed above.

The second deals with the misuse or destruction of "copyright management information." Section 1202 of the Copyright Act makes it illegal to remove or alter copyright management information conveyed along with a copyrighted work or to provide false copyright management information. Copyright management information includes information that identifies the authors, owners, or performers in a work, and the terms and conditions under which a work may be used. The intent of this section is to punish those who facilitate counterfeiting by stripping identifying information from a work or who falsely identify themselves as the authors of a work. The literal terms of the Act may go further, however, creating a quasi-moral right of attribution and ensuring that "clickwrap licenses" remain embedded in a computer program.

The final—and most controversial—part of the DMCA lies in its provisions granting a new form of legal protection to those who deploy technological measures to protect copyrighted works from unauthorized access, use, or copying. What one technology can do to protect digital content (e.g., music or motion pictures) from copying, another technology may be able to undo. During the legislative debate leading up to adoption of the DMCA, copyright owners insisted that they needed to be able to challenge those who circumvented technical measures used to protect digital forms of copyrighted works. Section 1201(a)(1)(A) forbids circumvention of effective technical measures used by copyright owners to protect access to their works. Sections 1201(a)(2) and 1201(b)(1) forbid development or distribution of technologies "primarily designed or produced for the purpose of circumventing a technological measure" used by copyright owners to protect their works, having "only limited commercially significant purpose or use other than to circumvent a technological measure," or "marketed . . . for use in circumventing a technological measure." (These subsections differ only in that (a)(2) pertains only to technologies for circumventing access controls and (b)(1) pertains to technologies that circumvent other technological measures. Notice, though, that there is no counterpart to 1201(a)(1)(A) to outlaw circumvention of, say, copy controls.) "Circumvention" means to "descramble a scrambled work, to decrypt an encrypted work, or otherwise avoid, bypass, remove, deactivate, or impair a technological measure." 17 U.S.C. §1201(a)(3).

This new statute marks a significant change in the balance between copyright owners and users in at least three respects. First, it reflects a rather striking decision to promote innovation by banning one class of innovations entirely—those that involve decryption technologies. If one thinks in terms of the competition between encryption technologies and decryption technologies as a sort of arms race, it can be said that the DMCA orders unilateral technological disarmament by the decrypters. Second, the statute changes the standard that has traditionally been applied to contributory infringement. The production of devices that facilitate infringement has always been illegal under copyright law, but only if the device produced is not "capable of a substantial noninfringing use." Sony Corp. v. Universal City Studios, 464 U.S. 417 (1984). The DMCA does not adopt this standard; instead, it adopts a broader definition of "illegal conduct," one that is closer to the dissent's "primary purpose or effect" test in *Sony*. The dissent in *Sony* would have applied that test to declare VCRs illegal. It remains to be seen what sorts of commercial devices will be swept into the DMCA's intermediate standard. Third, and perhaps most notable, the statute itself does not condition the illegality of circumvention on proof that the user violated the copyright laws. Nor does liability for making or distribution of a circumvention technology seem to turn on whether the defendant—or anyone else —has ever made an infringing copy or gotten unauthorized access to the copyrighted work being protected by the technical measure.

As the excerpt below indicates, Congress recognized the need to create some exceptions to the anticircumvention regulations.

Pamela Samuelson, *Intellectual Property and the Digital Economy: Why the Anti-Circumvention Regulations Need to Be Revised*
14 Berkeley Tech. L.J. 519 (1999)

. . . The DMCA ban on the act of circumventing technical protection systems is subject to seven very specific exceptions, as well as being qualified by several other subsections. In addition, it is subject to a two-year moratorium during which the Librarian of Congress is supposed to study the potential impact of the anticircumvention ban on noninfringing uses of copyrighted works which may lead to further limitations on the act-of-circumvention rule. While several of these exceptions and limitations respond to the gravest of concerns expressed by digital economy firms, they are still too narrowly crafted, as examples given below will reveal. Congress should have adopted a provision enabling courts to exempt acts of circumvention engaged in for other legitimate purposes. Courts interpreting section 1201 may either be forced to find liability in some situations in which it would be inappropriate to impose it or to stretch existing limitations. Congress may eventually need to revise this provision to recognize a broader range of exceptions.

The structure of the final DMCA anti-circumvention provision and its complexity resulted from the maximalist position with which the Administration and its

major copyright industry allies began the legislative struggle. Only when IT industry groups were able to identify particularized situations in which circumvention
was appropriate was there any legislative "give" on the issue, and then only to the
extent of that identified situation. As noted above, Clinton Administration officials
initially sought an almost unlimited ban of circumvention activities. The only exception to the circumvention ban in the Administration's favored legislation was an
authorization of circumvention of technical protection systems for legitimate law
enforcement, intelligence, and other governmental purposes. Without this exception, suspected Mafia bosses and terrorists, oddly enough, might have been able to
challenge attempted law enforcement or intelligence agency decryptions of their
records or communications under section 1201(a)(1).

The Administration's preferred bill also provided that nothing in section 1201
would "affect rights, remedies, limitations, or defenses to copyright infringement,
including fair use, under this title." This seemed to recognize that circumventing a
technical protection system for purposes of engaging in fair use or other noninfringing acts would be lawful, although it did not directly say so. Some representatives of major copyright industries who testified at a Congressional hearing on this
legislation expressed the view that fair use should not be an acceptable reason to
"break" a technical protection system used by copyright owners to protect their
works. Allan Adler, testifying on behalf of the Association of American Publishers,
for example, stated that "the fair use doctrine has never given anyone a right to
break other laws for the stated purpose of exercising the fair use privilege. Fair use
doesn't allow you to break into a locked library in order to make 'fair use' copies of
the books in it, or steal newspapers from a vending machine in order to copy articles and share them with a friend." The "breaking and entering" metaphor for
circumvention activities swayed some influential Congressmen in the debate over
anti circumvention regulations.

Courts should distinguish between circumvention aimed at getting unauthorized access to a work and circumvention aimed at making noninfringing uses of a
lawfully obtained copy. Section 1201(a)(1) is aimed at the former, not the latter.
Fair use, for example, would provide a poor excuse for breaking into a computer
system in order to get access to a work one wished to parody. However, if one had
already lawfully acquired a copy of the work, and it was necessary to bypass a technical protection system to make fair use of that copy, this would appear to be lawful
under section 1201(a)(1) and (c)(1). Take, for example, an act of circumvention
performed by Geoffery Nunberg, a friend of mine who works for Xerox's Palo Alto
Research Center. He was an expert witness in a lawsuit which successfully challenged the Washington Redskins' trademark on the ground that the word "redskins" is scandalous or disparaging. Nunberg decided it was necessary to take a clip
from an old Western movie to demonstrate derogatory uses of the term in context.
It was necessary for him to defeat a technical protection system adopted by the
owner of the copyright in this movie in order to make the clip for this purpose. If
section 1201(c)(1)'s preservation of fair use and other defenses to infringement are
to be given their plain meaning, it would seem that this sort of circumvention
should be permissible. Thus, if the clip from the movie qualifies as a fair use, the act
of circumvention may be privileged under section 1201(c)(1).

Although this section's apparent preservation of fair use was important, it did
not satisfy library and nonprofit groups who expressed substantial concern about
the impact that the anti-circumvention provisions would have on public access to

information. The only additional concession that the House Subcommittee on Intellectual Property thought should be made to concerns expressed by these groups was to create a special "shopping privilege" for them. This exception, which was included in the final DMCA, enables nonprofit library and educational institutions to circumvent technical protection systems to "make a good faith determination of whether to acquire a copy" of the work. Librarians and educators do not see much value in this provision because vendors of technically protected copyrighted works will generally have incentives to allow librarians and educators to have sufficient access to make acquisition decisions. Their broader concerns about the impact of anti-circumvention regulations on noninfringing uses fell on deaf ears in both the House and Senate Subcommittees on Intellectual Property.

Computer and software industry groups were initially unsuccessful in persuading Congress to create additional exceptions to the anti-circumvention rules and other changes to the anti-circumvention regulations to make them less harmful to legitimate activities in these industries. Not until the full Senate Judiciary Committee and the House Commerce Committee undertook their reviews of the legislation were concerns of these industry groups heeded. Out of the Senate Committee emerged three significant changes to the DMCA. The first was creation of a new exception to enable circumvention of technical protection systems for purposes of enabling a software developer to achieve interoperability among computer programs. The second was a provision clarifying that equipment manufacturers were under no obligation to specially design their products to respond to any particular technical measure used by those providing content for this equipment. The third was a provision indicating that section 1201 was not intended to broaden contributory or vicarious copyright liability.

. . . The Commerce version of the bill added a new exception to enable encryption research and the development of encryption-research tools. It also created two consumer-oriented exceptions, one to enable parents to circumvent access controls when necessary to protect their children from accessing harmful material on the Internet, and the other to enable circumvention to protect personal privacy. It also proposed a moratorium on the anti-circumvention rules so that a study could be conducted about the potential impact of anti-circumvention rules on fair use, the public domain, and other noninfringing uses of copyrighted works.

More clearly than the Judiciary Committees in either branch of Congress, the Commerce Committee recognized the unprecedented nature of the access right that was implicit in the act-of-circumvention provision of section 1201. "If left unqualified," said Congressman Bliley, "this new right . . . could well prove to be the legal foundation for a society in which information becomes available only on a 'pay-per-use' basis." To ensure this would not occur, the legislation was amended to enable librarians and educators to make a showing that the anti-circumvention provision was interfering with noninfringing uses of copyrighted materials and to seek an exemption from the ban. Insofar as such a showing could be made, the Commerce Committee thought that affected classes of works or of users should be exempt from section 1201(a)(1)(A). . . . The Commerce Committee review of the legislation also led to inclusion of a provision indicating that nothing in section 1201 "shall enlarge or diminish any rights of free speech or of the press for activities using consumer electronics, telecommunications, or computing products." This provision recognizes the potential impact of the anti-circumvention rule on free speech and free press interests. . . .

While the final version of the DMCA anti-circumvention provision responded to several significant concerns of the digital economy sector, it did so mainly by adopting specific exceptions. There are, however, many other legitimate reasons for circumventing technical protection systems that are not, strictly speaking, covered by the exceptions in the final bill. Five examples demonstrate that section 1201 should have an "or other legitimate purposes" exception to section 1201(a)(1).

Suppose, for example, that a copyright owner had reason to believe that an encrypted work contained an infringing version of one of its works. The only way to find out whether the copyright owner's suspicion is valid may be to circumvent the technical protection system to get access to the encrypted material. Even if its suspicions proved correct, the copyright owner would have violated section 1201(a)(1)(A) in the course of discovering this. There is no exception in section 1201 to protect this kind of decryption activity.

Or suppose that a content producer had licensed certain software that was essential to the development of its product (e.g., editing software used in the process of making motion pictures). In the course of a dispute about the performance quality of this software, the content producer might withhold payment of a royalty as a way of communicating its displeasure with the licensor's maintenance of the software. The software's licensor might then respond by activating a technical "self-help" system embedded in the software to stop the software from operating. To deal with this development, the licensee might well attempt to circumvent the self-help feature now blocking access to the software because the licensee needed to use the software to finish its movie and because it regarded itself as having a legitimate claim of licensor breach to justify holding back the royalty. However legitimate the claim or this activity, there is no exception to the anti-circumvention rule to protect the licensee in this situation.

Two further examples will illustrate the narrowness of certain existing privileges in the DMCA. Suppose, for example, that a firm circumvented a technical protection system to stop software it had licensed from monitoring certain uses of the software in ways not contemplated in the license agreement and which the licensee regarded as unwarranted and detrimental to its interests. Although there is a "personal privacy" exception in the DMCA, there is no general exception for circumventing to protect other confidentiality interests. Or suppose that a firm was considering making a multi-million dollar acquisition of a computer system whose producer asserted was highly secure. If this firm wished to test the veracity of the producer's assertions, without getting the producer's permission or over the producer's objection, it would seem to violate section 1201. Although there is a computer security testing exception in the Act, it only applies if one is already the owner or operator of the computer system being tested. It should be noted here that many security flaws discovered in widely deployed systems have been found by researchers who tested the system without permission of either the owner or manufacturer of such systems. These activities too are not covered by the computer security exception provided for in the DMCA.

Finally, because the DMCA recognizes that the anti-circumvention rules may have an impact on free speech and free press concerns, it may be worth considering an example of this sort. Suppose that an employee of a major chemical company gave a reporter a disk containing a digital copy of a report and several photographs pertaining to a major chemical spill that the company was trying to cover up. If information on the disk was technically protected and the employee was not authorized by the company to provide the information to the reporter, it would appear that the reporter would violate section 1201(a)(1) if he circumvented the technical protection system to get access to this information, even if consideration of free press and free speech interests might suggest that such a circumvention was justifiable.

One response to these examples might be to assert that copyright owners will generally not sue when these or other legitimate circumvention activities occur. However, in some of the examples given above, the technical protector might well have incentives to sue the circumventor. Given that there are serious criminal penalties for willfully violating section 1201, the overbreadth of this provision and the narrowness of existing exceptions will put many legitimate circumventors at unnecessary risk. If such suits are brought, courts may, of course, and probably will, find other ways to reach just results. They might, for example, decide that the "other defenses" provision of the anti-circumvention rule legitimized the circumvention, that some instances were within the spirit, even if not the letter, of an existing privilege, or that there was insufficient harm to the legitimate interests of the person challenging the circumvention activity to justify imposing liability. However, there should be a general purpose "or other legitimate purposes" provision in section 1201 so that courts will not have to thrash to reach appropriate results. This would add flexibility, adaptability, and fairness to the law. In many other parts of copyright law—with the fair use doctrine, for example, or the distinction between ideas and expressions—Congress has trusted the common law process to distinguish between legitimate and illegitimate activities. It could (and should) have done so with respect to circumvention legislation as well.

It would have been especially appropriate to adopt a general purpose "other legitimate purpose" provision because the anti-circumvention ban is an unprecedented provision for copyright law as to a significant new technology issue with which neither Congress nor the courts have much experience. The lack of a general purpose exception is particularly troubling in view of the harsh criminal and civil provisions in the statute, which may have a chilling effect on legitimate activities, including those affecting free speech. It could also put at risk some legitimate activities in the digital economy that will impede the growth of e-commerce, as will become more apparent in the next section. . . .

If Congress intended for circumvention of technical protection systems to be legal when done for legitimate purposes, it might seem obvious that Congress should be understood to have intended to enable users to effectuate the circumvention privileges it recognized. Although it will not always be necessary for a legitimate circumventor to make or use a circumvention technology to accomplish a privileged circumvention (e.g., enciphered text might be decoded by purely mental activity), most often this will be necessary. The deepest puzzle of section 1201 is whether Congress implicitly intended to allow the development and/or distribution of technologies necessary to accomplish legitimate circumvention activities, or whether, in essence, it created a number of meaningless privileges.

Seemingly relevant to addressing this question are some curious features of section 1201 that close study of this complex provision reveals. First, several exceptions to the anti-circumvention rule specifically authorize the creation of tools necessary to achieving a legitimate circumvention activity (e.g., the encryption research and interoperability privileges), while several others (e.g., the law enforcement privilege and the privacy privilege) do not. Secondly, while the interoperability privilege exempts necessary tools from both device provisions of section 1201, the encryption and security research privileges exempt tools only from the access-device provision, not from the control-device provision. Yet, it would seem that encryption and security research would often require testing both of access and of control components of technical protection systems. Thirdly, section 1201 contains no provision enabling the development or distribution of circumvention tools to enable fair use or other privileged uses in terrain which section 1201(a)(1)(A) doesn't reach (i.e., making fair uses of lawfully acquired copies). If Congress intended to recognize a right to "hack" a technical protection system to make fair uses, this right could be undermined if it could not be exercised without developing a tool to bypass the technical protection system or otherwise getting access to such a tool. Under some interpretations of section 1201(b)(1), development or distribution of such a tool would be unlawful.

Universal City Studios, Inc. v. Reimerdes
United States District Court for the Southern District of New York
111 F. Supp.2d 294 (S.D.N.Y. 2000)

KAPLAN, J.

Plaintiffs, eight major United States motion picture studios, distribute many of their copyrighted motion pictures for home use on digital versatile disks ("DVDs"), which contain copies of the motion pictures in digital form. They protect those motion pictures from copying by using an encryption system called CSS. CSS-protected motion pictures on DVDs may be viewed only on players and computer drives equipped with licensed technology that permits the devices to decrypt and play—but not to copy—the films.

Late last year, computer hackers devised a computer program called DeCSS that circumvents the CSS protection system and allows CSS-protected motion pictures to be copied and played on devices that lack the licensed decryption technology. Defendants quickly posted DeCSS on their Internet web site, thus making it readily available to much of the world. Plaintiffs promptly brought this action under the Digital Millennium Copyright Act (the "DMCA") to enjoin defendants from posting DeCSS and to prevent them from electronically "linking" their site to others that post DeCSS. Defendants responded with what they termed "electronic civil disobedience"—increasing their efforts to link their web site to a large number of others that continue to make DeCSS available. . . .

Defendant Eric Corley is viewed as a leader of the computer hacker community and goes by the name Emmanuel Goldstein, after the leader of the underground in George Orwell's classic, *1984*. He and his company, defendant 2600 Enterprises, Inc., together publish a magazine called *2600: The Hacker Quarterly*, which Corley founded in 1984, and which is something of a bible to the hacker community. The name "2600" was derived from the fact that hackers in the 1960's found that the transmission of a 2600 hertz tone over a long distance trunk connection gained access to "operator mode" and allowed the user to explore aspects of the telephone system that were not otherwise accessible. Mr. Corley chose the name because he regarded it as a "mystical thing," commemorating something that he evidently admired. Not surprisingly, *2600: The Hacker Quarterly* has included articles on such topics as how to steal an Internet domain name, access other people's e-mail, intercept cellular phone calls, and break into the computer systems at Costco stores and Federal Express. One issue contains a guide to the federal criminal justice system for readers charged with computer hacking. In addition, defendants operate a web site located at <http://www.2600.com> ("2600.com"), which is managed primarily by Mr. Corley and has been in existence since 1995.

Prior to January 2000, when this action was commenced, defendants posted the source and object code for DeCSS on the 2600.com web site, from which they could be downloaded easily. At that time, 2600.com contained also a list of links to other web sites purporting to post DeCSS. . . .

As the motion picture companies did not themselves develop CSS and, in any case, are not in the business of making DVD players and drives, the technology for making compliant devices, i.e., devices with CSS keys, had to be licensed to consumer electronics manufacturers. In order to ensure that the decryption technology did not become generally available and that compliant devices could not be used to copy as well as merely to play CSS-protected movies, the technology is licensed subject to strict security requirements. Moreover, manufacturers may not, consistent with their licenses, make equipment that would supply digital output that could be used in copying protected DVDs. Licenses to manufacture compliant devices are granted on a royalty-free basis subject only to an administrative fee. At the time of trial, licenses had been issued to numerous hardware and software manufacturers, including two companies that plan to release DVD players for computers running the Linux operating system.

With CSS in place, the studios introduced DVDs on the consumer market in early 1997. All or most of the motion pictures released on DVD were, and continue to be, encrypted with CSS technology. Over 4,000 motion pictures now have been released in DVD format in the United States, and movies are being issued on DVD at the rate of over 40 new titles per month in addition to rereleases of classic films. Currently, more than five million households in the United States own DVD players, and players are projected to be in ten percent of United States homes by the end of 2000.

DVDs have proven not only popular, but lucrative for the studios. Revenue from their sale and rental currently accounts for a substantial percentage of the movie studios' revenue from the home video market. Revenue from the home market, in turn, makes up a large percentage of the studios' total distribution revenue.

In late September 1999, Jon Johansen, a Norwegian subject then fifteen years of age, and two individuals he "met" under pseudonyms over the Internet, reverse engineered a licensed DVD player and discovered the CSS encryption algorithm and keys. They used this information to create DeCSS, a program capable of decrypting or "ripping" encrypted DVDs, thereby allowing playback on non-compliant computers as well as the copying of decrypted files to computer hard drives. Mr. Johansen then posted the executable code on his personal Internet web site and informed members of an Internet mailing list that he had done so. Neither Mr. Johansen nor his collaborators obtained a license from the DVD CCA. . . .

In the months following its initial appearance on Mr. Johansen's web site, DeCSS has become widely available on the Internet, where hundreds of sites now purport to offer the software for download. A few other applications said to decrypt CSS-encrypted DVDs also have appeared on the Internet.

In November 1999, defendants' web site began to offer DeCSS for download. It established also a list of links to several web sites that purportedly "mirrored" or offered DeCSS for download. The links on defendants' mirror list fall into one of three categories. By clicking the mouse on one of these links, the user may be brought to a page on the linked-to site on which there appears a further link to the DeCSS software. If the user then clicks on the DeCSS link, download of the software begins. This page may or may not contain content other than the DeCSS link. Alternatively, the user may be brought to a page on the linked-to site that does not itself purport to link to DeCSS, but that links, either directly or via a series of other pages on the site, to another page on the site on which there appears a link to the DeCSS software. Finally, the user may be brought directly to the DeCSS link on the linked-to site such that download of DeCSS begins immediately without further user intervention. . . .

The effect on plaintiffs of defendants' posting of DeCSS depends upon the ease with which DeCSS decrypts plaintiffs' copyrighted motion pictures, the quality of the resulting product, and the convenience with which decrypted copies may be transferred or transmitted.

As noted, DeCSS was available for download from defendants' web site and remains available from web sites on defendants' mirror list. Downloading is simple and quick—plaintiffs' expert did it in seconds. The program in fact decrypts at least some DVDs. Although the process is computationally intensive, plaintiffs' expert decrypted a store-bought copy of *Sleepless in Seattle* in 20 to 45 minutes. The copy is stored on the hard drive of the computer. The quality of the decrypted film is virtually identical to that of encrypted films on DVD. The decrypted file can be copied like any other.

The decryption of a CSS-protected DVD is only the beginning of the tale, as the decrypted file is very large—approximately 4.3 to 6 GB or more depending on the length of the film—and thus extremely cumbersome to transfer or to store on portable storage media. One solution to this problem, however, is DivX, a compression utility available on the Internet that is promoted as a means of compressing decrypted motion picture files to manageable size. . . .

The fact that DeCSS-decrypted DVDs can be compressed satisfactorily to 650 MB is very important. A writeable CD-ROM can hold 650 MB. Hence, it is entirely feasible to decrypt a DVD with DeCSS, compress and synchronize it with DivX, and then make as many copies as one wishes by burning the resulting files onto writeable CD-ROMs, which are sold blank for about one dollar apiece. Indeed, even if one wished to use a lower compression ratio to improve quality, a film easily could be compressed to about 1.3 GB and burned onto two CD-ROMs. But the creation of pirated copies of copyrighted movies on writeable CD-ROMs, although significant, is not the principal focus of plaintiffs' concern, which is transmission of pirated copies over the Internet or other networks. . . .

At trial, defendants repeated, as if it were a mantra, the refrain that plaintiffs, as they stipulated, have no direct evidence of a specific occasion on which any person decrypted a copyrighted motion picture with DeCSS and transmitted it over the Internet. But that is unpersuasive. Plaintiffs' expert expended very little effort to find someone in an IRC chat room who exchanged a compressed, decrypted copy of *The Matrix*, one of plaintiffs' copyrighted motion pictures, for a copy of *Sleepless in Seattle*. While the simultaneous electronic exchange of the two movies took approximately six hours, the computers required little operator attention during the interim. An MPAA investigator downloaded between five and ten DVD-sourced movies over the Internet after December 1999. At least one web site contains a list of 650 motion pictures, said to have been decrypted and compressed with DivX, that purportedly are available for sale, trade or free download. And although the Court does not accept the list, which is hearsay, as proof of the truth of the matters asserted therein, it does note that advertisements for decrypted versions of copyrighted movies first appeared on the Internet in substantial numbers in late 1999, following the posting of DeCSS.

The net of all this is reasonably plain. DeCSS is a free, effective and fast means of decrypting plaintiffs' DVDs and copying them to computer hard drives. DivX, which is available over the Internet for nothing, with the investment of some time and effort, permits compression of the decrypted files to sizes that readily fit on a writeable CD-ROM. Copies of such CD-ROMs can be produced very cheaply and distributed as easily as other pirated intellectual property. While not everyone with Internet access now will find it convenient to send or receive DivX'd copies of pirated motion pictures over the Internet, the availability of high speed network connections in many businesses and institutions, and their growing availability in homes, make Internet and other network traffic in pirated copies a growing threat.

These circumstances have two major implications for plaintiffs. First, the availability of DeCSS on the Internet effectively has compromised plaintiffs' system of copyright protection for DVDs, requiring them either to tolerate increased piracy or to expend resources to develop and implement a replacement system unless the availability of DeCSS is terminated. It is analogous to the publication of a bank vault combination in a national newspaper. Even if no one uses the combination to open the vault, its mere publication has the effect of defeating the bank's security system, forcing the bank to reprogram the lock. Development and implementation of a new DVD copy protection system, however, is far more difficult and costly than reprogramming a combination lock and may carry with it the added problem of rendering the existing installed base of compliant DVD players obsolete.

Second, the application of DeCSS to copy and distribute motion pictures on DVD, both on CD-ROMs and via the Internet, threatens to reduce the studios' revenue from the sale and rental of DVDs. It threatens also to impede new, potentially lucrative initiatives for the distribution of motion pictures in digital form, such as video-on-demand via the Internet.

In consequence, plaintiffs already have been gravely injured. As the pressure for and competition to supply more and more users with faster and faster network connections grows, the injury will multiply.

II.   The Digital Millennium Copyright Act . . .

B.   *Posting of DeCSS*

1.   Violation of Anti-Trafficking Provision

Section 1201(a)(2) of the Copyright Act, part of the DMCA, provides that:

> No person shall . . . offer to the public, provide or otherwise traffic in any technology . . . that—

(A)   is primarily designed or produced for the purpose of circumventing a technological measure that effectively controls access to a work protected under [the Copyright Act];

(B) has only limited commercially significant purpose or use other than to circumvent a technological measure that effectively controls access to a work protected under [the Copyright Act]; or

(C) is marketed by that person or another acting in concert with that person with that person's knowledge for use in circumventing a technological measure that effectively controls access to a work protected under [the Copyright Act].

In this case, defendants concededly offered and provided and, absent a court order, would continue to offer and provide DeCSS to the public by making it available for download on the 2600.com web site. DeCSS, a computer program, unquestionably is "technology" within the meaning of the statute. "Circumvent a technological measure" is defined to mean descrambling a scrambled work, decrypting an encrypted work, or "otherwise to avoid, bypass, remove, deactivate, or impair a technological measure, without the authority of the copyright owner," so DeCSS clearly is a means of circumventing a technological access control measure.[137] In consequence, if CSS otherwise falls within paragraphs (A), (B) or (C) of Section 1201(a)(2), and if none of the statutory exceptions applies to their actions, defendants have violated and, unless enjoined, will continue to violate the DMCA by posting DeCSS.

a.   Section 1201(a)(2)(A)

(1)   CSS Effectively Controls Access to Copyrighted Works

During pretrial proceedings and at trial, defendants attacked plaintiffs' Section 1201(a)(2)(A) claim, arguing that CSS, which is based on a 40-bit encryption key, is a weak cipher that does not "effectively control" access to plaintiffs' copyrighted works. They reasoned from this premise that CSS is not protected under this branch of the statute at all. Their post-trial memorandum appears to have abandoned this argument. In any case, however, the contention is indefensible as a matter of law.

First, the statute expressly provides that "a technological measure 'effectively controls access to a work' if the measure, in the ordinary course of its operation,

---

137. Decryption or avoidance of an access control measure is not "circumvention" within the meaning of the statute unless it occurs "without the authority of the copyright owner." 17 U.S.C. §1201(a)(3)(A). Defendants posit that purchasers of a DVD acquire the right "to perform all acts with it that are not exclusively granted to the copyright holder." Based on this premise, they argue that DeCSS does not circumvent CSS within the meaning of the statute because the Copyright Act does not grant the copyright holder the right to prohibit purchasers from decrypting. As the copyright holder has no statutory right to prohibit decryption, the argument goes, decryption cannot be understood as unlawful circumvention. Def. Post-Trial Mem. 10-13. The argument is pure sophistry. The DMCA proscribes trafficking in technology that decrypts or avoids an access control measure without the copyright holder consenting to the decryption or avoidance. *See* Judiciary Comm. Rep. at 17-18 (fair use applies "where the access is authorized"). Defendants' argument seems to be a corruption of the first sale doctrine, which holds that the copyright holder notwithstanding the exclusive distribution right conferred by Section 106(3) of the Copyright Act, 17 U.S.C. §106(3), is deemed by its "first sale" of a copy of the copyrighted work to have consented to subsequent sale of the copy. See generally 2 Nimmer §§8.11-8.12.

requires the application of information or a process or a treatment, with the authority of the copyright owner, to gain access to a work." One cannot gain access to a CSS-protected work on a DVD without application of the three keys that are required by the software. One cannot lawfully gain access to the keys except by entering into a license with the DVD CCA under authority granted by the copyright owners or by purchasing a DVD player or drive containing the keys pursuant to such a license. In consequence, under the express terms of the statute, CSS "effectively controls access" to copyrighted DVD movies. It does so, within the meaning of the statute, whether or not it is a strong means of protection.

This view is confirmed by the legislative history, which deals with precisely this point. The House Judiciary Committee section-by-section analysis of the House bill, which in this respect was enacted into law, makes clear that a technological measure "effectively controls access" to a copyrighted work if its *function* is to control access:

> The bill does define the *functions* of the technological measures that are covered—that is, what it means for a technological measure to 'effectively control access to a work' . . . and to 'effectively protect a right of a copyright owner under this title' . . . . The practical, common-sense approach taken by H.R. 2281 is that if, in the ordinary course of its operation, a technology actually works in the defined ways to control access to a work . . . then the 'effectiveness' test is met, and the prohibitions of the statute are applicable. This test, which focuses on the function performed by the technology, provides a sufficient basis for clear interpretation. . . .

Finally, the interpretation of the phrase "effectively controls access" offered by defendants at trial—viz., that the use of the word "effectively" means that the statute protects only successful or efficacious technological means of controlling access—would gut the statute if it were adopted. If a technological means of access control is circumvented, it is, in common parlance, ineffective. Yet defendants' construction, if adopted, would limit the application of the statute to access control measures that thwart circumvention, but withhold protection for those measures that can be circumvented. In other words, defendants would have the Court construe the statute to offer protection where none is needed but to withhold protection precisely where protection is essential. The Court declines to do so. Accordingly, the Court holds that CSS effectively controls access to plaintiffs' copyrighted works.

(2) DeCSS Was Designed Primarily to Circumvent CSS

As CSS effectively controls access to plaintiffs' copyrighted works, the only remaining question under Section 1201(a)(2)(A) is whether DeCSS was designed primarily to circumvent CSS. The answer is perfectly obvious. By the admission of both Jon Johansen, the programmer who principally wrote DeCSS, and defendant Corley, DeCSS was created solely for the purpose of decrypting CSS—that is all it does. Hence, absent satisfaction of a statutory exception, defendants clearly violated Section 1201(a)(2)(A) by posting DeCSS to their web site. . . .

Perhaps the centerpiece of defendants' statutory position is the contention that DeCSS was not created for the purpose of pirating copyrighted motion pictures. Rather, they argue, it was written to further the development of a DVD player that would run under the Linux operating system, as there allegedly were no Linux compatible players on the market at the time. The argument plays itself out in various ways as different elements of the DMCA come into focus. But it perhaps is useful to address the point at its most general level in order to place the preceding discussion in its fullest context. . . .

As the earlier discussion demonstrates, the question whether the development of a Linux DVD player motivated those who wrote DeCSS is immaterial to the question whether the defendants now before the Court violated the anti-trafficking provision of the DMCA. The inescapable facts are that (1) CSS is a technological means that effectively controls access to plaintiffs' copyrighted works, (2) the one and only function of DeCSS is to circumvent CSS, and (3) defendants offered and provided DeCSS by posting it on their web site. Whether defendants did so in order to infringe, or to permit or encourage others to infringe, copyrighted works in violation of other provisions of the Copyright Act simply does not matter for purposes of Section 1201(a)(2). The offering or provision of the program is the prohibited conduct—and it is prohibited irrespective of why the program was written, except to whatever extent motive may be germane to determining whether their conduct falls within one of the statutory exceptions.

2. Statutory Exceptions

Earlier in the litigation, defendants contended that their activities came within several exceptions contained in the DMCA and the Copyright Act and constitute fair use under the Copyright Act. Their post-trial memorandum appears to confine their argument to the reverse engineering exception. In any case, all of their assertions are entirely without merit.

a. Reverse Engineering

Defendants claim to fall under Section 1201(f) of the statute, which provides in substance that one may circumvent, or develop and employ technological means to circumvent, access control measures in order to achieve interoperability with another computer program provided that doing so does not infringe another's copyright and, in addition, that one may make information acquired through such efforts "available to others, if the person [in question] . . . provides such information solely for the purpose of enabling interoperability of an independently created computer program with other programs, and to the extent that doing so does not constitute infringement. . . ." They contend that DeCSS is necessary to achieve interoperability between computers running the Linux operating system and DVDs and that this exception therefore is satisfied. This contention fails.

First, Section 1201(f)(3) permits information acquired through reverse engineering to be made available to others only by the person who acquired the information. But these defendants did not do any reverse engineering. They simply took DeCSS off someone else's web site and posted it on their own.

Defendants would be in no stronger position even if they had authored DeCSS. The right to make the information available extends only to dissemination "solely for the purpose" of achieving interoperability as defined in the statute. It does not apply to public dissemination of means of circumvention, as the legislative history confirms. These defendants, however, did not post DeCSS "solely" to achieve interoperability with Linux or anything else.

Finally, it is important to recognize that even the creators of DeCSS cannot credibly maintain that the "sole" purpose of DeCSS was to create a Linux DVD player. DeCSS concededly was developed on and runs under Windows—a far more widely used operating system. The developers of DeCSS therefore knew that DeCSS could be used to decrypt and play DVD movies on Windows as well as Linux machines. They knew also that the decrypted files could be copied like any other unprotected computer file. Moreover, the Court does not credit Mr. Johansen's testimony that he created DeCSS solely for the purpose of building a Linux player. Mr. Johansen is a very talented young man and a member of a well known hacker group who viewed "cracking" CSS as an end it itself and a means of demonstrating his talent and who fully expected that the use of DeCSS would not be confined to Linux machines. Hence, the Court finds that Mr. Johansen and the others who actually did develop DeCSS did not do so solely for the purpose of making a Linux DVD player if, indeed, developing a Linux-based DVD player was among their purposes.

Accordingly, the reverse engineering exception to the DMCA has no application here. . . .

d. Fair Use . . .

The use of technological means of controlling access to a copyrighted work may affect the ability to make fair uses of the work. Focusing specifically on the facts of this case, the application of CSS to encrypt a copyrighted motion picture requires the use of a compliant DVD player to view or listen to the movie. Perhaps more significantly, it prevents exact copying of either the video or the audio portion of all or any part of the film. This latter point means that certain uses that might qualify as "fair" for purposes of copyright infringement—for example, the preparation by a film studies professor of a single CD-ROM or tape containing two scenes from different movies in order to illustrate a point in a lecture on cinematography, as opposed to showing relevant parts of two different DVDs—would be difficult or impossible absent circumvention of the CSS encryption. Defendants therefore argue that the DMCA cannot properly be construed to make it difficult or impossible to make any fair use of plaintiffs' copyrighted works and that the statute therefore does not reach their activities, which are simply a means to enable users of DeCSS to make such fair uses.

Defendants have focused on a significant point. Access control measures such as CSS do involve some risk of preventing lawful as well as unlawful uses of copyrighted material. Congress, however, clearly faced up to and dealt with this question in enacting the DMCA.

The Court begins its statutory analysis, as it must, with the language of the statute. Section 107 of the Copyright Act provides in critical part that certain uses of copyrighted works that otherwise would be wrongful are "not . . . infringement[s] of copyright." Defendants, however, are not here sued for copyright infringement. They are sued for offering and providing technology designed to circumvent technological measures that control access to copyrighted works and otherwise violating Section 1201(a)(2) of the Act. If Congress had meant the fair use defense to apply to such actions, it would have said so. Indeed, as the legislative history demonstrates, the decision not to make fair use a defense to a claim under Section 1201(a) was quite deliberate.

Congress was well aware during the consideration of the DMCA of the traditional role of the fair use defense in accommodating the exclusive rights of copyright owners with the legitimate interests of noninfringing users of portions of copyrighted works. It recognized the contention, voiced by a range of constituencies concerned with the legislation, that technological controls on access to copyrighted works might erode fair use by preventing access even for uses that would be deemed "fair" if only access might be gained. And it struck a balance among the competing interests.

The first element of the balance was the careful limitation of Section 1201(a)(1)'s prohibition of the act of circumvention to the act itself so as not to "apply to subsequent actions of a person once he or she has obtained authorized access to a copy of a [copyrighted] work. . . ." By doing so, it left "the traditional defenses to copyright infringement, including fair use, . . . fully applicable" provided "the access is authorized."

Second, Congress delayed the effective date of Section 1201(a)(1)'s prohibition of the act of circumvention for two years pending further investigation about how best to reconcile Section 1201(a)(1) with fair use concerns. Following that investigation, which is being carried out in the form of a rule-making by the Register of Copyright, the prohibition will not apply to users of particular classes of copyrighted works who demonstrate that their ability to make noninfringing uses of those classes of works would be affected adversely by Section 1201(a)(1).

Third, it created a series of exceptions to aspects of Section 1201(a) for certain uses that Congress thought "fair," including reverse engineering, security testing, good faith encryption research, and certain uses by nonprofit libraries, archives and educational institutions.

Defendants claim also that the possibility that DeCSS might be used for the purpose of gaining access to copyrighted works in order to make fair use of those works saves them under Sony Corp. v. Universal City Studios, Inc. But they are mistaken. *Sony* does not apply to the activities with which defendants here are charged. Even if it did, it would not govern here. *Sony* involved a construction of the Copyright Act that has been overruled by the later enactment of the DMCA to the extent of any inconsistency between *Sony* and the new statute. . . .

When *Sony* was decided, the only question was whether the manufacturers could be held liable for infringement by those who purchased equipment from them in circumstances in which there were many noninfringing uses for their equipment. But that is not the question now before this Court. The question here is whether the possibility of noninfringing fair use by someone who gains access to a protected copyrighted work through a circumvention technology distributed by the defendants saves the defendants from liability under Section 1201. But nothing in Section 1201 so suggests. By prohibiting the provision of circumvention technology, the DMCA fundamentally altered the landscape. A given device or piece of technology might have "a substantial noninfringing use, and hence be immune from attack under *Sony*'s construction of the Copyright Act—but nonetheless still be subject to suppression under Section 1201." Indeed, Congress explicitly noted that Section 1201 does not incorporate *Sony*.

The policy concerns raised by defendants were considered by Congress. Having considered them, Congress crafted a statute that, so far as the applicability of the fair use defense to Section 1201(a) claims is concerned, is crystal clear. In such circumstances, courts may not undo what Congress so plainly has done by "construing" the words of a statute to accomplish a result that Congress rejected. The fact that Congress elected to leave technologically unsophisticated persons who wish to make fair use of encrypted copyrighted works without the technical means of doing so is a matter for Congress unless Congress' decision contravenes the Constitution, a matter to which the Court turns below. Defendants' statutory fair use argument therefore is entirely without merit.

C. Linking to Sites Offering DeCSS

Plaintiffs seek also to enjoin defendants from "linking" their 2600.com web site to other sites that make DeCSS available to users. Their request obviously stems in no small part from what defendants themselves have termed their act of "electronic civil disobedience"—their attempt to defeat the purpose of the preliminary injunction by (a) offering the practical equivalent of making DeCSS available on their own web site by electronically linking users to other sites still offering DeCSS, and (b) encouraging other sites that had not been enjoined to offer the program. The dispositive question is whether linking to another web site containing DeCSS constitutes "offering [DeCSS] to the public" or "providing or otherwise trafficking" in it within the meaning of the DMCA. Answering this question requires careful consideration of the nature and types of linking.

Most web pages are written in computer languages, chiefly HTML, which allow the programmer to prescribe the appearance of the web page on the computer screen and, in addition, to instruct the computer to perform an operation if the cursor is placed over a particular point on the screen and the mouse then clicked. Programming a particular point on a screen to transfer the user to another web page when the point, referred to as a hyperlink, is clicked is called linking. Web pages can be designed to link to other web pages on the same site or to web pages maintained by different sites.

As noted earlier, the links that defendants established on their web site are of several types. Some transfer the user to a web page on an outside site that contains a good deal of information of various types, does not itself contain a link to DeCSS, but that links, either directly or via a series of other pages, to another page on the same site that posts the software. It then is up to the user to follow the link or series of links on the linked-to web site in order to arrive at the page with the DeCSS link and commence the download of the software. Others take the user to a page on an outside web site on which there appears a direct link to the DeCSS software and which may or may not contain text or links other than the DeCSS link. The user has only to click on the DeCSS link to commence the download. Still others may directly transfer the user to a file on the linked-to web site such that the download of DeCSS to the user's computer automatically commences without further user intervention.

The statute makes it unlawful to offer, provide or otherwise traffic in described technology. To "traffic" in something is to engage in dealings in it, conduct that necessarily involves awareness of the nature of the subject of the trafficking. To "provide" something, in the sense used in the statute, is to make it available or furnish it. To "offer" is to present or hold it out for consideration. The phrase "or otherwise traffic in" modifies and gives meaning to the words "offer" and "provide." In consequence, the anti-trafficking provision of the DMCA is implicated where one presents, holds out or makes a circumvention technology or device available, knowing its nature, for the purpose of allowing others to acquire it.

To the extent that defendants have linked to sites that automatically commence the process of downloading DeCSS upon a user being transferred by defendants' hyperlinks, there can be no serious question. Defendants are engaged in the functional equivalent of transferring the DeCSS code to the user themselves.

Substantially the same is true of defendants' hyperlinks to web pages that display nothing more than the DeCSS code or present the user only with the choice of commencing a download of DeCSS and no other content. The only distinction is that the entity extending to the user the option of downloading the program is the transferee site rather than defendants, a distinction without a difference.

Potentially more troublesome might be links to pages that offer a good deal of content other than DeCSS but that offer a hyperlink for downloading, or transferring to a page for downloading, DeCSS. If one assumed, for the purposes of argument, that the *Los Angeles Times* web site somewhere contained the DeCSS code, it would be wrong to say that anyone who linked to the *Los Angeles Times* web site, regardless of purpose or the manner in which the link was described, thereby offered, provided or otherwise trafficked in DeCSS merely because DeCSS happened to be available on a site to which one linked. But that is not this case. Defendants urged others to post DeCSS in an effort to disseminate DeCSS and to inform defendants that they were doing so. Defendants then linked their site to those "mirror" sites, after first checking to ensure that the mirror sites in fact were posting DeCSS or something that looked like it, and proclaimed on their own site that DeCSS could be had by clicking on the hyperlinks on defendants' site. By doing so, they offered, provided or otherwise trafficked in DeCSS, and they continue to do so to this day.

III. The First Amendment

Defendants argue that the DMCA, at least as applied to prevent the public dissemination of DeCSS, violates the First Amendment to the Constitution. They claim that it does so in two ways. First, they argue that computer code is protected speech and that the DMCA's prohibition of dissemination of DeCSS therefore violates defendants' First Amendment rights. Second, they contend that the DMCA is unconstitutionally overbroad, chiefly because its prohibition of the dissemination of decryption technology prevents third parties from making fair use of plaintiffs' encrypted works, and vague. They argue also that a prohibition on their linking to sites that make DeCSS available is unconstitutional for much the same reasons. . . .

B. *The Constitutionality of the DMCA's Anti-Trafficking Provision*

1. Defendants' Alleged Right to Disseminate DeCSS

Defendants first attack Section 1201(a)(2), the anti-trafficking provision, as applied to them on the theory that DeCSS is constitutionally protected expression and that the statute improperly prevents them from communicating it. Their attack presupposes that a characterization of code as constitutionally protected subjects any regulation of code to the highest level of First Amendment scrutiny. As we have seen, however, this does not necessarily follow.

Just as computer code cannot be excluded from the area of First Amendment concern because it is abstract and, in many cases, arcane, the long history of First Amendment jurisprudence makes equally clear that the fact that words, symbols and even actions convey ideas and evoke emotions does not inevitably place them beyond the power of government. The Supreme Court has evolved an analytical framework by which the permissibility of particular restrictions on the expression of ideas must [be] determined.

Broadly speaking, restrictions on expression fall into two categories. Some are restrictions on the voicing of particular ideas, which typically are referred to as content based restrictions. Others have nothing to do with the content of the expression—i.e., they are content neutral—but they have the incidental effect of limiting expression.

In general, "government has no power to restrict expression because of its message, its ideas, its subject matter, or its content. . . ." "Subject only to narrow and well-understood exceptions, [the First Amendment] does not countenance governmental control over the content of messages expressed by private individuals." In consequence, content based restrictions on speech are permissible only if they serve compelling state interests by the least restrictive means available.

Content neutral restrictions, in contrast, are measured against a less exacting standard. Because restrictions of this type are not motivated by a desire to limit the message, they will be upheld if they serve a substantial governmental interest and restrict First Amendment freedoms no more than necessary. . . .

Thus, the starting point for analysis is whether the DMCA, as applied to restrict dissemination of DeCSS and other computer code used to circumvent access control measures, is a content based restriction on speech or a content neutral regulation. Put another way, the question is the level of review that governs the DMCA's anti-trafficking provision as applied to DeCSS—the strict scrutiny standard applicable to content based regulations or the intermediate level applicable to content neutral regulations, including regulations of the nonspeech elements of expressive conduct.

Given the fact that DeCSS code is expressive, defendants would have the Court leap immediately to the conclusion that Section 1201(a)(2)'s prohibition on providing DeCSS necessarily is content based regulation of speech because it suppresses dissemination of a particular kind of expression. But this would be a unidimensional approach to a more textured reality and entirely too facile.

The "principal inquiry in determining content neutrality . . . is whether the government has adopted a regulation of speech because of [agreement or] disagreement with the message it conveys." The computer code at issue in this case, however, does more than express the programmers' concepts. It does more, in other words, than convey a message. DeCSS, like any other computer program, is a series of instructions that causes a computer to perform a particular sequence of tasks which, in the aggregate, decrypt CSS-protected files. Thus, it has a distinctly functional, non-speech aspect in addition to reflecting the thoughts of the programmers. It enables anyone who receives it and who has a modicum of computer skills to circumvent plaintiffs' access control system.

The reason that Congress enacted the anti-trafficking provision of the DMCA had nothing to do with suppressing particular ideas of computer programmers and everything to do with functionality—with preventing people from circumventing technological access control measures—just as laws prohibiting the possession of burglar tools have nothing to do with preventing people from expressing themselves by accumulating what to them may be attractive assortments of implements and everything to do with preventing burglaries. Rather, it is focused squarely upon the effect of the distribution of the functional capability that the code provides. Any impact on the dissemination of programmers' ideas is purely incidental to the overriding concerns of promoting the distribution of copyrighted works in digital form while at the same time protecting those works from piracy and other violations of the exclusive rights of copyright holders. . . .

This analysis finds substantial support in the principal case relied upon by defendants, *Junger v. Daley*. The plaintiff in that case challenged on First Amendment grounds an Export Administration regulation that barred the export of computer encryption software, arguing that the software was expressive and that the regulation therefore was unconstitutional. The Sixth Circuit acknowledged the expressive nature of computer code, holding that it therefore was within the scope of the First Amendment. But it recognized also that computer code is functional as well and said that "the functional capabilities of source code, particularly those of encryption source code, should be considered when analyzing the governmental interest in regulating the exchange of this form of speech." Indeed, it went on to indicate that the pertinent standard of review was that established in *United States v. O'Brien*, the seminal speech-versus-conduct decision. Thus, rather than holding the challenged regulation unconstitutional on the theory that the expressive aspect of source code immunized it from regulation, the court remanded the case to the district court to determine whether the *O'Brien* standard was met in view of the functional aspect of code.

Notwithstanding its adoption by the Sixth Circuit, the focus on functionality in order to determine the level of scrutiny is not an inevitable consequence of the speech-conduct distinction. Conduct has immediate effects on the environment. Computer code, on the other hand, no matter how functional, causes a computer to perform the intended operations only if someone uses the code to do so. Hence, one commentator, in a thoughtful article, has maintained that functionality is really "a proxy for effects or harm" and that its adoption as a determinant of the level of scrutiny slides over questions of causation that intervene between the dissemination of a computer program and any harm caused by its use. . . .

Society increasingly depends upon technological means of controlling access to digital files and systems, whether they are military computers, bank records, academic records, copyrighted works or something else entirely. There are far too many who, given any opportunity, will bypass those security measures, some for the sheer joy of doing it, some for innocuous reasons, and others for more malevolent purposes. Given the virtually instantaneous and worldwide dissemination widely available via the Internet, the only rational assumption is that once a computer program capable of bypassing such an access control system is disseminated, it will be used. And that is not all.

There was a time when copyright infringement could be dealt with quite adequately by focusing on the infringing act. If someone wished to make and sell high quality but unauthorized copies of a copyrighted book, for example, the infringer

needed a printing press. The copyright holder, once aware of the appearance of ·
infringing copies, usually was able to trace the copies up the chain of distribution,
find and prosecute the infringer, and shut off the infringement at the source.

In principle, the digital world is very different. Once a decryption program like
DeCSS is written, it quickly can be sent all over the world. Every recipient is capable not only of decrypting and perfectly copying plaintiffs' copyrighted DVDs, but
also of retransmitting perfect copies of DeCSS and thus enabling every recipient to
do the same. They likewise are capable of transmitting perfect copies of the decrypted DVD. The process potentially is exponential rather than linear. Indeed, the
difference is illustrated by comparison of two epidemiological models describing
the spread of different kinds of disease. In a common source epidemic, as where
members of a population contract a non-contagious disease from a poisoned well,
the disease spreads only by exposure to the common source. If one eliminates the
source, or closes the contaminated well, the epidemic is stopped. In a propagated
outbreak epidemic, on the other hand, the disease spreads from person to person.
Hence, finding the initial source of infection accomplishes little, as the disease continues to spread even if the initial source is eliminated. For obvious reasons, then, a
propagated outbreak epidemic, all other things being equal, can be far more difficult to control.

This disease metaphor is helpful here. The book infringement hypothetical is
analogous to a common source outbreak epidemic. Shut down the printing press
(the poisoned well) and one ends the infringement (the disease outbreak). The
spread of means of circumventing access to copyrighted works in digital form, however, is analogous to a propagated outbreak epidemic. Finding the original source
of infection (e.g., the author of DeCSS or the first person to misuse it) accomplishes nothing, as the disease (infringement made possible by DeCSS and the resulting availability of decrypted DVDs) may continue to spread from one person
who gains access to the circumvention program or decrypted DVD to another. And
each is "infected," i.e., each is as capable of making perfect copies of the digital file
containing the copyrighted work as the author of the program or the first person to
use it for improper purposes. The disease metaphor breaks down principally at the
final point. Individuals infected with a real disease become sick, usually are driven
by obvious self-interest to seek medical attention, and are cured of the disease if
medical science is capable of doing so. Individuals infected with the "disease" of
capability of circumventing measures controlling access to copyrighted works in
digital form, however, do not suffer from having that ability. They cannot be relied
upon to identify themselves to those seeking to control the "disease." And their
self-interest will motivate some to misuse the capability, a misuse that, in practical
terms, often will be untraceable.

These considerations drastically alter consideration of the causal link between
dissemination of computer programs such as this and their illicit use. Causation in
the law ultimately involves practical policy judgments. Here, dissemination itself
carries very substantial risk of imminent harm because the mechanism is so unusual
by which dissemination of means of circumventing access controls to copyrighted
works threatens to produce virtually unstoppable infringement of copyright. In
consequence, the causal link between the dissemination of circumvention computer
programs and their improper use is more than sufficiently close to warrant selection
of a level of constitutional scrutiny based on the programs' functionality.

Accordingly, this Court holds that the anti-trafficking provision of the DMCA as applied to the posting of computer code that circumvents measures that control access to copyrighted works in digital form is a valid exercise of Congress' authority. It is a content neutral regulation in furtherance of important governmental interests that does not unduly restrict expressive activities. In any case, its particular functional characteristics are such that the Court would apply the same level of scrutiny even if it were viewed as content based. Yet it is important to emphasize that this is a very narrow holding. The restriction the Court here upholds, notwithstanding that computer code is within the area of First Amendment concern, is limited (1) to programs that circumvent access controls to copyrighted works in digital form in circumstances in which (2) there is no other practical means of preventing infringement through use of the programs, and (3) the regulation is motivated by a desire to prevent performance of the function for which the programs exist rather than any message they might convey. One readily might imagine other circumstances in which a governmental attempt to regulate the dissemination of computer code would not similarly be justified. . . .

3. Overbreadth

Defendants' second focus is the contention that Section 1201(a)(2) is unconstitutional because it prevents others from making fair use of copyrighted works by depriving them of the means of circumventing plaintiffs' access control system. In substance, they contend that the anti-trafficking provision leaves those who lack sufficient technical expertise to circumvent CSS themselves without the means of acquiring circumvention technology that they need to make fair use of the content of plaintiffs' copyrighted DVDs. . . .

The copyrighted works at issue, of course, are motion pictures. People use copies of them in DVD and other formats for various purposes, and we confine our consideration to the lawful purposes, which by definition are noninfringing or fair uses. The principal noninfringing use is to play the DVD for the purpose of watching the movie—viewing the images and hearing the sounds that are synchronized with them. Fair uses are much more varied. A movie reviewer might wish to quote a portion of the verbal script in an article or broadcast review. A television station might want to broadcast part of a particular scene to illustrate a review, a news story about a performer, or a story about particular trends in motion pictures. A musicologist perhaps would wish to play a portion of a musical sound track. A film scholar might desire to create and exhibit to students small segments of several different films to make some comparative point about the cinematography or some other characteristic. Numerous other examples doubtless could be imagined. But each necessarily involves one or more of three types of use: (1) quotation of the words of the script, (2) listening to the recorded sound track, including both verbal and non-verbal elements, and (3) viewing of the graphic images.

All three of these types of use now are affected by the anti-trafficking provision of the DMCA, but probably only to a trivial degree. To begin with, all or substantially all motion pictures available on DVD are available also on videotape. In consequence, anyone wishing to make lawful use of a particular movie may buy or rent a videotape, play it, and even copy all or part of it with readily available equipment.

But even if movies were available only on DVD, as someday may be the case, the impact on lawful use would be limited. Compliant DVD players permit one to view or listen to a DVD movie without circumventing CSS in any prohibited sense. The technology permitting manufacture of compliant DVD players is available to anyone on a royalty-free basis and at modest cost, so CSS raises no technological barrier to their manufacture. Hence, those wishing to make lawful use of copyrighted movies by viewing or listening to them are not hindered in doing so in any material way by the anti-trafficking provision of the DMCA. Nor does the DMCA materially affect quotation of language from CSS-protected movies. Anyone with access to a compliant DVD player may play the movie and write down or otherwise record the sound for the purpose of quoting it in another medium.

The DMCA does have a notable potential impact on uses that copy portions of a DVD movie because compliant DVD players are designed so as to prevent copying. In consequence, even though the fair use doctrine permits limited copying of copyrighted works in appropriate circumstances, the CSS encryption of DVD movies, coupled with the characteristics of licensed DVD players, limits such uses absent circumvention of CSS. Moreover, the anti-trafficking provision of the DMCA may prevent technologically unsophisticated persons who wish to copy portions of DVD movies for fair use from obtaining the means of doing so. It is the interests of these individuals upon which defendants rely most heavily in contending that the DMCA violates the First Amendment because it deprives such persons of an asserted constitutional right to make fair use of copyrighted materials.

As the foregoing suggests, the interests of persons wishing to circumvent CSS in order to make lawful use of the copyrighted movies it protects are remarkably varied. Some presumably are technologically sophisticated and therefore capable of circumventing CSS without access to defendants' or other purveyors' decryption programs; many presumably are not. Many of the possible fair uses may be made without circumventing CSS while others, i.e., those requiring copying, may not. Hence, the question whether Section 1201(a)(2) as applied here substantially affects rights, much less constitutionally protected rights, of members of the "fair use community" cannot be decided *in bloc*, without consideration of the circumstances of each member or similarly situated groups of members. Thus, the prudential concern with ensuring that constitutional questions be decided only when the facts before the Court so require counsels against permitting defendants to mount an overbreadth challenge here. . . .

C. Linking

As indicated above, the DMCA reaches links deliberately created by a web site operator for the purpose of disseminating technology that enables the user to circumvent access controls on copyrighted works. The question is whether it may do so consistent with the First Amendment. . . .

Links are "what unify the [World Wide] Web into a single body of knowledge, and what makes the Web unique." They "are the mainstay of the Internet and indispensable to its convenient access to the vast world of information." They often are used in ways that do a great deal to promote the free exchange of ideas and information that is a central value of our nation. Anything that would impose strict liability on a web site operator for the entire contents of any web site to which the operator linked therefore would raise grave constitutional concerns, as web site operators would be inhibited from linking for fear of exposure to liability. And it is equally clear that exposing those who use links to liability under the DMCA might chill their use, as some web site operators confronted with claims that they have posted circumvention technology falling within the statute may be more inclined to remove the allegedly offending link rather than test the issue in court. Moreover, web sites often contain a great variety of things, and a ban on linking to a site that contains DeCSS amidst other content threatens to restrict communication of this information to an excessive degree.

The possible chilling effect of a rule permitting liability for or injunctions against Internet hyperlinks is a genuine concern. But it is not unique to the issue of linking. The constitutional law of defamation provides a highly relevant analogy. The threat of defamation suits creates the same risk of self-censorship, the same chilling effect, for the traditional press as a prohibition of linking to sites containing circumvention technology poses for web site operators. Just as the potential chilling effect of defamation suits has not utterly immunized the press from all actions for defamation, however, the potential chilling effect of DMCA liability cannot utterly immunize web site operators from all actions for disseminating circumvention technology. And the solution to the problem is the same: the adoption of a standard of culpability sufficiently high to immunize the activity, whether it is publishing a newspaper or linking, except in cases in which the conduct in question has little or no redeeming constitutional value.

In the defamation area, this has been accomplished by a two-tiered constitutional standard. There may be no liability under the First Amendment for defamation of a public official or a public figure unless the plaintiff proves, by clear and convincing evidence, that the defendant published the offending statement with knowledge of its falsity or with serious doubt as to its truth. Liability in private figure cases, on the other hand, may not be imposed absent proof at least of negligence under Gertz v. Robert Welch, Inc. A similar approach would minimize any chilling effect here.

The other concern—that a liability based on a link to another site simply because the other site happened to contain DeCSS or some other circumvention technology in the midst of other perfectly appropriate content could be overkill— also is readily dealt with. The offense under the DMCA is offering, providing or otherwise trafficking in circumvention technology. An essential ingredient, as explained above, is a desire to bring about the dissemination. Hence, a strong requirement of that forbidden purpose is an essential prerequisite to any liability for linking.

Accordingly, there may be no injunction against, nor liability for, linking to a site containing circumvention technology, the offering of which is unlawful under the DMCA, absent clear and convincing evidence that those responsible for the link (a) know at the relevant time that the offending material is on the linked-to site, (b) know that it is circumvention technology that may not lawfully be offered, and (c) create or maintain the link for the purpose of disseminating that technology. Such a standard will limit the fear of liability on the part of web site operators just as the *New York Times* standard gives the press great comfort in publishing all sorts of material that would have been actionable at common law, even in the face of flat denials by the subjects of their stories. And it will not subject web site operators to liability for linking to a site containing proscribed technology where the link exists for purposes other than dissemination of that technology.

In this case, plaintiffs have established by clear and convincing evidence that these defendants linked to sites posting DeCSS, knowing that it was a circumvention device. Indeed, they initially touted it as a way to get free movies, and they later maintained the links to promote the dissemination of the program in an effort to defeat effective judicial relief. They now know that dissemination of DeCSS violates the DMCA. An anti-linking injunction on these facts does no violence to the First Amendment. Nor should it chill the activities of web site operators dealing with different materials, as they may be held liable only on a compelling showing of deliberate evasion of the statute. . . .

COMMENTS AND QUESTIONS

1. The Second Circuit Court of Appeals affirmed Judge Kaplan's ruling in *Universal City Studios, Inc. v. Corley*, 273 F.3d 429 (2d Cir. 2001). The appellate court opinion concentrated on Corley's First Amendment defenses and agreed with Corley on two key issues: First, the court agreed that computer programs—even in object code form—are protected speech under the First Amendment. (See discussion in Chapter 13.) However, like Judge Kaplan, the Second Circuit concluded that the functionality of program code limited the degree of its First Amendment protection. Banning the functionality of circumvention technologies, such as DeCSS, was consistent with the First Amendment. Second, the court agreed that intermediate scrutiny applied to Corley's challenge to the DMCA anticircumvention rules. However, the court decided that Congress had tailored the DMCA narrowly enough to survive a constitutional challenge.

Concerning Corley's claim that the DMCA rules were unconstitutional because of their restrictive effects on fair use, the Second Circuit said this:

> We need not explore the extent to which fair use might have constitutional protection, grounded either on the First Amendment or the Copyright Clause, because whatever validity a constitutional claim might have as to an application of the DMCA that impairs fair use of copyrighted materials, such matters are far beyond the scope of this lawsuit for several reasons. In the first place, the Appellants do not claim to be making fair use of any copyrighted materials, and nothing in the injunction forbids them from making such fair use. . . .
>
> Second, as the District Court properly noted, to whatever extent the anti-trafficking provisions of the DMCA might prevent others from copying portions of DVD movies in order to make fair use of them, "the evidence as to the impact of the anti-trafficking provisions of the DMCA on prospective fair users is scanty and fails adequately to address the issues."
>
> Third, the Appellants have provided no support for their premise that fair use of DVD movies is constitutionally required to be made by copying the original work in its original format. . . . We know of no authority for the proposition that fair use, as protected by the Copyright Act, much less the Constitution, guarantees copying by the optimum method or in the identical format of the original. . . .

273 F.3d at 458-59.

Commentators disagree on whether the DMCA anticircumvention rules preserve some room for fair use hacking. See, e.g., *Samuelson, supra* (fair use preserved); Jane C. Ginsburg, From Having Copies to Experiencing Works: The Development of an Access Right in U.S. Copyright Law, forthcoming in Hugh Hansen, ed., U.S. Intellectual Property: Law and Policy (Sweet & Maxwell 2002) (1201(c) may permit some fair use circumventions); David Nimmer, A Riff on Fair Use in the Digital Millennium Copyright Act, 148 U. Penn. L. Rev. 673 (2000) (fair use not preserved). Some commentators argue that the DMCA anticircumvention rules are unconstitutional insofar as they foreclose fair uses. See, e.g., Neil Netanel, Locating Copyright Within the First Amendment Skein, 54 Stan. L. Rev. 1 (2001); Glynn S. Lunney, Jr., The Death of Copyright, 87 Virginia L. Rev. 813 (2001) (2001); Yochai Benkler, Free as the Air to Common Use: First Amendment Constraints on the Enclosure of the Public Domain, 74 N.Y.U. L. Rev. 354 (1999). See also Lawrence Lessig, Code and Other Laws of Cyberspace 132-38 (2000) (latent ambiguity in the U.S. Constitution as to whether limitations on copyright, such as fair use, are constitutionally required); Jane C. Ginsburg, Copyright and Control over New Technologies of Dissemination, 101 Colum. L. Rev. 1613 (2001) (copyright balance has shifted toward rightsholders with the advent of technical measures).

2. Computer scientist David Touretzky maintains a website, called "A Gallery of CSS Descramblers" at http://www-2.cs.cmu.edu/~dst/DeCSS/Gallery/ that contains numerous expressions of algorithms for descrambling the Content Scramble System, including one in haiku format and one in source code form. Does a website of this sort violate the DMCA? How would Judge Kaplan analyze such a claim? Consider also whether Professor Jane Ginsburg violated the DMCA anticircumvention rules when she linked to a website at which DeCSS was posted as part of her copyright course website in connection with her teaching of the *Reimerdes/Corley* case?

3. The Recording Industry Association of America sent a letter to Princeton Computer Science Professor Edward Felten and several coauthors asserting that presentation or publication of a paper these scientists had written about weaknesses in digital watermarking technologies that RIAA member firms planned to use to protect digital music would violate the DMCA anticircumvention rules. Is there anything in Judge Kaplan's *Reimerdes* decision that might have caused RIAA to conclude that such a claim would be viable?

4. Corley is not the only defendant in a DMCA anticircumvention case to have argued that the challenged software was lawful because it enabled fair uses. This defense was raised also in RealNetworks, Inc. v. Streambox, Inc., 2000 WL 127311 (W.D.Wash. 2000). RealNetworks offered its content industry customers a system for online delivery of digital content (e.g., sound recordings). Customers could set a digital "switch" to "stream" the content, or alternatively, set it to allow downloads. Streambox's VCR software enabled personal use copies to be made of content streamed with RealNetworks' software. The court concluded that the RealNetworks "digital handshake" authentication procedure, which the VCR software mimicked, was an access control system within the meaning of section 1201(a) and that the digital "switch," which the VCR ignored, was an effective technical measure within the meaning of section 1201(b). Because the VCR software bypassed both technical measures, it was held to violate both 1201(a)(2) and

1201(b)(1). The existence of substantial noninfringing uses for the VCR software was held to be irrelevant to liability under the anticircumvention rules.

5. The first criminal charges under the DMCA anticircumvention rules involve software designed to bypass security features of the Adobe Acrobat eBook Reader. A Russian company, ElcomSoft, developed its Advanced eBook Processor to enable Adobe's eBook users to convert eBook files to Adobe's PDF format. ElcomSoft sold copies of this program on the Internet. In July 2001, the FBI arrested Dmitry Sklyarov, an employee of ElcomSoft involved in developing the Advanced eBook Processor, as he was preparing to speak at a computer hacker conference in Las Vegas. The government charged Sklyarov and ElcomSoft with criminal violations of the DMCA, with penalties ranging up to five years' imprisonment and fines up to $2.25 million. The arrest outraged the computer science and civil liberties communities. The government eventually dropped the charges against Sklyarov (on condition that he testify against his employer), but the prosecution of ElcomSoft continues. ElcomSoft's motion to dismiss charges against it on various constitutional grounds was denied in United States v. Elcom, Ltd., 203 F. Supp.2d 1111 (N.D. Cal. 2002).

6. Less widely noticed than the *Corley* and *Sklyarov* cases, but potentially very significant, is a trial court decision in Sony Computer Entertainment of America, Inc. v. GameMasters, 87 F. Supp.2d 976 (N.D. Cal. 1999). Among other things, GameMasters sold game enhancement software that enabled Sony games country-coded for the Japanese market to play on U.S.-coded Sony platforms. Although concluding that the game enhancer program did not infringe any Sony copyrights under Lewis Galoob Toys, Inc. v. Nintendo of Am., Inc., 964 F.2d 965 (9th Cir. 1992), the court ruled that it violated section 1201(a)(2) because the program bypassed country codes for the games, which were, in the court's view, effective access control measures under the DMCA. Does this ruling give Sony an exclusive right to control the market for software to enhance the play of Sony games? Does it matter if Sony marketed a competing game enhancer program (as, in fact, it did)? Should GameMasters have raised an interoperability defense under section 1201(f)? Should GameMasters have charged Sony with misuse of DMCA anticircumvention rules, given that the software in question could not be used to make illegal copies of Sony programs?

7. Another lawsuit arising from posting DeCSS on the Internet was brought in January 2000 by the DVD Copy Control Association (DVD CCA). It charged Andrew Bunner, Andrew McLaughlin, and several others with trade secrecy misappropriation for posting DeCSS on the Internet, alleging that reverse engineering of CSS in violation of an anti–reverse engineering clause of a click-through license constituted trade secret misappropriation and that Bunner and his codefendants knew or should have known that DeCSS embodied or was derived from stolen CSS trade secrets when he posted this program on his website. This trial judge decided that DVD CCA was likely to succeed on the merits of this claim and issued a preliminary injunction, ordering Bunner and others to take DeCSS down from their website pending trial on the merits. See DVD Copy Control Ass'n v. McLaughlin, 2000 WL 48512 (Calif. Super. 2000). Bunner appealed. The California Court of Appeal, finding merit in Bunner's First Amendment defense, reversed. See DVD Copy Control Ass'n v. Bunner, 93 Cal. App.4th 648, 113 Cal. Rptr. 338 (2001). The court focused on the preliminary nature of the relief sought, which it concluded was an impermissible prior restraint on speech. The California Supreme

Court granted DVD CCA's request to hear the appeal in this case. That court's ruling will be posted on the casebook website when it becomes available.

8. The European Union has taken a very similar approach to regulating circumvention technologies in its Directive 2001/29/EC of the European Parliament and of the Council of 22 May 2001 on the harmonization of certain aspects of copyright and related rights in the information society. Official Journal L 167, 22/06/2001, 10-19, available at http://europa.eu.int/eur-lex/. Unlike the DMCA, the Directive does not distinguish between circumvention of access controls (illegal under section 1201(a)(1)(A)) and circumvention of other technical measures (not regulated under the DMCA). Interestingly, the EU Directive imposes an obligation on copyright owners and on member states of the EU to ensure that certain copyright exceptions can be exercised notwithstanding the rightsholders' use of technical measures. See Article 6(4) of the EU Directive. Dan L. Burk and Julie E. Cohen, Fair Use Infrastructure for Copyright Management Systems, 15 Harv. J.L. & Tech. 41 (2001), suggest that rightsholders should be able to bring claims for violating anticircumvention rules only if they have escrowed the keys to unlock technical measures so that users will be able to exercise fair use and other copyright exceptions. What do you think of this idea? What other means might be employed to ensure that users will be able to exercise fair use rights?

9. Among the many resources about digital rights management technologies are: Commission of the European Communities, Commission Staff Working Paper on Digital Rights: Background, Systems, and Assessments SEC 2002(197), Feb. 14, 2002, available at http://europa.eu.int/information_society/topics/multi/digital_rights/doc/drm_workingdoc.pdf; Daniel J. Gervais, Electronic Rights Management and Digital Identifier Systems, J. Electronic Publishing, March 1999, available at http://www.press.umich.edu/jep/04-03/gervais.html; Mark Stefik, Shifting the Possible: How Trusted Systems and Digital Property Rights Challenge Us to Rethink Digital Publishing, 12 Berkeley Tech. L.J. 137 (1997); Charles Clark, The Answer to the Machine is In the Machine, in The Future of Copyright in a Digital Environment (P. Bernt Hugenholtz, ed. 1996). For a critical perspective on DRM technologies, see, e.g., Julie E. Cohen, *Lochner* in Cyberspace: The New Economic Orthodoxy of "Rights Management," 97 Mich. L. Rev. 462 (1998).

10. Legislation to mandate installation of standard technical measures in all digital media devices was introduced into the U.S. Congress in 2002. See S. 2048: Consumer Broadband and Digital Television Promotion Act, 107th Cong., 2d Sess. (2002). This bill would give the Federal Communications Commission the power to issue rules imposing such mandates after hearing input from interested parties. The AHRA (discussed above) is a "precedent" for requiring standard technical measures to be installed in digital technologies. What are the pros and cons of such legislation?

PROBLEMS

Problem 10-1. BNN, the Washington Dispatch, and USA Total ("the companies") are all mainstream news organizations that provide news information to subscribers in a variety of media (such as newspapers or broadcast television). All have Web sites that provide anyone who uses the Internet with free access to some of their news stories, as well as other features designed specifically for Web users. The companies do not make subscription revenue from their Web pages but do sell some advertising to defray the costs of the pages. However, none of the companies shows a net profit on their pages. They maintain the page at least in part for image reasons. None of these organizations registers visitors to these Web sites or restrict visits in any way. However, BNN and the Washington Dispatch do make use of a file called "cookies.txt" that appears with modern Web browsers. By reading this file automatically, the companies can tell the server from which the browsing party is visiting, the Web site from which it has come, and the Web site it goes to next.

AlltheNews, Inc. (ANI) is a small start-up company that provides links to each of the major news organization Web pages on the Internet, including those of the companies described above. A link allows the user to jump seamlessly from ANI's site to any of the news organization sites. ANI's particular link uses "framing" technology to permit the linked site to be viewed as if it existed inside ANI's page, with a border provided by ANI. However, ANI has not in fact copied the companies' pages, but has merely sent a command to the user's Web browser instructing it to find the companies' pages and display them inside the frame. ANI sells advertising for its page. Its ads appear inside the border surrounding the frame.

The companies bring suit against ANI for copyright and trademark infringement. Who should prevail on each claim, and why?

Problem 10-2. The University of the Midwest (UM) runs one of the five largest Internet servers in the country. UM provides access to and forwards Usenet newsgroups. However, because of the limitations of server space, the system administrator at UM has decided not to carry all Usenet newsgroups. Instead, the UM server provides access only to about half of the newsgroups available on Usenet.

Playboy sues UM, arguing that it is liable for duplicating, distributing, and displaying numerous Playboy-copyrighted images posted to Usenet on its servers. Is UM a direct infringer? Would it affect the result if the UM system administrator made a conscious decision to allow the group alt.binaries.erotica.centerfolds (a group that has a large percentage of infringing Playboy material) to be part of the University's Usenet feed?

Problem 10-3. Kat, a law student using her University of Texas account, puts up a home page that includes links to several Web sites. One of those Web sites, run by Bismey Animation Conglomerate, Inc. (BAC), permits copying of its Web information only by those who have joined its "Computer Mouse Club" and have paid a fee to view the information. BAC warns users of its limited distribution policy once they have already accessed its Web page.

Byrd logs in to Kat's Web site from Finland. He follows Kat's link to the BAC Web page, causing a copy of the BAC page to be downloaded to his computer in Finland, even though he is not a member of the Club. He then distributes BAC's images widely in Finland.

Unable to obtain jurisdiction to sue Byrd, BAC files suit for copyright in-fringement against both Kat and the University of Texas, alleging both direct and contributory copyright infringement. What result?

Problem 10-4. ReplayTV recently introduced a digital video recorder (DVR), a digital version of the VCR. Thanks to digital technology, the Re-playTV 4500 offers consumers the ability to instantly skip over commercials with the click of a 30-second advance fast forward button. In addition, the large storage capacity of the ReplayTV 4500 hard drive enables consumers to store up to 60 hours of content, making archiving of content much more con-venient than on VCRs. Consumers can use an automated feature to bypass commercials automatically. A recent survey of DVR owners finds that 35 per-cent say they never watch commercials, while nearly 60 percent say they watch them only occasionally. The television industry fears that these capabilities will make advertisers much less willing to support their broadcasts. They sue to en-join sale of ReplayTV's DVR. How should the court rule on this case?

C. PATENT LAW

In recent years, software patents have met with increased acceptance in the patent system, as described in Chapter 3. Because of the perceived importance of the Internet and "e-commerce," an important subset of software patents now re-lates to the Internet. In this Section, we will describe some emerging trends in the law of Internet patents. We begin with patentability and then proceed to infringe-ment.

1. Patentability

The five major requirements of patentability are patentable subject matter; utility; novelty; nonobviousness; and enablement/written description.

Patentable subject matter has not been an important issue in the litigated cases involving Internet patents. There are two reasons for this. First, these cases have come along after the sea-change ushered in by State Street Bank and Trust Co. v. Signature Financial, Inc., 149 F.3d 1368 (Fed. Cir. 1998), which made it clear that both software and business method patents are permissible. Second, most of these are cases where *both parties* are members of Internet-related industries and hence can be expected to seek and hold Internet patents. There is therefore no incentive for an accused infringer to challenge patentability under the §101 patentable sub-ject matter requirement. In the *Netscape* case in the next paragraph, for example, the defendant Netscape Communications held 55 U.S. patents as of late 2002. The last thing Netscape would want to do is establish that all its own patents are invalid.

Most Internet-related patents would seem to have the level of utility required by the Patent Act. As to novelty, to date, there has been only limited case law on this issue. One exception is Netscape Communications Corp. v. Konrad, 295 F.3d 1315 (Fed. Cir. 2002), reproduced *supra* Chapter 3, which involved a series of patents for remote access to computer databases—an important function of the Internet. The Federal Circuit found that quasi-public demonstrations, together with offers involving commercial exploitation, invalidated the patents under the "on-sale" bar of 35 U.S.C. §102(b).

As to nonobviousness, the first Internet-related case to touch on nonobviousness was Amazon.com v. barnesandnoble.com.

≣
≣
≣ *Amazon.com, Inc. v. barnesandnoble.com, Inc.*
≣ *United States Court of Appeals for the Federal Circuit*
≣ *239 F.3d 1343 (Fed. Cir. 2001)*

CLEVENGER, Circuit Judge.

This is a patent infringement suit brought by Amazon.com, Inc. ("Amazon") against barnesandnoble.com, inc., and barnesandnoble.com LLC (together, "BN"). Amazon moved for a preliminary injunction to prohibit BN's use of a feature of its web site called "Express Lane." BN resisted the preliminary injunction on several grounds, including that its Express Lane feature did not infringe the claims of Amazon's patent, and that substantial questions exist as to the validity of Amazon's patent. The United States District Court for the Western District of Washington rejected BN's contentions [and granted a preliminary injunction.] BN brings its timely appeal from the order entering the preliminary injunction.

After careful review of the district court's opinion, the record, and the arguments advanced by the parties, we conclude that BN has mounted a substantial challenge to the validity of the patent in suit. Because Amazon is not entitled to preliminary injunctive relief under these circumstances, we vacate the order of the district court that set the preliminary injunction in place and remand the case for further proceedings.

I

This case involves United States Patent No. 5,960,411 ("the '411 patent"), which issued on September 28, 1999, and is assigned to Amazon. . . .

The '411 patent describes a method and system in which a consumer can complete a purchase order for an item via an electronic network using only a "single action," such as the click of a computer mouse button on the client computer system. Amazon developed the patent to cope with what it considered to be frustrations presented by what is known as the "shopping cart model" purchase system for electronic commerce purchasing events. In previous incarnations of the shopping cart model, a purchaser using a client computer system (such as a personal computer executing a web browser program) could select an item from an electronic catalog, typically by clicking on an "Add to Shopping Cart" icon, thereby placing the item in the "virtual" shopping cart. Other items from the catalog could be added to the shopping cart in the same manner. When the shopper completed the selecting process, the electronic commercial event would move to the check-out counter, so to speak. Then, information regarding the purchaser's identity, billing and shipping addresses, and credit payment method would be inserted into the transactional information base by the soon-to-be purchaser. Finally, the purchaser would "click" on a button displayed on the screen or somehow issue a command to execute the completed order, and the server computer system would verify and store the information concerning the transaction.

As is evident from the foregoing, an electronic commerce purchaser using the shopping cart model is required to perform several actions before achieving the ultimate goal of the placed order. The '411 patent sought to reduce the number of actions required from a consumer to effect a placed order. . . . How, one may ask, is the number of purchaser interactions reduced? The answer is that the number of purchaser interactions is reduced because the purchaser has previously visited the seller's web site and has previously entered into the database of the seller all of the required billing and shipping information that is needed to effect a sales transaction. Thereafter, when the purchaser visits the seller's web site and wishes to purchase a product from that site, the patent specifies that only a single action is necessary to place the order for the item. In the words of the written description, "once the description of an item is displayed, the purchaser need only take a single action to place the order to purchase that item." Col. 3, ll. 64-66.

The '411 patent has 26 claims, 4 of which are independent. . . . Although there are significant differences among the various independent and dependent claims in issue, for purposes of this appeal we may initially direct our primary focus on the "single action" limitation that is included in each claim. This focus is appropriate because BN's appeal attacks the injunction on the grounds that either its accused method does not infringe the "single action" limitation present in all of the claims, that the "single action" feature of the patent is invalid, or both.

We set forth below [claim 1], with emphasis added to highlight the disputed claim terms:

> 1. A method of placing an order for an item comprising:
> under control of a client system, displaying information identifying the item; and *in response to only a single action being performed,* sending a request to order the item along with an identifier of a purchaser of the item to a server system; under control of *a single-action ordering component* of the server system, receiving the request; retrieving additional information previously stored for the purchaser identified by the identifier in the received request; and generating an order to purchase the requested item for the purchaser identified by the identifier in the received request using the retrieved additional information; and *fulfilling the generated order* to complete purchase of the item whereby the item is ordered without using a *shopping cart ordering model.*

The district court interpreted the key "single action" claim limitation, which appears in each of the pertinent claims, to mean:

> The term "single action" is not defined by the patent specification. . . . As a result, the term "single action" as used in the '411 patent appears to refer to one action (such as clicking a mouse button) that a user takes to purchase an item once the following information is displayed to the user: (1) a description of the item; and (2) a description of the single action the user must take to complete a purchase order for that item.

With this interpretation of the key claim limitation in hand, the district court turned to BN's accused ordering system. BN's short-cut ordering system, called "Express

Lane," like the system contemplated by the patent, contains previously entered billing and shipping information for the customer. In one implementation, after a person is presented with BN's initial web page (referred to as the "menu page" or "home page"), the person can click on an icon on the menu page to get to what is called the "product page." BN's product page displays an image and a description of the selected product, and also presents the person with a description of a single action that can be taken to complete a purchase order for the item. If the single action described is taken, for example by a mouse click, the person will have effected a purchase order using BN's Express Lane feature. . . .

[The court concluded that under a proper claim interpretation, Amazon had made the showing that it is likely to succeed at trial on its infringement case. The court then turned to the issue of patent validity.]

The district court considered, but ultimately rejected, the potentially invalidating impact of several prior art references cited by BN. [W]e find that the district court committed clear error by misreading the factual content of the prior art references cited by BN and by failing to recognize that BN had raised a substantial question of invalidity of the asserted claims in view of these prior art references.

Validity challenges during preliminary injunction proceedings can be successful, that is, they may raise substantial questions of invalidity, on evidence that would not suffice to support a judgment of invalidity at trial. See, e.g., Helifix Ltd. v. Blok-Lok, Ltd., 208 F.3d 1339, 1352, 54 U.S.P.Q.2d 1299, 1308 (Fed. Cir. 2000). The test for invalidity at trial is by evidence that is clear and convincing. WMS Gaming, Inc. v. Int'l Game Tech., 184 F.3d 1339, 1355, 51 U.S.P.Q.2d 1385, 1396-97 (Fed. Cir. 1999). To succeed with a summary judgment motion of invalidity, for example, the movant must demonstrate a lack of genuine dispute about material facts and show that the facts not in dispute are clear and convincing in demonstrating invalidity. In resisting a preliminary injunction, however, one need not make out a case of actual invalidity. Vulnerability is the issue at the preliminary injunction stage, while validity is the issue at trial. The showing of a substantial question as to invalidity thus requires less proof than the clear and convincing showing necessary to establish invalidity itself. That this is so is plain from our cases. . . .

When the heft of the asserted prior art is assessed in light of the correct legal standards, we conclude that BN has mounted a serious challenge to the validity of Amazon's patent. We hasten to add, however, that this conclusion only undermines the prerequisite for entry of a preliminary injunction. Our decision today on the validity issue in no way resolves the ultimate question of invalidity. That is a matter for resolution at trial. It remains to be learned whether there are other references that may be cited against the patent, and it surely remains to be learned whether any shortcomings in BN's initial preliminary validity challenge will be magnified or dissipated at trial. All we hold, in the meantime, is that BN cast enough doubt on the validity of the '411 patent to avoid a preliminary injunction, and that the validity issue should be resolved finally at trial.

One of the references cited by BN was the "CompuServe Trend System." The undisputed evidence indicates that in the mid-1990s, CompuServe offered a service called "Trend" whereby CompuServe subscribers could obtain stock charts for a surcharge of 50 cents per chart. Before the district court, BN argued that this system anticipated claim 11 of the '411 patent. The district court failed to recognize the substantial question of invalidity raised by BN in citing the CompuServe Trend reference, in that this system appears to have used "single action ordering technology" within the scope of the claims in the '411 patent.

First, the district court dismissed the significance of this system partly on the basis that "[t]he CompuServe system was not a world wide web application." This distinction is irrelevant, since none of the claims mention either the Internet or the World Wide Web (with the possible exception of dependent claim 15, which mentions HTML, a program commonly associated with both the Internet and the World Wide Web). Moreover, the '411 patent specification explicitly notes that "[o]ne skilled in the art would appreciate that the single-action ordering techniques can be used in various environments other than the Internet." Col. 6, ll. 22-24.

More importantly, one of the screen shots in the record (reproduced [in Figure 10-1]) indicates that with the CompuServe Trend system, once the "item" to be purchased (i.e., a stock chart) has been displayed (by typing in a valid stock symbol), only a single action (i.e., a single mouse click on the button labeled "Chart ($ .50)") is required to obtain immediate electronic delivery (i.e., "fulfillment") of the item. Once the button labeled "Chart ($.50)" was activated by a purchaser, an electronic version of the requested stock chart would be transmitted to the purchaser and displayed on the purchaser's computer screen, and an automatic process to charge the purchaser's account 50 cents for the transaction would be initiated. In terms of the language of claims 2 and 11 in the CompuServe Trend system, the item to be ordered is "displayed" when the screen echoes back the characters of the stock symbol typed in by the purchaser before clicking on the ordering button.

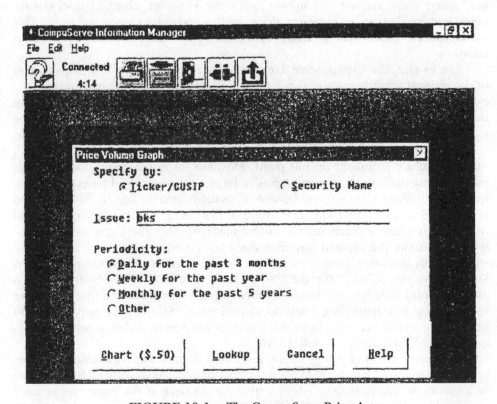

FIGURE 10-1. The CompuServe Prior Art.

The evidence before us indicates that the billing process for the electronic stock chart would not actually commence until the client system sent a message to the server system indicating that the electronic stock chart had been received at the client system. In its brief, Amazon argues that this feature of the CompuServe Trend system amounts to an additional "confirmation step necessary to complete the ordering process," and that the CompuServe Trend system therefore does not use "single action" technology within the scope of the claims in the '411 patent. However, all of the claims only require sending a *request* to order an item in response to performance of only a single action. In the CompuServe Trend system, this requirement is satisfied when a purchaser performs the single action of "clicking" on the button labeled "Chart ($.50)." The claims do not require that the billing process for the item must also be initiated in response to performance of the single action. Furthermore, in the CompuServe Trend system, the "action" of sending a message from the client system to the server system confirming successful reception of the electronic stock chart is performed automatically, without user intervention.

At oral argument, Amazon's counsel articulated three differences between the CompuServe Trend system and the claimed invention. First, Amazon's counsel repeated the district court's reasoning, and asserted that the CompuServe Trend system is not on the Internet or the World Wide Web. As mentioned above, the '411 patent specification indicates that this distinction is irrelevant.

Second, Amazon's counsel claimed that the CompuServe Trend system was different from the claims of the '411 patent because it required a user to "log in" at the beginning of each session, and therefore would not send the claimed "identifier" along with a request to purchase each item. However, claim 11 does not require transmission of an identifier along with a request to order an item. This requirement is found only in claims 1, 6, and 9, and their respective dependent claims.

On its face, the CompuServe Trend reference does not mention transmission of the claimed identifier along with a request to purchase each item. Nor does the evidence in the record at this stage indicate that the CompuServe Trend system transmitted such an identifier. BN has therefore not demonstrated that the CompuServe Trend reference anticipates the asserted claims of the '411 patent requiring transmission of such an identifier with the degree of precision necessary to obtain summary judgment on this point. However, as noted above, validity challenges during preliminary injunction proceedings can be successful on evidence that would not suffice to support a judgment of invalidity at trial. See *Helifix*, 208 F.3d at 1352, 54 USPQ2d at 1308. The record in this case is simply not yet developed to the point where a determination can be made whether the CompuServe Trend system transmits the claimed identifier along with a request to order an item, or whether this limitation is obvious in view of the prior art. For example, United States Patent No. 5,708,780 ("the '780 patent") (a reference cited by BN which is discussed more fully below), describes "forwarding a service request from the client to the server and appending a session identification (SID) to the request and to subsequent service requests from the client to the server within a session of requests." *See* '780 patent, col. 3, ll. 12-16.

Moreover, the '411 patent specification itself dismisses the distinction between ordering systems in which an identifier is transmitted along with each request to order an item, and systems in which a user logs in once at the beginning of each session. *See* '411 patent at col. 10, ll. 6-10 ("[T]he purchaser can be alternatively identified by a unique customer identifier that is provided by the customer when the customer initiates access to the server system and sent to the server system with each message.").

The final distinction drawn by Amazon's counsel between the claimed invention and the CompuServe Trend system was that—according to Amazon—the *only* reason that a purchaser would "call up" the screen would be to actually order an electronic stock chart, and that therefore an earlier action taken by a purchaser to invoke the screen should count as an extra purchaser action. According to this argument, the CompuServe Trend system would not meet the "single action" limitation because at least two actions would need to be taken to order an item: one action to invoke the ordering screen, and a second action to click on the ordering button. However, as the screen shot plainly indicates, a purchaser could use the display screen for purposes other than to order an electronic stock chart (*e.g.*, to "Lookup" a stock symbol). Furthermore, to the extent that Amazon argues that the CompuServe Trend fails to meet the "single action" limitation due to the "click" necessary to activate the stock chart ordering screen in the first place, Amazon also admits that BN's Express Lane feature fails to meet the same limitation because of the "click" required to proceed from a menu page to a product page when using the Express Lane feature.

As the CompuServe Trend stock chart ordering screen indicates, we note that once a purchaser types in a valid stock symbol, the screen displays both "information identifying the item" (*i.e.*, the stock symbol identifying the desired electronic stock chart) *and* an indication of the "single action" to be performed to order the identified item (*i.e.*, clicking on the button labeled "Chart ($.50)"). Therefore, the substantial question of invalidity raised by the CompuServe Trend reference is the same regardless of whether one considers claims explicitly requiring that both of these pieces of information be displayed (*i.e.*, claims 2 and 11) or claims requiring that only the "information identifying the item" be displayed (*i.e.*, claims 1, 6, and 9).

In view of the above, we conclude that the district court erred in failing to recognize that the CompuServe Trend reference raises a substantial question of invalidity. Whether the CompuServe Trend reference either anticipates and/or renders obvious the claimed invention in view of the knowledge of one of ordinary skill in the relevant art is a matter for decision at trial.

[The court also considered several other pieces of prior art that raised substantial questions of validity.]

Conclusion

While it appears on the record before us that Amazon has carried its burden with respect to demonstrating the likelihood of success on infringement, it is also true that BN has raised substantial questions as to the validity of the '411 patent. For that reason, we must conclude that the necessary prerequisites for entry of a preliminary injunction are presently lacking. We therefore vacate the preliminary injunction and remand the case for further proceedings.

Vacated and Remanded[.]

COMMENTS AND QUESTIONS

1. *Amazon.com* did establish the potential obviousness of Internet-era patents—in that case, Amazon.com's "1-click" Internet site shopping cart web software. But it is important to mention that the case was appealed after the grant of a preliminary injunction. Thus the court did *not* hold that Amazon.com's "1-click" patent was invalid for obviousness under 35 U.S.C. §103. It merely held that defendant barnesandnoble.com had established serious doubts about validity, and therefore the injunction should not have been granted.

Nevertheless, the case did add support to those who have argued that a large number of broad, early Internet-related patents may be invalid in light of prior art stemming from 1980s and 1990s-era "teletext" and "videotext" technology. Teletext is the broadcast transmission of signals which can be received and decoded by an electronic device such as a set-top box on a TV. "Videotext" systems are computer-based interactive systems that electronically deliver text, numbers, and graphics via telephone lines, two-way cable, or computer networks, either to a TV set or to a computer. The network-based implementation of videotext systems in the 1980s and (pre-Internet) 1990s involved the use of dedicated central computers and exclusive connections. See generally A. Alber, Videotex/Teletext Principles and Practices (New York: McGraw Hill 1985).

The CompuServe "Trend" System, source of the prior art reference that challenged the validity of Amazon.com's "1-click" patent, is an example of a 1990s-era videotext service. (See the case, Chapter 3, for an illustration of the screen display of the CompuServe system.) Despite the fact that vidoetext technology had only limited market acceptance, it generated a good deal of prior art, including a significant number of patents. More importantly, many of the software designers who worked on aspects of videotext systems have migrated to the Internet. Because of the worldwide reach of the Internet, these experts now constitute a large, accessible body of prior art experts. Defendants in infringement suits have now begun to tap into this resource.

A good example involves the case of Wang Laboratories, Inc. v. America Online, Inc., 197 F.3d 1377 (Fed. Cir. 1999) (see later this section). The patentee, Wang, held a patent on a videotext-era system for downloading "pages" of information from a central computer. One of the defendants, Netscape, Inc., solicited prior art from the community of programmers who contribute to the "Mozilla" web browser, which shares a significant amount of software code with Netscape's own browser. *See* Chris Oakes, Netscaping Seeing Tech Support, Wired News, April 24, 1998, available at http://www.wired.com/news/technology/0,1282,11905,00.html (Netscape seeking prior art to fend off patent infringement involving videotext-era patent held by Wang, Inc.).

According to the Mozilla.org web page, Mozilla programmers did indeed contribute useful prior art to the Netscape lawyers working on the case. See http://www.mozilla.org/legal/wang-dismissed.html:

> You guys blew away our lawyers. Tons of stuff came in, and *good* stuff. . . . It's really clear that the net can be an invaluable resource in fighting bogus claims.

For a proposal to formalize third-party involvement in prior art searching and provide rewards, see John R. Thomas, A Proposal for Patent Bounties, 2001 U. Ill. L.

Rev. 305. For a private effort aimed at the same result, which seems to have achieved at least some success, visit Bountyquest.com.

The final issue to consider centers on the universe of prior art to which the PTO and courts may look in considering nonobviousness. Unlike novelty, prior art for nonobviousness purposes is limited to so-called "analogous arts." This means that even if a reference from a completely "unrelated" art would make an invention obvious, that invention is not invalid under §103. This doctrine may have importance in the area of business method patents, where the growth in patent applications in the wake of *state Street Bank* has been tremendous. One recent comment notes that the doctrine of "analogous arts" should not be applied broadly in the area of Internet business method patents to cut down on the number of business method patents that simply claim an Internet version of an old business idea or practice. See Margo A. Bagley, Internet Business Model Patents: Obvious By Analogy, 7 Mich. Telecomm. & Tech. L. Rev. 253, 258 (2000-2001):

> [P]art of the solution [to the problem of invalid business method patents] lies in helping courts and the USPTO properly to define analogous art for a particular invention. To do so, judges and examiners must recognize the interchangeability of computer programming (i.e. "e-world" activities) to perform a function, with human or mechanical performance of the same function (i.e. "real world" activities). Such recognition is consistent with binding United States Supreme Court precedent and requires a reversal of the trend towards narrow analogous art definitions in the obviousness inquiry.

See also Glynn S. Lunney, Jr., E-Obviousness, 7 Mich. Telecomm. Tech. L. Rev. 363 (2001), available at http://www.mttlr.org/volseven/lunney.html (discussing the problem of the nonobviousness doctrine's application to business method patents).

2. Infringement

Interactive Gift Express, Inc. v. Compuserve, Inc.
United States Court of Appeals for the Federal Circuit
256 F.3d 1323 (Fed. Cir. 2001)

LINN, Circuit Judge.

Interactive Gift Express, Inc. ("IGE"), now known as E-Data, Corp., seeks review of a judgment of noninfringement of U.S. Patent No. 4,528,643 ("Freeny patent") entered by the United States District Court for the Southern District of New York on March 12, 1999. Because the district court erred as a matter of law in the construction of each of the five claim terms giving rise to IGE's noninfringement stipulation, we vacate and remand.

Background

A. The Freeny Patent

The Freeny patent is directed to a system for reproducing information in material objects at point of sale locations. Prior to the invention disclosed in the

Freeny patent, information disseminated to consumers in material objects, such as tape recordings, books, and records, was recorded onto the material objects at a central manufacturing facility, and the material objects were then shipped to remote retail locations for sale. These systems required centralized manufacturing facilities for reproducing the information in the material objects and extended distribution networks for distributing the material objects, once made, to various point of sale locations for sale to consumers. The manufacturing facilities and distribution networks represented substantial costs ultimately borne by consumers.

In such prior art systems, manufacturers had to estimate consumer demand for each new information-specific product and had to manufacture and ship quantities of material objects sufficient to meet the estimated demand at each retail location. Retailers had to make similar estimates to determine how many material objects for each information-specific product to order and keep in inventory. A low estimate of consumer demand resulted in unsatisfied customers and lost sales. On the other hand, high estimates left some material objects unsold, resulting in unrecouped costs.

To overcome these and other related problems, the Freeny patent provides a system for the distributed manufacture and sale of material objects at multiple locations directly serving consumers. The system includes a central control station, referred to in the Freeny patent as an "information control machine" or "ICM," and a plurality of remotely located manufacturing stations referred to as "information manufacturing machines" or "IMMs." At each IMM, a consumer selects the desired information and initiates a communication from the IMM to the ICM to gain authorization for copying of the selected information onto a desired type of material object. The consumer then waits for the IMM to receive the authorization, after which the selected information is copied by the IMM onto a blank material object. The invention can be used with a wide variety of information and material objects, such as music on cassettes and text on paper. Irrespective of the type of information and material object, the invention requires the purchase of the material object by the consumer, and the material object must contain information that was copied onto it at the point of sale location.

According to the Freeny patent, the information can be copied onto a selected type of material object whenever a consumer requests it. Consumer demand thus can be met without having to rely on manufacturing estimates and without having to bear the costs associated with overproduction, inventory control, shipping, and warehousing. The Freeny system also provides "for reproducing or manufacturing material objects at point of sale locations only with the permission of the owner of the information, thereby assuring that the owner of the information will be compensated in connection with such reproduction." Freeny patent, col. 4, ll. 8-13. The Freeny patent, in the description of the background of the invention, states that the invention overcomes the problem of "how to manufacture and distribute material objects embodying . . . information in an economical and efficient manner and in a manner which virtually assures that the owners of [the] information will be compensated in connection with the sale of such material objects." Freeny patent, col. 3, ll. 28-33.

Claim 1 of the Freeny patent is representative of the method claims at issue and defines the invention as follows:

> 1. A method for reproducing information in material objects utilizing information manufacturing machines located at point of sale locations, comprising the steps of:

providing from a source remotely located with respect to the information manufacturing machine the information to be reproduced to the information manufacturing machine, each information being uniquely identified by a catalog code;

providing a request reproduction code including a catalog code uniquely identifying the information to be reproduced to the information manufacturing machine requesting to reproduce certain information identified by the catalog code in a material object;

providing an authorization code at the information manufacturing machine authorizing the reproduction of the information identified by the catalog code included in the request reproduction code; and

receiving the request reproduction code and the authorization code at the information manufacturing machine and reproducing in a material object the information identified by the catalog code included in the request reproduction code in response to the authorization code authorizing such reproduction.

Freeny patent, col. 28, ll. 22-47.

Exemplary of the apparatus claims is claim 37, which reads as follows:

37. An apparatus for reproducing information in material objects at point of sale locations, comprising:

an information manufacturing machine located at a point of sale location for reproducing information in material objects, each information to be reproduced being uniquely identified by a catalog code and each information being received from a source remotely located with respect to the information manufacturing machine and each information being stored in the information manufacturing machine, the information manufacturing machine receiving a request reproduction code including a catalog code uniquely identifying the information to be reproduced and being adapted to provide an authorization code including the catalog code included in the request reproduction code, and the information manufacturing machine being adapted to reproduce the information identified by the catalog code in a material object in response to receiving the authorization code.

Freeny patent, col. 36, ll. 45-64.

B. The Accused Activities

The defendants are computer software and publishing companies and one retail bookstore. Plaintiff contends that the computer software and publishing companies infringe the Freeny patent by selling software or documents "online," that is, over the Internet and the World Wide Web. Plaintiff maintains that the retail bookstore infringes the Freeny patent by selling books that include a CD-ROM containing encrypted computer applications, access to which is not possible until the consumer retrieves a password. Plaintiff, through the construction it proffered in its Revised Claim Construction Report of November 12, 1996, has effectively conceded that none of the defendants are direct infringers.

With the one exception of the retail bookstore defendant, all of the accused systems distribute information directly to consumers' personal computers without using an intermediate retail location, the consumer instead dealing directly with a web-site over the Internet. Information is distributed and downloaded onto a consumer's own internal hard disk or other storage device without the purchase of any material object such as a floppy disk or CD-ROM.

In the case of the CD-ROMs sold to consumers by the retail bookstore defendant, if a consumer is interested in one or more of the encrypted programs contained on the CD-ROM, a password must first be requested. The password enables the consumer to decrypt the desired program and copy it for later use. As with the other accused systems, the CD-ROM product avoids the need for a consumer to purchase a material object, such as a floppy disk or a CD-ROM, because the decrypted data is copied directly onto the consumer's own storage device.

C. Proceedings Below

The district court limited discovery to claim construction matters and ordered IGE to file a binding claim construction report. There are five disputed claim limitations. IGE's binding report dealt with four of them: "point of sale location" (referred to in the report as "point of sale"); "material object"; "information manufacturing machine"; and "authorization code." The fifth is termed the "real-time transactions" limitation, arising out of an alleged requirement that certain steps of claim 1 be performed in order, and requiring that the information be provided to and stored at the IMM before the consumer requests it. Because there is no claim term directly associated with this "limitation" and IGE did not consider it to be a limitation, IGE did not provide an entry for it in its binding report. The report identified these four terms, and others not relevant to this appeal, as "technical terms . . . which are used differently from the normal usage in everyday language, but are defined in the patent as originally filed."

For each of these terms, the binding report provided what IGE termed a "simple definition" and also provided the location in the patent specification where these terms were defined. This information is as follows: (1) the simple definition of "point of sale" is "[t]he place at which the consumer or purchaser makes the purchase," and it is defined in the specification at "Col. 5, Lines 47-50"; (2) the simple definition of "material object" is "[a] paper with printed information, or a recording on a floppy disk, hard drive, or tape etc.," and it is defined in the specification at "Col. 4, Lines 36-59"; (3) the simple definition of "information manufacturing machine" is "[t]he computer system used by the consumer to make the point of sale purchase," and it is defined in the specification at "Col. 5, Lines 32-47, etc."; and (4) the simple definition of "authorization code" is "[t]his code is [*sic*] enables the information manufacturing machine (the consumers [*sic*—consumer's] computer system) to reproduce the electronic data in a material object," and it is defined in the specification at "Col. 6, Lines 1-23."

After receiving IGE's report and the parties' claim construction briefs, the court, on May 15, 1998, rendered an opinion and order construing the claims of the Freeny patent. See Interactive Gift Express, Inc. v. Compuserve Inc., 47 U.S.P.Q.2d 1797 (S.D.N.Y. 1998). The district court did not address invalidity. The district court's opinion contained a thorough and careful analysis of the Freeny patent and the relevant legal standards for claim construction. See *id*. The district court devoted most of its lengthy claim construction to the five disputed claim limitations. See *id*.

After the district court provided its claim construction of the five above-noted claim limitations, the parties entered into a Stipulated Order and Judgment ("Judgment"). The district court made no findings of fact regarding infringement. In the Judgment, IGE conceded that none of the defendants had in the past infringed, or was then infringing, any claim of the Freeny patent as construed by the court. See IGE Judgment, slip op. at 1. The Judgment stated specifically that "no method, system, or apparatus of any defendant includes any" of the five disputed claim limitations. *Id.*

In appealing the judgment, IGE challenges the district court's construction of each of the disputed claim limitations. Counsel for IGE acknowledged during the oral hearing before this court that in light of the stipulation entered into by the parties as part of the Judgment, and in view of the fact that the parties have stipulated not to what the accused methods or products are but only to what they are not, IGE must show that the district court was wrong in its construction of all five of the disputed claim limitations to prevail in this appeal.

Discussion

Analysis

In this opinion, we focus on the construction of the five disputed claim limitations as provided in the conclusions of the district court's claim construction, and upon which IGE's stipulations in the Judgment are premised. In construing claims, the analytical focus must begin and remain centered on the language of the claims themselves, for it is that language that the patentee chose to use to "particularly point[ ] out and distinctly claim[ ] the subject matter which the patentee regards as his invention." 35 U.S.C. §112, ¶2.

"It is well-settled that, in interpreting an asserted claim, the court should look first to the intrinsic evidence of record, i.e., the patent itself, including the claims, the specification and, if in evidence, the prosecution history. Such intrinsic evidence is the most significant source of the legally operative meaning of disputed claim language." Vitronics Corp. v. Conceptronic, Inc., 90 F.3d 1576, 1582 (Fed.Cir. 1996) (citation omitted). All intrinsic evidence is not equal however. See *id.* at 1582 (delineating a hierarchy among the intrinsic evidence).

First, we look to the claim language. Then we look to the rest of the intrinsic evidence, beginning with the specification and concluding with the prosecution history, if in evidence. If the claim language is clear on its face, then our consideration of the rest of the intrinsic evidence is restricted to determining if a deviation from the clear language of the claims is specified. A deviation may be necessary if "a patentee [has chosen] to be his own lexicographer and use terms in a manner other than their ordinary meaning." *Vitronics,* 90 F.3dat 1582, 39 U.S.P.Q.2d at 1576. A deviation may also be necessary if a patentee has "relinquished [a] potential claim construction in an amendment to the claim or in an argument to overcome or distinguish a reference." Elkay Mfg. Co. v. Ebco Mfg. Co., 192 F.3d 973, 979, 52 U.S.P.Q.2d 1109, 1113 (Fed. Cir. 1999). If however the claim language is not clear on its face, then our consideration of the rest of the intrinsic evidence is directed to resolving, if possible, the lack of clarity.

Resort to the specification is particularly important in this case because IGE has conceded that the claim limitations in dispute include technical terms that are defined in the specification. However, in looking to the specification to construe claim terms, care must be taken to avoid reading "limitations appearing in the specification . . . into [the] claims."

If the meaning of the claim limitations is apparent from the totality of the intrinsic evidence, then the claim has been construed. If however a claim limitation is still not clear, we may look to extrinsic evidence to help resolve the lack of clarity. Relying on extrinsic evidence to construe a claim is "proper only when the claim language remains genuinely ambiguous after consideration of the intrinsic evidence." Bell & Howell Document Mgmt. Prods. Co. v. Altek Sys., 132 F.3d 701, 706 (Fed.Cir. 1997).

Extrinsic evidence may always be consulted, however, to assist in understanding the underlying technology. But extrinsic evidence may never be used "for the purpose of varying or contradicting the terms in the claims." *Markman*, 52 F.3d at 981.

Although the district court provided a thorough and accurate description of the patent and of the relevant law, its claim construction impermissibly read limitations from the specification into each of the five disputed claim limitations. We treat each of these disputed claim limitations below, and then address the issues of waiver and judicial estoppel.

I. *Point of Sale Location*

The district court made several findings with regard to the construction of the expression "point of sale location." We address these findings below, agreeing with some and disagreeing with others.

1.

In response to the district court's request for binding definitions of the disputed terms, described earlier, IGE identified the passage at column 5, lines 47-50 as defining a point of sale location. That passage states that a point of sale location is "a location where a consumer goes to purchase material objects embodying predetermined or preselected information." Freeny patent, col. 5, ll. 47-50. The district court held this definition to be correct, and we agree. Clear support is provided for this definition in the Freeny patent specification at column 5, lines 47-50.

2.

The district court further held that, although point of sale locations are not restricted to retail locations, a home is not a point of sale location. *See Interactive Gift Express,* 47 U.S.P.Q.2d at 1810 & n. 9. IGE contends that the district court was wrong. IGE urges that a point of sale location is simply the location at which the consumer makes or effects a purchase. IGE argues that the concept of a home being a point of sale location is not new, citing home shopping networks, pay-per-view cable television, and home Internet shopping. IGE further argues that the specification defines a home as a point of sale location and discloses at least two embodiments in which the home is a point of sale location. IGE also argues that the prosecution history lists several transmission systems that could be adapted for use in the home. The appellees respond that IGE's asserted definition before the district court precludes a home from being a point of sale location, and that any references in the specification to homes as point of sale locations cannot overcome this definition. The appellees further respond that the rest of the intrinsic evidence, as well as the extrinsic evidence of standard dictionaries and references, supports the district court's construction.

We agree with IGE's position that a home is not precluded from being a point of sale location. Looking first, as we must, to the claim language itself, we find nothing precluding a home from being a point of sale location. See *Vitronics*, 90 F.3d at 1582. Except for requiring that an IMM be present, the independent claims are silent regarding the possible venues of a point of sale location.

Looking next to the specification, *see id.* at 1582, 90 F.3d 1576, we acknowledge the great likelihood that a point of sale location will not be a home, given that: (1) IGE's asserted definition, with which we agree, requires that a consumer go to a point of sale location "to purchase material objects," Freeny patent, col. 5, ll. 48-49; and (2) the specification requires, and IGE does not dispute, that the IMM be located at the point of sale location, *see, e.g.*, Freeny patent, col. 5, ll. 32-33, col. 12, ll. 66- 67. However, IGE's asserted definition, premised on the specification at column 5, lines 48 and 49, does not preclude a home from serving as a point of sale location, and the specification further describes a vending machine embodiment that could be utilized in a home. *See* Freeny patent, cols. 26-27. This intrinsic evidence unambiguously allows a home to serve as a point of sale location. Therefore, it is unnecessary to address IGE's arguments alleging that the prosecution history additionally supports our conclusion.

Given the lack of ambiguity in the intrinsic evidence, it would be improper to address any of the parties' arguments relating to extrinsic evidence, such as other examples of point of sale locations and standard references. See *Vitronics*, 90 F.3d at 1583 ("In those cases where the public record unambiguously describes the scope of the patented invention, reliance on any extrinsic evidence is improper."). * * *

II. *Material Object*

As with the term point of sale location, the district court made several findings with regard to the construction of the term "material object." We address these findings below, agreeing with some and disagreeing with others.

1.

The district court held that a material object is "a tangible medium or device in which information can be embodied, fixed, or stored, other than temporarily, and from which the information embodied therein can be perceived, reproduced, used or otherwise communicated, either directly or with the aid of another machine or device." Interactive Gift Express, 47 U.S.P.Q.2d at 1810. Although IGE admits in its brief to this court that a material object is a tangible medium, counsel for IGE argued to this court at the oral hearing that a material object is defined as the information itself and need not be a tangible medium. The appellees respond that the district court's construction is supported by the specification.

A material object cannot be the information itself, as IGE now argues. Examining first the claim language, claim 1, for example, requires that the information be reproduced in a material object. See Freeny patent, col. 28, ll. 22-23 (preamble to claim 1) and 44-45 (step four of claim 1). If the information itself is the material object, as IGE argues, then claim 1 would require the information to be reproduced in itself. Such a construction is illogical and does not accord with the plain import of the claim language.

Despite the plain language of the claims, we turn to the specification to discern whether IGE attributed a different meaning to the term material object. Examining the specification, it is clear that even the broadest definition of material object in the specification requires that a material object be a "medium or device in which information can be embodied or fixed." Freeny patent, col. 4, ll. 36-38. Thus, IGE's argument that the reproduced information itself constitutes the material object is not only illogical, but unsupported in the specification as well.

2.

The district court further held that a material object must be: (a) separate and distinct from the IMM, (b) removed from the IMM after purchase, and (c) intended for use away from the point of sale location. IGE argues that neither the claims nor the specification requires that a material object be separate and distinct from the IMM or intended for use at a location other than the point of sale location, and that these limitations were improperly read into the claims from the specification. The appellees respond that the district court's construction is supported by the specification. We agree with the district court on these three limitations, with one variation regarding point (c) above. On that point, we find that the material object could be intended for use at the point of sale location as long as it is on a device separate from the IMM.

Beginning with the claim language, we note that the preamble of claim 1, for example, describes a method in which IMMs are located at point of sale locations and in which information is reproduced in material objects utilizing the IMMs. See Freeny patent, col. 28, ll. 22-24. This language could be read to suggest that the material objects, which receive the reproduced information, are not part of the IMM and are intended to be purchased and removed from both the IMM and the point of sale location, but that reading is not clear from the claim itself. The claim later describes reproducing the information in a material object, but again there is no clear indication that the material object is or is not a separate and distinct item that is to be removed from the IMM after purchase and used on another device. See *id.* at col. 28, ll. 42- 45. Thus, we look to the specification for further guidance.

The Freeny patent envisions and discloses only material objects that are separate from the IMM and that can be purchased by the consumer and taken away from the IMM. See, e.g., Freeny patent, col. 13, ll. 25-48 (retail store embodiment), cols. 26-27 (vending machine embodiment). The emphasis of the specification on distribution and sale consistently reveals that the material objects are intended to be separate from the IMM, removed from the IMM, and used apart from the IMM. These three conditions . . . are fundamental to the meaning of a material object as clearly and consistently specified in the patent description.

IGE contends that "material object" should be construed so broadly as to include a hard disk that is internal to a personal computer. Although the specification describes numerous material objects, a hard disk, internal or otherwise, is never mentioned as a possibility. In fact, where a hard disk is discussed, it is in relation to the implementation of particular aspects of the IMM or the ICM and not as an example of a material object. See *id.* at col. 22, ll. 6-34. Any construction of the expression "material object" which encompasses a hard disk is not only not envisioned anywhere in the specification but is also inconsistent with the definition of a point of sale location asserted by IGE before the district court. Specifically, a consumer would not go to a point of sale location to purchase an internal hard disk embodying predetermined or preselected information.

3.

The district court also held that a material object "[m]ust be offered for sale independently from the information that may be reproduced onto the material object." *Interactive Gift Express,* 47 U.S.P.Q.2d at 1810. The district court applied this same limitation to a point of sale location. For the reasons discussed earlier with respect to a point of sale location, we again disagree with the district court's reading of this condition into the claims.

4.

Accordingly, we construe a material object to be a tangible medium or device in which information can be embodied, fixed, or stored, other than temporarily, and from which the information embodied therein can be perceived, reproduced, used or otherwise communicated, either directly or with the aid of another machine or device. A material object must be offered for sale, and be purchasable, at point of sale locations where at least one IMM is located. Further, a material object must be separate and distinct from the IMM, removed from the IMM after purchase, and intended for use on a device separate from the IMM either at the point of sale location or elsewhere. "Material object" does not encompass the hard disk component of a home personal computer. Finally, a material object need not be offered for sale independently from the information that may be reproduced onto the material object, that is, as a blank.

III. *Information Manufacturing Machine*

As with the term point of sale location, the district court made several findings with regard to the construction of the term IMM. For this term, however, we disagree with most of the district court's findings. We address each below.

1.

The district court required that the IMM functionality be divided into at least the following four "*separate and distinct* components: (a) a Manufacturing Control Unit, (b) a Master File Unit, (c) an Information Manufacturing Unit, and (d) a Reproduction Unit." *Interactive Gift Express,* 47 U.S.P.Q.2d at 1810 (emphasis added). IGE maintains that the district court improperly read the limitations of an embodiment into the claims. The appellees respond that these four components are required because Figure 1 of the Freeny patent, which contains these components, depicts the invention and not merely an embodiment of the invention. We agree with IGE.

Again, we turn first to the claim language itself. The independent claims do not recite any of these four components and do not convey any clear meaning of an IMM to one skilled in the art. The only limitations in the exemplary independent claims pertaining to the IMM relate to its placement at a point of sale location and to certain functions that it must perform, namely, storing information to be reproduced, receiving a request reproduction code, receiving an authorization code, and reproducing the requested information in a material object. See Freeny patent, col. 28, ll. 26-47 (claim 1), col. 36, ll. 47-64 (claim 37).

The specification describes an embodiment of the IMM containing the four components noted by the district court and performing the functions recited in the claims. See *id.* at col. 6, ll. 27-30, col. 9, l. 39—col. 10, l. 49. The disclosed embodiment of the IMM also performs the functions, not explicitly recited in either claim 1 or claim 37, of transmitting a request reproduction code and receiving and decoding encoded information. Of these, only five functions, namely, storing information to be reproduced, receiving and transmitting a request reproduction code, receiving an authorization code, and reproducing the requested information in a material object, are critical to the operation of the IMM as defined in the specification. See *id.* at col. 5, l. 21—col. 6, l. 23. As explained below, the receiving and decoding of encoded information is not essential to the present invention. There is no general description or definition of what constitutes an IMM other than this narrow functional definition presented in the specification. That is the only definition on which the public can rely, and it is therefore reasonable to conclude that an IMM must contain these five functions. To the extent that the district court's decision, by requiring all four components of the disclosed IMM to be present, requires more than these five critical functions to be performed by the IMM, it is in error.

COMMENTS AND QUESTIONS

1. It is clear that the Freeny patent recites an invention that long predates "e-commerce" as we know it. Should Freeny be given credit for envisioning "remote selling" broadening, claiming it generally, and asserting the patent against e-commerce defendants?

2. The plaintiff, now named "E-Data," unabashedly cites the Freeny patent as the company's only real asset. E-Data does not appear to make anything, sell anything, or do any research and development. Should this be relevant in determining the validity or scope of the Freeny patent?

3. Read the court's claim construction carefully. Imagine you are a major record label who wants to sell music over the Internet. You want to avoid the Freeny patent. Should you allow purchasers to download music directly to a CD disk in their computers? Or only to their hard drives? What if you advise the latter course, but some users transfer the files onto CDs? What if you know for a fact that many or even all users will do this? (These last two questions involve issues of contributory and willful infringement, see below).

4. For another case involving an earlier-era patent asserted against an Internet application, see Wang Laboratories, Inc. v. America Online Corp., 197 F.3d 1377 (Fed. Cir. 1999) (construing the term "frame" in a videotext-era patent as limited to pages encoded in character-based protocols, thus excluding bit-mapped protocols; finding no infringement of means-for claims under §112 ¶6, nor under the doctrine of equivalents).

≡ *British Telecommunications Plc. v. Prodigy*
≡ *Communications Corp.*
United States District Court for the Southern District of New York
217 F. Supp.2d 399, 2002 WL 1949225 (S.D.N.Y. Aug 22, 2002)

MCMAHON, J.

Plaintiff British Telecommunications ("BT") asserts that Defendant Prodigy Communications Corp. ("Prodigy"), through its business activities as an Internet Service Provider ("ISP"), directly infringes claims 3, 5, 6, and 7 (the "Asserted Claims") of U.S. Patent No. 4,873,662 (the "Sargent Patent" or "'662 Patent"). BT also alleges that Prodigy induces and contributes to infringement by Prodigy subscribers who infringe the Sargent patent by accessing the Internet through the Prodigy service.

The Court has already construed the claims of the patent in its *Markman* Opinion. British Telecommunications PLC v. Prodigy Communications Corp., 189 F. Supp.2d 101 (S.D.N.Y.2002) [*"British Telecomm I"*.] [This opinion set forth the text of several claims in the Sargent patent and established three interpretations relevant to the portion of the infringement opinion reproduced here. Claim 3 of the patent reads as follows, with key terms highlighted:

3. A digital information storage, retrieval and display system comprising:

a central computer means in which *plural blocks of information* are stored at respectively corresponding locations each of which locations is designated by a predetermined address therein by means of which a block can be selected, each of said blocks comprising *a first portion containing information for display and a second portion containing information not for display* but including *the complete address* for each of plural other blocks of information;
plural remote terminal means, each including (a) modem means for effecting input/output digital data communications with said central computer means via the telephone lines of a telephone network, (b) local memory means for locally storing digital data representing at least the first portion of the selected

block of information received via said modem means from the central computer and for processing digital data, (c) display means for visually displaying such a locally stored first portion of a block of information and (d) keypad means connected to communicate data to at least said local memory means for manual entry of keyed digital data; and

further memory means being provided as part of said local memory means at each of said remote terminal means for receiving and storing said second portion of the selected block of information in response to the selection of the block and when its respective first portion is transmitted thereto, said local memory means utilizing keyed digital data of less extent than any one of said complete addresses for another block of information but nevertheless uniquely indicative of one of the complete addresses contained in said second portion of the block of information which contains the first portion then being displayed for selectively accessing said further memory means and for supplying data to be transmitted by said modem means and indicative of the complete address of the next block of information which is to be retrieved and utilized for display purposes.

British Telecomm I, 189 F. Supp.2d 101, 111 (quoting '662 patent). . . .

For the reasons stated below, I find that as a matter of law, no jury could find that Prodigy infringes the Sargent patent, nor that Prodigy contributes to infringement of the Sargent patent, nor actively induces others to infringe that patent. I therefore grant Prodigy's motion for summary judgment. * * *

BT argues that Prodigy infringes the Sargent patent through its business activities as an Internet Service Provider. BT contends that Prodigy's web servers provide access to information in a manner that literally infringes the Sargent patent.

BT also alleges that the Internet infringes the Sargent patent and that Prodigy facilitates infringement by its subscribers by providing them with access to the Internet. BT contends that Prodigy contributorily infringes or actively induces the infringement of the Sargent patent by providing the necessary software and encouraging its subscribers to access pages of information from Web servers maintained by third parties. Therefore, BT argues, even if Prodigy's servers do not infringe the Sargent patent as a matter of law, summary judgment should be denied because Prodigy infringes the '662 patent by making and using infringing remote terminals. * * *

Prodigy is an Internet Service Provider ("ISP") that has supplied its customers with access to the Internet since October, 1996. Prodigy's services include dial-up access, and broadband DSL access service.

When a user dials in to the Prodigy system, the user's computer is assigned an IP address dynamically by Prodigy. An IP address is a unique binary number assigned to an interface connection of a computer to the Internet and is used by the other computers to send packets using the IP protocol to this computer. The member can then use the Web browser to retrieve Web pages from the Prodigy Web site or from other Web servers connected to the Internet.

BT contends that:

1. Each Web server on the Internet is a "central computer" as defined in the Sargent patent because each Web server has its own centralized data store.
2. HTML files qualify as "blocks of information" either literally or under the doctrine of equivalents.

3. Each URL address is a "complete address" within the meaning of the Court's construction of the term, either literally or under the doctrine of equivalents.

BT makes other arguments but it is not necessary to reach them because its failure to raise any disputed issue of fact as to these points means that Prodigy is entitled to judgment as a matter of law.

I. The Internet Does Not Infringe the Sargent Patent

A. *The Internet Has No "Central Computer"*

1. Literal Infringement

A "central computer" in the Sargent patent is:

> a single device, in one location. It is referred to as "central" because it is connected to numerous physically separate stations, called "remote terminals," by the telephone lines of a telephone network. So there is one computer, connected to many remote terminals. The central computer means in this patent thus serves as the hub of a digital information storage, retrieval and display system—and all of the remote terminals connect to it.
>
> The central computer stores information. The central computer contains a "main store." In the context of this patent, the main store is a mass information storage or memory device. An example of a main store is a magnetic disk, which is a rotating circular plate having a magnetizable surface on which information may be stored as a pattern of polarized spots on concentric recording tracks.
>
> The central computer contains an information database, which is "centralized" in the sense that all of the remote users can access it by accessing the central computer.

[*British Telecomm. I*, 189 F. Supp. 2d 109, 111-112.]

BT asserts that, while the Internet is made up of an enormous number of computers, each individual web server is a central computer in one location (i.e. central relative to the remote terminals within the meaning of the patent).

The cornerstone of this argument is BT's assertion that a central computer is not limited to a single computer as a matter of law. . . . The patent claims as construed clearly provide that the central computer is one device, in one location. Just as a circle has but one center, hub-and-spoke networks have only a single hub. There may be other circles with other centers, just as there may be other hub-and-spoke networks with other central computers or hubs. But each system (network) of the type claimed in the Sargent patent can have only one central computer. Therefore, viewing the Internet as a system (as BT asks me to do), it does not literally infringe the Sargent patent, because it contains no such central computer.

The central computer in the Sargent patent also contains an information database, which is "centralized" in the sense that all remote users can access it by accessing the central computer. [*British Telecomm I*, 189 F. Supp.2d 109, 112.] Prodigy argues that the Internet has no such "centralized data store," but rather, contains an extremely diffuse data storage architecture. According to Prodigy's expert, this distribution is the essence of the Internet, because it allows users to access information stored throughout a global network of networks of computers and storage devices that are loosely linked through adherence to an open group of protocols and standards adopted by the Internet community.

BT does not dispute that this is the case. It responds, however, that its argument is not that the Internet has a centralized data store, but that each Web server (or central computer, as BT would call it) has its own centralized data store because it has a main storage device for storing HTML files.

However, the claims of the '662 patent state that the centralized data store contains *all* of the blocks of information accessible by the remote terminals. [*British Telecomm. I*, 189 F. Supp.2d 109, 122.] BT does not dispute that there is no centralized data store for the Internet that contains all of the data remote users might care to access.

The Internet is a network of computers intertwined with each other in order to allow users around the world to exchange information. The whole purpose of the Internet is for the *sources* of information to be in many places rather than centralized. Any user can retrieve information that is stored on a Web server in any physical location, as long as that server is connected to the Web. For example, a Prodigy user does not have to rely on Prodigy to gather information from multiple sources and put it on its own server in order for a Prodigy customer to have access to the information. Rather, when Prodigy users connect to the Internet through Prodigy's system, users can access blocks of information located on remote systems, e.g. a computer in Alaska, rather than Prodigy's own computers in New York. This "network of networks" or "system of systems" allows users access to information from a variety of sources, in any location.

BT cites the general rule that addition to an accused apparatus of one or more features than the claim requires does not preclude a finding of infringement. But what BT characterizes as "additions" are fundamental differences in the nature of the claim elements. As it did during the *Markman* hearing, BT would have me exclude the word "central" from the construction of "central computer." The Court expressly rejected BT's interpretation by ruling that the Sargent patent claims a central computer that is a single computer with a centralized database. Because the Internet is not a computer network consisting of a centralized computer that stores all of the data accessible by remote terminals, Web servers on the Internet cannot literally infringe the '662 patent.

2. Doctrine of Equivalents

BT may not rely on the doctrine of equivalents to withstand Prodigy's motion for summary judgment. The doctrine of equivalents requires insubstantial differences between the patented invention and the accused product, as determined on an element-by-element basis. *Warner-Jenkinson*, 520 U.S. at 29-30. Whether the differences are insubstantial can be determined by the function-way-result test, which requires that the claimed and accused elements "perform substantially the same function in substantially the same way to obtain the same result." *Id.* at 40. In this case, the Internet fails the function-way-result test, because a central computer containing all of the data accessible by a remote terminal user operates in substantially different ways from the Internet.

A central computer, as claimed in the Sargent patent, has a one-to-one, hub and spoke relationship with numerous physically separate stations called remote terminals. The remote terminals are connected to the central computer by the telephone lines of a telephone network. All of the remote terminals connect to the central computer that has one centralized main store for storing information. As a result, a remote terminal in the Sargent patent does not identify in its communication protocol a computer with which it would like to communicate, for it communicates with only one central computer. In contrast, a computer operating on the Internet must at all times identify a specific computer with which it seeks to communicate, because not all of the remote users are connected to a single central source of information. If all Internet users were connected to Prodigy's Web server alone, BT's argument might have some force; but all Internet users are not connected to Prodigy. Instead, Internet users have access to multiple Web servers on the Internet that store information in various locations.

Indeed, the Internet is the very antithesis of a digital information storage system having a central computer. The opposite of a claim limitation cannot be considered its equivalent. Moore U.S.A. Inc. v. Standard Register Co., 229 F.3d 1091, 1106 (Fed.Cir. 2000). In *Moore,* the Federal Circuit held that a claim limitation reciting that an adhesive "extend[s] the majority of the lengths of said longitudinal marginal portions," could not be infringed either literally or under the doctrine of equivalents by a product having adhesive extending only a minority of a marginal portion (i.e. less than 50%)—even if it was almost a majority (e.g., 47.8%). *Id.* According to the Federal Circuit, "it would defy logic to conclude that a minority—the very antithesis of a majority—could be insubstantially different from a claim limitation requiring a majority." *Id.*

BT cannot dispute that any user throughout the world can access information stored in any of the millions of computers connected to the Internet. In contrast, the Sargent patent claims revolve around a central computer—a single device, in one location, with one main data store. The Internet, is, in short, an entirely different beast from the system described in the Sargent patent. Consequently, the Internet does not infringe the Sargent patent either literally or under the doctrine of equivalents. Prodigy is therefore entitled to summary judgment as a matter of law. . . .

C. The Internet Does Not Contain Blocks of Information as Required by the Sargent Patent

1. Literal Infringement

A key distinction between the '662 patent and the Prodigy Internet Service is the requirement of the '662 patent that information be stored as blocks of information. These blocks have special characteristics:

> Each block has a first portion and a second portion. These portions are separable, contiguous and co-stored sub-units. That means that the portions are stored together, and they are stored next to each other, yet they can be separated from each other. A block of information may contain very limited programming information, the purpose of

which is to reduce the complexity of keying required to communicate with the central computer.

The two parts of a block of information are the first portion and the second portion. The first portion of a block of information is intended for visual display on a remote terminal. The second portion is information not intended for display. The second portion contains the complete address for each of the other blocks of information referenced in the first portion. So if a block of information is referenced in the first portion, then the complete address for that block of information will be in the second portion. The second portion may also contain other information as well, such as information to influence the display or to reduce the complexity of keying required to communicate with the central computer. But it never contains information intended for display.

[*British Telecomm. I*, 189 F. Supp.2d 109, 116.]

Unlike the blocks of information required by the '662 patent, HTML code, which is the primary language of the World Wide Web and of the Prodigy Internet Service, does not use blocks. HTML code does not separate displayed information into a first sub-unit, and non-displayed information in a contiguous, separable second sub-unit. Rather, HTML code contains information to be displayed intermingled with other information concerning formatting and linking, such as URLs and anchors.

In HTML, hypertext references include each URL link adjacent to each phrase or image for display. For example, in the code,

<script>document.write(HTMLCacheArray[34];</script><A href='*http:// www.msnbc. com/modules/exports/ct—prodigy.a sp?/news/736921.asp*' target='— top'>**Yahoo! profits meet forecasts**</A><TD>

the information for display is shown in bold, and the URL is shown in italics. The first linking tag (which is referred to in HTML as an "anchor tag," and identified with the "<A"), is the information always for display associated with each URL. This information appears on the screen. The user can mouse this link, and click to activate it. The URL for each such component of displayed information is set forth in the HTML code immediately prior to the information for display. Consequently, URLs associated with information for display are not located contiguously and separably with a sub-unit of information not for display.

2. Doctrine of Equivalents

BT cannot rely on the doctrine of equivalents to withstand Prodigy's motion for summary judgment.

a. Application of the Doctrine of Equivalents is Barred with Respect to "Blocks of Information" Because the Applicant Made Unmistakable Assertions to Avoid the Prior Art

The doctrine of prosecution history estoppel prevents a patent owner from relying upon the doctrine of equivalents when the patent applicant relinquishes coverage of subject matter during the prosecution of the patent, either by amendment or argument. A patentee cannot invoke the doctrine of equivalents to "embrace a structure that was specifically excluded from the claims." Dolly, Inc. v. Spalding & Evenflo Cos., Inc., 16 F.3d 394, 400 (Fed.Cir. 1994).

During the prosecution of the Sargent patent, a new limitation was added to the phrase "blocks of information" in order to distinguish the Sargent patent from [several prior art] references. To distinguish [one such reference], for example, the Applicant cited to several of its narrowed claim limitations:

> For example, there is absolutely no suggestion anywhere in [the reference] that blocks of stored data should include a first portion containing information for display and a second portion containing information not for display but including the complete address for each of plural other blocks of information. Nor does [the reference] teach . . . manual entry of keyed digital data of less extent than any one complete address but nevertheless uniquely indicative of one of the complete addresses contained in the second portion of the block of information (which contains the first portion then being displayed).

Because BT relied on narrowing amendments to overcome prior art, equivalents are unavailable with respect to these claim limitations. *Warner Jenkinson*, 520 U.S. at 33. Thus, BT is barred from asserting that Prodigy's Internet service meets the above claim elements under the doctrine of equivalents.* * *

II. Contributory Infringement and Active Inducement

Because the Internet itself does not infringe the Sargent patent, Prodigy can not be liable for contributory infringement or active inducement for providing its users with access to the Internet. I therefore need not address BT's arguments concerning contributory infringement and active inducement in any detail.

Note on Contributory Infringement and Inducing Infringement

In neither the *Interactive Gift Express* nor the *British Telecomm* case were the defendants capable of directly infringing the claims in the patent. Each involved claims with limitations that are typically infringed only by end users. Obviously, the patentee in each case could not efficiently collect royalties from all end users. So they sued larger entities who, they alleged, were facilitating the infringement. The legal theory in the two cases was the same: contributory infringement or inducing infringement.

Contributory infringement under 35 U.S.C. §271(c) involves supplying a component or less than the full structure claimed in a patent, with knowledge that the component is specially adapted for use in a certain structure, together with knowledge that the structure is covered by a patent. See, e.g. Hewlett-Packard Co. v. Bausch & Lomb, Inc., 909 F.2d 1464 (Fed. Cir. 1990). Taking the elements of the Freeny patent, at issue in the *Interactive Gift Express* case, *supra*, notice that the defendants in that case were supplying some of the components of the claimed system—e.g., the "information manufacturing machines" described and claimed in the patent.

Active inducement of infringement under §271(b) involves acts that lead to infringement. A classic example is the sale of a product together with instructions for use intended to guide the buyer in performing the steps of a process patent. Again, the seller in this scenario must be aware of the process patent, and must intend to cause the buyer to perform acts that will constitute infringement. See Chiuminatta Concrete Concepts, Inc. v. Cardinal Indus., Inc., 145 F.3d 1303 (Fed.Cir. 1998).

Because many valuable Internet-era technologies involve end user activity of one kind or another, these doctrines may well come into play in future Internet patent infringement cases.

COMMENTS AND QUESTIONS

1. A related issue arises when some components of a claimed system are located outside the U.S. For example, would the sending of data produced by some offshore components of an infringing system be enough of an infringing act to constitute infringement of a U.S. patent? See generally Eli Lilly and Co. v. American Cyanamid Co., 82 F.3d 1568 (Fed. Cir. 1996) (affirming denial of preliminary injunction because process patent to pharmaceutical compounds was not infringed under 35 U.S.C. §271 by importation of a related compound produced by four-step chemical reaction; patented compound was likely "materially changed" in process of its conversion into the related compound prior to importation). With the decentralized nature of the Internet, it is a simple enough matter to base a computer program offshore and allow it to be accessed remotely from the U.S. Does the inherently territorial nature of patent law make it ill equipped to deal with such mobile infringers? For a prescient early discussion of the problem in the Internet context, see Dan L. Burk, Patents in Cyberspace: Territoriality and Infringement on Global Computer Networks, 68 Tulane L. Rev. 1 (1993).

Content Regulation

A. DEFAMATION

Zeran v. America Online
United States Court of Appeals for the Fourth Circuit
129 F.3d 327 (4th Cir. 1997)

WILKINSON, Chief Judge:

. . . On April 25, 1995, an unidentified person posted a message on an AOL bulletin board advertising "Naughty Oklahoma T-Shirts." The posting described the sale of shirts featuring offensive and tasteless slogans related to the April 19, 1995, bombing of the Alfred P. Murrah Federal Building in Oklahoma City. Those interested in purchasing the shirts were instructed to call "Ken" at Zeran's home phone number in Seattle, Washington. As a result of this anonymously perpetrated prank, Zeran received a high volume of calls, comprised primarily of angry and derogatory messages, but also including death threats. Zeran could not change his phone number because he relied on its availability to the public in running his business out of his home. Later that day, Zeran called AOL and informed a company representative of his predicament. The employee assured Zeran that the posting would be removed from AOL's bulletin board but explained that as a matter of policy AOL would not post a retraction. The parties dispute the date that AOL removed this original posting from its bulletin board.

On April 26, the next day, an unknown person posted another message advertising additional shirts with new tasteless slogans related to the Oklahoma City bombing. Again, interested buyers were told to call Zeran's phone number, to ask for "Ken," and to "please call back if busy" due to high demand. The angry, threatening phone calls intensified. Over the next four days, an unidentified party continued to post messages on AOL's bulletin board, advertising additional items including bumper stickers and key chains with still more offensive slogans. During this time period, Zeran called AOL repeatedly and was told by company representatives that the individual account from which the messages were posted would soon be closed. Zeran also reported his case to Seattle FBI agents. By April 30, Zeran was receiving an abusive phone call approximately every two minutes.

Meanwhile, an announcer for Oklahoma City radio station KRXO received a copy of the first AOL posting. On May 1, the announcer related the message's contents on the air, attributed them to "Ken" at Zeran's phone number, and urged the listening audience to call the number. After this radio broadcast, Zeran was inundated with death threats and other violent calls from Oklahoma City residents. Over the next few days, Zeran talked to both KRXO and AOL representatives. He also spoke to his local police, who subsequently surveilled his home to protect his safety. By May 14, after an Oklahoma City newspaper published a story exposing the shirt advertisements as a hoax and after KRXO made an on-air apology, the number of calls to Zeran's residence finally subsided to fifteen per day.

Zeran first filed suit on January 4, 1996, against radio station KRXO in the United States District Court for the Western District of Oklahoma. On April 23, 1996, he filed this separate suit against AOL in the same court. Zeran did not bring any action against the party who posted the offensive messages.[1] After Zeran's suit against AOL was transferred to the Eastern District of Virginia pursuant to 28 U.S.C. §1404(a), AOL answered Zeran's complaint and interposed 47 U.S.C. §230 as an affirmative defense. AOL then moved for judgment on the pleadings pursuant to Fed.R.Civ.P. 12(c). The district court granted AOL's motion, and Zeran filed this appeal.

II.

A.

Because §230 was successfully advanced by AOL in the district court as a defense to Zeran's claims, we shall briefly examine its operation here. Zeran seeks to hold AOL liable for defamatory speech initiated by a third party. He argued to the district court that once he notified AOL of the unidentified third party's hoax, AOL had a duty to remove the defamatory posting promptly, to notify its subscribers of the message's false nature, and to effectively screen future defamatory material. Section 230 entered this litigation as an affirmative defense pled by AOL. The company claimed that Congress immunized interactive computer service providers from claims based on information posted by a third party.

The relevant portion of §230 states: "No provider or user of an interactive computer service shall be treated as the publisher or speaker of any information provided by another information content provider." 47 U.S.C. §230(c)(1).[2] By its

---

1. Zeran maintains that AOL made it impossible to identify the original party by failing to maintain adequate records of its users. The issue of AOL's record keeping practices, however, is not presented by this appeal.

2. Section 230 defines "interactive computer service" as "any information service, system, or access software provider that provides or enables computer access by multiple users to a computer server, including specifically a service or system that provides access to the Internet and such systems operated or services offered by libraries or educational institutions." 47 U.S.C. §230(e)(2). The term "information content provider" is defined as "any person or entity that is responsible, in whole or in part, for the creation or development of information provided through the Internet or any other interactive computer

plain language, §230 creates a federal immunity to any cause of action that would make service providers liable for information originating with a third-party user of the service. Specifically, §230 precludes courts from entertaining claims that would place a computer service provider in a publisher's role. Thus, lawsuits seeking to hold a service provider liable for its exercise of a publisher's traditional editorial functions—such as deciding whether to publish, withdraw, postpone or alter content—are barred.

The purpose of this statutory immunity is not difficult to discern. Congress recognized the threat that tort-based lawsuits pose to freedom of speech in the new and burgeoning Internet medium. The imposition of tort liability on service providers for the communications of others represented, for Congress, simply another form of intrusive government regulation of speech. Section 230 was enacted, in part, to maintain the robust nature of Internet communication and, accordingly, to keep government interference in the medium to a minimum. In specific statutory findings, Congress recognized the Internet and interactive computer services as offering "a forum for a true diversity of political discourse, unique opportunities for cultural development, and myriad avenues for intellectual activity." *Id.* §230(a)(3). It also found that the Internet and interactive computer services "have flourished, to the benefit of all Americans, with a minimum of government regulation." *Id.* §230(a)(4). Congress further stated that it is "the policy of the United States . . . to preserve the vibrant and competitive free market that presently exists for the Internet and other interactive computer services, unfettered by Federal or State regulation." *Id.* §230(b)(2).

None of this means, of course, that the original culpable party who posts defamatory messages would escape accountability. While Congress acted to keep government regulation of the Internet to a minimum, it also found it to be the policy of the United States "to ensure vigorous enforcement of Federal criminal laws to deter and punish trafficking in obscenity, stalking, and harassment by means of computer." *Id.* §230(b)(5). Congress made a policy choice, however, not to deter harmful online speech through the separate route of imposing tort liability on companies that serve as intermediaries for other parties' potentially injurious messages.

Congress' purpose in providing the §230 immunity was thus evident. Interactive computer services have millions of users. See Reno v. ACLU, 117 S. Ct. at 2334 (noting that at time of district court trial, "commercial online services had almost 12 million individual subscribers"). The amount of information communicated via interactive computer services is therefore staggering. The specter of tort liability in an area of such prolific speech would have an obvious chilling effect. It would be impossible for service providers to screen each of their millions of postings for possible problems. Faced with potential liability for each message republished by their services, interactive computer service providers might choose to severely restrict the number and type of messages posted. Congress considered the weight of the speech interests implicated and chose to immunize service providers to avoid any such restrictive effect.

Another important purpose of §230 was to encourage service providers to self-regulate the dissemination of offensive material over their services. In this respect, §230 responded to a New York state court decision, Stratton Oakmont, Inc. v.

---

service." *Id.* §230(e)(3). The parties do not dispute that AOL falls within the CDA's "interactive computer service" definition and that the unidentified third party who posted the offensive messages here fits the definition of an "information content provider."

Prodigy Servs. Co., 1995 WL 323710 (N.Y. Sup.Ct. May 24, 1995). There, the plaintiffs sued Prodigy—an interactive computer service like AOL—for defamatory comments made by an unidentified party on one of Prodigy's bulletin boards. The court held Prodigy to the strict liability standard normally applied to original publishers of defamatory statements, rejecting Prodigy's claims that it should be held only to the lower "knowledge" standard usually reserved for distributors. The court reasoned that Prodigy acted more like an original publisher than a distributor both because it advertised its practice of controlling content on its service and because it actively screened and edited messages posted on its bulletin boards.

Congress enacted §230 to remove the disincentives to self-regulation created by the *Stratton Oakmont* decision. Under that court's holding, computer service providers who regulated the dissemination of offensive material on their services risked subjecting themselves to liability, because such regulation cast the service provider in the role of a publisher. Fearing that the specter of liability would therefore deter service providers from blocking and screening offensive material, Congress enacted §230's broad immunity "to remove disincentives for the development and utilization of blocking and filtering technologies that empower parents to restrict their children's access to objectionable or inappropriate online material." 47 U.S.C. §230(b)(4). In line with this purpose, §230 forbids the imposition of publisher liability on a service provider for the exercise of its editorial and self-regulatory functions.

B.

Zeran argues, however, that the §230 immunity eliminates only publisher liability, leaving distributor liability intact. Publishers can be held liable for defamatory statements contained in their works even absent proof that they had specific knowledge of the statement's inclusion. W. Page Keeton et al., Prosser and Keeton on the Law of Torts §113, at 810 (5th ed. 1984). According to Zeran, interactive computer service providers like AOL are normally considered instead to be distributors, like traditional news vendors or book sellers. Distributors cannot be held liable for defamatory statements contained in the materials they distribute unless it is proven at a minimum that they have actual knowledge of the defamatory statements upon which liability is predicated. *Id.* at 811 (explaining that distributors are not liable "in the absence of proof that they knew or had reason to know of the existence of defamatory matter contained in matter published"). Zeran contends that he provided AOL with sufficient notice of the defamatory statements appearing on the company's bulletin board. This notice is significant, says Zeran, because AOL could be held liable as a distributor only if it acquired knowledge of the defamatory statements' existence.

Because of the difference between these two forms of liability, Zeran contends that the term "distributor" carries a legally distinct meaning from the term "publisher." Accordingly, he asserts that Congress' use of only the term "publisher" in §230 indicates a purpose to immunize service providers only from publisher liability. He argues that distributors are left unprotected by §230 and, therefore, his suit should be permitted to proceed against AOL. We disagree. Assuming arguendo that Zeran has satisfied the requirements for imposition of distributor liability, this theory of liability is merely a subset, or a species, of publisher liability, and is therefore also foreclosed by §230.

The terms "publisher" and "distributor" derive their legal significance from the context of defamation law. Although Zeran attempts to artfully plead his claims as ones of negligence, they are indistinguishable from a garden variety defamation action. Because the publication of a statement is a necessary element in a defamation action, only one who publishes can be subject to this form of tort liability. Restatement (Second) of Torts §558(b) (1977); Keeton et al., *supra*, §113, at 802. Publication does not only describe the choice by an author to include certain information. In addition, both the negligent communication of a defamatory statement and the failure to remove such a statement when first communicated by another party—each alleged by Zeran here under a negligence label—constitute publication. Restatement (Second) of Torts §577; see also Tacket v. General Motors Corp., 836 F.2d 1042, 1046-47 (7th Cir. 1987). In fact, every repetition of a defamatory statement is considered a publication. Keeton et al., *supra*, §113, at 799.

In this case, AOL is legally considered to be a publisher. "[E]very one who takes part in the publication . . . is charged with publication." *Id*. Even distributors are considered to be publishers for purposes of defamation law:

> Those who are in the business of making their facilities available to disseminate the writings composed, the speeches made, and the information gathered by others may also be regarded as participating to such an extent in making the books, newspapers, magazines, and information available to others as to be regarded as publishers. They are intentionally making the contents available to others, sometimes without knowing all of the contents—including the defamatory content—and sometimes without any opportunity to ascertain, in advance, that any defamatory matter was to be included in the matter published.

Id. at 803. AOL falls squarely within this traditional definition of a publisher and, therefore, is clearly protected by §230's immunity.

Zeran contends that decisions like *Stratton Oakmont* and Cubby, Inc. v. CompuServe Inc., 776 F. Supp. 135 (S.D.N.Y. 1991), recognize a legal distinction between publishers and distributors. He misapprehends, however, the significance of that distinction for the legal issue we consider here. It is undoubtedly true that mere conduits, or distributors, are subject to a different standard of liability. As explained above, distributors must at a minimum have knowledge of the existence of a defamatory statement as a prerequisite to liability. But this distinction signifies only that different standards of liability may be applied within the larger publisher category, depending on the specific type of publisher concerned. See Keeton et al., *supra*, §113, at 799-800 (explaining that every party involved is charged with publication, although degrees of legal responsibility differ). To the extent that decisions like *Stratton* and *Cubby* utilize the terms "publisher" and "distributor" separately, the decisions correctly describe two different standards of liability. *Stratton* and *Cubby* do not, however, suggest that distributors are not also a type of publisher for purposes of defamation law.

Zeran simply attaches too much importance to the presence of the distinct notice element in distributor liability. The simple fact of notice surely cannot transform one from an original publisher to a distributor in the eyes of the law. To the contrary, once a computer service provider receives notice of a potentially defamatory posting, it is thrust into the role of a traditional publisher. The computer service provider must decide whether to publish, edit, or withdraw the posting. In this respect, Zeran seeks to impose liability on AOL for assuming the role for which §230 specifically proscribes liability—the publisher role.

Our view that Zeran's complaint treats AOL as a publisher is reinforced because AOL is cast in the same position as the party who originally posted the offensive messages. According to Zeran's logic, AOL is legally at fault because it communicated to third parties an allegedly defamatory statement. This is precisely the theory under which the original poster of the offensive messages would be found liable. If the original party is considered a publisher of the offensive messages, Zeran certainly cannot attach liability to AOL under the same theory without conceding that AOL too must be treated as a publisher of the statements.

Zeran next contends that interpreting §230 to impose liability on service providers with knowledge of defamatory content on their services is consistent with the statutory purposes outlined in Part IIA. Zeran fails, however, to understand the practical implications of notice liability in the interactive computer service context. Liability upon notice would defeat the dual purposes advanced by §230 of the CDA. Like the strict liability imposed by the *Stratton Oakmont* court, liability upon notice reinforces service providers' incentives to restrict speech and abstain from self-regulation.

If computer service providers were subject to distributor liability, they would face potential liability each time they receive notice of a potentially defamatory statement—from any party, concerning any message. Each notification would require a careful yet rapid investigation of the circumstances surrounding the posted information, a legal judgment concerning the information's defamatory character, and an on-the-spot editorial decision whether to risk liability by allowing the continued publication of that information. Although this might be feasible for the traditional print publisher, the sheer number of postings on interactive computer services would create an impossible burden in the Internet context. Cf. Auvil v. CBS 60 Minutes, 800 F. Supp. 928, 931 (E.D.Wash. 1992) (recognizing that it is unrealistic for network affiliates to "monitor incoming transmissions and exercise on-the-spot discretionary calls"). Because service providers would be subject to liability only for the publication of information, and not for its removal, they would have a natural incentive simply to remove messages upon notification, whether the contents were defamatory or not. See Philadelphia Newspapers, Inc. v. Hepps, 475 U.S. 767, 777, 106 S. Ct. 1558, 1564, 89 L. Ed.2d 783 (1986) (recognizing that fears of unjustified liability produce a chilling effect antithetical to First Amendment's protection of speech). Thus, like strict liability, liability upon notice has a chilling effect on the freedom of Internet speech.

Similarly, notice-based liability would deter service providers from regulating the dissemination of offensive material over their own services. Any efforts by a service provider to investigate and screen material posted on its service would only lead to notice of potentially defamatory material more frequently and thereby create a stronger basis for liability. Instead of subjecting themselves to further possible lawsuits, service providers would likely eschew any attempts at self-regulation.

More generally, notice-based liability for interactive computer service providers would provide third parties with a no-cost means to create the basis for future lawsuits. Whenever one was displeased with the speech of another party conducted over an interactive computer service, the offended party could simply "notify" the relevant service provider, claiming the information to be legally defamatory. In light of the vast amount of speech communicated through interactive computer services, these notices could produce an impossible burden for service providers, who would be faced with ceaseless choices of suppressing controversial speech or sustaining prohibitive liability. Because the probable effects of distributor liability on the vigor of Internet speech and on service provider self-regulation are directly contrary to §230's statutory purposes, we will not assume that Congress intended to leave liability upon notice intact. . . .

Blumenthal v. Drudge
United States District Court for the District of Columbia
992 F. Supp. 44 (D.D.C. 1998)

FRIEDMAN, J.

This is a defamation case revolving around a statement published on the Internet by defendant Matt Drudge. On August 10, 1997, the following was available to all having access to the Internet:

> The DRUDGE REPORT has learned that top GOP operatives who feel there is a double-standard of only reporting republican shame believe they are holding an ace card: New White House recruit Sidney Blumenthal has a spousal abuse past that has been effectively covered up.
>
> The accusations are explosive.
>
> There are court records of Blumenthal's violence against his wife, one influential republican, who demanded anonymity, tells the DRUDGE REPORT.
>
> If they begin to use [Don] Sipple and his problems against us, against the Republican Party . . . to show hypocrisy, Blumenthal would become fair game. Wasn't it Clinton who signed the Violence Against Women Act?
>
> [There goes the budget deal honeymoon.]
>
> One White House source, also requesting anonymity, says the Blumenthal wife-beating allegation is a pure fiction that has been created by Clinton enemies. [The First Lady] would not have brought him in if he had this in his background, assures the wellplaced staffer. This story about Blumenthal has been in circulation for years.
>
> Last month President Clinton named Sidney Blumenthal an Assistant to the President as part of the Communications Team. He's brought in to work on communications strategy, special projects themeing—a newly created position.
>
> Every attempt to reach Blumenthal proved unsuccessful.

Complaint, Ex. 4.

. . . Access to defendant Drudge's world wide web site is available at no cost to anyone who has access to the Internet at the Internet address of "www. drudgereport.com." The front page of the web site contains the logo "Drudge Report." Defendant Drudge has also placed a hyperlink on his web site that, when activated, causes the most recently published edition of the Drudge Report to be displayed. The web site also contains numerous hyperlinks to other on-line news publications and news articles that may be of interest to readers of the Drudge Report. In addition, during the time period relevant to this case, Drudge had developed a list of regular readers or subscribers to whom he e-mailed each new edition of the Drudge Report. By March 1995, the Drudge Report had 1,000 e-mail sub-scribers, and plaintiffs allege that by 1997 Drudge had 85,000 subscribers to his e-mail service.

In late 1996, defendant Drudge entered into a six-month licensing agreement with the publisher of "Wired" magazine. Under the agreement, the publisher of "Wired" had the right to receive and display future editions of the Drudge Report in "Hotwired," a new electronic Internet publication. In exchange, defendant Drudge received a bi-weekly royalty payment. In addition to the publication of the Drudge Report in "Hotwired," defendant Drudge continued to distribute each new edition via e-mail to his subscribers and via his world wide web site.

In late May or early June of 1997, at approximately the time when the "Wired" licensing agreement expired, defendant Drudge entered into a written license agreement with AOL. The agreement made the Drudge Report available to all members of AOL's service for a period of one year. In exchange, defendant Drudge received a flat monthly "royalty payment" of $3,000 from AOL. During the time relevant to this case, defendant Drudge has had no other source of in-come. Under the licensing agreement, Drudge is to create, edit, update and "oth-erwise manage" the content of the Drudge Report, and AOL may "remove content that AOL reasonably determine[s] to violate AOL's then standard terms of service." Drudge transmits new editions of the Drudge Report by e-mailing them to AOL. AOL then posts the new editions on the AOL service. Drudge also has continued to distribute each new edition of the Drudge Report via e-mail and his own web site.

Late at night on the evening of Sunday, August 10, 1997 (Pacific Daylight Time), defendant Drudge wrote and transmitted the edition of the Drudge Report that contained the alleged defamatory statement about the Blumenthals. Drudge transmitted the report from Los Angeles, California by e-mail to his direct subscrib-ers and by posting both a headline and the full text of the Blumenthal story on his world wide web site. He then transmitted the text but not the headline to AOL, which in turn made it available to AOL subscribers.

After receiving a letter from plaintiffs' counsel on Monday, August 11, 1997, Complaint, Ex. 6, defendant Drudge retracted the story through a special edition of the Drudge Report posted on his web site and e-mailed to his subscribers. At approximately 2:00 a.m. on Tuesday, August 12, 1997, Drudge e-mailed the re-traction to AOL which posted it on the AOL service. Defendant Drudge later pub-licly apologized to the Blumenthals.

Plaintiffs concede that AOL is a "provider . . . of an interactive computer ser-vice" for purposes of Section 230, and that if AOL acted exclusively as a provider of an interactive computer service it may not be held liable for making the Drudge Report available to AOL subscribers. See 47 U.S.C. §230(c)(1).

They also concede that Drudge is an "information content provider" because he wrote the alleged defamatory material about the Blumenthals contained in the Drudge Report. While plaintiffs suggest that AOL is responsible along with Drudge because it had some role in writing or editing the material in the Drudge Report, they have provided no factual support for that assertion. Indeed, plaintiffs affirma-tively state that "no person, other than Drudge himself, edited, checked, verified, or supervised the information that Drudge published in the Drudge Report." It also is apparent to the Court that there is no evidence to support the view originally taken by plaintiffs that Drudge is or was an employee or agent of AOL, and plain-tiffs seem to have all but abandoned that argument.

AOL acknowledges both that Section 230(c)(1) would not immunize AOL with respect to any information AOL developed or created entirely by itself and that there are situations in which there may be two or more information content providers responsible for material disseminated on the Internet—joint authors, a lyricist and a composer, for example. While Section 230 does not preclude joint liability for the joint development of content, AOL maintains that there simply is no evidence here that AOL had any role in creating or developing any of the information in the Drudge Report. The Court agrees. It is undisputed that the Blumenthal story was written by Drudge without any substantive or editorial involvement by AOL. AOL was nothing more than a provider of an interactive computer service on which the Drudge Report was carried, and Congress has said quite clearly that such a provider shall not be treated as a "publisher or speaker" and therefore may not be held liable in tort. 47 U.S.C. §230(c)(1). . . .

Plaintiffs [argue] that Section 230 of the Communications Decency Act does not provide immunity to AOL in this case because Drudge was not just an anonymous person who sent a message over the Internet through AOL. He is a person with whom AOL contracted, whom AOL paid $3,000 a month—$36,000 a year, Drudge's sole, consistent source of income—and whom AOL promoted to its subscribers and potential subscribers as a reason to subscribe to AOL. Furthermore, the license agreement between AOL and Drudge by its terms contemplates more than a passive role for AOL; in it, AOL reserves the "right to remove, or direct [Drudge] to remove, any content which, as reasonably determined by AOL . . . violates AOL's then-standard Terms of Service. . . ." By the terms of the agreement, AOL also is "entitled to require reasonable changes to . . . content, to the extent such content will, in AOL's good faith judgment, adversely affect operations of the AOL network."

In addition, shortly after it entered into the licensing agreement with Drudge, AOL issued a press release making clear the kind of material Drudge would provide to AOL subscribers—gossip and rumor—and urged potential subscribers to sign onto AOL in order to get the benefit of the Drudge Report. The press release was captioned: "AOL Hires Runaway Gossip Success Matt Drudge." It noted that "[m]averick gossip columnist Matt Drudge has teamed up with America Online," and stated: "Giving the Drudge Report a home on America Online (keyword: Drudge) opens up the floodgates to an audience ripe for Drudge's brand of reporting. . . . AOL has made Matt Drudge instantly accessible to members who crave instant gossip and news breaks."

Why is this different, the Blumenthals suggest, from AOL advertising and promoting a new purveyor of child pornography or other offensive material? Why should AOL be permitted to tout someone as a gossip columnist or rumor monger who will make such rumors and gossip "instantly accessible" to AOL subscribers, and then claim immunity when that person, as might be anticipated, defames another?

If it were writing on a clean slate, this Court would agree with plaintiffs. AOL has certain editorial rights with respect to the content provided by Drudge and disseminated by AOL, including the right to require changes in content and to remove it; and it has affirmatively promoted Drudge as a new source of unverified instant gossip on AOL. Yet it takes no responsibility for any damage he may cause. AOL is not a passive conduit like the telephone company, a common carrier with no control and therefore no responsibility for what is said over the telephone wires.

Because it has the right to exercise editorial control over those with whom it contracts and whose words it disseminates, it would seem only fair to hold AOL to the liability standards applied to a publisher or, at least, like a book store owner or library, to the liability standards applied to a distributor. But Congress has made a different policy choice by providing immunity even where the interactive service provider has an active, even aggressive role in making available content prepared by others.

In some sort of tacit quid pro quo arrangement with the service provider community, Congress has conferred immunity from tort liability as an incentive to Internet service providers to self-police the Internet for obscenity and other offensive material, even where the self-policing is unsuccessful or not even attempted. . . .

COMMENTS AND QUESTIONS

1. In *Zeran*, 47 U.S.C. section 230 gave AOL a complete defense to liability for defamatory postings even after Zeran had informed AOL of the offending statements. Congress is not always so kind to Internet service providers (ISPs), however. The safe harbor rules of the Digital Millennium Copyright Act (DMCA), particularly its "notice and take down" rules, discussed in Chapter 10 following the *Netcom* decision, are noticeably different from the exemption in the Communications Decency Act (CDA). The DMCA relieves ISPs from liability for infringing material of which they are unaware, but it also creates a duty to remove such material after they are informed of its existence—a duty that is backed up by the threat of ISP liability. Is there any principled reason for this difference? Is copyright infringement so different from defamation and similar torts that each requires different rules for ISP liability? Does the CDA exemption go too far?

2. Was the anonymous posting in *Zeran* defamatory?

3. Some commentators have suggested that the standard for what is considered defamatory should be different for Internet speech. Mike Godwin, in his book Cyber Rights: Defending Free Speech in the Digital Age 82-100 (1998) argues that defamation liability is unnecessary because the Internet makes it so much easier for people to respond to and cure misstatements or misimpressions made by others about them. A recent California case seemed to agree, although for different reasons than Godwin gave, indicating that the standard should be different because, in the context of a heated debate on the Internet, people expect statements to be hyperbole and emotional outburst, rather than assertions of fact. See Nicosia v. De Rooy, 1999 WL1128892 (N.D. Cal. July 7, 1999).

4. Both Zeran and Blumenthal were upset that AOL did not take defamatory material posted by users down fast enough. In other instances AOL has been criticized for taking down "uncivil" speech too quickly and arbitrarily enforcing the civility rules of its terms of service. What, if any, rights should users have to challenge termination of service for "civility" violations?

5. The *Zeran* and *Drudge* decisions and the CDA immunity provision have not been uniformly well received. One commentator questions whether the self-regulation by intermediaries the CDA provision hoped to induce will actually occur and suggests that courts would make sound decisions on intermediary liability issues. See, e.g., Susan Freiwald, Comparative Institutional Analysis in Cyberspace:

The Case of Intermediary Liability for Defamation, 14 Harv. J.L. & Tech. 569 (2001). However, other commentators have been more favorable toward the CDA immunity provision, including Matthew Schruers, The History and Economics of ISP Liability for Third Party Conduct, 88 Va. L. Rev. 205 (2002), who argues that economic analysis supports the CDA's total immunity. However, the European Union decided to place more responsibility on intermediaries than the U.S. Congress did by adopting a "notice and take down" approach to intermediary liability for Internet-based defamation, other violations of content regulations (such as hate speech), and copyright infringements. For a comparison of the U.S. and E.U. approaches to intermediary liability, see, e.g., Rosa Julia-Barcelo, On-line Intermediary Liability Issues: Comparing E.U. and U.S. Legal Frameworks, 22 Eur. Intell. Prop. Rev. 105 (2000).

6. Defamation is far from the only cause of action to which the CDA immunity provision has been applied to shield intermediaries from liability. See, e.g., Doe v. America Online, Inc., 783 So.2d 1010 (Fla. Sup. Ct. 2001) (Internet service provider was immune from liability for claim of negligence for allowing user to sell child pornography); Gentry v. eBay, Inc., 121 Cal. Rptr.2d 703 (Calif. Ct. App. 2002) (section 230 bars unfair competition and negligence claims against auction provider for inauthentic sports memorabilia); Schneider v. Amazon.com, Inc., 31 P.2d 37 (Wash. 2001) (section 230 bars action against intermediary for breach of contract); Jane Doe One v. Oliver, 755 A.2d 1000 (Conn. Super. Ct. 2000) (section 230 bars nuisance claim based on offensive speech); Patentwizard, Inc. v. Kinko's, Inc., 163 F. Supp.2d 1069 (D.S.D. 2001) (copy shop qualified for CDA immunity against state claims for negligence based on rental of Internet-accessible computers); Kathleen R. v. City of Livermore, 87 Cal. App.4th 684 (Cal. Ct. App. 2001) (public library qualified for CDA immunity as a provider of Internet services notwithstanding parent's suit complaining that the library had failed to shield her child from accessing indecent materials). However, the CDA immunity provision did not shield Internet service provider Mindspring from liability for a user's trademark infringement on a website hosted by Mindspring. See Gucci Am., Inc. v. Hall & Associates, 135 F. Supp.2d 409 (S.D.N.Y. 2001). Indeed, the statute makes it clear that it doesn't apply to intellectual property claims.

B. INDECENT OR OBSCENE COMMUNICATIONS

═══ *Reno v. American Civil Liberties Union*
Supreme Court of the United States
521 U.S. 844 (1997)

Justice STEVENS delivered the opinion of the Court.

At issue is the constitutionality of two statutory provisions enacted to protect minors from "indecent" and "patently offensive" communications on the Internet. Notwithstanding the legitimacy and importance of the congressional goal of protecting children from harmful materials, we agree with the three-judge District

Court that the statute abridges "the freedom of speech" protected by the First Amendment. . . .

II

The Telecommunications Act of 1996, Pub.L. 104-104, 110 Stat. 56, was an unusually important legislative enactment. As stated on the first of its 103 pages, its primary purpose was to reduce regulation and encourage the rapid deployment of new telecommunications technologies. The major components of the statute have nothing to do with the Internet; they were designed to promote competition in the local telephone service market, the multichannel video market, and the market for over-the-air broadcasting. The Act includes seven Titles, six of which are the product of extensive committee hearings and the subject of discussion in Reports prepared by Committees of the Senate and the House of Representatives. By contrast, Title V—known as the "Communications Decency Act of 1996" (CDA)—contains provisions that were either added in executive committee after the hearings were concluded or as amendments offered during floor debate on the legislation. An amendment offered in the Senate was the source of the two statutory provisions challenged in this case. They are informally described as the "indecent transmission" provision and the "patently offensive display" provision. . . .

The first, 47 U.S.C.A. §223(a) (Supp. 1997), prohibits the knowing transmission of obscene or indecent messages to any recipient under 18 years of age. It provides in pertinent part:

> (a) Whoever—
> > (1) in interstate or foreign communications— . . .
> > > (B) by means of a telecommunications device knowingly—
> > > > (i) makes, creates, or solicits, and
> > > > (ii) initiates the transmission of,
> > > any comment, request, suggestion, proposal, image, or other communication which is obscene or indecent, knowing that the recipient of the communication is under 18 years of age, regardless of whether the maker of such communication placed the call or initiated the communication; . . . .
> > (2) knowingly permits any telecommunications facility under his control to be used for any activity prohibited by paragraph (1) with the intent that it be used for such activity, shall be fined under Title 18, or imprisoned not more than two years, or both.

The second provision, §223(d), prohibits the knowing sending or displaying of patently offensive messages in a manner that is available to a person under 18 years of age. It provides:

> (d) Whoever—
> > (1) in interstate or foreign communications knowingly—
> > > (A) uses an interactive computer service to send to a specific person or persons under 18 years of age, or
> > > (B) uses any interactive computer service to display in a manner available to a person under 18 years of age,

any comment, request, suggestion, proposal, image, or other communication that, in context, depicts or describes, in terms patently offensive as measured by contemporary community standards, sexual or excretory activities or organs, regardless of whether the user of such service placed the call or initiated the communication; or

> (2) knowingly permits any telecommunications facility under such person's control to be used for an activity prohibited by paragraph (1) with the intent that it be used for such activity,

shall be fined under Title 18, or imprisoned not more than two years, or both.

The breadth of these prohibitions is qualified by two affirmative defenses. See §223(e)(5). One covers those who take "good faith, reasonable, effective, and appropriate actions" to restrict access by minors to the prohibited communications. §223(e)(5)(A). The other covers those who restrict access to covered material by requiring certain designated forms of age proof, such as a verified credit card or an adult identification number or code. §223(e)(5)(B).

III

On February 8, 1996, immediately after the President signed the statute, 20 plaintiffs filed suit against the Attorney General of the United States and the Department of Justice challenging the constitutionality of §§223(a)(1) and 223(d). A week later, based on his conclusion that the term "indecent" was too vague to provide the basis for a criminal prosecution, District Judge Buckwalter entered a temporary restraining order against enforcement of §223(a)(1)(B)(ii) insofar as it applies to indecent communications. A second suit was then filed by 27 additional plaintiffs, the two cases were consolidated, and a three-judge District Court was convened pursuant to §561 of the Act. After an evidentiary hearing, that Court entered a preliminary injunction against enforcement of both of the challenged provisions. Each of the three judges wrote a separate opinion, but their judgment was unanimous. . . .

The judgment of the District Court enjoins the Government from enforcing the prohibitions in §223(a)(1)(B) insofar as they relate to "indecent" communications, but expressly preserves the Government's right to investigate and prosecute the obscenity or child pornography activities prohibited therein. The injunction against enforcement of §§223(d)(1) and (2) is unqualified because those provisions contain no separate reference to obscenity or child pornography. . . .

IV

In arguing for reversal, the Government contends that the CDA is plainly constitutional under three of our prior decisions: (1) Ginsberg v. New York, 390 U.S. 629, 88 S. Ct. 1274, 20 L. Ed.2d 195 (1968); (2) FCC v. Pacifica Foundation, 438 U.S. 726, 98 S. Ct. 3026, 57 L. Ed.2d 1073 (1978); and (3) Renton v. Playtime Theatres, Inc., 475 U.S. 41, 106 S. Ct. 925, 89 L. Ed.2d 29 (1986). A close look at these cases, however, raises—rather than relieves—doubts concerning the constitutionality of the CDA.

In *Ginsberg*, we upheld the constitutionality of a New York statute that prohibited selling to minors under 17 years of age material that was considered obscene as to them even if not obscene as to adults. We rejected the defendant's broad submission that "the scope of the constitutional freedom of expression secured to a citizen to read or see material concerned with sex cannot be made to depend on whether the citizen is an adult or a minor." 390 U.S., at 636, 88 S. Ct., at 1279. In rejecting that contention, we relied not only on the State's independent interest in the well-being of its youth, but also on our consistent recognition of the principle that "the parents' claim to authority in their own household to direct the rearing of their children is basic in the structure of our society."

In four important respects, the statute upheld in *Ginsberg* was narrower than the CDA. First, we noted in *Ginsberg* that "the prohibition against sales to minors does not bar parents who so desire from purchasing the magazines for their children." *Id.*, at 639, 88 S. Ct., at 1280. Under the CDA, by contrast, neither the parents' consent—nor even their participation—in the communication would avoid the application of the statute. Second, the New York statute applied only to commercial transactions, *id.*, at 647, 88 S. Ct., at 1284-1285, whereas the CDA contains no such limitation. Third, the New York statute cabined its definition of material that is harmful to minors with the requirement that it be "utterly without redeeming social importance for minors." *Id.*, at 646, 88 S. Ct., at 1284. The CDA fails to provide us with any definition of the term "indecent" as used in §223(a)(1) and, importantly, omits any requirement that the "patently offensive" material covered by §223(d) lack serious literary, artistic, political, or scientific value. Fourth, the New York statute defined a minor as a person under the age of 17, whereas the CDA, in applying to all those under 18 years, includes an additional year of those nearest majority.

In *Pacifica*, we upheld a declaratory order of the Federal Communications Commission, holding that the broadcast of a recording of a 12-minute monologue entitled "Filthy Words" that had previously been delivered to a live audience "could have been the subject of administrative sanctions." 438 U.S., at 730, 98 S. Ct., at 3030 (internal quotations omitted). The Commission had found that the repetitive use of certain words referring to excretory or sexual activities or organs "in an afternoon broadcast when children are in the audience was patently offensive" and concluded that the monologue was indecent "as broadcast." *Id.*, at 735, 98 S. Ct., at 3033. The respondent did not quarrel with the finding that the afternoon broadcast was patently offensive, but contended that it was not "indecent" within the meaning of the relevant statutes because it contained no prurient appeal. After rejecting respondent's statutory arguments, we confronted its two constitutional arguments: (1) that the Commission's construction of its authority to ban indecent speech was so broad that its order had to be set aside even if the broadcast at issue was unprotected; and (2) that since the recording was not obscene, the First Amendment forbade any abridgement of the right to broadcast it on the radio.

In the portion of the lead opinion not joined by Justices Powell and Blackmun, the plurality stated that the First Amendment does not prohibit all governmental regulation that depends on the content of speech. *Id.*, at 742-743, 98 S. Ct., at 3036-3037. Accordingly, the availability of constitutional protection for a vulgar and offensive monologue that was not obscene depended on the context of the broadcast. *Id.*, at 744-748, 98 S. Ct., at 3037-3040. Relying on the premise that "of all forms of communication" broadcasting had received the most limited First Amendment protection, *id.*, at 748-749, 98 S. Ct., at 3039-3040, the Court concluded that the ease with which children may obtain access to broadcasts, "coupled with the concerns recognized in Ginsberg," justified special treatment of indecent broadcasting. *Id.*, at 749-750, 98 S. Ct., at 3040-3041.

As with the New York statute at issue in *Ginsberg*, there are significant differences between the order upheld in *Pacifica* and the CDA. First, the order in *Pacifica*, issued by an agency that had been regulating radio stations for decades, targeted a specific broadcast that represented a rather dramatic departure from traditional program content in order to designate when—rather than whether—it would be permissible to air such a program in that particular medium. The CDA's broad categorical prohibitions are not limited to particular times and are not dependent on any evaluation by an agency familiar with the unique characteristics of the Internet. Second, unlike the CDA, the Commission's declaratory order was not punitive; we expressly refused to decide whether the indecent broadcast "would justify a criminal prosecution." *Id.*, at 750, 98 S. Ct., at 3041. Finally, the Commission's order applied to a medium which as a matter of history had "received the most limited First Amendment protection," *id.*, at 748, 98 S. Ct., at 3040, in large part because warnings could not adequately protect the listener from unexpected program content. The Internet, however, has no comparable history. Moreover, the District Court found that the risk of encountering indecent material by accident is remote because a series of affirmative steps is required to access specific material.

In *Renton*, we upheld a zoning ordinance that kept adult movie theatres out of residential neighborhoods. The ordinance was aimed, not at the content of the films shown in the theaters, but rather at the "secondary effects"—such as crime and deteriorating property values—that these theaters fostered: "'It is th[e] secondary effect which these zoning ordinances attempt to avoid, not the dissemination of "offensive" speech.'" 475 U.S., at 49, 106 S. Ct., at 930 (quoting Young v. American Mini Theatres, Inc., 427 U.S. 50, 71, n. 34, 96 S. Ct. 2440, 2453, n. 34, 49 L. Ed.2d 310 (1976)). According to the Government, the CDA is constitutional because it constitutes a sort of "cyberzoning" on the Internet. But the CDA applies broadly to the entire universe of cyberspace. And the purpose of the CDA is to protect children from the primary effects of "indecent" and "patently offensive" speech, rather than any "secondary" effect of such speech. Thus, the CDA is a content-based blanket restriction on speech, and, as such, cannot be "properly analyzed as a form of time, place, and manner regulation." 475 U.S., at 46, 106 S. Ct., at 928. See also Boos v. Barry, 485 U.S. 312, 321, 108 S. Ct. 1157, 1163, 99 L. Ed.2d 333 (1988) ("Regulations that focus on the direct impact of speech on its audience" are not properly analyzed under *Renton*); Forsyth County v. Nationalist Movement, 505 U.S. 123, 134, 112 S. Ct. 2395, 2403, 120 L. Ed.2d 101 (1992) ("Listeners' reaction to speech is not a content-neutral basis for regulation").

These precedents, then, surely do not require us to uphold the CDA and are fully consistent with the application of the most stringent review of its provisions.

V

In Southeastern Promotions, Ltd. v. Conrad, 420 U.S. 546, 557, 95 S. Ct. 1239, 1245-1246, 43 L. Ed.2d 448 (1975), we observed that "[e]ach medium of expression . . . may present its own problems." Thus, some of our cases have recognized special justifications for regulation of the broadcast media that are not applicable to other speakers, see Red Lion Broadcasting Co. v. FCC, 395 U.S. 367, 89 S. Ct. 1794, 23 L. Ed.2d 371 (1969); FCC v. Pacifica Foundation, 438 U.S. 726, 98 S. Ct. 3026, 57 L. Ed.2d 1073 (1978). In these cases, the Court relied on the history of extensive government regulation of the broadcast medium, see, e.g., *Red Lion*, 395 U.S., at 399-400, 89 S. Ct., at 1811-1812; the scarcity of available frequencies at its inception, see, e.g., Turner Broadcasting System, Inc. v. FCC, 512 U.S. 622, 637-638, 114 S. Ct. 2445, 2456-2457, 129 L. Ed.2d 497 (1994); and its "invasive" nature, see Sable Communications of Cal., Inc. v. FCC, 492 U.S. 115, 128, 109 S. Ct. 2829, 2837-2838, 106 L. Ed.2d 93 (1989).

Those factors are not present in cyberspace. Neither before nor after the enactment of the CDA have the vast democratic fora of the Internet been subject to the type of government supervision and regulation that has attended the broadcast industry. Moreover, the Internet is not as "invasive" as radio or television. The District Court specifically found that "[c]ommunications over the Internet do not 'invade' an individual's home or appear on one's computer screen unbidden. Users seldom encounter content 'by accident.'" 929 F. Supp., at 844 (finding 88). It also found that "[a]lmost all sexually explicit images are preceded by warnings as to the content," and cited testimony that "'odds are slim' that a user would come across a sexually explicit sight by accident." *Ibid.*

We distinguished *Pacifica* in *Sable*, 492 U.S., at 128, 109 S. Ct., at 2837-2838, on just this basis. In *Sable*, a company engaged in the business of offering sexually oriented prerecorded telephone messages (popularly known as "dial-a-porn") challenged the constitutionality of an amendment to the Communications Act that imposed a blanket prohibition on indecent as well as obscene interstate commercial telephone messages. We held that the statute was constitutional insofar as it applied to obscene messages but invalid as applied to indecent messages. In attempting to justify the complete ban and criminalization of indecent commercial telephone messages, the Government relied on *Pacifica*, arguing that the ban was necessary to prevent children from gaining access to such messages. We agreed that "there is a compelling interest in protecting the physical and psychological well-being of minors" which extended to shielding them from indecent messages that are not obscene by adult standards, 492 U.S., at 126, 109 S. Ct., at 2836-2837, but distinguished our "emphatically narrow holding" in *Pacifica* because it did not involve a complete ban and because it involved a different medium of communication, *id.*, at 127, 109 S. Ct., at 2837. We explained that "the dial-it medium requires the listener to take affirmative steps to receive the communication." *Id.*, at 127-128, 109 S. Ct., at 2837. "Placing a telephone call," we continued, "is not the same as turning on a radio and being taken by surprise by an indecent message." *Id.*, at 128, 109 S. Ct., at 2837.

Finally, unlike the conditions that prevailed when Congress first authorized regulation of the broadcast spectrum, the Internet can hardly be considered a "scarce" expressive commodity. It provides relatively unlimited, low-cost capacity for communication of all kinds. The Government estimates that "[a]s many as 40 million people use the Internet today, and that figure is expected to grow to 200 million by 1999." This dynamic, multifaceted category of communication includes not only traditional print and news services, but also audio, video, and still images, as well as interactive, real-time dialogue. Through the use of chat rooms, any person with a phone line can become a town crier with a voice that resonates farther than it could from any soapbox. Through the use of Web pages, mail exploders, and newsgroups, the same individual can become a pamphleteer. As the District Court found, "the content on the Internet is as diverse as human thought." 929 F. Supp., at 842 (finding 74). We agree with its conclusion that our cases provide no basis for qualifying the level of First Amendment scrutiny that should be applied to this medium.

VI

Regardless of whether the CDA is so vague that it violates the Fifth Amendment, the many ambiguities concerning the scope of its coverage render it problematic for purposes of the First Amendment. For instance, each of the two parts of the CDA uses a different linguistic form. The first uses the word "indecent," 47 U.S.C.A. §223(a) (Supp. 1997), while the second speaks of material that "in context, depicts or describes, in terms patently offensive as measured by contemporary community standards, sexual or excretory activities or organs," §223(d). Given the absence of a definition of either term, this difference in language will provoke uncertainty among speakers about how the two standards relate to each other and just what they mean. Could a speaker confidently assume that a serious discussion about birth control practices, homosexuality, the First Amendment issues raised by the Appendix to our *Pacifica* opinion, or the consequences of prison rape would not violate the CDA? This uncertainty undermines the likelihood that the CDA has been carefully tailored to the congressional goal of protecting minors from potentially harmful materials.

The vagueness of the CDA is a matter of special concern for two reasons. First, the CDA is a content-based regulation of speech. The vagueness of such a regulation raises special First Amendment concerns because of its obvious chilling effect on free speech. See, e.g., Gentile v. State Bar of Nev., 501 U.S. 1030, 1048-1051, 111 S. Ct. 2720, 2731-2733, 115 L. Ed.2d 888 (1991). Second, the CDA is a criminal statute. In addition to the opprobrium and stigma of a criminal conviction, the CDA threatens violators with penalties including up to two years in prison for each act of violation. The severity of criminal sanctions may well cause speakers to remain silent rather than communicate even arguably unlawful words, ideas, and images. See, e.g., Dombrowski v. Pfister, 380 U.S. 479, 494, 85 S. Ct. 1116, 1125, 14 L. Ed.2d 22 (1965). As a practical matter, this increased deterrent effect, coupled with the "risk of discriminatory enforcement" of vague regulations, poses greater First Amendment concerns than those implicated by the civil regulation reviewed in Denver Area Ed. Telecommunications Consortium, Inc. v. FCC, 518 U.S. 727, 116 S. Ct. 2374, 135 L. Ed.2d 888 (1996).

The Government argues that the statute is no more vague than the obscenity standard this Court established in Miller v. California, 413 U.S. 15, 93 S. Ct. 2607, 37 L. Ed.2d 419 (1973). But that is not so. In *Miller*, this Court reviewed a criminal conviction against a commercial vendor who mailed brochures containing pictures of sexually explicit activities to individuals who had not requested such materials. *Id.*, at 18, 93 S. Ct., at 2611-2612. Having struggled for some time to establish a definition of obscenity, we set forth in *Miller* the test for obscenity that controls to this day:

(a) whether the average person, applying contemporary community standards would find that the work, taken as a whole, appeals to the prurient interest; (b) whether the work depicts or describes, in a patently offensive way, sexual conduct specifically defined by the applicable state law; and (c) whether the work, taken as a whole, lacks serious literary, artistic, political, or scientific value. *Id.*, at 24, 93 S. Ct., at 2615 (internal quotation marks and citations omitted).

Because the CDA's "patently offensive" standard (and, we assume arguendo, its synonymous "indecent" standard) is one part of the three-prong *Miller* test, the Government reasons, it cannot be unconstitutionally vague.

The Government's assertion is incorrect as a matter of fact. The second prong of the *Miller* test—the purportedly analogous standard—contains a critical requirement that is omitted from the CDA: that the proscribed material be "specifically defined by the applicable state law." This requirement reduces the vagueness inherent in the open-ended term "patently offensive" as used in the CDA. Moreover, the *Miller* definition is limited to "sexual conduct," whereas the CDA extends also to include (1) "excretory activities" as well as (2) "organs" of both a sexual and excretory nature.

The Government's reasoning is also flawed. Just because a definition including three limitations is not vague, it does not follow that one of those limitations, standing by itself, is not vague. Each of *Miller*'s additional two prongs—(1) that, taken as a whole, the material appeal to the "prurient" interest, and (2) that it "lac[k] serious literary, artistic, political, or scientific value"—critically limits the uncertain sweep of the obscenity definition. The second requirement is particularly important because, unlike the "patently offensive" and "prurient interest" criteria, it is not judged by contemporary community standards. See Pope v. Illinois, 481 U.S. 497, 500, 107 S. Ct. 1918, 1920-1921, 95 L. Ed.2d 439 (1987). This "societal value" requirement, absent in the CDA, allows appellate courts to impose some limitations and regularity on the definition by setting, as a matter of law, a national floor for socially redeeming value. The Government's contention that courts will be able to give such legal limitations to the CDA's standards is belied by *Miller*'s own rationale for having juries determine whether material is "patently offensive" according to community standards: that such questions are essentially ones of fact.

In contrast to *Miller* and our other previous cases, the CDA thus presents a greater threat of censoring speech that, in fact, falls outside the statute's scope. Given the vague contours of the coverage of the statute, it unquestionably silences some speakers whose messages would be entitled to constitutional protection. That danger provides further reason for insisting that the statute not be overly broad. The CDA's burden on protected speech cannot be justified if it could be avoided by a more carefully drafted statute.

VII

We are persuaded that the CDA lacks the precision that the First Amendment requires when a statute regulates the content of speech. In order to deny minors access to potentially harmful speech, the CDA effectively suppresses a large amount of speech that adults have a constitutional right to receive and to address to one another. That burden on adult speech is unacceptable if less restrictive alternatives would be at least as effective in achieving the legitimate purpose that the statute was enacted to serve.

In evaluating the free speech rights of adults, we have made it perfectly clear that "[s]exual expression which is indecent but not obscene is protected by the First Amendment." *Sable*, 492 U.S., at 126, 109 S. Ct., at 2836. See also Carey v. Population Services Int'l, 431 U.S. 678, 701, 97 S. Ct. 2010, 2024, 52 L. Ed.2d 675 (1977) ("[W]here obscenity is not involved, we have consistently held that the fact that protected speech may be offensive to some does not justify its suppression"). Indeed, *Pacifica* itself admonished that "the fact that society may find speech offensive is not a sufficient reason for suppressing it." 438 U.S., at 745, 98 S. Ct., at 3038.

It is true that we have repeatedly recognized the governmental interest in protecting children from harmful materials. See *Ginsberg*, 390 U.S., at 639, 88 S. Ct., at 1280; *Pacifica*, 438 U.S., at 749, 98 S. Ct., at 3040. But that interest does not justify an unnecessarily broad suppression of speech addressed to adults. As we have explained, the Government may not "reduc[e] the adult population . . . to . . . only what is fit for children." *Denver*, 518 U.S., at —, 116 S. Ct., at 2393 (internal quotation marks omitted) (quoting *Sable*, 492 U.S., at 128, 109 S. Ct., at 2837-2838). "[R]egardless of the strength of the government's interest" in protecting children, "[t]he level of discourse reaching a mailbox simply cannot be limited to that which would be suitable for a sandbox." Bolger v. Youngs Drug Products Corp., 463 U.S. 60, 74-75, 103 S. Ct. 2875, 2884-2885, 77 L. Ed.2d 469 (1983).

The District Court was correct to conclude that the CDA effectively resembles the ban on "dial-a-porn" invalidated in *Sable*. 929 F. Supp., at 854. In *Sable*, 492 U.S., at 129, 109 S. Ct., at 2838, this Court rejected the argument that we should defer to the congressional judgment that nothing less than a total ban would be effective in preventing enterprising youngsters from gaining access to indecent communications. *Sable* thus made clear that the mere fact that a statutory regulation of speech was enacted for the important purpose of protecting children from exposure to sexually explicit material does not foreclose inquiry into its validity. As we pointed out last Term, that inquiry embodies an "over-arching commitment" to make sure that Congress has designed its statute to accomplish its purpose "without imposing an unnecessarily great restriction on speech." *Denver*, 518 U.S., at —, 116 S. Ct., at 2385.

In arguing that the CDA does not so diminish adult communication, the Government relies on the incorrect factual premise that prohibiting a transmission whenever it is known that one of its recipients is a minor would not interfere with adult-to-adult communication. The findings of the District Court make clear that this premise is untenable. Given the size of the potential audience for most messages, in the absence of a viable age verification process, the sender must be charged with knowing that one or more minors will likely view it. Knowledge that, for instance, one or more members of a 100-person chat group will be minor—and therefore that it would be a crime to send the group an indecent message—would surely burden communication among adults.

The District Court found that at the time of trial existing technology did not include any effective method for a sender to prevent minors from obtaining access to its communications on the Internet without also denying access to adults. The Court found no effective way to determine the age of a user who is accessing material through e-mail, mail exploders, newsgroups, or chat rooms. 929 F. Supp., at

845 (findings 90-94). As a practical matter, the Court also found that it would be prohibitively expensive for noncommercial—as well as some commercial—speakers who have Web sites to verify that their users are adults. *Id.*, at 845-848 (findings 95-116). These limitations must inevitably curtail a significant amount of adult communication on the Internet. By contrast, the District Court found that "[d]espite its limitations, currently available user-based software suggests that a reasonably effective method by which parents can prevent their children from accessing sexually explicit and other material which parents may believe is inappropriate for their children will soon be widely available." *Id.*, at 842 (finding 73).

The breadth of the CDA's coverage is wholly unprecedented. Unlike the regulations upheld in *Ginsberg* and *Pacifica*, the scope of the CDA is not limited to commercial speech or commercial entities. Its open-ended prohibitions embrace all nonprofit entities and individuals posting indecent messages or displaying them on their own computers in the presence of minors. The general, undefined terms "indecent" and "patently offensive" cover large amounts of nonpornographic material with serious educational or other value. Moreover, the "community standards" criterion as applied to the Internet means that any communication available to a nation-wide audience will be judged by the standards of the community most likely to be offended by the message. The regulated subject matter includes any of the seven "dirty words" used in the *Pacifica* monologue, the use of which the Government's expert acknowledged could constitute a felony. See Olsen Test., Tr. Vol. V, 53:16-54:10. It may also extend to discussions about prison rape or safe sexual practices, artistic images that include nude subjects, and arguably the card catalogue of the Carnegie Library.

For the purposes of our decision, we need neither accept nor reject the Government's submission that the First Amendment does not forbid a blanket prohibition on all "indecent" and "patently offensive" messages communicated to a 17-year-old—no matter how much value the message may contain and regardless of parental approval. It is at least clear that the strength of the Government's interest in protecting minors is not equally strong throughout the coverage of this broad statute. Under the CDA, a parent allowing her 17-year-old to use the family computer to obtain information on the Internet that she, in her parental judgment, deems appropriate could face a lengthy prison term. See 47 U.S.C.A. §223(a)(2) (Supp. 1997). Similarly, a parent who sent his 17-year-old college freshman information on birth control via e-mail could be incarcerated even though neither he, his child, nor anyone in their home community, found the material "indecent" or "patently offensive," if the college town's community thought otherwise.

The breadth of this content-based restriction of speech imposes an especially heavy burden on the Government to explain why a less restrictive provision would not be as effective as the CDA. It has not done so. The arguments in this Court have referred to possible alternatives such as requiring that indecent material be "tagged" in a way that facilitates parental control of material coming into their homes, making exceptions for messages with artistic or educational value, providing some tolerance for parental choice, and regulating some portions of the Internet—such as commercial web sites—differently than others, such as chat rooms. Particularly in the light of the absence of any detailed findings by the Congress, or even hearings addressing the special problems of the CDA, we are persuaded that the CDA is not narrowly tailored if that requirement has any meaning at all.

VIII

In an attempt to curtail the CDA's facial overbreadth, the Government advances three additional arguments for sustaining the Act's affirmative prohibitions: (1) that the CDA is constitutional because it leaves open ample "alternative channels" of communication; (2) that the plain meaning of the Act's "knowledge" and "specific person" requirement significantly restricts its permissible applications; and (3) that the Act's prohibitions are "almost always" limited to material lacking redeeming social value.

The Government first contends that, even though the CDA effectively censors discourse on many of the Internet's modalities—such as chat groups, newsgroups, and mail exploders—it is nonetheless constitutional because it provides a "reasonable opportunity" for speakers to engage in the restricted speech on the World Wide Web. Brief for Appellants 39. This argument is unpersuasive because the CDA regulates speech on the basis of its content. A "time, place, and manner" analysis is therefore inapplicable. See Consolidated Edison Co. of N.Y. v. Public Serv. Comm'n of N.Y., 447 U.S. 530, 536, 100 S. Ct. 2326, 2332-2333, 65 L. Ed.2d 319 (1980). It is thus immaterial whether such speech would be feasible on the Web (which, as the Government's own expert acknowledged, would cost up to $10,000 if the speaker's interests were not accommodated by an existing Web site, not including costs for database management and age verification). The Government's position is equivalent to arguing that a statute could ban leaflets on certain subjects as long as individuals are free to publish books. In invalidating a number of laws that banned leafletting on the streets regardless of their content—we explained that "one is not to have the exercise of his liberty of expression in appropriate places abridged on the plea that it may be exercised in some other place." Schneider v. State of N.J. (Town of Irvington), 308 U.S. 147, 163, 60 S. Ct. 146, 151-152, 84 L. Ed. 155 (1939).

The Government also asserts that the "knowledge" requirement of both §§223(a) and (d), especially when coupled with the "specific child" element found in §223(d), saves the CDA from overbreadth. Because both sections prohibit the dissemination of indecent messages only to persons known to be under 18, the Government argues, it does not require transmitters to "refrain from communicating indecent material to adults; they need only refrain from disseminating such materials to persons they know to be under 18." Brief for Appellants 24.

This argument ignores the fact that most Internet fora—including chat rooms, newsgroups, mail exploders, and the Web—are open to all comers. The Government's assertion that the knowledge requirement somehow protects the communications of adults is therefore untenable. Even the strongest reading of the "specific person" requirement of §223(d) cannot save the statute. It would confer broad powers of censorship, in the form of a "heckler's veto," upon any opponent of indecent speech who might simply log on and inform the would-be discoursers that his 17-year-old child—a "specific person . . . under 18 years of age," 47 U.S.C.A. §223(d)(1)(A) (Supp. 1997)—would be present.

Finally, we find no textual support for the Government's submission that material having scientific, educational, or other redeeming social value will necessarily fall outside the CDA's "patently offensive" and "indecent" prohibitions. See also n. 37, *supra*. . . .

Justice O'CONNOR, with whom the Chief Justice joins, concurring in the judgment in part and dissenting in part.

I write separately to explain why I view the Communications Decency Act of 1996 (CDA) as little more than an attempt by Congress to create "adult zones" on the Internet. Our precedent indicates that the creation of such zones can be constitutionally sound. Despite the soundness of its purpose, however, portions of the CDA are unconstitutional because they stray from the blueprint our prior cases have developed for constructing a "zoning law" that passes constitutional muster. . . .

I

Our cases make clear that a "zoning" law is valid only if adults are still able to obtain the regulated speech. If they cannot, the law does more than simply keep children away from speech they have no right to obtain—it interferes with the rights of adults to obtain constitutionally protected speech and effectively "reduce[s] the adult population . . . to reading only what is fit for children." Butler v. Michigan, 352 U.S. 380, 383, 77 S. Ct. 524, 526, 1 L. Ed.2d 412 (1957). The First Amendment does not tolerate such interference. See *id.*, at 383, 77 S. Ct., at 526 (striking down a Michigan criminal law banning sale of books—to minors or adults—that contained words or pictures that "'tende[d] to . . . corrup[t] the morals of youth'"); *Sable Communications*, supra (invalidating federal law that made it a crime to transmit indecent, but nonobscene, commercial telephone messages to minors and adults); Bolger v. Youngs Drug Products Corp., 463 U.S. 60, 74, 103 S. Ct. 2875, 2884, 77 L. Ed.2d 469 (1983) (striking down a federal law prohibiting the mailing of unsolicited advertisements for contraceptives). If the law does not unduly restrict adults' access to constitutionally protected speech, however, it may be valid. In Ginsberg v. New York, 390 U.S. 629, 634, 88 S. Ct. 1274, 1277-1278, 20 L. Ed.2d 195 (1968), for example, the Court sustained a New York law that barred store owners from selling pornographic magazines to minors in part because adults could still buy those magazines.

The Court in *Ginsberg* concluded that the New York law created a constitutionally adequate adult zone simply because, on its face, it denied access only to minors. The Court did not question—and therefore necessarily assumed—that an adult zone, once created, would succeed in preserving adults' access while denying minors' access to the regulated speech. Before today, there was no reason to question this assumption, for the Court has previously only considered laws that operated in the physical world, a world that with two characteristics that make it possible to create "adult zones": geography and identity. See Lessig, Reading the Constitution in Cyberspace, 45 Emory L.J. 869, 886 (1996). A minor can see an adult dance show only if he enters an establishment that provides such entertainment. And should he attempt to do so, the minor will not be able to conceal completely his identity (or, consequently, his age). Thus, the twin characteristics of geography and identity enable the establishment's proprietor to prevent children from entering the establishment, but to let adults inside.

The electronic world is fundamentally different. Because it is no more than the interconnection of electronic pathways, cyberspace allows speakers and listeners to mask their identities. Cyberspace undeniably reflects some form of geography; chat rooms and Web sites, for example, exist at fixed "locations" on the Internet. Since users can transmit and receive messages on the Internet without revealing anything about their identities or ages, see Lessig, supra, at 901, however, it is not currently possible to exclude persons from accessing certain messages on the basis of their identity.

Cyberspace differs from the physical world in another basic way: Cyberspace is malleable. Thus, it is possible to construct barriers in cyberspace and use them to screen for identity, making cyberspace more like the physical world and, consequently, more amenable to zoning laws. This transformation of cyberspace is already underway. Lessig, *supra,* at 888-889. *Id.,* at 887 (cyberspace "is moving . . . from a relatively unzoned place to a universe that is extraordinarily well zoned"). Internet speakers (users who post material on the Internet) have begun to zone cyberspace itself through the use of "gateway" technology. Such technology requires Internet users to enter information about themselves—perhaps an adult identification number or a credit card number—before they can access certain areas of cyberspace, 929 F. Supp. 824, 845 (E.D.Pa. 1996), much like a bouncer checks a person's driver's license before admitting him to a nightclub. Internet users who access information have not attempted to zone cyberspace itself, but have tried to limit their own power to access information in cyberspace, much as a parent controls what her children watch on television by installing a lock box. This user-based zoning is accomplished through the use of screening software (such as Cyber Patrol or SurfWatch) or browsers with screening capabilities, both of which search addresses and text for keywords that are associated with "adult" sites and, if the user wishes, blocks access to such sites. *Id.,* at 839-842. The Platform for Internet Content Selection (PICS) project is designed to facilitate user-based zoning by encouraging Internet speakers to rate the content of their speech using codes recognized by all screening programs. *Id.,* at 838-839.

Despite this progress, the transformation of cyberspace is not complete. Although gateway technology has been available on the World Wide Web for some time now, *id.,* at 845; Shea v. Reno, 930 F. Supp. 916, 933-934 (S.D.N.Y. 1996), it is not available to all Web speakers, 929 F. Supp., at 845-846, and is just now becoming technologically feasible for chat rooms and USENET newsgroups, Brief for Federal Parties 37-38. Gateway technology is not ubiquitous in cyberspace, and because without it "there is no means of age verification," cyberspace still remains largely unzoned—and unzoneable. 929 F. Supp., at 846; *Shea, supra,* at 934. User-based zoning is also in its infancy. For it to be effective, (i) an agreed-upon code (or "tag") would have to exist; (ii) screening software or browsers with screening capabilities would have to be able to recognize the "tag"; and (iii) those programs would have to be widely available—and widely used—by Internet users. At present, none of these conditions is true. Screening software "is not in wide use today" and "only a handful of browsers have screening capabilities." *Shea, supra,* at 945-946. There is, moreover, no agreed-upon "tag" for those programs to recognize. 929 F. Supp., at 848; *Shea, supra,* at 945.

Although the prospects for the eventual zoning of the Internet appear promising, I agree with the Court that we must evaluate the constitutionality of the CDA as it applies to the Internet as it exists today. *Ante,* at 2349. Given the present state of cyberspace, I agree with the Court that the "display" provision cannot pass muster. Until gateway technology is available throughout cyberspace, and it is not in

1997, a speaker cannot be reasonably assured that the speech he displays will reach only adults because it is impossible to confine speech to an "adult zone." Thus, the only way for a speaker to avoid liability under the CDA is to refrain completely from using indecent speech. But this forced silence impinges on the First Amendment right of adults to make and obtain this speech and, for all intents and purposes, "reduce[s] the adult population [on the Internet] to reading only what is fit for children." *Butler*, 352 U.S., at 383, 77 S. Ct., at 526. As a result, the "display" provision cannot withstand scrutiny. Accord, *Sable Communications*, 492 U.S., at 126-131, 109 S. Ct., at 2836-2839; Bolger v. Youngs Drug Products Corp., 463 U.S., at 73-75, 103 S. Ct., at 2883-2885.

The "indecency transmission" and "specific person" provisions present a closer issue, for they are not unconstitutional in all of their applications. As discussed above, the "indecency transmission" provision makes it a crime to transmit knowingly an indecent message to a person the sender knows is under 18 years of age. 47 U.S.C.A. §223(a)(1)(B) (May 1996 Supp.). The "specific person" provision proscribes the same conduct, although it does not as explicitly require the sender to know that the intended recipient of his indecent message is a minor. §223(d)(1)(A). Appellant urges the Court to construe the provision to impose such a knowledge requirement, see Brief for Federal Parties 25-27, and I would do so. See Edward J. DeBartolo Corp. v. Florida Gulf Coast Building & Constr. Trades Council, 485 U.S. 568, 575, 108 S. Ct. 1392, 1397, 99 L. Ed.2d 645 (1988) ("[W]here an otherwise acceptable construction of a statute would raise serious constitutional problems, the Court will construe the statute to avoid such problems unless such construction is plainly contrary to the intent of Congress").

So construed, both provisions are constitutional as applied to a conversation involving only an adult and one or more minors—e.g., when an adult speaker sends an e-mail knowing the addressee is a minor, or when an adult and minor converse by themselves or with other minors in a chat room. In this context, these provisions are no different from the law we sustained in *Ginsberg*. Restricting what the adult may say to the minors in no way restricts the adult's ability to communicate with other adults. He is not prevented from speaking indecently to other adults in a chat room (because there are no other adults participating in the conversation) and he remains free to send indecent e-mails to other adults. The relevant universe contains only one adult, and the adult in that universe has the power to refrain from using indecent speech and consequently to keep all such speech within the room in an "adult" zone.

The analogy to *Ginsberg* breaks down, however, when more than one adult is a party to the conversation. If a minor enters a chat room otherwise occupied by adults, the CDA effectively requires the adults in the room to stop using indecent speech. If they did not, they could be prosecuted under the "indecency transmission" and "specific person" provisions for any indecent statements they make to the group, since they would be transmitting an indecent message to specific persons, one of whom is a minor. Accord, ante, at 2347. The CDA is therefore akin to a law that makes it a crime for a bookstore owner to sell pornographic magazines to anyone once a minor enters his store. Even assuming such a law might be constitutional in the physical world as a reasonable alternative to excluding minors completely from the store, the absence of any means of excluding minors from chat rooms in cyberspace restricts the rights of adults to engage in indecent speech in those rooms. The "indecency transmission" and "specific person" provisions share this defect.

But these two provisions do not infringe on adults' speech in all situations. And as discussed below, I do not find that the provisions are overbroad in the sense that they restrict minors' access to a substantial amount of speech that minors have the right to read and view. Accordingly, the CDA can be applied constitutionally in some situations. Normally, this fact would require the Court to reject a direct facial challenge. United States v. Salerno, 481 U.S. 739, 745, 107 S. Ct. 2095, 2100, 95 L. Ed.2d 697 (1987) ("A facial challenge to a legislative Act [succeeds only if] the challenger . . . establish[es] that no set of circumstances exists under which the Act would be valid"). Appellees' claim arises under the First Amendment, however, and they argue that the CDA is facially invalid because it is "substantially overbroad"— that is, it "sweeps too broadly . . . [and] penaliz[es] a substantial amount of speech that is constitutionally protected," Forsyth County v. Nationalist Movement, 505 U.S. 123, 130, 112 S. Ct. 2395, 2401, 120 L. Ed.2d 101 (1992). See Brief for Appellees American Library Association et al. 48; Brief for Appellees American Civil Liberties Union et al. 39-41. I agree with the Court that the provisions are overbroad in that they cover any and all communications between adults and minors, regardless of how many adults might be part of the audience to the communication.

This conclusion does not end the matter, however. Where, as here, "the parties challenging the statute are those who desire to engage in protected speech that the overbroad statute purports to punish . . . [t]he statute may forthwith be declared invalid to the extent that it reaches too far, but otherwise left intact." Brockett v. Spokane Arcades, Inc., 472 U.S. 491, 504, 105 S. Ct. 2794, 2802, 86 L. Ed.2d 394 (1985). There is no question that Congress intended to prohibit certain communications between one adult and one or more minors. See 47 U.S.C.A. §223(a)(1)(B) (May 1996 Supp.) (punishing "[w]hoever . . . initiates the transmission of [any indecent communication] knowingly that the recipient of the communication is under 18 years of age"); §223(d)(1)(A) (punishing "[w]hoever . . . send[s] to a specific person or persons under 18 years of age [a patently offensive message]"). There is also no question that Congress would have enacted a narrower version of these provisions had it known a broader version would be declared unconstitutional. 47 U.S.C. §608 ("If . . . the application [of any provision of the CDA] to any person or circumstance is held invalid, . . . the application of such provision to other persons or circumstances shall not be affected thereby"). I would therefore sustain the "indecency transmission" and "specific person" provisions to the extent they apply to the transmission of Internet communications where the party initiating the communication knows that all of the recipients are minors.

II

Whether the CDA substantially interferes with the First Amendment rights of minors, and thereby runs afoul of the second characteristic of valid zoning laws, presents a closer question. In *Ginsberg*, the New York law we sustained prohibited the sale to minors of magazines that were "harmful to minors." Under that law, a magazine was "harmful to minors" only if it was obscene as to minors. 390 U.S., at 632-633, 88 S. Ct., at 1276-1277. Noting that obscene speech is not protected by the First Amendment, Roth v. United States, 354 U.S. 476, 485, 77 S. Ct. 1304, 1309, 1 L. Ed.2d 1498 (1957), and that New York was constitutionally free to adjust the definition of obscenity for minors, 390 U.S., at 638, 88 S. Ct., at 1279-1280, the Court concluded that the law did not "invad[e] the area of freedom of expression constitutionally secured to minors." *Id.*, at 637, 88 S. Ct., at 1279. New York therefore did not infringe upon the First Amendment rights of minors. Cf. Erznoznik v. Jacksonville, 422 U.S. 205, 213, 95 S. Ct. 2268, 2274-2275, 45 L. Ed.2d 125 (1975) (striking down city ordinance that banned nudity that was not "obscene even as to minors").

The Court neither "accept[s] nor reject[s]" the argument that the CDA is facially overbroad because it substantially interferes with the First Amendment rights of minors. *Ante*, at 2348. I would reject it. Ginsberg established that minors may constitutionally be denied access to material that is obscene as to minors. As *Ginsberg* explained, material is obscene as to minors if it (i) is "patently offensive to prevailing standards in the adult community as a whole with respect to what is suitable . . . for minors"; (ii) appeals to the prurient interest of minors; and (iii) is "utterly without redeeming social importance for minors." 390 U.S., at 633, 88 S. Ct., at 1276. Because the CDA denies minors the right to obtain material that is "patently offensive"—even if it has some redeeming value for minors and even if it does not appeal to their prurient interests—Congress' rejection of the *Ginsberg* "harmful to minors" standard means that the CDA could ban some speech that is "indecent" (i.e., "patently offensive") but that is not obscene as to minors.

I do not deny this possibility, but to prevail in a facial challenge, it is not enough for a plaintiff to show "some" overbreadth. Our cases require a proof of "real" and "substantial" overbreadth, Broadrick v. Oklahoma, 413 U.S. 601, 615, 93 S. Ct. 2908, 2917-2918, 37 L. Ed.2d 830 (1973), and appellees have not carried their burden in this case. In my view, the universe of speech constitutionally protected as to minors but banned by the CDA—i.e., the universe of material that is "patently offensive," but which nonetheless has some redeeming value for minors or does not appeal to their prurient interest—is a very small one. Appellees cite no examples of speech falling within this universe and do not attempt to explain why that universe is substantial "in relation to the statute's plainly legitimate sweep." *Ibid.* That the CDA might deny minors the right to obtain material that has some "value," see *ante*, at 2347-2348, is largely beside the point. While discussions about prison rape or nude art, see *ibid.*, may have some redeeming education value for adults, they do not necessarily have any such value for minors, and under *Ginsberg*, minors only have a First Amendment right to obtain patently offensive material that has "redeeming social importance for minors," 390 U.S., at 633, 88 S. Ct., at 1276. There is also no evidence in the record to support the contention that "many [e]-mail transmissions from an adult to a minor are conversations between family members," *ante*, at 2341, n. 32, and no support for the legal proposition that such speech is absolutely immune from regulation. Accordingly, in my view, the CDA does not burden a substantial amount of minors' constitutionally protected speech.

Thus, the constitutionality of the CDA as a zoning law hinges on the extent to which it substantially interferes with the First Amendment rights of adults. Because the rights of adults are infringed only by the "display" provision and by the "indecency transmission" and "specific person" provisions as applied to communications involving more than one adult, I would invalidate the CDA only to that extent. Insofar as the "indecency transmission" and "specific person" provisions prohibit the use of indecent speech in communications between an adult and one or more minors, however, they can and should be sustained. The Court reaches a contrary conclusion, and from that holding that I respectfully dissent.

COMMENTS AND QUESTIONS

1. Would it be constitutional for Congress or state legislatures to enact a law that would prohibit minors from engaging in "indecent" speech with other minors? How would the authors of the majority and dissenting opinions in *Reno* answer that question?

2. In the aftermath of the *Reno* decision, Congress enacted the Child Online Protection Act (COPA). Section 1403(a) of this act, which is codified at 47 U.S.C. §231, provides that

[w]hoever knowingly and with knowledge of the character of the material, in interstate or foreign commerce by means of the World Wide Web, makes any communication for commercial purposes that is available to any minor and that includes any material that is harmful to minors shall be fined not more than $50,000, imprisoned not more than 6 months, or both.

COPA differs from the CDA in a number of respects. For one thing, COPA contains congressional findings about the need to protect children from harmful materials on the Internet. Second, it defines the term "harmful to minors" in a more precise way, as material that is obscene or that

(A) the average person, applying contemporary community standards, would find, taking the material as a whole and with respect to minors, is designed to appeal to, or is designed to pander to, the prurient interest;

(B) depicts, describes, or represents, in a manner patently offensive with respect to minors, an actual or simulated sexual act or sexual contact, an actual or simulated normal or perverted sexual act, or a lewd exhibition of the genitals or post-pubescent female breast; and

(C) taken as a whole, lacks serious literary, artistic, political, or scientific value for minors.

Third, COPA applies only to communications "for commercial purposes," a term that the statute also defines with some precision, apparently in the hope that this too might increase the likelihood that COPA will be adjudged constitutional.

The American Civil Liberties Union has challenged the constitutionality of COPA, arguing that even though this statute is narrower than the CDA provisions struck down in *Reno*, it nonetheless is not tailored narrowly enough to satisfy First Amendment standards, places unwarranted burdens on free speech, and will substantially chill protected expression. In ACLU v. Reno, 31 F. Supp. 2d 473 (E.D. Pa. 1999), the court issued a preliminary injunction to prohibit enforcement of COPA because of the likely success of the ACLU's First Amendment challenge. This decision is on appeal, however.

≡≡ *Ashcroft v. American Civil Liberties Union*
≡≡ United States Supreme Court
≡≡ *122 S. Ct. 1700 (2002)*

JUSTICE THOMAS: . . .

This case presents the narrow question whether the Child Online Protection Act's (COPA or Act) use of "community standards" to identify "material that is harmful to minors" violates the First Amendment. We hold that this aspect of COPA does not render the statute facially unconstitutional.

I

"The Internet . . . offer[s] a forum for a true diversity of political discourse, unique opportunities for cultural development, and myriad avenues for intellectual activity." 47 U.S.C. §230(a)(3) (1994 ed., Supp. V). While "surfing" the World Wide Web, the primary method of remote information retrieval on the Internet today, individuals can access material about topics ranging from aardvarks to Zoroastrianism. One can use the Web to read thousands of newspapers published around the globe, purchase tickets for a matinee at the neighborhood movie theater, or follow the progress of any Major League Baseball team on a pitch-by-pitch basis.

The Web also contains a wide array of sexually explicit material, including hardcore pornography. See, e.g., American Civil Liberties Union v. Reno, 31 F. Supp.2d 473, 484 (ED Pa. 1999). In 1998, for instance, there were approximately 28,000 adult sites promoting pornography on the Web. See H. R. Rep. No. 105-775, p. 7 (1998). Because "navigating the Web is relatively straightforward," Reno v. American Civil Liberties Union, 521 U.S. 844, 852 (1997), and access to the Internet is widely available in homes, schools, and libraries across the country, children may discover this pornographic material either by deliberately accessing pornographic Web sites or by stumbling upon them. See 31 F. Supp.2d at 476 ("A child with minimal knowledge of a computer, the ability to operate a browser, and the skill to type a few simple words may be able to access sexual images and content over the World Wide Web").

Congress first attempted to protect children from exposure to pornographic material on the Internet by enacting the Communications Decency Act of 1996 (CDA), 110 Stat:133. The CDA prohibited the knowing transmission over the Internet of obscene or indecent messages to any recipient under 18 years of age. See 47 U.S.C. §223(a). It also forbade any individual from knowingly sending over or displaying on the Internet certain "patently offensive" material in a manner available to persons under 18 years of age. See §223(d). The prohibition specifically extended to "any comment, request, suggestion, proposal, image, or other communication that, in context, depicted or described, in terms patently offensive as measured by contemporary community standards, sexual or excretory activities or organs." §223(d)(1). . . .

After our decision in Reno v. American Civil Liberties Union, Congress explored other avenues for restricting minors' access to pornographic material on the Internet. In particular, Congress passed and the President signed into law the Child Online Protection Act, 112 Stat. 2681-736 (codified in 47 U.S.C. §231 (1994 ed., Supp. V)). COPA prohibits any person from "knowingly and with knowledge of the character of the material, in interstate or foreign commerce by means of the World Wide Web, making any communication for commercial purposes that is available to any minor and that includes any material that is harmful to minors." 47 U.S.C. §231(a)(1).

Apparently responding to our objections to the breadth of the CDA's coverage, Congress limited the scope of COPA's coverage in at least three ways. First, while the CDA applied to communications over the Internet as a whole, including, for example, e-mail messages, COPA applies only to material displayed on the World Wide Web. Second, unlike the CDA, COPA covers only communications made "for commercial purposes." *Ibid.* And third, while the CDA prohibited "indecent" and "patently offensive" communications, COPA restricts only the narrower category of "material that is harmful to minors." *Ibid.*

Drawing on the three-part test for obscenity set forth in Miller v. California, 413 U.S. 15, 37 L. Ed. 2d 419, 93 S. Ct. 2607 (1973), COPA defines "material that is harmful to minors" as

> any communication, picture, image, graphic image file, article, recording, writing, or other matter of any kind that is obscene or that—
> (A) the average person, applying contemporary community standards, would find, taking the material as a whole and with respect to minors, is designed to appeal to, or is designed to pander to, the prurient interest;
> (B) depicts, describes, or represents, in a manner patently offensive with respect to minors, an actual or simulated sexual act or sexual contact, an actual or simulated normal or perverted sexual act, or a lewd exhibition of the genitals or post-pubescent female breast; and
> (C) taken as a whole, lacks serious literary, artistic, political, or scientific value for minors. 47 U.S.C. §231(e)(6).

Like the CDA, COPA also provides affirmative defenses to those subject to prosecution under the statute. An individual may qualify for a defense if he, "in good faith, has restricted access by minors to material that is harmful to minors (A) by requiring the use of a credit card, debit account, adult access code, or adult personal identification number; (B) by accepting a digital certificate that verifies age; or (C) by any other reasonable measures that are feasible under available technology." §231(c)(1). Persons violating COPA are subject to both civil and criminal sanctions. A civil penalty of up to $50,000 may be imposed for each violation of the statute. Criminal penalties consist of up to six months in prison and/or a maximum fine of $50,000. An additional fine of $50,000 may be imposed for any intentional violation of the statute. §231(a).

One month before COPA was scheduled to go into effect, respondents filed a lawsuit challenging the constitutionality of the statute in the United States District Court for the Eastern District of Pennsylvania. Respondents are a diverse group of organizations, most of which maintain their own Web sites. While the vast majority of content on their Web sites is available for free, respondents all derive income from their sites. Some, for example, sell advertising that is displayed on their Web sites, while others either sell goods directly over their sites or charge artists for the privilege of posting material. 31 F. Supp.2d at 487. All respondents either post or have members that post sexually oriented material on the Web. *Id.*, at 480. Respondents' Web sites contain "resources on obstetrics, gynecology, and sexual health; visual art and poetry; resources designed for gays and lesbians; information about books and stock photographic images offered for sale; and online magazines." *Id.*, at 484.

In their complaint, respondents alleged that, although they believed that the material on their Web sites was valuable for adults, they feared that they would be prosecuted under COPA because some of that material "could be construed as 'harmful to minors' in some communities. Respondents' facial challenge claimed, *inter alia,* that COPA violated adults' rights under the First and Fifth Amendments because it (1) "created an effective ban on constitutionally protected speech by and to adults"; (2) "[was] not the least restrictive means of accomplishing any compelling governmental purpose"; and (3) "[was] substantially overbroad." *Id.*, at 100-101.

The District Court granted respondents' motion for a preliminary injunction, barring the Government from enforcing the Act until the merits of respondents' claims could be adjudicated. 31 F. Supp.2d at 499. Focusing on respondents' claim that COPA abridged the free speech rights of adults, the District Court concluded that respondents had established a likelihood of success on the merits. *Id.*, at 498. The District Court reasoned that because COPA constitutes content-based regulation of sexual expression protected by the First Amendment, the statute, under this Court's precedents, was "presumptively invalid" and "subject to strict scrutiny." *Id.*, at 493. The District Court then held that respondents were likely to establish at trial that COPA could not withstand such scrutiny because, among other reasons, it was not apparent that COPA was the least restrictive means of preventing minors from accessing "harmful to minors" material. *Id.*, at 497.

The Attorney General of the United States appealed the District Court's ruling. American Civil Liberties Union v. Reno, 217 F.3d 162 (C.A.3 2000). The United States Court of Appeals for the Third Circuit affirmed. Rather than reviewing the District Court's "holding that COPA was not likely to succeed in surviving strict scrutiny analysis," the Court of Appeals based its decision entirely on a ground that was not relied upon below and that was "virtually ignored by the parties and the amicus in their respective briefs." *Id.*, at 173-174. The Court of Appeals concluded that COPA's use of "contemporary community standards" to identify material that is harmful to minors rendered the statute substantially overbroad. Because "Web publishers are without any means to limit access to their sites based on the geographic location of particular Internet users," the Court of Appeals reasoned that COPA would require "any material that might be deemed harmful by the most puritan of communities in any state" to be placed behind an age or credit card verification system. *Id.*, at 175. Hypothesizing that this step would require Web publishers to shield "vast amounts of material," *ibid.*, the Court of Appeals was "persuaded that this aspect of COPA, without reference to its other provisions, must lead inexorably to a holding of a likelihood of unconstitutionality of the entire COPA statute." *Id.*, at 174.

We granted the Attorney General's petition for certiorari, 532 U.S. 1037 (2001), to review the Court of Appeals' determination that COPA likely violates the First Amendment because it relies, in part, on community standards to identify material that is harmful to minors, and now vacate the Court of Appeals' judgment.

II . . .

Ending over a decade of turmoil, this Court in *Miller* set forth the governing three-part test for assessing whether material is obscene and thus unprotected by the First Amendment: "(a) Whether 'the average person, *applying contemporary community standards*' would find that the work, taken as a whole, appeals to the prurient interest; (b) whether the work depicts or describes, in a patently offensive way, sexual conduct specifically defined by the applicable state law; and (c) whether the work, taken as a whole, lacks serious literary, artistic, political, or scientific value." *Id.*, at 24 (internal citations omitted; emphasis added). . . .

III

The Court of Appeals [] concluded that this Court's prior community standards jurisprudence "has no applicability to the Internet and the Web" because "Web publishers are currently without the ability to control the geographic scope of the recipients of their communications." 217 F.3d at 180. We therefore must decide whether this technological limitation renders COPA's reliance on community standards constitutionally infirm.

A.

In addressing this question, the parties first dispute the nature of the community standards that jurors will be instructed to apply when assessing, in prosecutions under COPA, whether works appeal to the prurient interest of minors and are patently offensive with respect to minors. Respondents contend that jurors will evaluate material using "local community standards," Brief for Respondents 40, while petitioner maintains that jurors will not consider the community standards of any particular geographic area, but rather will be "instructed to consider the standards of the adult community as a whole, without geographic specification."

In the context of this case, which involves a facial challenge to a statute that has never been enforced, we do not think it prudent to engage in speculation as to whether certain hypothetical jury instructions would or would not be consistent with COPA, and deciding this case does not require us to do so. It is sufficient to note that community standards need not be defined by reference to a precise geographic area. See Jenkins v. Georgia, 418 U.S. 153, 157, 41 L. Ed. 2d 642, 94 S. Ct. 2750 (1974) ("A State may choose to define an obscenity offense in terms of 'contemporary community standards' as defined in *Miller* without further specification . . . or it may choose to define the standards in more precise geographic terms, as was done by California in *Miller*"). Absent geographic specification, a juror applying community standards will inevitably draw upon personal "knowledge of the community or vicinage from which he comes." *Hamling, supra,* at 105. Petitioner concedes the latter point, see Reply Brief for Petitioner 3-4, and admits that, even if jurors were instructed under COPA to apply the standards of the adult population as a whole, the variance in community standards across the country could still cause juries in different locations to reach inconsistent conclusions as to whether a particular work is "harmful to minors."

B.

Because juries would apply different standards across the country, and Web publishers currently lack the ability to limit access to their sites on a geographic basis, the Court of Appeals feared that COPA's "community standards" component would effectively force all speakers on the Web to abide by the "most puritan" community's standards. 217 F.3d at 175. And such a requirement, the Court of Appeals concluded, "imposes an overreaching burden and restriction on constitutionally protected speech." *Id.*, at 177.

In evaluating the constitutionality of the CDA, this Court expressed a similar concern over that statute's use of community standards to identify patently offensive material on the Internet. We noted that "the 'community standards' criterion as applied to the Internet means that any communication available to a nationwide audience will be judged by the standards of the community most likely to be offended by the message." *Reno*, 521 U.S. at 877-878. The Court of Appeals below relied heavily on this observation, stating that it was "not persuaded that the Supreme Court's concern with respect to the 'community standards' criterion has been sufficiently remedied by Congress in COPA." 217 F.3d at 174.

The CDA's use of community standards to identify patently offensive material, however, was particularly problematic in light of that statute's unprecedented breadth and vagueness. The statute covered communications depicting or describing "sexual or excretory activities or organs" that were "patently offensive as measured by contemporary community standards"—a standard somewhat similar to the second prong of *Miller's* three-prong test. But the CDA did not include any limiting terms resembling *Miller's* additional two prongs. See *Reno*, 521 U.S. at 873. It neither contained any requirement that restricted material appeal to the prurient interest nor excluded from the scope of its coverage works with serious literary, artistic, political, or scientific value. *Ibid.* The tremendous breadth of the CDA magnified the impact caused by differences in community standards across the country, restricting Web publishers from openly displaying a significant amount of material that would have constituted protected speech in some communities across the country but run afoul of community standards in others.

COPA, by contrast, does not appear to suffer from the same flaw because it applies to significantly less material than did the CDA and defines the harmful-to-minors material restricted by the statute in a manner parallel to the *Miller* definition of obscenity. See *supra*, at 5-6, 10. To fall within the scope of COPA, works must not only "depict, describe, or represent, in a manner patently offensive with respect to minors," particular sexual acts or parts of the anatomy, they must also be designed to appeal to the prurient interest of minors and "taken as a whole, lack serious literary, artistic, political, or scientific value for minors." 47 U.S.C. §231(e)(6).

These additional two restrictions substantially limit the amount of material covered by the statute. Material appeals to the prurient interest, for instance, only if it is in some sense erotic. Cf. Erznoznik v. Jacksonville, 422 U.S. 205, 213, 45 L. Ed. 2d 125, 95 S. Ct. 2268, and n. 10 (1975). Of even more significance, however, is COPA's exclusion of material with serious value for minors. See 47 U.S.C. §231(e)(6)(C). In *Reno*, we emphasized that the serious value "requirement is particularly important because, unlike the 'patently offensive' and 'prurient interest' criteria, it is not judged by contemporary community standards." 521 U.S. at 873 (citing Pope v. Illinois, 481 U.S. 497, 500, 95 L. Ed.2d 439, 107 S. Ct. 1918 (1987)). This is because "the value of [a] work [does not] vary from community to community based on the degree of local acceptance it has won." *Id.*, at 500. Rather, the relevant question is "whether a reasonable person would find . . . value in the material, taken as a whole." *Id.*, at 501. Thus, the serious value requirement "allows appellate courts to impose some limitations and regularity on the definition by setting, *as a matter of law,* a national floor for socially redeeming value." *Reno, supra,* at 873 (emphasis added), a safeguard nowhere present in the CDA.

C.

When the scope of an obscenity statute's coverage is sufficiently narrowed by a "serious value" prong and a "prurient interest" prong, we have held that requiring a speaker disseminating material to a national audience to observe varying community standards does not violate the First Amendment. In Hamling v. United States, 418 U.S. 87, 41 L. Ed.2d 590, 94 S. Ct. 2887 (1974), this Court considered the constitutionality of applying community standards to the determination of whether material is obscene under 18 U.S.C. §1461, the federal statute prohibiting the mailing of obscene material. Although this statute docs not define obscenity, the petitioners in *Hamling* were tried and convicted under the definition of obscenity set forth in Book Named "John Cleland's Memoirs of a Woman of Pleasure" v. Attorney General of Mass., 383 U.S. 413, 16 L. Ed.2d 1, 86 S. Ct. 975 (1966), which included both a "prurient interest" requirement and a requirement that prohibited material be "'utterly without redeeming social value.'" *Hamling, supra,* at 99 (quoting *Memoirs, supra,* at 418).

Like respondents here, the dissenting opinion in *Hamling* argued that it was unconstitutional for a federal statute to rely on community standards to regulate speech. Justice Brennan maintained that "national distributors choosing to send their products in interstate travels [would] be forced to cope with the community standards of every hamlet into which their goods [might] wander." 418 U.S. at 144. As a result, he claimed that the inevitable result of this situation would be "debilitating self-censorship that abridges the First Amendment rights of the people." *Ibid.*

This Court, however, rejected Justice Brennan's argument that the federal mail statute unconstitutionally compelled speakers choosing to distribute materials on a national basis to tailor their messages to the least tolerant community: "The fact that distributors of allegedly obscene materials may be subjected to varying community standards in the various federal judicial districts into which they transmit the materials does not render a federal statute unconstitutional." *Id.,* at 106.

Fifteen years later, *Hamling's* holding was reaffirmed in Sable Communications of Cal., Inc. v. FCC, 492 U.S. 115, 106 L. Ed.2d 93, 109 S. Ct. 2829 (1989). *Sable* addressed the constitutionality of 47 U.S.C. §223(b) (1982 ed., Supp. V), a statutory provision prohibiting the use of telephones to make obscene or indecent communications for commercial purposes. The petitioner in that case, a "dial-a-porn" operator, challenged, in part, that portion of the statute banning obscene phone messages. Like respondents here, the "dial-a-porn" operator argued that reliance on community standards to identify obscene material impermissibly compelled "message senders . . . to tailor all their messages to the least tolerant community." 492 U.S. at 124. Relying on *Hamling,* however, this Court once again rebuffed this attack on the use of community standards in a federal statute of national scope: "There is no constitutional barrier under *Miller* to prohibiting communications that are obscene in some communities under local standards even though they are not obscene in others. *If Sable's audience is comprised* of *different communities with different local standards, Sable ultimately bears the burden of complying with the prohibition on obscene messages.*" 492 U.S. at 125-126 (emphasis added).

The Court of Appeals below concluded that *Hamling* and *Sable* "are easily distinguished from the present case" because in both of those cases "the defendants had the ability to control the distribution of controversial material with respect to the geographic communities into which they released it" whereas "Web publishers have no such comparable control." 217 F.3d at 175-176. In neither *Hamling* nor *Sable*, however, was the speaker's ability to target the release of material into particular geographic areas integral to the legal analysis. In *Hamling*, the ability to limit the distribution of material to targeted communities was not mentioned, let alone relied upon, and in *Sable*, a dial-a-porn operator's ability to screen incoming calls from particular areas was referenced only as a supplemental point, see 492 U.S. at 125. In the latter case, this Court made no effort to evaluate how burdensome it would have been for dial-a-porn operators to tailor their messages to callers from thousands of different communities across the Nation, instead concluding that the burden of complying with the statute rested with those companies. See *id.*, at 126....

IV

The scope of our decision today is quite limited. We hold only that COPA's reliance on community standards to identify "material that is harmful to minors" does not *by itself* render the statute substantially overbroad for purposes of the First Amendment. We do not express any view as to whether COPA suffers from substantial overbreadth for other reasons, whether the statute is unconstitutionally vague, or whether the District Court correctly concluded that the statute likely will not survive strict scrutiny analysis once adjudication of the case is completed below. While respondents urge us to resolve these questions at this time, prudence dictates allowing the Court of Appeals to first examine these difficult issues.

JUSTICE KENNEDY, with whom JUSTICE SOUTER and JUSTICE GINSBURG join, concurring in the judgment.

I

If a law restricts substantially more speech than is justified, it may be subject to a facial challenge. Broadrick v. Oklahoma, 413 U.S. 601, 615, 37 L. Ed.2d 830, 93 S. Ct. 2908 (1973). There is a very real likelihood that the Child Online Protection Act (COPA or Act) is overbroad and cannot survive such a challenge. Indeed, content-based regulations like this one are presumptively invalid abridgements of the freedom of speech. See R. A. V. v. St. Paul, 505 U.S. 377, 382, 120 L. Ed.2d 305, 112 S. Ct. 2538 (1992). Yet COPA is a major federal statute, enacted in the wake of our previous determination that its predecessor violated the First Amendment. See Reno v. American Civil Liberties Union, 521 U.S. 844 (1997). Congress and the President were aware of our decision, and we should assume that in seeking to comply with it they have given careful consideration to the constitutionality of the new enactment. For these reasons, even if this facial challenge appears to have considerable merit, the Judiciary must proceed with caution and identify overbreadth with care before invalidating the Act.

In this case, the District Court issued a preliminary injunction against enforcement of COPA, finding it too broad across several dimensions. The Court of Appeals affirmed, but on a different ground. COPA defines "material that is harmful to minors" by reference to "contemporary community standards," 47 U.S.C. §231(e)(6) (1994 ed., Supp. V); and on the theory that these vary from place to place, the Court of Appeals held that the definition dooms the statute "without reference to its other provisions." American Civil Liberties Union v. Reno, 217 F.3d 162, 174 (CA3 2000). The Court of Appeals found it unnecessary to construe the rest of the Act or address the District Court's reasoning.

This single, broad proposition, stated and applied at such a high level of generality, cannot suffice to sustain the Court of Appeals' ruling. To observe only that community standards vary across the country is to ignore the antecedent question: community standards as to what? Whether the national variation in community standards produces overbreadth requiring invalidation of COPA, see *Broadrick*, *supra*, depends on the breadth of COPA's coverage and on what community standards are being invoked. Only by identifying the universe of speech burdened by COPA is it possible to discern whether national variation in community standards renders the speech restriction overbroad. In short, the ground on which the Court of Appeals relied cannot be separated from those that it overlooked.

The statute, for instance, applies only to "communication for commercial purposes." 47 U.S.C. §231(e)(2)(A). The Court of Appeals, however, did not consider the amount of commercial communication, the number of commercial speakers, or the character of commercial speech covered by the Act. Likewise, the statute's definition of "harmful to minors" requires material to be judged "as a whole." §231(e)(6)(C). The notion of judging work as a whole is familiar in other media, but more difficult to define on the World Wide Web. It is unclear whether what is to be judged as a whole is a single image on a Web page, a whole Web page, an entire multipage Web site, or an interlocking set of Web sites. Some examination of the group of covered speakers and the categories of covered speech is necessary in order to comprehend the extent of the alleged overbreadth.

The Court of Appeals found that COPA in effect subjects every Internet speaker to the standards of the most puritanical community in the United States. This concern is a real one, but it alone cannot suffice to invalidate COPA without careful examination of the speech and the speakers within the ambit of the Act. For this reason, I join the judgment of the Court vacating the opinion of the Court of Appeals and remanding for consideration of the statute as a whole. Unlike JUSTICE THOMAS, however, I would not assume that the Act is narrow enough to render the national variation in community standards unproblematic. Indeed, if the District Court correctly construed the statute across its other dimensions, then the variation in community standards might well justify enjoining enforcement of the Act. I would leave that question to the Court of Appeals in the first instance.

II . . .

The economics and technology of Internet communication differ in important ways from those of telephones and mail. Paradoxically, as the District Court found, it is easy and cheap to reach a worldwide audience on the Internet, see 31 F. Supp.2d at 482, but expensive if not impossible to reach a geographic subset, *id.*, at 484. A Web publisher in a community where avant garde culture is the norm may have no desire to reach a national market; he may wish only to speak to his neighbors; nevertheless, if an eavesdropper in a more traditional, rural community chooses to listen in, there is nothing the publisher can do. As a practical matter, COPA makes the eavesdropper the arbiter of propriety on the Web. And it is no answer to say that the speaker should "take the simple step of utilizing a [different] medium." *Ante,* at 19 (principal opinion of THOMAS, J.). "Our prior decisions have voiced particular concern with laws that foreclose an entire medium of expression. . . . The danger they pose to the freedom of speech is readily apparent—by eliminating a common means of speaking, such measures can suppress too much speech." City of Ladue v. Gilleo, 512 U.S. 43, 55, 129 L. Ed.2d 36, 114 S. Ct. 2038 (1994).

JUSTICE BREYER would alleviate the problem of local variation in community standards by construing the statute to comprehend the "Nation's adult community taken as a whole," rather than the local community from which the jury is drawn. *Ante,* at 1 (opinion concurring in part and concurring in judgment); see also *ante,* at 1-4 (O'CONNOR, J., concurring in part and concurring in judgment). There is one statement in a House Committee Report to this effect, "reflecting," JUSTICE BREYER writes, "what apparently was a uniform view within Congress." *Ante,* at 2. The statement, perhaps, reflects the view of a majority of one House committee, but there is no reason to believe that it reflects the view of a majority of the House of Representatives, let alone the "uniform view within Congress." *Ibid.*

In any event, we need not decide whether the statute invokes local or national community standards to conclude that vacatur and remand are in order. If the statute does incorporate some concept of national community standards, the actual standard applied is bound to vary by community nevertheless, as the Attorney General concedes. . . .

III

The question that remains is whether this observation *"by itself"* suffices to enjoin the Act. See *ante,* at 22. I agree with the Court that it does not. *Ibid.* We cannot know whether variation in community standards renders the Act substantially overbroad without first assessing the extent of the speech covered and the variations in community standards with respect to that speech.

First, the breadth of the Act itself will dictate the degree of overbreadth caused by varying community standards. Indeed, JUSTICE THOMAS sees this point and uses it in an attempt to distinguish the Communications Decency Act of 1996, which was at issue in *Reno.* See *ante,* at 13 ("The CDA's use of community standards to identify patently offensive material, however, was particularly problematic in light of that statute's unprecedented breadth and vagueness"); *ante,* at 14 ("The tremendous breadth of the CDA magnified the impact caused by differences in community standards across the country"). To explain the ways in which COPA is narrower than the CDA, JUSTICE THOMAS finds that he must construe sections of COPA elided by the Court of Appeals. Though I agree with the necessity for doing so, JUSTICE THOMAS' interpretation—undertaken without substantial arguments or briefing—is not altogether persuasive, and I would leave this task to the Court of

Appeals in the first instance. As this case comes to us, once it is accepted that we cannot strike down the Act based merely on the phrase "contemporary community standards," we should go no further than to vacate and remand for a more comprehensive analysis of the Act.

Second, community standards may have different degrees of variation depending on the question posed to the community. Defining the scope of the Act, therefore, is not relevant merely to the absolute number of Web pages covered, as JUSTICE STEVENS suggests, *post,* at 8-9 (dissenting opinion); it is also relevant to the proportion of overbreadth, "judged in relation to the statute's plainly legitimate sweep." *Broadrick,* 413 U.S. at 615. Because this issue was "virtually ignored by the parties and the amicus" in the Court of Appeals, 217 F.3d at 173, we have no information on the question. Instead, speculation meets speculation. On the one hand, the Court of Appeals found "no evidence to suggest that adults *everywhere* in America would share the same standards for determining what is harmful to minors." *Id.,* at 178. On the other hand, JUSTICE THOMAS finds "no reason to believe that the practical effect of varying community standards under COPA . . . is significantly greater than the practical effect of varying standards under federal obscenity statutes." *Ante,* at 20. When a key issue has "no evidence" on one side and "no reason to believe" [on] the other, it is a good indication that we should vacate for further consideration.

The District Court attempted a comprehensive analysis of COPA and its various dimensions of potential overbreadth. The Court of Appeals, however, believed that its own analysis of "contemporary community standards" obviated all other concerns. It dismissed the District Court's analysis in a footnote:

> We do not find it necessary to address the District Court's analysis of the definition of 'commercial purposes'; whether the breadth of the forms of content covered by COPA could have been more narrowly tailored; whether the affirmative defenses impose too great a burden on Web publishers or whether those affirmative defenses should have been included as elements of the crime itself; whether COPA's inclusion of criminal as well as civil penalties was excessive; whether COPA is designed to include communications made in chat rooms, discussion groups and links to other Web sites; whether the government is entitled to so restrict communications when children will continue to be able to access foreign Web sites and other sources of material that is harmful to them; what taken 'as a whole' should mean in the context of the Web and the Internet; or whether the statute's failure to distinguish between material that is harmful to a six year old versus a sixteen year old is problematic.

217 F.3d at 174, n. 19.

As I have explained, however, any problem caused by variation in community standards cannot be evaluated in a vacuum. In order to discern whether the variation creates substantial overbreadth, it is necessary to know what speech COPA regulates and what community standards it invokes.

It is crucial, for example, to know how limiting is the Act's limitation to "communication for commercial purposes." 47 U.S.C. §231(e)(2)(A). In *Reno,* we remarked that COPA's predecessor was so broad in part because it had no such limitation. 521 U.S. at 877. COPA, by contrast, covers a speaker only if:

> the person who makes a communication or offers to make a communication, by means of the World Wide Web, that includes any material that is harmful to minors, devotes

time, attention, or labor to such activities, as a regular course of such person's trade or business, with the objective of earning a profit as a result of such activities (although it is not necessary that the person make a profit or that the making or offering to make such communications be the person[']s sole or principal business or source of income).

47 U.S.C. §231(e)(2)(B).

So COPA is narrower across this dimension than its predecessor; but how much narrower is a matter of debate. In the District Court, the Attorney General contended that the Act applied only to professional panderers, but the court rejected that contention, finding "nothing in the text of the COPA . . . that limits its applicability to so-called commercial pornographers only." 31 F. Supp.2d at 480. Indeed, the plain text of the Act does not limit its scope to pornography that is offered for sale; it seems to apply even to speech provided for free, so long as the speaker merely hopes to profit as an indirect result. The statute might be susceptible of some limiting construction here, but again the Court of Appeals did not address itself to this question. The answer affects the breadth of the Act and hence the significance of any variation in community standards.

Likewise, it is essential to answer the vexing question of what it means to 'evaluate Internet material "as a whole," 47 U.S.C. §§231(e)(6)(A), (C), when everything on the Web is connected to everything else. As a general matter, "the artistic merit of a work does not depend on the presence of a single explicit scene. . . . The First Amendment requires that redeeming value be judged by considering the work as a whole. Where the scene is part of the narrative, the work itself does not for this reason become obscene, even though the scene in isolation might be offensive." *Ashcroft* v. *Free Speech Coalition*, 122 S. Ct. 1389, 1401 (2002). COPA appears to respect this principle by requiring that the material be judged "as a whole," both as to its prurient appeal, §231(e)(6)(A), and as to its social value, §231(e)(6)(C). It is unclear, however, what constitutes the denominator—that is, the material to be taken as a whole—in the context of the World Wide Web. See 31 F. Supp.2d at 483 ("Although information on the Web is contained in individual computers, the fact that each of these computers is connected to the Internet through World Wide Web protocols allows all of the information to become part of a single body of knowledge"); *id.*, at 484 ("From a user's perspective, [the World Wide Web] may appear to be a single, integrated system"). Several of the respondents operate extensive Web sites, some of which include only a small amount of material that might run afoul of the Act. The Attorney General contended that these respondents had nothing to fear from COPA, but the District Court disagreed, noting that the Act prohibits communication that "includes" any material harmful to minors. §231(a)(1). In the District Court's view, "it logically follows that [COPA] would apply to any Web site that contains only some harmful to minors material." 31 F. Supp.2d at 480. The denominator question is of crucial significance to the coverage of the Act. . . .

JUSTICE STEVENS, dissenting.

Appeals to prurient interests are commonplace on the Internet, as in older media. Many of those appeals lack serious value for minors as well as adults. Some are offensive to certain viewers but welcomed by others. For decades, our cases have recognized that the standards for judging their acceptability vary from viewer to viewer and from community to community. Those cases developed the requirement that communications should be protected if they do not violate contemporary community standards. In its original form, the community standard provided a shield for communications that are offensive only to the least tolerant members of society. Thus, the Court "has emphasized on more than one occasion that a principal concern in requiring that a judgment be made on the basis of 'contemporary community standards' is to assure that the material is judged neither on the basis of each juror's personal opinion, nor by its effect on a particularly sensitive or insensitive person or group." *Hamling* v. *United States*, 418 U.S. 87, 107, 41 L. Ed.2d 590, 94 S. Ct. 2887 (1974). In the context of the Internet, however, community standards become a sword, rather than a shield. If a prurient appeal is offensive in a puritan village, it may be a crime to post it on the World Wide Web. . . .

COPA not only restricts speech that is made available to the general public, it also covers a medium in which speech cannot be segregated to avoid communities where it is likely to be considered harmful to minors. The Internet presents a unique forum for communication because information, once posted, is accessible everywhere on the network at once. The speaker cannot control access based on the location of the listener, nor can it choose the pathways through which its speech is transmitted. By approving the use of community standards in this context, JUSTICE THOMAS endorses a construction of COPA that has "the intolerable consequence of denying some sections of the country access to material, there deemed acceptable, which in others might be considered offensive to prevailing community standards of decency." Manual Enterprises, Inc. v. Day, 370 U.S. 478, 488, 8 L. Ed.2d 639, 82 S. Ct. 1432 (1962).

If the material were forwarded through the mails, as in *Hamling*, or over the telephone, as in *Sable*, the sender could avoid destinations with the most restrictive standards. Indeed, in *Sable*, we upheld the application of community standards to a nationwide medium because the speaker was "free to tailor its messages . . . to the communities it *chooses* to serve," by either "hiring operators to determine the source of the calls . . . [or] arranging for the screening and blocking of out-of-area calls." 492 U.S. at 125 (emphasis added). Our conclusion that it was permissible for the speaker to bear the ultimate burden of compliance, *id.*, at 126, assumed that such compliance was at least possible without requiring the speaker to choose another medium or to limit its speech to what all would find acceptable. Given the undisputed fact that a provider who posts material on the Internet cannot prevent it from entering any geographic community, see *ante*, at 11, n. 6 (opinion of THOMAS, J.), a law that criminalizes a particular communication in just a handful of destinations effectively prohibits transmission of that message to all of the 176.5 million Americans that have access to the Internet, see *ante*, at 2, n. 2 (opinion of THOMAS, J.). In light of this fundamental difference in technologies, the rules applicable to the mass mailing of an obscene montage or to obscene dial-a-porn should not be used to judge the legality of messages on the World Wide Web.[2]

In his attempt to fit this case within the framework of *Hamling* and *Sable*, JUSTICE THOMAS overlooks the more obvious comparison—namely, the CDA

---

2. It is hardly a solution to say, as JUSTICE THOMAS suggests, *ante*, at 19, that a speaker need only choose a different medium in order to avoid having its speech judged by the least tolerant community. Our overbreadth doctrine would quickly become a toothless protection if we were to hold that substituting a more limited forum for expression is an acceptable price to pay. Since a content-based restriction is presumptively invalid, I would place the burden on parents to "take the simple step of utilizing a medium that enables," *ante*, at 19, them to avoid this material before requiring the speaker to find another forum.

invalidated in *ACLU I.* When we confronted a similar attempt by Congress to limit speech on the Internet based on community standards, we explained that because Web publishers cannot control who accesses their Web sites, using community standards to regulate speech on the Internet creates an overbreadth problem. "The 'community standards' criterion as applied to the Internet means that any communication available to a nationwide audience will be judged by the standards of the community most likely to be offended by the message." 521 U.S. at 877-878. Although our holding in *ACLU I* did not turn on that factor alone, we did not adopt the position relied on by JUSTICE THOMAS—that applying community standards to the Internet is constitutional based on *Hamling* and *Sable.*

JUSTICE THOMAS points to several other provisions in COPA to argue that any overbreadth will be rendered insubstantial by the rest of the statute. *Ante,* at 14-15. These provisions afford little reassurance, however, as they only marginally limit the sweep of the statute. It is true that, in addition to COPA's "appeals to the prurient interest of minors" prong, the material must be "patently offensive with respect to minors" and it must lack "serious literary, artistic, political, or scientific value for minors." 47 U.S.C. §231(e)(6). Nonetheless, the "patently offensive" prong is judged according to contemporary community standards as well, *ante,* at 11, n. 7 (opinion of THOMAS, J.). Whatever disparity exists between various communities' assessment of the content that appeals to the prurient interest of minors will surely be matched by their differing opinions as to whether descriptions of sexual acts or depictions of nudity are patently offensive with respect to minors. Nor does the requirement that the material be "in some sense erotic," see *ante,* at 15 (citing Erznoznik v. Jacksonville, 422 U.S. 205, 213, 45 L. Ed.2d 125, 95 S. Ct. 2268, and n. 10 (1975)), substantially narrow the category of images covered. Arguably every depiction of nudity—partial or full—is in some sense erotic *with respect to minors.*

Petitioner's argument that the "serious value" prong minimizes the statute's overbreadth is also unpersuasive. Although we have recognized that the serious value determination in obscenity cases should be based on an objective, reasonable person standard, Pope v. Illinois, 481 U.S. 497, 500, 95 L. Ed.2d 439, 107 S. Ct. 1918 (1987), this criterion is inadequate to cure COPA's overbreadth because COPA adds an important qualifying phrase to the standard Miller v. California, 413 U.S. 15, 37 L. Ed.2d 419, 93 S. Ct. 2607 (1973), formulation of the serious value prong. The question for the jury is not whether a reasonable person would conclude that the materials have serious value; instead, the jury must determine whether the materials have serious value *for minors.* Congress reasonably concluded that a substantial number of works, which have serious value for adults, do not have serious value for minors. Cf. *ACLU I,* 521 U.S. at 896 (O'CONNOR, J., concurring in judgment in part and dissenting in part) ("While discussions about prison rape or nude art . . . may have some redeeming educational value for *adults,* they do not necessarily have any such value for *minors*"). Thus, even though the serious value prong limits the total amount of speech covered by the statute, it remains true that there is a significant amount of protected speech within the category of materials that have no serious value for minors. That speech is effectively prohibited whenever the least tolerant communities find it harmful to minors.[5] While the objective

---

5. The Court also notes that the limitation to communications made for commercial purposes narrows the category of speech as compared to the CDA, *ante,* at 5. While it is certainly true that this condition limits the scope of the statute, the phrase "commercial purposes" is somewhat misleading. The

nature of the inquiry may eliminate any worry that the serious value determination will be made by the least tolerant community, it does not change the fact that, within the subset of images deemed to have no serious value for minors, the decision whether minors and adults throughout the country will have access to that speech will still be made by the most restrictive community. . . .

JUSTICE THOMAS acknowledges, and petitioner concedes, that juries across the country will apply different standards and reach different conclusions about whether particular works are harmful to minors. See *ante,* at 12-13. We recognized as much in *ACLU I* when we noted that "discussions about prison rape or safe sexual practices, artistic images that include nude subjects, and arguably the card catalog of the Carnegie Library" might offend some community's standards and not others, 521 U.S. at 878. In fact, our own division on that question provides further evidence of the range of attitudes about such material. See, e.g., *id.,* at 896 (O'CONNOR, J., concurring in judgment in part and dissenting in part). Moreover, amici for respondents describe studies showing substantial variation among communities in their attitudes toward works involving homosexuality, masturbation, and nudity.

Even if most, if not all, of these works would be excluded from COPA's coverage by the serious value prong, they illustrate the diversity of public opinion on the underlying themes depicted. This diversity of views surely extends to whether materials with the same themes, that do not have serious value for minors, appeal to their prurient interests and are patently offensive. There is no reason to think the differences between communities' standards will disappear once the image or description is no longer within the context of a work that has serious value for minors. Because communities differ widely in their attitudes toward sex, particularly when minors are concerned, the Court of Appeals was correct to conclude that, regardless of how COPA's other provisions are construed, applying community standards to the Internet will restrict a substantial amount of protected speech that would not be considered harmful to minors in many communities.

Whether that consequence is appropriate depends, of course, on the content of the message. The kind of hard-core pornography involved in *Hamling,* which I assume would be obscene under any community's standard, does not belong on the Internet. Perhaps "teasers" that serve no function except to invite viewers to examine hardcore materials, or the hidden terms written into a Web site's "metatags" in order to dupe unwitting Web surfers into visiting pornographic sites, deserve the same fate. But COPA extends to a wide range of prurient appeals in advertisements, online magazines, Web-based bulletin boards and chat rooms, stock photo galleries, Web diaries, and a variety of illustrations encompassing a vast number of messages that are unobjectionable in most of the country and yet provide no "serious value" for minors. It is quite wrong to allow the standards of a minority consisting of the

---

definition of commercial purposes, 47 U.S.C. §231(e)(2)(B), covers anyone who generates revenue from advertisements or merchandise, regardless of the amount of advertising or whether the advertisements or products are related to the images that allegedly are harmful to minors. As the District Court noted: "There is nothing in the text of the COPA, however, that limits its applicability to so-called commercial pornographers only; indeed, the text of COPA imposes liability on a speaker who knowingly makes any communication for commercial purposes 'that *includes any material* that is harmful to minors,'" App. to Pet. for Cert. 52a. In the context of the Internet, this is hardly a serious limitation. A 1998 study, for example, found that 83 percent of Web sites contain commercial content. Lawrence & Giles, Accessibility of Information of the Web, 400 Nature 107-109 (1999); Guernsey, Seek—but on the Web, You Might Not Find, N. Y. Times, July 8, 1999, p. G3. Interestingly, this same study found that only 1.5 percent of the 2.8 million sites cataloged contained pornographic content.

least tolerant communities to regulate access to relatively harmless messages in this burgeoning market.

In the context of most other media, using community standards to differentiate between permissible and impermissible speech has two virtues. As mentioned above, community standards originally served as a shield to protect speakers from the least tolerant members of society. By aggregating values at the community level, the *Miller* test eliminated the outliers at both ends of the spectrum and provided some predictability as to what constitutes obscene speech. But community standards also serve as a shield to protect audience members, by allowing people to self-sort based on their preferences. Those who abhor and those who tolerate sexually explicit speech can seek out like-minded people and settle in communities that share their views on what is acceptable for themselves and their children. This sorting mechanism, however, does not exist in cyberspace; the audience cannot self-segregate. As a result, in the context of the Internet this shield also becomes a sword, because the community that wishes to live without certain material not only rids itself, but the entire Internet of the offending speech.

In sum, I would affirm the judgment of the Court of Appeals and therefore respectfully dissent.

COMMENTS AND QUESTIONS

1. The Court in *Ashcroft v. ACLU* was remarkably split. Justice Thomas spoke for a majority of Justices only as to Parts I (background of the case), II (background on the First Amendment), and IV (remanding the case to the Third Circuit, asking it to analyze other constitutional issues). Justice O'Connor joined Part IIIB only. On what issues are members of the Court in the most agreement? On what issues are they most split? Assume for the sake of argument that the Third Circuit affirms the trial court that COPA is unconstitutionally overbroad; from what the Justices wrote here, how would you expect them to be inclined to vote on the ultimate question? Concerning less restrictive alternatives to COPA, consider the proposal in Lawrence Lessig, The Law of the Horse: What Cyberlaw Might Teach, 113 Harv. L. Rev. 501, 517-18 (1999) (suggesting that browsers might self-identify as children to whom different rules could be applied).

2. During the 2001-2002 term, the Court reviewed a First Amendment challenge to the Child Pornography Prevention Act of 1996, 18 U.S.C. sec. 2251 et seq., which extended the reach of federal child pornography laws by outlawing possession or distribution of sexually explicit images that appear to depict minors although they were actually produced by adults with the aid of specialized computer software without using any real children. The Supreme Court ruled 7-2 (Rehnquist and Scalia dissenting) that this legislation was unconstitutional in Ashcroft v. The Free Speech Coalition, 122 S. Ct. 1389 (2002). The Court had previously upheld prohibitions on the use of sexually explicit images of real children in New York v. Ferber, 458 U.S. 747 (1982) because of the perceived harm to children during the production process. Because CPPA would proscribe "a significant universe of speech that is neither obscene under *Miller* nor child pornography

under *Ferber*," the Court decided that the CPPA did not conform to First Amendment standards.

3. Another way to prevent children from being exposed to harmful materials on the Internet is for their parents to use filtering software that blocks access to sites that the software's developers rate as unsuitable for children. The World Wide Web Consortium (W3C) has developed a system to enable the tagging of Web sites, known as the Platform for Independent Content Selection (PICS), that can be used to automate filtering. Jonathan Weinberg discusses filtering and PICS in his article Rating the Net, 19 Hastings COMM/ENT L.J. 453 (1997):

> It is easy to understand the acclaim for filtering software. This software can do an impressive job at blocking access to sexually explicit material that a parent does not wish his or her child to see. The PICS standard for describing ratings systems is an important technical achievement, allowing the development and easy use of a variety of sophisticated rating schemes.

Id. at 455. However, Weinberg suggests that filtering and rating systems have their costs:

> It seems likely that a substantial number of adults, in the near future, will view the Internet through filters administered by blocking software. Intermediaries—employers, libraries, and others—will gain greater control over the things these adults read and see. Sites may be stripped out of the filtered universe because of deliberate political choices on the part of rating service administrators, and because of inaccuracies inherent in the ratings process.

Id. at 482.

Lawrence Lessig has also warned that ratings systems such as PICS are troublesome in part because they help to create an infrastructure that could enable censorship. See, e.g., Lawrence Lessig, Code and Other Laws of Cyberspace (2000).

As Weinberg points out, some libraries have decided to use filtering software for the computers through which they provide Internet access to their patrons. An association of library patrons and some individual patrons brought an action under 42 U.S.C. section 1983 to challenge their public library's use of Internet filtering software as an unconstitutional abridgement of freedoms protected by the First Amendment. In particular, they charged that the library's policy was a content-based restriction on access to the Internet and that it impermissibly barred them from accessing protected speech such as the Quaker Home page, the Zero Population Growth Web site, and an American Association of University Women of Maryland site. In Mainstream Loudoun v. Board of Trustees of the Loudoun County Library, 2 F. Supp.2d 783 (E.D. Va. 1998), the court ruled that the complaint had stated a viable claim against the library. Would the result have been different if the library had allowed adults to gain Internet access without filtering software and insisted on such software only when children wanted to have Internet access?

4. In 1999 Congress passed the Children's Internet Protection Act ("CIPA"), Pub. L. No. 106-554 that mandates the use of filtering technology in all public libraries and public schools which accept certain federal funding. The American Civil Liberties Union is representing the American Library Association, among others, in a First Amendment challenge to CIPA.

American Library Ass'n v. United States
United States District Court for the Eastern District of Pennsylvania
201 F. Supp.2d 401 (E.D. Pa. 2002)

BECKER, Chief Circuit Judge:

This case challenges an act of Congress that makes the use of filtering software by public libraries a condition of the receipt of federal funding. The Internet, as is well known, is a vast, interactive medium based on a decentralized network of computers around the world. Its most familiar feature is the World Wide Web (the "Web"), a network of computers known as servers that provide content to users. The Internet provides easy access to anyone who wishes to provide or distribute information to a worldwide audience; it is used by more than 143 million Americans. Indeed, much of the world's knowledge accumulated over centuries is available to Internet users almost instantly. Approximately 10% of the Americans who use the Internet access it at public libraries. And approximately 95% of all public libraries in the United States provide public access to the Internet.

While the beneficial effect of the Internet in expanding the amount of information available to its users is self-evident, its low entry barriers have also led to a perverse result—facilitation of the widespread dissemination of hardcore pornography within the easy reach not only of adults who have every right to access it (so long as it is not legally obscene or child pornography), but also of children and adolescents to whom it may be quite harmful. The volume of pornography on the Internet is huge, and the record before us demonstrates that public library patrons of all ages, many from ages 11 to 15, have regularly sought to access it in public library settings. There are more than 100,000 pornographic Web sites that can be accessed for free and without providing any registration information, and tens of thousands of Web sites contain child pornography.

Libraries have reacted to this situation by utilizing a number of means designed to insure that patrons avoid illegal (and unwanted) content while also enabling patrons to find the content they desire. Some libraries have trained patrons in how to use the Internet while avoiding illegal content, or have directed their patrons to "preferred" Web sites that librarians have reviewed. Other libraries have utilized such devices as recessing the computer monitors, installing privacy screens, and monitoring implemented by a "tap on the shoulder" of patrons perceived to be offending library policy. Still others, viewing the foregoing approaches as inadequate or uncomfortable (some librarians do not wish to confront patrons), have purchased commercially available software that blocks certain categories of material deemed by the library board as unsuitable for use in their facilities. Indeed, 7% of American public libraries use blocking software for adults. Although such programs are somewhat effective in blocking large quantities of pornography, they are blunt instruments that not only "underblock," i.e., fail to block access to substantial amounts of content that the library boards wish to exclude, but also, central to this litigation, "overblock," i.e., block access to large quantities of material that library boards do not wish to exclude and that is constitutionally protected.

Most of the libraries that use filtering software seek to block sexually explicit speech. While most libraries include in their physical collection copies of volumes such as *The Joy of Sex* and *The Joy of Gay Sex,* which contain quite explicit photographs and descriptions, filtering software blocks large quantities of other, comparable information about health and sexuality that adults and teenagers seek on the

Web. One teenager testified that the Internet access in a public library was the only venue in which she could obtain information important to her about her own sexuality. Another library patron witness described using the Internet to research breast cancer and reconstructive surgery for his mother who had breast surgery. Even though some filtering programs contain exceptions for health and education, the exceptions do not solve the problem of overblocking constitutionally protected material. Moreover, as we explain below, the filtering software on which the parties presented evidence in this case overblocks not only information relating to health and sexuality that might be mistaken for pornography or erotica, but also vast numbers of Web pages and sites that could not even arguably be construed as harmful or inappropriate for adults or minors.

The Congress, sharing the concerns of many library boards, enacted the Children's Internet Protection Act ("CIPA"), Pub. L. No. 106-554, which makes the use of filters by a public library a condition of its receipt of two kinds of subsidies that are important (or even critical) to the budgets of many public libraries—grants under the Library Services and Technology Act, 20 U.S.C. §9101 et seq. ("LSTA"), and so-called "E-rate discounts" for Internet access and support under the Telecommunications Act, 47 U.S.C. §254. LSTA grant funds are awarded, inter alia, in order to: (1) assist libraries in accessing information through electronic networks, and (2) provide targeted library and information services to persons having difficulty using a library and to underserved and rural communities, including children from families with incomes below the poverty line. E-rate discounts serve the similar purpose of extending Internet access to schools and libraries in low-income communities. CIPA requires that libraries, in order to receive LSTA funds or E-rate discounts, certify that they are using a "technology protection measure" that prevents patrons from accessing "visual depictions" that are "obscene," "child pornography," or in the case of minors, "harmful to minors." 20 U.S.C. §9134(f)(1)(A) (LSTA); 47 U.S.C. §254(h)(6)(B) & (C) (E-rate).

The plaintiffs, a group of libraries, library associations, library patrons, and Web site publishers, brought this suit against the United States and others alleging that CIPA is facially unconstitutional because: (1) it induces public libraries to violate their patrons' First Amendment rights contrary to the requirements of South Dakota v. Dole, 483 U.S. 203 (1987); and (2) it requires libraries to relinquish their First Amendment rights as a condition on the receipt of federal funds and is therefore impermissible under the doctrine of unconstitutional conditions. In arguing that CIPA will induce public libraries to violate the First Amendment, the plaintiffs contend that given the limits of the filtering technology, CIPA's conditions effectively require libraries to impose content-based restrictions on their patrons' access to constitutionally protected speech. According to the plaintiffs, these content-based restrictions are subject to strict scrutiny under public forum doctrine, see Rosenberger v. Rector & Visitors of Univ. of Va., 515 U.S. 819, 837 (1995), and are therefore permissible only if they are narrowly tailored to further a compelling state interest and no less restrictive alternatives would further that interest, see Reno v. ACLU, 521 U.S. 844, 874 (1997). The government responds that CIPA will not induce public libraries to violate the First Amendment, since it is possible for at least some public libraries to constitutionally comply with CIPA's conditions. Even if some libraries' use of filters might violate the First Amendment, the government submits that CIPA can be facially invalidated only if it is impossible for any public library to comply with its conditions without violating the First Amendment.

Pursuant to CIPA, a three-judge Court was convened to try the issues. Pub. L. No. 106-554. Following an intensive period of discovery on an expedited schedule to allow public libraries to know whether they need to certify compliance with CIPA by July 1, 2002, to receive subsidies for the upcoming year, the Court conducted an eight-day trial at which we heard 20 witnesses, and received numerous depositions, stipulations and documents. The principal focus of the trial was on the capacity of currently available filtering software. The plaintiffs adduced substantial evidence not only that filtering programs bar access to a substantial amount of speech on the Internet that is clearly constitutionally protected for adults and minors, but also that these programs are intrinsically unable to block only illegal Internet content while simultaneously allowing access to all protected speech.

As our extensive findings of fact reflect, the plaintiffs demonstrated that thousands of Web pages containing protected speech are wrongly blocked by the four leading filtering programs, and these pages represent only a fraction of Web pages wrongly blocked by the programs. The plaintiffs' evidence explained that the problems faced by the manufacturers and vendors of filtering software are legion. The Web is extremely dynamic, with an estimated 1.5 million new pages added every day and the contents of existing Web pages changing very rapidly. The category lists maintained by the blocking programs are considered to be proprietary information, and hence are unavailable to customers or the general public for review, so that public libraries that select categories when implementing filtering software do not really know what they are blocking.

There are many reasons why filtering software suffers from extensive over- and underblocking, which we will explain below in great detail. They center on the limitations on filtering companies' ability to: (1) accurately collect Web pages that potentially fall into a blocked category (e.g., pornography); (2) review and categorize Web pages that they have collected; and (3) engage in regular re-review of Web pages that they have previously reviewed. These failures spring from constraints on the technology of automated classification systems, and the limitations inherent in human review, including error, misjudgment, and scarce resources, which we describe in detail *infra* at 58-74. One failure of critical importance is that the automated systems that filtering companies use to collect Web pages for classification are able to search only text, not images. This is crippling to filtering companies' ability to collect pages containing "visual depictions" that are obscene, child pornography, or harmful to minors, as CIPA requires. As will appear, we find that it is currently impossible, given the Internet's size, rate of growth, rate of change, and architecture, and given the state of the art of automated classification systems, to develop a filter that neither underblocks nor overblocks a substantial amount of speech.

The government, while acknowledging that the filtering software is imperfect, maintains that it is nonetheless quite effective, and that it successfully blocks the vast majority of the Web pages that meet filtering companies' category definitions (e.g., pornography). The government contends that no more is required. In its view, so long as the filtering software selected by the libraries screens out the bulk of the Web pages proscribed by CIPA, the libraries have made a reasonable choice which suffices, under the applicable legal principles, to pass constitutional muster in the context of a facial challenge. Central to the government's position is the analogy it advances between Internet filtering and the initial decision of a library to determine which materials to purchase for its print collection. Public libraries have finite budgets and must make choices as to whether to purchase, for example, books on gardening or books on golf. Such content-based decisions, even the plaintiffs concede, are subject to rational basis review and not a stricter form of First Amendment scrutiny. In the government's view, the fact that the Internet reverses the acquisition process and requires the libraries to, in effect, purchase the entire Internet, some of which (e.g., hardcore pornography) it does not want, should not mean that it is chargeable with censorship when it filters out offending material.

The legal context in which this extensive factual record is set is complex, implicating a number of constitutional doctrines, including the constitutional limitations on Congress's spending clause power, the unconstitutional conditions doctrine, and subsidiary to these issues, the First Amendment doctrines of prior restraint, vagueness, and overbreadth. There are a number of potential entry points into the analysis, but the most logical is the spending clause jurisprudence in which the seminal case is South Dakota v. Dole, 483 U.S. 203 (1987). *Dole* outlines four categories of constraints on Congress's exercise of its power under the Spending Clause, but the only *Dole* condition disputed here is the fourth and last, i.e., whether CIPA requires libraries that receive LSTA funds or E-rate discounts to violate the constitutional rights of their patrons. As will appear, the question is not a simple one, and turns on the level of scrutiny applicable to a public library's content-based restrictions on patrons' Internet access. Whether such restrictions are subject to strict scrutiny, as plaintiffs contend, or only rational basis review, as the government contends, depends on public forum doctrine.

The government argues that, in providing Internet access, public libraries do not create a public forum, since public libraries may reserve the right to exclude certain speakers from availing themselves of the forum. Accordingly, the government contends that public libraries' restrictions on patrons' Internet access are subject only to rational basis review.

Plaintiffs respond that the government's ability to restrict speech on its own property, as in the case of restrictions on Internet access in public libraries, is not unlimited, and that the more widely the state facilitates the dissemination of private speech in a given forum, the more vulnerable the state's decision is to restrict access to speech in that forum. We agree with the plaintiffs that public libraries' content-based restrictions on their patrons' Internet access are subject to strict scrutiny. In providing even filtered Internet access, public libraries create a public forum open to any speaker around the world to communicate with library patrons via the Internet on a virtually unlimited number of topics. Where the state provides access to a "vast democratic forum[]," Reno v. ACLU, 521 U.S. 844, 868 (1997), open to any member of the public to speak on subjects "as diverse as human thought," *id*. at 870 (internal quotation marks and citation omitted), the state's decision selectively to exclude from the forum speech whose content the state disfavors is subject to strict scrutiny, as such exclusions risk distorting the marketplace of ideas that the state has facilitated. Application of strict scrutiny finds further support in the extent to which public libraries' provision of Internet access uniquely promotes First Amendment values in a manner analogous to traditional public fora such as streets, sidewalks, and parks, in which content-based restrictions are always subject to strict scrutiny.

Under strict scrutiny, a public library's use of filtering software is permissible only if it is narrowly tailored to further a compelling government interest and no less restrictive alternative would serve that interest. We acknowledge that use of filtering software furthers public libraries' legitimate interests in preventing patrons from accessing visual depictions of obscenity, child pornography, or in the case of minors, material harmful to minors. Moreover, use of filters also helps prevent patrons from being unwillingly exposed to patently offensive, sexually explicit content on the Internet. . . .

Narrow Tailoring . . .

The commercially available filters on which evidence was presented at trial all block many thousands of Web pages that are clearly not harmful to minors, and many thousands more pages that, while possibly harmful to minors, are neither obscene nor child pornography. Even the defendants' own expert, after analyzing filtering products' performance in public libraries, concluded that of the blocked Web pages to which library patrons sought access, between 6% and 15% contained no content that meets even the filtering products' own definitions of sexually explicit content, let alone the legal definitions of obscenity or child pornography, which none of the filtering companies that were studied use as the basis for their blocking decisions. Moreover, in light of the flaws in these studies, discussed in detail in our findings of fact above, these percentages significantly underestimate the amount of speech that filters erroneously block, and at best provide a rough lower bound on the filters' rates of overblocking. Given the substantial amount of constitutionally protected speech blocked by the filters studied, we conclude that use of such filters is not narrowly tailored with respect to the government's interest in preventing the dissemination of obscenity, child pornography, and material harmful to minors.

To be sure, the quantitative estimates of the rates of overblocking apply only to those four commercially available filters analyzed by plaintiffs' and defendants' expert witnesses. Nonetheless, given the inherent limitations in the current state of the art of automated classification systems, and the limits of human review in relation to the size, rate of growth, and rate of change of the Web, there is a tradeoff between underblocking and overblocking that is inherent in any filtering technology, as our findings of fact have demonstrated. We credit the testimony of plaintiffs' expert witness, Dr. Geoffrey Nunberg, that no software exists that can automatically distinguish visual depictions that are obscene, child pornography, or harmful to minors, from those that are not. Nor can software, through keyword analysis or more sophisticated techniques, consistently distinguish web pages that contain such content from web pages that do not.

In light of the absence of any automated method of classifying Web pages, filtering companies are left with the Sisyphean task of using human review to identify, from among the approximately two billion web pages that exist, the 1.5 million new pages that are created daily, and the many thousands of pages whose content changes from day to day, those particular web pages to be blocked. To cope with the Web's extraordinary size, rate of growth, and rate of change, filtering companies that rely solely on human review to block access to material falling within their category definitions must use a variety of techniques that will necessarily introduce substantial amounts of overblocking. These techniques include blocking every page of a Web site that contains only some content falling within the filtering companies' category definitions, blocking every Web site that shares an IP-address with a Web site whose content falls within the category definitions, blocking "loophole sites," such as anonymizers, cache sites, and translation sites, and allocating staff resources to reviewing content of uncategorized pages rather than re-reviewing pages, domain names, or IP-addresses that have been already categorized to determine whether their content has changed. While a filtering company could choose not to use these techniques, due to the overblocking errors they introduce, if a filtering company does not use such techniques, its filter will be ineffective at blocking access to speech that falls within its category definitions.

Thus, while it would be easy to design, for example, a filter that blocks only ten Web sites, all of which are either obscene, child pornography, or harmful to minors, and therefore completely avoids overblocking, such a filter clearly would not comply with CIPA, since it would fail to offer any meaningful protection against the hundreds of thousands of Web sites containing speech in these categories. As detailed in our findings of fact, any filter that blocks enough speech to protect against access to visual depictions that are obscene, child pornography, and harmful to minors, will necessarily overblock substantial amounts of speech that does not fall within these categories.

This finding is supported by the government's failure to produce evidence of any filtering technology that avoids overblocking a substantial amount of protected speech. Where, as here, strict scrutiny applies to a content-based restriction on speech, the burden rests with the government to show that the restriction is narrowly tailored to serve a compelling government interest. See *Playboy,* 529 U.S. at 816 ("When the Government restricts speech, the Government bears the burden of proving the constitutionality of its actions."); see also R.A.V. v. City of St. Paul, 505 U.S. 377, 382 (1992) ("Content-based regulations are presumptively invalid."). Thus, it is the government's burden, in this case, to show the existence of a filtering technology that both blocks enough speech to qualify as a technology protection measure, for purposes of CIPA, and avoids overblocking a substantial amount of constitutionally protected speech.

Here, the government has failed to meet its burden. Indeed, as discussed in our findings of fact, every technology protection measure used by the government's library witnesses or analyzed by the government's expert witnesses blocks access to a substantial amount of speech that is constitutionally protected with respect to both adults and minors. In light of the credited testimony of Dr. Nunberg, and the inherent tradeoff between overblocking and underblocking, together with the government's failure to offer evidence of any technology protection measure that avoids overblocking, we conclude that any technology protection measure that blocks a sufficient amount of speech to comply with CIPA's requirement that it "protect[] against access through such computers to visual depictions that are— (I) obscene; (II) child pornography; or (III) harmful to minors" will necessarily block substantial amounts of speech that does not fall within these categories. CIPA §1712 (codified at 20 U.S.C. §9134(f)(1)(A)). Hence, any public library's use of a software filter required by CIPA will fail to be narrowly tailored to the government's compelling interest in preventing the dissemination, through Internet terminals in public libraries, of visual depictions that are obscene, child pornography, or harmful to minors.

Where, as here, strict scrutiny applies, the government may not justify restrictions on constitutionally protected speech on the ground that such restrictions are necessary in order for the government effectively to suppress the dissemination of constitutionally unprotected speech, such as obscenity and child pornography. "The argument . . . that protected speech may be banned as a means to ban unprotected speech . . . turns the First Amendment upside down. The Government may not suppress lawful speech as the means to suppress unlawful speech." *Ashcroft,* 122 S. Ct. at 1404. This rule reflects the judgment that "[t]he possible harm to society in permitting some unprotected speech to go unpunished is outweighed by the possibility that protected speech of others may be muted . . . ." Broadrick v. Oklahoma, 413 U.S. at 612.

Thus, in *Ashcroft,* the Supreme Court rejected the government's argument that a statute criminalizing the distribution of constitutionally protected "virtual" child pornography, produced through computer imaging technology without the use of real children, was necessary to further the state's interest in prosecuting the dissemination of constitutionally unprotected child pornography produced using real children, since "the possibility of producing images by using computer imaging makes it very difficult for [the government] to prosecute those who produce pornography using real children." *Ashcroft,* 122 S. Ct. at 1404; see also *Stanley,* 394 U.S. at 567-58 (holding that individuals have a First Amendment right to possess obscene material, even though the existence of this right makes it more difficult for the states to further their legitimate interest in prosecuting the distribution of obscenity). By the same token, even if the use of filters is effective in preventing patrons from receiving constitutionally unprotected speech, the government's interest in preventing the dissemination of such speech cannot justify the use of the technology protection measures mandated by CIPA, which necessarily block substantial amounts of constitutionally protected speech.

CIPA thus resembles the Communications Decency Act, which the Supreme Court facially invalidated in Reno v. ACLU, 521 U.S. 844 (1997). Although on its face, the CDA simply restricted the distribution to minors of speech that was constitutionally unprotected with respect to minors, as a practical matter, given Web sites' difficulties in identifying the ages of Internet users, the CDA effectively prohibited the distribution to adults of material that was constitutionally protected with respect to adults. Similarly, although on its face, CIPA, like the CDA, requires the suppression of only constitutionally unprotected speech, it is impossible as a practical matter, given the state of the art of filtering technology, for a public library to comply with CIPA without also blocking significant amounts of constitutionally protected speech. We therefore hold that a library's use of a technology protection measure required by CIPA is not narrowly tailored to the government's legitimate interest in preventing the dissemination of visual depictions that are obscene, child pornography, or in the case of minors, harmful to minors.

For the same reason that a public library's use of software filters is not narrowly tailored to further the library's interest in preventing its computers from being used to disseminate visual depictions that are obscene, child pornography, and harmful to minors, a public library's use of software filters is not narrowly tailored to further the library's interest in protecting patrons from being unwillingly exposed to offensive, sexually explicit material. As discussed in our findings of fact, the filters required by CIPA block substantial numbers of Web sites that even the most puritanical public library patron would not find offensive, such as http://federo .com, a Web site that promotes federalism in Uganda, which N2H2 blocked as "Adults Only, Pornography," and http://www.vvm.com/~bond/home.htm, a site for aspiring dentists, which was blocked by Cyberpatrol as "Adult/Sexually Explicit." We list many more such examples in our findings of fact, see *supra,* and find that such erroneously blocked sites number in at least the thousands.

Although we have found large amounts of overblocking, even if only a small percentage of sites blocked are erroneously blocked, either with respect to the state's interest in preventing adults from viewing material that is obscene or child pornography and in preventing minors from viewing material that is harmful to minors, or with respect to the state's interest in preventing library patrons generally from being unwillingly exposed to offensive, sexually explicit material, this imprecision is fatal under the First Amendment. Cf. *Reno,* 521 U.S. at 874 ("[T]he CDA lacks the precision that the First Amendment requires when a statute regulates the content of speech."); *League of Women Voters,* 468 U.S. at 398 ("[E]ven if some of the hazards at which [the challenged provision] was aimed are sufficiently substantial, the restriction is not crafted with sufficient precision to remedy those dangers that may exist to justify the significant abridgement of speech worked by the provision's broad ban . . .").

While the First Amendment does not demand perfection when the government restricts speech in order to advance a compelling interest, the substantial amounts of erroneous blocking inherent in the technology protection measures mandated by CIPA are more than simply de minimis instances of human error. "The line between speech unconditionally guaranteed and speech which may legitimately be regulated, suppressed, or punished is finely drawn. Error in marking that line exacts an extraordinary cost." *Playboy,* 529 U.S. at 817 (internal quotation marks and citation omitted). Indeed, "precision of regulation must be the touchstone in an area so closely touching our most precious freedoms." Keyishian v. Bd. of Regents of the Univ. of the State of N.Y., 385 U.S. 589, 603 (1967) (internal quotation marks and citation omitted); see also Bantam Books, Inc. v. Sullivan, 372 U.S. 58, 66 (1963) ("The separation of legitimate from illegitimate speech calls for sensitive tools.") (internal quotation marks and citation omitted). Where the government draws content based restrictions on speech in order to advance a compelling government interest, the First Amendment demands the precision of a scalpel, not a sledgehammer. We believe that a public library's use of the technology protection measures mandated by CIPA is not narrowly tailored to further the governmental interests at stake.

Although the strength of different libraries' interests in blocking certain forms of speech may vary from library to library, depending on the frequency and severity of problems experienced by each particular library, we conclude, based on our findings of fact, that any public library's use of a filtering product mandated by CIPA will necessarily fail to be narrowly tailored to address the library's legitimate interests. Because it is impossible for a public library to comply with CIPA without blocking substantial amounts of speech whose suppression serves no legitimate state interest, we therefore hold that CIPA is facially invalid, even under the more stringent standard of facial invalidity urged on us by the government, which would require upholding CIPA if it is possible for just a single library to comply with CIPA's conditions without violating the First Amendment. . . .

Less Restrictive Alternatives

The constitutional infirmity of a public library's use of software filters is evidenced not only by the absence of narrow tailoring, but also by the existence of less restrictive alternatives that further the government's legitimate interests. See *Playboy*, 529 U.S. at 813 ("If a less restrictive alternative would serve the Government's purpose, the legislature must use that alternative."); *Sable*, 492 U.S. at 126 ("The Government may . . . regulate the content of constitutionally protected speech in order to promote a compelling interest if it chooses the least restrictive means to further the articulated interest.").

As is the case with the narrow tailoring requirement, the government bears the burden of proof in showing the ineffectiveness of less restrictive alternatives. "When a plausible, less restrictive alternative is offered to a content-based speech restriction, it is the Government's obligation to prove that the alternative will be ineffective to achieve its goals." *Playboy*, 529 U.S. at 816; see also *Reno*, 521 U.S. at 879 ("The breadth of this content-based restriction of speech imposes an especially heavy burden on the Government to explain why a less restrictive provision would not be as effective. . . ."); Fabulous Assocs., Inc. v. Pa. Pub. Util. Comm'n, 896 F.2d 780, 787 (3d Cir. 1990) ("We focus . . . on the more difficult question whether the Commonwealth has borne its heavy burden of demonstrating that the compelling state interest could not be served by restrictions that are less intrusive on protected forms of expression.") (internal quotation marks and citation omitted).

We find that there are plausible, less restrictive alternatives to the use of software filters that would serve the government's interest in preventing the dissemination of obscenity and child pornography to library patrons. In particular, public libraries can adopt Internet use policies that make clear to patrons that the library's Internet terminals may not be used to access illegal content. Libraries can ensure that their patrons are aware of such policies by posting them in prominent places in the library, requiring patrons to sign forms agreeing to comply with the policy before the library issues library cards to patrons, and by presenting patrons, when they log on to one of the library's Internet terminals, with a screen that requires the user to agree to comply with the library's policy before allowing the user access to the Internet.

Libraries can detect violations of their Internet use policies either through direct observation or through review of the library's Internet use logs. In some cases, library staff or patrons may directly observe a patron accessing obscenity and child pornography. Libraries' Internet use logs, however, also provide libraries with a means of detecting violations of their Internet use policies. These logs, which can be kept regardless whether a library uses filtering software, record the URL of every Web page accessed by patrons. Although ordinarily the logs do not link particular URLs with particular patrons, it is possible, using access logs, to identify the patron who viewed the Web page corresponding to a particular URL, if library staff discover in the access logs the URL of a Web page containing obscenity or child pornography. For example, David Biek, Director of Tacoma Public Library's main branch, testified that in the course of scanning Internet use logs he has found what looked like attempts to access child pornography, notwithstanding the fact that Tacoma uses Websense filtering software. In two cases, he communicated his findings to law enforcement and turned over the logs to law enforcement in response to a subpoena.

Once a violation of a library's Internet use policy is detected through the methods described above, a library may either issue the patron a warning, revoke the patron's Internet privileges, or notify law enforcement, if the library believes that the patron violated either state obscenity laws or child pornography laws. Although these methods of detecting use of library computers to access illegal content are not perfect, and a library, out of respect for patrons' privacy, may choose not to adopt such policies, the government has failed to show that such methods are substantially less effective at preventing patrons from accessing obscenity and child pornography than software filters. As detailed in our findings of fact, the underblocking that results from the size, rate of change, and rate of growth of the Internet significantly impairs the software filters from preventing patrons from accessing obscenity and child pornography. Unless software filters are themselves perfectly effective at preventing patrons from accessing obscenity and child pornography, "[i]t is no response that [a less restrictive alternative] . . . may not go perfectly every time." *Playboy,* 529 U.S. at 824; cf. Denver Area Educ. Telecomm. Consortium, Inc. v. FCC, 518 U.S. 727, 759 (1996) ("No provision . . . short of an absolute ban, can offer certain protection against assault by a determined child.").

The government has not offered any data comparing the frequency with which obscenity and child pornography is [*sic*] accessed at libraries that enforce their Internet use policies through software filters with the frequency with which obscenity and child pornography is [*sic*] accessed at public libraries that enforce their Internet use policies through methods other than software filters. Although the government's library witnesses offered anecdotal accounts of a reduction in the use of library computers to access sexually explicit speech when filtering software was mandated, these anecdotal accounts are not a substitute for more robust analyses comparing the use of library computers to access child pornography and material that meets the legal definition of obscenity in libraries that use blocking software and in libraries that use alternative methods. Cf. *Playboy,* 529 U.S. at 822 ("[T]he Government must present more than anecdote and supposition.").

We acknowledge that some library staff will be uncomfortable using the "tap-on-the-shoulder" method of enforcing the library's policy against using Internet terminals to access obscenity and child pornography. The Greenville County Library, for example, experienced high turnover among library staff when staff were required to enforce the library's Internet use policy through the tap-on-the-shoulder technique. Given filters' inevitable underblocking, however, even a library that uses filtering will have to resort to a tap-on-the-shoulder method of enforcement, where library staff observes a patron openly violating the library's Internet use policy, by, for example, accessing material that is obviously child pornography but that the filtering software failed to block. Moreover, a library employee's degree of comfort in using the tap-on-the-shoulder method will vary from employee to employee, and there is no evidence that it is impossible or prohibitively costly for public libraries to hire at least some employees who are comfortable enforcing the library's Internet use policy. . . .

Similar less restrictive alternatives exist for preventing minors from accessing material harmful to minors. First, libraries may use the tap-on-the-shoulder method when minors are observed using the Internet to access material that is harmful to minors. Requiring minors to use specific terminals, for example in a children's room, that are in direct view of library staff will increase the likelihood that library staff will detect minors' use of the Internet to access material harmful to minors. Alternatively, public libraries could require minors to use blocking software only if they are unaccompanied by a parent, or only if their parent consents in advance to their child's unfiltered use of the Internet. "A court should not assume that a plausible, less restrictive alternative would be ineffective; and a court should not presume parents, given full information, will fail to act." *Playboy*, 529 U.S. at 824.

In contrast to the "harmful to minors" statute upheld in Ginsberg v. New York, 390 U.S. 629 (1968), which permitted parents to determine whether to provide their children with access to material otherwise prohibited by the statute, CIPA, like the Communications Decency Act, which the Court invalidated in Reno, contains no exception for parental consent:

> [W]e noted in Ginsberg that "the prohibition against sales to minors does not bar parents who so desire from purchasing the magazines for their children." Under the CDA, by contrast, neither the parents' consent—nor even their participation—in the communication would avoid the application of the statute.

Reno, 521 U.S. at 865 (citation omitted); see also *Ginsberg*, 390 U.S. at 639 ("It is cardinal with us that the custody, care, and nurture of the child reside first in the parents, whose primary function and freedom include preparation for obligations the state can neither supply nor hinder." (quoting Prince v. Massachusetts, 321 U.S. 158, 166 (1944))). . . .

Finally, there are other less restrictive alternatives to filtering software that further public libraries' interest in preventing patrons from unwillingly being exposed to patently offensive, sexually explicit content on the Internet. To the extent that public libraries are concerned with protecting patrons from accidentally encountering such material while using the Internet, public libraries can provide patrons with guidance in finding the material they want and avoiding unwanted material. Some public libraries also offer patrons the option of using filtering software, if they so desire. Cf. Rowan v. Post Office Dept., 397 U.S. 728 (1970) (upholding a federal statute permitting individuals to instruct the Postmaster General not to deliver advertisements that are "erotically arousing or sexually provocative").

With respect to protecting library patrons from sexually explicit content viewed by other patrons, public libraries have used a variety of less restrictive methods. One alternative is simply to segregate filtered from unfiltered terminals, and to place unfiltered terminals outside of patrons' sight-lines and areas of heavy traffic. Even the less restrictive alternative of allowing unfiltered access on only a single terminal, well out of the line of sight of other patrons, however, is not permitted under CIPA, which requires the use of a technology protection measure on every computer in the library. See CIPA §1721(b)(6)(C) (codified at 47 U.S.C. §254(h)(6)(C)), CIPA §1712 (codified at 20 U.S.C. §9134(f)(1)(A)) (requiring a public library receiving E-rate discounts or LSTA grants to certify that it "has in place a policy of Internet safety that includes the operation of a technology protection measure with respect to any of its computers with Internet access . . . ." (emphasis added)); In re Federal-State Joint Board on Universal Service: Children's Internet Protection Act, CC Docket No. 96-45, Report and Order, FCC 01-120, ¶30 (Apr. 5, 2001) ("CIPA makes no distinction between computers used only by staff and those accessible to the public.").

Alternatively, libraries can use privacy screens or recessed monitors to prevent patrons from unwillingly being exposed to material viewed by other patrons. We acknowledge that privacy screens and recessed monitors suffer from imperfections as alternatives to filtering. Both impose costs on the library, particularly recessed monitors, which, according to the government's library witnesses, are expensive.

Moreover, some libraries have experienced problems with patrons attempting to remove the privacy screens. Privacy screens and recessed monitors also make it difficult for more than one person to work at the same terminal.

These problems, however, are not insurmountable. While there is no doubt that privacy screens and recessed terminals impose additional costs on libraries, the government has failed to show that the cost of privacy screens or recessed terminals is substantially greater than the cost of filtering software and the resources needed to maintain such software. Nor has the government shown that the cost of these alternatives is so high as to make their use prohibitive. With respect to the problem of patrons removing privacy screens, we find, based on the successful use of privacy screens by the Fort Vancouver Regional Library and the Multnomah County Public Library, that it is possible for public libraries to prevent patrons from removing the screens. Although privacy screens may make it difficult for patrons to work at the same terminal side by side with other patrons or with library staff, a library could provide filtered access at terminals that lack privacy screens, when patrons wish to use a terminal with others. Alternatively, a library can reserve terminals outside of patrons' sight lines for groups of patrons who wish unfiltered access.

We therefore conclude that the government has failed to show that the less restrictive alternatives discussed above are ineffective at furthering the government's interest either in preventing patrons from using library computers to access visual depictions that are obscene, child pornography, or in the case of minors, harmful to minors, or in preventing library patrons from being unwillingly exposed to patently offensive, sexually explicit speech.

Do CIPA's Disabling Provisions Cure the Defect?

The Government argues that even if the use of software filters mandated by CIPA blocks a substantial amount of speech whose suppression serves no legitimate state interest, and therefore fails strict scrutiny's narrow tailoring requirement, CIPA's disabling provisions cure any lack of narrow tailoring inherent in filtering technology. The disabling provision applicable to libraries receiving LSTA grants states that "[a]n administrator, supervisor, or other authority may disable a technology protection measure . . . to enable access for bona fide research or other lawful purposes." CIPA §1712(a)(2) (codified at 20 U.S.C. §9134(f)(3)). CIPA's disabling provision with respect to libraries receiving E-rate discounts similarly states that "[a]n administrator, supervisor, or other person authorized by the certifying authority . . . may disable the technology protection measure concerned, during use by an adult, to enable access for bona fide research or other lawful purpose." CIPA §1721(b) (codified at 47 U.S.C. §254(h)(6)(D)).

To determine whether the disabling provisions cure CIPA's lack of narrow tailoring, we must first determine, as a matter of statutory construction, under what circumstances the disabling provisions permit libraries to disable the software filters. It is unclear to us whether CIPA's disabling provisions permit libraries to disable the filters any time a patron wishes to access speech that is neither obscenity, child pornography, or in the case of a minor patron, material that is harmful to minors. Whether CIPA permits disabling in such instances depends on the meaning of the provisions' reference to "bona fide research or other lawful purpose." On the one hand, the language "to enable access for bona fide research or other lawful purpose" could be interpreted to mean "to enable access to all constitutionally protected material." As a textual matter, this reading of the disabling provisions is plausible. If a patron seeks access to speech that is constitutionally protected, then it is reasonable to conclude that the patron has a "lawful purpose," since the dissemination and receipt of constitutionally protected speech cannot be made unlawful.

Moreover, since a narrower construction of the disabling provision creates more constitutional problems than a construction of the disabling provisions that permits access to all constitutionally protected speech, the broader interpretation is preferable. "[I]f an otherwise acceptable construction of a statute would raise serious constitutional problems, and where an alternative interpretation of the statute is fairly possible, we are obligated to construe the statute to avoid such problems." INS v. St. Cyr, 121 S. Ct. 2271, 2279 (2001) (internal quotation marks and citations omitted). On the other hand, interpreting CIPA's disabling provisions to permit disabling for access to all constitutionally protected speech presents several problems. First, if "other lawful purpose" means "for the purpose of accessing constitutionally protected speech," then this reading renders superfluous CIPA's reference to "bona fide research," which clearly contemplates some purpose beyond simply accessing constitutionally protected speech. In general, "courts should disfavor interpretations of statutes that render language superfluous." Conn. Nat'l Bank v. Germain, 503 U.S. 249, 253 (1992).

Furthermore, Congress is clearly capable of explicitly specifying categories of constitutionally unprotected speech, as it did when it drafted CIPA to require funding recipients to use technology protection measures that protect against visual depictions that are "obscene," "child pornography," or, in the case of minors, "harmful to minors." CIPA §1712(a) (codified at 20 U.S.C. §9134(f)(1)(A)(i)(I)-(III)); CIPA §1721(b) (codified at 47 U.S.C. §254(h)(6)(B)(i)(I)-(III)). If Congress intended CIPA's disabling provisions simply to permit libraries to disable the filters to allow access to speech falling outside of these categories, Congress could have drafted the disabling provisions with greater precision, expressly permitting libraries to disable the filters "to enable access for any material that is not obscene, child pornography, or in the case of minors, harmful to minors," rather than "to enable access for bona fide research or other lawful purposes," which is the language that Congress actually chose.

At bottom, however, we need not definitively construe CIPA's disabling provisions, since it suffices in this case to assume without deciding that the disabling provisions permit libraries to allow a patron access to any speech that is constitutionally protected with respect to that patron. Although this interpretation raises fewer constitutional problems than a narrower interpretation, this interpretation of the disabling provisions nonetheless fails to cure CIPA's lack of narrow tailoring. Even if the disabling provisions permit public libraries to allow patrons to access speech that is constitutionally protected yet erroneously blocked by the software filters, the requirement that library patrons ask a state actor's permission to access disfavored content violates the First Amendment.

The Supreme Court has made clear that content-based restrictions that require recipients to identify themselves before being granted access to disfavored speech are subject to no less scrutiny than outright bans on access to such speech. In Lamont v. Postmaster General, 381 U.S. 301 (1965), for example, the Court held that a federal statute requiring the Postmaster General to halt delivery of communist propaganda unless the addressee affirmatively requested the material violated the First Amendment:

> We rest on the narrow ground that the addressee in order to receive his mail must request in writing that it be delivered. This amounts in our judgment to an unconstitutional abridgment of the addressee's First Amendment rights. The addressee carries an affirmative obligation which we do not think the Government may impose on him. This requirement is almost certain to have a deterrent effect, especially as respects those who have sensitive positions.

Id. at 307.

Similarly, in Denver Area Educational Telecommunications Consortium, Inc. v. FCC, 518 U.S. 727 (1996), the Court held unconstitutional a federal law requiring cable operators to allow access to patently offensive, sexually explicit programming only to those subscribers who requested access to the programming in advance and in writing. *Id.* at 732-33. As in *Lamont,* the Court in *Denver* reasoned that this content-based restriction on recipients' access to speech would have an impermissible chilling effect: "[T]he written notice requirement will . . . restrict viewing by subscribers who fear for their reputations should the operator, advertently or inadvertently, disclose the list of those who wish to watch the 'patently offensive' channel." *Id.* at 754; see also Fabulous Assocs., Inc. v. Pa. Pub. Util. Comm'n, 896 F.2d 780, 785 (3d Cir. 1990) (considering the constitutionality of a state law requiring telephone users who wish to listen to sexually explicit telephone messages to apply for an access code to receive such messages, and invalidating the law on the ground that "[a]n identification requirement exerts an inhibitory effect").

We believe that CIPA's disabling provisions suffer from the same flaws as the restrictions on speech in *Lamont, Denver,* and *Fabulous Associates.* By requiring library patrons affirmatively to request permission to access certain speech singled out on the basis of its content, CIPA will deter patrons from requesting that a library disable filters to allow the patron to access speech that is constitutionally protected, yet sensitive in nature. As we explain above, we find that library patrons will be reluctant and hence unlikely to ask permission to access, for example, erroneously blocked Web sites containing information about sexually transmitted diseases, sexual identity, certain medical conditions, and a variety of other topics. As discussed in our findings of fact, software filters block access to a wide range of constitutionally protected speech, including Web sites containing information that individuals are likely to wish to access anonymously.

That library patrons will be deterred from asking permission to access Web sites containing certain kinds of content is evident as a matter of common sense as well as amply borne out by the trial record. Plaintiff Emmalyn Rood, who used the Internet at a public library to research information relating to her sexual identity, testified that she would have been unwilling as a young teen to ask a librarian to disable filtering software so that she could view materials concerning gay and lesbian issues. Similarly, plaintiff Mark Brown stated that he would have been too embarrassed to ask a librarian to disable filtering software if it had impeded his ability to research surgery options for his mother when she was treated for breast cancer. As explained in our findings of fact, see *supra* at Subsection II.D.2.b, the reluctance of patrons to request permission to access Web sites that were erroneously blocked is further established by the low number of patron unblocking requests, relative to the number of erroneously blocked Web sites, in those public libraries that use software filters and permit patrons to request access to incorrectly blocked Web sites. Cf. *Fabulous Assocs.*, 896 F.2d at 786 ("On the record before us, there is more than enough evidence to support the district court's finding that access codes will chill the exercise of some users' right to hear protected communications.").

To be sure, the government demonstrated that it is possible for libraries to permit patrons to request anonymously that a particular Web site be unblocked. In particular, the Tacoma Public Library has configured its computers to present patrons with the option, each time the software filter blocks their access to a Web page, of sending an anonymous email to library staff requesting that the page be unblocked. Moreover, a library staff member periodically scans logs of URLs blocked by the filters, in an effort to identify erroneously blocked sites, which the library will subsequently unblock. Although a public library's ability to permit anonymous unblocking requests addresses the deterrent effect of requiring patrons to identify themselves before gaining access to a particular Web site, we believe that it fails adequately to address the overblocking problem.

In particular, even allowing anonymous requests for unblocking burdens patrons' access to speech, since such requests cannot immediately be acted on. Although the Tacoma Public Library, for example, attempts to review requests for unblocking within 24 hours, requests sometimes are not reviewed for several days. And delays are inevitable in libraries with branches that lack the staff necessary immediately to review patron unblocking requests. Because many Internet users "surf" the Web, visiting hundreds of Web sites in a single session and spending only a short period of time viewing many of the sites, the requirement that a patron take the time to affirmatively request access to a blocked Web site and then wait several days until the site is unblocked will, as a practical matter, impose a significant burden on library patrons' use of the Internet. Indeed, a patron's time spent requesting access to an erroneously blocked Web site and checking to determine whether access was eventually granted is likely to exceed the amount of time the patron would have actually spent viewing the site, had the site not been erroneously blocked. This delay is especially burdensome in view of many libraries' practice of limiting their patrons to a half hour or an hour of Internet use per day, given the scarcity of terminal time in relation to patron demand.

The burden of requiring library patrons to ask permission to view Web sites whose content is disfavored resembles the burden that the Supreme Court found unacceptable in *Denver,* which invalidated a federal law requiring cable systems operators to block subscribers' access to channels containing sexually explicit programming, unless subscribers requested unblocking in advance. The Court reasoned that "[t]hese restrictions will prevent programmers from broadcasting to viewers who select programs day by day (or, through 'surfing,' minute by minute). . . . ." *Denver,* 518 U.S. at 754. Similarly, in *Fabulous Associates*, the Third Circuit explained that a law preventing adults from listening to sexually explicit phone messages unless they applied in advance for access to such messages would burden adults' receipt of constitutionally protected speech, given consumers' tendency to purchase such speech on impulse. See *Fabulous Assocs.*, 896 F.2d at 785 (noting that officers of two companies that sell access to sexually explicit recorded phone messages "testified that it is usually 'impulse callers' who utilize these types of services, and that people will not call if they must apply for an access code").

In sum, in many cases, as we have noted above, library patrons who have been wrongly denied access to a Web site will decline to ask the library to disable the filters so that the patron can access the Web site. Moreover, even if patrons requested unblocking every time a site is erroneously blocked, and even if library staff granted every such request, a public library's use of blocking software would still impermissibly burden patrons' access to speech based on its content. The First Amendment jurisprudence of the Supreme Court and the Third Circuit makes clear that laws imposing content-based burdens on access to speech are no less offensive to the First Amendment than laws imposing content-based prohibitions on speech:

> It is of no moment that the statute does not impose a complete prohibition. The distinction between laws burdening and laws banning speech is but a matter of degree. The Government's content-based burdens must satisfy the same rigorous scrutiny as its content-based bans. . . . When the purpose and design of a statute is to regulate speech by reason of its content, special consideration or latitude is not afforded to the Government merely because the law can somehow be described as a burden rather than outright suppression.

United States v. Playboy Entm't Group, Inc., 529 U.S. 803, 812, 826 (2000) (invalidating a federal law requiring cable television operators to limit the transmission of sexually explicit programming to the hours between 10:00 P.M. and 6:00 A.M.); see also *Fabulous Assocs.*, 896 F.2d at 785 ("[H]ere . . . there is no outright prohibition of indecent communication. However, the First Amendment protects against government inhibition as well as prohibition.") (internal quotation marks and citation omitted).

Even if CIPA's disabling provisions could be perfectly implemented by library staff every time patrons request access to an erroneously blocked Web site, we hold that the content-based burden that the library's use of software filters places on patrons' access to speech suffers from the same constitutional deficiencies as a complete ban on patrons' access to speech that was erroneously blocked by filters, since patrons will often be deterred from asking the library to unblock a site and patron requests cannot be immediately reviewed. We therefore hold that CIPA's disabling provisions fail to cure CIPA's lack of narrow tailoring.

COMMENTS AND QUESTIONS

1. What level of scrutiny should the courts use in judging this legislation? If the Supreme Court used intermediate scrutiny instead of strict scrutiny, how would that affect the ultimate ruling on the merits?

2. The *ALA* case challenges the constitutionality of only the CIPA mandate of filtering technologies in public libraries. What differences between public schools and public libraries as institutions might be significant when courts analyze CIPA mandates for each?

3. The National Research Council issued a study committee report entitled *Youth, Pornography and the Internet* (2002), which concluded that "[t]here is no single or simple answer to controlling the access of minors to inappropriate material

on the Web. To date, most of the efforts to protect children from inappropriate sexually explicit material on the Internet have focused on technology-based tools such as filters and legal prohibitions or regulation. But the committee believes that neither technology nor policy can provide a complete—or even a nearly complete —solution. While both technology and public policy have important roles to play, social and educational strategies to develop in minors an ethic of responsible choice and the skills to effectuate these choices and to cope with exposure are foundational to protecting children from negative effects that may result from exposure to inappropriate material or experiences on the Internet."

4. Tensions may, of course, arise between the First Amendment and content regulation vis-à-vis other kinds of harmful information posted on the Internet than those that may be pornographic as to children. For example, the American Coalition of Life Activists posted information on a Web site concerning doctors who had performed abortions and distributed posters that, among other things, characterized abortionists as guilty of war crimes and arguably encouraged attacks on doctors who performed abortions. Four doctors and two health clinics, including Planned Parenthood of Willamette/Columbia, claimed these activities violated a federal law that protects those who work at reproductive clinics against threats of violence. A jury returned a verdict in favor of the physicians; the trial court enjoined this publication and ordered compensatory and punitive damages. In its first ruling on this matter, the Ninth Circuit Court of Appeals ruled that ACLA had engaged in First Amendment protected speech. See Planned Parenthood v. American Coalition of Life Activists, 244 F.3d 1007 (9th Cir. 2000). After rehearing the case en banc, a majority of the Ninth Circuit decided that ACLA's activities constituted a threat to the doctors and rejected ACLA's First Amendment defense. See Planned Parenthood v. American Coalition of Life Activists, 290 F.3d 1058 (9th Cir. 2002).

12

Privacy, Anonymity, and Encryption

A. STATUTORY AND COMMON LAW CLAIMS TO PROTECT ONLINE PRIVACY

The technical infrastructure of cyberspace makes it very inexpensive and easy to collect substantial amounts of information about individual users on the Internet. Many websites capture information about users by technological means, such as planting "cookies" on user hard drives, and monitor usage of their sites for various purposes (e.g., to decide which ads to direct to particular users, what prices to charge for products or services, or which among the firm's other products and services the user might be interested in). Whether this practice is or should be legal is the subject of much debate, as the case below indicates.

In re Pharmatrak, Inc. Privacy Litigation
United States District Court for Massachusetts
220 F. Supp.2d 4 (D. Mass. 2002)

TAURO, J.

Plaintiffs allege that Defendants "secretly intercepted and accessed Internet users' electronic communications with various health-related and medical-related Internet Web sites and secretly accessed their computer hard drives in order to collect private information about their Web browsing habits [and] confidential health information without their knowledge, authorization, or consent." Plaintiffs contend that the Pharmaceutical Defendants conspired with [Defendant] Pharmatrak to "collect and share this wrongfully obtained personal and sensitive information." This activity was allegedly accomplished through the use of "web bugs," "persistent cookies," and other devices. See Reno v. ACLU, 512 U.S. 844 (1997) (discussing the Internet); In re DoubleClick Inc. Privacy Litigation, 154 F. Supp.2d 497, 500-505 (S.D.N.Y. 2001) (discussing the Internet, the Web, cookies, and data collection). . . .

The Pharmaceutical Defendants hired Defendant Pharmatrak to monitor their corporate web sites and provide monthly analysis of web site traffic. Pharmatrak offered its clients two relevant products: NETcompare, which was designed to monitor activity across clients' web pages, and DRUGcompare, which was designed to monitor activity across disease categories and drug product pages. All of the Pharmaceutical Defendants purchased NETcompare, and Defendant Pharmacia may have licensed DRUGcompare during testing phases. Pharmatrak specifically represented to the Pharmaceutical Defendants that these products did not collect "personally identifiable information." Even though the Pharmaceutical Defendants may not have known precisely how Pharmatrak's software worked, Plaintiffs readily admit that "the Pharmaceutical Defendants did authorize Pharmatrak's presence upon their Web sites . . . " Pharmatrak's system operated through the use of HTML programming, JavaScript programming, cookies, and "web bugs." Each of the Pharmaceutical Defendants' web pages were programmed with Pharmatrak code, which allowed Pharmatrak to monitor web site activity. When a computer browser requested information from a Pharmaceutical Defendant's web page, the web page would send the requested information to the user, and the site's programming code would instruct the user's browser to contact Pharmatrak's web server and retrieve a "clear GIF" from it. A clear GIF is a one pixel-by-one pixel or two pixels-by-two pixels graphic image, and is sometimes called a web bug or a "pixel tag." The purpose of a clear GIF was to cause the user's computer browser to communicate directly with Pharmatrak's web server. Some communications may have also included code referencing JavaApplet, a software program that runs in a user's browser, or JavaScript, an Internet programming language.

Having caused the user's Internet browser to contact Pharmatrak, Pharmatrak then sent a cookie back to the browser. A cookie is an electronic file "attached" to a user's computer by a computer server. Plaintiffs concede that "[c]ookies generally perform many convenient and innocuous functions." Commonly, cookies are used to store users' preferences and other information, which allows users to easily access and utilize personalized services on the web or to maintain an online "shopping cart." Cookies also allow web sites to differentiate between users as they visit by assigning each individual browser a unique, randomly generated numeric or alphanumeric identifier. If an individual browser had already visited the "Pharmatrak-enabled" website, Pharmatrak would recognize the previously placed cookie and could therefore differentiate between a repeat visit and an initial visit. Pharmatrak programmed its cookies to expire after 90 days.

It is possible that many individual users were unaware that, in addition to their browser communicating with a Pharmaceutical Defendant's web site, it was also communicating with Pharmatrak. Plaintiffs allege that the JavaApplet used by Pharmatrak allowed Pharmatrak to monitor the length of time that a particular user viewed one of the Pharmaceutical Defendants' web pages. Plaintiffs also allege that the JavaScript programming allowed Pharmatrak to "intercept the full URL of the tracked Web page visited by the user," as well as "the full URL of the Web page visited by the Internet user *immediately prior* to the user's visit to the Pharmatrak-coded Web page. This prior Web page address is known as a 'referrer URL.'" According to Plaintiffs, Pharmatrak used JavaScript "to extract referring URLs from the client's history, thereby bypassing any security or privacy mechanisms put in place to control the flow of potentially sensitive data." The JavaScript and JavaApplet, therefore, also caused users' computer browsers to communicate with Pharmatrak's server while they intentionally communicated with the Pharmaceutical Defendants' servers.

Plaintiffs also assert that Pharmatrak was able to "Capture [] Personal Information Submitted by Internet Users to the Pharmaceutical Defendants' Web Sites." Users submitted this information in two ways. First, an individual could use the "POST" method, and voluntarily fill out an online form in order to register with the site, or to receive mailings, a rebate, or other information. For example, an individual wishing to view the full text of articles on nytimes.com must first register with the site, a process which requires the individual to volunteer certain information. Second, an individual using the "GET" method could perform an online search, resulting in a URL with search terms appended to it. The appended information is known as the "query string." For example, a person interested in Cornell Law School could perform a search resulting in the following URL: http://search.yahoo.com/bin/search?p=cornell+law+school. All of the material following the question mark (i.e. p=cornell+law+school) is known as the query string, and is "rich in useful content." Plaintiffs allege that Pharmatrak was able to intercept and collect detailed, specific information about individual users from the full URLs, and place the information into relational databases.

Plaintiffs' computer scientist, C. Matthew Curtin, and his company, Interhack, examined Pharmatrak's servers between December 17, 2001 and January 18, 2002, pursuant to the court's Order. The examination of Pharmatrak's logs "identified hundreds of people by name." Based on Curtin's analysis, Plaintiffs claim that Pharmatrak collected information which included: names, addresses, telephone numbers, dates of birth, sex, insurance status, medical conditions, education levels, and occupations. Pharmatrak also collected data about e-mail communications, including user names, e-mail addresses, and subject lines from e-mails. Although Plaintiffs submit no evidence that Pharmatrak collected, sorted, or assembled this information into detailed "profiles," other than the aggregate information it submitted to the Pharmaceutical Defendants, Curtin did build such profiles. Curtin also asserts that it would be possible to build detailed profiles of individuals using the data collected by Pharmatrak and matching it to "another data source, such as a telephone book." Again, however, there is no evidence that Pharmatrak ever attempted to do so.

In sum, Plaintiffs argue that "Pharmatrak's technology permits defendants to collect extensive, detailed information about plaintiffs and Class members." In addition to the personal information discussed above, the information collected allegedly included "Web sites the Internet users were at prior to the time they went to the Pharmaceutical Defendants' Web sites, questions they asked and typed in at those prior sites, information they entered while at the Pharmaceutical Defendants' web sites, and the types of computers they were using." . . .

Plaintiffs seek summary judgment against Defendants Pharmatrak and Glocal, and Defendants each seek summary judgment against Plaintiffs.

A.   Count I—The Wiretap Act

Title I of the Electronic Communication Privacy Act of 1986 ("ECPA"), Interception of Electronic Communications ("The Wiretap Act"), provides that:

> Except as otherwise specifically provided in this chapter[,] any person who—
>   (a) intentionally intercepts, endeavors to intercept, or procures any other person to intercept, any wire, oral, or electronic communication . . . shall be punished as provided in subsection (4) or shall be subject to suit as provided in subsection (5).

This criminal statute provides for a private right of action, and is subject [to] the following statutory exception:

> (d) It shall not be unlawful under this chapter for a person not acting under color of law to intercept a wire, oral, or electronic communication where such person is a party to the communication or where one of the parties to the communication has given prior consent to such interception unless such communication is intercepted for the purpose of committing any criminal or tortious act. . . .

. . .

Plaintiffs claim that "Pharmatrak intercepted plaintiffs' transmission of their personal information to the Pharmaceutical Defendants' Web sites without the express or implied consent of either plaintiffs or the Pharmaceutical Defendants." Despite the fact that the Pharmaceutical Defendants may have consented to Pharmatrak's assembly of anonymous, aggregate information, Plaintiffs insist that the web sites never consented to Pharmatrak's collection of personally identifiable information. Absent this specific consent, Plaintiffs argue, the Wiretap Act's statutory exception simply does not apply.

Pharmatrak concedes that the Pharmaceutical Defendants did not consent to the collection of personally identifiable information. According to Pharmatrak, however, the relevant inquiry is whether the Pharmaceutical Defendants consented to Pharmatrak's NETcompare *service*, i.e. the collection of data from the Pharmaceutical Defendants' web sites, regardless of how the service eventually operated. It is undisputed that the Pharmaceutical Defendants contracted with Defendant Pharmatrak to obtain data regarding their web sites, and that they proceeded to have the Pharmatrak code placed on the web sites. Pharmatrak, therefore, asserts that the statutory exception for consent has been met, and that it is entitled to summary judgment on the Wiretap Act claim.

In In re DoubleClick Inc. Privacy Litigation ("*DoubleClick*"), the Southern District of New York disposed of a multidistrict consolidated class action case pursuant to Rule 12(b)(6). There, the plaintiffs alleged that DoubleClick, an Internet advertising firm, placed cookies on their computers, thereby collecting "information that Web users, including plaintiffs and the Class, consider to be personal and private, such as names, e-mail addresses, home and business addresses, telephone numbers, searches performed on the Internet, Web pages or sites visited on the

Internet, and other communications and information that users would not ordinarily expect advertisers to be able to collect."

The *DoubleClick* court found that the web sites affiliated with DoubleClick were "'parties to the communication[s]' from plaintiffs and have given sufficient consent to DoubleClick to intercept them," despite the possibility that the plaintiffs may not have known that their computers were communicating with DoubleClick, and that the affiliated Web sites may not have fully understood the mechanisms of the DoubleClick service.

Having found consent, the *DoubleClick* court proceeded to analyze Section 2511(2)(d)'s "criminal" or "tortious" purpose requirement, which "is to be construed narrowly." The court noted that the evidence in the case suggested that DoubleClick's actions were motivated by legitimate business goals, and found an "utter lack of evidence that [DoubleClick's] intent was tortious. . . ." Because it found that DoubleClick acted with consent and without a tortious or criminal purpose, the court dismissed the plaintiffs' Wiretap Act claim.

In Chance v. Avenue A. Inc., 165 F. Supp.2d 1153 (W.D. Wash. 2001), the plaintiffs alleged that Avenue A had placed cookies on their computers, thus permitting the company to surreptitiously monitor plaintiffs' electronic communications. First, addressing consent, the court held that "[i]t is implicit in the web pages' code instructing the user's computer to contact Avenue A, either directly or via DoubleClick's server, that the web pages have consented to Avenue A's interception of the communication between them and the individual user." The court also found that the plaintiffs had presented no evidence that the defendants acted with a tortious or illegal purpose and, therefore, granted summary judgment on the claim to Avenue A.

In the present case, Plaintiffs concede that the Pharmaceutical Defendants consented to the placement of code for Pharmatrak's NETcompare service on their web sites. As was the case in DoubleClick and Avenue A, the web site Defendants (here, the Pharmaceutical Defendants) consented to the service of a web-monitoring company (Pharmatrak), and such consent precludes a claim under the Wiretap Act. The Pharmaceutical companies contracted with Pharmatrak, and authorized Pharmatrak to communicate with any users who contacted the Pharmaceutical Web sites. Despite Plaintiffs' valiant attempts to shift the inquiry, it is irrelevant for the purposes of the Wiretap Act whether the Pharmaceutical Defendants knew the precise mechanisms of Pharmatrak's service or not. It is sufficient that the Pharmaceutical Defendants were parties to communications with Plaintiffs and consented to the monitoring service provided by Defendant Pharmatrak.

Plaintiffs are also unable to demonstrate that Defendants acted with a tortious purpose. Plaintiffs have produced no evidence "'either (1) that the primary motivation, or (2) that a determinative factor in the actor [Pharmatrak's] motivation for intercepting the conversation was to commit a criminal [or] tortious . . . act.'" Without a showing of the requisite *mens rea*, Plaintiffs cannot succeed on their claim under the Wiretap Act.

Because the Pharmaceutical Defendants consented to Pharmatrak's NETcompare service, and because Plaintiffs are unable to present any evidence whatsoever of a tortious intent, Defendants are entitled to summary judgment on Count I of the Complaint.

B. Count II—Stored Communications Act

Title II of the ECPA, also known as the "Stored Wire and Electronic Communications and Transactional Records Act," "aims to prevent hackers from obtaining, altering, or destroying certain stored electronic communications." The statute provides:

> [W]hoever—(1) intentionally accesses without authorization a facility through which an electronic communication service is provided; or (2) intentionally exceeds an authorization to access that facility; and thereby obtains, alters, or prevents authorized access to a wire or electronic communication while it is in electronic storage in such system shall be punished as provided by subsection (b) of this section.

Plaintiffs acknowledge that §2701 was primarily designed to provide a cause of action against computer hackers, and argue that "Defendants' conduct of accessing data in plaintiffs' computers, including the content of plaintiffs' e-mails, constitutes electronic trespassing and falls squarely within the ambit of Section 2701."

Defendants disagree, and claim that they are entitled to summary judgment on at least two separate grounds: (1) Plaintiffs' computers are not facilities which provide electronic communications services, an essential element of §2701; and (2) any alleged access to "communications" was authorized.

Defendants are correct that an individual Plaintiff's personal computer is not a "facility through which an electronic communication service is provided" for the purposes of §2701. Plaintiffs find it noteworthy that "[p]ersonal computers provide consumers with the opportunity to access the Internet and send or receive electronic communications," and that "[w]ithout personal computers, most consumers would not be able to access the Internet or electronic communications." Fair enough, but without a telephone, most consumers would not be able to access telephone lines, and without televisions, most consumers would not be able to access cable television. Just as telephones and televisions are necessary devices by which consumers access particular services, personal computers are necessary devices by which consumers connect to the Internet. While it is possible for modern computers to perform server-like functions, there is no evidence that any of the Plaintiffs used their computers in this way. While computers and telephones certainly provide services in the general sense of the word, that is not enough for the purposes of the ECPA. The relevant *service* is Internet access, and the service is provided through ISPs or other servers, not [through] Plaintiffs' PCs.

Even if the court were to assume that Plaintiffs' computers are "facilities" under §2701, any access to stored communications was authorized and, thus, Defendants' conduct falls under the exception from liability created by §2701(c)(2). As was the case in *DoubleClick* and *Avenue A,* the Pharmaceutical Defendants are "users" under the ECPA. The *DoubleClick* court noted that, "in a practical sense, Web sites are among the most active 'users' of Internet access." As users, the Pharmaceutical Defendants could consent to Pharmatrak's interception of Plaintiffs' communications, and Plaintiffs cannot survive the motions for summary judgment "based solely on the naked allegation that defendant[s'] access was 'unauthorized.'"

Plaintiffs argue that this case is factually different from *DoubleClick*, because the Pharmaceutical Defendants did not know that Pharmatrak would collect the type and amount of personally identifiable information that it did. Even viewing this factual distinction in the light most favorable to Plaintiffs, the Pharmaceutical Defendants nonetheless authorized Pharmatrak to monitor electronic communications between the web sites and Plaintiffs. As discussed above [], the Pharmaceutical Defendants consented to the monitoring service provided by Defendant Pharmatrak in NETcompare, even if they were unaware that the program was able to identify personal information.

In addition, the ECPA does not prohibit Pharmatrak's actions with regard to the placing of cookies on Plaintiffs' computers. Section §2701 seeks to target communications which are in "electronic storage" incident to their transmission. This court agrees with the *DoubleClick* court that "Title II only protects electronic communications stored 'for a limited time' in the 'middle' of a transmission, i.e. when an electronic communication service temporarily stores a communication while waiting to store it." Even if such cookies were covered by the ECPA, Pharmatrak created and sent the cookies, and thus any accessing of the cookies by Pharmatrak at a later date would certainly be "authorized." Because Pharmatrak's cookies fall outside the scope of §2701, Plaintiffs' claim under that section must fail.

Finally, Plaintiffs persistently argue that the Pharmaceutical Defendants did not consent to the allegedly improper interception of personal information. If the Pharmaceutical Defendants did not consent to the alleged interception of personally identifiable information, then they could not have "intentionally access[ed] without authorization" any electronic communications. Without the necessary intent under this punitive statute, the Pharmaceutical Defendants cannot be held liable and are entitled to summary judgment.

Accordingly, all Defendants are entitled to summary judgment on Count II.

C. Count III—Computer Fraud and Abuse Act

The Computer Fraud and Abuse Act (CFAA) creates a claim against:

> (a) Whoever—. . . (2) intentionally accesses a computer without authorization or exceeds authorized access, and thereby obtains . . . (c) information from any protected computer if the conduct involved an interstate or foreign communication . . .

The CFAA limits recovery to those persons who suffer "damage or loss by reason of a violation" of the Act. Section 1030(e)(8) defines damage as "any impairment to the integrity or availability of data, a program, a system, or information, that—(A) causes loss aggregating at least $5,000 in value during any 1-year period to one or more individuals. . . ." Plaintiffs do not allege that their computers were physically damaged in any way, or that they suffered any damage resulting from the repair or replacement of their computer systems. Instead, Plaintiffs argue that their "sensible interpretation" of the CFAA allows recovery for a "cognizable 'loss,'" as distinct from economic damage, for the invasion of their privacy and the "concomitant loss of control over the dissemination of their private information." Plaintiffs stress that they allege both loss and damages, and that the damage threshold of $5,000 may be met by aggregating claims among individuals and over a one year period. The CFAA does not define "loss," and the First Circuit noted in EF Cultural Travel BV, et. al. v. Explorica that "[f]ew courts have endeavored to resolve the contours of damage and loss under the CFAA." In that case, the First Circuit explicitly agreed with the *DoubleClick* court, and concluded that the statute's use of "damage or loss" indicated a Congressional desire to allow recovery for more than purely physical damage. The First Circuit was careful to note, however, that it did not hold that any loss is compensable, and that "Congress could not have intended other types of loss to support recovery unless [the $5,000] threshold were met." Plaintiffs have not shown any evidence whatsoever that Defendants have caused them at least $5,000 of damage or loss. Even accepting Mr. Curtin's bald assertion that "[d]ata about people are valuable, marketable assets," Plaintiffs are unable to meet the statutory threshold. Any damage or loss under the CFAA may be aggregated across victims and across time, but only for a single act. Because Plaintiffs have not shown any facts that demonstrate damage or loss of over $5,000 for any single act of the Defendants, Defendants are entitled to summary judgment on Count III.

COMMENTS AND QUESTIONS

1. As the *Pharmatrak* case illustrates, persons who surf the Web may be ignorant of being monitored. Senators Edwards and Hollings introduced S. 197, the Spyware Control and Privacy Protection Act of 2001, in the 107th Congress to require firms to give notice if their software contains surveillance capabilities. The bill would also require disclosure of what information is being collected and to whom it will be sent. Firms would also have to provide information about how to disable spyware features. The bill would also require that users provide affirmative consent before spyware capabilities could be enabled. Violations of the law would give a private right of action to injured persons, allowing recovery of actual monetary losses or $2500 for each violation not to exceed $500,000. What are the pros and cons of such a bill? Would legislation of this sort have provided adequate relief to the plaintiffs here?

2. The European Union (EU) has adopted comprehensive privacy regulations to protect its citizens against unauthorized collection, processing, and reuse of personal data by third parties. See Directive 95/46/EC of the European Parliament and the Council, October 25, 1995, on the protection of individuals with regard to the processing of personal data and on the free movement of such data (Official Journal of the European Community, L281, Nov. 23, 1995). Article 6 of this Directive requires member states of the EU to provide, among other things, that personal data must be "(b) collected for specified, explicit, and legitimate purposes and not further processed in a way incompatible with those purposes." Article 7 goes on to provide that EU member states shall allow personal data to be processed only if: (a) the data subject has unambiguously given his consent; (b) the processing is necessary for the performance of a contract to which the data subject is a party or in order to take steps at the request of the data subject prior to entering into a contract; (c) the processing is necessary for compliance with a legal obligation, (d) the processing is necessary in order to protect the vital interests of the data subject; or (e) the processing is necessary for the performance of a task carried out in the public interest or in the exercise of official authority vested in . . . a third party to whom the data are disclosed. The Directive was meant to regulate data collection and

processing by nongovernmental actors (that is, by businesses and other organizations). Article 25 of the EU data protection directive provides that member states of the EU "shall provide that the transfer to a third country of personal data which are undergoing processing or are intended for processing after transfer may take place only if . . . the third country in question ensures an adequate level of protection" for personal data. More recently, the EU has issued Directive 2002/58/EC of the European Parliament and of the Council of 12 July 2002, concerning the processing of personal data and the protection of privacy in the electronic communications sector (Official Journal of the European Community L 201/37, July 31, 2002). The directive supplements other EU information privacy directives and updates EU privacy principles to apply to advanced digital technologies and the Internet. US and EU officials negotiated "safe harbor" rules allowing U.S. firms to collect and process data on Europeans as long as they comply with specified fair information privacy principles. See U.S. Department of Commerce, Safe Harbor Privacy Principles (July 21, 2000). What are the implications of the EU directive for pharmaceutical companies or for Pharmatrak as to EU citizens who might have visited Web sites surveilled by Pharmatrak's software?

3. During the 1990s, partly as a result of pressure from the EU and partly in order to stimulate the growth of e-commerce, U.S. government officials strongly urged firms to adopt "fair information practices" to protect online privacy and to post and abide by privacy policies on their websites. The Federal Trade Commission articulated five core privacy principles in Privacy Online: A Report to Congress (June 1998): (1) users should have notice of a firm's information practices before any personal information is collected from them, including what information is collected, by whom, and for what purposes, (2) users should have a choice about whether data can be collected about them and about whether such data can be disclosed to others or reused for other purposes, (3) users should be able to access information collected about them and to contest the accuracy of the information, (4) firms should take other reasonable measures to ensure that data collected is accurate and secure against unauthorized disclosures and access (e.g., by use of encryption to protect the information in transit or in a stored area), and (5) a simple means should exist to enforce fair information practices and obtain redress for grievances. Would adoption of these fair information practices have averted the online privacy complaint in the *Pharmatrak* case?

4. Under its authority to challenge unfair or deceptive practices in section 5 of the Federal Trade Commission Act, the Federal Trade Commission has initiated proceedings against firms for violating posted online privacy policies. For example, the FTC initiated charges against Toysmart.com after the firm went into bankruptcy because the bankruptcy trustee planned to sell the firm's customer lists (one of its few assets) in violation of its online privacy policy, which had promised consumers that any personal information collected by the firm would not be shared with third parties. See FTC Announces Settlement with Bankrupt Website, Toysmart.com, Regarding Alleged Privacy Policy Violations, available at http://www.ftc.gov/2000/07/toysmart2.htm.

5. The FTC has been active in reporting to Congress on cyberspace privacy-related issues. See, e.g., Federal Trade Commission, Self-Regulation and Online Privacy: A Report to Congress (July 1999). Among the other U.S.-government sponsored reports on privacy in the information age are these: Information Policy Committee, National Information Infrastructure Task Force, Options for Promot-

ing Privacy on the National Information Infrastructure (April 1997); Privacy Working Group, Information Infrastructure Task Force, Privacy and the National Information Infrastructure: Principles for Providing and Using Personal Information (1995); U.S. Dept of Commerce, N.T.I.A., Elements of Effective Self-Regulation for Protection of Privacy (Jan. 1998). The literature on cyberspace information privacy is vast. Among the works worth reading are: Fred M. Cate, Privacy in the Information Age (Brookings, 1997); Jerry Kang, Information Privacy in Cyberspace Transactions, 50 Stan. L. Rev. 1193 (1998); Joel R. Reidenberg, Privacy in the Information Economy: A Fortress or a Frontier for Individual Rights?, 44 Fed. Comm. L.J. 195 (1993); Frederick Schauer, Internet Privacy and the Public-Private Distinction, 38 Jurimetrics J. 555 (1998); Paul M. Schwartz, Privacy and the Economics of Personal Health Care Information, 76 Tex. L. Rev. 1 (1997); Paul M. Schwartz, Privacy and Democracy in Cyberspace, 52 Vand. L. Rev. 1609 (1999); Daniel J. Solove, Conceptualizing Privacy, 90 Cal. L. Rev. 1087 (2002). An especially good resource is Volume 52, issue 1, of the *Stanford Law Review* (May 2000) that features several articles and essays about cyberspace privacy issues by, among others, Anita L. Allen, Julie E. Cohen, Richard A. Epstein, A. Michael Froomkin, David G. Post, Jessica Litman, Pamela Samuelson, Eugene Volokh, Jonathan Weinberg, and Jonathan Zittrain. See also Whitfield Diffie and Susan Landau, Privacy on the Line: The Politics of Wiretapping and Encryption, Cambridge MA: MIT Press, 1998; Simson Garfinkel, Database Nation: The Death of Privacy in the 21st Century, Sebastopol CA: O'Reilly & Associates, 2000; Peter P. Swire and Robert E. Litan, None of Your Business: World Data Flows, Electronic Commerce, and the European Privacy Directive, Washington DC: Brookings Institution Press, 1998.

6. After the FTC documented Web sites' abusive practices of gathering considerable amounts of information from children about themselves and their families, Congress decided to enact the Children's Online Privacy Protection Act (COPPA). This Act requires Web site owners to get permission from parents before gathering information from children under the age of 13.

COPPA is typical of American-style information privacy laws. The Act was adopted only after some documented abuses had occurred and then was narrowly tailored to address those abuses. Similar is the Video Privacy Act, 18 U.S.C. §§2710-2711. Congress passed this Act to protect video rental records from unauthorized disclosures after information about Robert Bork's video choices were published in an effort to discredit his candidacy for the U.S. Supreme Court. A third example of sectoral privacy regulation is the Gramm-Leach-Bliley Act ("GLB Act") of 1999 (codified at 15 U.S.C. §§6801-09), which requires institutions providing financial products or services to individual consumers for personal, family, or household purposes to comply with certain privacy rules, mainly requiring disclosure about the firm's information privacy practices as to the sharing of personal data and giving consumers a chance to opt out. The Federal Trade Commission has published guidelines to help firms comply with this law: How to Comply with the Privacy of Consumer Financial Information Rule of the Gramm-Leach-Bliley Act: A Guide for Small Business from the Federal Trade Commission (July 2002), available at http://www.ftc.gov/bcp/conline/pubs/buspubs/glblong.htm. Many other examples of narrowly tailored, sector-based privacy laws can be found in Paul M. Schwartz & Joel R. Reidenberg, Data Privacy Law (1996). This book is a comprehensive study of U.S. information privacy laws, both state and federal. The Electronic Privacy Information Center provides a useful website for tracking privacy-related legislation pending before Congress. See http://www.epic.org/privacy/bill_track.html.

7. There are many reasons why the United States has not adopted comprehensive information privacy laws akin to those in the EU. For one thing, Americans are generally more trusting of the private sector and of the market than the Europeans. They think it is better for firms to adopt standards voluntarily and to abide by them rather than to have the government adopt strict rules, which the industry may ignore or subvert. Second, Americans tend to believe in the power of the mass media to hold private sector abuses in check. Third, Americans are inclined to think that technologies, such as the World Wide Web Consortium's Platform for Privacy Preferences, can contribute to solutions of problems created by technologies. In addition, even when Americans are considering government intervention, they are much more inclined than Europeans to engage in a cost-benefit analysis about regulatory alternatives. Identifying a market failure may suggest the need for government intervention, but Americans are more likely to go on to inquire whether possible unintended consequences of a proposed regulation will make the cure worse than the disease. Moreover, Americans are more inclined to adopt reactive rather than proactive regulations. That is, they are generally disinclined to regulate until problems have actually occurred, and they prefer to tailor regulatory solutions to those problems rather than to adopt broad regulations anticipating problems yet to arise. Finally, Americans are more prone to adopt regulations that give consumers information about private sector practices so that consumers can exercise their market power to shop for firms with good privacy policies. Once they have such information, Americans tend to think that the market will work things out. Consumers who are averse to reuses of their personal data will, in this view, shift their business to firms that respect their privacy preferences. Yet it must be said that the Direct Marketing Association is also a powerful lobbying organization, as are many of the organizations (such as the pharmaceutical companies) who use direct marketing techniques to reach their customers.

8. Efforts to use common law torts to protect electronic privacy have generally been unsuccessful. See also Dwyer v. American Express, 273 Ill. App. 3d 742, 652 N.E.2d 1351 (Ill. App. 1st Dist. 1995). Dwyer complained that American Express had breached his common privacy rights by compiling lists of his and other customers' buying habits and renting them to third parties. The court dismissed the complaint, saying that "[b]y using the American Express card, a cardholder is voluntarily, and necessarily, giving information to defendants that, if analyzed, will reveal a cardholder's spending habits and shopping preferences." Are there any limits to what American Express might do with customer data?

Smyth v. Pillsbury Co.
United States District Court for the Eastern District of Pennsylvania
914 F. Supp. 97 (E.D. Pa. 1996)

WEINER, J.

In this diversity action, plaintiff, an at-will employee, claims he was wrongfully discharged from his position as a regional operations manager by the defendant. Presently before the court is the motion of the defendant to dismiss pursuant to

Rule 12(b)(6) of the Federal Rules of Civil Procedure. For the reasons which follow, the motion is granted. . . .

Defendant maintained an electronic mail communication system ("e-mail") in order to promote internal corporate communications between its employees. Defendant repeatedly assured its employees, including plaintiff, that all e-mail communications would remain confidential and privileged. Defendant further assured its employees, including plaintiff, that e-mail communications could not be intercepted and used by defendant against its employees as grounds for termination or reprimand.

In October 1994, plaintiff received certain e-mail communications from his supervisor over defendant's e-mail system on his computer at home. In reliance on defendant's assurances regarding defendant's e-mail system, plaintiff responded and exchanged e-mails with his supervisor. At some later date, contrary to the assurances of confidentiality made by defendant, defendant, acting through its agents, servants and employees, intercepted plaintiff[']s private e-mail messages made in October 1994. On January 17, 1995, defendant notified plaintiff that it was terminating his employment effective February 1, 1995, for transmitting what it deemed to be inappropriate and unprofessional comments[1] over defendant's e-mail system in October, 1994.

As a general rule, Pennsylvania law does not provide a common law cause of action for the wrongful discharge of an at-will employee such as plaintiff. Pennsylvania is an employment at-will jurisdiction and an employer "may discharge an employee with or without cause, at pleasure, unless restrained by some contract." Henry v. Pittsburgh & Lake Erie Railroad Co., 139 Pa. 289, 297, 21 A. 157, 157 (1891). See also, Brown v. Hammond, 810 F. Supp. 644, 645 (E.D. Pa. 1993) (An employer's right to terminate an at-will employee is "virtually absolute"). . . .

Plaintiff claims that his termination was in violation of "public policy which precludes an employer from terminating an employee in violation of the employee's right to privacy as embodied in Pennsylvania common law."[2] In support for this proposition, plaintiff directs our attention to a decision by our Court of Appeals in Borse v. Piece Goods Shop, Inc., 963 F.2d 611 (3d Cir. 1992). In *Borse,* the plaintiff sued her employer alleging wrongful discharge as a result of her refusal to submit to urinalysis screening and personal property searches at her work place pursuant to the employer's drug and alcohol policy. After rejecting plaintiff's argument that the employer's drug and alcohol program violated public policy encompassed in the United States and Pennsylvania Constitutions, our Court of Appeals stated "our review of Pennsylvania law reveals other evidence of a public policy that may, under certain circumstances, give rise to a wrongful discharge action related to

---

1. Defendant alleges in its motion to dismiss that the e-mails concerned sales management and contained threats to "kill the backstabbing bastards" and referred to the planned Holiday party as the "Jim Jones Koolaid affair."

2. Although plaintiff does not affirmatively allege so in his Complaint or in his memorandum of law in opposition to defendant's motion to dismiss, the allegations in the Complaint might suggest that plaintiff is alleging an exception to the at-will employment rule based on estoppel, i.e. that defendant repeatedly assured plaintiff and others that it would not intercept e-mail communications and reprimand or terminate based on the contents thereof and plaintiff relied on these assurances to his detriment when he made the "inappropriate and unprofessional" e-mail communications in October 1994. The law of Pennsylvania is clear, however, that an employer may not be estopped from firing an employee based upon a promise, even when reliance is demonstrated. Paul v. Lankenau Hospital, 524 Pa. 90, 569 A.2d 346 (1990).

urinalysis or to personal property searches. Specifically, we refer to the Pennsylvania common law regarding tortious invasion of privacy." *Id*. at 620.

The Court of Appeals in *Borse,* observed that one of the torts which Pennsylvania recognizes as encompassing an action for invasion of privacy is the tort of "intrusion upon seclusion." As noted by the Court of Appeals, the Restatement (Second) of Torts defines the tort as follows:

> One who intentionally intrudes, physically or otherwise, upon the solitude or seclusion of another or his private affairs or concerns, is subject to liability to the other for invasion of his privacy, if the intrusion would be highly offensive to a reasonable person.

Restatement (Second) of Torts §652B. Liability only attaches when the "intrusion is substantial and would be highly offensive to the 'ordinary reasonable person.'" *Borse,* 963 F.2d at 621 (citation omitted). Although the Court of Appeals in *Borse* observed that "the Pennsylvania courts have not had occasion to consider whether a discharge related to an employer's tortious invasion of an employee's privacy violates public policy[,]" the Court of Appeals predicted that in any claim where the employee claimed that his discharge related to an invasion of his privacy "the Pennsylvania Supreme Court would examine the facts and circumstances surrounding the alleged invasion of privacy. If the court determined that the discharge was related to a substantial and highly offensive invasion of the employee's privacy, [the Court of Appeals] believe that it would conclude that the discharge violated public policy." *Id*. at 622. In determining whether an alleged invasion of privacy is substantial and highly offensive to a reasonable person, the Court of Appeals predicted that Pennsylvania would adopt a balancing test which balances the employee's privacy interest against the employer's interest in maintaining a drug-free workplace. *Id*. at 625. Because the Court of Appeals in *Borse* could "envision at least two ways in which an employer's drug and alcohol program might violate the public policy protecting individuals from tortious invasion of privacy by private actors[,]" *id*. at 626, the Court vacated the district court's order dismissing the plaintiff's complaint and remanded the case to the district court with directions to grant Borse leave to amend the Complaint to allege how the defendant's drug and alcohol program violates her right to privacy.

Applying the Restatement definition of the tort of intrusion upon seclusion to the facts and circumstances of the case sub judice, we find that plaintiff has failed to state a claim upon which relief can be granted. In the first instance, unlike urinalysis and personal property searches, we do not find a reasonable expectation of privacy in e-mail communications voluntarily made by an employee to his supervisor over the company e-mail system notwithstanding any assurances that such communications would not be intercepted by management. Once plaintiff communicated the alleged unprofessional comments to a second person (his supervisor) over an e-mail system which was apparently utilized by the entire company, any reasonable expectation of privacy was lost. Significantly, the defendant did not require plaintiff, as in the case of an urinalysis or personal property search[,] to disclose any personal information about himself. Rather, plaintiff voluntarily communicated the alleged unprofessional comments over the company e-mail system. We find no privacy interests in such communications.

In the second instance, even if we found that an employee had a reasonable expectation of privacy in the contents of his e-mail communications over the company e-mail system, we do not find that a reasonable person would consider the defendant's interception of these communications to be a substantial and highly offensive invasion of his privacy. Again, we note that by intercepting such communications, the company is not, as in the case of urinalysis or personal property searches, requiring the employee to disclose any personal information about himself or invading the employee's person or personal effects. Moreover, the company's interest in preventing inappropriate and unprofessional comments or even illegal activity over its e-mail system outweighs any privacy interest the employee may have in those comments.

COMMENTS AND QUESTIONS

1. In Bohach v. City of Reno, 932 F. Supp. 1232 (D. Nev. 1996), two police officers sued the City of Reno, claiming violations of their privacy rights in online communications, to stop an internal affairs investigation from getting access to, using, or disclosing messages they had sent to one another via the police department's network. The court concluded that Bohach and Catalano may have had a subjective expectation of privacy when using the network to communicate with one another (or else they would not have sent the indiscreet messages they did). However, they did not have an objectively reasonable expectation of privacy in the messages given the technical capabilities of the software (which regularly recorded traffic); policies of the department (which forbade use of the network to send certain kinds of messages, such as those in violation of antidiscrimination laws); and an announcement sent when the system was first installed informing users that messages would be "logged on the network."

2. Many employers regularly monitor Internet usage and e-mail communications by employees, which obviously reduces employee expectations of privacy. See United States v. Simons, 206 F.2d 392 (4th Cir. 2000).

3. Should firms at least be required to announce that they are engaged in monitoring of Internet-based communications before doing it? Why have legislative efforts to require announcement of such monitoring met with resistance in state legislatures?

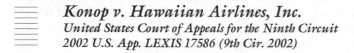

Konop v. Hawaiian Airlines, Inc.
United States Court of Appeals for the Ninth Circuit
2002 U.S. App. LEXIS 17586 (9th Cir. 2002)

BOOCHEVER, J.

Facts

Konop, a pilot for Hawaiian, created and maintained a website where he posted bulletins critical of his employer, its officers, and the incumbent union, Air Line Pilots Association ("ALPA"). Many of those criticisms related to Konop's opposition to labor concessions which Hawaiian sought from ALPA. Because

ALPA supported the concessions, Konop, via his website, encouraged Hawaiian employees to consider alternative union representation.

Konop controlled access to his website by requiring visitors to log in with a user name and password. He created a list of people, mostly pilots and other employees of Hawaiian, who were eligible to access the website. Pilots Gene Wong and James Gardner were included on this list. Konop programmed the website to allow access when a person entered the name of an eligible person, created a password, and clicked the "SUBMIT" button on the screen, indicating acceptance of the terms and conditions of use. These terms and conditions prohibited any member of Hawaiian's management from viewing the website and prohibited users from disclosing the website's contents to anyone else.

In December 1995, Hawaiian vice president James Davis asked Wong for permission to use Wong's name to access Konop's website. Wong agreed. Davis claimed he was concerned about untruthful allegations that he believed Konop was making on the website. Wong had not previously logged into the website to create an account. When Davis accessed the website using Wong's name, he presumably typed in Wong's name, created a password, and clicked the "SUBMIT" button indicating acceptance of the terms and conditions.

Later that day, Konop received a call from the union chairman of ALPA, Reno Morella. Morella told Konop that Hawaiian president Bruce Nobles had contacted him regarding the contents of Konop's website. Morella related that Nobles was upset by Konop's accusations that Nobles was suspected of fraud and by other disparaging statements published on the website. From this conversation with Morella, Konop believed Nobles had obtained the contents of his website and was threatening to sue Konop for defamation based on statements contained on the website.

After speaking with Morella, Konop took his website offline for the remainder of the day. He placed it back online the next morning, however, without knowing how Nobles had obtained the information discussed in the phone call. Konop claims to have learned only later from the examination of system logs that Davis had accessed the website using Wong's name.

In the meantime, Davis continued to view the website using Wong's name. Later, Davis also logged in with the name of another pilot, Gardner, who had similarly consented to Davis' use of his name. Through April 1996, Konop claims that his records indicate that Davis logged in over twenty times as Wong, and that Gardner or Davis logged in at least fourteen more times as Gardner. . . .

Discussion. . .

I. Electronic Communications Privacy Act Claims

We first turn to the difficult task of determining whether Hawaiian violated either the Wiretap Act, 18 U.S.C. §§2510-2522 (2000) or the Stored Communications Act, 18 U.S.C. §§2701-2711 (2000), when Davis accessed Konop's secure website. In 1986, Congress passed the Electronic Communications Privacy Act (ECPA), which was intended to afford privacy protection to electronic communications. Title I of the ECPA amended the federal Wiretap Act, which previously addressed only wire and oral communications, to "address[ ]the interception of . . .

electronic communications." S. Rep. No. 99-541, at 3 (1986). Title II of the ECPA created the Stored Communications Act (SCA), which was designed to "address[ ]access to stored wire and electronic communications and transactional records." *Id.*

As we have previously observed, the intersection of these two statutes "is a complex, often convoluted, area of the law." United States v. Smith, 155 F.3d 1051, 1055 (9th Cir. 1998). In the present case, the difficulty is compounded by the fact that the ECPA was written prior to the advent of the Internet and the World Wide Web. As a result, the existing statutory framework is ill-suited to address modern forms of communication like Konop's secure website. Courts have struggled to analyze problems involving modern technology within the confines of this statutory framework, often with unsatisfying results. See. e.g., Tatsuya Akamine, Note, Proposal for a Fair Statutory Interpretation: E-mail Stored in a Service Provider Computer Is Subject to an Interception Under the Federal Wiretap Act, 7 J.L. Pol'y 519, 521-29, 561-68 (1999) (criticizing the judiciary's interpretation of the ECPA). We observe that until Congress brings the laws in line with modern technology, protection of the Internet and websites such as Konop's will remain a confusing and uncertain area of the law.

A. The Internet and Secure Websites . . .

While most websites are public, many, such as Konop's, are restricted. For instance, some websites are password protected, require a social security number, or require the user to purchase access by entering a credit card number. The legislative history of the ECPA suggests that Congress wanted to protect electronic communications that are configured to be private, such as email and private electronic bulletin boards. See S. Rep. No. 99-541, at 35-36 ("This provision [the SCA] addresses the growing problem of unauthorized persons deliberately gaining access to . . . electronic or wire communications that are not intended to be available to the public."); H.R. Rep. No. 99-647 at 41, 62-63 (1986) (describing the Committee's understanding that the configuration of the electronic communications system would determine whether or not an electronic communication was readily accessible to the public). The nature of the Internet, however, is such that if a user enters the appropriate information (password, social security number, etc.), it is nearly impossible to verify the true identity of that user.

We are confronted with such a situation here. Although Konop took certain steps to restrict the access of Davis and other managers to the website,[3] Davis was

---

3. Specifically, Konop configured the website to allow access when a person typed in the correct web address, received the home page of his website, entered the name of an eligible person, created a password, and clicked the "SUBMIT" button indicating acceptance of the terms and conditions of use. In addition, Konop displayed the following language on the home page of his website:

> This is the gateway for NEWS UPDATES and EDITORIAL COMMENTS directed only toward Hawaiian Air's pilots and other employees, not including HAL management. By entering, you acknowledge and agree to the terms and conditions of use as specified below. You must read this entire page before entry. Others should simply find *something else* to do with their time.

> If you are already a registered user, you may fill in your name along with the other information required below, then enter the system. If you want to visit the system, and you belong to the authorized group, you must supply the proper information before you will be allowed to enter. Make note of the password you enter for your first visit, otherwise future visits may be delayed. Visits by others will be strictly prohibited.

nevertheless able to access the website by entering the correct information, which was freely provided to Davis by individuals who were eligible to view the website.

B. Wiretap Act

Konop argues that Davis' conduct constitutes an interception of an electronic communication in violation of the Wiretap Act. The Wiretap Act makes it an offense to "intentionally intercept[ ] . . . any wire, oral, or electronic communication." 18 U.S.C. §2511(1)(a). We must therefore determine whether Konop's website is an "electronic communication" and, if so, whether Davis "intercepted" that communication.

An "electronic communication" is defined as "any transfer of signs, signals, writing, images, sounds, data, or intelligence of any nature transmitted in whole or in part by a wire, radio, electromagnetic, photoelectronic or photooptical system." *Id.* §2510(12). As discussed above, website owners such as Konop transmit electronic documents to servers, where the documents are stored. If a user wishes to view the website, the user requests that the server transmit a copy of the document to the user's computer. When the server sends the document to the user's computer for viewing, a transfer of information from the website owner to the user has occurred. Although the website owner's document does not go directly or immediately to the user, once a user accesses a website, information is transferred from the website owner to the user via one of the specified mediums. We therefore conclude that Konop's website fits the definition of "electronic communication."

The Wiretap Act, however, prohibits only "interceptions" of electronic communications. "Intercept" is defined as "the aural or other acquisition of the contents of any wire, electronic, or oral communication through the use of any electronic, mechanical, or other device." *Id.* §2510(4). Standing alone, this definition would seem to suggest that an individual "intercepts" an electronic communication merely by "acquiring" its contents, regardless of when or under what circumstances the acquisition occurs. Courts, however, have clarified that Congress intended a narrower definition of "intercept" with regard to electronic communications.

In Steve Jackson Games, Inc. v. United States Secret Service, 36 F.3d 457 (5th Cir. 1994), the Fifth Circuit held that the government's acquisition of email messages stored on an electronic bulletin board system, but not yet retrieved by the intended recipients, was not an "interception" under the Wiretap Act. The court

---

Beneath this language, Konop provided boxes for a person's name, occupation, email address and password. Below the boxes were two buttons: one said "SUBMIT," the other said "CLEAR." The advisement continued:

All name and contact information will be kept strictly confidential. Any effort to defeat, compromise or violate the security of this website will be prosecuted to the fullest extent of the law.

WARNING!

The information contained herein is CONFIDENTIAL, and it is not intended for public dissemination! By requesting entry in the system, you must agree not to furnish any of the information contained herein to any other person or for any other use. Republication or redistribution of this information to any other person is strictly prohibited. Anyone found to disseminate this information to anyone other than those specifically named and allowed here will be banned from this website and held liable to prosecution for violation of the terms and conditions of use and for violation of this contract.

observed that, prior to the enactment of the ECPA, the word "intercept" had been interpreted to mean the acquisition of a communication contemporaneous with transmission. *Id.* at 460 (citing United States v. Turk, 526 F.2d 654, 658 (5th Cir. 1976)). The court further observed that Congress, in passing the ECPA, intended to retain the previous definition of "intercept" with respect to wire and oral communications, while amending the Wiretap Act to cover interceptions of electronic communications. See *Steve Jackson Games*, 36 F.3d at 462; S. Rep. No. 99-541, at 13; H.R. Rep. No. 99-647, at 34. The court reasoned, however, that the word "intercept" could not describe the exact same conduct with respect to wire and electronic communications, because wire and electronic communications were defined differently in the statute. Specifically, the term "wire communication" was defined to include storage of the communication, while "electronic communication" was not.[5] The court concluded that this textual difference evidenced Congress' understanding that, although one could "intercept" a *wire* communication in storage, one could not "intercept" an *electronic* communication in storage:

> Critical to the issue before us is the fact that, unlike the definition of "wire communication," the definition of "electronic communication" does not include electronic storage of such communications. . . . Congress' use of the word "transfer" in the definition of "electronic communication," and its omission in that definition of the phrase "any electronic storage of such communication" . . . reflects that Congress did not intend for "intercept" to apply to "electronic communications" when those communications are in "electronic storage."

Steve Jackson Games, 36 F.3d at 461-62; Wesley Coll. v. Pitts, 974 F. Supp. 375, 386 (D. Del. 1997) ("By including the electronic storage of wire communications within the definition of such communications but declining to do the same for electronic communications . . . Congress sufficiently evinced its intent to make acquisitions of electronic communications unlawful under the Wiretap Act only if they occur contemporaneously with their transmissions."), *aff'd*, 172 F.3d 861 (3d Cir. 1998); United States v. Reyes, 922 F. Supp. 818, 836 (S.D.N.Y. 1996) ("Taken together, the definitions thus imply a requirement that the acquisition of [electronic communications] be simultaneous with the original transmission of the data."); Bohach v. City of Reno, 932 F. Supp. 1232, 1236-37 (D. Nev. 1996) (requiring acquisition during transmission). The *Steve Jackson* Court further noted that the ECPA was deliberately structured to afford electronic communications *in storage* less protection than other forms of communication. See *Steve Jackson Games*, 36 F.3d at 462-64.

The Ninth Circuit endorsed the reasoning of *Steve Jackson Games* in United States v. Smith, 155 F.3d at 1051. The question presented in *Smith* was whether the Wiretap Act covered wire communications in storage, such as voicemail messages, or just wire communications in transmission, such as ongoing telephone conversations. Relying on the same textual distinction as the Fifth Circuit in *Steve Jackson Games*, we concluded that wire communications in storage could be "intercepted" under the Wiretap Act. We found that Congress' inclusion of storage in the

---

5. Until October 2001, "wire communication" was defined as "any aural transfer made in whole or in part through the use of facilities for the transmission of communications by the aid of wire, cable or other like connection between the point of origin and the point of reception . . . and *such term includes any electronic storage of such communication.* . . ." 18 U.S.C. §2510(1) (2000) (emphasis added).

definition of "wire communication" militated in favor of a broad definition of the term "intercept" with respect to wire communications, one that included acquisition of a communication subsequent to transmission. We further observed that, *with respect to wire communications only*, the prior definition of "intercept"—acquisition contemporaneous with transmission—had been overruled by the ECPA. *Smith*, 155 F.3d at 1057 n. 11. On the other hand, we suggested that the narrower definition of "intercept" was still appropriate with regard to electronic communications:

> In cases concerning "electronic communications" - the definition of which specifically includes "transfers" and specifically excludes "storage"—the "narrow" definition of "intercept" fits like a glove; it is natural to except non-contemporaneous retrievals from the scope of the Wiretap Act. In fact, a number of courts adopting the narrow interpretation of "interception" have specifically premised their decisions to do so on the distinction between §2510's definitions of wire and electronic communications.

Smith, 155 F.3d at 1057 (citations and alterations omitted).

We agree with the *Steve Jackson* and *Smith* courts that the narrow definition of "intercept" applies to electronic communications. Notably, Congress has since amended the Wiretap Act to eliminate storage from the definition of wire communication, see USA PATRIOT Act §209, 115 Stat. at 283, such that the textual distinction relied upon by the *Steve Jackson* and *Smith* courts no longer exists. This change, however, supports the analysis of those cases. By eliminating storage from the definition of wire communication, Congress essentially reinstated the pre-ECPA definition of "intercept"—acquisition contemporaneous with transmission—with respect to wire communications. See *Smith*, 155 F.3d at 1057 n. 11. The purpose of the recent amendment was to reduce protection of voice mail messages to the lower level of protection provided other electronically stored communications. *See* H.R. Rep. 107-236(I), at 158-59 (2001). When Congress passed the USA PATRIOT Act, it was aware of the narrow definition courts had given the term "intercept" with respect to electronic communications, but chose not to change or modify that definition. To the contrary, it modified the statute to make that definition applicable to voice mail messages as well. Congress, therefore, accepted and implicitly approved the judicial definition of "intercept" as acquisition contemporaneous with transmission.

We therefore hold that for a website such as Konop's to be "intercepted" in violation of the Wiretap Act, it must be acquired during transmission, not while it is in electronic storage.[6] This conclusion is consistent with the ordinary meaning of

---

6. The dissent, amici, and several law review articles argue that the term "intercept" must apply to electronic communications in storage because storage is a necessary incident to the transmission of electronic communications. See, e.g., Akamine, *supra*, at 561-65; Jarrod J. White, E-Mail@Work.Com: Employer Monitoring of Employee E-Mail, 48 Ala. L. Rev. 1079, 1083 (1997). Email and other electronic communications are stored at various junctures in various computers between the time the sender types the message and the recipient reads it. In addition, the transmission time of email is very short because it travels across the wires at the speed of light. It is therefore argued that if the term "intercept" does not apply to the *en route* storage of electronic communications, the Wiretap Act's prohibition against "intercepting" electronic communications would have virtually no effect. While this argument is not without appeal, the language and structure of the ECPA demonstrate that Congress considered and rejected this argument. Congress defined "electronic storage" as "any temporary, intermediate storage of a wire or electronic communication incidental to the electronic transmission thereof," 18 U.S.C. §2510(17)(A), indicating that Congress understood that electronic storage was an inherent part of

"intercept," which is "to stop, seize, or interrupt in progress or course before arrival." *Webster's Ninth New Collegiate Dictionary* 630 (1985). More importantly, it is consistent with the structure of the ECPA, which created the SCA for the express purpose of addressing "access to *stored* . . . electronic communications and transactional records." S. Rep. No. 99-541 at 3 (emphasis added). The level of protection provided stored communications under the SCA is considerably less than that provided communications covered by the Wiretap Act. Section 2703(a) of the SCA details the procedures law enforcement must follow to access the contents of stored electronic communications, but these procedures are considerably less burdensome and less restrictive than those required to obtain a wiretap order under the Wiretap Act. See *Steve Jackson Games*, 36 F.3d at 463. Thus, if Konop's position were correct and acquisition of a stored electronic communication were an interception under the Wiretap Act, the government would have to comply with the more burdensome, more restrictive procedures of the Wiretap Act to do exactly what Congress apparently authorized it to do under the less burdensome procedures of the SCA. Congress could not have intended this result. As the Fifth Circuit recognized in *Steve Jackson Games*, "it is most unlikely that Congress intended to require law enforcement officers to satisfy the more stringent requirements for an intercept in order to gain access to the contents of stored electronic communications." *Id.;* see also *Wesley Coll.*, 974 F. Supp. at 388 (same).

Because we conclude that Davis' conduct did not constitute an "interception" of an electronic communication in violation of the Wiretap Act, we affirm the district court's grant of summary judgment against Konop on his Wiretap Act claims.

C. Stored Communications Act

Konop also argues that, by viewing his secure website, Davis accessed a stored electronic communication without authorization in violation of the SCA. The SCA makes it an offense to "intentionally access[ ]without authorization a facility through which an electronic communication service is provided . . . and thereby obtain[ ] . . . access to a wire or electronic communication while it is in electronic storage in such system." 18 U.S.C. §2701(a)(1). The SCA excepts from liability, however, "conduct authorized . . . by a user of that service with respect to a communication of or intended for that user." 18 U.S.C. §2701(c)(2). The district court found that the exception in §2701(c)(2) applied because Wong and Gardner consented to Davis' use of Konop's website. It therefore granted summary judgment to Hawaiian on the SCA claim.

The parties agree that the relevant "electronic communications service" is Konop's website, and that the website was in "electronic storage." In addition, for the purposes of this opinion, we accept the parties' assumption that Davis' conduct constituted "access without authorization" to "a facility through which an electronic communication service is provided."

We therefore address only the narrow question of whether the district court properly found Hawaiian exempt from liability under §2701(c)(2). Section 2701(c)(2) allows a person to authorize a third party's access to an electronic

---

electronic communication. Nevertheless, as discussed above, Congress chose to afford stored electronic communications less protection than other forms of communication.

communication if the person is 1) a "user" of the "service" and 2) the communication is "of or intended for that user." See 18 U.S.C. §2701(c)(2). A "user" is "any person or entity who—(A) uses an electronic communications service; and (B) is duly authorized by the provider of such service to engage in such use." 18 U.S.C. §2510(13).

The district court concluded that Wong and Gardner had the authority under §2701(c)(2) to consent to Davis' use of the website because Konop put Wong and Gardner on the list of eligible users. This conclusion is consistent with other parts of the Wiretap Act and the SCA which allow intended recipients of wire and electronic communications to authorize third parties to access those communications. In addition, there is some indication in the legislative history that Congress believed "addressees" or "intended recipients" of electronic communications would have the authority under the SCA to allow third parties access to those communications. See H.R. Rep. No. 99-647, at 66-67 (explaining that "an addressee [of an electronic communication] may consent to the disclosure of a communication to any other person" and that "[a] person may be an 'intended recipient' of a communication . . . even if he is not individually identified by name or otherwise").

Nevertheless, the plain language of §2701(c)(2) indicates that only a "user" of the service can authorize a third party's access to the communication. The statute defines "user" as one who 1) *uses* the service and 2) is duly authorized to do so. Because the statutory language is unambiguous, it must control our construction of the statute, notwithstanding the legislative history. See United States v. Daas, 198 F.3d 1167, 1174 (9th Cir. 1999). The statute does not define the word "use," so we apply the ordinary definition, which is "to put into action or service, avail oneself of, employ." *Webster's* at 1299; *see Daas*, 198 F.3d at 1174 ("If the statute uses a term which it does not define, the court gives that term its ordinary meaning.").

Based on the common definition of the word "use," we cannot find any evidence in the record that Wong ever used Konop's website. There is some evidence, however, that Gardner may have used the website, but it is unclear when that use occurred. At any rate, the district court did not make any findings on whether Wong and Gardner actually used Konop's website—it simply assumed that Wong and Gardner, by virtue of being eligible to view the website, could authorize Davis' access. The problem with this approach is that it essentially reads the "user" requirement out of §2701(c)(2). Taking the facts in the light most favorable to Konop, we must assume that neither Wong nor Gardner was a "user" of the website at the time he authorized Davis to view it. We therefore reverse the district court's grant of summary judgment to Hawaiian on Konop's SCA claim. . . .

REINHART, J. dissenting:

. . . To read a contemporaneity requirement into the definition of "intercept" renders the prohibition against the electronic communication interception largely superfluous, and violates the precept against interpreting one provision of a statute to negate another. Intercept of electronic communications is defined as any "acquisition of the contents of any . . . electronic . . . communication through the use of any . . . device." 18 U.S.C. §2510 (4). The nature of electronic communication is that it spends infinitesimal amounts of time "en route," unlike a phone call. Therefore, in order to "intercept" an electronic communication, one ordinarily obtains one of the copies made en route or at the destination. These copies constitute "stored electronic communications," as acknowledged by the majority. 18 U.S.C. §2510(17)(A) ("'electronic storage' means . . . any temporary, intermediate storage of a wire or electronic communication incidental to the electronic transmission thereof"). If intercept is defined as solely contemporaneous acquisition, then in contravention of Congressional intent, at most all acquisitions of the contents of electronic communications would escape the intercept prohibition entirely. Jarrod J. White, Commentary, E-Mail@Work.Com: Employer Monitoring of Employee E-Mail, 48 Ala. L. Rev. 1079, 1083 (1997) ("Following the Fifth Circuit's rationale, [and excluding stored electronic communications from the intercept prohibition] there is only a narrow window during which an E-mail interception may occur— the seconds or milliseconds before which a newly composed message is saved to any temporary location following a send command. Therefore [assuming that stored communications are excluded from the intercept prohibition], interception of E-mail within the prohibition of the ECPA is virtually impossible."). . . .

[A] reading of the Wiretap Act that includes stored electronic communications in the statute's "intercept" prohibition is consistent with the nature of the technology at issue, leaves no unexplained statutory gaps, and renders none of the myriad provisions of either the Wiretap Act or the Stored Communications Act superfluous. Under such a reading, the Wiretap Act would prohibit the interception of electronic communications, both stored and en route, and subject violators to serious penalties. It would permit law enforcement to intercept such communications using a court order as indicated in §2516. (Whether or not it would preserve the use of other less savory techniques is a matter this court is not called upon to decide.) A court order can be obtained by state prosecutors in connection with any one of a number of enumerated crimes, and by any assistant United States attorney for the investigation of any federal felony. Wire communications are treated similarly with only minor exceptions (for example, authorization to intercept wire communications is only available for a finite, though extensive, list of federal crimes); this reading, consistent with Congressional intent as revealed in the legislative history of the statute, rejects the idea that stored electronic communications are afforded a lesser degree of protection from interception than stored wire communications.[2]

COMMENTS AND QUESTIONS

1. After *Konop* and *Steve Jackson Games*, what protection does the ECPA provide? Should Congress amend ECPA to provide an appropriate degree of protection to electronic communications? If so, how? Do you agree with the majority or with the dissent about the interpretation that should be given to the term "intercept"?

2. Critics of a firm, particularly employees, may prefer to post disparaging remarks pseudonymously or anonymously as an alternative to hosting a password-

---

2. In its interpretation of the term "intercept," the majority relies in part on legislative history from the USA PATRIOT Act. As the Supreme Court has cautioned, however, "'the views of a subsequent Congress form a hazardous basis for inferring the intent of an earlier one.'" Consumer Prod. Safety Comm'n v. GTE Sylvania, Inc., 447 U.S. 109, 117, 64 L. Ed.2d 766, 100 S. Ct. 2051 (1980) (quoting United States v. Price, 361 U.S. 304, 313, 4 L. Ed.2d 334, 80 S. Ct. 326 (1960). Such subsequent legislative history will "rarely override a *reasonable interpretation* of a statute that can be gleaned from its language and legislative history prior to its enactment." 447 U.S. at 118 n. 13 (emphasis added).

protected website, as Konop did. This strategy may broaden the audience for the critique. However, it does not ensure that the identities of the posters will necessarily be protected against disclosure since identity information is generally accessible through the posters' Internet service or access provider, as the cases below illustrate.

B. ONLINE ANONYMOUS SPEECH AND THE FIRST AMENDMENT

≡ *In re Subpoena Duces Tecum to America Online, Inc.*
≡ *Circuit Court of Fairfax County, Virginia*
≡ *52 Va. Cir. 26 (2000)*

KLEIN, J.

This matter is before the Court on America Online, Inc.'s ("AOL") Motion to Quash Subpoena seeking disclosure of identifying information for four AOL Internet service subscribers.

Plaintiff Anonymous Publicly Traded Company ("APTC") seeks to learn the identities of the subscribers so that it can properly name them as defendants in an action it has instituted in the State of Indiana. AOL asserts that the First Amendment rights of its subscribers preclude APTC from obtaining the relief it seeks in this Court. For the reasons set forth in this opinion, the Motion to Quash is denied. . . .

APTC argues that if the subpoena unreasonably burdens the First Amendment rights of the John Does, then the John Does are the proper parties to seek relief from the subpoena, not AOL. APTC's argument ignores longstanding precedent upholding the standing of third parties to seek vindication of First Amendment rights of others in situations analogous to the circumstances presented herein . . .

It cannot be seriously questioned that those who utilize the "chat rooms" and "message boards" of AOL do so with an expectation that the anonymity of their postings and communications generally will be protected. If AOL did not uphold the confidentiality of its subscribers, as it has contracted to do, absent extraordinary circumstances, one could reasonably predict that AOL subscribers would look to AOL's competitors for anonymity. As such, the subpoena duces tecum at issue potentially could have an oppressive effect on AOL.

Moreover, it is questionable whether all, or any, of the subscribers have received actual notice of the pendency of these proceedings or have the inclination or financial ability to defend against the subpoenas. As the Supreme Court has recognized, when the right to anonymity is at issue, "to require that [the right] be claimed by the members themselves would result in nullification of the right at the very moment of its assertion." NAACP v. Alabama, 357 U.S. at 459. Hence, this Court holds that AOL has standing to assert the First Amendment rights of the John Does.

As this Court has determined that the subpoena can have an oppressive effect on AOL, the sole question remaining is whether the subject subpoena is unreasonable in light of all the surrounding circumstances. Ultimately, this Court's ruling on the Motion to Quash must be governed by a determination of whether the issuance of the subpoena duces tecum and the potential loss of the anonymity of the John Does, would constitute an unreasonable intrusion on their First Amendment rights. In broader terms, the issue can be framed as whether a state's interest in protecting its citizens against potentially actionable communications on the Internet is sufficient to outweigh the right to anonymously speak on this ever-expanding medium. There appear to be no published opinions addressing this issue either in the Commonwealth of Virginia or any of its sister states. . . .

Inherent in the panoply of protections afforded by the First Amendment is the right to speak anonymously in diverse contexts. This right arises from a long tradition of American advocates speaking anonymously through pseudonyms, such as James Madison, Alexander Hamilton, and John Jay, who authored the *Federalist Papers* but signed them only as "Publius." In Talley v. California, 362 U.S. 60, 64, 4 L. Ed.2d 559, 80 S. Ct. 536 (1960), the Supreme Court recognized that "[a]nonymous pamphlets, leaflets, brochures and even books have played an important role in the progress of mankind," and held that the distribution of unsigned handbills urging a boycott of certain merchants, who were allegedly involved in discriminatory practices, fell within the ambit of the protections afforded by the First Amendment.

In McIntyre v. Ohio Elections Comm'n., 514 U.S. 334, 131 L. Ed.2d 426, 115 S. Ct. 1511 (1995), the Supreme Court again examined the breadth of the right to anonymity protected by First Amendment principles. Noting that famous works of literature had been penned by authors utilizing assumed names, the Court recognized that "[t]he decision in favor of anonymity may be motivated by fear of economic or official retaliation, by concern about social ostracism, or merely by a desire to preserve as much of one's privacy as possible." *McIntyre,* 514 U.S. at 341-42 (emphasis added). Specifically acknowledging that "the freedom to publish anonymously extends beyond the literary realm," the Supreme Court held in *McIntyre* that an Ohio law prohibiting distribution of anonymous campaign literature was constitutionally infirm. *Id.*

This Court must now decide whether the First Amendment right to anonymity should be extended to communications by persons utilizing chat rooms and message boards on the information superhighway. It is beyond question that thousands, perhaps millions, of people communicating by way of the Internet do so with a "desire to preserve as much of [their] privacy as possible." *McIntyre,* 514 U.S. at 342. "Through the use of chat rooms, any person with a phone line can become a town crier with a voice that resonates farther than it could from any soapbox. Through the use of Web pages, mail exploders, and newsgroups, the same individual can become a pamphleteer." Reno v. ACLU, 521 U.S. 844, 117 S. Ct. 2329, 2344, 138 L. Ed.2d 874 (1997). To fail to recognize that the First Amendment right to speak anonymously should be extended to communications on the Internet would require this Court to ignore either United States Supreme Court precedent or the realities of speech in the twenty-first century. This Court declines to do either and holds that the right to communicate anonymously on the Internet falls within the scope of the First Amendment's protections.

As AOL conceded at oral argument, however, the right to speak anonymously is not absolute. See *McIntyre,* 514 U.S. at 353 ("We recognize that a State's enforcement interest might justify a more limited identification requirement.")[.] In that the Internet provides a virtually unlimited, inexpensive, and almost immediate means of communication with tens, if not hundreds, of millions of people, the dangers of its misuse cannot be ignored. The protection of the right to communicate anonymously must be balanced against the need to assure that those persons who choose to abuse the opportunities presented by this medium can be made to answer for such transgressions. Those who suffer damages as a result of tortious or other actionable communications on the Internet should be able to seek appropriate redress by preventing the wrongdoers from hiding behind an illusory shield of purported First Amendment rights. . . .

Any defamatory statements made by one or more of the John Doe defendants would not be entitled to any First Amendment protection. Moreover, the release of confidential insider information, relating to a publicly traded company, through a medium such as the Internet, is no less pernicious than the libelous statements that fall outside the scope of First Amendment protections. In this age of communication in cyberspace, the potential dangers that could flow from the dissemination of such information increase exponentially as the proliferation of shareholder chat rooms continues unabated and more and more traders utilize the Internet as a means of buying and selling stocks. As such, the wrongful dissemination of such information through the Internet may also fall outside the scope of First Amendment protections. This Court, however, need not decide that question. Nor must it decide whether less than a compelling state interest might be sufficient to vitiate the anonymity of the John Does herein, because this Court finds that, under the circumstances of this case, the State of Indiana clearly has a compelling state interest to protect companies operating within its borders from such wrongful conduct. To rule otherwise would leave companies such as APTC virtually defenseless to this potentially virulent hazard.

Nonetheless, before a court abridges the First Amendment right of a person to communicate anonymously on the Internet, a showing, sufficient to enable that court to determine that a true, rather than perceived, cause of action may exist, must be made. AOL proposes that this Court adopt the following two prong test to determine when a subpoena request is reasonable and accordingly would require AOL to identify its subscribers: (1) the party seeking the information must have pleaded with specificity a prima facie claim that it is the victim of particular tortious conduct and (2) the subpoenaed identity information must be centrally needed to advance that claim. APTC responds that this Court should not, in any way, address the merits of its claim and should merely follow the procedures that APTC asserts are compelled by Va. Code §8.01-411. Although this Court agrees with AOL that APTC must establish that there is a legitimate basis to believe that it may have bona fide claims against the John Does before compliance with the subpoena duces tecum is ordered, it agrees with APTC that AOL's proposed test is unduly cumbersome. What is sufficient to plead a prima facie case varies from state to state and, sometimes, from court to court. This Court is unwilling to establish any precedent that would support an argument that judges of one state could be required to determine the sufficiency of pleadings from another state when ruling on matters such as the instant motion. . . .

Therefore, in lieu of the test proposed by AOL, this Court holds that, when a subpoena is challenged under a rule akin to Virginia Supreme Court Rule 4:9(c), a court should only order a non-party, Internet service provider to provide information concerning the identity of a subscriber (1) when the court is satisfied by the pleadings or evidence supplied to that court (2) that the party requesting the subpoena has a legitimate, good faith basis to contend that it may be the victim of conduct actionable in the jurisdiction where suit was filed and (3) the subpoenaed identity information is centrally needed to advance that claim. A review of the Indiana pleadings and the subject Internet postings satisfies this Court that all three prongs of the above-stated test have been satisfied as to the identities of the subscribers utilizing the four e-mail addresses in question.

In his December 22, 1999, correspondence to the Court, counsel for AOL argued that the methodology utilized by APTC in obtaining the AOL e-mail addresses in question is far from foolproof. This Court recognizes that the methodology may be less than totally certain and that some of the postings may turn out to be from persons who owe no fiduciary or contractual duty to APTC. Nonetheless, this Court finds that the compelling state interest in protecting companies such as APTC from the potentially severe consequences that could easily flow from actionable communications on the information superhighway significantly outweigh the limited intrusion on the First Amendment rights of any innocent subscribers. Hence, this Court finds that the instant subpoena duces tecum does not unduly burden the First Amendment rights of the John Does and is therefore not unreasonable in light of all the surrounding circumstances. Accordingly, AOL's Motion to Quash is denied in its entirety.

Doe v. 2TheMart.com Inc.
United States District Court for the Western District of Washington
140 F. Supp.2d 1088 (W.D. Wash. 2001)

ZILLY, J.

This matter comes before the Court on the motion of J. Doe (Doe) to proceed under a pseudonym and to quash a subpoena issued by 2TheMart.com (TMRT) to a local internet service provider, Silicon Investor/InfoSpace, Inc. (InfoSpace). The motion raises important First Amendment issues regarding Doe's right to speak anonymously on the Internet and to proceed in this Court using a pseudonym in order to protect that right.

Factual Background

There is a federal court lawsuit pending in the Central District of California in which the shareholders of TMRT have brought a shareholder derivative class action against the company and its officers and directors alleging fraud on the market. In that litigation, the defendants have asserted as an affirmative defense that no act or omission by the defendants caused the plaintiffs' injury. By subpoena, TMRT seeks to obtain the identity of twenty-three speakers who have participated anonymously on Internet message boards operated by InfoSpace. That subpoena is the subject of the present motion to quash.

InfoSpace is a Seattle based Internet company that operates a website called "Silicon Investor." The Silicon Investor site contains a series of electronic bulletin boards, and some of these bulletin boards are devoted to specific publicly traded companies. InfoSpace users can freely post and exchange messages on these boards. Many do so using Internet pseudonyms, the often fanciful names that people choose for themselves when interacting on the Internet. By using a pseudonym, a person who posts or responds to a message on an Internet bulletin board maintains anonymity.

One of the Internet bulletin boards on the Silicon Investor website is specifically devoted to TMRT. According to the brief filed on behalf of J. Doe, "to date, almost 1500 messages have been posted on the TMRT board, covering an enormous variety of topics and posters. Investors and members of the public discuss the latest news about the company, what new businesses it may develop, the strengths and weaknesses of the company's operations, and what its managers and its employees might do better." Past messages posted on the site are archived, so any new user can read and print copies of prior postings.

Some of the messages posted on the TMRT site have been less than flattering to the company. In fact, some have been downright nasty. For example, a user calling himself "Truthseeker" posted a message stating "TMRT is a Ponzi scam that Charles Ponzi would be proud of. . . . The company's CEO, Magliarditi, has defrauded employees in the past. The company's other large shareholder, Rebeil, defrauded customers in the past." Another poster named "Cuemaster" indicated that "they were dumped by their accountants . . . these guys are friggin liars . . . why haven't they told the public this yet??? Liars and criminals!!!!!" Another user, not identified in the exhibits, wrote "Lying, cheating, thieving, stealing, lowlife criminals!!!!" Other postings advised TMRT investors to sell their stock. "Look out below!!!! This stock has had it . . . get short or sell your position now while you still can." "They [TMRT] are not building anything, except extensions on their homes . . . bail out now."

TMRT, the defendant in the California lawsuit, issued the present subpoena to InfoSpace pursuant to Fed.R.Civ.P. 45(a)(2). The subpoena seeks, among other things, "all identifying information and documents, including, but not limited to, computerized or computer stored records and logs, electronic mail (E-mail), and postings on your online message boards," concerning a list of twenty-three InfoSpace users, including Truthseeker, Cuemaster, and the current J. Doe, who used the pseudonym NoGuano. These users have posted messages on the TMRT bulletin board or have communicated via the Internet with users who have posted such messages. The subpoena would require InfoSpace to disclose the subscriber information for these twenty-three users, thereby stripping them of their Internet anonymity.

InfoSpace notified these users by e-mail that it had received the subpoena, and gave them time to file a motion to quash. One such user who used the Internet pseudonym NoGuano now seeks to quash the subpoena.

NoGuano alleges that enforcement of the subpoena would violate his or her First Amendment right to speak anonymously. In response to the motion this Court issued a Minute Order directing the interested parties TMRT, InfoSpace, and NoGuano to file additional briefing. All interested parties filed briefing as directed and participated in oral argument.

Discussion . . .

The free exchange of ideas on the Internet is driven in large part by the ability of Internet users to communicate anonymously. If Internet users could be stripped of that anonymity by a civil subpoena enforced under the liberal rules of civil discovery, this would have a significant chilling effect on Internet communications and thus on basic First Amendment rights. Therefore, discovery requests seeking to identify anonymous Internet users must be subjected to careful scrutiny by the courts.

As InfoSpace has urged, "unmeritorious attempts to unmask the identities of online speakers . . . have a chilling effect on" Internet speech. The "potential chilling effect imposed by the unmasking of anonymous speakers would diminish if litigants first were required to make a showing in court of their need for the identifying information." "Requiring litigants to make such a showing would allow [the Internet] to thrive as a forum for speakers to express their views on topics of public concern." InfoSpace and NoGuano have accordingly urged this Court to "adopt a balancing test requiring litigants to demonstrate . . . that their need for identity information outweighs anonymous online speakers' First Amendment rights[.]"

In the context of a civil subpoena issued pursuant to Fed.R.Civ.P. 45, this Court must determine when and under what circumstances a civil litigant will be permitted to obtain the identity of persons who have exercised their First Amendment right to speak anonymously. There is little in the way of persuasive authority to assist this Court. However, courts that have addressed related issues have used balancing tests to decide when to protect an individual's First Amendment rights.

In Columbia Ins. Co. v. Seescandy.com, the plaintiff was unable to identify the defendants when filing the complaint. That complaint named J. Doe defendants, and alleged, *inter alia*, the infringement of a registered trademark when those defendants registered the "Seescandy.com" domain name. See *Seescandy.com*, 185 F.R.D. at 576. The J. Doe defendants had engaged in the allegedly tortious conduct entirely online, and anonymously. *Id.* at 578. The court considered whether to allow discovery to uncover the identity of the defendants so that they might be properly served and subject to the jurisdiction of the court. The court recognized the defendant's "legitimate and valuable right to participate in online forums anonymously or pseudonymously." *Id.*

Accordingly, the court ruled that four limiting principles would apply to such discovery. The court required that the plaintiff identify the individual with some specificity so the court could determine if they were truly an entity amenable to suit, and that the plaintiff identify all previous steps taken to locate the defendant, justifying the failure to properly serve. The *Seescandy.com* court imposed two other requirements that have direct relevance here. First, the plaintiff was required to show that the case would withstand a motion to dismiss, "to prevent abuse of this extraordinary application of the discovery process and to insure that plaintiff has standing[.]" *Id.* at 579-80. Second, the plaintiff was required to file a discovery request justifying the need for the information requested. *Id.* at 580. Therefore, the court required the plaintiff to demonstrate that the suit, and the resulting discovery sought, was not frivolous, and to demonstrate the need for the identifying information.

Similarly, in In re Subpoena Duces Tecum to America Online, Inc., 2000 WL 1210372, (Va.Cir.Ct. 2000), the court reviewed a subpoena seeking the identity of certain J. Doe defendants who had allegedly made defamatory statements and disclosed confidential information online. See *America Online, Inc.*, 2000 WL 1210372, *1. The Virginia court recognized the First Amendment right to Internet anonymity, and held that an Internet service provider could assert that right on behalf of its users. See *id.*, *5-6. The court applied a two part test determining whether the subpoena would be enforced. First, the court must be convinced by the pleadings and evidence submitted that "the party requesting the subpoena has a legitimate, good faith basis to contend that it may be the victim of conduct actionable in the jurisdiction where the suit was filed[.]" *Id.*, *8. Second, "the subpoenaed identity information [must be] *centrally needed to advance that claim.*" *Id.* (emphasis added). In that particular case, because the court concluded that the plaintiff had met these requirements, the discovery was allowed. The Virginia court concluded that the compelling state interest in protecting companies outweighed the limited intrusion on the First Amendment rights of any innocent Internet users. *Id.*

The courts in *Seescandy.com* and *America Online, Inc.* applied similar factors. Both required a showing of, at least, a good faith basis for bringing the lawsuit, and both required some showing of the compelling need for the discovery sought. In both cases, the need for the information was especially great because the information sought concerned J. Doe *defendants*. Without the identifying information, the litigation against those defendants could not have continued.

The standard for disclosing the identity of a non-party *witness* must be higher than that articulated in *Seescandy.com* and *America Online, Inc.* When the anonymous Internet user is not a party to the case, the litigation can go forward without the disclosure of their identity. Therefore, non-party disclosure is only appropriate in the exceptional case where the compelling need for the discovery sought outweighs the First Amendment rights of the anonymous speaker.

Accordingly, this Court adopts the following standard for evaluating a civil subpoena that seeks the identity of an anonymous Internet user who is not a party to the underlying litigation. The Court will consider four factors in determining whether the subpoena should issue. These are whether: (1) the subpoena seeking the information was issued in good faith and not for any improper purpose, (2) the information sought relates to a core claim or defense, (3) the identifying information is directly and materially relevant to that claim or defense, and (4) information sufficient to establish or to disprove that claim or defense is unavailable from any other source.[5]

This test provides a flexible framework for balancing the First Amendment rights of anonymous speakers with the right of civil litigants to protect their interests through the litigation discovery process. The Court shall give weight to each of

---

5. This Court is aware that many civil subpoenas seeking the identifying information of Internet users may be complied with, and the identifying information disclosed, without notice to the Internet users themselves. This is because some Internet service providers do not notify their users when such a civil subpoena is received. The standard set forth in this Order may guide Internet service providers in determining whether to challenge a specific subpoena on behalf of their users. However, this will provide little solace to Internet users whose Internet service company does not provide them notice when a subpoena is received.

these factors as the court determines is appropriate under the circumstances of each case. This Court is mindful that it is imposing a high burden. "But the First Amendment requires us to be vigilant in making [these] judgments, to guard against undue hindrances to political conversations and the exchange of ideas." *Buckley*, 525 U.S. at 192.

In the present case, TMRT seeks information it says will validate its defense that "changes in [TMRT] stock prices were *not* caused by the Defendants but by the illegal actions of individuals who manipulated the [TMRT] stock price using the Silicon Investor message boards." This Court must evaluate TMRT's stated need for the information in light of the four factors outlined above.

1. Was the subpoena brought in good faith?

This Court does not conclude that this subpoena was brought in bad faith or for an improper purpose. TMRT and its officers and directors are defending against a shareholder derivative class action lawsuit. They have asserted numerous affirmative defenses, one of which alleges that the defendants did not cause the drop in TMRT's stock value. TMRT could reasonably believe that the posted messages are relevant to this defense.

However, as originally issued the subpoena seeking the identity information was extremely broad. The subpoena would have required the disclosure of personal e-mails and other personal information that has no relevance to the issues raised in the lawsuit. This apparent disregard for the privacy and the First Amendment rights of the online users, while not demonstrating bad faith *per se*, weighs against TMRT in balancing the interests here.

2. Does the information sought relate to a core claim or defense?

Only when the identifying information is needed to advance core claims or defenses can it be sufficiently material to compromise First Amendment rights. If the information relates only to a secondary claim or to one of numerous affirmative defenses, then the primary substance of the case can go forward without disturbing the First Amendment rights of the anonymous Internet users.

The information sought by TMRT does not relate to a core defense. Here, the information relates to only one of twenty-seven affirmative defenses raised by the defendant, the defense that "no act or omission of any of the Defendants was the cause in fact or the proximate cause of any injury or damage to the plaintiffs." This is a generalized assertion of the lack of causation. Defendants have asserted numerous other affirmative defenses that go more "to the heart of the matter," such as the lack of material misstatements by the defendants, actual disclosure of material facts by the defendants, and the business judgment defense. Therefore, this factor also weighs in favor of quashing the subpoena.

3. Is the identifying information directly and materially relevant to a core claim or defense?

Even when the claim or defense for which the information is sought is deemed core to the case, the identity of the Internet users must also be materially relevant to that claim or defense. Under the Federal Rules of Civil Procedure discovery is normally very broad, requiring disclosure of any relevant information that "appears reasonably calculated to lead to the discovery of admissible evidence." Fed.R.Civ.P. 26(b)(1). But when First Amendment rights are at stake, a higher threshold of relevancy must be imposed. Only when the information sought is directly and materially relevant to a core claim or defense can the need for the information outweigh the First Amendment right to speak anonymously. See Los Angeles

Memorial Coliseum Comm'n, 89 F.R.D. at 494 (holding that a party seeking to enforce a subpoena to disclose non-party journalistic sources must demonstrate that the information is of "certain relevance.")

TMRT has failed to demonstrate that the identity of the Internet users is directly and materially relevant to a core defense. These Internet users are not parties to the case and have not been named as defendants as to any claim, cross-claim or third-party claim. Therefore, unlike in *Seescandy.com* and *America Online, Inc.,* their identity is not needed to allow the litigation to proceed.

According to the pleadings, the Internet user known as NoGuano has never posted messages on Silicon Investor's TMRT message board. At oral argument, TMRT's counsel conceded this point but stated that NoGuano's information was sought because he had "communicated" via the Internet with Silicon Investor posters such as Truthseeker. Given that NoGuano admittedly posted no public statements on the TMRT site, there is no basis to conclude that the identity of NoGuano and others similarly situated is directly and materially relevant to TMRT's defense.

As to the Internet users such as Truthseeker and Cuemaster who posted messages on the TMRT bulletin board, TMRT has failed to demonstrate that their identities are directly and materially relevant to a core defense. TMRT argues that the Internet postings caused a drop in TMRT's stock price. However, what was said in these postings is a matter of public record, and the identity of the anonymous posters had no effect on investors. If these messages did influence the stock price, they did so without *anyone* knowing the identity of the speakers.

TMRT speculates that the users of the InfoSpace website may have been engaged in stock manipulation in violation of federal securities law. TMRT indicates that it intends to compare the names of the InfoSpace users with the names of individuals who traded TMRT stock during the same period to determine whether any illegal stock manipulation occurred. However, TMRT's innuendos of stock manipulation do not suffice to overcome the First Amendment rights of the Internet users. Those rights cannot be nullified by an unsupported allegation of wrongdoing raised by the party seeking the information.

4. Is information sufficient to establish TMRT's defense available from any other source?

TMRT has failed to demonstrate that the information it needs to establish its defense is unavailable from any other source. The chat room messages are archived and are available to anyone to read and print. TMRT obtained copies of some of these messages and submitted them to this Court. TMRT can therefore demonstrate what was said, when it was said, and can compare the timing of those statements with information on fluctuations in the TMRT stock price. The messages are available for use at trial, and TMRT can factually support its defense without encroaching on the First Amendment rights of the Internet users.

COMMENTS AND QUESTIONS

1. How different are the tests enunciated in the *AOL* and *2TheMart* cases? Are the differences attributable to the fact that the plaintiffs in the *AOL* case are seeking disclosure of John Doe defendants and in the *2TheMart* case they are seeking disclosure of third-party witnesses? Which is the better test?

Should a court protect the anonymity of a John Doe defendant? If so, will the plaintiff have any possibility of redress? Should the ISP that permits anonymous posting be required to compensate the plaintiff for the harm the posting causes? Some have advocated such a rule, see I. Trotter Hardy, The Proper Legal Regime for Cyberspace, 55 U. Pitt. L. Rev. 993 (1994), though section 230 of the Communications Decency Act appears to foreclose such liability.

2. In Dendrite Int'l, Inc. v. Doe, 775 A.2d 756 (N.J. Super. App. Div. 2001), a New Jersey court announced several requirements before the court will order disclosure of the identity of anonymous posters of information on the Internet:

> We hold that when such an application is made, the trial court should first require the plaintiff to undertake efforts to notify the anonymous posters that they are the subject of a subpoena or application for an order of disclosure, and withhold action to afford the fictitiously named defendants a reasonable opportunity to file and serve opposition to the application. These notification efforts should include posting a message of notification of the identity discovery request to the anonymous user on the ISP's pertinent message board.
>
> The court shall also require the plaintiff to identify and set forth the exact statements purportedly made by each anonymous poster that the plaintiff alleges constitutes actionable speech.
>
> The complaint and all information provided to the court should be carefully reviewed to determine whether plaintiff has set forth a prima facie cause of action against the fictitiously named anonymous defendants. . . . [T]he plaintiff must produce sufficient evidence supporting each element of its cause of action, on a prima facie basis, prior to a court ordering the disclosure of the identity of the unnamed person.
>
> Finally, assuming the court concludes that the plaintiff has presented a prima facie cause of action, the court must balance the defendant's First Amendment right of anonymous free speech against the strength of the prima facie case presented and the necessity of the disclosure of the anonymous defendant's identity to allow plaintiff to properly proceed.

Does this standard go too far?

3. For a very helpful discussion of the tension between anonymity and accountability in cyberspace, see, e.g., Anne Wells Branscomb, Anonymity, Autonomy, and Accountability: Challenges to the First Amendment in Cyberspace, 104 Yale L.J. 1639 (1995).

4. The Electronic Privacy Communications Act requires Internet service providers to disclose the contents of an electronic communication to the government in response to a subpoena issued under the Federal Rules of Criminal Procedure or a warrant, but not otherwise. See 18 U.S.C. §2703. Should there be a similar requirement before ISPs disclose identity information to private parties?

McVeigh v. Cohen
United States District Court for the District of Columbia
983 F. Supp. 215 (D.D.C. 1998)

SPORKIN, District Judge.

. . . The Plaintiff, Senior Chief Timothy R. McVeigh, is a highly decorated seventeen-year veteran of the United States Navy who has served honorably and continuously since he was nineteen years old. At the time of the Navy's decision to discharge him, he was the senior-most enlisted man aboard the United States nuclear submarine U.S.S. Chicago.

On September 2, 1997, Ms. Helen Hajne, a civilian Navy volunteer, received an electronic mail ("email") message through the America Online Service ("AOL") regarding the toy-drive that she was coordinating for the Chicago crew members' children. The message box stated that it came from the alias "boysrch," but the text of the email was signed by a "Tim." Administrative Record ("AR") at 110. Through an option available to AOL subscribers, the volunteer searched through the "member profile directory" to find the member profile for this sender. The directory specified that "boysrch" was an AOL subscriber named Tim who lived in Honolulu, Hawaii, worked in the military, and identified his marital status as "gay." See AR at 111. Although the profile included some telling interests such as "collecting pics of other young studs" and "boy watching," it did not include any further identifying information such as full name, address, or phone number. . . .

Ms. Hajne proceeded to forward the email and directory profile to her husband, who, like Plaintiff, was also a noncommissioned officer aboard the U.S.S. Chicago. . . . [T]he Navy suspected the "Tim" who authored the email might be Senior Chief Timothy McVeigh. Before she spoke to the Plaintiff and without a warrant or court order, [the ship's principal legal adviser] . . . requested a Navy paralegal on her staff, Legalman First Class Joseph M. Kaiser, to contact AOL and obtain information from the service that could "connect" the screen name "boysrch" and accompanying user profile to McVeigh. See AR at 13. Legalman Kaiser called AOL's toll-free customer service number and talked to a representative at technical services. Legalman Kaiser did not identify himself as a Naval serviceman. According to his testimony at the administrative hearing, he stated that he was "a third party in receipt of a fax sheet and wanted to confirm the profile sheet, [and] who it belonged to." AR at 14. The AOL representative affirmatively identified Timothy R. McVeigh as the customer in question. See *id.* at 11-15.

Upon verification from AOL, Lieutenant Morean notified Senior Chief McVeigh that the Navy had obtained "some indication[ ] that he made a statement of homosexuality" in violation of §654(b)(2) of "Don't Ask, Don't Tell." AR at 27-28. In light of the Uniform Code of Military Justice prohibition of sodomy and indecent acts, she then advised him of his right to remain silent. See *id.* at 28, 30. . . . Shortly thereafter, in a memorandum dated September 22, 1997, the Navy advised Plaintiff that it was commencing an administrative discharge proceeding (termed by the Navy as an "administrative separation") against him. The reason stated was for "homosexual conduct, as evidenced by your statement that you are a homosexual." AR at 107.

On November 7, 1997, the Navy conducted an administrative discharge hearing before a three-member board. At the hearing, the Plaintiff made an unsworn oral statement that explained the substance of his email to Ms. Hajne, and thus by inference confirmed his authorship of the correspondence. See AR at 84. The Plaintiff presented evidence of a prior engagement to a woman and several other heterosexual relationships to rebut the presumption of homosexuality, pursuant to §654(b)(2). See AR at 82-84. This evidence was rejected by the Board. . . . At the conclusion of the administrative hearing, the board held that the government had sufficiently shown by a preponderance of the evidence that Senior Chief McVeigh had engaged in "homosexual conduct," a dischargeable offense. . . .

[The Court determined that McVeigh's discharge violated the Navy's "Don't Tell, Don't Pursue" policy.]

The . . . steps taken by the Navy in its "pursuit" of the Plaintiff were not only unauthorized under its policy, but likely illegal under the Electronic Communications Privacy Act of 1986 ("ECPA"). The ECPA, enacted by Congress to address privacy concerns on the Internet, allows the government to obtain information from an online service provider—as the Navy did in this instance from AOL—but only if a) it obtains a warrant issued under the Federal Rules of Criminal Procedure or state equivalent; or b) it gives prior notice to the online subscriber and then issues a subpoena or receives a court order authorizing disclosure of the information in question. See 18 U.S.C. §2703(b)(1)(A)-(B), (c)(1)(B).

In soliciting and obtaining over the phone personal information about the Plaintiff from AOL, his private on-line service provider, the government in this case invoked neither of these provisions and thus failed to comply with the ECPA. From the record, it is undisputed that the Navy directly solicited by phone information from AOL. Lieutenant Karin S. Morean, the ship's principal legal counsel and a member of the JAG corp, personally requested Legalman Kaiser to contact AOL and obtain the identity of the subscriber. See AR at 13. Without this information, Plaintiff credibly contends that the Navy could not have made the necessary connection between him and the user profile which was the sole basis on which to commence discharge proceedings.

The government, in its defense, contends that the Plaintiff cannot succeed on his ECPA claim. It argues that the substantive provision of the statute that Plaintiff cites, 18 U.S.C. §2703(c)(1)(B), puts the obligation on the online service provider to withhold information from the government, and not vice versa. In support of its position, Defendants cite to the Fourth Circuit opinion in Tucker v. Waddell, 83 F.3d 688 (4th Cir. 1996), which held that §2703(c)(1)(B) only prohibits the actions of online providers, not the government. Accordingly, Defendants allege that Plaintiff has no cause of action against the government on the basis of the ECPA.

Under the circumstances of this case, it is unlikely that the government will prevail on this argument. Section 2703(c)(1)(B) must be read in the context of the statute as a whole. In comparison, §2703(a) and (b) imposes on the government a reciprocal obligation to obtain a warrant or the like before requiring disclosure. It appears from the face of the statute that all of the subsections of §2703 were intended to work in tandem to protect consumer privacy. Even if, however, the government ultimately proves to be right in its assessment of §2703(c)(1)(B), the Plaintiff has plead §2703(a) and (b) as alternative grounds for relief. In his claim that the government, at the least, solicited a violation of the ECPA by AOL, the Court finds that there is likely success on the merits with regard to this issue. The government knew, or should have known, that by turning over the information without a warrant, AOL was breaking the law. Yet the Navy, in this case, directly solicited the information anyway. What is most telling is that the Naval investigator did not identify himself when he made his request. While the government makes much of the fact that §2703(c)(1)(B) does not provide a cause of action against the government, it is elementary that information obtained improperly can be suppressed where an individual's rights have been violated. In these days of "big brother," where through technology and otherwise the privacy interests of individuals from all walks of life are being ignored or marginalized, it is imperative that statutes explicitly protecting these rights be strictly observed.

The government has produced no evidence that would indicate that it would have proceeded without this information from AOL affirmatively linking the email to Senior Chief McVeigh. That the Plaintiff may have made incriminating statements at the subsequent administrative hearing does not bootstrap the Navy out of its legal dilemma of not only violating its own policy, but also a federal statute in its attempt to charge the Plaintiff with homosexuality. . . .

[The Court determined that McVeigh would suffer irreparable harm if his discharge was not halted by a preliminary injunction.]

IV. Public Interest

Certainly, the public has an inherent interest in the preservation of privacy rights as advanced by Plaintiff in this case. With literally the entire world on the world-wide web, enforcement of the ECPA is of great concern to those who bare the most personal information about their lives in private accounts through the Internet. In this case in particular, where the government may well have violated a federal statute in its zeal to brand the Plaintiff a homosexual, the actions of the Navy must be more closely scrutinized by this Court. It is disputed in the record exactly as to how the Navy represented itself to AOL when it requested information about the Plaintiff. The Defendants contend that Legalman Kaiser merely asked for confirmation of a fax sheet bearing Plaintiff's account. Plaintiff contends, and AOL confirms, however, that the Naval officer "misle[ad]" AOL's representative by "both failing to disclose the identity and purpose [of his request] and by portraying himself as a friend or acquaintance of Senior Chief McVeigh's." See AOL Statement on the Matter of Timothy McVeigh, Ct. Ex. 1. At the final injunction hearing, this issue should be fully explored. . . .

COMMENTS AND QUESTIONS

1. Does McVeigh have a viable cause of action against AOL for revealing his identity to the Navy or against the Navy for the deceptive manner in which it sought his identity from AOL?

Many opportunities exist for anonymous or pseudonymous communications or activities in cyberspace. While these communications and activities can be enriching, they can also be irresponsible and even illegal. The State of Georgia passed a law to prohibit anonymous and pseudonymous communications as a preventive measure against abusive uses of anonymity. This legislation was challenged as unconstitutionally vague and overbroad in ACLU v. Miller, 977 F. Supp. 1228 (N.D. Ga. 1997), and the court granted a preliminary injunction against its enforcement.

C. THIRD-PARTY LIABILITY FOR DISCLOSURE OF ILLEGALLY OBTAINED PRIVATE INFORMATION

Bartnicki v. Vopper
Supreme Court of the United States
532 U.S. 514 (2001)

JUSTICE STEVENS delivered the opinion of the Court. . . .

The suit at hand involves the repeated intentional disclosure of an illegally intercepted cellular telephone conversation about a public issue. The persons who made the disclosures did not participate in the interception, but they did know—or at least had reason to know—that the interception was unlawful. Accordingly, these cases present a conflict between interests of the highest order—on the one hand, the interest in the full and free dissemination of information concerning public issues, and, on the other hand, the interest in individual privacy and, more specifically, in fostering private speech. The Framers of the First Amendment surely did not foresee the advances in science that produced the conversation, the interception, or the conflict that gave rise to this action. It is therefore not surprising that Circuit judges, as well as the Members of this Court, have come to differing conclusions about the First Amendment's application to this issue. Nevertheless, having considered the interests at stake, we are firmly convinced that the disclosures made by respondents in this suit are protected by the First Amendment.

During 1992 and most of 1993, the Pennsylvania State Education Association, a union representing the teachers at the Wyoming Valley West High School, engaged in collective-bargaining negotiations with the school board. Petitioner Kane, then the president of the local union, testified that the negotiations were "'contentious'" and received "a lot of media attention." In May 1993, petitioner Bartnicki, who was acting as the union's "chief negotiator," used the cellular phone in her car to call Kane and engage in a lengthy conversation about the status of the negotiations. An unidentified person intercepted and recorded that call.

In their conversation, Kane and Bartnicki discussed the timing of a proposed strike, difficulties created by public comment on the negotiations, and the need for a dramatic response to the board's intransigence. At one point, Kane said: "'If they're not gonna move for three percent, we're gonna have to go to their, their homes . . . To blow off their front porches, we'll have to do some work on some of those guys. (PAUSES). Really, uh, really and truthfully because this is, you know, this is bad news. (UNDECIPHERABLE).'"

In the early fall of 1993, the parties accepted a non-binding arbitration proposal that was generally favorable to the teachers. In connection with news reports about the settlement, respondent Vopper, a radio commentator who had been critical of the union in the past, played a tape of the intercepted conversation on his public affairs talk show. Another station also broadcast the tape, and local newspapers published its contents. After filing suit against Vopper and other representatives of the media, Bartnicki and Kane (hereinafter petitioners) learned through discovery that Vopper had obtained the tape from Jack Yocum, the head of a local taxpayers' organization that had opposed the union's demands throughout the negotiations. Yocum, who was added as a defendant, testified that he had found the tape in his mailbox shortly after the interception and recognized the voices of Bartnicki and Kane. Yocum played the tape for some members of the school board, and later delivered the tape itself to Vopper.

In their amended complaint, petitioners alleged that their telephone conversation had been surreptitiously intercepted by an unknown person using an electronic device, that Yocum had obtained a tape of that conversation, and that he intentionally disclosed it to Vopper, as well as other individuals and media representatives. Thereafter, Vopper and other members of the media repeatedly published the contents of that conversation. The amended complaint alleged that each of the defendants "knew or had reason to know" that the recording of the private telephone conversation had been obtained by means of an illegal interception. Relying on both federal and Pennsylvania statutory provisions, petitioners sought actual damages, statutory damages, punitive damages, and attorney's fees and costs.

As we pointed out in Berger v. New York, 388 U.S. 41, 45-49, 18 L. Ed.2d 1040, 87 S. Ct. 1873 (1967), sophisticated (and not so sophisticated) methods of eavesdropping on oral conversations and intercepting telephone calls have been practiced for decades, primarily by law enforcement authorities. In *Berger*, we held that New York's broadly written statute authorizing the police to conduct wiretaps violated the Fourth Amendment. Largely in response to that decision, and to our holding in *Katz* v. *United States*, 389 U.S. 347, 19 L. Ed.2d 576, 88 S. Ct. 507 (1967), that the attachment of a listening and recording device to the outside of a telephone booth constituted a search, "Congress undertook to draft comprehensive legislation both authorizing the use of evidence obtained by electronic surveillance on specified conditions, and prohibiting its use otherwise. S. Rep. No. 1097, 90th Cong., 2d Sess., 66 (1968)." Gelbard v. United States, 408 U.S. 41, 78, 33 L. Ed.2d 179, 92 S. Ct. 2357 (1972) (Rehnquist, J., dissenting). The ultimate result of those efforts was Title III of the Omnibus Crime Control and Safe Streets Act of 1968, 82 Stat. 211, entitled Wiretapping and Electronic Surveillance.

One of the stated purposes of that title was "to protect effectively the privacy of wire and oral communications." *Ibid*. In addition to authorizing and regulating electronic surveillance for law enforcement purposes, Title III also regulated private conduct. One part of those regulations, §2511(1), defined five offenses punishable by a fine of not more than $10,000, by imprisonment for not more than five years, or by both. Subsection (a) applied to any person who "willfully intercepts . . . any wire or oral communication." Subsection (b) applied to the intentional use of devices designed to intercept oral conversations; subsection (d) applied to the use of the contents of illegally intercepted wire or oral communications; and subsection (e) prohibited the unauthorized disclosure of the contents of interceptions that were authorized for law enforcement purposes. Subsection (c), the original version of the provision most directly at issue in this case, applied to any person who "willfully discloses, or endeavors to disclose, to any other person the contents of any wire or oral communication, knowing or having reason to know that the information was obtained through the interception of a wire or oral communication in violation of this subsection." The oral communications protected by the Act were only those "uttered by a person exhibiting an expectation that such communication is not subject to interception under circumstances justifying such expectation." 18 U.S.C. §2510(2).

As enacted in 1968, Title III did not apply to the monitoring of radio transmissions. In the Electronic Communications Privacy Act of 1986, 100 Stat. 1848, however, Congress enlarged the coverage of Title III to prohibit the interception of "electronic" as well as oral and wire communications. By reason of that amendment, as well as a 1994 amendment which applied to cordless telephone communications, 108 Stat. 4279, Title III now applies to the interception of conversations over both cellular and cordless phones. Although a lesser criminal penalty may apply to the interception of such transmissions, the same civil remedies are available whether the communication was "oral," "wire," or "electronic," as defined by 18 U.S.C. §2510 (1994 ed. and Supp. V).

The constitutional question before us concerns the validity of the statutes as applied to the specific facts of this case. Because of the procedural posture of the case, it is appropriate to make certain important assumptions about those facts. We accept petitioners' submission that the interception was intentional, and therefore unlawful, and that, at a minimum, respondents "had reason to know" that it was unlawful. Accordingly, the disclosure of the contents of the intercepted conversation by Yocum to school board members and to representatives of the media, as well as the subsequent disclosures by the media defendants to the public, violated the federal and state statutes. Under the provisions of the federal statute, as well as its Pennsylvania analog, petitioners are thus entitled to recover damages from each of the respondents. The only question is whether the application of these statutes in such circumstances violates the First Amendment.

In answering that question, we accept respondents' submission on three factual matters that serve to distinguish most of the cases that have arisen under §2511. First, respondents played no part in the illegal interception. Rather, they found out about the interception only after it occurred, and in fact never learned the identity of the person or persons who made the interception. Second, their access to the information on the tapes was obtained lawfully, even though the information itself was intercepted unlawfully by someone else. Cf. Florida Star v. B. J. F., 491 U.S. 524, 536, 105 L. Ed.2d 443, 109 S. Ct. 2603 (1989) ("Even assuming the Constitution permitted a State to proscribe *receipt* of information, Florida has not taken this step"). Third, the subject matter of the conversation was a matter of public concern. If the statements about the labor negotiations had been made in a public arena—during a bargaining session, for example—they would have been newsworthy. This would also be true if a third party had inadvertently overheard Bartnicki making the same statements to Kane when the two thought they were alone.

We agree with petitioners that §2511(1)(c), as well as its Pennsylvania analog, is in fact a content-neutral law of general applicability. "Deciding whether a particular regulation is content based or content neutral is not always a simple task. . . . As a general rule, laws that by their terms distinguish favored speech from disfavored speech on the basis of the ideas or views expressed are content based." Turner Broadcasting System, Inc. v. FCC, 512 U.S. 622, 642-643, 129 L. Ed.2d 497, 114 S. Ct. 2445 (1994). In determining whether a regulation is content based or content neutral, we look to the purpose behind the regulation; typically, "government regulation of expressive activity is content neutral so long as it is '*justified* without reference to the content of the regulated speech.'" Ward v. Rock Against Racism, 491 U.S. 781, 791, 105 L. Ed.2d 661, 109 S. Ct. 2746 (1989).

In this case, the basic purpose of the statute at issue is to "protect the privacy of wire[, electronic,] and oral communications." S. Rep. No. 1097, 90th Cong., 2d

Sess., 66 (1968). The statute does not distinguish based on the content of the intercepted conversations, nor is it justified by reference to the content of those conversations. Rather, the communications at issue are singled out by virtue of the fact that they were illegally intercepted—by virtue of the source, rather than the subject matter.

On the other hand, the naked prohibition against disclosures is fairly characterized as a regulation of pure speech. Unlike the prohibition against the "use" of the contents of an illegal interception in §2511(1)(d), subsection (c) is not a regulation of conduct. It is true that the delivery of a tape recording might be regarded as conduct, but given that the purpose of such a delivery is to provide the recipient with the text of recorded statements, it is like the delivery of a handbill or a pamphlet, and as such, it is the kind of "speech" that the First Amendment protects. As the majority below put it, "if the acts of 'disclosing' and 'publishing' information do not constitute speech, it is hard to imagine what does fall within that category, as distinct from the category of expressive conduct." 200 F.3d at 120.

As a general matter, "state action to punish the publication of truthful information seldom can satisfy constitutional standards." Smith v. Daily Mail Publishing Co., 443 U.S. 97, 102, 61 L. Ed.2d 399, 99 S. Ct. 2667 (1979). More specifically, this Court has repeatedly held that "if a newspaper lawfully obtains truthful information about a matter of public significance then state officials may not constitutionally punish publication of the information, absent a need . . . of the highest order." *Id.*, at 103.

Accordingly, in New York Times Co. v. United States, 403 U.S. 713, 29 L. Ed.2d 822, 91 S. Ct. 2140 (1971) *(per curiam)*, the Court upheld the right of the press to publish information of great public concern obtained from documents stolen by a third party. In so doing, that decision resolved a conflict between the basic rule against prior restraints on publication and the interest in preserving the secrecy of information that, if disclosed, might seriously impair the security of the Nation. In resolving that conflict, the attention of every Member of this Court was focused on the character of the stolen documents' contents and the consequences of public disclosure. Although the undisputed fact that the newspaper intended to publish information obtained from stolen documents was noted in Justice Harlan's dissent, *id.*, at 754, neither the majority nor the dissenters placed any weight on that fact.

However, New York Times v. United States raised, but did not resolve the question "whether, in cases where information has been acquired *unlawfully* by a newspaper or by a source, government may ever punish not only the unlawful acquisition, but the ensuing publication as well." *Florida Star*, 491 U.S. at 535, n. 8. The question here, however, is a narrower version of that still-open question. Simply put, the issue here is this: "Where the punished publisher of information has obtained the information in question in a manner lawful in itself but from a source who has obtained it unlawfully, may the government punish the ensuing publication of that information based on the defect in a chain?" *Boehner*, 191 F.3d at 484-485 (Sentelle, J., dissenting). . . .

The Government identifies two interests served by the statute—first, the interest in removing an incentive for parties to intercept private conversations, and second, the interest in minimizing the harm to persons whose conversations have been illegally intercepted. We assume that those interests adequately justify the prohibition in §2511(1)(d) against the interceptor's own use of information that he or she acquired by violating §2511(1)(a), but it by no means follows that punishing disclosures of lawfully obtained information of public interest by one not involved in the initial illegality is an acceptable means of serving those ends.

The normal method of deterring unlawful conduct is to impose an appropriate punishment on the person who engages in it. If the sanctions that presently attach to a violation of §2511(1)(a) do not provide sufficient deterrence, perhaps those sanctions should be made more severe. But it would be quite remarkable to hold that speech by a law-abiding possessor of information can be suppressed in order to deter conduct by a non-law-abiding third party. Although there are some rare occasions in which a law suppressing one party's speech may be justified by an interest in deterring criminal conduct by another, this is not such a case.

With only a handful of exceptions, the violations of §2511(1)(a) that have been described in litigated cases have been motivated by either financial gain or domestic disputes. In virtually all of those cases, the identity of the person or persons intercepting the communication has been known. Moreover, petitioners cite no evidence that Congress viewed the prohibition against disclosures as a response to the difficulty of identifying persons making improper use of scanners and other surveillance devices and accordingly of deterring such conduct, and there is no empirical evidence to support the assumption that the prohibition against disclosures reduces the number of illegal interceptions.

Although this case demonstrates that there may be an occasional situation in which an anonymous scanner will risk criminal prosecution by passing on information without any expectation of financial reward or public praise, surely this is the exceptional case. Moreover, there is no basis for assuming that imposing sanctions upon respondents will deter the unidentified scanner from continuing to engage in surreptitious interceptions. Unusual cases fall far short of a showing that there is a "need of the highest order" for a rule supplementing the traditional means of deterring antisocial conduct. The justification for any such novel burden on expression must be "far stronger than mere speculation about serious harms." United States v. National Treasury Employees Union, 513 U.S. 454, 475, 115 S. Ct. 1003, 130 L. Ed.2d 964 (1995). Accordingly, the Government's first suggested justification for applying §2511(1)(c) to an otherwise innocent disclosure of public information is plainly insufficient.

The Government's second argument, however, is considerably stronger. Privacy of communication is an important interest, Harper & Row, Publishers, Inc. v. Nation Enterprises, 471 U.S. 539, 559, 85 L. Ed.2d 588, 105 S. Ct. 2218 (1985), and Title III's restrictions are intended to protect that interest, thereby "encouraging the uninhibited exchange of ideas and information among private parties . . . ." Moreover, the fear of public disclosure of private conversations might well have a chilling effect on private speech.

> In a democratic society privacy of communication is essential if citizens are to think and act creatively and constructively. Fear or suspicion that one's speech is being monitored by a stranger, even without the reality of such activity, can have a seriously inhibiting effect upon the willingness to voice critical and constructive ideas.

President's Commission on Law Enforcement and Administration of Justice, The Challenge of Crime in a Free Society 202 (1967).

Accordingly, it seems to us that there are important interests to be considered on *both* sides of the constitutional calculus. In considering that balance, we acknowledge that some intrusions on privacy are more offensive than others, and that the disclosure of the contents of a private conversation can be an even greater intrusion on privacy than the interception itself. As a result, there is a valid independent justification for prohibiting such disclosures by persons who lawfully obtained access to the contents of an illegally intercepted message, even if that prohibition does not play a significant role in preventing such interceptions from occurring in the first place.

We need not decide whether that interest is strong enough to justify the application of §2511(c) to disclosures of trade secrets or domestic gossip or other information of purely private concern. Cf. Time, Inc. v. Hill, 385 U.S. 374, 387-388, 17 L. Ed.2d 456, 87 S. Ct. 534 (1967) (reserving the question whether truthful publication of private matters unrelated to public affairs can be constitutionally proscribed). In other words, the outcome of the case does not turn on whether §2511(1)(c) may be enforced with respect to most violations of the statute without offending the First Amendment. The enforcement of that provision in this case, however, implicates the core purposes of the First Amendment because it imposes sanctions on the publication of truthful information of public concern.

In this case, privacy concerns give way when balanced against the interest in publishing matters of public importance. As Warren and Brandeis stated in their classic law review article: "The right of privacy does not prohibit any publication of matter which is of public or general interest." The Right to Privacy, 4 Harv. L. Rev. 193, 214 (1890). One of the costs associated with participation in public affairs is an attendant loss of privacy.

> Exposure of the self to others in varying degrees is a concomitant of life in a civilized community. The risk of this exposure is an essential incident of life in a society which places a primary value on freedom of speech and of press. 'Freedom of discussion, if it would fulfill its historic function in this nation, must embrace all issues about which information is needed or appropriate to enable the members of society to cope with the exigencies of their period.'

Time, Inc. v. Hill, 385 U.S. at 388 (quoting Thornhill v. Alabama, 310 U.S. 88, 102, 84 L. Ed. 1093, 60 S. Ct. 736 (1940)).

Our opinion in New York Times Co. v. Sullivan, 376 U.S. 254, 11 L. Ed.2d 686, 84 S. Ct. 710 (1964), reviewed many of the decisions that settled the "general proposition that freedom of expression upon public questions is secured by the First Amendment." *Id.*, at 269. Those cases all relied on our "profound national commitment to the principle that debate on public issues should be uninhibited, robust and wide-open," *New York Times,* 376 U.S. at 270. It was the overriding importance of that commitment that supported our holding that neither factual error nor defamatory content, nor a combination of the two, sufficed to remove the First Amendment shield from criticism of official conduct.

We think it clear that parallel reasoning requires the conclusion that a stranger's illegal conduct does not suffice to remove the First Amendment shield from speech about a matter of public concern. The months of negotiations over the proper level of compensation for teachers at the Wyoming Valley West High School were unquestionably a matter of public concern, and respondents were clearly engaged in debate about that concern. That debate may be more mundane than the Communist rhetoric that inspired Justice Brandeis' classic opinion in Whitney v. California, 274 U.S. at 372, but it is no less worthy of constitutional protection.

JUSTICE BREYER, with whom JUSTICE O'CONNOR joins, concurring.

. . . [T]he statutes, as applied in these circumstances, do not reasonably reconcile the competing constitutional objectives. Rather, they disproportionately interfere with media freedom. For one thing, the broadcasters here engaged in no unlawful activity other than the ultimate publication of the information another had previously obtained. They "neither encouraged nor participated directly or indirectly in the interception." No one claims that they ordered, counseled, encouraged, or otherwise aided or abetted the interception, the later delivery of the tape by the interceptor to an intermediary, or the tape's still later delivery by the intermediary to the media. Cf. 18 U.S.C. §2 (criminalizing aiding and abetting any federal offense). And, as the Court points out, the statutes do not forbid the receipt of the tape itself. *Ante*, at 9. The Court adds that its holding "does not apply to punishing parties for obtaining the relevant information *unlawfully*."

For another thing, the speakers had little or no *legitimate* interest in maintaining the privacy of the particular conversation. That conversation involved a suggestion about "blowing off . . . front porches" and "doing some work on some of these guys," thereby raising a significant concern for the safety of others. Where publication of private information constitutes a wrongful act, the law recognizes a privilege allowing the reporting of threats to public safety. See Restatement (Second) of Torts §595, Comment *g* (1977) (general privilege to report that "another intends to kill or rob or commit some other serious crime against a third person"); *id.*, §652G (privilege applies to invasion of privacy tort). Cf. Restatement (Third) of Unfair Competition §40, Comment *c* (1995) (trade secret law permits disclosures relevant to public health or safety, commission of crime or tort, or other matters of substantial public concern); Lachman v. Sperry-Sun Well Surveying Co., 457 F.2d 850, 853 (CA10 1972) (nondisclosure agreement not binding in respect to criminal activity); Tarasoff v. Regents of Univ. of Cal., 17 Cal. 3d 425, 436, 551 P.2d 334, 343-344, 131 Cal. Rptr. 14 (1976) (psychiatric privilege not binding in presence of danger to self or others). Even where the danger may have passed by the time of publication, that fact cannot legitimize the speaker's earlier privacy expectation. Nor should editors, who must make a publication decision quickly, have to determine present or continued danger before publishing this kind of threat.

Further, the speakers themselves, the president of a teacher's union and the union's chief negotiator, were "limited public figures," for they voluntarily engaged in a public controversy. They thereby subjected themselves to somewhat greater public scrutiny and had a lesser interest in privacy than an individual engaged in purely private affairs.

This is not to say that the Constitution requires anyone, including public figures, to give up entirely the right to private communication, i.e., communication free from telephone taps or interceptions. But the subject matter of the conversation at issue here is far removed from that in situations where the media publicizes truly private matters.

Thus, in finding a constitutional privilege to publish unlawfully intercepted conversations of the kind here at issue, the Court does not create a "public interest" exception that swallows up the statutes' privacy-protecting general rule. Rather, it finds constitutional protection for publication of intercepted information of a special kind. Here, the speakers' legitimate privacy expectations are unusually low, and the public interest in defeating those expectations is unusually high. Given these circumstances, along with the lawful nature of respondents' behavior, the statutes' enforcement would disproportionately harm media freedom. . . .

CHIEF JUSTICE REHNQUIST, with whom JUSTICE SCALIA and JUSTICE THOMAS join, dissenting.

Technology now permits millions of important and confidential conversations to occur through a vast system of electronic networks. These advances, however, raise significant privacy concerns. We are placed in the uncomfortable position of not knowing who might have access to our personal and business e-mails, our medical and financial records, or our cordless and cellular telephone conversations. In an attempt to prevent some of the most egregious violations of privacy, the United States, the District of Columbia, and 40 States have enacted laws prohibiting the intentional interception and knowing disclosure of electronic communications. The Court holds that all of these statutes violate the First Amendment insofar as the illegally intercepted conversation touches upon a matter of "public concern," an amorphous concept that the Court does not even attempt to define. But the Court's decision diminishes, rather than enhances, the purposes of the First Amendment: chilling the speech of the millions of Americans who rely upon electronic technology to communicate each day. . . .

Congress and the overwhelming majority of States reasonably have concluded that sanctioning the knowing disclosure of illegally intercepted communications will deter the initial interception itself, a crime which is extremely difficult to detect. It is estimated that over 20 million scanners capable of intercepting cellular transmissions currently are in operation, see Thompson, Cell Phone Snooping: Why Electronic Eavesdropping Goes Unpunished, 35 Am. Crim. L. Rev. 137, 149 (1997), notwithstanding the fact that Congress prohibited the marketing of such devices eight years ago, see 47 U.S.C. §302a(d). As Congress recognized, "all too often the invasion of privacy itself will go unknown. Only by striking at all aspects of the problem can privacy be adequately protected." S. Rep. No. 1097, at 69. . . .

The "dry up the market" theory, which posits that it is possible to deter an illegal act that is difficult to police by preventing the wrongdoer from enjoying the fruits of the crime, is neither novel nor implausible. It is a time-tested theory that undergirds numerous laws, such as the prohibition of the knowing possession of stolen goods. See 2 W. LaFave & A. Scott, Substantive Criminal Law §8.10(a), p. 422 (1986) ("Without such receivers, theft ceases to be profitable. It is obvious that the receiver must be a principal target of any society anxious to stamp out theft in its various forms"). We ourselves adopted the exclusionary rule based upon similar reasoning, believing that it would "deter unreasonable searches," Oregon v. Elstad, 470 U.S. 298, 306, 84 L. Ed.2d 222, 105 S. Ct. 1285 (1985), by removing an officer's "incentive to disregard [the Fourth Amendment]," Elkins v. United States, 364 U.S. 206, 217, 4 L. Ed.2d 1669, 80 S. Ct. 1437 (1960).

The same logic applies here and demonstrates that the incidental restriction on alleged First Amendment freedoms is no greater than essential to further the interest of protecting the privacy of individual communications. Were there no prohibition on disclosure, an unlawful eavesdropper who wanted to disclose the conversation could anonymously launder the interception through a third party and thereby avoid detection. Indeed, demand for illegally obtained private information would only increase if it could be disclosed without repercussion. The law against interceptions, which the Court agrees is valid, would be utterly ineffectual without these antidisclosure provisions. . . .

At base, the Court's decision to hold these statutes unconstitutional rests upon nothing more than the bald substitution of its own prognostications in place of the reasoned judgment of 41 legislative bodies and the United States Congress. The Court does not explain how or from where Congress should obtain statistical evidence about the effectiveness of these laws, and "since as a practical matter it is never easy to prove a negative, it is hardly likely that conclusive factual data could ever be assembled." *Elkins, supra,* at 218. Reliance upon the "dry up the market" theory is both logical and eminently reasonable, and our precedents make plain that it is "far stronger than mere speculation." United States v. Treasury Employees, 513 U.S. 454, 475, 115 S. Ct. 1003, 130 L. Ed.2d 964 (1995).

These statutes also protect the important interests of deterring clandestine invasions of privacy and preventing the involuntary broadcast of private communications. Over a century ago, Samuel Warren and Louis Brandeis recognized that "the intensity and complexity of life, attendant upon advancing civilization, have rendered necessary some retreat from the world, and man, under the refining influence of culture, has become more sensitive to publicity, so that solitude and privacy have become more essential to the individual." The Right to Privacy, 4 Harv. L. Rev. 193, 196 (1890). "There is necessarily, and within suitably defined areas, a . . . freedom *not* to speak publicly, one which serves the same ultimate end as freedom of speech in its affirmative aspect." Harper & Row, Publishers, Inc. v. Nation Enterprises, 471 U.S. 539, 559 (1985). One who speaks into a phone "is surely entitled to assume that the words he utters into the mouthpiece will not be broadcast to the world." Katz v. United States, 389 U.S. 347, 352, 19 L. Ed.2d 576, 88 S. Ct. 507 (1967).

These statutes undeniably protect this venerable right of privacy. Concomitantly, they further the First Amendment rights of the parties to the conversation. "At the heart of the First Amendment lies the principle that each person should decide for himself or herself the ideas and beliefs deserving of expression, consideration, and adherence." *Turner Broadcasting,* 512 U.S. at 641. By "protecting the privacy of individual thought and expression," United States v. United States Dist. Court for Eastern Dist. of Mich., 407 U.S. 297, 302, 32 L. Ed.2d 752, 92 S. Ct. 2125 (1972), these statutes further the "uninhibited, robust, and wide-open" speech of the private parties, New York Times Co. v. Sullivan, 376 U.S. 254, 270, 11 L. Ed.2d 686, 84 S. Ct. 710 (1964). Unlike the laws at issue in the *Daily Mail* cases, which served only to protect the identities and actions of a select group of individuals, these laws protect millions of people who communicate electronically on a daily basis. The chilling effect of the Court's decision upon these private conversations will surely be great: An estimated 49.1 million analog cellular telephones are currently in operation.

Although the Court recognizes and even extols the virtues of this right to privacy, these are "mere words," W. Shakespeare, Troilus and Cressida, act v, sc. 3, overridden by the Court's newfound right to publish unlawfully acquired information of "public concern," *ante,* at 10. The Court concludes that the private conversation between Gloria Bartnicki and Anthony Kane is somehow a "debate . . . . worthy of constitutional protection." *Ante,* at 20. Perhaps the Court is correct that "if the statements about the labor negotiations had been made in a public arena— during a bargaining session, for example—they would have been newsworthy." *Ante,* at 10. The point, however, is that Bartnicki and Kane had no intention of contributing to a public "debate" at all, and it is perverse to hold that another's unlawful interception and knowing disclosure of their conversation is speech "worthy of constitutional protection." The Constitution should not protect the involuntary broadcast of personal conversations. Even where the communications involve public figures or concern public matters, the conversations are nonetheless private and worthy of protection. Although public persons may have forgone the right to live their lives screened from public scrutiny in some areas, it does not and should not follow that they also have abandoned their right to have a private conversation without fear of it being intentionally intercepted and knowingly disclosed. . . .

COMMENTS AND QUESTIONS

1. While *Bartnicki* does not, of course, involve the Internet, the case has significant implications for Internet law because of the vast opportunities for republication of information enabled by the Internet. Vopper could as easily have posted the text of the intercepted call on the Internet as played it on the radio. Some who post allegedly illegally obtained information on the Internet may raise *Bartnicki* defenses if they, like Vopper, did not participate in wrongful acts in acquiring the information. For example, Andrew Bunner raised a First Amendment defense to a trade secret misappropriation claim made by the DVD Copy Control Association for posting a computer program known as DeCSS on his website. DVD-CCA alleged that DeCSS embodied or was substantially derived from trade secrets from its encryption program, the Content Scramble System (CSS). These secrets were allegedly misappropriated by a Norwegian teenager, Jon Johansen, when he reverse engineered CSS in violation of an antireverse engineering clause of a mass-market license. DVD-CCA argued that Bunner knew or should have known that DeCSS was the product of stolen trade secrets and consequently, that he too was engaged in trade secret misappropriation when he posted DeCSS on the web. The trial judge issued a preliminary injunction that was overturned on First Amendment grounds as a prior restraint on speech by the California Court of Appeal. See DVD Copy Control Ass'n v. Bunner, 93 Cal. App.4th 648, 113 Cal. Rptr. 338 (2001). The matter is pending before the California Supreme Court. Should Bunner win a *Bartnicki* defense?

2. Tensions between free speech/free press interests and information privacy interests are longstanding and well recognized. See, e.g., Time, Inc. v. Hill, 385 U.S. 374 (1967) in which the Supreme Court reversed an award of damages for invasion of privacy because false statements in an article about a past incident in the Hills' lives might have been made innocently or merely negligently. In order to safeguard constitutional free speech interests, the Court decided that publishers must have acted in reckless disregard of the truth or with knowledge of falsity of the information to be held liable for privacy invasions. Proposals for new restrictions on reuse and republication of personally identifiable information have led to renewed expressions of concern about the implications of such legislation for free speech and free press interests. See Richard A. Epstein, Privacy, Publication, and the First Amendment: The Dangers of First Amendment Exceptionalism, 52 Stan. L. Rev. 1003 (2000); Eugene Volokh, Freedom of Speech and Information Privacy: The Troubling Implications of a Right to Stop People from Speaking About You, 52 Stan. L. Rev. 1049 (2000).

3. Advances in technology have unquestionably made private information more vulnerable to interception and processing. Interception of cell phone conversations is relatively cheap and easy, and can be done without easy detection. As the *Bartnicki* case points out, outlawing privacy-invading technologies has not been very successful. Why? Would it help if Congress made the penalties more severe? Or should expectations of privacy simply diminish with every new technological advance?

D. FOURTH AMENDMENT AS APPLIED TO ONLINE PRIVACY

═══ *United States v. Slanina*
═══ United States Court of Appeals for the Fifth Circuit
═══ *283 F.3d 670 (5th Cir. 2002)*

BENAVIDES, J.

Slanina worked as the Fire Marshall for Webster, Texas for nine years. As Fire Marshall, his duties included public safety and fire prevention, fire inspections, review of city plans, enforcement of building codes, and handling of arson related calls. Additionally, he served as the Emergency Management Coordinator, concentrating on hurricanes and explosions. Slanina's immediate supervisor was Fire Chief Bruce Ure ("Ure"), who answered to the Public Safety Director, Mike Keller ("Keller"). As Public Safety Director, Keller was in charge of both the police and fire departments. Keller had once been Slanina's direct supervisor, but in November 1998 Keller and the City Manager, Roger Carlisle ("Carlisle"), decided to hire a full-time fire chief, selecting Ure for that position. Prior to Ure's arrival, Keller conducted Slanina's performance evaluations. Although Ure later assumed this responsibility, Keller maintained ultimate authority over Slanina's employment, including the review of his evaluations and any salary increases.

Prior to June 1999, Slanina's desk was located in City Hall, where he had a city-provided computer with Internet access but no connection to the city's intra-office network. When a new fire station was built, however, Slanina moved into his own office in the new station. He brought with him his old computer, but in the new fire station he had no Internet access or network connection. On Friday, June 11, 1999, Ryan Smith ("Smith"), the Management Information Systems Coordinator, began working to install the city network on the fire station computers. At around 5:00 P.M., Smith entered Slanina's new office with a grand master key and attempted to continue his work. The computer was turned on, but a screen saver was in place. Smith moved the mouse and discovered that the screen saver was protected by a password. To bypass the screen saver password, Smith restarted the computer. When he rebooted, however, Smith found that Slanina had installed a BIOS password. Without this password, Smith was unable to immediately access the computer's hard drive and could not install the network on Slanina's computer. Smith then contacted Ure to inform him of the problem, and Ure directed Smith to call Slanina and obtain the password.

Slanina had not come to work that Friday, as he was still recuperating from his recent surgery to have his wisdom teeth removed. Smith did not feel comfortable calling Slanina, so Ure himself phoned him. Ure informed Slanina that the computer technician was in his office attempting to install the network, but was unable to do so because of the password. Slanina initially balked, but after Ure indicated that Smith was already working overtime and that the job had to be completed that day, Slanina agreed to call Smith. On the phone with Smith, Slanina sounded nervous and hesitated before giving his password. He wanted to know exactly what Smith would do to his computer, and Smith promised that he was simply installing the network and configuring his computer to the server.

Having received the password, Smith then resumed his work on Slanina's computer. In order to complete the task, Smith had to walk between Slanina's office and the server room. Upon returning to the office, Smith unexpectedly encountered Slanina—just ten minutes after they had talked on the phone. Needless to say, Smith was surprised to see Slanina, his jaw still swollen from the surgery. Smith's suspicions were further aroused when after he left the room, Slanina jumped back on his computer. Finally, when Slanina asked how much longer the network installation process would take, Smith lied, telling him that it would be another "couple of hours." Smith overstated the time to give himself a chance to see if something was wrong.

When Slanina finally left, Smith saw that the email was running, but minimized on the screen. As Smith clicked on the email to close it, he noticed the presence of newsgroups. Three months earlier, Keller had told Smith that no one was permitted to have newsgroups on their computers, but the policy had not been disseminated to the fire station employees, including Slanina. Smith expanded the email to look further at the newsgroups and saw three titles suggesting the presence of pornography. It was widely known that employees were not allowed to have pornographic material on their computers. To further investigate, Smith clicked on one newsgroup title, "alt.erotica.xxx.preteen", and saw that about 25 of the approximately 60 files had been read. At that point, however, he did not view any of the files.

Before contacting Ure, Smith wanted to be certain that Slanina's computer did have pornographic material on it. He conducted a search for JPEG files, which contain photographic images, and GIF files, which are used for other graphic images. His search located one such file in the Recycle Bin, and Smith restored the file. When he saw that it contained an image of adult pornography, he printed the file and attempted to contact Slanina's superiors. Neither Ure nor Keller were available, though, and initially Smith was only able to reach the Assistant Fire Chief, Dean Spencer ("Spencer"). By the time Spencer arrived at the station, Smith had spoken to Ure, telling him that he had found child pornography on Slanina's computer. Ure instructed him to secure the office, so at 7:00 p.m. Smith changed the lock on the door, turned the computer off, and left.

The next day, Smith spoke again to Ure, who by now had contacted Keller at an FBI conference in South Padre Island. Keller told Ure and Smith to remove the computer from the fire station and place it in his office, which was located in the police station. When they went to Slanina's office, Smith showed Ure the pornography before removing the computer. On Sunday afternoon, Keller returned from his conference and contacted Smith and Ure, asking them to meet him in his office at 3:00 P.M. Once there, Keller instructed Smith and Ure to get what was needed to view the contents of Slanina's computer, as well as any Zip disk or drive in Slanina's office. Smith and Ure then returned to Slanina's office and retrieved the monitor and disks before rejoining Keller in his office. Smith showed Keller the picture of adult pornography he had printed on Friday night, and also pointed him to where he had found the image on the computer. With Smith's assistance, Keller searched material on the computer and Zip drive for about two hours, viewing explicit child pornography. Finally, Keller contacted City Manager Carlisle and informed him that child pornography had been discovered on Slanina's computer. Their discussion addressed the possibility of criminal violations as well as the misuse of city property. Human Resources was then contacted, and Keller indicated to Smith and Ure that they should notify the FBI the next day.

At 7:15 A.M. on Monday morning, Ure met Slanina in the parking lot as he arrived at work, milk and doughnuts in hand. Ure told Slanina that they needed to meet in Keller's office, and asked him to get into Ure's vehicle. Remembering that Slanina had undergone dental surgery the previous week, Ure asked him whether he had taken any medication that morning. Slanina said he had not, remarking that doing so would be a violation of city policy because he drove a city vehicle to work. In fact, though, he had taken medication, specifically the painkiller Vicodin. As they approached Keller's office at the police station, Slanina became visibly anxious, rocking back and forth. When they arrived, Slanina met Captain Ray Smiley ("Smiley") of the Internal Affairs Division and was furnished with a written copy of the Internal Affairs investigation. He was told that he would be suspended pending the investigation, which concerned the misuse of city property by obtaining child pornography with a city computer. Keller informed him that they had seized his computer and ordered Slanina to surrender his badge and city identification. . . .

The office and home computer equipment, drives, and disks were turned over to the FBI, which examined active files and recovered deleted files from the hard drives. Each computer had two hard drives. Child pornography was found on each hard drive, and all together these hard drives contained thousands of files with such images. In addition, news servers had been installed on both computers, set to search for images of preteen and child sex. Additionally, three zip disks were also searched. The Zip disk from Slanina's office contained more than one hundred files of child pornography. No child pornography was found on the two Zip disks recovered from Slanina's home.

On February 14, 2000, Slanina was indicted on two counts of possession of child pornography under 18 U.S.C. §§2252A(a)(5)(B), 2256. He moved to suppress all statements made by him to law enforcement officers and all evidence obtained from his office computer equipment and home computer equipment. At the conclusion of the suppression hearing, the district court denied the motion.

II. . . .

The threshold question in our Fourth Amendment analysis is whether Slanina had a "'constitutionally protected reasonable expectation of privacy.'" *California v. Ciraolo*, 476 U.S. 207, 211, 90 L. Ed.2d 210, 106 S. Ct. 1809 (1986) (quoting *Katz v. United States*, 389 U.S. 347, 360, 19 L. Ed.2d 576, 88 S. Ct. 507 (1967) (Harlan, J., concurring)). This analysis involves two questions: "(1) whether the defendant is able to establish an actual, subjective expectation of privacy with respect to the place being searched or items being seized, and (2) whether that expectation of privacy is one which society would recognize as reasonable." United States v. Gomez, 276 F.3d 694, 697 (5th Cir. 2001) (quoting United States v. Kye Soo Lee, 898 F.2d 1034, 1037-38 (5th Cir. 1990)). In the present case, Slanina clearly demonstrated a subjective expectation of privacy with respect to his office and office computer equipment. He had closed and locked the door to his office. To limit access to his computer files, he installed passwords, thereby making it more difficult for another person to get past the screen saver and reboot his computer. Cf. *Runyan*, 275 F.3d at 458 (holding that defendant exhibited subjective expectation of privacy in images of child pornography by storing them in containers away from plain view). Moreover, Slanina did not forfeit his expectation of privacy in the files by providing the BIOS password to Smith, as he gave Smith the password for the limited purpose of installing the network, not perusing his files.

Having determined that Slanina did exhibit a subjective expectation of privacy, we now must decide whether this expectation was objectively reasonable. The government notes that other city employees had a grand master key to Slanina's office. Furthermore, it claims that the city's need to develop network systems and upgrade equipment required complete computer access, and that Slanina's installation of the passwords did not change this situation. Finally, it points out that the computer was purchased by the city and that employees knew they were not allowed to use city computers to access and store pornography. Given these circumstances, the government contends, any expectation of privacy was unreasonable. We disagree.

Slanina had a private office at the new fire station, and the ability of a select few of his coworkers to access the office does not mean that the office was "so open to fellow employees or the public that no expectation of privacy is reasonable." O'Connor v. Ortega, 480 U.S. 709, 718, 94 L. Ed.2d 714, 107 S. Ct. 1492 (1987) (plurality). Moreover, even though network administrators and computer technicians necessarily had some access to his computer, there is no evidence that such access was routine. Cf. Leventhal v. Knapek, 266 F.3d 64, 74 (2d Cir. 2001) (finding that government employee's expectation of privacy was reasonable and noting that state agency's access to computer did not appear to be frequent, widespread, or extensive). The city did not disseminate any policy that prevented the storage of personal information on city computers and also did not inform its employees that computer usage and internet access would be monitored. See United States v. Simons, 206 F.3d 392, 398 (4th Cir. 2000) (holding that in light of employer policy to inspect and monitor Internet activity, employee had no reasonable expectation of privacy in files transferred from Internet). Accordingly, given the absence of a city policy placing Slanina on notice that his computer usage would be monitored and the lack of any indication that other employees had routine access to his computer, we hold that Slanina's expectation of privacy was reasonable.

Having concluded that Slanina had a reasonable expectation of privacy in his office and office computer equipment, we now must decide whether the warrantless search of them violated the Fourth Amendment. The government characterizes Smith and Keller's search as a reasonable employer search related to an investigation into workplace misconduct, and therefore not subject to the warrant requirement. Slanina, however, contends that the workplace exception does not apply in this case. He argues that once Smith contacted Ure, after finding only the newsgroup titles and the image of adult pornography, he effectively became an agent of the police. Under this theory, the subsequent search of the computer by Keller, in which images of child pornography were first discovered, was not an investigation into work-related misconduct. Rather, it was a criminal investigation performed by the police, and therefore subject to the warrant requirement.

In O'Connor v. Ortega, a plurality of the Supreme Court considered the constitutionality of a state hospital administrator's search of a doctor's desk and file cabinets pursuant to an investigation into noncriminal work-related misconduct. 480 U.S. at 712-13. Concluding that the doctor had a reasonable expectation of privacy, the Court nevertheless refused to apply the warrant requirement to the search. Instead, it held "that public employer intrusions on the constitutionally protected privacy interests of government employees for noninvestigatory, work-related purposes, as well as for investigations of work-related misconduct, should be judged by the standard of reasonableness under all the circumstances." 480 U.S. at 725-26. Specifically, such workplace searches must be reasonable both at the inception and in scope. *O'Connor*, 480 U.S. at 726.

Although *O'Connor* provides the starting point of our analysis, it does not end our inquiry, as the facts before us are distinguishable on at least two noteworthy points. First, in the present case, although Slanina's use of the city-provided computer equipment to access and store pornography certainly constituted workplace misconduct, it also violated criminal law. It cannot be said that by the time Keller, a law enforcement officer with expertise in child pornography investigations, searched Slanina's office computer, there was no criminal dimension to the investigation. The Supreme Court specifically excepted this situation from its holding in *O'Connor*, declining to "address the appropriate standard when an employee is being investigated for criminal misconduct or breaches of other nonwork-related or regulatory standards." *Id*. at 729 n.*. Second, the *O'Connor* Court suggested that its holding might not extend to the context of investigations into work-related misconduct by government employers who, like Keller, are also law enforcement officers. *See id*. at 724 (noting that while law enforcement officials are expected to learn the "niceties of probable cause . . . it is simply unrealistic to expect supervisors in most government agencies to learn the subtleties of the probable cause standard").

Other circuits, however, have shed light on this issue. In United States v. Simons, the Fourth Circuit considered the legality of a government employer's search of an employee's office for evidence of child pornography. The defendant was an employee of a division of the Central Intelligence Agency ("CIA") and was suspected of using his office computer to access pornography. With help from network administrators, the defendant's employer copied his hard drive from a remote location. 206 F.3d at 396. A criminal investigator from the CIA Office of the Inspector General ("OIG") was then contacted. *Id*. Upon viewing the copy of the hard drive, the investigator found images of child pornography. *Id*. Later the same day, the network administrator entered the defendant's office and seized the hard drive, replacing it with a copy. *Id*. A few days later, the FBI was called. *Id*. The defendant appealed his conviction for possession of child pornography, claiming that the search of his office by the network administrator violated the Fourth Amendment. The Fourth Circuit rejected this challenge, holding that the *O'Connor* standard applied to the office search. 206 F.3d at 400. Importantly, the court assumed that the purpose of the search was "to acquire evidence of criminal activity," *id*., which had been committed at the government office using government equipment. Nevertheless, it concluded, the *O'Connor* exception to the warrant requirement applied, observing that the government employer "did not lose its special need for the 'efficient and proper operation of the workplace,' merely because the evidence obtained was evidence of a crime." *Id.* (quoting *O'Connor*, 480 U.S. at 723).

We approve of the Fourth Circuit's reasoning in *Simons*, agreeing that *O'Connor*'s goal of ensuring an efficient workplace should not be frustrated simply because the same misconduct that violates a government employer's policy also happens to be illegal. See also 4 Wayne R. LaFave, Search and Seizure §10.3 (3d ed. 2002) (noting that cases upholding searches by government employers into criminal, work-related misconduct are fully consistent with the reasoning in *O'Connor*). There is an obvious distinction, however, between the facts confronted by the Fourth Circuit in *Simons* and the situation before us in the instant case. In *Simons*, the person conducting the search was a network administrator for the government employer, not a law enforcement official. By contrast, in the present case the critical search was performed by Keller, who was both a supervisor and a law enforcement officer. Therefore, we must also inquire whether the *O'Connor* exception should extend to the situation in which the criminal work-related misconduct is being investigated by an employer who is also a law enforcement officer. . . .

Our review of the relevant caselaw from our sister circuits leads us to the inescapable conclusion that Keller's search of Slanina's office computer equipment, including the hard drives and Zip disks, should be reviewed under the *O'Connor* standard. As an expert in child pornography investigations, Keller undoubtedly appreciated the possibility that the investigation into Slanina's misuse of city computer equipment might result in evidence of criminal violations. Nevertheless, any evidence of criminal acts was also proof of work-related misconduct. Once Smith and Ure uncovered evidence of work-related misconduct, the city did not lose its interest in being able to fully investigate such misconduct in a regular and efficient manner. The record evidence demonstrates that as of the time of Keller's search, the probe remained at least partly an investigation into employee misconduct. The subsequent involvement of the City Manager and human resources in the process attests to this characterization. To hold that a warrant is necessary any time a law enforcement official recognizes the possibility that an investigation into work-related misconduct will yield evidence of criminal acts would frustrate the government employer's interest in "the efficient and proper operation of the workplace." *O'Connor*, 480 U.S. at 723. We decline to impose such a burden on government employers. Therefore, in assessing the constitutionality of Keller's search, we apply the standard articulated in *O'Connor*.

Under *O'Connor*, a search by a government employer must be justified at its inception and reasonably related to the circumstances justifying the interference in the first place. *Id.* at 726. We have little difficulty concluding that Keller's search passes this test. At the inception of his search, Smith had already discovered titles of newsgroups suggesting the presence of child pornography on Slanina's computer. Smith had also found an image of adult pornography, which represented a violation of city policy. On this evidence alone, Keller was justified in conducting a full search of the computer and accompanying disks to look for evidence of misconduct. Moreover, the scope of the search was also reasonable. The computer had been provided to Slanina by the city, and any use of it to access pornography was a violation of city policy. Keller was entitled to determine the extent of Slanina's violations.

COMMENTS AND QUESTIONS

1. Fourth Amendment defenses have been raised in a number of Internet-related cases, including United States v. Charbonneau, 979 F. Supp. 1177 (S.D. Ohio 1997), which held that the defendant did not have a reasonable expectation of privacy for online exchanges of information in a private online chatroom where a government agent posing as a pedophile obtained child pornography from him. For a general discussion of the Fourth Amendment as applied to Internet searches, see Michael Adler, Note, Cyberspace, General Searches and Digital Contraband: The Fourth Amendment and the Net-Wide Search, 105 Yale L.J. 1093 (1996).

2. Kyllo v. United States, 121 S. Ct. 2038 (2001), addresses whether advances in surveillance technologies automatically reduce the scope of privacy rights individuals enjoy under the Fourth Amendment. In that case, the Supreme Court decided that the warrantless use of a thermal-imaging device aimed at a private home from a public street to detect relative amounts of heat within the home constituted a "search" within the meaning of the Fourth Amendment. It reversed Kyllo's conviction for manufacturing marijuana and remanded for further proceedings. Among other things, the Court stated:

> The *Katz* test—whether the individual has an expectation of privacy that society is prepared to recognize as reasonable—has often been criticized as circular, and hence subjective and unpredictable. See 1 W. LaFave, Search and Seizure §2.1(d), pp. 393-394 (3d ed. 1996). While it may be difficult to refine *Katz* when the search of areas such as telephone booths, automobiles, or even the curtilage and uncovered portions of residences are at issue, in the case of the search of the interior of homes—the prototypical and hence most commonly litigated area of protected privacy—there is a ready criterion, with roots deep in the common law, of the minimal expectation of privacy that exists, and that is acknowledged to be reasonable. To withdraw protection of this minimum expectation would be to permit police technology to erode the privacy guaranteed by the Fourth Amendment. We think that obtaining by sense-enhancing technology any information regarding the interior of the home that could not otherwise have been obtained without physical "intrusion into a constitutionally protected area" constitutes a search—at least where (as here) the technology in question is not in general public use. This assures preservation of that degree of privacy against government that existed when the Fourth Amendment was adopted. On the basis of this criterion, the information obtained by the thermal imager in this case was the product of a search. . . .
>
> Limiting the prohibition of thermal imaging to "intimate details" would not only be wrong in principle; it would be impractical in application, failing to provide "a workable accommodation between the needs of law enforcement and the interests protected by the Fourth Amendment," Oliver v. United States, 466 U.S. 170, 181 (1984). To begin with, there is no necessary connection between the sophistication of the surveillance equipment and the "intimacy" of the details that it observes—which means that one cannot say (and the police cannot be assured) that use of the relatively crude equipment at issue here will always be lawful. The Agema Thermovision 210 might disclose, for example, at what hour each night the lady of the house takes her daily sauna and bath—a detail that many would consider "intimate"; and a much more sophisticated system might detect nothing more intimate than the fact that someone left a closet light on. We could not, in other words, develop a rule approving only that through-the-wall surveillance which identifies objects no smaller than 36 by 36 inches, but would have to develop a jurisprudence specifying which home activities are "inti-

mate" and which are not. And even when (if ever) that jurisprudence were fully developed, no police officer would be able to know in advance whether his through-the-wall surveillance picks up "intimate" details—and thus would be unable to know in advance whether it is constitutional.

Under what circumstances might *Kyllo* be helpful for defendants in Internet-related cases?

3. In the aftermath of the Watergate scandal and the Nixon Administration's misuse of data about individuals in government records, Congress passed the Privacy Act of 1974 to establish statutory protections for personal data in the hands of federal agencies. Some state laws also protect personal data in government databases. For a discussion of the implications of the vast stores of personal data in government databases and limitations of existing privacy regulations, see, e.g., Daniel J. Solove, Access and Aggregation: Public Records, Privacy and the Constitution, 86 Minn. L. Rev. 1137 (2002); Daniel J. Solove, Digital Dossiers and the Dissipation of Fourth Amendment Privacy, 75 S. Cal. L. Rev. 1083 (2002). On occasion, Congress has insisted on protecting private information in the hands of state governments. The Driver's Privacy Protection Act, 18 U.S.C. §§2721-2725, forbids state motor vehicle agencies from "knowingly disclos[ing] or otherwise mak[ing] available to any person or entity personal information about any individual obtained by the department in connection with a motor vehicle record." 18 U.S.C. §2721(a). South Carolina challenged this law as a violation of the Tenth and Eleventh Amendments to the U.S. Constitution. The U.S. Supreme Court upheld the DPPA as an appropriate exercise of Congress' powers under the Commerce Clause in Reno v. Condon, 120 S. Ct. 666 (2001).

4. Since 1998, the FBI has been using its Carnivore system to intercept electronic mail and instant messaging information pertaining to suspects from Internet service providers (ISPs). The FBI installs Carnivore on the servers of the suspect's ISP after getting judicial authorization for its placement. Carnivore "sniffs" packets of data coming through the servers, and when it detects a message by or to the targeted suspect, Carnivore analyzes the content of the document. Among other things, it can be programmed to record messages containing certain words relevant to the investigation. The FBI claims that Carnivore examines only the contents of the suspect's e-mails. However, to filter out other messages, it necessarily analyzes routing codes that identify other users. The FBI likens Carnivore to pen register devices that keep track of numbers dialed by a suspect. The Supreme Court has held that a search warrant is not required for the government to install pen register devices, distinguishing between addressing information (e.g., telephone numbers dialed) and the content of communications (for which a search warrant must be obtained based on evidence of probable cause to believe a crime has been committed by the suspect). Privacy advocates have expressed concern about the potential for misuse of the Carnivore system because it can so easily be programmed to analyze and capture more information than a warrant may call for. Congress held hearings on the use of Carnivore in the summer of 2000, but the push for legislative limits on Carnivore lessened substantially after the terrorist attacks on the World Trade Center and the Pentagon in September 2001. In the aftermath of these attacks, Congress passed the USA PATRIOT (Uniting and Strengthening America by Providing Appropriate Tools Required to Intercept and Obstruct Terrorism) Act. Among other things, this law allows the government to collect addressing informa-

tion of electronic communications (e.g., e-mails) without a warrant, although to record or analyze the content of such electronic communications a warrant is required. The USA PATRIOT Act does not, however, define what the term "content" means in this context. Is the length of a message, information about attachments to email, or subject lines "content" or "address" information? When an Internet user types "google.com," this may be addressing information which the government can gather without a warrant, but what about information about the user's searches? As the *Pharmatrak* case indicates, search strings can be very information-rich. For a discussion of the implications of the USA PATRIOT Act for online privacy, concluding that the Act doesn't actually change existing privacy rules very much, see Orin S. Kerr, Internet Surveillance After the USA Patriot Act: The Big Brother That Isn't, 97 Nw. L. Rev. (forthcoming 2003).

5. Does the Fourth Amendment require a warrant before the government can decrypt an encrypted communication? Orin S. Kerr suggests not in his article The Fourth Amendment in Cyberspace: Can Encryption Create a "Reasonable Expectation of Privacy"?, 33 Conn. L. Rev. 503 (2001). However, Trulok v. Freeh, 275 F.3d 391 (4th Cir. 2002) suggests otherwise. Trulok sued FBI Director Freeh for damages on account of the FBI's warrantless search of password-protected files on his computer. The court was persuaded that this search was in violation of Trulok's Fourth Amendment rights, although ruling that the qualified immunity FBI agents enjoy precluded a damages award. Consider also United States v. Scarfo, 180 F. Supp.2d 572 (D.N.J. 2001), in which the FBI used keystroke-recording software to decipher the password for an encrypted file in its search for evidence of illegal gambling and loan sharking. Scarfo challenged the FBI's use of the software to capture other keystrokes as an unreasonable general search. The court ruled that the government's use of the keystroke-recording software did not violate the Fourth Amendment, even if it resulted in collection of more information than the warrant called for. See Raymond Shih Ray Ku, The Founder's Privacy: The Fourth Amendment and the Power of Technological Surveillance, 86 Minn. L. Rev. (2002).

E. ENCRYPTION POLICY

Bernstein v. United States Department of Justice
United States Court of Appeals for the Ninth Circuit
176 F.3d 1132 (9th Cir. 1999)

FLETCHER, Circuit Judge:

Government regulation of encryption was a subject of heated debate during the 1990s. The Defense Department, other intelligence agencies, and the FBI generally favored strong regulatory controls over encryption to enable national security, intelligence, and law enforcement officials to access encrypted communications or files and to keep strong encryption out of the hands of wrongdoers. The computer and software industry in the United States, along with civil liberties and privacy advocates, favored lessening export controls of encryption. Among other things, high technology industries pointed out that encryption was not as strictly regulated outside the U.S., that "strong" encryption was available elsewhere, and that U.S. restrictions on export of strong encryption only served to make U.S. industries less competitive in the world market. Civil liberties and privacy advocates were principally concerned about lessening restrictions on encryption because this technology was so useful for protecting private communications and stored information. See, e.g., Ian Goldberg, David Wagner, and Eric A. Brewer, Privacy-Enhancing Technologies for the Internet, IEEE COMPCON '97 (1997), available at http://www.cs.berkeley.edu/~daw/papers/privacy-compcon97-www/privacy-html.html. Although U.S. export control officials conceded that printed books and articles on encryption, even those that might contain source code forms of encryption programs, could lawfully be distributed without government permission, they were unwilling to reach the same conclusion about electronic forms of encryption programs. To export them, whether by posting them on the Internet or otherwise, government officials insisted that it was necessary to obtain an export control license beforehand. Several lawsuits challenged the license requirement of the export control regulations as applied to encryption software as an unconstitutional prior restraint on speech under the First Amendment. Although the Ninth Circuit withdrew the *Bernstein* decision, excerpted below, after the government changed the pertinent export regulations, the decision is nonetheless instructive because it addresses a question with broad implications for government regulation of computer programs in general and encryption programs in particular.

Background

Bernstein is currently a professor in the Department of Mathematics, Statistics, and Computer Science at the University of Illinois at Chicago. As a doctoral candidate at the University of California, Berkeley, he developed an encryption method —"a zero-delay private-key stream encryptor based upon a one-way hash function" —that he dubbed "Snuffle." Bernstein described his method in two ways: in a paper containing analysis and mathematical equations (the "Paper") and in two computer programs written in "C," a high-level computer programming language ("Source Code"). Bernstein later wrote a set of instructions in English (the "Instructions") explaining how to program a computer to encrypt and decrypt data utilizing a one-way hash function, essentially translating verbatim his Source Code into prose form.

Seeking to present his work on Snuffle within the academic and scientific communities, Bernstein asked the State Department whether he needed a license to publish Snuffle in any of its various forms. The State Department responded that Snuffle was a munition under the International Traffic in Arms Regulations ("ITAR"), and that Bernstein would need a license to "export" the Paper, the Source Code, or the Instructions. There followed a protracted and unproductive series of letter communications between Bernstein and the government, wherein Bernstein unsuccessfully attempted to determine the scope and application of the export regulations to Snuffle.

Bernstein ultimately filed this action, challenging the constitutionality of the ITAR regulations. The district court found that the Source Code was speech protected by the First Amendment, see Bernstein v. U.S. Department of State, 922

F. Supp. 1426 (N.D.Cal. 1996) (*"Bernstein I"*), and subsequently granted summary judgment to Bernstein on his First Amendment claims, holding the challenged ITAR regulations facially invalid as a prior restraint on speech, see Bernstein v. U.S. Department of State, 945 F. Supp. 1279 (N.D.Cal. 1996) (*"Bernstein II"*). . . .

Discussion

. . .

We begin by explaining what source code is. "Source code," at least as currently understood by computer programmers, refers to the text of a program written in a "high-level" programming language, such as "PASCAL" or "C." The distinguishing feature of source code is that it is meant to be read and understood by humans and that it can be used to express an idea or a method. A computer, in fact, can make no direct use of source code until it has been translated ("compiled") into a "low-level" or "machine" language, resulting in computer-executable "object code." That source code is meant for human eyes and understanding, however, does not mean that an untutored layperson can understand it. Because source code is destined for the maw of an automated, ruthlessly literal translator—the compiler—a programmer must follow stringent grammatical, syntactical, formatting, and punctuation conventions. As a result, only those trained in programming can easily understand source code.[11]

Also important for our purposes is an understanding of how source code is used in the field of cryptography. Bernstein has submitted numerous declarations from cryptographers and computer programmers explaining that cryptographic ideas and algorithms are conveniently expressed in source code.[12] That this should

---

11. It must be emphasized, however, that source code is merely text, albeit text that conforms to stringent formatting and punctuation requirements. For example, the following is an excerpt from Bernstein's Snuffle source code:

```
for (; ;)
(
uch = gtchr( );
if (!(n & 31))
(
for (i = 0; i<64; i++)
l[ ctr[i] ] = k[i] + h[n - 64 + i]    Hash512 (wm, wl, level, 8);
)
```

As source code goes, Snuffle is quite compact; the entirety of the Snuffle source code occupies fewer than four printed pages.

12. Source code's power to convey algorithmic information is illustrated by the declaration of MIT Professor Harold Abelson:

The square root of a number X is the number Y such that Y times Y equals X. This is declarative knowledge. It tells us something about square roots. But it doesn't tell us how to find a square root.

In contrast, consider the following ancient algorithm, attributed to Heron of Alexandria, for approximating square roots:

To approximate the square root of a positive number X,

— Make a guess for the square root of X.
— Compute an improved guess as the average of the guess and X divided by the guess.
— Keep improving the guess until it is good enough.

Heron's method doesn't say anything about what square roots are, but it does say how to approximate them. This is a piece of imperative "how to" knowledge.

be so is, on reflection, not surprising. As noted earlier, the chief task for cryptographers is the development of secure methods of encryption. While the articulation of such a system in layman's English or in general mathematical terms may be useful, the devil is, at least for cryptographers, often in the algorithmic details. By utilizing source code, a cryptographer can express algorithmic ideas with precision and methodological rigor that is otherwise difficult to achieve. This has the added benefit of facilitating peer review—by compiling the source code, a cryptographer can create a working model subject to rigorous security tests. The need for precisely articulated hypotheses and formal empirical testing, of course, is not unique to the science of cryptography; it appears, however, that in this field, source code is the preferred means to these ends.

Thus, cryptographers use source code to express their scientific ideas in much the same way that mathematicians use equations or economists use graphs. Of course, both mathematical equations and graphs are used in other fields for many purposes, not all of which are expressive. But mathematicians and economists have adopted these modes of expression in order to facilitate the precise and rigorous expression of complex scientific ideas. Similarly, the undisputed record here makes it clear that cryptographers utilize source code in the same fashion.[14]

In light of these considerations, we conclude that encryption software, in its source code form[15] and as employed by those in the field of cryptography, must be viewed as expressive for First Amendment purposes, and thus is entitled to the protections of the prior restraint doctrine. If the government required that mathematicians obtain a prepublication license prior to publishing material that included mathematical equations, we have no doubt that such a regime would be subject to scrutiny as a prior restraint. The availability of alternate means of expression, moreover, does not diminish the censorial power of such a restraint—that Adam Smith

[margin annotation: 1st amend]

Computer science is in the business of formalizing imperative knowledge—developing formal notations and ways to reason and talk about methodology. Here is Heron's method formalized as a procedure in the notation of the Lisp computer language:

```
(define (sqrtx)    (define (good-enough? guess)
(<(abs (-(square guess) x)) tolerance))
(define (improve guess)
(average guess (/ x guess)))
(define (try guess)
(if (good-enough? guess)
guess
(try (improve guess))))
(try 1))
```

14. Bernstein's Snuffle, in fact, provides an illustration of this point. By developing Snuffle, Bernstein was attempting to demonstrate that a one-way hash function could be employed as the heart of an encryption method. The Snuffle source code, as submitted by Bernstein to the State Department, was meant as an expression of how this might be accomplished. The Source Code was plainly not intended as a completed encryption product, as demonstrated by the fact that it was incomplete and not in a form suitable for final compiling. The Source Code, in fact, omits the hash function entirely—until combined with such a function and compiled, Snuffle is incapable of performing encryption functions at all.

Snuffle was also intended, in part, as political expression. Bernstein discovered that the ITAR regulations controlled encryption exports, but not one-way hash functions. Because he believed that an encryption system could easily be fashioned from any of a number of publicly-available one-way hash functions, he viewed the distinction made by the ITAR regulations as absurd. To illustrate his point, Bernstein developed Snuffle, which is an encryption system built around a one-way hash function.

15. We express no opinion regarding whether object code manifests a "close enough nexus to expression" to warrant application of the prior restraint doctrine. Bernstein's Snuffle did not involve object code, nor does the record contain any information regarding expressive uses of object code in the field of cryptography.

wrote Wealth of Nations without resorting to equations or graphs surely would not justify governmental prepublication review of economics literature that contain these modes of expression. . . .

The challenged EAR regulations explicitly apply to expression and place scientific expression under the censor's eye on a regular basis. In fact, there is ample evidence in the record establishing that some in the cryptography field have already begun censoring themselves, for fear that their statements might influence the disposition of future licensing applications. See, e.g., National Research Council, Cryptography's Role in Securing the Information Society 158 (1996) ("Vendors contended that since they are effectively at the mercy of the export control regulators, they have considerable incentive to suppress any public expression of dissatisfaction with the current process."). In these circumstances, we cannot conclude that the export control regime at issue is a "law of general application" immune from prior restraint analysis.[17]

Because the prepublication licensing scheme challenged here vests unbridled discretion in government officials, and because it directly jeopardizes scientific expression, we are satisfied that Bernstein may properly bring a facial challenge against the regulations. We accordingly turn to the merits. . . .

"[T]he protection even as to previous restraint is not absolutely unlimited." *Near*, 283 U.S. at 716. The Supreme Court has suggested that the "heavy presumption" against prior restraints may be overcome where official discretion is bounded by stringent procedural safeguards. See FW/PBS, 493 U.S. at 227 (plurality opinion of O'Connor, J.); Freedman v. Maryland, 380 U.S. 51, 58-59, 85 S. Ct. 734, 13 L. Ed.2d 649 (1965); *Kingsley Books*, 354 U.S. at 442-43; 11126 Baltimore Blvd. v. Prince George's County, 58 F.3d 988, 995 (4th Cir. 1995) (en banc). As our analysis above suggests, the challenged regulations do not qualify for this First Amendment safe harbor.[19] In Freedman v. Maryland, the Supreme Court set out three factors for determining the validity of licensing schemes that impose a

---

17. The government also argues that the EAR regulations are "laws of general application" because they are not purposefully aimed at suppressing any particular ideas that may be expressed in source code. With respect to this contention, the panel (including the dissenter) agree that the purpose of the regulations is irrelevant to prior restraint analysis. It is clear that a prior restraint analysis applies equally to content-neutral or content-based enactments. . . . Indeed, where unbridled discretion is vested in a governmental official, it is difficult to know whether a licensing regime is content-based or content-neutral. Accordingly, the government's purpose in censoring encryption source code is, at this stage of our First Amendment inquiry, beside the point. In other words, a prepublication licensing regime that has a chilling and censorial effect on expression is properly subject to facial attack as a prior restraint, whatever the purpose behind its enactment. See *Lakewood*, 486 U.S. at 759 (upholding facial attack against newsrack ordinance because of censorial effects, without discussing governmental purpose for enacting the ordinance).

19. The Supreme Court has also suggested that the presumption against prior restraints may be overcome where publication would directly and imminently imperil national security. See New York Times Co. v. United States, 403 U.S. 713, 730, 91 S. Ct. 2140, 29 L. Ed.2d 822 (1971) (Stewart, J., joined by White, J., concurring); *Near*, 283 U.S. at 716; see also United States v. The Progressive, Inc., 467 F. Supp. 990, 992 (W.D.Wis. 1979). In order to justify a prior restraint on national security grounds, the government must prove the publication would "surely result in direct, immediate, and irreparable damage to our Nation or its people." *New York Times*, 403 U.S. at 730 (Stewart, J., joined by White, J., concurring); see also *id*. at 726-27 (Brennan, J., concurring) (finding that national security is a sufficient interest only where there is "governmental allegation and proof that publication must inevitably, directly, and immediately cause the occurrence of an event kindred to imperiling the safety of a transport already at sea"); Burch v. Barker, 861 F.2d 1149, 1155 (9th Cir. 1988) ("Prior restraints are permissible in only the rarest of circumstances, such as imminent threat to national security.").

The government does not argue that the prior restraint at issue here falls within the extremely narrow class of cases where publication would directly and immediately imperil national security.

prior restraint on speech: (1) any restraint must be for a specified brief period of time; (2) there must be expeditious judicial review; and (3) the censor must bear the burden of going to court to suppress the speech in question and must bear the burden of proof. See 380 U.S. at 58-60. The district court found that the procedural protections provided by the EAR regulations are "woefully inadequate" when measured against these requirements. *Bernstein III*, 974 F. Supp. at 1308. We agree.

Although the regulations require that license applications be resolved or referred to the President within 90 days, see 15 C.F.R. §750.4(a), there is no time limit once an application is referred to the President. Thus, the 90-day limit can be rendered meaningless by referral. Moreover, if the license application is denied, no firm time limit governs the internal appeals process. See 15 C.F.R. §756.2(c)(1) (Under Secretary "shall decide an appeal within a reasonable time after receipt of the appeal."). Accordingly, the EAR regulations do not satisfy the first *Freedman* requirement that a licensing decision be made within a reasonably short, specified period of time. . . . The EAR regulatory regime further offends *Freedman*'s procedural requirements insofar as it denies a disappointed applicant the opportunity for judicial review.[21]

We conclude that the challenged regulations allow the government to restrain speech indefinitely with no clear criteria for review. As a result, Bernstein and other scientists have been effectively chilled from engaging in valuable scientific expression. Bernstein's experience itself demonstrates the enormous uncertainty that exists over the scope of the regulations and the potential for the chilling of scientific expression. In short, because the challenged regulations grant boundless discretion to government officials, and because they lack the required procedural protections set forth in *Freedman*, we find that they operate as an unconstitutional prior restraint on speech.[22] See *Lakewood*, 486 U.S. at 769-72 (holding that newsrack licensing ordinance was an impermissible prior restraint because it conferred unbounded discretion and lacked adequate procedural safeguards).

Concluding Comments

We emphasize the narrowness of our First Amendment holding. We do not hold that all software is expressive. Much of it surely is not. Nor need we resolve whether the challenged regulations constitute content-based restrictions, subject to the strictest constitutional scrutiny, or whether they are, instead, content-neutral restrictions meriting less exacting scrutiny. We hold merely that because the pre-publication licensing regime challenged here applies directly to scientific expression,

21. As noted earlier, the BXA enjoys essentially unbounded discretion under the EAR regulations in administering the license process. Accordingly, even if the challenged regulations provided for judicial review, the lack of explicit limits on the decisionmaker's discretion would likely make such review meaningless. In this sense, the presence of unbounded discretion itself may be considered fatal for purposes of prior restraint review. See *Lakewood*, 486 U.S. at 769-70 (striking down a licensing scheme where the mayor could merely claim that the license " 'is not in the public interest' when denying a permit application").

22. Our conclusion relating to the Source Code also resolves the status of the regulations as applied to the Instructions. Because the Instructions are essentially a translation of the Source Code into English, they are, if anything, nearer the heartland of the First Amendment. Consequently, to the extent the challenged regulations are unconstitutional as applied to the Source Code, they necessarily are unconstitutional as applied to the Instructions.

vests boundless discretion in government officials, and lacks adequate procedural safeguards, it constitutes an impermissible prior restraint on speech.

We will, however, comment on two issues that are entwined with the underlying merits of Bernstein's constitutional claims. First, we note that insofar as the EAR regulations on encryption software were intended to slow the spread of secure encryption methods to foreign nations, the government is intentionally retarding the progress of the flourishing science of cryptography. To the extent the government's efforts are aimed at interdicting the flow of scientific ideas (whether expressed in source code or otherwise), as distinguished from encryption products, these efforts would appear to strike deep into the heartland of the First Amendment. In this regard, the EAR regulations are very different from content-neutral time, place and manner restrictions that may have an incidental effect on expression while aiming at secondary effects.

Second, we note that the government's efforts to regulate and control the spread of knowledge relating to encryption may implicate more than the First Amendment rights of cryptographers. In this increasingly electronic age, we are all required in our everyday lives to rely on modern technology to communicate with one another. This reliance on electronic communication, however, has brought with it a dramatic diminution in our ability to communicate privately. Cellular phones are subject to monitoring, email is easily intercepted, and transactions over the internet are often less than secure. Something as commonplace as furnishing our credit card number, social security number, or bank account number puts each of us at risk. Moreover, when we employ electronic methods of communication, we often leave electronic "fingerprints" behind, fingerprints that can be traced back to us. Whether we are surveilled by our government, by criminals, or by our neighbors, it is fair to say that never has our ability to shield our affairs from prying eyes been at such a low ebb. The availability and use of secure encryption may offer an opportunity to reclaim some portion of the privacy we have lost. Government efforts to control encryption thus may well implicate not only the First Amendment rights of cryptographers intent on pushing the boundaries of their science, but also the constitutional rights of each of us as potential recipients of encryption's bounty. Viewed from this perspective, the government's efforts to retard progress in cryptography may implicate the Fourth Amendment, as well as the right to speak anonymously, see McIntyre v. Ohio Elections Comm'n, 514 U.S. 334, 115 S. Ct. 1511, 1524, 131 L. Ed.2d 426 (1995), the right against compelled speech, see Wooley v. Maynard, 430 U.S. 705, 714, 97 S. Ct. 1428, 51 L. Ed.2d 752 (1977), and the right to informational privacy, see Whalen v. Roe, 429 U.S. 589, 599-600, 97 S. Ct. 869, 51 L. Ed.2d 64 (1977). While we leave for another day the resolution of these difficult issues, it is important to point out that Bernstein's is a suit not merely concerning a small group of scientists laboring in an esoteric field, but also touches on the public interest broadly defined. . . .

COMMENTS AND QUESTIONS

1. The Ninth Circuit does not emphasize the point, but violations of the export control laws can be prosecuted as crimes. See 22 U.S.C. §2778. Should this affect the court's decision about the First Amendment issues in the case? Another cryptographer, Phil Zimmerman, spent years of his life under threats of criminal

prosecution because the Pretty Good Privacy (PGP) software he had written was available on Web sites outside the United States. Although these charges were eventually dropped by the government, Zimmermann continues to risk prosecution through his highly publicized (and unapologetic) distribution of PGP to political dissidents around the globe. See Douglas Hayward, So Arrest Me, Zimmermann Tells Feds, TechWeb News (May 19, 1997) http://www.techweb.com/se/direct-link.cgi?WIR1997051915.

2. Although the Ninth Circuit Court of Appeals withdrew its decision in *Bernstein*, see Bernstein v. United States, 192 F.3d 1308 (9th Cir. 1999), the decision has been influential nonetheless. Other courts have reached the same conclusion on the issue of whether computer programs enjoy First Amendment protection as speech. In Junger v. Daley, 209 F.3d 481 (6th Cir. 2000), a law professor was held to have a First Amendment right to post source code forms of encryption programs on his course Web site notwithstanding the export control laws. In Universal City Studios, Inc. v. Corley, 273 F.3d 429 (2d Cir. 2001), the Second Circuit Court of Appeals opined that computer programs, in both source and object code, enjoy First Amendment protection as expressive works, although it ruled that the scope of First Amendment protection may be limited because of the functionality of program code.

3. An interesting observation about export control laws is made in Lawrence Lessig, The Limits in Open Code: Regulatory Standards and the Future of the Net, 14 Berkeley Tech. L.J. 759 (1999). The U.S. government can easily regulate software companies that might wish to distribute products containing strong encryption features because they will be vulnerable to challenge if they export software exceeding current guidelines, or if they post code containing strong encryption on the company Web site. However, if a company posts open-source software on its site, persons outside the United States may be able to add strong encryption features to the posted code, and the U.S. government may be unable to do anything about this.

4. The Clinton Administration made repeated attempts to employ its commercial clout as a purchaser of computer systems to persuade the marketplace to accept computer chips that complied with certain escrow protocols that would enable the government, presumably upon a proper showing of necessity, to obtain access to encrypted information or communications. Because companies generally do not make one version of their products for the commercial marketplace and another to sell to the government, the Administration hoped that key escrow system technology would become a de facto norm, making it unnecessary for the government to seek legislation from the Congress that would mandate key escrow technologies. Widely known as the "Clipper chip" initiative, this effort met with considerable resistance from the commercial marketplace and from the cryptographic research community. For a narrative on this initiative and an expression of public policy concerns about it, see A. Michael Froomkin, It Came From Planet Clipper: The Battle Over Cryptographic Key "Escrow," 1996 U. Chi. Legal Forum 15 (1996).

5. Froomkin has also analyzed at length the constitutionality of a possible U.S. government mandate that key escrow systems be embedded in all computer systems. See A. Michael Froomkin, The Metaphor Is the Key: Cryptography, The Clipper Chip, and the Constitution, 143 U. Penn. L. Rev. 709 (1995). As the title

to his article suggests, the answer to the constitutional question is likely to depend on what metaphor the courts employ to judge the issue.

6. Countries differ in their policies regarding encryption software; yet it is clear that the global nature of the Internet today makes greater commonality in national encryption policies desirable. The Organization for Economic Cooperation and Development has developed guidelines for national policies. See OECD Cryptography Guidelines, http://www.oecd.org/dsti/sti/it/secur/prod/gd97-204 .pdf.

7. The National Research Council has published a report entitled Cryptography's Role in Securing the Information Society (Kenneth Dam & Herb Lin eds., 1996), which discusses the multidimensional importance of encryption in achieving a variety of societal objectives. For detailed consideration of the importance of encryption in fostering electronic commerce, see Stewart A. Baker & Paul Hurst, The Limits of Trust (1998); A. Michael Froomkin, Flood Control on the Information Ocean: Living with Anonymity, Digital Cash, and Distributed Databases, 15 J.L. & Comm. 395 (1996); A. Michael Froomkin, The Essential Role of Trusted Third Parties in Electronic Commerce, 75 Or. L. Rev. 49 (1996).

13

Unauthorized Access

A. SPAM

CompuServe Incorporated v. Cyber Promotions, Inc.
United States District Court for the Southern District of Ohio
962 F. Supp. 1015 (S.D. Ohio 1997)

GRAHAM, District Judge.

This case presents novel issues regarding the commercial use of the Internet, specifically the right of an online computer service to prevent a commercial enterprise from sending unsolicited electronic mail advertising to its subscribers.

Plaintiff CompuServe Incorporated ("CompuServe") is one of the major national commercial online computer services. It operates a computer communication service through a proprietary nationwide computer network. In addition to allowing access to the extensive content available within its own proprietary network, CompuServe also provides its subscribers with a link to the much larger resources of the Internet. This allows its subscribers to send and receive electronic messages, known as "e-mail," by the Internet. Defendants Cyber Promotions, Inc. and its president Sanford Wallace are in the business of sending unsolicited e-mail advertisements on behalf of themselves and their clients to hundreds of thousands of Internet users, many of whom are CompuServe subscribers. CompuServe has notified defendants that they are prohibited from using its computer equipment to process and store the unsolicited e-mail and has requested that they terminate the practice. Instead, defendants have sent an increasing volume of e-mail solicitations to CompuServe subscribers. CompuServe has attempted to employ technological means to block the flow of defendants' e-mail transmissions to its computer equipment, but to no avail.

921

This matter is before the Court on the application of CompuServe for a preliminary injunction which would extend the duration of the temporary restraining order issued by this Court on October 24, 1996 and which would in addition prevent defendants from sending unsolicited advertisements to CompuServe subscribers.

For the reasons which follow, this Court holds that where defendants engaged in a course of conduct of transmitting a substantial volume of electronic data in the form of unsolicited e-mail to plaintiff's proprietary computer equipment, where defendants continued such practice after repeated demands to cease and desist, and where defendants deliberately evaded plaintiff's affirmative efforts to protect its computer equipment from such use, plaintiff has a viable claim for trespass to personal property and is entitled to injunctive relief to protect its property.

I. . . .

Internet users often pay a fee for Internet access. However, there is no permessage charge to send electronic messages over the Internet and such messages usually reach their destination within minutes. Thus electronic mail provides an opportunity to reach a wide audience quickly and at almost no cost to the sender. It is not surprising therefore that some companies, like defendant Cyber Promotions, Inc., have begun using the Internet to distribute advertisements by sending the same unsolicited commercial message to hundreds of thousands of Internet users at once. Defendants refer to this as "bulk e-mail," while plaintiff refers to it as "junk e-mail." In the vernacular of the Internet, unsolicited e-mail advertising is sometimes referred to pejoratively as "spam."

CompuServe subscribers use CompuServe's domain name "CompuServe.com" together with their own unique alpha-numeric identifier to form a distinctive e-mail mailing address. That address may be used by the subscriber to exchange electronic mail with any one of tens of millions of other Internet users who have electronic mail capability. E-mail sent to CompuServe subscribers is processed and stored on CompuServe's proprietary computer equipment. Thereafter, it becomes accessible to CompuServe's subscribers, who can access CompuServe's equipment and electronically retrieve those messages.

Over the past several months, CompuServe has received many complaints from subscribers threatening to discontinue their subscription unless CompuServe prohibits electronic mass mailers from using its equipment to send unsolicited advertisements. CompuServe asserts that the volume of messages generated by such mass mailings places a significant burden on its equipment which has finite processing and storage capacity. CompuServe receives no payment from the mass mailers for processing their unsolicited advertising. However, CompuServe's subscribers pay for their access to CompuServe's services in increments of time and thus the process of accessing, reviewing and discarding unsolicited e-mail costs them money, which is one of the reasons for their complaints. CompuServe has notified defendants that they are prohibited from using its proprietary computer equipment to process and store unsolicited e-mail and has requested them to cease and desist from sending unsolicited e-mail to its subscribers. Nonetheless, defendants have sent an increasing volume of e-mail solicitations to CompuServe subscribers.

In an effort to shield its equipment from defendants' bulk e-mail, CompuServe has implemented software programs designed to screen out the messages and block their receipt. In response, defendants have modified their equipment and the messages they send in such a fashion as to circumvent CompuServe's screening software. Allegedly, defendants have been able to conceal the true origin of their messages by falsifying the point-of-origin information contained in the header of the electronic messages. Defendants have removed the "sender" information in the header of their messages and replaced it with another address. Also, defendants have developed the capability of configuring their computer servers to conceal their true domain name and appear on the Internet as another computer, further concealing the true origin of the messages. By manipulating this data, defendants have been able to continue sending messages to CompuServe's equipment in spite of CompuServe's protests and protective efforts.

Defendants assert that they possess the right to continue to send these communications to CompuServe subscribers. CompuServe contends that, in doing so, the defendants are trespassing upon its personal property. . . .

The Restatement §217(b) states that a trespass to chattel may be committed by intentionally using or intermeddling with the chattel in possession of another. Restatement §217, Comment e defines physical "intermeddling" as follows:

> . . . intentionally bringing about a physical contact with the chattel. The actor may commit a trespass by an act which brings him into an intended physical contact with a chattel in the possession of another[.]

Electronic signals generated and sent by computer have been held to be sufficiently physically tangible to support a trespass cause of action. Thrifty-Tel, Inc., v. Bezenek, 46 Cal.App.4th 1559, 1567, 54 Cal.Rptr.2d 468 (1996); State v. McGraw, 480 N.E.2d 552, 554 (Ind. 1985) (Indiana Supreme Court recognizing in dicta that a hacker's unauthorized access to a computer was more in the nature of trespass than criminal conversion); and State v. Riley, 121 Wash.2d 22, 846 P.2d 1365 (1993) (computer hacking as the criminal offense of "computer trespass" under Washington law). It is undisputed that plaintiff has a possessory interest in its computer systems. Further, defendants' contact with plaintiff's computers is clearly intentional. Although electronic messages may travel through the Internet over various routes, the messages are affirmatively directed to their destination.

Defendants, citing Restatement (Second) of Torts §221, which defines "dispossession", assert that not every interference with the personal property of another is actionable and that physical dispossession or substantial interference with the chattel is required. Defendants then argue that they did not, in this case, physically dispossess plaintiff of its equipment or substantially interfere with it. However, the Restatement (Second) of Torts §218 defines the circumstances under which a trespass to chattels may be actionable:

> One who commits a trespass to a chattel is subject to liability to the possessor of the chattel if, but only if,
>
> (a) he dispossesses the other of the chattel, or
> (b) the chattel is impaired as to its condition, quality, or value, or
> (c) the possessor is deprived of the use of the chattel for a substantial time, or
> (d) bodily harm is caused to the possessor, or harm is caused to some person or thing in which the possessor has a legally protected interest.

Therefore, an interference resulting in physical dispossession is just one circumstance under which a defendant can be found liable. Defendants suggest that "[u]nless an alleged trespasser actually takes physical custody of the property or physically damages it, courts will not find the 'substantial interference' required to maintain a trespass to chattel claim." (Defendant's Memorandum at 13). To support this rather broad proposition, defendants cite only two cases which make any reference to the Restatement. In Glidden v. Szybiak, 95 N.H. 318, 63 A.2d 233 (1949), the court simply indicated that an action for trespass to chattels could not be maintained in the absence of some form of damage. The court held that where plaintiff did not contend that defendant's pulling on her pet dog's ears caused any injury, an action in tort could not be maintained. *Id*. 63 A.2d at 235. In contrast, plaintiff in the present action has alleged that it has suffered several types of injury as a result of defendants' conduct. In Koepnick v. Sears Roebuck & Co., 158 Ariz. 322, 762 P.2d 609 (1988) the court held that a two-minute search of an individual's truck did not amount to a "dispossession" of the truck as defined in Restatement §221 or a deprivation of the use of the truck for a substantial time. It is clear from a reading of Restatement §218 that an interference or intermeddling that does not fit the §221 definition of "dispossession" can nonetheless result in defendants' liability for trespass. The *Koepnick* court did not discuss any of the other grounds for liability under Restatement §218.

A plaintiff can sustain an action for trespass to chattels, as opposed to an action for conversion, without showing a substantial interference with its right to possession of that chattel. *Thrifty-Tel, Inc.*, 46 Cal.App.4th at 1567, 54 Cal.Rptr.2d 468 (quoting Zaslow v. Kroenert, 29 Cal.2d 541, 176 P.2d 1 (Cal. 1946)). Harm to the personal property or diminution of its quality, condition, or value as a result of defendants' use can also be the predicate for liability. Restatement §218(b).

> An unprivileged use or other intermeddling with a chattel which results in actual impairment of its physical condition, quality or value to the possessor makes the actor liable for the loss thus caused. In the great majority of cases, the actor's intermeddling with the chattel impairs the value of it to the possessor, as distinguished from the mere affront to his dignity as possessor, only by some impairment of the physical condition of the chattel. There may, however, be situations in which the value to the owner of a particular type of chattel may be impaired by dealing with it in a manner that does not affect its physical condition. . . . In such a case, the intermeddling is actionable even though the physical condition of the chattel is not impaired.

The Restatement (Second) of Torts §218, Comment h. In the present case, any value CompuServe realizes from its computer equipment is wholly derived from the extent to which that equipment can serve its subscriber base. Michael Mangino, a software developer for CompuServe who monitors its mail processing computer equipment, states by affidavit that handling the enormous volume of mass mailings that CompuServe receives places a tremendous burden on its equipment. Defendants' more recent practice of evading CompuServe's filters by disguising the origin of their messages commandeers even more computer resources because CompuServe's computers are forced to store undeliverable e-mail messages and labor in vain to return the messages to an address that does not exist. To the extent that defendants' multitudinous electronic mailings demand the disk space and drain the processing power of plaintiff's computer equipment, those resources are not available to serve CompuServe subscribers. Therefore, the value of that equipment to

CompuServe is diminished even though it is not physically damaged by defendants' conduct.

Next, plaintiff asserts that it has suffered injury aside from the physical impact of defendants' messages on its equipment. Restatement §218(d) also indicates that recovery may be had for a trespass that causes harm to something in which the possessor has a legally protected interest. Plaintiff asserts that defendants' messages are largely unwanted by its subscribers, who pay incrementally to access their e-mail, read it, and discard it. Also, the receipt of a bundle of unsolicited messages at once can require the subscriber to sift through, at his expense, all of the messages in order to find the ones he wanted or expected to receive. These inconveniences decrease the utility of CompuServe's e-mail service and are the foremost subject in recent complaints from CompuServe subscribers. Patrick Hole, a customer service manager for plaintiff, states by affidavit that in November 1996 CompuServe received approximately 9,970 e-mail complaints from subscribers about junk e-mail, a figure up from approximately two hundred complaints the previous year. Approximately fifty such complaints per day specifically reference defendants. Defendants contend that CompuServe subscribers are provided with a simple procedure to remove themselves from the mailing list. However, the removal procedure must be performed by the e-mail recipient at his expense, and some CompuServe subscribers complain that the procedure is inadequate and ineffectual.

Many subscribers have terminated their accounts specifically because of the unwanted receipt of bulk e-mail messages. Defendants' intrusions into CompuServe's computer systems, insofar as they harm plaintiff's business reputation and goodwill with its customers, are actionable under Restatement §218(d).

The reason that the tort of trespass to chattels requires some actual damage as a prima facie element, whereas damage is assumed where there is a trespass to real property, can be explained as follows:

> The interest of a possessor of a chattel in its inviolability, unlike the similar interest of a possessor of land, is not given legal protection by an action for nominal damages for harmless intermeddlings with the chattel. In order that an actor who interferes with another's chattel may be liable, his conduct must affect some other and more important interest of the possessor. Therefore, one who intentionally intermeddles with another's chattel is subject to liability only if his intermeddling is harmful to the possessor's materially valuable interest in the physical condition, quality, or value of the chattel, or if the possessor is deprived of the use of the chattel for a substantial time, or some other legally protected interest of the possessor is affected as stated in Clause (c). Sufficient legal protection of the possessor's interest in the mere inviolability of his chattel is afforded by his privilege to use reasonable force to protect his possession against even harmless interference.

Restatement (Second) of Torts §218, Comment e. Plaintiff CompuServe has attempted to exercise this privilege to protect its computer systems. However, defendants' persistent affirmative efforts to evade plaintiff's security measures have circumvented any protection those self-help measures might have provided. In this case CompuServe has alleged and supported by affidavit that it has suffered several types of injury as a result of defendants' conduct. The foregoing discussion simply underscores that the damage sustained by plaintiff is sufficient to sustain an action for trespass to chattels. However, this Court also notes that the implementation of technological means of self-help, to the extent that reasonable measures are effective, is particularly appropriate in this type of situation and should be exhausted before legal action is proper. . . .

Defendants argue that plaintiff made the business decision to connect to the Internet and that therefore it cannot now successfully maintain an action for trespass to chattels. Their argument is analogous to the argument that because an establishment invites the public to enter its property for business purposes, it cannot later restrict or revoke access to that property, a proposition which is erroneous under Ohio law. See, e.g., State v. Carriker, 5 Ohio App.2d 255, 214 N.E.2d 809 (1964) (the law in Ohio is that a business invitee's privilege to remain on the premises of another may be revoked upon the reasonable notification to leave by the owner or his agents); Allstate Ins. Co. v. U.S. Associates Realty, Inc., 11 Ohio App.3d 242, 464 N.E.2d 169 (1983) (notice of express restriction or limitation on invitation turns business invitee into trespasser). On or around October 1995, CompuServe notified defendants that it no longer consented to the use of its proprietary computer equipment. Defendants' continued use thereafter was a trespass. Restatement (Second) of Torts §§252 and 892A(5); see also Restatement (Second) of Torts §217, Comment f ("The actor may commit a new trespass by continuing an intermeddling which he has already begun, with or without the consent of the person in possession. Such intermeddling may persist after the other's consent, originally given, has been terminated."); Restatement (Second) of Torts §217, Comment g.

Further, CompuServe expressly limits the consent it grants to Internet users to send e-mail to its proprietary computer systems by denying unauthorized parties the use of CompuServe equipment to send unsolicited electronic mail messages. This policy statement, posted by CompuServe online, states as follows:

> Compuserve is a private online and communications services company. CompuServe does not permit its facilities to be used by unauthorized parties to process and store unsolicited e-mail. If an unauthorized party attempts to send unsolicited messages to e-mail addresses on a CompuServe service, Compuserve will take appropriate action to attempt to prevent those messages from being processed by CompuServe. Violations of CompuServe's policy prohibiting unsolicited e-mail should be reported to . . .

Defendants Cyber Promotions, Inc. and its president Sanford Wallace have used plaintiff's equipment in a fashion that exceeds that consent. The use of personal property exceeding consent is a trespass. City of Amsterdam v. Daniel Goldreyer, Ltd., 882 F. Supp. 1273 (E.D.N.Y. 1995); Restatement (Second) of Torts §256. It is arguable that CompuServe's policy statement, insofar as it may serve as a limitation upon the scope of its consent to the use of its computer equipment, may be insufficiently communicated to potential third-party users when it is merely posted at some location on the network. However, in the present case the record indicates that defendants were actually notified that they were using CompuServe's equipment in an unacceptable manner. To prove that a would-be trespasser acted with the intent required to support liability in tort it is crucial that defendant be placed on notice that he is trespassing. . . .

In response to the trespass claim, defendants argue that they have the right to continue to send unsolicited commercial e-mail to plaintiff's computer systems under the First Amendment to the United States Constitution. The First Amendment states that "Congress shall make no law respecting an establishment of religion, or prohibiting the free exercise thereof; or abridging the freedom of speech, or of the press." The United States Supreme Court has recognized that "the constitutional guarantee of free speech is a guarantee only against abridgement by government, federal or state." Hudgens v. NLRB, 424 U.S. 507, 513, 96 S. Ct. 1029, 1033, 47 L. Ed.2d 196 (1976). Indeed, the protection of the First Amendment is not a shield against "merely private conduct." Hurley v. Irish-American Gay Group of Boston, 515 U.S. 557, —, 115 S. Ct. 2338, 2344, 132 L. Ed.2d 487 (1995) (citation omitted).

Very recently, in an action filed by Cyber Promotions, Inc. against America Online, Inc. ("AOL") the United States District Court for the Eastern District of Pennsylvania held that AOL, a company selling services that are similar to those of CompuServe, is private actor [sic]. Cyber Promotions, Inc. v. American Online, Inc., 948 F. Supp. 436, 443-44 (E.D.Pa. 1996). That case involved the question of whether Cyber Promotions had the First Amendment right to send unobstructed e-mail to AOL subscribers. The court held that Cyber Promotions had no such right and that, inter alia, AOL was not exercising powers that are traditionally the exclusive prerogative of the state, such as where a private company exercises municipal powers by running a company town. Id. at 442-43; Blum v. Yaretsky, 457 U.S. 991, 1004-05, 102 S. Ct. 2777, 2785-86, 73 L. Ed.2d 534 (1982); Marsh v. Alabama, 326 U.S. 501, 66 S. Ct. 276, 90 L. Ed. 265 (1946). This Court agrees with the conclusions reached by the United States District Court for the Eastern District of Pennsylvania.

In the present action, CompuServe is a private company. Moreover, the mere judicial enforcement of neutral trespass laws by the private owner of property does not alone render it a state actor. Rotunda & Nowak, Treatise on Constitutional Law §16.3, 546 (West 1992). Defendants do not argue that CompuServe is anything other than a private actor. Instead, defendants urge that because CompuServe is so intimately involved in this new medium it might be subject to some special form of regulation. Defendants cite Associated Press v. United States, 326 U.S. 1, 65 S. Ct. 1416, 89 L. Ed. 2013 (1945), and Turner Broadcasting Sys., Inc. v. FCC, 512 U.S. 622, 114 S. Ct. 2445, 129 L. Ed.2d 497 (1994), which stand for the proposition that when a private actor has a certain quantum of control over a central avenue of communication, then the First Amendment might not prevent the government from enacting legislation requiring public access to private property. No such legislation yet exists that is applicable to CompuServe. Further, defendants' discussion concerning the extent to which the Internet may be regulated (or should be regulated) is irrelevant because no government entity has undertaken to regulate the Internet in a manner that is applicable to this action. Indeed, if there were some applicable statutory scheme in place this Court would not be required to apply paradigms of common law to the case at hand.

In Lloyd Corp. v. Tanner, 407 U.S. 551, 92 S. Ct. 2219, 33 L. Ed.2d 131 (1972), protestors of the Vietnam War sought to pass out written materials in a private shopping center. Even though the customers of the shopping center were the intended recipients of the communication, the Supreme Court held that allowing the First Amendment to trump private property rights is unwarranted where there are adequate alternative avenues of communication. Id. at 567, 92 S. Ct. at 2228. The Supreme Court stated that:

> Although . . . the courts properly have shown a special solicitude for the guarantees of the First Amendment, this Court has never held that a trespasser or an uninvited guest

may exercise general rights of free speech on property privately owned and used non-discriminatorily for private purposes only.

Id. at 567-68, 92 S. Ct. at 2228. Defendants in the present action have adequate alternative means of communication available to them. Not only are they free to send e-mail advertisements to those on the Internet who do not use CompuServe accounts, but they can communicate to CompuServe subscribers as well through online bulletin boards, web page advertisements, or facsimile transmissions, as well as through more conventional means such as the U.S. mail or telemarketing. Defendants' contention, referring to the low cost of the electronic mail medium, that there are no adequate alternative means of communication is unpersuasive. There is no constitutional requirement that the incremental cost of sending massive quantities of unsolicited advertisements must be borne by the recipients. The legal concept in *Lloyd* that private citizens are entitled to enforce laws of trespass against would-be communicators is applicable to this case.

Defendants assert that CompuServe has assumed the role of a postmaster, to whom all of the strictures of the First Amendment apply, and that to allow it to enjoy a legally protected interest in its computer equipment in this context is to license a form of censorship which violates the First Amendment. However, such an assertion must be accompanied by a showing that CompuServe is a state actor. As earlier mentioned, defendants have neither specifically argued this point nor provided any evidence to support it. CompuServe is entitled to restrict access to its private property.

"The First and Fourteenth Amendments have never been treated as absolutes. Freedom of speech or press does not mean that one can talk or distribute where, when and how one chooses." Breard v. City of Alexandria, 341 U.S. 622, 642, 71 S. Ct. 920, 932, 95 L. Ed. 1233 (1951) (upholding local ordinances banning commercial solicitations over First Amendment objections) (footnote omitted). In Rowan v. U.S. Post Office Dept., 397 U.S. 728, 90 S. Ct. 1484, 25 L. Ed.2d 736 (1970) the United States Supreme Court held that the First Amendment did not forbid federal legislation that allowed addressees to remove themselves from mailing lists and stop all future mailings. The Court stated that the "mailer's right to communicate must stop at the mailbox of an unreceptive addressee . . . [t]o hold less would be to license a form of trespass[.]" *Id.* at 736-37, 90 S. Ct. at 1490.

In Tillman v. Distribution Sys. of America, Inc., 224 A.D.2d 79, 648 N.Y.S.2d 630 (1996) the plaintiff complained that the defendant continued to throw newspapers on his property after being warned not to do so. The court held that the defendant newspaper distributor had no First Amendment right to continue to throw newspapers onto the property of the plaintiff. After discussing the Supreme Court cases of *Rowan* and *Breard*, supra, the court pointed out that:

> The most critical and fundamental distinction between the cases cited above, on the one hand, and the present case, on the other, is based on the fact that here we are not dealing with a government agency which seeks to preempt in some way the ability of a publisher to contact a potential reader; rather, we are dealing with a reader who is familiar with a publisher's product, and who is attempting to prevent the unwanted dumping of this product on his property. None of the cases cited by the defendants stands for the proposition that the Free Speech Clause prohibits such a landowner from resorting to his common-law remedies in order to prevent such unwanted dumping. There is, in our view, nothing in either the Federal or State Constitutions which re-

quires a landowner to tolerate a trespass whenever the trespasser is a speaker, or the distributor of written speech, who is unsatisfied with the fora which may be available on public property, and who thus attempts to carry his message to private property against the will of the owner.

Id. 648 N.Y.S.2d at 635. The court concluded, relying on *Lloyd*, supra, that the property rights of the private owner could not be overwhelmed by the First Amendment. *Id.* 648 N.Y.S.2d at 636.

In the present case, plaintiff is physically the recipient of the defendants' messages and is the owner of the property upon which the transgression is occurring. As has been discussed, plaintiff is not a government agency or state actor which seeks to preempt defendants' ability to communicate but is instead a private actor trying to tailor the nuances of its service to provide the maximum utility to its customers.

Defendants' intentional use of plaintiff's proprietary computer equipment exceeds plaintiff's consent and, indeed, continued after repeated demands that defendants cease. Such use is an actionable trespass to plaintiff's chattel. The First Amendment to the United States Constitution provides no defense for such conduct. . . .

Finally, the public interest is advanced by the Court's protection of the common law rights of individuals and entities to their personal property. Defendants raise First Amendment concerns and argue that an injunction will adversely impact the public interest. High volumes of junk e-mail devour computer processing and storage capacity, slow down data transfer between computers over the Internet by congesting the electronic paths through which the messages travel, and cause recipients to spend time and money wading through messages that they do not want. It is ironic that if defendants were to prevail on their First Amendment arguments, the viability of electronic mail as an effective means of communication for the rest of society would be put at risk. In light of the foregoing discussion, those arguments are without merit. Further, those subscribing to CompuServe are not injured by the issuance of this injunction. Plaintiff has made a business decision to forbid Cyber Promotions and Mr. Wallace from using its computers to transmit messages to CompuServe subscribers. If CompuServe subscribers are unhappy with that decision, then they may make that known, perhaps by terminating their accounts and transferring to an Internet service provider which accepts unsolicited e-mail advertisements. That is a business risk which plaintiff has assumed.

Ferguson v. Friendfinders, Inc.
California Court of Appeal
115 Cal.Rptr.2d 258, 94 Cal.App.4th 1255 (2002)

HAERLE, J.

I. Introduction

Mark Ferguson (Ferguson) sued respondents for violating California law by sending him unsolicited e-mail advertisements that were allegedly deceptive and misleading. The superior court sustained a demurrer without leave to amend with respect to each of Ferguson's causes of action. In reaching its decision, the lower court found that section 17538.4 of the Business and Professions Code violates the dormant Commerce Clause of the United States Constitution.

In the published portion of this decision, we hold that section 17538.4 does not violate the dormant Commerce Clause. In the unpublished portion of this opinion, we conclude that the trial court erred by sustaining a demurrer without leave to amend as to each of Ferguson's causes of action except for the cause of action in which he purported to state a negligence claim.

II.   Statement of Facts

A.   *The Statute*

Section 17538.4 regulates conduct by persons or entities doing business in California who transmit unsolicited advertising materials. Section 17538.4, which originally applied only to faxed documents, was amended in 1998 to extend to electronic-mail (e-mail).

The statute defines "unsolicited e-mail documents" as "any e-mailed document or documents consisting of advertising material for the lease, sale, rental, gift offer, or other disposition of any realty, goods, services, or extension of credit" when the documents (a) are addressed to recipients who do not have existing business or personal relationships with the initiator and (b) were not sent at the request of or with the consent of the recipient. (§17538.4, subd. (e).)

Section 17538.4 requires that a "person or entity conducting business in this state" who causes an unsolicited e-mail document to be sent (1) establish a toll-free telephone number or valid sender operated return e-mail address that recipients may use to notify the sender not to e-mail further unsolicited documents; (2) include as the first text in the e-mailed document a statement informing the recipient of the toll-free number or return address that may be used to notify the sender not to e-mail any further unsolicited material; (3) not send any further unsolicited advertising material to anyone who has requested that such material not be sent; and (4) include in the subject line of each e-mail message "ADV:" as the first four characters or "ADV:ADLT" if the advertisement pertains to adult material. (§17538.4, subd. (a)-(g).)

Section 17538.4 applies to unsolicited e-mailed documents that are "delivered to a California resident via an electronic mail service provider's service or equipment located in this state." "Electronic mail service provider" is defined as "any business or organization qualified to do business in this state that provides individuals, corporations, or other entities the ability to send or receive electronic mail through equipment located in this state and that is an intermediary in sending or receiving electronic mail [e-mail]." (§17538.4, subd. (d).)

Section 17538.4 states that the section, or any part of it, shall become inoperative when "federal law is enacted that prohibits or otherwise regulates the transmission of unsolicited advertising by electronic mail." §17538.4, subd. (i).) Although Congress has considered several bills addressing this subject, federal law does not currently regulate the transmission of unsolicited advertising by electronic mail.

B. The Complaint

... On behalf of himself and all other persons similarly situated, Ferguson sued Friendfinders, Inc. and Conru Interactive, Inc., two California businesses located in Palo Alto, Andrew B. Conru, a California resident, and 50 doe defendants (jointly, respondents).

Ferguson alleged that respondents sent him and others unsolicited e-mail advertisements that did not comply with the requirement set forth in section 17538.4. Specifically, Ferguson alleged that "the subject lines of the email messages failed to begin with the characters 'ADV:'; the first line in the text of the e-mail messages failed to contain information about how recipients could have their email addresses removed from future advertising campaigns; the email messages failed to provide a valid return email address to which Plaintiffs could respond; and the headers of the email messages were altered to mask the identity of the sender." ...

C. Proceedings in the Lower Court

Respondents filed their demurrer to the complaint on March 3. ... Among other things, respondents alleged that the relief sought with respect to Ferguson's third and fourth causes of action "would constitute an unconstitutional interference with interstate commerce." In this regard, respondents argued that the Internet cannot be regulated by individual states because it is a national infrastructure without territorial boundaries.

[The Superior Court] sustained respondents' demurrer without leave to amend on the following ground: "California Business and Professions Code section 17538.4 unconstitutionally subjects interstate use of the Internet to inconsistent regulations, therefore violating the dormant Commerce Clause of the United States Constitution." Judgment was entered on July 17 and this timely appeal followed.

III. Discussion ...

A. Respondents Did Not Establish that Section 17538.4 is Unconstitutional

1. Scope of Review

The trial court found that respondents sustained their burden of proving that section 17538.4 is unconstitutional on its face. "A facial challenge to the constitutional validity of a statute or ordinance considers only the text of the measure itself, not its application to the particular circumstances of an individual." (Tobe v. City of Santa Ana (1995) 9 Cal. 4th 1069, 1084, 40 Cal. Rptr.2d 402, 892 P.2d 1145.) The challenger must " 'demonstrate that the act's provisions inevitably pose a present total and fatal conflict with applicable constitutional prohibitions.'" (*Ibid.*)

2. Dormant Commerce Clause

The Commerce Clause provides that "Congress shall have power . . . [t]o regulate commerce . . . among the several states. . . ." (U.S. Const., art. I, §8, cl. 3.) "[T]his affirmative grant of authority to Congress also encompasses an implicit or 'dormant' limitation on the authority of the States to enact legislation affecting interstate commerce." (Healy v. The Beer Institute (1989) 491 U.S. 324, 326, 109 S. Ct. 2491, 105 L. Ed.2d 275, fn. 1 (*Healy*).) In other words, the dormant commerce clause precludes state regulation in certain areas "even absent congressional action." (CTS Corp. v. Dynamics Corp. of America (1987) 481 U.S. 69, 87, 107 S. Ct. 1637, 95 L. Ed.2d 67.)

"[A]s the volume and complexity of commerce and regulation have grown in this country, the Court has articulated a variety of tests in an attempt to describe the difference between those regulations that the Commerce Clause permits and those regulations that it prohibits." (CTS Corp. v. Dynamics Corp. of America, *supra*, 481 U.S. at p. 87, 107 S. Ct. 1637.) Supreme Court authority establishes two primary lines of inquiry: "first, whether the ordinance discriminates against interstate commerce, and second, whether the ordinance imposes a burden on interstate commerce that is 'clearly excessive in relation to the putative local benefits'." (C & A Carbone, Inc. v. Town of Clarkstown (1994) 511 U.S. 383, 390, 114 S. Ct. 1677, 128 L. Ed.2d 399 (*C & A Carbone*).)

With respect to the first inquiry, regulations that discriminate against out-of-state actors are subject to "rigorous scrutiny." (*C & A Carbone, supra,* 511 U.S. at pp. 390-392, 114 S. Ct. 1677; see also CTS Corp. v. Dynamics Corp. of America, *supra,* 481 U.S. at p. 87, 107 S. Ct. 1637 ["The principal objects of dormant Commerce Clause scrutiny are statutes that discriminate against interstate commerce"].) "Discrimination against interstate commerce in favor of local business or investment is *per se* invalid, save in a narrow class of cases in which the municipality can demonstrate, under rigorous scrutiny, that it has no other means to advance a legitimate local interest. [Citation.]" (*C & A Carbone, supra,* 511 U.S. at p. 392, 114 S. Ct. 1677.)

This first level inquiry, which applies a strict scrutiny analysis, has been extended to state regulations that directly regulate interstate commerce. (See, e.g., *Healy, supra,* 491 U.S. at pp. 336-337, 109 S. Ct. 2491; Brown-Forman Distillers Corp. v. New York State Liquor Authority (1986) 476 U.S. 573, 579, 106 S. Ct. 2080, 90 L. Ed.2d 552; see also S.D. Myers, Inc. v. City and County of San Francisco (2001) 253 F.3d 461, 466-467.) State laws that regulate commerce occurring outside state borders have been found to offend the dormant Commerce Clause. (*Ibid.*)

The second inquiry, which is employed to evaluate regulations that do not discriminate against interstate commerce or directly regulate it, is a balancing test which requires that a court uphold a state regulation that serves an important public interest unless the benefits of that regulation are outweighed by the burden imposed on interstate commerce. (C & A Carbone, *supra,* 511 U.S. at pp. 390-392, 114 S. Ct. 1677; Pike v. Bruce Church, Inc. (1970) 397 U.S. 137, 142, 90 S. Ct. 844, 25 L. Ed.2d 174.) In the Court's own words, "[w]here the statute regulates even-handedly to effectuate a legitimate local public interest, and its effects on interstate commerce are only incidental, it will be upheld unless the burden imposed on such commerce is clearly excessive in relation to the putative local benefits."

(Pike v. Bruce Church, Inc., *supra,* 397 U.S. at p. 142, 90 S. Ct. 844; see also Edgar v. MITE Corp. (1982) 457 U.S. 624, 640, 102 S. Ct. 2629, 73 L. Ed.2d 269; People v. Hsu (2000) 82 Cal.App.4th 976, 982, 99 Cal. Rptr.2d 184.)

3. Strict Scrutiny Analysis

In the present case, respondents concede that section 17538.4 does not discriminate against out-of-state actors. The statute applies equally to in-state and out-of-state actors who (a) do business in California and (b) transmit unsolicited commercial e-mail (UCE) to a California resident, (c) via equipment located in California.

However, respondents contend that section 17538.4 directly regulates interstate commerce. Citing *Healy, supra,* 491 U.S. 324, 109 S. Ct. 2491, 105 L. Ed.2d 275, they argue that, when section 17538.4 is viewed in the context of Internet reality, the statute regulates beyond California's borders and that its extraterritorial reach violates the dormant Commerce Clause.

In *Healy,* the United States Supreme Court struck down provisions of a Connecticut statute that required out-of-state shippers of beer to affirm that their posted prices for products sold to Connecticut wholesalers were no higher than the prices at which those products were sold in States bordering Connecticut. The *Healy* Court found that Connecticut's price affirmation statute violated the dormant Commerce Clause because (1) it discriminated against brewers and shippers of beer engaged in interstate commerce and (2) it directly controlled commerce occurring wholly outside the State. (*Healy, supra,* 491 U.S. 324, 109 S. Ct. 2491, 105 L. Ed.2d 275.)

In support of the latter of these two holdings, the *Healy* Court identified several principles from prior cases "concerning the extraterritorial effects of state economic regulations. . . ." (*Healy, supra,* 491 U.S. at p. 336, 109 S. Ct. 2491.) First, a state statute that directly regulates commerce occurring wholly outside the boundaries of the State violates the Commerce Clause. (*Id.* at p. 336, 109 S. Ct. 2491.) Second, a state statute that directly "controls" commerce occurring wholly outside the boundaries of the State also violates the Commerce Clause. Third, to determine whether a statute impermissibly controls commerce outside the State, a court should evaluate the practical effect of the statute by considering "the consequences of the statute itself . . . [and] how the challenged statute may interact with the legitimate regulatory regimes of other States and what effect would arise if not one, but many or every, State adopted similar legislation." (*Ibid.*) Applying these principles, the *Healy* court found that Connecticut's price affirmation statute violated the dormant Commerce Clause because it had the practical effect of controlling beer prices in other States. (*Id.* at pp. 338-340, 109 S. Ct. 2491.)

Section 17538.4 does not violate the principles discussed in *Healy* because it does not directly regulate commerce occurring wholly outside the State. It expressly applies only when UCE is sent to a California resident by means of an electronic-mail service provider who has equipment in the State. Respondents contend, however, that the practical effect of section 17538.4 is to control commerce occurring wholly outside California because the geographic limitations set forth in section 17538.4 are ineffectual and, therefore, senders of UCE who do business in California must always comply with section 17538.4 regardless of the actual residence of the UCE recipient. Respondents offer several theories to support their claim that section 17538.4 has an impermissible extraterritorial reach.

First, respondents argue that the geographic limitations on the scope of section 17538.4 are ineffectual because of the very nature of the Internet. UCE is transmitted via the Internet which functions in cyberspace, a place respondents characterize as being "wholly insensitive to geographic distinctions." (Quoting American Libraries Association v. Pataki (S.D.N.Y. 1997) 969 F. Supp. 160, 170 (*Pataki*).) Thus, respondents maintain, an e-mail address simply does not logically correspond to a geographic residence.

The problem with this argument is that section 17538.4 does not regulate the Internet or Internet use per se. It regulates individuals and entities who (1) do business in California, (2) utilize equipment located in California and (3) send UCE to California residents. The equipment used by electronic-mail service providers does have a geographic location. And e-mail recipients are people or businesses who function in the real world and have a geographic residence.

Respondents mistakenly rely on *Pataki, supra,* 969 F. Supp. 160. In that case, the court found that a state law making it a crime to use a computer to disseminate obscene materials to a minor violated the dormant Commerce Clause. (*Id.* at p. 163.) The court found that the law regulated conduct occurring wholly outside the State and that its burden on interstate commerce exceeded its local benefit. (*Id.* at p. 169.) In reaching this conclusion, the *Pataki* court emphasized that the nature of the Internet, particularly its insensitivity to geographic distinctions, "makes it impossible to restrict the effects of the New York Act to conduct occurring within New York." (*Id.* at p. 177.) More generally, the court concluded that the Internet is an area of commerce "that must be marked off as a national preserve to protect users from inconsistent legislation that, taken to its most extreme, could paralyze development of the Internet altogether." (*Id.* at p. 169.)

Initially, we join the other California courts that have addressed this issue by rejecting *Pataki*'s holding that any State regulation of Internet use violates the dormant Commerce Clause. (See Hatch v. Superior Court (2000) 80 Cal.App.4th 170, 194-195, 94 Cal.Rptr.2d 453 [Penal Code section 288.2, which makes it a crime to transmit harmful matter over the Internet to a child, does not violate the Commerce Clause]; People v. Hsu, *supra,* 82 Cal.App.4th at p. 983, 99 Cal.Rptr.2d 184 [same].) "The Internet is undeniably an incident of interstate commerce, but the fact that communication thereby can affect interstate commerce does not automatically cause a state statute in which Internet use is an element to burden interstate commerce." (People v. Hsu, *supra,* 82 Cal.App.4th at p. 983, 99 Cal.Rptr.2d 184)

In any event, the *Pataki* court's conclusions about the extraterritorial effects of the New York law in that case do not apply to section 17538.4. The statute at issue in *Pataki* applied to *all Internet activity* and the court's comments about the absence of geographic sensitivity were made in that context. (*Pataki, supra,* 969 F. Supp. at p. 171.) As we have already explained, section 17538.4 does not regulate the Internet. It regulates e-mail users who send UCE to California residents via equipment located in California. These limitations distinguish section 17538.4 from the New York statute at issue in *Pataki* and avoid the problems which most concerned the *Pataki* court.

Respondents argue that, even if e-mail recipients do have geographic residences, it is simply not possible for senders of UCE to determine the residency of any particular e-mail recipient. Thus, respondents argue that the only way to avoid violating section 17538.4 is to comply with it in every instance. This argument has two fatal flaws. First, respondents ignore the second geographic limitation imposed by section 17538.4: it applies only when equipment located in the State is used. By limiting the scope of section 17538.4 to UCEs that are transmitted via equipment located in the State, our Legislature ensured that the statute would not reach conduct occurring "wholly" outside the State.

Second, the record does not support respondents' claim that it is impossible to determine the geographic residence of a UCE recipient. Both the Attorney General and Ferguson dispute this contention. They suggest that lists of e-mail addresses sorted by geographic residence exist already or can be created and utilized by senders of UCE. Respondents have offered no evidence supporting a contrary conclusion. Instead, they argue that "[t]ypically unsolicited email advertising is sent in 'bulk,' that is to lists of recipients processed by automation" and that "[t]here is no practical way to ascertain which addresses are California residents." That respondents consider section 17538.4's requirements inconvenient and even impractical does not mean that statute violates the Commerce Clause. Further, if respondents choose to comply with section 17538.4 all the time (so they can avoid having to determine whether they are corresponding with California residents via equipment located in California), that is their business decision. Such a business decision simply does not establish that section 17538.4 controls conduct occurring wholly outside California.

Respondents argue that, even if the residence of an e-mail recipient can be determined, section 17538.4 reaches commerce occurring wholly outside the State because it applies to a California resident who receives and/or opens his or her UCE while in a location outside California. This very argument was rejected by the Supreme Court of Washington in State v. Heckel (2001) 143 Wash.2d 824, 24 P.3d 404 (*Heckel*), a case upholding a statute analogous to section 17538.4 against a dormant Commerce Clause challenge. Like the Washington statute at issue in *Heckel*, section 17538.4 does not purport to regulate when or where UCE recipients may read their e-mail. And, the question posed by this hypothetical—whether the statute must or should be construed to apply to State residents when they are out of state—is a "jurisdictional question not at issue in this case." (*Heckel, supra,* 24 P.3d at p. 412.)

Respondents argue that another practical effect of section 17538.4 is that it conflicts with statutes regulating UCE that have been enacted by other states. Notwithstanding the fact that, to date, at least 18 states have enacted laws regulating UCE (*Heckel, supra,* 24 P.3d at pp. 411-412), respondents have identified only one actual conflict pertaining to one requirement imposed by section 17538.4. Section 17538.4, subdivision (g), requires that the subject line of the UCE include "ADV:ADLT" as its first eight characters if the message contains adult information. Respondents contend this requirement directly conflicts with a Pennsylvania statute which requires that the first nine characters of a subject line of a UCE containing explicit sexual materials be "ADV ADULT" if the UCE is transmitted to a person "within the Commonwealth." (See 18 Pa. Cons.Stat. section 5903(A.1).)

Respondents' argument that section 17538.4 conflicts with Pennsylvania law fails at its base because they have not established that the geographic limitations imposed by section 17538.4 are ineffectual. In other words, although respondents have found a minor distinction between California and Pennsylvania law, they have not shown that a UCE sender would ever face a situation in which he or she was required to comply with both laws at the same time.[4] The Commerce Clause protects against inconsistent regulations in order to prevent "the projection of one state regulatory regime into the jurisdiction of another." (*Healy, supra,* 491 U.S. at pp. 336-337, 109 S. Ct. 2491.) Respondents have not established that section 17538.4 has such an effect.

We conclude that section 17538.4 does not discriminate against or directly regulate or control interstate commerce. Therefore, section 17538.4 does not violate the Commerce Clause if it serves a legitimate local public interest and if the burden it imposes on interstate commerce is not excessive when viewed in light of its local benefits.

4. The Balancing Test

a. The State Interest

As noted, section 17538.4 regulates the amount of UCE sent to residents of the State by establishing and enforcing a mechanism for residents to have their names removed from UCE mailing lists. It also regulates the content of UCE sent to State residents by imposing truthfulness and disclosure requirements on UCE senders.

Like traditional paper "junk" mail, UCE can be annoying and waste time. But courts and commentators have acknowledged that UCE causes many additional problems. (See, e.g., *Heckel, supra,* 143 Wash.2d 824, 24 P.3d 404; CompuServe Inc. v. Cyber Promotions, Inc. (S.D.Ohio 1997) 962 F. Supp. 1015, 1022; America Online Inc. v. IMS. (E.D.Va. 1998) 24 F. Supp.2d 548, 550; Goldsmith & Sykes, The Internet and the Dormant Commerce Clause (2001) 110 Yale L.J. 785 (hereafter, The Internet and the Dormant Commerce Clause); Whang, An Analysis of California's Common and Statutory Law Dealing with Unsolicited Commercial Electronic Mail: An Argument for Revision (2000) 37 San Diego L. Rev. 1201 (hereafter, An Argument for Revision); Sorkin, Technical and Legal Approaches to Unsolicited Electronic Mail (2001) 35 U.S.F. L. Rev. 325 (hereafter, Technical and Legal Approaches).)

These additional problems have developed because UCE is easy and inexpensive to create, but difficult and costly to eliminate. UCE, often referred to as "spam," can be and usually is sent to many recipients at one time at little or no cost to the sender. Since the cost of sending unsolicited bulk e-mail is "negligible[,]" spammers "have little incentive to consume resources in an efficient manner." (Technical and Legal Approaches, *supra,* at p. 338.) Studies indicate that 10 to 30 percent of all e-mail sent on a given day consists of UCE. (An Argument for Revision, *supra,* at pp. 1202-1203.)

---

4. Assuming that an originator of UCE faced a legal challenge because it complied with the subject line requirement of one state's law, but not the other's, we would expect that the doctrine of substantial compliance would be utilized to defend against a legal challenge to that usage. (Cf. Asdourian v. Araj (1985) 38 Cal.3d 276, 283-284, 211 Cal. Rptr. 703, 696 P.2d 95.)

In contrast, the costs created by UCE are substantial. Internet Service Providers (ISPs), incur significant business related costs accommodating bulk e-mail advertising and dealing with the problems it creates. ISPs attempt to defray those costs by charging higher fees to their customers. Individuals who receive UCE can experience increased Internet access fees because of the time required to sort, read, discard and attempt to prevent future sending of UCE. If the individual undertakes this process at work, his or her employer suffers the financial consequences of the wasted time. (See An Argument for Revision, *supra*, at p. 1203.)

The financial harms caused by the proliferation of UCE have been exacerbated by the use of deceptive tactics which are used to disguise the identity of the UCE sender and the nature of his or her message. Such deceptive tactics increase the already significant costs that UCE imposes on Internet users. (See generally, *Heckel, supra*, 24 P.3d at pp. 409-411.) For example, by disguising the nature and origin of their messages, spammers evade attempts to filter out their messages and force ISPs to incur additional costs attempting to return messages to non-existent addresses or otherwise dispose of undeliverable messages. Likewise, e-mail recipients cannot easily identify unwanted UCE or promptly or effectively contact senders of such messages to request that future mailings not be sent. Furthermore, by using fraudulent domain names and return e-mail addresses, senders misdirect responses to their messages to innocent third parties who can suffer serious economic consequences. (*Ibid.*)

This "cost-shifting" from senders of deceptive UCE to Internet businesses and e-mail users "has been likened to sending junk mail with postage due or making telemarketing calls to someone's pay-per-minute cellular phone." (*Heckel, supra*, 24 P.3d at p. 410.) As noted above, the *Heckel* court found that a Washington law regulating UCE did not violate the dormant Commerce Clause. Among other things, the Washington statute prohibits deceptive subject line descriptions and misrepresentation of the sender's identity. (*Id*. at p. 407.) In upholding these provisions, the *Heckel* court found that states have a substantial interest in preventing the cost-shifting which is inherent in the sending of deceptive UCE. (*Id*. at p. 410.)

We agree with the *Heckel* court that protecting a state's citizens from the economic damage caused by deceptive UCE constitutes a "'legitimate local purpose.'" (*Heckel, supra*, 24 P.3d at p. 410.) In addition, we find that deceptive UCE poses non-economic dangers as well. Deceptive UCE can be difficult if not impossible to identify without opening the message itself. Having to take that extra step can be more than a waste of time and money. Studies indicate that UCE often contains offensive subject matter, is a favored method for pursuing questionable if not fraudulent business schemes, and has been successfully used to spread harmful computer viruses. (An Argument for Revision, *supra*, at p. 1203 & fn. 9.)

We find that California has a substantial legitimate interest in protecting its citizens from the harmful effects of deceptive UCE and that section 17538.4 furthers that important interest. By requiring disclosure of the advertising and/or adult nature of an unsolicited e-mail in the subject line, section 17538.4 establishes a quick and simple way of identifying UCE without having to read it first. By requiring establishment and disclosure of a legitimate procedure for responding to a UCE, section 17538.4 holds UCE senders accountable for their actions. And, by requiring that senders of UCE honor requests that future mailings not be sent to recipients who do not want them, section 17538.4 protects California residents from all of the potential harms associated with unwanted UCE.

b. The Burden on Interstate Commerce

We must next consider whether the burden that section 17538.4 imposes on interstate commerce outweighs the benefits of that statute.

To the extent that section 17538.4 requires truthfulness in advertising, it does not burden interstate commerce at all "but actually 'facilitates it by eliminating fraud and deception.'" (*Heckel, supra,* 24 P.3d at p. 411.) Further, as the *Heckel* court found, "'truthfulness requirements . . . make spamming unattractive to many fraudulent spammers, thereby reducing the volume of spam.'" (*Ibid.,* quoting The Internet and the Dormant Commerce Clause, *supra,* at p. 819.) Nor do the statute's affirmative disclosure requirements impose any appreciable burden on senders of UCE. As the Attorney General has observed, the cost of placing particular letters in the subject line of the e-mail and including a valid return address in the message itself "is appreciably zero in terms of time and expense." Finally, respondents do not identify any burden on interstate commerce arising from the requirement that an express request to be eliminated from a UCE sender's mailing list must be honored. Any conceivable burden clearly does not outweigh the local benefits of section 17538.4.

We conclude that the burdens imposed on interstate commerce by section 17538.4 are minimal and do not outweigh the statute's benefits. Therefore, respondents have failed to carry their burden of proving that section 17538.4 violates the dormant Commerce Clause.

COMMENTS AND QUESTIONS

1. A number of states—Washington, Virginia, and California among them—have passed laws to regulate "spam." Each state has approached the problem in a slightly different manner. In Washington, for example, the law prohibits the falsification of email headers and the creation of misleading subject lines in commercial electronic mail messages. This prohibition applies both to messages that are sent *from* computers within the state and to messages that are sent *to* email addresses that the spammer knows are held by Washington residents. The spammer is imputed with the knowledge that the account is held by a Washington resident if that information would have been available if a request had been made to the registered owner of the domain name contained in the recipient's email address. The California law requires that "opt-out" information be clearly placed in all unsolicited commercial email messages, and further requires that an opt-out request be honored.

How should spam be defined? Must it be commercial, or can nonprofit groups and individuals be guilty of spamming too? Must it be "bulk" email? Suppose a company repeatedly sends messages to a few hundred people on a targeted mailing list. Is that bulk email? Does it matter whether the company has some reason to put people on a list, like a prior business relationship?

These definitional concerns raise another issue, presented by the juxtaposition of *CompuServe* and *Ferguson.* Should spam be regulated by a statute, which presumably would set out a clear definition of the banned practice, or by common law theories like trespass to chattels? What are the merits and problems with each approach? Note that the scope of the Internet trespass cases is significantly broader than spam, and we discuss them in detail in Section C of this chapter.

2. "Netiquette" norms about acceptable and unacceptable behavior on computer networks evolved in an era when these networks were used largely by technically sophisticated researchers at universities and industry laboratories. This included norms against sending chain letters and other unsolicited bulk email over the network. The Internet Engineering Task Force has decided to publish netiquette guidelines to help "newbie" users and network administrators to become acquainted with these norms. See Network Working Group, Netiquette Guidelines, Request for Comments Doc. 1855 (last revised October 1995) http://sunsite. cnlab-switch.ch/ftp/doc/standard/rfc/18xx/1855.

What, if any, deference should be given to netiquette rules in legal disputes? At least one court has decided that netiquette rules against spam may provide an ISP with a justification for terminating service to a spammer even when the ISP's terms of service do not expressly prohibit spam. See, e.g., Carl Kaplan, An Argument for 'Netiquette' Holds Up in Court, N.Y. Times, July 16, 1999, http://www.nytimes.com/library/tech/99/07/ cyber/cyberlaw/16law.html. The case discussed in Kaplan's article is 1267623 Ontario Inc. v. Nexx Online Inc. [1999] O.J. No. 2246 (Ont. Sup. Ct.). For an argument that judicial deference to netiquette may not always be appropriate, see Mark A. Lemley, The Law and Economics of Internet Norms, 73 Chi.-Kent L. Rev. 1257 (1999).

Some who object to spam believe that netiquette norms, laws, and litigation are inadequate ways to stop spam. One innovative idea for controlling spammers comes from Paul Vixie. He publishes a list of ISPs from which spam emanates and relies on the voluntary actions of ISP subscribers to his list to block mailings from the offending ISPs. Vixie has published a justification for this private action: The Realtime Blackhole List's Rationale, http://maps.vix.com/rbl/rationale.html. An ISP will have the incentive to root out spam in its system if it gets on Vixie's list because suddenly none of its users will be able to send or receive email from other host computers connected to the Internet. Is this laudable private action or vigilantism run amok? Cf. David E. Sorkin, Technical and Legal Approaches to Unsolicited Electronic Mail, 35 U.S.F. L. Rev. 325 (2001) (arguing that legal solutions to spam are replacing technical solutions over time).

3. AOL has had a great deal of experience with spammers and has been innovative in the legal claims that it makes against them. Trespass was only one of five causes of action that AOL brought against a spammer who had sent more than 60 million messages to AOL users. It also charged the spammer with a violation of section 43(a) of the Lanham Act because the spammer's mail falsely designated the origin of its spam as aol.com, thus implying that AOL had approved the sending of these messages. In addition, AOL charged the spammer with dilution of the AOL trademark, alleging that its mark had been tarnished by being associated with the defendant's spam. AOL agreed to voluntary dismissal of two other claims in its original complaint—one alleging violation of the federal Computer Fraud and Abuse Act and the other a violation of the Virginia Computer Crimes Act—if the court granted summary judgment in its favor on the other three claims. A federal judge did grant summary judgment on these claims in America Online Inc. v. IMS, 48 U.S.P.Q.2d 1857 (E.D. Va. 1998). The trespass and civil violations of these two criminal statutes raise questions about whether spamming should be criminalized.

4. *Ferguson* concludes that the California anti-spam statute does not violate the commerce clause because it does not "directly" burden out-of-state commerce. The court reasons that the statute is limited to email sent to California residents via computer equipment located in California. But how significant a restriction is that really? Many California residents—including all those who receive email at work—receive email using California equipment. How can a putative spammer tell whether its email will be sent to a California resident using California equipment? Is there any way to do so short of emailing the person to find out where they live and work? (Presumably such an email would also violate the statute.)

The court seems unsympathetic to the dilemma of spammers. It suggests that a law does not violate the dormant commerce clause merely because it adds significantly to the burden of compliance. But isn't the dormant commerce clause designed to prevent exactly such a burden?

Can *Ferguson* and *Heckel* be reconciled with *Pataki*, discussed in the opinion? What if the New York statute had forbidden making indecent information available to New York residents? Would it survive commerce clause scrutiny under the rationale of *Ferguson*? Should it? Other cases have divided on the constitutionality of banning Internet sales in order to favor local distributors. Compare Ford Motor Co. v. Texas Department of Transportation, 264 F.3d 493 (5th Cir. 2001) (Texas ban on direct Internet car sales did not violate commerce clause) with Santa Fe Natural Tobacco v. Spitzer, 2001 WL 636441 (S.D.N.Y. June 8, 2001) (New York ban on Internet tobacco sales violates dormant commerce clause).

For an early and perceptive articulation of the dormant commerce clause issue, see Dan L. Burk, Federalism in Cyberspace, 28 Conn. L. Rev. 1095 (1996). For a more recent and more skeptical treatment, see Jack L. Goldsmith & Alan O. Sykes, The Internet and the Dormant Commerce Clause, 110 Yale L.J. 785 (2001). One commentator suggests that we can find middle ground between *Pataki* and the spam cases. See Michelle Armond, State Internet Regulation and the Dormant Commerce Clause, 17 Berkeley Tech. L.J. 379 (2002).

5. *CompuServe* concludes that application of the doctrine of trespass to chattels to speech by spammers does not implicate the First Amendment because CompuServe is a private party, not a government actor. Does this result make sense? Isn't CompuServe invoking the power of the government to enjoin speech? Under the court's reading of the First Amendment, why should there be any constitutional restrictions on defamation suits?

B. TRESPASS TO CHATTELS

≡≡≡ *eBay, Inc. v. Bidder's Edge, Inc.*
United States District Court for the Northern District of California
100 F. Supp.2d 1058 (N.D. Cal. 2000)

WHYTE, District Judge.

Plaintiff eBay, Inc.'s ("eBay") motion for preliminary injunction was heard by the court on April 14, 2000. The court has read the moving and responding papers and heard the argument of counsel. For the reasons set forth below, the court preliminarily enjoins defendant Bidder's Edge, Inc. ("BE") from accessing eBay's computer systems by use of any automated querying program without eBay's written authorization.

I. Background

eBay is an Internet-based, person-to-person trading site. eBay offers sellers the ability to list items for sale and prospective buyers the ability to search those listings and bid on items. The seller can set the terms and conditions of the auction. The item is sold to the highest bidder. The transaction is consummated directly between the buyer and seller without eBay's involvement. A potential purchaser looking for a particular item can access the eBay site and perform a key word search for relevant auctions and bidding status. eBay has also created category listings that identify items in over 2500 categories, such as antiques, computers, and dolls. Users may browse these category listing pages to identify items of interest.

Users of the eBay site must register and agree to the eBay User Agreement. Users agree to the seven page User Agreement by clicking on an "I Accept" button located at the end of the User Agreement. The current version of the User Agreement prohibits the use of "any robot, spider, other automatic device, or manual process to monitor or copy our web pages or the content contained herein without our prior expressed written permission." It is not clear that the version of the User Agreement in effect at the time BE began searching the eBay site prohibited such activity, or that BE ever agreed to comply with the User Agreement.

eBay currently has over 7 million registered users. Over 400,000 new items are added to the site every day. Every minute, 600 bids are placed on almost 3 million items. Users currently perform, on average, 10 million searches per day on eBay's database. Bidding for and sales of items are continuously ongoing in millions of separate auctions.

A software robot is a computer program which operates across the Internet to perform searching, copying and retrieving functions on the web sites of others. A software robot is capable of executing thousands of instructions per minute, far in excess of what a human can accomplish. Robots consume the processing and storage resources of a system, making that portion of the system's capacity unavailable to the system owner or other users. Consumption of sufficient system resources will slow the processing of the overall system and can overload the system such that it will malfunction or "crash." A severe malfunction can cause a loss of data and an interruption in services.

The eBay site employs "robot exclusion headers." A robot exclusion header is a message, sent to computers programmed to detect and respond to such headers, that eBay does not permit unauthorized robotic activity. Programmers who wish to comply with the Robot Exclusion Standard design their robots to read a particular data file, "robots.txt," and to comply with the control directives it contains. . . .

eBay identifies robotic activity on its site by monitoring the number of incoming requests from each particular IP [(Internet Protocol)] address[.] Once eBay identifies an IP address believed to be involved in robotic activity, an investigation into the identity, origin and owner of the IP address may be made in order to determine if the activity is legitimate or authorized. If an investigation reveals unauthorized robotic activity, eBay may attempt to ignore ("block") any further requests from that IP address. Attempts to block requests from particular IP addresses are not always successful.

Organizations often install "proxy server" software on their computers. Proxy server software acts as a focal point for outgoing Internet requests. Proxy servers conserve system resources by directing all outgoing and incoming data traffic through a centralized portal. . . . Information requests sent through such proxy servers cannot easily be traced back to the originating IP address and can be used to circumvent attempts to block queries from the originating IP address. Blocking queries from innocent third party proxy servers is both inefficient, because it creates an endless game of hide-and-seek, and potentially counterproductive, as it runs a substantial risk of blocking requests from legitimate, desirable users who use that proxy server. . . .

BE does not host auctions. BE is an auction aggregation site designed to offer on-line auction buyers the ability to search for items across numerous on-line auctions without having to search each host site individually. As of March 2000, the BE web site contained information on more that five million items being auctioned on more than one hundred auction sites. BE also provides its users with additional auction-related services and information. The information available on the BE site is contained in a database of information that BE compiles through access to various auction sites such as eBay. When a user enters a search for a particular item at BE, BE searches its database and generates a list of every item in the database responsive to the search, organized by auction closing date and time. Rather than going to each host auction site one at a time, a user who goes to BE may conduct a single search to obtain information about that item on every auction site tracked by BE. It is important to include information regarding eBay auctions on the BE site because eBay is by far the biggest consumer to consumer on-line auction site. . . .

[The parties attempted to agree on terms for BE's access to the eBay site, but were unable to do so]. As a result, eBay attempted to block BE from accessing the eBay site; by the end of November, 1999, eBay had blocked a total of 169 IP addresses it believed BE was using to query eBay's system. BE elected to continue crawling eBay's site by using proxy servers to evade eBay's IP blocks.

Approximately 69% of the auction items contained in the BE database are from auctions hosted on eBay. BE estimates that it would lose one-third of its users if it ceased to cover the eBay auctions.

The parties agree that BE accessed the eBay site approximate 100,000 times a day. eBay alleges that BE activity constituted up to 1.53% of the number of requests received by eBay, and up to 1.10% of the total data transferred by eBay during certain periods in October and November of 1999. BE alleges that BE activity constituted no more than 1.11% of the requests received by eBay, and no more than 0.70% of the data transferred by eBay. . . . eBay has not alleged any specific incremental damages due to BE activity.

It appears that major Internet search engines, such as Yahoo!, Google, Excite and AltaVista, respect the Robot Exclusion Standard.[5]

---

5. BE appears to argue that this cannot be the case because searches performed on each of these search engines will return results that include eBay web pages. However, this does not establish that these sites do not respect robot exclusion headers. There are numerous ways in which search engines can obtain information in compliance with exclusion headers, including; obtaining consent, abiding by the robot[s].txt file guidelines, or manually searching the sites. BE did not present any evidence of any site ever complaining about the activities of any of these search engines.

eBay now moves for preliminary injunctive relief preventing BE from accessing the eBay computer system based on nine causes of action: trespass, false advertising, federal and state trademark dilution, computer fraud and abuse, unfair competition, misappropriation, interference with prospective economic advantage and unjust enrichment. However, eBay does not move, either independently or alternatively, for injunctive relief that is limited to restricting how BE can use data taken from the eBay site.[6] . . .

III. Analysis

A. *Balance of Harm*

According to eBay, the load on its servers resulting from BE's web crawlers represents between 1.11% and 1.53% of the total load on eBay's listing servers. eBay alleges both economic loss from BE's current activities and potential harm resulting from the total crawling of BE and others. In alleging economic harm, eBay's argument is that eBay has expended considerable time, effort and money to create its computer system, and that BE should have to pay for the portion of eBay's system BE uses. eBay attributes a pro rata portion of the costs of maintaining its entire system to the BE activity. However, eBay does not indicate that these expenses are incrementally incurred because of BE's activities, nor that any particular service disruption can be attributed to BE's activities. eBay provides no support for the proposition that the pro rata costs of obtaining an item represent the appropriate measure of damages for unauthorized use. In contrast, California law appears settled that the appropriate measure of damages is the actual harm inflicted by the conduct:

> Where the conduct complained of does not amount to a substantial interference with possession or the right thereto, but consists of intermeddling with or use of or damages to the personal property, the owner has a cause of action for trespass on case, and may recover only the actual damages suffered by reason of the impairment of the property or the loss of its use.

Zaslow v. Kroenert, 29 Cal.2d 541, 551, 176 P.2d 1 (1946). Moreover, even if BE is inflicting incremental maintenance costs on eBay, potentially calculable monetary damages are not generally a proper foundation for a preliminary injunction. See e.g., Sampson v. Murray, 415 U.S. 61, 90, 94 S. Ct. 937, 39 L. Ed.2d 166 (1974). Nor does eBay appear to have made the required showing that this is the type of extraordinary case in which monetary damages may support equitable relief. . . .

eBay's allegations of harm are based, in part, on the argument that BE's activities should be thought of as equivalent to sending in an army of 100,000 robots a day to check the prices in a competitor's store. This analogy, while graphic, appears inappropriate. Although an admittedly formalistic distinction, unauthorized robot intruders into a "brick and mortar" store would be committing a trespass to real property. There does not appear to be any doubt that the appropriate remedy for

---

6. The bulk of eBay's moving papers and declarations address the alleged misuse of the eBay mark and the information BE obtains from the eBay computers. The court does not address the facts specific to these claims, nor the merits of these claims.

an ongoing trespass to business premises would be a preliminary injunction. *See e.g.,* State v. Carriker, 5 Ohio App.2d 255, 214 N.E.2d 809, 811-12 (1964) (interpreting Ohio criminal trespass law to cover a business invitee who, with no intention of making a purchase, uses the business premises of another for his own gain after his invitation has been revoked); General Petroleum Corp. v. Beilby, 213 Cal. 601, 605, 2 P.2d 797 (1931). More importantly, for the analogy to be accurate, the robots would have to make up less than two out of every one-hundred customers in the store, the robots would not interfere with the customers' shopping experience, nor would the robots even be seen by the customers. Under such circumstances, there is a legitimate claim that the robots would not pose any threat of irreparable harm. However, eBay's right to injunctive relief is also based upon a much stronger argument.

If BE's activity is allowed to continue unchecked, it would encourage other auction aggregators to engage in similar recursive searching of the eBay system such that eBay would suffer irreparable harm from reduced system performance, system unavailability, or data losses. BE does not appear to seriously contest that reduced system performance, system unavailability or data loss would inflict irreparable harm on eBay consisting of lost profits and lost customer goodwill. Harm resulting from lost profits and lost customer goodwill is irreparable because it is neither easily calculable, nor easily compensable and is therefore an appropriate basis for injunctive relief. *See, e.g.,* People of California ex rel. Van De Kamp v. Tahoe Reg'l Planning Agency, 766 F.2d 1316, 1319 (9th Cir. 1985). Where, as here, the denial of preliminary injunctive relief would encourage an increase in the complained of activity, and such an increase would present a strong likelihood of irreparable harm, the plaintiff has at least established a possibility of irreparable harm.

In the patent infringement context, the Federal Circuit has held that a preliminary injunction may be based, at least in part, on the harm that would occur if a preliminary injunction were denied and infringers were thereby encouraged to infringe a patent during the course of the litigation. *See* Atlas Powder Co. v. Ireco Chemicals, 773 F.2d 1230, 1233 (Fed.Cir. 1985). In the absence of preliminary injunctive relief, "infringers could become compulsory licensees for as long as the litigation lasts." *Id.* The Federal Circuit's reasoning is persuasive. "The very nature of the patent right is the right to exclude others. . . . We hold that where validity and continuing infringement have been clearly established, as in this case, immediate irreparable harm is presumed. To hold otherwise would be contrary to the public policy underlying the patent laws." Smith Int'l, Inc. v. Hughes Tool Co., 718 F.2d 1573, 1581 (Fed.Cir. 1983) (footnotes omitted). Similarly fundamental to the concept of ownership of personal property is the right to exclude others. See Kaiser Aetna v. United States, 444 U.S. 164, 176, 100 S. Ct. 383, 62 L. Ed.2d 332 (1979) (characterizing "the right to exclude others" as "one of the most essential sticks in the bundle of rights that are commonly characterized as property"). If preliminary injunctive relief against an ongoing trespass to chattels were unavailable, a trespasser could take a compulsory license to use another's personal property for as long as the trespasser could perpetuate the litigation.

BE correctly observes that there is a dearth of authority supporting a preliminary injunction based on an ongoing to trespass to chattels. In contrast, it is black letter law in California that an injunction is an appropriate remedy for a continuing trespass to real property. See Allred v. Harris, 14 Cal.App.4th 1386, 1390, 18 Cal. Rptr.2d 530 (1993) (citing 5 B.E. Witkin, Summary of California Law, Torts §605

(9th ed. 1988)). If eBay were a brick and mortar auction house with limited seating capacity, eBay would appear to be entitled to reserve those seats for potential bidders, to refuse entrance to individuals (or robots) with no intention of bidding on any of the items, and to seek preliminary injunctive relief against non-customer trespassers eBay was physically unable to exclude. The analytic difficulty is that a wrongdoer can commit an ongoing trespass of a computer system that is more akin to the traditional notion of a trespass to real property, than the traditional notion of a trespass to chattels, because even though it is ongoing, it will probably never amount to a conversion. The court concludes that under the circumstances present here, BE's ongoing violation of eBay's fundamental property right to exclude others from its computer system potentially causes sufficient irreparable harm to support a preliminary injunction. . . .

If eBay's irreparable harm claim were premised solely on the potential harm caused by BE's current crawling activities, evidence that eBay had licensed others to crawl the eBay site would suggest that BE's activity would not result in irreparable harm to eBay. However, the gravamen of the alleged irreparable harm is that if BE is allowed to continue to crawl the eBay site, it may encourage frequent and unregulated crawling to the point that eBay's system will be irreparably harmed. There is no evidence that eBay has indiscriminately licensed all comers. Rather, it appears that eBay has carefully chosen to permit crawling by a limited number of aggregation sites that agree to abide by the terms of eBay's licensing agreement. "The existence of such a [limited] license, unlike a general license offered to all comers, does not demonstrate a decision to relinquish all control over the distribution of the product in exchange for a readily computable fee." Ty, Inc. v. GMA Accessories, Inc., 132 F.3d 1167, 1173 (7th Cir. 1997) (discussing presumption of irreparable harm in copyright infringement context). eBay's licensing activities appear directed toward limiting the amount and nature of crawling activity on the eBay site. Such licensing does not support the inference that carte blanche crawling of the eBay site would pose no threat of irreparable harm. . . .

B. *Likelihood of Success* . . .

1. Trespass

Trespass to chattels "lies where an intentional interference with the possession of personal property has proximately cause[d] injury." Thrifty-Tel v. Bezenek, 46 Cal.App.4th 1559, 1566, 54 Cal. Rptr.2d 468 (1996). Trespass to chattels "although seldom employed as a tort theory in California" was recently applied to cover the unauthorized use of long distance telephone lines. *Id.* Specifically, the court noted "the electronic signals generated by the [defendants'] activities were sufficiently tangible to support a trespass cause of action." *Id.* at n. 6. Thus, it appears likely that the electronic signals sent by BE to retrieve information from eBay's computer system are also sufficiently tangible to support a trespass cause of action.

In order to prevail on a claim for trespass based on accessing a computer system, the plaintiff must establish: (1) defendant intentionally and without authorization interfered with plaintiff's possessory interest in the computer system; and (2) defendant's unauthorized use proximately resulted in damage to plaintiff. See

Thrifty-Tel, 46 Cal.App.4th at 1566, 54 Cal. Rptr.2d 468; see also Itano v. Colonial Yacht Anchorage, 267 Cal.App.2d 84, 90, 72 Cal. Rptr. 823 (1968) ("When conduct complained of consists of intermeddling with personal property 'the owner has a cause of action for trespass or case, and may recover only the actual damages suffered by reason of the impairment of the property or the loss of its use.' ") (quoting Zaslow v. Kroenert, 29 Cal.2d 541, 550, 176 P.2d 1 (1946)). Here, eBay has presented evidence sufficient to establish a strong likelihood of proving both prongs and ultimately prevailing on the merits of its trespass claim.

a.   BE's Unauthorized Interference

eBay argues that BE's use was unauthorized and intentional. eBay is correct. BE does not dispute that it employed an automated computer program to connect with and search eBay's electronic database. BE admits that, because other auction aggregators were including eBay's auctions in their listing, it continued to "crawl" eBay's web site even after eBay demanded BE terminate such activity.

BE argues that it cannot trespass eBay's web site because the site is publicly accessible. BE's argument is unconvincing. eBay's servers are private property, conditional access to which eBay grants the public. eBay does not generally permit the type of automated access made by BE. In fact, eBay explicitly notifies automated visitors that their access is not permitted. "In general, California does recognize a trespass claim where the defendant exceeds the scope of the consent." Baugh v. CBS, Inc., 828 F. Supp. 745, 756 (N.D.Cal. 1993).

Even if BE's web crawlers were authorized to make individual queries of eBay's system, BE's web crawlers exceeded the scope of any such consent when they began acting like robots by making repeated queries. See City of Amsterdam v. Daniel Goldreyer, Ltd., 882 F. Supp. 1273, 1281 (E.D.N.Y. 1995) ("One who uses a chattel with the consent of another is subject to liability in trespass for any harm to the chattel which is caused by or occurs in the course of any use exceeding the consent, even though such use is not a conversion."). Moreover, eBay repeatedly and explicitly notified BE that its use of eBay's computer system was unauthorized. The entire reason BE directed its queries through proxy servers was to evade eBay's attempts to stop this unauthorized access. The court concludes that BE's activity is sufficiently outside of the scope of the use permitted by eBay that it is unauthorized for the purposes of establishing a trespass. See Civic Western Corp. v. Zila Industries, Inc., 66 Cal.App.3d 1, 17, 135 Cal. Rptr. 915 (1977) ("It seems clear, however, that a trespass may occur if the party, entering pursuant to a limited consent, . . . proceeds to exceed those limits . . .") (discussing trespass to real property).

eBay argues that BE interfered with eBay's possessory interest in its computer system. Although eBay appears unlikely to be able to show a substantial interference at this time, such a showing is not required. Conduct that does not amount to a substantial interference with possession, but which consists of intermeddling with or use of another's personal property, is sufficient to establish a cause of action for trespass to chattel. See *Thrifty-Tel*, 46 Cal.App.4th at 1567, 54 Cal. Rptr.2d 468 (distinguishing the tort from conversion). Although the court admits some uncertainty as to the precise level of possessory interference required to constitute an intermeddling, there does not appear to be any dispute that eBay can show that BE's conduct amounts to use of eBay's computer systems. Accordingly, eBay has made a strong showing that it is likely to prevail on the merits of its assertion that BE's use of eBay's computer system was an unauthorized and intentional interference with eBay's possessory interest.

b. Damage to eBay's Computer System

A trespasser is liable when the trespass diminishes the condition, quality or value of personal property. See CompuServe, Inc. v. Cyber Promotions, 962 F. Supp. 1015 (S.D. Ohio 1997). The quality or value of personal property may be "diminished even though it is not physically damaged by defendant's conduct." *Id*. at 1022. The Restatement offers the following explanation for the harm requirement:

> The interest of a possessor of a chattel in its inviolability, unlike the similar interest of a possessor of land, is not given legal protection by an action for nominal damages for harmless intermeddlings with the chattel. In order that an actor who interferes with another's chattel may be liable, his conduct must affect some other and more important interest of the possessor. Therefore, one who intentionally intermeddles with another's chattel is subject to liability only if his intermeddling is harmful to the possessor's materially valuable interest in the physical condition, quality, or value of the chattel, or if the possessor is deprived of the use of the chattel for a substantial time, or some other legally protected interest of the possessor is affected. . . . Sufficient legal protection of the possessor's interest in the mere inviolability of his chattel is afforded by his privilege to use reasonable force to protect his possession against even harmless interference.

Restatement (Second) of Torts §218 cmt. e (1977).

eBay is likely to be able to demonstrate that BE's activities have diminished the quality or value of eBay's computer systems. BE's activities consume at least a portion of plaintiff's bandwidth and server capacity. Although there is some dispute as to the percentage of queries on eBay's site for which BE is responsible, BE admits that it sends some 80,000 to 100,000 requests to plaintiff's computer systems per day. Although eBay does not claim that this consumption has led to any physical damage to eBay's computer system, nor does eBay provide any evidence to support the claim that it may have lost revenues or customers based on this use, eBay's claim is that BE's use is appropriating eBay's personal property by using valuable bandwidth and capacity, and necessarily compromising eBay's ability to use that capacity for its own purposes. See *CompuServe*, 962 F. Supp. at 1022 ("any value [plaintiff] realizes from its computer equipment is wholly derived from the extent to which that equipment can serve its subscriber base.").

BE argues that its searches represent a negligible load on plaintiff's computer systems, and do not rise to the level of impairment to the condition or value of eBay's computer system required to constitute a trespass. However, it is undisputed that eBay's server and its capacity are personal property, and that BE's searches use a portion of this property. Even if, as BE argues, its searches use only a small amount of eBay's computer system capacity, BE has nonetheless deprived eBay of the ability to use that portion of its personal property for its own purposes. The law recognizes no such right to use another's personal property. Accordingly, BE's actions appear to have caused injury to eBay and appear likely to continue to cause injury to eBay. If the court were to hold otherwise, it would likely encourage other auction aggregators to crawl the eBay site, potentially to the point of denying effective access to eBay's customers. If preliminary injunctive relief were denied, and other aggregators began to crawl the eBay site, there appears to be little doubt that the load on eBay's computer system would qualify as a substantial impairment of condition or value. California law does not require eBay to wait for such a disaster before applying to this court for relief. The court concludes that eBay has made a strong showing that it is likely to prevail on the merits of its trespass claim, and that there is at least a possibility that it will suffer irreparable harm if preliminary injunctive relief is not granted. eBay is therefore entitled to preliminary injunctive relief. . . .

COMMENTS AND QUESTIONS

1. The tort of trespass to chattels traditionally requires proof not just that the defendant "intermeddled" with a chattel but that the defendant's use actually caused injury to the chattel or injured the owner by depriving it of the benefit of using the chattel. The chattel in this case is eBay's server, so the Restatement approach would seem to require proof that eBay's servers were damaged, or at least that eBay lost the use of its servers. But eBay could not prove either of those things. eBay's servers did not crash, nor did they need more frequent repair because Bidder's Edge sent a large number of requests to the servers. Nor was eBay deprived of the use of the server. eBay customers weren't kicked out, nor did they have their requests delayed, by reason of Bidder's Edge's use.

Judge Whyte's opinion points to two sorts of injury attributable to Bidder's Edge's conduct. First, Judge Whyte pointed out that when Bidder's Edge sent its flood of requests (normally in the middle of the night), it used just over 1% of eBay's capacity. The court worried that if dozens of other companies sent similar bulk requests at exactly the same time, eBay's server could crash. Second, Judge Whyte seemed to undo the injury requirement altogether by concluding that any use of the plaintiff's server was necessarily an interference with eBay's exclusive right of control, even if the use didn't prevent eBay from doing whatever it wanted with its server. Significantly, it is the second rationale that every subsequent court has pointed to in finding trespass to chattels even absent any possible injury to the chattel itself.

Does *eBay*'s analysis of injury make sense? Or is the court really applying the rather different tort of trespass to land, which punishes intermeddling directly whether or not there is injury? See Dan L. Burk, The Trouble With Trespass, 4 J. Sm. & Emerging Bus. L. 27 (2000) (criticizing trespass cases for confusing the two doctrines).

2. Might eBay have anticompetitive motives for preventing Bidder's Edge from truthfully reporting the prices of various goods on different auction sites? If auction aggregators don't exist, it becomes harder for consumers to comparison-shop, and they may just buy from the auction site with the largest brand name—eBay. Law professors opposed to the *eBay* decision made this point on appeal:

> Established online merchants have a substantial incentive to use the doctrine of trespass to interfere with the flow of price and product information on the Internet. The district court's decision places the flow of information within their control, as it allows them to circumscribe the use of tools that gather information and present the re-

sults in a usable format. These tools are essential to make the process of gathering information both feasible and useful to the average consumer. Without information about online alternatives, competition on the Internet will be reduced. Like eBay, many sites may have a motive to prevent such competition. eBay would rather not have a site like Bidder's Edge tell consumers that they can get the same product cheaper at a competing auction site. Similarly, online sellers of music, books, videos, toys and countless other sites that don't have the lowest prices won't want to participate in a price-comparison service. This is especially true of companies like eBay with large market shares, because they may believe that they could shut down a data aggregator altogether by choosing not to participate. Such companies will instead rely on their strong brand name to keep consumers coming to their site—and ignorant of the cheaper prices or better service that may be available elsewhere. The district court's opinion gives these companies the power to block such a price-comparison service altogether. While the promise of ecommerce is to improve consumer information and lower transaction costs, under a trespass theory many of those benefits will disappear.[4]

http://www.law.berkeley.edu/institutes/bclt/pubs/lemley/bedgeami.pdf. Is this a fair criticism? Should the doctrine of trespass to chattels take the plaintiff's motive into account?

3. While the trespass to chattels cause of action has only recently been applied to the Internet, a number of recent decisions have used the tort to permit the owners of servers to prevent unwanted access. These cases fall into two basic categories. One set of cases—including *eBay*—involve a Web site owner's attempt to limit or prevent access to data the Web site owner has itself made open to the public.[1] In addition to *eBay*, courts in Register.com, Inc. v. Verio, Inc., 126 F. Supp.2d 238 (S.D.N.Y. 2000) and Oyster Software, Inc. v. Forms Processing, 2001 WL 1736382 (N.D. Cal. Dec. 6, 2001) have held that a public Web site can prevent automated access, even to information (such as the WHOIS database in *Verio*) that the Web site is obligated to make available to the public. These courts have not required any proof of burden on the server. Rather, they have followed the second theory in *eBay*, holding that any access to the server deprived the Web site owner of its right of dominion.

The second set of cases involves not the collection of data from a Web site but the sending of data to a mail server. The first applications of trespass to chattels to the Internet involved spam. See CompuServe, Inc. v. Cyber Promotions, Inc., 962 F. Supp. 1015 (S.D. Ohio 1997); America Online v. National Health Care Discount, Inc., 174 F. Supp.2d 890 (N.D. Iowa 2001). In these cases, the court found that bulk e-mail was overwhelming the servers of the plaintiff Internet service providers, and the court concluded that sending such bulk email trespassed on the ISP servers. In Intel Corp. v. Hamidi, 114 Cal. Rptr.2d 244 (Ct. App. 2001), *review granted* (Cal. 2002), the court expanded the rationale of the spam cases by eliminating the requirement of burden on the servers. In that case, the court en-

---

4. Consumers can obtain price information in the physical world by reading advertisements and catalogs, or using existing comparison-shopping products like *Consumer Reports*. While in theory a store might be legally justified in excluding anyone who works for *Consumer Reports* from entering their store or buying their products, as a practical matter it would be difficult for them to do so. eBay, by contrast, has found in its trespass theory a perfect mechanism for preventing information-gathering.

1. The protection of information *not* open to the public—private or password-controlled servers—present a different set of issues. The Computer Fraud and Abuse Act, 18 U.S.C. §1030, precludes unauthorized access to a networked computer, and there is no need to apply trespass to preclude such conduct.

joined Hamidi, a former employee of Intel, from sending e-mails to current Intel employees complaining about the company. While there was clearly no harm to or burden on the servers, the court concluded that injury was not required, and in any event could be met by proof that Intel employees spent company time reading the e-mails.

After *Verio* and *Intel*, can you think of any electronic transmission to a public server that doesn't require advance permission?

One court has rejected a trespass to chattels claim. Ticketmaster Corp. v. tickets.com, 2000 Copyright L. Decs. ¶28,146 (C.D. Cal. Aug. 10, 2000). In *Ticketmaster*, the court concluded that tickets.com was not trespassing on Ticketmaster's server by "scraping" the data from the Ticketmaster server, and then linking directly to places on the Ticketmaster site where users could buy tickets to various events.[2] The court was skeptical of the entire theory of trespass to chattels as applied to the Internet, but it distinguished *eBay* on the ground that Ticketmaster could not show actual harm to its servers.

4. Many of the cases decided under the rubric of trespass to chattels could also be decided under other statutes. For example, many state laws now ban spam. See, e.g., Cal. Bus. & Prof. Code §17538.4. And many of the data cases, such as *eBay* and *Ticketmaster*, are really efforts to protect uncopyrightable data by creating a new form of intellectual property law. The intuitive case for protection of data compilations may motivate courts to rule for the plaintiffs on a trespass theory in order to effectively create a form of intellectual property for data protection. Does this result make sense? Or should the courts be careful to avoid undermining copyright law's limits? Note that copyright law may preempt state torts that create copyright-like rights within the constitutional field of copyright. See *Ticketmaster, supra*, in which the court held various state torts preempted by federal copyright law.

5. The broad application of trespass to the Internet effectively creates a consent standard for using the Internet. Web sites and even e-mail recipients have an effective veto over the sending or collecting of data. Rather than simply deciding to make information open to the public or keep it private, a Web site owner can declare that information is public but that particular specified individuals are barred from using it.

Understanding the trespass cases in this light puts the focus on how those declarations are made and communicated. In some cases, such as *eBay*, this is not much of an issue: It was quite clear to Bidder's Edge that eBay objected to its collection of data from the eBay Web site. But in other cases, courts have held that terms and conditions placed on a Web site—or even the use of an automated Robot Exclusion Header—constitute sufficient notice that a particular user is unwanted.

Does it make sense to give a Web site owner the right to post an announcement excluding certain users or anyone who would make certain uses? The alternative is for the Web site owner to rely on technical blocking alternatives. For example, after Ticketmaster lost its case, it reconfigured its Web site to block deep links from tickets.com. Should the courts stay out of such disputes and let the parties engage in their own technological competition? Or will the result be a wasteful technological "arms race"?

---

2. Presumably the linking claim would have to be based on some theory of contributory trespass, since it is Ticketmaster customers rather than tickets.com who are actually sending data to the Ticketmaster site.

6.   The concept of trespass in cyberspace depends heavily on a conception of a Web site or mail server as "property" from which, as with land, the owner ought to have the right to exclude others. But a number of commentators have challenged the metaphor of an Internet site as a "place" akin to land. See, e.g., Dan Hunter: Cyberspace as Place and the Tragedy of the Digital Anticommons, 91 Calif. L. Rev. __ (forthcoming 2003); Mark A. Lemley, Place and Cyberspace, 91 Calif. L. Rev. __ (forthcoming 2003); Maureen A. O'Rourke, Property Rights and Competition on the Internet: In Search of an Appropriate Analogy, 16 Berkeley Tech. L.J. 561 (2001). Hunter suggests that the metaphor is psychologically quite powerful, but troubling as a policy matter. Lemley argues that courts can and should focus on the ways the Internet is *not* like land. He also points out that treating the Internet like land does not necessarily mean that the owner should get an absolute right to exclude others. In the real world, the law gives many different sorts of rights of varying strengths to land. Similarly, a court might decide that an absolute right of exclusion is not the right legal analogy.

In this regard, it is worth considering Dan Burk's argument that nuisance, not trespass, is the right analogy from real property:

> [T]he correct property theory might be nuisance to web sites, rather than trespass. Nuisance lies only if the cost of the intrusive activity outweighs the benefit. The "muddy" nature of nuisance would allow computer owners on the Net to exclude unreasonably costly uses of their servers, while allowing access for socially beneficial uses, even if the server owner might otherwise object. Stated differently, nuisance would authorize computer owners to legally "defect" from the network when necessary to avoid wasteful negative network externalities, but require them to remain legally networked when necessary to generate beneficial positive network externalities. Of course, the server owner always would have the option of physically disconnecting from the network to avoid objectionable uses, so long as he was willing to forgo the positive benefits of the network as well. Presumably, proper application of the nuisance standard would make this drastic action unattractive on average to rational server owners, as they would be shielded from marginally detrimental uses, while enjoying marginally beneficial network advantages.

Burk, *supra*, at 53.

Are property principles relevant to the Internet at all? If so, how should a court decide which analogy is the right one to apply?

PROBLEMS

Problem 13.1:   Infoplex is a search engine. In order to run a comprehensive search engine, Infoplex must collect and index data from over one billion Web sites. In order to keep its search engine up-to-date, Infoplex must revisit those pages at least once a week, and often more frequently. To do this, Infoplex uses automated software robots called "spiders." These spiders crawl the Web, automatically downloading all of the information on all of the Web sites they can find. Because of the practical impossibility of entering into contracts with the owners of all these Web sites—among other things, millions of new pages are added each year—Infoplex has configured its spiders to collect any data it can from any site that is open to the public.

Do any of the following plaintiffs have a claim against Infoplex for trespass to chattels based on its indexing of their sites?

1. Site A, which has a written "terms of use" statement precluding any collection of all or substantially all of its data by any for-profit company.

2. Site B, which uses a Robot Exclusion Header in the source code of its Web page. Such a header signals to robots that they are not welcome on the site. Not all robots recognize or respect such a header, though, and Infoplex has configured its robots to ignore such headers.

3. Site C, an Internet service provider that has sent a letter to the general counsel of Infoplex demanding that Infoplex pay it $1,000 per month for the right to index any of its customers' pages.

C. COMPUTER CRIMES

United States v. Morris
United States Appeals Court for the Second Circuit
928 F.2d 504 (2d Cir. 1991)

JON O. NEWMAN, Circuit Judge:

. . . In the fall of 1988, Morris was a first-year graduate student in Cornell University's computer science Ph.D. program. Through undergraduate work at Harvard and in various jobs he had acquired significant computer experience and expertise. When Morris entered Cornell, he was given an account on the computer at the Computer Science Division. This account gave him explicit authorization to use computers at Cornell. Morris engaged in various discussions with fellow graduate students about the security of computer networks and his ability to penetrate it.

In October 1988, Morris began work on a computer program, later known as the INTERNET "worm" or "virus." The goal of this program was to demonstrate the inadequacies of current security measures on computer networks by exploiting the security defects that Morris had discovered. The tactic he selected was release of a worm into network computers. Morris designed the program to spread across a national network of computers after being inserted at one computer location connected to the network. Morris released the worm into INTERNET, which is a group of national networks that connect university, governmental, and military computers around the country. The network permits communication and transfer of information between computers on the network.

Morris sought to program the INTERNET worm to spread widely without drawing attention to itself. The worm was supposed to occupy little computer operation time, and thus not interfere with normal use of the computers. Morris programmed the worm to make it difficult to detect and read, so that other programmers would not be able to "kill" the worm easily.

Morris also wanted to ensure that the worm did not copy itself onto a computer that already had a copy. Multiple copies of the worm on a computer would make the worm easier to detect and would bog down the system and ultimately cause the computer to crash. Therefore, Morris designed the worm to "ask" each computer whether it already had a copy of the worm. If it responded "no," then the worm would copy onto the computer; if it responded "yes," the worm would not duplicate. However, Morris was concerned that other programmers could kill the worm by programming their own computers to falsely respond "yes" to the question. To circumvent this protection, Morris programmed the worm to duplicate itself every seventh time it received a "yes" response. As it turned out, Morris underestimated the number of times a computer would be asked the question, and his one-out-of-seven ratio resulted in far more copying than he had anticipated. The worm was also designed so that it would be killed when a computer was shut down, an event that typically occurs once every week or two. This would have prevented the worm from accumulating on one computer, had Morris correctly estimated the likely rate of reinfection.

Morris identified four ways in which the worm could break into computers on the network:

(1) through a "hole" or "bug" (an error) in [SENDMAIL], a computer program that transfers and receives electronic mail on a computer;

(2) through a bug in the "finger d[a]emon" program, a program that permits a person to obtain limited information about the users of another computer;

(3) through the "trusted hosts" feature, which permits a user with certain privileges on one computer to have equivalent privileges on another computer without using a password; and

(4) through a program of password guessing, whereby various combinations of letters are tried out in rapid sequence in the hope that one will be an authorized user's password, which is entered to permit whatever level of activity that user is authorized to perform.

On November 2, 1988, Morris released the worm from a computer at the Massachusetts Institute of Technology. MIT was selected to disguise the fact that the worm came from Morris at Cornell. Morris soon discovered that the worm was replicating and reinfecting machines at a much faster rate than he had anticipated. Ultimately, many machines at locations around the country either crashed or became "catatonic." When Morris realized what was happening, he contacted a friend at Harvard to discuss a solution. Eventually, they sent an anonymous message from Harvard over the network, instructing programmers how to kill the worm and prevent reinfection. However, because the network route was clogged, this message did not get through until it was too late. Computers were affected at numerous installations, including leading universities, military sites, and medical research facilities. The estimated cost of dealing with the worm at each installation ranged from $200 to more than $53,000.

Morris was found guilty, following a jury trial, of violating 18 U.S.C. §1030(a)(5)(A). He was sentenced to three years of probation, 400 hours of community service, a fine of $10,050, and the costs of his supervision.

I. The Intent Requirement in Section 1030(a)(5)(A)

Section 1030(a)(5)(A), covers anyone who

(5) intentionally accesses a Federal interest computer without authorization, and by means of one or more instances of such conduct alters, damages, or destroys

information in any such Federal interest computer, or prevents authorized use of any such computer or information, and thereby

(A) causes loss to one or more others of a value aggregating $1,000 or more during any one year period; . . .

Procedure

The District Court concluded that the intent requirement applied only to the accessing and not to the resulting damage. Judge Munson found recourse to legislative history unnecessary because he considered the statute clear and unambiguous. However, the Court observed that the legislative history supported its reading of section 1030(a)(5)(A).

Morris argues that the Government had to prove not only that he intended the unauthorized access of a federal interest computer, but also that he intended to prevent others from using it, and thus cause a loss. . . .

The first federal statute dealing with computer crimes was passed in 1984, Pub.L. No. 98-473 (codified at 18 U.S.C. §1030 (Supp. II 1984)). The specific provision under which Morris was convicted was added in 1986, Pub.L. No. 99-474, along with some other changes. The 1986 amendments made several changes relevant to our analysis.

Mental State

First, the 1986 amendments changed the scienter requirement in section 1030(a)(2) from "knowingly" to "intentionally." See Pub.L. No. 99-474, section 2(a)(1). The subsection now covers anyone who

(2) intentionally accesses a computer without authorization or exceeds authorized access, and thereby obtains information contained in a financial record of a financial institution, or of a card issuer as defined in section 1602(n) of title 15, or contained in a file of a consumer reporting agency on a consumer, as such terms are defined in the Fair Credit Reporting Act (15 U.S.C. 1681 et seq.).

According to the Senate Judiciary Committee, Congress changed the mental state requirement in section 1030(a)(2) for two reasons. Congress sought only to proscribe intentional acts of unauthorized access, not "mistaken, inadvertent, or careless" acts of unauthorized access. S.Rep. No. 99-432, 99th Cong., 2d Sess. 5 (1986), *reprinted in* 1986 U.S.Code Cong. & Admin.News 2479, 2483 [hereinafter Senate Report].

Also, Congress expressed concern that the "knowingly" standard "might be inappropriate for cases involving computer technology." *Id.* The concern was that a scienter requirement of "knowingly" might encompass the acts of an individual "who inadvertently 'stumble[d] into' someone else's computer file or computer data," especially where such individual was authorized to use a particular computer. *Id.* at 6, 1986 U.S.Code Cong. & Admin.News at 2483. The Senate Report concluded that "[t]he substitution of an 'intentional' standard is designed to focus Federal criminal prosecutions on those whose conduct evinces a clear intent to enter, without proper authorization, computer files or data belonging to another." *Id.*, U.S.Code Cong. & Admin.News at 2484. Congress retained the "knowingly" standard in other subsections of section 1030. See 18 U.S.C. §1030(a)(1), (a)(4).

This use of a mens rea standard to make sure that inadvertent accessing was not covered is also emphasized in the Senate Report's discussion of section 1030(a)(3) and section 1030(a)(5), under which Morris was convicted. Both subsections were designed to target "outsiders," individuals without authorization to access any federal interest computer. Senate Report at 10, U.S.Code Cong. & Admin.News at 2488. The rationale for the mens rea requirement suggests that it modifies only the "accesses" phrase, which was the focus of Congress's concern in strengthening the scienter requirement.

The other relevant change in the 1986 amendments was the introduction of subsection (a)(5) to replace its earlier version, subsection (a)(3) of the 1984 act, 18 U.S.C. §1030(a)(3) (Supp. II 1984). The predecessor subsection covered anyone who

> knowingly accesses a computer without authorization, or having accessed a computer with authorization, uses the opportunity such access provides for purposes to which such authorization does not extend, and by means of such conduct knowingly uses, modifies, destroys, or discloses information in, or prevents authorized use of, such computer, if such computer is operated for or on behalf of the Government of United States and such conduct affects such operation.

The 1986 version changed the mental state requirement from "knowingly" to "intentionally," and did not repeat it after the "accesses" phrase, as had the 1984 version. By contrast, other subsections of section 1030 have retained "dual intent" language, placing the scienter requirement at the beginning of both the "accesses" phrase and the "damages" phrase. See, e.g., 18 U.S.C. §1030(a)(1).

Morris notes the careful attention that Congress gave to selecting the scienter requirement for current subsections (a)(2) and (a)(5). Then, relying primarily on comments in the Senate and House reports, Morris argues that the "intentionally" requirement of section 1030(a)(5)(A) describes both the conduct of accessing and damaging. As he notes, the Senate Report said that "[t]he new subsection 1030(a)(5) to be created by the bill is designed to penalize those who intentionally alter, damage, or destroy certain computerized data belonging to another." Senate Report at 10, U.S.Code Cong. & Admin.News at 2488. The House Judiciary Committee stated that "the bill proposes a new section (18 U.S.C. 1030(a)(5)) which can be characterized as a 'malicious damage' felony violation involving a Federal interest computer. We have included an 'intentional' standard for this felony and coverage is extended only to outside trespassers with a $1,000 threshold damage level." H.R.Rep. No. 99-612, 99th Cong.2d Sess. at 7 (1986). A member of the Judiciary Committee also referred to the section 1030(a)(5) offense as a "malicious damage" felony during the floor debate. 132 Cong.Rec. H3275, 3276 (daily ed. June 3, 1986) (remarks of Rep. Hughes).

[handwritten margin note: Morris Argument]

The Government's argument that the scienter requirement in section 1030(a)(5)(A) applies only to the "accesses" phrase is premised primarily upon the difference between subsection (a)(5)(A) and its predecessor in the 1984 statute. The decision to state the scienter requirement only once in subsection (a)(5)(A), along with the decision to change it from "knowingly" to "intentionally," are claimed to evince a clear intent upon the part of Congress to apply the scienter requirement only to the "accesses" phrase, though making that requirement more difficult to satisfy. This reading would carry out the Congressional objective of protecting the individual who "inadvertently 'stumble[s] into' someone else's computer file." Senate Report at 6, U.S.Code Cong. & Admin.News at 2483.

The Government also suggests that the fact that other subsections of section 1030 continue to repeat the scienter requirement before both phrases of a subsec-

[handwritten margin note: Gov'ts Argument]

tion is evidence that Congress selectively decided within the various subsections of section 1030 where the scienter requirement was and was not intended to apply. Morris responds with a plausible explanation as to why certain other provisions of section 1030 retain dual intent language. Those subsections use two different mens rea standards; therefore it is necessary to refer to the scienter requirement twice in the subsection. For example, section 1030(a)(1) covers anyone who

> (1) knowingly accesses a computer without authorization or exceeds authorized access, and by means of such conduct obtains information that has been determined by the United States Government pursuant to an Executive order or statute to require protection against unauthorized disclosure for reasons of national defense or foreign relations, or any restricted data . . . with the intent or reason to believe that such information so obtained is to be used to the injury of the United States, or to the advantage of any foreign nation.

Since Congress sought in subsection (a)(1) to have the "knowingly" standard govern the "accesses" phrase and the "with intent" standard govern the "results" phrase, it was necessary to state the scienter requirement at the beginning of both phrases. By contrast, Morris argues, where Congress stated the scienter requirement only once, at the beginning of the "accesses" phrase, it was intended to cover both the "accesses" phrase and the phrase that followed it.

There is a problem, however, with applying Morris's explanation to section 1030(a)(5)(A). As noted earlier, the predecessor of subsection (a)(5)(A) explicitly placed the same mental state requirement before both the "accesses" phrase and the "damages" phrase. In relevant part, that predecessor in the 1984 statute covered anyone who "knowingly accesses a computer without authorization, . . . and by means of such conduct knowingly uses, modifies, destroys, or discloses information in, or prevents authorized use of, such computer. . . ." 18 U.S.C. §1030(a)(3) (Supp. II 1984). This earlier provision demonstrates that Congress has on occasion chosen to repeat the same scienter standard in the "accesses" phrase and the subsequent phrase of a subsection of the Computer Fraud Statute. More pertinently, it shows that the 1986 amendments adding subsection (a)(5)(A) placed the scienter requirement adjacent only to the "accesses" phrase in contrast to a predecessor provision that had placed the same standard before both that phrase and the subsequent phrase.

Despite some isolated language in the legislative history that arguably suggests a scienter component for the "damages" phrase of section 1030(a)(5)(A), the wording, structure, and purpose of the subsection, examined in comparison with its departure from the format of its predecessor provision persuade us that the "intentionally" standard applies only to the "accesses" phrase of section 1030(a)(5)(A), and not to its "damages" phrase.

II. The Unauthorized Access Requirement in Section 1030(a)(5)(A)

Section 1030(a)(5)(A) penalizes the conduct of an individual who "intentionally accesses a Federal interest computer without authorization." Morris contends that his conduct constituted, at most, "exceeding authorized access" rather than the "unauthorized access" that the subsection punishes. Morris argues that there was insufficient evidence to convict him of "unauthorized access," and that even if the evidence sufficed, he was entitled to have the jury instructed on his "theory of defense."

We assess the sufficiency of the evidence under the traditional standard. Morris was authorized to use computers at Cornell, Harvard, and Berkeley, all of which were on INTERNET. As a result, Morris was authorized to communicate with other computers on the network to send electronic mail (SEND MAIL), and to find out certain information about the users of other computers (finger d[a]emon). The question is whether Morris's transmission of his worm constituted exceeding authorized access or accessing without authorization.

The Senate Report stated that section 1030(a)(5)(A), like the new section 1030(a)(3), would "be aimed at 'outsiders,' i.e., those lacking authorization to access any Federal interest computer." Senate Report at 10, U.S.Code Cong. & Admin.News at 2488. But the Report also stated, in concluding its discussion on the scope of section 1030(a)(3), that it applies "where the offender is completely outside the Government, . . . or where the offender's act of trespass is interdepartmental in nature." *Id.* at 8, U.S.Code Cong. & Admin.News at 2486.

Morris relies on the first quoted portion to argue that his actions can be characterized only as exceeding authorized access, since he had authorized access to a federal interest computer. However, the second quoted portion reveals that Congress was not drawing a bright line between those who have some access to any federal interest computer and those who have none. Congress contemplated that individuals with access to some federal interest computers would be subject to liability under the computer fraud provisions for gaining unauthorized access to other federal interest computers. See, e.g., *id.* (stating that a Labor Department employee who uses Labor's computers to access without authorization an FBI computer can be criminally prosecuted).

The evidence permitted the jury to conclude that Morris's use of the [SENDMAIL] and finger d[a]emon features constituted access without authorization. While a case might arise where the use of [SENDMAIL] or finger d[a]emon falls within a nebulous area in which the line between accessing without authorization and exceeding authorized access may not be clear, Morris's conduct here falls well within the area of unauthorized access. Morris did not use either of those features in any way related to their intended function. He did not send or read mail nor discover information about other users; instead he found holes in both programs that permitted him a special and unauthorized access route into other computers.

Moreover, the jury verdict need not be upheld solely on Morris's use of [SENDMAIL] and finger d[a]emon. As the District Court noted, in denying Morris's motion for acquittal,

> Although the evidence may have shown that defendant's initial insertion of the worm simply exceeded his authorized access, the evidence also demonstrated that the worm was designed to spread to other computers at which he had no account and no authority, express or implied, to unleash the worm program. Moreover, there was also evidence that the worm was designed to gain access to computers at which he had no account by guessing their passwords. Accordingly, the evidence did support the jury's conclusion that defendant accessed without authority as opposed to merely exceeding the scope of his authority.

In light of the reasonable conclusions that the jury could draw from Morris's use of [SENDMAIL] and finger d[a]emon, and from his use of the trusted hosts feature and password guessing, his challenge to the sufficiency of the evidence fails.

Morris endeavors to bolster his sufficiency argument by contending that his conduct was not punishable under subsection (a)(5) but was punishable under subsection (a)(3). That concession belies the validity of his claim that he only exceeded authorization rather than made unauthorized access. Neither subsection (a)(3) nor (a)(5) punishes conduct that exceeds authorization. Both punish a person who "accesses" "without authorization" certain computers. Subsection (a)(3) covers the computers of a department or agency of the United States; subsection (a)(5) more broadly covers any federal interest computers, defined to include, among other computers, those used exclusively by the United States, 18 U.S.C. §1030(e)(2)(A), and adds the element of causing damage or loss of use of a value of $1,000 or more. If Morris violated subsection (a)(3), as he concedes, then his conduct in inserting the worm into the INTERNET must have constituted "unauthorized access" under subsection (a)(5) to the computers of the federal departments the worm reached, for example, those of NASA and military bases.

To extricate himself from the consequence of conceding that he made "unauthorized access" within the meaning of subsection (a)(3), Morris subtly shifts his argument and contends that he is not within the reach of subsection (a)(5) at all. He argues that subsection (a)(5) covers only those who, unlike himself, lack access to any federal interest computer. It is true that a primary concern of Congress in drafting subsection (a)(5) was to reach those unauthorized to access any federal interest computer. The Senate Report stated, "[T]his subsection [(a)(5)] will be aimed at 'outsiders,' i.e., those lacking authorization to access any Federal interest computer." Senate Report at 10, U.S.Code Cong. & Admin.News at 2488. But the fact that the subsection is "aimed" at such "outsiders" does not mean that its coverage is limited to them. Congress understandably thought that the group most likely to damage federal interest computers would be those who lack authorization to use any of them. But it surely did not mean to insulate from liability the person authorized to use computers at the State Department who causes damage to computers at the Defense Department. Congress created the misdemeanor offense of subsection (a)(3) to punish intentional trespassers into computers for which one lacks authorized access; it added the felony offense of subsection (a)(5) to punish such a trespasser who also causes damage or loss in excess of $1,000, not only to computers of the United States but to any computer within the definition of federal interest computers. With both provisions, Congress was punishing those, like Morris, who, with access to some computers that enable them to communicate on a network linking other computers, gain access to other computers to which they lack authorization and either trespass, in violation of subsection (a)(3), or cause damage or loss of $1,000 or more, in violation of subsection (a)(5).

Morris also contends that the District Court should have instructed the jury on his theory that he was only exceeding authorized access. The District Court decided that it was unnecessary to provide the jury with a definition of "authorization." We agree. Since the word is of common usage, without any technical or ambiguous meaning, the Court was not obliged to instruct the jury on its meaning. See, e.g., United States v. Chenault, 844 F.2d 1124, 1131 (5th Cir. 1988) ("A trial court need not define specific statutory terms unless they are outside the common understanding of a juror or are so technical or specific as to require a definition.").

An instruction on "exceeding authorized access" would have risked misleading the jury into thinking that Morris could not be convicted if some of his conduct could be viewed as falling within this description. Yet, even if that phrase might have applied to some of his conduct, he could nonetheless be found liable for doing what the statute prohibited, gaining access where he was unauthorized and causing loss.

Additionally, the District Court properly refused to charge the jury with Morris's proposed jury instruction on access without authorization. That instruction stated, "To establish the element of lack of authorization, the government must prove beyond a reasonable doubt that Mr. Morris was an 'outsider,' that is, that he was not authorized to access any Federal interest computer in any manner." As the analysis of the legislative history reveals, Congress did not intend an individual's authorized access to one federal interest computer to protect him from prosecution, no matter what other federal interest computers he accesses.

══
══
══   **United States v. Riggs**
     United States District Court for the Northern District of Illinois
     739 F. Supp. 414 (N.D. Ill. 1990)

BUA, District Judge.

... In about September 1988, Neidorf and Riggs devised and began implementing a scheme to defraud Bell South Telephone Company ("Bell South"), which provides telephone services to a nine-state region including Alabama, Georgia, Mississippi, Tennessee, Kentucky, Louisiana, North Carolina, South Carolina, and Florida. The objective of the fraud scheme was to steal Bell South's computer text file which contained information regarding its enhanced 911 (E911) system for handling emergency calls to policy, fire, ambulance, and other emergency services in municipalities. The text file which Riggs and Neidorf planned to steal specifically details the procedures for installation, operation, and maintenance of E911 services in the region in which Bell South operates. Bell South considered this file to contain valuable proprietary information and, therefore, closely guarded the information from being disclosed outside of Bell South and its subsidiaries. Riggs and Neidorf wanted to obtain the E911 text file so it could be printed in a computer newsletter known as "PHRACK" which Neidorf edited and published.

In about December 1988, Riggs began the execution of the fraud scheme by using his home computer in Decatur, Georgia, to gain unlawful access to Bell South's computer system located at its corporate headquarters in Atlanta, Georgia. After gaining access to Bell South's system, Riggs "downloaded" the text file, which described in detail the operation of the E911 system in Bell South's operating region. Riggs then disguised and concealed his unauthorized access to the Bell South system by using account codes of persons with legitimate access to the E911 text file.

Pursuant to the scheme he had devised with Neidorf, Riggs then transferred the stolen computer text file to Neidorf by way of an interstate computer data network. Riggs stored the stolen text file on a computer bulletin board system[4] located

4. A computer bulletin board system is a computer program that simulates an actual bulletin board by allowing computer users who access a particular computer to post messages, read existing messages, and delete messages. The messages exchanged may contain a wide variety of information,

in Lockport, Illinois, so as to make the file available to Neidorf. The Lockport bulletin board system was used by computer "hackers" as a location for exchanging and developing software tools and other information which could be used for unauthorized intrusion into computer systems. Neidorf, a twenty-year-old student at the University of Missouri in Columbia, Missouri, used a computer located at his school to access the Lockport computer bulletin board and thereby receive the Bell South E911 text file from Riggs. At the request of Riggs, Neidorf then edited and retyped the E911 text file in order to conceal the fact that it had been stolen from Bell South. Neidorf then "uploaded" his revised version of the stolen file back onto the Lockport bulletin board system for Riggs' review. To complete the scheme, in February 1989, Neidorf published his edited edition of Bell South's E911 text file in his PHRACK newsletter.

B. Charges

The current indictment asserts seven counts. Count I charges that Riggs committed wire fraud in violation of 18 U.S.C. §1343 by transferring the E911 text file from his home computer in Decatur, Georgia to the computer bulletin board system in Lockport, Illinois. Count II charges both Riggs and Neidorf with violating §1343 by causing the edited E911 file to be transferred from a computer operated by Neidorf in Columbia, Missouri, to the computer bulletin board system in Lockport, Illinois. Counts III and IV assert that by transferring the E911 text file via an interstate computer network, Riggs and Neidorf violated the National Stolen Property Act, 18 U.S.C. §2314, which prohibits interstate transfer of stolen property. Finally, Counts V-VII charge Riggs and Neidorf with violating §1030(a)(6)(A) of the Computer Fraud and Abuse Act of 1986, 18 U.S.C. §1030(a)(6)(A), which prohibits knowingly, and with intent to defraud, trafficking in information through which a computer may be accessed without authorization.

II. Discussion

A. Motion to Dismiss Count II

Neidorf claims that Count II of the indictment is defective because it fails to allege a scheme to defraud, one of the necessary elements for a wire fraud claim under 18 U.S.C. §1343. See Lombardo v. United States, 865 F.2d 155, 157 (7th Cir.) (holding that the two elements of a wire fraud claim under §1343 are a scheme to defraud and the use of wire communications in furtherance of the scheme), *cert. denied*, 491 U.S. 905, 109 S. Ct. 3186, 105 L. Ed.2d 695 (1989). All Count II charges, says Neidorf, is that he received and then transferred a computer text file, not that he participated in any scheme to defraud.

including stolen credit card numbers, confidential business information, and information about local community events. See Note, Computer Bulletin Board Operator Liability for User Misuse, 54 Fordham L.Rev. 439, 439-41 & nn. 1-11 (1988); see also Jensen, An Electronic Soap Box: Computer Bulletin Boards and the First Amendment, 39 Fed.Com.L.J. 217 (1987); Morrison, Electronic Bulletin Board System Prover BBS, 13 Legal Econ. 44 (1987); Soma, Smith & Sprague, Legal Analysis of Electronic Bulletin Board Activities, 7 W. New Engl.L.Rev. 571 (1985).

Unsurprisingly, Neidorf's reading of the indictment is self-servingly narrow. The indictment plainly and clearly charges that Neidorf and Riggs concocted a fraud scheme, the object of which was to steal the E911 text file from Bell South and to distribute it to others via the PHRACK newsletter. The indictment also clearly alleges that both Riggs and Neidorf took action in furtherance of the fraud scheme. Riggs allegedly used fraudulent means to access Bell South's computer system and then disguised his unauthorized entry. Neidorf allegedly furthered the scheme by redacting from the E911 text file references to Bell South and other information which would reveal the source of the E911 file, transmitting the redacted file back to the Lockport bulletin board for Riggs review, and publishing the redacted text file in the PHRACK newsletter for others' use. Moreover, both Neidorf and Riggs allegedly used coded language, code names, and other deceptive means to avoid the detection of their fraud by law enforcement officials. These allegations sufficiently set forth the existence of a scheme to defraud, as well as Neidorf's participation in the scheme. See McNally v. United States, 483 U.S. 350, 358, 107 S. Ct. 2875, 2880-81, 97 L. Ed.2d 292 (1987) (where the Court, quoting Hammerschmidt v. United States, 265 U.S. 182, 188, 44 S. Ct. 511, 512, 68 L. Ed. 968 (1924), held that "to defraud" as used in the mail fraud statute simply means "wronging one in his property rights by dishonest methods or schemes" usually by "the deprivation of something of value by trick, deceit, chicane, or overreaching"); see also Carpenter v. United States, 484 U.S. 19, 108 S. Ct. 316, 320-21, 98 L. Ed.2d 275 (1987) (applying *McNally* to the wire fraud statute, the Court held that a *Wall Street Journal* columnist participated in a scheme to defraud chargeable under §1343 where he executed a plan under which he disclosed confidential financial information to an investor in exchange for a share of the investor's profits from that information).

Neidorf also argues that Count II is deficient because it fails to allege that he had a fiduciary relationship with Bell South. To support this position, Neidorf relies on cases such as United States v. Richter, 610 F. Supp. 480 (N.D.Ill. 1985), and United States v. Dorfman, 532 F. Supp. 1118 (N.D.Ill. 1981). In each of those cases, as well as other similar cases cited by Neidorf, the court held that where a wire fraud charge is based on the deprivation of an intangible right, such as the right to honest and fair government or the right to the loyal service of an employee, the government must allege the existence of a fiduciary relationship between the defendant and the alleged victim to state a charge under §1343.

In the instant case, however, the wire fraud charge is not based on the deprivation of an intangible right. The government charges Riggs and Neidorf with scheming to defraud Bell South out of property—the confidential information contained in the E911 text file. The indictment specifically alleges that the object of defendants' scheme was the E911 text file, which Bell South considered to be valuable, proprietary, information. The law is clear that such valuable, confidential information is "property," the deprivation of which can form the basis of a wire fraud charge under §1343. See *Carpenter*, 108 S. Ct. at 320; see also United States v. Keane, 852 F.2d 199, 205 (7th Cir.), *cert. denied*, 490 U.S. 1084, 109 S. Ct. 2109, 104 L. Ed.2d 670 (1989). Therefore, Neidorf's argument misconstrues the wire fraud charge against him. Cases such as *Richter* and *Dorfman* are wholly inapposite.[7]

7. Moreover, to the extent that prior case law such as *Dorfman* and *Richter* held that a mail fraud or a wire fraud charge can be based on the deprivation of intangible rights so long as a fiduciary relationship exists between the victim and the defendant, those cases are no longer good law. The Supreme

As further support for his argument that fiduciary relationship between himself and Bell South must be alleged to state a wire fraud charge against him, Neidorf analogizes his role in the alleged scheme to that of an "innocent tippee" in the securities context, such as the defendants in Dirks v. Securities Exchange Commission, 463 U.S. 646, 103 S. Ct. 3255, 77 L. Ed.2d 911 (1983), and Chiarella v. United States, 445 U.S. 222, 100 S. Ct. 1108, 63 L. Ed.2d 348 (1980). This analogy, however, is fallacious. Those cases involved individuals who come upon information lawfully; the question in each of those cases was whether, once possessing that information, the individual had a duty to disclose it. In the instant case, in contrast, Neidorf is alleged to have planned and participated in the scheme to defraud Bell South. Although Riggs allegedly was the one who actually stole the E911 text file from Bell South's computer system, the government alleges that Neidorf was completely aware of Riggs' activities and agreed to help Riggs conceal the theft to make the fraud complete. Therefore, in no way can Neidorf be construed as being in a similar situation to the innocent tippees in *Dirks* and *Chiarella*. As a result, the court rejects his argument that Count II is defective for failing to allege a fiduciary duty between himself and Bell South. Neidorf's motion to dismiss Count II is accordingly denied.

B. *Motion to Dismiss Counts III and IV*

Counts III and IV charge Riggs and Neidorf with violating 18 U.S.C. §2314, which provides, in relevant part:

> Whoever transports, transmits, or transfers in interstate or foreign commerce any goods, wares, merchandise, securities or money, of the value of $5000 or more, knowing the same to have been stolen, converted or taken by fraud . . . [s]hall be fined not more than $10,000 or imprisoned not more than ten years, or both.

The government concedes that charging Neidorf under §2314 plots a course on uncharted waters. No court has ever held that the electronic transfer of confidential, proprietary business information from one computer to another across state lines constitutes a violation of §2314. However, no court has addressed the issue. Surprisingly, despite the prevalence of computer-related crime, this is a case of first impression. The government argues that reading §2314 as covering Neidorf's conduct in this case is a natural adaptation of the statute to modern society. Conversely, Neidorf contends that his conduct does not fall within the purview of §2314 and that the government is seeking an unreasonable expansion of the statute. He urges the court to dismiss the charge on two grounds.

Court expressly rejected the notion that such a charge can be based on the deprivation of an intangible right—fiduciary relationship or not—in McNally v. United States, 483 U.S. 350, 107 S. Ct. 2875, 97 L. Ed.2d 292 (1987). See Carpenter v. United States, 484 U.S. 19, 108 S. Ct. 316, 320, 98 L. Ed.2d 275 (1987). The *McNally* Court ruled that a mail fraud charge must be based on the deprivation of property. *Id.* However, the property which forms the basis for a wire fraud or mail fraud charge can be "intangible" property. See Bateman v. United States, 875 F.2d 1304, 1306 & n. 2 (7th Cir. 1989); see also United States v. Barber, 881 F.2d 345, 348 (7th Cir. 1989), *cert. denied*, 495 U.S. 922, 110 S. Ct. 1956, 109 L. Ed.2d 318 (1990). This distinction between intangible property and intangible rights has somewhat muddled the ruling in *McNally. Id.*

Tranfer Across state lines

Neidorf's first argument is that the government cannot sustain a §2314 charge in this case because the only thing which he allegedly caused to be transferred across state lines was "electronic impulses." Neidorf maintains that under the plain language of the statute, this conduct does not come within the scope of §2314 since electronic impulses do not constitute "goods, wares, or merchandise."

The court is unpersuaded by Neidorf's disingenuous argument that he merely transferred electronic impulses across state lines. Several courts have upheld §2314 charges based on the wire transfer of fraudulently obtained money, rejecting the arguments of the defendants in those cases that only electronic impulses, not actual money, crossed state lines. For example, in United States v. Gilboe, 684 F.2d 235 (2d Cir. 1982), *cert. denied*, 459 U.S. 1201, 103 S. Ct. 1185, 75 L. Ed.2d 432 (1983), the court held, in affirming a §2314 conviction based on the wire transfer of funds:

> The question whether [§2314] covers electronic transfers of funds appears to be one of first impression, but we do not regard it as a difficult one. Electronic signals in this context are the means by which funds are transported. The beginning of the transaction is money in one account and the ending is money in another. The manner in which the funds were moved does not affect the ability to obtain tangible paper dollars or a bank check from the receiving account. If anything, the means of transfer here were essential to the fraudulent scheme.

Id. at 238. Other circuits have followed the reasoning in *Gilboe*. See United States v. Kroh, 896 F.2d 1524, 1528-29 (8th Cir. 1990); United States v. Goldberg, 830 F.2d 459, 466-67 (3d Cir. 1987); United States v. Wright, 791 F.2d 133, 135-37 (10th Cir. 1986); see also United States v. Kenngott, 840 F.2d 375, 380 (7th Cir. 1987) (citing *Gilboe* with approval). In all of these cases, the courts held that money was transferred across state lines within the meaning of §2314 because funds were actually accessible in one account prior to the transfer, and those funds were actually accessible in an out-of-state account after the transfer. The courts refused to accept the superficial characterization of the transfers as the mere transmittal of electronic impulses.

Similarly, in the instant case, Neidorf's conduct is not properly characterized as the mere transmission of electronic impulses. Through the use of his computer, Neidorf allegedly transferred proprietary business information—Bell South's E911 text file. Like the money in the case dealing with wire transfers of funds, the information in the E911 text file was accessible at Neidorf's computer terminal in Missouri before he transferred it, and the information was also accessible at the Lockport, Illinois computer bulletin board after Neidorf transferred it. Therefore, under *Gilboe*, *Kroh*, *Wright*, and *Goldberg*, the mere fact that the information actually crossed state lines via computer-generated electronic impulses does not defeat a charge under §2314.

The question this case presents, then, is not whether electronic impulses are "goods, wares, or merchandise" within the meaning of §2314, but whether the proprietary information contained in Bell South's E911 text file constitutes a "good, ware, or merchandise" within the purview of the statute. This court answers that question affirmatively. It is well-settled that when proprietary business information is affixed to some tangible medium, such as a piece of paper, it constitutes "goods, wares, or merchandise" within the meaning of §2314. See United States v. Greenwald, 479 F.2d 320, 322 (6th Cir.) (documents containing valuable chemical

ISSUE

formulae are "goods, wares, or merchandise" under §2314), *cert. denied*, 414 U.S. 854, 94 S. Ct. 154, 38 L. Ed.2d 104 (1973); United States v. Bottone, 365 F.2d 389, 393 (2d Cir.) (copies of documents describing a manufacturing process of patented drugs constitute a "good" under §2314), *cert. denied*, 385 U.S. 974, 87 S. Ct. 514, 17 L. Ed.2d 437 (1966); United States v. Lester, 282 F.2d 750, 754-55 (3d Cir. 1960) (copies of geophysical maps identifying oil deposits come within the purview of §2314), *cert. denied*, 364 U.S. 937, 81 S. Ct. 385, 5 L. Ed.2d 368 (1961); United States v. Seagraves, 265 F.2d 876 (3d Cir. 1959) (same facts as in *Lester*).

Therefore, in the instant case, if the information in Bell South's E911 text file had been affixed to a floppy disk, or printed out on a computer printer, then Neidorf's transfer of that information across state lines would clearly constitute the transfer of "goods, wares, or merchandise" within the meaning of §2314. This court sees no reason to hold differently simply because Neidorf stored the information inside computers instead of printing it out on paper. In either case, the information is in a transferrable, accessible, even salable form.

Tangible Form [margin annotation]

Neidorf argues in his brief that a §2314 charge cannot survive when the "thing" actually transferred never takes tangible form. A few courts have apparently adopted this position. For example, in United States v. Smith, 686 F.2d 234 (5th Cir. 1982), the court held that a copyright does not fit within the definition of "goods, wares, or merchandise" under §2314. The court ruled that in order to come within that definition, "[t]he 'thing' or 'item' must have some sort of tangible existence; it must be in the nature of 'personal property or chattels.'" *Id.* at 241. Similarly, in *Bottone, supra,* where the court held that copies of documents describing a manufacturing process for a patented drug constitute "goods, wares, or merchandise" under §2314, the court opined:

> To be sure, where no tangible objects were ever taken or transported, a court would be hard pressed to conclude that "goods" had been stolen and transported within the meaning of §2314; the statute would presumably not extend to the case where a carefully guarded secret was memorized, carried away in the recesses of a thievish mind and placed in writing only after a [state] boundary had been crossed.

365 F.2d at 393.

No tangibility Requirement [margin annotation]

Nevertheless, this court is not entirely convinced that tangibility is an absolute requirement of "goods, wares, or merchandise" under §2314. Congress enacted §2314 to extend the National Motor Vehicle Theft Act to cover all stolen property over a certain value ($5000) which is knowingly transported across state lines. See Dowling v. United States, 473 U.S. 207, 218-20, 105 S. Ct. 3127, 3133-35, 87 L. Ed.2d 152 (1985). In line with this broad congressional intent, courts have liberally construed the term "goods, wares, or merchandise" as "a general and comprehensive designation of such personal property and chattels as are ordinarily the subject of commerce." See United States v. Whaley, 788 F.2d 581, 582 (9th Cir.) (quoting *Seagraves,* 265 F.2d at 880), *cert. denied*, 479 U.S. 962, 107 S. Ct. 458, 93 L. Ed.2d 404 (1986). Reading a tangibility requirement into the definition of "goods, wares, or merchandise" might unduly restrict the scope of §2314, especially in this modern technological age. For instance, suppose the existence of a valuable gas, used as an anesthetic, which is colorless, odorless, and tasteless—totally imperceptible to the human senses. If this gas is stored in a tank in Indiana, and a trucker hooks up to the tank, releases the valuable gas into a storage tank on his truck, and then takes the gas to Illinois to sell it for a profit, is there no violation of §2314 simply because the gas is not technically tangible? This court is reluctant to believe that any court would construe §2314 so narrowly.

In any event, this court need not decide that issue to resolve this case, for even if tangibility is a requirement of "goods, wares or merchandise" under §2314, in this court's opinion the computer-stored business information in this case satisfies that requirement. Although not printed out on paper, a more conventional form of tangibility, the information in Bell South's E911 text file was allegedly stored on computer. Thus, by simply pressing a few buttons, Neidorf could recall that information from computer storage and view it on his computer terminal. The information was also accessible to others in the same fashion if they simply pressed the right buttons on their computer. This ability to access the information in viewable form from a reliable storage place differentiates this case from the mere memorization of a formula and makes this case more similar to cases like *Greenwald*, *Bottone*, *Seagraves*, and *Lester*, where proprietary information was also stored, but in a more traditional manner—on paper. The accessibility of the information in readable form from a particular storage place also makes the information tangible, transferable, salable and, in this court's opinion, brings it within the definition of "goods, wares, or merchandise" under §2314.

In order to sustain a charge against Neidorf under §2314, however, the government cannot simply allege that Neidorf transferred "goods, wares, or merchandise" across state boundaries; the government must also allege that Neidorf executed the transfer knowing the goods were "stolen, converted or taken by fraud." This requirement forms the basis for Neidorf's second challenge to Counts III and IV. Relying on Dowling v. United States, 473 U.S. 207, 105 S. Ct. 3127, 87 L. Ed.2d 152 (1985), Neidorf maintains that the §2314 charges should be dismissed because the "things" he allegedly transferred are not the type of property which is capable of being "stolen, converted or taken by fraud."

In *Dowling*, the government charged the defendant with violating §2314 by shipping "bootleg" and "pirated"[10] phonorecords across state lines. *Id.* at 212, 105 S. Ct. at 3130-31. The government argued that the shipments came within §2314 because the phonorecords embodied performances of copyrighted musical compositions which the defendant had no right to distribute. *Id.* at 214-15, 105 S. Ct. at 3131-32. The Court framed the issue in the case as follows:

> Dowling does not contest that he caused the shipment of goods in interstate commerce, or that the shipments had sufficient value to meet the monetary requirement. He argues, instead, that the goods shipped were not "stolen, converted or taken by fraud."
>
> . . . We must determine, therefore, whether phonorecords that include the performance of copyrighted musical compositions for the use of which no authorization has been sought or royalties paid are consequently "stolen, converted or taken by fraud" for purposes of §2314.

Id. at 214-16, 105 S. Ct. at 3131-32. The Court ruled that while the holder of a copyright possesses certain property rights which are protectible and enforceable

---

10. A "bootleg" phonorecord is an unauthorized copy of a commercially unreleased performance. A "pirated" phonorecord is an unauthorized copy of a performance already commercially released. *Dowling*, 473 U.S. at 209-10 n. 2, 105 S. Ct. at 3129 n. 2.

under copyright law, he does not own the type of possessory interest in an item of property which may be "stolen, converted or taken by fraud." *Id*. at 216-18, 105 S. Ct. at 3132-34. Thus, the Court held that §2314 does not apply to interstate shipments of "bootleg" and "pirated" phonorecords whose unauthorized distribution infringes on valid copyrights. *Id*. at 228-29, 105 S. Ct. at 3138-39.

Neidorf also cites United States v. Smith, 686 F.2d 234 (5th Cir. 1982), to support his argument. Like *Dowling*, *Smith* held that copyright infringement is not the equivalent of theft or conversion under §2314. *Id*. at 241. The instant case, however, is distinguishable from *Dowling* and *Smith*. This case involves the transfer of confidential, proprietary business information, not copyrights. As *Dowling* and *Smith* recognized, the copyright holder owns only a bundle of intangible rights which can be infringed, but not stolen or converted. The owner of confidential, proprietary business information, in contrast, possesses something which has clearly been recognized as an item of property. *Carpenter*, 108 S. Ct. at 320; *Keane*, 852 F.2d at 205. As such, it is certainly capable of being misappropriated, which, according to the indictment, is exactly what happened to the information in Bell South's E911 text file.

In his final gasp, Neidorf points out that in *Dowling*, the Court based its ruling partly on the fact that Congress passed the Copyright Act to deal exclusively with copyright infringements. The Court reasoned that applying §2314 to the infringement of copyrights would result in an unnecessary and unwarranted intrusion into an area already governed by the Copyright Act. 473 U.S. at 221-26, 105 S. Ct. at 3135-38. Neidorf makes a similar argument in this case. He notes that Congress has enacted a statute—the Computer Fraud and Abuse Act ("CFAA"), 18 U.S.C. §1030—which is specifically designed to address computer-related crimes, such as unauthorized computer access. Neidorf claims that the enactment of the CFAA precludes a finding that §2314 reaches his alleged conduct in this case.

The problem with Neidorf's argument, however, is that he does not cite, and this court is unable to find, anything in the legislative history of the CFAA which suggests that the statute was intended to be the exclusive law governing computer-related crimes, or that its enactment precludes the application of other criminal statutes to computer-related conduct. Therefore, the court rejects Neidorf's claim that applying §2314 to the instant case would undermine the Congressional intent behind the CFAA. Similarly, the court rejects Neidorf's bald assertion that the legislative history behind §2314 supports his argument. Nothing in the legislative history of §2314 prevents the court from finding that the information in Bell South's E911 text file was "stolen, converted or taken by fraud" as that term is used in §2314. Accordingly, Neidorf's motion to dismiss Counts III and IV is denied. . . .

COMMENTS AND QUESTIONS

1. The break-in to Bell South computers and subsequent appropriation of E911 information also led to a seizure of computers, files, and equipment from the offices of Steve Jackson Games (SJG). Secret Service agents believed that a copy of the E911 information was being stored on a bulletin board system on the company's computers in an account of the alleged perpetrator. Steve Jackson Games successfully sued the U.S. Secret Service for violating its rights under the Electronic

Communications Privacy Act. See Steve Jackson Games v. United States Secret Service, 816 F. Supp. 432 (W.D.Tex. 1993).

Yet, the case was not a total victory for SJG. The trial court had decided that the seizure of the SJG computer that contained the private electronic mail that had been sent to (stored on) the bulletin board but not read (retrieved) by the intended recipients did not constitute an unlawful "intercept" under the Federal Wiretap Act. The judge reasoned that because the Secret Service's acquisition of the contents of the electronic communications was not contemporaneous with the transmission of those communications, it had not "intercepted" them. The Fifth Circuit affirmed the lower court on this issue. See Steve Jackson Games v. United States Secret Service, 36 F.3d 457 (5th Cir. 1994). Most courts have followed *Steve Jackson Games* in reading the ECPA's definition of "intercept" narrowly, and applying only the lesser protections afforded against accessing "stored" communications. See Konop v. Hawaiian Airlines, discussed in Chapter 12, *supra.*

2. Two lawyers with considerable experience prosecuting computer crimes have offered an explanation as to why these crimes may be more difficult than traditional crimes for prosecutors to deal with. See Scott Charney & Kent Alexander, Computer Crime, 45 Emory L.J. 931, 940-941 (1996):

> The shift from a corporeal environment—where items are stored in a tangible form that can be physically carried, such as information written on paper—to an intangible, electronic environment means that computer crimes, and the methods used to investigate them, are no longer subject to traditional rules and constraints. Consider, for example, the way the crimes of theft and criminal mischief have changed. Before the advent of computer networks, the ability to steal information or damage property was to some extent determined by physical limitations. A burglar could only break so many windows and burglarize so many homes in a week. During each intrusion, he could take away only what he could carry. While this conduct is by no means trivial, the amount of property he could steal or the amount of damage he could cause was restricted by physical limitations.
>
> In the information age, these limitations no longer apply. Criminals seeking information stored in networked computers with dial-in access can access that information from virtually anywhere in the world. The quantity of information that can be stolen, or the amount of damage that can be caused by malicious programming code, may be limited only by the speed of the network and the criminal's equipment. Moreover, such conduct can very easily occur across state and national borders.
>
> The lack of physical boundaries not only creates opportunities for criminals, but raises novel issues for law enforcement personnel. For example, when agents seek a search warrant, Rule 41 of the Federal Rules of Criminal Procedure requires that they seek the warrant in the district where the property to be searched is located. In other words, if agents wish to search a file cabinet in lower Manhattan in New York City, they would apply for a warrant in the Southern District of New York.
>
> But suppose an informant indicates that she was working on her computer in lower Manhattan and saw that her company was keeping a second set of books in an effort to defraud shareholders and the Internal Revenue Service. Based upon this information, agents might get a warrant from the Southern District, enter the office, and copy this critical evidence. Although this would appear to be a straightforward case, what if the informant's computer was part of a local area network (LAN) whose server —the computer on which these records were stored—was actually located in New Jersey? Would a warrant issued in New York support such a seizure? Or suppose the offending company was a multinational corporation and the server was located in a

foreign country? What would be the international ramifications of executing a search on a foreign computer system without consulting that country's authorities?

The other major impact caused by the shift to intangibles is that many of the existing theft, damage, and extortion laws protect physical property. Thus, new crimes may need to be defined.

3. Computer crimes have given rise to some very interesting and well-written books. Among them are: Katie Hafner & John Markoff, Cyberpunk: Outlaws and Hackers on the Computer Frontier (1995); John Markoff & Tustomu Shimomura, Takedown: The Pursuit and Capture of Kevin Mitnick, America's Most Wanted Computer Outlaw by the Man Who Did It (1996); Bruce Sterling, The Hacker Crackdown: Law and Disorder on the Electronic Frontier (1993); Clifford Stoll, The Cuckoo's Egg: Tracking a Spy Through the Maze of Computer Espionage (1995).

4. Even when miscreants do not intend to commit computer crimes, they may use computers or other information technologies in the course of their endeavors. Because of this, law enforcement officials have sought legislative and voluntary industry adoption of technical infrastructures to enable them to engage in surveillance for law enforcement purposes. These officials have sometimes been successful in these efforts. See Communications Assistance for Law Enforcement Act, 47 U.S.C. §§1002-1005; Federal Communications Commission, Rep. No. ET-98-8, FCC Proposes Rules to Meet Technical Requirements of CALEA (Oct. 22, 1998). Some commentators express concerns about this and similar developments, in part because of their implications for privacy. See, e.g., Susan A. Friewald, Uncertain Privacy: Communications Attributes After the Digital Telephony Act, 69 S. Cal. L. Rev. 949 (1996).

5. In the wake of the events of September 11, 2001, Congress passed the USA PATRIOT Act, which expands the government's power to conduct surveillance and intelligence-gathering activity. The Act also creates a series of new computer crimes directed specifically at terrorism. For a discussion of the Act, see Orin S. Kerr, Internet Surveillance After the USA Patriot Act: The Big Brother That Isn't, 97 Nw. L. Rev. (forthcoming 2003).

6. The last several years have seen a steady growth in the number of computer crimes. Viruses have proliferated and grown more sophisticated. Fighting viruses is made more difficult by the growing number of executable files attached to e-mails. Computer hacking has also gotten easier, with the proliferation of "scripts" that enable even those with minimal technical knowledge to exploit weaknesses in computer security systems. Law enforcement authorities have increased their workload correspondingly. One author estimates that nearly 1000 cases are pending under the CFAA alone. A. Hugh Scott, Computer and Intellectual Property Crime: Federal and State Law 75 (2001).

Whether the increase in computer crime represents a new sort of illegal activity, or merely the transfer of existing criminal behavior to the new online environment, has been the matter of some debate. Katyal argues that the answer is a bit of both. He concludes that much about computer crime is indeed old wine in new bottles. Nonetheless, he identifies three differences between computer crime and other sorts of crime: (1) Computers reduce the cost of criminal activity, thus encouraging it; (2) computer crimes involve the unwitting participation of third parties such as ISPs and involuntary hosts for DDOS attacks; and (3) computer crimes (and law enforcement activities as well) are largely invisible to the public, and thus not subject to the traditional constraints of social norms. Neal Kumar Katyal, Criminal Law in Cyberspace, 149 U. Pa. L. Rev. 1003 (2001).

7. The CFAA has grown steadily in scope since it was first enacted. Originally passed to protect the federal government's computers from attack, the definition of a "protected computer" under the Act was expanded to cover any computer "which is used in interstate or foreign commerce or communication." 28 U.S.C. §1030(e)(2)(B). In the Internet age, this means any computer that can be connected to the Internet. Further while many provisions of the CFAA are quite narrowly tailored to particular harms, some are much broader. Section 1030(a)(4) makes it illegal to "access a protected computer without authorization or exceed authorized access" with an intent to defraud if the defendant obtains anything of value thereby. Even broader is section 1030(a)(2)(C), which makes it a crime to "intentionally access a protected computer without authorization or exceed authorized access" and obtain "information from any protected computer if the conduct involved an interstate or foreign communication." There is no requirement of obtaining value or causing harm, nor of deception. Accessing a computer from out of state and obtaining information without access is itself a crime under this provision.

For a discussion of the remarkable breadth of the CFAA, see Orin S. Kerr, The Troubling Trigger of Cybercrime (working paper 2002).

What does it mean to "exceed authorized access"? Suppose that an employee damages files that she is clearly entitled to access in the course of her job. Has she "exceeded authorized access" because the employer would have objected to the damage if it had known? Cf. Briggs v. State, 1998 WL 19913 (Md. 1998) (holding that an employee didn't violate a state "unauthorized access" law by locking up employer data with passwords, but not ruling on the question of exceeding authorized access).

Note on Civil Uses of the CFAA

While the Computer Fraud and Abuse Act was intended as a criminal law designed to punish computer hackers, the statute also creates a civil cause of action for anyone injured by unauthorized access to a networked computer. Victims can obtain injunctive relief and can also obtain monetary relief for economic loss in excess of $5,000. 28 U.S.C. §1030(g), (e)(8). Courts have generally held that this $5,000 includes not just damage to computers, but other economic loss occasioned by the illegal activity. See EF Cultural Travel BV v. Explorica, Inc., 274 F.3d 577 (1st Cir. 2001). And in 2001 Congress amended section 1030 to provide that lost profits were compensable under certain sections of the CFAA. 28 U.S.C. §1030(e)(11).

The goal of the civil remedies was to permit those injured by computer hackers or computer viruses to have some form of redress. And indeed, some courts have issued injunctions against computer hackers. See, e.g., YourNetDating LLC v. Mitchell, 88 F. Supp. 2d 870 (N.D. Ill. 2000). Because of the broad scope of the CFAA, however, its civil provisions have been used not just in cases involving computer hackers, but in all sorts of legal disputes between competitors. For example, in Register.com, Inc. v. Verio, Inc., 126 F. Supp.2d 238 (S.D.N.Y. 2000), the court found a violation of the CFAA by a marketing company that accessed the plaintiff's publicly available Web site and collected data that were free for everyone to use. The court held that the defendant had violated the plaintiff's terms and conditions of use (posted on the Web site, but not included in a clickwrap license), and so had "exceeded authorized access" in violation of section 1030(a)(2)(C). The result was to turn what was really a breach of contract claim—and a fairly weak one at that—into a tort and indeed potentially a crime.[3]

The civil provisions of the CFAA have been used in a variety of other disputes as well, some quite far removed from computer hacking. The plaintiffs in In re Pharmatrak Privacy Litigation, discussed in Chapter 12, *supra,* claimed that the defendants' collection of personally identifiable information about them from pharmaceutical company Web sites violated the CFAA. The court rejected the claim, but only because it concluded that the plaintiffs could not show $5,000 worth of actual economic loss from the use of their personal information. The court appeared to accept the plaintiffs' claim that taking information from the pharmaceutical companies' Web sites violated the CFAA. *Accord* In re Intuit Privacy Litigation, 138 F. Supp.2d 1272 (C.D. Cal. 2001). And in North Texas Preventive Imaging LLC v. Eisenberg, 1996 WL 1359212 (C.D. Cal. Aug. 19, 1996), the court held that a purchaser of software could state a claim under the CFAA against the vendor, who had included a "logic bomb" in an upgrade disk that let the vendor disable the software if the purchaser did not continue to pay. See also Shaw v. Toshiba Am. Info. Sys., 91 F. Supp.2d 926 (E.D. Tex. 1999) (sale of defective floppy disk controllers that damaged data on computers in which they are installed could violate the CFAA).[4]

The breadth of the CFAA means that it may also be used in cases that involve the theft of trade secrets using a computer. For example, in Shurgard Storage Center v. Safeguard Self Storage, Inc., 119 F. Supp.2d 1121, 1125 (W.D. Wash. 2000), the court held that an employee exceeded his authorization and therefore violated the CFAA when he "sent an e-mail to a competitor containing his employer's information."

COMMENTS AND QUESTIONS

1. Should the CFAA include a civil cause of action at all? Should it apply to the broader provisions of the statute, such as §1030(a)(2)(C) and (a)(4)? Or does application of the CFAA permit plaintiffs to bypass the elements of other civil claims? For example, in order to show misappropriation of trade secrets Shurgard would need to demonstrate that the information its employee took was in fact a secret. But there is no such requirement in the CFAA.

2. While the CFAA is the federal statute that most specifically targets computer crime, there is a host of other statutes that can be brought to bear against computer hackers. First, all 50 states and the District of Columbia have their own statutes targeting computer crime. For a complete list, see A. Hugh Scott, Com-

---

3. By contrast, some state statutes, such as Tex. Penal Code §33.01, require that the victim make it clear that access is unauthorized and have a security system in place before access can trigger the criminal law.

4. Sale of defective computer goods more commonly presents ordinary issues of tort and contract law. For a proposed expansion of tort law to create a cause of action against those who run insecure computer systems that can be hijacked by hackers in "distributed denial of service" attacks, see Stephen E. Henderson & Matthew E. Yarbrough, Suing the Insecure?: A Duty of Care in Cyberspace, 32 N. Mex. L. Rev. 11 (2002).

puter and Intellectual Property Crime: Federal and State Statutes (2001). These state statutes are designed to cover much of the same conduct prohibited in the CFAA. State statutes are potentially subject to preemption, however, particularly if they are applied to prohibit the copying of copyrightable information. See, e.g., Rosciszewski v. Arete Assocs., 1 F.3d 225 (4th Cir. 1993).

Second, there is a host of specific federal statutes that target particular types of conduct that may occur either online or offline, but that have been used to catch computer criminals. Among the more significant are:

- The Economic Espionage Act, 18 U.S.C. §1831 *et seq.*, makes it illegal to steal trade secrets by various means, either for private use or on behalf of a foreign government.
- The No Electronic Theft Act, 17 U.S.C. §506(a), passed in 1997, amended existing criminal laws against copyright infringement to punish those who committed copyright infringement with no purpose of financial gain if the aggregate loss to the copyright owner exceeded $1,000. The purpose of the Act was to change the result in cases like United States v. LaMacchia, 871 F. Supp. 535 (D. Mass. 1994), which held that a defendant did not commit a crime unless he acted for purposes of financial gain.
- State and federal gambling statutes make it illegal to transmit bets in foreign or interstate commerce. See 18 U.S.C. §1084. While Congress has tried and failed to prohibit Internet gambling specifically, the courts have held that online gambling is illegal in most states, and that online gambling that occurs between the U.S. and another country violates federal law. See, e.g., United States v. Cohen, 260 F.3d 68 (2d Cir. 2001) (convicting a defendant of running a sports betting service in Antigua—where gambling is legal—because his clients placed bets from states where gambling was illegal).
- The Child Sexual Exploitation and Pornography statute, 18 U.S.C. §2251 *et seq.*, has been used to catch a number of defendants guilty of both possessing and distributing child pornography. Prosecution of child pornography in the computer context raises at least two interesting issues. First, part of the justification for punishing even the mere possession of child pornography is that such pornography not only is morally offensive but necessarily relies on injury to children. That rationale is undercut in the case of digitally altered child pornography, which appears to but does not actually depict sexual acts with children. In Ashcroft v. Free Speech Coalition, 122 S. Ct. 1389 (2002), the Court struck down a law banning possession of virtual child pornography, concluding that it must be treated like obscene material involving adults (for which creation and distribution, but not mere possession, can be made illegal). Second, the definition of "possession" has become murkier in the computer era. Pop-up Internet sites and automatic background downloads make it possible that a computer user may unwittingly end up with child pornography on his computer after having been "mousetrapped" into a series of porn sites. In United States v. Tucker, 150 F. Supp.2d 1263 (D. Utah 2001), *aff'd* 305 F.3d 1193 (10th Cir. 2002), the defendant admitted that he had viewed child pornography online, but claimed that he did not know that the images were downloaded to his computer, and therefore did not knowingly "possess" them within the meaning of the statute. The court rejected the defense because it concluded that the defendant was computer-savvy and likely knew of the existence of the files, based

in part on their location on his computer. But it held open the possibility that a defendant who did not knowingly store illegal files on his computer might not violate the law.

Third, there are a number of catch-all statutes that can be applied to online activity. Notable here are the mail and wire fraud statutes, 18 U.S.C. §§1341, 1343, and the National Stolen Property Act, 18 U.S.C. §2314-2315. While these statutes are quite broadly written, there is some question as to how well they apply to computer crimes. Pooley, Lemley, and Toren note these limitations in James H. A. Pooley et al., Understanding the Economic Espionage Act of 1996, 5 Tex. Intell. Prop. L. Rev. 177 (1997):

> The ITSP provides, in pertinent part, as follows:
>
> > Whoever transports, transmits, or transfers in interstate or foreign commerce any goods, wares, merchandise, securities or money, of the value of $5,000 or more, knowing the same to have been stolen, converted or taken by fraud . . .
> > Shall be fined not more than $10,000 or imprisoned not more than ten years, or both.
>
> This statute was enacted by Congress in 1934 to fill an enforcement gap in the National Motor Vehicle Theft Act. Both statutes were intended to aid the states in their detection and punishment of criminals who sought to evade state authorities by fleeing in stolen vehicles or with stolen property over state lines. However, since ITSP was drafted at a time when information did not have the economic value it has today and at a time when information could not be quickly copied and instantaneously transmitted to any location in the world, it is not particularly well suited to deal with the theft of intangible property, such as trade secrets. Moreover, in light of United States v. Brown,[6] it is uncertain whether ITSP can be used to charge a person with theft of trade secrets where no tangible property was transferred across state lines. In other words, *Brown* casts serious doubt on whether the phrase "goods, wares and merchandise" contained in section 2314 covers intangible property.
>
> The grand jury indicted Brown for violating section 2314 by transporting computer programs, software and source code interstate from Georgia to New Mexico. Brown moved to dismiss the indictment arguing that under United States v. Dowling,[7] the government failed to allege that he transferred in interstate commerce "physical goods, wares [or] merchandise" within the meaning of section 2314. The government admitted that it would not be able to prove that the defendant made a copy of the source code using, for example, the company's hard disk or that the defendant had in his possession any tangible property belonging to the company. The trial court ruled that the source code by itself "is not the type of property which is contemplated . . . within the language of the statute, goods, wares or merchandise."
>
> The appellate court agreed, citing *Dowling*. In *Dowling*, the defendant was convicted of violating section 2314 following his interstate distribution of bootleg Elvis Presley records. The Supreme Court reversed the conviction and held that it was not Congress' intention that ITSP function as a criminalization of copyright infringement. The Supreme Court emphasized that its decision did not deal with a situation in which the initial procurement was accomplished by theft or fraud and that the courts have never required that the items stolen and transported remain in entirely unaltered form. The Court emphasized, however, that:

6. 925 F.2d 1301 (10th Cir. 1991).
7. 473 U.S. 207 (1985).

[T]hese cases and others prosecuted under §2314 have always involved physical 'goods, wares [or] merchandise' that have themselves been 'stolen, converted or taken by fraud.' This basic element comports with the common-sense meaning of the statutory language: by requiring that the 'goods, wares [or] merchandise' be 'the same' as those 'stolen, converted or taken by fraud' the provision seems clearly to contemplate a physical identity between the items unlawfully obtained and those eventually transported, and hence some prior physical taking of the subject goods.[8]

The *Brown* court, quoting this language, held that "[p]urely intellectual property" such as the source code appropriated by the defendants is not the type of property covered by section 2314: "It can be represented physically, such as through writing on a page, but the underlying, intellectual property itself, remains intangible" and, thus, "cannot constitute goods, wares, merchandise which have been stolen, converted or taken within the meaning of sections 2314 or 2315." The *Brown* court also stated that the United States v. Riggs decision [reprinted above] was in error in light of the Supreme Court's decision in *Dowling. . . .*

An analysis of the two decisions strongly suggests that *Brown* and not *Riggs* was correctly decided. In particular, if the *Riggs* rationale was followed it would lead to some clearly unintended results. Specifically, the *Riggs* court opined that it was not necessary to resolve whether or not the E911 file constitutes goods, wares or merchandise, since the defendant and others had the ability to "access the information in viewable form from a reliable storage place which also makes the information tangible, transferable, salable and, in this court's opinion brings it within the definition of 'goods, wares, or merchandise' under section 2314." Here, the *Riggs* court was arguably elevating form over substance. In other words, there is no doubt that defendants Riggs and Neidorf misappropriated the computerized text file. However, section 2314 is not directed towards the act of theft, but to criminalize interstate *transfer* of stolen goods, wares or merchandise. The computer text file was transmitted across interstate lines by Riggs in the form of electronic signals and only became tangible property when the electronic signals were printed on paper. Thus, the court in *Riggs* did not address the real issue, whether purely intangible property is goods, wares or merchandise, but instead determined that the acts of the defendants should be covered by section 2314 because logically, most types of stolen intangible property should not be treated differently from stolen tangible property. If this reasoning were applied to *all* intangible property, it would lead to results clearly not foreseen or intended by Congress. For example, accessing a computer from out of state would necessarily involve the transfer of property across state lines—there would be no difference, in other words, between "access" and "transfer". Further, section 2314 would apply under certain circumstances, to the interstate transportation of patent-infringing goods. In other words, if a person "steals" an invention that is protected by a patent and then ships in interstate commerce an article manufactured in accord with the stolen patented specifications, he or she could be successfully prosecuted under §2314 according to the reasoning of the *Riggs* court. Congress surely did not intend to criminalize patent infringement through the back door.

Pooley et al. are more sanguine about the use of the wire fraud statute:

The broader scope results from the use of the word "property" in section 1341 and section 1343 as compared to the far narrower phrase "goods, wares and merchandise"

8. 473 U.S. at 216.

used in section 2314. For example, in United States v. Seidlitz,[9] the defendant used his knowledge of his former employer's computer system to enter the computer system and download computer data. The appellate court upheld the trial court's determination that the software qualified as property within the meaning of the wire fraud statute. The court held that the software was a trade secret, even though similar programs were in the public domain, because defendant's former employer had invested substantial sums to modify the system for his own needs, it was of competitive value and the employer took steps to prevent persons other than clients and employees from using the system. Accordingly, there was sufficient evidence from which a jury could conclude that information stored in the computer system was "property" as used in section 1343.

Nonetheless, they point out that not all conduct of interest will meet the requirements of this statute either.

3. Computer crime cases raise a host of procedural issues as well. Many of these have to do with the application of the Fourth Amendment to searches and seizures of computers. See, e.g., United States v. Kennedy, 81 F. Supp.2d 1103 (D. Kan. 2000) (search of defendant's online computer files by an anonymous caller and the ISP he alerted did not trigger the Fourth Amendment prohibition against unreasonable searches and seizures). These cases in turn depend on the existence of a reasonable expectation of privacy, an issue discussed in detail in Chapter 12, *supra*.

United States v. Ivanov
United States District Court for the District of Connecticut
175 F. Supp.2d 367 (D. Conn. 2001)

THOMPSON, District Judge.

Defendant Aleksey Vladimirovich Ivanov ("Ivanov") has been indicted, in a superseding indictment, on charges of conspiracy, computer fraud and related activity, extortion and possession of unauthorized access devices. Ivanov has moved to dismiss the indictment on the grounds that the court lacks subject matter jurisdiction. Ivanov argues that because it is alleged that he was physically located in Russia when the offenses were committed, he can not be charged with violations of United States law. For the reasons set forth below, the defendant's motion is being denied.

I. Background

Online Information Bureau, Inc. ("OIB"), the alleged victim in this case, is a Connecticut corporation based in Vernon, Connecticut. It is an "e-commerce" business which assists retail and Internet merchants by, among other things, hosting their websites and processing their credit card data and other financial transactions. In this capacity, OIB acts as a financial transaction "clearinghouse", by aggregating and assisting in the debiting or crediting of funds against each account for thousands of retail and Internet purchasers and vendors. In doing so, OIB collects and

9. 589 F.2d 152 (4th Cir. 1978).

maintains customer credit card information, merchant account numbers, and related financial data from credit card companies and other financial institutions.

The government alleges that Ivanov "hacked" into OIB's computer system and obtained the key passwords to control OIB's entire network. The government contends that in late January and early February 2000, OIB received from Ivanov a series of unsolicited e-mails indicating that the defendant had obtained the "root" passwords for certain computer systems operated by OIB. A "root" password grants its user access to and control over an entire computer system, including the ability to manipulate, extract, and delete any and all data. Such passwords are generally reserved for use by the system administrator only.

The government claims that Ivanov then threatened OIB with the destruction of its computer systems (including its merchant account database) and demanded approximately $10,000 for his assistance in making those systems secure. It claims, for example, that on February 3, 2000, after his initial solicitations had been rebuffed, Ivanov sent the following e-mail to an employee of OIB:

> [name redacted], now imagine please Somebody hack you network (and not notify you about this), he download Atomic software with more than 300 merchants, transfer money, and after this did 'rm-rf/'[1] and after this you company be ruined. I don't want this, and because this i notify you about possible hack in you network, if you want you can hire me and im allways be check security in you network. What you think about this?

The government contends that Ivanov's extortionate communications originated from an e-mail account at Lightrealm.com, an Internet Service Provider based in Kirkland, Washington. It contends that while he was in Russia, Ivanov gained access to the Lightrealm computer network and that he used that system to communicate with OIB, also while he was in Russia. Thus, each e-mail sent by Ivanov was allegedly transmitted from a Lightrealm.com computer in Kirkland, Washington through the Internet to an OIB computer in Vernon, Connecticut, where the e-mail was opened by an OIB employee.

The parties agree that the defendant was physically located in Russia (or one of the other former Soviet Bloc countries) when, it is alleged, he committed the offenses set forth in the superseding indictment.

The superseding indictment comprises eight counts. Count One charges that beginning in or about December 1999, or earlier, the defendant and others conspired to commit the substantive offenses charged in Counts Two through Eight of the indictment, in violation of 18 U.S.C. §371. Count Two charges that the defendant, knowingly and with intent to defraud, accessed protected computers owned by OIB and by means of this conduct furthered a fraud and obtained something of value, in violation of 18 U.S.C. §§2, 1030(a)(4) and 1030(c)(3)(A). Count Three charges that the defendant intentionally accessed protected computers owned by OIB and thereby obtained information, which conduct involved interstate and foreign communications and was engaged in for purposes of financial gain and in furtherance of a criminal act, in violation of 18 U.S.C. §§2, 1030(a)(2)(C) and 1030(c)(2)(B). Counts Four and Five do not pertain to this defendant.

---

1. An individual with "root access" who inputs the UNIX command "rm-rf/" will delete all files on the network server, including all operating system software.

Count Six charges that the defendant transmitted in interstate and foreign commerce communications containing a threat to cause damage to protected computers owned by OIB, in violation of 18 U.S.C. §§1030(a)(7) and 1030(c)(3)(A). Count Seven charges that the defendant obstructed, delayed and affected commerce, and attempted to obstruct, delay and affect commerce, by means of extortion by attempting to obtain property from OIB with OIB's consent, inducing such consent by means of threats to damage OIB and its business unless OIB paid the defendant money and hired the defendant as a security consultant, in violation of 18 U.S.C. §1951(a). Count Eight charges that the defendant, knowingly and with intent to defraud, possessed unauthorized access devices, which conduct affected interstate and foreign commerce, in violation of 18 U.S.C. §§1029(a)(3).

II. Discussion

The defendant and the government agree that when Ivanov allegedly engaged in the conduct charged in the superseding indictment, he was physically present in Russia and using a computer there at all relevant times. Ivanov contends that for this reason, charging him under the Hobbs Act, 18 U.S.C. §1951, under the Computer Fraud and Abuse Act, 18 U.S.C. §1030, and under the access device statute, 18 U.S.C. §1029, would in each case require extraterritorial application of that law and such application is impermissible. The court concludes that it has jurisdiction, first, because the intended and actual detrimental effects of Ivanov's actions in Russia occurred within the United States, and second, because each of the statutes under which Ivanov was charged with a substantive offense was intended by Congress to apply extraterritorially.

A. The Intended and Actual Detrimental Effects of the Charged Offenses Occurred Within the United States

As noted by the court in United States v. Muench, 694 F.2d 28 (2d Cir. 1982), "[t]he intent to cause effects within the United States . . . makes it reasonable to apply to persons outside United States territory a statute which is not expressly extraterritorial in scope." *Id.* at 33. "It has long been a commonplace of criminal liability that a person may be charged in the place where the evil results, though he is beyond the jurisdiction when he starts the train of events of which that evil is the fruit." United States v. Steinberg, 62 F.2d 77, 78 (2d Cir. 1932). "[T]he Government may punish a defendant in the same manner as if [he] were present in the jurisdiction when the detrimental effects occurred." Marc Rich & Co., A.G. v. United States, 707 F.2d 663, 666 (2d Cir. 1983).

The Supreme Court has quoted with approval the following language from Moore's International Law Digest:

> The principle that a man, who outside of a country willfully puts in motion a force to take effect in it, is answerable at the place where the evil is done, is recognized in the criminal jurisprudence of all countries. And the methods which modern invention has furnished for the performance of criminal acts in that manner has made this principle one of constantly growing importance and of increasing frequency of application.

Ford v. United States, 273 U.S. 593, 623, 47 S. Ct. 531, 71 L. Ed. 793 (1927). Moreover, the court noted in *Rich* that:

> [I]t is certain that the courts of many countries, even of countries which have given their criminal legislation a strictly territorial character, interpret criminal law in the sense that offences, the authors of which at the moment of commission are in the territory of another State, are nevertheless to be regarded as having been committed in the national territory, if one of the constituent elements of the offence, and more especially its effects, have taken place there. *The S.S. Lotus,* 1927 P.C.I.J., ser. A, No. 10, at 23, *reprinted in* 2 Hudson, World Court Reports, 23, 38 (1935).

Rich, 707 F.2d at 666.

Here, all of the intended and actual detrimental effects of the substantive offenses Ivanov is charged with in the indictment occurred within the United States. In Counts Two and Three, the defendant is charged with accessing OIB's computers. Those computers were located in Vernon, Connecticut. The fact that the computers were accessed by means of a complex process initiated and controlled from a remote location does not alter the fact that the accessing of the computers, i.e. part of the detrimental effect prohibited by the statute, occurred at the place where the computers were physically located, namely OIB's place of business in Vernon, Connecticut.

Count Two charges further that Ivanov obtained something of value when he accessed OIB's computers, that "something of value" being the data obtained from OIB's computers. In order for Ivanov to violate §1030(a)(4), it was necessary that he do more than merely access OIB's computers and view the data. See United States v. Czubinski, 106 F.3d 1069, 1078 (1st Cir. 1997) ("[M]erely viewing information cannot be deemed the same as obtaining something of value for purposes of this statute." . . . "[T]his section should apply to those who steal information through unauthorized access. . . . "). The indictment charges that Ivanov did more than merely gain unauthorized access and view the data. Ivanov allegedly obtained root access to the OIB computers located in Vernon, Connecticut. Once Ivanov had root access to the computers, he was able to control the data, e.g., credit card numbers and merchant account numbers, stored in the OIB computers; Ivanov could copy, sell, transfer, alter, or destroy that data. That data is intangible property of OIB. See Carpenter v. United States, 484 U.S. 19, 25, 108 S. Ct. 316, 98 L. Ed.2d 275 (1987) (noting that the "intangible nature [of confidential business information] does not make it any less 'property' protected by the mail and wire fraud statutes."). "In determining where, in the case of intangibles, possession resides, the measure of control exercised is the deciding factor." New York Credit Men's Ass'n v. Mfrs. Disc. Corp., 147 F.2d 885, 887 (2d Cir. 1945).

At the point Ivanov gained root access to OIB's computers, he had complete control over that data, and consequently, had possession of it. That data was in OIB's computers. Since Ivanov possessed that data while it was in OIB's computers in Vernon, Connecticut, the court concludes that he obtained it, for purposes of §1030(a)(4), in Vernon, Connecticut. The fact that Ivanov is charged with obtaining OIB's valuable data by means of a complex process initiated and controlled from a remote location, and that he subsequently moved that data to a computer located in Russia, does not alter the fact that at the point when Ivanov first possessed that data, it was on OIB's computers in Vernon, Connecticut.

Count Three charges further that when he accessed OIB's computers, Ivanov obtained information from protected computers. The analysis as to the location at which Ivanov obtained the information referenced in this count is the same as the analysis as to the location at which he obtained the "something of value" referenced in Count Two. Thus, as to both Counts Two and Three, it is charged that the balance of the detrimental effect prohibited by the pertinent statute, i.e., Ivanov's obtaining something of value or obtaining information, also occurred within the United States.

Count Six charges that Ivanov transmitted a threat to cause damage to protected computers. The detrimental effect prohibited by §1030(a)(7), namely the receipt by an individual or entity of a threat to cause damage to a protected computer, occurred in Vernon, Connecticut because that is where OIB was located, where it received the threat, and where the protected computers were located. The analysis is the same as to Count Seven, the charge under the Hobbs Act.

Count Eight charges that Ivanov knowingly and with intent to defraud possessed over ten thousand unauthorized access devices, i.e., credit card numbers and merchant account numbers. For the reasons discussed above, although it is charged that Ivanov later transferred this intangible property to Russia, he first possessed it while it was on OIB's computers in Vernon, Connecticut. Had he not possessed it here, he would not have been able to transfer it to his computer in Russia. Thus, the detrimental effect prohibited by the statute occurred within the United States.

Finally, Count One charges that Ivanov and others conspired to commit each of the substantive offenses charged in the indictment. The Second Circuit has stated that "the jurisdictional element should be viewed for purposes of the conspiracy count exactly as we view it for purposes of the substantive offense. . . ." United States v. Blackmon, 839 F.2d 900, 910 (2d Cir. 1988) (internal citations and quotation marks omitted). See also United States v. Kim, 246 F.3d 186, 191, n. 2 (2d Cir. 2001) (noting that jurisdiction over a conspiracy charge depends upon jurisdiction over the underlying substantive charge). Federal jurisdiction over a conspiracy charge "is established by proof that the accused planned to commit a substantive offense which, if attainable, would have violated a federal statute, and that at least one overt act has been committed in furtherance of the conspiracy." United States v. Giordano, 693 F.2d 245, 249 (2d Cir. 1982). Here, Ivanov is charged with planning to commit substantive offenses in violation of federal statutes, and it is charged that at least one overt act was committed in furtherance of the conspiracy. As discussed above, the court has jurisdiction over the underlying substantive charges. Therefore, the court has jurisdiction over the conspiracy charge, at a minimum, to the extent it relates to Counts Two, Three, Six, Seven or Eight.

Accordingly, the court concludes that it has subject matter jurisdiction over each of the charges against Ivanov, whether or not the statutes under which the substantive offenses are charged are intended by Congress to apply extraterritorially, because the intended and actual detrimental effects of the substantive offenses Ivanov is charged with in the indictment occurred within the United States.

B. Intended Extraterritorial Application

The defendant's motion should also be denied because, as to each of the statutes under which the defendant has been indicted for a substantive offense, there is clear evidence that the statute was intended by Congress to apply extraterritorially. This fact is evidenced by both the plain language and the legislative history of each of these statutes.

There is a presumption that Congress intends its acts to apply only within the United States, and not extraterritorially. However, this "presumption against extraterritoriality" may be overcome by showing "clear evidence of congressional intent to apply a statute beyond our borders. . . ." U.S. v. Gatlin, 216 F.3d 207, 211 (2d Cir. 2000). "Congress has the authority to enforce its laws beyond the territorial boundaries of the United States. Whether Congress has in fact exercised that authority in [a particular case] is a matter of statutory construction." Equal Employment Opportunity Comm. v. Arabian American Oil Co., 499 U.S. 244, 248, 111 S. Ct. 1227, 113 L. Ed.2d 274 (1991) (internal citations omitted) (*"ArAmCo "*).

The defendant is charged with substantive offenses in violation of 18 U.S.C. §1951, 18 U.S.C. §1030 and 18 U.S.C. §1029, and with conspiracy in violation of 18 U.S.C. §371. . . .

2. 18 U.S.C. §1030: The Computer Fraud and Abuse Act

The Computer Fraud and Abuse Act ("CFAA") was amended in 1996 by Pub. L. No. 104-294, 110 Stat. 3491, 3508. The 1996 amendments made several changes that are relevant to the issue of extraterritoriality, including a change in the definition of "protected computer" so that it included any computer "which is used in interstate *or foreign* commerce or communication." 18 U.S.C. §1030(e)(2)(B) (emphasis added). The 1996 amendments also added subsections (a)(2)(C) and (a)(7), which explicitly address "interstate or foreign commerce", and subsection (e)(9), which added to the definition of "government entity" the clause "any foreign country, and any state, province, municipality or other political subdivision of a foreign country".

The plain language of the statute, as amended, is clear. Congress intended the CFAA to apply to computers used "in interstate or foreign commerce or communication." The defendant argues that this language is ambiguous. The court disagrees. The Supreme Court has often stated that "a statute ought, upon the whole, to be so construed that, if it can be prevented, no clause, sentence, or word shall be superfluous, void, or insignificant." Regions Hosp. v. Shalala, 522 U.S. 448, 467, 118 S. Ct. 909, 139 L. Ed.2d 895 (1998) (internal citations and quotation marks omitted). In order for the word "foreign" to have meaning, and not be superfluous, it must mean something other than "interstate". In other words, "foreign" in this context must mean international. Thus, Congress has clearly manifested its intent to apply §1030 to computers used either in interstate or in foreign commerce.

The legislative history of the CFAA supports this reading of the plain language of the statute. The Senate Judiciary Committee issued a report explaining its reasons for adopting the 1996 amendments. S.Rep. No. 357, 104th Congr., 2d Sess. (1996). In that report, the Committee specifically noted its concern that the statute as it existed prior to the 1996 amendments did not cover "computers used in foreign communications or commerce, despite the fact that hackers are often foreign-based." *Id.* at 4. The Committee cited two specific cases in which foreign-based hackers had infiltrated computer systems in the United States, as examples of the kind of situation the amendments were intended to address:

For example, the 1994 intrusion into the Rome Laboratory at Grifess Air Force Base in New York, was perpetrated by a 16-year-old hacker in the United Kingdom. More recently, in March 1996, the Justice Department tracked down a young Argentinean man who had broken into Harvard University's computers from Buenos Aires and used those computers as a staging ground to hack into many other computer sites, including the Defense Department and NASA.

Id. at 4-5. Congress has the power to apply its statutes extraterritorially, and in the case of 18 U.S.C. §1030, it has clearly manifested its intention to do so. . . .

4. 18 U.S.C. §371: The Conspiracy Statute

The Second Circuit has recently noted that where the court has jurisdiction over the underlying substantive criminal counts against a defendant, the court also has jurisdiction over the conspiracy counts. See *Kim,* 246 F.3d at 191, n. 2. A court may "infer[ ] the extra-territorial reach of conspiracy statutes on the basis of a finding that the underlying substantive statute reached extra-territorial offenses, even though the conspiracy charges came under separate code sections. . . ." United States v. Evans, 667 F. Supp. 974, 981 (S.D.N.Y. 1987) (internal quotation marks and citations omitted). See also United States v. Yousef, 927 F. Supp. 673, 682 (S.D.N.Y. 1996) ("Extraterritorial jurisdiction over a conspiracy charge depends on whether extraterritorial jurisdiction exists as to the underlying substantive crime.") Because the court finds that each of the underlying substantive statutes in this case was intended by Congress to apply extraterritorially, it also finds that it has jurisdiction over the conspiracy charge.

IV. Conclusion

For the reasons set forth above, the defendant's Motion to Dismiss for Lack of Subject Matter Jurisdiction is hereby DENIED.

It is so ordered.

COMMENTS AND QUESTIONS

1. Is it really plausible to say that Ivanov possessed the information "in Connecticut," triggering the U.S. computer crime laws? Isn't the court's real holding that U.S. law can be applied to conduct that occurs outside the United States as long as the victim resides in the United States? Is that the right result as a policy matter? Note that the Russian government has recently indicted U.S. law enforcement officials for conducting a computer crime investigation that involved hacking into the computer of a suspected criminal in Russia. If what Ivanov did violates U.S. law, does it follow that Russian law must apply to "hackbacks" from the United States?

2. The 2001 USA PATRIOT Act expanded the reach of the CFAA to explicitly cover computers located outside the United States that affect interstate or foreign commerce or communication. Does this suggest that the court was correct in

Ivanov? Or does it suggest on the contrary that the old version of the Act should not have reached conduct that occurred on a Russian computer?

3. An alternative to extraterritorial application of U.S. laws is to conclude some sort of international treaty on computer crime. In late 2001, the Council of Europe concluded a comprehensive Convention on Cybercrime, E.T.S. 185 (Nov. 23, 2001) (the "Budapest Convention"). The Budapest Convention requires member states to prohibit unauthorized access to computers, interception of data, and computer-related fraud. It also provides for the punishment of specific offenses such as distribution of child pornography and copyright infringement.

14

Electronic Commerce

A. BACKGROUND ON ELECTRONIC COMMERCE

Electronic commerce is big business. A few years ago, ecommerce was an interesting concept, but there was not much substance to it. By 1999, it had become the hottest thing around. Not only were consumers buying an enormous volume of goods over the Internet, but business-to-business ecommerce had taken off as well. Even with the .com collapse of 2001, economic transactions over the Internet have continued to increase.

The "law of electronic commerce" is a vague and poorly defined thing. In some senses, it is no different from the law of commerce generally. Contract disputes, tax issues, and payment systems each have their own legal infrastructure, and in large part applying law to ecommerce is simply a matter of applying those rules to a new environment. At this writing, there are very few reported ecommerce cases, but that doesn't mean there is no law.

Ecommerce is not all old wine in new bottles, however. Some truly interesting new developments have begun to challenge the law in a variety of ways. In this section, we introduce the reader to a number of these challenges. Because of the embryonic state of development of the law of ecommerce, this section offers more speculation—and less law—than any other part of the book.

We begin with some ideas about how ecommerce might differ from traditional business models.

*J. Bradford De Long & A. Michael
Froomkin, The Next Economy?*
Deborah Hurley et al., eds., Internet Publishing and Beyond: The
Economics of Digital Information and Intellectual Property
(Cambridge, MIT Press, 1999)

. . . "Technological" Prerequisites of the Market

Modern technologies are beginning to undermine the features that make the Invisible Hand of the market system an effective and efficient system for organizing production and distribution. The case for the market system has always rested on three pillars: call the first excludability, the ability of sellers to force consumers to become buyers and thus to pay for what they use; call the second rivalry, a structure of costs in which two cannot partake as cheaply as one, and in which producing enough for two million people uses up at least twice as many resources as producing enough for one million people; call the third transparency, that individuals can see clearly what they need and what is for sale so that they truly know what they wish to buy.

All three of these pillars fit the economy of Adam Smith's day pretty well. They fit much of today's economy pretty well too—although the fit for the telecommunications and information processing industries is less satisfactory. They will fit tomorrow's economy less well than today's. And there is every indication that they will fit the twenty-first century economy relatively poorly. As we look at developments along the leading technological edge of the economy, we can see what used to be second-order "externality" corrections to the Invisible Hand becoming first-order phenomena. And we can see the Invisible Hand of the competitive market working less and less well in an increasing number of areas. This result is particularly surprising when one considers that most economic theory suggests that things which make information cheaper and more accessible should generally reduce friction in competitive markets, not gum up the works.

Excludability

In information-based sectors of the next economy the owner of a commodity will no longer be able to easily and cheaply exclude others from using or enjoying the commodity. Digital data is cheap and easy to copy. Methods exist to make copying more difficult, but they add expense and complexity. Without excludability the relationship between producer and consumer is much more a gift-exchange than a purchase-and-sale relationship. The appropriate paradigm is then an NPR fund-raising drive. There is no reason to presume that non-excludable commodities will get into the hands of the consumers who value them the most. And—with compensation to the producer determined not by the purchase-and-sale exchange of money for value but by the user's feelings of moral obligation to the producer—there is no reason to expect that production will be as high as it should be to maximize social welfare.

If goods are not excludable then rather than sell things, people simply help themselves. If the taker feels like it, he or she may make a "pledge" to support the producer. Perhaps the average pledge will be large enough that producers cover their costs. Many people seem to feel a moral obligation to tip cabdrivers and waiters and to contribute to National Public Radio. But without excludability it is hard to believe that the (voluntary) payments as a matter of grace from consumers to producers will be large enough to encourage the optimal level of production. Indeed, most of what we call "rule of law" consists of a legal system that enforces excludability—such enforcement of excludability ("protection of my property rights," even when the commodity is simply sitting there unused and idle) is one of the few tasks that the theory of laissez-faire allows the government.

Excludability does not exist in a Hobbesian state of nature: the laws of physics do not prohibit people from sneaking in and taking your things. So the police and the judges exist to enforce it, through penalties for breach of contract and damage awards for theft of intellectual property. The importance of this "artificial" creation of excludability is rarely remarked on: fish are supposed to rarely remark upon the water in which they swim.

We can see how an absence of excludability can warp a market and an industry by taking a brief look at the history of network television. During its three-channel heyday in the 1960s and 1970s, North American network television was available to anyone with an antenna and a receiver because broadcasters lacked the means of preventing the public from getting the signals for free. Free access was, however, accompanied by scarce bandwidth, and by government allocation of the scarce bandwidth to producers.

The absence of excludability for broadcast television did not destroy the television broadcasting industry. Broadcasters couldn't charge for what they were truly producing, but broadcasters worked out that they could charge for something else: the attention of the program-watching consumers during commercials. Rather than paying money directly, the customers of the broadcast industry merely had to endure the commercials (or get up and leave the room; or channel-surf) if they wanted to see the show.

This solution prevented the market for broadcast programs from collapsing: it allowed broadcasters to charge someone for something. But it left its imprint on the industry. Charging-for-advertising does not lead to the same invisible hand guarantee of productive optimum as does charging for product. In the case of network television, audience attention to advertisements was more-or-less unconnected with audience involvement in the program.

This created a bias toward lowest-common-denominator programming. Consider two programs, one of which will fascinate 500,000 people, and the other of which 30 million people will watch as slightly preferable to watching their ceiling. The first might well be better for social welfare: the 500,000 with a high willingness-to-pay might well, if there was a way to charge them, collectively outbid the 30 million apathetic potential watchers. Thus a network able to collect revenues from interested viewers would broadcast the first program, seeking the applause (and the money) of the dedicated and forgoing the eye-glazed semi-attention of the mass.

But the process breaks down when the network obtains revenue by selling commercials to advertisers. The network can offer advertisers either 500,000 or 30 million viewers. How influenced the viewers will be by the commercials depends relatively little on how much they like the program. As a result, charging-for-advertising gives every incentive to broadcast what a mass audience would tolerate. It gives no incentive to broadcast what a niche audience would love.

As bandwidth becomes cheaper, these problems become less important: one particular niche program may well be worth broadcasting when the mass audience has become sufficiently fragmented by the viewability of multiple clones of bland programming. Until then, however, expensive bandwidth combined with the absence of excludability meant that broadcasting revenues depended on the viewer numbers rather than the intensity of demand. Non-excludability helped ensure that broadcast programming would be "a vast wasteland."

In the absence of excludability, there is no reason to presume that industries today and tomorrow will be able to avoid analogous distortions: the absence of excludability leaves potential users with no effective way to make the market system notice how strong their demand is and exactly what their demand is for.

Rivalry

In the information-based sectors of the next economy the use or enjoyment of the information-based commodity will no longer necessarily involve rivalry. With most tangible goods, if Alice is using a particular good, Bob cannot be. Charging the ultimate consumer the good's cost of production or the free market price provides the producer with an ample reward for his or her effort. It also leads to the appropriate level of production: social surplus (measured in money) is not maximized by providing the good to anyone whose final demand for a commodity is too weak to wish to pay the cost for it that a competitive market would require.

But if goods are non-rival—if two can consume as cheaply as one—then charging a per-unit price to users artificially restricts distribution: to truly maximize social welfare you need a system that supplies everyone whose willingness to pay for the good is greater than the marginal cost of producing another copy. And if the marginal cost of reproduction of a digital good is near-zero, that means almost everyone should have it for almost free.

However, charging price equal to marginal cost almost surely leaves the producer bankrupt, with little incentive to maintain the product except the hope of maintenance fees, and no incentive whatsoever to make another one except that warm fuzzy feeling one gets from impoverishing oneself for the general good. . . .

A good economic market is characterized by competition to limit the exercise of private economic power, by price equal to marginal cost, by the return to investors and workers corresponding to the social value added of the industry, and by appropriate incentives for innovation and new product development. These seem impossible to achieve all at once in markets for non-rival goods—and digital goods are certainly non-rival.

Transparency

In the information-based sectors of the next economy—indeed, in many sectors of the economy today—the purchase of a good will no longer be transparent. The Invisible Hand assumed that purchasers know what it is that they want and what they are buying. If purchasers need first to figure out what they want and what they are buying, there is no good reason to presume that their willingness to pay corresponds to its true value to them.

Adam Smith's pinmakers sold a good that was small, fungible, low-maintenance and easily understood. Alice could buy her pins from Gerald today, and from Henry tomorrow. But today's purchaser of, say, a suite of software programs is faced with needs and constraints that a metric designed to explain the market for pins may leave us poorly prepared to understand. The market for software "goods" is almost never a market for today's tangible goods, but rather for a bundle of present goods, future goods, and future services. The initial purchase is not a complete transaction in itself, but rather a down payment on the establishment of a relationship.

Once the relationship is established, both buyer and seller find themselves in different positions. Adam Smith's images are less persuasive in the context of services—especially bespoke services which require deep knowledge of the customer's wants and situation (and of the maker's capabilities)—which are not, by their nature[,] fungible or easily comparable.

When Alice shops for a software suite, she not only wants to know about its current functionality—something notoriously difficult to figure out until one has had days or weeks of hands-on experience—but she also needs to have some idea of the likely support that the manufacturer will provide. Is the line busy at all hours? Is it a toll call? Do the operators have a clue? Will next year's corporate downsizing lead to longer holds on support calls?

Worse, what Alice really needs to know cannot be measured at all before she is committed: learning how to use a software package is an investment she would prefer not to repeat. Since operating systems change frequently, and interoperability needs changes even more often, Alice needs to have a prediction about the likely upgrade path for her suite. This, however, turns on unknowable and barely guessable factors: the health of the corporation, the creativity of the software team, the corporate relationships between the suite seller and other companies.

Some of the things Alice wants to know, such as whether the suite works [ ] quickly enough on her computer, are potentially measurable at least—although one rarely finds a consumer capable of measuring them before purchase, or a marketing system designed to accommodate such a need. You buy the shrink-wrapped box at a store, take it home, unwrap the box—and find that the program is incompatible with your hardware, your operating system, or one of the six programs you bought to cure defects in the hardware or the operating system. . . .

The economics of information is frequently invoked to adjust the traditional neoclassical paradigm to model for the consumer's decision as to whether it pays to attempt to acquire these facts: for example, one can hypothesize that Alice's failure to acquire the necessary information is evidence of the high cost of the investigation compared to the expected value of what it might reveal. So adjusted the basic model retains descriptive power. But its explanatory power is limited. . . .

Out on the Cybernetic Frontier . . .

As a first step toward discerning what new theories of the new markets might look like if new visions do turn out to be necessary, or how old ones should be adjusted, it seems sensible to examine how enterprises and entrepreneurs are already reacting to the fact of widespread market failure. The hope is that experience along the frontiers of electronic commerce will serve as a good guide to what pieces of the theory are likely to be most important, and will suggest areas in which further development might have a high rate of return.

The Market for Software (Shareware, Public Betas and More)

We noted above that the market for modern, complex products is anything but transparent. While one can think of services, such as medicine, which are particularly opaque to the buyer, today it is difficult to imagine a more opaque product than software. Indeed, when one considers the increasing opacity of products in the context of the growing importance of services to the economy, it suggests that transparency is and will become a particularly important issue in the next economy.

Consumers' failure to acquire full information about the software they buy certainly demonstrates that acquiring the information must be expensive. In response to this cost, social institutions have begun to spring up to get around the shrink-wrap dilemma. The first was so-called shareware: you download the program, if you like the program you send its author some money, and maybe in return you get a manual, access to support, or an upgraded version. Shareware dealt with the information acquisition problem by turning the purchase-and-sale of software into a gift-exchange relationship, more akin to an NPR fund raising drive. ("Is this station worth just fifty cents a week to you? Then call . . .") The benefit to try-before-you-buy is precisely that it makes the process more transparent. The cost is that try-before-you-buy often turns out to be try-use-and-don't-pay.

The next stage beyond shareware has been the evolution of the institution of the "public beta." This public beta is a time-limited (or bug-ridden) version of the product: users can investigate the properties of the public beta version to figure out if the product is worthwhile. But to get the permanent (or the less bug-ridden) version, they have to pay.

Yet a third is the "dual track" version: Eudora shareware versus Eudora Professional. Perhaps the hope is that users of the free low-power version will some day become richer, or less patient, or find they have greater needs. At that point they will find it least disruptive to switch to a product that looks and feels familiar, that is compatible with their habits, and their existing files. In effect (and if the sellers are lucky), the free version captures them as future customers before they are even aware they are future buyers.

The developing free-public-beta industry is a way of dealing with the problem of lack of transparency. It is a relatively benign development, in the sense that it involves competition through distribution of lesser versions of the ultimate product. An alternative would be (say) the strategy of constructing barriers to compatibility: the famous examples in the computer industry come from the 1970s when the Digital Equipment Corporation made non-standard cable connectors; from the mid-1980s when IBM attempted to appropriate the entire PC industry through the PS/2 line; and from the late 1980s when Apple Computers used a partly ROM-based operating system to exclude clones. Perhaps the main reason that the free-public-beta strategy is now dominant is the catastrophic failure of both IBM's PS/2 and Apple's ROM-based strategies of exclusion based on non-compatibility—even though they were both near-successes.

ShopBots (*BargainFinder*)

Predictions abound as to how software will use case- and rule-based thinking to do your shopping for you, advise you on how to spend your leisure time, and in general organize your life for you. But that day is still far in the future. So far we have only the crude prototype of the knowledge-scavenging virtual robot, the automated comparison shopper.

Yet, the online marketplace so far has had an ambiguous reaction to the advent of the automated comparison shopper. BargainFinder is one of the first such—and highly experimental—Internet-based agents. BargainFinder does just one thing. Perhaps it does it too well.

The user enters the details of a music compact disk she might like to purchase. BargainFinder interrogates several online music stores that might offer to sell them. It then reports back the prices in a tidy table that makes comparison shopping easy. The system is not completely transparent: it is not always possible to discern the vendor's shipping charges without visiting the vendor's web site. But as Bargain-Finder's inventors say, "it is still only an experiment."

Most economists, be they Adam Smithian classicists, neo-classical Austrians, or more modern economics of information mavens, would agree with the proposition that a vendor in a competitive market selling a standardized product—for one Tiger Lily CD is as good as another—would want customers to know as much as possible about what the vendor offers for sale, and the prices at which the goods are available.

The reason for this near-consensus is that in a competitive market every sale at the offer price should be welcome: all are made at a markup over marginal cost. Thus all online CD retailers ought to have wanted to be listed by BargainFinder, if only because every sale that went elsewhere when they had the lowest price was lost profit.

Not so. A significant fraction of the merchants regularly visited by Bargain-Finder were less than ecstatic. They retaliated by blocking the agent's access to their otherwise publicly-available data. Currently (March 1997), one third of the merchants targeted by the BargainFinder (three out of nine) continue to lock out its queries. One, CDNow, did so for frankly competitive reasons. The other two said that the costs of large numbers of "hobbyist" queries were too great for them. Meanwhile, seven additional merchants have asked to be listed.

One possible explanation for the divergence between the economic theorist's prediction that every seller should want to be listed by BargainFinder and the apparent outcome is the price gouging story. In this story, stores blocking Bargain-Finder tend to charge higher than normal prices because they are able to take advantage of consumer ignorance of cheaper alternatives. The stores are gouging buyers by taking advantage of relatively high costs of search.

In this case BargainFinder and its successors are indeed valuable developments. They will make markets more efficient and lower prices. This is entirely possible, although one need not go quite as far as one writer who suggested that the entire world economy is made up of such great pricing inefficiencies that the change to an information economy will drastically reduce inflation.

Another possibility is the kindly service story. Stores blocking BargainFinder tend to charge higher than normal prices because they provide additional service or convenience. If commerce becomes increasingly electronic and impersonal (or if "personal" comes to mean "filtered through fiendishly clever software agents"), this sort of humanized attention will become increasingly expensive. To the extent that this additional service or convenience can be provided automatically, things are less clear.

In a sometimes forgotten classic, The Joyless Economy, Tibor Scitovsky noted that the advent of mass production of furniture seemed to cause the price of hand-carved chairs to increase, even as the demand for them shrank. As consumers switched to less costly (and less carefully made, one-size-fits-all) mass-produced furniture, carvers became scarce. Soon only the rich could engage their services. If the kindly service story is right, the rise of the commodity market in turn creates a risk that the economy will become yet more "joyless": mass tastes will be satisfied cheaply as specialty tastes become ever more a luxury.

On the other hand the rise of ShopBots such as BargainFinder offers an opportunity for consumers to aggregate their preferences on worldwide scale. As it becomes increasingly easy for consumers to communicate their individualized preferences to manufacturers and suppliers, and increasingly easy to tailor goods to individual tastes—be it a CD that only has the tracks you like, customized blue jeans, or a car manufactured just in time to your specifications—personalized goods may become the norm, putting the "joy" back into the economy. Some signs of this were visible even before the information revolution: lower costs of customization ha[ve] already undermined one of Scitovsky's examples, as fresh-baked bread makes its comeback at many supermarkets and specialty stores.

In either the price gouging or kindly service stories, the advent of Bargain-Finder presents CD retailers with a dilemma: If they join in, they contribute towards turning the market for CDs into a commodity market with competition only on price. If they act "selflessly" and stay out, in order to try to degrade Bargain-Finder's utility (and preserve their higher average markup), they must hope that their competitors will understand their long-run self-interest in the same way. But overt communication in which all sellers agreed to block BargainFinder would, of course, violate the Sherman Act. And without a means of retaliation to "punish" players who do not pursue the collusive long-run strategy of blocking Bargain-Finder, the collapse of the market into a commodity market with only price competition appears likely.

Indeed, if the strategy was to undermine BargainFinder by staying away, it appears to be failing. CD retailers are unblocking BargainFinder and more are clamoring to join. Whether or not this is an occasion for joy depends on which explanation above is closer to the truth. The growth of the bookstore chain put the local bookshop out of business, just as the growth of supermarkets killed the corner grocer. Not everyone considers this trend to be a victory, despite the lower prices. A human element has been lost, and a "personal service" element that may have led to a better fit between purchaser and purchase has been lost as well.

So far, the discussion has operated on the basis of the assumption that CD merchants would have an incentive to block BargainFinder if they charge higher than normal prices. Strangely, some merchants may have had an incentive to block it if they charged lower than normal prices. As we all know, merchants sometimes advertise a "loss leader," and offer to sell a particular good at an unprofitable price. Merchants do this in order to lure consumers into the store where they either may be attracted to more profitable versions of the same good (leading, in the extreme case, to "bait and switch"), or in the hope that the consumer will spy other, more profitable goods to round out the market basket.

You can explain this merchant behavior in different ways, either by talking about the economics of information, locational utility, myopic consumers generalizing incorrectly on the basis of a small number of real bargains, or about temporary monopolies caused by the consumer's presence in this store as opposed to another store far away. It may be that merchants blocking BargainFinder did not want consumers to be able to exploit their loss leaders without having to be exposed to the other goods offered simultaneously. Without this exposure the loss leaders would not lure buyers to other, higher-profit items, but would simply be losses. The merchant's ability to monopolize the consumer's attention for a period may be the essence of modern retailing; the reaction to BargainFinder, at least, suggests that this is what merchants believe. The growing popularity of frequent buyer and other loyalty programs also suggests that getting and keeping customer attention is important to sellers.

Interestingly, this explanation works about equally well for the kindly service and loss leader explanations, which are the two stories that are consistent with the assumption that the CD market was relatively efficient before BargainFinder came along.

Browsing Is Our Business (CDNow)

More important and perhaps more likely is the possibility that the Bargain-Finder and other ShopBots threaten merchants who are in the browsing assistance business. Some online merchants are enthusiastically attempting to fill the role of personal shopping assistant. Indeed, some of the most successful online stores have adapted to the new marketplace by inverting the information equation.

Retail stores in meatspace ("meatspace" being the part of life that is not cyberspace) provide information about available products—browsing and information acquisition services—that consumers find valuable and are willing to pay for either in time and attention or in cash. Certainly meatspace shopping is conducive to unplanned, impulse purchases, as any refrigerator groaning under kitchen magnets will attest. Retail stores in cyberspace may exacerbate this: what, after all, is a store in cyberspace but a collection of information?

CDNow, for example, tailors its virtual storefront to what it knows of a customer's tastes based upon her past purchases. In addition to dynamically altering the storefront on each successive visit, CDNow also offers to send shoppers occasional email information about new releases that fit their past buying patterns.

One can imagine stores tailoring what they present to what they presume to be the customer's desires, based on demographic information available about the customer even before the first purchase. Tailoring might extend beyond showcasing different wares: taken to the logical extreme it would include some form of price discrimination based on facts known about the customer's preferences, or on demographic information thought to be correlated with preferences. (The U.S. and other legal systems impose constraints on the extent to which stores may generalize from demographic information: for example, stores that attempt race-based, sex-based, or other types of invidious price variation usually violate U.S. law.)

A critical microeconomic question in all this is how consumers and manufacturer/sellers exchange information in this market. Both consumers and sellers have an interest in encouraging the exchange of information: in order to provide what the consumer wants, the sellers need to know what is desired and how badly it is wanted; consumers need to know what is on offer where, and at what price. A ShopBot may solve the consumer's problem of price, but it will not tell him about an existing product of which he is unaware. Similarly, CDNow may reconfigure its store to fit customer profiles, but without some external source of information about customers this takes time, and requires repeat visitors.

Indeed, it requires that customers come in through the front door: all the reconfiguration in the world will not help CDNow if customers are either unaware that they would enjoy its products, or if the customers' only relationship with CDNow is via a ShopBot.

The retail outlet in the average mall can plausibly be described as a mechanism for informing consumers about product attributes. The merchant gives away product information in the hopes that consumers will make purchases. Physical stores, however, have fixed displays and thus must provide more or less identical information to every customer. Anyone who looks in the window, anyone who studies the product labels, or even the product catalogs, receives the same sales pitch.

It may be that the dynamic storefront story is the Internet's substitute for the kindly service story. If so, then the rise of agent-based shopping may well be surprisingly destructive. It raises the possibility of a world in which retail shops providing valuable services are destroyed by an economic process that funnels a large percentage of consumer sales into what become commodity markets without middlemen: people use the high-priced premium cyberstore to browse, but then use BargainFinder to purchase.

To appreciate the problem, consider Bob, an online merchant who has invested a substantial amount in a large and easy to use "browsing" database that combines your past purchases, current news, new releases, and other information to present you with a series of choices and possible purchases that greatly increase your chances of coming across something interesting. After all, a customer enters seeking not a particular title, and not a random title, but a product that he or she would like. What is being sold is the process of search and information acquisition that leads to the judgment that this is something to buy. A good online merchant would make the service of "browsing" easy—and would in large part be selling that browsing assistance.

In this browsing is our business story there is a potential problem: browsing assistance is not excludable. Unless Bob charges for his services (which is likely to discourage most customers and especially the impulse purchaser), there is nothing to stop Alice from browsing merchant Bob's website to determin[e] the product she wants, and then using BargainFinder to find the cheapest source of supply. BargainFinder will surely find a competitor with lower prices because Bob's competitor will not have to pay for the database and the software underlying the browsing assistance.

If so, then projects like BargainFinder will have a potentially destructive application, for many online stores will be easy to turn into commodity markets once the process of information acquisition and browsing is complete. It would be straight-forward to run a market in kitchen gadgets along the lines of the BargainFinder, even if much of the market for gadgets involves finding solutions to problems one was not consciously aware one had: first free-ride off of one of the sites that provides browsing assistance to discover what you want, then open another window and access BargainFinder to buy it. Students and other people with more time than money have been using this strategy to purchase stereo components for decades: draw on the sales expertise of the premium store, then buy from the warehouse. But the scope and ease of this strategy is about to become much greater.

To merchants providing helpful shopping advice, the end result will be as if they spent all their time in their competitors' discount warehouse, pointing out goods that the competitors' customers ought to buy. The only people who will pay premium prices for the physical good—and thus pay for browsing and information services—will be those who feel under a gift-exchange moral obligation to do so: the "sponsors" of NPR.

Collaborative Filtering (FireFly)

Collaborative filtering provides part of the answer to the information exchange problem. It also provides another example of how information technology changes the way that consumer markets will operate. In their simplest form, collaborative filters such as FireFly bring together consumers to exchange information about their preferences. The assumption is that if Alice finds that several other readers—each of whom also likes Frisch, Kafka, Kundera and Klima but gets impatient with James and Joyce—tends to like William Gass, the odds are good that Alice might enjoy Gass's On Being Blue, too.

In the process of entering sufficient information about her tastes to prime the pump, Alice adds to the database of linked preference information. In helping herself, Alice helps others. In this simplest form, the collaborative filter helps Alice find out about new books she might like. The technology is applicable to finding potentially congenial CDs, news, web sites, software, travel, financial services and restaurants—as well as to helping Alice find people who share her interests. Indeed, each of these is a service currently available or soon to be offered via FireFly.

At the next level of complexity, the collaborative filter can be linked to a ShopBot. Once Alice has decided that she will try On Being Blue she can find out who will sell it to her at the best price.

The really interesting development, however, comes when Alice's personal preference data is available to every merchant Alice visits. (Leave aside for a moment who owns this data, and the terms on which it becomes available.) A shop like CDNow becomes able to tailor its virtual storefront to a fairly good model of Alice's likely desires upon her first visit. CDNow may use this information to showcase its most enticing wares, or it may use it to fine tune its prices to charge Alice all that her purse will bear—or both.

Whichever is the case, shopping will not be the same.

Once shops acquire the ability to engage in price discrimination, consumers will of course seek ways of fighting back. One way will be to shop anonymously, and see what price is quoted when no consumer data is proffered. Consumers can either attempt to prevent merchants and others from acquiring the transactional data that could form the basis of a consumer profile, or they can avail themselves of anonymizing intermediaries who will protect the consumer against the merchant's attempt to practice perfect price discrimination by aggregating data about the seller's prices and practices. In this model, a significant fraction of cyber commerce will be conducted by software agents who will carry accreditation demonstrating their credit-worthiness, but will not be traceable back to their progenitors.

Thus potential legal constraints on online anonymity may have more far-reaching consequences than their obvious effect on unconstrained political speech. . . .

COMMENTS AND QUESTIONS

1. DeLong and Froomkin present a rather dystopian vision of electronic commerce, in which economic changes threaten important social values and upset economic assumptions with little clear idea of what will replace them. By contrast, a more positive view of electronic commerce would focus on the benefits it does offer:

- New opportunities for reducing transactions costs between buyers and sellers. The eBay auction site is a prime example of a site that facilitates transactions that would probably not occur in real space. An even greater reduction in distribution costs is possible when the goods can be distributed electronically over the network itself. And marketing costs may decline—or at least change—because of Internet search technologies.
- A model closer to perfect competition. While deLong and Froomkin worry about the effects of an exclusive focus on price, the Internet can also facilitate better-informed comparison about non-price attributes like performance, service, reliability, etc. The creation of comparison sites may simply represent the disaggregation of product information from product sales in certain industries.
- The ability to take advantage of economies of scale and scope. In part because they eliminate geography, companies like amazon.com and CDNow can list a range of titles that most Americans would never have access to in a local store. Far from "mainstreaming" product choice, for some products the Internet may support a greater diversity than previous marketing channels ever could.

2. The background to electronic commerce is not entirely a function of the economics of the goods and services provided. It is also a function of infrastructure —meaning both the bandwidth needed to support a large number of transactions and a secure framework for transactions to take place. On the former, see Jeffrey MacKie-Mason & Hal Varian, Some Economics of the Internet, *in* Networks, Infrastructure and the New Task for Regulation 107 (1997); Howard A. Shelanski, The Speed Gap: Broadband Infrastructure and Electronic Commerce, 14 Berkeley Tech. L.J. 721 (1999). For a variety of perspectives on the subject, see Lee W. McKnight & Joseph P. Bailey, Internet Economics (1997). The latter is discussed in more detail *infra*.

3. For a business-oriented look at electronic commerce, see Soon-Yong Choi et al., The Economics of Electronic Commerce (1997).

B. ONLINE CONTRACTS AND PAYMENTS

≡ *In re RealNetworks, Inc., Privacy Litigation*
United States District Court for the Northern District of Illinois
2000 WL 631341 (N.D. Ill. 2000)

KOCORAS, J.

Before the Court is [*sic*] Intervenor David Keel's additional arguments in support of Plaintiffs' opposition to arbitration. For the reasons set forth below, the Court rejects Intervenor's additional arguments.

Background

Plaintiffs Michael Lieschke, Robert Jackson, and Todd Simon (collectively, the "Plaintiffs"), both on behalf of a class of Illinois plaintiffs and individually, brought suit against Defendant RealNetworks, Inc. ("RealNetworks") under federal and common law. Plaintiffs allege trespass to property and privacy, claiming that Real-Networks' software products secretly allowed RealNetworks to access and intercept users' electronic communications and stored information without their knowledge or consent. Previously, this Court considered and granted RealNetworks' motion to stay this matter and enforce arbitration, finding that the End User License Agreement (the "License Agreement") required arbitration of this dispute. See Lieschke v. RealNetworks, Inc., No. 99C 7274, 99 C 7380, 2000 WL 198424 (N.D. Ill. Feb. 11, 2000). Subsequently, this Court allowed Intervenor David Keel (the "Intervenor") to file his additional arguments in support of Plaintiffs' opposition to arbitration in order to raise certain arguments not presented to the Court when it decided the arbitration issue. It is these arguments that the Court presently addresses.

RealNetworks offers free basic versions of two products, RealPlayer and Real-Jukebox, for users to download from RealNetworks' site on the World-Wide Web. These products allow users to see and hear audio and video available on the Internet and to download, record, and play music.

Before a user can install either of these software packages, they must accept the terms of RealNetworks' License Agreement, which appear on the user's screen. Paragraph 10 of the Agreement includes the following clause:

> This License Agreement shall be governed by the laws of the State of Washington, without regard to conflicts of law provisions, and you hereby consent to the exclusive jurisdiction of the state and federal courts sitting in the State of Washington. Any and all unresolved disputes arising under this License Agreement shall be submitted to arbitration in the State of Washington.

Defendant cites this clause as binding authority for its assertions that arbitration is required. Intervenor, on the other hand, argues that this clause does not operate to require arbitration for several reasons. First, Intervenor contends that the License Agreement, including the arbitration requirement, does not constitute a "writing." Second, Intervenor claims that Ninth Circuit decisional law controls the construction of the arbitration provision and dictates that the arbitration clause be read narrowly to preclude enforcement in this action. Finally, Intervenor argues that the arbitration provision is unenforceable because it is unconscionable.

Discussion

Although national policy encourages arbitration of disputes, submission to arbitration is consensual, not coercive. See Mastrobuono v. Shearson Lehman Hutton, Inc., 514 U.S. 52, 57, 62, 115 S. Ct. 1212, 1216, 1218, 131 L. Ed.2d 76 (1995). Thus, a court cannot force a party to arbitrate unless that party has entered into a contractual agreement to do so. See First Options of Chicago, Inc. v. Kaplan, 514 U.S. 938, 943, 115 S. Ct. 1920, 131 L. Ed.2d 985 (1995); AT & T Technologies v. Communications Workers of America, 475 U.S. 643 648 (1986). In order to determine whether the parties intended to submit to arbitration, a court reviews the contract at issue. See *AT & T Technologies,* 475 U.S. at 648. In so doing, a court employs the standard methods of contract interpretation, using state-law principles. See *Mastrobuono,* 514 U.S. at 54; Perry v. Thomas, 482 U.S. 483, 492 (1987); *First Options of Chicago,* 514 U.S. at 944. Ambiguities, however, are resolved in favor of arbitration. See Mastrobuono, 514 U.S. at 62.

A party contesting the submission of the claim to arbitration must clearly show that the presumption of arbitrability does not apply. See Int'l Union of Operating Engineers, Local Union 103 v. Indiana Const. Corp., 13 F.3d 253, 255-56 (7th Cir. 1994). A claim will be deemed to be arbitrable if an arbitration clause is capable of any interpretation that a claim is covered. See *id.* If parties have a contract providing for arbitration of some issues, questions concerning the scope of issues subject to arbitration should be resolved in favor of arbitration. See Miller v. Flume, 139 F.3d 1130, 1136 (7th Cir. 1998).

I. Writing Requirement

Intervenor claims that the License Agreement, including the arbitration provision, does not constitute a writing as required by the Federal Arbitration Act (the "FAA") and the Washington Arbitration Act (the "WAA") in order to be enforced. According to Intervenor, the License Agreement is an electronic agreement, and electronic agreements do not satisfy the "written" agreement provisions of the FAA and the WAA. Moreover, Intervenor asserts that even if some electronic agreements are acceptable, RealNetworks' electronic agreement is not because a user cannot print or save it. RealNetworks does not dispute that the arbitration provision must be written in order to be enforceable. Rather, RealNetworks argues that its License Agreement, including the arbitration provision, constitute[s] a writing and that it may be printed and saved.

Both the Intervenor and RealNetworks agree that Congress intended the FAA to apply only to written contracts. Because the terms in the statute must be given their plain meaning and do not explicitly allow for an "electronic" agreement, Intervenor reasons that an electronic communication cannot satisfy the writing requirement, but only a written one can. However, this only begs the question, what is a written agreement? Although contract terms must be given their plain and ordinary meaning, the Court is unconvinced that the plain and ordinary meaning of "writing" or "written" necessarily cannot include any electronic writings. See Williams v. Taylor, 120 S. Ct. 1479, 1488 (2000) (words will be interpreted as taking their ordinary, contemporary, common meaning).

Courts frequently look to dictionaries in order determine the plain meaning of words and particularly examine how a word was defined at the time the statute was drafted and enacted. The FAA was enacted in 1925. See Cortez Byrd Chips, Inc. v. Bill Harbert Construction Co., 120 S. Ct. 1331, 1333 (2000). As now, words had several different definitions. In relevant part, at the time, Webster's Dictionary defined "writing" as:

1. The act or art of forming letters or characters on paper, wood, stone, or other material, for the purpose of recording the ideas which characters and words express, or of communicating them to others by visible signs. 2. Anything written or printed; anything expressed in characters or letters. See Webster's Dictionary (1913).

Webster's defined "written" as the participle of write, which it defined as:

1. To set down, as legible characters; to form the conveyance of meaning; to inscribe on any material by a suitable instrument; as, to write the characters called letters; to write figures. See *id*.

A legal dictionary at the time provided that "The word 'written,' used in a statute, may include printing and any other mode of representing words and letters." See Pope, Benjamin, W., Legal Definitions, Callaghan and Co. (1920). Thus, although the definition of a writing included a traditional paper document, it did not exclude representations of language on other media. Because electronic communications can be letters or characters formed on the screen to record or communicate ideas, be visible signs, and can be legible characters that represent words and letters as well as form the conveyance of meaning, it would seem that the plain meaning of the word "written" does not exclude all electronic communications. That being said, the Court does not now find that all electronic communications may be considered "written." Rather, the Court examines the contract at issue in this action and finds that its easily printable and storable nature is sufficient to render it "written."

The Court rejects Intervenor's contention that the License Agreement is not printable and storable. Intervenor asserts that RealNetworks affirmatively inhibits users from printing or storing the License Agreement by failing to provide a conspicuous "print" or "save" button on the pop-up License Agreement window. However, Intervenor is incorrect in its assertions because the License Agreement may rather easily be printed and is automatically stored on the user's hard drive despite the absence of the "print" and "save" buttons. In fact, there exists more than one way to print the License Agreement. First, before the user has even accepted the License Agreement, the user can right click his mouse over the text of the License Agreement, select all, and copy and paste it onto any word processing program. Since using the right click function is too specialized for Intervenor, he even has the option to simply click and drag the cursor over the text of the License Agreement in order to highlight it and then copy and paste the License Agreement onto any word processing program. Moreover, users have yet another way of printing the License Agreement. After a user accepts the License Agreement, it is automatically downloaded and saved to the user's hard drive. The user can then click on the License Agreement, listed separately as either "RealJukeBox License Agreement" or "RealPlayer License Agreement," depending on the product, and easily print out either agreement from the file pull down menu. Thus, Intervenor's assertion that the License Agreement cannot be saved, retrieved, or printed is incorrect. Moreover, once installed, the License Agreement is not hidden, as Intervenor claims, but is listed as prominent and separate icons under "Real" on the "Start" menu. Although any computer use can be intimidating, the process of printing the License Agreement is no more difficult or esoteric than many other basic computer functions, and the melodrama and over exaggeration with which Intervenor describes the alleged impossibility of printing the License Agreement is disingenuous.

Finally, Intervenor points to Congress' present day discussions about electronic communications in arguing that the FAA's and WAA's writing requirement cannot be satisfied by an electronic communication. However, the modern congressional discussions that Intervenor points to do not serve as evidence of Congress' intent when it enacted the FAA in 1925. That Congress may now, with some hindsight on the advance of electronic communication, explicitly provide for written and electronic agreements in new legislation, does not mean that Congress in 1925 excluded electronic communications from the category of written communications by not explicitly providing for it. Rather, "New words may be designed to fortify the current rule with a more precise text that curtails uncertainty." See ProCD, Inc. v. Zeidenberg, 86 F.3d 1447, 1452 (7th Cir. 1996). Modern Congress' discussions indicate that it was, in fact, the "uncertain" legal effect of an electronic record or an electronic signature that prompted Congress to consider the "Electronic Signatures in Global and National Commerce Act," to which Intervenor cites. See House Report No. 106- 341(I), September 27, 1999. Moreover, it seems that the License Agreement would, nevertheless, constitute a writing even for purposes of Congress' discussions today because the License Agreement may be printed and stored. See 145 Cong. Rec. S14881-01, at *S14884, November 19, 1999.

Thus, the License Agreement, including the arbitration provision, is a written agreement. . . .

Conclusion

For the reasons set forth above, the Court rejects Intervenor's additional arguments in support of Plaintiffs' opposition to arbitration.

COMMENTS AND QUESTIONS

1. Does the Real Networks license give a fair opportunity to retain a copy? Should a reasonable consumer be expected to highlight the contract terms and

copy them into a word processing program? To search their computer for files automatically downloaded without notice?

2. In Sea-Land Serv. v. Lozen, Int'l, 285 F.3d 808 (9th Cir. 2002), the court accepted an email with an electronic .sig file as evidence that the representation contained in the email was made by the signatory. The court didn't consider whether it formed a binding contract, however, but merely concluded that it was evidence that could qualify as the admission of a party under the hearsay rules.

3. Courts have had to adapt the rules of contract law to new technology before. They have had no difficulty in concluding that the telegraph and the fax are both "writings" within the meaning of the Statute of Frauds, but that a telephone conversation is not. Does the Internet present any more difficulty than the fax or the telegraph? See R.J. Robertson, Electronic Commerce on the Internet and the Statute of Frauds, 49 S.C. L. Rev. 787 (1998).

Note on Electronic Signature Legislation

As electronic commerce has boomed, the importance of the electronic contracting has increased, even as the legal status of electronic contracts has been subject to a certain degree of uncertainty. The basic issues of contract law—offer and acceptance, and in certain circumstances a written contract and signatures of the parties—pose new problems when executed through new technologies such as email and web forms. Courts have attempted to resolve some of these problems through application of traditional contract rules and the U.C.C., but the continued threat of inconsistent treatment has also led legislatures to revise contract statutes.

The ALI and the NCCUSL attempted to modify UCC, particularly Article 2, to cover electronic licensing specifically, but they failed to reach agreement on key provisions. The NCCUSL continued to work on its model and eventually released the Uniform Computer Information Transactions Act (UCITA). Among UCITA's many provisions are ones recognizing the validity of electronic assent and digital signatures. However, UCITA has thus far been one of the least successful pieces of model legislation. It has been adopted in only two states, and several states have adopted anti-UCITA "bomb shelter" statutes. Further, UCITA is at best an incomplete solution to the problem of electronic contracting, because it applies only to licenses of software and related digital information. So, as questions arise regarding offer and acceptance in an electronic setting, most courts continue to apply the traditional rules of UCC article 2 and the Restatement (Second) of Contracts, adapting them as best as possible to the new regimes. For a fuller discussion of those offer and acceptance issues, see Chapter 6, *supra*.

Issues stemming from the Statute of Frauds' writing and signature requirements, however, have followed a different path. While some courts have applied the writing and signature requirements to electronic transactions under the UCC, the uncertainty within the UCC led to numerous legislative attempts to clarify the validity of electronic records and signatures. Model codes, state governments, and the federal government have all attempted to create some legal certainty in the realm of electronic records and signatures. Now, with the passage in 2000 of the Electronic Signatures in Global and National Commerce Act ("E-Sign") and the wide adoption of the Uniform Electronic Transactions Act ("UETA"), some basic questions have begun to be resolved.

The concern over whether electronic transactions were valid under the Statute of Frauds was potentially a very large barrier to electronic commerce. The Statute of Frauds requires that certain contracts must be recorded in writing and signed by the parties to indicate the parties' intentions. U.C.C. §2-201(1) (1998). The Statute covers practically all major sale contracts, including contracts requiring more than a year to perform, and contracts for the sale of real property, personal property, securities, or goods greater than $500.

States had a clear interest in facilitating these contracts, and as ecommerce began to expand, states began to pass enabling legislation. In 1994, Utah became the first state to pass a digital signature enabling law, and California followed shortly thereafter. Utah and California established a pattern of states drafting digital signature laws unique to their state. Unique features came in one or more of three different flavors. First, some laws specified or favored one technology over others, while other laws were technology-neutral. Utah, for example, favored one particular technology for digital signatures, while California was technology-neutral. Other states, such as Alaska and Georgia, did not specify a particular technology but nevertheless specified that any acceptable technology must include some validation of identity. Second, some laws were broadly applicable, while other laws were designed to enable digital signatures and records only in particular circumstances. The Alabama Electronic Tax Return Filing Act, for example, enabled electronic records and signatures for tax returns. Ala. Code §§40-30-1 to 40-30-6 (2000). Finally, some states passed enabling legislation that included significant consumer protections, such as requiring companies to seek affirmative consent from consumers before providing notices electronically. Considering all the varieties of legislation validating electronic signatures and records, as of August 2002, Massachusetts was the only state that had not passed any legislation validating electronic signatures. See McBride, Baker & Coles, E-Commerce: Legislative Tables: Laws Authorizing Signatures, available at http://www.mbc.com/ecommerce/ (last visited September 4, 2002).

As Jane Winn has observed, many of these specific statutes failed precisely because they attempted to anticipate the direction of technological change and commercial behavior rather than react to existing patterns of behavior. Jane Kaufman Winn, Open Systems, Free Markets, and Regulation of Internet Commerce, 72 Tulane L. Rev. 1177 (1998). Thus, many "digital signature" statutes were written in the mid-1990s on the assumption that no one would engage in commercial transactions online without secure public-key encryption, and that third party "certification authorities" would spring up to serve the market for verification of strangers' public keys. None of this happened, however, leaving states like Utah with complex regulatory schemes governing nonexistent practices and entities. See Jane K. Winn, The Emperor's New Clothes: The Shocking Truth About Digital Signatures and Internet Commerce, 37 Idaho L. Rev. 353 (2001).

In the face of this confusion, the NCCUSL drafted a very successful model electronic records and signatures act, the Uniform Electronic Transactions Act (1999) ("UETA"). UETA decreed parity between electronic and paper records in a technology-neutral fashion. UETA has served as the model for many states to revise or finally pass digital signature enabling legislation. However, while UETA has created greater consistency regarding the technology-neutral provisions and its intended scope, at least among new legislation, states continued to adapt UETA with consumer protection provisions that vary from state to state.

Perhaps the most significant effort at harmonization is the federal Electronic Signatures in Global and National Commerce Act, Pub. L. 106-229, 114 Stat. 464 (2000) (codified at 15 U.S.C. §§7001 et seq.) (E-Sign), which became effective on October 1, 2000. E-Sign broadly authorized state and federal government acceptance of electronic documents and signatures in interstate and foreign commerce. Amid all this confusion and proliferation of legislation, E-Sign provides some certainty: Federal and state governments will accept electronic documents and signatures for interstate and international commerce. But E-Sign did not resolve all the ambiguities, since it allows both states and regulatory agencies to preempt and interpret E-Sign. The following sections will discuss UETA, E-Sign, and the impacts of preemption, and briefly touch on comparable developments in the European Union.

UETA

The fundamental rule of UETA is set forth in Section 7, which establishes parity between electronic records and authorizations and print records and signatures. Section 7 establishes that records, signatures, and contracts may not be denied legal effect or enforceability solely because they are in electronic form or because an electronic record was used in their formation. Section 7 then positively asserts that if a law requires a signature or a written record, an electronic record or electronic signature satisfies the law.

The NCCUSL intended UETA to be read very broadly, within the narrow confines of Section 7's parity rule. UETA was intended to affect *only* the efficacy of electronic signatures and records, but it was intended to apply to electronic signatures and records in a wide array of situations. Thus, the drafters took pains to ensure that UETA was technology-neutral and applied broadly across technologies. The UETA definitions of "electronic," "electronic record," "electronic signature," and so forth are sufficiently broad to cover telephony as well as computer records; digital as well as analog formats; "click-wrap" mouse-clicks and e-mail signature files. An "electronic signature," for example, includes an "electronic sound, symbol, or process attached to or logically associated with a record and executed or adopted by a person with the intent to sign the record," and an "electronic record" is any record "created, generated, sent, communicated, received, or stored by electronic means." UETA §2. UETA goes so far as to say that the medium is "irrelevant" and that "the critical element is the intent[]" to sign the record. UETA §2, Cmt. 6. This broad ambit is an important part of UETA's goal of furthering uniformity among the states, since it precludes the possibility of states adopting multiple, conflicting technical standards.

The scope of UETA, while "inherently limited" to "transactions related to business, commercial (including consumer) and governmental matters" (UETA §3, Cmt. 1) is also in reality rather broad: UETA applies to "electronic records and electronic signatures relating to a transaction" (UETA §3(a)). The model statute includes only a few listed exceptions (wills, trusts, codicils; the UCITA; and most portions of the UCC). UETA §3(b). The statute does include a provision for states to exempt laws of their own choosing, but concludes in Comment 9 that "exclusion of additional areas was not warranted." Despite the warnings, the "exclusion of additional areas" has been a significant point for modification of UETA within the states. UETA has been highly successful, adopted in some form in 38 of the states within just three years. However, some states have made very substantial modifications to UETA to satisfy consumer protection concerns. California, for instance, included additional consumer protections for notices regarding insurance, mortgage foreclosure, and utility cutoffs. For a general discussion of uniformity in state electronic commerce legislation, see Larry E. Ribstein and Bruce H. Kobayashi, State Regulation of Electronic Commerce, 51 Emory L.J. 1 (2002).

While UETA generally took a minimalist approach, the statute does include some depth in its treatment of electronic records. Sections 9 through 20 all provide basic rules for the interpretation of electronic records in a contract context. Section 9 concerns attribution, specifying that rules that govern attribution in print contexts will also govern attribution in an electronic context. Section 10 covers the effect of change or error in the contract. Section 11 deals with notarization, an important area for contracting, specifying that the same kinds of information attached to print notarizations must also be attached or associated to electronic notarizations. Section 14 allows electronic agents, authorized to act for their users, to enter into contracts even without their users' express knowledge. Section 15 specifies how the time and place of sending and receipt are determined. Finally, Sections 12 and 13 concern the retention of electronic records and their admissibility as evidence.

Additionally, UETA included two sections on creation, receipt, retention, and distribution of electronic records by government agencies. Section 17 generally leaves the creation and retention of electronic records and the conversion of written records to electronic format up to the agencies. Likewise, Section 18 is broadly deferential to agency determinations of whether and how to accept electronic records and signatures. These sections should be read in conjunction with clauses 12(f) and (g), which specify that electronic records satisfy legal recordkeeping requirements but permit agencies to impose additional requirements for the retention of a record.

The basic consumer protections in UETA are scant, in keeping with its generally minimalist approach. Both parties must agree to engage in business electronically, but such consent need not be explicit; it can be inferred from "context and environment, including the parties' conduct." UETA §5. In the comments, the drafters explained that explicit permission might be burdensome to the parties. UETA §5, Comment 3. Parties are permitted to change their minds and return to nonelectronic contracting. UETA §5. UETA does provide for states to develop their own statutory exclusions but urges against it. UETA §3; see also §3 comments. UETA requires that the records be "capable of retention," a positive consumer protection, but undercuts the requirement by defining "not capable of retention" as an affirmative action on the part of the sender to "inhibit the ability of the recipient to print or store" the record. UETA §8. And finally, UETA allows individuals' electronic agents to enter into contracts even without the individuals' knowledge; this feature has also been construed as potentially harmful to consumers. UETA §14. This overall lack of consumer protections was remedied in some states, as already discussed, and also in the federal digital signatures bill, E-Sign.

E-Sign

After considerable debate, the Electronic Signatures in Global and National Commerce Act of 1990 ("E-Sign") was enacted in 2000. 15 U.S.C. §7001 et seq. E-Sign was modeled on UETA but differs from it in significant ways. Those differences, in combination with E-Sign's elaborate preemption scheme, provide an additional inducement for states to pass an unmodified UETA. E-Sign was enacted to cover interstate and international transactions; to provide a certain amount of harmony among the states by providing a floor for recognition of electronic contracts and signatures; and, on some level, to encourage states to adopt UETA in an unmodified form. The general scope of E-Sign is somewhat larger than UETA, effectively covering all transactions relating to personal property and services. E-Sign included consumer protections left out of UETA but did not include many of the contract interpretation clauses. UETA, by contrast, covers only transactions within an individual state's jurisdiction, and although it was intended to produce uniformity, it has been adopted in nonuniform fashions across the states. E-Sign therefore apparently preempts many states' older digital signature bills and nonconforming UETA statutes. However, states that have passed UETA or a similarly technologically neutral law may preempt E-Sign, and the differences between UETA and E-Sign may provide incentives to the states to do so.

Both E-Sign and UETA recognize electronic records and documents as legally equivalent to written records. The fundamental rule is laid out in Title I of E-Sign:

> [W]ith respect to any transaction in or affecting interstate or foreign commerce—(1) a signature, contract or other record relating to such transaction may not be denied legal effect, validity, or enforceability solely because it is in electronic form; and (2) a contract relating to such transaction may not be denied legal effect, validity, or enforceability solely because an electronic signature or electronic record was used in its formation.

15 U.S.C. §7001(a). Title I of E-Sign defines "record" and "signature" broadly, specifying that nearly any electronic means of recording information may constitute a "record" and that nearly any evidence of an intent to sign a record may constitute a "signature." An electronic record is "a contract or other record created, generated, sent, communicated, received or stored by electronic means." 15 U.S.C. §7006(4). An electronic signature is "an electronic sound, symbol, or process attached to or logically associated with a contract or other record and executed or adopted by a person with the intent to sign the record." 15 U.S.C. §7006(5). Compare UETA's definitions, §2, which are almost identical.

Like UETA, E-Sign is technology-neutral, meaning that the law does not specify the details of particular technologies which will be acceptable. Furthermore, neither E-Sign nor UETA require or prefer technologies that validate the identity of the parties. However, the parties themselves are not prevented from negotiating and transacting for particular technologies, such as public key encryption or digital signatures.

UETA and E-Sign are also alike in that both specify that the laws merely establish legal parity between electronic documents and signatures and their paper counterparts. They neither address the underlying validity of the contract nor change the fundamental rules and balances within the contract.

Despite these important similarities, there are some differences. E-Sign includes all the consumer protection provisions from UETA but strengthens some and adds others. Title I requires that parties affirmatively consent to transact electronically, and that there must be confirmation of consumers' ability to do so. While UETA also requires that both parties agree to transact electronically, in

UETA such consent need not be explicit and may be inferred from the parties' actions. UETA also has no access test. In fact, UETA explicitly found that it would be counterproductive to require explicit consent, apparently under the reasoning that it would be an unnecessary inconvenience for the consumer. The drafters of E-Sign, cognizant of that complaint, mandated the Federal Trade Commission and the Department of Commerce to evaluate the consumer consent and notification provisions. In June 2001, the agencies submitted a report finding that the benefits of the explicit consent provision outweighed the burdens and recommending that the provision remain in place.

E-Sign allows contracts between electronic agents but requires that the actions of the electronic agent must be "legally attributable" to the person for that person to be bound. 15 U.S.C. §7001(h). UETA, by contrast, had no such requirement and, in fact, would allow contracts to be formed without any human awareness at all.

E-Sign, like UETA, was made inapplicable to wills, codicils, and testaments. E-Sign also excluded family law procedures, which were not even mentioned in UETA's comments, and court notices and pleadings. Finally, E-Sign excluded various consumer notices such as mortgage foreclosure, termination of utilities, insurance benefits, and product recall notices. Many of these had been the subject of similar variances from UETA in the states.

E-Sign also omits some important UETA provisions, including basic contracting rules that deal with mistakes, determine attribution of electronic signatures, cover unsecured electronic promissory notes or documents of title, and set guidelines for determining when a message was deemed sent or received.

For a detailed analysis of E-Sign, see Jonathan E. Stern, Note, The Electronic Signatures in Global and National Commerce Act, 16 Berkeley Tech. L.J. 391 (2001).

Preemption in E-Sign

E-Sign contains a detailed preemption section, requiring preemption of state laws that conflict with E-Sign, but allowing states to evade preemption either by adopting UETA unmodified or by adopting a similar technology-neutral law that does not conflict with E-Sign. E-Sign's preemption section was designed with great deference to UETA, and in many ways serves as encouragement for states to adopt UETA.

According to 15 U.S.C. §7002, states may "modify, limit or supersede" the provisions of 15 U.S.C. §7001 with respect to state law, *if* they adopt the official version of UETA, or another law that specifies alternative procedures or requirements for the use or acceptance of electronic records or signatures so long as it is technology-neutral and is "consistent" with the substantive provisions of the Act. State laws adopted after June 30, 2000, must make specific reference to E-Sign. This detailed preemption clause is in contrast with the usual clause, which preempts "inconsistent" state laws. Here, E-Sign preempts laws that might otherwise not be wholly "inconsistent," but also does not preempt UETA-based laws even where those laws would be inconsistent. It should be noted, however, that even in states that adopt the official UETA, federal writing and signature requirements are still governed by E-Sign. The effect of these preemption provisions is to preclude states from changing UETA in ways that do not match the rules set forth in E-Sign.

International Legislation

Like UETA and E-Sign, the base provisions in the European Electronic Signatures Directive also specify that signatures cannot be discriminated against solely because they are electronic. European Directive on a Community Framework for Electronic Signatures (Electronic Signatures Directive), Council Directive 99/93/EC, 2000 O.J. (L 13) 12, adopted December 1999. However, unlike UETA and E-Sign, the Directive distinguishes between "advanced electronic signatures" and generic electronic signatures. "Advanced electronic signatures" include additional guarantees of authenticity from third-party certification service providers (CSPs) and are favored under the Directive. Generic electronic signatures cannot be denied *solely* because they are electronic, but advanced electronic signatures benefit from a presumption of admissibility under the Directive. Other Directives address consumer protection provisions covered in E-Sign and to a lesser extent UETA. The Distance Contracts Directive attempts to provide broad protections for consumers, giving them the right to know terms in advance of signing, cancellation rights, etc. European Directive on the Protection of Consumers in Respect of Distance Contracts, Council Directive 97/7/EC of 20 May 1997 on the Protection of Consumers in Respect of Distance Contracts. Generally, the European Union is on the same path as the United States regarding electronic signatures and contracts, which should not be surprising, since an international model law, the UNCITRAL Model Law on Electronic Commerce, served as the basis both for UETA and for similar laws in Europe.

PROBLEM

Problem 14-1: Vendoco is a seller of widgets. SmallCo has purchased widgets in the past from Vendoco and from others, but has no standing purchase order with Vendoco. One day, Vendoco receives an email from the address jsmith@smallco.com that reads "To Whom It May Concern: Please send 1,000 widgets by overnight delivery to SmallCo's offices COD for a total price of $50,000. Thanks, Jane." There is no .sig file on the email, but Vendoco has dealt with Jane Smith before, and knows that she is a purchasing agent for SmallCo. Vendoco ships the order.

The next day, Jane Smith calls Vendoco to ask why she has received 1,000 widgets. She denies ever sending the email.

Have Vendoco and SmallCo formed a contract?

Jane Kaufman Winn, The Emerging Law of Electronic Commerce

4. Payment Transactions

Payment systems were among the first commercial transaction systems to migrate to an electronic environment. In 1957, paper checks were first imprinted with the magnetic ink character recognition line on the bottom that permitted the check processing system to be automated. In the late 1960s, banks began experimenting with automated teller machines and secure systems for wire transfers of funds. At the same time, the use of credit cards rapidly proliferated. In 1970, in response to widespread criticism of aggressive tactics on the part of card issuers to expand rapidly the use of credit cards while at the same time severely limiting card issuer liability, Congress enacted a comprehensive scheme of consumer protections for card holders that remains in effect today. The law governing electronic funds transfers dates from 1978, when consumer protections were passed by Congress that applied to transactions such as ATM withdrawals. Outside the realm of consumer payment systems, in 1989, the ULC formalized a law governing wholesale wire transfers, UCC Article 4A, which has now been adopted in all 50 states.

In the late 1990s, all large-scale payment systems in the US had been adapted to operate within secure networked mainframe computer systems operated by regulated financial institutions. As a result, Internet-based payment systems have faced formidable competition and have not been able to establish any significant market share. Many standard developing organizations and technology vendors are competing to achieve a dominant position in the Internet payment arena, but it is unclear which, if any, of the current competitors will ultimately prevail. First Virtual, the first commercial Internet e-cash system, began operations in 1995 amid great fanfare, but ceased payment system operations in 1998 due to lack of market share. Likewise, Internet micropayment technology seemed very promising in the mid-1990s, but by 1998 commercial products such as Millicent were still not enjoying widespread acceptance. Just as it is hard to predict who will be the winners among these emerging technologies, it is also unclear how the existing large-scale mainframe-based payment systems will adapt to these new competitive forces.

4.1 Credit Card Transactions

Credit cards, used in combination with the SSL protocol supported by the end user's browser, have proven to be the payment system of choice for retail Internet electronic commerce. The SSL protocol works within a very simple public key infrastructure, and provides a secure channel for communication of information between the end user's browser and the e-commerce server. Early concerns over the lack of security for Internet communications led MasterCard and Visa each to begin work on designing a much more complex public key infrastructure that would provide digital signature certificates to card holders, merchants, acquiring banks and issuing banks. These projects later merged into the Secure Electronic Transaction (SET) standard. The SET standard offers a much higher level of security than the SSL standard by adding new safeguards against fraud and unauthorized use of credit card information. In order to do so, however, it will have to place heavy demands on existing credit card transaction processing infrastructure and may require the execution of complex cryptographic algorithms that exceed the processing capacity of the average end user's system. These and other problems have slowed down the rate of adoption of the SET standard and progress in further refining the standard. While work on the more sophisticated and complex SET standard has progressed slowly, the SSL protocol has become the de facto standard for security for retail Internet commerce today.

Although the SSL standard provides only minimal security for payments transactions over the Internet, the existing legal and technical framework of the credit card system supplements those protections to produce an Internet payment system that meets the current minimum requirements of merchants, end users and financial institutions. The only segment of the credit card system that uses the Internet as a medium of communication is the transmission of the cardholder's account number to the Internet merchant. From the merchant's e-commerce server, information about authorized charges [is] transmitted to the merchant's acquiring bank in the same manner as they would be transmitted by a telephone or mail order merchant. The rights and obligations between the merchant, the merchant's acquiring bank and the cardholder's issuing bank are set by private contracts between the parties.

Consumers considering whether to use the Internet to make purchases can limit their risk of loss due to fraud by using their credit card as a form of payment because federal regulations limit consumer liability for unauthorized charges to $50. This limit applies whether the card is used in a face-to-face transaction, in a telephone or mail order transaction, or in an Internet transaction. The Federal Reserve Board, the federal agency charged with oversight of consumer credit card regulations, has stated that merchants who accept credit card information in transactions in which the merchant does not have the opportunity to inspect the credit card cannot contest a consumer's later claim that a particular charge transaction was unauthorized. This rule was developed in the mail order and telephone order context, and applies equally to the Internet context.

A merchant considering accepting payment by credit card from an Internet retail site must first be satisfied that it has found a way to minimize the risk of fraud and error associated with credit card use, because the merchant will not be allowed to pass those costs on to the consumer, or in most cases, the merchant's acquiring bank. A merchant may decide that it nevertheless makes sense to accept credit cards as a payment device for Internet commerce given the lack of practical alternatives, the increased volume of sales that are likely to result, and the fact that the credit card issuer, not the merchant, assumes the risk of payment default by the card holder.

Consumers also enjoy access to dispute resolution services provided by credit card issuers in the event that the consumer has a dispute with the Internet merchant regarding the goods or services purchased. Under certain circumstances, federal regulations require card issuers to investigate and resolve cardholder complaints about goods and services purchased by credit card. Current business practice among card issuers has considerably expanded the use of this dispute resolution service to include more transactions than are covered by federal regulation. From the consumer perspective, the use of a credit card as a payment mechanism substantially reduces the risk of being forced either to pay for unacceptable goods or services ordered over the Internet, or to submit to the jurisdiction of a remote forum in order to dispute the value of goods and services purchased over the Internet.

4.2 Electronic Funds Transfers

If some of the new technologies for payments under development are ultimately successful, it is possible they will be outside the scope of existing laws, including consumer protection regulations. Unless and until regulators intervene, such systems would be regulated by contracts among the parties. Wholesale funds transfer systems in the US evolved largely outside of any existing regulatory framework for over a decade before a formal body of law was established to govern the rights and obligations of the parties. The law that now addresses wholesale wire transfers is UCC Article 4A. Article 4A is a very significant development in the law of electronic commerce because it was one of the first bodies of law to consider in depth how the use of electronic authentication systems should be regulated.

In the US, financial institutions operate a wholesale wire transfer system for large scale business to business funds transfers. These systems, which include the Fedwire operated by the Federal Reserve system, and the New York Clearing House for Interbank Payment Systems (CHIPS), transfer in excess of one trillion dollars per day. These systems began operations in the early 1970s, and operate largely among banks and their major corporate customers. Before the adoption of Article 4A, the only law that applied to these systems beyond private contracts among the participants were Federal Reserve Board Operating Circulars, for transfers that used the Fedwire, and the operating rules of CHIPS, for transfers that used CHIPS. Many aspects of these transactions were not covered by any organized body of law, however, and it was possible for disputes to arise between parties which were not clearly governed by any contract or operating system rule.

Banks providing wire transfer services were not particularly concerned about the lack of formal law governing the wholesale funds transfer system until some litigated cases in the 1980s raised issues that the banks found troubling. One such issue that drove the banks to the ULC to support the Article 4A drafting process was a litigated case in which a bank failed to make a funds transfer on the date requested by its customer. The court suggested that a bank making an error in handling a wire transfer might be held liable for the lost profits from any business deal the transferor lost due to the delay. Banks were unwilling to accept liability beyond the time value of the funds while they were delayed due to the error. Because a funds transfer might pass through several banks on the way from transferor to transferee, it was not possible for a bank to be certain that it would always be protected against liability by a preexisting contractual relationship with the disgruntled transferor. The only way to guarantee a limit to the bank's liability would be by statute. After considerable debate in the drafting process, the representatives of the banks' customers agreed to this limitation.

Banks and their customers shared a commitment to keeping the price of funds transfer services low, and expanding liability for the banks would have a necessary consequence of forcing banks to raise the price of funds transfer services or to leave the market. Bank customers agreed that it was more efficient for customers to accept responsibility for monitoring the proper execution of funds transfers when large profits were at stake than to put the banks in the position of insuring all their customers against any risk of bank error in executing transfers. Many bank customers were operating a level of sophistication that was equivalent to the banks themselves, and so in a context in which no consumers were involved, the customer could reasonably be expected to assume some responsibility for the operation of the system in exchange for lower prices.

Another major point of contention between the banks and their customers was how responsibility for unauthorized funds transfers should be allocated. The banks initially took the position that unauthorized funds transfers could only occur as a result of carelessness by their customers because banks had adequate security procedures in place, but their customers were unwilling to accept this analysis. After heated debate, a complex compromise was worked out dividing liability for unauthorized funds transfers between the bank and the customer. The initial allocation of liability was on the bank, but the bank could shift the risk of liability to the customer if the bank and the customer agreed on a "commercially reasonable security procedure" that would be used to initiate funds transfers. A "commercially reasonable" security procedure is one that is adapted to the customer's situation, in light of the amount, type and volume of funds transfers the customer makes, the customer's business and other factors. If the bank can prove that it complied with the security procedure agreed upon with the customer, then the bank cannot be held liable for an unauthorized funds transfer executed from the customer's account. The only exception to this rule arises in the unlikely event that the customer can prove that the unauthorized funds transfer did not originate with any person or facility under the customer's control. In that case, which would include funds transfers executed by hackers penetrating the security of the system from outside the customer's facilities, the bank must bear the risk of loss.

Article 4A takes a very different approach to liability issues than the consumer protection regulations that apply to credit card transactions. With credit cards, the consumer is presumed to be incapable of making any significant contribution to reducing the risk of loss due to unauthorized use of the card, and so is exonerated from almost all liability as a result. Card issuers, merchants and acquiring banks bear almost all risk of fraud and error, and as a result have an incentive to invest in the most sophisticated antifraud technology available. In the wholesale funds transfer environment, however, many bank customers are operating at a level of sophistication equivalent to that of the banks, and are required to be active participants in the design and maintenance of the security of the funds transfer system. Even though the loss allocation rules in each system point in opposite directions, Article 4A and the credit card system are each examples of commercial law that has been adapted very successfully to different categories of payment system. . . .

6. Conclusion

Existing commercial law can be adapted to new electronic commerce technologies in a manner that simplifies and supports business practice if changes are made in light of present commercial reality. There are many successful examples of technology neutral commercial law, such as the Article 4A concept of a "security procedure" and the Article 8 concept of a "security entitlement," that are flexible enough to accommodate many different forms of technology. Business practices in Internet commerce may not yet be well enough established for commercial law to capture and reflect the standard default terms the parties might expect to operate in the absence of explicit contract terms. Until a body of business practices develops to guide the direction of legislation, transacting parties should carefully consider how risks are allocated by private agreement.

If Congress and state legislatures leap in too quickly to promote promising technologies, chances are great that the result will be greater inefficiency, not less. Legislators should not be in the business of trying to guess the winners in the current competition among technologies for Internet commerce. If Congress and state legislatures cannot refrain from acting in this area, however, they should limit their intervention to protecting less sophisticated parties from possible overreaching by more sophisticated parties. The model of credit card consumer protection offers a promising model for legislation that promotes electronic commerce without dictating any technological choices. Credit card consumer protection regulations shelter less sophisticated parties from fraud and error risks they cannot control while forcing more sophisticated parties to invest in security procedures to reduce such risks as much as possible. This type of legislation can help to make the entire system operate more efficiently than it would if transactions were governed simply by standard form contracts drawn up by card issuers.

COMMENTS AND QUESTIONS

1.   Credit card laws allocate responsibility for unauthorized charges in a way that is very protective of consumers. Should online payment legislation do the same thing?

2.   Closely related to the question of digital signatures is the feasibility of new forms of electronic currency such as "electronic cash." A variety of electronic cash systems have been developed. While they differ in technical details, each operates much like a prepaid phone card or "chit" that a consumer buys from a bank or other institution. In this case, though, the "card" is nothing more than an encrypted number. Once credited with a certain sum, the consumer can use that number to pay for goods or services. The key difference between electronic cash and other forms of Internet payments systems is that the merchant can verify that the cash is valid without ever learning the identity of the buyer. Unlike the data trails left by credit cards, therefore, electronic cash can preserve anonymity in commercial transactions—just as paper currency does in the real world. For a discussion of electronic cash, see A. Michael Froomkin, Flood Control on the Information Ocean: Living With Anonymity, Digital Cash, and Distributed Databases, 15 J.L. & Com. 395 (1996).

At this writing, electronic cash has not gained widespread acceptance. Electronic cash is cumbersome, which may deter many people from using it. Consumers have turned out not to mind paying for goods over the Internet by credit card, perhaps because they value their privacy less than many scholars suppose. And different forms of electronic cash are generally not exchangeable or compatible with each other. Because electronic payment systems have the characteristics of a network market, the absence of either a clear market leader or an open standard may deter the broad acceptance needed to start the ball rolling. See Mark A. Lemley, Standardizing Government Standard-Setting Policy for Electronic Commerce, 14 Berkeley Tech. L.J. 745, 754-756 (1999).

If electronic cash does gain acceptance, it may herald a fundamental change in the way currencies operate. Kerry Macintosh has argued that electronic cash may open a wedge for private (rather than government-issued) currencies. See Kerry Lynn Macintosh, How to Encourage Global Electronic Commerce: The Case for Private Currencies on the Internet, 11 Harv. J.L. & Tech. 733 (1998); Kerry Lynn Macintosh, The New Money, 14 Berkeley Tech. L.J. 659 (1999). For a more skeptical view, see Jane Kaufman Winn, Clash of the Titans: Regulating the Competition Between Established and Emerging Electronic Payment Systems, 14 Berkeley Tech. L.J. 675 (1999).

Is electronic cash a good thing? As in the debates we saw earlier over encryption and anonymity, society must trade off its citizens' interest in privacy against the risk that anonymity can be used to evade the law. For a discussion of financial cryptography and anonymity, see Peter Swire, The Uses and Limits of Financial Cryptography: A Law Professor's Perspective, http://www.osu.edu/units/law/swire.htm.

Note on International Harmonization and Electronic Commerce

With its Framework for Global Electronic Commerce, the Clinton Administration has sought to set the agenda for Internet governance worldwide. The leading user of the Internet, the United States hopes to persuade the rest of the world to adopt the American legal and policy approach to ecommerce so that its rules will become the global norms. Although the European Union (EU) has championed initiatives on personal data protection and on the sui generis law to protect the contents of databases in the international arena, most countries have been in a reactive mode toward U.S. policy initiatives. With the U.S. digital economy growing at a rapid pace, there is a natural tendency among Americans to think that the rest of the world would benefit by adopting American legal and policy initiatives. It is fair for other countries to consider whether this in fact is so.

An obvious fact about the Internet is the global character of its reach. While it is unquestionably true that a great deal of trade is international, the physicality of tangible goods, such as automobiles, vacuum cleaners, and television sets, makes it easy to apply territory-based rules to them. United States law can easily be applied to a transaction based in the United States, but what law applies if unlawful information (e.g., pornography or copyright infringement) is uploaded to a computer in the United States but downloaded in Japan or Belgium? If two electronic agents, one representing a U.S. client and one representing a Japanese client, "meet" in cyberspace and exchange messages, and the U.S. electronic agent thinks a contract has been formed, whose law will determine which jurisdiction's law will be used to judge the validity and terms of the contract? It is readily apparent that laws may vary from nation to nation on such an issue. These variations may interfere with the growth of electronic commerce as well as other desired objectives. The question is: how can nations work together to find enough common ground on the private law of the Internet to promote ecommerce and other beneficial exchanges of information?[1]

Complete harmonization of laws may be desirable to promote Internet commerce, but harmonizing diverse legal rules can be a tediously slow process. Consider, for example, that almost a decade of meetings preceded the diplomatic conference at which the WIPO Copyright Treaty was concluded. An alternative to harmonization may be to form guidelines for countries to employ as they formulate the specifics of their own legal rules on a topic. The Organization for Economic Cooperation and Development (OECD) has been active in promoting this form of international cooperation. Guidelines may not lead to uniformity, however, in part

---

1. For a discussion of the issues that arise in the international context, see Steven Hoffer, World Cyberspace Law (1999).

because countries that endorse guidelines sometimes do not actually implement them. Guidelines may also be implemented in inconsistent ways. Yet even inconsistent implementations of rules based on guidelines may be better than the chaos of complete disharmony. Differences in national culture and legal traditions may make it difficult to attain consensus on the fine details of legal rules on an international basis. Nevertheless, international efforts, such as those undertaken by the United Nations Commission on International Trade Law (UNCITRAL), offer some promise for evolving harmonized rules to promote electronic commerce over the Internet.

Another way to achieve harmony on a global scale may be for one nation to propose legal rules that it urges all nations to adopt. This may be a faster path to harmonization than the laborious consensus process that typifies the treatymaking process. Both the United States and the EU have used this approach to international lawmaking for the Internet, in particular as to global electronic commerce. The U.S. White Paper on Intellectual Property and the National Information Infrastructure, for example, proposed digital copyright rules virtually identical to the treaty proposals the Administration submitted to WIPO at more or less the same time. The United States hoped for, and largely got, a "first mover" advantage by proposing these rules, for the draft treaty considered in 1996 in Geneva largely reflected the U.S. positions. The Clinton Administration's proposed rules became the baseline for discussion, even if they were ultimately transformed in the course of the U.S. legislative and international treatymaking process.

Despite the many initiatives to develop consensus on the law of the Internet, some dangers clearly lurk in the international arena. Some arise from the ability of major multinational firms to engage in what Professor Froomkin describes as "regulatory arbitrage," in which a firm plays some nations off against others as a way to get acceptance of rules that the multinational firm prefers. Also dangerous are potential races to the bottom (that is, contests over which nation will adopt the least restrictive rules and attract the most commercial activity as a result), or races to the top (who can adopt the toughest rules that will become a baseline for applying pressure to get international adoption by others?). Much as countries might like to take some time to think through what laws they think should be used to regulate the Internet, there is a sense of urgency about putting in place a legal and policy infrastructure to promote electronic commerce and other exchanges of information via the Internet. The fear is that those who wait too long will be left behind in the global information economy. Perhaps this fear can have constructive consequences in motivating countries to work together to achieve the minimum level of consensus needed for electronic commerce to flourish. Whether that will happen remains to be seen, however.

C. INTERNET TAXATION

≡≡ *Internet Tax Freedom Act*

Sec. 1101. Moratorium.

(a) Moratorium.—No State or political subdivision thereof shall impose any of the following taxes during the period beginning on October 1, 1998, and ending 3 years after the date of the enactment of this Act—

(1) taxes on Internet access, unless such tax was generally imposed and actually enforced prior to October 1, 1998; and

(2) multiple or discriminatory taxes on electronic commerce.

(b) Preservation of State and Local Taxing Authority.—Except as provided in this section, nothing in this title shall be construed to modify, impair, or supersede, or authorize the modification, impairment, or superseding of, any State or local law pertaining to taxation that is otherwise permissible by or under the Constitution of the United States or other Federal law and in effect on the date of enactment of this Act.

(c) Liabilities and Pending Cases.—Nothing in this title affects liability for taxes accrued and enforced before the date of enactment of this Act, nor does this title affect ongoing litigation relating to such taxes.

(d) Definition of Generally Imposed and Actually Enforced.—For purposes of this section, a tax has been generally imposed and actually enforced prior to October 1, 1998, if, before that date, the tax was authorized by statute and either—

(1) a provider of Internet access services had a reasonable opportunity to know by virtue of a rule or other public proclamation made by the appropriate administrative agency of the State or political subdivision thereof, that such agency has interpreted and applied such tax to Internet access services; or

(2) a State or political subdivision thereof generally collected such tax on charges for Internet access.

(e) Exception to Moratorium.—

(1) In general.—Subsection (a) shall also not apply in the case of any person or entity who knowingly and with knowledge of the character of the material, in interstate or foreign commerce by means of the World Wide Web, makes any communication for commercial purposes that is available to any minor and that includes any material that is harmful to minors unless such person or entity has restricted access by minors to material that is harmful to minors—

(A) by requiring use of a credit card, debit account, adult access code, or adult personal identification number;

(B) by accepting a digital certificate that verifies age; or

(C) by any other reasonable measures that are feasible under available technology.

(2) Scope of exception.—For purposes of paragraph (1), a person shall not be considered to [be] making a communication for commercial purposes of material to the extent that the person is—

(A) a telecommunications carrier engaged in the provision of a telecommunications service;

(B) a person engaged in the business of providing an Internet access service;

(C) a person engaged in the business of providing an Internet information location tool; or

(D) similarly engaged in the transmission, storage, retrieval, hosting, formatting, or translation (or any combination thereof) of a communication made by another person, without selection or alteration of the communication. . . .

(f) Additional Exception to Moratorium.—

(1) In general.—Subsection (a) shall also not apply with respect to an Internet access provider, unless, at the time of entering into an agreement with a customer for the provision of Internet access services, such provider offers such customer (either for a fee or at no charge) screening software that is designed to permit the customer to limit access to material on the Internet that is harmful to minors.

[Definitions relating specifically to subsections (e) and (f) have been omitted.]

[Sections 1102 and 1103 establish a commission to study the problem and report back to Congress.]

Sec. 1104.   Definitions.

For the purposes of this title:

(1) Bit tax.—The term "bit tax" means any tax on electronic commerce expressly imposed on or measured by the volume of digital information transmitted electronically, or the volume of digital information per unit of time transmitted electronically, but does not include taxes imposed on the provision of telecommunications services.

(2) Discriminatory tax.—The term "discriminatory tax" means—

(A) any tax imposed by a State or political subdivision thereof on electronic commerce that—

(i) is not generally imposed and legally collectible by such State or such political subdivision on transactions involving similar property, goods, services, or information accomplished through other means;

(ii) is not generally imposed and legally collectible at the same rate by such State or such political subdivision on transactions involving similar property, goods, services, or information accomplished through other means, unless the rate is lower as part of a phase-out of the tax over not more than a 5-year period;

(iii) imposes an obligation to collect or pay the tax on a different person or entity than in the case of transactions involving similar property, goods, services, or information accomplished through other means;

(iv) establishes a classification of Internet access service providers or online service providers for purposes of establishing a higher tax rate to be imposed on such providers than the tax rate generally applied to providers of similar information services delivered through other means; or

(B) any tax imposed by a State or political subdivision thereof, if—

(i) except with respect to a tax (on Internet access) that was generally imposed and actually enforced prior to October 1, 1998, the sole ability to access a site on a remote seller's out-of-State computer server is considered a factor in determining a remote seller's tax collection obligation; or

(ii) a provider of Internet access service or online services is deemed to be the agent of a remote seller for determining tax collection obligations solely as a result of—

(I) the display of a remote seller's information or content on the out-of-State computer server of a provider of Internet access service or online services; or

(II) the processing of orders through the out-of-State computer server of a provider of Internet access service or online services.

(3) Electronic commerce.—The term "electronic commerce" means any transaction conducted over the Internet or through Internet access, comprising the sale, lease, license, offer, or delivery of property, goods, services, or information, whether or not for consideration, and includes the provision of Internet access.

(4) Internet.—The term "Internet" means collectively the myriad of computer and telecommunications facilities, including equipment and operating software, which comprise the interconnected world-wide network of networks that employ the Transmission Control Protocol/Internet Protocol, or any predecessor or successor protocols to such protocol, to communicate information of all kinds by wire or radio.

(5) Internet access.—The term "Internet access" means a service that enables users to access content, information, electronic mail, or other services offered over the Internet, and may also include access to proprietary content, information, and other services as part of a package of services offered to users. Such term does not include telecommunications services.

(6) Multiple tax.—

(A) In general.—The term "multiple tax" means any tax that is imposed by one State or political subdivision thereof on the same or essentially the same electronic commerce that is also subject to another tax by another State or political subdivision thereof (whether or not at the same rate or on the same basis), without a credit (for example, a resale exemption certificate) for taxes paid in other jurisdictions.

(B) Exception.—Such term shall not include a sales or use tax imposed by a State and 1 or more political subdivisions thereof on the same electronic commerce or a tax on persons engaged in electronic commerce which also may have been subject to a sales or use tax thereon.

(C) Sales or use tax.—For purposes of subparagraph (B), the term "sales or use tax" means a tax that is imposed on or incident to the sale, purchase, storage, consumption, distribution, or other use of tangible personal property or services as may be defined by laws imposing such tax and which is measured by the amount of the sales price or other charge for such property or service. . . .

Sec. 1201. Declaration That Internet Should Be Free of New Federal Taxes.

It is the sense of Congress that no new Federal taxes similar to the taxes described in section 1101(a) should be enacted with respect to the Internet and Internet access during the moratorium provided in such section. . . .

Sec. 1203. Declaration That the Internet Should Be Free of Foreign Tariffs, Trade Barriers, and Other Restrictions.

(a) In General.—It is the sense of Congress that the President should seek bilateral, regional, and multilateral agreements to remove barriers to global electronic commerce through the World Trade Organization, the Organization for Economic Cooperation and Development, the Trans-Atlantic Economic Partnership, the Asia Pacific Economic Cooperation forum, the Free Trade Area of the America, the North American Free Trade Agreement, and other appropriate venues.

(b) Negotiating Objectives.—The negotiating objectives of the United States shall be—

(1) to assure that electronic commerce is free from—

(A) tariff and nontariff barriers;

(B) burdensome and discriminatory regulation and standards; and

(C) discriminatory taxation; and

(2) to accelerate the growth of electronic commerce by expanding market access opportunities for—

(A) the development of telecommunications infrastructure;

(B) the procurement of telecommunications equipment;

(C) the provision of Internet access and telecommunications services; and

(D) the exchange of goods, services, and digitalized information. . . .

COMMENTS AND QUESTIONS

1. After heated debate, Congress extended the moratorium on Internet taxation until 2006. See Christopher J. Schafer, Federal Legislation Regarding Taxation of Internet Sales Transactions, 16 Berkeley Tech. L.J. 415 (2001). It is likely that this extension will effectively make the moratorium permanent, as retailers and consumers come to rely on the tax-free nature of electronic commerce.

2. The stated goal of the Internet Tax Freedom Act (ITFA) is to prohibit discriminatory taxation against electronic commerce sellers and multiple or overlapping taxation between different jurisdictions. Such taxation might occur, for example, where a seller located in one jurisdiction sells a product into another jurisdiction, and both jurisdictions seek to impose sales tax on the transaction. It would indeed seem unfair to permit such double taxation. But how likely is that? In the modern world, lots of commerce takes place across borders. Can't we deal with electronic commerce tax issues in the same way we have dealt with other transborder issues?

Indeed, the tax law is actually *more* favorable to electronic commerce than to other types of transactions. The Supreme Court has held that interstate commerce is not subject to state sales tax at all by the seller's state. Mail order catalogs, for example, don't charge tax on out-of-state purchases. (In theory, the recipient is supposed to remit local tax to the state of receipt, but that rule is almost never enforced.) Presumably, the ITFA would preserve this state of affairs for electronic commerce. Further, electronic commerce may make it possible for some companies to relocate to tax havens to avoid paying income tax or various other kinds of taxes. Finally, the ITFA provides that no new taxes can be imposed on electronic commerce for a three-year period, even if corresponding taxes are imposed on other sorts of commerce.

Although the initial wave of ecommerce was conducted by companies that specialized in Internet sales, more and more electronic commerce is conducted by regular, "bricks and mortar" companies that have ventured online. These "clicks and mortar" sites sell both online and in stores around the country. How should they be treated for tax purposes? As the prevalence of clicks and mortar sites grows, it may be harder to sustain a distinction between taxable sales in the physical world and tax-free Internet sales.

3. There is a growing literature on the taxation problems posed by electronic commerce. See, e.g., David Hardesty, Taxation of Electronic Commerce (1999); David L. Forst, Old and New Issues in the Taxation of Electronic Commerce, 14 Berkeley Tech. L.J. 711 (1999). For arguments against the tax moratorium, see Arthur J. Cockfield, Designing Tax Policy for the Digital Biosphere: How the Internet Is Changing Tax Laws, 34 Conn. L. Rev. 333 (2002); Arthur J. Cockfield, Transforming the Internet into a Taxable Forum: A Case Study in E-Commerce Taxation, 85 Minn. L. Rev. 1171 (2001).

4. While the reach of the ITFA is domestic, much of the electronic commerce tax problem is international in scope. The statute suggests ways to negotiate favorable tax treatment for electronic commerce, but the United States cannot legislate in this area alone. Whether the rest of the world will follow its model remains to be seen.

15

Internet Governance

The legal problems in regulating the Internet that we have discussed have led a number of commentators to suggest that existing law is ill-suited to solving the problems of Internet governance. Alternative proposals take a variety of forms, from suggesting that the Net be treated as its own jurisdiction to endorsing some sort of international governance structure. Whether the Internet really needs new governance models and what those models might be are disputed questions.

David R. Johnson & David G. Post, And How Shall the Net Be Governed? A Meditation on the Relative Virtues of Decentralized, Emergent Law
Coordinating the Internet 62 (Brian Kahin & James Keller eds., 1997)

Introduction

Now that lots of people use (and plan to use) the internet, many—governments, businesses, techies, users and system operators (the "sysops" who control ID issuance and the servers that hold files)—are asking how we will be able to

(1) establish and enforce baseline rules of conduct that facilitate reliable communications and trustworthy commerce, and
(2) define, punish and prevent wrongful actions that trash the electronic commons or impose harm on others.

In other words, how will Cyberspace be governed, and by what right?

1019

By creating a new global, border-disregarding, place that cannot readily be controlled by any existing sovereign . . . the net weakens many of the institutions that we have come to rely on for a solution to the basic problems of collective action—the selection of means by which individuals coordinate and order their interactions so as to achieve what they believe is a greater good. Thus, the very nature and growing importance of the net calls for a fundamental re-examination of the institutional structure within which rulemaking—at least as applicable to the activities conducted solely on the net—takes place. As more fully discussed below, that re-examination might lead us to conclude that the net allows the problem of collective action to be solved by a new, decentralized process that does not closely resemble those we have used in the past to pass laws and enforce behavioral norms.

Questions about whether and how the net shall be governed are now arising most pointedly in connection with the issuance of domain names (like "ibm.com"). Domain names are translated by means of lookup tables distributed across the net into the IP addresses (like "123.45.67.89") that determine how messages are routed over the net. Because domain names are easier to remember than long strings of numbers, and because top level domains are often used in email addresses (like "fred@ibm.com"), they have become a particularly valuable form of "virtual real estate". Yet, despite their value and importance, it is far from clear who (if anyone) has the authority to determine who has the right to use any particular domain name (and on what terms and conditions they have that right), or to establish the basic structure of the domain name system—the combination of technical standards and trade practices pursuant to which domain names are registered and the associated lookup tables are distributed across the net.

As described in RFC 1591 (available at http://ds.internic.net/rfc/rfc1591.txt), the Internet Assigned Numbers Authority (IANA)

> is responsible for the overall coordination and management of the Domain Name System (DNS), and especially the delegation of portions of the name space called top-level domains. . . .

Although both IANA and InterNIC (which has delegated the DNS administration to Network Solutions, Inc. (NSI), a private company) receive US government funds for their operation, no contract, constitution, or treaty gives either these bodies or the US Government the right to set policy regarding domain names on the global network. Nor do these bodies have any obviously valid claim to make the exclusive delegation of registration duties. The financial support provided by the US Government has not given it ownership of any intellectual property or physical asset essential (other than in the very short term) to the operation of a domain name system. To the contrary, domain name look up tables function because local hosts point their domain name servers at these tables; a form of custom, and not "law," dictates the particular root servers to which local hosts point for this information.

The current uncertainty regarding governance of the domain name system extends to much more than the technical standards governing domain name registration and selection of root servers. Basic economic and policy questions remain unanswered. At present, NSI (with NSF's blessing) demands payment for registration of domain names. But, again, no statute or international convention—nor even a universal acceptance of trade practice—clearly legitimizes NSI's right to charge that fee (or justifies any particular amount that might be charged). Nor is there any obvious source of guidance regarding what other conditions (such as a promise to abide by particular laws, to resolve disputes in a specified manner, or to waive certain claims) may be imposed as a prerequisite to domain name registration. Thus, no one can now say that any given condition must, may, or may not be imposed as a minimum requirement for this particular passport to "netizenship". Nor do any of the many different private and governmental organizations that are currently discussing a range of questions in this area—e.g., how many "top level domains" should be allowed, whether multiple registries should be allowed to compete, and what duties might reasonably be imposed on those who operate registries—have an uncontested or clearly legitimate claim to the authority to decide these matters unilaterally.

These questions are of crucial strategic importance, despite the uncertainty surrounding them, because only through an IP address and an association of that address with a findable reference, whether through a domain name or a directory, can an individual meaningfully enter Cyberspace in the first instance. An IP address block and a Domain Name are necessary to become a sysop offering access to the net. Domain name based email addresses are the essence of online identity for individual users. Dispensers of those virtual addresses thus stand at the border checkpoint between the virtual and the non-virtual world, and the contract pursuant to which one receives a domain name or other online ID can potentially serve as the means—perhaps the most effective means—by which the most basic rights and obligations of all Cyberspace participants can be specified.

Thus, although the current domain name policy debate appears to apply primarily to ministerial duties performed by a registry, for the purpose of avoiding duplicative names, the contracts entered into with such a registry (and any associated subsidiary contracts through which individual users contract with the domain name/address-holder to obtain access to the net) could prove of primary importance in determining both the degree of freedom and the level of order on the net.

Why Must the Net Be "Governed" at All?

Some may ask why the net must be "governed" at all? Even the three judge Federal court in Philadelphia that threw out the Communications Decency Act on First Amendment grounds seemed thrilled by the "chaotic" and seemingly ungovernable character of the net. And the net now prospers precisely because of its decentralized architecture and the absence of centralized rule-making authority. Everyone who can buy a computer and has access to the global telephone network is free to establish a node on the net. Everyone is free to create editorial value by pointing to others' creations. New users connect by agreement with any nearby node or by getting an email address from any commercial or non-commercial supplier. Lots of systems have lots of different rules governing the behavior of users, and users—at least in most countries—are free to leave any system whose rules they find oppressive. Some systems demand full identification from users; some allow or even encourage anonymity. Some impose editorial controls to create "kid friendly" or "lawyer friendly" environments; others act more like common carriers who accept all comers. Some require and enforce promises to abide by traditional copyright laws; others require all participants to waive claims that interfere with redistribution of the materials users post online. And, up until now, access by sysops to domain names and IP addresses that make it possible to settle new territory in Cyberspace has not been conditioned on any required promises to comply with (or to require users to comply with) specific laws or behavioral standards. That has, to be sure, left sysops free to impose their own rules on end users. But the diversity of differing venues on the net, and the ability of users to decide where to visit (and where not to visit) and with whom to communicate, has tended both to keep sysop tyranny in check and to limit the adverse impact of wrongdoing by individual users.

This decentralized decision-making has helped to make it possible for large numbers of people with different goals to get interconnected. But the problem of collective action remains and, indeed, grows more urgent as the net becomes larger and more complex. Anarchy, after all, has costs. It just won't do for packets, for example, to be systematically misrouted. People won't trust their important commercial and private dealings to a network where a domain name might be translated to a different IP address depending on where the message happens to originate. Nor, indeed, will large numbers of users visit online spaces if they encounter systematic fraud or vandalism or other activities they view as harmful or antisocial. There are activities that, when permitted even in only a few online venues, impose costs on all others, and against which individuals may want to protect themselves. Spamming is a form of wrongdoing that may be beyond the capacity (or desire) of a particular local sysop to control but that can make lots of users of lots of other systems miserable. The same could be said of launching destructive code. Some web pages may invade your privacy on contact. Some parts of the electronic forest path may even be conducive to highway robbery. As the global village transforms itself into a complex electronic city, crime cannot be far behind. If the natural result of decentralized activities on the net were the development of unpredictable technical environments and unsafe social spaces, then calls for top down, centralized forms of collective action would become louder and more persuasive. Thus, even with respect to activities that take place solely on the net, we face the questions whether and how to generate and enforce rules to control anti-social users and the sysops who tolerate them.

Moreover, the net can be used to facilitate communications among individuals whose online actions impose harm even on those who only frequent the nonvirtual world. Most real world communities will want to be assured that the net will not be used systematically to undercut their security. Online tax havens could harm the physical infrastructure of local communities that lose tax revenues. Online conspiracies to commit violence in the real world will surely draw a response from the potential victims. Accordingly, both users of the net and all of those affected by their actions will likely demand some form of "governance" or "order" that prevents wrongdoing. The key question now posed, in connection with the domain name system and derivatively with respect to every other aspect of online interaction, is whether that governance must take the traditional form of centralized, top down lawmaking or whether, instead, the nature of the net allows decentralized creation of another, very different, form of public order.

Competing Models

There are four basic competing models for the governance of the global net.

First, existing territorial sovereigns can simply seek to extend their jurisdiction, and to amend their laws as necessary, to attempt to govern all actions on the net that have substantial impacts on their own citizenry.

Second, sovereigns can enter into multi-lateral international agreements to establish new and uniform rules specifically applicable to conduct on the net.

Third, a new international organization can attempt to establish new rules—and new means of enforcing those rules and of holding those who make the rules accountable to appropriate constituencies.

Fourth, de facto rules may emerge as a result of the complex interplay of individual decisions by domain name and IP address registries (regarding what conditions to impose on possession of an online address), by sysops (regarding what local rules to adopt, what filters to install, what users to allow to sign on, and with which other systems to connect) and by users (regarding which personal filters to install and which systems to patronize).

We believe that, in part because of serious problems with the first three, traditional models, and in part because of the surprising ability of decentralized action to address serious problems that might previously have been thought to require "top down" centralized law making by a sovereign with a monopoly on the authorized use of force, the net may well be capable of being "governed" primarily by the fourth method—a mechanism that Tom Bell (following Hayek) calls "polycentric law" and that we will call "decentralized, emergent law." The decentralized, emergent form of collective action involves voluntary acceptance of standards (or, as the Internet Engineering Task Force motto would have it: "rough consensus and working code"). Despite the fears of those who cannot conceive of order as arising from anything other than top down, hierarchical control, this is not a process that necessarily leads to chaos and anarchy. To the contrary, the technical protocols of the net have in effect created a complex adaptive system that produces a type of order that does not rely on lawyers, court decisions, statutes, or votes. We will argue that the same decentralized decisionmaking that created the net at a technical level may be able to create a workable and, indeed, empowering and just form of order even at the highest level of the protocol stack—the realm of rules applicable to the collective social evaluation and governance of human behavior.

Because decentralized action may well be capable of generating responsible self-regulation of the net, those who propose other forms of collective action might be best advised to hold off any efforts to achieve top down control—lest they prematurely preempt the growth of what might be the most efficient and empowering form of net governance. Existing sovereigns need not waive their ultimate power to take action to protect the well-being of their citizens, of course. But they should sensibly defer action to see whether the collective actions of domain name registries, sysops and users produces a set of operational rules that provides reasonable protection for the vital interests they are charged to protect. If the net is allowed to develop a responsible self-regulatory structure, by means of decentralized, emergent law making, and if this new mechanism proves up to the task of building a productive and non-predatory order, then all concerned will have saved the large resources that might otherwise have been spent trying, perhaps without similar success, to impose rules from a centralized source. . . .

Can Net Policies and Rules Be Made and
Enforced without Centralized Decision-Making?

We certainly do not mean to suggest that the governance models sketched out above will have, or that they should have, no impact on the net. Merely to suggest that there are "problems" with implementation of any or all of these models, is not to prove that they are inadequate for any of the tasks at hand; after all, proponents of representative democracy are fond of saying that while it is a terrible system, it's better than any known alternative. The fundamental question is whether, at least for the global electronic communications network, the fourth governance model of decentralized and emergent law-making might have significant advantages over the alternative models and should be looked at as the presumptively primary source of online order.

Consider what makes the net work. The net itself solves an immensely difficult collective action problem: how to get large numbers of individual computer networks, running diverse operating systems, to communicate with one another for the common good. And, yet, the net is really nothing more than a set of voluntary standards regarding message transmission, routing, and reception. There is not now and never was a central governmental body that decreed or voted to adopt a law stating that TCP/IP is required to be used by those wishing to communicate electronically on a global scale, or that HTTP is required to be used if you wish to communicate over a particular portion of the global network (the World Wide Web). If you connect to a neighboring host and send out packets of data that conform to the protocol, your messages can be heard by others who have adopted the protocol. All are free to decline to follow the standard and to obey some other protocol, and they will communicate only to those who, literally, speak their language. Many people and groups have, in fact, seceded (or declined to join) the global net, forming local area, or proprietary wide area, networks.

The "rule-making" process for baseline protocols of the net had none of the vices of centralized, top down, bureaucratic or political, governance. The rules instead evolved from the decentralized decisions by individuals to adopt a promising standard because it served their own interests. To be sure, the successful rules were created by individuals and small groups and they spread more quickly as a result of some government funded innovation and communications. But they did not stem from or rely in any way on the law of a geographically defined territory. They did not require any agreement among representatives of sovereign nations. And they did not require the creation of a new policy-making apparatus that required an international bureaucracy or that faced questions regarding the accountability of decisionmakers to particular constituencies. Minorities are protected by their right to propose inconsistent rules and, indeed, to follow those alternative rules if they believe the benefits of doing so outweigh the costs. Enforcement of a predominant rule set stems naturally from uncoordinated, decentralized decisions.

[Johnson and Post respond to a number of possible objections to their scheme and then suggest that some role remains for national law.]

Nevertheless, one might postulate some activities online that threaten most "real world" citizens and that are not even tolerated and protected by any geographic state. Imagine, for example, a host computer based in international waters, using wireless technology to broadcast messages that enable terrorist groups to make chemical weapons and coordinate an attack. In such a case, the small net "community" that patronized that online venue would be, in effect, at war with both the remainder of the online world and the authorities and citizens of the real world as well. Any scheme for responsible self-regulation of the net must deal, conceptually, with this kind of "hard case." The decentralized, emergent form of order deals with this kind of case by conceding that, at this extreme, the national sovereigns may exercise force to defend their interests—just as sysops and users may use their own electronic form of force (their prerogatives to banish users or to leave a particular system) to set boundaries on others' otherwise uncontrollable wrongdoing.

Because the net does have real impacts on the real world, it can best hope to preserve its decentralized, emergent character if it "renders unto Caesar what is Caesar's". If online commercial transactions radically undermine the tax system needed to build the physical infrastructure, territorial governments may be entitled to defend that core interest by shutting down host sites specially designed to facilitate such transactions. Perhaps the sysops who facilitate online transactions should anticipate this problem and create a centralized means for online commerce to pay a fair tax, to a single collector, as a means of discouraging more disruptive and potentially duplicative enforcement proceedings by local authorities. In the face of such responsible action by the net itself, local authorities would be more likely to recognize that they do not possess a writ that automatically runs to all areas of the net, and that they should not seek to set the rules governing online interactions that don't seriously negatively impact the tangible world they govern.

It bears remembering that the users of the net and the policy-setting inhabitants of the "real world" most affected by online activities are, to a first approximation, the same people. As a group, netizens will not want to support activities that threaten core values they share as citizens of the tangible world. There are lots of novel issues that arise from the ability of electronic messages to cross territorial borders—but those issues will be resolved in part by means of the ability of every user and system to filter out unwanted messages, and, in part, by means of the ability of such cross-border communications to bring the world into close agreement about core values. . . .

Domain Name Policy as a Key First Problem for Collective Action—Revisited

To determine whether the combination of decentralized decision-making and better communications between real world authorities and virtual communities could lead to a workable form of governance for the net, let's examine more closely the current core hard case: the policies governing creation of new top level domains. If there is any question on which there at first appears to be a need for strong centralized rule, it's the question of how domain names are issued and how they are translated into IP numbers. The Domain Name System determines where your data packets are sent. If two separate registries both issued a "right" to use "ibm.com", and mapped this domain name to different IP addresses, and if half of the net derived its DNS lookup tables from each of these two incompatible regimes, massive confusion would ensue. If different registries impose differing conditions on access to net real estate or online identity, then there will be no single definition of "netizenship"—and wrongdoers (by someone's definition) could seek out the most tolerant regimes. Because of their mnemonic character, certain domain names and domain name uses are already being challenged as infringing of trademark rights deemed vital by companies who sell branded products. And there are now or soon will be lots of other questions that implicate the potentially intense and conflicting interests of particular communities: Can a registry charge for the use of a domain name? How much? And what decision-making process governs the expenditure of the money? May "indecent" domain names be registered? Must those who use domain names agree to resolve their disputes by arbitration? Agree to abide by copyright laws? Issue email addresses only to identifiable users? The domain name system thus already poses stark questions regarding the relationship between any self-regulatory system for the net and the powers of existing legislatures and courts.

There is reason to believe that even these challenging and contentious issues can be resolved by decentralized, emergent decision-making. For example, even the apparently fatal conflict between inconsistent domain name registration systems seems likely to be avoided without top down controls. Most users and sysops are interested in accurate routing of messages. They will want to connect to the DNS sources that most other people use. The confusing dual and inconsistent system hypothesized above is unstable (or, rather, could never arise in the first place) because the most widely used of the two systems would soon attract virtually all of the traffic (or all of the connections from downstream systems). Thus, the successful deployment of two incompatible versions of a top level domain, or two widely distributed yet incompatible sets of lookup tables, is about as likely as the simultaneous growth in one country of two languages that have the same words mapped onto different meanings. Because people look to reliable sources for their information, good data drive out bad. Network economies, and the creation of order from positive returns to information structure, save the day. Thus, while it is physically possible and currently lawful for system operators to create a mess by pointing their domain name resolving software at multiple incompatible sources, that nightmare scenario probably won't occur and need not be prohibited by legislation of any kind.

Similarly, there is good reason to believe that some combination of domain name registries and domain name holders will impose rules, in connection with issuance of access to the net, that reflect widespread agreement regarding what constitutes wrongful action. And there is reason to think that the actions of users in selecting the online venues they visit and support will in general keep such regulation from becoming either too oppressive or too lax. The online public will band together to electronically shun tyrants and detectable crooks. (We may need to worry more about due process, to protect unpopular minorities from mobs, than law enforcement.) Dens of thieves—and packets of data sent from known dens of thieves—can generally be avoided online. If your concern is privacy, you can avoid web sites that don't post verifiable tokens indicating that they observe rules that you deem satisfactory. If you don't want certain sites to link to your web page, you can use software code to preclude such links. No matter what your policy goal, acting through the filtering power of sysops and users is much more likely to produce rapid and effective results than lobbying for the enactment of some rule by a new transnational legislative body.

To be sure, no decentralized, emergent lawmaking scheme of this kind could be 100% effective. But substantial consensus is, operationally and practically, quite important even when total compliance cannot be achieved (as, by the way, is always the case, even under centralized law enforcement regimes run by non-democratic sovereigns). The reason is, again, that screening applicants for IDs and filtering out known sources of wrongful messages reduces the impact of wrongdoing even when it does not put the wrongdoer totally out of business. Trademark infringement tolerated on web pages in a small corner of the net, and filtered out by most responsible sysops once they are on notice of the problem, simply cannot cause very much confusion.

In contrast, efforts to use traditional top down, centralized lawmaking to solve the problems posed by the domain name system seem very likely to fail in more brittle ways. Take the question whether the establishment of alternative top level domains should be allowed. In the context of decentralized, emergent law, this question is decided in the marketplace—by multiple independent decisions whether to register with a new purported provider of a ".biz" domain or whether to point a local domain name server at another root lookup table. If, in contrast, the US were to purport to exercise its powers to prohibit the establishment of alternative top level domains, it would simply fail to attain jurisdiction over the actions of some host provider operating entirely outside the US. Perhaps the US could effectively prohibit all US hosts from pointing their local domain name servers at that remote root table, but the First Amendment might constrain such restrictions, which in any event would look silly if they contrasted with practices in other countries and the desires of the US market. If the US instead sought to negotiate a new treaty agreement governing the establishment of new top level domains, it would likely still be defining the shape of the bargaining table while the issue was decided, de facto, by engineering decisions. If it sought to delegate decisions on top level domain structure to a new international organization, it would face unanswerable questions about how to compel compliance with that organization's decisions by private actors. And even if most countries agreed to defer to and enforce the decisions of such an organization, there would be a serious question how to assure that its decisions reflected the needs and preferences of all participants in net based commerce. The best indicator of those needs and preferences would be the independent actions by sysops and users to accept a new standard. Traditional law making processes become, in the context, a counterproductive extra loop that at most delays or misdirects decisions otherwise likely to evolve rapidly from a decentralized process. . . .

COMMENTS AND QUESTIONS

1. Is it in fact difficult or impossible to apply existing law to the Internet? Has the development of case law since this article was written (in 1996) offered any more evidence about how well existing law and existing legal systems can handle the challenges posed by the Internet?

Johnson and Post develop their ideas in a number of other articles with similar themes. David Johnson & David Post, Chaos Prevailing on Every Continent: A New Theory of Decentralized Decision-Making in Complex Systems, 73 Chi.-Kent L. Rev. 1055 (1999); David R. Johnson & David Post, Law and Borders—The

Rise of Law in Cyberspace, 48 Stan. L. Rev. 1367 (1996); David G. Post, Governing Cyberspace, 43 Wayne L. Rev. 155 (1996); David G. Post, Anarchy, State and the Internet: An Essay on Law-Making in Cyberspace, 1995 J. Online L. art. 3.

For challenges to the Johnson and Post methodology, see Jack Goldsmith, Against Cyberanarchy, 65 U. Chi. L. Rev. 1199 (1998); Jack Goldsmith, Regulation of the Internet: Three Persistent Fallacies, 73 Chi.-Kent L. Rev. 1119 (1999); Neil Weinstock Netanel, Cyberspace Self-Governance; A Skeptical View From Liberal Democratic Theory, 88 Cal. L. Rev. 395 (2000). For other takes on how the Internet challenges traditional theories of governance, see, e.g., James Boyle, Foucault in Cyberspace: Surveillance, Sovereignty, and Hard-Wired Censors, 66 U. Cin. L. Rev. 177 (1997); Dan L. Burk, The Market for Digital Piracy, *in* Borders in Cyberspace 205 (Brian Kahin & Charles Nesson eds., 1998); Dan L. Burk, Virtual Exit in the Global Information Economy, 73 Chi.-Kent L. Rev. 943 (1999); A. Michael Froomkin, The Internet as a Source of Regulatory Arbitrage, *in* Borders in Cyberspace 129 (Brian Kahin & Charles Nesson eds., 1998); I Trotter Hardy, The Proper Legal Regime for "Cyberspace," 55 U. Pitt. L. Rev. 993 (1994).

2. Internet governance can't be decided only by focusing on the defects of the current system, of course. One must also propose a superior alternative. Does the Johnson/Post model of private ordering work for the Internet? How will it deal with conduct online that has effects offline? With nonconsensual torts online?

One way to explore the limits of the Johnson/Post model is to use the example they chose—the domain name system—as a case study for Internet governance. Johnson and Post suggest that no one need govern the domain name system, because strong network effects mean that everyone will soon coalesce around the same registry. But one might reasonably wonder what would happen to those stranded in the losing registry, and what constrains the power of a single (presumably private) registry once it has been established as an Internet standard. For a very different account of the structure of the domain name system, see the following excerpt adapted from Mark A. Lemley & David McGowan, Legal Implications of Network Economic Effects, 86 Calif. L. Rev. 479 (1998):

> The Internet, like the telephone network, exhibits a strong form of network effects—the network *is* the product in a very real sense. Given the parallels between the two, one might expect the Internet to exhibit the same market structure as the telephone network. But it does not. The Internet looks nothing like the old Bell System, with a single regulated corporation in charge of all the connections. In fact, it doesn't even look like the new, streamlined model of telephone competition, in which various large network owners will be forced to interconnect on government-set (and government-enforced) terms. Rather, the Internet appears (at least at first glance) to be an example of working anarchy—it consists of millions of different entities around the globe, public and private, which connect together in a patchwork network of uncertain provenance.
>
> How can this be? The answer is twofold. First, the Internet is not composed entirely of its own set of lines connecting one Internet user to the next, though some Internet specific "backbone" wires do exist. Rather, the Internet piggybacks on existing communications technology, notably the wire telephone network, using available space to send distributed packets of information from place to place. As a result, no one can fairly be said to have "built" the Internet in the physical sense, though of course a number of people built early pieces of it, and United States government agencies such

as the National Science Foundation and the Defense Advanced Research Projects Agency contributed parts of the network backbone.

Second, and more important, the Internet itself is nothing more than a relatively simple set of computer protocols (commonly called TCP/IP today) governing the interchange of data. In other words, what we think of as "the Internet" is really only a published, nonproprietary interface standard. Anyone who uses the standard to transmit data from their computer is "on" the Internet; anyone who doesn't use the standard is not. The success of the Internet is due largely to its spectacularly successful interoperability. It did not drive out its competitors in the "computer networking" market so much as subsume them. In the mid-1980s, one could participate in computer networking by joining one of approximately 50,000 bulletin board systems (or BBS's), or one of the fledgling online service providers like Prodigy or Compuserve, or (depending on where one worked) one of the private networks of military or academic computers. Each of these computer networks was largely incompatible with the others, with the result that joining a bulletin board let you communicate only with other members of that bulletin board. Interconnection protocols beginning with Usenet and SMTP allowed messages to be transferred between different groups of networked computers. As the communications technology between networks became more seamless, people began to think of themselves as on the Internet itself, rather than connected to a private computer networking group which could itself exchange data with other private groups. From a perspective of network economic effects, the Internet is a tremendous success story because it allows different and often incompatible computer systems to communicate with each other, expanding the size of the network without requiring purchase from the standards owner.

Things are not quite as simple as this, however. TCP/IP does not do everything automatically and without supervision, any more than do the stock exchanges, often cited as the most efficient of "unregulated" markets. Rather, there are a wide variety of rulemaking groups that enforce standards on the Internet. For example, technical standards (including updates or changes to the TCP/IP protocol) are set by the Internet Engineering Task Force (IETF), itself a voluntary body with no "official" authority over the Internet beyond the willingness of Internet users to adopt the changes it proposes. Further "rules" are created by the code written both into the Internet protocols and that written into privately owned programs like Netscape Navigator, Microsoft Internet Explorer, and Sun's Java that operate on the Internet.

For our purposes, though, the best example of the role of network effects in Internet governance has to do with domain names. InterNIC (and the private company Network Solutions, Inc.) set rules for addressing, mapping the "domain names" commonly used to identify people on the Net to the numeric IP address that is actually registered to a particular server. For addressing to work, someone must maintain a list of valid IP addresses and their aliases, and everyone on the Internet must work from that list, so that a user who types in "www.ibm.com" will find the computer identified with that alias. Network Solutions (NSI) has performed this function for several years now with respect to certain of the international top level domains, or iTLDs, like ".com". The list of names and matching IP addresses are entered into a series of "root domain name servers" or DNSs. The servers are themselves updated regularly. If your name is on the list, you can be found on the Internet. If not, anyone who types that name into their browser or mail program will not be able to reach you.

Obviously, therefore, the DNS servers are central to the functioning of the Internet. And if you want your name to have a DNS entry, the only obvious way to get it is to request that NSI put it there. But NSI is a private entity; it is not at all clear what authority they have to "run" the Internet, or indeed who might be able to give them that authority. NSI took over operation of the domain name registration system based on a contract from the U.S. National Science Foundation. That contract will expire in 1998; NSF has already indicated that they do not intend to renew it.

So what happens to the DNS servers? Consider several possible outcomes. First, NSI may decide to keep administering the DNS system, and the courts may decide it has a right to do so. If this occurs, control over the network will effectively have been placed in the hands of a single private entity, which will become the *de facto* standard-setter. In theory, NSI could be displaced from this position by market competition—someone else could set up a competing, incompatible domain name server, and if enough users of the Internet (and therefore of the NSI DNS system) switched to this incompatible system, the owners of the new server would become the new market leader. In practice, network effects make this unlikely, because a "competing Internet" that few people are using will not be attractive to those already on the current Internet. Indeed, some halting efforts toward such an alternate DNS system have so far been unsuccessful. While NSI's control over DNS might also be displaced by hacking, any such unauthorized access to the DNS servers is likely to be illegal.

A second possibility is that NSI will get to keep its control over DNS, but that some legal constraint will be imposed on its discretion in running the DNS system. There have been suggestions that the government should play a fundamental role in compelling access to NSI's domain name servers. Indeed, litigation on this issue has already begun. In a complaint filed in March of 1997 against NSI, a company called PGP Media alleged that NSI's failure to incorporate PGP-registered domains violated the antitrust laws. The claim is that NSI's configuration file "is the central (and essential) technical bottle-neck facility for the Domain Name Registration Market," and the plaintiffs seek "extremely limited and narrowly tailored injunctive relief to compel NSI to add reference in the Configuration File on the NSI Root Nameservers so that PGP may compete with NSI in the Domain Name Registration Market for Domain Name registrations." The fact that this claim was even filed pays tribute to the growing confusion over precisely who should have authority to "issue" domain names.

Finally, the government could decide to remove NSI's control over domain name registration entirely, replacing it either with a de novo open system of private registration, or even a system of government registration. In February 1997, the International Ad Hoc Committee (IAHC), a nongovernmental Internet advisory group set up to study the issue, recommended the creation of seven new "generic top-level domains (gTLDs)," to be administered on a global basis by "multiple competing registrars" overseen by a (private) Council of Registrars and a (private) DNS Policy Oversight Committee. The international nature of this approach is an important indication that one cannot merely say "the government" will establish a new policy. While the IAHC report was prepared under the informal auspices of the World Intellectual Property Organization, and the "Memorandum of Understanding" it establishes is deposited with the International Telecommunications Union, there is no governmental or international legal authority behind the proposal, a fact which has upset both the United States and the European Union. Indeed, the Memorandum of Understanding declares that it is agreed to by "The Internet Community," an ethereal entity if ever there was one. NSI probably has no enforceable legal obligation to comply with a dictate from such a body, though of course the body's rules might well end up being incorporated into national or international law. Alternatively, whatever private group claims authority over Internet domain names is undoubtedly subject to existing national laws, at least if the country applying those laws has jurisdiction.

This last alternative seems to have prevailed. The United States, after writing a competing report, merged its proposal with the IAHC's in 1998. Under this revised proposal, administration of the domain name *registry*, and coordination with competing domain name *registrars*, will be managed by a non-profit corporation called ICANN, to be governed by members chosen from a variety of groups interested in the process. While neither the structure of ICANN nor the domain name rules it will create were clear at this writing, it seems likely that the new domain name system will include multiple gTLDs, and that numerous registrars will be licensed to register domain names within these gTLDs (though all the names will be kept in a single registry, under the control of ICANN).

From an economic perspective, there is clearly value to be had in a shared rather than monopolistic top-level domain system. Internet domain names are valuable things; one generic domain name was recently sold for over $100,000. NSI currently charges only [$35] per year per domain name, up from $0 a few years ago. But an NSI freed of governmental constraints on its pricing policy probably has significant power to raise the price of domain names, either across the board or by price discriminating. Competition among domain name registrars would constrain such power, particularly if (as the IAHC report recommends) competing registrars could register names within a single TLD. If IBM can choose to obtain rights to "ibm.com" from either NSI or from a competitor such as PGP, it will be able to shop effectively for the lowest registration price, and price should approach marginal cost.[344]

On the other hand, administering such a competitive system will be more difficult than running the current system. Someone must control access to the DNS root servers; either one of the registrars must be trusted to give nondiscriminatory access to the servers, or some governmental body will have to police interconnections, as is done in the telephone industry. Some provision will also have to be made for preventing conflicting registrations, and the interaction between trademark law and domain name registrations will become more complex. These functions don't necessarily have to be carried out by a government—government regulation of Internet traffic in any form makes a lot of people nervous and would also subject the administrator to constitutional restraints in the US that do not now exist—but they will have to be accomplished somehow if domain name registration is to be competitive rather than proprietary. The existing system—one based on consensus—appears unlikely to survive very long.

3. Since these articles were written, the debate over governance of the domain name system has shifted focus to ICANN—the non-profit corporation organized at the behest of both the "Internet community" and the U.S. government to oversee the transition to competition in the provision of domain names. ICANN has come in for a great deal of public criticism, both for the secrecy of its decision-making processes and for its substantive decision to require alternative dispute resolution in trademark cases. Among the most prominent critics is Michael Froomkin. He has challenged the legitimacy of the U.S. government's decision to delegate control over the DNS to ICANN, has attacked ICANN for its secret and undemocratic processes, and has pointed to systematic flaws in ICANN's largest project: its procedures for resolving trademark disputes and creating new top-level domains. See A. Michael Froomkin, Wrong Turn in Cyberspace: Using ICANN to Route Around the APA and the Constitution, 50 Duke L.J. 17 (2000); A. Michael Froomkin, ICANN's "Uniform Dispute Resolution Policy"—Causes and (Partial) Cures, 67 Brook. L. Rev. 605 (2002). See also Jonathan Weinberg, ICANN and the Problem of Legitimacy, 50 Duke L.J. 187 (2000). But see Joe Sims & Cynthia

---

344. By contrast, a competing top-level domain which cannot register ".com" domains might find itself handicapped by the convenience effect of the widespread use of the .com TLD. IBM may be less likely to switch to a competing domain name registrant if the TLD they use is an unfamiliar one, since part of the value of having a name like "ibm.com" is that those who want to visit the site for the first time can easily guess the name.

L. Bauerly, A Response to Professor Froomkin: Why ICANN Does Not Violate the APA or the Constitution, 6 J. Sm. & Emerging Bus. L. 65 (2002). It is certainly the case that ICANN has acted slowly in adding new top-level domains, though whether that is a good or bad thing may depend on one's perspective. And though ICANN originally promised to turn control over to directors elected from the Internet community at large, more recently it has announced its intention to rely only on directors appointed by various interest groups.

What does Froomkin's argument suggest about Internet governance? Is there any way to create a private body that is representative of the Internet, has legitimacy, and can make decisions in an efficient manner? Or is Froomkin correct that we may fall back in the final analysis on law as the ultimate arbiter of Internet rules?

4. A different strand of legal thought on the Internet has focused not on the choice between existing law and Internet self-determination, but on things outside of law that constrain human behavior online. In particular, an important and growing body of legal scholarship has focused attention on the role of "code" in setting quasi-legal rules on the Net. See, e.g., Lawrence Lessig, Code and Other Laws of Cyberspace (2000); Lawrence Lessig, Reading the Constitution in Cyberspace, 45 Emory L.J. 869 (1996); Lawrence Lessig, Intellectual Property and Code, 11 St. John's J. Legal Commentary 635 (1996); Lawrence Lessig, The Constitution of Code: Limitations on Choice-Based Critiques of Cyberspace Regulation, 5 CommLaw Conspectus 181 (1997); David Post, Bargaining in the Shadow of the Code: File Caching, Copyright, and Contracts Evolving in Cyberspace (working paper 1997); Joel R. Reidenberg, Governing Networks and Rule-Making in Cyberspace, 45 Emory L.J. 911 (1996); Joel R. Reidenberg, Lex Informatica: The Formulation of Information Policy Rules Through Technology, 76 Tex. L. Rev. 553 (1998).

The basic idea here is that the way the architecture of the Internet is constructed both enables and constrains behavior. Because the Internet does not require identification of a person or a location, for example, anonymity and geographical indeterminacy are possible in Internet space. By contrast, if a particular rule or behavior is built into the system, it may foreclose people from certain actions even if the law would otherwise permit them. If the Internet Protocol were set to bar framing another party's Web page, for example, the copyright cases on framing simply wouldn't arise, whether or not framing would be legal under copyright law.

For a concrete example of "code-based regulation," see the Digital Telephony Act of 1994, Pub. L. No. 103-414, 108 Stat. 4279; see also Susan Freiwald, Uncertain Privacy: Communication Attributes After the Digital Telephony Act, 69 S. Cal. L. Rev. 949 (1996). The Digital Telephony Act required telephone companies to modify their network architecture to enable access by law enforcement to the communications of private parties.

5. As Lessig's book notes, law and code are not all that constrain behavior in cyberspace. Behavior is also a function of the market (what I can do is limited by what I can afford), and of social norms, or netiquette. There is significant literature on the sociology of online behavior, and some attention has been given to informal social sanctions like "flaming" that are used to punish or reward behavior. For a skeptical discussion of Internet norms in the legal context, see Mark A. Lemley, The Law and Economics of Internet Norms, 73 Chi.-Kent L. Rev. 1257 (1999). For a discussion of what constitutes "private" ordering in cyberspace, see Margaret

Jane Radin & R. Polk Wagner, The Myth of Private Ordering: Rediscovering Legal Realism in Cyberspace, 73 Chi.-Kent L. Rev. 1295 (1999).

6. Although much has been made of the dispute over whether government regulation or self-governance is appropriate for the Internet, talk of government regulation begs the question, "which government?" The Internet is inherently global in scope, and its regulation by any one territorial government is likely to cause problems. Some of those problems are evident in the *Yahoo* case discussed in Chapter 9. How should the Internet be regulated when national laws differ substantively? The obvious extremes—that parties should be liable for conduct everywhere their Web site can be accessed, or that they should be liable only where they (or perhaps their servers) are located—both have insurmountable problems. Subjecting anyone who ventures onto the Internet to liability for transgressing the laws of any nation in the world reduces all speech and commerce to the least common denominator. No one could put anything on a Web page that was not simultaneously acceptable to the governments of France, China, and Iran. Conversely, if countries cannot regulate foreign Internet conduct based on its domestic effects, unscrupulous users are likely to flock to "data havens" from which they can freely pirate copyrighted works, sell obscene material, defame others, and the like.

The rules of jurisdiction and choice of law discussed in Chapter 9 may offer one intermediate solution. We may be able to apply existing legal rules to determine that liability is appropriate in some jurisdictions but not others, based on the nature of the actor and the conduct in each particular case. But those legal rules were designed for a world in which worldwide distribution of products was something done by sophisticated corporations who could be expected to learn and abide by the laws of various foreign jurisdictions. Arguably they will not apply too well to the Internet.

The alternative is to eliminate substantive legal diversity, either by a treaty harmonizing laws or by submitting Internet disputes to some sort of world governing body. While there are periodic efforts at harmonizing particular areas of law, and substantial progress has been made in areas such as copyright, true international governance is decidedly unlikely in the foreseeable future.

Glossary

For more definitions, the authors of this textbook recommend PHILLIP E. MAR-
GOLIS, COMPUTER & INTERNET DICTIONARY (Random House Webster's 1999).

ACPA (Anticybersquatting Consumer Protection Act) A law passed by Congress in 1999 to protect trademark holders from domain name squatters who
use a domain name in bad faith in commerce. The ACPA provides for cancellation and/or transfer of the domain name and statutory damages.

Algorithm A procedure for solving a given type of mathematical problem. Most
computer programs employ algorithms to calculate the appropriate response to a
user request or to locate and manipulate data in memory.

Analog A method of representing information in a continuous and linear format.
For example, the hands of a clock represent the time as continuously varying
angles instead of as a discrete numeric sum, as a **digital** watch would.

Application Program A computer program primarily designed for **end users** and
made to run on top of an **operating system**. Typical applications include word
processors, spreadsheets, database programs, communication programs, and web
browsers.

Application Programming Interface (API) A set of **routines, protocols**, and
tools for building software **applications** in order to ensure their compatibility
with specific **operating systems** or other **applications**.

Architecture The overall structure and function of a hardware or software computer system, usually defined by the minimum **standards** a component must
meet in order to achieve compatibility with the system.

Arithmetic Logic Unit (ALU) One of the two main components of the **CPU**,
primarily responsible for performing arithmetic and logical operations.

ARPA The U.S. Defense Department's Advanced Research Project Agency.
ARPA was the organization responsible for originally creating the **Internet**.

Backward-compatible Compatible with earlier models or versions of the same product. Often a key feature for new computers or programs necessary in order to retain user loyalty and perpetuate **network effects**.

Bandwagon Standardization A process of **standardization** whereby subsequent entrants to the market adopt the standard of an existing firm.

Bandwidth The amount of data that can be transmitted from one device to another over a given amount of time. For digital devices, bandwidth is usually measured in bits per second (bps) or bytes per second. For analog devices, bandwidth is usually measured in cycles per second, or Hertz (Hz). Bandwidth is the most common way to gauge the speed of a system's **Internet** access.

BBS (Bulletin Board System) A computer-based message center that allows users to access it remotely and to post text messages for others to read either chronologically or by subject matter.

Berne Convention An international convention that sets minimum standards for copyright protection.

Binary Code A code based on two unique digits (usually 1s and 0s) used by computers to store data and implement instructions.

BIOS (Basic Input/Output System) A set of essential software routines that test hardware at startup, start the **operating system**, and support transfer of data among hardware devices. BIOS is typically stored in **ROM**.

Black Box Analysis A process of **reverse engineering** whereby the analyst tests the software by feeding it instructions or commands and recording the results. While this process does not reveal the actual code of the program, it can often uncover the logical structure of the program.

C++ One of the most popular modern programming languages.

Caching The process of storing information from an external source (e.g., a disk or the Internet) in a computer's memory so that it can be accessed repeatedly at a faster pace by the **CPU**.

CDA (Communications Decency Act) A law passed by Congress in 1996 which attempted, among other things, to protect minors from "indecent" and "patently offensive" communications over the **Internet**. A majority of the content restrictions were subsequently invalidated by the Supreme Court in 1997. The CDA also included provisions which explicitly exempted **OSPs** from liability for online defamation.

Central Processing Unit (CPU) The main component of a computer system responsible for performing calculations and instructing the system on how to function. A CPU typically consists of (1) an arithmetic logic unit (**ALU**), which performs arithmetic and logical operations and (2) the **control unit**, which gathers instructions from memory and decodes and executes them.

Child Pornography Prevention Act (CPPA) A law passed by Congress in 1996 to attack the rise of computerized or "virtual" child pornography.

Clickwrap Licenses **Mass-market licenses** that often appear during the installation of a program or at the entrance to a web page, requiring the user to click on a button (and thus manifest assent to the license) in order to proceed with use of the program or site.

Compilation The process of converting **source code** to **object code**. Decompilation converts **object code** back to **source code**.

Computer-Human Interaction (CHI) An interdisciplinary field combining education, graphic art, industrial design, industrial management, computer science, mechanical engineering, psychology, artificial intelligence, linguistics, information science and sociology to understand how human beings process information so that products can better be designed to enhance useability.

Control Unit One of the two main components of the **CPU**. The control unit is primarily responsible for gathering instructions from memory and decoding and executing them.

CONTU (Commission on New Technological Uses of Copyright) A national commission formed by Congress in the late 1970s to recommend the proper application of copyright law to new technologies.

COPA (Child Online Protection Act) Congress' second attempt to limit the access of minors to offensive content on the **Internet** after major provisions of the **CDA** were struck down by the Supreme Court.

COPPA (Children's Online Privacy Protection Act) A law passed by Congress requiring website owners to get permission from parents before gathering information from children under the age of 13.

Copyleft Coined by Richard Stallman of the Free Software Foundation, copyleft licenses are a form of **open source license** where all licensees are required to promise not to incorporate the software in a commercial product and to pass it on, even if embedded in a large program, to others free of use restrictions.

Cyberspace A metaphor for the nonphysical realm created by computer systems. Generally used to refer to the "place" where online interactions and communications occur.

Cybersquatter An individual who registers a **domain name** in order to deprive the trademark owner of it, or in order to sell it, or confuse customers.

Data Structure In programming, a scheme used to organize related pieces of information. Examples include data organized as a set of files, lists, arrays, records, trees, or tables.

Database A collection of information organized so that a computer program can quickly search, retrieve, and sort the data for display.

De Facto Standard A standard adopted by a majority of users without any effort at coordination from industry groups or the government.

Decryption The process of translating **encrypted** data into readable data, often utilizing complex **algorithms**.

Digital   A method of representing information as a discrete value. For example, a digital watch represents the time as specific numbers, as opposed to **analog** watch hands, which represent time through continuous and linear movement.

DMCA (Digital Millennium Copyright Act)   The most recent and comprehensive change to U.S. Copyright law. Passed in 1998, the DMCA extends copyright protection in many areas of technology, including the prevention of **TPM circumvention**.

Domain Name   A name used to identify one or more **IP addresses**. Domain names are most often used in **URLs** to help web browsers find specific sites on the **Internet**. A typical domain name consists of a word or phrase followed by a **TLD** such as .com, .org, or .net.

DOS (Disk Operating System)   A generic term for early PC **operating systems**. The most popular version, MS-DOS, was originally developed by Microsoft for IBM.

Electronic Commerce (E-Commerce)   Using the Internet to sell goods or services.

Emulation Software   A program with the ability to imitate another program or device. For example, some programs allow Apple Macintosh computers to emulate the Windows **operating system** and run Windows **applications**.

Encryption   The process of translating data into a secret code, often utilizing complex **algorithms** to carry out the translation. To reverse the process and read the data, one must **decrypt** the code.

End-to-End (e2e)   A description of the architecture of the Internet offered by Reed, Saltzer, and Clark, in which the network carries all compliant packets and the "intelligence" of the network is built into the ends rather than into the network itself.

End Users   Customers who purchase finished products from vendors (as opposed to **OEMs**/developers, who purchase products in order to modify, improve, bundle, or integrate them with other products).

EPC (European Patent Convention)   The convention that established the **EPO** and set the rules for patentability in the European Union.

EPO (European Patent Office)   The governmental agency in Europe in charge of receiving and processing patent applications and issuing patents.

ESign (Electronic Signatures in Global and National Commerce Act)   A law passed by Congress in 2000 to create legal parity between electronic records and signatures and their print counterparts. ESign was modeled after UETA and preempts most non-UETA state digital signature laws.

Filtering   The process of screening incoming content to a computer and eliminating specific selections based on subject matter. Most commonly used to filter out **spam** or offensive sexual, political, or violent material.

Framing   The process of displaying content from different web pages so that it appears to the user to be within the "frame" of the original page.

Freeware Software distributed for free. Often subject to an **open source license**.

GNU (GNU's Not Unix!) An operating system distributed by the Free Software Foundation as a free alternative to Unix; also called GNU/Linux or Linux for the developer of its kernel, Linus Torvalds.

GPL (General Public License) The license developed by the Free Software Foundation to freely distribute GNU and other software. One of a variety of free and open source licenses enjoying currency, GPL's hallmark is that it requires any code incorporating GPL code also to incorporate the GPL, a feature that has been described as "viral."

Graphical User Interface (GUI) A method of displaying information about an **operating system** or **application** and receiving commands from users based on visual images, such as **icons**, pointers, a desktop, windows, and menus.

Gray Market A marketplace where goods are bought internationally and then re-sold to customers domestically, usually at a price far below the domestic price. Products entering a country from a gray market are also known as parallel imports.

HREF (Hypertext Reference Link) An **HTML** instruction **linking** text or graphics to another document or website.

HTML (Hyper Text Markup Language) The programming language used to create documents on the World Wide Web.

HTTP (Hyper Text Transfer Protocol) The **protocol** used by the World Wide Web to define how data is formatted and transmitted.

I/O (Input/Output) Device A device whose primary purpose is inputting or extracting data from a computer, such as a floppy disk drive.

ICANN (Internet Corporation for Assigned Names and Numbers) A non-profit corporation formed in 1998 to administer **IP address** allocation, **protocol** parameter assignment, **domain name** system management, and **root server system** management functions.

Icon A small picture that represents an object or program on a computer screen. Icons are typically a central feature of **graphical user interfaces** (GUIs).

Independent Software Vendors (ISVs) A company that produces software un-affiliated with a particular hardware product.

Information Technology Using computers and networks to manage, process, and communicate information.

Infrastructure The physical **architecture** of a **network**.

Integrated Circuit Also known as a chip, an integrated circuit is a small device made out of a **semiconductor** material containing transistors and other electronic components.

Internet A global **network** of millions of computers, originally developed by **ARPA**.

Internet Engineering Task Force (IETF) The main standards organization for the **Internet**. The IETF is a large international body of network designers, operators, vendors, and researchers working to expand and improve the way the **Internet** functions.

InterNIC (Internet Network Information Center) A consortium, involving the National Science Foundation, AT&T, General Atomics, and Network Solutions, Inc. (**NSI**), whose purpose is to register **domain names**, provide a directory of **Internet** domains to the public, and give general support and information to the Internet community. Until recently, NSI had primary authority as part of InterNIC to register all **domain names**.

Interoperability Designing a computer component so that it is compatible with (i.e., works with) other components.

IP Address A numerical identification used to locate a specific computer on the **Internet**. For example, 1.206.40.130.

ISP (Internet Service Provider) A company that provides access to the **Internet**, usually through local phone lines. For example, America Online (AOL).

Java An **object-oriented** programming language developed by Sun Microsystems that allows a single **application** to run on any **operating system**. Use of Java programs has become especially common on the **Internet**.

Linking The process of using **HTML** to allow text or graphics on a web page to refer to another web page or document, whereby clicking on the link takes the user to that page or document directly.

Local Area Network (LAN) A **network** in which all components are located within a relatively small fixed geographic area, often within one building.

Logic Bomb A "lockout" feature implemented in software programs whereby the program will shut down unless it receives a new "key" from the programmer on a regular basis. Often used to police and enforce license payments from customers.

Market Failure The inability of a free market to meet the needs of all its consumers and suppliers without generating externalities.

Mass-market Licenses Also known as End User License Agreements. Often found in **shrinkwrap** or **clickwrap** form, these licenses are non-negotiated agreements issued in identical form to all customers without variance in terms.

Metatag A special **HTML** instruction embedded in the code of a web page to provide web browsers with information about who created the page, how often it is updated, what subjects it concerns, and keywords that correspond to its content. **Search engines** often use metatags to properly catalogue web pages.

Microprocessor A synonym for **CPU**.

MP (Madrid Protocol) A recent revision of the **MTA**.

MTA (Madrid Trademark Agreement) An international treaty allowing trademark owners to file a single application in a member country and use that single application to secure rights in all other member countries.

Natural Language Language used by humans to communicate, as opposed to a computer language such as **Java**. Often used to refer to the ability of certain search programs to take human or "natural" language questions and convert them into computer-language inquiries.

NCCUSL (National Conference of Commissioners on Uniform State Laws) A national group of state representatives working to unify state laws.

NDA (Non-Disclosure Agreement) A written contract limiting the right of the signatories to discuss or utilize any information they receive that is covered by the agreement. Often used by companies when seeking financing, in forming joint ventures, or entering licensing agreements with other companies. Also used by companies with departing employees in order to maintain trade secrets.

Netiquette A contraction of **Internet** etiquette, netiquette represents an informal set of social norms that define acceptable and unacceptable behavior on computer **networks**.

Network A system connecting two or more compatible points to each other. For example, the telephone network; the **Internet**.

Network Effects See **Network Externalities**.

Network Externalities The increase or decrease in utility or satisfaction that a consumer of a product derives from every additional consumer's use of that product.

Network Market A market for products that exhibit **network externalities**.

Nonexcludability A characteristic of a **public good** whereby the creator of the good is unable to prevent those who do not pay for the good from consuming it.

Nonrivalrous A characteristic of a **public good** whereby additional consumers of the good do not deplete the supply of the good available to others.

NSI (Network Solutions, Inc.) The original company in charge of registering **domain names**.

Object Code Written instructions for a program in a form readable by computers. Usually translated or "**compiled**" from **source code**, the human-readable form most often used by programmers.

Object-Oriented Programming A special type of programming that combines **data structures** with functions to create reusable "objects." Once an object is created, it can be used in several different files or applications (e.g., using an arrow to show the position of a mouse pointer).

OEMs (Original Equipment Manufacturers) Companies that sell customized computers to **end users**, usually packaging or bundling hardware and software components from multiple third-party manufacturers.

Open Source License A license, typically used for software products, that allows anyone to have access to the source code of the product and to use or build on the code in any way they wish as long as they make their results equally available free of charge and under the same open source license conditions.

Operating System The main computer program that loads into memory when a computer is first powered up. The operating system serves as the foundation for running other computer programs called **applications**. Operating systems generally perform basic tasks, such as recognizing input from the keyboard or mouse, sending output to the display screen, keeping track of files and directories, and controlling **peripheral** devices such as disk drives and printers.

OSP (Online Service Provider) See **ISP**.

PCT (Patent Cooperation Treaty) An international treaty signed in 1970 which allows a patent applicant in a member country to delay subsequent member country applications for up to 30 months while still maintaining her original priority date.

Peer-to-Peer Network (p2p) A network **architecture** that enables individual users to connect directly to other individual users' computers; used for direct personal file sharing, as in Napster, Gnutella, etc.

Peripheral Any external device attached to a computer, such as a monitor, keyboard, disk drive, mouse, or printer.

PICS (Platform for Independent Content Selection) A system developed by the World Wide Web Consortium to enable the tagging of websites in order to **filter** out objectionable content automatically.

Protocol An agreed-upon format for transmitting data between two devices.

PTO (Patent and Trademark Office) The governmental agency in the United States in charge of receiving and processing patent and trademark applications and issuing patents and trademark registrations.

Public Good A good which benefits all members of society whether they pay for it or not. For example, national military defense. Private markets generally undersupply public goods because producers cannot reap the marginal value of their investment in providing such goods.

Public-key Cryptography A cryptographic system involving two uniquely correlated **algorithmic** keys—a public key available to any user and a private or secret key available only to select individuals, usually the recipients of confidential messages. The sender of a message can protect its contents by **encrypting** it with the recipient's public key. The recipient can then **decrypt** the message using the corresponding private key, thus ensuring the security of the message.

Random-Access Memory (RAM) A type of computer memory in which any memory location can be accessed independently (as opposed to sequentially). Unlike **ROM**, RAM loses its contents when its power supply is turned off. RAM is most commonly used to store **operating system**, **application**, and data files when loaded into memory from a hard drive or other peripheral.

Read-Only Memory (ROM) A type of computer memory which can contain pre-recorded data. The data stored in the ROM, unlike **RAM**, cannot normally be reset or erased, even when its power supply is turned off. ROM is most commonly used to store a computer's start-up programs and diagnostic applications.

Reverse Engineering   The process of uncovering how a component or **application** functions by analyzing the final product.

Root Server System   A **network** of thirteen servers that supply the world with official domain name information.

Schematic   A model or diagram showing each part of a product.

SDMI (Secure Digital Music Initiative)   An effort by the U.S. recording industry to create a uniform method of distributing music in **digital** format with a security system to prevent unauthorized access or duplication. See also **TPM**.

Search Engine   A website that collects and catalogues the content of web pages, allowing users to input key words or queries and then generating a list of the sites with the highest correlation to the inquiry based on a matching **algorithm**. For example, Alta Vista and Excite are common **Internet** search engines.

Semiconductor   A material that acts as both a poor conductor of electricity and a poor insulator, primarily used to manufacture computer chips. For example, silicon or germanium.

Shareware   A method of distributing software based on an honor system. Distribution is free, with the author requesting payment from the user if she likes the product and chooses to continue using it regularly. Payment often assures service support and free upgrades.

Shrinkwrap Licenses   A **mass-market license** enclosed within the shrinkwrapped box in which a product is sold. A typical shrinkwrap license will declare that by opening the shrinkwrap, the user assents to the terms of the license, even though many consumers are not able to read the license until after they open the box.

Site Licenses   Licenses that require payment based on the number of computers in which the program is installed.

Source Code   Written instructions for a program in a form readable by humans. Must be translated or "**compiled**" into **object code** in order to be executed by a computer.

Spam   Unsolicited commercial communications, originally via Usenet but today usually via electronic mail.

Standards   Specific technology that is adopted for use in a particular industry for a particular purpose. Standards can be adopted either by a recognized organization (e.g., **IETF**), by government decree, or **de facto** when a majority of users chooses on their own to employ the technology.

Subroutine   The section of a program that performs a particular task.

Switching Costs   The cost of converting or replacing a **standard**. For example, the time it takes to learn the features of a new word processing application after having already learned those associated with an old one.

TCP/IP (Transmission Control Protocol/Internet Protocol)   The collection of communications **protocols** used to connect computers to the **Internet** and transmit data.

TLD (Top-Level Domain)   The suffix attached to **Internet domain names**, such as .com, .net, or .org.

TPM Circumvention   The process of either disabling or deceiving a **TPM** in order to access or duplicate the content or program protected.

TPMs (Technological Protection Measures)   Security devices that attempt to prevent duplication and unauthorized access to copyrighted works, often some form of **encryption**-based software.

TRIPs (Agreement on Trade-Related Aspects of Intellectual Property Rights) An international treaty, signed in 1994, which relies on national treatment and nondiscrimination principles to set minimum standards for international protection of intellectual property.

UCITA (Uniform Computer Information Transactions Act)   A statute proposed by **NCCUSL** that would expand the role of state contract law in governing transactions in computer information.

UDRP (Uniform domain name Dispute Resolution Process)   A mandatory administrative process established and managed by ICANN to resolve domain name disputes between domain name holders and trademark holders who claim that domain names are identical or confusingly similar to their trademarks and are being used in bad faith.

UETA (Uniform Electronic Transactions Act)   Model legislation, finalized in 1999 by the NCCUSL, that creates legal parity between electronic records and signatures and their print counterparts.

URL (Uniform Resource Locator)   The location of a specific web page or document on the **Internet**. URLs begin with the **protocol** they use (e.g., **HTTP**) and are usually listed as a file name within a sub-directory of a **domain name**. For example, http://www.law.berkeley.edu/BCLT

User Friendly   A general term referring to any feature that makes a computer easier to use, especially for novice users. For example, help screens, Graphical User Interfaces (**GUI**s), and menus.

UTSA (Uniform Trade Secrets Act)   A model law promulgated by **NCCUSL** intended to unify state trade secrecy laws throughout the United States. To date, UTSA has been adopted in one form or another by 40 states and the District of Columbia.

Vaporware   A sarcastic term used to describe computer products that have been announced and advertised but are either never released or are not yet under development at the time the announcement is made. Sometimes used to suggest the existence of anti-competitive strategies by large dominant companies, such as Microsoft, where the announcements and advertising are solely meant to intimidate smaller competitors and discourage venture capital investment in competing products.

WIPO (World Intellectual Property Organization)   A specialized agency of the United Nations responsible for the promotion of the protection of intellectual property throughout the world through cooperation among countries, and for the administration of various multilateral treaties dealing with the legal and administrative aspects of intellectual property.

WTO (World Trade Organization) The international organization responsible for enforcing the provisions of the **TRIPs** agreement.

WYSIWYG (What-You-See-Is-What-You-Get) A method by which documents appear on the screen exactly as they will look when printed.

Table of Cases

Major cases are in italics.

Table of Statutes

Uniform Acts

Uniform Commercial Code

Uniform Computer Information Transactions Act

Uniform Electronic Transactions Act

Uniform Trade Secrets Act

Index